Commercial Litigation in Anglophone Africa:

The law relating to civil jurisdiction, enforcement of foreign judgments and interim remedies

Commercial Litigation in Anglophone Africa:

The law relating to civil jurisdiction, enforcement of foreign judgments and interim remedies

SECOND EDITION

Andrew J Moran, KC

BCL (Oxon), LLB (Lond)
One of His Majesty's Counsel
Master of the Bench of Middle Temple

&

Anthony J Kennedy

BCL, BA (Oxon)
Barrister

juta

Commercial Litigation in Anglophone Africa:
The law relating to civil jurisdiction, enforcement of foreign judgments and interim remedies

First published 2018
Second Edition 2022

www.juta.co.za

ISBN: 978 1 48515 0 435

Project Specialist: Fuzlin Toffar
Editor: James Ryan
Proofreader: Mary-Ann Emanuel
Indexer: Lexinfo
Typeset: Elinye Ithuba DTP & Print Solutions (Pty) Ltd

PREFACE TO THE SECOND EDITION

The four years since the first edition of this book have seen many important developments in the law in most of the 16 English-speaking jurisdictions addressed, which are reflected in the updated text. Some of these developments are mentioned below.

The Roman-Dutch common-law jurisdictions have seen South African courts further entrench the principles of *forum non conveniens* into the civil law of jurisdiction, with one judge at first instance deciding that those principles now form part of the law of South Africa (although quite how this regime interacts with the existing law relating to the *rationes jurisdictiones* and attachment to found or confirm jurisdiction remains unexplored by the courts). South Africa has also seen significant developments to the law of *mandament van spolie* and, for the first time, has recognised the availability of anti-suit interdict relief. The Supreme Court of Eswatini has now confirmed that attachment of property is required where a *peregrinus* is sued by an *incola* of that jurisdiction. The same Supreme Court has also held that foreign judgments may be enforced in Eswatini pursuant to the common law. In Zimbabwe, the Supreme Court considered and stated the principles on the basis of which interim interdict relief may be granted. Important developments to the law relating to submission to the jurisdiction and *mandament van spolie* were made by the courts in Namibia.

In the common-law jurisdictions, the jurisdictional implications of the Companies Act 2019 in Ghana are set out in the text relating to that jurisdiction. The High Court of Ghana also held (for what seems to be the first time) that it had the power to make an anti-suit injunction. In Zambia, the Supreme Court confirmed the *lacuna* principle pursuant to which the Zambian rules of court may be supplemented by the English Rules of the Supreme Court where no available domestic procedural rule exists. Zambia also saw the introduction of a number of significant amendments to the rules of the High Court effecting service of process and jurisdiction over foreign companies and these changes are reflected in the text. The court in Kenya further developed the jurisprudence relating to the enforcement of foreign judgments and third-party disclosure orders.

Since the first edition went to print a number of reviews of the book have been published, notably, thoughtful and constructive reviews by Ada Ordor and others in (2019) 136 *South African Law Journal* 587–93 and by Chukwuma Okoli in (2020) 16 *Journal of Private International Law* 189–203. The authors take this opportunity to express their thanks to both Ordor and others and Okoli for the trouble and consideration taken by them in their reviews of the first edition.

Both reviews have contributed greatly to the second edition of the book: each chapter now contains a section on anti-suit injunctions or interdicts (as the case may be); and we have endeavoured to place emphasis on the domestic law of each English-speaking jurisdiction in preference to the law of other jurisdictions, where this has been practicable (the availability of sources is still problematic with many of the jurisdictions covered).

The authors thank Richard Frimpong Oppong and Chukwuma Okoli for their generous help in locating various sources otherwise inaccessible to them and Esther Kilimba of Clyde & Co., Tanzania, for her help in accessing primary legislation in that jurisdiction.

The authors are conscious that certain English-speaking jurisdictions have been omitted from consideration, namely, Anglophone Cameroon and Rwanda. The reason for this is that, at present and, in relation to Cameroon, despite the heroic efforts of Michael A. Yanou in his 2015 work, *Practice and Procedure in Civil Matters in the Courts of Records in Anglophone Cameroon*, there is simply insufficient material, either at all or in the English language, to provide a helpful account of the law in those jurisdictions relating to the subjects addressed in this book. This is a matter to be revisited, hopefully, in later editions when the position is clearer.

The authors once again thank their editor and publisher at Juta and Company (Pty) Ltd, James Ryan and Stephen Allcock for their support and forbearance.

We have stated the law, as we understand it, as at 31 March 2022.

AJM
AJK

PREFACE TO THE FIRST EDITION

On 4 January 1962, in the course of a speech to mark the opening of the Ghana Law School in Accra, President Kwame Nkrumah highlighted the importance of lawyers to a developing state. President Nkrumah stated that lawyers were first needed to assist ordinary men and women with their everyday legal problems, and secondly, and perhaps most importantly, lawyers were needed 'in the service of the state, to deal with treaties and commercial agreements and with questions of private and public international law'. The President also emphasised the importance of Ghanaian lawyers becoming acquainted with the law of other African countries and 'constantly increasing inter-African economic and cultural relations'. These sentiments have become even more relevant to lawyers in both private practice and public service throughout Africa over the course of the past fifty years.

The economic development of Africa in recent decades has not gone unremarked upon. Trade within Africa and trade between African countries and other major trading blocs such as the European Union, the United States of America and, more recently, China, have increased. The Africa Economic Outlook 2017 (African Development Bank, The Organisation for Economic Cooperation and Development, United Nations Development Programme) notes that Africa's current population is approximately one billion people, that its expanding middle class is estimated at 350 million, and that by 2050 Africa is projected to host approximately 20% of the world's population. The African Economic Outlook 2017 also notes that Africa's growing population is expected to lead to a rise in consumer spending from USD 680 billion in 2008 to USD 2.2 trillion by 2030.

With increased intra and extra-continental trade and increased continental consumption, inevitably the scope for the occurrence of commercial disputes has expanded and will only continue to expand. An increasing number of these disputes will possess international, cross-border characteristics and it is with these that this work is concerned.

Lawyers on the continent (and, for present purposes, specifically in Anglophone jurisdictions) will need to be in a position to advise their clients on notoriously difficult questions, such as: when a court may lawfully be seised of an international commercial dispute; when a party must arrest a person or attach property as security for a claim in order to seise a court with jurisdiction; what pre-trial remedies are available to a party to an international dispute (for example, asset-freezing orders, search and seize orders, third-party disclosure orders); and, in the event a party obtains a judgment against a person, whether and where that judgment is enforceable.

Not only will lawyers and law students in these jurisdictions need to be familiar with these (and other related) matters regarding the jurisdictions within which they practise, but increasingly they will need to be informed, following President Nkrumah's admonition to Ghanaian lawyers, of the law of other African jurisdictions.

It is hoped that this work will be of benefit in enabling lawyers (and law students) to equip themselves to advise clients on international disputes.

It is also hoped that this work will be of use to judges sitting in Anglophone jurisdictions deciding cases in which an issue or issues of law arise where the court considers that it may be of benefit to see how judges in other Anglophone jurisdictions have disposed of the issue in question.

More generally, lawyers outside the continent advising clients engaged or intending to engage in trade with African countries, and such businesses themselves, may wish to forearm themselves for the potential challenges awaiting litigants in Anglophone Africa.

The authors wish to express their thanks to the librarians at the Bodleian Law Library, University of Oxford; in London, the Institute of Advanced Legal Studies (where special mention is due to Hester Swift for her encyclopaedic knowledge of African sources and her tenacity in hunting down even the most obscure references); the School of Oriental and African Studies; Lincoln's Inn Library and the British Museum Library. In addition, the authors thank their editor and publisher at Juta Press, Tessa Botha and Stephen Allcock, for their support and forbearance.

The authors also wish to express a debt of gratitude to Professor Adrian Briggs of St Edmund Hall, University of Oxford, who, at different times, tutored them both in private international law and without whose example and inspiration this work would, probably, not have been written.

We have endeavoured to state the law as it was on 1 January 2018.

AJM
AJK

NOTES ON CITATION

Note on the citation of case law in this work

With respect to judicial authorities, in some of the jurisdictions under consideration, the authors have provided a reference only to an online report of the cited judgment. In certain jurisdictions, for example Kenya, this is common practice: law reporting is now undertaken predominantly online (in Kenya, the Electronic Kenyan Law Reports appear to be the main resource). Even in jurisdictions where both hardcopy and online reports are available, where it has proved difficult to obtain the hardcopy report, the electronic report has instead been cited. Otherwise, the authors have provided orthodox hardcopy references to judicial authorities.

In this regard, by reason of the sometimes restricted availability of copies of judicial and academic authorities, the authors have provided, where appropriate, citations from judicial and academic authorities of somewhat greater length than is, perhaps, conventional. It is hoped that this will be of assistance to readers where the source of the citation is either not generally available or available only at prohibitive expense.

Note on the citation of statutory material in this work

The authors note that in several of the jurisdictions under consideration, as a matter of domestic jurisprudence, the orthodoxy is to cite statutes by reference to the title of the chapter of the codified version of the laws in which they appear, along with the number of that chapter ('CAP' references, omitting the year of enactment). In this work, the authors refer to the relevant statute by its title and the year of its enactment in order to present a clearer picture of the law which was in force at a particular point in time. The authors do, however, also provide the reference to the number of the chapter in which the statute may be found in the codified version of the laws of the relevant jurisdiction for the sake of completeness.

Note on the placement of Eswatini in this work

Despite the renaming of Swaziland as Eswatini, in the interests of editorial simplicity, the placement of the chapter covering this jurisdiction has remained the same in this edition as in the first edition of this work.

TABLE OF CONTENTS

TABLE OF CASES

Page

B

Page

Page

Page

Page

Page

Page

Page

G

Page

K

Page

Page

M

Page

Page

Page

N

Page

Page

Page

Page

Page

Page

T

Page

V

W

Page

Z

TABLE OF LEGISLATION

ESWATINI

Rules

GERMANY

GHANA

Legislative Instrument

Ordinance

Rules

LESOTHO

Orders

Rules

MALAWI

Orders

MYANMAR

Statutes

Year	No	Title	Page
		NAMIBIA	
		Proclamation	
1981	R222	Proclamation	
		s 21(1)	288
		Rules	
2014		Rules of the High Court of Namibia	282, 310, 314, 331, 334, 348
		Rule 4	282
		Rule 7(1), (2), (5), (6), (7), (8), (11)	282
		Rule 8	320
		Rule 9	320, 348
		Rule 8(2), (3)	282
		Rule 8(4), (9)	283
		Rule 9(1), (2), (3), (4)	283
		Rule 11	284
		Rule 11(1)	284, 285
		Rule 11(1)(b)	283
		Rule 11(2), (3), (5), (6)	285
		Rule 11(7)	286
		Rule 12(1), (2)	283
		Rule 12(4), (5)	284
		Rule 13	283
		Rule 21(2)	330
		Rule 25	331
		Rule 40	330
		Rule 45	282
		Rule 48	330
		Rule 65(1), (2), (3)	328
		Rule 65(4)	328, 331
		Rule 65(5)(b)	329
		Rule 65(6)	329
		Rule 65(7), (8)	328
		Rule 66(1)	331
		Rule 66(1)(a), (b)	329
		Rule 66(1)(c)	330
		Rule 66(2)	330, 331
		Rule 66(4)	330
		Rule 67(1)	331
		Rule 67(1)(a), (b)	331
		Rule 67(2)	331
		Rule 69(1)	330
		Rule 70(1)	331

SIERRA LEONE

Orders

TANZANIA

Order

Ordinance

Regulations

Rules

THE GAMBIA

Orders

Ordinance

Year	No	Title	Page
		Rules	
2009		High Court (Amendment) Rules	724, 725, 739, 742
		Rule 3	725
		Rule 3(2)	739, 742
		Rule 3(3)	739
		Rule 3(7)	740
		Rule 4(3)(a)	739
1924	2	Reciprocal Enforcement of Judgments Rules	751
		Rule 2	753
		Rule 3	753
		Rule 4	753
		Rule 5	753
		Rule 6	754
		Rule 7	755
		Rule 10	755
		Rule 11	755
		Rule 13	755
		Rule 14	755
		Rules of the High Court	725, 728, 731, 735, 739, 745
		Order II, r 1(2)	725
		Order II, r 9	739
		Order V, r 1(1)	725
		Order VIII, r 1	725
		Order VIII, r 2	726
		Order VIII, r 3	726
		Order VIII, r 4	726
		Order VIII, r 5	726
		Order VIII, r 6	726
		Order VIII, r 7	726
		Order VIII, r 8	728–729, 730, 732, 734, 744, 747
		Order VIII, r 8(2)	728
		Order VIII, r 8(e)	736, 738
		Order VIII, r 8(e)(i)–(iii)	744
		Order VIII, r 8(f)	738
		Order VIII, r 9	729, 730, 732, 745
		Order VIII, r 10(1), (2)	733
		Order VIII, r 10(3)	734
		Order X, r 1	772
		Order X, r 2	773
		Order X, r 3	773
		Order X, r 5(1)	773
		Order X, r 6	773
		Order XI	772

UGANDA

Orders

Rules

UNITED KINGDOM

Rules

ZANZIBAR

Decrees

Rules

CONVENTIONS

TREATIES

Chapter 1

BOTSWANA

1.1 Jurisdiction

In common with other Roman-Dutch law jurisdictions, the connecting factor of greatest significance in the application of the rule determining whether a Botswanan court may assume jurisdiction over a dispute is the status of the parties to the dispute as an *incola* or *peregrinus* of Botswana. These rules are examined below.

1.1.1 Commencing proceedings where the defendant is within the jurisdiction

Pursuant to the Rules of the High Court 2011[1] ('the Rules') every action where service is to be effected within the Republic of Botswana shall be commenced by a writ of summons, petition of notice of motion ('originating process') signed by the Registrar of the High Court and date-stamped with the stamp of the court.[2] Service of any process on a person may be effected by delivering a copy to the person personally and, where that person refuses to accept delivery, by leaving the copy in full view of the person or by leaving a copy at the place of residence or business of the person.[3] In case of difficulty the plaintiff may apply to a judge for leave to effect substituted service on the defendant.[4]

---

[1] Published by the Chief Justice in the exercise of his powers under s 28 of the High Court Act 1975 (Act 21 of 1974 and Act 2 of 1975) on 12 January 2011 (SI 1 of 2011). The correct domestic citation of this provision is 'High Court Act [chapter 04:02]' of the Laws of Botswana, 2013. In this regard, the reader is referred to the 'Note on the citation of statutory material in this work', which appears at the end of the 'List of Statutory Material Cited' at the beginning of this work.

[2] Order 6, r 1(1). Where an action is commenced by writ of summons that writ shall be 'in Form 2 to Schedule 1' to the Rules, with such 'variations as the circumstances require' and shall be endorsed with the particulars of claim, signed by the plaintiff or his attorney, which particulars shall state truly and concisely the nature and the grounds of the cause of action and the relief sought: Order 6, rr 5 and 7. An exception to this rule is process for the arrest of the defendant.

[3] Order 8, r 2(2)(a) and (b); additional methods of service are prescribed by sub-rules (c)–(k).

[4] Order 8, r 3.

After service upon him of the writ of summons (or other originating process) the defendant is required to enter an appearance[5] within 14 days if he is resident or, in the case of a company, has its principal place of business within a radius of 100 km of the Registry out of which the writ was issued or 21 days in all other cases.[6]

1.1.2 Commencing proceedings where the defendant is outside the jurisdiction

Order 10 of the Rules makes provision for edictal citation, or service of process out of the jurisdiction.

Order 10, rule 1 provides that no process or document by which proceedings are instituted shall be served outside the Republic of Botswana except by leave of the judge.

Any person wishing to obtain leave to serve process out of the jurisdiction must make an application to the judge setting out concisely the nature and extent of his claim, the grounds on which it is based and on which the judge has jurisdiction to entertain the claim, and also the manner of service which the judge is asked to authorise.[7]

In *Lifelinx Insurance Agencies (Pty) Ltd v Chikowe*,[8] Makhwade J held that proceedings issued and served outside the jurisdiction other than in compliance with Order 6 rule 9 and Order 10 of the Rules were irregular proceedings issued without the authority of the court and would be set aside.

1.1.2.1 Incolae *and* peregrini

For the purposes of the application of its civil jurisdiction rules, inter alia, Botswanan law differentiates between those persons who are *incolae* and those who are *peregrini*. However, the authorities which have considered the appropriate test to be employed in order to determine whether a person is an *incola* or a *peregrinus* have not been wholly successful in fashioning a clear test.

---

[5] Which is entered by completing a memorandum of appearance in accordance with Order 9, r 1(3).

[6] Order 6, r 12.

[7] Order 10, r 2(1). On such an application: 'The judge may make such order as to the manner of service as to him seems meet and shall further order the time within which notice of intention to defend is to be given or any other steps to be taken by the person to be served.' Order 10, r 2(3). On service of a document in a foreign country, see Order 8, rr 4 and 6.

[8] [2006] 2 BLR 435 (HC).

In *Misroame v Motsisi*,[9] the terms *peregrinus* and *incola* were considered in the context of an application by a defendant for security for costs. Gweke-Dako J stated:[10]

> 'Under Roman law, legal status was largely based on nationality. One was either a Roman citizen, i.e. *civis municeps* and therefore entitled to all legal rights, or one was a *peregrinus* (a foreigner) and as such debarred from enjoying certain rights. Apart from this, the terms "peregrinus" and "incola", both of which were handed down by the Romans, have not been defined with any precision. Under Roman-Dutch law as originally practised in Holland, nationality was also used as the test. This has largely disappeared and the distinction between *peregrine* and *incolae* appeared to have given way and [became one] based on domicile, meaning actual permanent or indefinite residence, *cum animus manendi*,[11] i.e. an intention to remain permanently or indefinitely.'

The judge further noted that: the terms *incola* and *peregrinus* had not been defined in Botswanan law;[12] it had not been expressly decided whether domicile or residence was the criterion to be applied in determining whether a person is a *peregrinus*; and that there were authorities supporting domicile as the test, a combination of domicile and residence of a reasonably permanent character as the test and also residence alone as the test.[13] The judge held[14] that the trend favoured using a test of residence provided there was some 'acceptable evidence of some permanence or settled nature about it'. This chimes with the test employed for that purpose in other Roman-Dutch law jurisdictions.[15]

It is unclear how far more recent authority supports the aforementioned trend away from domicile and towards residence. As such, the test to be employed in Botswana to determine whether a natural person is an *incola* or a *peregrinus* remains unsettled. In *Healthcare Management Services (Pty) Ltd v Smith*,[16] the defendant was admitted to the plaintiff hospital and received treatment there. On her discharge, she failed to settle her account. The plaintiff brought an urgent application for the arrest of the defendant *tanquam suspectus de fuga* (which will be dealt with in

---

9 [1994] BLR 313 (HC).

10 Ibid 320G–321A.

11 As for the authorities which elucidate the meaning to be given to this expression for the purposes of jurisdiction, see *Kenyon v Kenyon and Jenkins* [1974] 1 BLR 2 (High Court: Aguda CJ) and *Dance v Dance (2)* [1976] 2 BLR 43 (CA) (Maisels P; Milne and Doyle JJA), *per* Milne JA at 44. For the development of the law on domicile, see Forsyth *Private International Law* 5 ed 145, fn 99 (and the authorities therein cited) and 149, fn 115 (and the authorities therein cited).

12 [1994] BLR 313 at 322H.

13 Ibid 322H–323C.

14 Ibid 323A–B. The judge cited *Kallos & Sons (Pty) Ltd v Mavromati* [1946] WLD 312, a decision on an application for security for costs, in support of this and further referred to the test of ordinary residence contained in O 23 r 1 of the English Rules of the Supreme Court (the Order concerned with security for costs).

15 See, in this respect, the test employed in the courts of Namibia (*Kahan v Lidchi* [2000] NAHC 19 30 May 2000 (NAHC) (Levy AJ)) and Zimbabwe (*African Distillers v Zietkiewicz* 1980 ZLR 135 (Beck J)).

16 [1996] BLR 301 (HC).

greater depth below). The defendant opposed the application on the bases that no application *ad fundandam jurisdictionem* had been brought to found jurisdiction and there was insufficient evidence of her intention to leave the jurisdiction.

In contrast to the decision in *Misroame v Motsisi* (which arose in the context of an application for security for costs), the question for the court in *Healthcare Management* was over the existence (and potential exercise of) the court's jurisdiction. As Aboagye J explained:[17] 'An arrest *ad fundandam jurisdictionem* is an attachment of the person or property of one who is domiciled and resident in a foreign country in order to make him amenable to the jurisdiction of the court.' The judge found that on the evidence the defendant was an *incola* and not a *peregrinus* because her husband had a four-year contract of employment with the Spar Supermarket chain, she had a residency permit and she had stated that she had a settled intention to remain in the jurisdiction. Aboagye J,[18] relying on the decision in *Graham v Phillips*,[19] held: 'A peregrine is a person who is neither domiciled nor resident within the area of jurisdiction of the court and it has been held that either domicile or residence within the area or jurisdiction of the court, of some permanent or settled nature, is sufficient to constitute a person an *incola*.'

It is unfortunate that Aboagye J's attention appears not to have been drawn to the decision in *Misroame v Motsisi*.[20] Had it been, the test to determine whether a person is an *incola* or a *peregrinus* may have been further clarified. From a doctrinal and jurisprudential point of view, the fact that there are several authorities which support different tests is unfortunate. From a practical point of view, however, and taken in the light of the authorities, such as they are, it would appear that, for jurisdictional purposes, a natural person will be considered an *incola* if they are domiciled in Botswana or are resident in Botswana, where that residence is of a permanent or settled nature.[21]

Turning to the categorisation of legal persons, in *Silverstone (Pty) Ltd v Lobatse Clay Works (Pty) Ltd*[22] the plaintiff was a company incorporated in Botswana. The plaintiff had its registered office in Botswana but no shareholders who were resident in Botswana; the plaintiff's administrative centre was outside the jurisdiction. The plaintiff brought an action for the return of certain equipment in the possession of the defendant and the defendant applied for the attachment of the equipment to confirm jurisdiction alleging that the plaintiff was a *peregrinus*

---

[17] Ibid 306B–C, quoting Herbstein and Van Winsen *Civil Practice of the Superior Courts of South Africa* 3 ed.

[18] Ibid 306D–E.

[19] 1966 (1) SA 556, a decision of the High Court in Salisbury, Southern Rhodesia (Davies J).

[20] There is no reference to the decision in *Misroame v Motsisi* in Aboagye J's judgment, at any rate.

[21] This view is supported by the decision in [2008] 2 BLR 540 (HC) (Kirby J), where, at para [10], the judge referred to both the 'domicile' and 'residence' of the parties in reaching the view that both were peregrines.

[22] [1996] BLR 190 (CA) (Amissah JP; Schreiner and Tebbutt JJA).

and did not have any property apart from the equipment with which to satisfy any judgment in the defendant's favour.[23] At first instance the court granted the attachment.[24] On appeal, the court held: a company, like a natural person, could have more than one place of residence[25] and a company could also have a place of residence at its registered office;[26] the plaintiff was an *incola* of Botswana on the basis of its residence;[27] the plaintiff was also domiciled in Botswana because it was incorporated and had its registered office in Botswana and it was an *incola* on the basis of *ratione* domicile.[28] In consequence, no attachment of the *incola* plaintiff's assets could be made.[29]

Hence, it is the case that, when determining whether a legal person is an *incola* or a *peregrinus* for the purposes of jurisdiction, the court will adopt the same test as that which it uses when asking the same question about a natural person.

1.1.2.2 *The jurisdictional significance of attachment*

By way of preliminary observation, in giving the judgment of the court in *Silverstone (Pty) Ltd v Lobatse Clay Works (Pty) Ltd*,[30] Tebbutt JA[31] stated:[32]

> 'The doctrine of effectiveness is an essential feature of jurisdiction. A judgment would not be effective if it should yield an empty result and that would occur if judgment were obtained against a foreign *peregrinus* who owned no assets in the country in which judgment is given against him. The attachment of an asset of his within the jurisdiction would however, render the judgment effective since execution could then be levied against it. The attachment would then make the *peregrinus* amenable to the court's jurisdiction. However, such attachment could only be made against assets of a *peregrinus*.'

The judge expressed his agreement with the statement of Nienaber AJA in *Ewing McDonald & Co Ltd v M & M Products Co*:[33]

---

[23] The basis of the defendant's application for an attachment of the equipment was to confirm jurisdiction in support of arbitration proceedings commenced under the agreement between the parties. In the light of the court's finding that the plaintiff was an *incola*, the court declined to decide whether attachment was available in respect of an arbitration.

[24] The reasons why first instance judge, Lesetedi AgJ, reached that conclusion are set out in the judgment of Tebbutt JA, at [1996] BLR 190, 193C–G.

[25] [1996] BLR 190, 198C.

[26] Ibid 200D–E.

[27] Ibid.

[28] Ibid 200E et seq.

[29] Ibid 204D.

[30] [1996] BLR 190.

[31] With whom Schreiner JA and Amissah JP agreed.

[32] [1996] BLR 190 at 203.

[33] 1991 (1) SA 252 (A) (Van Heerden and Smalberger JJA and Nicholas, Friedman and Nienaber AJJA).

> 'While effectiveness may be the rationale for jurisdiction, it is not necessarily the criterion for its existence. It is true that effectiveness is ... "the basic principle of jurisdiction in our law"... But it is as true that "effectiveness does not per se confer jurisdiction on a Court".'[34]

The doctrine of effectiveness has traditionally occupied a central place in the law of the Republic of South Africa. The observations cited above suggest that it has been similarly thought of in Botswanan courts. The recent developments in the law of South Africa on the role of, and place for, the doctrine of effectiveness in that jurisdiction may well exercise an influence on the continued development and application of the doctrine, such as it is, in Botswana.[35]

1.1.2.2.1 Where the plaintiff and the defendant are both *incolae*

Where both the parties to a dispute are *incolae*, no jurisdictional problems arise. The dispute is a purely domestic one over which the court has jurisdiction.

1.1.2.2.2 Where the plaintiff is an *incola* and the defendant is a *peregrinus*

Here, it would appear that an attachment of the *peregrinus* defendant's property is necessary in order for the plaintiff to establish jurisdiction. In *Dominion Earthworks v Pieter Lodewickus Bezuidenhout*,[36] the court confirmed the decision of the High Court for an attachment of certain plant and machinery to found jurisdiction in circumstances where the plaintiff was an *incola* of Botswana and the defendant a *peregrinus*. The plaintiff was an individual who had been appointed by the defendant to manage certain road building works in Botswana. The defendant was a company registered and carrying on business in South Africa. On the plaintiff's application *ex parte* for an attachment of certain of the defendant's plant and machinery to found jurisdiction for a money claim and for an interim interdict prohibiting the defendant from disposing of that property, the plaintiff claimed that he was an *incola* of Botswana and that the defendant was a *peregrinus*. The plaintiff argued that he was entitled to have the property of the defendant attached in order to found or confirm jurisdiction. The court at first instance granted the plaintiff the relief sought by way of a rule *nisi* calling on the defendant to show cause why the rule ought not to be confirmed at the return date. The defendant put in affidavit evidence in which, inter alia, it denied that the plaintiff was an *incola* (on the basis that the plaintiff was a resident of South Africa and

---

[34] The court thus followed the approach of (the majority of) the South African Appellate Division in *Bisonboard Ltd v K Braun Woodworking Machinery (Pty) Ltd* 1991 (1) SA 482 (A).

[35] For a more in-depth analysis of the doctrine of effectiveness, the reader is referred to the first section of the chapter on the Republic of South Africa.

[36] [1964–1967] BLR 267 (CA) (Roper P, Schreiner and Hathorn JJA).

only temporarily present in Botswana) but admitted that it was a *peregrinus*. The court at first instance dismissed the defendant's contention, held that jurisdiction was well founded on the basis of an attachment of assets and (it seems) continued the interim relief.

On appeal the defendant sought permission to withdraw the admission that it was a *peregrinus* in order to contend that it was an *incola* and thus its property ought not to have been attached so as to found jurisdiction. The Court of Appeal refused the defendant permission to withdraw its admission on the basis that the defendant had not placed on record an explanation of how the admission came to be made and the reasons for seeking to withdraw it.[37]

It would appear that plural attachment of a *peregrinus* defendant's property is permissible. In *Semele v Montanus*,[38] the *incola* plaintiff applied to attach certain property to found jurisdiction in an action sought to be commenced by edictal citation (service out of the jurisdiction). Attachment of two of the items which the plaintiff sought to attach had already been authorised to found jurisdiction in a suit by one plaintiff and attachment of the third item had also already been authorised to found jurisdiction in a suit by a second plaintiff. Edwards J held that plural attachment was possible in such circumstances. The judge[39] held, in reliance on *Thermo Radiant Oven Sales (Pty) Ltd v Nelspruit Bakeries (Pty) Ltd*:[40]

> 'The principle of effectiveness has been considerably eroded by the established practice of attaching (in cases where a single action is to be instituted) property whose value is trifling when compared with the plaintiff's claim. In the case referred to it was also noted that jurisdiction continues to subsist even after the extinction of the attachment on which it was initially founded.'[41]

In *Bigzy Holdings (Pty) Ltd v Eso Management (Pty) Ltd*,[42] the *incola* plaintiff applied for attachment *ad confirmandam jurisdictionem* of certain of the *peregrinus* defendants' motor vehicles. The vehicles themselves were outside the jurisdiction. The order was granted by way of a rule *nisi* to the effect that the vehicles be seized at any border post they used to enter or exit the jurisdiction or wherever they may be found within the jurisdiction. Certain of the defendants contended that they had submitted to the jurisdiction and that the court could not grant

---

37 Ibid 270, *per* Hathorn JA.

38 [1977] BLR 110 (HC) (Edwards J).

39 Having first referred to the principle set out in Herbstein and Van Winsen's *Civil Practice of Superior Courts* 2 ed 28, that jurisdiction depends on the power of the court to give an effective judgment and having observed that that principle 'is not in any full sense applied unless the value of the property attached is sufficient to satisfy the judgment in each of the actions to found jurisdiction in which it has been attached'.

40 1969 (2) SA 295 (A) (Steyn CJ; Ogilvie Thompson, Botha, Potgieter and Jansen JJA).

41 [1977] BLR 110. Owing to various defects in the application, the judge ordered that the plaintiffs in the two prior actions should have the opportunity of being heard before the attachment in the instance case was made.

42 [2002] 2 BLR 125 (HC) (Lesetedi J).

an attachment in such circumstances because the submission conferred on the court the jurisdictional powers which had, prior to the submission, been lacking. The plaintiff contended that mere submission without an attachment was not sufficient to confer an otherwise lacking jurisdiction as no effectiveness in implementing the court's decision in the action would have been established.

Lesetedi J held that a submission to the jurisdiction by a *peregrinus* defendant was sufficient to give the court jurisdiction without an attachment of property *ad confirmandam jurisdictionem.* The judge also determined that where there had been a submission to the jurisdiction prior to an application for an order of attachment to confirm jurisdiction, the court would not grant the order because the court's jurisdiction would already have been secured and the court would not thereafter concern itself with whether any judgment which might have been given would be effective or not. However, it was held that a submission after the attachment had been made was too late and the court would not set aside the attachment in such circumstances.

Referring to various South African authorities the judge[43] outlined the principles relevant to jurisdiction in the instant case (as a recent statement of the law, the passage bears extended citation):

> 'In the present context jurisdiction means that power vested in the court by law to adjudicate upon, determine and dispose of a matter. See *Ewing McDonald & Co. Ltd v M & M Products* [1991] 1 S.A. 252 (A). By disposing of a matter, it is included in the court's power to put its decisions into execution, i.e. to enforce its judgments. Such power is both in extent and character territorial, it being confined within the boundaries and over subjects or subject matter associated with the court's decreed territory. The object of the principle is that judgments should be given where they can be enforced or given effect because judgments which cannot be enforced are illusory. As pointed out by Viljoen JA in *Veneta Mineraria Spa v Carolina Collieries (Pty.) Ltd* ... "A court can only be said to have jurisdiction in a matter if it has power not only of taking cognisance of the suit but also of giving effect to its judgment." This has led to what is commonly referred to as the doctrine or principle of effectiveness. In a claim based on contract, the court will under the common law and practice under it, therefore exercise jurisdiction upon any one of the following grounds, namely, ratione domicilii; ratione rei sitae and ratione contractus. The last ground refers either to where the contract has been entered into or where it has to be performed within the jurisdiction. See the *Veneta Mineraria* case supra at p. 890F quoting Kotze J in *Brooks v Maquassi Halls Ltd.* [1914] C.P.D. 371. Kotze J went on to state:
>
> > "But in order to exercise jurisdiction under either the second or third ground which I have mentioned, the practice has always been to grant an arrest either of the property or the person of the debtor as *fundandam jurisdictionem* [sic], and in this way the debtor or his property, to use the expressive language of the Dutch lawyers becomes

[43] Ibid 129A–131A.

> bankvast. There is, therefore, always something against which, in the event of the judgment being in favour of the plaintiff, the decree of the court can operate, and not amount to a mere nullity, for the court, like nature, should do nothing in vain."

It has been warned however that "effectiveness" should not be given too literal an interpretation. Potgieter JA. aptly put the warning in *Thermo Radiant Oven Sales Ltd v Nelspruit Bakeries (Pty) Ltd* [1969] 2 S.A. 295 at p. 309F thus:

> "It should, I consider, not be equated with a guarantee that in every case the judgment of the case would be satisfied completely."

Such a warning is sound for even in an action against an *incola* defendant, there is no guarantee that when execution is levied against his possessions, such possessions may not satisfy the judgment, yet the court exercises its jurisdiction even if the *incola* defendant is impecunious.

It is for that reason that in modern times the value of the property to be attached does not always bear a relationship to the claim. It can be quite nominal. In this regard Herbstein and Van Winsen's *The Civil Practice of the Supreme Court of South Africa* (4 ed) p. 92 also points out the anomaly of the term "effectiveness" and the need for the principle not to be given too literal a meaning in these words:

> "It appears the only reason why ... courts still require an attachment to found jurisdiction is to enable the court to give a judgment which has some effect even though ultimately the judgment may in many cases be only partly satisfied and the effectiveness of the judgment fictional to the extent that it is not satisfied."

The principle of effectiveness is however not the sole basis of jurisdiction. There is also the principle of submission. See *American Flag plc v Great African T-Shirt Corp CC* [2000] 1 S.A. 356 (W). There are situations where a peregrine defendant or respondent voluntarily submits to the jurisdiction which he would otherwise not be subject and by so doing, confers jurisdiction on such court. Such a person cannot afterwards be heard to say that the court has no jurisdiction over him. See *Pollack on Jurisdiction by Pistorius* (2[d] ed.) at p. 7 ...

But is submission alone without attachment sufficient to confer jurisdiction on a court in an action by an *incola* plaintiff against a *peregrinus* defendant? It appears from South African cases that the courts there have for over a century made dicta to the effect that actions by *incolae* against peregrine defendants are entertained solely on the ground of consent to jurisdiction ...

Pollack on Jurisdiction op cit at p. 8, also states, more in point, that:

> "Modern South African law does not, however, require the arrest of the person of the defendant or the attachment of his goods in addition to submission in those cases where, ordinarily, such arrest or attachment would be necessary to confirm the court's jurisdiction."

The above appear to me to be sound law and there is not reason why this court should not follow the same principles.'

1.1.2.2.3 Where the plaintiff and the defendant are both *peregrini*

Generally, in proceedings in Botswana, where both parties are *peregrini*, an attachment of property will be insufficient to confer jurisdiction on the court. In addition, the plaintiff must establish a *ratio jurisdictionis* in order to seize the court with jurisdiction over the dispute. (An exception to this would appear to be where an order for attachment is made in a dispute between *peregrini* which is being litigated outside the jurisdiction.)

In *Pretorius v Sweiger*,[44] the plaintiff *peregrinus* applied *ex parte* for an order for the attachment of the person of the defendant *peregrinus* and of certain money and other moveable property alleged to belong to him. The defendant was at the time of the application not within the jurisdiction. The plaintiff was a judgment creditor pursuant to a foreign judgment and contended that the presence within the jurisdiction of money and other property conferred jurisdiction on the court as the *forum res sitae* and that the attachment of property was sought to confirm that jurisdiction. Dismissing the application Edwards J found that there was no evidence that the assets within the jurisdiction were in any way identifiable with the money which the plaintiff claimed from the defendant and held that where one *peregrinus* had a money claim contracted abroad against another *peregrinus* the fact that the latter had assets within the jurisdiction did not constitute the court the *forum res sitae* for the purpose of the claim (*forum rei sitae* being an established *ratio jurisdictionis*).

In *Martex Trading (Pty) Ltd v Yannoulis (No 2)*,[45] the applicant applied to attach certain property of the respondent *peregrinus* who had left the jurisdiction after service of the writ of summons on him. Livesey Luke CJ held[46] that the court had jurisdiction to attach property to found or confirm jurisdiction in such circumstances but that 'it is well established that the court does not lightly allow property to be attached either to found or confirm jurisdiction' and that it was incumbent on the plaintiff to provide evidence of the nature, value and location of the property which it was sought to be attached. Evidence of the nature of the property was required in order to determine whether any of it was perishable or whether any of it was exempt from execution by law; evidence of the value of the property was necessary in order to satisfy the court that it is saleable value or so that it may know its value as compared with the value of the claim; and evidence as to the location of the property was required so as to eliminate any mistake as to the identity of the property.

---

[44] [1979–1980] BLR 124 (HC).

[45] [1991] BLR 346 (HC) (Livsey-Luke CJ). See also [1991] BLR 330 (HC) (Livsey-Luke CJ).

[46] [1991] BLR 346F–G.

On the question of the value of the property the judge cited[47] with apparent approval the judgment of Beadle CJ in the Southern Rhodesian (as it was then) case of *Ex parte Mor-Tal Construction Co (Pvt) Ltd*,[48] where it was stated:[49]

> 'The Court will want to know the value of the property which is sought to be attached, because, while the value of the property might be a quite irrelevant consideration in deciding whether or not the Court has jurisdiction, it is a most important consideration in deciding whether the Court in the exercise of its discretion can equitably order an attachment of the property to be made. Obviously if the property sought to be attached greatly exceeds the value of the claim, that would be a factor to be taken into account in refusing an attachment. Similarly, in reverse, if the value of the property sought to be attached was insignificant compared with the value of the claim, there again the necessity for attachment might not appear to arise.'

The judge also appeared to agree with the statement of principle by Beadle CJ in the subsequent case of *Ex parte Farrar*,[50] that usually the court had to be satisfied that the attachment was necessary for some other purpose, such as preventing the court's order from being *brutum fulmen*, and that evidence would usually be required to show that there is a likelihood that the respondent would remove the property from the jurisdiction if leave to attach is not given.

In *Pascoe v Botswana Ash Pty Ltd*,[51] the second defendant objected *in limine* that the court lacked jurisdiction to entertain the plaintiff's action against him because at the time the action was commenced both he and the plaintiff were peregrines of Botswana, both being resident and domiciled in South Africa, and he had no assets in Botswana. Kirby J dismissed the claim against the second defendant on the ground that where the claim sounded in money and both the plaintiff and defendant were *peregrini*, there had to be a recognised *ratio jurisdictionis*, as well as an arrest or attachment. Any arrest or attachment merely to found jurisdiction would not be sufficient.

In this regard, Kirby J stated:[52]

> 'It has been repeatedly held that whether or not the court has jurisdiction over the cause of action (where, for example, as here, the cause of action arose within the jurisdiction), an attachment or arrest is essential for the exercise of jurisdiction over a peregrine defendant. The court must have the power to enforce its judgment before it will assume or exercise jurisdiction.'

47 Ibid 347H–348B.
48 1962 (2) SA 664 (SR).
49 Ibid 665F–H.
50 1973 (1) SA 231 (R).
51 [2008] 2 BLR 540 (HC) (Kirby J).
52 Ibid 543E–G.

Having referred to *Bigzy Holdings (Pty) Ltd v Eso Management (Pty)*,[53] Kirby J held:[54]

> 'The position in such a case [where both parties are *peregrini*] was neatly summarised by Nienaber A.JA. in *Ewing McDonald & Co. Ltd. v M & M Products Co.* [1991] 1 S.A. 252 (A) at p, 258. He held that before the court will assume jurisdiction in respect of claims sounding in money, where both the plaintiff and the defendant are peregrine, both a recognised *ratio jurisdictionis* as well as an arrest or attachment are essential. Any arrest or attachment must necessarily be one *ad confirmandum jurisdictionem*. That accords with my view with the approach which should be adopted in Botswana as well.'

In *Concorde Leasing Corp Ltd v TPR (Pty) Ltd*,[55] an action between two peregrines, the plaintiff applied *ex parte* for the attachment of certain property (a motor grader) in the possession of the defendant pending determination of an action which it intended to bring in South Africa against the defendant *peregrinus*.[56] The plaintiff was a leasing company which had let the grader to the defendant pursuant to the terms of a lease agreement; the defendant was using the property within Botswana for the purposes of its business. The plaintiff alleged that the defendant had breached the terms of the lease. The plaintiff further alleged that it had cancelled the lease and proposed to commence proceedings against the defendant in South Africa for repossession of the property. The plaintiff alleged that, if the defendant was allowed to remain in possession of the grader pending the outcome of the intended action in South Africa, the grader would deteriorate in value and might be damaged. Edwards J held that he had jurisdiction to grant an order for the attachment of the property notwithstanding that both the plaintiff and the defendant were peregrines and that the proposed action was in a foreign court.[57] On the facts he held that such an order of attachment was appropriate to preserve the grader *pendente lite*. The judge made an order that a rule *nisi* should issue, calling upon the defendant to show cause why the grader should not be attached pending determination of an action to be instituted by the plaintiff against the defendant in the Supreme Court of South Africa and that the rule *nisi* should operate as an interim attachment.[58]

---

[53] [2002] 2 BLR 125 (HC) (Lesetedi J) 130–1. Kirby J determined, at [2008] 2 BLR 540 at 543H, that this case 'confirmed the general requirement of effectiveness, but distinguished cases in which the defendant submits to the jurisdiction of the court' which was not the position in the case before him.

[54] [2008] 2 BLR 540 at 543H–544C.

[55] [1979–1980] BLR 122 (HC).

[56] It appears from the report that the plaintiff had not at the time of the application commenced proceedings in the Republic of South Africa against the defendant.

[57] Referring to *Kibe v Mphoko* 1958 (1) SA 364 (O) 366–7, where the operation of a bank account was interdicted.

[58] The judge also ordered that the plaintiff should institute the action in South Africa within ten days, failing which the attachment should cease to operate.

1.1.2.3 Rationes jurisdictiones

There is no suggestion that the law in Botswana differs from the law in the Republic of South Africa on the acceptable *rationes jurisdictiones*. While more in-depth treatment is afforded the *rationes jurisdictiones* in the chapter on the Republic of South Africa,[59] the basic position may be summarised by reference to the judgment of the Supreme Court of the Cape in *Einwald v The German West African Co.*[60] There, De Villiers CJ stated:[61]

> 'What then are the grounds upon which the jurisdiction of this Court can be exercised, in respect of any contract over any defendant without his consent, express or implied? The grounds are threefold: *viz* by virtue of the defendant's domicile being here, by virtue of the contract either having been entered into here or having to be performed here, and by virtue of the subject matter in an action *in rem* being situated in this Colony.'

Added to these are the place of the delict and cases which concern property. The principal connecting factors for jurisdictional purposes which result are: *ratio domicilii (actor sequitur forum rei)*; *ratio contractus*; *ratio delictus*; and *ratio rei sitae.*[62] To this list may also be added *ratio causa continentia.*

1.1.2.3.1 *Ratio domicilii* (*actor sequitur forum rei*)

Ratio domicilii expresses the principle of Roman-Dutch law that the fundamental basis of jurisdiction is that a plaintiff should sue a defendant at the defendant's place of domicile or, as has become the case, residence (*actor sequitur forum rei*). There is nothing to suggest that the Botswanan courts would treat this issue any differently to the courts in the Republic of South Africa.[63]

---

[59] To which the reader is referred.

[60] (1887) 5 SC 86 (De Villiers CJ).

[61] Ibid 91.

[62] Different authors treat the organisation of this subject in different ways. Peté *et al Civil Procedure* 2 ed (2011) (70ff), discuss the subject under the headings *ratione domicilii, ratione res gestae, ratione rei sitae* and then claims relating to property and claims sounding in money. In Schulze *On Jurisdiction and the Recognition and Enforcement of Foreign Money Judgments* (2005), the discussion (at 1–15) revolves around domicile and the bases for assumption of jurisdiction over *incolae* and *peregrini*. In Kelbrick *Civil Procedure in South Africa* 2 ed (2012), the subject is analysed (at 42–3, paras [84–6]) in terms of claims in money and property. Forsyth *Private International Law* 5 ed (2012) discusses (at 205–6) residence and domicile, the various *rationes jurisdictionis* and then claims in money or property. Herbstein and Van Winsen *The Civil Practice of the High Courts of South Africa* 5 ed (2009) (Cillers, Loots and Nel), discusses (at 67–81) the subject under the topic headings: claims in money, property (and status). Pistorius *Pollak on Jurisdiction* 2 ed (1993), arranges the discussion under the topic headings money claims and property claims. There are merits in all of these approaches.

[63] Accordingly, for a more detailed treatment of this issue, the reader is referred to the corresponding discussion in the chapter on the Republic of South Africa.

1.1.2.3.2 *Ratio contractus*

There is nothing to suggest that the Botswanan courts would treat this issue any differently to the courts in the Republic of South Africa. Accordingly, a court where: (1) the contract was concluded (the *locus contractus*); (2) the contract is to be performed in whole or in part (the *locus solutionis*); and (3) the contract was breached in the manner relied upon by the plaintiff in Botswana, may, *ratio contractus*, exercise jurisdiction.[64]

1.1.2.3.3 *Ratio delicti commissi*

A court may have jurisdiction by reason of a *ratio delicti commissi* in the event that a delict was committed or occurred within its area of jurisdiction. Again, there is nothing to suggest that the Botswanan courts treat this issue any differently to the courts in the Republic of South Africa.[65]

1.1.2.3.4 *Ratio rei sitae*

The location of movable or immovable property within the area of jurisdiction of a court will confer on that court jurisdiction by reason of a *ratio rei sitae*: it is the court of the place where the property is situated. Again, there is nothing to suggest that the Botswanan courts treat this issue any differently to the courts in the Republic of South Africa.[66]

1.1.2.3.5 *Ratio causa continentia*

There is nothing to suggest that the courts in Botswana treat the *causa continentia* doctrine differently to the courts in the Republic of South Africa. The *causa continentia* rule is one that permits a court to assume jurisdiction in a case in which, but for the application of the rule, it might not have jurisdiction over the entirety of the dispute or over a particular defendant. The application of the rule is intended to avoid a 'multiplicity of proceedings and the possibility of conflicting judgments on the same cause and allows for the more convenient disposition of cases'.[67] Pistorius states[68] that in order to apply 'it must be established that there

---

[64] Given that there is nothing to suggest that the courts in Botswana treat this issue any differently to the courts in the Republic of South Africa, the reader is referred to the corresponding discussion in the chapter on South Africa for a more detailed treatment of this issue.

[65] Accordingly, for a more detailed treatment of this issue, the reader is referred to the corresponding discussion in the chapter on the Republic of South Africa.

[66] Accordingly, for a more detailed treatment of this issue, the reader is referred to the corresponding discussion in the chapter on the Republic of South Africa.

[67] Pistorius *Pollak on Jurisdiction* 2 ed (1993) 25.

[68] Ibid 26.

is no other forum which has jurisdiction in respect of all the defendants on other recognised grounds of jurisdiction'.[69]

1.1.2.4 *Submission to the jurisdiction*

Botswanan law recognises submission to the jurisdiction as a basis of jurisdiction over a dispute in certain circumstances.

Generally, submission may take one of two forms. First, unilateral submission, whereby a party against whom proceedings have been commenced takes a step in, and so participates in, the proceedings, which as a matter of Botswanan law renders him amenable to the jurisdiction of the Botswanan courts. Second, consensual submission, whereby the parties agree prior to or subsequent to a dispute arising to submit to the jurisdiction of the Botswanan courts.

1.1.2.4.1 Submission by participating in existing proceedings

Once served with process out of the jurisdiction Order 9 rule 5 of the Rules provides that the defendant to an action may, at any time before entering an appearance, or, if he has entered a conditional appearance, within 14 days after entering that appearance, apply to the judge for an order setting aside the writ of summons or its service on him, or declaring that the writ of summons has not been duly served on him, or discharging any order giving leave to serve the writ of summons on him out of the jurisdiction. A defendant may enter a conditional appearance with the leave of the judge.[70] A conditional appearance is treated for all purposes as an unconditional appearance unless the judge otherwise orders or the defendant applies to the judge for an order under Order 9 rule 5 discharging any order giving leave to serve the writ of summons on him out of the jurisdiction or otherwise setting aside service of the writ of summons on him.[71]

In the light of these provisions, it is highly likely that, where the defendant applies, either before entering an appearance or having entered a conditional appearance which is treated as a conditional appearance by the judge, for the relevant order, he will, in so doing, not be taken to have submitted to the jurisdiction of the court.

That said, there appears to be no reported authority which addresses the question which steps in the proceedings are sufficient for a defendant to be regarded as having submitted to the jurisdiction. In *Becco Botswana (Pty) Ltd v*

---

[69] Given, as we have said, that there is nothing to suggest that the courts in Botswana treat this issue any differently to the courts in the Republic of South Africa, the reader is referred to the corresponding discussion in the chapter on South Africa for a more detailed treatment of this issue.

[70] Order 9 r 4(1).

[71] Order 9 r 4(2).

Diamond Manufacturing Botswana (Pty) Ltd,[72] proceedings arose out of a contract which contained an arbitration clause. The plaintiff issued those proceedings on 10 November 1982; the defendant filed a notice of appearance to defend on 1 February 1983 and filed a request for further and better particulars on 15 February to which the plaintiff served a response on 27 April 1983. In June 1983, the defendant filed a motion seeking a stay of proceedings in favour of arbitration. O'Brien Quinn CJ held: (1) the filing of a request for further and better particulars formed, together with the reply to that request, part of the pleadings in the proceedings;[73] (2) the defendant had taken a step in the proceedings by filing a request for further and better particulars;[74] and (3) although the defendant could not apply for a stay of the proceedings using section 6 of the Arbitration Act 1959,[75] he was entitled to raise the defence that the case ought to be decided by arbitration and that could be done by special preliminary plea.[76]

As regards the second finding, O'Brien Quinn CJ stated:[77]

> 'The analogy to be drawn from that decision of the Supreme Court of Nigeria is that if the defendant, by taking an action when he could have done so, was held to have taken a step in the proceedings, then in the instant case, the defendant, by requesting further particulars which ... is part of the pleadings, a fortiori, he should be held to have taken a step in the proceedings and thus put himself outside the scope of section 6(1) of the Arbitration Act. I, too, would adopt the dicta of Ridley J in *Austin and Whiteley Ltd. v S. Bowley & Son* (1913) 108 L.T. 921: "In my opinion what is intended by a step in the proceedings is some step which indicates an intention on the part of a party to the proceedings that he desires that the action should proceed and has no desire that the matter should be referred to arbitration." In my opinion the defendant could have made this application immediately after entering appearance to defend but, by requesting further particulars, he indicated an intention that he desired that the action should proceed and that he had no desire that the matter should be referred to arbitration.'

In a subsequent case, *BM Packaging (Pty) Ltd v PPC Botswana (Pty) Ltd*,[78] in which *Becco Botswana* appears not to have been cited, the defendant registered an appearance to defend and then filed its plea denying the claim and at the same time counterclaimed (although the report is unclear as to the nature of this counterclaim – it contains only one reference to it). The defendant also

---

[72] [1983] BLR 288 (HC) (O'Brien Quinn CJ).

[73] Considering and following the Natal case of *Dinath v Du Toit NO* 1969 (4) SA 165 (N) (Harcourt J).

[74] Considering and applying by analogy the decision of the Supreme Court of Nigeria in *Nigerian Produce Marketing Co Ltd v Compagnie Noga D'Importation et D'Exportation SA* [1971] 2 ALR Comm 211 (Lewis and Madarikan JJSC; Sowemimo AgJSC).

[75] Proclamation 75 of 1959 (now Cap 06:01 of the Laws of Botswana, 2013).

[76] Applying *Rhodesian Railways Ltd v Mackintosh* [1932] AD 359 (Wessels ACJ).

[77] [1983] BLR 288 at 293E–G.

[78] [1998] BLR 309 (HC) (Mosojane J).

filed a special plea contending that the plaintiff was obliged to have recourse to the arbitration clause in the agreement between them and that the proceedings should be stayed. The plaintiff contended that the defendant had taken steps in the proceedings subsequent to the delivery of its appearance to defend and was thereby prevented from relying on the arbitration clause. Mosojane J held[79] that the preponderance of authority was to the effect that a defendant did not take a step in the proceedings by filing a defence containing a special plea relying on the clause.

1.1.2.4.2 Submission by agreement

1.1.2.4.2.1 *Jurisdiction clauses*

In *Ropace Botswana (Pty) Ltd v Dawson and Fraser (Pty) Ltd*[80] Lesetedi J refused an application for summary judgment and followed *BM Packaging* in recognising that the defendant could rely in its defence on an arbitration clause in its agreement with the plaintiff which, if proved, would constitute a ground for a stay of proceedings.[81]

In circumstances where a *peregrinus* plaintiff sues a *peregrinus* defendant, and the cause of action arises within the court's area of jurisdiction, the Botswanan courts have encountered the same difficulties faced by the courts in South Africa.[82] Briefly, in South Africa, it has been held that, in the circumstances currently under consideration, submission by either the *peregrinus* plaintiff or *peregrinus* defendant or both of them does not found jurisdiction.[83]

Despite the fact that courts in Botswana have often found decisions by the courts of South Africa to be of useful persuasive authority when pronouncing on Botswanan law,[84] it would appear that the South African view, at least as stated in the previous paragraph, has been rejected.[85] In *MAK (Pty) Ltd v St Paul Insurance Co SA Ltd*,[86] the Botswanan High Court[87] concluded that, where all

---

[79] Ibid 315E–316B.

[80] [2001] 1 BLR 479 (HC) (Lesetedi J).

[81] It is also the case that, in the context of an interlocutory application for declaratory relief the courts have enforced an arbitration clause by ordering a stay of proceedings and making an order referring the dispute to arbitration: *Building Construction 2000 v Ralebala* [2007] 3 BLR 762 (HC) (Dingake J).

[82] A fuller summary of which difficulties is provided in the chapter on the Republic of South Africa.

[83] *Veneta Mineraria Spa v Carolina Collieries (Pty) Ltd* 1985 (3) SA 633 (D). See also Kiggundu *Private International Law in Botswana: Cases and Materials* 2 ed 169.

[84] *MAK (Pty) Ltd v St Paul Insurance Co SA Ltd* [2007] 1 BLR 210 (HC) (Marumo J).

[85] Ibid 218–19.

[86] [2007] 1 BLR 210 (HC) (Marumo J).

[87] Albeit relying on South African authority (*Jamieson v Sabingo* 2002 (4) SA 49 (SCA)) where the South African Supreme Court was confronted with an action by a 'local *incola*' plaintiff against a defendant *peregrinus*. See further: *Hay Management Consultants (Pty) Ltd v P3 Management Consultants (Pty) Ltd* 2005 (2) SA 522 (SCA), approving the decision in *American Flag plc v Great African T-Shirt Corp* 2000 (1) SA 356 (W) and the relevant

the parties before the court were peregrines and had entered into a jurisdiction agreement conferring jurisdiction upon the courts of Botswana, the Botswanan courts should have jurisdiction. Marumo J stated:[88]

> 'There are of course important public policy considerations behind the requirement of effectiveness in court judgments. Court processes should not be reduced to mere academic exercises. But there are equally important public policy considerations behind the requirement that parties should be held to their contracts. I am unable to conceive of any reason in this age of intense international trade involving cross-border transactions, as well as the existence of efficient mechanism for the international enforcement of judgments why peregrini parties who have by their own agreement submitted themselves to the jurisdiction of a court should not be held to their obligations in terms of their agreement.'

While the remarks of Marumo J cited above are undoubtedly obiter dicta,[89] it is submitted that they strike the right note and should be followed. Such an approach chimes with the approach which Botswanan courts seem to take with respect to arbitration clauses (they appear to have regard to such clauses and endeavour to give effect to them). However, in the absence of a reported decision which is directly on point, the position is not free from all doubt.[90]

1.1.2.4.2.2 Domicilum citandi et executandi *clauses*

As a matter of South African law, the use of a *domicilium citandi et executandi* clause[91] in an agreement may, in particular where the defendant is a foreign *peregrinus*, indicate submission.[92] There is no reason to think that the courts in Botswana would employ a different approach.

---

section of the chapter on the Republic of South Africa in this work. By way of explanation, it should be noted that South African law distinguishes between a 'local *incola*' (ie an *incola* of the relevant Division of the South African High Court), a 'local *peregrinus*' (ie an *incola* of the Republic of South Africa but a *peregrinus* of the relevant Division of the South African High Court) and a 'foreign *peregrinus*' (ie a *peregrinus* of the Republic of South Africa). Botswanan law simply distinguishes between an *incola* and a *peregrinus* of Botswana as a whole.

[88] [2007] 1 BLR 210, 218A–D. After saying this, the judge went on to reject the reasoning of the South African court in *Mineraria*, at least 'insofar as it may be read to exclude jurisdiction even where effectiveness can be achieved by means other than the attachment of the person or goods of a peregrinus defendant to confirm jurisdiction', in favour of the approach in *Jamieson*.

[89] The defendant in *MAK* initially disputed the jurisdiction of the Botswanan court but then abandoned its objection (see [2007] 1 BLR 210, 219A).

[90] Especially in the light of previous comments by the Botswana High Court on this subject. See, for instance: *Pretorius v Sweiger II* [1979–1980] BLR 129 (HC) (Edwards J), where it was said, at 130: 'the time of the court should not be taken up with disputes, having nothing to do with Botswana, between persons neither domiciled nor resident' in Botswana.

[91] A clause which sets out an address where formal notices in relation to the contract (such as a demand for payment or a threat to cancel) or a summons in litigation arising out of the contract, can be served.

[92] *Hay Management Consultants (Pty) Ltd v P3 Management Consultants (Pty) Ltd* 2005 (2) SA 522 (SCA), *per* Heher JA (Scott, Cameron and Conradie JJA and Patel AJA agreeing) para [15]; where the clause was regarded as 'a significant factor' as was the choice of South African law as the proper law (para [14]).

1.1.2.5 *The jurisdictional significance of arrest of the person*

In Botswana, as opposed to the Republic of South Africa (where it has been held that arrest of the person so as to found or confirm the jurisdiction is unconstitutional),[93] it is still theoretically possible that arrest of the person can provide a basis to found or confirm the court's jurisdiction. Indeed, a court in Botswana may still grant interim relief in the form of arrest *tanquam suspectus de fuga*[94] and, on that basis, it is logical to conclude that arrest of the person may still found or confirm the jurisdiction of the court.

1.2 Enforcement of Foreign Judgments

Under Botswanan law, a foreign judgment may be enforced by way of ordinary action at common law or under the regime contained in the Judgments (International Enforcement) Act 1981.[95]

1.2.1 Enforcement at common law

The basic law of Botswana is to be found in the General Law Proclamation 1909,[96] the General Law (Cape Statutes) Revision Proclamation 1959[97] and the Botswana Independence Act 1966.[98] Section 2 of the General Law Proclamation provides that: 'The laws in force in the Colony of the Cape of Good Hope on 10th day of June, 1891 shall *mutatis mutandis* and so far as not inapplicable be the laws in force and to be observed in [Botswana].'

Section 3(d) of the General Law (Cape Statutes) Revision Proclamation 1959 made clear that it[99] did not affect the

---

[93] *Bid Industrial Holdings (Pty) Ltd v Strang* 2008 (3) SA 355 (SCA) (Howie P, Nugent, Ponnan, Maya JJA and Malan AJA).

[94] As to which, see further below under the sub-heading 'Arrest of individuals *tanquam suspectus de fuga*' in the 'Interim Remedies' section of this chapter.

[95] Act 16 of 1981 (now Cap 11:04 of the Laws of Botswana, 2013).

[96] Proclamation 36 of 1909. So far as material for present purposes, s 2 of the 1909 Proclamation amended s 19 of a Proclamation issued on 10 June 1891 by the High Commissioner for Botswana, which had provided: 'In all suits, actions, or proceedings, civil or criminal, the law to be administered shall, as nearly as the circumstances of the country will permit, be the same as the law for the time being in force in the colony of the Cape of Good Hope: Provided that no Act passed after this date by the Parliament of the Colony of the Cape of Good Hope shall be deemed to apply to the said territory.'

[97] Proclamation 2 of 1959 (now Cap 14:04 of the Laws of Botswana, 2013).

[98] Upon which the Constitution of Botswana, which became effective on 30 September 1966, has not built.

[99] And, principally s 2 thereof, which provided that: 'All laws enacted by the legislative authority of the Colony of the Cape of Good Hope, in force in [Botswana] by virtue of the General Law Proclamation (No 36 of 1909) other than: a) laws which, notwithstanding that they may have been made before the 10th day of June 1891, have been applied to the Territory or to anything in the Territory, by some other Proclamation;

> 'continued application of the Roman Dutch common law in the Territory or of any other laws other than the enactments of the legislative authority of the Colony of the Cape of Good Hope which were in force in the Colony of the Cape of Good Hope on the tenth day of June, 1891, and were in force in [Botswana] at the commencement of this Proclamation'.

On 30 September 1966, Botswana gained independence from Great Britain by virtue of the Botswana Independence Act 1966. Section 2 of the 1966 Act provides that:

> 'On and after the appointed day all law which, whether being a rule of law or a provision of an Act of Parliament or of any other enactment or instrument whatsoever, is in force on that day or has been passed or made before that day and comes into force thereafter, shall, unless and until provision to the contrary is made by Parliament or some other authority having power in that behalf, have the same operation in relation to Botswana, and persons and things belonging to or connected with Botswana, as it would have apart from this subsection if on the appointed day the Bechuanaland Protectorate had been renamed Botswana but there had been no change in its status.'

In the light of those provisions, it appears that Roman-Dutch law is the common law in Botswana, which fact has not been changed by Botswana's independence. This view has been confirmed by the High Court decision in *Dow v Law Society of Botswana*.[100]

In discerning the content of the common law, and generally, the Botswanan courts often refer to, and find highly persuasive, decisions given by courts in the Republic of South Africa.[101] However, it appears that Botswanan courts do not consider themselves bound, as a matter of course, by the way in which South African courts presently interpret and apply Roman-Dutch common law.[102]

In summary, therefore, it appears to be the case that Botswanan courts consider South African decisions – in so far as those decisions interpret and apply Roman-Dutch common law – to be of significant persuasive weight but not binding upon them.

---

and b) the laws specified [in the third column of the schedule to the Proclamation] shall no longer be in force in Botswana.'

[100] [2008] 3 BLR 56 (HC) (Kirby J), para [31].

[101] As explained by Van Niekerk: 'The application of South African law in the courts of Botswana' (2004) *CILSA* 37(3) 312, especially 319–22 in the context of private law. See further: *Chicole v Attorney-General* [1997] BLR 244 (HC) (Cotran J); *Bank of Botswana v Dineo* [1995] BLR 645 and *Makwati v The State* [1996] BLR 682 (CA) (Schreiner, Steyn and Tebbutt JJA) 687, *per* Schreiner JA, where reliance was placed on the decision of a court in the Republic of South Africa in *R v Koning* 1953 (3) SA 220 (T) (Ramsbottom J) to substantiate the conclusion that the appellant was guilty of manslaughter rather than murder.

[102] *The State v Gofhamodimo* [1984] BLR 119 (CA). See further: *Kgoboki v The State* [1985] BLR 380 (HC) (Murray J) 401 and the decision of the Court of Appeal in *Trans Lobatse (Pty) Ltd v Marsh; Mahajan v Trans Lobatse (Pty) Ltd* [1997] BLR 77 (Aguda, Steyn and Tebbutt JJA).

Against that background, the enforcement of foreign judgments pursuant to the common law in Botswana may be considered.[103] In *Design Unit (Pty) Ltd v Tuli Lodge (Pty) Ltd*,[104] Edwards J held that the meaning of a foreign judgment is a matter to be ascertained by applying the usual rules of construction. In an action for provisional sentence the applicant plaintiff sought to enforce a default judgment granted by the Supreme Court of South Africa against a company incorporated in Botswana and having its registered office in Gaborone bearing the same name as the defendant in the Botswanan enforcement proceedings. The respondent contended that the judgment debtor was a South African company of the same name and having its principal place of business in Johannesburg. In construing the South African judgment as concerning the South African company of the same name, Edwards J followed the South African case of *Firestone South Africa (Pty) Ltd v Genticuro AG*[105] where Trollip JA stated:[106] 'The basic principles applicable to construing documents also apply to the construction of a court's judgment or order: the court's intention is to be ascertained primarily from the language of the judgment or order as construed according to the usual well-known rules.'

In *Pretorius v Sweiger (II)*,[107] Edwards J considered an application for judgment in an action for payment of money. The amount claimed was alleged to represent the agreed price of goods sold and delivered and, it appears from the report, the sum also represented (presumably as a claim in the alternative) the amount for which a foreign judgment had been granted. It seems that the judge dismissed the application in so far as it was based on the enforcement of the judgment on the grounds that: (1) the order was in a foreign language and no translation had been supplied; (2) the order had not been authenticated; and (3) there was no averment that the judgment was a final one. (The judge then dismissed the application in so far as it was based on the claim for the price of goods sold and delivered on the ground that the court lacked jurisdiction to hear the claim because the parties were *peregrini* and no other basis for jurisdiction appeared: (1) the plaintiff was 'of Windhoek, Namibia'; (2) the respondent was a South African citizen and lived in Transvaal; (3) no basis for jurisdiction *ratione rei sitae*, *rei gestae* or *contractus* was alleged: 'The time of the Court should not be taken up with disputes, having

---

[103] As to which, certain difficulties may present themselves to a *peregrinus* foreign judgment creditor who is seeking to enforce the foreign judgment against the *peregrinus* judgment debtor. As has been explained above, in order for the Botswanan court to have jurisdiction, the judgment creditor must be able to point to a *ratio jurisdictionis*, which condition he may find difficult to satisfy in the context of actions seeking to enforce a foreign judgment. See further: Frimpong Oppong 'Recognition and enforcement of foreign judgments in Commonwealth African countries' (2014) XV *Yearbook of Private International Law* 365, 370.

[104] [1979–1980] BLR 136 (HC) (Edwards J).

[105] 1977 (4) SA 298 (A) (Trollip, Rabie, Muller, Corbett and De Villiers JJA).

[106] Ibid 298D–E.

[107] [1979–1980] BLR 129 (HC) (Edwards J).

nothing to do with Botswana, between parties neither resident nor domiciled here.' It is not clear what the outcome would have been had the foreign judgment not possessed the defects identified by the judge.)

The plaintiff in *Accurist (SA) (Pty) Ltd v Jan Jacob van Zyl*[108] was the assignee of a South African judgment and sought provisional sentence against the defendant for the judgment debt. The summons claimed an amount in terms of an order of the Supreme Court of South Africa dated 28 November 1975. It was not stated in the summons and it was not apparent from any document exhibited to the summons that the judgment was final. Further, there was evidence that the South African judgment had become superannuated three years after it had been granted. Corduff J refused to grant provisional sentence and held that it must appear from the face of record that the judgment relied on was final and in the instant case it appeared that the judgment was provisional. Further, he held that if a judgment has become superannuated it could not support an action in Botswana. Applying South African procedural law he found that the judgment had become superannuated in 1978, at the expiry of three years after it had been granted.

In *Cloete v Brink*[109] Nganunu J refused to recognise and enforce a South African judgment which the plaintiff had obtained against the defendant from the magistrate's court for the District of Pretoria on the basis that neither the plaintiff nor the defendant were residents of Botswana. The judge[110] rejected an argument that the defendant had submitted to the jurisdiction:

> 'it is a well-known principle of Roman Dutch law that jurisdiction can by prorogation be extended, the defendant's action in submitting or acquiescing to the jurisdiction should be clearly made and if it is being inferred this must be from factors which must only lead to the inference that he intended to submit to the jurisdiction and leave no room for any other inference. See *Du Preez v Philip-King* 1963 (1) S.A. 801.'

The judge further held:[111]

> 'The provisional summons has not shown that this action has anything to do with Botswana or demonstrate that any of the parties are residents in Botswana. In such a case it seems obvious to me that the court is being asked to assume jurisdiction on a matter which may well have nothing to do with this country and of which this court can give no effective implementation after judgment is granted. In a situation of this type a court in Botswana is entitled to refuse to assume jurisdiction even assuming, without deciding so, that the South African judgment does not fall under Act 11:04 [the Judgments (International Enforcement) Act], but that nevertheless it ought to be recognised as a judgment of a competent court.'

---

[108] [1982] 1 BLR 1 (HC) (Corduff J).

[109] [1996] BLR 224 (HC) (Nganunu J).

[110] Ibid 227A–B.

[111] Ibid 227G–H.

The question whether the magistrate's court for the District of Pretoria was a 'superior court' for the purposes of the Judgments (International Enforcement) Act was left open. That said, *Cloete* confirms (as does the next authority cited) that there exists a residual jurisdiction to enforce foreign judgments at common law if the Judgments (International Enforcement) Act does not apply to the judgment in question.

In *Barclays Bank of Swaziland v Koch*[112] the plaintiff sought to enforce a judgment of the High Court of Swaziland against a resident of Botswana. Nganunu CJ noted the plaintiff's position that the judgment was not one registered under section 3 of the Judgments (International Enforcement) Act (without deciding whether it was possible to register a judgment under that section because no order had been published specifying the countries to which section 3 applies) and that it sought to enforce the judgment by way of the provisional sentence procedure provided by the High Court Rules. The judge stated:[113]

> 'common law permits the enforcement of such judgments indirectly through the expeditious procedure of a provisional sentence summons. Certain conditions must, however, be satisfied by a litigant who proposes to take advantage of that procedure. The main points to be satisfied as far as they are relevant to this case are that the judgment must be final and conclusive ... In addition all documents necessary to prove the judgment must be in order and the judgment relied upon as a cause of action should be annexed.'

Nganunu CJ found that the summons for provisional sentence did not attach the judgment itself and that there was no explanation offered for that omission, although the summons did attach the Registrar's certificate (presumably of the High Court of Swaziland) that a judgment had been granted and that it was final and unsatisfied and no appeal had been brought from it. Notwithstanding this certificate, the judge refused the application: 'In my judgment the actual judgment of the court is required to be enclosed and certified by the relevant officer of the court' (and if in a foreign language it must be translated by a sworn translator of the court, although the judge did not specify which court the translator should be authorised by: presumably the foreign court or the Botswana court).[114] The reason for this is that the judgment might disclose that it was based on a cause of action contrary to public policy in Botswana, thereby preventing it from being recognised and enforced in Botswana.

It is noteworthy that in the passage cited above Nganunu CJ relied on the decision of the South African Appellate Division in *Jones v Krok*.[115] There the

---

112 [1997] BLR 1294 (HC) (Nganunu J).

113 Ibid 1297D–G.

114 Ibid 1298A–D.

115 1995 (1) SA 677 (A).

court formulated the principles for enforcement of a foreign judgment at common law as follows:[116]

> 'the present position in South Africa is that a foreign judgment is not directly enforceable, but constitutes a cause of action and will be enforced by our Courts provided (i) that the court which pronounced the judgment had jurisdiction to entertain the case according to the principles recognised by our law with reference to the jurisdiction of foreign courts (sometimes referred to as "international jurisdiction or competence"); (ii) that the judgment is final and conclusive in its effect and has not become superannuated; (iii) that the recognition and enforcement of the judgment by our Courts would not be contrary to public policy; (iv) that the judgment was not obtained by fraudulent means; (v) that the judgment does not involve the enforcement of a penal or revenue law of the foreign State; and (vi)...'.

It is likely that this formulation will be adopted by the Botswanan court.

While foreign matrimonial decrees are not enforceable under the Judgments (International Enforcement) Act, foreign divorce decrees are recognisable and enforceable under the common law provided they meet the common-law principles for recognition of foreign judgments.[117] Only the decrees granted by the courts of the domicile of the parties at the time of their marriage will be recognised in Botswana (a married woman takes on the domicile of her husband on marriage).[118]

Proof of a foreign judgment for the purposes of court proceedings in Botswana is by means of the production of authenticated copies of the judgment purporting to be sealed with the seal of the foreign court.[119]

1.2.2 Enforcement pursuant to statute

1.2.2.1 *The regime for enforcement pursuant to statute*

The preamble to the Judgments (International Enforcement) Act 1981 ('the 1981 Act')[120] states that the 1981 Act is one

> 'to consolidate and amend the law relating to the enforcement in Botswana of judgments given in countries which accord reciprocal treatment to judgments given in Botswana, for facilitating the enforcement in other countries of judgments given in Botswana and for other purposes connected therewith'.

---

[116] Ibid 685B–D.

[117] *Mtui v Mtui* [2000] 1 BLR 406 (HC) (Lisimba J), where a Tanzanian divorce decree was recognised and enforced and the parties' assets situated in Botswana were divided according to Botswanan domestic law: *Gyimah v The Attorney General, ex p Gyimah* [2010] 1 BLR 646 (HC) (Motswagole J).

[118] *Egner v Egner* [1974] 2 BLR 5, *per* Aguda CJ at 6.

[119] *T Shouten's Imports (Pty) Ltd v Wintercom Botswana (Pty) Ltd* [1984] BLR 111 (HC) (Hannah ACJ); and ss 2 and 3 of the Evidence (Commonwealth and Foreign Acts of State and Judgments) Act 1910 (1973 rev) (HCN 68 of 1910, now Cap 10:03 of the Laws of Botswana, 2013).

[120] (Act 16 of 1981) (now Cap 11:04 of the Laws of Botswana, 2013).

In accordance with generally accepted tenets of statutory interpretation, an Act to consolidate and amend is to be interpreted 'like any other statute, namely by giving primacy to the ordinary meaning of their provisions read in context'.[121]

The 1981 Act is divided into three parts. Part I contains the short title to the Act. Part II concerns judgments generally and Part III concerns maintenance orders (defined in section 13(1) as 'an order, other than an order of affiliation, for the periodic payment of sums of money towards the maintenance of the wife of other dependents of the person against whom the order is made ...').[122] The focus of the analysis below is on Part II.

Section 9 of the 1981 Act provides: 'No proceedings for the recovery of a sum payable under a foreign judgment, being a judgment to which this Part applies, other than proceedings by way of registration of the judgment, shall be entertained by any court in Botswana.' Thus foreign judgments within Part II of the 1981 Act are enforceable exclusively through the procedures set out in that Part and are unenforceable otherwise.

Section 2 of the 1981 Act, entitled 'Interpretation', defines the term 'judgment' as follows: 'a judgment or order given or made by a court in any civil proceedings or a judgment or order given or made by a court in any criminal proceedings for the payment of a sum of money in respect of compensation or damages to an injured party ...' and includes an arbitration award if the award has become enforceable in the same manner as a judgment.

It is unclear whether the section 2 definition of the term 'judgment' embraces a judgment for the costs of the judgment creditor incurred in obtaining the judgment abroad. If, for example, the judgment creditor had obtained nominal damages for a breach of contract in the proceedings abroad but had also obtained judgment for substantial costs, would this be a 'judgment' within the meaning of section 2? Such a costs judgment would certainly be a judgment for 'a sum of money'. However, whether a costs judgment would be a judgment 'in respect of compensation or damages to an injured party' is less clear. An award of the costs of litigation is not, without abuse of language, an award of 'damages'. The ordinary meaning of the term 'compensation' is the action of making amends for something, specifically 'money given to compensate for loss or injury'.[123]

---

[121] Bell and Engle *Cross on Statutory Interpretation* 3 ed (1995) 7; Bennion *Bennion on Statutory Interpretation* 5 ed (2008) 605 s 211(4). In *Farrell v Alexander* [1976] 2 All ER 721 (Lord Wilberforce, Viscount Dilhorne and Lords Simon, Edmund-Davies and Russell), Lord Wilberforce stated (at 726b–c): 'self-contained statutes, whether consolidating the previous law, or doing so with amendments, should be interpreted, if reasonably possible, without recourse to antecedents, and ... the recourse should only be had when there is a real and substantial difficulty or ambiguity which classical methods of construction cannot resolve.'

[122] Part III concerns only maintenance, that is, the payment of money and not other matrimonial orders such as custody of children: *Mthethwa v Lebang* [1990] BLR 615 (HC) (Aboagye J). Certain matrimonial decrees are enforceable at common law: see *Mtui v Mtui* [2000] 1 BLR 406 (HC).

[123] *The New Shorter Oxford English Dictionary.*

A legitimate reading of these words is that an award of compensation means a sum awarded to compensate for the primary loss or injury suffered by the judgment creditor which formed the subject of the action in the foreign court and not the costs incurred in pursuing the action and in ultimately obtaining compensation for the original wrong.

However, the better view is, perhaps, that the term 'judgment' in section 2 covers a foreign judgment which includes, in addition to any element of damages or compensation for the primary wrong in respect of which the foreign proceedings were commenced, a sum representing the costs of bringing those proceedings in order to recover the damages or compensation in respect of which the judgment was pronounced, such a sum being one awarded to compensate for the loss of the expenditure in vindicating the judgment creditor's rights. The reasons for preferring this construction are, inter alia, as follows. First, the definition of 'judgment' in section 2 is of sufficient amplitude to include a judgment containing (whether expressly or not) an element in respect of the costs of the foreign proceedings.[124] Second, such a construction achieves the overriding aim of the 1981 Act in giving reciprocal effect to foreign judgments within Botswana where the 1981 Act itself does not clearly exclude any costs element of a foreign judgment from enforcement. Third, a foreign judgment may or may not itself distinguish between the parts of the sum awarded representing costs and damages and in cases where the distinction could not be drawn it would be surprising if the legislature had intended a foreign judgment not to be a 'judgment' within the meaning of the 1981 Act, with the result that the entire judgment was unenforceable.

The matter is not, however, free from doubt.

What is perhaps reasonably free from doubt is that the section 2 definition of 'judgment' excludes judgments for multiple damages, penal damages, exemplary damages and awards not representing compensation in the sense set out above. The dictionary definition of 'damages' is: 'A sum of money claimed or awarded in compensation for loss or injury.'[125] As a matter of ordinary English the terms 'compensation' and 'damages' import the notion of indemnity or a weighing of the loss against the balancing award of money.[126] It is unlikely that a Botswanan court would find that a foreign judgment, which on the evidence was or contained an award of multiple damages or some other penal element, was a 'judgment' for the purposes of section 2 of the 1981 Act. Whether the court could 'blue pencil'

---

124 This construction is also consistent with ss 26 ('Liberal construction') and 27 ('Positive interpretation favoured') of the Interpretation Act 1984 (Act 20 of 1984, now Cap 01:04 of the Laws of Botswana, 2013).

125 *The New Shorter Oxford English Dictionary.*

126 This notion of the loss being in balance with the award is consistent with the Latinate etymology of the word 'compensation' which derives from *cum* meaning with or jointly or together and *pendere* meaning to weigh.

the offending element of the judgment from the genuinely compensatory element is unclear. In cases where the foreign court has itself distinguished between the elements of its judgment, then the proper course might be to permit enforcement of the compensatory element while declining to enforce the punitive element. In cases where the foreign court has not distinguished between the offending and inoffensive elements of its judgment, it would seem that the judgment as a whole is not within the definition of a 'judgment' for the purposes of section 2 of the 1981 Act.[127]

A judgment enforceable under Part II of the 1981 Act is not otherwise enforceable in Botswana. Thus a judgment in respect of costs only (on the assumption that the views expressed above are incorrect) may be enforceable at common law.

Section 3 of the 1981 Act, entitled 'Application of Part II', provides that where the President of Botswana is satisfied that if the benefits of Part II are extended to the superior courts of another country, substantial reciprocity of treatment will be assured then he or she may by statutory instrument order:[128] (1) that Part II shall extend to that country; and (2) that such courts of that country as are specified in the order shall be the superior courts of that country for the purposes of Part II.

A judgment of a superior court of a country to which Part II is extended is a judgment to which Part II applies if the following cumulative conditions are satisfied: (1) it is final and conclusive between the parties (notwithstanding any appeal against the judgment); (2) the judgment is for a sum of money and not for a sum in respect of taxes, other charges of like nature or a fine or penalty; and (3) the judgment is given after the coming into operation of the order extending Part II to the superior courts of that country.

Section 4 of the 1981 Act, entitled 'Continuance of existing provisions', provides that Part II 'also extends to every country to which the United Kingdom Judgments Act applied immediately before the commencement of this Part'. The term 'the United Kingdom Judgments Act' is not defined in section 2 of the 1981 Act nor is it referred to in the Interpretation Act 1984. The United Kingdom has only one statute entitled 'Judgments Act' which is the Judgments Act 1838, the operation of which is confined to England and Wales.

---

[127] Such a judgment might well be one which in any event falls within the public policy defence afforded by s 7(1)(a)(v) of the 1981 Act: see *Dicey, Morris and Collins on the Conflict of Laws* 15 ed (2012) rule 51 at 737; paras 14–157.

[128] To date, it seems that no such order has been made: See further *Barclays Bank of Swaziland v Koch* [1997] BLR 1294 (HC) in which the plaintiff contended that it could not register its judgment under the 1981 Act because no order under s 3 had been published specifying the countries to which that section applied. Nganunu CJ declined to deal with this point, deciding the case instead on the plaintiff's compliance with the requirements of the provisional sentence procedure.

The United Kingdom Acts which are concerned with the enforcement of foreign judgments within the United Kingdom are the Administration of Justice Act 1920 and the Foreign Judgments (Reciprocal Enforcement) Act 1933.[129] These Acts permit enforcement within the United Kingdom of judgments made by courts in a variety of Commonwealth and other countries such as Gambia, Kenya, Lesotho, Malawi and Israel. It is unclear whether the reference in section 4 of the 1981 Act is to either or both of these Acts, although, if it is not, then it is difficult to understand to what the reference might be. Legislative clarification of this point is desirable.

Section 4(2) further provides that the President may by statutory instrument declare, as regards any country, that it is a country to which section 4(1) applies and may specify which of the courts of that country are superior courts for the purposes of Part II of the 1981 Act.[130]

1.2.2.2 *Procedure for registration*

Section 5 contains provisions concerning the registration of foreign judgments with the Botswana High Court. A judgment creditor has six years from the date of the foreign judgment or the date of the last judgment in the foreign proceedings if there was an appeal, to have the judgment registered in the High Court.

A judgment shall not be registered either if it has been wholly satisfied or it could not be enforced by execution in the country of the original court. Subject to the provisions of section 7 relating to the setting aside of a registered judgment, registration of a foreign judgment means that it may be enforced as if it were a judgment of the Botswana court: proceedings may be taken on the judgment; the sum for which the judgment is registered carries interest; and the registering court has the same control over the execution of a registered judgment. If expressed in foreign currency, the judgment is registered in Pula at the rate of exchange obtaining at the date of the judgment of the original court. The judgment may also be registered for the reasonable costs of and incidental to registration. Under section 5(4) execution shall not issue on the judgment so long as under the 1981 Act and the rules of court made under it[131] 'it is competent for any party to make an application to have the registration of the judgment set aside' or, where an application is made, that application has been finally determined.

[129] The Civil Jurisdiction and Judgments Act 1982, Regulation (EU) 1215/2012 and the Lugano Convention on jurisdiction and the recognition and enforcement of judgments in civil and commercial matters 2007 (OJ L 147, 10 June 2009) are concerned with the arrangements for enforcement of judgments within the United Kingdom itself and within the European Union and European Free Trade Association respectively.

[130] As far as can be ascertained, no such statutory instrument has been made under s 4(2) to date.

[131] As to which see below.

It seems to the authors that the former bar to execution should be construed as requiring a challenge to the judgment to be issued within a reasonable time or within such time as the registering court directs on registration, otherwise the terms of section 5(4) might permit a judgment debtor to frustrate the execution of a registered judgment by simply doing nothing but assert that he is a party competent to make an application to have the judgment set aside while not taking any steps to do so.

Section 6 contains provisions for the making of rules of court for various purposes relating to the objects of Part II of the 1981 Act: (1) for the giving of security for costs by persons applying for registration of a judgment; (2) for the matters to be proved on an application for the registration of a judgment and for regulating the mode of providing those matters; (3) for the service on the judgment debtor of notice of the registration of the judgment; (4) for the fixing of the period within which an application may be made to have the registration set aside; (5) for the method by which any question under Part II of the 1981 Act whether a foreign judgment can be enforced by execution in the foreign court or the interest payable under the judgment under the law of the foreign court is to be determined; (6) for any other matter which under Part II is to be prescribed.[132]

1.2.2.3 *Setting aside registration*

Section 7 sets out those cases in which a registered judgment must or may be set aside.[133] The registration of a judgment *must* be set aside if the registering court is satisfied (section 7(1)(a)) that: (1) the judgment is not one to which Part II applies; (2) the courts in the country of origin had no jurisdiction in the case; (3) the judgment debtor did not receive sufficient notice in the original proceedings to enable him to defend those proceedings; (4) the judgment was obtained by fraud;[134] (5) the enforcement of the judgment would be contrary to public policy

---

[132] So far as can be ascertained from the Botswana Rules of the High Court 2011 (SI 1 of 2011), no such rules relating to foreign judgments have yet been made. (For example, the language of O 57 'Security for Costs', appears not to cover a case of the enforcement of a foreign judgment by registration because O 57(1) envisages the jurisdiction being triggered by the 'commencement of proceedings' which is not an act which is apt to describe the registration of a judgment in accordance with s 5(1) of the 1981 Act.)

[133] The provisions of s 7 are materially identical to the terms of s 4 of the United Kingdom Foreign Judgments (Reciprocal Enforcement) Act 1933. Accordingly, authorities decided under the English 1933 Act may prove of use to the construction of s 7 of the 1981 Act.

[134] See *Dicey, Morris and Collins on the Conflict of Laws* 15 ed (2012) rule 50 at 727; *Owens Bank Ltd v Bracco* [1992] 2 AC 443 (HL) (E), in which it was held that the fraud defence was not limited to fraud which was extraneous or collateral to the dispute which the foreign court determined and applied equally to fraud which was intrinsic to the foreign proceedings. The fraud defence is therefore broad: 'if the fraud upon the foreign court consists in the fact that the plaintiff has induced that court by fraud to come to a wrong conclusion, you can reopen the whole case even although you will have in this court to go into the very facts which were investigated and which were in issue in the foreign proceedings': *per* Lindley LJ in *Vadala v Lawes*

of the country of the registering court;[135] or (6) the rights under the judgment are not vested in the person applying for registration.

Section 7(2) sets out three deeming provisions relating to the jurisdiction of the courts of the country in which the judgment was obtained. First, the foreign court is deemed to have had jurisdiction in actions *in personam* where the judgment debtor: (1) submitted to the jurisdiction of the court by voluntarily appearing in the proceedings; (2) was a plaintiff or counterclaimant in the proceedings; (3) had agreed to submit to the jurisdiction of the court before proceedings; (4) at the time of the proceedings was resident in or, if a legal person, had its principal place of business in the country of the relevant foreign court; (5) had an office or place of business in the country of the relevant foreign court. Second, in the case of actions where the subject-matter is immovable property or an action *in rem* of which the subject was movable property, if the property was at the time of the proceedings situated in the country of the relevant foreign court. Third, in all other cases, if the jurisdiction of the original court is recognised by the registering court.

Section 7(3) provides that the courts of the country of the original court shall not be deemed to have had jurisdiction if: (1) the subject-matter of the proceedings was immovable property outside the country of the original court; or (2) the bringing of proceedings in the original court was contrary to an agreement under which the dispute was to be settled otherwise than by proceedings in the courts of the country of that court except where the judgment debtor: submitted by entering an appearance; was a plaintiff or a counterclaimant; agreed to submit to the jurisdiction; or where the foreign court is otherwise recognised as having jurisdiction by the registering court; or (3) the judgment debtor had immunity from the jurisdiction of the foreign court under public international law and did not submit to the jurisdiction of the foreign court.

Section 7(1)(b) provides that the registration of a judgment may be set aside if the registering court is satisfied that the matter in dispute in the proceedings

---

(1890) 25 QBD 310, CA at 316–17. This line of English authority has not been followed in Canada and New South Wales, Australia (see *Dicey, Morris and Collins* op cit). The fraud defence is likely to be identical with that available under the common law.

[135] See *Dicey, Morris and Collins on the Conflict of Laws* 15 ed (2012) rule 51, at 735: such as recognising and enforcing a judgment obtained in breach of an injunction not to proceed in a foreign court (see the authorities cited in *Dicey, Morris and Collins* op cit 736 fn 562). The denial of natural justice defence provided by s 7(1)(a)(iii), failure to receive any or any adequate notice of proceedings, may also be characterised as a public policy defence. It may be that other natural justice defences can be accommodated within the public policy defence. (*Habib Bank Ltd v Ahmed* [2001] EWCA Civ 1270, [2002] 1 Lloyd's Rep 444, is cited by Briggs in *Civil Jurisdiction and Judgments* 6 ed (2015) 790 para 7.92, as an example of such a case, *sed quaere* whether it is a true example: in *Habib Bank* the Court of Appeal in allowing an appeal against registration found that the judge at first instance had failed to give sufficient reasons for dismissing a fraud on the court argument advanced by the judgment debtor rather than identifying any offence to English public policy in the proceedings in Pakistan.)

in the foreign court had previously been the subject of a final and conclusive judgment by a court having jurisdiction in the matter. Section 8(1), which is set out below, provides a further discretionary ground for setting aside registration.

Section 8 makes provision for the powers of the registering court on an application to set aside registration. Sub-section (1) provides that if on an application to set aside the registration of a judgment the plaintiff satisfied the court either that an appeal is pending or that he is entitled and intends to appeal against the judgment, the court may set aside the registration of the judgment, or adjourn the application to set aside registration on such terms as it thinks fit until after the expiration of such period as appears to the court to be reasonable to enable the judgment debtor to take the steps necessary to have the appeal disposed of.

If the reason for setting aside registration is that the judgment is not enforceable by execution in the country of origin this does not prevent a further application when the judgment becomes enforceable.[136]

Where a judgment is set aside solely because at the date of the application for registration the judgment had been partly satisfied, the court may, on the application of the judgment creditor, order judgment to be registered for the balance outstanding.[137]

Section 10 addresses the recognition of foreign judgments in Botswana and provides that, subject to limited exceptions set out in sub-section (2), a judgment to which Part II applies (or would have applied if the judgment had not been satisfied) whether registered or not shall be recognised in any court in Botswana as conclusive as between the parties thereto in all proceedings founded on the same cause of action and may be relied on by way of defence or counterclaim in any such proceedings.

Section 11 deals with the power of the President by statutory instrument to exclude the judgments of the courts of a country from Part II where the recognition of Botswana judgments by that country is 'substantially less favourable' than the recognition by that country of Botswanan judgments. Section 12 deals with the issuing to Botswana judgment creditors of certified copies of judgments which are entered in the High Court.

---

[136] Section 8(2).

[137] Section 8(3).

1.3 Interim Remedies

1.3.1 Jurisdiction to grant interim remedies

Interim relief is available[138] in Botswana and may be granted: on an interlocutory application at a hearing pre-trial conducted in conformity with procedural steps provided for in the relevant provision in the Rules; on an urgent application on notice to the respondent to that application; or on an *ex parte* application without notice to the respondent to that application. Urgent applications on notice and *ex parte* applications without notice for interim relief represent significant departures from the Rules and will be granted only if certain conditions are met.

1.3.2 Procedure

Order 12 of the Rules makes provision for the making of applications to the court. Every application (with the exception of petitions) shall be made on notice of motion supported by an affidavit setting out the facts on which the plaintiff relies for his relief.[139] At the hearing of the application the Rules provide that the judge may grant or dismiss the application or grant interim relief.[140] The Rules do not specify what interim relief is available to a plaintiff/applicant.

It is not apparent from the reported authorities whether the jurisdiction of the court extends to granting pre-action interim relief but the wording of the relevant Rule would seem to be of sufficient breadth to accommodate such an application.

1.3.2.1 *Urgency*

The jurisdiction of the court to entertain urgent applications on notice and *ex parte* applications without notice for interim relief is set out in Order 12, rule 12 of the Rules, which provides, inter alia:

> '(1) In urgent applications the court or a judge may dispense with the forms and service provided for in these Rules and may dispose of such matters at such time and place and in such a manner, and in accordance with such procedure (which shall as far as practicable be in terms of these Rules) as it seems meet.
>
> (2) In every affidavit or petition filed in support of any application under sub-rule (1) the plaintiff shall set forth explicitly the circumstances which he avers render the matter urgent and the reasons why he claims that he could not be afforded substantial redress at a hearing in due course.'

---

[138] This is made clear by s 95(5) of the Botswana Constitution 1966 (as amended), which provides: 'The High Court shall have jurisdiction to supervise any civil or criminal proceedings before any subordinate court or any court martial and may make such orders, issue such writs and give such directions as it may consider appropriate for the purpose of ensuring that justice is duly administered by any such court.'

[139] Rule 1.

[140] Order 12, r 4(3).

An urgent application is made by notice of motion and supported by affidavit evidence and must be accompanied by a certificate of urgency signed by the plaintiff's attorney confirming that the case is one of urgency as deposed to by his client indicating the reasons for the urgency such that the normal rules as to the time for service and sitting times of the court can be dispensed with.

The requirement for a certificate of urgency is one imposed by a practice direction given by the Registrar.[141]

In *Letsoalo v Lesuma Trading Co (Pty) Ltd*,[142] Nganunu J held[143] that, in signing such a certificate, the attorney is acting in a dual capacity:

> 'Firstly, as an officer of the court and, secondly, as the guardian of the interests of his client. The attorney signing the certificate should act in good faith, bearing in mind that the court should treat such a certificate seriously. The affidavit supporting the case must make out a case for urgency and the signed certificate does not ipso facto establish urgency.'

The judge also observed[144] that urgency is a matter of degree:

> 'The Rules of Court and the established procedures should only be dispensed with to the extent necessitated by the urgency of the matter. Urgency has degrees and where a matter, though urgent, is not desperately urgent so as to require immediate court attention a litigant is required to comply with the Rules to the extent possible and to move the court in a reasonable manner and not a desperate hurry.'

In *Letsoalo* itself the urgent application was made on 22 June 1993 for hearing the same day and was opposed. The basis for the urgency in the application was that the defendant had allegedly unlawfully dispossessed the plaintiff of his Nissan 1 Tonner V6 and that had prejudiced the plaintiff in the running of his business. In dismissing the application for, among other grounds, want of urgency, the judge stated:[145] 'I do get the impression that some attorneys have taken the view that the signed certificate ipso facto establishes urgency. That is obviously not so.'

Four years after his decision in *Letsoalo*, in *Big Game Development Co (Botswana) (Pty) Ltd v De Kock*,[146] Nganunu J considered it necessary on an urgent application to re-emphasise the observations he had made regarding the making of certificates of urgency:[147]

---

[141] This practice direction is referred to in the judgment of Nganunu J in *Late Our Properties (Pty) Ltd v First National Bank of Botswana Ltd* [1997] BLR 618 (HC). In that case the certificate of urgency stated: 'I have read the aforesaid affidavit ... and hereby certify that the applicants' special circumstances render the application urgent and calls for the rules relating to the time to be dispensed with.' No urgency was established by the applicants in that case.

[142] [1993] BLR 214 (HC) (Nganunu J).

[143] Ibid 216.

[144] Ibid in the headnote.

[145] Ibid 216.

[146] [1997] BLR 301 (HC) (Nganunu J).

[147] Ibid 305C–F.

'The urgency rules are a clear departure from the general requirement that all litigants must be given an opportunity to defend their causes, and this is secured by the Rules regarding service of process, notices and the *dies* allowed them to do so. Some urgency may not require complete suspension of and departure from all such rules in order to afford adequate justice to the person initiating the proceedings. Urgency is relative. It is important that practitioners must not abuse this exceptional practice for the simple reason that it deprives the opposite party of their usual rights and upsets the orderly despatch of court business. Constant and persistent disturbance of court and judges' schedules results in chaos. Practice has shown that the rule is quite clearly abused and practitioners have resorted to signing certificates of urgency not because of any urgency but to gain an advantage of one type or another to which their clients are then not entitled. The advantage that practitioners most often aim at is to have their cases heard before the time they could have otherwise been heard if they follow the ordinary rules. This may be because the courts are congested, but jumping the queue, as it were, is not conducive to proper disposal of other cases nor fair to opponents. So abridgement to the rules should be made for just cause and any allegation of urgency must meet the requirements of subrule (2).'

In that case the judge found that there were no reasons why shortened but more reasonable periods of service would not have been appropriate.[148]

In *Auto Rhine (Pty) Ltd v Zentek Electronics Botswana (Pty) Ltd*,[149] Mosojane J considered an urgent application where the applicant (the defendant in the substantive proceedings) sought an order for a rule *nisi* requiring the respondent (the plaintiff in the substantive proceedings) to show cause why a default judgment previously obtained by the respondent should not be discharged and the applicant granted leave to defend the previous proceedings and suspend the attachment by the deputy sheriff pursuant to the default judgment of the applicant's tools of trade. The applicant contended that the summons on which default judgment had been obtained had never been served on him. The urgency alleged related to the threatened seizure by the deputy sheriff of the attached property which the applicant stated was vital to the operation of the company and that removal of the property would result in loss of revenue. The judge found that the application had been made promptly and that the fear that the deputy sheriff would return and remove the property was not unfounded. The judge further found that no prejudice had been established by the respondent in the ordering of a rule *nisi* pending determination of the allegations concerning the default judgment.

---

148 The *Big Game* case suggests that the courts will consider urgency not as an absolute value but a relative one justifying varying degrees of departure from the Rules, depending on the degree of urgency. However, in practice urgent applications tend to be all or nothing to be heard within days of the notice of motion being issued rather than in compliance with a timetable representing a graduated departure from the Rules.

149 [1997] BLR 1309 (HC) (Mosojane J).

The judge then considered the respondent's contention that the fact that the applicant might suffer financial loss unless the matter was heard immediately did not bring a case within the embrace of urgency.[150] In rejecting this argument the judge stated:[151]

> 'A large proportion of the cases I have seen so far coming before the courts in this country on [an] urgent basis involve matters of interest to commerce and business in one form or another and the loss or retention of revenue. It just depends from which angle the argument is presented and what is really at stake, and I cannot accept as a general rule that matters of threatened financial loss cannot be argued before the courts in an urgent application. I would have thought that commercial interests and revenue form the bulk of litigation in the courts and do find their way quite prominently into urgent applications. Should these be rejected out of hand? I do not agree.'

The judge found that the application was urgent.

Urgency was also found in *Hinton v Fair Deal Wooden Windows (Pty) Ltd*,[152] where the court made an order on an urgent application for the tenant of certain premises to be evicted from those premises. Sarkodie-Mensah AJ stated:[153]

> 'The question of urgency must be adjudicated upon taking the circumstances and the apparent harm likely to be caused to the [plaintiff] into consideration. In proceeding by way of urgency, what the [plaintiff] is asking the court to do is to dispense with the forms and service provided for in the rules and to dispose of the matter at such short notice and in a manner and in accordance with procedures as would meet the justice of the case. In doing so, the [plaintiff] is seeking to ruffle the feathers of the court and he must have very good reasons for so doing.'

In the instant case the plaintiff made the application two days after the defendant's lease expired and the plaintiff had a tenant ready to take up occupation of the premises but was being prevented from doing so by the former tenant in possession.

Where the urgency of the application is as a result of the plaintiff's own conduct in failing to raise in earlier proceedings issues of the ownership of a particular property in respect of which the plaintiff then sought urgent interim relief in later proceedings, the application in later proceedings was not found to be urgent.[154]

---

[150] An argument which may have read across into the test for urgency a consideration which is taken into account in the decision whether to grant an interim interdict (where the question whether the applicant can be recompensed at trial for any financial loss caused to him by the interdict not being granted arises).

[151] [1997] BLR 1309 at 1313H–1314A.

[152] [2006] 1 BLR 142 (HC) (Sarkodie-Mensah AJ).

[153] Ibid 144A–C.

[154] *Makome Syndicate v Masowe Syndicate* [2002] 1 BLR 442 (HC) (Lesetedi J) in which the applicant (the defendant in the substantive proceedings) sought to set aside an eviction order made in earlier proceedings and sought an order restraining the respondents (the plaintiffs in the substantive proceedings) from watering their livestock at a borehole allegedly owned by certain of the applicants: 'The [defendant] applicants have

Delay in the bringing of an allegedly urgent application may count against the application being accepted as urgent for the purposes of Order 12, rule 12. In *Carlton Motors (Pty) Ltd v Stanbic Bank Botswana*[155] the plaintiffs in earlier proceedings had entered judgment in default of appearance against the defendants on 2 September 2002 and a warrant of execution over the movable property of the defendants was issued the same day. The plaintiffs made an attachment of the defendants' property on 2 October 2002. The defendants were aware by mid-October 2002 that the judgment in default had been entered yet delayed until early March 2003 in bringing an application to have the judgment rescinded, at which time the deputy sheriff had not yet taken steps to remove the attached property. The court held that the defendants' application did not satisfy the requirements of Order 12, rule 12, and observed:[156]

> 'It is upon a party against whom judgment has been granted to expeditiously take steps to have the said judgment set aside if it contests the validity of such judgment. Such a party cannot sit on its rights over an extended period of time only to come to court on a certificate of urgency at such a late stage when there is not even precipitative action on the part of the other side.'

To similar effect are *CBS Advertising Agency (Pty) Ltd v Lebopo Engineering (Pty) Ltd*[157] (where a delay of five months in making an application was fatal); *Norbundi Pty Ltd v Botswana Building Society*[158] (where the application was made in July 2010 in respect of a judgment entered in November 2007); *Malele v Registrar of Trade Unions*[159] where no complaint had been made about the matters in issue for five years and the claim itself was weak); and *Collins Newman & Co v Geniuspoint Investments (Pty) Ltd*[160] (where a delay of seven months was fatal).

Further it has been held:[161] 'Urgency must be made out of the facts which by themselves render a matter urgent. In other words, it must be an objective assessment of the facts which render a matter urgent.' This statement was made in the context of an application which was said by the plaintiff to be urgent for reasons which were mistaken when assessed objectively.

Raisi v Chairman Limkokwing University[162] illustrates the breadth of the discretion conferred on the court by Order 12, rule 12. The plaintiff brought an

for some considerable time been aware of the dispute and were not diligent enough to present their case properly in the first instance.'

[155] [2003] 1 BLR 307 (HC) (Lesetedi J).

[156] Ibid 311D–E.

[157] [2007] 2 BLR 533 (HC) (Walia J).

[158] [2010] 3 BLR 305 (HC) (Tshosa J).

[159] [2011] 2 BLR 887 (HC) (Garekwe J).

[160] [2018] 2 BLR 140 (HC) (Leburu J).

[161] *Botswana Ash (Pty) Ltd v Zuzumbe (Pty) Ltd* [2003] 1 BLR 58 (HC) 62 (Monthe AJ); followed in *Ndlera v Voice of Power Ministries International* (unreported) 6 February 2013 (HC) (Tau J).

[162] [2010] 3 BLR 171 (HC) (Leburu AJ).

urgent application seeking an order reviewing and setting aside a decision made in disciplinary proceedings brought against him by the defendant by which the plaintiff was dismissed from his employment with the defendant. The plaintiff's uncontested evidence was that he was an expatriate who had a wife and two children to support and that he had financial obligations and no other source of income other than his employment with the defendant. Leburu AJ, citing *Carlton Motors* and *Botswana Ash*, dismissed the application on the ground that it was not urgent because the plaintiff had 'failed to adduce explicit facts which render this matter urgent'. The brief report does not reveal the financial circumstances of the plaintiff. For example, it does not appear what, if any, savings the plaintiff or his family might have had available to them to see them through to a substantive hearing of his complaint in due course or whether the plaintiff's job prospects were such that he could have found alternative employment without too much difficulty. Further, there is no analysis of the strengths of the plaintiff's case against the defendant. As a decision simply on the facts as they appear from the report, it seems harsh.

On occasion, the urgency of an application is assumed and the question whether an application brought on an urgent basis is indeed urgent is not separately considered.[163]

These authorities establish that the test for whether an application is urgent, for the purposes of Order 12, rule 12, is a broad test which takes into account: any delay in the bringing of the application; the nature of the issues in the case; what, if any, prejudice will be suffered by the defendant; and what, if any, loss will be suffered by the plaintiff if the procedures set out in the Rules are not departed from in the particular case. Doubtless the range of factors to be taken into account is not closed and each case will be considered on its merits.

The decision of Kirby J in *Kgosiencho v Sechele*[164] ('the *Sechele* case') represents an elaboration of this broad test, introducing into it elements of the requirements considered on an *ex parte* application for relief where quite different considerations obtain. The *Sechele* case concerned an attempt by certain members of the royal family to prevent the burial of the late Mokgallagadi Sechele, the regent of the Bakwena tribe. The notice of motion seeking the interim order preventing the burial scheduled for Saturday 7 October 2000 (and a final order preventing burial in the Royal graveyard at Molepolole) was filed on the morning of Thursday 5 October. The case was heard *inter partes* by Kirby J on Friday 6 October and he

[163] *Pule v Lobatse Town Council* [2006] 1 BLR 481 (HC) which concerned the validity of the removal of an elected deputy mayor of Lobatse and his imminent replacement by way of a vote by the council. Newman J did not separately consider whether the applicant's application was urgent and the respondents did not contend otherwise.

[164] [2000] 2 BLR 344 (HC).

gave judgment the same day noting that:[165] 'This judgment has been prepared in considerable haste and it is not as full as it would otherwise have been.' The judge stated[166] that in urgent applications 'of this nature' the following conditions were required to be satisfied:

> '(1) An adequate basis of urgency should be laid in order to dispense with the normal time limits; (2) Proper evidence of the authority and locus standi of the [plaintiff] must be furnished; (3) Full and honest disclosure must be made by the [plaintiff] of all facts relevant to the issue, including circumstances adverse to the [plaintiff] which are within the [plaintiff's] knowledge. This is especially so if very short notice is given, due to the circumstances; (4) Reasonable notice must be given to parties who may be adversely affected by the order sought unless the circumstances render this impossible; (5) The [plaintiff] must show substantial prejudice or potential prejudice if the order is not granted as a matter of urgency.'

In setting out these five requirements in such general terms, Kirby J appears to have intended that they should apply to all urgent applications and not simply the one of which he was seised. In formulating these requirements as he did, the judge introduced into the test for urgency under Order 12, rule 12 a requirement of disclosure which is a characteristic of *ex parte* applications and had not previously been a requirement of urgent applications which are *inter partes.*

The judge cited no authority in support of the application of these five requirements to urgent applications in general and the application of requirements (3), (4) and (5) does not even appear to have been argued by counsel for the respondents.

Kirby J refused the application on the basis that of the five requirements he set out only the first, the requirement of urgency, had been satisfied.

In *African Alliance Botswana Ltd v Botswana Public Officers' Pension Fund*[167] ('the *African Alliance* case'), Kirby J considered an urgent application for an interim order setting aside the cancellation of a management agreement. In dismissing the application the judge, inter alia, relied on his decision in the *Sechele* case and stated:[168]

> 'The [plaintiff] must show an adequate basis for urgency, rendering compliance with the usual rules inappropriate, and that he will suffer substantial actual or potential prejudice if the order sought is not urgently granted. He must also make full and honest disclosure of all relevant facts including those that may be prejudicial to him. Finally he must give reasonable notice of the proceedings to affected parties unless the circumstances render that impossible or impracticable.'

---

[165] Ibid 349C.

[166] Ibid 346G–347B.

[167] [2007] 3 BLR 391 (HC).

[168] Ibid 394H–395A.

The judge found that none of these requirements had been satisfied.

The *African Alliance* case was cited in *Malele v Registrar of Trade Unions*[169] by Garekwe J in formulating a statement of the test under Order 12, rule 12, which included the requirement that the plaintiff make 'full and honest disclosure of all relevant facts including those that may be prejudicial to him'. Garekwe J then repeated this formulation in *JH Zikhale Motorway Pty Ltd v Thipe Transport Holdings.*[170]

It is unusual to impose on the plaintiff in an *inter partes* application (ie the party making the application) a duty of full disclosure of all facts relevant to the matter in issue before the court. A conventional view of adversarial proceedings would dictate that it is for each party to pursue its own interests and defend its own position without the advantage of assistance from the other party by reason of a requirement imposed by the court that that other party should render such assistance.

The rationale of the requirement in *ex parte* applications (which type of applications are explored in more depth below) that the plaintiff is under a duty of full and frank disclosure of all material facts (and law) relevant to the application is that the judge is hearing the application in the absence of the defendant/respondent to that application. This raises the prospect of the court making an order on a false basis and so the court imposes the duty of disclosure on the plaintiff to ensure so far as possible that the order is not made on a false basis. The penalty for breach of the duty of disclosure is the discharge of the order. This rationale is wholly absent in the case of an urgent application conducted *inter partes.*

It may be that the circumstances in which the urgent application was made in the *Sechele* case led Kirby J to treat it as if it were an *ex parte* application and by doing so apply a more stringent test than that which had previously been applied to urgent applications. If so, then this is entirely understandable, given that those circumstances included the following: counsel for the plaintiffs accepted that in issuing the application on Thursday 5 October the plaintiffs intended to apply *ex parte* but that the Registrar required the plaintiffs to serve the motion on the defendants; and the motion was served on the defendants on Thursday night for the hearing on Friday morning. As Kirby J observed, this meant 'effectively leaving the [defendants] one night during which to brief attorneys and prepare, if so advised, their papers in opposition'.[171]

[169] [2011] 2 BLR 887 (HC).

[170] [2011] 2 BLR 950 (HC).

[171] [2000] 2 BLR 344 (HC), 348D. It is noteworthy that in two cases in which the *Sechele* case has been cited and followed, the applications under consideration were *ex parte* applications (even though they were characterised by the judge in each case, Dambe J, as urgent applications): *Sutai Construction Machinery Repair*

If not, then the *Sechele* case should be confined to its own facts and the test applied to urgent applications should remain the broad test outlined above.

Similar points can be made regarding the *African Alliance* case.

It is, therefore, unfortunate that the *African Alliance* case has been followed in two recent decisions of the High Court and it is to be hoped that orthodoxy will reassert itself and that the test for urgency under Order 12, rule 12 will return to that set out in the cases referred to earlier.

1.3.2.2 Ex parte *applications*

Applications may be made *ex parte*[172] and a person against whom an *ex parte* order is made may anticipate the return day on giving not less than 24 hours' notice.[173]

If the court accedes to the *ex parte* application, it grants a rule *nisi* usually operating as an interim interdict and on the return date the defendant must show cause why the interim interdict should not be continued to trial or other determination of the cause.[174]

The test for the granting of such an application was set out in *Moerane v Phiri*[175] in which the plaintiff applied by way of notice of motion for an interim order in the form of a rule *nisi* requiring the defendant to show cause why a deputy sheriff should not take into his possession a certain vehicle. The underlying allegation was that the plaintiff alleged he had sold the vehicle to the defendant and, having paid the plaintiff a deposit for the vehicle and received delivery of it, the defendant had failed to pay the balance due under the sale agreement. The application for an interim order was filed on 22 April 1998 and the motion was moved *ex parte* before the Registrar on 4 May 2000. On the same day the plaintiff issued a writ of summons seeking payment of the balance of the purchase price of the vehicle and costs.

The Registrar made the order sought and by the return day (22 May 1998) the defendant had been served with the order (but not the notice of motion and founding affidavit) and the deputy sheriff had seized the vehicle. In June 1998 the plaintiff served his writ of summons on the defendant. The rule *nisi* was extended from time to time until it came before Horn Ag J on 23 August 2000.

Pty Ltd v Landscape Decorators Pty Ltd [2011] 1 BLR 19 (HC); and *Experience Count Pty Ltd v Owhin Estates Pty Ltd* [2011] 1 BLR 200 (HC), see below.

172 Order 12, r 4.

173 Order 12, r 8.

174 This contrasts with the position in other jurisdictions, for example, England, where the hearing on the return date is a renewed application by the applicant for the relief granted *ex parte*.

175 [2000] 2 BLR 219 (HC) (Horn Ag J).

Horn Ag J approved[176] the test for the making of an order *ex parte* as set out in *Republic Motors (Pvt) Ltd v Lytton Road Service Station (Pvt) Ltd*:[177]

> 'The procedure of approaching the Court *ex parte* should be sparingly employed and carefully disciplined by the existence of factors of such urgency, or of well-founded apprehension of perverse conduct on the part of the [defendant] who is informed beforehand that resort will be had to the assistance of the Court, that the course of justice stands in danger of frustration unless temporary curial intervention can be unilaterally obtained.'

In dismissing the application with costs, the judge agreed with submissions by the defendant's counsel that: (1) the plaintiff had not established a *prima facie* right to possess the vehicle; (2) the plaintiff had been guilty of material non-disclosure in that he had failed to inform the court that he had facilitated the transfer of the vehicle to the respondent's name which was highly relevant because the plaintiff contended that ownership of the vehicle did not pass on delivery; (3) no good reason had been given in the founding affidavit to justify the application being made *ex parte*. On the third point the judge stated:[178]

> 'I am of the opinion that the application for confirmation must fail. In my view the invocation of *ex parte* proceedings without notice to the [defendant] constituted, in the circumstances of this case, a gross abuse of the process of the court not only because no grounds were stated for the alleged belief from the [plaintiff] that the [defendant] would conceal the motor car if he had notice of the application but also because the application was totally misconceived and this would have been apparent if the [defendant] had been given an opportunity to oppose the grant of the rule.'[179]

It does not appear that the plaintiff in the case gave or was required to give any undertakings to the court: (1) to serve the notice of motion and founding affidavit forthwith; or (2) in the event that the court found that the rule ought not to have been granted to indemnify and pay the defendant for any loss or damage he may have suffered by reason of the rule having been granted.[180]

The *Moerane* case illustrates the desirability of the cross-undertaking as to damages generally. The defendant, an aspiring taxi driver, had been deprived of the use of the vehicle from June 1998 to early September 2000, well over two years, during which time not only was he unable to turn it to commercial use (or alternatively, he was unable to resell the car and thereby avoid suffering over two years' depreciation in its value), but also the physical condition of the vehicle would inevitably have deteriorated through non-use.

---

176 Ibid 224E.

177 1971 (2) SA 516 (R) (Beck J).

178 [2000] 2 BLR 219 at 225B–C.

179 Indeed, in commencing his judgment, the judge had described the case as 'one of the worst cases I have come across of a litigant snatching an order obtained on an *ex parte* application'.

180 The absence of a cross-undertaking as to damages further meant that the question whether that undertaking should be fortified by a payment into court did not arise.

In *First National Bank of Botswana Ltd v Ditshotlo (Practice Note)*,[181] heard shortly after the *Moerane* case, Horn Ag J refused to extend a rule *nisi* granted *ex parte* expressing the view:[182] 'I am not prepared to "rubber stamp" orders for creditors to seize from their debtors, without notice, property which they have leased or sold to the debtor.' The judge emphasised again that what was required for this sort of procedure were facts satisfying the test set out in the *Republic Motors* case he relied on in the *Moerane* case.

In *First National Bank of Botswana Ltd v Taimu*,[183] the court discharged a rule *nisi*, which had been made *ex parte*, on the return date. The plaintiff (for these purposes, the party seeking the order), who had delayed for seven months before bringing the application, wanted to obtain possession of a vehicle; the vehicle was in the possession of the defendant. Chatikobo J found that the order had been made without disclosure of all material facts in that the judge making the order had not been informed that, as the plaintiff knew, the defendant had indicated his willingness to continue making payments for the vehicle and had drawn a cheque in favour of the plaintiff for a sum attributable to the lease payments. The judge held[184] that those making *ex parte* applications had to 'observe the utmost good faith' when disclosing material to the court and that if an order was made and 'it appears that material facts have been kept back, whether wilfully and mala fides or negligently', the court had a discretion to discharge the order.[185]

It is not clear whether this disclosure test includes a requirement that the plaintiff and his advisers should ensure that all reasonable enquiries have been made of all those whom it might be thought would have in their possession facts material to the application before the duty can be said to have been discharged. The better view is that it does, thereby ensuring, in principle at least, that the quality of the information available to the court on an application is maximised.

The test for the grant of *ex parte* application appears from the authorities to be as follows: (1) whether the plaintiff has a *prima facie* right of a sort which is amenable to protection by interim relief; (2) whether there are present in relation to the plaintiff's right 'factors of such urgency, or of well-founded apprehension of perverse conduct on the part of the respondent' such that interim relief should be granted; (3) if the plaintiff is able to establish (1) and (2) then the court has a discretion whether or not to make the order sought and in assessing the exercise

181 [2000] 2 BLR 233 (HC).

182 Ibid 234F–G.

183 [2003] 1 BLR 409 (HC).

184 Ibid 413H–414A, approving passages from Herbstein and Van Winsen *The Civil Practice of the Supreme Court of South Africa* 4 ed 367 to like effect.

185 To the same effect are *B & E International (Botswana) (Pty) Ltd v Ed-u-Compt (Pty) Ltd* [2005] BWHC 115 (Tafa Ag J) and, in the context of an *ex parte* application for an order mandament van spolie, *Yardstick Services (Pty) Ltd v Feune (Pty) Ltd* [2017] 2 BLR 466 (HC) (Dube AJ).

of this discretion the court will take into account such matters as delay in the making of the application. The plaintiff has a duty to make disclosure in good faith to the court of matters which are material to the court's decision. As has already been noted, if this duty is breached then the court has a discretion to discharge the order (if made) at the return date or any earlier hearing.

Since the cases referred to above were decided, the principles on which relief might be granted *ex parte* have been elaborated upon in two decisions of Dambe J in 2011 in which *Moerane v Phiri* and *First National Bank of Botswana Ltd v Taimu* were not cited. Instead of following the principles set out in the case referred to above, more recently the five-stage test set out in the judgment of Kirby J in the *Sechele* case (also quoted in full above) has been applied.

As has been mentioned earlier, the *Sechele* case is an example of an urgent application (which departed from earlier authority in its consideration of the test to be applied to Order 12, rule 12). The *Sechele* case is not an example of an *ex parte* application (as demonstrated by the fourth stage of the test set out in *Sechele*).

In *Sutai Construction Machinery Repair Pty Ltd v Landscape Decorators Botswana Pty Ltd*,[186] Dambe J considered the case of an *ex parte* application seeking to place certain of the defendant's immovable property under attachment *securitatem debiti* pending determination of the plaintiff's money claim against the defendant. In dismissing the application, the judge found that stages (1)–(4) of the test in the *Sechele* case were not satisfied.

He also found that the fifth stage of the *Sechele* test (that the plaintiff must show substantial prejudice or potential prejudice should the order not be granted as a matter of urgency) was not satisfied, a finding undoubtedly open to him on the facts. In doing so the judge stated:[187]

> 'An anti dissipation order is a common law remedy. Its purpose is to prevent (the intended defendant) who could be shown prima facie (a) to have no bona fide defence against an apparently valid claim by the [plaintiff] (b) who has assets within the jurisdiction and (c) who has the intention to defeat the [plaintiff's] claim or to render it hollow by secreting his assets.'

These additional reasons advanced by the judge for the dismissing of the plaintiff's claim are obiter dicta because the judge had already dismissed the application by reference to the first four stages of the *Sechele* test. However, this passage from the judgment might be taken to have been intended as a statement of principle for use in future cases. If so, then the observations set out below may be made.[188]

First, as regards point (a) in the passage, this appears to require a plaintiff (ie the party seeking an anti-dissipation order) to show that the defendant has no

[186] [2011] 1 BLR 19 (HC).

[187] Ibid 24A–B.

[188] For the sake of completeness, historically injunctions are equitable relief, not common-law relief.

bona fide defence to an apparently valid claim. This applies too stringent a test for the plaintiff. It is surely too much to expect at an interlocutory stage a plaintiff to show that the defendant has no *bona fide* defence. It is quite correct to focus on the calibre of the plaintiff's claim but if that claim is *prima facie* a good claim, or at least not a bad one, it cannot be correct to require the claimant to proceed and negative any defence which the defendant might have available.

Second, as regards point (b) in the passage, there would seem to be no reason in principle why the court cannot make an order against a defendant subject to its jurisdiction in respect of assets of that defendant wherever they are located. In the modern era, when considering the movement of money across national boundaries, it is highly artificial to regard sums standing to the credit of the defendant in a bank account in Switzerland or New York as being somehow outside the control of the defendant and, through the defendant, the court. It is unnecessary to limit the power of the court to make an order preventing dissipation only to those of the defendant's assets as are physically located within Botswana.

Third, as regards point (c), it is quite correct that the touchstone of an anti-dissipation order is to prevent a defendant conducting his affairs in such a way as to render any judgment which the plaintiff may obtain against him otiose. It is that intention which makes the defendant's conduct amenable to the anti-dissipation jurisdiction. A defendant conducting his affairs in a normal fashion ought not to be the subject of that jurisdiction.

A few months later, in March 2011, Dambe J followed the *Sechele* case once again in *Experience Count Pty Ltd v Owhin Estates Pty Ltd*,[189] where the plaintiff applied *ex parte* for an order requiring the defendant to deliver up to him geysers and thermal fluid for domestic heating appliances which the plaintiff had supplied to him and for which he had not been paid or, alternatively, to restrain the defendant from installing the geysers. The plaintiff had earlier, in December 2010, obtained summary judgment against the defendant for the purchase price of the geysers, which judgment the defendant had failed to satisfy. The plaintiff had caused the issue of a writ of execution and had instructed the deputy sheriff to execute that writ. The deputy sheriff had issued a *nulla bona* return after failing to find any movable or immovable property belonging to the defendant. Before the judge, it was held that ownership in the geysers had passed to the defendant under the contract of sale and that the deputy sheriff had been wrong to issue a return of *nulla bona* in respect of the defendant's movable property and that the deputy sheriff could still therefore attach that property. As regards the question whether the geysers would accede to the land if they were to be installed (relief upon as a ground of urgency for the application) the judge found that there was insufficient evidence to support this contention.

---

[189] [2011] 1 BLR 200 (HC).

1.3.3 Interim interdicts

The conditions necessary for interim relief by way of an interim interdict were considered by Maisels ACJ in *Makolaba v Nwaka*.[190] In reliance on the South African decision in *Webster v Mitchell*,[191] he held that 'where a [plaintiff, the party applying for the interdict] established a prima facie, but not a clear right, the test for granting an interdict is where the balance of convenience lies'. In a dispute over the use of a borehole, the judge assumed that the plaintiff had a *prima facie* right to the borehole but proceeded to discharge the rule *nisi* which the plaintiff had obtained restraining the defendants from using the borehole on the ground that the balance of convenience did not favour the continuation of the relief because: first, the defendant had been using the borehole to water his 600-head herd of cattle for over a year and, if he was denied the use of the borehole, the cattle would die of thirst; second, the plaintiff himself stated that he had agreed to sell the borehole for R1,300 and thus the measure of his loss was in that sum and there was no evidence to show that the defendant was not in a position to pay that sum; and, third, there had been a lengthy delay in bringing the proceedings.

The broad test laid down in *Makolaba* was considered and elaborated upon in *Plumstead Furnishers (Pty) Ltd v Modern Home (Pty) Ltd*.[192] In *Plumstead*, Hannah J held that, on the return date of a rule *nisi* calling upon the defendants to show cause why a temporary interdict restraining certain construction work should not be continued pending decision in the plaintiff's action for ejectment:[193]

> 'At this stage it is sufficient if the [plaintiff] establishes: (a) a prima facie right, even though open to some doubt; (b) a well grounded apprehension of irreparable injury to itself; (c) the absence of ordinary remedy; and also that on a balance of convenience it is better to grant an interdict than not.'

The judge found that the evidence before him on the return date failed to establish a *prima facie* case and he discharged the rule *nisi*.[194]

In *Spectra Botswana (Pty) Ltd v First National Bank of Botswana Ltd*[195] the court was concerned with the construction of an on-demand performance bond. The plaintiff undertook the design, supervision and construction of the second defendant's new headquarters in Gaborone for a fixed price of P53 million pursuant to an agreement dated 12 December 1991. Under this agreement the plaintiff was required to enter into 'a deed of suretyship' with the

[190] [1968–1970] BLR 25 (HC).
[191] 1948 (1) SA 1186 (Clayden J).
[192] [1983] BLR 122 (HC).
[193] Ibid 124B–D.
[194] A similar test was applied by Martin Horwitz Ag J in *Mokone v Mokone* [1989] BLR 394 (HC).
[195] [1995] BLR 210 (CA) (Aguda, Lord Cowie (or Lord Wylie, the report mentions both judges) and Tebbutt JJA).

second defendant which itself required the plaintiff to arrange for a guarantee of 10% of the fixed price. The plaintiff arranged for the first defendant bank to issue a guarantee to the second defendant in the sum of P5.3 million. On 26 June 1992 the bank issued a guarantee to the second defendant which contained the following wording:

> 'We ... undertake to pay you the said amount of P5,300,000 on receipt of a written demand from you to do so and which demand may be made by you if [in your opinion and sole discretion] the said contractor fails or neglects to commence with the works on the date prescribed in the contract, or if he fails to proceed therewith or if he for any reason fails or neglects to complete the service in accordance with the terms and conditions of the contract or the insolvency laws in force within Botswana. Subject to the above ... the said demand can be made by you at any stage.'

Shortly after the plaintiff had commenced work on site it had received payments in the total sum of P12 million. Early in 1992 the general manager of the second defendant was killed in an accident and the board of the second defendant was reconstituted. On 4 June 1992 the acting general manager of the second defendant wrote to the plaintiff informing it that the board had been advised that the agreement was *ultra vires* the second defendant and was 'invalid and without any force and effect' and demanded repayment of the P12 million paid to date. (The second defendant also made an allegation that the plaintiff had paid a bribe to an official and purported to cancel the agreement on that ground.) On the same day the second defendant wrote to the bank demanding payment under the guarantee. On 27 August 1992 the plaintiff made an urgent application to Horwitz J for an interim interdict restraining the bank from paying. The judge refused the application.

The Court of Appeal dismissed the plaintiff's appeal from Horwitz J's decision. Approving *Makolaba*,[196] *Moisakamo v Moisakamo*[197] (see below) and *Plumstead Furnishers*,[198] Tebbutt JA[199] confirmed that the law on interim interdicts in Botswana and the Republic of South Africa was the same. The judge further cited and approved[200] Corbett J's statement of the requisites for an interim interdict in *LF Boshoff Investments (Pty) Ltd v Cape Town Municipality*:[201]

> 'Briefly these requisites are that the [plaintiff] for such temporary relief must show:
>
> *(a)* that the right which is the subject matter of the main action and which he seeks to protect by means of interim relief is clear or, if not clear, is *prima facie* established though open to some doubt;

196 [1968–1970] BLR 25 (HC) (Maisels ACJ).

197 [1979–1980] BLR 131 (HC).

198 [1983] BLR 122.

199 [1995] BLR 210, at 214. Both Aguda and Lord Cowie/Wylie JJA agreed with Tebbutt JA.

200 Ibid 214.

201 1969 (2) SA 256 (C) (Corbett J).

> *(b)* that, if the right is only *prima facie* established, there is a well-grounded apprehension of irreparable harm to the [plaintiff] if the interim relief is not granted and he ultimately succeeds in establishing his right;
>
> *(c)* that the balance of convenience favours the granting of interim relief; and
>
> *(d)* that the [plaintiff] has no other satisfactory remedy.'

Tebbutt JA stated he was prepared to assume that the plaintiff had a right which 'is not clear but is prima facie established, though open to some doubt' (he also adopted the language of Lord Diplock in *American Cyanamid Co v Ethicon Ltd*,[202] that the plaintiff had 'a good arguable claim' to the right he sought to protect).

The judge stated that the correct approach to the requirements for an interim interdict was not to consider them in isolation but to view them on an inter-related basis. The judge found that there was insufficient evidence to discharge the onus on the plaintiff of showing irreparable harm if the interdict were not granted. He also found that inter-related to the question of irreparable harm was the question whether the plaintiff had alternative remedies. On that question the judge held that if, as the plaintiff contended, the guarantee had been wrongly paid (in bad faith) then the plaintiff would have claims for damages against the second defendant, which was a substantial company with fixed assets of about P635 million and/or the bank. There was, therefore, another satisfactory remedy.

The meaning of a right *prima facie* established for the purposes of interim relief was considered by Newman J in *Pule v Lobatse Town Council*[203] where he followed guidance provided in *Webster v Mitchell*[204] (which, as Newman J stated, had been followed in *Plumstead Furnishers*, which had itself been approved in *Spectra Botswana*) in which Clayden J stated:[205]

> 'If the phrase used were "*prima facie case*" what the Court would have to consider would be whether the [plaintiff] had furnished proof which, if uncontradicted and believed at the trial, would establish his right. In the grant of a temporary interdict, apart from prejudice involved, the first question for the Court in my view is whether, if interim protection is given, the [plaintiff] could ever obtain the rights he seeks to protect. *Prima facie* that has to be shown. The use of the phrase "*prima facie* established though open to some doubt" indicates I think that more is required than merely to look at the allegations of the [plaintiff], but something short of a weighing up of the probabilities of conflicting versions is required. The proper manner of approach I consider is to take the facts as set out by the [plaintiff], together with any facts set out by the [defendant] which the [plaintiff] cannot dispute, and to consider whether, having regard to the inherent probabilities, the [plaintiff] could on those facts obtain relief at a trial. The facts set up in contradiction by the [defendant] should then be considered. *If serious*

---

202 [1975] AC 396, HL (Lord Diplock, Viscount Dilhorne and Lords Cross, Salmon and Edmund-Davies).

203 [2006] 1 BLR 481 (HC).

204 1948 (1) SA 1186.

205 Ibid 1189.

> *doubt is thrown on the case of the [plaintiff] he could not succeed in obtaining temporary relief, for his right, prima facie* established, may only be open to "some doubt". But if there is mere contradiction, or unconvincing explanation, the matter should be left to trial and the right be protected in the meanwhile, subject of course to the respective prejudice in the grant or refusal of interim relief.'

Importantly, Clayden J also proceeded to consider the case where temporary relief was considered but there was the prospect of harm being caused to the defendant by reason of the grant of such relief:[206]

> 'Although the grant of a temporary interdict interferes with a right which is apparently possessed by the [defendant], the position of the [defendant] is protected because, although the [plaintiff] sets up a case which *prima facie* establishes that the [defendant] has not the right apparently exercised by him, the test whether or not temporary relief is to be granted is the harm which will be done. And in a proper case it might well be that no relief would be granted to the [plaintiff] except on conditions which would compensate the [defendant] for interference with his right, should the [plaintiff] fail to show at the trial that he was entitled to interfere.'

In *Webster v Mitchell*, Clayden J was considering a claim by the plaintiff that he was the owner of a racehorse in the possession of the defendant, who was the horse's trainer. The judge applied the principles which he stated and found that, although there was a doubt about whether the plaintiff was the owner of the racehorse, because he had caused it to be registered in the name of the trainer, having regard to all the facts the plaintiff's right was *prima facie* established.

The judge then addressed the question of the harm which might be suffered by either party were the possession and control of the horse to be transferred to the plaintiff or remain with the trainer pending resolution of the issue of ownership and observed that the harm would be equal on both sides in the event of transfer or retention of possession and control. However, the order sought by the plaintiff was simply that the trainer be restrained from alienating, dealing with and racing the horse prior to determination of the issue of ownership. The judge found that this form of order might cause the defendant harm, but not as much harm as would be caused to the plaintiff by permitting the defendant to exercise full rights of ownership pending the action.

> 'Normally the Court acts on the balance of convenience. If there is greater possible prejudice to the [defendant] an interim interdict will be refused. See *Crossfield & Son Ltd v Crystallizers Ltd* (1925, W.L.D. 216, at p. 223); if, though there is prejudice to the [defendant], that prejudice is less than that of the [plaintiff] the interdict will be granted, subject, if they can be imposed, to conditions which will protect the [defendant].'[207]

---

[206] Ibid 1189–90.

[207] Ibid 1192–3.

In *Webster v Mitchell* the terms in which the interdict was sought safeguarded the interests of the defendant while minimising the potential harm to the plaintiff and the interdict was granted in those terms (with some refinements).

In *Pule v Lobatse Town Council*, Newman J decided the case on the balance of convenience, holding that it tilted in favour of the town council being permitted properly to fulfil its functions pending resolution of the issue whether the mayor had been removed lawfully.

Spectra Botswana was applied by the Court of Appeal in *Vancouver Consolidated Investments (Pty) Ltd v Ministry of Education*[208] and followed by Kirby J in *Sidhu v Singh*[209] (where *Pule v Lobatse Town Council* does not appear to have been cited to the court).

For the sake of completeness, in *Sidhu v Singh* the judge referred[210] to the first requirement for interim relief set out in *Spectra Botswana*, that the plaintiff show a right *prima facie* established, and referred[211] to a refinement of that requirement set out by the South African Supreme Court of Appeal in *Simon NO v Air Operations of Europe.*[212] This refinement is in materially identical terms to the elucidation of the expression 'a right *prima facie* established' set out in *Webster v Mitchell* and set out above.

Sidhu v Singh was followed in *Simply Botswana (Pty) Ltd v Global Media InCorp (Pty) Ltd.*[213]

On the authorities it can be stated that the requirements for an interim interdict in Botswana are the four requirements approved by the Court of Appeal in *Spectra Botswana* with the subsequent explanation of the first of those requirements as set out in *Pule v Lobatse Town Council.*[214]

Hence, for the avoidance of doubt, a plaintiff seeking such temporary relief must show that:

(1) the right which is the subject-matter of the main action and which he seeks to protect by means of interim relief is clear or, if not clear, is *prima facie* established, though open to some doubt. This latter phrase means that the court should consider the facts as set out by the plaintiff, together with any

[208] [2008] 1 BLR 270 (CA) (Moore, Lord Coulsfield and Ramodibedi JJA).

[209] [2010] 2 BLR 565 (HC).

[210] Ibid 568D–H.

[211] Ibid.

[212] 1999 (1) SA 217 (SCA) (Smalberger, Howie, Plewman, Streicher JAA and Ngoepe AJA) 228H.

[213] (Unreported) 1 April 2013 (HC) (Tau J).

[214] A similar approach was followed by Sapire AJ in *In re Peermont Global (Botswana) Pty Ltd v Racewood Investments (Pty) Ltd* [2006] 1 BLR 80 (HC), in a case involving an interim interdict successfully sought by the holder of a gaming licence against a clandestine unlicensed gaming operation. The judge found that the applicant had the relevant *locus standi* to bring proceedings because the relevant gaming legislation was enacted partly with the object of protecting licensees against unlicensed operators.

facts set out by the defendant which the plaintiff cannot dispute, and assess whether, having regard to the inherent probabilities, the plaintiff could on those facts obtain relief at a trial. The facts set up in contradiction by the defendant should then be considered. If serious doubt is thrown on the case of the plaintiff he could not succeed in obtaining temporary relief, because his right, *prima facie* established, may only be open to 'some doubt' but not to serious doubt;

(2) if the right is only *prima facie* established, there is a well-grounded apprehension of irreparable harm to the plaintiff if the interim relief is not granted and he ultimately succeeds in establishing his right;

(3) the balance of convenience favours the granting of interim relief; and

(4) the plaintiff has no other satisfactory remedy.

An interim interdict may be mandatory in character. In *Mascom Wireless Botswana Pty Ltd v Say Hello Pty Ltd*,[215] the court allowed an appeal out of time against an order of Sarkodie-Mensah J (made on the application of the defendant) by which she declared the plaintiff telecommunications network licensee to have been in breach of an agreement to supply transmission time to the defendant service provider and ordered that the plaintiff should continue to perform all its obligations under its agreement with the defendant and in particular to provide transmission time to the defendant. The plaintiff's appeal was allowed on the grounds that there had been no breach of contract as declared by the judge at first instance and the plaintiff had continued to supply the defendant with transmission time on a cash basis in any event. Absent these two considerations, the court did not suggest that the granting of a mandatory interdict pending trial would have been wrong in law.

An interim interdict will issue against the government in an appropriate case. In *Medical Rescue International Botswana Ltd v Attorney-General*,[216] the court held unanimously that an interim interdict could be granted to preserve the status quo in applications for judicial review (the application itself was referred back to the High Court for determination).

An interim interdict will likewise issue against emanations of the government such as national or local government agencies. In *Lodges of Botswana (Pty) Ltd v Tawana Land Board and Botswana Tourism Organisation*[217] the Court of Appeal allowed an appeal from the decision of Dambe J dismissing the plaintiff's application for an urgent interim interdict restraining the defendants from ordering it to vacate two safari camps pending review of the defendants' decisions on the plaintiff's bid for the tender to operate the two safari camps.

---

[215] [2008] 3 BLR 182 (CA) (Tebbutt JP, Lord Coulsfield and Foxcroft JJA).

[216] [2006] 1 BLR 516 (CA) (Tebbutt JP, Zietsman, Grosskopf, McNally and Chinhengo JJA).

[217] (Unreported) 1 February 2013 (CA) (Lord Abernethy, Gaongalelwe and Foxcroft JJA).

The wilful disobedience to an interim interdict (as with any order of the court) is potentially a contempt of court and punishable by imprisonment or a fine or both upon the bringing of committal proceedings by the aggrieved party. In *The Evangelical Lutheran Church in Southern Africa v Phillip Jeremiah Robinson*,[218] an interim interdict was made by Edwards J on the application of the appellant. The appellant then brought committal proceedings against the first respondent on the ground that he had wilfully disobeyed the interim interdict. On the committal application the first respondent contended that the appellant had had and continued to have no *locus standi* to bring the original application for the interim interdict. Corduff J agreed with the respondent's submission and held that the appellant had no legal personality such as enabled it to commence legal proceedings and dismissed the contempt application. Allowing the appellant's appeal, the court held, inter alia, that regardless of the status of the appellant, the respondent was bound to comply with the order of Edwards J once made and that the order could not be challenged until the contempt was purged (*per* Kentridge JA, giving the lead judgment and relying on the English authority *Hadkinson v Hadkinson*[219]).

1.3.4 Freezing orders/Anti-dissipation interdicts

The jurisdiction of the court to make an anti-dissipation interdict was recognised in *Moisakamo v Moisakamo*,[220] where Edwards J considered a rule *nisi* calling upon the defendant to show cause why he should not be interdicted from disposing of or dealing with certain property pending the determination of review proceedings in which the plaintiff sought the setting aside of a division of matrimonial property made by a chief. The judge held:[221]

> 'Unless the [plaintiff's] intended proceedings for the division of property acquired by the parties during the marriage can be regarded as vindicatory or quasi-vindicatory she cannot obtain an interdict if she does not prove an actual or well-grounded apprehension that if no interdict is granted she will suffer irreparable loss.'

The judge stated[222] that the plaintiff's claim could be viewed as quasi-vindicatory in nature but discharged the rule *nisi* on the grounds that it was for the plaintiff to specify the property she intended to claim or to set out why she should be excused from specifying it and that she had done neither. The judge also held[223] that the plaintiff had not shown a well-grounded apprehension of irreparable loss.

---

218 [1982] 1 BLR 215 (CA) (Maisels P, Aguda and Kentridge JJA).

219 [1952] 2 All ER 567, CA, *per* Romer LJ, cited in [1982] 1 BLR 215 at 219–20.

220 [1979–1980] BLR 131 (HC).

221 Ibid 132.

222 Ibid 134.

223 Ibid 133.

The circumstances in which an anti-dissipation interdict may be granted received fuller consideration in *Cerimele Construction Co (Botswana) (Pty) Ltd v Joint Venture Morteo-Condotee SCRL*,[224] in which the plaintiff applied for an interdict restraining the defendant, a construction company incorporated in Italy, from disposing of or removing its assets from Botswana pending arbitration proceedings between the parties. The plaintiff contended that it had a claim for over P7 million arising out of a sub-contract between it and the defendant and that it feared that the defendant *peregrinus* would leave the jurisdiction without paying. Gaefele AgJ considered whether under Botswanan law the relief sought was available (*Moisakamo v Moisakamo* appears not to have been brought to the court's attention). On the evidence before him the judge found that the plaintiff had not established that the defendant intended to remove its assets with a view to defeating the plaintiff's claim. The judge held 'without deciding' that an anti-dissipation interdict[225] was not available in aid of arbitration proceedings.

In considering the test to be applied in Botswana for the grant *pendente lite* of an anti-dissipation interdict, the judge followed the decision of Stegmann J in the South African case *Knox D'Arcy Ltd v Jamieson*,[226] in which, on an *ex parte* application, the judge granted an anti-dissipation interdict and stated:[227]

> 'The essential purpose of the interdict in question is to prevent a person (the intended defendant), who can be shown *prima facie*
>
> *(a)* to have no *bona fide* defence against an apparently valid claim by another (the plaintiff);
>
> *(b)* to have assets within the jurisdiction of the Court (today, within the area of any Division of the Supreme Court of South Africa); and
>
> *(c)* to have an intention to defeat the plaintiff's claim, or to render it hollow, by secreting his (the intended defendant's) assets in any of a number of ways (for example, by apparently or actually disposing of them or by removing them beyond the jurisdiction of the Court)
>
> from successfully defeating the ends of justice, provided that the plaintiff can show a well-grounded apprehension of irreparable loss.'

In *Knox D'Arcy* the plaintiffs also sought an ancillary order to the anti-dissipation interdict that the defendants within three days of service of the interdict make an affidavit disclosing every asset held by them within the Republic of South Africa or anywhere else in the world (relying on decisions on the English courts in which such disclosure orders had been made). Stegmann J stated:[228]

---

224 [1995] BLR 399 (HC).

225 This being the term used in preference to the English *Mareva* injunction.

226 1994 (3) SA 700 (W).

227 Ibid 706B–D.

228 Ibid 709C–E.

> 'the English Courts have also accepted that if a Mareva injunction is likely to be rendered ineffectual or unworkable without discovery of certain facts or documents, the Court has an inherent common-law power to make such orders for discovery of facts or documents as may be necessary to ensure that the injunction will be effectual and workable ... The last mentioned approach appears to me to be entirely consistent with our own legal principles.'

The judge made an ancillary order requiring the defendants to disclose their assets in the Republic of South Africa, but left open the question whether the court had jurisdiction to make such an order in respect of the defendants' assets worldwide.

Stegmann J described the relief sought as potentially oppressive and the procedure whereby the order was sought as open to serious abuses. He made the order subject to a number of safeguards: the plaintiffs were required to give an undertaking that they would make good all damage caused by the interdict in the event that they failed to establish their case at trial (although no fortification on this undertaking was ordered by way, for example, of a payment into court or the lodging of security); an exception was made to the interdict in respect of living expenses and legal expenses; it was also ordered that funds should be made available so that the defendants could carry on their business; the order was made subject to a maximum limit (R15 million) which was stated in the body of the order. The judge also permitted the plaintiffs to delay service of the order for up to 21 days so that they could be afforded an opportunity to seek parallel relief from the courts of Switzerland and England.

In *Cerimele Construction* Gaefele Ag J further observed that, on the facts of a particular case, the guidelines, set out by Lord Denning MR in the English Court of Appeal in *Third Chandris Shipping Corp v Unimarine SA*[229] for the appropriate exercise of the relevant discretionary powers, could be adopted with any necessary modifications. These guidelines are as follows:

> '(i) The plaintiff should make full and frank disclosure of all matters in his knowledge which are material for the judge to know ... (ii) The plaintiff should give particulars of his claim against the defendant, stating the ground of his claim and the amount thereof, and fairly stating the points made against it by the defendant. (iii) The plaintiff should give some grounds for believing that the defendants have assets here ... (iv) The plaintiff should give some grounds for believing that there is a risk of the assets being removed before the judgment or award is satisfied ... (v) The plaintiffs must, of course, give an undertaking in damages, in case they fail in their claim or the injunction turns out to be unjustified. In a suitable case this should be supported by a bond or security: and the injunction only granted on it being given, or undertaken to be given.'[230]

[229] [1979] 2 All ER 972 CA (Lord Denning MR, Lawton and Cumming-Bruce LJJ), at 984–5.

[230] *Cerimele Construction* was followed in *PGM Building Construction (Pty) Ltd v Mosojane, Phumaphi & Co* [1995] BLR 722 (HC) (Gaefele Ag J), where the application was dismissed for lack of evidence of a risk of

Subsequent authorities in which *Cerimele Construction* was not cited have applied a different test for the granting of an anti-dissipation interdict.

In *Kamogelo v Motlhagodi*[231] Nganunu J applied the test for the granting of an interim interdict to an application for an anti-dissipation interdict. The plaintiff was required to show:

> '(a) a prima facie right; (b) a well-grounded apprehension of harm or in fact an existing harm if the relief is not granted; (c) that the balance of convenience favours the granting of an interim interdict; and (d) that the [plaintiff] has no other satisfactory remedy.'

The judge refused the application because the balance of convenience did not favour the defendant being prevented from managing and dealing with the property in question.

In *Standard Chartered Bank of Botswana Ltd v Jotia*,[232] Mosojane J considered a rule *nisi* obtained by the plaintiff bank freezing the account of the defendant. The judge stated that the relief claimed was a temporary interdict and the question was whether the requisites for such relief had been established. Referring to the judgment of Clayden J in *Webster v Mitchell*[233] and *Makolaba v Nwaka*[234] he held that the plaintiff needed to establish a *prima facie* right and a well-grounded apprehension of irreparable harm if the relief is not granted, that there was no adequate alternative remedy and that the balance of convenience favoured the continuation of the interdict. The judge also stated:[235]

> 'Where however the [plaintiff's] claim against the [defendant] is for damages and the [plaintiff] lays no claim to any property held by the [defendant] as his but establishes that the property is about to be transferred in order to defeat a judgment he hopes to get in an action for damages, he can succeed in getting an interdict if he can show that the [defendant] has no bona fide defence to his action and that the object of the transfer of the assets is to defeat his claim.'

The judge proceeded to find that the plaintiff's claim in the case was delictual in nature and was for damages and thus fell into that category of claim.[236] However, the judge did not then consider whether the defendant 'has no bona fide defence' but instead held that the plaintiff had established 'a prima facie right of claim'.

---

dissipation and in *Galeforolwe v Golden Fruit (Pty) Ltd* [2015] BLR 131 (HC) (Sechele J), where the interdict was refused but the respondent was ordered to pay the proceeds of a disposal of real property into an account in the name of the applicant pending determination of the dispute *PGM Building Construction* was itself applied in *Ideatank (Pty) Ltd v Southern District Council & anr* [2018] 2 BLR 310 (HC) (Tafa J).

[231] [1997] BLR 218 (HC).

[232] [1999] 2 BLR 1 (HC).

[233] 1948 (1) SA 1186.

[234] [1968–1970] BLR 25.

[235] [1999] 2 BLR 1 at 8B–C.

[236] As opposed to a claim for specific property, a vindicatory action, where the applicant must show not only a *prima facie* right of ownership of the property but also that there is a direct connection between the claim and the property itself before he can obtain an interdict.

Applying the temporary interdict test the judge continued the interdict, freezing the defendant's bank account.

In *Sethole v O D Drilling*,[237] Leburu AJ followed *Kamogelo v Motlhagodi* and dismissed the application for an anti-dissipation interdict on the ground that the plaintiff had failed to show a *prima facie* right.

There appear, therefore, to be two bases on which the grant of an anti-dissipation interdict has been considered in Botswana: first, on the basis of the test set out in *Knox D'Arcy v Jamieson* supplemented by the guidelines for the exercise of the discretion as described in *Third Chandris Shipping v Unimarine*; and/or second, on the basis of the interim interdict test as set out in *Webster v Mitchell* and *Makolaba v Nwaka*.

1.3.5 Search and seize orders[238]

It appears that the Botswanan courts are cognisant of the fact that courts in other countries (principally England) have developed, at common law, a jurisdiction whereby which an interdict may be granted to ensure that vital evidence is preserved for use at a subsequent trial.[239]

However, there is an absence of reported authority dealing with the question of whether the Botswanan courts have the jurisdiction to grant such an order and, if they do, the principles upon which that jurisdiction will be exercised.

In these circumstances, and given the affinity of the Botswanan legal system with that of the Republic of South Africa, it is likely that the Botswanan courts will be guided by the reported authorities and academic commentary in South Africa. For the sake of completeness, set out below is a synopsis of the position which the South African courts have adopted with respect to search and seize orders.[240]

The remedy was described by the Appellate Division in *Shoba v Officer Commanding, Temporary Police Camp, Wagendrift Dam; Maphanga v Officer Commanding, SA Police Murder & Robbery Unit, Pietermaritzburg*,[241] where Corbett CJ (giving the judgment of the court) held:[242]

---

[237] [2010] 3 BLR 398 (HC).

[238] The reader is directed to Peté et al *Civil Procedure* 2 ed (2011) 415–17; Herbstein and Van Winsen *The Civil Practice of the High Courts of South Africa* 5 ed (2009) 1495–515; Prest *The Law and Practice of Interdicts* (1996) 172–98 and to the relevant section in the chapter on the Republic of South Africa.

[239] See, in this respect, *Botswana Railways Organisation v Setsogo* [1996] BLR 112 (CA) (Amissah JP Aguda, Steyn, Tebbutt and Hoexter JJA).

[240] For a more in-depth discussion of the South African court's approach to the grant of this relief, the reader is referred to the relevant section of the chapter on the Republic of South Africa.

[241] 1995 (4) SA 1 (A) (Corbett CJ, EM Grosskopf, Nestadt, and Steyn JJA and Nicholas AJA).

[242] Ibid 15F–J, following the acceptance of the practice *obiter* in *Universal City Studios Inc v Network Video (Pty) Ltd* 1986 (2) SA 734 (A), *per* Corbett JA (as he then was) 755A–C.

> 'At this point it is necessary to give a decision in regard to what was left open in both the Universal City Studios case supra and Jafta's case supra, *viz* whether an Anton Piller order directed at the preservation of evidence should be accepted as part of our practice. In my view, it should; and I would define what a [plaintiff] for such an order, obtained in camera and without notice to the [defendant], must prima facie establish, as the following:
>
> (1) That he, the [plaintiff], has a cause of action against the [defendant] which he intends to pursue;
>
> (2) that the [defendant] has in his possession specific (and specified) documents or things which constitute vital evidence in substantiation of [plaintiff's] cause of action (but in respect of which [plaintiff] cannot claim a real or personal right); and
>
> (3) that there is a real and well-founded apprehension that this evidence may be hidden or destroyed or in some manner be spirited away by the time the case comes to trial or to the stage of discovery.'[243]

1.3.6 Third-party disclosure orders

There is no reported authority in Botswana on the question whether a Botswanan court can make an order compelling a person who is not a party to proceedings to give disclosure.[244] In the absence of such authority, it is likely, given the close relationship between the two legal systems, that the Botswanan courts will be guided by the approach which the South African courts take with respect to the grant of such relief.[245]

1.3.7 Anti-suit interdicts (injunctions)

An anti-suit interdict (injunction) is an order restraining the injunction defendant from either commencing or continuing proceedings outside Botswana in breach of a legal or equitable right on the part of the injunction plaintiff not to pursue

[243] Applying these principles to the facts, Corbett CJ held (at 21F–H): 'As to the factual merits, it seems to me that the applicant established (i) a strong *prima facie* case of having been assaulted and tortured while in police custody; (ii) that he intended to pursue against the second respondent a civil action arising from such assault and torture; (iii) that, if it existed, the torture apparatus would be vital evidence in such a civil action; and that there was a real and well-founded apprehension that such apparatus, if it existed, would be hidden or destroyed before the matter came to trial. This was hardly in dispute. In my opinion, the Court *a quo* should, therefore, have granted an Anton Piller order in this case.'

[244] As a matter of English law, a court may make such an order: *Norwich Pharmacal Co v Customs & Excise Comrs* [1974] AC 133 (HL(E)) (Lords Reid and Morris, Viscount Dilhorne and Lords Cross and Kilbrandon).

[245] The South African authorities which deal with the availability of this type of relief, and the circumstances in which said relief will be granted, are not easy to reconcile so as to produce a coherent body of law. For the reasons more fully set out when dealing with this particular topic in the chapter on the Republic of South Africa, it is submitted that a South African court would, in principle, be willing to grant a party the type of relief currently under discussion.

litigation outside Botswana or, conversely, restraining the injunction defendant from commencing or continuing proceedings inside Botswana in breach of a legal or equitable right on the part of the injunction plaintiff to have the dispute between the parties litigated in a jurisdiction other than Botswana.[246]

There is no reported judicial authority in Botswana on whether or not an anti-suit injunction is a remedy available to the courts in Botswana. That said, the courts of Ghana,[247] Nigeria[248]and, crucially, for present purposes, the Republic of South Africa[249] have concluded that this form of relief is available in those jurisdictions. Given the affinity which exists between the legal systems in place in Botswana and the Republic of South Africa, it is likely that the Botswana courts will be guided by the approach which the South African courts take with respect to this relief.[250]

1.3.8 *Mandament van spolie*

A spoliation order is an order whereby a person who has unlawfully deprived another person of possession of a thing is ordered to restore that person to possession of that thing.[251] The remedy is a summary remedy and the person who dispossessed another cannot defend the application by contending that the person who was dispossessed was not entitled to be in possession of the thing in the first place.

The court will restore possession before deciding upon entitlement to possession and the competing claims to entitlement to possession.

The object is to prevent people taking the law into their own hands by taking possession of things in advance of the legal rights to the thing being determined by a court.[252]

---

[246] In similar vein, an anti-anti-suit injunction is an order restraining the injunction defendant from commencing or continuing proceedings to restrain the injunction plaintiff from applying to restrain the injunction defendant from commencing or continuing proceedings. The leading works on this topic are: Raphael *The Anti-Suit Injunction* 2 ed (2019) and Briggs *Civil Jurisdiction and Judgments* 7 ed (2021), chapter 28. It is also conceptually possible to obtain similar relief in the context of arbitration but such relief is outside the scope of this work.

[247] *Quantum Oil Terminals Ltd v International Finance Corp* (H Ct) (Asiedu J, Suit No: Misc/00228/17, rulings of 8 January 2018 and 23 February 2018).

[248] *United Bank for Africa Plc v Coker* (1996) 4 NWLR 239 (CA) (Muhammad, Ayoola and Pats-Acholonu JJCA).

[249] *Vedanta Resources Holdings Limited v ZCCM Investment Holdings PLC* 2019 JDR 1425 (GJ) (Adams J).

[250] For further guidance on the principles which a South African court would apply when asked to grant an anti-suit interdict, the reader is referred to the relevant section of the chapter on the Republic of South Africa.

[251] In *Moloi v Naledi Motors (Pty) Ltd* [2018] 3 BLR 203 (HC), Radijeng J held that an extinguished lien over a motor vehicle in respect of the outstanding costs of one set of repairs to that vehicle could not form the basis for a defence to a subsequent claim by the owner of the vehicle for a spoliation order in respect of the same vehicle in relation to a later set of repairs.

[252] This has been made very clear by the High Court of Botswana in *Mandandi v Mandandi* [2003] 2 BLR 88 (HC) (Marumo J). At 89G–90A, Marumo J stated that the 'fundamental purpose of the remedy is to restore

A Botswanan court may grant this type of relief.[253] It may do so where the plaintiff proves, on the balance of probabilities, that: (1) he was in peaceful and undisturbed possession of the thing; and (2) he was forcibly dispossessed of that thing.[254]

1.3.9 Arrest of individuals *tanquam suspectus de fuga*

Order 15, rule 1 of the Rules provides:

> '(1) Where a plaintiff proves to the satisfaction of the Registrar that he has a good cause of action against the defendant to the amount of P40,000 or more, and there is good ground for believing that the defendant is about to leave Botswana and that the absence of the defendant from Botswana will materially prejudice the plaintiff in the prosecution of his claim, the Registrar may issue a writ of arrest directing the defendant to be arrested and held to bail to answer the plaintiff's claim.'[255]

Sub-rule (2) provides that the application must be supported by an affidavit setting out all facts which would justify the Registrar in issuing, or refusing to issue, the writ of arrest, in particular:

> '*(a)* the sum alleged to be due to the plaintiff by the defendant, when it became due and the cause thereof;
>
> *(b)* whether or not the plaintiff holds any security for the alleged debt and, if he does, the nature and value thereof;
>
> *(c)* that the deponent believes that the defendant is about to remove from Botswana and the grounds for such belief; and
>
> *(d)* the steps, if any, which the plaintiff has already taken to enforce his claim.'

---

possession following unlawful deprivation of the same. It has absolutely nothing to do with ownership. It is no more and no less than a possessory remedy available to any possessor, including an unlawful possessor, in order to prevent members of the public taking the law into their own hands. Consequently, a court considering an application for spoliation will not concern itself with ownership of the property in issue. That is an irrelevant consideration. It will simply confine itself to the issues of possession and the deprivation thereof.'

[253] *Mandandi v Mandandi* [2003] 2 BLR 88 (HC) (Marumo J); affirmed by *JM Masala Transport (Pty) Ltd v Seabelo Express* [2006] 2 BLR 424 (HC) (Tafa Ag J).

[254] *Mandandi v Mandandi* [2003] 2 BLR 88 at 89H–90A.The judge adopted as correct the test posited by the South African High Court in *Kramer v Trustees Christian Coloured Vigilance Council, Grassy Park* 1948 (1) SA 748 (C) (Herbstein J). These requirements were then affirmed in *JM Masala Transport*.

[255] The writ of arrest is addressed to and executed by the sheriff of Botswana or his deputy: O 15, r 2, Sch 1 form 7. If the defendant does not satisfy the claim or provide security, the plaintiff may apply for confirmation of the arrest on the return day and unless sufficient cause to the contrary is shown, the judge shall confirm the arrest and order the return of the defendant to prison but shall also make such orders as he sees fit for the speedy determination of the proceedings between the parties with the writ of arrest standing as a writ of summons in the case: O 15, r 13. Order 53 also provides for imprisonment for debt of a judgment debtor on the application of a judgment creditor. No maximum term of imprisonment is prescribed.

The wording of Order 15 is such that it empowers the Registrar to issue a writ of arrest pre-judgment in a cause or matter.[256] Sub-rule (1) refers to the absence of the defendant from the jurisdiction materially prejudicing the plaintiff in 'the prosecution of his claim', the clear implication of which is that the writ of arrest procedure is available to a plaintiff during the pendency of his claim prior to judgment.

The wording in other parts of Order 15 renders it likely that the writ of arrest is also available pre-issue of proceedings. The defendant may avoid arrest and imprisonment by giving reasonable security by bond or obligation or by satisfying the claim.[257] Sub-rule (8) provides that if a bond has been given by the arrested defendant as security for the claim then 'the plaintiff shall proceed with his action precisely as if there had been no arrest and the writ of arrest shall in that case stand as a writ of summons in the action'. Pursuant to Order 6, rule 1(1), every action is begun by writ of summons (or petition of notice of motion). It would seem to follow that a plaintiff may apply for and be granted a writ of arrest prior to issuing a writ of summons commencing the action and in the event that the defendant is arrested and a bond is given for his appearance, then the writ of arrest shall stand as the originating process in the action.

It is not clear from the terms of sub-rules (1) and (2) whether the writ of arrest is available for debt claims only or whether it is available for damages claims in addition. Sub-rule (1) refers to the Registrar having to be satisfied that the plaintiff has 'a good cause of action against a defendant to the amount of P40,000 or more' without stating whether the cause of action is for debt or for a claim for an unliquidated sum such as claim for damages. The term 'cause of action' is of great amplitude and is apt to cover *any* set of facts for which the law may give a remedy[258] including a damages claim.

However, the references in sub-rule (2) to the facts which would justify the Registrar issuing the writ of arrest are to 'the sum alleged to be due the plaintiff' and 'the alleged debt' in which the use of the definite article suggests that the writ of arrest is confined to circumstances where the plaintiff is claiming a liquidated sum. Further references in Order 15 lend support to such an interpretation: rule 5(1) refers to 'The sum of money or other thing demanded'; and rule 6(1) refers to 'the sum of money or thing mentioned'.

---

[256] Though the Registrar may require the plaintiff to give security for any damages that may be caused by the issuing of the writ of arrest: O 15, r 4.

[257] Order 15, rr 6(1) and 7; Sch 1, forms 8 and 9, the bond is given to the sheriff and is assignable by him to the plaintiff.

[258] '"Cause of action" has been held from the earliest time to mean every fact which is material to be proved to entitle the plaintiff to succeed – every fact which the defendant would have a right to traverse', *Cooke v Gill* (1873) LR 8 CP 107, at 116 *per* Brett J; also *per* Diplock LJ in *Letang v Cooper* [1965] 1 QB 232, CA (E), at 242–3: 'A cause of action is simply a factual situation the existence of which entitles one person to obtain from the court a remedy against another person.'

Although these references raise the prospect that the writ of arrest might be confined to cases of debt or other liquidated claims and cases of claims in respect of particular property, the breadth of the terms in which rule 1(1) (the operative part of Order 15) is drafted suggest that the better view is that a writ of arrest may issue in support of any claim and that the references to debt or claims in respect of 'the sum of money' or thing demanded in the subsequent rules of Order 15 are illustrations of claims in respect of which a writ of arrest may issue and are not intended to cut down the breadth of the remedy provided for by Order 15, rule 1(1).

The predecessor Order of the High Court to Order 15 was considered in *International Voluntary Services v John Beck*,[259] where the respondent to the application had obtained a writ of arrest against a British national who had been employed in Botswana on a contract basis and whose intention it was to leave for South Africa when his contract ended at the end of August 1982. The respondent's action was in respect of an alleged debt and proceedings had been issued over a year earlier in July 1981, during which period the plaintiff did not seek to leave Botswana. The plaintiff employee sought the discharge of the writ. Referring to certain South African authorities Hannah J held:[260]

> 'The procedure set out in Order 9 has its origin in the Roman-Dutch law and, in my opinion, it would be wrong not to take cognisance of the manner in which a similar procedure in South Africa, both under common law and rules of court, is operated.
>
> In my judgment, to obtain a writ of arrest under Order 9 a plaintiff must prove as a necessary part of the prejudice he claims he will suffer, that the defendant, in removing himself from the jurisdiction of the Court, intends to evade his obligations arising under any judgment the plaintiff may in due course obtain against him. It is not, of course, necessary that there should be direct proof of such an intention; it is sufficient if there are circumstances from which such an intention is the proper inference. Various factors must be considered and each case will turn on its own facts.'

The court found that there was no basis for the inference that the plaintiff intended to leave Botswana for South Africa in order to evade any obligation which might eventually arise under a judgment of the Botswanan court.

It must be noted that since the decision in *International Voluntary Services*, the position in South Africa has changed. In *Malachi v Cape Dance Academy International (Pty) Ltd*,[261] the Constitutional Court considered the question whether arrest of an individual *tanquam suspectus de fuga* was unconstitutional.

---

259 [1982] 2 BLR 12 (HC).

260 Ibid 14; to the same effect is *B & E International (Botswana) (Pty) Ltd v Ed-u-Compt (Pty) Ltd* [2005] BWHC 115 (Tafa Ag J).

261 2010 (6) SA 1 (CC) (Ngcobo CJ, Moseneke DCJ and Cameron, Froneman, Jafta, Khampepe, Nkabinde, Skweyiya, Van der Westhuizen and Yacoob JJ). Mogoeng J gave the judgment of the court.

The Constitutional Court held that the limitation on freedom represented by an order of arrest *tanquam suspectus de fuga* was not justifiable in terms of section 36 of the Constitution of the Republic of South Africa, 1996. In doing so the court found that: the provisions struck at debtors who could not pay as well as those who could, but refused to, pay and were thus overbroad;[262] arrest *tanquam suspectus de fuga* had historically been regarded as an extraordinary remedy and a high financial threshold for a claim had been applied to it which had, over the decades, become devalued to the point where the threshold for an order was R40 'probably the cost of two small chickens';[263] and comparable jurisdictions had done away with arrest and detention that aims to prevent flight or to recover debts.[264]

While it is the case that, currently, in Botswana, arrest of an individual *tanquam suspectus de fuga* is a remedy which the court appears to be able to grant, it remains to be seen whether the Botswanan authorities follow the approach which the courts in the Republic of South Africa now take. In this regard, it is noteworthy that the Rules make provision for the arrest and imprisonment of a defaulting judgment debtor. Order 53 contains the detailed provisions for the making of an application for an order for personal attachment. Rule 1(1) provides:

> 'Where the Sheriff or his deputy has made a return of nulla bona or not sufficient goods on a writ of execution, the judgment creditor may cause to be issued a summons commanding the judgment debtor to pay the amount of the judgment, and, unless he does so, to show cause at a time and place stated why an order for personal attachment should not be made.'

The courts have made such arrest and imprisonment orders without, apparently, considering them unconstitutional.[265]

---

[262] Ibid para [38], as with those in *Coetzee v Government of South Africa* 1995 (4) SA 631 (CC).

[263] Ibid para [41].

[264] The judge, Mogoeng J, in fns 11 and 56, cited various examples of this including a supposed power of arrest to prevent a defendant fleeing the jurisdiction available to the English courts and a supposed power in the English court to grant security (attachment) for the plaintiff's claim in the form of a *Mareva* injunction. In so concluding the judge relied on Aird 'The Scottish arrestment and the English freezing order' (2002) 51 *ICLQ* 155. However, it appears that the judge may not have had the article properly explained to him or may have been misled by the article itself in that: (1) there is no existing power of arrest in the English court, the examples cited by Aird are of the making of passport orders where the defendant's passport is retained by the court (or the plaintiff's solicitors) but the defendant is neither arrested nor imprisoned or otherwise detained; and (2) the *Mareva* injunction does not provide security for the plaintiff's claim in the sense used in the article 'security effective even against the insolvency of the [defendant]' (at 157) but merely preserves assets pending judgment – if another creditor seeks enforcement of a debt prior to the plaintiff obtaining judgment and that debt exhausts the sums subject to the *Mareva* injunction, the plaintiff can do nothing about it.

[265] *Tours of Africa (Pty) Ltd v First National Bank of Botswana Ltd* [2018] 3 BLR 272 (CA), *per* Walia JA at 275A–H; *Masire v Seropela* [2017] 1 BLR 432 (Motswagole J).

Chapter 2

GHANA

2.1 Jurisdiction

The bases on which a Ghanaian court may assume jurisdiction over a cause or matter are statutory in origin.

The fundamental means by which a Ghanaian court is seised of jurisdiction over a defendant at the suit of a plaintiff is by service of process on the defendant.[1]

The High Court (Civil Procedure) Rules 2004[2] ('the High Court Rules') distinguish between service within and service outside the jurisdiction.

Generally, civil proceedings are commenced by the filing of a writ of summons.[3]

2.1.1 Service where the defendant is within the jurisdiction

In domestic cases the writ is issued by being sealed by the Registrar to the High Court.[4]

Order 7 makes provision for service within the jurisdiction. The default rule is that a defendant must be served personally with any document that is required to be served.[5] Provision is also made for substituted service in specified circumstances.[6] Order 7 contains further provisions addressing particular instances of service such as service on partnerships,[7] service on corporations and companies,[8] service

---

[1] No real connection is required between the defendant and Ghana for a plaintiff to seise the Ghanaian court of jurisdiction over the defendant through service of process within the jurisdiction: *Tafa & Co (Ghana) Ltd v Tafa & Co Ltd* [1977] 1 GLR 422 (H Ct) (Edusai J), where the judge stated (at 425): 'The presence of a foreigner within this jurisdiction is sufficient for service of a writ on him. Jurisdiction in my view is granted upon territorial dominion and any person who is within the territorial dominion owes obedience to its sovereign power and therefore must be obedient to its laws and to the jurisdiction of its courts.'

[2] Made by CI 47. The rules are made pursuant to the power conferred on the Rules of Court Committee by s 80 of the Courts Act 1993 (this appears as Act 459 of the Laws of Ghana, 2004).

[3] Order 2, r 2 and r 3(1) provides that the writ must be as in Form 1 to the Schedule to the High Court Rules (the writ must contain certain basic information about the claim and the parties). A writ is valid in the first instance for a period of 12 months (O 2, r 9(1)). Order 71, r 2 provides that, where a party wishes to enforce a foreign judgment pursuant to statute, an application for such enforcement must be made by notice of motion (the authors are grateful to Bobby Banson of Robert Smith & Adelaide Law, Accra, Ghana, for bringing this to their attention).

[4] Order 2, r 7(1).

[5] Order 7, r 2(1). Service must be effected by the bailiff or a process server registered with the court or a party may direct service (O 7, r 1).

[6] Order 7, r 6.

[7] Order 7, r 4(2)(b).

[8] Order 7, r 4(2)(c) and r 5, which make provision for service of a body corporate at its registered office or by service on the body corporate's chairman, president, managing director or other similar officer. In addition, the Ghana Companies Act 2019 (Act 992), s 291 provides that a document may be served on a company by sending it to the official email address of the company registered with the Registrar of Companies (as provided for by s 122(1) of the 2019 Act) or by sending the document to the facsimile machine of the company or by service on the director of the company required (by s 182(1) of the 2019 Act) to be resident in Ghana or on a member of the company.

on the local agent of a principal who is out of the jurisdiction[9] and service of the writ pursuant to the terms of a contract.[10]

The Companies Act 2019 broadens the circumstances in which the Ghanaian High Court may take jurisdiction over a claim brought against companies not formed under the laws of Ghana but which have (or in certain circumstances, had) an established place of business within Ghana.

Chapter Five of the 2019 Act makes provision for 'external companies'. Section 329(2) defines an external company as, 'a body corporate formed outside the Republic which, has an established place of business in the country'.

Section 329(3) defines an established place of business as

> 'a branch, management, share, transfer or registration office, factory, mine, or any other fixed place of business, but does not include an agency unless the agent has, and habitually exercises, a general authority to negotiate and conclude contracts on behalf of the body corporate or maintains a stock of merchandise from which the agent regularly fills orders on behalf of the body corporate'.

Within one month of the establishment of a place of business, an external company is required to deliver to the Registrar of companies, inter alia, the address of the principal place of business and the name and address in Ghana of a process agent, authorised to accept service of process on behalf of the external company.[11]

Documentation (including process) 'shall be sufficiently served' on an external company by: delivery to an electronic address provided by it to the Registrar of companies; delivery or postage to the person last registered as the external company's process agent, even if the agent refuses to accept service or the company has ceased to maintain a place of business in Ghana; or by sending the document to the facsimile machine of the company.[12]

---

[9] Order 7, r 13: '(1) Where the Court is satisfied on an ex-parte application: (a) that a contract has been entered into in Ghana with or through an agent who resides or carries on business in Ghana or a body corporate that has its registered office or place of business in Ghana; and (b) that the principal for whom the agent was acting at the time the contract was entered into was neither a person residing nor carrying on business in Ghana or a corporate body having a registered office or place of business in Ghana; and (c) that at the time of the application: (i) the agent's authority has not been revoked; or (ii) the agent is still in business relation with the principal, the Court may make an order authorising service of the writ beginning an action relating to the contract, to be effected on the agent instead of the principal.'

[10] Order 7, r 14: 'Where (a) a contract contains a term to the effect that the Court shall have jurisdiction to hear and determine any action in respect of the contract or, apart from any such term, the Court has jurisdiction to hear and determine any such action; and (b) the contract provides that in the event of any action in respect of the contract being commenced the process by which it is commenced may be served on the defendant or on any other person on behalf of the defendant as may be specified in the contract or in such manner or at such place, whether in or outside Ghana, as may be so specified, then, if an action in respect of the contract is commenced and the writ is served in accordance with the contract, the writ shall, subject to Order 8, be deemed to have been duly served on the defendant.'

[11] Section 330(1)(b) of the 2019 Act.

[12] Section 333(1) of the 2019 Act.

Where the registration of the name and address of a process agent has not been effected by the external company (or the agent has died or, if a corporate agent, it has been dissolved), the company 'shall be sufficiently served' by: delivery to a place of business of the company in Ghana; or, if the company has ceased to have a place of business in Ghana, by delivery to the registered office or principal place of business in the company's country of incorporation.[13]

Thus, the Companies Act 2019 has extended the circumstances in which a company may be served provided for in Order 7 of the High Court Rules, to include, inter alia: service on an agent who formerly had but, at the time of service, no longer has authority to accept service on behalf of the company; and a company which once had but, at the time of service, no longer has a place of business in Ghana.

In the latter case, it seems that section 333(3) provides a way around the provisions requiring leave for service of process outside the jurisdiction provided for in Order 8 rule 3 of the High Court Rules ('process ... shall be sufficiently served on the company if delivered or sent by post to ... the registered office or principal place of business of the company in the country of incorporation').

2.1.2 Service where the defendant is outside the jurisdiction

In cases where the plaintiff wishes to serve the writ outside the jurisdiction, the rules provide as follows:[14] 'No writ, notice of which is to be served out of the jurisdiction, shall be *issued* without leave of the Court as provided in Order 8' (emphasis provided).

Order 8 makes provision for service outside the jurisdiction and Order 8, rule 3 prescribes an exclusive set of grounds on which the Ghanaian court may assume jurisdiction over a person present outside the jurisdiction.

Order 8, rule 3[15] provides:

'(1) Service out of the jurisdiction of notice of a writ may be effected with leave of the Court in the following cases

(*a*) if the whole subject-matter of the action begun by the writ is immovable property situate within the jurisdiction (with or without rents or profits) or the perpetuation of testimony relating to any such property;

---

13 Section 333(2) and (3) of the 2019 Act.

14 Order 2, r 7(5).

15 The rule of the English Rules of the Supreme Court regulating service out of the jurisdiction prior to 1999 (when the Civil Procedure Rules came into effect) was O XI. Under the Rules of the Supreme Court 1883 and the Rules of the Supreme Court 1965, which superseded the 1883 Rules, O XI, r 1, provided for service out of the jurisdiction. The terms of the Ghanaian O 8, r 3 are materially identical to the Rules of the Supreme Court 1883, save that the Ghanaian High Court Rules include O 8, r 3(1)(m), which is absent from the 1883 Rules.

(*b*) if an act, deed, will, contract, obligation or liability affecting immovable property situate within the jurisdiction is sought to be construed, rectified, set aside or enforced in the action begun by the writ;

(*c*) if in the action begun by the writ relief is sought against a person domiciled or ordinarily resident within the jurisdiction;

(*d*) if the action begun by the writ is for the administration of the estate of a person who died domiciled within the jurisdiction or for any relief or remedy which might be obtained in any such action;

(*e*) if the action begun by the writ is for the execution, as to property situated within the jurisdiction, of the trusts of a written instrument, being trusts that ought to be executed according to the laws of this country and of which the person to be served with the writ is a trustee, or for any relief or remedy which might be obtained in any such action;

(*f*) if the action begun by the writ is brought against a defendant not domiciled or ordinarily resident within the jurisdiction to enforce, rescind, dissolve, annual (sic) or otherwise affect a contract, or to recover damages or obtain other relief in respect of the breach of a contract which

(i) was made within the jurisdiction; or

(ii) was made by or through an agent trading or residing within the jurisdiction on behalf of a principal trading or residing out of the jurisdiction; or

(iii) is by its terms, or by implication governed by the laws of this country;

(*g*) if the action begun by the writ is brought against a defendant not domiciled or ordinarily resident within the jurisdiction, in respect of a breach

(i) committed within the jurisdiction of a contract made within or out of the jurisdiction; and

(ii) notwithstanding the fact that the breach is preceded or accompanied by a breach committed out of the jurisdiction that renders impossible the performance of so much of the contract as ought to have been performed within the jurisdiction;

(*h*) if the action begun by the writ is founded on a tort committed within the jurisdiction;

(*i*) if in the action begun by the writ, an injunction is sought that orders the defendant to do or refrain from doing anything within the jurisdiction (whether or not damages are also claimed in respect of a failure to do or the doing of that thing);

(*j*) if the action begun by the writ is properly brought against a person duly served within the jurisdiction, but a person out of the jurisdiction is a necessary or proper party to it;

(*k*) if the action begun by the writ is by a mortgagee of immovable property situated within the jurisdiction and seeks the sale of the property, foreclosure of the mortgage or delivery by the mortgagor of possession of the property but not an order for payment of any moneys due under the mortgage;

(l) if the action begun by the writ is by a mortgagor of immovable property situate within the jurisdiction and seeks redemption of the mortgage, discharge of the mortgage or delivery by the mortgagee of possession of the property but not a personal judgment; or

(m) if the action begun by the writ is in respect of a contract which contains a term to the effect that the Court shall have jurisdiction to hear and determine any action in respect of the contract.'[16]

2.1.2.1 *Procedure*[17]

Order 8, rule 1 states the basic rule that no writ shall be served out of the jurisdiction save with the leave of the court.

Order 8, rule 2(1) provides:

> 'An application for the grant of leave under rule 1(2) shall be supported by an affidavit stating the grounds on which the application is made and stating that in the deponent's belief, the plaintiff has a good cause of action, and showing in what place or country the defendant is or may probably be found.'[18]

Rule 2(2) provides that the court shall not grant leave unless it is made sufficiently to appear to the court: '(a) that the case is a proper one for service out of the jurisdiction; and (b) that the case falls within one of the provisions of rule 3.'

It appears that, where a plaintiff intends to serve a writ outside the jurisdiction, a failure to apply for leave to issue a writ before issuing the writ itself is treated as a fundamental error and will render the writ null and void.[19] Where, however, the plaintiff does not intend to serve the writ out of the jurisdiction, no leave is needed to issue the writ, even where the defendant is resident outside the jurisdiction.[20]

---

[16] It will be noted that there is no provision made for the court to permit service of the writ on a defendant who is present out of the jurisdiction if the action is one to enforce a foreign judgment; Frimpong Oppong 'Recognition and enforcement of foreign judgments in Commonwealth African countries' (2014) XV *Yearbook of Private International Law* 365, 372. See also *NML Capital v Republic of Argentina*, Suit No RPC/343/12 (unreported) 2012 (HC) and *Republic v High Court (Commercial Division) Accra, ex parte Attorney General, NML Capital and the Republic of Argentina*, Civil Motion No J5/10/2013 (unreported) 2013 (Sup Ct, Ghana). By way of comparison, see the English Civil Procedure Rules, PD 6B, para 3.1(10).

[17] Order 58 sets out special rules governing 'commercial claims', as defined (at O 58, r 2). Commercial actions are commenced in the same way as other actions (O 58, r 3(1)).

[18] In *Shirlstar Container Transport Ltd v Kadas Shipping Co* [1989–90] 1 GLR 401 (H Ct) Laptey J held (at 410) that it was in that case sufficient if the statement of claim and writ of summons disclosed the grounds.

[19] *Lokko v Lokko* [1991] 2 GLR 184 (CA) (Essiem, Ofori-Boateng and Adjabeng JJA), *per* Ofori-Boateng JA (giving the judgment of the court) 188. (The court cited the Supreme Court decision in *Mosi v Bagyina* [1963] 1 GLR 337 (Van Lare, Mills-Odoi and Akufo-Addo JJSC) 346–8, *per* Akufo-Addo JSC, as authority for the proposition that a writ issued in breach of the relevant rule of court is void.)

[20] *Lokko v Lokko*, at 189. In the *Lokko* case, the defendant was resident in New York, USA, when the writ was issued. However, the defendant had retained solicitors in Ghana who received service on the defendant's behalf and entered an appearance.

In *Shirlstar Container Transport Ltd v Kadas Shipping Co*,[21] a modification was made to the general rule that a writ intended for service outside the jurisdiction which is issued without leave is void. Accordingly, in cases where there are multiple defendants, some of whom reside within the jurisdiction and others of whom reside outside the jurisdiction, the plaintiff is entitled to issue the writ prior to the court's granting him leave to serve notice of the writ on those defendants resident outside the jurisdiction.[22]

It also seems that a writ issued for service outside the jurisdiction that contains claims some of which are within Order 8, rule 3, and some of which are not within that rule, is not a writ within Order 8 and is void and cannot be saved by the striking out of the claims not within rule 3.[23]

As a matter of Ghanaian law, the proper test for the court to apply on an application for leave to issue and serve out of the jurisdiction was set out in *Signal Oil and Gas Co v Bristow Helicopters Ltd*,[24] where Griffiths-Randolph J stated:[25]

> 'The position therefore is that although this court has the party [sic, 'power'] to grant leave for the issue of a writ of summons for service on a party resident outside its jurisdiction, it does so sparingly ... the [plaintiff] has to furnish plausible evidence to convince the court that he has a good cause of action, or that there is a real issue to be tried, but not that the case will succeed: vide *Ellinger v. Guinness, Mahon & Co., Frankfurter Bank A.-G. And Metall Gesellschaft A.-G.* [1939] 4 All ER 16; and to satisfy the court that the other party does not have a proper defence to the claim.'

Once the plaintiff has satisfied the court to the required standard that he is within one or more of the relevant gateways under Order 8, rule 3, the court has power to grant the plaintiff leave to serve the defendant out of the jurisdiction. Whether the court exercises this power is a matter of discretion. As mentioned above, the court must be satisfied that the case is a proper one for service out of the jurisdiction. The discretion must be exercised 'sparingly'.[26] However, there is little recent guidance in the Ghanaian authorities on the matters that the court should take into account in exercising that discretion.

---

[21] [1989–90] 1 GLR 401 (H Ct) (Laptey J).

[22] Ibid 408, *per* Lamptey J who stated that it would be 'unfair and unjust to contend that [O 2, r 7(5)] should be religiously complied with, if the failure to so comply with that rule would lead to the whole of the writ of summons being invalidated'. The judge found support for this result in *Bawa v Oyegoke* [1977] 2 GLR 412 (Taylor J), at 414.

[23] *Eboe v Eboe* [1962] 1 GLR 453 (Sup Ct) (Korsah CJ, Sarkodee-Adoo and Aduma-Bossman JJSC). Allowing the defendant's appeal, the Supreme Court held (at 457) that the court did not have power to grant leave to issue a writ containing claims not within the predecessor to O 8, r 3.

[24] [1976] 1 GLR 371 (H Ct); Frimpong Oppong *Private International Law in Commonwealth Africa* (2013) 51.

[25] [1976] 1 GLR 371 at 375.

[26] *Signal Oil and Gas Co v Bristow Helicopters Ltd* [1976] 1 GLR 371.

In *Signal Oil and Gas Co*,[27] Griffiths-Randolph J considered the question whether leave to serve out of the jurisdiction should be granted in an application where the cause of action was in tort. In that case a helicopter had been involved in an accident in Ghana in which the plaintiffs' employee had been killed. The helicopter had been let to the plaintiffs pursuant to a contract made outside the jurisdiction and the helicopter had been manufactured and maintained in Italy. The defendants were foreign companies domiciled and ordinarily resident outside Ghana. Refusing leave to issue and serve the writ outside the jurisdiction, the judge stated:[28]

> 'since the contract ... on which the claim was based was executed in another country, where also the plans were drawn up, the parties have their establishments outside Ghana, and not only was the gear box whose manufacture was said to be defective made in Italy, but also the maintenance and repair of the helicopter were carried outside the Republic, but it was only the accident that occurred here, the tort was committed outside Ghana which therefore cannot be said to be the most appropriate or convenient venue for this action'.

The decision was informed by the English authorities that the judge cited on the meaning of Order XI, rule 1(ee) of both the then Ghanaian Rules of the High Court and the English Rules of the Supreme Court,[29] which were to the effect that damage suffered within the jurisdiction was insufficient for leave to be granted to issue and serve out; what was required was that the tort should have been committed within the jurisdiction. Nonetheless, the passage quoted above does demonstrate that the appropriateness or convenience of the forum was an influential consideration at the time.

The framework within which the Ghanaian courts consider the grant of leave to serve out of the jurisdiction is derived from earlier English rules of court.[30]

[27] [1976] 1 GLR 371 (H Ct); Frimpong Oppong *Private International Law in Commonwealth Africa* (2013) 51.

[28] [1976] 1 GLR 371 at 378. However, it should be noted that in *Wachter v Harlley* [1968] GLR 1069 (H Ct) (Charles Crabbe J), the court considered an application to dismiss an action based on a tort committed outside the jurisdiction in Switzerland where the defendant's connection with Ghana was simply that he had been served within the jurisdiction. The defendant did not apply for a stay of the Ghanaian proceedings on the ground that Ghana was not an appropriate forum, and the judge did not refer to the point either. The argument concerned the proper law of the tort.

[29] Under the Rules of the Supreme Court 1883 (1961 ed), the corresponding sub-rule was in identical terms and was also numbered O XI, r 1(ee): '(ee) The action is founded on a tort committed within the jurisdiction.' This sub-rule was subsequently amended in England by the Rules of the Supreme Court 1965, which superseded the 1883 Rules, where O XI, r 1(f) provided: 'The claim is founded on a tort and the damage was sustained, or resulted from an act committed, within the jurisdiction.' In Ghana, the position remains that the tort must have been committed within the jurisdiction (see O 8, r 3(h), above).

[30] As noted above, the rule of the English Rules of the Supreme Court regulating service out of the jurisdiction prior to 1999 (when the Civil Procedure Rules came into effect) was O XI. Under the Rules of the Supreme Court 1883 and the Rules of the Supreme Court 1965, which superseded the 1883 Rules, O XI, r 1, provided for service out of the jurisdiction. The terms of the Ghanaian O 8, r 3 are materially identical to the Rules of the Supreme Court 1883, save that the Ghanaian High Court Rules include O 8, r 3(1)(m), which is absent from the 1883 Rules.

In view of this affinity with earlier English rules of court, it is likely that when considering the matters discussed in this section, a Ghanaian court may derive some assistance from the English authorities. Set out below therefore is guidance which is drawn from the English authorities in which the equivalent rules have been considered.

The English equivalents of Order 8, rules 2 and 3 have been the subject of judicial consideration at the highest level in England. In *Seaconsar Far East Ltd v Bank Markazi Jomhouri Islami Iran*,[31] the House of Lords considered the interaction of Order XI, rules 1(1) and 4, of the Rules of the Supreme Court (the equivalent to Order 8, rules 2 and 3). Lord Goff (with whom the other Lords agreed) reviewed the authorities on the question what a plaintiff under Order XI was required to show on an application for leave to serve a writ out of the jurisdiction and found that the plaintiff was required to show, first, that the cause of action deposed to in the evidence in support of the application fell within the provisions of rule 1(1) and, second, that on the merits of the case there was a serious question to be tried. On the question of the standard to which these issues were required to be shown, Lord Goff stated:[32]

> 'A judge faced with a question of leave to serve proceedings out of the jurisdiction under Order 11 will in practice have to consider both (1) whether jurisdiction has been sufficiently established, on the criterion of the good arguable case laid down in Korner's case, under one of the paragraphs of rule 1(1), and (2) whether there is a serious issue to be tried, so as to enable him to exercise his discretion to grant leave, before he goes on to consider the exercise of that discretion, with particular reference to the issue of forum conveniens.'

The first of these matters was held to correspond to the requirement in Order XI, rule 4, that 'no such leave shall be granted unless it shall be made sufficiently to appear to the Court or Judge that the case is a proper one for service out of the jurisdiction under this Order'[33] and the second was a threshold requirement for the merits of the plaintiff's claim.[34]

---

[31] [1994] 1 AC 438, (HL (E)) (Lords Templeman, Griffiths, Goff, Browne-Wilkinson and Mustill).

[32] At 456H–457B. See also the decision of the Privy Council in *Altimo Holdings and Investment Ltd v Kyrgyz Mobil Tel Ltd* [2012] 1 WLR 1804 (Lord Phillips PSC and Lords Mance, Collins, Kerr and Clarke JJSC), *per* Lord Collins at para [71], confirming this statement of principle.

[33] *Seaconsar* at 451A–B, 452A–B, 453D–G.

[34] *Seaconsar* at 452D–E, 455A–C, 456G–H. Notwithstanding the separate treatment of the English O XI, r 4, in *Seaconsar* and the earlier authorities referred to therein, it is unclear whether the amendment in 1883 of O XI, r 3 (under the Rules of Court contained in Sch 1 to the Supreme Court of Judicature Act 1875) by the introduction of an expanded O XI, r 4, in the 1883 Rules of Court, was intended to produce this result. At the time the leading textbook on the Rules took the view that the amendment to include the wording 'no such leave shall be granted unless it shall be made sufficiently to appear to the Court or Judge that the case is a proper one for service out of the jurisdiction under this Order' was merely an amplification of the previous rule (see Wynne Baxter *Judicature Acts & Rules 1873–1883* 5 ed (1883) 176–7).

Thus, considering the English authorities, it is suggested that, analytically, it would be helpful to determine applications for leave to serve process out of the jurisdiction by applying the following, four-component approach.[35]

(1) *The formal requirements.* Has the plaintiff produced evidence satisfying the formal requirements of Order 8, rule 2 (or English Order XI, rule 4)? This requires the plaintiff in his affidavit in support of the application to set out: (a) the belief of the deponent that the plaintiff has a good cause of action; (b) the place or country the defendant is or probably may be found; and (c) the grounds on which the application is made.

(2) *The sufficiency requirement.* Under the English Order XI, rule 4, it was held in the *Seaconsar* case that the words 'and no such leave shall be granted unless it shall be made sufficiently to appear to the Court or Judge that the case is a proper one for service out of the jurisdiction under this Order' introduced a sufficiency requirement (or, in other words, a degree of proof requirement) such that the plaintiff must show that there is a good arguable case[36] that the case falls within one of the gateways under Order XI, rule 1(1).

---

[35] As summarised in the English *Supreme Court Practice 1965* (1999 ed) 93–4, paras 11/1/9–11/1/12. The commentary referred to in the *Supreme Court Practice* refers to three elements; in the text above the present authors include four elements, the additional element being the formal requirements of English r 4 and Ghanaian r 2.

[36] In *Canada Trust v Stolzenberg (No 2)* [2002] 1 AC 1 (HL(E)) (Lords Steyn, Hoffmann, Cooke, Hope and Hobhouse), *per* Lord Steyn (with whom the other Lords agreed) 13F, the House of Lords appeared to approve passages from the judgment of Waller LJ in the Court of Appeal in the same case ([1998] 1 WLR 547) including the following (at 555F–G): 'It is also right to remember that the "good arguable case" test, although obviously applicable to the ex parte stage, becomes of most significance at the inter partes stage where two arguments are being weighed in the interlocutory context which, as I have stressed, must not become a "trial". "Good arguable case" reflects in that context that one side has a much better argument on the material available. It is the concept which the phrase reflects on which it is important to concentrate, i.e. of the court being satisfied or as satisfied as it can be having regard to the limitations which an interlocutory process imposes that factors exist which allow the court to take jurisdiction.' In *Goldman Sachs International v Novo Banco SA* [2018] 1 WLR 3683 (Lords Mance, Sumption and Hodge, Lady Black and Lord Lloyd-Jones), the UK Supreme Court further clarified the correct understanding of the test in the *Canada Trust* case. Lord Sumption (with whom all the other members of the court agreed and in reliance on his own judgment in *Brownlie v Four Seasons Holdings Incorporated* [2018] 1 WLR 192) stated at para [9]: 'For the purpose of determining an issue about jurisdiction, the traditional test has been whether the claimant had "the better of the argument" on the facts going to jurisdiction. In *Brownlie v Four Seasons Holdings Inc* [2018] 1 WLR 192, para 7, this court reformulated the effect of that test as follows: "(i) that the claimant must supply a plausible evidential basis for the application of a relevant jurisdictional gateway; (ii) that if there is an issue of fact about it, or some other reason for doubting whether it applies, the court must take a view on the material available if it can reliably do so; but (iii) the nature of the issue and the limitations of the material available at the interlocutory stage may be such that no reliable assessment can be made, in which case there is a good arguable case for the application of the gateway if there is a plausible (albeit contested) evidential basis for it."'

(3) *The merits requirement.* The plaintiff must demonstrate that there is a serious issue to be tried on the merits of the claim upon which the claimant relies. Lord Goff in *Seaconsar* stated[37] as follows:

> 'The court cannot resolve disputed questions of fact on affidavit evidence; and it is consistent with the statement of the law by Lord Davey that if, at the end of the day, there remains a substantial question of fact or law or both, arising on the facts disclosed by the affidavits, which the plaintiff bona fide desires to try, the court should, as a rule, allow the service of the writ. If this approach is correct, the standard of proof in respect of the cause of action can broadly be stated to be whether, on the affidavit evidence before the court, there is a serious question to be tried.'

(4) *The court's discretion.* Once the above matters are established by the plaintiff, the court will proceed to consider the exercise of its discretion to allow service out of the jurisdiction. The court's discretion is exercised cautiously. As was stated by Pearson J in *Société Générale de Paris v Dreyfus Brothers*:[38]

> 'But of course it becomes a very serious question, and ought always to be considered a very serious question, whether or not, even in a case like that, it is necessary for the jurisdiction of the Court to be invoked, and whether this Court ought to put a foreigner, who owes no allegiance here, to the inconvenience and annoyance of being brought to contest his rights in this country, and I for one say, most distinctly, that I think this Court ought to be exceedingly careful before it allows a writ to be served out of the jurisdiction.'

The exercise of the court's discretion is dealt with below under the sub-heading '*Forum non conveniens*'. Order 8, rules 4–11 contain ancillary provisions regarding such matters as the time within which a defendant must enter an appearance after service of process on him,[39] the procedure to be adopted for service where a convention governs the means of service[40] and dispensing with the need for personal service outside the jurisdiction.[41]

2.1.2.2 *Bases for service out of the jurisdiction*

The bases on which the court may grant permission which are of particular significance for present purposes are discussed below.

(1) Relief is sought against any person domiciled, or ordinarily resident, within the jurisdiction.

[37] *Seaconsar* 452C–D.

[38] (1885) 29 Ch D 239 at 242–3; cited with approval by Lord Goff in *Seaconsar* at 455D.

[39] Rule 4.

[40] Rule 6.

[41] Rule 5(3). A person may be served in any way in accordance with the laws of the country in which service is effected or in a way prescribed by a Civil Procedure Convention.

The term 'person' in Order 8, rule 3(c), includes any natural or legal person.[42]

There is little Ghanaian judicial authority on the meaning of the term 'domicile' for the purposes of the application of Order 8, rule 3(c). It is likely, given the willingness of the Ghanaian courts to look to English law for the meaning of terms inherited from colonial times, that the Ghanaian courts will adopt the jurisprudence applicable in English law regarding the terms 'domicile' for the purposes of determining jurisdiction over a person.[43] Under the English Rules of the Supreme Court upon which Order 8, rule 3, of the High Court Rules appears to have been based,[44] 'domicile' was defined as follows:[45]

> 'In general the domicile of a person is in the country in which he has his permanent home (see Dicey, *Conflict of Laws*, 7th ed., Chap. 6), the country in which his habitation is fixed without any present intention of removing (*Re Craignish*, [1892] 3 Ch. 180, C.A.; *Huntly v. Gaskell*, [1906] A.C. 56; *Casdagli v. C.*, [1919] A.C. 145). No person can at any time be without a domicile or have more than one domicile. The domicile of origin remains until a new domicile of choice has been adopted (*Bell v. Kennedy* (1868), L.R. 1 Sc. App. 307, H.L.; *Udny v. Udny* (1869), ibid, 441, H.L., *Winans v. A.-G.*, [1904] A.C. 287, H.L.).'

The Ghanaian courts have jurisdiction on the basis of residency 'within the jurisdiction'.[46]

The Ghanaian courts will assume jurisdiction over a legal person if, at the commencement of the action, business is being carried out by it at some definite and more or less permanent place in Ghana: *Ackerman v Societe Generale de Compensation*.[47] Subsequently, in *Tafa & Co (Ghana) Ltd v Tafa & Co Ltd*,[48] the same judge (Edusei J) as decided the *Ackerman* case decided that the fact that business was carried on within Ghana by a legal person gave the courts jurisdiction over that person – the need for a 'more or less permanent place of business' was not referred to.

---

42 Section 32(1) of the Interpretation Act 1960 (this appears as CA 4 of 2004 in the Laws of Ghana, 2004). Legal persons incorporated under the laws of foreign jurisdictions will be recognised by the Ghanaian courts as having capacity to sue and be sued: *Edusei v Diners Club Suisse SA* [1982–83] GLR 809 (CA) (Francois, Mensa Boison and Abban JAA).

43 See generally on the meaning of 'domicile', *Dicey, Morris and Collins on The Conflict of Laws* 15 ed (2012) vol 1, r 34 para 6R-001.

44 As noted above, the rule of the English Rules of the Supreme Court regulating service out of the jurisdiction prior to 1999 (when the Civil Procedure Rules came into effect) was O XI. Under the Rules of the Supreme Court 1883 and the Rules of the Supreme Court 1965, which superseded the 1883 Rules, O XI, r 1 provided for service out of the jurisdiction where the defendant was domiciled or ordinarily resident within the jurisdiction.

45 Rules of the Supreme Court 1883 (1961 ed) 144.

46 As noted above, mere presence is sufficient: *Tafa & Co (Ghana) Ltd v Tafa & Co Ltd* [1977] 1 GLR 422 (H Ct) (Edusei J, at 425).

47 [1967] GLR 212 (H Ct) (Edusei J at 214).

48 [1977] 1 GLR 422 (H Ct) (Edusei J at 425).

The Court of Appeal considered the question of what is required for the Ghanaian court to assume jurisdiction over a legal person in *Sanyo Electric Trading v Quacoopome*.[49] The principles on the basis of which a legal person was domiciled in Ghana for the purposes of the court's jurisdiction were formulated as follows:[50]

> 'As a general rule a person domiciled in a contracting state shall, whatever his nationality, be sued in the courts of that state. The domicile of the plaintiff in such cases is usually irrelevant. A legal person is said to be domiciled in a state if it has its seat in that state or country, that is to say, if either (a) it was incorporated in that state or country and has its registered office therein; or (b) its central management or control is exercised there. It is trite learning that mere physical presence is not sufficient. The defendant must be actually domiciled in the state or country for any legal action instituted against it to be maintainable jurisdictionally.'

This formulation seems to be based on the traditional definition of the 'domicile' of a legal person under the early English Rules of the Supreme Court:[51]

> 'A corporation is domiciled where it is registered, if the law requires it to be registered, and if it does not it is domiciled in the country by whose law it is incorporated (*Dicey*, Conflict of Laws, 7th ed., p. 477). A corporation is "resident" and "ordinarily resident" where its central management and control is exercised ...'.

Whether a foreign corporation is present within the jurisdiction through the presence of an agent appears to be a matter on which there is no judicial authority in Ghana. The position in England is set out in *The Lalandia*;[52] Langton J stated:[53]

> 'Now taking these various tests, the test of making or selling contracts and the test of Lord Wrenbury in the Okura case of whether the defendants are acting "by" a person or "through" a person, and the value to be attached to whether the rent is paid by the foreign corporation or whether the agent in this country has the right or not to make any independent contract and has any discretion of his own—applying all these various tests as best I can to the present case, it seems to me that Escombe, McGrath & Co. fall upon the side of the line of *agents who carry on their own business and not the business of the foreign corporation* ... I have to make up my mind *whether the foreign corporation is really here, in the sense that it has somebody doing its business here who is not doing primarily his own business*, and I think Escombe, McGrath & Co. on the evidence are primarily doing their own business and only in a secondary sense doing the business of the East Asiatic Company' (emphasis provided).

It is likely that a Ghanaian court would follow this statement of principle (as has the Nigerian Supreme Court).[54]

---

49 [2001–02] 2 GLR 198 (CA) (Omari-Sasu, Ansah and Asiamah JJA).

50 Ibid *per* Asiamah JA at 204.

51 Rules of the Supreme Court 1883 (1961 ed) 145.

52 [1933] P 56.

53 Ibid.

54 Followed in Nigeria *In re. Gresham Life Assurance Society (Nigeria) Ltd* [1973] (1) ALR Comm 215 (Sup Ct) (at the time the equivalent today of the Nigerian Federal Court of Appeal; Elias CJ, Fatayi-Williams and Ibekwe JJSC).

(2) The action is one brought against the defendant to enforce ... or otherwise effect a contract or to recover damages or other relief for or in respect of a breach of a contract:

(a) made within the jurisdiction, or

(b) made by or through an agent trading or residing within the jurisdiction on behalf of a principal trading or residing out of the jurisdiction, or

(c) by its terms or by implication to be governed by the law in force in the jurisdiction, or

If the action begun by the writ is brought against a defendant not domiciled or ordinarily resident within the jurisdiction, in respect of a breach

(a) committed within the jurisdiction of a contract wherever made, within or out of the jurisdiction; and

(b) notwithstanding the fact that the breach is preceded or accompanied by a breach out of the jurisdiction which renders impossible the performance of so much of the contract as ought to have been performed within the jurisdiction.

It is likely that, in the apparent absence of Ghanaian authority on the construction and application of Order 8, rule 3(f) and (g), a Ghanaian court will be guided by the academic and judicial authorities on the construction and application of the (former) equivalent provision in the English Rules of the Supreme Court.[55]

A concise statement of the law is as follows[56] (and should be adapted substituting 'Ghana' for 'England'):

'(i) **Where a contract is made in England**

11-181

If the parties enter into negotiations by correspondence from different countries, the contract is made where the letter of acceptance is posted. But in commercial transactions today communication by telephone, telex, fax and electronic mail is much more common than by post. It is now well established, following the decision of the Court of Appeal in *Entores v. Miles Far East Corporation* (which was approved by the House of Lords) [*Brinkibon Ltd v. Stahag Stahl und Stahlwarenhandelsgesellschaft mbH* [1983] 2 AC 34]) that if the parties use "instantaneous" means of communication such as telephone, fax or electronic mail, the contract is made where the acceptance is communicated to the offeror. It has been held that if a contract made in England contains a submission to arbitration in a foreign country, an action in England at common law to enforce the foreign arbitration award is within this part of the clause. The contract must actually be made in England as that phrase is understood in English law. It is not sufficient if it merely says that it shall be

[55] Order XI, r 1(e) respectively: Rules of the Supreme Court 1883 (1961 ed) and O XI, r 1(d) and (e) of the Rules of the Supreme Court 1965.

[56] *Dicey, Morris and Collins on The Conflict of Laws* 15 ed (2012) vol 1, r 34 paras 11-181–11-187.

deemed to be so made, though this may be sufficient to make it one which is governed by English law. A contract may be made in England within the meaning of this clause although it was preceded by a less formal agreement made abroad, or if it was originally made in England, but amended abroad.

(ii) **Where a contract is made by or through an agent trading or residing in England**

11-182

The clause says "by or through" an agent, not "by" an agent. Hence the case is within the clause, although the agent has no authority to make contracts on behalf of his foreign principal, but only has authority to obtain orders and transmit them to his principal for acceptance or rejection. This part of the clause is designed to bring within Rule 34 foreigners who transact business in England by or through agents, and consequently it does not apply where the agent's principal is the claimant. Hence a claimant cannot invoke clause (6)(ii) where the contract was made by or through his agent.

11-183

If proceedings are brought by consignees of a cargo against foreign ship-owners under the bills of lading, the case is not within this part of the clause if the charterparty (but not the bills of lading) was made by or through agents of the shipowners in England, even though it refers to the bills of lading and was made by charterers acting on behalf of the consignees. It may be otherwise, however, if the charterers are identical with the consignees...

(iii) **Where a contract is governed by English law**

11-186

...

11-187

Although the fact that a contract is governed by English law is an important factor in the exercise of the discretion under this head in favour of the English forum, it is not conclusive. This head of jurisdiction was described as exorbitant in *Amin Rasheed Shipping Corp v. Kuwait Insurance Co*, where the House of Lords held that in the circumstances it was not appropriate for the English court to determine a dispute involving a marine insurance policy governed by English law when the Kuwaiti courts were the forum conveniens. Until that decision it was generally thought that the fact that a contract was governed by English law was in itself sufficient to justify leave. But now the claimant has a heavier burden. In *Amin Rasheed* Lord Diplock suggested that, in order to justify leave under this head, the plaintiff had to show that justice could not be obtained by him in the foreign court, or could only be obtained at excessive cost, delay or inconvenience. But it was subsequently held that Lord Diplock was merely giving examples, and was not providing an exhaustive list, of the relevant factors. The court has to consider all factors, and the fact that English law is the applicable law may be of great importance, or it may be of little consequence as seen in the context of the whole case. Thus if there is likely to be no dispute on matters of law or construction, or if the law of the foreign forum is substantially the same as English law, the fact that English law is the applicable law will be of little weight. But where an issue of English public policy arises in relation to a contract which is (or may be) governed by English law, it is desirable that it should be decided by the English court; conversely, where the foreign court may apply its own public policy to defeat a claim based on a contract governed by English law, that too is a reason for the English court taking jurisdiction. If the claimant has alternative remedies in contract and tort upon the same facts, he can choose his remedy.'

(3) The action is founded on tort or other civil wrong committed within the jurisdiction.

There is little authority in Ghana on the construction and application of Order 8, rule 3(h). As noted above,[57] in *Wachter v Harlley*,[58] the court considered an application to dismiss an action based on a tort committed outside the jurisdiction in Switzerland where the defendant's connection with Ghana was simply that he had been served within the jurisdiction (and thus the case fell outside the scope of what is now Order 8, rule 3(h)). The case concerned allegedly defamatory comments made in Switzerland. The defendant did not apply for a stay of the Ghanaian proceedings on the ground that Ghana was not an appropriate forum, and the judge did not refer to the point either. The argument concerned the proper law of the tort. In this case, had the plaintiff applied for leave to issue a writ for service out of the jurisdiction, the application ought to have been refused.

In *Signal Oil and Gas Co v Bristow Helicopters Ltd*,[59] for example, an application for leave to issue a writ for service out of the jurisdiction was refused on the basis that, although the damage had occurred within the jurisdiction, the tort itself had not and the case was therefore not within what is now Order 8, rule 3(h).

As with the construction and application of Order 8, rule 3(f) and (g), it is likely that, in the apparent absence of Ghanaian authority on the subject, a Ghanaian court will be guided by the academic and judicial authorities on the construction and application of the (former) equivalent provision in the English Rules of the Supreme Court on the question when is a tort committed within the jurisdiction.[60]

A statement of the law is as follows:[61]

'11-212

... As both the Privy Council [in *Distillers Co (Bio-chemicals) Ltd v. Thompson* [1971] AC 458] and the Supreme Court of Canada [*Moran v. Pyle National (Canada) Ltd* (1973) 43 D.L.R. (3d) 239] have pointed out, the competing theories for the determination of the

[57] [1968] GLR 1069 (H Ct) (Charles Crabbe J).

[58] [1968] GLR 1069 (H Ct) (Charles Crabbe J).

[59] [1976] 1 GLR 371; Frimpong Oppong *Private International Law in Commonwealth Africa* (2013) 51.

[60] Order XI, r 1(ee) and 1(f) respectively: Rules of the Supreme Court 1883 (1961 ed) and 1965.

[61] *Dicey, Morris and Collins on the Conflict of Laws* 15 ed (2012) vol 1, r 34 paras 11-212–11-213.

place of a tort have been that (i) all ingredients of the cause of action must have occurred within the jurisdiction, or (ii) the last ingredient, the event which completes a cause of action, must have occurred within the jurisdiction, or (iii) the act which the defendant committed must have occurred within the jurisdiction.

11-213

In *Distillers Co Ltd v Thompson* the Privy Council adopted the test of the place where in substance the act or omission occurred which gave the plaintiff his cause of action. So that where the essence of the complaint was failure to warn the consumer of the dangers of a product (rather than the faulty manufacture of the product) the cause of action was held to have arisen at the place where the failure to warn occurred; and the torts of negligent and fraudulent misrepresentation, where the negligent or fraudulent statement was communicated from one country to another, were held to have been committed where the statement was received and acted upon. Prior to the adoption of that test, but consistently with it, it had been held that the tort of defamation was committed where the defamatory statements were published and not where they were posted or uttered.'

2.1.2.3 *Submission to the jurisdiction*

Two circumstances must be distinguished under the title submission to the jurisdiction. First, where submission is alleged because the defendant has entered an appearance in existing proceedings in Ghana. Second, where the defendant has agreed (usually by contractual provision) to submit to the jurisdiction of the court in advance of a dispute arising.

2.1.2.3.1 Submission by appearance

It is well established in Ghana that an appearance entered by a party solely to contest the jurisdiction of the court is not a voluntary submission to the jurisdiction of the court. In *Sanyo Electric Trading v Quacoopome*,[62] the defendant argued before the Court of Appeal that the court below had no jurisdiction over it. In acceding to that argument, the Court of Appeal accepted that the defendant, in entering a conditional appearance to contest the jurisdiction of the court, had not submitted to the jurisdiction.[63]

In *Moubarak v Holland West Afrika Lijn*,[64] the contract provided for the application of the law of the Netherlands and for all actions under the contract to be brought before the courts of Amsterdam 'and no other court shall have jurisdiction ... unless the carrier ... voluntarily submits himself thereto'. The defendant was the carrier and the beneficiary of this clause. On being

[62] [2001–02] 2 GLR 198 (CA) (Omari-Sasu, Ansah and Asiamah JJA).

[63] Order 9, r 7 of the 2004 rules makes provision for the entering of a conditional appearance.

[64] (1953) 14 WACA 262 (W African Court of Appeal) (Foster-Sutton P, Coussey JA and Korsah J).

served with a writ of summons which specified a return date, the defendant did not apply for stay of proceedings but instead the defendant filed a defence. Notwithstanding that the defence pleaded the point that the court did not have jurisdiction, the Court of Appeal held that the defendant had submitted to an order for pleadings and had taken a step in the proceedings such as amounted to a submission to the jurisdiction.[65]

It seems that a defendant may submit to the jurisdiction by posting a bail bond to secure his release, initially having been arrested pursuant to what is now Order 73 of the rules as an absconding defendant. In *Wachter v Harlley*,[66] the court stated:[67]

> 'On 17 June 1967, an absconding warrant to arrest the defendant was issued against the defendant. This shows that he was within the jurisdiction of the court. The order for the issue of a warrant was made at 9:40am and by 12:40pm, that is, within three hours of the issue of the warrant, the defendant had been brought to court. Before the court, counsel for the defendant stated that the defendant was prepared to offer bail for his appearance before the court. Eventually a bail bond was executed. In my view the conduct on the part of the defendant means that he has submitted to the jurisdiction of the courts of Ghana in respect of this particular matter and he cannot be heard to dispute that submission. As far as one can see, there was no protest ...'.

It is not clear what sort of protest would have ensured that the defendant remained able to contend that he had not submitted to the jurisdiction by executing a bail bond to secure his liberty. This places a defendant in such circumstances in an invidious position.

After entering a conditional appearance in accordance with the Rules, the defendant ought promptly to raise the objection on which he relies, failing which the court may treat the appearance as unconditional and the court must at all times ensure that a conditional appearance is entered for a genuine reason and not merely to delay the proceedings.

2.1.2.3.2 Submission by agreement

2.1.2.3.2.1 *Jurisdiction clauses*

The courts in Ghana will have regard to jurisdiction clauses in favour of foreign courts or arbitration proceedings[68] and endeavour to give effect to them.

---

[65] The *Moubarak* case was followed in *Polimex Co Ltd v BBC Builders & Engineers Co Ltd* [1968] GLR 168 (H Ct) (Edusei J), where the defendant did not enter a conditional appearance and did not otherwise protest the jurisdiction of the court. This, combined with steps in filing of additional issues for the summons for directions and filing a defence and counterclaim, amounted to submission.

[66] [1968] GLR 1069 (H Ct) (Charles Crabbe J).

[67] Ibid 1075.

[68] For example, in *Fattal v Fattal* [1999–2000] 1 GLR 331 (CA) (Lamptey, Wood and Brobbey JJA), a stay of proceedings in Ghana was granted in a partnership dispute where the partnership agreement contained

In *CILE v Chiavelli*,[69] proceedings had been commenced in Ghana for recovery of certain sums alleged as being the value of the plaintiff's goods sold by the defendants. The defendants objected to the jurisdiction on the basis that the parties had contracted for disputes between them to be settled in Italy: 'For every dispute only the forum of the judicial authority in Modena is competent.'[70] The contract between the parties was entered into in Italy and was in the Italian language. Granting the defendants' application (and striking out the claim) Amissah JA stated:[71]

> 'With the exception of the oblique references to agreements to submit disputes to the jurisdiction of the English courts made by Lord Phillimore in the *Kwik Hoo Tong Handel Maatschappij* case (at pp. 609-610), direct authorities on contractual agreements to submit to a particular court as opposed to an arbitration in a particular country are not easy to find. But I think the principle should be the same. Just as parties to contracts regularly and freely opt to submit their disputes to arbitration and effect is given to their option, so, I think, should effect be given to such an expressed intention of the parties if they opt that their disputes should be submitted only to the judicial authority of a particular place. And the case for this is even stronger if, as in the present case, the judicial authority in question is one so closely connected with the place and the language in which the contract was made.'[72]

In *CILE v Black Star Line*,[73] decided by Amissah JA three weeks after his judgment in the *Chiavelli* case, the judge declined to give effect to a jurisdiction clause in favour of the English courts. The court found that: the defendant was a Ghanaian company; the dispute concerned the alleged improper detention of goods in Ghana by the defendant; those goods were alleged to be collecting 'vast rents' for the government of Ghana; the defendant had raised the jurisdiction clause very late in the proceedings such that there had been several adjournments and the calling of some evidence in the case; to stay the proceedings in favour of England would be in effect to instruct the plaintiff to forego his rights because by the time the case was heard in England the value of the rents taken by the government of Ghana would exceed the value of the goods. In the circumstances the court declined to give effect to the jurisdiction clause.

---

an arbitration clause and this notwithstanding that the defendants had entered an appearance and had filed defences.

[69] [1967] GLR 651 (H Ct) (Amissah JA).

[70] Notwithstanding that the defendants appear to have filed defences to the plaintiff's claims.

[71] [1967] GLR 651, 656.

[72] After the court's decision in *CILE v Black Star Line* [1967] GLR 744 (H Ct) (Amissah JA), the plaintiff in the *Chiavelli* case returned, in mid-February 1968, to argue another point why the court should not strike the case out and remit it to the court in Modena. The court's decision dismissing this attempt is reported at [1968] GLR 160. Amissah JA did not accept that the *Black Star Line* case was relevant and restated the principle: 'It is not impossible, nor is it even unusual, for a court with undoubted jurisdiction in a case to decline to exercise it in deference to a court of a foreign country also with jurisdiction in the case.'

[73] [1967] GLR 744 (H Ct) (Amissah JA).

In *Fan Milk Ltd v State Shipping Corp*,[74] the court considered an action in contract where the plaintiff was a Ghanaian company carrying on business in Ghana, the defendant was a statutory corporation established under the laws of Ghana and financed by the government, the vessel carrying the goods alleged to have been delivered damaged was a Ghanaian registered vessel and the goods were delivered in Ghana. The defendant contended that the proceedings should be stayed in favour of England because the bill of lading contained a jurisdiction clause in favour of the English courts. Relying on the English Court of Appeal decision in *Cargo lately laden on board the ship or vessel Fehmarn v The Fehmarn (Owners), The Fehmarn*,[75] the court held:[76]

> 'Reasonableness, therefore, is usually the criterion for deciding whether or not a jurisdiction clause ought to be honoured, and what is reasonable is a question of fact for the court. As I have said the parties are a Ghanaian company and a Ghanaian corporation, the goods were delivered in Ghana. Ghanaian law and English law on the matter do not differ in any material particular. I do not think this is a proper case to stay proceedings.'

The Fehmarn was followed and applied by Brandon J (as he then was) in *Owners of cargo lately laden on board the ship or vessel Eleftheria v The Eleftheria (Owners), The Eleftheria*,[77] where he considered the earlier authorities and set out a statement of the principles applicable to an application for a stay of proceedings where there was a jurisdiction clause relied on by the party seeking the stay. Brandon J's statement of the principles has since been accepted as the authoritative statement in this area by courts in other Anglophone African jurisdictions.[78]

In *The Eleftheria* the jurisdiction clause provided: 'Any dispute arising under this bill of lading shall be decided in the country where the carrier has his principal place of business [Greece].' The owners of cargo on board the *Eleftheria* commenced proceedings in England and the shipowners applied for a stay of those proceedings. In staying the proceedings in favour of the Greek courts Brandon J set out the principles on the basis of which a stay may be granted:[79]

> '(1) Where plaintiffs sue in England in breach of an agreement to refer disputes to a foreign court, and the defendants apply for a stay, the English court, assuming the claim to be otherwise within its jurisdiction, is not bound to grant a stay but has a discretion whether to do so or not. (2) The discretion should be exercised by granting a stay unless strong cause for not doing so is shown. (3) The burden of proving such strong cause is on the plaintiffs. (4) In exercising its discretion the court should take into account all the circumstances of the particular case. (5) In particular, but without prejudice to (4), the following matters,

[74] [1971] 1 GLR 238 (H Ct) (Hayfron-Benjamin J).
[75] [1958] 1 WLR 159 (Lord Denning, Hodson and Morris LJJ).
[76] [1971] 1 GLR 238, 242.
[77] [1970] P 94; [1969] 1 Lloyd's Rep 237 (QBD, Comm Ct).
[78] See, by way of example, *Nika Fishing Co Ltd v Lavina Corp* [2008] 16 NWLR 509 (Sup Ct, Nigeria).
[79] [1970] P 94 at 99G–100C.

> where they arise, may properly be regarded:—(a) In what country the evidence on the issues of fact is situated, or more readily available, and the effect of that on the relative convenience and expense of trial as between the English and foreign courts, (b) Whether the law of the foreign court applies and, if so, whether it differs from English law in any material respects, (c) With what country either party is connected, and how closely, (d) Whether the defendants genuinely desire trial in the foreign country, or are only seeking procedural advantages, (e) Whether the plaintiffs would be prejudiced by having to sue in the foreign court because they would: (i) be deprived of security for their claim; (ii) be unable to enforce any judgment obtained; (iii) be faced with a time-bar not applicable in England; or (iv) for political, racial, religious or other reasons be unlikely to get a fair trial.'

It is likely that *The Eleftheria* will be regarded as authoritative in Ghanaian courts when confronted with a jurisdiction clause that is controversial in its application to the facts.[80]

2.1.2.3.2.2 *Application for service out of the jurisdiction based on a jurisdiction clause*

In the English Rules of the Supreme Court,[81] Order XI, rule 1(1)(d)(i)–(iv), the sub-rule governing service out of the jurisdiction in cases concerned with contract, provides as follows: 'The claim is made to enforce ... a contract which ... (iv) contains a term to the effect that the High Court shall have jurisdiction to hear and determine any action in respect of the contract.' This additional provision was included in the English rules in order to reverse the decision of the Court of Appeal in *British Wagon Co Ltd v Gray*.[82]

The High Court Rules, Order 8, rule 3(m) contains the equivalent provision: 'if the action begun by the writ is in respect of a contract which contains a term to the effect that the Court shall have jurisdiction to hear and determine any action in respect of the contract.'

Where the defendant is not present within the jurisdiction and where the agreement between the parties contains a jurisdiction clause in favour of the Ghanaian courts, an order may be made for service of the defendant out of the jurisdiction.

---

[80] Adopting such an approach, of course, would demonstrate a divergence between the law of Ghana and the law of England on this point. English law now adopts an approach which accords greater respect to the jurisdiction clause: *Donohue v Armco Inc* [2002] 1 All ER 749 (HL (E)) (Lords Bingham, Mackay, Nicholls, Hobhouse and Scott), where Lord Bingham, at 754G–J, held: 'Where the dispute is between two contracting parties, A and B, and A sues in a non-contractual forum, and A's claims fall within the scope of the exclusive jurisdiction clause in their contract, and the interests of other parties are not involved, effect will in all probability be given to the clause.'

[81] Rules of the Supreme Court 1965 (the successor provision to O XI, r 2(a) of the Rules of the Supreme Court 1883 (1960 ed), introduced by amendment in 1920).

[82] [1896] 1 QB 35.

2.1.2.4 Lis alibi pendens

The approach of the Ghanaian courts to concurrent proceedings concerning the same subject-matter and parties within and outside the jurisdiction is not entirely clear. In *Fattal v Fattal*,[83] Wood JA commented on the concurrence of proceedings in Ghana and Lebanon as follows (after finding that neither the parties nor the remedies sought in the two sets of proceedings were identical):

> 'Finally on the question of the forum conveniens, I find the plaintiff counsel's argument to which the defendant provided no answers unassailable. When the issue of the forum conveniens, or the forum competents, that is the forum for the determination of this suit was raised before the learned trial judge, he decided in favour of the North Lebanon court for the sole reason that the case in Lebanon is very likely to be completed and judgment delivered before the case in Ghana does. He thus concluded that since "there is a possibility of conflicting judgments being given by the two courts, it will be an abuse of the legal process of the court to allow the proceedings in the two courts to go on at the same time".
>
> The mere fact of the pendency of a similar suit (even if found to be so), is not a criteria for determining the forum conveniens.'

From this passage it seems tolerably clear that the court will be concerned to identify the *forum conveniens* as a critical step in determining whether, on the assumption the two sets of proceedings are the same, the Ghanaian court will take steps to prevent the proceedings outside the jurisdiction from continuing.

There would appear to be no reason why a Ghanaian court could not order a party subject to its personal jurisdiction to stay proceedings commenced by that party outside the jurisdiction between the same parties and concerning the same subject-matter. Order 25, rule 1(1) provides:

> 'The Court may grant an injunction by an interlocutory order in all cases in which it appears to the Court to be just or convenient to do so, and the order may be made either unconditionally or upon such terms and conditions as the Court considers just.'

These words are of sufficient amplitude to embrace an application for an anti-suit injunction.

2.1.2.5 Forum non conveniens

As noted at section 2.1.2.1 above, the final stage in the court's analysis when determining whether to permit service out is to consider whether, in the exercise of its discretion, the court should permit service out. In other words, the court must consider whether Ghana is the *forum conveniens.*

---

[83] [1999–2000] 1 GLR 331, 350.

It appears that Ghanaian courts consider it appropriate to take into account considerations of convenience when deciding whether to grant leave to issue and serve out of the jurisdiction (or whether to grant a stay of proceedings already commenced). Indeed, and as mentioned above in *Signal Oil and Gas Co v Bristow Helicopters Ltd*,[84] Griffiths-Randolph J refused leave to issue and serve the writ outside the jurisdiction, stating:[85]

> 'since the contract ... on which the claim was based was executed in another country, where also the plans were drawn up, the parties have their establishments outside Ghana, and not only was the gear box whose manufacture was said to be defective made in Italy, but also the maintenance and repair of the helicopter were carried outside the Republic, but it was only the accident that occurred here, the tort was committed outside Ghana which therefore cannot be said to be the most appropriate or convenient venue for this action.'

This decision demonstrates that at the stage of deciding whether or not to grant leave to issue a writ for service out of the jurisdiction, a major factor informing the court's discretion is whether Ghana is the appropriate forum for the hearing and determination of the action.

In adopting this approach, the Ghanaian courts seem to have followed that which, historically, English courts have adopted. English courts seemed always to have held that a major factor in the exercise of the discretion to grant leave to serve out of the jurisdiction or to stay proceedings already served out of the jurisdiction was whether the English proceedings were vexatious and oppressive. The expression 'vexatious and oppressive' bore a wide meaning and extended to considerations related to the comparative convenience of proceedings in England as opposed to a particular foreign forum. For example, in *Logan v Bank of Scotland (No 2)*,[86] the Court of Appeal granted an application staying proceedings served as of right in England in favour of Scotland. Sir Gorell Barnes P stated:[87]

> 'Now, it is true that the Courts of this country have not gone so far as to express themselves upon the question of convenience in terms similar to those used in the Scotch cases, though, as I have already noticed, it may be doubted whether there is any substantial difference between the two. Yet it seems to me clear that the inconvenience of trying a case in a particular tribunal may be such as practically to work a serious injustice upon a defendant and be vexatious. This would probably not be so if the difference of trying

[84] [1976] 1 GLR 371 (H Ct) (Griffiths-Randolph J); Frimpong Oppong *Private International Law in Commonwealth Africa* (2013) 51.

[85] At 378. However, it should be noted that in *Wachter v Harlley* [1968] GLR 1069, the court considered an application to dismiss an action based on a tort committed outside the jurisdiction in Switzerland where the defendant's connection with Ghana was simply that he had been served within the jurisdiction. The defendant did not apply for a stay of the Ghanaian proceedings on the grounds that Ghana was not an appropriate forum, and the judge did not refer to the point either. The argument concerned the proper law of the tort.

[86] [1906] 1 KB 141 (CA) (Sir Gorell Barnes, President, Collins MR, and Romer LJ).

[87] Ibid 151–2. This was a decision under the 1883 Rules of the Supreme Court.

> in one country rather than in another were merely measured by some extra expense; but where the difficulty for the defendant of trying in the country in which the action is brought is such that it is impracticable to properly try the case by reason of the difficulty of procuring the attendance of busy men as witnesses, and keeping them during trial, and of having to deal with masses of books, documents, and papers which are not in the country where the action is brought, and of dealing with law foreign to the tribunal, it appears to me that a case of vexation in some circumstances may be made out if the plaintiff chooses to sue in that country rather than in that where everybody is and where all the witnesses and material for the trial are.'

In *Spiliada Maritime Corp v Cansulex Ltd*,[88] the House of Lords decided:[89]

> 'The basic principle is that a stay will only be granted on the ground of forum non conveniens where the court is satisfied that there is some other available forum, having competent jurisdiction, which is the appropriate forum for the trial of the action, i.e. in which the case may be tried more suitably for the interests of all the parties and the ends of justice.'

The English courts will, therefore, refuse leave to issue and serve a writ out of the jurisdiction or (in a case where leave has been granted but the defendant enters a conditional appearance) will stay English proceedings if England is not the *forum conveniens*.[90]

2.2 Enforcement of Foreign Judgments

It seems that under Ghanaian law a foreign judgment may be enforced in Ghana either under the statutory regime set out in Part V of the Courts Act 1993 or at common law.

---

[88] [1987] AC 460 (Lords Keith, Templeman, Griffiths, Mackay and Goff).

[89] Ibid 476C, *per* Lord Goff, with whom the other Lords of Appeal agreed (Lord Templeman delivering a concurring opinion). A decision under the 1965 Rules of the Supreme Court.

[90] See, generally, *Dicey, Morris and Collins on the Conflict of Laws* 15 ed (2012) vol 1, r 38(2) and (3) para 12-007 et seq; r 38 states the modern English law as follows, inter alia: '(2) ... an English court has power to order a stay of proceedings on the basis that England is an inappropriate forum (forum non conveniens) if: (a) the defendant shows there to be another court with competent jurisdiction which is clearly or distinctly more appropriate than England for the trial of the action, and (b) it is not unjust that the claimant be deprived of the right to trial in England. (3) In considering whether to assume jurisdiction in any of the cases mentioned in Rule 34 (service out of the jurisdiction with the permission of the court) the court will generally require the claimant to show England to be the most appropriate forum for the trial of the claim.' See further *Vedanta Resources plc v Lungowe* [2020] AC 1045 (SC) (Lady Hale, Lords Wilson and Hodge, Lady Black and Lord Briggs), [66]–[70].

2.2.1 Enforcement at common law

There is a consensus among commentators that enforcement at common law is available for judgment creditors in Ghana. Frimpong Oppong states:[91]

> 'English law was introduced into the Ghanaian legal system through the Supreme Court Ordinance of 1876. Section 14 of the Ordinance provided that:
>
> > "the common law, the doctrines of equity, and Statutes of general application which were in force in England at the date when the colony obtained a local legislature, that is to say, on the 24th of July 1874, shall be in force within the jurisdiction of the court."
>
> The Ordinance made the common law part of the laws of the then Gold Coast (now Ghana). Through it the body of law known as private international law, including the rules on recognition and enforcement of judgments at common law, became part of the laws of Ghana.'

By 1874 the basic English law principles of enforcement at common law had been settled and it is to be expected that a Ghanaian court will have regard to developments in the English common law that have occurred since that time.[92]

These principles are conveniently set out in *Dicey, Morris and Collins on the Conflict of Laws*:[93]

> '**Rule 42**
>
> (1) Subject to the Exceptions hereinafter mentioned and to Rule 62 (international conventions), a foreign judgment in personam given by the court of a foreign country with jurisdiction to give that judgment in accordance with the principles set out in Rules 43 to 46, and which is not impeachable under any of Rules 49 to 54, may be enforced by a claim or counterclaim for the amount due under it if the judgment is
>
> *(a)* for a debt, or definite sum of money (not being a sum payable in respect of taxes or other charges of a like nature or in respect of a fine or other penalty); and

[91] (2005) 31 (4) *Commonwealth Law Bulletin* 19. See also Amankwah 'Ghanaian law: Its evolution and interaction with English law' (1970) 4 *Cornell International Law Journal* 37. The common-law regime does not appear to be much used or known about in the profession in Ghana: see, for example, *Republic v Mallet, ex p Braun* [1975] 1 GLR 68, where a judgment of a West German court was unsuccessfully sought to be enforced under the 1993 Act (because the 1993 Act does not extend to Germany); it does not appear that the common-law route was considered. Frimpong Oppong warns Ghanaian lawyers ('Recognition and enforcement of foreign judgments in Ghana' (2005) 31 (4) *Commonwealth Law Bulletin* 19 at 31): 'If international clients cannot be assured of reliable legal advice in this area of the law due to its neglect, it will not augur well for Ghana's efforts at promoting commercial dealings with it.'

[92] However, it must be remembered that O 8, r 3 of the High Court Rules does not allow the Ghanaian court to permit service of a writ on a defendant who is present outside the jurisdiction where the action is one to enforce a foreign judgment; Frimpong Oppong 'Recognition and enforcement of foreign judgments in Commonwealth African countries' (2014) XV *Yearbook of Private International Law* 365, 372 and, specifically, fn 31. See also *NML Capital v Republic of Argentina*, Suit No RPC/343/12 (unreported) 2012 (HC) and *Republic v High Court (Commercial Division) Accra, ex p Attorney General, NML Capital and the Republic of Argentina*, Civil Motion No J5/10/2013 (unreported) 2013 (Sup Ct, Ghana).

[93] 15 ed (2012) vol 1 para 14R-020.

(*b*) final and conclusive,

but not otherwise.

Provided that a foreign judgment may be final and conclusive, though it is subject to an appeal, and though an appeal against it is actually pending in the foreign country where it was given.

(2) A foreign judgment given by the court of a foreign country with jurisdiction to give that judgment in accordance with the principles set out in Rules 43 to 46, which is not impeachable under any of Rules 49 to 54 and which is final and conclusive on the merits, is entitled to recognition at common law and may be relied on in proceedings in England.

(3) No proceedings may be brought by a person on a cause of action in respect of a judgment which has been given in his favour in proceedings between the same parties or their privies in a court in another part of the United Kingdom or in a court in an overseas country unless that judgment is not enforceable according to clause (1), or not entitled to recognition according to clause (2), of this Rule.'

In order for its judgment to be enforceable the foreign court must have possessed international competence to determine the case. Before considering, however, the circumstances in which a foreign court will be considered at common law to have such international competence, it is necessary to consider, in this context, the meaning of the word 'court'. In the *Mba* case,[94] the applicant sought from the High Court an order to enforce a judgment of the Economic Community of West African States (ECOWAS) against the Republic of Ghana. While the High Court ultimately rejected the application based on its interpretation of the effect of the statutory regime by which the judgments of foreign courts can be enforced in Ghana (as discussed in more detail below) and so did not have to consider, explicitly, whether the judgment of the ECOWAS court could be enforced at common law, the court did seem to be of the view that the ECOWAS court was indeed a court, properly so called.[95] In consequence, it is strongly arguable that the judgments of such courts ought, in principle, to be capable of being enforced at common law, so long as the other relevant requirements of enforcement are met.[96] It is to be hoped that the courts of Ghana have an opportunity to consider this line of argument in the near future. If they do, the authors submit that

[94] *In the Matter of an Application to Enforce the Judgment of the Community Court of Justice of the ECOWAS against the Republic of Ghana and in the Matter of Chude Mba v The Republic of Ghana,* Suit No. HRCM/376/15 (unreported) 2 February 2016 (Suurbaareh JA).

[95] Ibid p 7 of the ruling.

[96] Frimpong Oppong 'The High Court of Ghana declines to enforce an ECOWAS Court judgment' (2017) 25 *African Journal of International and Comparative Law* 127, 131. See also, for a wider context, Frimpong Oppong and Niro 'Enforcing judgments of international courts in national courts' (2014) 5 *Journal of International Dispute Settlement* 344.

the jurisprudence of South African courts[97] may, in particular, provide useful guidance as to the approach which the common law ought to take when faced with a request to enforce the judgment of an international tribunal.

Returning, then, to the circumstances in which, as a matter of common law, a foreign court will have been internationally competent, it will have been so in the following cases:[98] (1) if the person against whom the judgment was given was, at the time the proceedings were instituted, present in the foreign country; or (2) if the person against whom the judgment was given was the claimant, or counterclaimed, in the proceedings in the foreign court; or (3) if the person against whom the judgment was given submitted to the jurisdiction of that court by voluntarily appearing in the proceedings; or (4) if the person against whom the judgment was given had, before the commencement of the proceedings, agreed, in respect of the subject-matter of the proceedings, to submit to the jurisdiction of that court or of the courts of that country.

Among the established defences to an action at common law on a foreign judgment are the following: (1) where the foreign judgment was procured by either (a) fraud on the part of the party in whose favour the judgment is given, or (b) fraud on the part of the court pronouncing the judgment;[99] (2) the enforcement or recognition of the foreign judgment would be contrary to public policy;[100] and (3) where the proceedings in which the foreign judgment was obtained were contrary to the rules of natural justice.[101]

2.2.2 Enforcement pursuant to statute

2.2.2.1 *The regime for enforcement pursuant to statute*

As mentioned above, the statutory regime for enforcement of foreign judgments in Ghana is set out in Part V of the Courts Act 1993 ('the 1993 Act').

The 1993 Act is a transposition[102] of the provisions of the United Kingdom Foreign Judgments (Reciprocal Enforcement) Act 1933 and, as a result, it is to be expected that a Ghanaian court when construing the terms of the 1993 Act will refer to judicial and academic authorities on the construction of these provisions of the 1933 Act.[103]

---

[97] By way of example, the Constitutional Court of the Republic of South Africa in *Government of the Republic of Zimbabwe v Fick* 2013 (5) SA 325 developed the common law of that country so as to render the orders of the Tribunal of the Southern African Development Community enforceable.

[98] *Dicey, Morris and Collins on the Conflict of Laws* 15 ed (2012) vol 1, r 43 para 14R-054.

[99] Ibid r 50 para 14R-137.

[100] Ibid r 51 para 14R-152.

[101] Ibid r 52 para 14R-162.

[102] There are some differences in drafting, however. In addition, there is some modernising language and some further sub-division of clauses into sub-sections in the 1993 Act.

[103] In particular, reference should be made to: *Dicey, Morris and Collins on the Conflict of Laws* 15 ed (2012) vol 1, paras 14R183–14-195; Briggs *Civil Jurisdiction and Judgments* 7 ed (2021) paras 35.01-35.10.

The 1993 Act applies to jurisdictions to which sections 81–88[104] of Part V of the 1993 Act have been extended by legislative instrument.[105] At the present time these countries are as follows: Brazil; France; Israel; Italy; Japan; Lebanon; Senegal; Spain; the United Arab Republic;[106] and the United Kingdom.[107]

A brief summary of the principal provisions of the 1993 Act is set out below.

2.2.2.2 *Procedure for registration*

The procedure for registration is as follows:[108] a judgment creditor under a foreign judgment[109] may apply to the High Court in Ghana[110] for registration of the judgment; the procedure for registration is prescribed by the procedure rules of the appropriate court – in the case of the High Court these are the rules made pursuant to section 98 of the Act; an application for registration 'shall' be made within six years of the date of either the foreign judgment itself or the determination of any appeal or review proceedings in respect of the foreign judgment.[111]

---

[104] The sections within Part V concerned with the reciprocal enforcement of judgments.

[105] See the Foreign Judgments and Maintenance Orders (Reciprocal Enforcement) Instrument 1993 (LI 1575), Sch 1. The reciprocal enforcement of maintenance orders has been extended to: Switzerland; the United Kingdom; the Australian states of Queensland, Tasmania and Western Australia; and the Canadian provinces of Alberta, British Colombia, Newfoundland, North-west Territories, Nova Scotia, Ontario and Prince Edward Island.

[106] A political union between Egypt and Syria which existed between 1958 and 1961 and not thereafter.

[107] In *Mba,* Suit No. HRCM/376/15 (unreported) 2 February 2016, the High Court, relying on the decision of the Supreme Court in *Republic v High Court (Commercial Division) Accra, ex p Attorney General and NML Capital Ltd*, Civil Motion No. J5/10/2013 (unreported) (Date-Bah, Dotse, Yeboah, Gbadegbe and Akamba JJSC), correctly determined that the 1993 Act had not been extended to the ECOWAS Community Court, such that judgments of that court could not be enforced via the procedure set out in the 1993 Act. It is also, on a first blush basis, difficult to see how the statutory regime could be extended so as to encompass judgments of, say, the ECOWAS Community Court, to the use of the word 'country' in s 81 of the 1993 Act. For further context, see Frimpong Oppong 'The High Court of Ghana declines to enforce an ECOWAS Court judgment' (2017) 25 *African Journal of International and Comparative Law* 127, 130–1.

[108] Section 82.

[109] It has been held by the Court of Appeal in England that the 1920 Act does not permit registration of a judgment given by a court in one state in an action to enforce a judgment given by a court in another state: *Strategic Technologies Pte Ltd v Procurement Bureau of the Republic of China Ministry of National Defence* [2020] EWCA Civ 1604 (David Richards, Males and Elisabeth Laing LJJ). The definition of 'judgment' in s 12(1) of the 1920 Act is materially identical to the definition in s 11(1) of the 1933 Act and so the decision in *Strategic Technologies* will probably apply to the 1933 Act as well.

[110] Section 82(1).

[111] Section 82(2). The six-year period is derived from s 2(1) of the Foreign Judgments (Reciprocal Enforcement) Act 1933. There is a difference in the language used in the 1993 Act and the 1933 Act: the terms of s 82(2) of the 1993 Act are mandatory and clearly impose a limit on the court, removing any discretion to permit registration outside the six-year period: see *Yankson v Mensah* [1976] 1 GLR 355 (H Ct) where Edusei J agreed with this conclusion (at 375). In the 1933 Act the language used in relation to the six-year period is permissive ('may apply ... within six years'): Briggs *Civil Jurisdiction and Judgments* 7 ed (2021) para 35.10.

Section 82(3)[112] makes the registration of the foreign judgment discretionary, 'The High Court may, subject to proof of the prescribed matters and to other provisions of this Act, order the judgment to be registered.' These prescribed matters are set out in section 81(2)[113] of the 1993 Act; the foreign judgment must: (1) be final and conclusive; (2) be a money judgment not being a sum in respect of taxes or a fine or other penalty; and (3) it is given after the coming into force of the instrument extending sections 81–88 of the 1993 Act to the jurisdiction of the foreign court.

Section 82(7) provides that, regardless of the currency in which the foreign judgment was issued, the judgment must be registered in the currency of Ghana based on the exchange rate prevailing at the foreign judgment of the original court.[114]

2.2.2.3 *Setting aside registration*

Section 83(1)(a)[115] of the 1993 Act provides that in certain prescribed circumstances the court *must* set aside registration of the foreign judgment.[116] These circumstances are that:

(1) the judgment is not a judgment to which the 1993 Act applies or was registered in contravention of any previous provisions of the 1993 Act; or

(2) the original court had no jurisdiction in the case; or

(3) the judgment debtor, being the defendant in the proceedings in the original court, did not, although process may have been duly served on him in accordance with the law of the country of the original court, receive notice of those proceedings in sufficient time to enable him to defend the proceedings and did not appear;[117] or

---

[112] The equivalent to s 2(1) of the 1933 Act.

[113] The equivalent to s 1(2) of the 1933 Act.

[114] This provision has not proved popular with the courts. It has been characterised as a provision which encourages contract-breaking and fraud (because of volatility in the exchange rate of the *cedis*, it pays Ghanaian counterparties to delay payment until the debt in the foreign currency is worth far less than at the time of contracting). In *Broderick v Northern Engineering Product* [1991] 2 GLR 88 (H Ct), Brobbey J confirmed that the sub-section should be given its natural meaning and that it was not the proper function of a judge deliberately to misinterpret the express terms of a statute in order to achieve the result he desired. However, at common law and in domestic proceedings, a Ghanaian court may award damages in a foreign currency: *Royal Dutch Airlines (KLM) v Farmex Ltd* [1989–90] 1 GLR 46 (CA) (Osei-Hwere (dissenting), Lamptey and Essiem JJA), *per* Essiem J at 61–2. This conclusion was upheld when the case came before the Supreme Court: [1989–90] GLRD 266 para 136 (Adade Ag CJ, Wuaku, Amua-Sekyi (dissenting), Aikins and Edward Wiredu JJSC).

[115] The equivalent to s 4(1)(a) of the 1933 Act.

[116] The exclusionary provisions of the 1933 Act were based on the common law: 'The grounds of jurisdiction in the 1933 Act were deliberately framed so as to reproduce the rules of the common law as closely as possible', *Dicey, Morris and Collins on the Conflict of Laws* 15 ed (2012) vol 1, para 14-190.

[117] In *Ashurst Morris Crisp v Renner* (1931–7) Div Ct 107, Aitken J held that although the judgment debtor had been served with the English High Court writ in Accra and had not appeared in the English proceedings,

(4) the judgment was obtained by fraud;[118] or

(5) the enforcement of the judgment would be contrary to public policy in Ghana.[119]

Under section 83(1)(b)[120] the judgment *may* be set aside if the court is satisfied that the matter in dispute in the proceedings in the original court had previously been the subject of a final conclusive judgment by a court having jurisdiction in the matter.

The question whether the foreign court had jurisdiction is determined exhaustively[121] by the deeming provisions of section 83(2)(a).[122] The foreign court is deemed to have had jurisdiction in the case of a judgment in an action *in personam* if:

(1) the judgment debtor, being a defendant in the original court, submitted to the jurisdiction of that court by voluntarily appearing in the proceedings otherwise than for the purpose of protecting, or obtaining the release of property seized, or threatened with seizure, in the proceedings or of contesting the jurisdiction of that court; or

(2) the judgment debtor was the plaintiff in, or counter-claimed in, the proceedings in the original court; or

(3) the judgment debtor, being a defendant in the original court, had before the commencement of the proceedings agreed, in respect of the subject-

the judgment was enforceable against him because he had instructed his solicitors to file a defence in the proceedings.

[118] The equivalent to s 4(1)(a)(iv) of the 1933 Act. The rules related to setting aside a foreign judgment obtained by fraud are comprehensively set out in *Dicey, Morris and Collins on the Conflict of Laws* 15 ed (2012) vol 1, r 50 paras 14R-137–14-145. In *The Conflict of Laws*, para 14-191, it is stated of the fraud provisions of the 1933 Act: 'The provisions with regard to fraud and public policy are the same as the common law rules. In particular, the common law rule that a foreign judgment can be impeached for fraud even though no newly discovered evidence is produced, and even though the fraud was alleged in the foreign proceedings, applies to enforcement and recognition under the 1933 Act. In *Owens Bank Ltd v Bracco* [1992] 2 AC 443 the House of Lords held that the fraud exception in the Administration of Justice Act 1920 was subject to the same rule, and indicated (obiter) that the same must be so under the 1933 Act.' *Owens Bank* has not been followed in certain Commonwealth jurisdictions (eg Canada in *Beals v Saldanha* [2003] 3 SCR 416, (2003) 234 DLR 4th 1; and New South Wales in *Keele v Findley* (1991) 21 NSWLR 444 (NSWSC); but in *Close v Arnot* (unreported) 21 November 1997 (NSW), the Common Law Division distinguished *Keele v Findley* and applied the traditional English standard of fraud in respect of a foreign judgment in a case where the defendant had, for good reason, allowed foreign proceedings to go undefended. A Ghanaian court would not be bound by the *Owens Bank* decision.

[119] The equivalent to s 4(1)(a)(v) of the 1933 Act. The relevant rule in *The Conflict of Laws* is at r 51, paras 14R-152–14-158.

[120] The equivalent to s 4(1)(b) of the 1933 Act.

[121] *Société Co-opérative Sidmetal v Titan International Ltd* [1966] 1 QB 828; *Sharps Commercials Ltd v Gas Turbines Ltd* [1956] NZLR 819 (a decision on the identically worded New Zealand Act).

[122] The equivalent to s 4(2)(a) of the 1933 Act.

matter of the proceedings, to submit to the jurisdiction of that court or of the courts of the country of that court; or

(4) the judgment debtor, being a defendant in the original court, was at the time when the proceedings were instituted resident in, or being a body corporate had its principal place of business in, the country of that court; or

(5) the judgment debtor, being a defendant in the original court, had an office or place of business in the country of that court and the proceedings in that court were in respect of a transaction effected through or at that office or place.

Section 83(2)(b)[123] relates to property and provides that the foreign court has jurisdiction in proceedings relating to movable or immovable property if that property was situated in the foreign country when proceedings were commenced.

Section 83(2)(c) provides that in any other case the foreign court will be deemed to have had jurisdiction if the jurisdiction of the foreign court is recognised under the law of Ghana.[124]

Section 83(3) provides that the courts of the country of the original court shall be deemed not to have had jurisdiction if the subject-matter of the proceedings was immovable property outside the jurisdiction of the original court, or the original proceedings were brought in breach of an arbitration clause (settled otherwise than in proceedings in the courts of the country of that court), or the defendant was immune from suit under the rules of public international law.

Enforcement of a judgment at common law is not available if the foreign judgment is one that is registrable under the 1993 Act.[125]

---

[123] The equivalent to s 4(2)(b) of the 1933 Act.

[124] The equivalent to s 4(2)(c) of the 1933 Act. It remains undecided whether this provision would entitle a court to recognise a basis for the jurisdiction of the foreign court not expressly provided for in the Act but available at common law, such as the presence of the defendant in the jurisdiction of the foreign court at the time of the commencement of proceedings. The discussion of this provision in *Dicey, Morris and Collins on The Conflict of Laws* 15 ed (2012) vol 1, para 14-190, suggests that this is not the case; in *Société Co-opérative Sidmetal v Titan International Ltd* [1966] 1 QB 828, Widgery J held (at 850C–D) that an action *in personam* not within s 4(2)(a) was also excluded from s 4(2)(c): 'It seems to me that an action *in personam* does not fall within subsection (2) unless it satisfies one or other of the conditions in paragraph (a). As I read the section, no action *in personam* could fall within paragraph (c) at all because all such actions are excluded by the terms of paragraph (c).'

[125] Section 85 of the 1993 Act provides: 'No proceedings for the recovery of a sum payable under a foreign judgment, being a judgment to which this Sub-Part applies other than proceedings by way of registration of the judgment, shall be entertained by any court in Ghana.' See also *Yankson v Mensah* [1976] 1 GLR 355 (H Ct), where Edusei J confirmed (at 375) that a registrable judgment could not be enforced other than by the Courts Act 1971 (as the 1993 Act was then) notwithstanding that the judgment creditor had registered the judgment outside the six-year period provided for and that the judgment was, for that reason, invalidly registered. Frimpong Oppong has criticised this decision stating (*Private International Law in Commonwealth Africa* (2013) 535, fn 4) that it is not an evasion of the Act to seek to enforce a registrable judgment at common

On an application for enforcement of a foreign judgment, the High Court Rules, Order 71 applies. The applicant may apply *ex parte* for registration of the judgment. The application must be supported by affidavit evidence accompanied by an authenticated copy of the judgment. The court may order the applicant to give security for the costs of the application for registration. Notice of registration must be given personally to the judgment debtor and if he is out of the jurisdiction the notice may be served without leave under Order 8, rule 3. If he wishes to set aside registration, the judgment debtor must apply for the registration to be set aside (the time limit for this application appears from the notice of registration).

2.3 Interim Remedies

2.3.1 Jurisdiction to grant interim remedies

The jurisdiction of the High Court to grant injunctions is statutory:

> 'The Court may grant an injunction by an interlocutory order in all cases in which it appears to the Court to be just or convenient to do so, and the order may be made either unconditionally or upon such terms and conditions as the Court considers just.'[126]

Although there is no reported authority directly in point, it is likely that, in order for a Ghanaian court to make an interlocutory order in a cause, the court must have jurisdiction over the substantive dispute between the parties.[127]

2.3.2 Procedure for application

The rules governing interlocutory applications in the High Court are set out in Order 19. Applications are made by motion[128] supported by affidavit evidence[129] and, except where the rules otherwise provide, must be made on notice to the party effected.[130] Usually three clear days' notice of an application is required but the court may give leave for a period of notice less than that provided for in the rules.[131]

---

law. However, the clear terms of s 85 suggest that this view is incorrect and that registration is the only means of enforcement in Ghana.

[126] High Court Rules, O 25, r 1(1). The rules are made pursuant to the power conferred on the Rules of Court Committee by s 80 of the Courts Act 1993.

[127] Such was the position in the United Kingdom prior to the passing of s 25 of the Civil Jurisdiction and Judgments Act 1982 which now empowers courts in the United Kingdom to grant relief in aid of proceedings outside the jurisdiction (*Siskina (Owners of cargo lately on board) v Distos Compania Naviera SA, The Siskina,* [1979] AC 210 (HL(E))).

[128] Order 19, r 1(1).

[129] Order 19, r 4 (O 20 sets out provisions as to the form and contents of the affidavit).

[130] Order 19, r 1(3).

[131] Order 19, r 2.

Order 19, rule 3, allows for an application to be made *ex parte* but on condition that: 'The applicant shows to the satisfaction of the Court good reason for making the application ex-parte and the precise nature of the irreparable damage or serious mischief which will be occasioned by proceeding in the ordinary way.'

Order 25 makes provision for applications for injunctive relief. An application may be made *ex parte* but the applicant must satisfy the court that applying on notice will occasion irreparable damage or serious mischief.[132] An order made *ex parte* lasts no longer than ten days after which it lapses unless the court makes a further order.[133]

Order 25, rule 9, enshrines in the rules the requirement for an applicant for an injunction to give a cross-undertaking as to damages:

> '(1) Where an application is made under rules 1 and 2 of this Order the Court shall, if the application is opposed, require, before making an order, that the applicant shall give an undertaking to the person opposing the application to pay any damages that person may suffer as a result of the grant of the application if it turns out in the end that the applicant was not entitled to the order.
>
> (2) The giving of an undertaking required under subrule (1) shall be a precondition to the making of any order under rules 1 and 2 of this order.'

Although the terms of Order 25, rule 9(1), suggest that the court's power to require the applicant for an injunction to give a cross-undertaking in damages is confined to applications on notice,[134] it is likely that a court would construe the terms of rule 9(2) as being of sufficient amplitude to extend to an *ex parte* application.

It appears that Ghanaian courts use the terms 'interim' and 'interlocutory' in relation to injunctions interchangeably (unlike the apparently rigid distinction maintained by Nigerian courts).[135] Here the term 'interlocutory' is used to describe all pre-trial injunctions (*ex parte* or *inter partes*).

2.3.3 Interlocutory injunctions generally

In deciding whether to grant an application for an interlocutory injunction, the Ghanaian courts follow English law principles. In *Pountney v Doegah*,[136]

[132] Order 25, r 1(7) and (8). Sub-r (8) reproduces the words contained in O 19, r 3.

[133] Order 25, r 1(9).

[134] The provisions of r 9(1) operate where the application is opposed. On an *ex parte* application there will be no opposition.

[135] *Kotoye v Central Bank of Nigeria* [1989] 1 NWLR 419, (Sup Ct, Nigeria) (Nnamani, Karibi-Whyte, Agbaje, Nnaemeka-Agu and Craig JJSC); although in *Ghana Private Road Transport Union of the Trades Union Congress v Danful* [1995–96] 1 GLR 20 (H Ct), Gbadegbe J sought to draw this distinction. It seems the distinction is usually ignored by the courts.

[136] [1987–88] 1 GLR 111 (CA) (Abban, Osei-Hwere and Wuaku JJA).

the plaintiff sought an interlocutory injunction to restrain the defendant from building on land that the plaintiff contended she had been allocated by the Lands Commission. Allowing the plaintiff's appeal from the court at first instance, the court applied the principles set out in two leading English authorities. Abban JA stated:[137]

> 'It seems to me that the contents of these two documents—the affidavit of Mr Kilba and the statement of defence—rather showed that the plaintiff-appellant had, on the face of it, a better claim to the disputed plot than the defendant-respondent. In other words, the plaintiff-appellant's claim was not vexatious but had a legal basis. That is, the plaintiff-appellant had a legal right which could be asserted either at law or in equity and so the court could grant an injunction in protection of that right. "It is a fundamental rule that the court will only grant an injunction at the suit of a private individual to support a legal right": per Lord Denning MR in *Thorne v. British Broadcasting Corporation* [1957] 1 W.L.R. 1104 at 1109, C.A.
>
> There is no rule requiring the plaintiff to establish a *prima facie* case. The rule is that the court must be satisfied that the plaintiff's case is not frivolous and once that has been established then the governing consideration is the balance of convenience: see *American Cyanamid Co. v. Ethicon Ltd.* [1975] A.C. 396, H.L. Clearly on the showing of Mr. Kilba, that condition was satisfied by the plaintiff-appellant.'

The court granted an interlocutory injunction restraining the defendant from continuing building work until the determination of the action.[138]

The decision in *Pountney v Deogah* was endorsed by the Supreme Court of Ghana in *Yehans International Ltd v Tsuru & anr*,[139] in which the plaintiff landowner obtained an interlocutory injunction against the defendants restraining them from changing the nature of the land in dispute. The defendants' appeal to the Court of Appeal was dismissed. On appeal to the Supreme Court, Yeboah JSC (giving the judgment of the court), dismissed the defendants' appeal and stated the basic principles governing an application for an interlocutory injunction as follows:

> '1. That the status quo should as much as possible be maintained.
>
> 2. That the court should ensure that the successful party does not have a hollow victory at the end of the day.
>
> 3. That the order does not work greater inconvenience to either party than is reasonably or absolutely necessary.
>
> 4. That the question of hardship to either party must be seriously considered.'[140]

---

[137] Ibid 115.

[138] In *Food Specialties Ghana Ltd v Technicas de Multiconstruction SA* [1987-88] 1 GLR 25, [1987-88] GLRD 4 (CA) (Abban, Osei-Hwere and Wuaku JJA), the court relied on English authority in dismissing an appeal from the grant of an interlocutory injunction: *Hoffman-La Roche v Secretary of State for Trade & Industry* [1975] AC 295 at 355 (HL) *per* Lord Wilberforce; and *Woollerton & Wilson Ltd v Richard Costain Ltd* [1970] 1 WLR 411 at 413.

[139] [2011] GHASC 27 (Brobbey, Ansah, Owusu, Yeboah and Bonnie JJSC).

[140] Endorsing the Court of Appeal's judgment on this point.

The decision of the House of Lords relied on by the courts in both *Pountney v Doegah* and *Yehans International Ltd v Tsuru*, is *American Cyanamid Co v Ethicon Ltd*,[141] in which Lord Diplock gave the leading opinion of the House of Lords (with which the other Lords agreed). The opinion of Lord Diplock is generally taken as establishing a test comprising two elements:

(1) 'The court ... must be satisfied that the claim is not frivolous or vexatious; in other words, that there is a serious issue to be tried';[142]

'... unless the material available to the court at the hearing of the application for an interlocutory injunction fails to disclose that the plaintiff has any real prospect of succeeding in his claim for a permanent injunction at the trial, the court should go on to consider whether the balance of convenience lies in favour of granting or refusing the interlocutory relief that is sought';[143]

(2) On the balance of convenience:[144]

'... the governing principle is that the court should first consider whether, if the plaintiff were to succeed at the trial in establishing his right to a permanent injunction, he would be adequately compensated by an award of damages for the loss he would have sustained as a result of the defendant's continuing to do what was sought to be enjoined between the time of the application and the time of the trial. If damages in the measure recoverable at common law would be adequate remedy and the defendant would be in a financial position to pay them, no interlocutory injunction should normally be granted, however strong the plaintiff's claim appeared to be at that stage. If, on the other hand, damages would not provide an adequate remedy for the plaintiff in the event of his succeeding at the trial, the court should then consider whether, on the contrary hypothesis that the defendant were to succeed at the trial in establishing his right to do that which was sought to be enjoined, he would be adequately compensated under the plaintiff's undertaking as to damages for the loss he would have sustained by being prevented from doing so between the time of the application and the time of the trial. If damages in the measure recoverable under such an undertaking would be an adequate remedy and the plaintiff would be in a financial position to pay them, there would be no reason upon this ground to refuse an interlocutory injunction.

It is where there is doubt as to the adequacy of the respective remedies in damages available to either party or to both, that the question of balance of convenience arises. It would be unwise to attempt even to list all the various matters which may need to be taken into consideration in deciding where the balance lies, let alone to suggest the relative weight to be attached to them. These will vary from case to case.

Where other factors appear to be evenly balanced it is a counsel of prudence to take such measures as are calculated to preserve the status quo.'

---

[141] [1975] AC 396 (HL(E)) (Lord Diplock, Viscount Dilhorne and Lords Cross, Salmon and Edmund-Davies).

[142] Ibid 407G.

[143] Ibid 408A–B.

[144] Ibid 408B–G.

These, then, are the principles cited and relied on by the Court of Appeal and the Supreme Court in Ghana and that a Ghanaian court will follow in considering whether to grant an interlocutory injunction.[145]

2.3.4 Freezing orders

While it would appear that the freezing order is, conceptually at least, a remedy known to Ghanaian law,[146] there is still no reported authority which determines the question whether a Ghanaian court would grant an order by way of injunction for the purpose of freezing assets of the defendant to proceedings to ensure that he does not dissipate them prior to the conclusion of the proceedings. For the reasons referred to above, it is to be expected that, should the opportunity arise, this form of relief will be recognised in Ghana.

The English Court of Appeal has set down the following guidance on when a *Mareva* injunction should be granted. Hence, in *Mareva Compania Naviera v International Bulk Carriers SA*,[147] Lord Denning[148] stated that:

> 'In my opinion that principle applies to a creditor who has a right to be paid the debt owing to him, even before he has established his right by getting judgment for it. If it appears that the debt is due and owing, and there is a danger that the debtor may dispose of his asserts so as to defeat it before judgment, the court has jurisdiction in a proper case to grant an interlocutory judgment so as to prevent him disposing of those assets.'

In *Third Chandris Shipping Corp v Unimarine SA*,[149] Lord Denning MR[150] provided this further guidance:

> 'The guidelines
>
> In endeavouring to set out some guidelines, I have had recourse to the practice of many other countries which have been put before us. They have been most helpful. These are the points which those who apply for it should bear in mind. (i) The Plaintiff should make full and frank disclosure of all matters in his knowledge which are material for the judge to know... (ii) The Plaintiff should give particulars of his claim against the Defendant, stating the ground of his claim and the amount thereof, and fairly stating the points made against it by the Defendant. (iii) The Plaintiff should give some grounds for believing that the Defendants have assets here ...The existence of a bank account in England is enough, whether it is in overdraft or not. (iv) The Plaintiff should give some grounds for believing

[145] Although the first part of the test was misstated in *Bilson v Rawlings* [1993–94] 2 GLR 413 (H Ct), where Essilfie-Bondzie J stated that the plaintiff needed to show a strong *prima facie* case.

[146] See s 23A of the Anti-Money Laundering Act 2008 (Act 749), inserted by s 7 of the Anti-Money Laundering (Amendment) Act 2017 (Act 874); *The Republic v High Court (Financial Division 2) Accra* [2017] GHASC 10 (and the case law cited therein).

[147] [1980] 1 All ER 213 (CA) (Lord Denning MR, Roskill and Ormrod LJJ; 23 June 1975).

[148] Ibid 215b.

[149] [1979] 2 All ER 972 (CA) (Lord Denning MR, Lawton and Cumming-Bruce LJJ; 10 May 1979).

[150] Ibid 984g–985d.

that there is a risk of the assets being removed before the judgment or award is satisfied. The mere fact that the Defendant is abroad is not by itself sufficient. No one would wish any reputable foreign company to be plagued with a *Mareva* injunction simply because it has agreed to London arbitration. But there are some foreign companies whose structure invites comment. We often see in this court a corporation which is registered in a country where the company law is so loose that nothing is known about it, where it does no work and has no officers and no assets. Nothing can be found out about the membership, or its control, or its assets, or the charge on them. Judgment cannot be enforced against it. There is no reciprocal enforcement of judgments. It is nothing more than a name grasped from the air, as elusive as the Cheshire cat. In such cases the very fact of incorporation there gives some ground for believing there is a risk that, if judgment or an award is obtained, it may go unsatisfied. Such registration of such companies may carry many advantages to the individuals who control them but they may suffer the disadvantage of having a *Mareva* injunction granted against them. The giving of security for a debt is a small price to pay for the convenience of such a registration. Security would certainly be required in New York. So also it may be in London. Other grounds may be shown for believing there is a risk. But some such should be shown. (v) The Plaintiffs must, of course, give an undertaking in damages, in case they fail in their claim or the injunction turns out to be unjustified. In a suitable case this should be supported by a bond or security: and the injunction only granted on it being given, or undertaken to be given.'

2.3.5 Search and seize orders

In Ghana, the availability of *Anton Piller* relief (as originally developed[151]) has been placed on a statutory basis. Section 47 of the Copyright Act 2005[152] provides, inter alia:

'(1) A person whose rights under this Act are in imminent danger of being infringed or are being infringed upon may initiate civil proceedings in the High Court ...

(2) On an *ex parte application*, the Court may make an order in chambers for the inspection or removal from the defendant's premises of copyright infringing materials which constitute evidence of infringement by the defendant.'

Thus a plaintiff with a claim for infringement of copyright may apply for an *Anton Piller* order. There appears to be no judicial consideration of these provisions.

There is no reported authority whether an application for such an order outside the context of infringement of copyright would be granted by a Ghanaian court (for example, where the plaintiff has strong grounds to believe that the defendant has in his possession confidential information in the form of lists of the plaintiff's clients, for example, to which no copyright may apply and which the plaintiff fears will be destroyed prior to the discovery process and trial). However, as with

[151] *Anton Piller KG v Manufacturing Processes Ltd* [1976] Ch 55 (CA) (Lord Denning MR, Ormrod and Shaw LJJ), was itself a copyright infringement case.

[152] This appears as Act 690 of the Laws of Ghana, 2004.

the original *Anton Piller* decision, the root of the court's jurisdiction to grant injunctive relief is statutory and formulated in terms which would have been familiar to the court in the *Anton Piller* case itself (where it is just and convenient to make an order). It is to be expected that a Ghanaian court will develop such remedies as and when appropriate.

In England, *Anton Piller* relief at common law may be granted in cases in which the pre-conditions set out by Ormrod LJ in the *Anton Piller* case itself have been applied. Those pre-conditions are as follows:[153]

> 'There are three essential pre-conditions for the making of such an order, in my judgment. First, there must be an extremely strong *prima facie* case. Secondly, the damage, potential or actual, must be very serious for the [plaintiff]. Thirdly, there must be clear evidence that the defendants have in their possession incriminating documents or things, and that there is a real possibility that they may destroy such material before any application inter partes can be made.'

2.3.6 Third-party disclosure orders

There is no authority on the question whether a Ghanaian court may, apart from the established post-issuing of proceedings and pre-trial procedures whereby a third party may be served with a witness summons requiring his attendance at court in order to give evidence and/or to produce documents,[154] order a person not a party to the proceedings to give disclosure. Such a power is available to the English courts in the form of a *Norwich Pharmacal* order[155] whereby an innocent third party caught up in a tort may be ordered to disclose the name or other identity of the tortfeasor.

In *Norwich Pharmacal Co v Customs and Excise Comrs*, the English House of Lords[156] set out the following principle:

> 'That if through no fault of his own a person gets mixed up in the tortious acts of others so as to facilitate their wrong-doing he may incur no personal liability but he comes under a duty to assist the person who has been wronged by giving him full information and disclosing the identity of the wrongdoers ... [It does not matter] whether he became so mixed up by voluntary action on his part or because it was his duty to do what he did. It may be that if this causes him expense the person seeking the information ought to reimburse him. But justice requires that he should co-operate in righting the wrong if he unwittingly facilitated its perpetration.'

---

[153] *Anton Piller KG v Manufacturing Processes Ltd* [1976] Ch 55 (CA) (Lord Denning MR, Ormrod and Shaw LJJ), *per* Ormrod LJ at 62A.

[154] High Court Rules 2004, O 38, rr 10–13.

[155] *Norwich Pharmacal Co v Customs & Excise* [1974] AC 133 (HL(E)) (Lords Reid and Morris, Viscount Dilhorne and Lords Cross and Kilbrandon).

[156] Ibid 175, *per* Lord Reid.

More recent authority[157] has clarified the conditions which the plaintiff must satisfy in order to obtain such relief:

> 'The three conditions to be satisfied for the court to exercise the power to order *Norwich Pharmacal* relief are:
>
> i) a wrong must have been carried out, or arguably carried out, by an ultimate wrongdoer;
>
> ii) there must be the need for an order to enable action to be brought against the ultimate wrongdoer; and
>
> iii) the person against whom the order is sought must: (a) be mixed up in so as to have facilitated the wrongdoing; and (b) be able or likely to be able to provide the information necessary to enable the ultimate wrongdoer to be sued.'

If the plaintiff satisfies all of those conditions, the English court will then go on to exercise its discretion. In doing so, it must keep in mind the proper scope of *Norwich Pharmacal* relief: the jurisdiction cannot be used for wide-ranging discovery or the gathering of evidence, but is strictly confined to necessary information.[158]

2.3.7 Anti-suit injunctions

An anti-suit injunction is an order restraining the injunction defendant from either commencing or continuing proceedings outside Ghana in breach of a legal or equitable right on the part of the injunction plaintiff not to pursue litigation outside Ghana or, conversely, restraining the injunction defendant from commencing or continuing proceedings inside Ghana in breach of a legal or equitable right on the part of the injunction plaintiff to have the dispute between the parties litigated in a jurisdiction other than Ghana.[159]

In *Quantum Oil Terminals Ltd v International Finance Corp*,[160] the Ghanaian High Court acknowledged that it had the power to grant an anti-suit injunction. The court first determined that the injunction plaintiff and the injunction defendant

[157] *Ramilos Trading Ltd v Valentin Mikhaylovich Buyanovsky* [2016] EWHC 3175 (Comm) (H Ct) (Flaux J), citing, at para [11], *Mitsui & Co Ltd v Nexen Petroleum* [2005] EWHC 625 (Ch), [2005] 3 All ER 511 at [21] (H Ct) (Lightman J).

[158] *Ramilos Trading Ltd v Valentin Mikhaylovich Buyanovsky* [2016] EWHC 3175 (Comm) (H Ct) (Flaux J) para [46].

[159] In similar vein, an anti-anti-suit injunction is an order restraining the injunction defendant from commencing or continuing proceedings to restrain the injunction plaintiff from applying to restrain the injunction defendant from commencing or continuing proceedings. The leading works on this topic are: Raphael *The Anti-Suit Injunction* 2 ed (2019) and Briggs *Civil Jurisdiction and Judgments* 7 ed (2021), ch 28. It is also conceptually possible to obtain similar relief in the context of arbitration but such relief is outside the scope of this work.

[160] Suit No: Misc/00228/17 (unreported) 8 January 2018 and 23 February 2018 (H Ct) (Asiedu J).

had agreed that the courts of Ghana had jurisdiction to determine disputes arising out of the various contracts into which they had entered. The court then dismissed the injunction defendant's argument that the parties had only entered into a non-exclusive jurisdiction agreement (with the consequence, as argued by the injunction defendant, that the injunction defendant had reserved the right to bring proceedings elsewhere). Ultimately, the court was of the view that the correct characterisation of the jurisdiction agreement was not determinative; instead, to the extent that the parties had chosen the law of Ghana to govern their contractual relationship, 'no court in any jurisdiction is better placed to construe and apply the laws of the Republic of Ghana than a Ghanaian court of competent jurisdiction'. In consequence, therefore, the High Court, for what appears to be the first time in its history,[161] granted the anti-suit injunction sought.

It is respectfully submitted that the Ghanaian High Court was correct to determine that it could, in principle, grant the relief sought by the injunction plaintiff in *Quantum Oil Terminals*. Indeed, as noted at section 2.3.1 above, the jurisdiction of the High Court to grant injunctions is statutory and may be exercised in all cases where it is 'just and convenient' to do so.

That said, the reasoning of the court in support of the conclusion that it ought, on the facts, grant an anti-suit injunction is, with respect, more difficult. That reasoning is very brief. Indeed, contrary to the court's conclusion and for the reasons which are set out in more detail below, it is submitted that the construction of the jurisdiction agreement between the parties was of far greater importance than the court allowed. It is to be hoped that the (correct) conclusion in *Quantum Oil Terminals* that the Ghanaian High Court has the power to grant an anti-suit injunction will provide a springboard for the further clarification of the circumstances in which such relief may be granted.

In the expectation, therefore, that Ghanaian courts will have the opportunity in the future to consider further the circumstances in which anti-suit relief may be granted, it may be of assistance to set out the principles which English courts have formulated and which English courts apply when asked to grant anti-suit relief. After all, the statutory basis upon which Ghanaian courts may grant an anti-suit injunction is identical to that upon which their English counterparts exercise that jurisdiction and there is a very close affinity between Ghanaian law and English law in this regard.[162] It is to be anticipated, therefore, that a Ghanaian

[161] R Frimpong Oppong 'Reforming Private International Law in African Countries: Looking Inward and Outward' in Jan L Neels and Eesa A. Fredericks (eds) *Commercial Private International Law in Southern Africa – Comparative and International Perspectives. Essays in Honour of Professor Christopher F Forsyth QC* (forthcoming, on file with the authors).

[162] It is worth noting that the High Court of South Africa in *Vedanta Resources Holdings Ltd v ZCCM Investment Holdings plc* 2019 JDR 1425 (GJ) paras [11], [54] and [56] (Adams J) and the High Court of Nigeria

court before which an application is brought for an anti-suit injunction may well pay close attention to English authorities in setting out the principles upon which an anti-suit injunction may be granted in Ghana. Set out below, in summary, are the principles of English law governing the grant of an anti-suit injunction.

The Ghanaian court must have personal jurisdiction over the injunction defendant. The court may be seised either by service on the defendant within the jurisdiction or service out of the jurisdiction with the leave of the court.[163]

The injunction plaintiff must assert a cause of action for relief. Usually, the injunction plaintiff will contend that the injunction defendant is committing a wrong by bringing or proposing to bring proceedings in a foreign court. This will require the plaintiff to characterise the conduct of the defendant as the breach of a legal or equitable right.

A legal right may, and often will, be based on a right not to be sued in a foreign jurisdiction arising out of an exclusive jurisdiction clause in favour of the courts of Ghana (thereby making it clear that, contrary to the reasoning of the court in *Quantum Oil Terminals*, the correct construction of the jurisdiction agreement between the parties is significant). An equitable right may be the right not to be sued in a foreign jurisdiction and may be the corollary of an equitable wrong which is that it is oppressive and vexatious and therefore unconscionable for the injunction defendant to commence or continue proceedings against the injunction plaintiff in a foreign jurisdiction.

The prime example of a cause of action based on a legal right not to be sued in a foreign jurisdiction is where the parties have agreed expressly that the courts of Ghana should have exclusive jurisdiction over disputes arising out of the contract (which can be a substantive contract or a settlement agreement) between them.[164] In such a case proof of the underlying cause of action is likely to be a sufficient condition for the grant of the relief and that good reason would need to be shown why the discretion to order an injunction should not be exercised.[165]

The principal example of a cause of action based on an equitable wrong is where proceedings brought abroad by the defendant are oppressive and vexatious.

---

in *Zenith Global Merchant Ltd v Zhongfu International Investment (Nig) FZE* (2017) All FWLR 1837, 1924 (Akinyemi J) have also referred to English principles in a similar context.

[163] The substantive law and procedure for which in Ghana has been set out above.

[164] The contract may be a substantive contract or a settlement agreement and the dispute resolution provisions may be exclusively in favour of the courts of Ghana or may be in favour of arbitration: *British Airways Board v Laker Airways Ltd* [1985] AC 58 (HL (E)) (Lords Diplock, Fraser, Scarman, Roskill and Brightman), *per* Lord Diplock at p 81C–E. For the purposes of comparison, see *Quantum Oil Terminals* Suit No: Misc/00228/17 (unreported) 8 January 2018 and 23 February 2018 (H Ct) (Asiedu J).

[165] *The Angelic Grace* [1995] 1 Lloyd's Rep 87 (CA) (Neill, Leggatt and Millett LJJ), *per* Millett LJ at p 96, col 2, and Neill LJ at p 97, col 1; *Donohue v Armco Inc* [2000] 1 Lloyd's Rep 579 (CA) (Stuart-Smith, Brooke and Sedley LJJ), where it was stated that 'strong reasons' (*per* Stuart-Smith LJ at para 35) or 'strong cause' (*per* Brooke LJ at paras 59 and 60) would be required to deny an injunction.

An example of such conduct is illustrated by the decision of the Privy Council in *SNI Aerospatiale v Lee Kui Jak*[166] where a resident of Brunei had been killed in a helicopter crash and his widow (and her brother-in-law, as co-administrator of his estate), the respondent plaintiffs in the appeal to the Privy Council, had commenced proceedings in Brunei and had subsequently been persuaded to sue in Texas instead. The appellant defendant applied for an anti-suit injunction restraining the plaintiffs from proceeding against it in Texas. The Privy Council allowed the defendant's appeal, held that an injunction ought to be granted restraining the respondents from proceeding in Texas and remitted the matter to the Brunei courts.

Transposing the findings of the Privy Council to Ghana, it was held that an anti-suit injunction would be granted if: (1) pursuit of the foreign proceedings is vexatious or oppressive; (2) Ghana is the natural forum for the resolution of the dispute; and (3) the injunction does not deprive the defendant of advantages in the foreign jurisdiction of which it would be unjust to deprive him.[167]

Other examples of equitable wrongs which may attract an anti-suit injunction are: undermining the jurisdiction of the Ghanaian court;[168] vexatious conduct by relying on foreign procedural laws;[169] wrongfully undermining a Ghanaian judgment;[170] or enforcement of a foreign judgment wrongfully obtained.[171]

2.3.8 Other interlocutory relief

2.3.8.1 *Interim preservation of property*

Order 25, rule 2 provides:

> '(1) On the application of any party to a cause or matter the Court may make an order for the detention, custody or preservation of any property which is the subject-matter of the cause or matter or in respect of which any question may arise in the action, or may order the inspection of any such property in the possession of a party.

---

[166] [1987] AC 871 (PC (Brunei)) (Lords Keith, Griffiths, MacKay and Goff and Sir John Megaw).

[167] Lord Goff (giving the opinion of the Privy Council) p 896F–H. That the court to which the application is made should be the natural forum for the resolution of the dispute was repeated by the House of Lords in *Airbus Industrie GIE v Patel* [1999] 1 AC 119 (HL (E)) (Lords Goff, Slynn, Steyn, Clyde and Hutton), *per* Lord Goff (with whom the other Lords agreed) pp 138G–H and 140H–141B.

[168] For example, by commencing bankruptcy proceedings outside the jurisdiction when such proceedings are in progress in Ghana: *SNI Aerospatiale v Lee Kui Jak* [1987] AC 871, *per* Lord Goff at pp 892G–893B.

[169] By seeking to depose witnesses in the USA where those witnesses would be subject to cross-examination in proceedings in Ghana, for example: *Omega Group Holdings Ltd v Kozeny* [2002] CLC 132.

[170] By commencing proceedings outside the jurisdiction for declaratory relief designed to frustrate the enforcement of a Ghanaian judgment in that jurisdiction: *Masri v Consolidated Contractors International (UK) Ltd (No 3)* [2009] QB 503 (CA).

[171] Where the foreign judgment was obtained through fraud and perjury: *Ellerman Lines Ltd v Read* [1928] 2 KB 144 (CA), *per* Scrutton LJ at pp 152–3.

(2) To enable an order under subrule (1) to be carried out the Court may by the order authorise any person to enter upon any land or building in the possession of any party to the cause or matter.

(3) Where the right of a party to a specific fund is disputed, the Court may, on the application of a party to the cause or matter, order the fund to be paid into court or otherwise secured.

(4) An order under this rule may be made on such terms as the Court considers just.

(5) Unless the Court otherwise directs, a defendant may not apply for such an order before the defendant files appearance.'

In *Vanderpuye v Nartey*,[172] the Court of Appeal considered the requirements for an interim preservation of property order. Amissah JA (giving the judgment of the court), cited the decision of the House of Lords in *American Cyanamid* and followed it, stating:[173] 'The governing principle should be whether on the face of the affidavits there is need to preserve the status quo in order to avoid irreparable damage to the applicant and provided his claim is not frivolous or vexatious.'

In *In re: Yendi Skins Affairs; Yakubu II v Abdulai*,[174] in considering interlocutory orders concerning personal status, the Supreme Court, without expressly citing *American Cyanamid*, decided the appeal by applying a balance of convenience test to the case.

The Court of Appeal has subsequently set out at length certain of the considerations that should be taken into account when a court is invited to make an interim preservation of property order:[175]

'*(a)* As decided in *Garrard v. Edge & Sons* (1889) 58 LJ Ch 397, CA, the order must be made against the person in possession or custody of the property in dispute. See also *Wilder v Wilder and Charters (No 2)* (1912) 56 SJ 571, CA.

(b) The property must be the subject-matter of the suit. Thus in *Scott v. Mercantile Accident Insurance Co* (1892) 8 TLR 431 the lower court made an order that certain jewellery should remain in the custody of the police. An appeal against this order was allowed because it was admitted on the evidence that the property was not the subject-matter of the action, but that only a question might arise about it in the cause or matter.

(c) It was held in *Leney & Sons, Ltd v. Callingham & Thompson* [1908] KB 79 at 84, CA, per Farwell LJ that:

> "... the question of the exercise of the judicial discretion was always based, and is still based, upon this, that there is property in dispute to some interest in which the plaintiff shows a *prima facie* title; and preservation is ensured until the rights of the parties can be finally determined."

---

172 [1977] 1 GLR 428 (CA) (Amissah, Kingsley-Nyinah and Hayfron-Benjamin JJA).

173 Ibid 432.

174 [1984–86] 2 GLR 231 (Sup Ct) (Adade, Francois JJSC; Osei-Hwere, Amua-Sekyi and Ampiah JJA).

175 *General Development Co Ltd v Rad Forest Products Ltd* [1999–2000] 2 GLR 178 (CA) (Benin, Ansah and Amonoo-Monney JJA), *per* Benin JA at pp 182–3.

(d) The case of *Chaplin v. Barnett* (1912) 28 TLR 256, CA decides that the order will be granted so long as there is something which ought to be done to ensure the security of the property.

(e) An order will be made in order to preserve the subject-matter of the suit from destruction: see *Strelley v. Pearson* (1880) 15 Ch D 113 where the court granted an order restraining the defendant from ceasing to pump water of a mine for the sole purpose of preventing the mine from destruction.

(f) The court will also grant an order in court to preserve the subject-matter from depreciation physically or in value. So if it is established that it is necessary to do so the court will grant it; hence an order was made in the case of *Steamship New Orleans Co v. London and Provincial Marine and General Insurance Co* [1909] 1 KB 943, CA that a ship lying in a port in Singapore be brought to England for preservation there. However an order may not be made if it will cause undue hardship in carrying it out or will serve no useful purpose.

These grounds are by no means exhaustive; other grounds may unfold due to a particular case under consideration.'

As with interlocutory injunctions, the provisions of Order 25, rule 9, apply to interim preservation of property orders.

2.3.8.2 *Arrest of an absconding defendant*

Finally, the High Court Rules 2004, Order 73, provides for arrest of a defendant in certain circumstances:

'ARREST OF ABSCONDING DEFENDANT

Rule 1—Defendant leaving the Jurisdiction; Application for Security

(1) A plaintiff may at the institution of an action or at any time before final judgment, make an application *ex parte* supported by an affidavit to the Court for an order that security be taken for the appearance of the defendant to answer any judgment that may be given against the defendant in the action where the amount involved in the action exceeds ¢5million, and

(a) the defendant has disposed of or removed all or part of the property of the defendant from the country; or

(b) the defendant is about to leave the country.

(2) Where the Court is satisfied that the provisions in paragraph *(a)* or *(b)* of subrule (1) have been substantiated and that the execution of any judgment in the action against the defendant is likely to be obstructed or delayed, it may issue a warrant to bring the defendant before the Court to show cause why the defendant should not give good and sufficient bail for the defendant's appearance.

Rule 2—Bail for Appearance

Where the defendant fails to show cause, the Court shall order the defendant to give bail for the defendant's appearance at any time while the action is pending until the execution or satisfaction of any judgment that may be given against the defendant in the action, and the surety shall undertake to pay any money that may be adjudged to be paid by the defendant in the action, in default of the appearance of the defendant.

Rule 3—Deposit in Lieu of Bail

A deposit of money or other valuable property by the defendant sufficient to satisfy the claim and costs of the action may be accepted by the Court in lieu of bail.

Rule 4—Committal in Default of Security or Deposit

Where the defendant fails to furnish security or to provide sufficient security the defendant may

(a) be committed to custody until the determination of the action; or

(b) if the judgment is against the defendant, until the execution of the order if the Court so orders

except that the Court may at any time release the defendant upon reasonable cause being shown and upon terms such as security or other matters of relevance.'

Brobbey JSC, in a seminar paper on civil enforcement of judgments,[176] states:

'Rules on civil imprisonment in the High Court and Circuit Court and summons to show cause in the district court permit imprisonment of a judgment debtor who does not pay his debts. Those rules are inconsistent with article 14(1) of the 1992 Constitution. To the extent that they are inconsistent with the constitution, they should be considered as void: See article 1(2) of the Constitution. Simply stated, civil imprisonment and summons to show cause are revoked and inapplicable under any circumstance to enforce the payment of debt.'

Article 14(1) of the 1992 Constitution provides:

'(1) Every person shall be entitled to his personal liberty and no person shall be deprived of his personal liberty except in the following cases and in accordance with procedure permitted by law —

(a) in execution of a sentence or order of a court in respect of a criminal offence of which he has been convicted; or

(b) in execution of an order of a court punishing him for contempt of court; or

(c) for the purpose of bringing him before a court in execution of an order of a court; or

(d) in the case of a person suffering from an infectious or contagious disease, a person of unsound mind, a person addicted to drugs or alcohol or a vagrant, for the purpose of his care or treatment or the protection of the community; or

(e) for the purpose of the education or welfare of a person who has not attained the age of eighteen years; or

[176] Brobbey JSC *Enforcement of Judgment and Orders by Justice of the Supreme Court.*

(*f*) for the purpose of preventing the unlawful entry of that person into Ghana, or of effecting the expulsion, extradition or other lawful removal of that person from Ghana or for the purpose of restricting that person while he is being lawfully conveyed through Ghana in the course of his extradition or removal from one country to another; or

(*g*) upon reasonable suspicion of his having committed or being about to commit a criminal offence under the laws of Ghana.'

The provisions of Order 73 do not appear to fit comfortably within any of sub-paragraphs (1)*(a)*–*(g)* of article 14(1) of the Constitution. There must be serious doubt as to whether an order for the arrest of a defendant in the circumstances contemplated by Order 73 is lawful.

Chapter 3

KENYA

3.1 Jurisdiction

The bases on which a Kenyan court may assume jurisdiction over a cause or matter are statutory in origin.

The means by which a Kenyan court is seised of jurisdiction over a defendant at the suit of a plaintiff is by service of process on the defendant.[1]

The Civil Procedure Rules 2010 (High Court) ('the High Court Rules')[2] distinguish between service within and service outside the jurisdiction.

All civil proceedings are commenced by presenting a 'plaint' to the court.[3] Once a suit has been filed through the presenting of a plaint, 'a summons shall issue to the defendant ordering him to appear within the time specified therein'.[4]

3.1.1 Service where the defendant is within the jurisdiction

Personal service of a summons on a person present within Kenya establishes jurisdiction as of right over that person.

A summons is usually served on an individual by personal service.[5]

A summons is served on a company in one of the ways prescribed by the rules,[6] inter alia: by service on the secretary, director or other principal officer of the company; by leaving it at the registered offices of the company; or by leaving it at the place where the company carries on business.

On the question whether a company carries on business within Kenya for the purposes of service under the rules, the Court of Appeal in *Riddlesbarger v Robson*[7] adopted the following passage from Dicey *The Conflict of Laws* 6 ed (1949):

> 'Apart, however, from cases such as this, a corporation can be treated as being present in England for the purpose of serving a writ upon it when the company carries on business in England. The question whether a corporation is carrying on business here is one of

[1] Order 5, rr 1 and 8. No real connection is required between the defendant and Kenya for a plaintiff to seise the Kenyan court with jurisdiction over the defendant through service within the jurisdiction: *Riddlesbarger v Robson* [1958] EA 375 (CA) (Sir Kenneth O'Connor P, Briggs V-P and Forbes JA), where a defendant was served with proceedings at Eastleigh Airport, Nairobi, while he was in transit through Kenya. Forbes JA stated (at 379I): 'in an action in personam, provided the defendant is within the territory, for however short a time, the court has jurisdiction.'

[2] Legal Notice 151 of 2010. The High Court Rules are made pursuant to the power conferred on the Rules Committee by s 81 of the Civil Procedure Act 1924 (Act 43 of 1948, now Cap 21 of the Laws of Kenya, 2010). In this regard, the reader is referred to the 'Note on the citation of statutory material in this work', which appears at the end of the 'List of Statutory Material Cited' at the beginning of this work.

[3] Order 3, r 1(1). Order 4 sets out the prescribed contents of the plaintiff's plaint.

[4] Order 5, r 1(1). The summons is signed by a judge or officer appointed by a judge and the defendant must be given not less than ten days to appear.

[5] Order 5, r 8(1); as mentioned above, this may be a transient presence.

[6] Order 5, r 3.

[7] [1958] EA 375 (CA) (Sir Kenneth O'Connor P, Briggs V-P and Forbes JA), *per* Forbes JA at 387H–388A.

> fact not always easy to determine. A foreign railway company, for example, may perform part of its business, say the selling of tickets, in London, without necessarily carrying on business there. The answer to the question whether it does or does not carry on business in England depends upon whether or not the agent who sells the tickets makes a contract for the foreign company, or merely sells the tickets as part of his own business. This is substantially a question as to the relation of the agent towards the foreign company. In order, further, that a foreign corporation may be treated as being in England, the requirements of Order IX, R8 as to the service of a writ in England on a corporate body must be complied with.'

However, transactions undertaken by a foreign company through an agent present within the jurisdiction do not necessarily establish a presence on the part of that foreign company or that the foreign company is carrying on business within Kenya for the purposes of establishing jurisdiction through service of a summons on that agent. In *Re: Lowenthal and Air France*,[8] in a case concerned with enforcement in Kenya of a judgment given against the defendant by the High Court of Zambia, the Kenyan court considered whether the Zambian court had international jurisdiction. Prior to the issuing of proceedings in Zambia the defendant company had ceased to transact business there. The plaintiff had served proceedings on an employee of an independent company that represented the defendant company commercially in Zambia. The defendant did not appear in the proceedings and the resultant judgment was registered *ex parte* in Kenya. The defendant applied to set the registration of the judgment aside. The question for the Kenyan court was whether the defendant had been 'duly served with the process of the original court'. Rudd J held[9] that the agent of the defendant in Zambia did no more than the business of a forwarding agent, forwarding orders for confirmation or rejection by the defendant: 'This does not amount in law to the transaction of business by Air France in Zambia through Miss Hurter for the purpose of establishing Air France's presence or residence in Zambia through Miss Hurter or her company.' The same approach is likely to be followed in a purely domestic, Kenyan context.

Whether a foreign corporation is present within the jurisdiction through the agency of another person was considered in England in *The Lalandia*,[10] where Langton J stated:[11]

> 'Now taking these various tests, the test of making or selling contracts and the test of Lord Wrenbury in the Okura case of whether the defendants are acting "by" a person or "through" a person, and the value to be attached to whether the rent is paid by the foreign corporation or whether the agent in this country has the right or not to make any

[8] [1966] 2 ALR Comm 301 (H Ct) (Rudd J).

[9] Ibid 305:6–9.

[10] [1933] P 56.

[11] Ibid 66–7.

> independent contract and has any discretion of his own—applying all these various tests as best I can to the present case, it seems to me that Escombe, McGrath & Co. fall upon the side of the line of *agents who carry on their own business and not the business of the foreign corporation* ... I have to make up my mind *whether the foreign corporation is really here, in the sense that it has somebody doing its business here who is not doing primarily his own business*, and I think Escombe, McGrath & Co. on the evidence are primarily doing their own business and only in a secondary sense doing the business of the East Asiatic Company' (emphasis provided).

It is likely that a Kenyan court would be guided by this statement of principle (as the Nigerian Supreme Court has been)[12] when considering whether a company is present or carrying on business within Kenya for the purposes of establishing jurisdiction as of right over that company.

Whether a foreign company without a place of business carries on business within Kenya is highly fact-sensitive. In the context of the strict rules regarding notification of insurance claims in accordance with the terms of an insurance policy, it has been observed (obiter) that 'there is nothing to prevent a foreign company which has no place of business in Kenya carrying on business here'.[13] For the purposes of service pursuant to Order 5, rule 3(b)(iii),[14] it is likely that the court will require something more than a purely ethereal presence (such as advertising reach combined with selling through the internet and postal delivery of goods); the court, for example, will require a physical address from which business is conducted such that service or substituted service can be effected on a location.

3.1.2 Service where the defendant is outside the jurisdiction

3.1.2.1 *Procedure*

Order 5, rule 21[15] makes provision for service outside the jurisdiction. It prescribes an exclusive set of grounds on which the Kenyan court may assume jurisdiction over a person present outside the jurisdiction.

[12] Followed in Nigeria: *In re Gresham Life Assurance Society (Nigeria) Ltd* [1973] (1) ALR Comm 215 (Sup Ct; at the time the equivalent today of the Nigerian Federal Court of Appeal) (Elias CJ, Fatayi-Williams and Ibekwe JJSC).

[13] *Kanti & Co Ltd v Oriental Fire and General Insurance Co Ltd* [1973] 1 EA 203 (CA), *per* Spry VP at 204D.

[14] Which permits service 'if there is no registered office and no registered postal address of the corporation, by leaving it at the place where the corporation carries on business'.

[15] The rule of the English Rules of the Supreme Court regulating service out of the jurisdiction prior to 1999 (when the English Civil Procedure Rules came into effect) was O XI. Under the Rules of the Supreme Court 1883 and the Rules of the Supreme Court 1965, which superseded the 1883 Rules, O XI, r 1, provided for service out of the jurisdiction. The terms of the Kenyan O 5, r 21, are materially identical to the Rules of the Supreme Court 1883, save that the former includes O 5, r 21(e)(iv), which is absent from the 1883 Rules.

Order 5, rule 21 provides:

> 'Service out of Kenya of a summons or notice of a summons may be allowed by the court whenever—
>
> *(a)* the whole subject-matter of the suit is immovable property situate in Kenya (with or without rents and profits);
>
> *(b)* any act, deed, will, contract, obligation or liability affecting immovable property situate in Kenya is sought to be construed, rectified, set aside, or enforced in the suit;
>
> *(c)* any relief is sought against any person domiciled or ordinarily resident in Kenya;
>
> *(d)* the suit is for the administration of the personal estate of a deceased person who at the time of his death was domiciled in Kenya, or for the execution (as to property situate in Kenya) of the trusts of any written instrument, of which the person to be served is a trustee, which ought to be executed according to the law of Kenya;
>
> *(e)* the suit is one brought to enforce, rectify, rescind, dissolve, annul, or other-wise affect a contract or to recover damages or other relief for or in respect of the breach of a contract—
>
> (i) made in Kenya; or
>
> (ii) made by or through an agent trading or residing in Kenya on behalf of a principal trading or residing out of Kenya; or
>
> (iii) by its terms or by its legislation to be governed by the Laws of Kenya; or
>
> (iv) which contains a provision to the effect that any Kenyan court has jurisdiction to hear and determine that suit in respect of that contract,
>
> or is brought in respect of a breach committed in Kenya, of a contract, wherever made, even though such a breach was preceded or accompanied by a breach out of Kenya which rendered impossible the performance of the part of the contract which ought to have been performed in Kenya; or
>
> *(f)* the suit is founded on a tort committed in Kenya;
>
> *(g)* any injunction is sought as to anything to be done in Kenya, or any nuisance in Kenya is sought to be prevented or removed, whether damages are or are not also sought in respect thereof; or
>
> *(h)* any person out of Kenya is a necessary or proper party to a suit properly brought against some other person duly served in Kenya.'[16]

An application for leave to serve a summons or notice of a summons outside the jurisdiction should be brought by application using the procedure set out in Order 51, rule 1.[17]

---

[16] It will be noted that there is no provision made for the court to permit service of the writ on a defendant who is present out of the jurisdiction if the action is one to enforce a foreign judgment; Frimpong Oppong 'Recognition and enforcement of foreign judgments in Commonwealth African countries' (2014) XV *Yearbook of Private International Law* 365, 372. By way of comparison, see the English Civil Procedure Rules, PD6B, para 3.1(10).

[17] Which provides: 'All applications to the court shall be by motion and shall be heard in open court unless the court directs the hearing to be conducted in chambers or unless the rules expressly provide.'

Order 51, rule 3 provides that no motion should be made without notice to 'the parties affected thereby'. Rule 3 sets out exceptions to this general rule in terms of 'irreparable harm or serious mischief' should notice be given.[18] It will be unusual for an applicant for leave to serve out of the jurisdiction to be in a position to contend that he will suffer irreparable harm or serious mischief by putting the prospective defendant on notice of the application. However, the practice is that such applications are made *ex parte* without notice to the prospective defendant and this practice is justifiable on practical grounds that the application in question is to initiate proceedings against a person not present within the jurisdiction, and to require notice of the application to be given to that person might itself require an application to serve the notice of the application out of the jurisdiction (if the court wished to retain control of the service of court documents overseas, as it surely would).

Order 5, rule 25, makes provision for the evidence required in support of an application to serve out of the jurisdiction. The application must be supported:

> 'by affidavit or other evidence, stating that in the belief of the deponent the plaintiff has a good cause of action, and showing in what place or country such defendant is or probably may be found, and whether such defendant is a Commonwealth citizen or a British protected person or not, and the grounds on which the application is made; and no such leave shall be granted unless it is made sufficiently to appear to the court that the case is a proper one for service out of Kenya under this Order.'

(The significance of the distinction between a Commonwealth or British protected person or not is that, in the former case, defendants who are citizens of countries specified in section 95(3) of the Constitution[19] will be served with the summons itself,[20] whereas all other defendants are served with notice of the summons and not the summons itself.)[21]

---

[18] 'Provided, however, that the court, if satisfied that the delay caused by proceeding in the ordinary way would or might entail irreparable or serious mischief, may make any order *ex parte* upon such terms as to costs or otherwise, and subject to such undertaking, if any, as to the court seems just, and any party affected by such order may move to set it aside.'

[19] Being, the United Kingdom and Colonies, Canada, Australia, New Zealand, India, Sri Lanka, Ghana, Malaysia, Nigeria, Cyprus, Sierra Leone, Tanzania, Jamaica, Trinidad and Tobago, Uganda, Malawi, Malta, Zambia, The Gambia, Singapore, Guyana, Botswana, Lesotho, Barbados, Eswatini, Mauritius, Zimbabwe, and any other country prescribed by the Kenyan Parliament.

[20] Order 5, r 27.

[21] Order 5, r 28. The reasons for this are rooted in English legal history: a summons is a command from the sovereign and it was thought discourteous to serve such a command on a person not resident in the United Kingdom and not a British subject; thus, a notice of the summons was served instead (see *Nanjibhai Prabhudas & Co Ltd v Standard Bank Ltd* [1968] EA 670 (CA) (Sir Charles Newbold P, Sir Clement de Lestang V-P and Law JA), *per* Sir Charles Newbold P at 683C–E; the origin of the rule is s 19 of the English Common Law Procedure Act 1852; after the repeal of the 1852 Act, the rule was incorporated into the Rules of the Supreme Court; *Westman v Aktiebolaget Ekmans Mekaniska Snickarefabrick* (1876) 1 Ex D 237).

The framework within which the Kenyan courts consider the grant of leave to serve out of the jurisdiction is derived from earlier English rules of court.[22] It would be unsurprising therefore were a Kenyan court to seek guidance on the interpretation of these rules in the English authorities and that guidance is set out, where appropriate, below.

The English equivalents of Kenyan Order 5, rules 21 and 25 have been the subject of judicial consideration at the highest level in England. In *Seaconsar Far East Ltd v Bank Markazi Jomhouri Islami Iran*,[23] the House of Lords considered the interaction of Order XI, rules 1(1) and 4 of the Rules of the Supreme Court (the equivalent to Order 5, rules 21 and 25). Lord Goff (with whom the other Lords agreed) reviewed the authorities on the question what a plaintiff under Order XI was required to show on an application for leave to serve a writ out of the jurisdiction and found that the plaintiff was required to show, first, that the cause of action deposed to in the evidence in support of the application fell within the provisions of rule 1(1) and, second, that on the merits of the case there was a serious question to be tried. On the question of the standard to which these issues were required to be shown, Lord Goff stated:[24]

> 'A judge faced with a question of leave to serve proceedings out of the jurisdiction under Order 11 will in practice have to consider both (1) whether jurisdiction has been sufficiently established, on the criterion of the good arguable case laid down in *Korner's* case, under one of the paragraphs of rule 1(1), and (2) whether there is a serious issue to be tried, so as to enable him to exercise his discretion to grant leave, before he goes on to consider the exercise of that discretion, with particular reference to the issue of forum conveniens.'

The first of these matters was held to correspond to the requirement in Order XI, rule 4 that 'no such leave shall be granted unless it shall be made sufficiently to appear to the Court or Judge that the case is a proper one for service out of the jurisdiction under this Order'[25] and the second was a threshold requirement for the merits of the plaintiff's claim.[26]

---

[22] As noted above, the rule of the English Rules of the Supreme Court regulating service out of the jurisdiction prior to 1999 (when the English Civil Procedure Rules came into effect) was O XI. Under the Rules of the Supreme Court 1883 and the Rules of the Supreme Court 1965, which superseded the 1883 Rules, O XI, r 1, provided for service out of the jurisdiction. The terms of the Kenyan O 5, r 21, are materially identical to the Rules of the Supreme Court 1883, save that the former includes O 5, r 21(e)(iv), which is absent from the 1883 Rules.

[23] [1994] 1 AC 438 (HL(E)) (Lords Templeman, Griffiths, Goff, Browne-Wilkinson and Mustill).

[24] At 456H–457B. See also the decision of the Privy Council in *Altimo Holdings and Investment Ltd v Kyrgyz Mobil Tel Ltd* [2012] 1 WLR 1804 (Lord Phillips PSC and Lords Mance, Collins, Kerr and Clarke JJSC), *per* Lord Collins para [71], confirming this statement of principle.

[25] *Seaconsar* 451A–B, 452A–B, 453D–G.

[26] *Seaconsar* 452D–E, 455A–C, 456G–H. Notwithstanding the separate treatment of the English O XI, r 4, in *Seaconsar* and the earlier authorities referred to therein, it is unclear whether the amendment in 1883 of O XI, r 3 (under the Rules of Court contained in Sch 1 to the Supreme Court of Judicature Act 1875) by

Thus a four-component approach is used in deciding applications for leave to serve out of the jurisdiction.[27]

(1) *The formal requirements.* Has the plaintiff produced evidence satisfying the formal requirements of Order 5, rule 25 (or English Order XI, rule 4)? This requires the plaintiff in his affidavit in support of the application to set out: (a) the belief of the deponent that the plaintiff has a good cause of action; (b) the place or country the defendant is or probably may be found; (c) whether the defendant is a Commonwealth citizen or a British protected person or not; and (d) the grounds on which the application is made.

(2) *The sufficiency requirement.* Under the English Order XI, rule 4 it was held in the *Seaconsar* case that the words 'and no such leave shall be granted unless it shall be made sufficiently to appear to the Court or Judge that the case is a proper one for service out of the jurisdiction under this Order' introduced a sufficiency requirement (or, in other words, a degree of proof requirement) such that the plaintiff must show that there is a good arguable case[28] that the case falls within one of the gateways under Order XI, rule 1(1).

---

the introduction of an expanded O XI, r 4, in the 1883 Rules of Court, was intended to produce this result. At the time the leading textbook on the Rules took the view that the amendment to include the wording: 'No such leave shall be granted unless it shall be made sufficiently to appear to the Court or Judge that the case is a proper one for service out of the jurisdiction under this Order', was merely an amplification of the previous rule (see Wynne Baxter *Judicature Acts & Rules 1873–1883* 5 ed (1883) 176–7).

[27] As summarised in the English *Supreme Court Practice 1965* (1999 ed) 93–4, paras 11/1/9–11/1/12. The commentary referred to in the *Supreme Court Practice* refers to three elements; in the text above, the present authors include four elements, the additional element being the formal requirements of English r 4 and Kenyan r 25.

[28] In *Canada Trust v Stolzenberg (No 2)* [2002] 1 AC 1 (HL(E)) (Lords Steyn, Hoffmann, Cooke, Hope and Hobhouse), *per* Lord Steyn (with whom the other Lords agreed) 13F, the House of Lords appeared to approve passages from the judgment of Waller LJ in the Court of Appeal in the same case ([1998] 1 WLR 547) including the following (at 555F–G): 'It is also right to remember that the "good arguable case" test, although obviously applicable to the ex parte stage, becomes of most significance at the inter partes stage where two arguments are being weighed in the interlocutory context which, as I have stressed, must not become a "trial". "Good arguable case" reflects in that context that one side has a much better argument on the material available. It is the concept which the phrase reflects on which it is important to concentrate, i.e. of the court being satisfied or as satisfied as it can be having regard to the limitations which an interlocutory process imposes that factors exist which allow the court to take jurisdiction.' In *Goldman Sachs International v Novo Banco SA* [2018] 1 WLR 3683, the UK Supreme Court (Lords Mance, Sumption and Hodge, Lady Black and Lord Lloyd-Jones) further clarified the correct understanding of the test in the *Canada Trust* case. Lord Sumption (with whom all the other members of the court agreed and in reliance on his own judgment in *Brownlie v Four Seasons Holdings Incorporated* [2018] 1 WLR 192), stated, at para [9]: 'For the purpose of determining an issue about jurisdiction, the traditional test has been whether the claimant had "the better of the argument" on the facts going to jurisdiction. In *Brownlie v Four Seasons Holdings Inc* [2018] 1 WLR 192, para 7, this court reformulated the effect of that test as follows: "(i) that the claimant must supply a plausible evidential basis for the application of a relevant jurisdictional gateway; (ii) that if there is an issue of fact about it, or some other reason for doubting whether it applies, the court must take a view on the material available if it can reliably do so; but (iii) the nature of the issue and the limitations of the material available

In *Assanand and Sons (Uganda) Ltd v East African Records Ltd*,[29] the Court of Appeal determined that whether the case is within one or more of the gateways under Order 5, rule 21 will be a matter for the court to decide on the evidence, applying the principles set out below when the gateways are considered in greater detail. It is clear, however, that the plaintiff must strictly meet the requirements of rule 21:[30]

> 'A mere assertion by the plaintiff that the court has jurisdiction is not enough. The rule requires the *facts* showing that the court has jurisdiction to be stated. The objects of this requirement would seem to be, first, that the court should be able to exercise some critical foundation and to draw a reasonable inference that if the facts alleged are established, it would appear to have jurisdiction and second, that the defendant should know what facts were alleged and have an opportunity of controverting them, if desired. In the present case, the defendant (appellant) never, from first to last, had any document served upon it which set out the facts upon which the plaintiff (respondent) relied to give the Kenya court jurisdiction over a Uganda company; and notwithstanding that a printed heading on the plaintiffs plaint form ... required not only that the facts constituting the cause of action, but where it arose and "facts showing jurisdiction" to be set out, no facts showing that the court had jurisdiction were set out. The plaint was quite obviously deficient in an essential respect.' (emphasis in original)

(3) *The merits requirement*. The plaintiff must demonstrate that there is a serious issue to be tried on the merits of the claim upon which the claimant relies. Lord Goff in *Seaconsar* stated[31] as follows:

> 'The court cannot resolve disputed questions of fact on affidavit evidence; and it is consistent with the statement of the law by Lord Davey that if, at the end of the day, there remains a substantial question of fact or law or both, arising on the facts disclosed by the affidavits, which the plaintiff bona fide desires to try, the court should, as a rule, allow the service of the writ. If this approach is correct, the standard of proof in respect of the cause of action can broadly be stated to be whether, on the affidavit evidence before the court, there is a serious question to be tried.'

(4) *The court's discretion*. Once the above matters are established by the plaintiff, the court will proceed to consider the exercise of its discretion to allow service out of the jurisdiction. The court's discretion is exercised cautiously. As was stated by Pearson J in *Société Générale de Paris v Dreyfus Brothers*:[32]

---

at the interlocutory stage may be such that no reliable assessment can be made, in which case there is a good arguable case for the application of the gateway if there is a plausible (albeit contested) evidential basis for it."'

29 [1959] 1 EA 360 (CA) (Sir Kenneth O'Connor P, Forbes V-P and Windham JA).

30 Ibid 364D–F.

31 *Seaconsar* 452C–D.

32 (1885) 29 Ch D 239 at 242–3; cited with approval by Lord Goff in *Seaconsar* at 455D.

> 'But of course it becomes a very serious question, and ought always to be considered a very serious question, whether or not, even in a case like that, it is necessary for the jurisdiction of the Court to be invoked, and whether this Court ought to put a foreigner, who owes no allegiance here, to the inconvenience and annoyance of being brought to contest his rights in this country, and I for one say, most distinctly, that I think this Court ought to be exceedingly careful before it allows a writ to be served out of the jurisdiction.'

The exercise of the court's discretion is dealt with below under the sub-heading '*Forum non conveniens*'.

3.1.2.2 *Bases for service out of the jurisdiction*

The bases on which the court may grant permission which are of particular significance for present purposes are discussed below.

(1) Relief is sought against any person domiciled, or ordinarily resident, within the jurisdiction.

The term 'person' in Order 5, rule 21(c) includes any natural or legal person.[33]

There is little Kenyan judicial authority on the meaning of the term 'domicile' for the purposes of the application of Order 5, rule 21(c). It is likely, given the willingness of the Kenyan courts to look to English law for the meaning of terms inherited from colonial times, that the Kenyan courts will adopt the jurisprudence applicable in English law regarding the terms 'domicile' for the purposes of determining jurisdiction over a person.[34] Under the English Rules of the Supreme Court upon which Order 5, rule 21 of the Civil Procedure Rules appears to have been based,[35] 'domicile' was defined as follows:[36]

> 'In general the domicile of a person is in the country in which he has his permanent home (see Dicey, *Conflict of Law*, 7th ed., Chap. 6), the country in which his habitation is fixed without any present intention of removing (*Re Craignish*, [1892] 3 Ch. 180, C.A.; *Huntly v. Gaskell*, [1906] A.C. 56; *Casdagli v. C.*, [1919] A.C. 145). No person can at any time be without a domicile or have more than one domicile. The domicile of origin remains until a new domicile of choice has been adopted (*Bell v. Kennedy* (1868), L.R. 1 Sc. App. 307, H.L.; *Udny v. Udny* (1869), ibid., 441, H.L., *Winans v. A.-G.*, [1904] A.C. 287, H.L.).'

[33] Section 3(1) of the Interpretation and General Provisions Act 1956 (Act 7 of 1956, Act 39 of 1956, now Cap 2 of the Laws of Kenya, 2012 (rev 2014)).

[34] See generally on the meaning of 'domicile', *Dicey, Morris and Collins on the Conflict of Laws* 15 ed (2012) vol 1, r 34, para 6R-001.

[35] As noted above, the rule of the English Rules of the Supreme Court regulating service out of the jurisdiction prior to 1999 (when the Civil Procedure Rules came into effect) was O XI. Under the Rules of the Supreme Court 1883 and the Rules of the Supreme Court 1965, which superseded the 1883 Rules, O XI, r 1 provided for service out of the jurisdiction where the defendant was domiciled or ordinarily resident within the jurisdiction.

[36] Rules of the Supreme Court 1883 (1960 ed) 144.

The Kenyan courts have jurisdiction on the basis of ordinary residence within Kenya (as noted above, transient presence is also sufficient). Whether a person is ordinarily resident in Kenya is a question of fact to be determined in all the circumstances of the case.[37]

As regards the domicile and ordinary residence of a company, these concepts do not appear to have been the subject of judicial analysis in the Kenyan courts. As a guide to the meaning of these terms, the Kenyan courts may look to the traditional definition of the 'domicile' and 'residence' of a legal person under the English Rules of the Supreme Court[38] (from which Order 5, rule 21 of the Civil Procedure Rules 2010 is derived):

> 'A corporation is domiciled where it is registered, if the law requires it to be registered, and if it does not it is domiciled in the country by whose law it is incorporated (Dicey, *Conflict of Laws*, 7th ed., p. 477). A corporation is "resident" and "ordinarily resident" where its central management and control is exercised ...'.

(2) The action is one brought to enforce, rectify, rescind, dissolve, annul, or otherwise affect a contract or to recover damages or other relief for or in respect of the breach of a contract:

- (a) made in Kenya; or
- (b) made by or through an agent trading or residing in Kenya on behalf of a principal trading or residing out of Kenya; or
- (c) by its terms or by its legislation to be governed by the Laws of Kenya; or
- (d) which contains a provision to the effect that any Kenyan court has jurisdiction to hear and determine that suit in respect of that contract,

or is brought in respect of a breach committed in Kenya, of a contract, wherever made, even though such a breach was preceded or accompanied by a breach out of Kenya which rendered impossible the performance of the part of the contract which ought to have been performed in Kenya.

The place where a contract was made was considered by the Court of Appeal in *Karachi Gas Co Ltd v Issaq*[39] in which, by correspondence written in both Kenya and Pakistan, a contract was concluded for the sale by the plaintiff, a Kenyan resident, to the defendant, a company incorporated in Pakistan, of 100,000 feet of

---

[37] In *Donnebaum v Mikolaschek* [1964] EA 645, Rudd J found that the defendant had ceased to be ordinarily resident in Kenya a matter of two days prior to the commencement of proceedings, thereby depriving the Kenyan courts of jurisdiction in the case.

[38] Rules of the Supreme Court 1883 (1960 ed) 145.

[39] [1965] EA 42 (CA) (Newbold Ag V-P and Spry and Duffus JJA). Cited and followed in *Nairobi Projector Services Ltd v Kabuleeta* [2006] eKLR 55 (H Ct) (Visram J).

pipes f.o.b.[40] Mombasa, Kenya. The plaintiff was also to arrange for the relevant export permit and the defendant was to arrange for the relevant import licences. After certain delays the defendant repudiated the contract by refusing to accept delivery of the pipes f.o.b. Mombasa. The plaintiff commenced proceedings in Kenya and obtained an order granting him leave to serve the defendant outside the jurisdiction in Pakistan. The defendant applied to have that order set aside on the basis, inter alia, that the court had no jurisdiction because the proper law of the contract was Pakistan law and not Kenyan law.

On the question where the contract was made, the majority of the court[41] applied 'the postal rule'[42] and held that the contract had been made in Kenya as this was the country from which the plaintiff had posted his acceptance of the defendant's counter-offer.[43]

The court also held[44] that the proper law of the contract (or that part of it relevant for the purposes of the appeal)[45] was Kenyan law because, inter alia: the contract had been made in Kenya; the goods subject of the contract were in Kenya at the time the contract was made; delivery of those goods was to be made in Kenya; the language of the contract was in English; and the terms were terms familiar in English contracts of sale.

Finally, the court found that there had been a breach of the contract in Kenya because the defendant refused to accept delivery of the goods f.o.b. Mombasa, where both the plaintiff's and defendant's obligations regarding delivery and acceptance were due to be performed.[46]

It has been asserted: 'A contract wholly entered into and performed outside Kenya gives the courts no jurisdiction, even if the defendant actually resides in Kenya.'[47] It is submitted that this cannot be a correct statement of the law because

---

[40] Free (or freight) on board, ie, the plaintiff's obligations were to deliver the pipes to the ship's railing; the defendant was to arrange for marine freight, insurance and unloading.

[41] Duffus JA at 49H–I and Spry JA at 55G–I.

[42] The rule of English conflict of laws is that a contract is made in the country where the acceptance is *posted*; in cases of instantaneous communications, telex, fax, email, etc, the contract is made in the country where the communication is *received* (*Entores Ltd v Miles Far East Corp* [1955] 2 QB 327 (CA, England) (Denning, Birkett and Parker LJJ); see further below.

[43] A further example of the fact that a contract made in Kenya provided the court with jurisdiction is *African Mercantile Co Ltd v Patel* (1927–28) 11 KLR 69 (H Ct) (Stephens J), where the defendant was in India but the contract had been made in Kenya.

[44] [1965] EA 42 CA, *per* Newbold Ag V-P at 54A–D and Spry JA at 56A–57C, applying the 'system of law with which the transaction has its closest and most real connection' test.

[45] Ibid *per* Duffus JA at 49I–50A.

[46] As regards the place of performance, in *Kenya School of Flying v ACE INA UK Ltd* [2005] eKLR 55 (H Ct) (Waweru J), it was held, inter alia, that an insurance policy placed and issued in London was due to be performed in England and not Kenya where an insured event had occurred. (A contract case and not a tort case – for which it is cited in Frimpong Oppong *Private International Law in Commonwealth Africa* (2013) 55 fn 36.)

[47] Frimpong Oppong *Private International Law in Commonwealth Africa* (2013) 54 fn 31; citing *Sunrise Travel and Tours Ltd v Wanjigi* [2002] LLR 5933.

residence within Kenya by a defendant will always give the plaintiff the right to serve that defendant when he is present within the jurisdiction and will also give the plaintiff a basis on which to apply to the court for leave to serve that defendant outside the jurisdiction if he is not present within the jurisdiction, in each case regardless of the nature of the underlying cause of action (with the exception of a cause of action concerning title to foreign land).[48]

It is likely that, in the apparent absence of further Kenyan authority on the construction and application of Order 5, rule 21(e), a Kenyan court will have regard to the academic and judicial authorities on the construction and application of the (former) equivalent provision in the English Rules of the Supreme Court.[49]

A concise statement of the law is as follows:[50]

> '(i) **Where a contract is made in England**
>
> **11-181**
>
> If the parties enter into negotiations by correspondence from different countries, the contract is made where the letter of acceptance is posted. But in commercial transactions today communication by telephone, telex, fax and electronic mail is much more common than by post. It is now well established, following the decision of the Court of Appeal in *Entores v. Miles Far East Corp* (which was approved by the House of Lords [*Brinkibon Ltd v. Stahag Stahl und Stahlwarenhandelsgesellschaft mbH* [1983] 2 AC 34]) that if the parties use "instantaneous" means of communication such as telephone, fax or electronic mail, the contract is made where the acceptance is communicated to the offeror. It has been held that if a contract made in England contains a submission to arbitration in a foreign country, an action in England at common law to enforce the foreign arbitration award is within this part of the clause. The contract must actually be made in England as that phrase is understood in English law. It is not sufficient if it merely says that it shall be deemed to be so made, though this may be sufficient to make it one which is governed by English law. A contract may be made in England within the meaning of this clause although it was preceded by a less formal agreement made abroad, or if it was originally made in England, but amended abroad.

[48] Frimpong Oppong elsewhere cites the *Sunrise Travel* case for a different proposition: 'The court suggested that in an era of increased globalization it would be a good thing for defendants to be sued where they are domiciled' (see Frimpong Oppong 'A decade of private international law in African courts 1997–2007' (2008) X *YPIL* 367 at 404 fn 180). Further, in Frimpong Oppong *Private International Law in Commonwealth Africa* (2013) 54 fn 31, *Georgina Ngina v Inter Freight East Africa Ltd* [2006] eKLR (civil case 564 of 2006; 14 June 2006) is cited for the proposition: 'Nor does it matter that the underlying transaction was entered into outside the jurisdiction, in this instance, via a contract made in Kigali, Rwanda.' While this is undoubtedly the case, it is important to note that the *Ngina* case was not concerned with service outside the jurisdiction. There, Osiemo J found that the defendant (within the jurisdiction) was properly sued as the agent of the principal.

[49] Order XI, r 1(e) respectively: Rules of the Supreme Court 1883 (1961 ed) and O XI, r 1(d) and (e) of the Rules of the Supreme Court 1965.

[50] *Dicey, Morris and Collins on the Conflict of Laws* 15 ed (2012) vol 1, r 34, paras 11-181–11-187.

(ii) **Where a contract is made by or through an agent trading or residing in England**

11-182

The clause says "by or through" an agent, not "by" an agent. Hence the case is within the clause, although the agent has no authority to make contracts on behalf of his foreign principal, but only has authority to obtain orders and transmit them to his principal for acceptance or rejection. This part of the clause is designed to bring within Rule 34 foreigners who transact business in England by or through agents, and consequently it does not apply where the agent's principal is the claimant. Hence a claimant cannot invoke clause (6)(ii) [Order 5, rule 21(e)(ii)] where the contract was made by or through his agent.

11-183

If proceedings are brought by consignees of a cargo against foreign ship-owners under the bills of lading, the case is not within this part of the clause if the charterparty (but not the bills of lading) was made by or through agents of the shipowners in England, even though it refers to the bills of lading and was made by charterers acting on behalf of the consignees. It may be otherwise, however, if the charterers are identical with the consignees...

(iii) **Where a contract is governed by English law**

11-186

...

11-187

Although the fact that a contract is governed by English law is an important factor in the exercise of the discretion under this head in favour of the English forum, it is not conclusive. This head of jurisdiction was described as exorbitant in *Amin Rasheed Shipping Corp v Kuwait Insurance Co*, where the House of Lords held that in the circumstances it was not appropriate for the English court to determine a dispute involving a marine insurance policy governed by English law when the Kuwaiti courts were the forum conveniens. Until that decision it was generally thought that the fact that a contract was governed by English law was in itself sufficient to justify leave. But now the claimant has a heavier burden. In *Amin Rasheed* Lord Diplock suggested that, in order to justify leave under this head, the plaintiff had to show that justice could not be obtained by him in the foreign court, or could only be obtained at excessive cost, delay or inconvenience. But it was subsequently held that Lord Diplock was merely giving examples, and was not providing an exhaustive list, of the relevant factors. The court has to consider all factors, and the fact that English law is the applicable law may be of great importance, or it may be of little consequence as seen in the context of the whole case. Thus if there is likely to be no dispute on matters of law or construction, or if the law of the foreign forum is substantially the same as English law, the fact that English law is the applicable law will be of little weight. But where an issue of English public policy arises in relation to a contract which is (or may be) governed by English law, it is desirable that it should be decided by the English court; conversely, where the foreign court may apply its own public policy to defeat a claim based on a contract governed by English law, that too is a reason for the English court taking jurisdiction. If the claimant has alternative remedies in contract and tort upon the same facts, he can choose his remedy.'

(3) The action is founded on tort or other civil wrong committed within the jurisdiction.

In *Donnebaum v Mikolaschek*,[51] in a case concerning a libel published in Austria, the court found that the plaint presented to and filed by the court did not allege a republication in Kenya of the original libel published in Vienna or that the defendant authorised any such republication. The affidavit filed in support of the application for leave to serve outside the jurisdiction in Tanganyika did allege a republication in Kenya, but did not allege that the defendant was responsible for that republication. The court set aside the order granting leave to serve out of the jurisdiction.

There is, however, little reported authority on the meaning and application of Order 5, rule 21(f) and, as with the construction and application of Order 5, rule 21(e), it is likely that a Kenyan court will have regard to the academic and judicial authorities on the construction and application of the (former) equivalent provision in the English Rules of the Supreme Court on the question when is a tort committed within the jurisdiction.[52]

A statement of the law is as follows:[53]

> **'11-212**
>
> ... As both the Privy Council [in *Distillers Co (Bio-chemicals) Ltd v Thompson* [1971] AC 458] and the Supreme Court of Canada [*Moran v Pyle National (Canada) Ltd* (1973) 43 D.L.R. (3d) 239] have pointed out, the competing theories for the determination of the place of a tort have been that (i) all ingredients of the cause of action must have occurred within the jurisdiction, or (ii) the last ingredient, the event which completes a cause of action, must have occurred within the jurisdiction, or (iii) the act which the defendant committed must have occurred within the jurisdiction.
>
> **11-213**
>
> In *Distillers Co Ltd v Thompson* the Privy Council adopted the test of the place where in substance the act or omission occurred which gave the plaintiff his cause of action. So that where the essence of the complaint was failure to warn the consumer of the dangers of a product (rather than the faulty manufacture of the product) the cause of action was held to have arisen at the place where the failure to warn occurred; and the torts of negligent and fraudulent misrepresentation, where the negligent or fraudulent statement was communicated from one country to another, were held to have been committed where the statement was received and acted upon. Prior to the adoption of that test, but consistently with it, it had been held that the tort of defamation was committed where the defamatory statements were published and not where they were posted or uttered.'

---

[51] [1964] EA 645 (H Ct) (Rudd J).

[52] Order XI, r 1(ee) and 1(f) respectively: Rules of the Supreme Court 1883 (1961 ed) and 1965.

[53] *Dicey, Morris and Collins on the Conflict of Laws* 15 ed (2012) vol 1, r 34, paras 11-212–11-213.

3.1.2.3 *Submission to the jurisdiction*

Two circumstances must be distinguished under the title submission to the jurisdiction. First, where submission is alleged in extant proceedings in Kenya. Second, where the defendant has agreed (usually by contractual provision) to submit to the jurisdiction of the court in advance of a dispute arising.

3.1.2.3.1 Submission by appearance

It is well established in Kenya that an appearance entered by a party solely to contest the jurisdiction of the court is not a voluntary submission to the jurisdiction of the court.[54]

In *Nanjibhai Prabhudas & Co Ltd v Standard Bank Ltd*,[55] the defendant, who had been served in Uganda with Kenyan proceedings, entered an unconditional appearance and then filed a motion to set aside service of those proceedings (as opposed to the order granting leave to serve him out of the jurisdiction) and for an extension of time for the service of his defence. The Court of Appeal held that he had entered an unconditional appearance by issuing the motion that was the subject of the appeal. Sir Charles Newbold P stated:[56]

> 'In my view, where a defendant chooses to enter an unconditional appearance in proceedings in the court, he must be taken, save in the exceptional circumstances such as where he contemporaneously files a notice of motion to set aside the proceedings to which he entered an appearance, to have waived any irregularity in the process to which he enters an appearance and thus accepts the jurisdiction of the court ... The circumstances of this case, in any event, show no ground for treating the irregularities which occurred as entitling the defendant to set aside the service. If a defendant objects to any process on the ground of an irregularity, it is his duty to take immediate action to have it set aside. In this case the defendant, having entered an unconditional appearance, took out the motion which is the subject of this appeal; but in spite of being aware that there was other process designed to obtain for the plaintiff summary judgment on the summons to which an unconditional appearance had been entered, the defendant not only took no part in that process but set down this notice of motion for a date long after the other process would be heard and determined. Action of that nature on the part of the defendant results in a position in which he can expect very little sympathy from the courts.'

---

[54] *Fonville v Kelly III* [2002] 1 EA 71 (H Ct), *per* Githinji J at 78d–e: 'Notwithstanding the order for leave to serve out of jurisdiction [sic], a foreign defendant who is served has a right to contest the jurisdiction of the court by entering a conditional appearance and thereafter making an application to set aside the service or to strike out the suit for want of jurisdiction.'

[55] [1968] EA 670 (CA) (Sir Charles Newbold P, Sir Clement de Lestang V-P and Law JA), *per* Sir Charles Newbold P at 683C–E.

[56] Ibid 684C–G.

After entering a conditional appearance in accordance with the Rules, the defendant ought promptly therefore to raise the objection on which he relies, failing which the court may treat the appearance as unconditional.

3.1.2.3.2 Submission by agreement

3.1.2.3.2.1 *Jurisdiction clauses*

The courts in Kenya will have regard to jurisdiction clauses in favour of foreign jurisdictions or arbitration proceedings and endeavour to give effect to them. However, although the court retains discretion to disregard the foreign jurisdiction clause in favour of the Kenyan courts, an arbitration clause must be given effect if a party to the agreement seeks a stay of court proceedings.[57]

In *Ronning v Société Navale Chargeurs Delmas Vieljeux, The François Vieljeux*,[58] the Court of Appeal considered an appeal by the plaintiff, owner of cargo aboard *The François Vieljeux*, in its action against the defendants, carrier/shipowner of *The François Vieljeux* and the carrier's agent. The vessel, having embarked from Mombasa, had become a total loss. One issue in the case was whether and to what extent the master of the vessel had been negligent in failing to inspect adequately the stowage of cargo in the hold, the movement of which was alleged to have been a contributory factor to the foundering and loss of the vessel. The carriers entered a conditional appearance and applied, inter alia, for a stay of the proceedings in favour of the courts of France on the basis that the bill of lading under which the cargo was shipped contained a jurisdiction clause in favour of the courts of the country where the carrier had his principal place of business, in this case France. The judge at first instance (Kneller J) granted the stay sought by the carriers relying on the principles set out by Brandon J (as he then was) in *Owners of cargo lately laden on board the ship or vessel Eleftheria v The Eleftheria (Owners), The Eleftheria*,[59] where he considered earlier authorities and set out a statement of the principles applicable to an application for a stay of proceedings where there was a jurisdiction clause relied on by the party seeking the stay. Brandon J's statement of the principles has since been accepted as the authoritative statement in this area by courts in other Anglophone African jurisdictions.[60]

In *The Eleftheria* the jurisdiction clause provided: 'Any dispute arising under this bill of lading shall be decided in the country where the carrier has his principal

---

[57] Section 6(1) Arbitration Act 1995 (Act 4 of 1995, without a Cap number in the Laws of Kenya, 2010), unless the court finds: the clause is null and void, inoperative or incapable of being performed; or there is in fact no dispute between the parties within the clause.

[58] [1987] Revue de Droit Uniforme 537, [1976–85] 1 EA 513, [1982–88] 1 KAR 398 (CA) (Hancox JA and Nyarangi and Chesoni Ag JJA).

[59] [1970] P 94; [1969] 1 Lloyd's Rep 237 (QBD, Comm Ct).

[60] *Nika Fishing Co Ltd v Lavina Corp* [2008] 16 NWLR 509 (Sup Ct, Nigeria).

place of business [Greece]' (a clause identical in terms to the clause in *The François Vieljeux*). The owners of cargo on board *The Eleftheria* commenced proceedings in England and the shipowners applied for a stay of those proceedings. In staying the proceedings in favour of the Greek courts Brandon J set out the principles on the basis of which a stay may be granted:[61]

> '(1) Where plaintiffs sue in England in breach of an agreement to refer disputes to a foreign court, and the defendants apply for a stay, the English court, assuming the claim to be otherwise within its jurisdiction, is not bound to grant a stay but has a discretion whether to do so or not. (2) The discretion should be exercised by granting a stay unless strong cause for not doing so is shown. (3) The burden of proving such strong cause is on the plaintiffs. (4) In exercising its discretion the court should take into account all the circumstances of the particular case. (5) In particular, but without prejudice to (4), the following matters, where they arise, may properly be regarded:—(a) In what country the evidence on the issues of fact is situated, or more readily available, and the effect of that on the relative convenience and expense of trial as between the English and foreign courts, (b) Whether the law of the foreign court applies and, if so, whether it differs from English law in any material respects, (c) With what country either party is connected, and how closely, (d) Whether the defendants genuinely desire trial in the foreign country, or are only seeking procedural advantages, (e) Whether the plaintiffs would be prejudiced by having to sue in the foreign court because they would: (i) be deprived of security for their claim; (ii) be unable to enforce any judgment obtained; (iii) be faced with a time-bar not applicable in England; or (iv) for political, racial, religious or other reasons be unlikely to get a fair trial.'

By a majority, the Court of Appeal in *Ronning* dismissed the plaintiff's appeal stating that the grant of a stay was a matter within the discretion of the judge at first instance and that he had correctly formulated the test to be applied and had arrived at the right conclusion.[62] The principles set out in *The Eleftheria* must be taken to represent Kenyan law on the question whether a stay of proceedings should be granted on the basis of a jurisdiction clause in favour of a foreign jurisdiction.

In *United India Insurance Co Ltd v East African Underwriters (Kenya) Ltd*,[63] the Court of Appeal followed[64] the principles governing applications for a stay of proceedings on the basis of a jurisdiction clause as expounded less than a year earlier by the Court of Appeal in *The François Vieljeux*. The defendants in the *United India Insurance* case applied for a stay of the plaintiff's Kenyan proceedings

---

[61] [1970] P 94 at 99G–100C.

[62] Ibid *per* Hancox JA at 581 and Nyarangi Ag JA at 582. Chesoni Ag JA delivered a powerful dissenting judgment and would have allowed the appeal (at 596) and removed the stay permitting the proceedings to continue in Kenya. However, Chesoni Ag JA did not appear to dissent from the application of the principles set out in *The Eleftheria* (at 587, 590 and 595).

[63] [1982–88] 1 KAR 639 (CA) (Madan, Kneller and Hancox JJA).

[64] Ibid *per* Madan JA at 642, Kneller JA at 646–7 and Hancox JA at 649.

on the basis of an exclusive jurisdiction clause in favour of the courts of Bombay (now, Mumbai). The court upheld the decision of the judge at first instance not to stay the proceedings, inter alia, because: the evidence of fact in the case was located in Kenya, as were all the known witnesses; the breaches of duty occurred within Kenya; the grant of the stay would require the witnesses to travel to Bombay 'at enormous expense';[65] witnesses refusing to travel would not be compellable; the cost of a trial in Bombay would be 'staggering';[66] and the two corporate defendants that were incorporated in India had divested themselves of any immediate interest in the suit by having assigned that interest to a defendant that was incorporated and domiciled in Kenya.[67]

3.1.2.3.2.2 *Application for service out of the jurisdiction based on a jurisdiction clause*

In the English Rules of the Supreme Court,[68] Order XI, rule 1(1)(d)(i)–(iv), the sub-rule governing service out of the jurisdiction in cases concerned with contract, provides as follows: 'The claim is made to enforce ... a contract which ... (iv) contains a term to the effect that the High Court shall have jurisdiction to hear and determine any action in respect of the contract.' This additional provision was included in the English rules in order to reverse the decision of the Court of Appeal in *British Wagon Co Ltd v Gray*.[69]

The Kenyan Civil Procedure Rules 2010, Order 5, rule 21(e)(i)–(iv) contains the equivalent provision: 'The suit is one brought to enforce ... a contract ... which contains a provision to the effect that any Kenya court has jurisdiction to hear and determine that suit in respect of that contract.'

Where the defendant is not present within the jurisdiction, and where the agreement between the parties contains a jurisdiction clause in favour of the Kenyan courts, an order may be made for service of the defendant out of the jurisdiction.

---

[65] Ibid *per* Madan JA at 643.

[66] Ibid.

[67] The principles set down in *The François Vieljeux* and the *United India Insurance* case have since been followed by Kenyan courts on numerous occasions: *Friendship Container Manufacturers Ltd v Mitchell Cotts Ltd* [2001] 2 EA 338 (H Ct) (Mbaluto J); *Fonville v Kelly III* [2002] 1 EA 71 (H Ct) (Githinji J); *Raytheon Aircraft Credit Corp v Air Al-Faraj Ltd* [2005] 2 KLR 47 (CA) (Tunoi, Githinji and Onyango Otieno JJA); *Valentine Investment Co v Federal Republic of Germany* [2006] eKLR (H Ct) (Khaminwa J); *Five Forty Aviation Ltd v Lufthansa Technik Aero Alzey Gmbh* [2011] eKLR (H Ct) (Kimondo J); *Health & Water Foundation v Intervita Onlus* [2015] eKLR (H Ct) (Mabeya J).

[68] Rules of the Supreme Court 1965 (the successor provision to O XI, r 2(a), of the Rules of the Supreme Court 1883 (1960 ed), introduced by amendment in 1920).

[69] [1896] 1 QB 35.

3.1.2.4 Lis alibi pendens

There seems to be little authority from the Kenyan courts on the question of concurrent proceedings concerning the same subject-matter and parties within and outside the jurisdiction. The issue arose in *Owens v Owens*,[70] in the context of divorce proceedings taking place in England and Kenya. However, because the court did not consider that there was any prospect of inconsistent decrees being made by the courts there was no proper discussion of the principles applicable where inconsistent decisions are a real possibility.

There is a statutory provision that touches on the subject, however. The Civil Procedure Act 1924, section 6, provides:

> 'Stay of suit
>
> No court shall proceed with the trial of any suit or proceeding in which the matter in issue is also directly and substantially in issue in a previously instituted suit or proceeding between the same parties, or between parties under whom they or any of them claim, litigating under the same title, where such suit or proceeding is pending in the same or any other court having jurisdiction in Kenya to grant the relief claimed.
>
> *Explanation* – The pendency of a suit in a foreign court shall not preclude a court from trying a suit in which the same matters or any of them are in issue in such suit in such foreign court.'

This 'Explanation' provided after section 6 confirms that a Kenyan court may entertain proceedings while parallel proceedings are in progress elsewhere.

Frimpong Oppong states:[71]

> 'In appropriate proceedings, the Kenyan court may exercise discretion and stay proceedings in favour of a foreign court. The onus for establishing a strong reason for avoiding the jurisdiction of the Kenyan courts is on the party who seeks to avoid that jurisdiction and that burden is a heavy one. In exercising its discretion, the court should take into account all circumstances of the particular case, such as: the country where the evidence on the issues of fact is situated or more readily available; whether and how differently the law of the foreign country applies; with what country either party is connected and how closely; whether the defendant genuinely desires trial in the foreign country or is only seeking a procedural advantage, and whether the plaintiff would be prejudiced by having to sue in a foreign country. The mere fact that proceedings are pending abroad is not enough to compel the court to stay proceedings – an important consideration is the danger of inconsistent judgments.'

However, the authority cited in support of this statement of the law (*United India Insurance Co Ltd v East African Underwriters (Kenya) Ltd*)[72] concerned an

[70] [1959] EA 909 (CA) (Forbes Ag P, Windham JA and Sir Owen Corrie Ag JA).

[71] *Private International Law in Commonwealth Africa* (2013) 93–4.

[72] [1982–88] 1 KAR 639 (CA) (Madan, Kneller and Hancox JJA).

application for a stay of proceedings in the presence of a jurisdiction clause where no proceedings were on foot in a foreign jurisdiction and not an application for a stay of proceedings in a case where proceedings are (or will be) pursued in a different jurisdiction.

In considering whether to order a stay of domestic proceedings in favour of proceedings in a foreign court, the Kenyan courts may well look to the approach adopted by the English courts in this regard. In *de Dampierre v de Dampierre*,[73] the House of Lords held that where a stay of English proceedings is sought on the basis that there are parallel proceedings in another jurisdiction the principles of *forum non conveniens* enunciated in *Spiliada Maritime Corp v Cansulex Ltd*[74] (which are dealt with more fully below), apply. Thus in *de Dampierre*, a case concerning parallel divorce proceedings in France and England, the court considered the connections between the parties and the two jurisdictions and the appropriateness of proceedings in France rather than in England and concluded that the English proceedings should be stayed:[75]

> 'Here it is beyond dispute that there are very strong factors connecting the case with France, whereas now there are practically none connecting the case with England. Neither party suggests that New York is the appropriate forum. It follows that *prima facie* the courts of France clearly provide the appropriate jurisdiction for the resolution of the dispute, so that a stay should be granted unless justice requires otherwise. In considering the question, the [judge at first instance] ... did indeed invoke the authority of one of the earlier authorities on the inherent jurisdiction, relying as he did on the much-quoted dictum of Lord Diplock in *MacShannon v. Rockware Glass Ltd.* [1978] A.C. 975, 812. He recognised the undoubted "Frenchness" of the marriage and the spouses, but considered that the wife's absence from what he described as the "harsh" French regime and her presence in the more "benevolent" regime which prevails here, plainly afforded a juridical advantage to her and that, following Lord Diplock's approach, this must outweigh the "Frenchness" of the marriage of the spouses and point to the conclusion that England was the more appropriate jurisdiction for the dissolution of the marriage.'

And:[76]

> 'The weight to be given to what has been called a "legitimate personal or juridical advantage" was considered by your Lordships' House in the *Spiliada* case [1987] A.C. 460, 482-484. The conclusion there reached was that, having regard to the underlying principle, the court should not, as a general rule, be deterred from granting a stay of proceedings simply because the plaintiff in this country will be deprived of such an advantage, provided that the court is satisfied that substantial justice will be done in the appropriate forum overseas. Reference was made, in particular, to cases concerning discovery where, as is

---

73 [1988] AC 92 (HL(E)) (Lords Keith, Brandon, Templeman, Ackner and Goff).

74 [1987] AC 460 (HL(E)).

75 Ibid *per* Lord Goff at 109E–H.

76 Ibid 110B–F.

> well known, there is a spectrum of systems of discovery applicable in various jurisdictions; and the opinion was expressed that, generally speaking, injustice cannot be said to be done if a party is compelled to accept one of these well recognised systems of discovery in another forum. If I follow that approach in the circumstances of the present case, I find that French matrimonial law contains provisions for "compensation" which, unlike our own, place emphasis upon the question whether the breakdown of the marriage was due to the exclusive fault of one of the parties, providing (subject to an important exception) that a party so at fault is deprived of the right to an award of compensation. Such an approach is no longer acceptable in this country, though it bears a close resemblance to the principles applicable here not so very long ago. But it is evidently still acceptable in a highly civilised country with which this country has very close ties of friendship, not least nowadays through our common membership of the European Community; and I find it impossible to conclude that, objectively speaking, justice would not be done if the wife was compelled to pursue her remedy for financial provision under such a regime in the courts of a country which provide, most plainly, the natural forum for the resolution of this matrimonial dispute.'

Thus what is required is a balancing of the various factors in the case to ascertain in which jurisdiction the case is most appropriately decided.

In this context, the basis on which a Kenyan court may grant an application for an anti-suit injunction to prevent to continuation of proceedings outside the jurisdiction is not entirely clear. Section 63(e) of the Civil Procedure Act 1924 (as amended), provides: 'In order to prevent the ends of justice from being defeated, the court may, *if it is so prescribed* ... (e) make such other interlocutory orders as may appear to the court to be just and convenient' (emphasis provided). Section 2 of the 1924 Act defines 'prescribed' as meaning 'prescribed by rules' and the term 'rules' is also defined in section 2 as meaning 'rules and forms made by the Rules Committee to regulate the procedure of courts'. The powers of the Rules Committee to make rules are contained in section 81 of the 1924 Act. The most recent iteration of the High Court Rules is the Civil Procedure Rules 2010.

The applicable provision of the Civil Procedure Rules, Order 40, 'Temporary Injunctions and Interlocutory Orders', does not appear to be applicable to a case where an anti-suit injunction is sought in a case other than one involving a breach of contract.

On an application to enforce a jurisdiction clause by way of an anti-suit injunction, a party may rely on Order 40, rule 2(1), which provides:

> 'In any suit for restraining the defendant from committing a breach of contract or other injury of any kind, whether compensation is claimed in the suit or not, the plaintiff may, at any time after the commencement of the suit, and either before or after judgment, apply to the court for a temporary injunction to restrain the defendant from committing the breach of contract or injury complained of, or any injury of a like kind arising out of the same contract or relating to the same property or right.'

In cases where a stay of domestic proceedings is sought in the absence of a jurisdiction clause in favour of a foreign forum, perhaps a better basis on which to proceed is by reliance on section 3A of the 1924 Act which provides: '**Saving of inherent powers of court** Nothing in this Act shall limit or otherwise affect the inherent power of the court to make such orders as may be necessary for the ends of justice or to prevent abuse of the process of the court.' It is submitted that, in appropriate circumstances, a Kenyan court could take the view that the pursuit of concurrent domestic proceedings and foreign proceedings was an abuse of its process and/or inimical to the ends of justice and that it should stay its own proceedings in order to bring such conduct to an end.

3.1.2.5 Forum non conveniens

The Kenyan courts have yet to consider whether the doctrine of *forum non conveniens* forms part of the law of Kenya. It is, of course, open to the Kenyan courts to disavow the recognition of the modern doctrine of *forum non conveniens*. However, it is submitted, that a form of the doctrine was introduced into or recognised as forming part of the law of Kenya by section 3(1) of the Judicature Act 1967 which makes provision for the 'Mode of exercise of jurisdiction' of the High Court, inter alia:

> 'The jurisdiction of the High Court, the Court of Appeal and of all subordinate courts shall be exercised in conformity with –
>
> *(a)* the Constitution;
>
> *(b)* *[all written laws and certain scheduled Acts of the United Kingdom Parliament]*;
>
> *(c)* subject thereto and so far as those written laws do not extend or apply, the substance of the common law, the doctrines of equity and the Statutes of general application in force in England on the 12th August, 1897, and the procedure and practice observed in court of justice in England on that date ...'.

A species of the doctrine of *forum non conveniens* was recognised in England prior to the 1897 cut-off date provided for by section 3(1)(c) of the 1967 Act, as is demonstrated in the case law set out below.

Historically, the English courts seemed always to have held that a major factor in the exercise of the discretion to grant leave to serve out of the jurisdiction or stay proceedings already served out of the jurisdiction was whether the English proceedings were vexatious and oppressive. The expression 'vexatious and oppressive' bore a wide meaning and extended to considerations related to the comparative convenience of proceedings in England as opposed to a particular foreign forum. For example, in *Logan v Bank of Scotland (No. 2)*,[77] the Court of

---

[77] [1906] 1 KB 141 CA (Sir Gorell Barnes, President, Collins MR, and Romer LJ).

Appeal granted an application staying proceedings served as of right in England in favour of Scotland. Sir Gorell Barnes P stated:[78]

> 'Now, it is true that the Courts of this country have not gone so far as to express themselves upon the question of convenience in terms similar to those used in the Scotch cases, though, as I have already noticed, it may be doubted whether there is any substantial difference between the two. Yet it seems to me clear that the inconvenience of trying a case in a particular tribunal may be such as practically to work a serious injustice upon a defendant and be vexatious. This would probably not be so if the difference of trying in one country rather than in another were merely measured by some extra expense; but where the difficulty for the defendant of trying in the country in which the action is brought is such that it is impracticable to properly try the case by reason of the difficulty of procuring the attendance of busy men as witnesses, and keeping them during trial, and of having to deal with masses of books, documents, and papers which are not in the country where the action is brought, and of dealing with law foreign to the tribunal, it appears to me that a case of vexation in some circumstances may be made out if the plaintiff chooses to sue in that country rather than in that where everybody is and where all the witnesses and material for the trial are.'

In *Logan v Bank of Scotland (No. 2)*, Sir Gorell Barnes P relied on English authority dating back to 1882[79] for the proposition of law that England had an analogous doctrine to the Scottish law doctrine of *forum non conveniens*. By virtue of the provisions of section 3(1)(c) of the 1967 Act, this doctrine forms part of the law of Kenya also.

The modern expression of the English doctrine of *forum non conveniens* appears in *Spiliada Maritime Corp v Cansulex Ltd, The Spiliada*.[80] The House of Lords elaborated upon these principles and decided that the doctrine of *forum non conveniens* applied to cases not only where leave is sought for service of a writ outside the jurisdiction or where service has been effected and a stay of the proceedings is sought (or an order that service of the writ is set aside) but extended the doctrine to cases where proceedings had been commenced as of right by service within the jurisdiction:[81]

> 'The basic principle is that a stay will only be granted on the ground of forum non conveniens where the court is satisfied that there is some other available forum, having competent jurisdiction, which is the appropriate forum for the trial of the action, i.e. in which the case may be tried more suitably for the interests of all the parties and the ends of justice.'

---

[78] At 151–2. This was a decision under the 1883 Rules of the Supreme Court.

[79] *Peruvian Guano Co v Bockwoldt* (1883) 23 Ch D 225 (CA) (Jessel MR, Lindley and Bowen LJJ), *per* Jessel MR at p 230.

[80] [1987] AC 460 (Lords Keith, Templeman, Griffiths, Mackay and Goff).

[81] At 476C, *per* Lord Goff, with whom the other Lords of Appeal agreed (Lord Templeman delivering a concurring opinion). A decision under the 1965 Rules of the Supreme Court.

The English courts will, therefore, refuse leave to serve a writ out of the jurisdiction or, in a case where leave has been granted or the defendant is served as of right within the jurisdiction but the defendant enters a conditional appearance and applies for a stay of the proceedings, will stay English proceedings if England is not the *forum conveniens*.[82] The principles applicable in both of these circumstances are set out in greater detail below.

Where an application is made for leave to serve a writ out of the jurisdiction, the following principles apply[83] (using Kenya and not England as the jurisdictional base):

(1) The plaintiff must show good reason why service of process on a foreign defendant should be permitted and, in considering this question, the court must take into account the nature of the dispute, the legal and practical issues involved, such questions as local knowledge, availability of witnesses and their evidence, and expense.

(2) Lord Goff in *The Spiliada* added that the fundamental question (as it is in cases of staying of actions on *forum non conveniens* grounds, see below) was to identify the forum in which the case could suitably be tried for the interests of all the parties and for the ends of justice. To justify the exercise of the discretion to grant leave to serve a writ outside the jurisdiction, the plaintiff has to show that Kenya is clearly the appropriate forum for the trial of the action. But where the parties have contractually agreed on Kenya as the forum which they prefer, the court will normally assume jurisdiction.

Where a writ has been served as of right within the jurisdiction or with leave outside the jurisdiction and the defendant applies to set aside service of the writ or to stay the proceedings, the principles applied to such an application are as follows:[84]

(1) In general the legal burden of proof rests on the defendant to persuade the court to exercise its discretion to grant a stay, although the evidential burden will rest on a party who seeks to establish the existence of matters

[82] See, generally, *Dicey, Morris and Collins on the Conflict of Laws* 15 ed (2012) vol 1, r 38(2) and (3) para 12-007 et seq; r 38 states the modern English law as follows, inter alia: '(2) ... an English court has power to order a stay of proceedings on the basis that England is an inappropriate forum (forum non conveniens) if: (a) the defendant shows there to be another court with competent jurisdiction which is clearly or distinctly more appropriate than England for the trial of the action, and (b) it is not unjust that the claimant be deprived of the right to trial in England. (3) In considering whether to assume jurisdiction in any of the cases mentioned in Rule 34 (service out of the jurisdiction with the permission of the court) the court will generally require the claimant to show England to be the most appropriate forum for the trial of the claim.' See further *Vedanta Resources plc v Lungowe* [2020] AC 1045 (SC) (Lady Hale, Lords Wilson and Hodge, Lady Black and Lord Briggs), [66]–[70].

[83] See *Dicey, Morris and Collins on the Conflict of Laws* 15 ed (2012) vol 1, r 38(3), para 12-053 et seq.

[84] Ibid r 38(2), para 12-030 et seq.

which will assist him in persuading the court to exercise its discretion in his favour.

(2) If the court is satisfied by the defendant that there is another available forum which is clearly a more appropriate forum for the trial of the action, the burden will shift to the plaintiff to show that there are special circumstances by reason of which justice requires that the trial should nevertheless take place in Kenya.

(3) The burden on the defendant is not just to show that Kenya is not the natural or appropriate forum, but to establish that there is another forum which is clearly or distinctly more appropriate than the Kenyan forum; accordingly, where (as in some commercial disputes) there is no particular forum which can be described as the natural forum, there will be no reason to grant a stay.

(4) The court will look to see what factors there are which point in the direction of another forum as being the 'natural forum', ie that with which the action has the most real and substantial connection. These will include factors affecting convenience or expense (such as availability of witnesses) and such other factors as the law governing the transaction and the places where the parties reside or carry on business, and also whether the claim is part of a larger overall dispute which would be damaged by being fragmented.

(5) If the court concludes at that stage that there is no other available forum which is clearly more appropriate for the trial of the action, the court will ordinarily refuse a stay.

(6) If, however, the court concludes that there is some other available forum which *prima facie* is clearly more appropriate, it will ordinarily grant a stay unless there are circumstances by reason of which justice requires that a stay should not be granted. In that enquiry, the court will consider all the circumstances of the case, including circumstances which go beyond those taken into account when considering connecting factors with other jurisdictions.

(7) A stay will not be refused simply because the plaintiff will thereby be deprived of 'a legitimate personal or juridical advantage', provided that the court is satisfied that substantial justice will be done in the available appropriate forum.

It is likely that a Kenyan court will have regard to these principles in considering the exercise of its discretion both to grant leave to serve a writ out of the jurisdiction and in considering any application to set aside service of a writ served outside the jurisdiction or stay proceedings where it is contended that a different jurisdiction is the appropriate jurisdiction for resolution of the dispute.

In exercising its discretion, the court must keep in mind the fact that the incidence of the burden of proof differs depending on the type of application under consideration: on an application for leave to serve out of the jurisdiction, the legal and evidential burden of proof is on the plaintiff; whereas, on an application to set aside service of a writ or to stay proceedings commenced as of right by service within the jurisdiction, the legal burden of proof is on the defendant to those proceedings but, as noted above, an evidential burden remains with the party who is seeking to persuade the court of a matter that may influence the court in exercising its discretion in that party's favour.

Order 5, rules 26–31 contain ancillary provisions regarding such matters as the time within which a defendant must enter an appearance after service of process on him[85] and the means by which service is to be effected outside the jurisdiction, including substituted service if appropriate.[86]

As the application for leave to serve outside the jurisdiction is made *ex parte*, there is a duty on the plaintiff to make full and frank disclosure of all material facts. In *Donnebaum v Mikolaschek*,[87] Farrell J held,[88] citing an English authority, *The Hagen*,[89] that there had not been full and frank disclosure on the plaintiff's (second) application to serve outside the jurisdiction and that this alone would justify the setting aside of the order granted to serve the defendant outside the jurisdiction.

In *The Hagen*, the English Court of Appeal also set out the following cautionary observation:[90]

> 'During these present sittings Vaughan Williams L.J. and myself have on more than one occasion had to consider Order XI [the equivalent to Order 5, rule 21 of the Civil Procedure Rules 2010], and we have had many authorities discussed and fully considered by the Court, and the conclusion to which the authorities led us I may put under three heads. First we adopted the statement of Pearson J., in *Societe Générale de Paris v. Dreyfus Brothers*, that "it becomes a very serious question, and ought always to be considered a very

[85] Rule 26.

[86] *Patel v Mart* (1954) 27 KLR 40, that the defendant, in respect of whom leave to serve out of the jurisdiction in Tanganyika was granted, was on safari, was not a sufficient reason to make an order for substituted service. There must be an inability to effect prompt service such as, for example, that the defendant is evading service.

[87] [1966] EA 25 (H Ct) (Farrell J). This was the plaintiff's second attempt to seise the Kenyan court with jurisdiction. The first attempt was dismissed by Rudd J in September 1964: [1964] EA 645.

[88] Ibid 28A.

[89] [1908] P 189 (CA) (Lord Alverstone CJ and Farwell and Kennedy LJJ), *per* Farwell LJ at 201: 'The second point which we considered established by the cases was this, that, if on the construction of any of the sub-heads of Order xi. there was any doubt, it ought to be resolved in favour of the foreigner; and the third is that, inasmuch as the application is made *ex parte*, full and fair disclosure is necessary, as in all *ex parte* applications, and a failure to make such full and fair disclosure would justify the Court in discharging the order, even although the party might afterwards be in a position to make another application.'

[90] Ibid *per* Farwell LJ at 201.

> serious question, whether or not, even in a case like that, it is necessary for the jurisdiction of the Court to be invoked, and whether this Court ought to put a foreigner, who owes no allegiance here, to the inconvenience and annoyance of being brought to contest his rights in this country, and I for one say, most distinctly, that I think this Court ought to be exceedingly careful before it allows a writ to be served out of the jurisdiction".'

There can be little doubt that a Kenyan court would assent to these observations.

3.2 Enforcement of Foreign Judgments

Under Kenyan law a foreign judgment may be enforced in Kenya either at common law or under the statutory regime set out in the Foreign Judgments (Reciprocal Enforcement) Act 1984[91] and the Civil Procedure Act 1924.

3.2.1 Enforcement at common law

Enforcement and recognition of a foreign judgment at common law was recently considered by the Court of Appeal in *Shah v Haria*,[92] in which Githinji JA, giving the judgment of the court, set out in great detail the principles applicable to the enforcement of a foreign judgment at common law. The case concerned an attempt to enforce in Kenya a judgment of the Federal Supreme Court of Ethiopia dated 17 January 2005 by which the plaintiff was awarded the birr equivalent of damages in the sum of US$250,000. In or around May 2007 the plaintiff filed a plaint in the High Court of Kenya claiming the Kenyan shilling equivalent of the Ethiopian birr sum outstanding. The defendants entered a defence that contended, inter alia, an Ethiopian judgment was not enforceable in Kenya because of the absence of any reciprocal enforcement agreement between Kenya and Ethiopia. The plaintiff applied for summary judgment on his claim based on the Ethiopian judgment.

The court referred[93] to section 3(1) of the Judicature Act 1967 (see also section 3.1.2.5, above) which makes provision for the 'Mode of exercise of jurisdiction' of the High Court, inter alia:

> 'The jurisdiction of the High Court, the Court of Appeal and of all subordinate courts shall be exercised in conformity with –

---

[91] Act 4 of 1984 (now Cap 43 of the Laws of Kenya, 2010). In *Italframe Ltd v Mediterranean Shipping Co* [1986] eKLR; Civil Appeal 18 of 1985 (Hancox JA; Platt and Gachuhi AgJJA) the Court of Appeal held, relying on the preamble to the 1984 Act, that the 'basic principle upon which neighbouring or other states provide for the enforcement of foreign judgments, is one of the reciprocity and the advantage to be gained therefrom'.

[92] [2016] eKLR; Civil Appeal 147 of 2009 (Githinji, Mohammed and Otieno-Odek JJA; judgment on appeal dated 26 February 2016; judgment at first instance dated 27 January 2009).

[93] Ibid para [20].

(a) the Constitution;

(b) *[all written laws and certain scheduled Acts of the United Kingdom Parliament]*;

(c) subject thereto and so far as those written laws do not extend or apply, the substance of the common law, the doctrines of equity and the Statutes of general application in force in England on the 12th August, 1897, and the procedure and practice observed in court of justice in England on that date ...'.

Against that background the court held that[94] 'a foreign judgment is enforceable in Kenya as a claim in common law'. The court proceeded to set out the applicable principles, derived from English law. It is not proposed to paraphrase this important statement of the law; instead, the relevant passages[95] from Githinji JA's judgment are set out below:

> 'The common law principles on enforcement of foreign judgments were extensively elaborated in the case of *Adams & Others –v- Cape Industrials PLC*, (1990) Ch. 433. The principles are:
>
> *(a)* Where a foreign court of competent jurisdiction has adjudicated a certain sum to be due from one person to another, a legal obligation arises to pay that sum, on which an action of debt to enforce the judgment may be maintained. (See Park B. in *Williams –v- Jones* (1845) 13 M. & W. 628, 633 as quoted in *Adams & Others –v- Cape Industrials* [sic, 'Industries'] *PLC*, (1990) Ch. 433 at 513.
>
> *(b)* In deciding whether the foreign court was one of competent jurisdiction, courts will apply not the law of the foreign court itself but English rules of private international law. The competence of the foreign court is competence of the court in an international sense – i.e. its territorial competence over the subject-matter and over the defendant. Its competence or jurisdiction in any other sense is not material. (See Lindley M.R. in *Pemberton –v- Hughes* (1899) 1 Ch. 781,791).
>
> *(c)* In *Emanuel –v- Symon*, (1908) 1 KB 302, Buckley L.J. said that in actions in personam there are five cases in which the courts of England will enforce a foreign judgment. These are: (i) where the defendant is a subject of the foreign country in which the judgment was obtained; (ii) where he was resident in the foreign country when the action began; (iii) where the defendant in the character of plaintiff has selected the forum in which he is afterwards sued; (iv) where the defendant has voluntarily appeared and (v) where the defendant has contracted to submit himself to the forum in which the judgment was obtained.
>
> *(d)* If a foreign judgment is to be enforced against a corporation, it must be shown that at the relevant time, the corporation was carrying on business and it was doing so at a definite and to some reasonable extent, permanent place in the foreign country. (See *Adams & Others –v- Cape Industrials PLC*, (1990) Ch. 433 at 512).

[94] Ibid *per* Githinji JA (giving the judgment of the court) para [22].

[95] Ibid.

(e) It is only the judgment of a foreign court recognized as competent by English law which will give rise to an obligation on the part of the defendant to obey it. The onus is on the plaintiff seeking to enforce the foreign judgment to prove the competence of such court to assume jurisdiction; the evidentiary burden may shift during trial. (See *Adams & Others –v- Cape Industrials PLC*, (1990) Ch. 433 at 550).

(f) The principle that a foreign court has jurisdiction to give an in personam judgment[96] if the judgment debtor, the defendant in the foreign court, submitted to the jurisdiction of the foreign court is well settled.

(g) A foreign judgment obtained in circumstances that are contrary to natural justice does not give rise to any obligation of obedience enforceable at common law.

(h) If a judgment is pronounced by a foreign court over persons within its jurisdiction and in a matter in which it is competent to deal, English courts will never investigate the propriety of the proceedings in the foreign court, unless they offend substantial justice. Where no substantial justice is offended, all that the English court shall look into is the finality of the judgment and the competence of the foreign court to entertain the sort of case which it did deal with and its competence to require the defendant to appear before it. (See *Pemberton –v- Hughes*, (1899) 1 Ch 781,790-791 as per Lindley M.R). Mere procedural irregularity, on the part of the foreign court according to its own rules, is not a ground of defence to enforcement of the foreign judgment. (See *Adams & others –v- Cape Industrials PLC*, (1990) Ch. 433 at 567).

(i) A defendant, shown to have been subject to the jurisdiction of a foreign court, cannot seek to persuade English court to examine the correctness of the judgment whether on the facts or as to the application by the foreign court of its own law. A foreign judgment is not impeachable merely because it is manifestly wrong. (See *Goddard –v- Gray*, L.R. 6 Q.B. 139).

(j) A judgment of a foreign court having jurisdiction over the parties and subject-matter – i.e. having jurisdiction to summon the defendants before it and to decide such matters as it has decided – cannot be impeached on merits but can be impeached if the proceedings, the method by which the court comes to a final decision, are contrary to English views of substantial justice.'

One observation may be made about this statement of the law and that is in relation to point *(c)*(i) above that an English court will enforce a foreign judgment where the defendant is a subject of the foreign country in which the judgment was obtained. English law has never recognised the jurisdiction of a foreign court on the basis that the defendant was a subject or citizen of that country. English law will recognise the jurisdiction of a foreign court on bases (ii)–(v), but not (i).[97]

---

[96] In *Pattni v Ali* [2007] 2 AC 85 (PC) (Lords Bingham and Walker, Lady Hale and Lords Carswell and Mance), the judgment creditor sought to enforce in the Isle of Man a Kenyan judgment. The judgment debtors argued that the Kenyan judgment was *in rem* in nature, rather than *in personam*. The Privy Council rejected this argument, holding that the material parts of the Kenyan judgment were *in personam* in nature.

[97] See *Dicey, Morris and Collins on the Conflict of Laws* 15 ed (2012) vol 1, r 43, paras 14R-054–055 and 14-085.

Applying those principles, Githinji JA set out[98] the requirements for a foreign judgment from a non-designated jurisdiction to be enforced in Kenya:

'*(a)* A party must file a plaint at the High Court of Kenya providing a concise statement of the nature of the claim, claiming the amount of the judgment debt, supported by a verifying affidavit, list of witnesses and bundle of documents intended to be relied upon. A certified copy of the foreign judgment should be exhibited to the Plaint.[99]

(b) It is open to a defendant to challenge the validity of the foreign judgment under the grounds set out in Section 9 of the *Civil Procedure* Act.[100]

(c) A judgment creditor is entitled to summary judgment under Order 36 unless the defendant judgment debtor can satisfy the Court that there is a real prospect of establishing at trial one of the grounds set out in Section 9 of the Civil Procedure Act.

(d) If the foreign judgment creditor is successful after trial, the judgment creditor will have the benefit of a High Court judgment and the judgment creditor will be entitled to use the procedures of the Kenyan courts to enforce the foreign judgment which will now be executed as a Kenyan judgment.

(e) The money judgment in the foreign judgment must be final and conclusive. It may be final and conclusive even though it is subject to an appeal. Under Section 9 of the Civil Procedure Act, a foreign judgment is conclusive as to any matter thereby directly adjudicated upon between the same parties or between parties under whom they or any of them claim, litigating under the same title except:

(i) where it has not been pronounced by a court of competent jurisdiction;

(ii) where it has not been given on the merits of the case;

(iii) where it appears on the face of the proceedings to be founded on an incorrect view of international law or a refusal to recognize the law of Kenya in cases in which such law is applicable;

---

[98] [2016] eKLR para [23] of the judgment.

[99] It is to be noted that this requirement does not fully elucidate what is to happen when the plaintiff – the foreign judgment creditor – wishes to enforce that judgment against a defendant who is present outside the jurisdiction. It must be remembered that O 5, r 21 of the High Court Rules does not allow the Kenyan court to permit service of the writ on a defendant who is present outside the jurisdiction where the action is one to enforce a foreign judgment; Frimpong Oppong 'Recognition and enforcement of foreign judgments in Commonwealth African countries' (2014) XV *Yearbook of Private International Law* 365, 371–2.

[100] Which provides: '9. *When foreign judgment not conclusive* A foreign judgment shall be conclusive as to any matter thereby directly adjudicated upon between the same parties or between parties under whom they or any of them claim, litigating under the same title, except—

(a) where it has not been pronounced by a court of competent jurisdiction;

(b) where it has not been given on the merits of the case;

(c) where it appears on the face of the proceedings to be founded on an incorrect view of international law or a refusal to recognize the law of Kenya in cases in which such law is applicable;

(d) where the proceedings in which the judgment was obtained are opposed to natural justice;

(e) where it has been obtained by fraud;

(f) where it sustains a claim founded on a breach of any law in force in Kenya.'

(iv) where the proceedings in which the judgment was obtained are opposed to natural justice;

(v) where it has been obtained by fraud; or

(vi) where it sustains a claim founded on a breach of any law in force in Kenya.'

This statement of the law relating to enforcement at common law of foreign judgments in Kenya may now be taken as the authoritative statement of the law in this area.[101]

Among the more important defences to an action at common law on a foreign judgment are the following: (1) where the foreign judgment was procured by fraud either, (a) fraud on the part of the party in whose favour the judgment is given, or (b) fraud on the part of the court pronouncing the judgment;[102] (2) where the proceedings in which the foreign judgment was obtained were contrary to the rules of natural justice.[103]

3.2.2 Enforcement pursuant to statute

3.2.2.1 *The regime for enforcement pursuant to statute*

As mentioned above, the statutory regime for enforcement of foreign judgments in Kenya is found in the Foreign Judgments (Reciprocal Enforcement) Act 1984 ('the 1984 Act') and section 9 of the Civil Procedure Act 1924 ('the 1924 Act').[104]

---

[101] See too the statement of the common law in *Dicey, Morris and Collins on the Conflict of Laws* 15 ed (2012) vol 1, rr 42–54, as applied in *Raw Bank Plc v Yusuf Omar* [2020] eKLR (High Court of Mombasa) (Chepkwony J).

[102] *Dicey, Morris and Collins on the Conflict of Laws* 15 ed (2012) vol 1, r 50, para 14R-137, 'A foreign judgment, on the other hand, can be impeached for fraud even though no newly discovered evidence is produced and even though the fraud might have been, and was, alleged in the foreign proceedings' (para 14-139).

[103] *Dicey, Morris and Collins on the Conflict of Laws* 15 ed (2012) vol 1, r 52, para 14R-162. Referring to the decision in *Adams v Cape Industries plc* [1990] Ch 433, it is stated (para 14-164): 'The Court of Appeal held that the defence of breach of natural justice was not limited to the requirements of due notice of the hearing to a litigant and opportunity to put a case to the foreign court. It confirmed that the basic question was that stated in *Pemberton v. Hughes*, namely whether there was a procedural defect which constituted a breach of the English court's view of substantial justice, which would depend on the nature of the proceedings under consideration. The principle was applied in *Masters v. Leaver*, where the Court of Appeal considered that a substantial failure to follow its own procedure for an assessment of damages meant that proceedings before a Texas court had led to a judgment in denial of substantial justice.'

[104] In Kenya, there is no equivalent statutory regime in place to that which exists in Uganda, Malawi, Tanzania or Zanzibar. Taking each jurisdiction in turn, in Uganda, s 3 of the Judgments Extension Act 1908 allows for the enforcement of a warrant for the civil arrest of a defendant emanating from a court in Kenya, Malawi or Tanzania (but not Zanzibar). It would appear that, with respect to the civil arrest of a defendant, a similar regime is in place in Malawi: s 3 of the Nyasaland Judgments Extension Ordinance 1912, as amended, allows a judge sitting in the High Court in that country to 'execute a warrant for the arrest of the defendant where the warrant has been issued in' Kenya, Uganda, Tanzania or Zanzibar (and see further the discussion of this Ordinance in the relevant part of the chapter on Malawi). In Tanzania, s 3 of the Judgments Extension Act 1921 allows a judge, inter alia, to indorse or execute a warrant issued by the High Court of Kenya,

While the overall scheme and particular parts of the 1984 Act are recognisable as having been derived from the United Kingdom Foreign Judgments (Reciprocal Enforcement) Act 1933, the 1984 Act is a substantially redrafted and extended version of the 1933 Act. Accordingly, when a Kenyan court is engaged in the process of construing the terms of the 1984 Act, it is likely that judicial and academic authorities on the construction of these provisions of the 1933 Act[105] will be of limited use and will need to be treated with caution.

On the other hand, section 9 of the 1924 Act shares some of the same provisions as section 4(1)(a) of the 1933 Act (such as those relating to the defence of fraud) and a Kenyan court may look to English authority for the meaning of provisions common to both statutes. Section 9 of the 1924 Act provides that a foreign judgment[106] shall be conclusive as to the matters adjudicated upon between the same parties or parties claiming under them save in six instances (as to which, see below).

The 1984 Act applies to jurisdictions to which the 1984 Act has been extended by Order.[107] At the present time these countries are as follows: Australia, Malawi, Seychelles, Tanzania, Uganda, Zambia, the United Kingdom and the Republic of Rwanda.

A brief summary of the principal provisions of the 1984 Act is set out below.

The 1984 Act applies to various types of judgment[108] including a judgment or order: in civil proceedings whereby a sum of money is payable, including a lump sum as financial provision for or maintenance of a spouse or former spouse of a child; in civil proceedings whereby movable property is ordered to be delivered to a person; an order for compensation for damage to an injured person made in criminal proceedings; for an interim payment if that order is final and

---

Malawi, Zanzibar or Uganda. In Zanzibar, s 3 of the Judgments Extension Decree 1908, as amended by s 2 of the Judgments Extension (Amendment) Decree 1921, allows a judge, inter alia, to indorse or execute a warrant issued by the High Court of the Colony and Protectorate of Kenya, 'Nyasaland' (Malawi), the 'Tanganyika Territory' (Tanzania) or Uganda. As appears further below, the statutory regime in Kenya has not been extended to any one of Uganda, Malawi, Tanzania or Zanzibar.

[105] In particular, reference should be made to: *Dicey, Morris and Collins on the Conflict of Laws* 15 ed (2012) vol 1, paras 14R183–14-195; Briggs *Civil Jurisdiction and Judgments* 7 ed (2021) paras 35.01–35.10.

[106] It should be noted that, in *Gathuna v African Orthodox Church of Kenya* [1982] eKLR; Civil Appeal 4 of 1982 (Law and Miller AJJ, Kneller AgJA), the Court of Appeal held that a judgment of the Holy Synod of the Apostolic and Patriarchal Throne of Greek Orthodox Patriarchate of Alexandria was not a judgment to which the 1924 Act applied because it fell outside the meaning given to the term 'foreign judgment' by s 2 of the 1924 Act.

[107] Section 13 of the 1984 Act; see the Foreign Judgments (Reciprocal Enforcement) (Extension of Act) Order 1984 (LN 135 of 1984, LN 301 of 1991), Sch.

[108] Section 3(1). In *Arthur Gatungu Gathuna v African Orthodox Church of Kenya* [1982] eKLR, the Court of Appeal held that a judgment of the Holy Synod Apostolic and Patriarchal Throne of the Greek Orthodox Patriarchate Metropolitan of Alexandria was not a foreign judgment for the purposes of enforcement in Kenya under the 1924 Act.

conclusive.[109] A judgment is final and conclusive despite the fact that an appeal is pending against it or that it may still be subject to an appeal in the relevant foreign court.[110]

Section 3(3) sets out 13 types of judgment to which the 1984 Act does not apply, inter alia, a judgment or order: for a sum in respect of tax, a fine or penalty; in respect of exemplary, multiple or punitive damages; for periodic payment of financial provision for a spouse or child; for custody or guardianship of a child; where the judgment was procured in breach of a jurisdiction agreement and where the defendant did not submit to the jurisdiction of the foreign court; where the judgment of the designated country was in fact a judgment given in another country.

The foreign court is deemed to have had international jurisdiction for the purposes of the 1984 Act if,[111] inter alia: the defendant submitted to the jurisdiction of the foreign court by voluntarily appearing in the proceedings; the judgment debtor was plaintiff in or counterclaimed in the foreign proceedings; the defendant agreed in writing to submit to the jurisdiction of the foreign court; the judgment debtor was at the time the foreign proceedings were instituted habitually resident in or, if a legal person, was incorporated in or had its principal place of business in the foreign jurisdiction; the judgment debtor had at the time the foreign proceedings were instituted an office or place of business in or, if a legal person, had a branch in the foreign jurisdiction and the proceedings were in respect of a transaction effected or an occurrence arising from business carried out by, through or at that office or branch; the judgment debtor was conducting business in the foreign jurisdiction, had appointed an agent there to receive service of process in respect of that business and the proceedings in the foreign court were in respect of a transaction effected in connection with, or of an occurrence arising from, that business; in the case of a contract, the obligation which was the subject of the proceedings was, or was to be, wholly or mainly performed in the foreign jurisdiction; in the case of actions *in rem* or determining the rights of ownership, use or possession in immovable property or tangible movable property, the property in question was at the institution of the proceedings situated in the foreign jurisdiction; and in the case of an action to recover damages for physical injury to or death of a person or damage to tangible property, the circumstance which gave rise to the injury or death or damage occurred within the foreign jurisdiction or the injury or damage was suffered in that jurisdiction.

A foreign court is deemed *not* to have had jurisdiction in the circumstances set out in section 4(2) where: under Kenyan private international law rules,

---

[109] Section 3(2).

[110] Section 3(2).

[111] Section 4(1)(a)–(i).

a court other than the relevant foreign court had exclusive jurisdiction over the matter; the defendant appeared conditionally or otherwise for all or any of three purposes, (1) to contest the jurisdiction of the court, or (2) to invite the court in its discretion not to exercise its jurisdiction; or (3) to protect, or obtain the release of, property seized or threatened with seizure in those proceedings; where the judgment debtor was entitled to immunity from the jurisdiction of the foreign court under the rules of public international law and did not appear other than to contest the jurisdiction of the court.

3.2.2.2 *Procedure for registration*

Under section 5(1) a judgment creditor may apply *ex parte* to register the foreign judgment within six years of the date of the judgment[112] or, if there has been an appeal, the date of the last judgment in the case.[113] On such an application the court may either not allow the application in which case the court will direct a summons to be issued so that the application is then heard *inter partes* or may allow the application and order that notice of the registration of the foreign judgment be given to the judgment debtor. If the foreign judgment is expressed in a foreign currency it may be registered in the equivalent sum in Kenyan shillings at the exchange rate prevailing at the date of registration.[114] Execution of a judgment registered on an *ex parte* application is stayed automatically for 14 days after the date on which the judgment debtor is served with notice of the registration.

The court shall not register a foreign judgment if either it has been wholly satisfied or it could not be enforced by execution in the country of the foreign court.[115]

A judgment debtor may apply for registration of the foreign judgment to be set aside or reduced in amount on any of the grounds set out in section 10, subsections (2), (3) and (4) and on such an application the court may set aside the foreign judgment or reduce it in amount.[116]

---

[112] The six-year period is derived from s 2(1) of the United Kingdom Foreign Judgments (Reciprocal Enforcement) Act 1933. As in the 1933 Act, the language used in the 1984 Act in relation to the six-year period is permissive ('may apply ... within six years'): Briggs *Civil Jurisdiction and Judgments* 7ed (2021) para 35.10 .

[113] Section 5(4) sets out the documentation which is required on an application to register a foreign judgment.

[114] Section 7. It is not clear how this section is intended to operate in practice. If a judgment creditor sees an exchange rate advantage in having the foreign judgment registered in the currency in which it is expressed, this may disadvantage the judgment debtor unfairly depending on the time at which it is converted into local currency. Doubtless the court retains discretion to regulate any such unfairness on the application of either party.

[115] In *Herman Phillip Steyn v Charles Thys* [2011] eKLR (H Ct) (13 October 2005), the judgment debtor had filed an appeal in the foreign court (Tanzania) and that court had stayed execution of the judgment. The Kenyan court held that the judgment did not therefore fall within the 1984 Act (s 6(2)(b)).

[116] No appeal lies to the Court of Appeal from a decision at first instance to set aside or not to set aside a foreign judgment (or any other decision made by the High Court under the 1984 Act other than a decision

3.2.2.3 *Setting aside registration*

Sub-section (2) sets out 29 grounds on which a foreign judgment may be set aside. These include:

(1) the judgment is not one to which the 1984 Act applies;

(2) the judgment was registered in contravention of the 1984 Act;

(3) the foreign court had no international jurisdiction to adjudicate on the matter the subject of the judgment;[117]

(4) the judgment debtor did not appear in the foreign court and the jurisdiction of that court was based on a jurisdiction clause that is invalid under Kenyan rules of private international law;

(5) the cause of action on which the foreign judgment was given had already been the subject of a final and conclusive judgment by a court having jurisdiction to adjudicate on that cause of action;

(6) the cause of action adjudicated upon by the foreign court had since become the subject of a final and conclusive judgment by a Kenyan court which is irreconcilable with the foreign judgment;

(7) the judgment debtor, being the defendant in the original proceedings, either (1) was not served with the process of the original court *or* (2) was served but did not receive notice of the proceedings in sufficient time to enable him to defend those proceedings *and* in the case of (1) or (2) either (a) did not appear or (b) appeared only (i) to contest the jurisdiction, (ii) to invite the court in its discretion not to exercise its jurisdiction or (iii) to protect or obtain the release of property seized or threatened with seizure in those proceedings;[118]

(8) the judgment was obtained by fraud, other than fraud which was, or could have been, put in issue by the judgment debtor in the proceedings of the foreign court or an appeal therefrom;[119]

---

to register or a decision refusing to register a foreign judgment): *Patel v Bank of Baroda* [2001] eKLR (CA) (Tunoi, Lakha and Keiwua JJA; 13 July 2001). (The statements in Frimpong Oppong *Private International Law in Commonwealth Africa* (2013) 368 fn 79 and in Bwonwonga *Civil Procedure in Kenya* (2012) 146 para 465, that a decision not to set aside registration may be appealed, are incorrect.)

[117] This ground also appears in s 9(a) of the 1924 Act.

[118] There are eight variations in this ground: (1) combined with (a) or any one (or more) of (b)(i)–(iii); and (2) in the same combinations.

[119] This provision rids Kenyan law of the highly unsatisfactory English common-law approach to fraud in this context, 'A foreign judgment, on the other hand, can be impeached for fraud even though no newly discovered evidence is produced and even though the fraud might have been, and was, alleged in the foreign proceedings.' (*Dicey, Morris and Collins on the Conflict of Laws* 15 ed (2012) vol 1, r 50, para 14R-137 and para 14-139). However, s 9 of the 1924 Act provides: '9. *When foreign judgment not conclusive* A foreign judgment shall be conclusive as to any matter thereby directly adjudicated upon between the same parties or between

(9) Kenyan private international law would have applied certain mandatory provisions of Kenyan domestic law to the proceedings and the foreign judgment disregards those provisions in some material respect;[120]

(10) the foreign court in reaching its judgment decided one of the matters set out at section 3(3)(c)–(k) but a Kenyan court applying its private international law rules would have decided that question differently;[121]

(11) the foreign judgment had been taken on appeal and reversed or discharged or otherwise set aside;

(12) the judgment debtor is a person entitled to immunity from the jurisdiction of the Kenyan High Court under the laws of public international law;

(13) the rights under the judgment are not vested in the person applying for registration; and

(14) enforcement of the judgment would be contrary to Kenyan public policy.[122]

---

parties under whom they or any of them claim, litigating under the same title, except ... (e) where it has been obtained by fraud.' It is unclear how these two provisions interrelate. It is submitted that the correct view is that the 1924 Act has been derogated by the 1984 Act and that, in respect of a registrable judgment, to the extent that fraud which was or could have been put in issue in the foreign proceedings cannot be relied upon as a ground to set aside (or impeach the conclusiveness of the foreign judgment – which amounts to the same thing in the context) the foreign judgment. The English common-law approach to fraud would, however, by virtue of s 9 of the 1924 Act, appear to continue in force in respect of foreign judgments that fall outside the 1984 Act.

[120] Section 9(c) of the 1924 Act makes similar provision: '9. *When foreign judgment not conclusive* A foreign judgment shall be conclusive as to any matter thereby directly adjudicated upon between the same parties or between parties under whom they or any of them claim, litigating under the same title, except ... (c) where it appears on the face of the proceedings to be founded on an incorrect view of international law or a refusal to recognize the law of Kenya in cases in which such law is applicable.'

[121] This provision produces a further nine grounds on which a foreign judgment may be set aside: if the Kenyan court would have decided a question relating to any of the following matters differently: s 3(3)(c) periodic payments to a spouse, former spouse or child or other dependant person; (d) rights to matrimonial property; (e) custody or guardianship of children; (f) administration of the affairs of a person lacking capacity; (g) succession or administration of estates of the deceased whereby money is payable or movables deliverable; (h) in a matter of social security or public assistance where a sum of money is payable by or to a public authority; (i) corporate bankruptcy; (j) damage, death or injury caused by occurrences involving nuclear matter or ionising radiation; and (k) where the foreign proceedings were brought in breach of a jurisdiction clause and the defendant to them did not counterclaim or submit the jurisdiction of the court (although it is difficult to envisage a situation where s 10(2)(j) would apply when s 3(3)(k) did not render the foreign judgment non-registrable under the 1984 Act).

[122] Section 9(c) of the 1924 Act makes similar provision: '9. *When foreign judgment not conclusive* A foreign judgment shall be conclusive as to any matter thereby directly adjudicated upon between the same parties or between parties under whom they or any of them claim, litigating under the same title, except— (d) where the proceedings in which the judgment was obtained are opposed to natural justice.' This provision approximates to s 10(2)(n) of the 1984 Act. In *East African Development Bank v Dari Ltd*, the High Court at Nairobi (Okwany J) held: 'The mandate of the court did not extend to reviewing, interrogating or analysing the said judgment in order to determine if the procedure the court adopted was proper or if the judge who presided over the case ought to have recused himself from hearing the case. The issues of recusal of the judge, the alleged fraud ... were matters which fell to the jurisdiction of the English court where the judgment

Section 10(3) provides that an application may be made to set aside registration of a foreign judgment to the extent that its enforcement would require payment of sums in excess of monetary limits of liability imposed by any Kenyan statute that applies under Kenyan rules of private international law.[123]

Section 10(4) provides that the High Court may set aside a foreign judgment to the extent that the total sums awarded, including costs, are 'substantially in excess' of what would have been awarded by the High Court itself on the basis of the findings of law and fact made by the foreign court.

Under section 11 an application may also be made to set aside the registration of a foreign judgment on any of the bases set out below. On an application under sub-section (1) or (2) the court may set aside the foreign judgment or adjourn the application for a reasonable period[124] to enable the foreign proceedings to be resolved. Hence, a judgment debtor may apply to set aside the registration of a foreign judgment if:

(1) an appeal is pending against the foreign judgment; or

(2) the judgment debtor is entitled to and intends to appeal against the judgment; or

(3) the matter in relation to which the foreign judgment was given is the same as that in respect of which proceedings were instituted in Kenya before they were instituted in the foreign court and the Kenyan proceedings are still pending.[125]

In addition to these provisions of the 1984 Act for the setting aside or adjustment of the sums due under a foreign judgment, the 1924 Act provides that a foreign judgment shall not be treated as conclusive[126] in six instances. To the extent that these instances do not overlap with those set out in the 1984 Act, they are as follows:

debtors should have presented their concerns.' In this case, the judgment debtors had contested the action (and the non-recusal of the judge) in England.

[123] Unlike sub-s (2) of s 10, sub-s (3) does not contain the wording, 'a registered judgment *may* be set aside' (emphasis provided), suggesting that the court has no discretion in the matter if a domestic mandatory statutory limit applies to the judgment. It seems that the judgment must then be set aside to that extent, ie, to the extent it exceeds the mandatory statutory limit.

[124] For 'a reasonable period' rather than 'pending disposal of the proceedings', so as to ensure that control of the timing does not lie in the judgment debtor's hands.

[125] The section does not make clear whether the court has discretion to set aside a foreign judgment in these circumstances. It is submitted that the court would not have such discretion because, inter alia: (1) if the legislature had intended to confer discretion it would have made that clear; and (2) the unenforceability of a foreign judgment obtained after proceedings had commenced in Kenya would act as a disincentive on parties to engage in forum-shopping.

[126] And therefore is not registrable under the 1984 Act (see s 3(2)(b) of the 1984 Act).

(1) where the foreign judgment was not given on the merits of the case;[127]

(2) where the foreign judgment appears to have been founded on an incorrect view of international law;[128]

(3) where the proceedings in which the judgment was obtained are opposed to natural justice;[129] and

(4) where it sustains a claim founded on a breach of any law in force in Kenya.[130]

3.3 Interim Remedies

3.3.1 Jurisdiction to grant interim remedies

The jurisdiction of the High Court to grant injunctions is statutory. Section 63 of the Civil Procedure Act 1924 (as amended), provides:

> 'In order to prevent the ends of justice from being defeated, the court may, if it is so prescribed –
>
> *(a)* issue a warrant to arrest the defendant and bring him before the court to show cause why he should not give security for his appearance, and if he fails to comply with any order for security commit him to prison;
>
> *(b)* direct the defendant to furnish security to produce any property belonging to him and to place the same at the disposal of the court or order the attachment of any property;
>
> *(c)* grant a temporary injunction and in case of disobedience commit the person guilty thereof to prison and order that his property be attached and sold;
>
> *(d)* appoint a receiver of any property and enforce the performance of his duties by attaching and selling his property;
>
> *(e)* make such other interlocutory orders as may appear to the court to be just and convenient.'

As noted above (at section 3.1.2.4), section 2 of the 1924 Act defines 'prescribed' as meaning 'prescribed by rules' and the term 'rules' is also defined in section 2 as meaning 'rules and forms made by the Rules Committee to regulate the procedure of courts'. The powers of the Rules Committee to make rules are contained in section 81 of the 1924 Act. The most recent iteration of the High Court Rules is the Civil Procedure Rules 2010.

---

[127] Section 9(b). In *Singh v Singh* [1936–37] 17 KLR 82, 83 Webb J determined that the judgment of the foreign court would be one 'on the merits' where the matter of controversy between the parties was 'the subject of direct adjudication' in the foreign court.

[128] Section 9(c).

[129] Section 9(d). As noted above, there is likely to be a substantial overlap between this provision and s 10(2)(n).

[130] Section 9(f).

The relevant provisions of the Civil Procedure Rules are Order 39, 'Arrest and Attachment before Judgment', and Order 40, 'Temporary Injunctions and Interlocutory Orders'.

The rules governing interlocutory applications in the High Court are set out in Order 51. All applications are made by motion and are heard in open court, unless the court otherwise directs or the rules themselves so provide.[131]

Although there is no authority directly in point, it is likely that in order for a Kenyan court to make an interlocutory order in a cause, it is necessary that the court has jurisdiction over the substantive dispute between the parties.[132]

3.3.2 Procedure for application

All applications by motion must be made on notice to the other party except that,

> 'The court, if satisfied that the delay caused by proceeding in the ordinary way would or might entail irreparable or serious mischief, may make any order ex parte upon such terms as to costs or otherwise, and subject to such undertaking, if any, as to the court seems just, and any party affected by such order may move to set it aside.'[133]

A notice of motion must be supported by affidavit evidence if evidence is relied on and the notice of motion must state the basis on which the motion is made.[134]

Order 40, rule 4, makes express provision for *ex parte* applications for interlocutory injunctions:

> '(1) Where the court is satisfied for reasons to be recorded that the object of granting the injunction would be defeated by the delay, it may hear the application *ex parte.*
>
> (2) An *ex parte* injunction may be granted only once for not more than fourteen days and shall not be extended thereafter except once by consent of parties or by the order of the court for a period not exceeding fourteen days.
>
> (3) In any case where the court grants an *ex parte* injunction the applicant shall within three days from the date of issue of the order serve the order, the application and pleading on the party sought to be restrained. In default of service of any of the documents specified under this rule, the injunction shall automatically lapse.
>
> (4) All applications under this order shall be heard expeditiously and in any event within sixty days from the date of filing unless the court for good reason extends the time.'

---

[131] Order 51, r 1.

[132] Such was the position in England prior to the passing of s 25 of the Civil Jurisdiction and Judgments Act 1982 which now empowers courts in England to grant relief in aid of proceedings outside the jurisdiction (*Siskina (Owners of cargo lately on board) v Distos Compania Naviera SA, The Siskina* [1979] AC 210 (HL(E)).

[133] Order 51, r 3.

[134] Order 51, r 4. Detailed provision for affidavits is made in O 19.

3.3.3 Interlocutory injunctions generally

Order 40, 'Temporary Injunctions and Interlocutory Orders', makes provision for certain specified types of interlocutory orders as set out in rules 1, 2 and 10.

A feature of Order 40 is that the rules which confer power on the court to make interlocutory orders as specified are expressly predicated on the basis that proceedings have already been instituted at the time the application is made. This is the consequence of rules 1, 2 and 10, containing words to the effect that interlocutory injunctions may only be granted 'in a suit', that is, after proceedings have commenced.

Order 40 empowers the court to make an interlocutory injunction: (1) protecting property in dispute in proceedings; (2) enjoining the defendant to the proceedings from removing or disposing of his property with a view to obstructing or delaying the plaintiff from executing any judgment he may obtain in the suit; (3) restraining the defendant from committing a breach of contract or other wrong; and (4) for the detention, preservation or inspection of property the subject-matter of the dispute.

Injunctions of type (1) and (2)

Order 40, rule 1, provides:

> 'Where in any suit it is proved by affidavit or otherwise—
>
> *(a)* that any property in dispute in a suit is in danger of being wasted, damaged, or alienated by any party to the suit, or wrongfully sold in execution of a decree; or
>
> *(b)* that the defendant threatens or intends to remove or dispose of his property in circumstances affording reasonable probability that the plaintiff will or may be obstructed or delayed in the execution of any decree that may be passed against the defendant in the suit,
>
> the court may by order grant a temporary injunction to restrain such act, or make such other order for the purpose of staying and preventing the wasting, damaging, alienation, sale, removal, or disposition of the property as the court thinks fit until the disposal of the suit or until further orders.'

Rule 1, therefore, contains the power to make an order, (1) preserving property in dispute in the suit or, (2) restraining a defendant from disposing of his property in order to obstruct or delay the plaintiff in executing any judgment he may obtain against the defendant.

Injunction type (1)

Although there is little Kenyan authority on the principles applicable to this type of injunction, a decision of the High Court in *JMW v PMO*[135] held that

[135] [2014] eKLR (H Ct) (Musyoka J; 20 June 2014).

the applicable principles were those set out by the Uganda Court of Appeal in *Giella v Cassman Brown & Co Ltd*,[136] where Spry V-P (giving the judgment of the court) stated:[137]

> 'The conditions for the grant of an interlocutory injunction are now, I think, well settled in East Africa. First, an applicant must show a *prima facie* case with a probability of success. Secondly, an interlocutory injunction will not be normally granted unless the applicant might otherwise suffer irreparable injury, which would not adequately be compensated by an award of damages. Thirdly, if the court is in doubt, it will decide an application on the balance of convenience.'

In *JMW v PMO*, the court further held that the meaning of the expression 'prima facie case with a probability of success' was as held by the Court of Appeal in *Mrao v First American Bank of Kenya Ltd*:[138]

> 'So what is a *prima facie* case? I would say that in civil cases it is a case in which on the material presented to the court a tribunal properly directing itself will conclude that there exists a right which has apparently been infringed by the opposite party as to call for an explanation or rebuttal from the latter.'

The principles set out in *Giella v Cassman Brown & Co Ltd* must, therefore, be taken as representing Kenyan law on the granting of an interlocutory injunction where the court is empowered to make such an order.

In order to obtain a type (1) injunction, therefore, the plaintiff will need to show a *prima facie* case with a probability of success that: 'Any property in dispute in a suit is in danger of being wasted, damaged, or alienated by any party to the suit, or wrongfully sold in execution of a decree'; and that if the order is refused the plaintiff might suffer irreparable injury, which would not adequately be compensated by an award of damages.

The wording of Order 40, rule 1(a) is inapposite to cover an application for *Anton Piller*-type relief, inter alia, because rule 1(a) is confined to cases where property that is the subject of the dispute is at risk, as opposed to an *Anton Piller* case where the risk is the destruction of evidence.

It is likely that, as with any interlocutory injunction, an undertaking as to damages will be required of the plaintiff as a condition of the order.[139]

---

[136] [1973] EA 358 (CA) (Sir William Duffus P, Spry V-P and Law JA).

[137] Ibid 360E–F.

[138] [2003] KLR 125 (CA) (Kwach, Bosire and O'Kubasu JJA), *per* Bosire JA at 137:10–14 (misquoted by the judge in *JMW v PMO*). There, the Court of Appeal set out the passage quoted above from *Giella v Cassman Brown & Co Ltd* and described the principles set out there as well settled (*per* Bosire JA at 135:42–136:11).

[139] *Shah v Devji* [1965] EA 91 (H Ct) (Rudd J) 94A; *Chatur Radio Service v Pronogram Ltd* [1994] eKLR (CA) (Gicheru, Muli and Omolo JJA).

Injunction type (2)

The plaintiff may obtain an injunction restraining a defendant from disposing of the defendant's property in order to obstruct or delay the plaintiff in executing any judgment the plaintiff may obtain against the defendant. Such an injunction is generally referred to by the Kenyan courts as a *Mareva* injunction[140] or freezing order.

Some confusion has arisen in the Kenyan authorities regarding the correct rule of the Civil Procedure Rules under which to make a *Mareva* order. It appears that the courts consider the appropriate rule under which to make a *Mareva* order is that contained in Order 39, rule 5, relating to attachment of property. Indeed the courts appear to have gone further and to have assimilated the principles on which a *Mareva* order is granted with the terms of Order 39, rule 5.

As will be seen below, where Order 39 is addressed in greater detail, this approach is fundamentally flawed: Order 39, rule 5 deals with security for the plaintiff's claim and is a proprietary remedy, whereas Order 40, rule 1(b) does not purport to grant the plaintiff security and operates solely *in personam* over the defendant.

The correct rule under which to make an application for a *Mareva* injunction is Order 40, rule 1(b).

The Kenyan courts have demonstrated a willingness to adopt the principles of English practice regarding the grant of *Mareva* relief.[141] In *International Air Transport Association v Akarim Agencies Co Ltd*,[142] the court adopted the statement of the conditions for the grant of a *Mareva* injunction set out in the English textbook, *Goode on Commercial Law*:[143]

> 'The grant of a freezing injunction is governed by principles quite distinct from those laid down for ordinary interim injunctions.... Before granting a freezing injunction the court will usually require to be satisfied that;
>
> *(a)* The [plaintiff] has "a good arguable case" based on a pre-existing cause of action;
>
> *(b)* The claim is one over which the court has jurisdiction;
>
> *(c)* The defendant appears to have assets within the jurisdiction;
>
> *(d)* There is a real risk that those assets will be removed from the jurisdiction or otherwise dissipated if the injunction is not granted; and

---

[140] After the title of the English authority in which such orders were first approved at appellate level: *Mareva Compania Naviera SA v International Bulkcarriers SA* [1975] 2 Lloyd's Rep 509 (CA) (Lord Denning MR, Ormrod and Roskill LJJ).

[141] See *Kanduyi Holdings Ltd v Balm Kenya Foundation* [2013] eKLR (H Ct) (Gikonyo J); *Cleopatra Kama Mugyenyi v Aispan* [2016] eKLR, Employment and Labour Relations Ct (Nelson J).

[142] [2014] eKLR (H Ct) (Gikonyo J; orders stayed pending an appeal).

[143] 4 ed (2010) 1287 para [31] of the judgment.

(e) There is a balance of convenience in favour of granting the injunction;

(f) The Court can also order disclosure of documents or the administration of requests for further information to assist the claimant in ascertaining the location of the defendant's assets.'

The judge in the *International Air Transport Association* case then confirmed[144] that the test for 'arguable case', 'has been assigned a meaning within the context of [a] freezing order and has been adopted with approval by many courts in Kenya'. That meaning is that set out by Mustill J in *The Niedersachsen*:[145] 'A case which is more than barely capable of serious argument, and yet not necessarily one which the Judge believes to have a better than 50 per cent. chance of success.'

The principles on which the Kenyan courts will act on an application for a *Mareva* injunction appear, therefore, to be clear and well settled.[146]

Injunctions of type (3)

The third type of injunction authorised by the Civil Procedure Rules is an order restraining the defendant from committing a breach of contract or other wrong.

This is the classic *quia timet* interlocutory injunction for the grant of which the Kenyan courts have adopted[147] the test set out by the Uganda Court of Appeal in *Giella v Cassman Brown & Co Ltd*,[148] by Spry V-P.[149]

---

[144] [2014] eKLR para [32] of the judgment, quoting (a little inaccurately) the passage from *The Niedersachsen* relied on.

[145] [1983] 2 Lloyd's Rep 600 at 605, col 1.

[146] Although some departures from principle do occur: in the *Aidspan* case Nelson J appeared to require proof 'beyond peradventure' that the defendant was removing assets or dissipating them with the intention of depriving the plaintiff of the chance to enforce her judgment. This is too high a standard and the usual balance of probabilities ought to apply. In the *International Air Transport Association* case itself the judge reverted (para [34]) to the language of 'arguable case' rather than the requirement he had earlier referred to of 'good arguable case'. It should be noted that in *Mcdouglas Kagwa v Weekly Review Ltd* [1992] eKLR, the Court of Appeal (Masime, Gicheru and Kwach JJA) appear to have decided that a *Mareva* injunction, 'cannot be issued against defendants who are permanently settled in Kenya and have their assets here'. The report of this decision is very brief and the authorities cited by the court do not support this proposition. It is probably best regarded as *per incuriam*.

[147] See the decision of the Court of Appeal in *Mrao v First American Bank of Kenya Ltd* [2003] KLR 125 (CA) (Kwach, Bosire and O'Kubasu JJA). There the Court of Appeal set out the passage quoted above from *Giella v Cassman Brown & Co Ltd* and described the principles set out there as well settled (*per* Bosire JA at 135:42–136:11). There are occasional departures from this orthodoxy, however. In *Jan Bolden Nielsen v Herman Philipus Steyn* [2012] eKLR (H Ct) (Mabeya J), the court (emboldened by the decision in *Suleiman v Amboseli Resort Ltd*, see below) stated that it 'is not necessarily bound to the three principles set out in the *Giella v. Cassman Brown* case. The court may look at the circumstances of the case generally and the overriding objective of the law.' The judge in *Zubeidi v Kibaiya* [2014] eKLR (H Ct) (Gikonyo J), citing the *Nielsen* case, also appears not to have regarded himself as bound by the decision in *Giella v Cassman Brown & Co Ltd*. However, the Court of Appeal has more recently reaffirmed in *Kinyua Koech Ltd v Nairobi Homes (Mombasa) Ltd* [2015] eKLR (Okwengu, Makhandia and Sichale JJA) that the correct principles are those set out in *Giella*. That orthodoxy appears to have reasserted itself is evidenced by *Wanjua v Gathuni Tea Factory Co Ltd* [2016] eKLR (H Ct) (Mativo J).

[148] [1973] EA 358 (CA) (Sir William Duffus P, Spry V-P and Law JA).

[149] Ibid 360E–F.

The grant of an injunction is made in the exercise of the court's discretion and the plaintiff must show: (1) a *prima facie* case with a probability of success;[150] (2) without the grant of the injunction the plaintiff might suffer irreparable injury for which damages would not be adequate compensation; and (3) if the court is in doubt it will decide the case on the balance of convenience.

In *Giella v Cassman Brown & Co Ltd*, the defendant's appeal against an order made enforcing a covenant in restraint of trade was allowed because: first, the court considered the plaintiff company's claim to enforce the undertaking 'very doubtful' and the plaintiff had only a 'possibility of success'; and, second, because the plaintiff had failed to demonstrate that damages would not be an adequate remedy.[151]

As a postscript to the above, after the decision in *Giella v Cassman Brown & Co Ltd* was reported in 1973, the House of Lords handed down the decision in *American Cyanamid Co v Ethicon Ltd*,[152] in which Lord Diplock gave the lead opinion (with which the other Lords agreed). Given the willingness of the Kenyan courts to have regard to English authority in this area, it may be of benefit to set out briefly the principles established in the *American Cyanamid* case.

The opinion of Lord Diplock is generally taken as establishing a test comprising two elements:

(1) 'The court ... must be satisfied that the claim is not frivolous or vexatious; in other words, that there is a serious issue to be tried';[153]

'unless the material available to the court at the hearing of the application for an interlocutory injunction fails to disclose that the plaintiff has any real prospect of succeeding in his claim for a permanent injunction at the trial, the court should go on to consider whether the balance of convenience lies in favour of granting or refusing the interlocutory relief that is sought';[154]

---

[150] In *Suleiman v Amboseli Resort Ltd* [2004] 2 KLR 589 (H Ct) (Ojwang Ag J), the court granted an injunction notwithstanding that the plaintiff had failed to establish a *prima facie* case (at 606:1–4) and made the order on the basis that it was better to safeguard and maintain the status quo for greater justice than to let the status quo be disrupted by not granting an injunction. The judge embellished the test in *Giella v Cassman Brown & Co Ltd* in the following way (at 607:9–11): 'The Court, in responding to prayers for interlocutory injunctive relief, should always opt for the lower rather than the higher risk of injustice.'

[151] In *Orawo v Mistry* [1988] eKLR (H Ct) (Mbogholi-Msagha, the court granted an injunction restraining the first and second defendants from registering the transfer of a certain parcel of land, about which there was a dispute, to the third defendant. An injunction was refused in *Kiponda v The Independent Electoral and Boundaries Commission* [2013] eKLR (Chief Magistrate Shikanda; 31 May 2013): the plaintiff applied for an order restraining the second defendant from assuming office, and undertaking any functions as the Ganda Ward County Assembly Representative; the plaintiff failed to show that he would suffer irreparable loss or harm from the second defendant continuing in office until his election petition had been determined at a full hearing.

[152] [1975] AC 396 (HL(E)) (Lord Diplock, Viscount Dilhorne and Lords Cross, Salmon and Edmund-Davies).

[153] Ibid 407G.

[154] Ibid 408A–B.

(2) On the balance of convenience:[155]

'the governing principle is that the court should first consider whether, if the plaintiff were to succeed at the trial in establishing his right to a permanent injunction, he would be adequately compensated by an award of damages for the loss he would have sustained as a result of the defendant's continuing to do what was sought to be enjoined between the time of the application and the time of the trial. If damages in the measure recoverable at common law would be adequate remedy and the defendant would be in a financial position to pay them, no interlocutory injunction should normally be granted, however strong the plaintiff's claim appeared to be at that stage. If, on the other hand, damages would not provide an adequate remedy for the plaintiff in the event of his succeeding at the trial, the court should then consider whether, on the contrary hypothesis that the defendant were to succeed at the trial in establishing his right to do that which was sought to be enjoined, he would be adequately compensated under the plaintiff's undertaking as to damages for the loss he would have sustained by being prevented from doing so between the time of the application and the time of the trial. If damages in the measure recoverable under such an undertaking would be an adequate remedy and the plaintiff would be in a financial position to pay them, there would be no reason upon this ground to refuse an interlocutory injunction.

It is where there is doubt as to the adequacy of the respective remedies in damages available to either party or to both, that the question of balance of convenience arises. It would be unwise to attempt even to list all the various matters which may need to be taken into consideration in deciding where the balance lies, let alone to suggest the relative weight to be attached to them. These will vary from case to case.

Where other factors appear to be evenly balanced it is a counsel of prudence to take such measures as are calculated to preserve the status quo.'

Kenyan courts are cognisant of the test set down by the House of Lords in the *American Cyanamid* case.[156] Courts in Nigeria and Ghana have clarified their own law by reference to the decision in *American Cyanamid* itself. It may be that, were this area to be revisited by the Supreme Court of Kenya, that court would also have regard to the clarification offered by the *American Cyanamid* principles and the decisions of courts in Nigeria and Ghana where those principles have been applied.

---

155 Ibid 408B–G.

156 See, by way of example, *Wanjua v Gathuni Tea Factory Co Ltd* [2016] eKLR (H Ct) (Mativo J). There, Mativo J, in considering the first limb of the test from *Giella* and *Mrao*, stated that the elements of the test set down by the *American Cyanamid* case had been 'reiterated in numerous cases in Kenya'. The judge appeared to see little difference between the plaintiff's needing to demonstrate a '*prima facie* case with a probability of success' according to the test from *Giella* and the plaintiff's needing to show a 'serious issue to be tried' according to the test from *American Cyanamid*.

Injunctions of type (4)

The fourth type of order is that provided for by Order 40, rule 10: for the detention, preservation or inspection of property the subject-matter of the dispute.

An application for this type of injunction may be made by 'any party to a suit' (plaintiff or defendant or third party) for 'the detention, preservation, or inspection of any property which is the subject matter of such suit, or as to which any question may arise therein'.[157] The property must be the subject-matter of the suit or a question must arise in the suit relating to the property.

The court has power under Order 40 to 'authorise any person to enter upon or into any land or building in the possession of any other party to such suit' for the purpose of taking observations, samples or performing experiments for the purpose of obtaining information or evidence for the suit.[158]

As with the first type of injunction looked at above, the wording of Order 40, rule 1(a) is inapposite to cover an application for *Anton Piller*-type relief, inter alia, because rule 10(1) is confined to cases where property that is the subject of the dispute in the suit or as regards which a question arises in the suit and observations, samples or experiments are needed for the purpose of the suit. An *Anton Piller* case is where the risk is of the destruction of evidence.

Apart from these four instances contained in the High Court Rules, the Kenyan court, in accordance with section 63(e) of the 1924 Act can make any order as may appear to it to be just and convenient and it is to be expected that, in doing so, the Kenyan court will apply the test set out in *Giella v Cassman Brown & Co Ltd*.[159]

3.3.4 Freezing orders

As mentioned above, some confusion has arisen as to the correct demarcation between the effect of Order 39, rule 5 and the Kenyan court's power to make a *Mareva* or freezing injunction. This is addressed further below when Order 39 is discussed.

At present, however, it is sufficient to observe that the Kenyan court has the power to make a *Mareva* injunction in an appropriate case, pursuant to section 3A of the 1924 Act (see section 3.1.2.4 above).[160] In cases where a plaintiff wishes to obtain disclosure of the defendant's assets, both within Kenya and worldwide,

---

157 Order 40, r 10(1)(a).

158 Order 40, r 10(1)(b) and (c).

159 [1973] EA 358 (CA) (Sir William Duffus P, Spry V-P and Law JA).

160 See, by way of example, *UBA Kenya Bank Ltd v Magotsi* [2015] eKLR, Industrial Ct (Nduma J). There, the court made it clear that *Mareva* relief could be awarded by a Kenyan court (though the judge refused to grant the relief sought on the facts of the case).

an application for a *Mareva* injunction will be more efficacious, whereas the court appears not to have the power to order such disclosure under Order 39, rule 5.

The English Court of Appeal has set down the following guidance on when a *Mareva* injunction should be granted. This guidance may be[161] of some benefit to a Kenyan court when considering the grant of this type of relief. Hence, in *Mareva Compania Naviera v International Bulk Carriers SA*,[162] Lord Denning[163] stated that:

> 'In my opinion that principle applies to a creditor who has a right to be paid the debt owing to him, even before he has established his right by getting judgment for it. If it appears that the debt is due and owing, and there is a danger that the debtor may dispose of his assets so as to defeat it before judgment, the court has jurisdiction in a proper case to grant an interlocutory judgment so as to prevent him disposing of those assets.'

In *Third Chandris Shipping Corp v Unimarine SA*,[164] Lord Denning[165] provided this further guidance:

> 'The guidelines
>
> In endeavouring to set out some guidelines, I have had recourse to the practice of many other countries which have been put before us. They have been most helpful. These are the points which those who apply for it should bear in mind. (i) The Plaintiff should make full and frank disclosure of all matters in his knowledge which are material for the judge to know... (ii) The Plaintiff should give particulars of his claim against the Defendant, stating the ground of his claim and the amount thereof, and fairly stating the points made against it by the Defendant. (iii) The Plaintiff should give some grounds for believing that the Defendants have assets here ...The existence of a bank account in England is enough, whether it is in overdraft or not. (iv) The Plaintiff should give some grounds for believing that there is a risk of the assets being removed before the judgment or award is satisfied. The mere fact that the Defendant is abroad is not by itself sufficient. No one would wish any reputable foreign company to be plagued with a *Mareva* injunction simply because it has agreed to London arbitration. But there are some foreign companies whose structure invites comment. We often see in this court a corporation which is registered in a country where the company law is so loose that nothing is known about it, where it does no work and has no officers and no assets. Nothing can be found out about the membership, or its control, or its assets, or the charge on them. Judgment cannot be enforced against it. There is no reciprocal enforcement of judgments. It is nothing more than a name grasped from the air, as elusive as the Cheshire cat. In such cases the very fact of incorporation there gives some ground for believing there is a risk that, if judgment or an award is obtained, it may go unsatisfied. Such registration of such companies may carry many advantages

[161] And is: see *UBA Kenya Bank Ltd v Magotsi* and *Beta Healthcare International Ltd v Grace Mumbi Githaiga* [2016] eKLR (H Ct, Commercial and Admiralty Division) (Kariuki J), paras [33]–[34].

[162] [1980] 1 All ER 213 (CA) (Lord Denning MR, Roskill and Ormrod LJJ).

[163] Ibid 215b.

[164] [1979] 2 All ER 972 (CA) (Lord Denning MR, Lawton and Cumming-Bruce LJJ).

[165] Ibid 984g–985d.

to the individuals who control them but they may suffer the disadvantage of having a *Mareva* injunction granted against them. The giving of security for a debt is a small price to pay for the convenience of such a registration. Security would certainly be required in New York. So also it may be in London. Other grounds may be shown for believing there is a risk. But some such should be shown. (v) The Plaintiffs must, of course, give an undertaking in damages, in case they fail in their claim or the injunction turns out to be unjustified. In a suitable case this should be supported by a bond or security: and the injunction only granted on it being given, or undertaken to be given.'

3.3.5 Search and seize orders

In Kenya, the availability of *Anton Piller* relief (as originally posited)[166] has been placed on a statutory basis. The Copyright Act 2001,[167] section 37 provides, inter alia:

'**Anton Piller orders**

(1) If a person has *prima facie* evidence that his right has been infringed by another party and he satisfies the court or competent authority that *prima facie*—

(a) he has a cause of action against another person which he intends to pursue;

(b) the other person has, in his possession, documents infringing copies or other things of whatsoever nature which constitute evidence of great importance in substantiation of that cause of action; and

(c) there is the real and well-founded apprehension that the documents, infringing copies or other things may be hidden, destroyed or rendered inaccessible before discovery can be made in the usual way,

the court or competent authority as the case may be, may make such order as it considers necessary or appropriate to secure the preservation of the documents, copies or things as evidence.

(2) An order made under subsection (1) may be granted *ex parte*.'

Thus, a plaintiff with a claim for infringement of copyright may apply for an *Anton Piller* order.[168] There appears to be no judicial consideration of these statutory provisions. However, a number of points may be made:

(1) The statutory provisions differ from the test set out in the *Anton Piller* case itself in the following respects:

(a) the *Anton Piller* case requires 'an extremely strong *prima facie* case'[169] whereas the 2001 Act requires simply a *prima facie* case;

---

[166] [1976] Ch 55 (CA) (Lord Denning MR, Ormrod and Shaw LJJ), was itself a copyright infringement case.

[167] Act 12 of 2001.

[168] Section 37 of the Copyright Act 2001 applies *only* to copyright and related rights as defined in the Act (Pt III of the Act, ss 22–33).

[169] [1976] Ch 55, *per* Ormrod LJ at 62A.

(b) the *Anton Piller* case requires 'the damage, potential or actual, must be very serious for the plaintiff'[170] whereas the 2001 Act contains no such requirement; instead, the Act requires that *prima facie* the plaintiff must show that the documents or other material in the possession of the defendant 'constitute evidence of great importance in substantiation of that cause of action';

(c) finally, the *Anton Piller* case requires 'clear evidence that the defendants have in their possession incriminating documents or things, and that there is a real possibility that they may destroy such material before any application *inter partes* can be made'[171] whereas the Act requires that *prima facie* 'there is the real and well-founded apprehension that the documents, infringing copies or other things may be hidden, destroyed or rendered inaccessible before discovery can be made in the usual way'.

The 2001 Act appears, therefore, to be weaker in its protection for a defendant and to make it comparatively easier for a plaintiff to obtain *Anton Piller* relief.

(2) Although no express provision is made in section 37, it is to be expected that a court making an order under the 2001 Act will require as a condition for the making of the order an undertaking as to damages to be given by the plaintiff.[172]

(3) Again, although no express provision is made in section 37, it is to be expected that a court making an *Anton Piller* order will impose similar conditions on the order as are provided for in the English Civil Procedure Rules, such as for the attendance of an independent supervising solicitor.[173]

The Kenyan authorities appear also to decide that the courts have power at common law to make an *Anton Piller* order in cases other than those involving the infringement of copyright.[174] In these cases, the courts have applied the test set

---

170 Ibid.

171 Ibid.

172 See *Chatur Radio Service v Pronogram Ltd* [1994] eKLR (CA) (Gicheru, Muli and Omolo JJA); *Mumias Sugar Co Ltd v Option Two* [2014] eKLR (H Ct) (Gikonyo J) para [27].

173 See the English CPR at Part 25, Practice Direction 25A, para 7: www.justice.gov.uk/courts/procedure-rules/civil/rules/part25/pd_part25a#7.1.

174 *Montana (K) Ltd v Anthony Maina Kara* [2006] eKLR (H Ct) (Kasango J; trademark dispute); *John Boniface Maina v Safaricom Ltd* [2013] eKLR (H Ct) (Kimondo J; copyright infringement, where s 37 was mentioned but the *Anton Piller* order was made applying the common-law test in the *Anton Piller* case itself); *Mathenge v Njoroge* [2013] eKLR (H Ct) (Waweru J; administration of a deceased's estate) *Mumias Sugar Co Ltd v Option Two* [2014] eKLR (H Ct) (Gikonyo J; trademark dispute).

out by Ormrod LJ in the *Anton Piller* case itself. That test sets out the following pre-conditions for the making of an order:[175]

> 'There are three essential pre-conditions for the making of such an order, in my judgment. First, there must be an extremely strong prima facie case. Secondly, the damage, potential or actual, must be very serious for the [plaintiff]. Thirdly, there must be clear evidence that the defendants have in their possession incriminating documents or things, and that there is a real possibility that they may destroy such material before any application inter partes can be made.'

The juridical basis for making such orders, as was noted above, is contained in section 63 of the Civil Procedure Act 1924 (as amended). The 1924 Act also preserves for the inherent jurisdiction of the court in the following terms:

> **'3A. Saving of inherent powers of the court**
>
> Nothing in this Act shall limit or otherwise affect the inherent powers of the court to make such orders as may be necessary for the ends of justice or to prevent abuse of the process of the court.'

The courts, therefore, retain the power to develop further forms of relief to cater for circumstances other than those contemplated by the four types of injunction and the *Anton Piller* relief under the 2001 Act and at common law referred to above.

3.3.6 Third-party disclosure orders

There is no judicial authority directly on the question whether a Kenyan court may, apart from the established post-issuing of proceedings and pre-trial procedures, whereby a third party may be served with a witness summons requiring his attendance at court in order to give evidence and/or to produce documents,[176] order a person not a party to the proceedings to give disclosure.[177] (Although section 3A of the 1924 Act provides a statutory basis for such a power; see sections 3.1.2.4 and 3.3.5 above.) Such a power is available to the English courts in the form of a *Norwich Pharmacal* order[178] whereby an innocent third party caught up in a tort may be ordered to disclose the name or other identity of the tortfeasor. In *Waiguru v Google Inc*,[179] a *Norwich Pharmacal* order was the subject of an application by the plaintiff. The judge did not find that he did not have power to make such an order (although for other reasons the order was not made).

---

[175] *Anton Piller KG v Manufacturing Processes Ltd* [1976] Ch 55 (CA) (Lord Denning MR, Ormrod and Shaw LJJ), *per* Ormrod LJ at 62A.

[176] Order 16, r 1.

[177] In *George Fondo v Said Ali Omar* [2021] eKLR (Environment and Land Court at Malinidi) (Olola J), the court recognised, obiter, the *Norwich Pharmacal* jurisdiction, but on the facts of the case the need to make an order did not arise.

[178] *Norwich Pharmacal Co v Customs & Excise* [1974] AC 133 (HL(E)) (Lords Reid and Morris, Viscount Dilhorne and Lords Cross and Kilbrandon).

[179] [2014] eKLR (H Ct) (Lenaola J).

In *Norwich Pharmacal Co v Customs and Excise Comrs*, the House of Lords[180] set out the following principle:

> 'That if through no fault of his own a person gets mixed up in the tortious acts of others so as to facilitate their wrong-doing he may incur no personal liability but he comes under a duty to assist the person who has been wronged by giving him full information and disclosing the identity of the wrongdoers... [It does not matter] whether he became so mixed up by voluntary action on his part or because it was his duty to do what he did. It may be that if this causes him expense the person seeking the information ought to reimburse him. But justice requires that he should co-operate in righting the wrong if he unwittingly facilitated its perpetration.'

More recent authority[181] has clarified the conditions which the plaintiff must satisfy in order to obtain such relief:

> 'The three conditions to be satisfied for the court to exercise the power to order *Norwich Pharmacal* relief are:
>
> (i) a wrong must have been carried out, or arguably carried out, by an ultimate wrongdoer;
>
> (ii) there must be the need for an order to enable action to be brought against the ultimate wrongdoer; and
>
> (iii) the person against whom the order is sought must: (a) be mixed up in so as to have facilitated the wrongdoing; and (b) be able or likely to be able to provide the information necessary to enable the ultimate wrongdoer to be sued.'

If the plaintiff satisfies all of those conditions, the English court will then go on to exercise its discretion. In doing so, it must keep in mind the proper scope of *Norwich Pharmacal* relief: the jurisdiction cannot be used for wide-ranging discovery or the gathering of evidence, but is strictly confined to necessary information.[182]

3.3.7 Anti-suit injunctions

An anti-suit injunction is an order restraining the injunction defendant from either commencing or continuing proceedings outside Kenya in breach of a legal or equitable right on the part of the injunction plaintiff not to pursue litigation outside Kenya or, conversely, restraining the injunction defendant from commencing or continuing proceedings inside Kenya in breach of a legal or

---

180 [1974] AC 133, *per* Lord Reid at 175.

181 *Ramilos Trading Ltd v Valentin Mikhaylovich Buyanovsky* [2016] EWHC 3175 (Comm) (H Ct) (Flaux J) citing, at para [11], *Mitsui v Nexen Petroleum* [2005] EWHC 625 (Ch); [2005] 3 All ER 511 at [21] (H Ct) (Lightman J).

182 *Ramilos Trading Ltd v Valentin Mikhaylovich Buyanovsky* [2016] EWHC 3175 (Comm) (H Ct) (Flaux J) para [46].

equitable right on the part of the injunction plaintiff to have the dispute between the parties litigated in a jurisdiction other than Kenya.[183]

There can be little doubt that the Kenyan court is invested with the power to make such an order (see section 3A of the 1924 Act and sections 3.1.2.4 and 3.3.5 above). However, there appears to be no reported authority in which a Kenyan court has been invited to consider whether and, if so, on what principles such an injunction may be made.

It may be of some assistance to set out the principles which English courts have formulated and which English courts apply when asked to grant anti-suit relief. After all, the statutory basis upon which a Kenyan court may grant an injunction (in this context an anti-suit injunction) is identical to that upon which their English counterparts exercise that jurisdiction and there is a very close affinity between Kenyan law and English law in this regard.[166] It is to be anticipated, therefore, that a Kenyan court before which an application is brought for an anti-suit injunction may well pay close attention to the English authorities in setting out the principles upon which an anti-suit injunction may be granted in Kenya. Set out below, in summary, are the principles of English law governing the grant of an anti-suit injunction.

The Kenyan court must have personal jurisdiction over the injunction defendant. The court may be seised either by service on the defendant within the jurisdiction or service out of the jurisdiction with the leave of the court.[184]

The injunction plaintiff must assert a cause of action for relief. Usually, the injunction plaintiff will contend that the injunction defendant is committing a wrong by bringing or proposing to bring proceedings in a foreign court. This will require the plaintiff to characterise the conduct of the defendant as the breach of a legal or equitable right.

A legal right may, and often will, be based on a right not to be sued in a foreign jurisdiction arising out of an exclusive jurisdiction clause in favour of the courts of Kenya. An equitable right may be the right not to be sued in a foreign jurisdiction and may be the corollary of an equitable wrong which is that it is oppressive and vexatious and therefore unconscionable for the injunction defendant to commence or continue proceedings against the injunction plaintiff in a foreign jurisdiction.

---

[183] In similar vein, an anti-anti-suit injunction is an order restraining the injunction defendant from commencing or continuing proceedings to restrain the injunction plaintiff from applying to restrain the injunction defendant from commencing or continuing proceedings. The leading works on this topic are: Raphael *The Anti-Suit Injunction* 2 ed (2019) and Briggs *Civil Jurisdiction and Judgments* 7 ed (2021), ch 28. It is also conceptually possible to obtain similar relief in the context of arbitration but such relief is outside the scope of this work.

[184] The substantive law and procedure for which in Kenya has been set out above.

The prime example of a cause of action based on a legal right not to be sued in a foreign jurisdiction is where the parties have agreed expressly that the courts of Kenya should have exclusive jurisdiction over disputes arising out of the contract (which can be a substantive contract or a settlement agreement) between them.[185] In such a case proof of the underlying cause of action is likely to be a sufficient condition for the grant of the relief and that good reason would need to be shown why the discretion to order an injunction should not be exercised.[186]

The principal example of a cause of action based on an equitable wrong is where proceedings brought abroad by the defendant are oppressive and vexatious. An example of such conduct is illustrated by the decision of the Privy Council in *SNI Aerospatiale v Lee Kui Jak*,[187] where a resident of Brunei had been killed in a helicopter crash and his widow (and her brother-in-law, as co-administrator of his estate), the respondent plaintiffs in the appeal to the Privy Council, had commenced proceedings in Brunei and had subsequently been persuaded to sue in Texas instead. The appellant defendant applied for an anti-suit injunction restraining the plaintiffs from proceeding against it in Texas. The Privy Council allowed the defendant's appeal, held that an injunction ought to be granted restraining the respondents from proceeding in Texas and remitted the matter to the Brunei courts.

Transposing the findings of the Privy Council to Kenya, it was held that an anti-suit injunction would be granted if: (1) pursuit of the foreign proceedings is vexatious or oppressive; (2) Kenya is the natural forum for the resolution of the dispute; and (3) the injunction does not deprive the defendant of advantages in the foreign jurisdiction of which it would be unjust to deprive him.[188]

Other examples of equitable wrongs which may attract an anti-suit injunction are: undermining the jurisdiction of the Kenyan court;[189] vexatious conduct

[185] The contract may be a substantive contract or a settlement agreement and the dispute resolution provisions may be exclusively in favour of the courts of Kenya or may be in favour of arbitration: *British Airways Board v Laker Airways Ltd* [1985] AC 58 (HL (E)) (Lords Diplock, Fraser, Scarman, Roskill and Brightman), *per* Lord Diplock at p 81C–E.

[186] *The Angelic Grace* [1995] 1 Lloyd's Rep 87 (CA) (Neill, Leggatt and Millett LJJ), *per* Millett LJ at p 96, col 2, and Neill LJ at p 97, col 1; *Donohue v Armco Inc* [2000] 1 Lloyd's Rep 579 (CA) (Stuart-Smith, Brooke and Sedley LJJ), where it was stated that 'strong reasons' (*per* Stuart-Smith LJ at para 35) or 'strong cause' (*per* Brooke LJ at para 59 and 60) would be required to deny an injunction.

[187] [1987] AC 871 (PC (Brunei)) (Lords Keith, Griffiths, MacKay and Goff and Sir John Megaw).

[188] Lord Goff (giving the opinion of the Privy Council) p 896F–H. That the court to which the application is made should be the natural forum for the resolution of the dispute was repeated by the House of Lords in *Airbus Industrie GIE v Patel* [1999] 1 AC 119 (HL (E)) (Lords Goff, Slynn, Steyn, Clyde and Hutton), *per* Lord Goff (with whom the other Lords agreed) pp 138G–H and 140H–141B.

[189] For example, by commencing bankruptcy proceedings outside the jurisdiction when such proceedings are in progress in Kenya: *SNI Aerospatiale v Lee Kui Jak* [1987] AC 871, *per* Lord Goff at pp 892G–893B.

by relying on foreign procedural laws;[190] wrongfully undermining a Kenyan judgment;[191] or enforcement of a foreign judgment wrongfully obtained.[192]

3.3.8 Other interlocutory relief

3.3.8.1 *Arrest of an absconding defendant*

The Civil Procedure Rules 2010, Order 39, rule 1, 'Where defendant may be called upon to furnish security for appearance', provides for arrest of a defendant in certain circumstances:

> 'Where at any stage of a suit, other than a suit of the nature referred to in paragraphs (a) to (d) of section 12 of the Act, the court is satisfied by affidavit or otherwise—
>
> *(a)* that the defendant with intent to delay the plaintiff, or to avoid any process of the court, or to obstruct or delay the execution of any decree that may be passed against him—
>
> (i) has absconded or left the local limits of the jurisdiction of the court; or
>
> (ii) is about to abscond or leave the local limits of the jurisdiction of the court; or
>
> (iii) has disposed of or removed from the local limits of the jurisdiction of the court his property or any part thereof; or
>
> *(b)* that the defendant is about to leave Kenya under circumstances affording reasonable probability that the plaintiff will or may thereby be obstructed or delayed in the execution of any decree that may be passed against the defendant in the suit,
>
> the court may issue a warrant to arrest the defendant and bring him before the court to show cause why he should not furnish security for his appearance:
>
> Provided that the defendant shall not be arrested if he pays to the officer entrusted with the execution of the warrant any sum specified in the warrant as sufficient to satisfy the plaintiff's claim; and such sum shall be held in deposit by the court until the suit is disposed of or until the further order of the court.'

The Act referred to in the first clause of rule 1 is the Civil Procedure Act 1924, section 12(a)–(d) of which makes provision for suits: (a) for the recovery of immovable property; (b) for the partition of immovable property; (c) for the foreclosure, sale or redemption in the case of a mortgage of or charge upon immovable property; and (d) for the determination of any other right to or interest in immovable property.

---

[190] By seeking to depose witnesses in the USA where those witnesses would be subject to cross-examination in proceedings in Kenya, for example: *Omega Group Holdings Ltd v Kozeny* [2002] CLC 132.

[191] By commencing proceedings outside the jurisdiction for declaratory relief designed to frustrate the enforcement of a Kenyan judgment in that jurisdiction: *Masri v Consolidated Contractors International (UK) Ltd (No 3)* [2009] QB 503, CA.

[192] Where the foreign judgment was obtained through fraud and perjury: *Ellerman Lines Ltd v Read* [1928] 2 KB 144 (CA), *per* Scrutton LJ at pp 152–3.

Order 39, rule 1 entitles a plaintiff to apply to the court for the arrest of the defendant in the two sets of circumstances set out in the rule: (1) the defendant is about to abscond domestically and/or dissipate property; or (2) the defendant is about to leave Kenya. What the plaintiff must show in order to obtain an arrest of the defendant differs in each of these circumstances.

In the first, the plaintiff must show that the defendant is acting 'with *intent* to delay the plaintiff, or to avoid any process of the court, or to obstruct or delay the execution of any decree that may be passed against him' (emphasis provided).

In the second, the plaintiff does not need to show the defendant is acting with any particular intent; the plaintiff simply needs to show that the fact of the defendant's departure from Kenya may result in a 'reasonable probability that the plaintiff will or may thereby be obstructed or delayed in the execution of any decree that may be passed against the defendant in the suit' (as to the meaning of this provision see: *Fernandes v Commercial Bank of Africa Ltd*[193] below).

An arrest of the defendant in the first case will be considerably more difficult for a plaintiff to achieve than it will in the second case.

Once arrested, the consequences for the defendant are the same in either of these cases: the warrant operates as an order *nisi* and the defendant is required to show why he should not be ordered to provide security for his appearance. (The proviso to this is contained in the final paragraph of rule 1; in order to avoid arrest in the first place, the defendant may elect to pay the entirety of the plaintiff's claim which is then held on deposit pending the conclusion of the proceedings.)

If the defendant fails to show cause then the court has no discretion and must order that he pay into court a sum sufficient to meet the plaintiff's claim.[194]

There is no reason to doubt that the use of the term 'security' is intended to mean that the plaintiff's claim is secured on the sums paid by the defendant to ensure his release from arrest, that is, the sums paid over are retained free from claims by third parties. (The provisions of Order 39, rule 10, preserving the rights of prior creditors and judgment creditors to attached property apply to property attached pursuant to rule 6 and not to security given under rules 1 and 2.) For the purposes of rule 1 (and rule 5), encumbered property would not comprise 'security' as provided for by that rule (and rule 5).

---

[193] [1969] EA 482 (H Ct) (Mosdell J).

[194] Rule 2 is entitled 'Security' and provides: 'Where the defendant fails to show such cause the court shall order him either to deposit in court money or other property sufficient to answer the claim against him, or to furnish security for his appearance at any time when called upon while the suit is pending and until satisfaction of the decree that may be passed against him in the suit.' Arrangements may be made for security to be provided by a surety. Where the defendant fails to provide security he may be committed to prison for a period not exceeding six months (O 39, r 4).

In *Fernandes v Commercial Bank of Africa Ltd*,[195] the court considered an action for malicious prosecution based on the defendant's use of what was then Order 38, rule 1 (the predecessor to Order 39, rule 1). Dismissing the claim the court held, inter alia: (1) what is necessary under rule 1(b) is delay after judgment has been given (pre-judgment delay being addressed by rule 1(a));[196] (2) if a defendant remains outside Kenya permanently or for a protracted period, execution of any judgment is likely to be obstructed or delayed; the judgment in such a case could not have been executed, for example, by the defendant's 'committal to civil gaol';[197] (3) what the plaintiff must show on an application under rule 1(b) is 'reasonable and probable cause' for believing that the defendant's departure may obstruct or delay execution of the judgment the plaintiff may obtain. The court stated the test as follows:[198]

> 'An honest belief based upon a full conviction, founded on reasonable grounds, of the existence of a state of circumstances which assuming them to be true would reasonably lead an ordinary prudent and cautious man placed in the position of the [plaintiff] to the conclusion that the [defendant] was about to leave Kenya under circumstances affording reasonable probability that the [plaintiff] will or may thereby be obstructed or delayed in the execution of any decree that may be passed against the [defendant] in the suit.'

In formulating this test the judge did not expressly distinguish between sub-rules (a) and (b); however, from the context it is clear he had in mind sub-rule (b).

3.3.8.2 *Attachment of property*

Order 39, rule 5, 'Where defendant may be called upon to furnish security for production of property', provides for the attachment of the defendant's property in specified circumstances:

> '(1) Where at any stage of a suit the court is satisfied, by affidavit or otherwise, that the defendant, with intent to obstruct or delay the execution of any decree that may be passed against him—
>
> *(a)* is about to dispose of the whole or any part of his property;
>
> *(b)* is about to remove the whole or any part of his property from the local limits of the jurisdiction of the court,
>
> the court may direct the defendant, within a time to be fixed by it, either to furnish security, in such sum as may be specified in the order, to produce and place at the disposal of the court, when required, the said property or the value of the same, or such portion thereof as may be sufficient to satisfy the decree, or to appear and show cause why he should not furnish security.

---

[195] [1969] EA 482 (H Ct) (Mosdell J).

[196] Ibid 492F–G.

[197] Ibid 492G.

[198] Ibid 491F–G.

> (2) The plaintiff shall, unless the court otherwise directs, specify the property required to be attached and the estimated value thereof.
>
> (3) The court may also in the order direct the conditional attachment of the whole or any portion of the property so specified.'

Rule 5 requires the plaintiff to show that the defendant, in disposing of his property or removing it from the local jurisdiction of the court, is acting 'with *intent* to obstruct or delay the execution of any decree that may be passed against him' (emphasis provided).

When the plaintiff establishes the matters required for an order under rule 5, the court may then direct the defendant to do one of three things: (1) furnish security in the sum specified in the order; (2) produce for the order of the court the property that the defendant was disposing of or removing from the local jurisdiction of the court; or (3) appear to show cause why he should not be ordered to provide security.

Order 39, rule 6, provides:

> 'Where the defendant fails to show cause why he should not furnish security, or fails to furnish the security required, within the time fixed by the court, the court may order that the property specified, or such portion thereof as appears sufficient to satisfy any decree which may be passed in the suit, be attached.'

As with Order 39, rule 1, there is no reason to doubt that the use of the term 'security' in rules 5 and 6, is intended to mean that the plaintiff's claim is secured on the sums paid by the defendant to secure his release from arrest, that is, the sums paid over is retained free from claims by third parties.

The provisions of Order 39, rule 10, preserving the rights of prior creditors and judgment creditors to attached property apply to property attached pursuant to rule 6 after security for the plaintiff's claim has not been given by the defendant as ordered, and not to security given under rule 5.

More generally on the construction and meaning of Order 39, rules 1, 2, 5 and 6, some confusion appears to have developed in the authorities on the effect of Order 39, in particular Order 39, rule 5. In *Kanduyi Holdings Ltd v Balm Kenya Foundation*,[199] the judge stated[200] that Order 39, rules 5 and 6, 'could be said [to be] and is a statutory codification of an interlocutory relief commonly known as *Mareva* injunction or freezing order in the UK. The principle was laid down in the case of *Mareva Compania Navierra* [sic] *SA v. International Bulk Carriers SA* [1975] 2 Lloyds Rep 509' and[201] '[a]ccordingly, Order 39 Rules 5 and 6 of the

---

199 [2013] eKLR (H Ct) (Gikonyo J).

200 Ibid para [21].

201 Ibid para [22].

CPR should operate within known dimensions of law drawing from the above case and other judicial precedents on the subject.'[202]

However, this is fundamentally to misunderstand the nature of these provisions. Unlike a *Mareva* injunction, Order 39, rules 1 and 5 are intended to give the plaintiff security for his claim in the circumstances specified in those rules, whereas a *Mareva* injunction does not give the applicant security over the assets frozen by the order. Further, Order 39, rules 1 and 5 operate (in effect) *in rem* (property or money must be produced), whereas a *Mareva* injunction operates *in personam*.

The equivalent provision to Order 39, rule 5 appears in the Indian Civil Procedure Code.[203] In *Sardar Govindrao Mahadik v Devi Sahai*,[204] the Indian Supreme Court stated:[205]

> 'The sole object behind the order levying attachment before judgment is to give an assurance to the plaintiff that his decree if made would be satisfied. It is a sort of guarantee against the decree becoming infructuous for want of property available from which the plaintiff can satisfy the decree.'

This correctly states the effect of Order 39, rule 5, the object of which is to provide security for the plaintiff.

[202] A view repeated by the same judge in *International Air Transport Association v Akarim Agencies Co Ltd* [2014] eKLR (H Ct) (Gikonyo J; orders stayed pending an appeal), paras [22] and [31]; and *Cleopatra Kama Mugyenyi v Aispan* [2016] eKLR (Employment and Labour Relations Ct) (Nelson J) para [12]. *Kanduyi* was cited with apparent approval in *Beta Healthcare International Ltd v Grace Mumbi Githaiga* [2016] eKLR (H Ct) (Commercial and Admiralty Division) (Kariuki J), para [22].

[203] Order 38, r 5. The relevant parts of the Code dates back to at least 1908.

[204] [1982] 1 SCC 237, AIR 1982 SC 989, [1982] 2 SCR 186 (Indian Sup Ct) (Desai DA). See generally, Takwani *Civil Procedure* 5 ed (2003) 224–8.

[205] [1982] 2 SCR 186 at 223C–D.

Chapter 4

LESOTHO

4.1 Jurisdiction

4.1.1 Commencing proceedings where the defendant is within the jurisdiction

The provisions of the High Court Rules 1980 ('the Rules')[1] state that domestic proceedings in Lesotho are commenced by summons in which the defendant is given a specified time to enter an appearance (depending on how far he lives from the office of the Registrar) and that such summons must contain a short statement of the facts relied on by the plaintiff.[2]

Where the defendant wishes to defend the claim, he must give notice of his intention to do so by entering an appearance at the office of the Registrar. The defendant does not waive any jurisdictional objection by entering an appearance.[3]

Fourteen days after the defendant has entered an appearance, the plaintiff must serve his declaration in which he must set out the nature of his claim, the conclusions of law that he contends are derived from the facts pleaded and the remedy he seeks.[4]

4.1.2 Commencing proceedings where the defendant is outside the jurisdiction

Pursuant to rule 5, the leave of the court is required for any originating process to be served outside the jurisdiction.

On an application for leave to serve outside of the jurisdiction the plaintiff must set out the nature and extent of his claim, the grounds on which it is based, the grounds on which the court is alleged to have jurisdiction over the claim and the manner of service which the court is asked to authorise.[5]

---

[1] Legal Notice 9 of 1980. The High Court Rules were made pursuant to the power to make such rules conferred upon the Chief Justice by the High Court Act 1978 (Act 5 of 1978) s 16.

[2] Rule 18.

[3] Rule 19.

[4] Rule 21.

[5] Rule 5(2).

On the application the court may make such order as to the manner of service as it considers appropriate and shall also order the time within which the defendant should enter an appearance.

4.1.2.1 Incolae *and* peregrini

As with other jurisdictions which have a Roman-Dutch legal system, a court's power to assume jurisdiction over a defendant rests on the character of the defendant. To that end, it is necessary to distinguish between a defendant who is an *incola* and one who is a *peregrinus*.

There does not appear to be any reported authority dealing directly with the question of how the courts in Lesotho determine whether a person is an *incola* or a *peregrinus*. In consequence, it is likely that a court in Lesotho would employ the same test as is employed by the courts in the Republic of South Africa.[6]

In this regard, South African law distinguishes between *incolae* and *peregrini* in the following manner:[7]

> '(1) an *incola* is a person who is either domiciled (in the technical sense) or resident within the area of the jurisdiction of the court, provided that the residence is of some permanent or settled nature; and (2) a *peregrinus* is a person who is neither domiciled nor resident ... within the area of the jurisdiction of the court.'

4.1.2.2 *The jurisdictional significance of attachment*

Rule 6 makes provision for attachment of property and arrest of the person to found or confirm the jurisdiction. In this section, attachment of a defendant's property so as to found or confirm the jurisdiction of the Lesotho court is considered. Further below,[8] the jurisdictional significance of arrest of the person is examined.

---

[6] The authors take this view because of the strong affinity between the law as applied in South Africa and the law applied in Lesotho. As the High Court stated in *Mokhethi v Lesotho National General Ins Co Ltd* [2006] LSHC 151 (HC) (Majara J), in the context of the normal requirement for a *peregrinus* to provide security for costs when suing an *incola*: 'Most of the authorities quoted to this Court regarding this issue are South African ones which are highly persuasive in our jurisdiction.' For a fuller treatment of the meaning given to the terms '*domiciled*' and '*resident*' in South African law, the reader is referred to the chapter on the Republic of South Africa.

[7] Herbstein and Van Winsen *The Civil Practice of the High Courts of South Africa* 5 ed (2009) 69. It should be noted that the South African term 'local *peregrinus*' (used to describe one who is a *peregrinus* of that division of the High Court but still a resident of the Republic itself) is not known in Lesotho law. Hence, in Lesotho, there are only *incolae* and *peregrini*.

[8] Under the heading 'The jurisdictional significance of arrest of the person'.

4.1.2.2.1 Where the plaintiff and the defendant are both *incolae*

Where both the parties to a dispute are *incolae*, no jurisdictional problems arise. The dispute is a purely domestic one over which the court has jurisdiction.

4.1.2.2.2 Where the plaintiff is an *incola* and the defendant is a *peregrinus*

Rule 6(1) makes provision for the attachment of property: 'The court may on application grant leave for property of a *peregrinus* which is in Lesotho to be attached in order to give the court jurisdiction in an action which the [plaintiff] intends to bring against such *peregrinus*.'

For such an order to be made the plaintiff must satisfy the court of the matters in sub-rule (2):

> '(a) that he has a *prima facie* cause of action against the *peregrinus* and (b) that the property sought to be attached is the property of the *peregrinus* or that the *peregrinus* has some right in the property, and (c) that the [plaintiff] himself is an *incola* of Lesotho and that the [defendant] is a *peregrinus*'.[9]

Sub-rule (2) confirms that the advantages of attachment of property to found or confirm jurisdiction are confined to residents of Lesotho (with the consequence that the rule does not apply to a *peregrinus* plaintiff).[10]

It is important to note that, in the circumstances currently under consideration, it is apparently not incumbent on the plaintiff to have to show, additionally, that a *ratio jurisdictionis*[11] (or cause of action) relevantly connected with Lesotho exists.

In the situation currently under discussion, it is also necessary to consider the question of what property of a *peregrinus* defendant can be attached by an *incola* plaintiff. The court considered this question in *Moggee & du Toit v Makhoza*.[12] In this case, the *peregrinus* was a judgment creditor who had sought to enforce in Lesotho a South African judgment against the *incola* judgment debtor. The *incola* debtor paid a sum falling just short of the judgment debt to the Registrar of the High Court. At the same time the *incola* debtor applied *ex parte* to attach that

---

[9] As to which, see *Maphike v Pierre-Yves Sachet* [2019] LSCA 35 (CA) (Damaseb, Chinhengo and Mtshiya AJJA).

[10] Once an order for attachment is granted, the court will expect the plaintiff to proceed diligently and apply for leave to sue by edictal citation and serve the summons or run the risk of the attachment being discharged: *Association of Chinese Merchants and Manufacturers of Lesotho v Pen He* [1999] LSHC 111 (HC), where Monapathi J discharged the attachment in view of the plaintiff's dilatory conduct. Sub-rules (3)–(7) then contain various ancillary provisions dealing with, inter alia, disputes as to the ownership of property that has been attached and the protection of third-party interests.

[11] *Lepota v Hyland* [1991] LSHC 77 (HC), where Lehohla J held (transcript, p 7), following *The Estate of Brownstein v Commissioner for Inland Revenue* 1957 (3) SA 512 (A): 'An *incola* is held to be capable of suing a *peregrinus* after attachment *ad fundandam jurisdictionem*, regardless of where the cause of action arose.' *Rationes jurisdictiones* are discussed further below, under the sub-heading of the same name.

[12] [1985] LSHC 66 (HC).

sum *ad fundandam jurisdictionem* in an action against the *peregrinus* for damages in which the *incola* debtor claimed a sum in excess of the judgment debt. The Acting High Court judge, Mr DS Levy, in discharging the order for attachment of the sum paid to the Registrar, held[13] that, while a debt owed to a *peregrinus* in the hands of any third party is always capable of attachment, the *peregrinus* did not have any right to the sum paid by the *incola* to the Registrar,[14] such that attachment of that property was not possible in this case.

It was contended by the *incola* that the court had discretion whether to discharge the order for attachment notwithstanding the finding that the *peregrinus* did not have a right to the sum paid to the Registrar. The judge appears[15] to have assumed, *arguendo*, that he had discretion whether to discharge the order and exercised[16] that discretion in favour of discharging the order for attachment on the basis that if the *incola* was permitted to continue proceedings in Lesotho on the basis of the attachment he would have the advantage of an eight-year period of prescription for the debt sued upon,[17] whereas if jurisdiction was declined and he was required to proceed in South Africa, the debt would be subject to a three-year period of prescription and to permit the proceedings to continue in Lesotho would therefore cause 'grave prejudice' to the *peregrinus* where that state of affairs had been brought about by the *incola* himself.

This decision suggests that the court has discretion to permit proceedings against a *peregrinus* to continue, notwithstanding that there is no valid attachment by the *incola* of the property or the person of the *peregrinus*.

4.1.2.2.3 Where the plaintiff and the defendant are both *peregrini*

Rule 6 has been strictly construed. In *Burger v Ocrim SAP*,[18] the plaintiff *peregrinus* ('Burger', a South African entity) made an urgent application against, inter alia, the first defendant *peregrinus* ('Ocrim', an Italian company) seeking to attach Ocrim's property in the hands of the second and third defendants (both of which were *incolae*) in order to confirm the jurisdiction of the court. Ocrim and the second defendant had entered into a contract by which Ocrim was to supply plant and equipment for a project known as the Maseru Maize Mill and Silo Complex ('the Complex'). Ocrim and Burger entered into a sub-contract whereby Burger was

---

[13] Ibid 4–5 of the transcript.

[14] Similarly, in *Midmacor (Pty) Ltd v Zakhura Brothers (Pty) Ltd* [1995] LSHC 20 (HC) and also at [1995] LSCA 89 (HC) (it is unclear why the same decision is reported in two series or reports as having been given on two separate dates: the correct date is 23 June 1995), the court (BP Cullinan CJ) refused to attach property which had been let by a third party to the defendant.

[15] Ibid 5 of the transcript.

[16] Ibid 5–6.

[17] There is a lack of clarity in the transcript as to whether the *incola*'s action was for damages, debt or both.

[18] [1986] LSHC 55 (HC).

to carry out parts of the main contract. Burger commenced work on the Complex in April 1985 and moved equipment and personnel onto the site. Burger also undertook manufacturing work for the project at its premises in South Africa. In April 1986 Ocrim unlawfully terminated the sub-contract. Molai J refused Burger's application on the ground that rule 6 only authorised attachment of the property of a *peregrinus* by an *incola* and not by another *peregrinus*.[19]

As a matter of the literal construction of rule 6, the decision in *Burger* is undoubtedly correct; however, the outcome hardly seems just. The result of the decision was that Burger could not bring proceedings against Ocrim in Lesotho, notwithstanding that the sub-contract was to be performed in Lesotho (and South Africa); the proper law of the sub-contract may well have been (absent a choice of law clause) Lesotho law (or South African); any relevant witnesses would probably have been present in Lesotho or South Africa; and relevant documentation would similarly have been present in Lesotho and South Africa. Burger, it seems, was left to pursue its remedies against Ocrim in Italy.[20]

In *Burger v Ocrim SAP* it was not argued that (and, generally, it is unclear whether) the common law was superseded by rule 6 entirely or whether there is scope for the courts to develop the common law by allowing departures in appropriate cases from the jurisdictional rules contained in rule 6.[21] *Burger*'s case is a good example of one where some flexibility in the application of jurisdictional rules would have resulted in the proceedings being heard in Lesotho because Lesotho was the most appropriate jurisdiction in which to resolve the dispute.

The way in which the Lesotho courts have dealt with situations involving a plaintiff *peregrinus* and at least one *incola* defendant is also instructive when seeking to make sense of the court's wider approach in the situation currently under consideration. By way of illustration, shortly after the *Burger* case was decided, the court in *Bateman v G Govoni Imports & Exports (Pty) Ltd*,[22] seems to have departed from the orthodox position.

In *Bateman*, the plaintiff *peregrinus* applied both for leave to sue the first defendant *peregrinus* by edictal citation by having the summons served on it in South Africa and for an order attaching the second defendant *incola*'s property as security for the plaintiff's claim. The orders sought were made and on the return

[19] Ibid 6–7 of the transcript.

[20] This decision also creates certain difficulties to a *peregrinus* foreign-judgment creditor who is seeking to enforce the foreign judgment against a *peregrinus* judgment debtor. See further below under the heading 'Enforcement of Foreign Judgments' and Frimpong Oppong: 'Recognition and enforcement of foreign judgments in Commonwealth African countries' (2014) XV *Yearbook of Private International Law* 365, 370.

[21] The Supreme Court of Appeal in South Africa has taken this path in order to mitigate the unfairness of a strict application of the jurisdictional attachment rules: *Bid Industrial Holdings (Pty) Ltd v Strang* 2008 (3) SA 355 (SCA) (Howie P; Nugent, Ponnan, Maya JJA and Malan AJA).

[22] [1987] LSHC 18 (HC).

date the second defendant *incola*, relying on the *Burger* case, sought the discharge of the order attaching its property as security for the plaintiff's claim on the basis that rule 6 did not permit the attachment of the property of an *incola* on the application of a *peregrinus*. Kheola ACJ refused the second defendant's application on the following grounds: first,[23] the application was not brought pursuant to rule 6 and so the *Burger* case was not relevant;[24] second,[25] the plaintiff's application for security for his claim was made in order to ensure the effectiveness of any judgment he might ultimately obtain; third,[26] attachment prior to judgment was permissible where 'this is done in order to prevent the debtor from disposing of his property before the creditor has obtained judgment against him thereby defeating the creditor's claim'; fourth, the court would not interfere with a party's right over its property unless 'good cause' was shown;[27] and fifth,[28] the judge held that the plaintiff had shown good cause because the second defendant was 'losing money and making no profit' and that it could not be ruled out that the second defendant could close down.

On its face, the *Bateman* case is authority for the following propositions: first, the Lesotho courts have jurisdiction to entertain proceedings brought by a *peregrinus* against another *peregrinus* in the absence of attachment of property; second, a *peregrinus* may obtain an order for attachment of the property of an *incola* defendant as security for his claim if he shows 'good cause'.

The first proposition is an unorthodox statement of Roman-Dutch rules on jurisdiction where conventionally an attachment of property is a necessary precondition of the court's jurisdiction to entertain an action against a *peregrinus*.

The second proposition seems to establish a form of order that falls short of the exacting requirements of a freezing order or anti-dissipation interdict,[29] where proof of dissipation is usually necessary, and which can operate to the prejudice of third-party creditors of the person whose property is attached on the application of the *peregrinus* plaintiff. It is also in conflict with a decision of Guni J in *Thusanang Bahoebi Multipurpose Cooperative Society v Nhlapo*,[30] where

---

[23] Ibid 3–4 of the transcript.

[24] At p 3 of the transcript, the Acting Chief Justice also observed that in *Burger*, '[t]he application was dismissed on the ground that Burger was a *peregrinus* and had no right in law to attach the property of an *incola* of Lesotho in order to give the court jurisdiction. The court already had jurisdiction on the ground that the [defendant] was an *incola* of Lesotho.' However, this is to misstate and/or misunderstand the decision in *Burger* where the property which was sought to be attached was that of the first defendant, Ocrim SAP, an Italian company, and the court did not have jurisdiction on the ground that Ocrim was an *incola* because it was not.

[25] Ibid 4 of the transcript.

[26] Ibid.

[27] Ibid.

[28] Ibid 5.

[29] Which form of interim remedy is discussed in greater detail below, in the section of this chapter headed 'Interim Remedies'.

[30] [1996] LSHC 42 (HC) (14 March 1996).

the plaintiff sought an attachment of the defendant's property as security for its claim and the application was refused on the basis that there is no provision in the Rules for attachment of property before judgment as security for the plaintiff's claim. The *Bateman* decision was not cited to the court in the *Thusanang* case.

In the light of the reported authorities, the principles upon which a court in Lesotho may order attachment of property in cases between *peregrini* are, unfortunately, unclear. On the face of it, one of two possible approaches may be taken in the future:

(1) the courts may decide that the *Burger* case is authoritative. In these circumstances, it would appear that a *peregrinus* plaintiff cannot sue a *peregrinus* defendant in Lesotho: rule 6 only allows an *incola* plaintiff to attach the property of a *peregrinus* defendant; or

(2) the courts may decide that the *Bateman* case is authoritative. In these circumstances, a *peregrinus* plaintiff would be able to sue a *peregrinus* defendant in Lesotho: there is no need to attach property in order to confer jurisdiction on the court.

If the approach set out in (1) above seems too hostile to litigation exclusively between *peregrini* being conducted in Lesotho, the approach set out in (2) above, when considered in conjunction with the fact that the plaintiff apparently does not need to show a *ratio jurisdictionis*,[31] does not state clearly what, in fact, does give the Lesotho court jurisdiction over the defendant. As a result, there is a clear need for a decision by the Court of Appeal on this matter.

4.1.2.3 Rationes jurisdictiones

In the light of the inconsistent nature of the judicial pronouncements on the subject, it is not wholly clear whether the plaintiff needs to show the existence of a *ratio jurisdictionis* in order to secure the jurisdiction of the Lesotho court. Accordingly, the material which appears in this section has been included for the sake of completeness; should the Lesotho court decide that a plaintiff does not need to show the existence of a *ratio jurisdictionis* in order to secure the jurisdiction of the court, there will be no need to consider such *rationes* in any depth.

At present there is nothing to suggest that the *rationes jurisdictiones* themselves which could exist in Lesotho (as distinct from the question of whether it is necessary to make appeal to them at all in order to found or confirm the jurisdiction of the Lesotho court) are any different to those which are known to the law of South Africa. While more in-depth treatment is afforded the *rationes jurisdictiones* in the chapter on the Republic of South Africa,[32] the basic position may be summarised

---

[31] Which concept is considered under the sub-heading '*Rationes jurisdictiones*' below.

[32] To which the reader is referred.

by reference to the judgment of the Supreme Court of the Cape Colony in *Einwald v The German West African Co.*[33] There, De Villiers CJ stated:[34]

> 'What then are the grounds upon which the jurisdiction of this Court can be exercised, in respect of any contract over any defendant without his consent, express or implied? The grounds are threefold: *viz* by virtue of the defendant's domicile being here, by virtue of the contract either having been entered into here or having to be performed here, and by virtue of the subject matter in an action *in rem* being situated in this Colony.'

Added to these are the place of the delict and cases which concern property. The principal connecting factors for jurisdictional purposes which result are: *ratio domicilii (actor sequitur forum rei)*; *ratio contractus*; *ratio delictus*; and *ratio rei sitae.*[35] To this list may also be added *ratio causa continentia.*

4.1.2.3.1 *Ratio domicilii* (*actor sequitur forum rei*)

Ratio domicilii expresses the principle of Roman law that the fundamental basis of jurisdiction is that a plaintiff should sue a defendant at the defendant's place of domicile or, as has become the case, residence (*actor sequitur forum rei*). There is nothing to suggest that the Lesotho courts would treat this issue any differently to the courts in the Republic of South Africa.[36]

4.1.2.3.2 *Ratio contractus*

There is nothing to suggest that the Lesotho courts would treat this issue any differently to the courts in the Republic of South Africa. Accordingly, a court where: (1) the contract was concluded (the *locus contractus*); (2) the contract is to be performed in whole or in part (the *locus solutionis*); or (3) the contract was breached in the manner relied upon by the plaintiff in Lesotho may, *ratio contractus*, exercise jurisdiction.[37]

---

[33] (1887) 5 SC 86 (De Villiers CJ).

[34] Ibid 91.

[35] Different authors treat the organisation of this subject in different ways. Peté et al *Civil Procedure* 2 ed (2011) (at 70ff), discuss the subject under the headings *ratione domicilii, ratione res gestae, ratione rei sitae* and then claims relating to property and claims sounding in money. In Schulze *On Jurisdiction and the Recognition and Enforcement of Foreign Money Judgments* 2005, the discussion (at 1–15) revolves around domicile and the bases for assumption of jurisdiction over *incolae* and *peregrini*. In Kelbrick *Civil Procedure in South Africa* 2 ed (2012), the subject is analysed (at 42–3; paras 84–6) in terms of claims in money and property. Forsyth *Private International Law* 5 ed (2012) discusses (at 205–46) residence and domicile, the various *rationes jurisdictionis* and then claims in money or property. Herbstein and Van Winsen *The Civil Practice of the High Courts of South Africa* 5 ed (2009) discusses (at 67–81) the subject under the topic headings claims in money, property (and status). Pistorius *Pollak on Jurisdiction* 2 ed (1993), arranges the discussion under the topic headings money claims and property claims. There are merits in all of these approaches.

[36] Accordingly, for a more detailed treatment of this issue, the reader is referred to the corresponding discussion in the chapter on South Africa.

[37] Given that there is nothing to suggest that the courts in Lesotho treat this issue any differently to the courts in the Republic of South Africa, the reader is referred to the corresponding discussion in the chapter on South Africa for a more detailed treatment of this issue.

4.1.2.3.3 *Ratio delicti commissi*

A court may have jurisdiction by reason of a *ratio delicti commissi* in the event that a delict was committed or occurred within its area of jurisdiction. Again, there is nothing to suggest that the Lesotho courts would, if a plaintiff had to show the existence of a *ratio jurisdictionis* in order to secure the jurisdiction of the Lesotho court, treat this issue any differently to the way in which courts in the Republic of South Africa treat it.[38]

4.1.2.3.4 *Ratio rei sitae*

The location of movable or immovable property within the area of jurisdiction of a court will confer on that court jurisdiction by reason of a *ratio rei sitae*: it is the court of the place where the property is situated. Again, there is nothing to suggest that the Lesotho courts treat this issue any differently to the courts in the Republic of South Africa.[39]

4.1.2.3.5 *Ratio causa continentia*

The *causa continentia* rule is one that permits a court to assume jurisdiction in a case in which, but for the application of the rule, it might not have jurisdiction over the entirety of the dispute or over a particular defendant. Again, there is nothing to suggest that the Lesotho courts would, if a plaintiff had to show the existence of a *ratio jurisdictionis* in order to secure the jurisdiction of the Lesotho court, treat this issue any differently to the way in which the courts in the Republic of South Africa treat it. The application of the rule is intended to avoid a 'multiplicity of proceedings and the possibility of conflicting judgments on the same cause and allows for the more convenient disposition of cases'.[40] Pistorius states[41] that in order to apply 'it must be established that there is no other forum which has jurisdiction in respect of all the defendants on other recognised grounds of jurisdiction'.[42]

---

[38] Accordingly, for a more detailed treatment of this issue, the reader is referred to the corresponding discussion in the chapter on the Republic of South Africa.

[39] Accordingly, for a more detailed treatment of this issue, the reader is referred to the corresponding discussion in the chapter on the Republic of South Africa.

[40] Pistorius *Pollak on Jurisdiction* 2 ed (1993) 25.

[41] Ibid 26.

[42] Given, as has been said, that there is nothing to suggest that the courts in Lesotho treat this issue any differently to the courts in the Republic of South Africa, the reader is referred to the corresponding discussion in the chapter on South Africa for a more detailed treatment of this issue.

4.1.2.4 *Submission to the jurisdiction*

Lesotho law recognises submission to the jurisdiction as a basis for the assumption of jurisdiction over a dispute in certain circumstances.

Generally, submission may take one of two forms. First, unilateral submission, whereby a party against whom proceedings have been commenced takes a step in the proceedings which as a matter of Lesotho law renders him amenable to the jurisdiction of the Lesotho courts. Second, consensual submission, whereby the parties agree prior to or subsequent to a dispute arising to submit to the jurisdiction of the Lesotho courts.

4.1.2.4.1 Submission by participating in existing proceedings

In the case of unilateral consent, questions will be directed at whether the acts of the party (usually the defendant) amounted to a submission to the jurisdiction or not. The plaintiff must bear the onus of showing that the relevant acts amounted to a submission to the jurisdiction of the Lesotho court.

There is an absence of reported authority in Lesotho as to when a court will consider that a party against whom proceedings have been commenced has taken a step in those proceedings so as to render him amenable to the Lesotho court's jurisdiction. It is submitted that, in the light of the close relationship between the law of Lesotho and the law of South Africa, courts in Lesotho will have regard to the guidance issued by the courts in the Republic of South Africa when confronted with such matters.

The courts in South Africa have determined that, in the following cases, the defendant's actions were held to evidence submission:[43] (1) pleading to the merits; (2) filing a counterclaim; (3) requesting a postponement or agreeing to a postponement without objection; (4) demanding security; (5) appointing an agent authorised to be sued; (6) attending an enquiry into his financial position and agreeing to pay a judgment debt in instalments; (7) accepting appointment as an executor or executrix; (8) delay in taking an objection to the jurisdiction of the court before trial; (9) submission may be made orally to the court by counsel acting for the defendant.[44]

A case where the plaintiff may be found to have submitted to the jurisdiction is where the plaintiff brings a claim and the defendant responds with a claim in reconvention over which claim the court would not ordinarily have jurisdiction to entertain that claim against the plaintiff.[45]

---

[43] Pistorius *Pollak on Jurisdiction* 2 ed (1993) 11, authorities at fns 35–41 and 45.

[44] *Agro-Grip (Pty) Ltd v Ayal* 1999 (3) SA 126 (W) 128F–G.

[45] Pistorius *Pollak on Jurisdiction* 2 ed (1993) 65–7; *Mediterranean Shipping Co v Speedwell Shipping Co Ltd* 1986 (4) SA 329 (D), *per* Van Heerden J at 333H: 'The court in which a plaintiff brings his action also has

The following acts have been held not to constitute submission:[46] (1) the entry of an appearance to defend: 'a defendant is entitled to take this step in order to plead want of jurisdiction but his failure to take any further steps may imply consent'; (2) the failure to enter an appearance to defend; (3) the appointment of an agent under a general power of attorney; (4) a submission to arbitration in another country did not constitute submission to the courts of that country; (5) a letter (enclosing an affidavit) from an attorney acting for the defendant but not the attorney of record.

4.1.2.4.2 Submission by agreement

4.1.2.4.2.1 *Jurisdiction clauses*

An otherwise valid and enforceable exclusive jurisdiction clause may be disregarded on the grounds of public policy. In *Khotle v Metropolitan Life Insurance*,[47] Acting High Court judge Mr DS Levy, considered an employment contract containing an exclusive jurisdiction clause in favour of the magistrate's court in the District of the Cape or the Supreme Court of South Africa (Cape Provincial Division). The plaintiff was a resident of Lesotho who had contracted to act as an insurance agent in Lesotho for the defendant, the head office of which was in Cape Town. The judge held[48] that the proper law of the contract was South African law. The defendant contended that the plaintiff's action should be dismissed in favour of the courts of the Cape. The judge dismissed the defendant's application on the basis that certain provisions of Lesotho employment legislation (the Employment Act 1967)[49] would not be applied were the action to be heard in the Cape[50] and that:[51]

> 'In the result an employee of the First Defendant who is a citizen of Lesotho and whose employment is in Lesotho exclusively, would be deprived of the protection otherwise afforded to him by the Act which in its scope governs all master and servant relationships

jurisdiction to entertain a defendant's counterclaim even should the action be withdrawn'; *Birkett v Birkett* 1953 (4) SA 445 (T), *per* Dowling J at 451H: 'There is the further fact that not only has the applicant [ie the plaintiff on the counterclaim] expressly submitted to the jurisdiction of this Court, but in seeking the jurisdiction of this Court he has thereby submitted himself to the jurisdiction of the Court in respect of any counterclaim, adjudication upon which is not dependent on the domicile of the [plaintiff].' Where the defendant claims in reconvention (as noted above) he will have submitted: Pistorius *Pollak on Jurisdiction* 2 ed (1993) 11, authorities at fn 36.

[46] Pistorius *Pollak on Jurisdiction* 2 ed (1993) 10, authorities at fns 25–9.

[47] [1985] LSHC 77 (HC) (Levy AJ). The decision was cited with approval in *Komane v City Express Stores* [2006] LSLAC 9 (LAC) (Mosito J) para [22]. This was a decision of the Labour Appeal Court, dealing with clauses which forced Lesotho workers to attend disciplinary hearings in South Africa.

[48] Ibid 4–5 of the transcript.

[49] Act 22 of 1967.

[50] Ibid 6 of the transcript.

[51] Ibid.

> in Lesotho. I consider this consequence ... to be contrary to public policy and a circumvention ... of Clause 11 of the Act. I accordingly find Clause 15 of the agreement to be null and void and unenforceable.'

The judge observed[52] that this conclusion meant that the plaintiff was saved from having

> 'at great personal expense and with considerable inconvenience to institute action in Cape Town where he is a foreigner and may be obliged to find security for the Defendant's costs with the possible total frustration of his action whereas the employer has its branch office in Maseru where the whole dispute has arisen'.

Clearly the court had sympathy with the plaintiff's position. However, the possibility of respecting the contractual rights of the parties and pre-empting any difficulties the plaintiff might face in the Cape by staying the plaintiff's proceedings in Lesotho on terms that the defendant should not seek security for costs in any proceedings in the Cape was not considered by the court (or suggested by counsel for the defendant).

4.1.2.4.2.2 Domicilium citandi et executandi *clauses*

By including a *domicilium citandi et executandi* clause in their contract, a party may nominate an address to which formal notices in relation to the contract (such as a demand for payment or a threat to cancel) or the service of process in litigation arising out of the contract can be served. There is nothing to suggest that the law in Lesotho on *domicilium citandi et executandi* clauses differs from the law of the Republic of South Africa on the subject. In consequence, the use of such a clause (nominating an address for service, as described above, in Lesotho) may, in particular where the defendant is a *peregrinus*, indicate submission to the jurisdiction of the Lesotho courts.[53]

4.1.2.5 *The jurisdictional significance of arrest of the person*

Rule 6(8) provides for arrest of the person to found or confirm jurisdiction: 'On the application of an *incola* of Lesotho the court may order the arrest of a *peregrinus* who is temporarily within the jurisdiction of the court.' Sub-rule (8) sets out a number of conditions to which the making of an order for arrest is subject: (1) the plaintiff must show that he has a good cause of action against the *peregrinus*; (2) the plaintiff must produce a certificate by an advocate or attorney certifying that in

---

[52] Ibid 6–7.

[53] See, by way of comparison, the decision of the South African Supreme Court in *Hay Management Consultants (Pty) Ltd v P3 Management Consultants (Pty) Ltd* 2005 (2) SA 522 (SCA), *per* Heher JA (Scott, Cameron and Conradie JJA and Patel AJA agreeing) para [15], where the clause was regarded as 'a significant factor' as was the choice of South African law as the proper law (para [14]).

the opinion of the advocate or attorney the plaintiff has a good cause of action against the *peregrinus*; (3) the court must order a warrant of arrest to be addressed to the sheriff in accordance with form E of Schedule 1 to the Rules;[54] (4) the sheriff shall bring the *peregrinus* to court as soon as possible and if the *peregrinus* gives security for the claim or for his continued presence in Lesotho 'as may seem to the court to be adequate' the *peregrinus* shall be immediately released.

The standard for arrest of a person (a good cause of action) is therefore a higher standard than that required for an attachment of property (where only a *prima facie* case need be demonstrated). Upon a successful application and subsequent arrest of a defendant, there is little in sub-rule (8) to provide guidance to the court or practitioners (or arrestees) as to the amount or type of security that will ensure the release of the defendant. It is unsatisfactory that, where the liberty of the individual is concerned, the conditions for the release of the defendant are so heavily reliant on the exercise of the discretion of an individual judge.

It would appear that the Lesotho courts have yet to follow the lead of the South African Supreme Court of Appeal in abolishing judicial arrest to found or confirm the jurisdiction of the court.[55]

4.2 Enforcement of Foreign Judgments

A foreign judgment may be enforced in Lesotho either at common law (though this is a matter of some controversy) or under the statutory regime set out in the Reciprocal Enforcement of Judgments Proclamation 1922.[56]

[54] Form E is in rule *nisi* form commanding the sheriff to arrest the defendant and bring him before the court on a specified date for the defendant 'to show cause why he should not be committed to prison and detained pending delivery of the judgment of the Court in an action wherein the plaintiff claims ... from the defendant unless he shall give security to the satisfaction of the court that he will abide such judgment or remain within the jurisdiction of the Court until such judgment is delivered'. The burden of proof on the question of the liberty of the defendant is therefore on the defendant himself.

[55] *Maphike v Pierre-Yves Sachet* [2019] LSCA 35 (CA), where such jurisdictional arrest was sought and no comment made on its abolition. By contrast, the Supreme Court of Appeal of South Africa reached a contrary conclusion in the light of provisions of the Constitution of the Republic of South Africa, 1996, in particular s 12, relating to personal liberty corresponding to provisions in the Lesotho Constitution, 1993 (viz s 6 of the Lesotho Constitution; s 12 of the South African Constitution provides, '(1) Everyone has the right to freedom and security of the person, which includes the right - (a) not to be deprived of freedom arbitrarily or without just cause; (b) not to be detained without trial...'): *Bid Industrial Holdings (Pty) Ltd v Strang* 2008 (3) SA 355 (SCA).

[56] Proclamation 2 of 1922.

4.2.1 Enforcement at common law

The basic law of Lesotho is to be found in the General Law Proclamation 1884[57] ('the 1884 Proclamation') and the Constitution of Lesotho 1993 ('the Constitution').[58]

The 1884 Proclamation provides, inter alia:

> 'In all suits, actions or proceedings, civil or criminal, the law to be administered shall, as nearly as the circumstances of the country will permit, be the same as the law for the time being in force in the Colony of the Cape of Good Hope ... and provided further that no law enacted by the legislative authority of the Colony of the Cape of Good Hope, or any legislative authority succeeding thereto in the Cape of Good Hope, shall have effect in Basutoland unless it is included in the First Schedule or the Third Schedule to the Law Revision Proclamation [Proclamation 12 of 1960], or has been specially applied therein by the Legislature of Basutoland.'

Thus, as at 29 May 1884 (the date on which the Proclamation came into force), the law applicable to the jurisdiction of what was then Basutoland was the law 'for the time being in force in the Colony of the Cape of Good Hope'. The 1884 Proclamation remained in force as at the date of Lesotho's independence.

Lesotho was granted independence by means of the United Kingdom Parliament Lesotho Independence Act 1966, section 1 of which provided: 'On 4th October 1966 (in this Act referred to as "the appointed day") the territory which immediately before that day constitutes the Colony of Basutoland shall cease to form part of Her Majesty's dominions and shall become an independent kingdom under the name of Lesotho.'

Section 2 of the 1966 Act made provision for the continuity of existing laws:

> 'Subject to the following provisions of this Act, on and after the appointed day all law which, whether being a rule of law or a provision of an Act of Parliament or of any other enactment or instrument whatsoever, is in force on that day or has been passed or made before that day and comes into force thereafter, shall, unless and until provision to the contrary is made by Parliament or some other authority having power in that behalf, have the same operation in relation to Lesotho, and persons and things belonging to or connected with Lesotho, as it would have apart from this subsection if on the appointed day Basutoland has been renamed Lesotho but there had been no change in its status.'

---

[57] Proclamation 2B of 1884.

[58] The official editorial note on the Lesotho Legal Information Institute website (https://lesotholii.org/ls/legislation/num-act/1993/1) reads as follows: 'The Revised Draft of a Constitution for Lesotho was published as Government Notice No. 12 of 1993 on 5 February 1993. That revised draft was then amended by Government Notice No. 211 of 1993, published on 27 March 1993. By virtue of section 5 of the Lesotho Constitution (Commencement) Order, 1993 (Order No. 5 of 1993) as amended by the Lesotho Constitution (Commencement) (Amendment) Order, 1993 (Order No. 16 of 1993), the draft constitution came into operation as the Constitution of Lesotho on 2 April 1993, following the appointment on 1 April 1993 of a Prime Minister Designate.'

Further provision was made for the independent Lesotho by the Lesotho Independence Order 1966,[59] article 3 of which provided that the Constitution set out in the Schedule to the Order would come into effect at the commencement of the Order.[60]

The Constitution in the Schedule to the Order made no specific provision regarding the law of Lesotho as at the date of independence (presumably because this had already been addressed in section 2 of the 1966 Act) and the 1993 Constitution did not alter this position.

At independence, therefore, the law of Lesotho was the law 'for the time being in force in the Colony of the Cape of Good Hope' as provided for by the 1884 Proclamation. The question arises, precisely what body of law does section 2 receive into Lesotho law? Is it the law of the Cape as at 29 May 1884, or as at the date in 1909 when the Cape ceased to be an independent colony,[61] or as at 4 October 1966 when Lesotho became an independent state, or the law administered at the present time in the Cape Province of the Republic of South Africa?

A number of sources lend support to the construction of section 2 that it imported into Lesotho law the law of the Cape as it stood at 29 May 1884.

In *Khatala v Khatala*,[62] a decision of the Basutoland Court of Appeal[63] on the applicability of Roman-Dutch law to a marriage entered into in accordance with both Christian and Basuto rites, the court discussed the correct construction of section 2 of the 1884 Proclamation. Giving the judgment of the court, Schreiner JA stated[64] (emphasis provided): 'The proviso to section 12 [sic, 2] of Proclamation No. 26 [sic, 2B] of 1884 applies *the then existing law* of the Cape of Good Hope to Basutoland.' However, the judgment contains no analysis or reasoning to support this conclusion and further the statement was not necessary for decision in the case and is obiter.

In *Motsamai Pholo v The Principal Chief of Mokhotlong*,[65] the petitioner applied by motion for a declaration of right but did not apply for any additional relief. Benson CJ dismissed the application, holding that, although such an application was permitted in South Africa by reason only of a change in the law effected in that jurisdiction by the General Law Amendment Act 1935: 'The law regarding Declarations of Rights in Basutoland is governed by the common law of South Africa as it was prior to the 29th May 1884.'[66]

---

[59] United Kingdom SI 1172 of 1966.
[60] Immediately before the 4 October 1966 ('the appointed day' provided for by s 1 of the 1966 Act).
[61] Pursuant to the South Africa Act 1909.
[62] [1963–66] 10 HCTLR 97.
[63] Watkin Williams P, Schreiner and Murray JJA.
[64] Ibid 99.
[65] [1963–66] 10 HCTLR 188 (Basutoland High Court).
[66] Ibid 189C–D.

At the other end of the spectrum of potential constructions is one that holds that section 2 refers to the *living* law of the Cape Colony, now Cape Province, as it was after 29 May 1884. This construction too has some academic[67] and judicial[68] support. Poulter states:[69] 'The common law to be administered in Lesotho is basically the common law in force in the Cape Province of the Republic of South Africa today, and not that applied in 1909.' JH Pain expresses the view[70] that the 1884 Proclamation 'introduces a timeless reception of the Roman-Dutch common law' and, in a footnote to that passage, further states, '[t]his has always been assumed by the courts in Lesotho. There is no reported case where South African decisions have been departed from' and asserts that the decision of Benson CJ in *Motsamai Pholo v The Principal Chief of Mokhotlong*,[71] 'is not correct'.

In *R v Khopiso Lerotholi*,[72] certain of the accused were charged with murder and others with being accessories after the fact. At trial, Willan CJ was required to decide whether English law provided the legal test for criminal liability as an accessory after the fact or whether South African law did so. The judge held[73] that South African law bound him and that he should follow the principles of Roman-Dutch law set out in the South African Appellate Division in *R v Mlooi*.[74]

An intermediate construction, that the law of the Cape Colony imported into Lesotho by the 1884 Proclamation was the law as it stood on 29 May 1884 but that the Lesotho courts should have regard to the law of the Cape Province as it has developed since that date, following it where appropriate, also has some academic[75] and judicial[76] support.

> 'We cannot, and need not, review the actual legal history of Lesotho over the past 86 years [from 1884]. We need not even fix the point at which that system was cut loose from its mooring at the Cape and left to navigate alone – by dead reckoning to pursue the metaphor – with occasional guidance from the Cape's successor systems. It is enough to conclude that this position has been reached without doing violence to the words of the 1884 Proclamation. This seems to me to be the correct position and to be the

---

[67] Poulter 'The common law in Lesotho' [1969] 13 *JAL* 127; Palmer and Poulton *The Legal System of Lesotho* (1972); see also JH Pain 'The reception of English and Roman-Dutch law in Africa with reference to Botswana, Lesotho and Swaziland' (1978) 11 *CILSA* 137.

[68] *R v Khopiso Lerotholi* [1926–53] 1 HCTLR 320 (Basutoland High Court).

[69] 'The common law in Lesotho' [1969] 13 *JAL* 127 at 131; a view repeated in Palmer and Poulton *The Legal System of Lesotho* (1972) 53.

[70] 'The reception of English and Roman-Dutch law in Africa with reference to Botswana, Lesotho and Swaziland' (1978) 11 *CILSA* 137 at 165 and fn 130.

[71] [1963–66] 10 HCTLR 188 (Basutoland High Court).

[72] [1926–53] 1 HCTLR 320 (Basutoland High Court).

[73] Ibid 326A–B.

[74] [1925] AD 131.

[75] Beardsley 'The common law in Lesotho' [1970] 14 *JAL* 198 at 200; Sanders 'Legal dualism in Lesotho, Botswana, Swaziland: A general survey' [1985] 1 *LLJ* 47 at 48.

[76] *Mathenjwa v R* [1970–76] SLR 25 (CA) (Schreiner P, Caney and Milne JJA).

> only position that is consistent both with the 1884 Proclamation and with the fact and necessity of the operation of an independent national legal system in Lesotho whose premises ... are radically different from those of the Cape Colony's successor.'[77]

This intermediate position has received some judicial approval. In *Mathenjwa v R*,[78] in the Eswatini Court of Appeal, Schreiner P stated:[79]

> 'If this conclusion involves a departure from the law as now established in the Republic of South Africa this is to be deplored, for it is much to be desired that the law of Southern Africa should in essentials be uniform. But we are obliged to apply what we understand to be the law of Swaziland [now Eswatini], even if divergence from the law of the foundation member of the South African Law Association is the result.'

Eswatini has a similar (though not identical) reception provision to that of Lesotho.

As a matter of authority, the decisions in *Motsamai Pholo v The Principal Chief of Mokhotlong*[80] and *R v Khopiso Lerotholi*[81] appear to be conflicting on the question of the proper construction of the 1884 Proclamation. Academic authorities are similarly divided in their opinion on this question.

Returning to the language of the Proclamation, as at 29 May 1884, the law applicable to the jurisdiction of what was then Basutoland was the law '*for the time being* in force in the Colony of the Cape of Good Hope' (emphasis provided). Applying orthodox canons of statutory construction and giving the words their ordinary meaning,[82] the expression '*for the time being*' is usually taken to mean, 'at the present time or the actual time in question'.[83] This approach would support the construction that the 1884 Proclamation was intended to incorporate the law of the Cape Colony as at 29 May 1884, leaving the Lesotho courts free to develop

---

[77] Beardsley 'The common law in Lesotho' [1970] 14 *JAL* 198, 200.

[78] [1970–76] SLR 25 (CA) (Schreiner P, Caney and Milne JJA).

[79] Ibid 29H.

[80] [1963–66] 10 HCTLR 188 (Basutoland High Court).

[81] [1926–53] 1 HCTLR 320 (Basutoland High Court).

[82] *Cross on Statutory Interpretation* 3 ed (1995) 31–3; *Craies on Legislation* 10 ed (2012) 701 para 17.1.1 (where the 'cardinal rule' that the words in a statute should be given their ordinary meaning is said to date back to the times of Henry VIII and a statute of 1536). In this regard, there is no need to consult legal dictionaries in order to determine the meaning of words in a statute (as one of the proponents of the living law construction does in his article referred to above: Poulter 'The common law in Lesotho' [1969] 13 *JAL* 127 at 130 fn 2).

[83] *The Chambers Dictionary*; *Oxford English Dictionary*, 'Before in various uses ... Of time'; *Collins English Dictionary* 'for the moment'. However, a contrary view of the meaning of the phrase 'for the time being' was taken by the UK House of Lords in *Department for Environment, Food and Rural Affairs v ASDA Stores Ltd* [2003] UKHL 71, [2004] 1 All ER 268, *per* Lord Nicholls para [18], p 273 (with whom Lords Hoffmann, Hobhouse, Millett and Walker agreed). That case concerned the construction of amendments to a UK Act that were intended to import into UK law EEC/EU food produce grading rules. The House of Lords held that Community grading rules could be expected to change over time and that the use in the relevant legislation of the phrase 'for the time being' was intended to reflect that (thereby rendering the UK in compliance with its obligations under the Treaty of Rome).

the common law of Lesotho without being tied to a foreign system of law. It is submitted that this is a preferable outcome to the living law construction and accommodates the sentiments expressed by the proponents of the intermediate position reflecting and respecting Lesotho's judicial and political independence.

The matter will not, however, finally be resolved until authoritatively determined by the Lesotho Court of Appeal.

Against that background, it is a matter of some conjecture whether a foreign judgment must be enforced using the Reciprocal Enforcement of Judgments Proclamation[84] ('the 1922 Proclamation'); there is doubt as to whether a judgment creditor may seek enforcement of the foreign judgment pursuant to the common law.[85]

According to the High Court's decision in *ABSA Bank Ltd v Latela*,[86] it would appear that there is no mechanism for enforcement of a foreign judgment pursuant to the common law. There, the plaintiff sought to enforce a judgment given by a magistrate's court in Bloemfontein (albeit only in so far as that judgment related to costs). Having set out[87] her view that the enforcement of foreign judgments was governed by the 1922 Proclamation, the judge concluded,[88] inter alia, that because South Africa was not a country to which that Proclamation applied, the application should be rejected.

The logical conclusion of the High Court's reasoning in this case is that it is only possible to enforce a foreign judgment pursuant to the terms of the 1922 Proclamation. That this is so is reinforced by Guni J's own words:[89]

> 'Because [the plaintiff] ignored all the relevant provisions of the Proclamation 2B of 1922, [it] must have elected to proceed under another law which [it] has chosen not to disclose before this court. I am not aware of any other law which authorises this court to recognise foreign judgements. My search revealed that no such other law authorising this court to recognise foreign judgements, exists.'

Hence, if the 1922 Proclamation does not apply (because, say, the country from which the judgment emanates is not covered by the Proclamation), it is apparently not possible to enforce the foreign judgment: there is no enforcement at common law.

---

[84] 2 of 1922.

[85] *ABSA Bank Ltd v Latela* [2004] LSHC 47 (HC) (Guni J). Indeed, the Commonwealth Secretariat appear to take the view that a judgment creditor may not seek enforcement of the foreign judgment using the common law: 'Commonwealth Practice in the Recognition of Foreign Judgments' (2009) 35 *Commonwealth Law Bulletin* 345, 346.

[86] Ibid.

[87] Ibid 2 of the transcript.

[88] Ibid 4–5.

[89] Which appear at p 2 of the transcript.

Such a conclusion is unfortunate and, it is submitted, erroneous as a matter of principle and as a matter of authority.

As a matter of authority, the wording of the 1922 Proclamation does not mandate the conclusion that enforcement of a foreign judgment must be pursuant to the 1922 Proclamation or not at all.[90] In addition, the High Court in *Adam v Adam*[91] had previously indicated that enforcement under the common law was a perfectly legitimate course of action to take (especially when dealing with a judgment from a country which was not covered by the 1922 Proclamation). Hence, in *Adam v Adam*, in the context of an attempt to enforce a final order for divorce made by the Supreme Court of the Cape of Good Hope Provincial Division, Maqutu J stated:[92] 'The Republic of South Africa is not among the countries with which Lesotho enjoys a reciprocal enforcement of judgment status ... This problem is not insurmountable because it can be dealt with through the Common Law', thereby indicating that enforcement pursuant to the common law represented a legitimate course of action for the plaintiff to take. The decision in *Adam* was not cited to or by the court in the *ABSA* case; accordingly, no reason was given for departing from *Adam*.

Similarly, as a matter of principle, preventing enforcement of a foreign judgment which meets the relevant criteria (as set out below) at common law unnecessarily inhibits the development of this area of law. There is little sense, it is submitted, in preventing, *in toto*, enforcement of judgments emanating from courts in countries to which the provisions of the 1922 Proclamation do not extend.[93]

If it is correct that enforcement of foreign judgments pursuant to common law is accepted in Lesotho,[94] it is submitted that the common-law position would likely reflect that which is currently in force in South Africa.

---

[90] Indeed, the English legislation on which the 1922 Proclamation is based sits comfortably alongside enforcement at common law.

[91] *Adam v Adam* [1994] LSCA 183 (HC) (Maqutu J). This case, like *Latela*, dealt with an attempt to enforce a judgment from a court in South Africa.

[92] Ibid 4–5 of the transcript.

[93] In *ABSA Bank Ltd v Latela* [2004] LSHC 47 (HC) (Guni J), the plaintiff did not specify the law pursuant to which it wished to enforce the South African judgment in Lesotho, such that the judge was left to conclude that enforcement was sought pursuant to the terms of the 1922 Proclamation. Judged against the criteria set out in the 1922 Proclamation, the application was defective: the judgment was not one of a superior court in a designated country. The plaintiff's approach to the application may well be thought to indicate its view that enforcement at common law was permissible: it made no attempt to comply with the provisions of the 1922 Proclamation (perhaps because it was not seeking enforcement pursuant thereto). All the same, it is regrettable that the decision in *Adam* was not cited to the High Court.

[94] In which case, there may also be a need to reform the law of jurisdiction so as to alter the circumstances in which a Lesotho court has jurisdiction over a dispute between two peregrines. Given the uncertainties over the jurisdictional conditions which may or may not need to be satisfied where the action is between two peregrines (as to which, see the discussion of the decision in *Burger v Ocrim SAP* [1986] LSHC 55 (HC) and

The basis on which the South African court will enforce a foreign judgment was, insofar as presently relevant, set out by Corbett CJ in *Jones v Krok*:[95]

> 'the present position in South Africa is that a foreign judgment is not directly enforceable, but constitutes a cause of action and will be enforced by our Courts provided (i) that the court which pronounced the judgment had jurisdiction to entertain the case according to the principles recognised by our law with reference to the jurisdiction of foreign courts (sometimes referred to as "international jurisdiction or competence"); (ii) that the judgment is final and conclusive in its effect and has not become superannuated; (iii) that the recognition and enforcement of the judgment by our Courts would not be contrary to public policy; (iv) that the judgment was not obtained by fraudulent means; [and] (v) that the judgment does not involve the enforcement of a penal or revenue law of the foreign State....'

The plaintiff in an action to enforce a foreign judgment by ordinary action may seek to obtain provisional sentence[96] in the action or summary judgment or may proceed to prove the case at trial.

The question of the finality of a judgment in the context of an appeal against the foreign judgment was addressed by Corbett CJ in *Jones v Krok*,[97] where he set out the following rules:[98]

> '(1) The fact that the judgment is subject to appeal or even that an appeal is pending in the foreign jurisdiction does not affect the finality of the judgment, provided that in all other respects it is final and conclusive.
>
> (2) Where, however, it is shown that the judgment is subject to such an appeal or that such an appeal is pending, the Court in this country which is asked to enforce the judgment enjoys a discretion and in the exercise thereof may, instead of giving judgment in favour of the plaintiff, stay the proceedings pending the final determination of the appeal or appeals in the foreign jurisdiction.
>
> (3) Although the onus of proving that a foreign judgment is final and conclusive rests upon the party seeking to enforce it ... it seems to me that, where this onus has been discharged, it is up to the defendant to place before the Court the facts relating to the impending appeal and such other relevant facts as may persuade the Court to exercise its discretion in favour of granting a stay of proceedings.
>
> (4) In exercising this discretion the Court may take into account all relevant circumstances, including (but not confined to) whether an appeal is actually pending, the consequences to the defendant if judgment be given in favour of plaintiff and thereafter

Bateman v G Govoni Imports & Exports (Pty) Ltd [1987] LSHC 18 (HC) above), the present state of the law may make it unduly burdensome for a *peregrinus* foreign judgment creditor who is seeking to enforce the foreign judgment against the *peregrinus* judgment debtor to do that. See further: Frimpong Oppong 'Recognition and enforcement of foreign judgments in Commonwealth African countries' (2014) XV *Yearbook of Private International Law* 365, 370–1.

[95] 1995 (1) SA 677 (AD), *per* Corbett JA (giving the judgment of the court) 685B–D.

[96] Ibid *per* Corbett CJ 685F.

[97] Ibid *per* Corbett CJ (giving the judgment of the court) 689B–693C.

[98] Ibid 692B–G.

> (possibly after the judgment has been satisfied) the appeal succeeds in the foreign jurisdiction and whether the defendant is pursuing the right of appeal genuinely and with due diligence. As a rule, however, the Court will refuse to assess the merits and demerits of the appeal and its prospects of success in the foreign Court.'

4.2.2 Enforcement pursuant to statute

4.2.2.1 *The regime for enforcement pursuant to statute*

The enforcement of foreign judgments in Lesotho is governed by the 1922 Proclamation[99] and the Reciprocal Enforcement of Judgments Rules of Court 1923.[100]

The 1922 Proclamation makes provision for a system of registration of foreign judgments,[101] the purpose of which is to domesticate the foreign judgment and render it enforceable in Lesotho as if it were a judgment of the Lesotho court.[102]

4.2.2.2 *Procedure for registration*

Where a judgment has been obtained in the courts of a territory to which the 1922 Proclamation applies, the judgment creditor may apply to the Lesotho court to have that judgment registered. The application must be made within 12 months of the date of the judgment or such longer period as the court may allow. The court may then order the judgment to be registered with the consequence that it may then be enforced as if it were a judgment of the Lesotho court. The Lesotho court may only allow registration if 'in all the circumstances ... it is just and convenient'[103] to do so. Registration is, therefore, ultimately a matter of discretion.

The procedure for registration of a foreign judgment under the 1922 Proclamation is set out in the Reciprocal Enforcement of Judgments Rules of

---

[99] 2 of 1922. By a High Commissioner's Notice (96 of 1922) the Proclamation was extended to Bechuanaland Protectorate, Swaziland, Southern Rhodesia, Northern Rhodesia, Zanzibar Protectorate, Nyasaland Protectorate, Kenya Colony and Protectorate, New Zealand, Western Australia, Tanganyika Territory, Uganda, New South Wales, Victoria, North Australia and Central Australia.

[100] High Commissioner's Notice 50 of 1923, hereafter cited as 'REJ rule/REJ r'.

[101] Section 3.

[102] Section 3(3). The provisions of the 1922 Proclamation correspond very closely to legislation of the United Kingdom (the Administration of Justice Act 1920) on which the 1922 Proclamation was based. In particular, ss 2, 3, 4, 5 and 6 are effectively transpositions of, respectively, ss 12(1), 9, 10, 11 and 14 of the Administration of Justice Act 1920. It is to be expected that a Lesotho court will refer to judicial and academic authorities on the construction of these provisions of the 1920 Act when deciding questions on the construction of corresponding provisions of the 1922 Proclamation. The House of Lords has held that the provisions of the 1920 Act 'have to be construed with reference to the common law as understood in 1920': *Owens Bank Ltd v Bracco* [1992] 2 AC 443 (HL (E)), *per* Lord Bridge (giving the leading speech with which Lords Griffiths, Ackner, Goff and Browne-Wilkinson agreed) 488E–F. Lord Bridge also set out a brief legislative history of the 1920 Act at 488B–E. See also: *Dicey, Morris and Collins on the Conflict of Laws* 15 ed (2012) vol 1, paras 14R-173–14-181; A Briggs *Civil Jurisdiction and Judgments* 7 ed (2021) paras 35.01–35.10.

[103] Section 3(1).

Court.[104] An application is made for registration; an order granting leave to register may then be made; written notice of registration must then be served on the judgment debtor advising him of his right to seek to set aside the order granting leave and of the time within which such an application must be made.

The application may be made *ex parte* or by summons and, if made *ex parte*, the court may direct that a summons be issued.[105] The application must be supported by an affidavit setting out the facts regarding the judgment, exhibiting the judgment or a verified or otherwise authenticated copy and stating that to the best of the deponent's information and belief, the judgment creditor is entitled to enforce the judgment and that the judgment does not fall within any of the cases to which section 3(2) refers (that there is no defence to the registration).[106]

Section 3(2) of the 1922 Proclamation provides for a number of defences to registration:

(1) The original court acted without jurisdiction.[107] For the purposes of the 1922 Proclamation the foreign court has international jurisdiction for the purposes of the registration of its judgments if the judgment debtor was ordinarily resident or carrying on business within the jurisdiction of that court.[108] In *Sfeir & Co v National Insurance Co of New Zealand*,[109] it was held that a New Zealand insurance company was not carrying on business in Ghana by reason only of retaining an agent in Ghana having authority limited to bind the company by settlements of claims arising in Ghana under its policies issued elsewhere: the business carried on by the agents was the agents' own and not the company's.[110]

(2) The judgment debtor did not voluntarily appear and neither submitted nor agreed to the jurisdiction of the foreign court where the foreign court did not otherwise have jurisdiction.[111]

(3) The judgment debtor was not duly served with the process of the foreign court. There is some judicial authority under the corresponding provisions of the 1920 Act that 'duly served' means served in accordance with the law of the foreign court whose document it was.[112]

---

104 High Commissioner's Notice 50 of 1923.

105 REJ r 1.

106 REJ r 2.

107 Section 3(2)(a).

108 Presence within the foreign jurisdiction is not sufficient to give the foreign court international jurisdiction over the defendant for the purposes of the 1922 Proclamation.

109 [1964] 1 Lloyd's Rep 330.

110 Ibid 339, col 1, *per* Mocatta J.

111 Section 3(2)(b).

112 *Sfeir & Co v National Insurance Co of New Zealand* [1964] 1 Lloyd's Rep 330, *per* Mocatta J at 341, col 1.

(4) The judgment of the foreign court was obtained by fraud.[113] Fraud here bears a broad meaning reflecting the English common law as it was in 1920. A judgment debtor may set aside the registration of a foreign judgment if he can persuade the court that the judgment was obtained by fraud. It is irrelevant in this context that the foreign court has already considered and determined against the judgment debtor the same questions of fact on which the judgment debtor seeks to rely in the Lesotho court in order to set aside the registration of the foreign judgment. There is no requirement that the facts relied on as establishing fraud should not have been discoverable with the exercise of reasonable diligence at the time the proceedings in the foreign court took place. However undesirable it may seem, the position is clear under the 1920 Act and therefore under the 1922 Proclamation: a judgment debtor may effectively relitigate before the Lesotho court issues of fraud already determined against him in the foreign court by the very judgment which the judgment creditor seeks to enforce in Lesotho.[114]

(5) The judgment debtor satisfies the court that an appeal is pending or that he is entitled to appeal the foreign judgment and intends to do so. No doubt the court could place conditions on the setting aside of the registration of the foreign judgment such that any appeal was prosecuted expeditiously.

(6) The foreign judgment was in respect of a cause of action that for reasons of public policy or some similar reason could not have been entertained by the Lesotho court.

(7) The judgment debtor satisfies the court that for some other reason it is not just and convenient to register the judgment or that it is just and convenient to set aside registration.

Where an order giving leave to register the judgment is made, said order must state the time period within which the judgment debtor may apply to set aside the registration (at least 14 days, depending on the distance of the judgment debtor's ordinary residence from Maseru).[115] If the application was by summons

[113] Section 3(2)(d).

[114] *Owens Bank Ltd v Bracco* [1992] 2 AC 443 (HL (E)), *per* Lord Bridge at 489B–H. The rules relating to setting aside a foreign judgment obtained by fraud are comprehensively set out in *Dicey, Morris and Collins on the Conflict of Laws* 15 ed (2012) vol 1, r 50, paras 14R-137–14-145; the position in English law has not been followed in certain Commonwealth jurisdictions (eg Canada in *Beals v Saldanha* [2003] 3 SCR 416, (2003) 234 DLR (4th) 1; and New South Wales in *Keele v Findley* (1991) 21 NSWLR 444 (NSWSC) and plainly it would be open to a Lesotho court to do so also; but in *Close v Arnot* (unreported) 21 November 1997 (NSW), the Common Law Division distinguished *Keele v Findley* and applied the traditional English standard of fraud in respect of a foreign judgment in a case where the defendant had, for good reason, allowed foreign proceedings to go undefended).

[115] REJ r 6.

the order must be served on the judgment debtor but if the application was made *ex parte*, service of the order is not required.[116]

Notice in writing of registration of the judgment must be served on the judgment debtor within a reasonable time after the registration and such notice must state that the judgment debtor is entitled to apply to set aside registration and must also state the number of days for applying to set aside registration limited by the order giving leave to register the judgment.[117]

4.2.2.3 *Setting aside registration*

The judgment debtor may apply by summons for registration to be set aside and the court may order that the registration be set aside unconditionally or on terms if the court is satisfied that: the case falls within one of the cases under section 3(2) of the 1922 Proclamation; or it is not just and convenient to register the judgment; or 'for any other sufficient reasons'.[118]

4.3 Interim Remedies

4.3.1 Jurisdiction to grant interim remedies

Section 2 of the High Court Act 1978 provides that the High Court for Lesotho shall have

> 'unlimited jurisdiction to hear and determine any civil or criminal proceedings under any law in force in Lesotho [and] in its discretion and at the instance of any interested person, power to inquire into and determine any existing, future or contingent right or obligation, notwithstanding that such person cannot claim any relief consequential upon the determination'.

It seems that the Lesotho courts will grant interim remedies pursuant to the inherent jurisdiction of the court. The discussion below sets out the various types of interim remedy which may be granted in Lesotho, focusing, in particular, on the grant of: interim interdicts, freezing orders/anti-dissipation interdicts and search and seizure orders.

4.3.2 Procedure for application

Rule 8 of the Rules provides that every application to court shall be brought on notice of motion supported by an affidavit setting out the facts upon which the plaintiff relies. Applications may be made *inter partes* on notice, *ex parte* or *ex parte* on an urgent basis.

---

116 REJ r 5.

117 REJ r 9.

118 REJ r 12.

Inter partes applications are made on notice. The correct procedure for seeking interim relief is to make an application on notice of motion supported by affidavit evidence setting out the right for which protection is claimed and the facts supporting the granting of that relief.[119] Sub-rules (8)–(17) contain detailed provision for such matters as the service of evidence in response to an application and the making of counter-applications.

4.3.2.1 *Urgency*

An application for interim relief may also be made *ex parte*[120] on an urgent basis.[121] However, the Court of Appeal in *BP Lesotho (Pty) Ltd v Moloi*[122] emphasised the exceptional nature of such applications. Grosskopf JA stated:[123] 'This Court and the High Court have warned time and again against the launching of such applications and against the granting of orders without notice to [defendants/] respondents.'

In delivering this admonishment Grosskopf JA cited, inter alia, *Commander of the Lesotho Defence Force v Matela*,[124] where Gauntlett JA stated:[125]

> 'I pause to note that the frequency with which interdicts and other orders are sought by counsel, and granted by the High Court, without notice to parties cited as [defendants/] respondents is a matter for concern. As a general rule, basic considerations of fairness and the need to prevent the administration of justice being brought into disrepute require appropriate notice to be given. Orders should only be granted without notice where this is rigorously justified (where, for instance, there is extreme urgency or the need to prevent the order from being frustrated where any prior notice could well have that effect). Legal practitioners who continue to disregard these requirements must expect costs orders to be made *de bonis propriis* in appropriate cases.'

---

[119] The High Court Rules, r 8. The summons procedure (r 18) is used for actions in which relief (including interdictory relief) is claimed. The two procedures are quite distinct. In general, application proceedings provide interim and urgent relief: *per* Maqutu J in *Jiao v Motebang* [2008] LSHC 57 (HC) (28 September 2008) para [2].

[120] The High Court Rules, r 8(4) and (22). Applications made *ex parte* must be filed with the Registrar two days before the day on which it is set down to be heard. A person having an interest in an application made *ex parte* may himself issue an application for leave to oppose, supported by an affidavit (if he learns of the *ex parte* application by its appearance on the roll for hearing or otherwise).

[121] Sub-rule (22) makes provision for urgent applications. In such applications the court may dispense with the forms and provisions as to service contained in the Rules. The affidavit supporting an urgent application must set out the circumstances that are alleged to render the application urgent and the reasons why the deponent claims substantial relief could not be afforded in a hearing in accordance with the Rules. An urgent application must also be accompanied by a certificate of an advocate or attorney which sets out that the advocate or attorney 'has considered the matter and that he bona fide believes it to be a matter for urgent relief'.

[122] [2006] LSCA 3 (CA) (Steyn P, Grosskopf JA and Nomngcongo J).

[123] Ibid para [8] and the authorities to which the judge referred therein.

[124] [1999] LLR 13 (CA) (Steyn P, Leon and Gauntlett JJA).

[125] Ibid 16.

In the *BP Lesotho* case, the Court of Appeal also emphasised that any delay on the part of the plaintiff in making the application would generally be fatal to the contention that the application was urgent.[126]

4.3.3 Interim interdicts

In *A-G of Lesotho v Swissbourgh Diamond Mines (Pty) Ltd*,[127] the Court of Appeal[128] set out the principles governing the granting of interim interdicts in Lesotho.[129] Steyn JA (giving the judgment of the court) stated:[130]

> 'The requisites for the granting of an interim interdict in South African law is [sic] well known. The seminal judgment in *Setlogelo v. Setlogelo* 1914 AD 221 laid down these requirements in a form adopted by both Appellants' and Respondents' counsel. Erasmus et al points [sic] out in their work *Superior Court Practice* at EB-1.2 that the practice of the South African courts concerning the applicability of "the strength of case" as a threshold test is ambivalent. Indeed, refinements have been made from time to time but the approach as formulated by the Court of Appeal in *Setlogelo* has received consistent endorsement.
>
> In the case of an interlocutory interdict the requirements an Applicant [/plaintiff] must establish can be summarised thus:
>
> 1. A prima facie right;
> 2. a well grounded apprehension of irreparable harm;
> 3. a balance of convenience in favour of the granting of interim relief; and
> 4. the absence of any other satisfactory remedy.
>
> It is also clear that these factors should not be assessed "separately or in isolation" (Erasmus op cit E8-9) but in conjunction with one another ... there can be no doubt as to the overriding discretionary nature of the remedy. Whilst such discretion must always be exercised judicially, no comprehensive strictures can be laid down which can be held to exclude this discretion ... That delay on the part of the applicant [/plaintiff] is a consideration to which regard can be had in exercising the court's discretion is also clear.'[131]

---

[126] On the original application the applicant plaintiff had not disclosed when he became aware of the fact (closure of the respondent's business in Lesotho) allegedly giving rise to the urgency of the application. It subsequently transpired that the plaintiff had known about the fact for six months prior to the application being made.

[127] Appeal 38 of 1994 (CA); [1995–96] LLR & LB 173.

[128] Mahomed P, Steyn, Browde, Kotze and Leon JJA.

[129] Settling authoritatively what had previously been unsettled law: compare the different tests formulated by the same tribunal in *Manong v Manong* [1974–75] LLR 282 (HC), *per* Cotran J at 283F–284B and *Russell v De Freitas* [1974–75] LLR 393 (HC), *per* Cotran ACJ at 396B.

[130] [1995–96] LLR & LB 173 at 182.

[131] *Setlogelo v Setlogelo* 1914 AD 221 (Lord de Villiers CJ, Innes JA and Maasdorp AJA), was a case where an interlocutory application had been made by the plaintiff but the effect of the application was to seek a final interdict (see Lord de Villiers CJ at 226; the application was in substance an application for a *mandament van spolie*). The principles set out in *Setlogelo* are applicable to final interdicts and are that the plaintiff must show (*per* Innes JA at 227): (1) a clear right; (2) injury actually committed or reasonably apprehended; and (3) the

The decision in the *Swissbourgh* case was applied and developed further in *Tsapane v Chaba*,[132] where Lehohla J accepted[133] the submission that the Court of Appeal in *Swissbourgh* had endorsed a threshold test of balance of convenience, 'in the case of interlocutory interdict ... the threshold test has with development of our law shifted from prima facie right that it used to be. The balance of convenience has since been elevated to being the core test.'[134]

In considering whether to grant an interim interdict the court will be astute to examine the nature of the relief claimed on an interim basis to ascertain whether it is in effect final relief rather than interim relief which is sought.[135] In *Wool Wagon (Pty) Ltd v Lesotho National General Insurance Co Ltd*,[136] the plaintiffs made an application for an interdict (rather than seeking an interdict by action using the summons procedure followed by pleadings) ostensibly on an interim basis. The plaintiffs were insured under a material damage policy issued by the defendant. The plaintiffs had submitted claims that had been neither declined nor accepted by the defendant. The plaintiffs sought an order at an interlocutory stage that the defendant make a decision on whether to accept the claims. Hlajoane AJ characterised the application as one by which the plaintiffs sought final relief not interim relief and, applying the test for a final interdict in *Setlogelo*, dismissed the application on the grounds, inter alia, that there was no 'clear right' to a decision on liability[137] and that there was a dispute of fact as to whether the plaintiffs had furnished the required proof to support their claim.[138]

---

absence of similar protection by any other ordinary remedy. The statement of the effect of *Setlogelo* in the Lesotho Court of Appeal in *Swissbourgh* should be read in this context.

132 [2001] LSHC 130 (HC).

133 Ibid 11–12 of the transcript.

134 The *Tsabane* case was followed and applied in the Labour Court of Lesotho in *Mokitimi v Central Bank of Lesotho* LC/23/13; and the *Swissbourgh* case was reaffirmed by the Court of Appeal in *BP Lesotho (Pty) Ltd v Moloi* [2006] LSCA 3 (CA) (Steyn P, Grosskopf JA and Nomngcongo J). The *Swissbourgh* case has recently been applied again by the High Court in *Lemphane Diamond Mine v Minister of Mining* [2022] LSHC 08 (HC) (Mathaba J).

135 As in the *Setlogelo* case itself, see above.

136 [2002] LSCA 63 (HC).

137 On this aspect of the case the judge's reasoning is less than satisfactory: the judge found that there was a 'right to be given a reply of whether to accept or deny liability by the [defendant]'. On the undisputed facts, that right had been infringed by the defendant.

138 Maqutu J reached the same conclusion applying the *Setlogelo* test for a final interdict in *Jiao v Motebang* [2008] LSHC 57 (HC); the *Setlogelo* test has also been applied in the Lesotho Labour Court: *Lesotho Workers Union v Zinyathi Trading (Pty) Ltd* [2013] LSLC 20.

4.3.4 Freezing orders/Anti-dissipation interdicts

In *BP Lesotho (Pty) Ltd v Moloi*,[139] the Court of Appeal recognised the jurisdiction to make a *Mareva* injunction[140] and confirmed the principles on which such an injunction would be granted. Relying on the South African case of *Knox D'Arcy v Jamieson*,[141] the Lesotho Court of Appeal held:[142] 'a [plaintiff] may in an appropriate case, and pending the outcome of an action for damages, bring an interlocutory interdict to restrain a [defendant] from concealing or getting rid of his assets with the intention of defeating the [plaintiff's] claim'.

In *Knox D'Arcy*, EM Grosskopf JA (giving the judgment of the court) stated:[143]

> 'The question which arises from this approach is whether a plaintiff need show a particular state of mind on the part of the [defendant], ie that he is getting rid of the funds, or is likely to do so, with the intention of defeating the claims of creditors. Having regard to the purpose of this type of interdict, the answer must be, I consider, yes, except possibly in exceptional cases. As I have said, the effect of the interdict is to prevent the [defendant] from freely dealing with his own property to which the plaintiff lays no claim. Justice may require this restriction in cases where the [defendant] is shown to be acting mala fide with the intent of preventing execution in respect of the plaintiff's claim. However, there would not normally be any justification to compel a [defendant] to regulate his bona fide expenditure so as to retain funds in his patrimony for the payment of claims (particularly disputed ones) against him. I am not, of course, at the moment dealing with special situations which might arise, for instance, by contract or under the law of insolvency.'

And:[144]

> 'The purpose of the interdict is not to be a substitute for the claim for damages but to reinforce it - to render it more effective. And the question whether the claim is a satisfactory remedy in the absence of an interdict would normally answer itself. Except where the [defendant] is a Croesus, a claim for damages buttressed by an interdict of this sort is always more satisfactory for the plaintiff than one standing on its own feet. The question of an alternative remedy accordingly does not arise in this sort of case. The interdict with which we are dealing is sui generis. It is either available or it is not. No other remedy can really take its place (except, possibly, in certain circumstances attachments or arrests).'

The remedy is *sui generis* and is not an alternative to some other remedy. The plaintiff must therefore show that the defendant is dissipating his assets with a view to defeating the plaintiff's claim in the event the plaintiff succeeds.[145]

---

[139] [2006] LSCA 3 (CA) (Steyn P, Grosskopf JA and Nomngcongo J).

[140] In *Lebelo v Lebelo* [1976] LLR 206 (HC), Mofokeng J (at 209) had described the existence of such a jurisdiction as 'absurd'.

[141] 1996 (4) SA 348 (A) (EM Grosskopf, Nestadt, FH Grosskopf, Harms and Scott JJA).

[142] *BP Lesotho (Pty) Ltd v Moloi* [2006] LSCA 3, para [11].

[143] *Knox D'Arcy Ltd v Jamieson* 1996 (4) SA 348 at 372G–I.

[144] Ibid 373B–E.

[145] A practical and common-sense approach is to be taken to the evidence: *Lagoon Beach Hotel (Pty) Ltd v Lehane* 2016 (3) SA 143 (SCA) (Navsa, Cachalia, Leach, Tshiqi and Willis JJA), *per* Leach JA, giving the judgment of the court, at para [15].

Although EM Grosskopf JA left open the possibility of a *bona fide* transaction amounting to dissipation, the cases where this is capable of proof will be rare, as he appeared to confirm when endorsing a statement in the English Court of Appeal in *Polly Peck International plc v Nadir (No 2)*,[146] to the effect that a freezing order is not intended to alter a defendant's ordinary conduct:[147]

> 'The contention is that the [defendants'] business set-up was such that profits were earned by the Netherlands company. This resulted in money earned in this country being sent overseas, which rendered it likely that there would be no assets to attach in South Africa if a judgment were to be obtained against the respondents. As I stated above, there may be exceptional circumstances in which even a bona fide disposition of assets may be interdicted, but in my view this is not that sort of case. First, this was not the petitioners' [i.e. plaintiffs'] case on the papers. There they pinned their colours to the mast of the intentional secreting of assets. But, in any event, the facts of this case do not require that the [defendants] should be interdicted from dealing with their own assets. The [defendants] have a corporate structure which results in money leaving this country. They adopted this structure for good business reasons and, on the assumption underlying this contention, are using it in good faith for that purpose. No authority in our law has been quoted in support of the petitioners' contention that an interdict may be granted in a case like this, nor could I find any. In English law, which, it would seem, inspired the application in the present case, a *Mareva* injunction would not be available in a case like the present. As was stated in *Polly Peck International plc v Nadir and Others (No 2)* [1992] 4 All ER 769 (CA) at 785g–h:
>
> > "It is not the purpose of a Mareva injunction to prevent a defendant acting as he would have acted in the absence of a claim against him."'

The burden of proof is on the plaintiff to make out the requirements of the order and the standard of proof would seem to be the establishing of a *prima facie* case that the requirements are made out.[148]

A freezing order does not give the plaintiff any priority over the frozen assets in preference to other creditors in insolvency.[149]

On the facts of the *Moloi* case such an interdict was, however, not available because the plaintiff had

> 'failed at the outset to make out a case that he has well-founded claims for damages against the appellant. But of greater importance is his failure to show that the [defendant] was getting rid of its funds and assets, or is likely to do so, with the intention of defeating the claims of [the plaintiff].'[150]

---

146 [1992] 4 All ER 769.

147 *Knox D'Arcy Ltd v Jamieson* 1996 (4) SA 348 at 377A–E.

148 Ibid 373E–H. Although EM Grosskopf JA also seems to have considered (at 378J–379B) that the balance of convenience approach might be applied to this type of application.

149 Ibid 372A–C.

150 *BP Lesotho (Pty) Ltd v Moloi* [2006] LSCA 3 para [11].

The court allowed the bank's appeal and dismissed the plaintiff's application.

The *Moloi* case was followed and applied by Chaka-Makhooane J in *Tigele v Pile Enterprises*,[151] a case involving breaches of company directors' fiduciary duties.

4.3.5 Search and seize orders

There is little reported authority in Lesotho on the question whether the Lesotho courts have jurisdiction to make search and seize orders.

In *The Commissioner of the Lesotho Mounted Police Services v Standard Bank Lesotho Ltd*,[152] the court was concerned with the question whether it had power to make an order that the respondents to the Commissioner's application (three of whom were banks) hand over to the police the originals of 'all bank records in their possession' relating to the fourth respondent company. The application was made under the legislation that limited such disclosure to specified types of documents[153] and under the inherent jurisdiction of the court. The court rejected the application both because the order sought was wider than the statutory provision relied on and also on the basis that the exercise of the court's inherent jurisdiction did not empower the court to make substantive law. On the question of the court's inherent jurisdiction, the judge set out, with apparent approval, submissions by counsel for the banks, inter alia, that the South African courts had held that the court had no power to make an *Anton Piller* order.[154]

Later, in *Mahlakeng v Southern Sky (Pty) Ltd*,[155] the plaintiffs contended that they had brought the application on an urgent basis 'because of the existence of some real and well-founded apprehension that the [defendant] would destroy their evidence before trial'. In disposing of this contention, the court stated that the South African case of *Eiser v Vuna Health Care (Pty) Ltd*[156] 'explains instances of granting *Anton Piller* orders whose main purpose is to preserve evidence to be used'. Although the point was not expressly made, it appears reasonably clear that the judge found that the plaintiffs' contention failed because it did not fall within the recognised scope of an *Anton Piller* order and not because the court had no power to make such an order.

---

[151] [2010] LSHC 15 (HC).

[152] [2000] LSHC 2 (HC) (Cullinan AJ).

[153] The relevant legislation, the Criminal Procedure and Evidence Act (Act 9 of 1981), s 247(2), refers only to 'bank ledgers, day-books, cash-books or other account books' (derived from the definition of 'banker's books' in the United Kingdom Bankers Books Evidence Act 1879).

[154] The South African authority of *Cerebos Food Corp v Diverse Foods SA* 1984 (4) SA 149 (T) was relied on for this proposition (Transvaal Provincial Division) (Boshoff JP and Dijkhorst and O'Donovan JJ). However, the law in South Africa had, in this respect, moved on: see *Shoba v Officer Commanding, Temporary Police Camp, Wagendrift Dam; Maphanga v Officer Commanding, SA Police Murder & Robbery Unit, Pietermaritzburg* 1995 (4) SA 1 (A) (Corbett CJ, EM Grosskopf, Nestadt and Steyn JJA and Nicholas AJA). The reader is referred to the discussion of these authorities in the chapter on the Republic of South Africa.

[155] [2003] LSHC 79 (HC) (Hlajoane J).

[156] 1998 (3) SA 139 (W), Witwatersrand Local Division) (Wunsh J).

In *Eiser v Vuna Health Care (Pty) Ltd* itself,[157] the judge followed the South African Appellate Division decision in *Shoba v Officer Commanding, Temporary Police Camp, Wagendrift Dam; Maphanga v Officer Commanding, SA Police Murder & Robbery Unit, Pietermaritzburg*[158] in concluding that *Anton Piller* relief was available. In view of these developments in South African law since the decision in *The Commissioner of the Lesotho Mounted Police Services v Standard Bank Lesotho Ltd*,[159] which confirm the jurisdiction of the South African courts to make an *Anton Piller* order, it is likely that a Lesotho court would prefer the approach of Hlajoane J in the *Mahlakeng* case to that of Cullinan AJ in the *Standard Bank* case and make an *Anton Piller* order in an appropriate case.

In *Shoba*, Corbett CJ (giving the judgment of the court) held:[160]

> 'At this point it is necessary to give a decision in regard to what was left open in both the Universal City Studios case supra and Jafta's case supra, viz whether an *Anton Piller* order directed at the preservation of evidence should be accepted as part of our practice. In my view, it should; and I would define what a [plaintiff] plaintiff for such an order, obtained in camera and without notice to the [defendant], must prima facie establish, as the following:
>
> (1) That he, the [plaintiff], has a cause of action against the [defendant] which he intends to pursue;
>
> (2) that the [defendant] has in his possession specific (and specified) documents or things which constitute vital evidence in substantiation of [plaintiff's] cause of action (but in respect of which the [plaintiff] cannot claim a real or personal right); and
>
> (3) that there is a real and well-founded apprehension that this evidence may be hidden or destroyed or in some manner be spirited away by the time the case comes to trial or to the stage of discovery.'[161]

---

[157] Ibid.

[158] 1995 (4) SA 1 (A) (Corbett CJ, EM Grosskopf, Nestadt and Steyn JJA and Nicholas AJA). See 15G and 18B–C.

[159] [2000] LSHC 2 (HC) (Cullinan AJ).

[160] 1995 (4) SA 1 (A) 15F–J, following the acceptance of the practice obiter in *Universal City Studios Inc v Network Video (Pty) Ltd* 1986 (2) SA 734 (A), *per* Corbett JA (as he then was) 755A–C. The principles set out in *Shoba* are the settled principles on which a search and seize order is made in the Republic of South Africa: *Viziya Corp v Collaborit Holdings (Pty) Ltd* 2019 (3) SA 173 (SCA) (Wallis, Saldulker, Mathopo and Van der Merwe JJA and Rogers AJA, *per* Mathopo, giving the judgment of the court), at para [22]. For a full account of the principles which a South African court will apply when deciding whether to grant this type of relief, the reader is referred to the chapter on the Republic of South Africa.

[161] Applying these principles to the facts, Corbett CJ held (ibid 21F–H): 'As to the factual merits, it seems to me that the [plaintiff] established (i) a strong *prima facie* case of having been assaulted and tortured while in police custody; (ii) that he intended to pursue against the second [defendant] a civil action arising from such assault and torture; (iii) that, if it existed, the torture apparatus would be vital evidence in such a civil action; and that there was a real and well-founded apprehension that such apparatus, if it existed, would be hidden or destroyed before the matter came to trial. This was hardly in dispute. In my opinion, the Court *a quo* should, therefore, have granted an *Anton Piller* order in this case.'

As regards the requirement that the evidence at which the order is directed should be 'vital evidence', Corbett CJ stated:[162] 'I have used the words "vital evidence" in the sense of being evidence of great importance to the [plaintiff's] case.'

4.3.6 Third-party disclosure orders

There appears to be no reported judicial authority in which a Lesotho court has made an order requiring a third party to give information or documents prior to the commencement of proceedings.

The position in South Africa is as set out below and it is to be supposed that this will be influential in the future development of Lesotho law.

In *Kinekor Films (Pty) Ltd v B A Adami Films (Pty) Ltd*,[163] allowing the plaintiff's appeal, the court made an order compelling the defendant to disclose the identity of the source of the films in its possession of which the plaintiff was the copyright owner, with a view to the plaintiff bringing proceedings against those persons. Giving the judgment of the full bench of the Eastern Cape Division, Eksteen J held[164] that it was

> 'clear that the person or persons from whom the [respondent] had obtained the infringing copies of the films were, in the same way, infringing the [plaintiffs] copyright by supplying such films to the respondent, and that the [plaintiff] would therefore, *prima facie*, have a cause of action against such suppliers. Such an action however cannot be brought unless the [plaintiff] knows who the person or persons are who are acting in breach of its copyright. It says that it does not know who these persons are, and the obvious place to seek this information is from the [defendant] who must be aware of their identity. To deny the [plaintiff] the relief it seeks would in my view not be in the interests of justice but would rather afford an unwarranted protection of the infringers of the [plaintiff's] copyright in the pursuit of their illegal activity.'

In *Roamer Watch Co SA v African Textile Distributors*,[165] Cilliers AJ drew a distinction[166] between two types of disclosure cases: first, those where

> 'the [plaintiff] seeks to proceed against an unincorporated body or the officials of an unincorporated or incorporated body, and seeks disclosure of the names of the appropriate persons to cite from another person who is possessed of this information by virtue of his being an official of that body or standing in some other similar relation to that body';

and second,[167] those where the plaintiff 'is concerned to obtain the name of a party whom he is unable to identify and against whom he may have a cause of action'.

---

162 Ibid 15J–16B.
163 1976 (4) SA 935 (E) (Eksteen, Kannemeyer and De Wet JJ).
164 Ibid 939G–J.
165 1980 (2) SA 254 (W).
166 Ibid 281F–G.
167 Ibid 281H–I.

In the latter situation, the plaintiff is seeking discovery of the name from a party who may have sound commercial or other reasons for being reluctant to disclose it. Cilliers AJ stated[168] that in the second case the plaintiff would need to indicate at least the following in the papers filed for hearing:

(1) A *bona fide* belief in his right of action against the party whose name he seeks to be disclosed and that he has reasonable grounds for believing that he has such a claim against such party. Here the strength of the plaintiff's case against the unknown alleged wrongdoer is relevant to the exercise of the court's discretion.

(2) There is no other complete remedy. Another appropriate remedy may consist either of an adequate claim against a party who is known to him in respect of the same damages which the plaintiff claims to have suffered, or in another procedural remedy to establish the same information which he seeks from the respondent.

(3) The defendant is able to supply such information.

In *Cerebos Food Corp v Diverse Foods SA (Pty) Ltd*,[169] giving the judgment of the full bench of the Transvaal Provincial Division, Van Dijkhorst J held that[170] 'neither in the Roman law nor the Roman-Dutch law nor in our law as laid down by the Appellate Division is there any authority for an order that a defendant disclose the names or particulars of sources and retail outlets'.

However, the court in the *Cerebos Food* case also held[171] that South African courts had no jurisdiction to make *Anton Piller* orders (defined by the court as[172] 'orders for the attachment of documents and other things can be granted where no right is claimed to them except that they should be preserved and produced as evidence in an intended Court action'). However, the Appellate Division in *Shoba v Officer Commanding, Temporary Police Camp, Wagendrift Dam; Maphanga v Officer Commanding, SA Police Murder & Robbery Unit, Pietermaritzburg*,[173] subsequently held this decision to have been wrong. The authority of the *Cerebos Food* case on ancillary orders and disclosure orders must therefore be doubted.[174] Indeed,

---

168 Ibid 282A–D.

169 1984 (4) SA 149 (T) (Boshoff JP and Van Dijkhorst and O'Donovan JJ).

170 Ibid 168A–B.

171 See the passages at 170H–I and 173E–F.

172 Ibid 168B–C.

173 1995 (4) SA 1 (A) (Corbett CJ, EM Grosskopf, Nestadt, and Steyn JJA and Nicholas AJA).

174 In addition, the decision in *Roamer Watch Co SA v African Textile Distributors* 1980 (2) SA 254 (W) appears not to have been cited to the court in *Cerebos Food*. Further the Appellate Division assumed, without deciding the question, that a court may order a non-party to furnish information required by the applicant for the purpose of litigation: *Krygkor Pensioenfonds v Smith* 1993 (3) SA 459 (A), where a divorcee was entitled to part of her former husband's pension; he refused to pay her and she applied, inter alia, for an order requiring the pension fund to inform her as to her husband's pension. The Appellate Division held (at 462A–B):

this was seemingly confirmed by the Gauteng Local Division in *Nampak Glass (Pty) Ltd v Vodacom (Pty) Ltd*,[175] where the court held that *Norwich Pharmacal* relief should be recognised and that doing so was 'an appropriate development ... and the requirements of English law, suitably adapted, serve well enough to provide an effective remedy'.[176]

The better view, therefore, is that the Lesotho court has power to make an order requiring a third party to disclose the identity of a wrongdoer.[177]

4.3.7 Anti-suit interdicts (injunctions)

An anti-suit interdict (injunction) is an order restraining the injunction defendant from either commencing or continuing proceedings outside Lesotho in breach of a legal or equitable right on the part of the injunction plaintiff not to pursue litigation outside Lesotho or, conversely, restraining the injunction defendant from commencing or continuing proceedings inside Lesotho in breach of a legal or equitable right on the part of the injunction plaintiff to have the dispute between the parties litigated in a jurisdiction other than Lesotho.[178]

'The Appellate Division had authoritatively affirmed that it was entitled to adapt its procedures in the interests of justice; that it could be accepted for the purposes of the present case (without so deciding) that a Court in appropriate circumstances had the jurisdiction to order a party against whom an applicant had no cause of action and who was not a party or intended party to litigation with the applicant, to supply the required information.' This goes further than previous authority in this area by extending the range of disclosure from the identity of a wrongdoer to 'information' generally. Referring to both documents and information, Wunsh J in *Eiser v Vuna Health Care (Pty) Ltd* 1998 (3) SA 139 (W), stated (at 148A–B): 'Our Courts have an inherent jurisdiction to come to the assistance of a litigant who, before proceedings are instituted, requires information from a third party, which is sparingly exercised (*Krygkor Pensioenfonds v Smith* 1993 (3) SA 459 (A)) and there are a few instances where a would-be opponent has been ordered to disclose documents before the institution of proceedings as in *Durban and District African Football Association v Dhludhla & Others* 1961 (3) SA 892 (D).'

[175] 2019 (1) SA 257 (GJ) (Unterhalter J).

[176] At para 20. In practice this form of order, requiring disclosure of identity or information to assist a prospective plaintiff, had been made by the courts: *BL v FL* 2015 (4) SA 271 (FB), Tsatsi AG, where an order was made against a husband's pension administrator requiring disclosure of financial information so that his former wife could ascertain whether the husband had complied with the court order dealing with their divorce which had made provision for 50% of the husband's pension to be paid to her.

[177] The authorities cited in this section predate the enactment of s 32 of the Constitution of the Republic of South Africa, 1996, which provision appears to confirm that courts in the Republic of South Africa have the jurisdiction to make third-party disclosure orders.

[178] In a similar vein, an anti-anti-suit injunction is an order restraining the injunction defendant from commencing or continuing proceedings to restrain the injunction plaintiff from applying to restrain the injunction defendant from commencing or continuing proceedings. The leading works on this topic are: Raphael *The Anti-Suit Injunction* 2 ed (2019) and Briggs *Civil Jurisdiction and Judgments* 7 ed (2021), ch 28. It is also conceptually possible to obtain similar relief in the context of arbitration but such relief is outside the scope of this work.

There is no reported judicial authority in Lesotho on whether or not an anti-suit interdict is a remedy available to the courts in Lesotho. That said, the courts of Ghana,[179] Nigeria[180] and, crucially, for present purposes, the Republic of South Africa[181] have concluded that this form of relief is available in those jurisdictions. Given the affinity which exists between the legal systems in place in Lesotho and the Republic of South Africa, it is likely that the Lesotho courts will be guided by the approach which the South African courts take with respect to this relief.[182]

4.3.8 *Mandament van spolie*

A spoliation order[183] is an order whereby a person who has unlawfully deprived another person of possession of a thing is ordered to restore that person to possession of that thing. As the Lesotho Court of Appeal[184] has recently stated, the 'justification underlying the grant of a *mandament van spolie* is that no person is entitled to take the law into his own hands'. The remedy is a summary remedy and the person who dispossessed another cannot defend the application by contending that the person who was dispossessed was not entitled to be in possession of the thing in the first place.

What is clear from the reported case law[185] is that the Lesotho courts pay very close attention to the way in which the South African courts have developed and applied the principles underpinning this particular remedy. Hence, the application for a spoliation order is usually made *ex parte* and the plaintiff needs to

179 *Quantum Oil Terminals Ltd v International Finance Corp* Suit No: Misc/00228/17 (unreported) 8 January 2018 and 23 February 2018 (H Ct) (Asiedu J).

180 *United Bank for Africa Plc v Coker* (1996) 4 NWLR 239 (CA) (Muhammad, Ayoola and Pats-Acholonu JJCA).

181 *Vedanta Resources Holdings Ltd v ZCCM Investment Holdings plc* 2019 JDR 1425 (GJ) (Adams J).

182 For further guidance on the principles which a South African court would apply when asked to grant an anti-suit interdict, the reader is referred to the relevant section of the chapter on the Republic of South Africa.

183 Peté et al *Civil Procedure* 2 ed (2011) 423–5.

184 *Chen Zheng Hong v Gu Kingxin* [2020] LSCA 44 (SC) (Mosito P, Chinhengo and Van Der Westhuizen AJJA).

185 See, *inter alia*, *Commissioner of Sales Tax v Magistrate's Berea (Mr Murenzi)* [2001] LSCA 57 (HC) (Monapathi J); *Kolobe v Hoohlo* [2004] LSHC 23; *Lefeta v Mafereka* [1995] LSCA 22 (HC) (Maqutu J); *Khororo v Tanki Fiee* (1982-1984) LLR 215 (Mofokeng J).

prove on the balance of probabilities that: (1) he was in peaceful and undisturbed possession of the thing;[186] and (2) he was forcibly dispossessed of that thing.[187]

Ordinarily, of course, the plaintiff will ask the court to make a spoliation order against the defendant because the defendant dispossessed the plaintiff of the property in question. However, in *Chen Zheng Hong v Gu Kingxin*,[188] the Lesotho Court of Appeal held, obiter, but correctly it is submitted, that the plaintiff 'need not … as part of his case prove [the defendant] had acquired possession of the property'. South African decisions[189] dealing with termination of access to a company email server and access to a flow of water demonstrate the accuracy of this proposition.

However, it is submitted that the Lesotho Court of Appeal's obiter statement in *Chen Zheng Hong* cannot be elevated to a general statement of the law governing spoilation orders, not least because the South African authorities which support the proposition are concerned with the 'exercise of actions usually flowing from servitudes'.[190] In *Chen Zheng Hong* itself, the plaintiff was a director of the third defendant company. The plaintiff fell out with the other directors (the first and second defendants) and the defendants suspended the plaintiff from office and despoiled him of access to the office rooms he was using. The Court of Appeal upheld the High Court's decision to grant a spoliation order in these circumstances. It is submitted that the Court of Appeal's conclusion on the facts is understandable, in that it ensured that the question whether the plaintiff had a right to possession of the office was determined later on in time, obviating

[186] The plaintiff need not show that he was entitled to possession nor that his possession was lawful. He need only show that he was in de facto possession: *Zulu v Minister of Works KwaZulu* 1992 (1) SA 181 (D), *per* Thirion J at 187E–H: 'The *mandament van spolie* is a possessory remedy by which a person who has been illicitly deprived of his possession is restored to his possession before the merits of the dispute regarding the lawfulness of his possession are enquired into. An applicant [ie the plaintiff] for a spoliation order has to prove that he had possession ... *mandament van spolie* is not concerned with the protection or restoration of rights at all. Its aim is to restore the factual possession of which the *spoliatus* has been unlawfully deprived. The question of the lawfulness of the spoliatus' possession is not enquired into at all.' In that case, a Zulu prince failed to succeed in obtaining a spoliation order in respect of a supply of water to his property that had been cut off by the water company. (Although incorporeal rights may be the subject of a spoliation order: *Nienaber v Stuckey* 1946 AD 1049 (Greenberg and Schreiner JJA and Davis AJA), *per* Greenberg JA at 1056–7, giving the example of servitutal rights of way, where the holder does not have exclusive possession of the land, but can obtain relief against dispossession by spoliation.)

[187] For a comprehensive survey of the principles applied by courts in the Republic of South Africa when dealing with applications for spoilation orders, the reader is referred to the relevant section in the chapter on the Republic of South Africa.

[188] [2020] LSCA 44 (SC).

[189] See, by way of example, *Blendrite v Moonisami* 2021 (5) SA 61 (SCA) (Navsa, Mocumie and Dlodlo JJA and Gorven and Ledwaba AJJA), *per* Gorven AJA, giving the judgment of the court, at paras [10]–[16] and the authorities cited therein.

[190] Ibid para [10] and, outside that context, it can be a defence to a spoilation application to show that the property is no longer in the hands of the defendant: *Monteiro v Diedricks* 2021 (3) SA 482 (SCA) (Dambuza, Schippers and Plasket JJA and Goosen and Mabindla-Boqwana AJJA).

the need for the plaintiff to take matters into his own hands in the interim. Yet, it is not clear that the language in which the Court of Appeal couched its obiter statement was entirely apposite given the facts of the case before it and it is equally unclear that the conclusion reached is supportable by reference to the aforementioned South African authorities.

Where the court grants a spoilation order, it will restore possession – ie return matters to the *status quo ante*. It will then hear the competing claims as to entitlement to possession, before deciding which party has the better right to possess the property in question.

Finally, in the South African case of *Outdoor Network v The Passenger Rail Agency of South Africa*,[191] the court considered an application for a final interdict to restrain threatened spoliation. The plaintiffs were lessees of land from the defendants for the purpose of placing advertising billboards on that land. The defendants terminated the leases and threatened to remove the plaintiff's structures. The plaintiffs claimed that they had a right to possession that was in immediate risk of being interfered with. Boruchowitz J rejected the application finding that the plaintiff did not satisfy the criteria for a final interdict set out in *Setlogelo v Setlogelo*[192] and in the course of doing so stated:[193]

> '23 Where the *mandament van spolie* is relied on, the possession which must be proved is not possession in the juridical sense; it is enough if the holding by the applicant [ie the plaintiff] is with the intention of securing some benefit for himself. The lawfulness or injustice of the possession is irrelevant. Thus, even a thief or robber is entitled to avail himself of the *mandament*. Also, a lessee who is deprived of the use of and enjoyment of premises is entitled to invoke the *mandament* to have the use and enjoyment restored to him even though he is not a possessor in the juristic sense.
>
> 24 If mere factual possession, irrespective of how it was obtained, was sufficient to establish a clear right, even a thief or mala fide possessor would be entitled to obtain a final interdict. There can be no justification for the protection by means of an interdict of illicitly or illegally obtained possession.
>
> 25 The *mandament van spolie* cannot be invoked to prohibit a threatened spoliation; it is only available to a de facto possessor who has been despoiled ...'.

The plaintiffs could not show a clear right that was about to be infringed and thus did not satisfy the first criterion in the *Setlogelo* case. Neither could the plaintiffs show that they had been dispossessed and thus a spoliation order was not available to them. In light of what has been said above about the highly persuasive nature of South African authorities on this subject in Lesotho, it is to be expected that the Lesotho courts would follow this decision if presented with the same facts.

[191] Case 2013/26064 (unreported) 30 May 2014 (Gauteng Local Division).

[192] 1914 AD 221.

[193] Ibid paras [23]–[25] of the judgment.

4.3.9 Arrest of individuals *tanquam suspectus de fuga*

In *Mahmood v Zakhura Brothers (Pty) Ltd*,[194] the High Court considered the nature of this relief and concluded:[195]

> 'It is a relief available to a creditor who on reasonable grounds suspects that a debtor against whom he has instituted an action or intends instituting action for the recovery of the debt, is about to [flee] from the jurisdiction of the court in order to escape responsibility for the debt. (Herbstein and Van Winsen: the Civil Practice of the High Courts of South Africa, 3rd edition p113). It is available at common Law as well under statute.'

Rule 7 of the Lesotho High Court Rules makes provision for arrest of the person *tanquam suspectus de fuga*. The person seeking the arrest of a (putative) defendant must submit a writ of arrest[196] to the Registrar of the High Court for his signature.

The draft writ of arrest must be accompanied by an affidavit made by the plaintiff or his agent from his personal knowledge that must set out, inter alia: the cause of action; that the defendant is indebted to the plaintiff (or that the plaintiff has suffered damage as a result of the defendant's acts); that the plaintiff has insufficient security for the debt (or damages); that the deponent believes that the defendant is about to or is making preparations to depart from Lesotho, setting out the grounds for that belief.

On his arrest (or thereafter) the defendant is entitled to give the sheriff adequate security by bond or obligation and the sheriff shall permit the defendant to go free.

If the defendant does not satisfy the plaintiff's claim or provide adequate security, the plaintiff may on the return day for the writ of arrest apply for confirmation of the arrest and the court may, 'unless sufficient cause to the contrary is shown', order the return of the defendant to prison.

Sub-rule (15) provides that if judgment is ultimately given against the defendant then he shall be 'entitled to his release and discharge from such arrest'.

In *Mahmood*,[197] the High Court was required to consider the effect of an equivalent provision to rule 7 of the Lesotho High Court Rules in section 18 of the Subordinate Courts Act 1988,[198] which made provision for the arrest of

---

194 [2020] LSHC 2 (HC) (Banyane AJ).

195 Ibid para [21].

196 Rule 7(2) specifies that the writ should be in accordance with Form F, Sch 1 to the Rules, which commands the sheriff to arrest the defendant and bring him before the court on a specified day 'and to abide the judgment of the Court ... or to show cause why he should not be ordered to abide the judgment of the Court or furnish security for his further presence within its jurisdiction until its judgment has been delivered ...or failing the due provision of such security why he should not be committed to prison and detained pending the judgment of this Court ...'.

197 [2020] LSHC 2 (HC).

198 Act 9 of 1988; s 18 to be read in conjunction with r 54 of the Subordinate Courts Rules 1996.

a defendant *tanquam suspectus de fuga*. In the course of the judgment, Banyane AJ made reference[199] to the decision of the South African Constitutional Court in *Malachi v Cape Dance Academy International (Pty) Ltd*,[200] and endorsed the comments of Mogoeng J (giving the judgment of the court), who stated:[201] 'The object of the arrest "is to ensure that [the potential debtor] remains within the jurisdiction of the court until the court has given judgment in the matter."'

However, in *Mahmood*, Banyane AJ did not comment on the fact that the South African Constitutional Court in *Malachi* abolished arrest *tanquam suspectus de fuga* in the Republic of South Africa. The absence of such comment was likely because the constitutionality of this relief as a matter of Lesotho law was not argued before the High Court. Hence, there is nothing in the judgment in *Mahmood* which gives the impression that arrest of a defendant *tanquam suspectus de fuga* is unconstitutional and so unavailable in Lesotho.

Even so, given the close affinity between the law of the Republic of South Africa and the law in Lesotho, it is worth setting out the reasoning of the judgment of the Constitutional Court in *Malachi*, if only so as to stimulate debate of the question as to whether this form of relief is, in fact, unconstitutional in Lesotho. Hence, in so far as relevant, Mogoeng J held:

> '[32] The object of the arrest "is to ensure that [the potential debtor] remains within the jurisdiction of the court until the court has given judgment in the matter." As soon as judgment is given, a debtor would, however, be free to catch the next flight to any foreign destination even if this is done to evade payment and no realisable asset exists in the country, from the proceeds of which payment may be effected. Arrest does not, therefore, ensure the satisfaction of the judgment debt. Admittedly, the unfairly exerted pressure of incarceration may at times force the arrestee to pay the debt or provide security. But, that does not detract from the fact that the arrest does not necessarily render the judgment any more executable or beneficial to the creditor than would have been the case had the debtor left the country. It simply limits the fundamental right to freedom of the person for no just reason.
>
> [33] The order for the arrest of persons *tanquam suspectus de fuga* under the impugned provisions is ordinarily made at the time when their civil liability has not yet been established. Their debt is only alleged on affidavit, often in an urgent application brought ex parte. The potential debtor is often only afforded the opportunity to resist the severe curtailment of the right to freedom, by the order, on the return date. Potentially the detention may endure for as long as the action is pending. The effect of this deprivation was more aptly captured in *Segal v Diners Club South Africa* where we are warned that "[i]f the debtor has been wrongly deprived of his

---

199 [2020] LSHC 2 (HC), para [23].

200 2010 (6) SA 1 (CC) (Ngcobo CJ, Moseneke DCJ, Cameron, Froneman, Jafta, Khampepe, Nkabinde, Skweyiya, Van der Westhuizen, Yacoob and Mogoeng JJ).

201 Ibid para [32].

> freedom it cannot be put right in the subsequent suit. The harm is irreparable." Nothing can undo the degrading effect of incarceration, particularly if the order were [sic] obtained *ex parte*. This is the position in which the plaintiff in this matter found herself for 16 days.
>
> [34] Since there is no legal basis for the imprisonment of someone who has been found civilly liable, it is inconceivable that any legal justification can ever exist for putting behind bars a person whose civil liability is yet to, or will possibly never, be proven. Although an order for arrest is granted by a court, the intervention of the judicial process cannot legitimise the deprivation of freedom, since the arrest may stem from a debt which has itself not been established through the judicial process. I therefore conclude that there is no just cause for the arrest in terms of the impugned provisions.'

It remains to be seen whether the courts of Lesotho would follow the approach of the South African Constitutional Court, were they asked to do so.

Chapter 5

LIBERIA

The Republic of Liberia emerged out of the settlement of large numbers of freed and free-born African Americans between about 1822 and 1847 in the area that became known as Liberia.[1] Uniquely in the colonial history of Africa, Liberia itself peaceably declared its independence, on 26 July 1847. The first President of Liberia, Joseph Jenkins Roberts, was a wealthy free-born African American from Virginia. The African American settlers of Liberia brought with them American

[1] This movement of African Americans was primarily at the instigation of an organisation called 'The Society for the Colonization of Free People of Color of America', founded in 1816 ('the American Colonization Society'; 'the ACS'). The ACS was a peculiar alliance between American slave-owning interests and American abolitionists who shared an interest in removing freed and free-born African Americans from the USA to Africa. In the former case, this was because the increase in the number of freed and free-born African Americans at the time was considered a threat to the institution of slavery. In the latter case, because abolitionists believed the life chances of African Americans would be greater outside the USA than inside.

influences, including a republican constitution bearing strong similarities to that of the United States of America.

In view of the historical background of Liberia, it is unsurprising that, again uniquely for an African nation, Liberia's laws have a strong affinity with United States Federal law principles.

5.1 Jurisdiction

The Liberian Civil Procedure Law 1972 ('the CPL') contains the relevant provisions that regulate civil jurisdiction in Liberia.

Paragraph 1.1 of the CPL provides:

> '§ 1.1. Application of Civil Procedure Law.
>
> The Civil Procedure Law shall govern the procedure in all civil actions and special proceedings before all judges and in all courts in the judicial branch of the Government, except where the procedure is regulated by inconsistent statutes or rules adopted in conformity therewith.'

The CPL comprises, therefore, an overarching code governing procedure in all civil actions in Liberia.

The root of the jurisdiction of the Liberian courts is service of process on the defendant. As long ago as 1908 the Liberian Supreme Court held in *Maurice v Diggs*:[2]

> 'If the judgment or decree of a court were rendered against one without summons or warning of the suit, both personal and real property would truly be insecure and innumerable evils created in communities. For this reason a judgment or decree is not only voidable but void where there is want of jurisdiction over subject matter or over the parties to the action or some of them. A court in pronouncing a judgment or decree in such cases acts without jurisdiction if there is want of jurisdiction over the parties, in that regular process has not been served upon them thereby bringing them within the jurisdiction of the court.'

Chapter 3 of the CPL concerns the commencement of actions and jurisdiction.

5.1.1 Service where the defendant is within the jurisdiction

Paragraphs 3.31–33 provide that a civil action is commenced by filing a complaint or petition with the clerk of the court; once the complaint is filed, the clerk must

[2] (1908) 2 LLR 3 at 4–5. Cited with approval and followed in *Tubman v Murdoch* (1934) 4 LLR 179, *per* Grimes CJ at 183–4, where the judge stated, 'This principle, so settled by our own Supreme Court twenty-six years ago, is so much in harmony with the rule in vogue in all other jurisdictions the decisions of which are available to us, that we could well refrain from citing other authority.' The decision in *Tubman v Murdoch* was itself cited with approval and followed by Pierre CJ in *Seton v Azango* (1971) 20 LLR 674 at 675–6.

issue a writ of summons at once; the summons is directed at the ministerial officer of the court in which the action is brought and must contain the details of the parties' names and addresses, the time within which the defendant must appear and defend and various other instructions.

Paragraph 3.37 provides: 'All process of courts of record may be served anywhere within the Republic of Liberia', and that service within Liberia but outside the issuing court's county must be effected by the ministerial officer of the court of the county, district or territory where the person to be served is located.

Paragraph 3.38 contains provisions concerning the manner of personal service.

Personal service on a natural person must be made, inter alia, 'by reading and delivering'[3] the summons to the person to be served or a person designated by the person to be served as his agent for service in writing, provided certain conditions of registering that agent have been satisfied.

A partnership must be served 'by reading and personally delivering' the summons within Liberia to: any partner; an agent for service (registered in the same way as with an individual); or if the partnership is under suit under a common name, reading and personally delivering the summons within Liberia to an officer or general or managing agent.

Service on an unincorporated association in a suit against it in its common name is effected 'by reading and personally delivering' the summons within Liberia to an officer or general or managing agent or agent registered to accept service.

Service within Liberia on a domestic or foreign corporation must be effected 'by reading and personally delivering' the summons to an officer or general or managing agent or to any other agent authorised by appointment or by statute to received service of process.

Further provision is made for service on foreign corporations by the Associations Law 1977, by which[4] a foreign corporation authorised to do business in Liberia must designate a registered agent in Liberia upon whom process against the corporation may be served. The manner of service is that provided by the CPL.[5] Where the foreign corporation fails to register or maintain an agent in Liberia or where the agent resigns or the foreign corporation is not authorised to do business in Liberia, the Minister of Foreign Affairs of Liberia is deemed to be the agent of the corporation for the purposes of service of process.[6]

---

[3] Although the rules are silent on the point and although there seems to be no authority on the question, it is thought that notifying the person to whom the summons is delivered that what is being delivered is a summons is sufficient. It would be too much to expect the defendant passively to wait as the ministerial officer reads out the contents of the summons.

[4] § 3.1.

[5] § 3.2.

[6] §§ 3.2 and 3.3.

5.1.2 Service where the defendant is outside the jurisdiction

5.1.2.1 *Procedure*

Paragraph 3.39 makes provision for service outside the jurisdiction:

> 'The following persons may be served with summons outside Liberia in the same manner as if such service were made within Liberia and with the same jurisdictional effect as if the summons were delivered within Liberia:
>
> *(a)* A person domiciled in Liberia;
>
> *(b)* A person subject to the jurisdiction of the courts of Liberia under sections 3.1, 3.2, or 3.3 of this title.
>
> Such service outside Liberia may be made by a ministerial officer of a court in the jurisdiction where service is made or by any attorney, solicitor, barrister, or equivalent who is duly qualified to serve a summons in such jurisdiction.'

Although paragraph 3.39 is unclear on the point, it is likely that service outside the jurisdiction must be effected as personal service: a person may be served in 'the same manner' as if service were within Liberia, that is, personal service.

5.1.2.2 *Bases for service out of the jurisdiction*

Paragraph 3.39 does not expressly reserve to the court a residuary discretion whether to permit service out of the jurisdiction notwithstanding that the requirements of sub-paragraphs (a) or (b) have been satisfied. The wording of paragraph 3.39 suggests that service out of the jurisdiction is as of right.

Paragraph 3.39 therefore permits service out of the jurisdiction in four sets of circumstances, which are set out below. Added to these are the provisions of paragraph 12.9 of the Associations Law 1977, which sets out a number of additional heads of jurisdiction and these additional heads are set out below as the fifth set of circumstances.

Circumstance (1): where the defendant is domiciled in Liberia

The CPL does not appear to contain a definition of 'domicile', and it is thought that Liberian law would follow the well-established common-law understanding in defining domicile as follows:[7]

> 'The notion which lies at the root of the concept of domicile is that of permanent home. "By domicile we mean home, the permanent home; and if you do not understand your permanent home I am afraid that no illustration drawn from foreign writers or foreign languages will very much help you to it." A person may be said to have his home

[7] *Dicey, Morris and Collins on the Conflict of Laws* 15 ed (2012) vol 1, r 4, para 6-004; quoting from *Whicker v Hume* (1858) 7 HLC 124, 160. United States law is to similar effect: *Merriam-Webster Legal Dictionary* defines 'domicile' as, 'a person's fixed, permanent and principal home for legal purposes'.

> in a country if he resides in it without any intention of at present removing from it permanently or for an indefinite period. But a person does not cease to have his home in a country merely because he is temporarily resident elsewhere; and a person who has formed the intention of leaving a country does not cease to have his home in it until he acts according to that intention.'

The 'domicile' of a legal person has been described as follows:[8]

> 'A corporation is domiciled where it is registered, if the law requires it to be registered, and if it does not it is domiciled in the country by whose law it is incorporated (Dicey, *Conflict of Laws*, 7th ed., p. 477). A corporation is 'resident' and 'ordinarily resident' where its central management and control is exercised'.

The term '*ordinarily resident*' has been explained as follows:[9]

> 'It has sometimes been said that "ordinary residence" means nothing more or less than "residence", but it is submitted that the better view is that the adjective does add something, an element of continuity, order, or settled purpose.'

Circumstance (2): paragraph 3.1 of the CPL

Paragraph 3.1 of the CPL provides:

> '§ 3.1: Personal jurisdiction over nondomiciliary who has been in Liberia.
>
> A nondomiciliary who has been in Liberia shall be subject to the jurisdiction of Liberian courts in the same manner as if he were a domiciliary of Liberia.'

The meaning of this provision is unclear. The phrase 'nondomiciliary who has been in Liberia', might be taken literally to mean, 'a person who does not have a permanent home in Liberia but who at any point in the past was present in Liberia' is subject to the jurisdiction of the Liberian courts.

However, it is thought that this cannot be what is intended by paragraph 3.1. If it were, it would mean, for example, that a French businessman who visited Liberia in his youth will be potentially subject to the jurisdiction of the Liberian courts until his death (and possibly after).

A more coherent construction would be that a person present in Liberia at the time the matters with which the proceedings are concerned arose is subject to the jurisdiction of the Liberian courts where that person is no longer within the jurisdiction.

---

[8] English Rules of the Supreme Court, 1883 (1960 ed) 145. The same meaning followed through to the 1965 Rules of the Supreme Court.

[9] *Dicey, Morris and Collins on the Conflict of Laws* 15 ed (2012) vol 1, para 6-160.

Circumstance (3): paragraph 3.2 of the CPL

Paragraph 3.2 of the CPL provides:

> '§ 3.2. Personal jurisdiction over nondomiciliary through acts within Liberia.
>
> After proper service of summons, a court may exercise jurisdiction over a nondomiciliary, even though he has not been in Liberia, as to a claim arising from any of the acts enumerated in this section in the same manner as if he were a domiciliary, if, in person or through an agent, he
>
> *(a)* Transacts any business within Liberia or makes a contract with a person in Liberia which is to be performed there, or
>
> *(b)* Commits a tortuous [sic] act within Liberia, or
>
> *(c)* Owns, uses, or possesses any real property situated within Liberia.'

The bases on which a person may be served out of the jurisdiction are set out in sub-paragraphs (a)–(c) if a claim arises:

(a) (i) from a business transaction within Liberia undertaken by the defendant; or

(ii) from a business transaction within Liberia undertaken by the defendant's agent; or

(iii) a contract is concluded by the defendant with a person in Liberia which is to be performed in Liberia; or

(iv) a contract is concluded by the defendant's agent with a person in Liberia which is to be performed in Liberia.

It is unclear what is meant by 'transacts business' in this context, whether this amounts to using a Liberian bank in respect of a contract to be performed overseas between foreign parties, for example.

(b) (i) from a tortious act committed by the defendant within Liberia; or

(ii) from a tortious act committed by the defendant's agent within Liberia.

This head of jurisdiction appears to exclude a party seeking to seise the court of jurisdiction in circumstances where the tort in question was committed overseas, but the damage was suffered in Liberia.

(c) from the defendant's direct or indirect (through an agent) ownership, use or possession of real property situated within Liberia.

In this case it appears that the right to proceed against the foreign defendant does not arise where the acts are not those of his agent in Liberia but are acts committed by, for example, a lessee of the defendant or some other holder of a legal right in the defendant's real property in Liberia.

Circumstance (4): paragraph 3.3 of the CPL

Paragraph 3.3 provides:

> '§ 3.3. Personal jurisdiction over domiciliaries and nondomiciliaries in certain kinds of actions.
>
> After proper service of summons, a court may exercise personal jurisdiction over a person in the following actions:
>
> *(a)* To annul a marriage or for divorce, if the marital status is subject to adjudication in Liberian courts;
>
> *(b)* Affecting the possession of, interest in, or title to, real or personal property within Liberia;
>
> *(c)* In which a levy upon property of the defendant has been made within Liberia pursuant to an order of attachment or a chattel has been seized in an action to recover a chattel.
>
> The provisions of this section are applicable to any defendant whether a domiciliary or nondomiciliary.'

The bases on which a person may be served out of the jurisdiction are set out in sub-paragraphs (a)–(c) where:

(a) the defendant's marital status is subject to the jurisdiction of the Liberian courts.

Sub-paragraph (a) refers back to Liberian law on the question whether the marital status in question is subject to the jurisdiction of the Liberian courts, but without making clear the basis on which that status is subject to the jurisdiction of the Liberian courts.

(b) affecting the possession of, interest in or title to real or personal property within Liberia.

Sub-paragraph (b) is of sufficient breadth to embrace actions brought in respect of the plaintiff's 'possession of, interest in, or title to, real or personal property within Liberia' or that of the defendant.

Sub-paragraph (b) appears also to overlap with paragraph 3.2(c) in so far as the action concerns the defendant who owns or possesses real property in Liberia.

(c) where the action concerns a levy on the defendant's property within Liberia that has been made by way of an attachment or a chattel has been seized in a possession action.

The form of attachment in this sub-paragraph must be a pre-service attachment; otherwise, for the purposes of paragraph 3.39, the defendant would already be a party and, therefore, the attachment would be post-action.[10]

---

[10] The CPL, para 7.16, provides for an application for an attachment prior to service of the summons.

Circumstance (5): paragraph 12.9 of the Associations Law

Paragraph 12.9 provides:

> '§ 12.9. Actions or Special Proceedings Against Foreign Corporations.
>
> 1. By resident of Liberia or domestic corporation. Subject to the limitations with regard to personal jurisdiction contained in sections 3.2 or 3.3 of the Civil Procedure Law, an action or special proceeding against a foreign corporation may be maintained by a resident of Liberia or by a domestic corporation of any type or kind.
> 2. By another foreign corporation or nonresident. Except as otherwise provided in this chapter, an action or special proceeding against a foreign corporation may be maintained in Liberia by another foreign corporation of any type or kind or by a nonresident in the following cases only:
>   *(a)* Where the action is brought to recover damages for the breach of a contract made or to be performed within Liberia, or relating to property situated within Liberia at the time of the making of the contract;
>   *(b)* Where the cause of action arose within Liberia, except where the object of the action or special proceeding is to affect the title of real property situated outside Liberia;
>   *(c)* Where the subject matter of the litigation is situated within Liberia;
>   *(d)* Where the action or special proceeding is based on a liability for acts done within Liberia by a foreign corporation;
>   *(e)* Where the defendant is a foreign corporation doing business in Liberia, subject to the provisions of paragraph 3.
> 3. Dismissal for inconvenience to parties. Any action upon a cause of action not arising out of business transacted or activities performed within Liberia brought against a foreign corporation by a nonresident of Liberia or a foreign corporation may in the discretion of the Liberian court be dismissed if it appears that the convenience of the parties would be better served by an action brought in some other jurisdiction.'

Sub-paragraph 12.9.1 would appear to confirm that a Liberian resident or domestic corporation may bring an action against a foreign corporation as provided in the CPL at paragraphs 3.2 and 3.3.

Sub-paragraph 12.9.2 prescribes the circumstances in which a foreign corporation or a non-resident may bring an action against a foreign corporation (only) and confines those circumstances to five causes of action:

(1) an action for damages for breach of a contract made in Liberia or to be performed in Liberia or relating to real or personal property situated in Liberia at the time the contract was made;

(2) where the cause of action arose in Liberia except where the cause of action concerns real property outside Liberia;

(3) where the subject-matter of the action is situated in Liberia (the wording used is of sufficient amplitude to extend to choses in action and choses in possession);

(4) where the cause of action is based on acts performed within Liberia by a foreign corporation (for example, acts comprising part of a claim in civil conspiracy undertaken at a meeting in Monrovia);

(5) where the defendant is a foreign corporation doing business in Liberia.[11]

Sub-paragraph 12.9.3 contains provisions broadly reflective of the *forum non conveniens* doctrine, such that the court may dismiss the action if it is more appropriate that the action be brought elsewhere.

5.1.2.3 *Submission to the jurisdiction*

Two circumstances must be distinguished under the title submission to the jurisdiction. First, where submission is alleged in extant proceedings in Liberia. Second, where the defendant has agreed (usually by contractual provision) to submit to the jurisdiction of the court in advance of a dispute arising.

5.1.2.3.1 Submission by appearance

In domestic cases the Liberian courts accept that the entering of an appearance by a party amounts to submission to the jurisdiction.

Paragraph 3.61, 'Appearance by defendant defined', of the CPL defines an appearance by the defendant as follows: 'Service of an answer or a notice of appearance or the making by the defendant of a motion constitutes an appearance by him.'

A defendant may, however, appear solely to contest the jurisdiction of the court as paragraph 3.63 makes clear: 'An appearance of the defendant is equivalent to personal service of the summons upon him, unless an objection to jurisdiction of the person is asserted by motion under section 1.1.2(1)(b) or in the answer and is upheld by the court.'[12]

In *King v Williams*,[13] Bey-Solow J gave the opinion of the Supreme Court and held:[14]

> 'The general rule is that if a defendant, though not served with process, takes such a step in an action, or seeks such relief at the hands of the court as is consistent only with the proposition that the court has jurisdiction of the cause and of his person, he therefore

[11] Para 12.2 defines what is not doing business in Liberia.

[12] *New York Karpeh v James T Manning* (1936) 5 LLR 162 (Sup Ct), *per* Grimes CJ at 169.

[13] (1925) 2 LLR 523 (Sup Ct) (Johnson CJ, Witherspoon and Bey-Solow JJ).

[14] Ibid 525.

> submits himself to the jurisdiction of the court, and is bound by its action as fully as if he had been regularly served with process. Likewise if a defendant has been served with process, any objection he may have to the irregularity of the service, must be made promptly, otherwise his failure to appear and object will amount to a waiver of his right to do so. Where a party to a judicial proceeding admits by some act or conduct the jurisdiction of the court, he may not thereafter deny the jurisdiction, especially where the assumption of a contrary position would be to the prejudice of another party who has acquiesced in the position formerly taken. A court which is competent to decide its own jurisdiction in a given case may determine that question at anytime in the proceedings of the cause, whenever that fact is made to appear to its satisfaction, either before or after judgment.'

This approach was followed in *Coleman v Coope*[15] and the decision itself was cited and followed in *Sesay v Republic of Liberia*.[16]

5.1.2.3.2 Submission by agreement

5.1.2.3.2.1 *Jurisdiction clauses*

Jurisdiction clauses are generally treated as a means of submission by agreement. There is, however, a dearth of authority in Liberia on the attitude of the courts to the enforcement of jurisdiction clauses.

An analogy may be drawn between treatment of jurisdiction clauses and treatment of arbitration clauses, on which there is judicial authority in Liberia. The analogy is inexact however, because under paragraph 7.6 of the Commercial Code 2010,[17] where there is an arbitration agreement and a party commences an action, the other party may apply to the court to refer the action to arbitration and, if satisfied that the matter is one in respect of which there is an arbitration agreement, the court 'shall ... refer the matter to arbitration'. The terms of the Code suggest that there is no discretion to decline to refer to arbitration.

However, in considering arbitration clauses, the courts have made clear statements in support of parties' contractual autonomy which, when read across to the context of enforcement of jurisdiction clauses, leads to the conclusion that the courts will not merely have regard to such clauses but will enforce them unless there is a good reason for not doing so.

In *Chicri Bros v Isuzu Motors*,[18] the court upheld an arbitration clause and referred the matter to arbitration. In doing so the court relied, inter alia, on Chapter III, article 25 of the 1986 Constitution which provides: 'Obligation of contract shall be guaranteed by the Republic and no laws shall be passed which might impair this right.' This decision was followed in *KML v Metzger*.[19]

---

[15] (1955) 12 LLR 226 (Sup Ct), *per* Russell CJ at 230.

[16] (1956) 12 LLR 306 (Sup Ct), *per* Pierre J at 312.

[17] Title 7 – Liberian Code of Law Revised.

[18] (2000) 40 LLR 128 (Sup Ct), *per* Morris J.

[19] (2004) 42 LLR 216 (Sup Ct), *per* Cooper CJ.

Liberian law affords the sanctity of contracts special precedence. It was stated by Bank J in *Minister of Lands, Mines and Energy v Liberty Gold and Diamond Co*:[20]

> 'One of the core values upon which Liberia's economic system is built is respect for the sanctity of contracts. So strong was the conviction of the framers of the Liberian Constitution that the nation and its Government should show respect for the sanctity of contracts that they embedded in that most sacred document a provision that obligated the Government to respect the principle of sanctity of contracts, without reference to whether the contract was between the Government and a private individual or between two private individuals, natural or legal. Article 25 of the Constitution expressed that conviction in the following words: "Obligation of contract shall be guaranteed by the Republic and no laws shall be passed which might impair this right." LIB. CONST., ART 25 (1986).'

It is to be expected, therefore, that a Liberian court will give effect to a jurisdiction clause agreed freely by the parties to the contract, subject always to the court retaining a discretion to intervene when the interests of justice demand it should.

In this regard, it is of some significance that certain African jurisdictions have adopted the five principles set out in an English Commercial Court decision as suitable limiting principles to party autonomy in this area.

The five principles were outlined by Brandon J (as he then was) in *Owners of cargo lately laden on board the ship or vessel Eleftheria v The Eleftheria (Owners), The Eleftheria*.[21] (Brandon J's statement of the principles has since been accepted in other common-law jurisdictions as the authoritative statement in this area.[22])

In *The Eleftheria* the jurisdiction clause provided: 'Any dispute arising under this bill of lading shall be decided in the country where the carrier has his principal place of business [Greece].' The owners of cargo on board the *Eleftheria* commenced proceedings in England and the shipowners applied for a stay of those proceedings. In staying the proceedings in favour of the Greek courts Brandon J set out the principles on the basis of which a stay may be granted:[23]

> '(1) Where plaintiffs sue in England in breach of an agreement to refer disputes to a foreign court, and the defendants apply for a stay, the English court, assuming the claim to be otherwise within its jurisdiction, is not bound to grant a stay but has a discretion whether to do so or not. (2) The discretion should be exercised by granting a stay unless strong cause for not doing so is shown. (3) The burden of proving such strong cause is on the plaintiffs. (4) In exercising its discretion the court should take into account all the circumstances of the particular case. (5) In particular, but without prejudice to (4), the following matters, where they arise, may properly be regarded:—(a) In what country

---

[20] [2014] LRSC 5 (Sup Ct).

[21] [1970] P 94; [1969] 1 Lloyd's Rep 237 (QBD, Comm Ct).

[22] *Aratra Potato Co Ltd v Egyptian Navigation Co (The El Amria)* [1981] 2 Lloyd's Rep 119 (CA, Eng); *Anraj Fish Products Industries Ltd v Hyundai Merchant Marine Co Ltd* [2000] ILPr 717 (Fed Ct, Can); *Nika Fishing Co Ltd v Lavina Corp* [2008] 16 NWLR 509 (Sup Ct, Nigeria).

[23] [1970] P 94 at 99G–100C.

> the evidence on the issues of fact is situated, or more readily available, and the effect of that on the relative convenience and expense of trial as between the English and foreign courts, (b) Whether the law of the foreign court applies and, if so, whether it differs from English law in any material respects, (c) With what country either party is connected, and how closely, (d) Whether the defendants genuinely desire trial in the foreign country, or are only seeking procedural advantages, (e) Whether the plaintiffs would be prejudiced by having to sue in the foreign court because they would: (i) be deprived of security for their claim; (ii) be unable to enforce any judgment obtained; (iii) be faced with a time-bar not applicable in England; or (iv) for political, racial, religious or other reasons be unlikely to get a fair trial.'

It may well be that as and when a Liberian court comes to consider the matter *de novo*, these principles may provide some helpful guidance.

5.1.2.3.2.2 *Application for service out of the jurisdiction based on a jurisdiction clause*

As has been explained above, the CPL and the Associations Law together exhaustively set out the circumstances in which a person may be served with a summons outside of Liberia. In those provisions, no mention is made of a plaintiff having a right to serve out based on there being a jurisdiction clause for the courts of Liberia in a contract, or a jurisdiction agreement for the courts of Liberia between the plaintiff and the defendant. Accordingly, it is unsurprising that there is no Liberian authority on the question of whether a plaintiff can make an application for service out of a summons on a defendant out of the jurisdiction on this basis.

5.2 Enforcement of Foreign Judgments

5.2.1 Enforcement at common law

Liberia has not passed legislation enabling the courts to recognise and enforce foreign judgments. Recognition and enforcement of foreign judgments is a matter for common-law rules and it appears that recognition and enforcement of a foreign judgment will be granted as a matter of comity between nations subject to certain evidential requirements contained in the CPL.

The CPL provisions regarding the enforcement of a foreign judgment concern the admissibility in evidence of the foreign judgment:[24]

[24] These paragraphs appear in the CPL at Part II 'Trial Procedure', Chapter 25 'Evidence', the provisions concern matters such as judicial notice of facts, hearsay evidence, competency of witnesses, etc – all provisions concerned with adjectival law.

'§ 25.12. Foreign judgments.

A foreign judgment in a case in which the defendant did not appear although a party thereto shall not be admissible against him; but if any person appeared on his behalf in the case, the foreign judgment shall be admissible unless he shows that the appearance was without his authority ...

§ 25.13. Proof of jurisdiction of court.

In all cases in which the judgment of a court of limited jurisdiction or of a foreign court is sought to be introduced in evidence, the jurisdiction of such court must be proved to extend to the case in which the judgment was given.'

The application of the provisions of the CPL was considered in *Turner v Burnette*,[25] where the plaintiff/appellant former wife was a citizen of the USA who had married a Liberian national in 1964. In 1966 they had a child together in Liberia, who was also a Liberian national. In 1968 the couple separated and the plaintiff returned to the USA with the child. In 1970 the plaintiff sued for divorce in the Circuit Court of Cook County, Illinois, and the court granted a decree dissolving the marriage and granting custody of the child to the plaintiff. Both plaintiff and defendant remarried. In 1974, the defendant visited the USA and abducted the child and took him to Liberia.[26] The plaintiff followed and issued a writ of *habeas corpus* in order to secure the return of the child.

The judge framed the question before him as follows:[27]

'The question is whether in a habeas corpus proceeding attacking the right of a father to retain possession of his minor child, a Liberian court, operating upon the principle of comity, must give recognition to an Illinois decree awarding custody of the child to his mother, when that decree is obtained by the mother in an ex parte divorce action in an Illinois court which had no personal jurisdiction over the father.'

The judge stated that the Liberian law relating to the 'admissibility of foreign judgments' was to be found in paragraphs 25.12 and 25.13 and that, because the defendant did not appear before the Illinois court and contended that he had been neither summoned nor had an opportunity to be heard by the Illinois court, the Illinois judgment was not admissible against him.

With respect to the portion of the Illinois judgment that concerned the dissolution of the marriage, the judge held that while the decree could be attacked on the grounds of jurisdiction and lack of due process, it nonetheless bound the defendant because an estoppel arose by reason of the defendant's remarriage in reliance on the divorce decree that prevented the defendant from denying the validity of the decree.

---

[25] (1975) 24 LLR 212 (Sup Ct) (Henries J).

[26] Ibid. At the time, Liberian law granted custody of the children of a marriage to the husband.

[27] Ibid 215.

However, the defendant was not bound by that part of the decree that granted custody to the plaintiff because the defendant was not personally served with process and did not appear before the Illinois court. (In so holding the court was influenced by United States authorities on the doctrine of 'divisible divorce', whereby a court may gain jurisdiction over a defendant on the basis of constructive notice in respect of the divorce itself, but not gain jurisdiction over the defendant where there are separable personal rights, such as custody of minors, in the absence of personal service or voluntary appearance.) For this reason the Illinois court did not have jurisdiction over the defendant and the decree was not admissible under paragraphs 25.12 and 25.13.

Importantly for present purposes, the judge appeared to accept[28] the following statement of principle regarding the circumstances where comity would lead the court to recognise and enforce a foreign judgment:

> 'In *Hilton v. Guyot,* supra, at 143, the United States Supreme Court said: "Comity, in the legal sense, is neither a matter of absolute obligation on the one hand, nor of mere courtesy and good will, upon the other. But it is the recognition which one nation allows within its territory to the legislative, executive or judicial acts of another nation, having due regard both to the international duty and convenience, and to the rights of its own citizens, or of other persons who are under the protection of its laws." See also 47 AM. JUR., 2d, Judgments, § 1215. It is also stated in 16 AM. JUR., 2d, Conflict of Laws, § 5, that "in considering the question of comity, it should also be borne in mind that the recognition of foreign laws cannot be claimed as a right but only as a favor or courtesy. The application of comity does not rise [sic] to the effect of establishing an imperative rule of law; it has the power to persuade but not command. Comity being voluntary, and not obligatory, rests in the discretion of the tribunal of the forum and is governed by certain more or less widely recognized rules." Generally, greater force and dignity will be given to the judgments of foreign courts when parties have had their day in a court of competent jurisdiction, after due service of process or after entry of appearance, and have had a full and impartial hearing upon the merits of their case; unless it can be shown that the proceedings were tainted with fraud.'

It seems, therefore, that any foreign judgment may be enforceable in Liberia at common law as a matter of comity between nations. The procedure appears to be that a suit is commenced on the foreign judgment, in the same way as an action is commenced at common law in other jurisdictions.

Whether the foreign judgment is admissible against the defendant as a matter of the law of *evidence* is regulated by paragraphs 25.12 and 25.13 of the CPL. If the foreign judgment is not admissible, because the defendant did not appear or because the foreign court lacked jurisdiction, the judgment will not be recognised or enforced.

---

[28] Ibid 217–18: citing the United States Supreme Court decision in *Hilton v Guyot* [1895] USSC 185, 159 US 113 (1895); and also the *American Jurisprudence* 2 ed (1962).

Even then, as a matter of comity, the Liberian court may decline to recognise or enforce a judgment admitted into evidence against the defendant on the grounds that it was obtained by fraud, for example, or that the foreign proceedings offended Liberian notions of natural justice.

As demonstrated by the *Turner* case, the Liberian courts look to United States jurisprudence in ascertaining and developing the law of Liberia.[29]

The classical statement of United States principle appears in the Supreme Court decision cited by the judge in the *Turner* case, *Hilton v Guyot*:[30]

> 'In view of all the authorities upon the subject, and of the trend of judicial opinion in this country and in England, following the lead of Kent and Story, we are satisfied that, where there has been opportunity for a full and fair trial abroad before a court of competent jurisdiction, conducting the trial upon regular proceedings, after due citation or voluntary appearance of the defendant, and under a system of jurisprudence likely to secure an impartial administration of justice between the citizens of its own country and those of other countries, and there is nothing to show either prejudice in the court, or in the system of laws under which it was sitting, or fraud in procuring the judgment, or any other special reason why the comity of this nation should not allow it full effect, the merits of the case should not, in an action brought in this country upon the judgment, be tried afresh, as on a new trial or an appeal, upon the mere assertion of the party that the judgment was erroneous in law or in fact. The defendants, therefore, cannot be permitted, upon that general ground, to contest the validity or the effect of the judgment sued on.'

It should be noted that this regime for the recognition and enforcement of foreign judgments is generally considered to be reasonably progressive and liberal. Referring to the various schemes for the recognition and enforcement of foreign judgment in operation in various countries and regions of the world, the Permanent Bureau of the Hague Conference on Private International Law stated: 'The current state of affairs is unsatisfactory in itself, but might have been more tolerable if all the countries in the world had a recognition and enforcement regime as receptive to foreign judgments as, for example, that of the US.'[31]

In the USA it is state law and not federal law that governs the recognition and enforcement of foreign judgments.[32] The principles applicable to the recognition and enforcement of foreign judgments vary slightly from state to state, but it seems generally accepted that United States common law on this subject is codified in uniform legislation.[33] The Uniform Enforcement of Foreign Money-Judgments Recognition Act ('the Uniform Act') was prepared by the United

---

[29] The Liberian legal information institute, Liberlii, has on its website a link entitled 'US Jurisprudence' that links to the Worldlii page for the USA.

[30] 159 US 113 (1895), *per* Justice Gray delivering the opinion of the court at 202–3.

[31] *Some Reflections of the Permanent Bureau on a General Convention on Enforcement of Judgments*, Preliminary draft 17 (May 1992), quoted in Newman *Enforcement of Money Judgments* (1999) USA-3, fn 2.

[32] In the federal courts, state law is applied to the recognition and enforcement of foreign judgments.

[33] Newman *Enforcement of Money Judgments* (1999) USA-5, USA-24.

States Uniform Law Commissioners in 1962 and has since been enacted by 32 states, including New York, California, Texas, Illinois, Massachusetts, Ohio and Michigan. Recognition and enforcement is by way of an action on the foreign judgment.

The codified common-law principles may be summarised as follows: a United States court will not review the merits of the foreign judgment; a United States court *will* generally enforce a final foreign money judgment that is enforceable where rendered *unless*:[34]

(1) The court of origin did not have jurisdiction over the defendant.

A foreign judgment will be denied enforcement if the court of origin did not have personal jurisdiction over the defendant and may be denied enforcement if the court of origin did not have jurisdiction over the subject-matter.

(a) *Personal jurisdiction.* A United States court will usually assume that the court of origin had personal jurisdiction unless the defendant raises the issue. A United States court must refuse enforcement if the court of origin did not have personal jurisdiction, (i) under its own laws, and (ii) in accordance with international concepts of jurisdiction. As regards (ii), recent decisions applying the Uniform Act look to whether the defendant had 'minimum contacts' with the country of origin.[35] Section 5 of the Uniform Act sets out six (non-exhaustive) bases that meet the minimum contacts test: (1) service in the foreign state (unless that forum was a seriously inconvenient forum for the proceedings); (2) voluntary appearance in the foreign proceedings (save where it was to protect property seized or threatened with seizure or to contest the jurisdiction of the foreign court); (3) a prior agreement to submit to the jurisdiction of the foreign court; (4) domicile in the foreign jurisdiction, including incorporation or principal place of business there; (5) a business office in the foreign country that is related to the cause of action; or (6) operation of a vehicle or plane on the foreign country that is related to the cause of action.

(b) *Subject-matter jurisdiction* (see also below). United States courts usually presume the jurisdiction of the foreign court over the subject-matter of the original cause of action and challenges on this basis are rare.

(2) The court of origin lacked fair procedures.

[34] Ibid USA-25–45; s 4 of the Uniform Act.

[35] *Ackerman v Levine* 788 F 2d 830 (2d Cir 1986).

(3) The court of origin did not have subject-matter jurisdiction over the original cause of action.

(4) The defendant did not receive adequate notice of the court of origin's proceedings.

The defendant must show that he did not receive actual notice of the proceedings or that the method of service was not reasonable. The defendant must also have had sufficient notice to allow him to defend the proceedings. If the defendant raises a question as to the adequacy of the notice, in assessing which the United States court will consider whether the service of process satisfied: (1) US standards of due process, which is an enquiry as to the reasonableness of the method of service; and (2) the foreign country's requirements as to service.

(5) The cause of action on which the foreign judgment is based or the judgment itself violates the public policy of the USA or of the particular state.

United States courts may accede to a public policy defence where: (1) the judicial system under which the judgment was rendered lacked fair procedures;[36] or (2) the judgment itself violates or is based on a claim that violates federal or state public policy. Examples of the former are a judiciary dominated by the political branches of government, prevention of a party from obtaining counsel or witnesses or documents or prevention of a party from appealing the decision. Examples of the latter are rare, one being a Luxembourg judgment that purported to reduce the judgment creditor's United States federal taxes by 77%.[37]

(6) The judgment was obtained by fraud.

In the USA the fraud must be 'extrinsic fraud' rather than 'intrinsic fraud'. The former refers to action by the judgment creditor that deprived the judgment debtor of an adequate opportunity to present his case to the foreign court, whereas intrinsic fraud relates to matters such as false testimony or forged documents that could have been litigated in the foreign court. The difference has been stated as follows: '[T]he fraud must relate to matters other than issues that could have been litigated and must be a fraud on the court.'[38]

---

[36] In *British Midland Ltd v International Travel Inc* 497 F 2d 869 (9th Cir 1974), the court held that English civil procedure did not 'outrageously depart from our notions of civilized jurisprudence'.

[37] *Overseas Inns SA v United States* 6895 F Supp 968 (ND Tex 1988).

[38] *Fairchild, Arabatzis & Smith, Inc v Prometco (Produce & Metals) Co* 470 F Supp 610, 615 (SDNY 1979).

(7) The judgment conflicts with another final judgment.

In the case of two inconsistent foreign judgments, the United States courts will usually enforce the last in point of time.[39]

(8) The court of origin's proceedings were contrary to an agreement between the parties to submit the dispute to a different forum or to arbitration.

If the parties have agreed to an exclusive forum for the resolution of disputes the United States courts may, but are not obliged to, deny enforcement. A forum selection defence is unlikely to be sustained where the judgment debtor participated in the foreign proceedings (other than for the purposes of disputing the jurisdiction or contesting the seizure of property).

(9) The court of origin was a seriously inconvenient forum.

This defence was not available at common law but was added by the Uniform Act, section 4(b)(6): '(b) A foreign judgment need not be recognised if ... (6) in the case of jurisdiction based only on personal service, the foreign court was a seriously inconvenient forum for the trial of the action.' This defence is only available if the jurisdiction of the foreign court was based solely on personal service. This ground for denying enforcement is rarely successful[40] because it usually requires the United States court to find that the foreign court should have dismissed or stayed the proceedings on the basis that it was not a convenient forum.

(10) A defence exists that would prevent enforcement of a United States judgment under the same circumstances.

If the defendant establishes (1) or (2) above, the United States court is required to deny enforcement. If any one or more of (3)–(10) is established, the court has discretion to deny enforcement. A United States court may decide to enforce a judgment in whole or part or not at all.

As mentioned above, given the affinity between Liberian and United States law, it is likely that in considering and developing the Liberian common law of recognition and enforcement of foreign judgments, the Liberian courts will be influenced by the state of the United States common law.

---

[39] *Ackerman v Ackerman* 517 F Supp 614 (SDNY 1981).

[40] *Bank of Nova Scotia v Tschabold Equipment Ltd* 754 P 2d 1290 (Wash, 1988), holding that this defence to enforcement was not available where jurisdiction was based not only on personal service but also on the defendant's transaction of business in Canada and voluntary appearance before the Canadian court (the judgment debtor had been served out of the jurisdiction in Washington State; voluntary appearance was established by the judgment debtor applying to the Canadian court to strike out the judgment creditor's statement of claim and by corresponding with the court setting out various defences to the claim).

5.2.2 Enforcement pursuant to statute

As has been noted above, Liberia has not yet passed legislation enabling the courts to recognise and enforce foreign judgments.

5.3 Interim Remedies

5.3.1 Jurisdiction to grant interim remedies

Chapter 7 of the CPL, 'Provisional Remedies', provides:[41]

> '§ 7.1. Kinds of provisional remedies.
>
> The provisional remedies include attachment, arrest, injunction, receivership, and notice of pendency. On a motion for a provisional remedy, the plaintiff shall state whether any other provisional remedy has been secured or sought in the same action against the same defendant, and the court may require the plaintiff to elect between those remedies to which he would otherwise be entitled. For this purpose, seizure of a chattel in an action to recover a chattel is a provisional remedy.'

5.3.2 Attachment of property[42]

Paragraph 7.11 of the CPL deals with attachment:

> '§ 7.11. Grounds for attachment.
>
> An order of attachment may be granted in any action where the plaintiff has demanded and where there is reasonable ground for believing that he would be entitled, in whole or in part, or in the alternative to a money judgment against one or more defendants, when
>
> *(a)* The defendant is a foreign corporation or not a domiciliary of the Republic; or
>
> *(b)* The defendant is domiciled in the Republic and cannot be personally served despite diligent efforts to do so; or
>
> *(c)* The defendant, with intent to defraud his creditors or to avoid service of summons, has departed or is about to depart from the Republic, or keeps himself concealed therein; or
>
> *(d)* The defendant, with intent to defraud his creditors, has assigned, disposed of or secreted property, or removed it from the Republic or is about to do any of these acts; or

---

[41] The CPL makes provision for receivership and notice of pendency. Receivership (CPL, §7.81) is unlikely to be an attractive interim remedy given that attachment achieves much the same ends but without the receiver's costs. Notice of pendency (CPL, §7.91) is a useful means of fixing the public at large with constructive notice of the plaintiff's proceedings against the defendant and ensuring that anyone dealing with the defendant's real property is bound by the proceedings after the filing of the notice of pendency.

[42] A survey of US law on this subject is to be found in Newman *Attachment of Assets* 2 ed 2016, USA-1–USA-32.

> *(e)* The action is one for a money judgment enforceable under subchapter B of chapter 44 [which refers to a money judgment or order directing the payment of money, including costs].
>
> The definition of the term money judgment in section 41.1 is applicable to this section [a money judgment is an interlocutory or final judgment or any part thereof, for a sum of money or directing the payment of a sum of money].'

In order for a plaintiff to obtain an attachment over the defendant's property, therefore, the plaintiff is required to show:

(1) a reasonable ground for believing the plaintiff would be entitled to a money judgment; and

(2) one or more of five matters:

   (a) The defendant is a foreign corporation or not a domiciliary of Liberia.

   Whether the defendant is a foreign corporation is self-explanatory. The term 'domicile' has been explained above as meaning, in the context of a legal person, where the central management or control is exercised.

   (b) The defendant is domiciled in Liberia but cannot be personally served despite diligent efforts to do so.

   Again, this is self-explanatory; what amounts to diligent efforts will be fact-sensitive and will depend on all the circumstances of the case.

   (c) The defendant has departed or is about to depart from Liberia and is about to or has done so 'with intent to defraud his creditors or to avoid service of summons'.[43] Under this sub-paragraph, the plaintiff must show not only that the defendant is about to leave or has left Liberia but also that the defendant's actions were undertaken with a particular intent. In the usual case this intent will need to be inferred from the facts available to the plaintiff. Proof of intent to defraud (or to avoid service) is, nonetheless, a high hurdle to negotiate and cogent evidence will be required in order for the court to reach a conclusion on this matter.

   (d) The defendant has or is about to dissipate his assets 'with intent to defraud his creditors'. Again, cogent evidence will be required to establish the necessary intent.

[43] The sub-paragraph also refers to a defendant who 'keeps himself concealed', but this seems to add little to the second ground.

(e) The fifth matter under paragraph 7.11 is that the action brought by the plaintiff is 'one for a money judgment enforceable under subchapter B of chapter 44'. That subchapter concerns:

> '§ 44.21. Applicability of subchapter.
>
> A money judgment or order directing the payment of money or any part of such judgment or order, including an order to pay costs, may be enforced as prescribed in this subchapter ...'.

The five sub-paragraphs of paragraph 7.11 are alternatives and so sub-paragraph 7.11(e) appears to empower a Liberian court to grant an attachment where: (1) there is a reasonable ground for believing the plaintiff would be entitled to a money judgment; and (2) the plaintiff's action is one for a money judgment enforceable under the money judgment provisions of chapter 44B of the CPL.

Sub-paragraph 7.11(e) seems to add little to the first requirement in paragraph 7.11 described above. The logic of this is that an attachment is available in *any* case where the claim may reasonably result in a money judgment enforceable under the money judgment provisions of the CPL.

The advantage of an attachment over other forms of interlocutory relief that operate *in personam* is that the attachment gives the plaintiff security in the thing attached. Paragraph 7.13 makes this plain:

> '§ 7.13. Attaching creditor's rights in personal property.
>
> Where a clerk of court has delivered a writ of attachment to a sheriff, the plaintiff's rights in a debt owed to the defendant or in an interest of the defendant in personal property against which debt or property a judgment may be enforced, are superior to the extent of the amount of the attachment to the rights of any transferee of the debt or property, except:
>
> *(a)* A transferee who acquired the debt or property before it was levied upon for fair consideration or without knowledge of the order of attachment; or
>
> *(b)* A transferee who acquired the debt or property for fair consideration after it was levied upon without knowledge of the levy and while such debt or property was not in the possession of the sheriff.'

The exceptions to the superiority of the plaintiff's interest in the defendant's attached property are in favour of transferees of the property in question for fair consideration without knowledge of the attachment and before the property was reduced to the possession of the sheriff.

In *UMC Corp v AMS Inc*,[44] the court stated:

> 'It is common knowledge that an order of attachment is granted in an action where the plaintiff has demanded, and where he reasonably believes that he would be entitled to a money judgment against a defendant. Rev. Code 1:7.11. It follows then that there must be a main suit in which a money judgment is expected, and the object of the attachment is to seize property as a security pending the final determination of the main suit and to satisfy the judgment thereof.'

---

[44] (1976) 25 LLR 267 (Sup Ct) (Pierre CJ).

An application for an attachment is made by notice of motion under paragraph 10.1 of the CPL with an affidavit in support[45] deposing to the material facts on the basis of which the application is made. It is a mandatory requirement under paragraph 17.15(2) that the plaintiff give a bond 'in an amount equal to one and one half-times the amount demanded in the complaint that the plaintiff shall pay to the defendant all legal costs and damages which may be sustained by reason of the attachment'. In the *UMC* case the Supreme Court stated 'that requiring a bond in attachment proceedings is mandatory, and not within the discretion of a judge to entertain the suit without a bond. This is so elementary that we cannot perceive how any judge could have allowed omission of such a legal requirement.'

An order for an attachment may be made *ex parte*,[46] but the defendant must be served with a writ of summons as well as the writ of attachment if the court is to have jurisdiction over the defendant.[47]

Sub-paragraphs 7.18–7.21 deal with the mechanics of the sheriff levying on real or personal property in execution of the attachment. Attachments are ranked in priority in the order in which they were delivered to the officer who levied upon the property.

Paragraph 7.24 contains far-reaching disclosure provisions:

> '§ 7.24. Disclosure.
>
> Upon motion of any interested person, at any time after the granting of an order of attachment and prior to final judgment in the action, upon such notice as the court may direct, the court may order disclosure by any person of information regarding any property in which the defendant has an interest or any debt owing to the defendant.'

The powers of the court under paragraph 7.24 to order disclosure of information regarding the defendant's assets are not confined to the parties to the proceedings or even their privies, but extends to 'any person' including third parties such as banks. The plaintiff would need to show that, *prima facie*, the person against whom such a disclosure application is made has in his possession relevant information regarding the defendant's assets.

5.3.3 Arrest of the person

Chapter 7 of the CPL, 'Provisional Remedies', provides:

> '§ 7.41. Grounds for arrest.
>
> An order for arrest as a provisional remedy may be granted only where the plaintiff has demanded, and where there is reasonable ground for believing that he would be entitled to
>
> *(a)* A judgment requiring payment of a sum of money, failure to satisfy which through execution will subject the judgment debtor to imprisonment under section 44.71(2);

---

[45] CPL, §7.15.

[46] CPL, §7.16.

[47] *Pentee v Zoe* (1997) 38 LLR 485 (Sup Ct).

> *(b)* A judgment requiring payment of a sum of money failure to pay which may be punishable as a contempt under section 44.71(3); or
>
> *(c)* A judgment requiring the performance of an act, neglect or refusal to perform which would be punishable by the court as a contempt under section 44.71(4);
>
> and where the defendant is not a resident of the Republic or is about to depart therefrom, by reason of which nonresidence or departure there is danger that such judgment will be rendered ineffectual.'

Arrest of the person is permissible in three cases in each one of which the plaintiff must also show that the defendant is not a resident of Liberia[48] or is a resident and is about to leave the jurisdiction and that because of the defendant's non-residence or imminent departure there is a danger that the judgment will be rendered ineffectual:

(1) Paragraph 44.71(2) concerns five specific proceedings, each carrying a degree of moral opprobrium, where arrest is available as a means of execution if the judgment debtor cannot or will not pay the amount due:

> '2. *Judgments enforceable by imprisonment if execution not satisfied.* Judgments in any of the following actions shall be enforceable by execution, but if the judgment debtor cannot or will not pay the full amount of the judgment together with interest and costs, the sheriff shall arrest him and the court shall order him imprisoned for a period sufficiently long to liquidate the full amount of the judgment, interest, and costs at the rate of twenty-five dollars per month:
>
> *(a)* Adultery;
>
> *(b)* Seduction of wife or child;
>
> *(c)* Illegally taking away or harboring a wife or child or ward under twenty-one years of age;
>
> *(d)* Enticing an incompetent away from his legally appointed trustee or guardian; or
>
> *(e)* Injury to the reputation when the words spoken or written are actionable per se.'

(2) Paragraph 44.71(3) concerns two types of proceedings where relationships of trust and confidence or family relations are at issue: fiduciary/trust duties; and duties to support a wife, child or other dependent:

[48] In *Kamil Saab v Bharwanoy Inc* (1974) 23 LLR 425 (Sup Ct) (Henries J), where the court held that a foreign national residing legally in Liberia and engaged in business in Liberia is a domiciliary of Liberia and an order for attachment made against such a foreign national on the sole ground that he is not a domiciliary is in error.

> '3. *Money judgments enforceable by contempt.* Any of the following money judgments may be enforced by contempt proceedings:
>
> *(a)* Against a trustee or a person acting in a fiduciary relationship for the payment of a sum of money for a default or dereliction of his duty; or
>
> *(b)* For the support of a wife, child, or other dependent.'

(3) Sub-paragraph 44.71(4) is concerned with any other judgments and provides that such judgment may be enforced by: ministerial officer of the court (such as signing a conveyance where the defendant refuses to do so); appointment of a receiver of the defendant's property where the defendant refuses to comply with the judgment; where title to the defendant's real property is vested in another person; or where the defendant is in contempt.

> '*Other judgments.* Any interlocutory or final judgment or order, or any part thereof, not enforceable under section 44.21 or paragraph 1, 2, or 3 of this section may be enforced by one of the following methods:
>
> *(a)* Directing the act to be done at the cost of the disobedient party by the ministerial officer of the court or by some other person appointed by the court; and the act when so done shall have the same effect as if done by the disobedient party; or
>
> *(b)* On application of the party entitled to performance, appointment of a receiver of property of the disobedient party under section 44.72 to compel compliance with the judgment; or
>
> *(c)* On judgment of a court of record, if real property is within the county, entering a judgment divesting the title of any party and vesting it in another person in lieu of directing a conveyance thereof; and such judgment when probated in the office of the clerk of the probate court and recorded in the office of the Registrar of Deeds shall have the effect of a conveyance executed in due form of law; or
>
> *(d)* Adjudging the disobedient party in contempt and punishing him as provided in section 44.73.'

Paragraph 44.73 makes provision for enforcement through contempt proceedings.

In *Al-Haj Massaquoi v Joe Munah*,[49] the Supreme Court held that, on his arrest, a defendant may secure his discharge by giving a bond with one or more sureties.[50] The amount of bail required of a defendant should not ordinarily exceed $100.[51]

[49] (1945) 9 LLR 53 (Sup Ct) (Russell J).

[50] The case also decided that where, having secured an attachment, a plaintiff wishes to increase the amount in an attachment beyond $100.00, he should exhibit evidence showing the additional damage he alleged he has suffered so that the court can make an assessment of any further sum to be attached.

[51] *Churchill Thomas v Gabriel L Dennis* (1936) 5 LLR 92 (Sup Ct) (Russell J). Whether this is still good law after 80 years is a moot point. Article 21(d)(ii) of the Liberian Constitution prohibits excessive bail. It is unlikely that this figure, which may have seemed reasonable in 1936, will be considered reasonable today.

In all cases it should be recalled:[52]

> 'This Court has said, in *Halaby v. Farhart*, 7 LLR 129, 130 (1941), that attachment is a harsh remedy and is to be resorted to only in cases where other remedies would be insufficient. An attorney who invokes the remedy must see to it that every statutory requirement is literally complied with, and should not proceed until he has satisfied himself that sufficient statutory grounds exist for the writ of attachment and that he can produce sufficient evidence to prove his allegations. This statement still holds true. Issuance of the writ of attachment depends upon compliance with statute, and not on the discretion of the court or a mere making of a motion. The statutory grounds must be alleged and proven and sworn to by affidavit before the writ can issue.'

5.3.4 Preliminary injunctions

Paragraph 7.61 makes provision for the granting of a preliminary injunction where certain requirements are satisfied:

> '§ 7.61. Grounds for preliminary injunction.
>
> A preliminary injunction may be granted in any action where it appears that the defendant threatens or is about to do, or is doing or procuring or suffering to be done, an act in violation of the plaintiff's rights respecting the subject of the action, and tending to render the judgment ineffectual, or in any action where the plaintiff has demanded and would be entitled to a judgment restraining the defendant from the commission or continuance of an act which, if committed or continued during the pendency of the action, would produce injury to the plaintiff.'

Paragraph 7.61 deals with two situations: first, conduct on the part of the defendant that may render a judgment in the plaintiff's favour ineffectual; and, second, where the plaintiff claims an injunction as a remedy in the proceedings and seeks an order protecting him from damage by reason of the defendant's conduct pending the outcome of the proceedings.

In either case an injunction will not lie if the applicant has an adequate remedy at law, by way of damages or by defending the proposed action.[53]

An application for a preliminary injunction under paragraph 7.61 must be made on notice to the defendant[54] and is made by motion under paragraph 10.1 supported by affidavit evidence setting out the plaintiff's claim and the basis

---

[52] *Kamil Saab v Bharwanoy Inc* (1974) 23 LLR 425 (Sup Ct) (Henries J), at 428. See also Russell J in *Churchill Thomas v Gabriel L Dennis* (1936) 5 LLR 92, 'The law does not favor the arrest of defendants in civil actions, and hence all statutes which permit a defendant in a civil suit to be arrested must be construed strictly. For, a man's liberty is too sacred to be wantonly restrained.'

[53] *Francis v Menzo Salami Bros* (1954) 11 LLR 422 (Sup Ct) (Shannon J): where the applicant applied for an injunction to restrain the respondent instituting an action for debt, the court held that the applicant had an adequate remedy at law: he could defend the action.

[54] CPL, §7.62.

for the injunction under paragraph 7.61.[55] On the hearing of the application, if the court is minded to make the order sought, the plaintiff is required to give a bond to secure the defendant against any losses he may suffer as a result of the injunction if it appears subsequently that he ought not to have been enjoined.[56]

Paragraph 7 also makes separate provision for a temporary restraining order that may be sought without notice to the defendant. Sub-paragraph 7.64 provides:

> '§ 7.64. Temporary restraining order.
>
> 1. *Prerequisites for issuance.* If, on a motion for a preliminary injunction, the plaintiff shall show that immediate and irreparable injury, loss, or damages will result unless the defendant is restrained before a hearing can be had, a temporary restraining order may be granted without notice. Prior to the granting of a motion for a temporary restraining order, the plaintiff shall give a bond in an amount to be fixed by the court, to the effect that the plaintiff, if it is finally determined that he was not entitled to a restraining order, will pay all damages and costs which may be incurred by any party who is found to have been wrongfully restrained.'

The plaintiff must show by affidavit evidence on an application by motion that he will suffer immediate and irreparable harm (for which damages would not be an effective remedy)[57] unless the defendant is temporarily restrained from undertaking the conduct alleged to be harmful to the plaintiff.[58]

The temporary restraining order is a precursor to the hearing of an application *inter partes* for a preliminary injunction. A temporary restraining order may not last more than ten days (unless good cause is shown). The court on the hearing of the application for a temporary restraining order shall set the hearing date for the preliminary injunction application at the earliest possible time.

The function of a preliminary injunction is not to provide a remedy for a wrong already committed but to provide preventive relief pending the hearing

---

[55] CPL, §7.63.

[56] CPL, §7.63(3), 'the plaintiff shall give a bond'.

[57] *Thompson v Cooper* (1959) 13 LRSC 3 (Sup Ct) (Wilson CJ), at 355, on the meaning of irreparable harm: 'As ordinarily used the term means that which cannot be repaired, restored, or adequately compensated for in money, or where the compensation cannot be safely measured. ... Where, however, there is a full, complete and adequate remedy in a court of law for an injury, it is not irreparable; and if full compensation can be obtained by damages in an action in that form, equity will not apply the extraordinary remedy by injunction.'

[58] Reflecting the position at common law: *Cooper v Macintosh* (1944) 8 LLR 400 (Sup Ct) (Barclay J), 'To warrant the allowance of a writ of injunction it must clearly appear that some act has been done, or is threatened, which will produce irreparable injury to the party asking an injunction. Unless this be made to appear, an injunction should be denied. If, however, the injury threatened be irreparable, chancery will interfere by injunction. An injury is irreparable either from its own nature, as when the party injured cannot be adequately compensated therefor in damages or when the damages which may result therefrom cannot be measured by any certain pecuniary standard, or when it is shown that the party must respond is insolvent, and for that reason incapable of responding in damages.'

of the main action:[59] 'An action of injunction is not a possessory action, but one of a restraining or prohibitive character.'

A plaintiff seeking an injunction to restrain the invasion of real property must prove his title or interest in the property. A bare assertion that the plaintiff is the lawful owner of certain land without stating the nature and character of the alleged ownership will not give a right in law or equity; instead, a sufficient title must be shown.[60]

An injunction binds those with actual notice of it and it is not necessary that a third party should be a party to the suit or served with a copy of the order. A person who has actual notice of the injunction and disobeys it is in contempt of court.[61]

5.3.5 Freezing orders and search and seize orders

In certain other common-law jurisdictions in Africa, the courts have adopted two forms of English interlocutory relief, the *Mareva* injunction and the *Anton Piller* order.

The former is an order that operates *in personam* against the respondent (usually the defendant to the proceedings) and which restrains the respondent from dealing with his assets up to a certain amount save than in the ordinary course of business.

No security is provided to the applicant by reason of the making of the injunction. On the granting of a *Mareva* injunction the applicant will be required to give an undertaking as to damages and frequently this is ordered to be fortified by a payment into court or by the provision of a bank guarantee supporting the undertaking.

An *Anton Piller* order is a search and seize order that entitles the applicant, subject to some stringent safeguards, to enter the respondent's property and search for named items of evidence prior to their feared destruction by the respondent.

---

[59] *Tubman v Murdoch* (1934) 4 LLR 179 (Sup Ct) (Grimes CJ); cited in *James E Johnson v John W Powell* (1934) 4 LLR 221 (Sup Ct) (Dixon J). Also, *Young v Embree* (1936) 5 LLR 242 (Sup Ct) (Grimes CJ), 'injunction does not lie where title to real property is an issue involved'.

[60] *Moore v Mensah* (1953) 11 LLR 339 (Sup Ct) (Shannon J).

[61] *Porte v Dennis* (1947) 9 LLR 214 (Sup Ct) (Grimes CJ), where the Secretary of State was summoned to show cause why he should not be held in contempt of court for having issued a passport to the applicant's wife in the knowledge that the court had ordered that no passport should be issued.

Neither of these forms of relief appears to date to have made its way into Liberian practice.[62] As things stand, therefore, the remedies set out in paragraph 7 of the CPL must be taken comprehensively to represent current Liberian law on interim relief.[63]

[62] In the USA it seems the *Mareva* injunction is historically unavailable for reasons relating to the date at which United States federal law is taken to have received the common law and principles of equity law from English law, being 1789, the date of the US Judiciary Act: *Grupo de Mexicano de Desarrollo v Alliance Bond Fund* 27 US 308 (1999) (Sup Ct) (Rehnquist CJ, Scalia, O'Connor, Kennedy and Thomas JJ in the majority; Ginsburg, Stevens, Souter and Breyer JJ dissenting in part). The majority opinion was delivered by Scalia J; however, there are passages in the opinion that suggest the majority may have misunderstood the nature of *Mareva* relief, that it does not give security to the applicant and that the respondent may continue to deal with his assets for all legitimate purposes (see, in particular, p 327 where Scalia J quoted from the previous decision of the Supreme Court in *De Beers Consol Mines, Ltd v United States* 325 US 212 (1945), that the effect of such an injunction was to 'impose an injunction on him, indefinite in duration, disabling him to use so much of his funds or property as the court deems necessary for security or compliance with its possible decree'. This is not the effect of a *Mareva* injunction, which does not disable the respondent from the use of his property or provide security for the applicant. For these reasons it would be open to a Liberian court to look at the jurisdiction to grant *Mareva* relief without regard to the decision of the United States Supreme Court in the *Grupo de Mexicano* case.

[63] The principles upon which *Mareva* and *Anton Piller* relief is granted are stated elsewhere in this work.

Chapter 6

MALAWI

6.1 Jurisdiction

The Courts Act 1958[1] ('the 1958 Act') makes provision, inter alia, for the rules governing jurisdiction and interim remedies in Malawi. (The enforcement of foreign judgments is addressed in greater detail below.) The most significant provisions of the 1958 Act for present purposes are referred to below.

Section 29 of the 1958 Act (as amended), entitled 'Practice and Procedure of the High Court', provides, inter alia:

> 'Save as otherwise provided in this Act, the practice and procedure of the High Court shall, so far as local circumstances admit, be the practice and procedure (including the practice and procedure relating to execution) provided in the Rules of the Supreme Court, 1999.'

Thus, the default position in Malawi was that the Rules of the Supreme Court 1965, 1999 edition ('the RSC'), the rules that governed the practice and procedure of the High Court of England and Wales until they were superseded in 1999 with new Civil Procedure Rules, governed the practice and procedure of the Malawi High Court.

On 1 September 2016 the Courts (Amendment) Act 2016[2] ('the 2016 Act') received the assent of the President of Malawi and, it appears, came into force on the same date.[3] The 2016 Act provided for certain amendments to the 1958 Act that effected a number of important changes to the structure of the High Court and the civil procedure rules. Most significantly, for present purposes, reliance on the RSC has been abandoned and replaced with a new code of civil procedure, the Courts (High Courts) (Civil Procedure) Rules ('the 2017 Rules').[4]

---

[1] Act 1 of 1958. The correct domestic citation of this provision is 'Courts [chapter 03:02]' of the Laws of Malawi, 2010. In this regard, the reader is referred to the 'Note on the citation of statutory material in this work', which appears at the end of the 'List of Statutory Material Cited' at the beginning of this work.

[2] Act 23 of 2016. The 2016 Act does not yet appear to have been allocated a Cap number.

[3] See, in this regard: *Chiutsi v National Bank of Malawi (Order)* [2016] MWHC 605 (Nyirenda J).

[4] Reference No D. 3:02, Ministry of Justice and Constitutional Affairs – 20 July 2015 (date of publication; yet to pass into law). That notice concerned draft rules bearing the year 2016. These draft rules are reproduced in substance by the 2017 Rules. That the 2017 Rules mark a significant departure from the previous regime is illustrated by, for example, the institution of mandatory mediation for all proceedings (O 13, rr 1–11). The 2017 Rules do not appear yet to have been Gazetted as required by O 1 r 2. As of May 2017, there were opposing judicial views as to whether the RSC applied or whether the new regime applied: see *Chiutsi v National Bank of Malawi* [2016] MWHC 605, where the judge seemingly indicated that rules of civil procedure formerly in place 'are no longer in operation'; by contrast, in *Columbia Commonwealth University Ltd v National Council For Higher Education (Order)* [2017] MWHC 115 (Tembo J), where the originating summons was dated 14 April 2017, the High Court made reference to the RSC in terms which indicate the rules therein contained were still in force in Malawi.

Section 7 of the 2016 Act provides:

> 'Section 29 of the principal Act [the 1958 Act] is repealed and replaced as follows—
>
> **29**. The practice and procedure of the High Court shall be provided in the rules of procedure made by the Chief Justice under section 67 [of the 1958 Act].'

The 2016 Act makes provision[5] for the High Court to sit in five divisions: the Civil, Commercial, Criminal, Family and Probate Divisions. The Act also removes the power of the Chief Justice to make rules, 'for the purpose of varying, supplementing, revoking or replacing the Rules of the Supreme Court'.[6]

As from 1 September 2016, therefore, as a matter of law the RSC ceased to apply as the rules of practice and procedure for the Malawi High Court.

The 2017 Rules came into force on a date appointed by the Chief Justice and published in the *Gazette*.[7] The 2017 Rules apply to all applications made after the commencement date.[8]

Order 1, rule 5(2), sets out the following rules of interpretation applicable to the 2017 Rules:

> 'The Court shall seek to give effect to the overriding principal objective whenever it—
>
> *(a)* exercises any power conferred on it by these Rules; or
>
> *(b)* interprets any written law, rules and regulations.'

The overriding principal objective is set out at Order 1, rule 5(1):

> 'The overriding objective of these Rules is to deal with proceedings justly and this includes –
>
> *(a)* ensuring that the parties are on an equal footing;
>
> *(b)* saving expenses;
>
> *(c)* dealing with a proceeding in ways which are proportionate to the—
>
> (i) amount of money involved;
>
> (ii) importance of the case; and
>
> (iii) complexity of the issues;
>
> *(d)* ensuring that a proceeding is dealt with expeditiously and fairly; and
>
> *(f)* allocating to a proceeding an appropriate share of the Court's resources, while taking into account the need to allocate resources to other proceedings.'

---

[5] Ibid s 3 inserting a new s 6A into the 1958 Act.

[6] Ibid s 9 by deleting sub-s (2) from s 67 of the 1958 Act.

[7] Order 1 r 2, see above. The authors have been unable to determine the exact date on which the appointed date was gazetted. As at May 2017, the RSC was, it appears, still being applied: see the reference to O 29 in the judgment of Kenyatta Nyirenda J in *Mike Appel & Gatto Ltd v General Motors South Africa (Pty) Ltd* [2017] MWHC 112.

[8] Order 35, r 9.

The overriding objective in Order 1, rule 5(1), of the 2017 Rules corresponds very closely to the language used in Part 1.1 of the English Civil Procedure Rules (1999) ('the CPR'), which replaced the RSC. In England, principally because the new rules are premised on the overriding objective, the CPR was (and is) treated as an entirely new code of civil procedure and citation of authorities on the RSC, even on areas that appear in both codes, is not only discouraged but is said generally to be irrelevant to the proper interpretation of the CPR.

In interpreting the 2017 Rules it is to be expected that the Malawian courts may have regard to the approach adopted by the English courts in interpreting the CPR. The English Court of Appeal in *Biguzzi v Rank Leisure plc*,[9] addressed criticism of the judge at first instance that he failed to have regard to decisions under the RSC when reaching a decision on a similar area of procedural law under the CPR. Lord Woolf MR stated:[10] 'I do not accept the criticisms of the judge with regard to his approach to the previous authorities. Indeed far from criticising the judge, I would commend his approach' and[11] 'Earlier authorities are no longer generally of any relevance once the C.P.R. applies.'

What follows below is an exposition of the new regime under the 2017 Rules.

Under the 2017 Rules, the fundamental means by which a Malawian court is seised of jurisdiction over a defendant at the suit of a plaintiff is by service of process on the defendant and, as previously, the 2017 Rules distinguish between service within and service outside the jurisdiction.

6.1.1 Service where the defendant is within the jurisdiction

Service of a person present within the jurisdiction will give the court jurisdiction over that person.

A company is present within the jurisdiction if it has its registered offices within the jurisdiction or if it has its principal place of business in Malawi or if it has offices in Malawi (in which case process may be served at the principal office).[12]

The Companies Act 1986[13] makes provision for the registration of domestic companies and also makes provision for 'external companies'. The latter provisions will bear upon the question whether a foreign company is present within the jurisdiction for the purposes of service of process.

[9] [1999] 1 WLR 1926 (CA) (Lord Woolf MR, Brooke and Walker LJJ).

[10] Ibid 1932B.

[11] Ibid 1934G–H.

[12] Order 8, r 18(1).

[13] The Companies Act 1986 (Act 18 of 1986, Cap 46:03 of the Laws of Malawi, 2010), for a domestic company: ss 127 (registered office), 137 (service of documents on a company at its registered office) and 143 (the requirement that at least half the directors of a company and no less than three should be resident in Malawi). For an external company: s 311.

The term 'external company' is defined in section 306(2) as 'a body corporate formed outside Malawi which establishes or maintains an established place of business in Malawi'.

A foreign company will be 'present' in Malawi for the purposes of service if it has established or if it maintains an established place of business in Malawi.

The term 'established place of business' is defined in section 306(3) as follows:

> 'For the purposes of this Part, the expression "established place of business", in relation to a body corporate, means a branch, management, share transfer, or registration office or a factory, mine, or other fixed place of business, but does not include an agency unless the agent has, and habitually exercises, a general authority to negotiate and conclude contracts on behalf of the body corporate or maintains a stock of merchandize belonging to that body corporate from which he regularly fills orders on its behalf:
>
> Provided that—
>
> *(a)* a body corporate shall not be deemed to have an established place of business in Malawi merely because it carries on business dealings in Malawi through a broker or general commission agent acting in the ordinary course of his business as such; and
>
> *(b)* the fact that the body corporate has a subsidiary which is incorporated, resident or carrying on business in Malawi, whether through an established place of business or otherwise, shall not of itself constitute the place of business of that subsidiary an established place of business of that body corporate.'

Section 307(1)(b)(vii) requires an external company to appoint a 'documentary agent' who is 'authorized by the company to accept service of process and other documents on its behalf'. The documentary agent must have a residential address in Malawi.

Section 311 provides for service of process and other documents on an external company. Section 311(1) provides:

> '(1) Any writ or document shall be sufficiently served on an external company if delivered or sent by post to the person last registered as the documentary agent of the company, pursuant to subparagraph (vii) of section 307 (1) (b), at his last known registered address, even if the documentary agent refuses to accept service or the company has ceased to maintain an established place of business in Malawi:
>
> Provided that this subsection shall not apply to service of a document—
>
> *(a)* if the company was struck off the Register of External Companies, pursuant to section 320, more than six years prior to such service;
>
> *(b)* if the person last registered as documentary agent is dead, or, in the case of a body corporate, dissolved.'

Where the foreign company does not have a registered documentary agent or that agent is no longer available, the company may be served with process at 'any established place of business of the company in Malawi, or, if the company has ceased to have any established place of business in Malawi, to the registered office or principal place of business of the company in the country of its incorporation'.[14] The latter will need the leave of the court pursuant to Order 8, rule 30(2).

The question whether a foreign corporation is present within the jurisdiction through the presence of an agent appears to be a matter on which there is no judicial authority in Malawi. The position in England is set out in *The Lalandia*,[15] where Langton J stated:[16]

> 'Now taking these various tests, the test of making or selling contracts and the test of Lord Wrenbury in the Okura case of whether the defendants are acting "by" a person or "through" a person, and the value to be attached to whether the rent is paid by the foreign corporation or whether the agent in this country has the right or not to make any independent contract and has any discretion of his own—applying all these various tests as best I can to the present case, it seems to me that Escombe, McGrath & Co. fall upon the side of the line of *agents who carry on their own business and not the business of the foreign corporation* ... I have to make up my mind *whether the foreign corporation is really here, in the sense that it has somebody doing its business here who is not doing primarily his own business*, and I think Escombe, McGrath & Co. on the evidence are primarily doing their own business and only in a secondary sense doing the business of the East Asiatic Company' (emphasis provided).[17]

The courts are likely to have this statement of principle in mind in determining whether a foreign corporation is present through an agent for the purposes of service of process under section 36(3).

Service of a summons on the defendant must be effected personally[18] within three months[19] of issue (by the Registrar) unless either it is not practical for the party to serve the document personally (in which case an order for substituted service may be made)[20] or the court orders that the summons may be served in another way.[21]

---

14 Section 311(2).

15 [1933] P 56.

16 Ibid 66–7.

17 Followed in Nigeria in *In re: Gresham Life Assurance Society (Nigeria) Ltd* [1973] (1) ALR Comm 215 (Sup Ct, at the time the equivalent today of the Nigerian Federal Court of Appeal) (Elias CJ, Fatayi-Williams and Ibekwe JJSC). See further in this respect the relevant section of the chapter on Nigeria.

18 Order 8, rr 3 and 17.

19 Order 7, r 25(1). Confusingly, O 5, r 1, requires the commencement of proceedings by the filing of a summons 'in Form 1'. Form 1, contained in Sch 1 to the 2017 Rules, states that the summons is to be served within four calendar months or, if permission is required to serve outside the jurisdiction, within six months. It seems likely that a court would apply the three-month period in O 7, rather than the four-month period in Form 1.

20 Order 8, rr 3(a) and 20.

21 Order 8, r 3(b).

6.1.2 Service where the defendant is outside the jurisdiction

6.1.2.1 *Procedure*

Order 8, rule 30(1), provides that a party may apply to the court for an order that a summons in the court be served outside Malawi.

Rule 30(2) sets out the circumstances in which such an order may be made. It is of considerable significance that the provisions in rule 30(2) empowering the court to permit service out of the jurisdiction are in mandatory terms, 'The Court *shall* ... order that a summons or other process be served outside Malawi ...' (emphasis provided) if the plaintiff is able to pass through one or more of the gateways provided for in rule 30(2). This provision appears to exclude discretion in the court to refuse permission to serve process out of the jurisdiction where the plaintiff has passed through one or more of the gateways in rule 30(2).[22] (See further discussion of this point below.)

Rule 30(2) provides for service out of the jurisdiction in the following circumstances:

> 'The Court shall, on application, order that a summons or other process be served outside Malawi where the Court is satisfied that the party seeking permission has a good and arguable case for relief sought by the party in the proceeding, and—
>
> *(a)* the claim concerns land in Malawi;
>
> *(b)* an Act of Parliament, deed, will, contract, obligation or liability affecting land in Malawi is sought to be interpreted, rectified, set aside or enforced;
>
> *(c)* the claim is against a person who is domiciled or ordinarily resident in Malawi;
>
> *(d)* the claim is for the administration of an estate of a person who was domiciled in Malawi at the date of the person's death;
>
> *(e)* the claim is for the execution of a trust, the person to be served is a trustee, and the trust concerns property in Malawi;
>
> *(f)* the claim concerns a contract made in Malawi or governed by the law of Malawi;
>
> *(g)* the claim is based on a breach of contract committed in Malawi, whether or not the contract was made in Malawi;
>
> *(h)* the claim is based on a tort committed in Malawi;
>
> *(i)* the claim is for damage suffered in Malawi, whether or not the tort causing the damage happened in Malawi;
>
> *(j)* the claim is for an amount payable under any law to a public institution in Malawi;
>
> *(k)* the proceeding is brought against a person in Malawi and the other person outside Malawi is a necessary party to the proceeding;

[22] Contrast the provisions of RSC O 11, r 1(1), where the wording is simply that service out of the jurisdiction is permissible with the leave of the court if the plaintiff passes through one of the gateways. This wording preserves the court's discretion to refuse leave if, for example, England is not the *forum conveniens*.

(l) the proceeding is for an injunction ordering the person to do or not do anything in Malawi whether or not damages are claimed; or

(m) for any other reason the Court is satisfied that it is necessary for the claim to be served on a person outside Malawi.'[23]

The scheme of rule 30(2) is, therefore, that the plaintiff must establish two matters: (1) a good and arguable case for the relief claimed; and (2) that the claim passes through one or more of the 13 gateways set out at rule 30(2)(a)–(m). Once the court determines that the plaintiff has a good and arguable case and that the claim passes through one or more of the 13 gateways then 'The Court shall ... order that' the summons be served outside the jurisdiction.

On an application to serve out of the jurisdiction the court may give directions extending the time for service of the summons and for filing a response or defence to the claim.[24] The plaintiff must make a statement under oath evidencing service on the defendant.[25]

The 2017 Rules make no special provision for the defendant subsequently to enter a conditional appearance. However, it is thought that the defendant should make an application pursuant to Order 10, rule 1, at the earliest opportunity for a declaration that the court does not have jurisdiction over him and an order staying the proceedings.

A number of observations may be made regarding the new regime.

First, unlike the position under the previous regime,[26] there would appear to be no discretion in the court to refuse permission to serve out of the jurisdiction on the basis, for example, that Malawi is not the appropriate jurisdiction for the resolution of the dispute.

It does not follow from this, however, that, once the defendant has been served outside the jurisdiction, the defendant cannot apply for the proceedings to be stayed on the basis that Malawi is not the appropriate forum for the resolution of the dispute between the parties and that some other forum is the more appropriate one. It is to be expected that, applying the overriding objective as they are obliged to do, the courts will have regard to the principles set out in *Spiliada Maritime Corp v Cansulex Ltd*,[27] where the House of Lords decided:[28]

---

[23] It will be noted that there is no express provision made for the court to permit service of the writ on a defendant who is present out of the jurisdiction if the action is one to enforce a foreign judgment; Frimpong Oppong 'Recognition and enforcement of foreign judgments in Commonwealth African countries' (2014) XV *Yearbook of Private International Law* 365, 372. By way of comparison, see the English Civil Procedure Rules, PD 6B, para 3.1(10).

[24] Order 8, r 32.

[25] Order 8, r 33.

[26] Where the plaintiff had to satisfy the court that the case was a 'proper one' for service out.

[27] [1987] AC 460 (HL(E)) (Lords Keith, Templeman, Griffiths, Mackay and Goff).

[28] Ibid 476C, *per* Lord Goff, with whom the other Lords of Appeal agreed (Lord Templeman delivering a concurring opinion). A decision under the 1965 Rules of the Supreme Court.

> 'The basic principle is that a stay will only be granted on the ground of forum non conveniens where the court is satisfied that there is some other available forum, having competent jurisdiction, which is the appropriate forum for the trial of the action, i.e. in which the case may be tried more suitably for the interests of all the parties and the ends of justice.'

On this basis the English courts will stay English proceedings if England is not the *forum conveniens.*[29]

Second, unlike the position under the previous rules, the 2017 Rules do not make provision for permission to be granted for service out of the jurisdiction where the plaintiff relies on a jurisdiction clause (this point is addressed further below).

Third, again, unlike the position under the previous rules, the 2017 Rules do not make provision for permission to be granted for service out of the jurisdiction where the plaintiff seeks to enforce a foreign judgment or an arbitration award against the defendant in Malawi (where the defendant has assets in Malawi, but resides outside the jurisdiction, for example).

Fourth, unlike the RSC,[30] the 2017 Rules do not provide for service out of the jurisdiction in respect of a contract made by or through an agent trading or residing within the jurisdiction on behalf of a principal trading or residing out of the jurisdiction.

Despite these differences, the framework within which the Malawian courts consider the grant of leave to serve out of the jurisdiction resembles, albeit now to a lesser extent, the English Rules of the Supreme Court.[31] Malawian courts may therefore be guided by English authorities on aspects of the application of the 2017 Rules.

---

[29] See, generally, *Dicey, Morris and Collins on the Conflict of Laws* 15 ed (2012) vol 1, r 38(2) and (3), para 12-007 et seq; r 38 states the modern English law as follows, inter alia: '(2) ... an English court has power to order a stay of proceedings on the basis that England is an inappropriate forum (forum non conveniens) if: (a) the defendant shows there to be another court with competent jurisdiction which is clearly or distinctly more appropriate than England for the trial of the action, and (b) it is not unjust that the claimant be deprived of the right to trial in England. (3) In considering whether to assume jurisdiction in any of the cases mentioned in Rule 34 (service out of the jurisdiction with the permission of the court) the court will generally require the claimant to show England to be the most appropriate forum for the trial of the claim.'

[30] RSC, O XI, r 1(1)(d)(ii) and (iv).

[31] The rule of the English Rules of the Supreme Court regulating service out of the jurisdiction prior to 1999 (when the Civil Procedure Rules came into effect) was O XI. Under the Rules of the Supreme Court 1883 and the Rules of the Supreme Court 1965, which superseded the 1883 Rules, O XI, r 1, provided for service out of the jurisdiction.

6.1.2.2 *Bases for service out of the jurisdiction*

The bases on which the court may grant permission which are of particular significance for present purposes are discussed below.

(1) Relief is sought against any person domiciled, or ordinarily resident, within the jurisdiction

The term 'person' in Order 8, rule 30(2)(c) includes any natural or legal person.[32]

It is likely, given the affinity of Malawi and English law, that the Malawian courts will look to the jurisprudence applicable in English law regarding the meaning of the terms 'domicile' and 'ordinary residence' for the purposes of determining jurisdiction over a person.[33]

Domicile has been authoritatively described in the following terms:[34]

> 'The notion which lies at the root of the concept of domicile is that of permanent home. "By domicile we mean home, the permanent home; and if you do not understand your permanent home I am afraid that no illustration drawn from foreign writers or foreign languages will very much help you to it." A person may be said to have his home in a country if he resides in it without any intention of at present removing from it permanently or for an indefinite period. But a person does not cease to have his home in a country merely because he is temporarily resident elsewhere; and a person who has formed the intention of leaving a country does not cease to have his home in it until he acts according to that intention.'

It may also be of relevance to note that 'domicile' was defined in the RSC as follows:[35]

> 'In general the domicile of a person is in the country in which he has his permanent home (see Dicey, *Conflict of Laws*, 7th ed., Chap. 6), the country in which his habitation is fixed without any present intention of removing (*Re Craignish*, [1892] 3 Ch. 180, C.A.; *Huntly v. Gaskell*, [1906] A.C. 56; *Casdagli v. C.*, [1919] A.C. 145). No person can at any time be without a domicile or have more than one domicile. The domicile of origin remains until a new domicile of choice has been adopted (*Bell v. Kennedy* (1868), L.R. 1 Sc. App. 307, H.L.; *Udny v. Udny* (1869), ibid, 441, H.L., *Winans v. A.-G.*, [1904] A.C. 287, H.L.).'

---

[32] Section 2(1) of the General Interpretation Act 1966 (Act 36 of 1966, now Cap 01:01 of the Laws of Malawi, 2010).

[33] See generally on the meaning of 'domicile', *Dicey, Morris and Collins on the Conflict of Laws* 15 ed (2012) vol 1, r 4, para 6-004.

[34] Ibid para 6R-001, quoting from *Whicker v Hume* (1858) 7 HLC 124, 160.

[35] The Rules of the Supreme Court 1883 (1960 ed) 144. Under the Rules of the Supreme Court 1883 and the Rules of the Supreme Court 1965, which superseded the 1883 Rules, O XI, r 1, provided for service out of the jurisdiction where the defendant was domiciled or ordinarily resident within the jurisdiction. Although the 2016 Rules are a new code, there is no reason to suppose that a concept such as 'domicile' has changed its meaning.

The 'domicile' of a legal person has been described as follows:[36]

> 'A corporation is domiciled where it is registered, if the law requires it to be registered, and if it does not it is domiciled in the country by whose law it is incorporated (Dicey, *Conflict of Laws*, 7th ed., p. 477). A corporation is "resident" and "ordinarily resident" where its central management and control is exercised ...'.

The term 'ordinarily resident' has been explained as follows:[37]

> 'It has sometimes been said that "ordinary residence" means nothing more or less than "residence," but it is submitted that the better view is that the adjective does add something, an element of continuity, order, or settled purpose.'

It is likely that a company will be regarded as ordinarily resident in Malawi if it satisfies the conditions for presence within the jurisdiction.[38]

(2) The claim concerns a contract made in Malawi or governed by the law of Malawi or the claim is based on a breach of contract committed in Malawi whether or not the contract was made in Malawi

It is likely that, in the apparent absence of Malawian authority on the construction and application of Order 8, rule 30(2)(f) and (g), a Malawian court will be guided by the academic and judicial authorities on the construction and application of the (former) equivalent provision in the RSC.[39]

A concise statement of the law is as follows[40] (and should be adapted substituting 'Malawi' for 'England'):

> '(i) **Where a contract is made in England**
>
> **11-181**
>
> If the parties enter into negotiations by correspondence from different countries, the contract is made where the letter of acceptance is posted. But in commercial transactions today communication by telephone, telex, fax and electronic mail is much more common than by post. It is now well established, following the decision of the Court of Appeal in *Entores v Miles Far East Corp* (which was approved by the House of Lords [*Brinkibon Ltd v. Stahag Stahl und Stahlwarenhandelsgesellschaft mbH* [1983] 2 AC 34]) that if the parties use "instantaneous" means of communication such as telephone, fax or electronic mail, the contract is made where the acceptance is communicated to the offeror. It has been held that if a contract made in England contains a submission to arbitration in a foreign country, an action in England at common law to enforce the foreign arbitration award is within this part of the clause. The contract must actually be made in England as that phrase is understood in English law. It is not sufficient if it merely says that it shall be

[36] Rules of the Supreme Court, 1883 (1960 ed) 145. The same meaning followed through to the 1965 Rules of the Supreme Court.

[37] *Dicey, Morris and Collins on the Conflict of Laws* 15 ed (2012) vol 1, para 6-160.

[38] Which conditions have been set out above.

[39] Order XI, r 1(d) and (e) of the Rules of the Supreme Court 1965.

[40] *Dicey, Morris and Collins on The Conflict of Laws* 15 ed (2012) vol 1, r 34, paras 11-181–11-187.

deemed to be so made, though this may be sufficient to make it one which is governed by English law. A contract may be made in England within the meaning of this clause although it was preceded by a less formal agreement made abroad, or if it was originally made in England, but amended abroad.

(iii) **Where a contract is governed by English law**

11-186

...

11-187

Although the fact that a contract is governed by English law is an important factor in the exercise of the discretion under this head in favour of the English forum, it is not conclusive. This head of jurisdiction was described as exorbitant in *Amin Rasheed Shipping Corp v Kuwait Insurance Co*, where the House of Lords held that in the circumstances it was not appropriate for the English court to determine a dispute involving a marine insurance policy governed by English law when the Kuwaiti courts were the *forum conveniens*. Until that decision it was generally thought that the fact that a contract was governed by English law was in itself sufficient to justify leave. But now the claimant has a heavier burden. In *Amin Rasheed* Lord Diplock suggested that, in order to justify leave under this head, the plaintiff had to show that justice could not be obtained by him in the foreign court, or could only be obtained at excessive cost, delay or inconvenience. But it was subsequently held that Lord Diplock was merely giving examples, and was not providing an exhaustive list, of the relevant factors. The court has to consider all factors, and the fact that English law is the applicable law may be of great importance, or it may be of little consequence as seen in the context of the whole case. Thus if there is likely to be no dispute on matters of law or construction, or if the law of the foreign forum is substantially the same as English law, the fact that English law is the applicable law will be of little weight. But where an issue of English public policy arises in relation to a contract which is (or may be) governed by English law, it is desirable that it should be decided by the English court; conversely, where the foreign court may apply its own public policy to defeat a claim based on a contract governed by English law, that too is a reason for the English court taking jurisdiction. If the claimant has alternative remedies in contract and tort upon the same facts, he can choose his remedy.'

As mentioned above, unlike the RSC,[41] the 2017 Rules do not provide for service out of the jurisdiction in respect of a contract made by or through an agent trading or residing within the jurisdiction on behalf of a principal trading or residing out of the jurisdiction. It would appear, therefore, that where a foreign defendant is trading by or through an agent in Malawi, the court has no power to grant permission to a plaintiff to serve that foreign defendant outside the jurisdiction on the basis that the contract was made by or through an agent within the jurisdiction.[42]

[41] RSC, O XI, r 1(1)(d)(ii) and (iv).

[42] It was held in *Union International Insurance Co Ltd v Jubilee Insurance Co Ltd* [1991] 1 WLR 415 (QBD, Comm Ct) (Phillips J), that the provisions of the equivalent parts of O XI of the Rules of the Supreme Court 1965 did not apply to plaintiffs.

(3) The action is founded on a tort committed within the jurisdiction or the damage caused by that tort is suffered within the jurisdiction

There is no reported judicial authority in Malawi on the construction and application of Order 8, rule 30(2)(h).

As with the construction and application of Order 8, rule 30(2)(f) and (g), it is likely that, in the absence of Malawian authority on the subject, a Malawian court will be guided by the academic and judicial authorities on the construction and application of the (former) equivalent provision in the English Rules of the Supreme Court on the question when is a tort committed within the jurisdiction.[43]

A statement of the law is as follows:[44]

> **'11-212**
>
> As both the Privy Council [in *Distillers Co (Bio-chemicals) Ltd v. Thompson* [1971] AC 458] and the Supreme Court of Canada [*Moran v. Pyle National (Canada) Ltd* (1973) 43 D.L.R. (3d) 239] have pointed out, the competing theories for the determination of the place of a tort have been that (i) all ingredients of the cause of action must have occurred within the jurisdiction, or (ii) the last ingredient, the event which completes a cause of action, must have occurred within the jurisdiction, or (iii) the act which the defendant committed must have occurred within the jurisdiction.
>
> **11-213**
>
> In *Distillers Co Ltd v Thompson* the Privy Council adopted the test of the place where in substance the act or omission occurred which gave the plaintiff his cause of action. So that where the essence of the complaint was failure to warn the consumer of the dangers of a product (rather than the faulty manufacture of the product) the cause of action was held to have arisen at the place where the failure to warn occurred; and the torts of negligent and fraudulent misrepresentation, where the negligent or fraudulent statement was communicated from one country to another, were held to have been committed where the statement was received and acted upon. Prior to the adoption of that test, but consistently with it, it had been held that the tort of defamation was committed where the defamatory statements were published and not where they were posted or uttered.'

On the question whether relevant damage was suffered in Malawi, the editors of *The Conflict of Laws* state:[45]

> **'11-216**
>
> Damage sustained within the jurisdiction must refer to recoverable damage, including recoverable economic loss. In Canada and Australia, similar wording has been held to apply to consequential pecuniary damage sustained in the forum flowing from physical injury caused outside the forum, and these decisions have been followed in England. The fact that the centre of the claimant's business is within the jurisdiction does not necessarily

---

[43] Order XI, r 1(ee) and 1(f) respectively: Rules of the Supreme Court 1883 (1961 ed) and 1965.

[44] *Dicey, Morris and Collins on the Conflict of Laws* 15 ed (2012) vol 1, r 34, paras 11-212–11-213.

[45] Ibid para 11-216.

> mean that the economic damage is sustained there. In the second part of the formula, "an act committed within the jurisdiction" also extends to negligent omissions such as a failure to give adequate warning about the dangers of a product. In the *Metall und Rohstoff* case it was held that, for the purposes of each part of the formula, it is not necessary that all of the damage be sustained within the jurisdiction, or that all of the acts be committed within the jurisdiction. Some significant damage must have occurred in England; or the damage (wherever sustained) must result from substantial and efficacious acts committed within the jurisdiction, irrespective of whether or not other substantial and efficacious acts have been committed elsewhere.'

(4) For any other reason the Court is satisfied that it is necessary for the claim to be served on a person outside Malawi

Sub-rule 30(2)(m) did not appear in the RSC that preceded the 2017 Rules. The wording of the sub-rule presents some challenges of construction.

The words, 'for any *other* reason' (emphasis provided), must be taken to refer to the preceding 12 bases for granting permission to serve out of the jurisdiction, otherwise the qualification of 'reason' but the adjective 'other' would deprive the latter of meaning.

As for the circumstances in which the court can be satisfied that it is 'necessary' for the claim to be served out of the jurisdiction, these circumstances are unlikely to relate to some characteristic of the defendant that makes it 'necessary' to serve him outside the jurisdiction because either: (1) the situation would already be covered by sub-rule 30(2)(k) which provides for service out of the jurisdiction on a 'necessary party'; or (2) if service out of the jurisdiction is necessary because the defendant is outside the jurisdiction then the provision is unnecessary because it is already catered for in the preceding provisions.

It is difficult to divine the imperative that could satisfy a court that service outside the jurisdiction is 'necessary' or, for that matter, the matters of which the court must be satisfied in order to conclude that service out of the jurisdiction is 'necessary'.

It is submitted that sub-rule 30(2)(m) may be given meaning by construing it so that the court has power to grant permission to serve out of the jurisdiction in the case of a claim that does not fall within any other gateway under rule 30(2) but where Malawi is so plainly the appropriate forum for the resolution of the dispute that, in conformity to the overriding objective, it is 'necessary' in order to secure that objective that a claim not otherwise justiciable in Malawi should nonetheless be resolved in Malawi. In other words, sub-rule 30(2)(m) provides the court with a *forum conveniens* basis on which to assume jurisdiction. If so, this is a welcome development and may help to avoid some injustices. For example, if a Malawian domiciliary is injured in a road traffic accident by a Tanzanian road haulier employed by a Tanzanian road haulage company outside the jurisdiction in Zambia and the witnesses to the accident were the passengers in the car, all Malawian domiciliaries, then it would make little sense to refuse the injured party permission to serve outside the jurisdiction in Tanzania when all the witnesses lived within the jurisdiction. In such circumstances a court could be satisfied that in order to ensure '(a) ... that the parties are on an equal footing; [and] (b) saving expenses', it was necessary that the defendant should be served in Tanzania.

6.1.2.3 *Submission to the jurisdiction*

Two circumstances must be distinguished under the title submission to the jurisdiction. First, where submission is alleged in extant proceedings in Malawi. Second, where the defendant has agreed (usually by contractual provision) to submit to the jurisdiction of the court in advance of a dispute arising (or possibly afterwards also).

6.1.2.3.1 Submission by appearance

A summary of the common-law principles is set out below. In the absence of Malawian authority on the subject,[46] it is likely that a court will have regard to the established principles at common law.

A party who voluntarily appears in proceedings in which he has been served outside the jurisdiction will be held to have submitted to the jurisdiction of the court. Further:[47]

> **'11-130**
>
> Submission has been inferred when the defendant applied to strike out part of the claim. It has also been inferred when the defendant filed affidavits and appeared through counsel to argue the merits on the claimant's application for an injunction; or when the defendant consented inter partes to the continuance of a freezing injunction without reserving his right to contest the jurisdiction; or when he sought to set aside a committal order and gave an undertaking and submitted evidence; when he moved to set aside a default judgment and at the same time applied for an order that the plaintiff deliver a statement of claim; and when he applied for an order for security for costs. The clear trend of the modern authorities is that the defendant will not be regarded as having submitted by making an application in the proceedings, provided that he has specifically reserved his objection to the jurisdiction.'

---

[46] Under the previous version of the Rules of Court, an acknowledgement of service by the defendant without more was regarded as submission to the jurisdiction: *Sacranie t/a Textilewear v Ali* [1997] 2 MLR 245 (Mtambo J) 247e.

[47] *Dicey, Morris and Collins on the Conflict of Laws* 15 ed (2012) vol 1, r 32, generally paras 11-125–11-133.

As noted above, whilst the 2017 Rules do not provide for a particular procedure to challenge the jurisdiction of the court, the same result can be achieved by an application under Order 10, rule 1, for a declaration that the court does not have jurisdiction and an order staying the proceedings in Malawi in favour of another forum.

6.1.2.3.2 Submission by agreement

6.1.2.3.2.1 *Jurisdiction clauses*

The courts in Malawi will endeavour to give effect to jurisdiction clauses in favour of foreign jurisdictions or arbitration proceedings.

Mirza v AMI (Malawi) Ltd[48] concerned a contractual dispute. The plaintiff purchased goods in Dubai and arranged for them to be shipped by the defendant to Malawi. The goods were discharged in Mozambique and were then damaged in transit to Malawi. The plaintiff brought proceedings in Malawi and the defendant contended that the bill of lading for the goods contained an exclusive jurisdiction clause in favour of the courts of Antwerp. The judge, relying on section 103(2) of the Constitution, stated: 'The Judiciary shall have jurisdiction over all issues of judicial nature and shall have exclusive authority to decide whether an issue is within its competence' (underlining in original), and adopted the five principles outlined by Brandon J (as he then was) in *Owners of cargo lately laden on board the ship or vessel Eleftheria v The Eleftheria (Owners), The Eleftheria.*[49] Brandon J's statement of the principles has since been accepted in other jurisdictions as the authoritative statement in this area.[50]

In *The Eleftheria* the jurisdiction clause provided 'Any dispute arising under this bill of lading shall be decided in the country where the carrier has his principal place of business [Greece].' The owners of cargo on board the *Eleftheria* commenced proceedings in England and the shipowners applied for a stay of those proceedings. In staying the proceedings in favour of the Greek courts Brandon J set out the principles on the basis of which a stay may be granted:[51]

> '(1) Where plaintiffs sue in England in breach of an agreement to refer disputes to a foreign court, and the defendants apply for a stay, the English court, assuming the claim to be otherwise within its jurisdiction, is not bound to grant a stay but has a discretion whether to do so or not. (2) The discretion should be exercised by granting a stay unless strong cause for not doing so is shown. (3) The burden of proving such strong cause is on the plaintiffs. (4) In exercising its discretion the court should take into account all the circumstances of

---

48 [2007] MWHC 116.

49 [1970] P 94; [1969] 1 Lloyd's Rep 237 (QBD, Comm Ct).

50 *Aratra Potato Co Ltd v Egyptian Navigation Co (The El Amria)* [1981] 2 Lloyd's Rep 119 (CA, Eng); *Anraj Fish Products Industries Ltd v Hyundai Merchant Marine Co Ltd* [2000] ILPr 717 (Fed Ct, Can); *Nika Fishing Co Ltd v Lavina Corp* [2008] 16 NWLR 509 (Sup Ct, Nigeria).

51 [1970] P 94 at 99G–100C.

> the particular case. (5) In particular, but without prejudice to (4), the following matters, where they arise, may properly be regarded:—(a) In what country the evidence on the issues of fact is situated, or more readily available, and the effect of that on the relative convenience and expense of trial as between the English and foreign courts, (b) Whether the law of the foreign court applies and, if so, whether it differs from English law in any material respects, (c) With what country either party is connected, and how closely, (d) Whether the defendants genuinely desire trial in the foreign country, or are only seeking procedural advantages, (e) Whether the plaintiffs would be prejudiced by having to sue in the foreign court because they would: (i) be deprived of security for their claim; (ii) be unable to enforce any judgment obtained; (iii) be faced with a time-bar not applicable in England; or (iv) for political, racial, religious or other reasons be unlikely to get a fair trial.'

In *Mirza v AMI*, the court dismissed the plaintiff's claim on the ground that the plaintiff had sued the agent and not the principal. Nonetheless, in order to reach this conclusion, the judge must have decided that he had jurisdiction in the matter so, as a matter of law, the judge's approval of the decision of Brandon J forms part of the ratio of the case. It is to be expected that *The Eleftheria* will be treated as authoritative in Malawian courts in the future.

As regards arbitration clauses, section 6(1) of the Arbitration Act 1967[52] provides:

> 'If any party to an arbitration agreement, or any person claiming through or under him, commences any legal proceedings in any court against any other party to the agreement, or any person claiming through or under him, in respect of any matter agreed to be referred, any party to those legal proceedings may at any time after appearance, and before delivering any pleadings or taking any other steps in the proceedings, apply to that court to stay the proceedings, and that court, if satisfied that there is no sufficient reason why the matter should not be referred in accordance with the agreement, and that the applicant was, at the time when the proceedings were commenced, and still remains, ready and willing to do all things necessary to the proper conduct of the arbitration, may make an order staying the proceedings.'

Thus, a party may submit to the jurisdiction of the court and by doing so deprive himself of the benefit of an arbitration clause. On the application of the beneficiary of an arbitration clause for a stay of the court proceedings, the court has discretion whether to stay proceedings and refer the matter to arbitration or not.

6.1.2.3.2.2 *Application for service out of the jurisdiction based on a jurisdiction clause*

One question that arises is the statutory basis on which a Malawian court may assume jurisdiction over a cause where the plaintiff in Malawi applies for service on the putative defendant out of the jurisdiction based on a jurisdiction clause in an agreement.

---

[52] Act 26 of 1967 (now Cap 6:03 of the Laws of Malawi, 2010).

In the English RSC,[53] Order XI, rule 1(1)(d)(i)–(iv), the sub-rule governing service out of the jurisdiction in cases concerned with contract, contained an additional sub-sub-paragraph which provided as follows: 'The claim is made to enforce ... a contract which ... (iv) contains a term to the effect that the High Court shall have jurisdiction to hear and determine any action in respect of the contract.' This additional provision was included in the English rules in order to reverse the decision of the Court of Appeal in *British Wagon Co Ltd v Gray*.[54]

The position at common law is stated by the editors of *The Conflict of Laws* as follows:[55]

> **'11-131**
>
> Submission may also be inferred from the terms of a contract. At common law, the mere agreement of the parties that the court was to have jurisdiction to determine disputes arising out of a contract between them was insufficient by itself to give the court jurisdiction, because the defendant could not be legally served with process if he was out of England. But if one party to the contract nominated an agent resident in England to accept service of process on his behalf, he was deemed to submit to the jurisdiction, and service could be effected on the agent in accordance with the contract.'

Where the defendant is not present within the jurisdiction and where no other provision of the 2017 Rules, Order 8, rule 30(2) is applicable to the case, the question is whether the Malawian court has power to order service out of the jurisdiction solely on the basis that the agreement between the parties contains a jurisdiction clause in favour of the Malawian courts. It would seem not and in such a case there would be no basis on which the Malawian court could validly make an order for service of the defendant out of the jurisdiction.

6.1.2.4 Lis alibi pendens

The approach of the Malawian courts to concurrent proceedings concerning the same subject-matter and parties within and outside the jurisdiction is not clear. It is likely, however, that a Malawian court, acting as directed by the overriding objective would entertain an application to stay Malawian proceedings in favour of proceedings being pursued overseas and would do so if, on balance, the aims of the overriding objective were to be met by a stay of the Malawian proceedings.

---

[53] Rules of the Supreme Court 1965 introduced by amendment in 1920.

[54] [1896] 1 QB 35 (CA), where a party sought leave to serve the putative defendant in Scotland. Leave was refused because the basis on which it was sought was a jurisdiction clause in favour of the English courts and there was no provision in the rules allowing for service out in those circumstances. Lord Esher MR stated (at 36): 'The Court can take no notice of such an agreement, and can only order service of the writ in the manner allowed by the rules, and not in any other manner upon which the parties may agree.'

[55] *Dicey, Morris and Collins on the Conflict of Laws* 15 ed (2012) vol 1, r 32.

There would appear to be no reason why a Malawian court could not order a party subject to its personal jurisdiction to stay proceedings commenced by that party outside the jurisdiction between the same parties and concerning the same subject-matter. Order 10, rule 27 provides: 'The Court may, on application, grant an injunction by an interlocutory order when it appears to the Court to be just and convenient to do so, and the order may be made unconditionally or on such terms or conditions as the Court considers just.' These words are of sufficient amplitude to embrace an application for an anti-suit injunction.

6.1.2.5 Forum non conveniens

As has been noted when considering the regime provided for by the 2017 Rules and, specifically, when considering sub-rule 30(2)(m), it appears that the principle of *forum non conveniens* is known to Malawian law. The reader is referred to those passages for a more detailed discussion of the *forum non conveniens* principle.

6.2 Enforcement of Foreign Judgments

Under Malawian law certain foreign judgments may be enforced in Malawi pursuant to one of a number of statutes or, save where said statutes prohibit, at common law.

6.2.1 Enforcement at common law

Enforcement of a foreign judgment at common law is available for judgment creditors in Malawi.

English law was introduced into Malawi, at that time a constituent part of the British Central Africa Protectorate, by means of the Africa Order in Council 1889, section 13 of which provided that civil and criminal jurisdiction

> 'should, so far as circumstances admitted, be exercised upon the principles of and in conformity with the substance of the law for the time being in force in and for England and with the powers vested in and according to the course of procedure and practice observed by and before Courts of Justice and Justices of the Peace in England according to their respective jurisdictions and authorities'.

Section 15(2) of the British Central Africa Order in Council 1902,[56] relating to that part of central Africa covered by the Africa Order in Council 1889 which became modern-day Malawi, continued the regime applicable under section 13 of the 1889 Order in Council to the new British Central Africa Protectorate.

---

[56] Made on 11 August 1902, gazetted on 31 October 1902.

By the Nyasaland Order in Council 1907,[57] the British Central Africa Protectorate was redesignated the Nyasaland Protectorate, a governor was appointed and an executive council and legislative council were established, with the latter having power to make ordinances. The 1907 Order in Council preserved in all other respects the provisions of the British Central Africa Order in Council 1902.

Also in 1907, by the Nyasaland Order in Council 1907 (No 2),[58] section 15(2) of the British Central Africa Order in Council 1902 was revoked and substituted as follows:

> 'Such civil and criminal jurisdiction shall, so far as circumstances admit, be exercised in conformity with the substance of the common law, doctrines of equity, and statutes of general application in force in England, on the eleventh day of August, one thousand nine hundred and two, and with the powers vested in, and according to the procedure and practice observed by and before Courts of Justice, and Justices of the Peace in England, according to their respective jurisdictions and authorities at that date, save in so far as the same may at any time before the commencement of this Order have been, or hereafter may be, modified or amended by or under the authority of any Order of His Majesty in Council, or by any Ordinance or Ordinances passed in and for the Protectorate.'

Thus, the law in force in Malawi as at 1902 was, inter alia, the common law as at that time.

By 1902 the basic English law principles of enforcement of a foreign judgment at common law had been settled and these represent the law applicable in Malawi as at 1902. It is to be expected that a Malawian court will also have regard to developments in the English common law that have occurred since that time in applying the 1902 common-law principles.[59]

This statement reflects the statements of principle from the Malawian courts on this subject. In *Heyns v Demetriou*,[60] where Mwaungulu J stated: 'This Court's jurisdiction over foreign judgments is statutory and common law.' The judge held, setting aside the registration of the judgment, that the judgment creditor could proceed with a claim at common law.

---

[57] Made on 6 July 1907, gazetted on 21 October 1907.

[58] Made on 21 December 1907, gazetted on 29 February 1908.

[59] However, it should be remembered that O 8, r 30(2) of the 2016 Rules does not allow the Malawi court to permit service of the writ on a defendant who is present outside the jurisdiction where the action is one to enforce a foreign judgment.

[60] (Unreported) 10 September 2001 (H Ct) (Mwaungulu J).

These principles are conveniently set out in *Dicey, Morris and Collins on the Conflict of Laws*:[61]

> **'Rule 42**
>
> (1) Subject to the Exceptions hereinafter mentioned and to Rule 62 (international conventions), a foreign judgment in personam given by the court of a foreign country with jurisdiction to give that judgment in accordance with the principles set out in Rules 43 to 46, and which is not impeachable under any of Rules 49 to 54, may be enforced by a claim or counterclaim for the amount due under it if the judgment is
>
> *(a)* for a debt, or definite sum of money (not being a sum payable in respect of taxes or other charges of a like nature or in respect of a fine or other penalty); and
>
> *(b)* final and conclusive,
>
> but not otherwise.
>
> Provided that a foreign judgment may be final and conclusive, though it is subject to an appeal, and though an appeal against it is actually pending in the foreign country where it was given.
>
> (2) A foreign judgment given by the court of a foreign country with jurisdiction to give that judgment in accordance with the principles set out in Rules 43 to 46, which is not impeachable under any of Rules 49 to 54 and which is final and conclusive on the merits, is entitled to recognition at common law and may be relied on in proceedings in England.
>
> (3) No proceedings may be brought by a person on a cause of action in respect of a judgment which has been given in his favour in proceedings between the same parties or their privies in a court in another part of the United Kingdom or in a court in an overseas country unless that judgment is not enforceable according to clause (1), or not entitled to recognition according to clause (2), of this Rule.'

In order for its judgment to be enforceable the foreign court must have possessed international competence to determine the case. As a matter of common law a foreign court will have been internationally competent in the following cases:[62] (1) if the person against whom the judgment was given was, at the time the proceedings were instituted, present in the foreign country; or (2) if the person against whom the judgment was given was the claimant, or counterclaimed, in the proceedings in the foreign court; or (3) if the person against whom the judgment was given submitted to the jurisdiction of that court by voluntarily appearing in the proceedings; or (4) if the person against whom the judgment was given had, before the commencement of the proceedings, agreed, in respect of the subject-matter of the proceedings, to submit to the jurisdiction of that court or of the courts of that country.[63]

---

[61] 15 ed (2012) vol 1, para 14R-020.

[62] *Dicey, Morris and Collins on the Conflict of Laws* 15 ed (2012) vol 1, r 43, para 14R-054.

[63] It was stated by Mwaungulu J in *Heyns v Demetriou* (unreported) 10 September 2001 (H Ct) that if the defendant agrees to submit to the court's jurisdiction he is deemed to have agreed to submit to that court's

To this list may be added a fifth ground posited by Mwaungulu J in *Heyns v Demetriou*,[64] where, citing the decision of the English Court of Appeal in *Emmanuel v Symon*,[65] the judge stated and apparently accepted that a further basis for the jurisdiction of the foreign court would be 'where the defendant is a subject of the foreign country in which the judgment has been obtained'. As a basis for the jurisdiction of the foreign court, this has been doubted.[66]

Among the established defences to an action at common law on a foreign judgment are the following: (1) where the foreign judgment was procured by fraud, either (a) fraud on the part of the party in whose favour the judgment is given or (b) fraud on the part of the court pronouncing the judgment;[67] (2) the enforcement or recognition of the foreign judgment would be contrary to public policy;[68] and (3) where the proceedings in which the foreign judgment was obtained were contrary to the rules of natural justice.[69]

6.2.2 Enforcement pursuant to statute

6.2.2.1 *The regimes for enforcement pursuant to statute*

The relevant statutes for the purposes of enforcement in Malawi of a foreign judgment are: (1) the British and Colonial Judgments Ordinance 1922[70] ('the

procedure rules and is bound by the judgment, even though he may not have had notice of the proceedings. The most recent edition of *Dicey, Morris and Collins on the Conflict of Laws* 15 ed (2012) vol 1, para 14-080, departs from this approach and states that the ultimate question is whether there has been a substantial injustice and the court may take into account, inter alia, whether the foreign court provides an opportunity for the foreign judgment to be set aside.

[64] (Unreported) 10 September 2001 (H Ct) (Mwaungulu J).

[65] [1908] 1 KB 302.

[66] *Dicey, Morris and Collins on the Conflict of Laws* 15 ed (2012) vol 1, r 43, para 14-085: 'There is a long chain of dicta extending from 1828 to 1948 suggesting that the courts of a foreign country might have jurisdiction over a person if he was a subject or citizen of that country. But there is no actual decision which supports this proposition. *Douglas v Forrest* [(1882) 4 Bing 686] goes nearest to a decision to this effect. But that is a very old case, and the judgment dwells also on the fact that the defendant retained property in the foreign country-an alternative basis of jurisdiction which would not now be acknowledged as adequate. It is evident that nationality is quite inappropriate as a basis of jurisdiction when the defendant is, e.g. a British citizen or an American citizen, or an Australian citizen since in these cases the political unit (or State) does not coincide with the law district (or country). Citizenship does not serve to identify them with any particular law district, such as England or New York or Victoria, within a composite State such as the United Kingdom, the United States or Australia. Moreover, the question whether a person is a national of a given state is a matter for the law of that State. As a connecting factor, therefore, nationality is not subject to the control or definition of the *lex fori*; and as the law of the given State may deem a person to be a national, or deny nationality, on grounds which are objectionable in English eyes, nationality would constitute too unpredictable a basis for jurisdiction. Nationality as a basis of jurisdiction has been doubted by three High Court judges, and definitely rejected by the Irish High Court. It cannot therefore safely be relied upon today.'

[67] *Dicey, Morris and Collins on the Conflict of Laws* 15 ed (2012) vol 1, r 50, para 14R-137.

[68] Ibid r 51, para 14R-152.

[69] Ibid r 52, para 14R-162.

[70] Ordinance 3 of 1922. The complete Ordinance appears as Cap 15 in the Laws of Nyasaland, 1957. The complete Ordinance has, however, been omitted from the most recent publication of the Laws of Malawi

1922 Ordinance'), (2) the Nyasaland Judgments Extension Ordinance 1912[71] ('the 1912 Extension Ordinance') and (3) the Service of Process and Enforcement of Judgments Act 1957[72] ('the 1957 Service Act').

Proclamations by the Governor have extended the 1922 Ordinance to judgments from the superior courts of the Seychelles,[73] Basutoland (now Lesotho), Eswatini,[74] Somaliland[75] (British Somaliland, modern-day Republic of Somaliland, an autonomous region of Somalia), New South Wales,[76] the British Solomon Islands[77] and the Gilbert and Ellis Islands.[78]

The 1912 Extension Ordinance applies to decrees for any debt, damages or costs obtained or entered up in courts in Kenya, Uganda, Tanganyika (now Tanzania), Northern Rhodesia (now Zambia) and Zanzibar.

The 1957 Service Act provides for service in Malawi of civil or criminal process and the enforcement of civil judgments emanating from Zambia and Southern Rhodesia (now Zimbabwe).

6.2.2.1.1 British and Colonial Judgments Ordinance 1922

As will become apparent below, the 1922 Ordinance is a transposition of the applicable provisions of the United Kingdom Administration of Justice Act 1920. It is to be expected therefore that a Malawian court will have regard to (although not, of course, be bound by) decisions of the English courts, in particular, and the commentary by academics on the interpretation of the 1920 Act of the United Kingdom Parliament.[79] The principal provisions of the 1922 Ordinance are referred to below.

(2010). Volume XI of the 2010 publication indicates that it has been omitted pursuant to s 9 of the Revision of the Laws Act (Act 15 of 1968, now Cap 1.02 of the Laws of Malawi, 2010). The omission of the complete Ordinance is not an indication that it has been repealed.

[71] Ordinance 7 of 1912. It was amended by the Judgments Extension (Amendment) Ordinance 4 of 1922. The complete Ordinance appears as Cap 14 in the Laws of Nyasaland, 1957. The complete Ordinance has, however, been omitted from the most recent publication of the Laws of Malawi (2010). Volume XI of the 2010 publication indicates that it has been omitted pursuant to s 9 of the Revision of the Laws Act (Cap 01.02 of the Laws of Malawi, 2010). The omission of the complete Ordinance is not an indication that it has been repealed.

[72] Act 4 of 1956 (now Cap 04:04 of the Laws of Malawi).

[73] Government Notice 47 of 1924.

[74] Government Notice 4 of 1925.

[75] Government Notice 33 of 1925.

[76] Government Notice 156 of 1925.

[77] Government Notice 150 of 1957.

[78] Ibid.

[79] The relevant parts of *Dicey, Morris and Collins on the Conflict of Laws* 15 ed (2012) on the application of the 1920 Act are as follows: r 53, paras 14R-173–14-181.

By section 2, the Ordinance applies to any judgments[80] or orders in any civil proceedings providing for the payment of a sum of money, and includes awards in arbitration proceedings[81] if these can, under the law in force where they are made, be enforced in the same manner as judgments.[82]

Section 3 of the Ordinance provides that where a judgment has been obtained from the High Court in England or Ireland or the Court of Session in Scotland, the judgment creditor may apply to the High Court in Malawi at any time within 12 months after the date of the judgment to have the judgment registered and on such an application the court may, 'if in all the circumstances of the case it thinks it just and convenient that the judgment should be enforced in [Malawi]', order the judgment to be registered.[83]

6.2.2.1.1.1 *Procedure for registration*

Section 4[84] provides that no judgment shall be registered if:

(1) the original court acted without jurisdiction;

(2) the judgment debtor[85] was neither (a) carrying on business[86] nor ordinarily resident within the jurisdiction; (b) did not voluntarily appear or otherwise submit or agree to the jurisdiction of the court;

(3) the defendant was not duly served with the proceedings and did not appear notwithstanding that he was ordinarily resident or carrying on business within the jurisdiction or had agreed to submit to the jurisdiction of the court;

(4) the judgment was obtained by fraud;[87]

---

[80] It has been held by the Court of Appeal in England that the 1920 Act does not permit registration of a judgment given by a court in one state in an action to enforce a judgment given by a court in another state: *Strategic Technologies Pte Ltd v Procurement Bureau of the Republic of China Ministry of National Defence* [2020] EWCA Civ 1604 (David Richards, Males and Elisabeth Laing LJJ). The definition of 'judgment' in s 12(1) of the 1920 Act is materially identical to the definition in s 11(1) of the 1933 Act and so the decision in *Strategic Technologies* will probably apply to the 1933 Act as well.

[81] In *Bauman, Hinde and Co v David Whitehead & Sons* Appeal 17 of 1998 (unreported) (Malawi Supreme Court of Appeal), the court dismissed contentions that the arbitrators in that case had acted without jurisdiction (a ground for refusing or setting aside registration under s 4(a) of the 1922 Ordinance). The court reached this conclusion by reviewing the evidence in support of the existence of an agreement containing an arbitration clause as alleged by the plaintiff.

[82] The equivalent of s 12(1) of the 1920 Act.

[83] The equivalent of s 9(1) of the 1920 Act.

[84] The equivalent of s 9(2) of the 1920 Act.

[85] Being a legal or natural person.

[86] It has been held by an English court that a New Zealand insurance company did not carry on business in a country (in that case, Ghana) merely because it maintained agents there with limited powers: *Sfeir & Co v National Insurance Co of New Zealand Ltd* [1964] 1 Lloyd's Rep 330 (QBD).

[87] Fraud is determined by reference to the common-law principles on fraud: *Owens Bank Ltd v Bracco* [1992] 2 AC 443 (HL (E)), where it was held that s 9(2) of the 1920 Act was to be construed as having adopted

(5) the judgment debtor satisfies the court that an appeal is pending or that he is entitled and intends to appeal against the judgment;

(6) the judgment was in respect of a cause of action which for reasons of public policy or some other similar reasons could not have been entertained by the Malawian court.

Section 5[88] provides that, once registered, the judgment is of the same force and effect as if it had been originally obtained in Malawi.

Section 10[89] provides that where the Governor is satisfied that reciprocal provisions have been made in any other Commonwealth country, he may declare that the 1922 Ordinance extends to the judgments obtained in the superior courts of that jurisdiction. The 1922 Ordinance has been extended to the jurisdictions referred to above.

Section 9[90] provides that provision may be made by rules of court for regulating the practice and procedure of proceedings under the Ordinance.

The Ordinance contains no provisions dealing with recognition of foreign judgments (as opposed to their enforcement). In the ordinary course the recognition of a foreign judgment would be addressed by a reference to common-law principles.[91]

Rules of court were made under section 9 of the Ordinance (the British and Colonial Judgments Rules; 'the 1922 Rules'), and follow a familiar pattern: an application to register a registrable judgment may be made *ex parte* or by

---

the approach of the common-law courts to the finality of a foreign judgment; that, accordingly, there was no requirement, as there was in the case of an action to set aside an English judgment on the ground of fraud, that the fraud should be established by fresh evidence that had not been available to the defendant at trial and could not with reasonable diligence have been discovered by him before judgment had been delivered. This decision, in effect, permits a defendant to relitigate matters already disposed of before the foreign court. The position is the same under the English 1933 Act. The rules relating to setting aside a foreign judgment obtained by fraud are comprehensively set out in *Dicey, Morris and Collins on the Conflict of Laws* 15 ed (2012) vol 1, r 50, paras 14R-137–14-145. There, at para 14-191, it is stated of the fraud provisions of the 1933 Act: 'The provisions with regard to fraud and public policy are the same as the common law rules. In particular, the common law rule that a foreign judgment can be impeached for fraud even though no newly discovered evidence is produced, and even though the fraud was alleged in the foreign proceedings, applies to enforcement and recognition under the 1933 Act. In *Owens Bank Ltd v Bracco* [[1992] 2 AC 443] the House of Lords held that the fraud exception in the 1920 Act was subject to the same rule, and indicated *(obiter)* that the same must be so under the 1933 Act.' *Owens Bank* has not been followed in certain Commonwealth jurisdictions (eg Canada in *Beals v Saldanha* [2003] 3 SCR 416, (2003) 234 DLR (4th) 1; and New South Wales in *Keele v Findley* (1991) 21 NSWLR 444 (NSWSC); but in *Close v Arnot* (unreported) 21 November 1997 (NSW), the Common Law Division distinguished *Keele v Findley* and applied the traditional English standard of fraud in respect of a foreign judgment in a case where the defendant had, for good reason, allowed foreign proceedings to go undefended). A Malawian court would not be bound by the *Owens Bank* decision.

88 The equivalent of s 9(3) of the 1920 Act.

89 The equivalent of s 14 of the 1920 Act.

90 The equivalent of s 11 of the 1920 Act.

91 *Dicey, Morris and Collins on the Conflict of Laws* 15 ed (2012) vol 1, r 53, para 14-180.

originating summons; the application must be supported by an affidavit exhibiting the judgment and stating that, to the best of the deponent's belief, the judgment creditor is entitled to enforce the judgment and the judgment does not fall within any of the exceptions set out in section 4 of the Ordinance; the application itself is for leave to register the judgment and any order granting leave must state the time within which the judgment debtor should raise any objection by way of an application to set aside registration, such application being by summons.

6.2.2.1.1.2 *Setting aside registration*

By section 6 of the 1922 Ordinance, the 1922 Judgments Rules are to provide (and do so provide) for service on the judgment debtor of notice of registration of a judgment. The 1922 Rules[92] also enable the High Court, on the application of a judgment debtor (made by way of summons) to set aside registration of a judgment on such terms as the court sees fit. A writ of execution may be issued after the time provided for in the order, granting that leave to register the judgment has expired without an objection being raised by the defendant.

6.2.2.1.2 Nyasaland Judgments Extension Ordinance 1912

The 1912 Extension Ordinance sets out a special regime in respect of decrees for any debt, damages or costs obtained or entered up in the High Court of Kenya, the High Court of Uganda, the High Court of Tanzania or the High Court of Zanzibar or any court subordinate to any of those courts.

Section 2 of the 1912 Extension Ordinance provides that: where a decree has been obtained or entered up in any of the courts set out in the previous paragraph

> 'for any debt, damages or costs and where it is desired that such decree shall be executed upon the person or property of the defendant[93] [ie the judgment debtor] in [Malawi], such decree may be transferred to [the High Court of Malawi] for execution and the provisions in force in such court for the execution of decrees shall apply in the same manner as if such decree had been entered up [in the High Court].'

All proceedings shall, and may be, had and taken as if the decree had been a decree originally obtained in the High Court and all the reasonable costs and charges with regard to the transfer and execution of such decree shall be recovered in like manner as if the same were part of the original decree.

---

92 Made by way of Government Notice 187 of 1922.

93 The 1912 Extension Ordinance refers to execution against both the property and person of the judgment debtor, but s 19.6(c) of the Constitution of Malawi (1994), enshrining the right not to be imprisoned for an inability to fulfil contractual obligations, has probably ended the practice of arrest for debt.

Section 3 of the 1912 Ordinance provides as follows:[94]

> 'Where any warrant is issued by the [High Court of Kenya], the High Court of Uganda, the High Court ofTanzania or the [High Court of Zanzibar], or in any Court subordinate to such Courts ... for the arrest of a defendant in a civil case either before or after judgment, a Judge of the High Court shall have power (a) to endorse and execute such warrant, (b) to issue before such endorsement a provisional warrant for the arrest of the defendant, upon the receipt of such telegraphic or other information under such circumstances as would in his opinion justify the issue of a warrant if the circumstances had arisen within his jurisdiction:
>
> Provided that a person arrested under such provisional warrant shall be discharged unless the original warrant is produced and endorsed within such reasonable time as may seem requisite:
>
> Provided also that no such warrant shall be endorsed or executed unless the warrant or information from the Court desiring the arrest is accompanied by an intimation that such Court indemnifies the High Court against all such costs, charges and expenses to be incurred by the High Court.'

6.2.2.1.3 Service of Process and Enforcement of Judgments Act 1957

This is an Act the intention of which was to provide for the service in Malawi of civil or criminal process and the enforcement of civil judgments emanating from Zambia and Southern Rhodesia (modern-day Zimbabwe). Part IV concerns the enforcement of judgments, which is defined as 'any judgment or order whereunder a sum of money is payable given or made in a court in any civil proceedings' but excluding a maintenance order for a husband's wife or child or other dependants, and also an arbitration award if enforceable in the country in which it was made.

6.2.2.1.3.1 *Procedure for registration*

The procedure in the Act is as follows: the judgment creditor may, within 12 months of the date of the original judgment, register the certificate of the foreign

[94] It would appear that, with respect to the civil arrest of a defendant, a similar regime is in place in Uganda – see s 3 of the Judgments Extension Act 1908 and the relevant part of the chapter on Uganda. In Tanzania, s 3 of the Judgments Extension Act 1921 allows a judge, inter alia, to indorse or execute a warrant issued by the High Court of the High Court of Kenya, or of Malawi or of Zanzibar or of Uganda. In Zanzibar, s 3 of the Judgments Extension Decree 1908, as amended by s 2 of the Judgments Extension (Amendment) Decree 1921 allows a judge, inter alia, to indorse or execute a warrant issued by the High Court of the Colony and Protectorate of Kenya, or of 'Nyasaland' (Malawi) or of the 'Tanganyika Territory' (Tanzania) or of Uganda. In Kenya, there is no equivalent regime in place. There, enforcement of a foreign judgment pursuant to statute is governed by the Foreign Judgments (Reciprocal Enforcement) Act 1984. That Act does not make reference to 'warrants of arrest' and, in any event, only applies to jurisdictions to which it has been extended by Order; it has not yet been extended to any one of Uganda, Malawi, Tanzania or Zanzibar.

judgment by the production of the certificate to the High Court of Malawi or a subordinate court of Malawi depending on whether the judgment is from the foreign High Court or subordinate court; the 12-month limit on registration may be extended with the leave of the registering court; the judgment certificate is then registered in a 'Register of Southern Rhodesian and Zambia Judgments'; the court in Malawi must be satisfied that the registration is 'reasonable and justifiable'; the judgment creditor must then, prior to execution, file an affidavit with the court in Malawi at which the certificate is registered, stating the amount for which execution is proposed; the registering court may, however, on the application of the judgment debtor, (1) stay proceedings on terms as to giving security and/or making an application to set aside the judgment, (2) grant other relief as the court deems fit.

6.2.2.1.3.2 *Setting aside registration*

The grounds on which the judgment may be set aside are not specified in the 1957 Service Act.

6.3 Interim Remedies

6.3.1 Jurisdiction to grant interim remedies

The jurisdiction of the Malawi High Court to grant injunctions is statutory: 'The Court may, on application, grant an injunction by an interlocutory order when it appears to the Court to be just and convenient to do so, and the order may be made unconditionally or on such terms or conditions as the Court considers just.'[95]

6.3.2 Procedure for application

The rules governing interlocutory applications in the High Court are set out in Order 10. Applications are made in Form 4[96] supported by a sworn statement setting out the facts that support the relief sought[97] and, except where the rules otherwise provide, must be made on notice to the party effected.[98] Usually two clear days' notice of an application is required, but the court may give leave for a period of notice less than that provided for in the rules.[99]

Order 10, rule 5, allows for an application to be made *ex parte* if:

---

95 2017 Rules, O 10, r 27.
96 Order 10, r 1.
97 Order 10, r 4(b).
98 Order 10, r 5.
99 Order 10, r 6.

> '(a) the matter is so urgent that the Court decides the application in a proceeding should be dealt with in the absence of the other party; or (b) the Court orders, for good reason, that there is no need to serve it on the other party'.

One such good reason will surely be that to serve it on the other party may lead to the purpose of the application for the injunction becoming frustrated.[100]

Applications made *ex parte* are subject to a duty of full disclosure or good faith. If relevant facts (or law) are not disclosed on the application, this provides a basis for the discharge of the injunction.[101]

Order 10, rule 7, reverses the usual rule that proceedings must be conducted in open court:[102]

> 'An application for an interlocutory order made during a proceeding is not to be dealt with in open court unless- (a) it is in the public interest that the matter be dealt with in open court; or (b) the Court is of the opinion for good reason that the matter should be dealt with in open court.'

6.3.3 Interlocutory injunctions generally

Although there is no authority directly in point, it is likely that, in order for a Malawian court to make an interlocutory order in a cause, it is necessary that the court has jurisdiction over the substantive dispute between the parties.[103] To this extent the 2017 rules have extinguished the jurisdiction of the Malawian courts

---

[100] Under the previous rules it had been held that in cases of urgency an *ex parte* injunction should only be granted until the *inter partes* hearing and then, if the court was satisfied that it should be extended in its duration, an interim injunction should be granted until trial or further order; at trial, if appropriate to the case, a permanent injunction might then be granted: *Bata Shoe Co v Shore Rubber* [2000] MWHC 12 (H Ct), *per* Mwaungulu J – the terminology used in Malawi is, therefore, *ex parte* injunction, interim injunction (or interlocutory injunction, made *inter partes*) and permanent injunction.

[101] *Mike Appel & Gatto Ltd v General Motors South Africa (Pty) Ltd* [2017] MWHC 112, *per* Kenyatta Nyirenda J.

[102] Section 60 of the Courts Act 1958 provides: 'In exercise of its jurisdiction, powers and authorities the proceedings of every court shall, except as otherwise provided by any other law for the time being in force, be carried on in an open court to which the public generally may have access: Provided that any court shall have power to hear any matter or proceeding or any part thereof in camera if, in the opinion of the presiding Judge, or magistrate, it is expedient in the interest of justice or propriety or for other sufficient reason so to do.' Section 67 of the 1958 Act empowers the Chief Justice to make rules of court: 'The Chief Justice may make rules of court prescribing anything which, under this Act, may be or is to be prescribed and generally for the better carrying out of the purposes of this Act.' It is a moot point whether by reversing the rule regarding hearings in open court contained in s 60, the rule committee acted *ultra vires* the power in s 67 by making the rule contained in O 10, r 7.

[103] Such was the position in the United Kingdom prior to the passing of s 25 of the Civil Jurisdiction and Judgments Act 1982 which now allows courts in the United Kingdom to grant relief in aid of proceedings outside the jurisdiction (*Siskina (Owners of cargo lately on board) v Distos Compania Naviera SA, The Siskina*, [1979] AC 210 (HL (E))).

to grant interim relief in aid of overseas proceedings where the Malawian court has no jurisdiction over the substantive dispute between the parties.[104]

Order 10, rule 8(1) permits an application for an interlocutory injunction to be made before proceedings have commenced, subject to certain requirements. Sub-rule 8(2) provides that the court may make such an order if satisfied '(a) the applicant has a serious question to be tried and, if the evidence brought by the applicant remains as it is, the applicant is likely to succeed; and (b) the balance of convenience favours the making of the order'.

Sub-rule 8(2) sets out the test to be applied on an application for an interlocutory injunction before the commencement of proceedings. The test to be applied on other applications for interlocutory injunctions after the commencement of proceedings is not set out in Order 10. However, as a matter of principle, the test for the granting of an interlocutory injunction ought to be the same whether the application is made before or after proceedings are commenced (subject to the requirements that appear in Order 10, rule 8(1) concerning the provision of reasons why the order should be made prior to the commencement of proceedings).

The test set out in sub-rule 8(2) is also very close to the test for the making of an interlocutory injunction in English law.[105] It is submitted that the test set out in sub-rule 8(2) is the test applicable to all applications for interlocutory injunctions whether made before or after the commencement of proceedings.

---

[104] The RSC empowered the English court to make such an order in aid of foreign proceedings: RSC 1965 (1999 ed), O 29, r 8A (SI 415 of 1997). Because the 2016 Rules do not reproduce this provision of the RSC, the position in Malawi appears to have reverted to that under the common law as stated in *The Siskina* (reverted because s 29(b) of the Courts Act 1958 would not have prevented the right of a party to apply for interim relief in aid of foreign proceedings because s 25 of the Civil Jurisdiction and Judgments Act 1982 does not 'relate solely to procedure' within the meaning of s 29(b) of the 1958 Act and thus was not excluded from operation by the proviso contained in s 29(b)).

[105] Under the previous rules the test applicable was the test under English law: RSC, O 29; Chilenga *Civil Procedure in Malawi* 2011 at para 244 (and see further below). See, by way of example: *Mobil Oil (Malawi) Ltd v Leonard Mutsinze* Civil Cause No 1510 of 1992 (unreported) where Chatsika J stated that: 'the principles upon which an application for an injunction will be considered are set out in Order 29/1/2 and 29/1/3 of the Rules of the Supreme Court and were succinctly elucidated in the case of *American Cyanamid Co v Ethicon Limited* (1975) AC 396. Before an injunction can be granted, it must be established that the applicant has a good claim to the right he seeks to protect. The court does not decide the claim on the evidence contained in the affidavits. A good claim is said to have been established if the applicant shows that there is a serious point to be decided. When these principles have been established, the Court exercises its discretion on the balance of convenience. In deciding the question of the balance of convenience the Court will consider whether damages will be a sufficient remedy for the mischief which is complained of and even if it considers that damages will be a sufficient remedy, it must further consider and decide whether the defendant or wrong doer shall be able to pay such damages.' The judgment in *Mobile Oil* was cited with approval by the High Court in *Govati v BP Malawi Ltd* [2003] MWHC 114 (Phiri J).

The test in English law for the making of an interlocutory injunction was set out by the House of Lords in *American Cyanamid Co v Ethicon Ltd*,[106] in which Lord Diplock gave the opinion of the House of Lords (with which the other Lords agreed). The opinion of Lord Diplock is generally taken as establishing a test comprising two elements:

(1) 'The court ... must be satisfied that the claim is not frivolous or vexatious; in other words, that there is a serious issue to be tried';[107]

'... unless the material available to the court at the hearing of the application for an interlocutory injunction fails to disclose that the plaintiff has any real prospect of succeeding in his claim for a permanent injunction at the trial, the court should go on to consider whether the balance of convenience lies in favour of granting or refusing the interlocutory relief that is sought';[108]

(2) On the balance of convenience:[109]

'... the governing principle is that the court should first consider whether, if the plaintiff were to succeed at the trial in establishing his right to a permanent injunction, he would be adequately compensated by an award of damages for the loss he would have sustained as a result of the defendant's continuing to do what was sought to be enjoined between the time of the application and the time of the trial. If damages in the measure recoverable at common law would be adequate remedy and the defendant would be in a financial position to pay them, no interlocutory injunction should normally be granted, however strong the plaintiff's claim appeared to be at that stage. If, on the other hand, damages would not provide an adequate remedy for the plaintiff in the event of his succeeding at the trial, the court should then consider whether, on the contrary hypothesis that the defendant were to succeed at the trial in establishing his right to do that which was sought to be enjoined, he would be adequately compensated under the plaintiff's undertaking as to damages for the loss he would have sustained by being prevented from doing so between the time of the application and the time of the trial. If damages in the measure recoverable under such an undertaking would be an adequate remedy and the plaintiff would be in a financial position to pay them, there would be no reason upon this ground to refuse an interlocutory injunction.

It is where there is doubt as to the adequacy of the respective remedies in damages available to either party or to both, that the question of balance of convenience arises. It would be unwise to attempt even to list all the various matters which may need to be taken into consideration in deciding where the balance lies, let alone to suggest the relative weight to be attached to them. These will vary from case to case.

Where other factors appear to be evenly balanced it is a counsel of prudence to take such measures as are calculated to preserve the status quo.'

---

[106] [1975] AC 396, (HL (E)) (Lord Diplock, Viscount Dilhorne and Lords Cross, Salmon and Edmund-Davies).

[107] Ibid 407G.

[108] Ibid 408A–B.

[109] Ibid 408B–G.

These, then, are the principles that a Malawian court will follow in considering whether to grant an interlocutory injunction.[110]

Where an interlocutory mandatory injunction is sought: 'The case has to be unusually strong and clear before the mandatory injunction can be granted at the interlocutory stage ... courts require a high probability that the plaintiff's claim will succeed.'[111]

6.3.4 Freezing orders[112]

The courts in Malawi may grant a freezing injunction (such relief having previously been available under the RSC). This form of relief has been renamed in the 2017 Rules and is now called a 'freezing injunction'. The relevant rules are at Order 10, rules 10–16.[113] A freezing injunction is defined[114] as an 'order ... restraining a person from removing assets from Malawi or dealing with assets in or outside Malawi'.

A court may make a freezing injunction in two circumstances:[115] (1) where the court has given judgment in favour of the applicant (ie the plaintiff) and the freezing injunction is ancillary to the judgment; and (2) where the court is satisfied that: (a) the applicant (ie the plaintiff) has a good and arguable case; and (b) a judgment or order in the matter or its enforcement is likely to involve the assets; and (c) the assets are likely to be removed from Malawi or dealing with them should be restrained.

---

[110] Under the previous rules of court this was the test applied by the Malawian courts: *Press & Shire Clothing v Banda* [1995] 1 MLR 192 (H Ct), *per* Nyirenda J at 197H and 198B (a case where an injunction was granted restraining the defendant from interfering with the plaintiff's business by excluding the plaintiff from premises the latter rented from the defendant); *Kawaye v Fungatira* [1997] 1 MLR 352 (H Ct), *per* Mwaungulu J at 353g and 355f–g (an injunction was granted restraining the defendant from continuing to build on a plot of land that the second plaintiff had allegedly allocated to the first plaintiff, until the issue of ownership of the plot had been resolved); *Bata Shoe Co v Shore Rubber* [2000] MWHC 12 (H Ct), *per* Mwaungulu J.

[111] *Agricultural Development and Marketing Corp v Bina Kakusa* [2000] MWHC 7 (H Ct), *per* Mwaungulu J, relying on the English Court of Appeal decision in *Locabail Int Finance Ltd v Agroexport* [1986] 1 WLR 657 (the *Bina Kakusa* case concerned a mandatory injunction requiring the defendant former employee to return the plaintiff's vehicle; the injunction was discharged by the judge who found that the employer's remedy in damages was adequate).

[112] The formulation of the test for the granting of such an injunction expressed in Chilenga *Civil Procedure in Malawi* (2011) paras 247–50, must be taken to have been superseded by the 2016 Rules.

[113] The Constitution (1994), s 28, provides: '1. Every person shall be able to acquire property alone or in association with others. 2. No person shall be arbitrarily deprived of property.' Order 10, rr 10–16, would not offend s 28.2 because: (1) the defendant is not 'deprived' of his property, the nature of a freezing order is that restrictions are placed upon the use the defendant can make of his property; (2) no deprivation takes place at the time of the execution of the injunction, because the defendant's title is not interfered with; and (3) if there is deprivation, it is not arbitrary because of the procedures set out in the 2016 Rules.

[114] Order 10, r 11.

[115] Order 10, r 12.

Rules 13 of the 2017 Rules provides that a freezing injunction may be sought at three points in time: (1) 'Where a proceeding has commenced'; (2) 'Where the proceedings have not commenced'; and (3) 'Where the application is made in any other case'. These provisions are a little difficult to reconcile. It is difficult to conceive the situation contemplated by sub-rule (3), where the adjective 'other' qualifies the noun 'case' and, therefore, plainly refers back to the cases in sub-rules (1) and (2), meaning that sub-rule (3) must refer to cases other than (1) and (2). However, cases (1) and (2) neatly describe all the cases in which the court is empowered to make a freezing injunction.[116]

In applications under sub-rule (1), the plaintiff must: describe the assets, their value and location; and include the name and address of the owner of the assets, if known, and the identity of anyone else who may be affected by the order.

In applications under sub-rule (2), the plaintiff must state: the name and address of anyone else likely to be a defendant; the basis of the plaintiff's claim; the amount or nature of the claim; what has been done to recover the amount of the claim or to get the relief claimed; and any possible defence to the claim.

Sub-rule (3) sets out a number of matters that should be addressed in an application 'in any other case'. As has been noted above, the drafting of this sub-rule is problematic. It is perhaps best understood as setting out the matters that should be addressed in any application for a freezing injunction (that is, an application made under sub-rule (1) or (2)).[117] If understood in this way, it is a requirement that an application under sub-rules (1) or (2), as applicable (that is, *all* applications for a freezing injunction), must set out:

(a) how the assets to be subject of the order will form part of any judgment or its enforcement;

(b) what will be done to preserve the assets;

(c) where the application has not been made on notice, the reason for this;

(d) an undertaking as to damages that may be caused to the defendant or potential defendant, or anyone else who may be adversely affected, if the order is made; and

(e) a sworn statement in support of the application and a draft freezing order.

[116] Either proceedings have been commenced or they have not. The circumstances are binary. Further, as noted above, the court appears not to be empowered to make a freezing injunction in cases where proceedings will not be issued in Malawi at all (because they are ongoing elsewhere and/or because proceedings cannot be issued in Malawi). Sub-rule (3) also cannot refer to the post-judgment situation because, *ex hypothesi*, proceedings have been commenced (sub-r (1)), otherwise no judgment can have been rendered in the first place.

[117] This involves reading the phrase 'in any other case' as meaning 'in any case'. This is the approach, it is submitted, that the courts should adopt in the construction of this sub-rule.

The following observations may be made on these requirements:

(a) Sub-rule (a) appears designed to ensure that the assets subject to the freezing injunction are owned legally or beneficially by the putative judgment debtor; thus, evidence will be required on any application establishing a proprietary connection between the putative judgment debtor and the assets (assets not owned legally or beneficially by the judgment debtor will not be available for execution).

(b) The meaning of rule 13(3)(b) is unclear; the sub-rule requires the plaintiff to set out what will be done to preserve the assets. However, as rule 11 makes clear, the freezing injunction operates *in personam* as against the defendant (or the defendant's proxy) and restrains the defendant from removing the assets from Malawi or dealing with assets in or outside Malawi. Thus, it is not clear how a plaintiff will be able to set out what will be done to preserve the assets when the assets will not be under the plaintiff's direct control. Perhaps the sub-rule is best taken as requiring the plaintiff to indicate to the court whether a monitoring regime is desired whereby the defendant must report to the plaintiff and to the court any expenditure said to be in the ordinary course of business or for personal or legal expenses so that the depletion of the assets may be monitored.

(c) Sub-rule (c) requires a plaintiff to explain why the application was not made on notice to the defendant. Evidence of urgency, combined with evidence that if the defendant is put on notice there is a real risk that the freezing injunction may be frustrated, will satisfy this requirement.

(d) The undertaking as to damages is the 'price' of the injunction and is a standard term unless the circumstances are exceptional (or unless the relief is sought after judgment). It may also be that the court will require the undertaking to be 'fortified', in an appropriate case, by the payment by the plaintiff of a sum into court.[118]

(e) The contents of the sworn statement referred to in sub-rule (e) are further, non-exhaustively, set out in rule 13(4), which provides (in effect) that matters (a)–(c) above must be supported by sworn evidence. Rule 13(4) provides: (a) the plaintiff must show why he believes there is a risk of dissipation of the defendant's assets; (b) if the plaintiff is a judgment creditor, why he believes the judgment may be frustrated in the absence of a freezing order; (c) where proceedings have not been commenced and the name and/or address of the defendant owner of the assets is unknown, what has been done to find that information; and (d) in any other case,

[118] As was the position under the RSC, O 29.

(i) how the assets will form part of the judgment or order (replicating sub-rule 3(a)); (ii) what will be done to preserve the assets (replicating sub-rule 3(b)); (iii) if the application has not been made on notice, the reasons for this (replicating sub-rule 3(c)).

Rules 14, 15 and 16 make provision for: the service of the order granting the freezing injunction in cases where the name and address of the owner of the assets is not known; for the fixing of a return date; the filing of a summons in cases where the proceedings have not been commenced; and for the varying or setting aside of a freezing injunction.

6.3.5 Search and seize orders[119]

In Malawi, the availability of search and seize orders (*Anton Piller* relief[120]) is dealt with in Order 10, rules 17–26 (such relief having previously been available under the RSC). This form of relief has been renamed in the 2017 Rules and is now called a 'seizing injunction'.[121]

Rule 17 empowers the court to 'make an order (the "seizing injunction") authorizing an applicant to seize documents and objects in the possession of another person'. The order may be made without notice to the defendant and, where the matter is 'extremely urgent', before proceedings have been commenced.[122]

Rule 19 sets out the five conditions that must be satisfied before the court may make a seizing injunction:

(1) the order is required to preserve evidence (documents and/or objects);

(2) there is 'a real possibility' that unless the order is made the defendant or potential defendant will destroy, alter or conceal that evidence or remove the evidence from Malawi;

---

[119] The formulation of the test for the granting of such an injunction expressed in Chilenga *Civil Procedure in Malawi* (2011) paras 251–4, must be taken to have been superseded by the 2016 Rules. Further, the decision in *Societe Bic SA v AL Jugal Investments* [2008] MWHC 157 (H Ct), *per* Twea J, must now read as subject to the new rules.

[120] Named after *Anton Piller KG v Manufacturing Processes Ltd* [1976] Ch 55 (CA) (Lord Denning MR, Ormrod and Shaw LJJ), a copyright infringement case.

[121] Although the Constitution 1994, at s 21, enshrines a right to privacy which might be thought to prohibit the making of this kind of order, s 44.2 of the Constitution permits departures from certain of the human rights in Ch IV as follows, 'No restrictions or limitations may be placed on the exercise of any rights and freedoms provided for in this Constitution other than those prescribed by law, which are reasonable, recognized by international human rights standards and necessary in an open and democratic society.' Doubtless the Rules Committee would have had these provisions in mind when drafting the seizure order provisions and must have concluded that the provisions of s 44.2 had been satisfied.

[122] Order 10, r 18.

(3) the plaintiff has 'a good and arguable case';

(4) if the documents and/or objects are not seized there is a likelihood of 'serious potential or actual harm' to the plaintiff's interests;

(5) there is 'clear evidence' that the documents and/or objects are in the defendant's possession.[123]

Rule 20 sets out seven particulars that the plaintiff must supply on the application: a description of the things to be covered by the injunction; the address of the premises to be searched; the basis of the plaintiff's claim; ancillary matters such as proposals for service on the defendant and the attendance of an independent practitioner (see further rule 22 below); an undertaking as to damages; a sworn statement in support of the application; and a draft order.

The matters that must be covered by the sworn statement are set out in rule 21 and relate to the facts supporting the applicant's case under (1)–(5) above.

Rule 22 contains important ancillary matters which the order 'shall include', such as provisions as to: the appointment of an independent legal practitioner to supervise the execution of the order; the making of a record of the documents and/or objects seized; the manner of storage of those things; the time for copying and returning the things seized.

The court may also order[124] the defendant to give any information stated in the order and include a further order in the seizing injunction restraining the defendant for no more than seven days from telling another person about the seizing injunction save for the purpose of obtaining legal advice.

Order 10 further makes provision for the appointment of a receiver or property owned by the defendant as an ancillary order under a seizing injunction. The property over which such an order may be made is not confined to the real evidence that is the object of the seizing injunction (there would be no purpose in such an order as the seizure of evidence is catered for in the seizing injunction itself). Instead, although the rule does not make it explicit, the circumstances in which a receiver may be appointed will be very rare and will relate to situations where the defendant's business or assets may be run down, prior to any judgment. The intention in appointing a receiver is to ensure the security of the assets

---

[123] The original *Anton Piller* requirements were formulated by Ormrod LJ in that case as follows (at 62A–B): 'There are three essential pre-conditions for the making of such an order, in my judgment. First, there must be *an extremely strong prima facie case*. Secondly, *the damage*, potential or actual, *must be very serious* for the applicant. Thirdly, there must be *clear evidence* that the defendants have in their possession incriminating documents or things, and that there is a real possibility that they may destroy such material before any application *inter partes* can be made' (emphasis provided). As can be seen, there is a very close correlation between the requirements as originally articulated in the *Anton Piller* case and the terms of O 10, r 19. The one main difference is that the quality of the applicant's case has been reduced from an extremely strong *prima facie* case to a good and arguable case, thereby making the applicant's task in persuading the court somewhat easier.

[124] Order 10, r 23.

against which the plaintiff may wish to execute judgment (for example a company pension fund where there are real doubts about the integrity of the officers of the company in their dealings with the pension fund).

6.3.6 Third-party disclosure orders

There is no reported authority on the question whether, under the 2017 Rules, a Malawian court may, apart from the established post-issuing of proceedings and pre-trial procedures whereby a third party may be served with a witness summons requiring his attendance at court in order to give evidence and/or to produce documents,[125] order a person not a party to the proceedings to give disclosure of, for example, the identity for a tortfeasor.

Under the RSC such a power was available to the English courts in the form of a *Norwich Pharmacal* order[126] whereby an innocent third party caught up in a tort may be ordered to disclose the name or other identity of the tortfeasor and the power remains available under the English CPR notwithstanding that the CPR contains no specific provision catering for such orders.

It is likely that a Malawian court would consider that the terms of Order 10, rules 1 and 27, are of sufficient amplitude to justify the granting of this type of relief.

In *Norwich Pharmacal Co v Customs and Excise Comrs*, the English House of Lords[127] set out the following principle:

> 'That if through no fault of his own a person gets mixed up in the tortious acts of others so as to facilitate their wrong-doing he may incur no personal liability but he comes under a duty to assist the person who has been wronged by giving him full information and disclosing the identity of the wrongdoers ... [It does not matter] whether he became so mixed up by voluntary action on his part or because it was his duty to do what he did. It may be that if this causes him expense the person seeking the information ought to reimburse him. But justice requires that he should co-operate in righting the wrong if he unwittingly facilitated its perpetration.'

---

[125] 2016 Rules, O 17, rr 31–5 and rr 49–54.

[126] *Norwich Pharmacal Co v Customs & Excise* [1974] AC 133 (HL(E)) (Lords Reid and Morris, Viscount Dilhorne and Lords Cross and Kilbrandon).

[127] Ibid 175, *per* Lord Reid.

More recent authority[128] has clarified the conditions which the plaintiff must satisfy in order to obtain such relief:

> 'The three conditions to be satisfied for the court to exercise the power to order Norwich Pharmacal relief are:
>
> i) a wrong must have been carried out, or arguably carried out, by an ultimate wrongdoer;
>
> ii) there must be the need for an order to enable action to be brought against the ultimate wrongdoer; and
>
> iii) the person against whom the order is sought must: (a) be mixed up in so as to have facilitated the wrongdoing; and (b) be able or likely to be able to provide the information necessary to enable the ultimate wrongdoer to be sued.'

If the plaintiff satisfies all of those conditions, the English court will then go on to exercise its discretion. In doing so, it must keep in mind the proper scope of *Norwich Pharmacal* relief: the jurisdiction cannot be used for wide-ranging discovery or the gathering of evidence, but is strictly confined to necessary information.[129]

6.3.7 Anti-suit injunctions

An anti-suit injunction is an order restraining the injunction defendant from either commencing or continuing proceedings outside Malawi in breach of a legal or equitable right on the part of the injunction plaintiff not to pursue litigation outside Malawi or, conversely, restraining the injunction defendant from commencing or continuing proceedings inside Malawi in breach of a legal or equitable right on the part of the injunction plaintiff to have the dispute between the parties litigated in a jurisdiction other than Malawi.[130]

There is currently no reported decision of a Malawian court which confirms that an anti-suit injunction is a remedy available in Malawi. However, when the matter arises for decision in Malawi, it is to be expected that a Malawian court

---

[128] *Ramilos Trading Ltd v Valentin Mikhaylovich Buyanovsky* [2016] EWHC 3175 (Comm) (H Ct) (Flaux J), citing, at para [11], *Mitsui v Nexen Petroleum* [2005] EWHC 625 (Ch); [2005] 3 All ER 511 at [21] (H Ct) (Lightman J).

[129] *Ramilos Trading Ltd v Valentin Mikhaylovich Buyanovsky* [2016] EWHC 3175 (Comm) (H Ct) (Flaux J) para [46].

[130] In similar vein, an anti-anti-suit injunction is an order restraining the injunction defendant from commencing or continuing proceedings to restrain the injunction plaintiff from applying to restrain the injunction defendant from commencing or continuing proceedings. The leading works on this topic are: Raphael The Anti-Suit Injunction 2 ed (2019) and Briggs Civil Jurisdiction and Judgments 7 ed (2021), ch 28. It is also conceptually possible to obtain similar relief in the context of arbitration but such relief is outside the scope of this work.

will find that it has jurisdiction to grant this relief pursuant to Order 10, rules 1 and 27 of the 2017 Rules.

In the expectation, therefore, that Malawian courts will be prepared to grant this form of relief, it may be of assistance to set out the principles which English courts have formulated and which English courts apply when asked to grant anti-suit relief. After all, the statutory basis upon which Malawian courts may grant an anti-suit injunction is identical to that upon which their English counterparts exercise that jurisdiction and there is a very close affinity between Malawian law and English law in this regard.[131] It is to be anticipated, therefore, that a Malawian court before which an application is brought for an anti-suit injunction may well pay close attention to the English authorities in setting out the principles upon which an anti-suit injunction may be granted in Malawi. Set out below, in summary, are the principles of English law governing the grant of an anti-suit injunction.

The Malawian court must have personal jurisdiction over the injunction defendant. The court may be seised either by service on the defendant within the jurisdiction or service out of the jurisdiction.[132]

The injunction plaintiff must assert a cause of action for relief. Usually, the injunction plaintiff will contend that the injunction defendant is committing a wrong by bringing or proposing to bring proceedings in a foreign court. This will require the plaintiff to characterise the conduct of the defendant as the breach of a legal or equitable right.

A legal right may, and often will, be based on a right not to be sued in a foreign jurisdiction arising out of an exclusive jurisdiction clause in favour of the courts of Malawi. An equitable right may be the right not to be sued in a foreign jurisdiction and may be the corollary of an equitable wrong which is that it is oppressive and vexatious and therefore unconscionable for the injunction defendant to commence or continue proceedings against the injunction plaintiff in a foreign jurisdiction.

The prime example of a cause of action based on a legal right not to be sued in a foreign jurisdiction is where the parties have agreed expressly that the courts of Malawi should have exclusive jurisdiction over disputes arising out of the contract (which can be a substantive contract or a settlement agreement) between them.[133] In such a case proof of the underlying cause of action is likely to be a

---

[131] It is worth noting that the High Court of South Africa in *Vedanta Resources Holdings Ltd v ZCCM Investment Holdings plc* 2019 JDR 1425 (GJ) at para [11], [54] and [56] (Adams J) and the High Court of Nigeria in *Zenith Global Merchant Ltd v Zhongfu International Investment (Nig) FZE* (2017) All FWLR 1837, 1924 (Akinyemi J) have also referred to English principles in a similar context.

[132] The substantive law and procedure for which in Malawi has been set out above.

[133] The contract may be a substantive contract or a settlement agreement and the dispute resolution provisions may be exclusively in favour of the courts of Malawi or may be in favour of arbitration:

sufficient condition for the grant of the relief and that good reason would need to be shown why the discretion to order an injunction should not be exercised.[134]

The principal example of a cause of action based on an equitable wrong is where proceedings brought abroad by the defendant are oppressive and vexatious. An example of such conduct is illustrated by the decision of the Privy Council in *SNI Aerospatiale v Lee Kui Jak,*[135] where a resident of Brunei had been killed in a helicopter crash and his widow (and her brother-in-law, as co-administrator of his estate), the respondent plaintiffs in the appeal to the Privy Council, had commenced proceedings in Brunei and had subsequently been persuaded to sue in Texas instead. The appellant defendant applied for an anti-suit injunction restraining the plaintiffs from proceeding against it in Texas. The Privy Council allowed the defendant's appeal, held that an injunction ought to be granted restraining the respondents from proceeding in Texas and remitted the matter to the Brunei courts.

Transposing the findings of the Privy Council to Malawi, it was held that an anti-suit injunction would be granted if: (1) pursuit of the foreign proceedings is vexatious or oppressive; (2) Malawi is the natural forum for the resolution of the dispute; and (3) the injunction does not deprive the defendant of advantages in the foreign jurisdiction of which it would be unjust to deprive him.[136]

Other examples of equitable wrongs which may attract an anti-suit injunction are: undermining the jurisdiction of the Malawian court;[137] vexatious conduct by relying on foreign procedural laws;[138] wrongfully undermining a Malawian judgment;[139] or enforcement of a foreign judgment wrongfully obtained.[140]

British Airways Board v Laker Airways Ltd [1985] AC 58 (HL (E)) (Lords Diplock, Fraser, Scarman, Roskill and Brightman), per Lord Diplock at p 81C–E.

[134] *The Angelic Grace* [1995] 1 Lloyd's Rep 87 (CA) (Neill, Leggatt and Millett LJJ), per Millett LJ at p 96, col 2, and Neill LJ at p 97, col 1; *Donohue v Armco Inc* [2000] 1 Lloyd's Rep 579 (CA) (Stuart-Smith, Brooke and Sedley LJJ), where it was stated that 'strong reasons' (per Stuart-Smith LJ at para 35) or 'strong cause' (per Brooke LJ at paras 59 and 60) would be required to deny an injunction.

[135] [1987] AC 871 (PC (Brunei)) (Lords Keith, Griffiths, MacKay and Goff and Sir John Megaw).

[136] Lord Goff (giving the opinion of the Privy Council) at p 896F–H. That the court to which the application is made should be the natural forum for the resolution of the dispute was repeated by the House of Lords in *Airbus Industrie GIE v Patel* [1999] 1 AC 119 (HL (E)) (Lords Goff, Slynn, Steyn, Clyde and Hutton), per Lord Goff (with whom the other Lords agreed) at pp 138G–H and 140H–141B.

[137] For example, by commencing bankruptcy proceedings outside the jurisdiction when such proceedings are in progress in Malawi: *SNI Aerospatiale v Lee Kui Jak* [1987] AC 871, per Lord Goff at pp 892G–893B.

[138] By seeking to depose witnesses in the USA where those witnesses would be subject to cross-examination in proceedings in Malawi, for example: *Omega Group Holdings Ltd v Kozeny* [2002] CLC 132.

[139] By commencing proceedings outside the jurisdiction for declaratory relief designed to frustrate the enforcement of a Malawian judgment in that jurisdiction: *Masri v Consolidated Contractors International (UK) Ltd* (No 3) [2009] QB 503 (CA).

[140] Where the foreign judgment was obtained through fraud and perjury: *Ellerman Lines Ltd v Read* [1928] 2 KB 144 (CA), per Scrutton LJ at pp 152–3.

6.3.8 Other interlocutory relief

6.3.8.1 *Arrest of an absconding defendant*

The Courts Act 1958, section 13, provides for the civil arrest of a defendant in certain circumstances:

> '**Arrest before judgment**
>
> (1) If, in any civil action or suit, the High Court is satisfied by evidence on oath that the plaintiff has a good cause of action and that the defendant, with intent to obstruct, defeat or delay the claim of the plaintiff, is about to leave Malawi or has disposed of or has removed or is about to remove his property or any part thereof out of Malawi, the High Court may, upon application made by the plaintiff at any time after the issue of the writ, issue a warrant to bring the defendant before the High Court to show cause why he should not give security for his appearance to the satisfaction of the High Court.
>
> (2) If the defendant fails to show cause or fails to give such security as may be ordered, the High Court may commit him to custody until the determination of the action or suit or execution of the judgment, provided that it may release him at any time on such terms as it may think just.'

The Constitution of Malawi 1994,[141] section 200 provides:

> 'Except in so far as they are inconsistent with this Constitution, all Acts of Parliament, common law and customary law in force on the appointed day shall continue to have force of law, as if they had been made in accordance with and in pursuance of this Constitution: Provided that any laws currently in force may be amended or repealed by an Act of Parliament or be declared unconstitutional by a competent court.'

The question arises whether this power of civil arrest in section 13 of the 1958 Act survives the enactment of the Constitution.

Section 15 of the Constitution provides:

> 'The human rights and freedoms enshrined in this Chapter shall be respected and upheld by the executive, legislature and judiciary and all organs of the Government and its agencies and, where applicable to them, by all natural and legal persons in Malawi and shall be enforceable in the manner prescribed in this Chapter.'

Section 18 provides: 'Every person has the right to personal liberty.'

Section 19.6(c) provides: 'Subject to this Constitution, every person shall have the right to freedom and security of person, which shall include the right not to be- ... (c) imprisoned for inability to fulfill [sic] contractual obligations.'

Given the breadth of the provisions in section 13(1) of the 1958 Act, which permit arrest of the defendant and contemplate his incarceration under section 13(2) for such time as it takes to dispose of the plaintiff's claim, and in

141 In force 18 May 1994: s 212.1.

view of the fact that imprisonment for failure to fulfil contractual obligations is expressly prohibited by the Constitution, it is submitted that civil imprisonment of a defendant for any cause of action is unlawful under the Constitution and will be declared to be so by the courts as and when the occasion arises.

6.3.8.2 *Attachment of assets*

The Courts Act 1958, section 14, provides for the attachment of a defendant's assets before judgment in certain circumstances:

> '**Attachment before judgment**
>
> (1) If, in any civil action or suit, the High Court is satisfied by evidence on oath that the plaintiff has a good cause of action and that the defendant, with intent to obstruct, defeat or delay the execution of any judgment that may be given against him, has disposed or is about to dispose of his property or any part thereof or has removed or concealed or made away with or handed over to others any of his property, the High Court may, upon application made by the plaintiff at any time after the issue of the writ, order the defendant to furnish security for such amount, not exceeding the claim and costs in the action or suit, as to the High Court may seem fit, or in default may direct that any property of the defendant be attached until further order.
>
> (2) No attachment under this section shall prejudice the claims of any person not a party to the suit.'

Section 14 travels over much the same ground as the 2017 Rules, Order 10, rules 10–16, the provisions regulating the making of freezing injunctions.

It is not proposed to discuss this provision further because there would appear to be no particular merit in making an application under section 14 as opposed to one under Order 10, rules 10–16. This is because section 14(2) makes it clear that the beneficiary of an order under section 14 does not acquire security in the property attached and that feature of section 14 deprives it of any advantage over the usual freezing injunction procedure.

Chapter 7

NAMIBIA

7.1 Jurisdiction

Litigation in Namibia must be conducted according to the provisions of the Rules of the High Court of Namibia[1] ('the High Court Rules'). The plaintiff has the onus of proving the jurisdiction of the court.[2]

7.1.1 Commencing proceedings where the defendant is within the jurisdiction

A plaintiff who wishes to institute an action in Namibia against a defendant may make a claim by suing out of the office of the registrar a combined summons.[3] A legal practitioner, or the party himself if he sues in person, must sign the summons and every other pleading.[4] A summons will be considered properly issued when the registrar date stamps it with the official court stamp and uniquely numbers it for identification purposes.[5] After the combined summons has been signed, stamped and numbered by the registrar, it must be returned to the plaintiff or, if represented, to his legal practitioner, for the purposes of service.[6]

Any document initiating proceedings must be served by the sheriff and service of such process may be effected using any of the ways set out in rule 8(2) or (3).

---

[1] Made pursuant to s 39 of the High Court Act 1990 (Act 16 of 1990). The Rules of the High Court were last amended in 2014: see GN 4 of 2014.

[2] *Cabinet of the Transitional Government of South West Africa v Dagnin* 1990 NR 14 (Levy J) 18B. This is true whether the case is a domestic one or one with an international aspect, though, in former cases, proving the jurisdiction of the court should be easier for the plaintiff.

[3] Rule 7(1). The combined summons must be as near as is possible to the example in Form 1. Further detail is provided in r 7(5) and (6).

[4] Rule 45. Rule 7(1) itself is said to be 'subject to rule 4'. Rule 45 specifies in some detail the appropriate form which pleadings should take. See further in relation to particulars of claim, r 7(7) and (8).

[5] Rule 7(2).

[6] Rule 7(11).

Provision is also made for alternative methods of service to be employed.[7] Service of any process may then be proved using any of the mechanisms contained in rule 9(1).[8]

7.1.2 Commencing proceedings where the defendant is outside the jurisdiction

A party wishing to serve process on a defendant outside the jurisdiction must obtain permission to do so from the court.[9] However, service out of the jurisdiction by way of edictal citation does not confer jurisdiction on the court. Instead, it is necessary to demonstrate that the court has jurisdiction before leave to sue by edictal citation will be granted. In practice, therefore, an application for attachment of property and an application for permission to serve process out of the jurisdiction by way of edictal citation are likely to be made, *ex parte*, at the same time.[10]

When making an application for permission to serve process outside Namibia, the plaintiff must set out concisely the: (1) nature and extent of his claim; (2) the grounds on which it is based and on which the court has jurisdiction to entertain the claim;[11] and (3) the manner of service which the court is asked to authorise.[12]

---

[7] Rule 8(4) and (9). Substituted service is the subject of detailed treatment in r 13.

[8] The document which serves as proof of service must, together with the served process or document, without delay be furnished to the person at whose request service was effected: r 9(2). Within five days from receipt of the document which serves as proof of service and the process or document referred to in r 9(2), the person on whose request service was effected must file with the registrar each such document on behalf of the person who effected service: r 9(3). Whenever the court is not satisfied as to the effectiveness of the service, it may order any further steps that it considers practicable and reasonable to be taken: r 9(4).

[9] Rule 12(1) of the Rules of the High Court: 'A person may not serve any process or document outside Namibia whereby proceedings are instituted in the court whether the address of the person to be served is known or not, except by leave of the court granted in terms of this rule and subject to rule 11(1)(b).' It is submitted that this conclusion was not (and indeed could not be) altered by the decision in *Labuschagne v Gaerdes* [2014] NAHCMD 277 (HC) (Hoff J), which decision is explored in more depth below. There, the judge did not make any reference to the requirement that the plaintiff would have to obtain leave to serve, by way of edictal citation, process on the defendant in Angola (where the defendant was ordinarily resident). This omission should not, it is submitted, be taken as an indication that the *incola* plaintiff does not have to comply with this requirement. The case dealt exclusively with the question whether the applicant was entitled to an order for attachment, which order would confirm the court's jurisdiction. The institution of the action, and the consequent (potential) need to serve process outside Namibia, formed the next stage of the litigation, with which the court had not yet become concerned.

[10] *Kahan v Lidchi* [2000] NAHC 19.

[11] This requirement is of longstanding in the law of South West Africa and, now, Namibia. By way of example, in *Cabinet of the Transitional Government of South West Africa v Dagnin* 1990 NR 14, 17G–I, Levy J, referring to *Girdwood v Theron* 1913 CPD 859 (Gardiner AJ) said that 'a summons directed against a person should state the grounds on which the Court has jurisdiction. This principle has been consistently followed.' Levy J also (at 17F–G) held that a 'summons which does not set forth particulars showing that the Court has jurisdiction is bad and liable to dismissal'.

[12] Rule 12(2).

Where the manner of service proposed is other than personal service, the plaintiff must also set out in his application the last known whereabouts of the person to be served and the inquiries made to ascertain his present whereabouts.[13]

Where the court receives an application in the terms set out above, it may make an order as to the manner of service and

> 'order the time in which notice of intention to defend is to be given and any other step that the person to be served must take and if service by publication is ordered, the service may be on Form 2 approved and signed by the registrar'.[14]

A plaintiff wishing to obtain leave to effect service out of the jurisdiction of any document other than one by which proceedings are instituted may make an application in the terms set out above or 'request leave at any case management conference'.[15] If the plaintiff chooses to make the application at a case management conference, '[n]o papers need to be filed in support of the request and the court may act on such information as may be given from the bar or given in any other manner as it may require and may make an order.'

The service of any order which is obtained in terms of these rules must be effected in the manner set out in rule 11.[16] This rule is concerned with the service of process outside of Namibia. Hence, service of process or any document in a foreign country must be effected:

> '*(a)* where there is no law in that country prohibiting such service or the authorities of that country have not interposed any objection to such service by—
>
> (i) the head of any Namibian diplomatic or consular mission in that foreign country authorised to serve such process or document;
>
> (ii) any foreign diplomatic or consular officer of the foreign country to Namibia who attends to the service of process or documents on behalf of Namibia in that foreign country;
>
> (iii) an official signing as or on behalf of the head of the department dealing with the administration of justice in that foreign country and is authorised under the law of that country to serve process or document; or
>
> *(b)* where the foreign country is a designated country in terms of legislation which provides for the reciprocal service of civil process[17] in terms of that legislation.'[18]

---

[13] Ibid.

[14] Rule 12(4).

[15] Ibid.

[16] See further, r 12(5).

[17] As to which, see the Reciprocal Service of Civil Process Act 1994 (Act 27 of 1994), particularly s 4 thereof. To date, it appears that only the Republic of South Africa has become a 'designated' country for the purposes of the Act, which designation occurred on 15 June 1995 and appears in the *Government Gazette* of the same date. The list of 'designated countries' for the purposes of the Reciprocal Service of Civil Process Act therefore mirrors the list of 'designated countries' for the Enforcement of Foreign Civil Judgments Act 1994 (Act 28 of 1994), which is dealt with below.

[18] Rule 11(1).

Where any process or document is to be served in accordance with these provisions, it must be delivered to the registrar together with revenue stamps to the value of N$250 affixed to it, except that no revenue stamps are required where service is effected on behalf of the Government of Namibia.[19]

Additionally, when serving any process of court or any other document in a foreign country, the plaintiff, where the official language or one of the official languages of the foreign country is not English, must provide a sworn translation (into an official language of the foreign country or part of the foreign country) of the process or document which is to be served. This translation should accompany a certified copy of the process or document.[20]

As in domestic cases, it is necessary for the party wishing to effect service to prove that service. However, the rules on proof of service of process or any document are difficult to construe. Rule 11(5), which seeks to make special provision for service effected in the Republic of South Africa, provides that service of process or any document in that country is proved:

> '*(a)* where service has been effected by a sheriff, by the return of service of that sheriff; [or]
>
> *(b)* where service has been effected by any other person, in the manner described in subrule (6).'

This approach is, however, slightly confusing. Sub-rule 6 deals with service of any process or document in a foreign country *other* than a 'designated country' under the Reciprocal Service of Civil Process Act 1994 (ie the Republic of South Africa) and the Republic of South Africa where the service has been effected by a sheriff. *Prima facie*, therefore, sub-rule (6) appears not to be designed to cater for service in the Republic of South Africa at all. Be that as it may, it seems that the intention of rule 11(5) is that, where service has been effected by any person either in a country other than South Africa or in South Africa by a person other than a sheriff, such service is proven by:

> 'A certificate duly authenticated in terms of the laws of the country of the person effecting service in terms of subrule (1) in which he or she—
>
> *(a)* identifies himself or herself that he or she is authorised under the law of that country to serve process or document therein;
>
> *(b)* states that the process or document in question has been served as required by the law of that country and sets out the manner and the date of such service; and
>
> *(c)* affirms that the law of the country concerned permits him or her to serve process of the court or documents or that there is no law in that country prohibiting such service and that the authorities of that country have not interposed any objection to the service.'

---

[19] Rule 11(3).

[20] Rule 11(2).

It is of importance for the plaintiff to ensure that the court can be satisfied that effective service of process or of the document in question has, in fact, taken place. Where the court is not so satisfied 'it may order such further steps to be taken as it considers practicable and reasonable'.[21]

Where a summons is served outside Namibia, the time allowed for entering an appearance shall not be less than 21 days.[22]

7.1.2.1 Incolae *and* peregrini

The rules which govern the question whether the court has jurisdiction in a particular case differ depending on the identity of the parties to that case (and, in the main, though not exclusively, upon the identity of the defendant). Hence, it is necessary to distinguish between those defendants who are *incolae* of Namibia and those who are *peregrini.*

When assessing the status of a natural person, and despite some authority to the contrary,[23] it would appear to be the case that the High Court considers a *peregrinus* to be one who is neither domiciled nor resident within the court's territorial jurisdiction.[24]

With respect to legal persons, a foreign company may be found, on the balance of probabilities, to be 'resident'[25] in the jurisdiction. The Supreme Court of Namibia, in *Mahe Construction v Seasonaire*,[26] concluded that a company, even if it were a foreign company, could, in principle, be considered to be resident in Namibia in certain circumstances.[27] The crucial consideration seemed to be that the foreign company was 'not merely carrying on some of its business within the Court's jurisdiction but ... has substantial operations in Namibia'.[28] On the facts

---

21 Rule 11(7).

22 Section 24 of the High Court Act.

23 *Kahan v Lidchi* [2000] NAHC 19 (Levy AJ), where it was held that anyone residing within the geographical boundaries of Namibia, even if that residence was not indefinite, was an *incola* of Namibia, even if they were neither a citizen of, nor domiciled in, Namibia. A *peregrinus*, by contrast, was said to be someone not so residing. Such an approach obviously puts the concept of 'residence' at the heart of the distinction between an *incola* and a *peregrinus.*

24 *Schiebler v Kiss* 1985 (3) SA 489 (SWA) (Strydom J) and, more recently, *Van Wyk v Matrix Mining (Pty) Ltd* [2020] NAHCNLD 109 (January J), at para [36].

25 As provided for by s 16 of the High Court Act 1990. If a company is found to be resident, it will also be found to have the *locus standi* to be sued.

26 2002 NR 398 (SC) (Strydom CJ; O'Linn and Choma AJA). The plaintiff entered into a subcontract with the defendant (who had entered into a contract with a South African company) in respect of work to be done on a hospital in Windhoek. Thereafter, the South African company was placed into provisional liquidation and the building work on the hospital was suspended. At the time, the defendant was alleged to owe some N$433,000 to the plaintiff. The defendant denied its liability and the plaintiff sued.

27 Ibid 405D–I, endorsing the conclusion of the court below: 2002 NR 53 (Hannah J). The Supreme Court went on to endorse the decisions in *Appleby (Pty) Ltd v Dundas Ltd* 1948 (2) SA 905 (E) (Hoexter J) 911; *Ochs v Kolmanskop Diamond Mines Ltd* 1921 SWA 8 and *Wright v Stuttaford & Co* 1929 EDL 10, 37.

28 2002 NR 398 at 405G–H.

of the case, operations (undertaken from an office) in Namibia were carried out for the better part of a year and the defendant found it necessary to open a bank account with First National Bank in Windhoek.[29] The submission that the court did not have jurisdiction on the basis of residence was rejected.

The High Court, in *Namibia Bunker Services (Pty) Ltd v ETS Katanga Futur*,[30] had the opportunity to provide further clarity on the circumstances in which a foreign company can be considered to be resident in Namibia. The company in question was registered in the Democratic Republic of Congo, where it also had its principal place of business. In arguing that it had a 'consistent presence'[31] in Namibia, the company sought to rely on the fact that: (1) its sales manager visited Namibia regularly, at intervals of at least once every two months, to attend to issues arising out of the contract into which it had entered with a Namibian company; (2) there was a consistent flow of the company's goods through Walvis Bay; (3) Walvis Bay was the only convenient and cost-effective port through which the company could channel its goods; and (4) pursuant to its agreement with the Namibian company, it had to make payment in Namibia.

The High Court rejected this submission[32] but did not say why. That is to be regretted, given that the test demands a nuanced approach to be applied on the facts of each case: 'substantial' is a word which is opaque unless explained. It does appear, however, that the cumulative impact of the factors outlined in the previous paragraph was assessed and found wanting by the judge.

From these two judgments, it may be the case that, in order to satisfy the substantiality requirement, operations carried on in the jurisdiction cannot be transient. The use of office premises in the jurisdiction, from which operations are managed, for the better part of a year, has a degree of permanence to it that the mere movement of goods belonging to a company, or the infrequent visitation of a member of its staff, do not possess. If this is the case, it is unfortunate that neither the Supreme Court nor the High Court has yet taken the opportunity to spell it out.

7.1.2.2 *The jurisdictional significance of attachment*

The above distinction between those classed as *incolae* and those classed as *peregrini* of Namibia is of importance when considering whether it is necessary for the plaintiff to attach the defendant's property in order to found or confirm the jurisdiction of the court in Namibia. As with most other countries which have

---

29 Ibid.

30 [2014] NAHCMD 197 (HC) (Van Niekerk J). The High Court did not refer to the decision of the Supreme Court in *Mahe*. Van Niekerk J did, however, refer to *Ochs* and *Appleby* (and so applied the same test).

31 [2014] NAHCMD 197 para [36].

32 Ibid para [39].

a Roman-Dutch law system, attachment of the defendant's property[33] (where permissible) is central to the court's ability to take jurisdiction. Against this background, the various situations in which a Namibian court may be asked to take jurisdiction are considered below.

7.1.2.2.1 Where the plaintiff and the defendant are both *incolae*

Where both the parties to a dispute are *incolae*, no jurisdictional problems arise. The dispute is a purely domestic one over which the court has jurisdiction.

In *Schiebler v Kiss*,[34] the High Court of South West Africa was confronted with an attempt to attach property belonging to the defendant (who was an *incola*) in order to confirm jurisdiction. In summary, the plaintiff had obtained a rule *nisi* against the defendant whereby he was authorised to attach, in order to confirm jurisdiction, assets which belonged to the defendant. On the return date, the defendant raised an objection *in limine* to the confirmation of the order on the basis that he was domiciled within the jurisdiction of the court, such that attachment could not be made.

Ultimately, there was no disagreement between the parties as to the validity of the defendant's objection. The plaintiff instead argued that, on previous occasions, the court had been willing to order attachment of an *incola*'s property to ensure that the judgment of the court would be effective, which attachment was of the same species as an attachment to confirm jurisdiction.

The court rejected the plaintiff's submission and refused to make the rule *nisi* final. As can be seen from the headnote,[35] the court referred to section 21(1) of Proclamation R222 of 1981, which prohibited a court from ordering attachment of property in order to found jurisdiction against an *incola* defendant and was prepared to extend this to cases where the plaintiff sought attachment to confirm jurisdiction as well.

After obtaining independence, the Namibian legislature has specifically endorsed the view that it is neither necessary nor permissible to attach the property of an *incola* defendant:[36] the Namibian court has jurisdiction over all

---

[33] Or, potentially, arrest of the defendant's person, as to which, see further below, under the sub-heading 'The jurisdictional significance of arrest of the person'.

[34] 1985 (3) SA 489 (SWA) (Strydom J).

[35] Ibid. The rest of the judgment is reported only in Afrikaans.

[36] The prohibition applies irrespective of whether the case is brought in the High Court or the magistrate's court. As to the former, s 25 of the High Court Act provides that: 'No attachment of person or property to found jurisdiction shall be ordered by the High Court against any person residing in Namibia', while s 30bis of the Magistrates' Courts Act 1944 states: 'The court may order attachment of person or property to found or confirm jurisdiction against any person who does not reside in the Republic, in respect of an action within its jurisdiction, where the claim or the value of the matter in dispute amounts to at least forty rand, exclusive of any costs in respect of the recovery thereof, and may grant an order allowing service of any process in such

those persons residing in Namibia without the need for an attachment of a person's property first.

7.1.2.2.2 Where the plaintiff is an *incola* and the defendant is a *peregrinus*

Where the defendant is a *peregrinus*, attachment of property to found or confirm jurisdiction[37] is essential. In *SOS-Kinderdorf International v Effie Lentin Architects*,[38] default judgment had been entered against the *peregrinus* defendant in the substantive proceedings, which default judgment the defendant then ought to rescind. Frank J approached the question by pointing out that the defendant's *peregrinus* status meant that 'even if the court has jurisdiction upon one or other of the common law grounds it is still necessary for an incola ... plaintiff to attach the property ... to [secure] the jurisdiction already possessed by the court'.[39]

In *Labuschagne v Gaerdes*,[40] the Namibian High Court offered some guidance on what an *incola* plaintiff has to show in order to obtain attachment[41] of a *peregrinus* defendant's property. The plaintiff originally approached the court on an urgent and *ex parte* basis seeking an order for the attachment of certain vehicles, which belonged to the defendants, either for the purposes of founding or confirming the court's jurisdiction.[42] The court granted the plaintiff a temporary interdict in the form of a rule *nisi*. The question for Hoff J was whether to confirm the rule *nisi* pending the determination of the action which the plaintiff intended to commence.

In coming to the conclusion that the rule *nisi* should be so extended, Hoff J stated as follows:[43]

> '[A plaintiff] needs to prove in an application such as the present one that the [plaintiff] is an *incola* of this Court and that the [defendant] is a *peregrinus*, secondly that the [plaintiff] has a *prima facie* case and thirdly that the property to be attached belongs to the [defendant].'

Addressing the elements of Hoff J's statement separately:

---

action to be effected in such manner as may be stated in such order.' See further in this respect *Sylvie McTeer Properties v Kuhn* [2017] NASC (SC) (Maritz JA, Chomba and Damaseb AJA).

[37] Namibian courts tend to elide, or at least often fail to distinguish between, the concepts of attachment in order to found jurisdiction and attachment in order to confirm jurisdiction. As to the important differences between the two concepts, see the treatment of this issue in the chapter on the Republic of South Africa and the authorities cited in relation thereto.

[38] 1990 NR 300 (HC) (Frank J).

[39] 1990 NR 300 (HC) 300I–301A, citing *Thermo Radiant Oven Sales (Pty) Ltd v Nelspruit Bakeries (Pty) Ltd* 1969 (2) SA 295 (A), 300D and 311E.

[40] *Labuschagne v Gaerdes* [2014] NAHCMD 277 (HC) (Hoff J).

[41] That attachment is necessary in this case has recently been confirmed by the Supreme Court in *Sylvie McTeer Properties v Kuhn* [2017] NASC (SC) (Maritz JA, Chomba and Damaseb AJA).

[42] Ibid para [1].

[43] Ibid para [21].

(i) 'the [plaintiff] is an *incola* and the [defendant] is a *peregrinus*'

The judge did not cite any authority for this proposition and neither defined nor referred to any authority providing a definition of the terms '*incola*' and '*peregrinus*'.[44] On the facts, there was no dispute as to the defendants being *peregrini*. When making this statement, it is likely that the judge was cognisant of the prohibition on the attachment of property belonging to an *incola* to found or confirm jurisdiction, as set out in section 25 of the High Court Act 1990.

(ii) 'the [plaintiff] has a *prima facie* case'

In determining the correct meaning of '*prima facie*' case in this context, Hoff J[45] referred (with apparent approval) to two South African authorities.

First, Hoff J cited *Butler v Banimar Shipping Co SA*,[46] seemingly for the proposition that

> 'the term *prima facie* as applied in this sort of case bears a meaning different from that which it is commonly known to bear in other contexts. It means here that the [plaintiff] must tender evidence which, if accepted, will establish a cause of action - the fact that such evidence is in dispute does not disentitle the [plaintiff] to the desired attachment.'

It would appear, therefore, that at this juncture, the court is not entitled to go into the merits of the application.[47]

Second, Hoff J cited *Hülse-Reuter v Gödde*[48] in order to explain why the test which the plaintiff has to satisfy is of such a 'low level', viz: 'The primary object of an attachment is to establish jurisdiction, once that is done the case of action will in due course have to be established in accordance with the ordinary standard of proof in subsequent proceedings.'

For these reasons, Hoff J felt that he did not have to decide the disputed issue of ownership over the goods at issue in the substantive case and hence confirmed the rule *nisi*.

(iii) 'the property to be attached belongs[49] to the [defendant]'[50]

The necessity of such a requirement is plain.

---

[44] The lack of any attempt to define these terms may well signify the acceptance by the courts of the approach towards definition set out by the High Court in *Kahan*.

[45] [2014] NAHCMD 277 para [22].

[46] 1978 (4) SA 753 (SE) 753F (Howie AJ) and the authorities therein referenced.

[47] 1978 (4) SA 753 (SE) 759.

[48] 2001 (4) SA 1336 (SCA) 1343G–H (Scott JA).

[49] Which includes having a beneficial interest in the property: *Bourgwells Ltd (Owners of MFV Ofelia) v Shepalov* 1998 NR 307.

[50] There can be little doubt that the plaintiff is also expected to meet this requirement when both parties are *peregrini*.

The test which the plaintiff has to satisfy in order to show that the property in question belongs to the defendant was first set out in *Slabber v Blanco.*[51] There, Muller AJ stated as follows:

> 'The general principle ... has been expressed by Van Wyk J in *Stellenbosch Farmers' Winery Ltd v. Stellenvale Winery (Pty) Ltd* 1957 (4) SA 234 (C) at 235E to be:
>
> > "Where there is a dispute as to the facts a final interdict should only be granted in notice of motion proceedings if the facts as stated by the [defendants] together with the admitted facts in the [plaintiff's] affidavits justify such an order ... Where it is clear that the facts, though not formally admitted, cannot be denied, they must be regarded as admitted."
>
> In *Plascon-Evans Paints Ltd v Van Riebeeck Paints (Pty) Ltd*,[52] a decision of the South African Appellate Division, Corbett JA (as he then was) refined the principle in the *Stellenbosch Farmers*' case in the following manner after accepting the basic principle as expressed by Van Wyk J in the passage quoted above:[53]
>
> > "It seems to me however, that this formulation of the general rule and particularly the second sentence thereof, requires some clarification and, perhaps, qualification.
> >
> > It is correct that, where in proceedings on notice of motion disputes of fact have arisen on the affidavits, a final order, whether it be an interdict or some other form of relief, may be granted if those facts averred in the [plaintiff's] affidavits which have been admitted by the [defendant], together with the facts alleged by the [defendant], justify such an order. The power of the Court to give such final relief on the papers before it is, however, not confined to such a situation. In certain instances, the denial by the [defendant] *of a fact alleged by the* [plaintiff] may not be such as to raise a real, genuine or bona fide dispute of fact ... If in such a case the [defendant] has not availed himself of his right to apply for the deponents concerned to be called for cross-examination ... and the court is satisfied as to the inherent credibility of the [plaintiff's] factual averment, it may proceed upon the basis of the correctness thereof and include this fact among those upon which it determines whether the [plaintiff] is entitled to the final relief which he seeks ... Moreover, there may be exceptions to this general rule as, for example, where the allegations or denials of the [defendant] are so far-fetched or clearly untenable that the court is justified in rejecting them merely on the papers".'

The Namibian High Court has more recently affirmed the continued application of the rules set out in *Slabber*. In *Namibia Bunker Services (Pty) Ltd v ETS Katanga Futur*,[54] the court had to determine whether to make final the rule *nisi* which the plaintiff had been granted and, by which, it had been able to attach property in the jurisdiction. One of the questions which arose was whether the defendant owned the property in question. Van Niekerk J held[55] that 'the onus is on the

---

51 1991 NR 404 (HC) (Muller AJ) 410 et seq.

52 1984 (3) SA 623 (A) (Corbett, Miller and Nicholas JJA and Galgut and Howard AJJA).

53 At 234G–235D.

54 [2014] NAHCMD 197 (HC) (Van Niekerk J).

55 Ibid para [49].

[plaintiff] to establish on a balance of probabilities that the [defendant] is the owner or has some other attachable interest in the property'.[56] She continued:[57]

> 'On the return day of a rule nisi authorising attachment and if the [plaintiff] seeks confirmation of the rule, the relief claimed is final in nature. Should there be a dispute of fact on any issue, e.g. ownership of the property attached, that needs to be proved on a balance of probabilities, the test to be applied is the well-known rule laid down in *Stellenbosch Farmers' Winery Ltd v Stellenvale Winery (Pty) Ltd* 1957 (4) SA 234 (C) at 235E-G and refined in *Plascon-Evans Paints Ltd v Van Riebeeck Paints (Pty) Ltd* 1984 (3) SA 623 (A) at 634G-635G (see generally *Slabber v Blanco and Others* 1991 NR 404 (HC)).'

Thus, the plaintiff will have to prove, on the balance of probabilities, that the property sought to be attached belongs to the defendant and the test applied will be that set out in the *Plascon-Evans Paints* case.

7.1.2.2.3 Where the plaintiff and the defendant are both *peregrini*

Where both parties are *peregrini*, it will still be necessary (but will not be sufficient)[58] for a plaintiff to attach the defendant's property in order to secure the jurisdiction of the court. The plaintiff will need to rely on a cause of action which arose within the court's jurisdiction (a *ratio jurisdictionis*), as well as on the attachment of the defendant's property within the jurisdiction.[59] To put the point another way, unless the plaintiff can show that the cause of action arose within the jurisdiction of the court, the court will not make an order allowing the plaintiff to attach the defendant's property (and hence will not give the plaintiff leave to serve process on the defendant out of the jurisdiction by way of edictal citation, should that be required).[60]

In adopting this position, the law of Namibia mirrors the common law of the Republic of South Africa.[61] Hence, where both parties are *peregrini*, the plaintiff may rely on one of the following (principal) *rationes jurisdictiones* in order to

---

56 For which proposition, the judge cited: *Lendalease Finance (Pty) Ltd v Corporacion De Mercadeo Agricola* 1976 (4) SA 464 (A) 489B–C; *Italtrafo SpA v Electricity Supply Commission* 1978 (2) SA 705 (W) 709A–B; *Tsung v Industrial Development Corp of SA Ltd* 2006 (4) SA 177 (SCA) 182D.

57 [2014] NAHCMD 197 para [49].

58 See the section immediately below.

59 *Kahan v Lidchi* [2000] NAHC 19.

60 Ibid. The decision in *Kahan* has recently been confirmed by the High Court in *Namibia Bunker Services (Pty) Ltd v ETS Katanga Futur* [2014] NAHCMD 197, where Van Niekerk J, para [39], stated: 'Where, as in this case, an *incola* wishes to sue a peregrine defendant to enforce a claim sounding in money, it is still necessary for the *incola* plaintiff to attach the property of the *peregrinus* to confirm jurisdiction even if the Court has jurisdiction based thereon that the cause of action arose within the Court's jurisdiction (*Thermo Radiant Oven Sales (Pty) Ltd v. Nelspruit Bakeries (Pty) Ltd* 1969 (2) SA 295 (A) at 300D and 311E; *SOS-Kinderdorf International v. Effie Lentin Architects* 1990 NR 300 (HC) at 302I-303A); *SOS Kinderdorf International v. Effie Lentin Architects* 1992 NR 390 (HC) 401I).'

61 See *Van Wyk v Matrix Mining (Pty) Ltd* [2020] NAHCNLD 109 (January J), at para [37]. In addition, see Forsyth *Private International Law* 5 ed (2012) 224: 'If the plaintiff, as well as the defendant, is a foreign

prove that the cause of action arose within the jurisdiction. These are considered immediately below.

7.1.2.3 Rationes jurisdictions

There is no Namibian judicial or academic authority for the suggestion that the law with respect to the *rationes jurisdictions* themselves differs from the law in the Republic of South Africa. While more in-depth treatment is afforded the *rationes jurisdictions* in the chapter on South Africa,[62] the basic position may be summarised by reference to the judgment of the Supreme Court of the Cape Colony in *Einwald v The German West African Company*.[63] There, De Villiers CJ stated:[64]

> 'What then are the grounds upon which the jurisdiction of this Court can be exercised, in respect of any contract over any defendant without his consent, express or implied? The grounds are threefold: *viz* by virtue of the defendant's domicile being here, by virtue of the contract either having been entered into here or having to be performed here, and by virtue of the subject matter in an action *in rem* being situated in this Colony.'

Added to these are the place of the delict and cases which concern property. The principal connecting factors for jurisdictional purposes which result are: *ratio domicilii (actor sequitur forum rei)*; *ratio contractus*; *ratio delictus*; and *ratio rei sitae*.[65] To this list may also be added *ratio causa continentia*.

7.1.2.3.1 *Ratio domicilii* (*actor sequitur forum rei*)

Ratio domicilii expresses the principle of Roman law that the fundamental basis of jurisdiction is that a plaintiff should sue a defendant at the defendant's place or domicile or, as has become the case, residence (*actor sequitur forum rei*). There is nothing to suggest that the Namibian courts would treat this issue any differently to the courts in the Republic of South Africa.[66]

---

peregrine, he may apply for an order of attachment only if the cause of action arose within the court's area' and the substantive discussion of this point in the chapter on the Republic of South Africa.

[62] To which the reader is referred.

[63] (1887) 5 SC 86 (De Villiers CJ).

[64] Ibid 91.

[65] Different authors treat the organisation of this subject in different ways. Peté et al *Civil Procedure* 2 ed (2011) 70ff discuss the subject under the headings *ratione domicilii*, *ratione res gestae*, *ratione rei sitae* and then claims relating to property and claims sounding in money. In Schulze *On Jurisdiction and the Recognition and Enforcement of Foreign Money Judgments* (2005), the discussion (at 1–15) revolves around domicile and the bases for assumption of jurisdiction over *incolae* and *peregrini*. In Kelbrick *Civil Procedure in South Africa* 2 ed (2012) the subject is analysed (at 42–3; paras [84–6]) in terms of claims in money and property. Forsyth *Private International Law* 5 ed (2012) discusses (at 205–46) residence and domicile, the various *rationes jurisdictionis* and then claims in money or property. Herbstein and Van Winsen *The Civil Practice of the High Courts of South Africa* 5 ed (2009) discusses (at 67–81) the subject under the topic headings claims in money, property (and status). Pistorius *Pollak on Jurisdiction* 2 ed (1993) arranges the discussion under the topic headings money claims and property claims. There are merits in all of these approaches.

[66] Accordingly, for a more detailed treatment of this issue, the reader is referred to the corresponding discussion in the chapter on the Republic of South Africa.

7.1.2.3.2 *Ratio contractus*

There is nothing to suggest that the Namibian courts would treat this issue any differently to the courts in the Republic of South Africa. Accordingly, a court where: (1) the contract was concluded (the *locus contractus*); (2) the contract is to be performed in whole or in part (the *locus solutionis*); or (3) the contract was breached in the manner relied upon by the plaintiff in Namibia may, *ratio contractus*, exercise jurisdiction.[67]

7.1.2.3.3 *Ratio delicti commissi*

A court may have jurisdiction by reason of a *ratio delicti commissi* in the event that a delict was committed or occurred within its area of jurisdiction. Again, there is nothing to suggest that the Namibian courts treat this issue any differently to the courts in the Republic of South Africa.[68]

7.1.2.3.4 *Ratio rei sitae*

The location of movable or immovable property within the area of jurisdiction of a court will confer on that court jurisdiction by reason of a *ratio rei sitae*: it is the court of the place where the property is situated. Again, there is nothing to suggest that the Namibian courts treat this issue any differently to the courts in the Republic of South Africa.[69]

7.1.2.3.5 *Ratione causa continentia*

The *causa continentia* rule permits a court to assume jurisdiction in a case in which, but for the application of the rule, it might not have had jurisdiction over the entirety of the dispute or over a particular defendant. The application of the rule is intended to avoid 'a multiplicity of proceedings and the possibility of conflicting judgments on the same cause and allows for the more convenient disposition of cases'.[70]

---

[67] Given that there is nothing to suggest that the courts in Namibia treat this issue any differently to the courts in the Republic of South Africa, the reader is referred to the corresponding discussion in the chapter on the Republic of South Africa for a more detailed treatment of this issue.

[68] Accordingly, for a more detailed treatment of this issue, the reader is referred to the corresponding discussion in the chapter on the Republic of South Africa.

[69] Accordingly, for a more detailed treatment of this issue, the reader is referred to the corresponding discussion in the chapter on the Republic of South Africa.

[70] Pistorius *Pollak on Jurisdiction* 2 ed (1993) 25. For a fuller discussion of the rule, the reader is referred to the chapter on the Republic of South Africa.

That the rule is known to, and employed in, Namibian courts is confirmed by *New York Shipping v EMMI Equipment (Pty) Ltd*,[71] a decision of the South West African Division of the High Court. The first defendant had drawn two promissory notes, both of which were payable at the Netherlands Bank in Windhoek. The first defendant was within the jurisdiction of the court but the second defendant, the payee, who had signed as an indorser, and the plaintiff, were both resident in South Africa (as were the majority of the other parties who signed as co-debtors *in solidum* and/or sureties). The plaintiff brought proceedings in (then) South West Africa and the defendants objected to the jurisdiction of the court.

Relying[72] upon the decision of the South African Appellate Division in *Roberts Construction v Willcox Bros (Pty) Ltd*,[73] Muller J referred to the *causa continentia* rule being available for use in circumstances where 'several debtors, jointly liable for the same debt, are within different areas of jurisdiction. According to the *continentia* rule, they should nevertheless be amenable to the jurisdiction of a single court.' While acknowledging[74] that the 'limits within which the *continentia* rule should apply in modern law were not laid down in the *Roberts Construction Co* case', Muller J held that the 'the present case before this court appears to be pre-eminently a case in which the rule can and should be applied'.

In circumstances where the *causa continentia* doctrine does not apply, it is submitted that the position adopted by the Namibian courts is less than satisfactory. Indeed, in *Joseph & Snyman v Freedom Square*,[75] the High Court recently confirmed the need to attach the property of *peregrini* in order to join them to the action in question. The plaintiff and the defendant were both *incolae*.[76] The plaintiff sued for sums due under a contract of mandate (agency) which it alleged that one Rau had negotiated and signed with it on behalf of the defendant. While the defendant denied any contract of mandate existed, it also applied to join two third-parties (Rau and Redefine Properties Ltd, both of whom were resident in South Africa) to the action contending that if there were liability for the commission sums, the liability was that of the third parties. The plaintiff opposed the application on the basis that the court did not have jurisdiction, because no attachment of the third parties' property had taken place.[77]

---

[71] 1968 (1) SA 355 (SWA). The continued application of the rule, and the legitimacy of the conclusion reached in the case, has not been doubted in Namibian post-independence.

[72] Ibid 364A.

[73] 1962 (4) SA 326 (AD) 335 and 336.

[74] *New York Shipping Co* 1968 (1) SA 355 (SWA) 364H.

[75] [2015] NAHCMD 161.

[76] This point is not immediately clear from the judgment. However, from the authors' subsequent researches, it appears to be the case.

[77] And the plaintiff contended that such attachment was necessary, even if, as the defendant alleged, the cause of action had arisen within the jurisdiction.

Miller AJ agreed with the plaintiff's contention. Having found that the third parties had not submitted to the jurisdiction of the court, Miller AJ held that attachment was necessary to found or confirm that jurisdiction and, given that such attachment had not taken place, the court did not have the necessary jurisdiction over the third parties.[78]

While it is the case that the *causa continentia* doctrine was not relied upon *arguendo*, the result reached appears contrary to the principle that all relevant parties should be before the court so as to avoid, inter alia, a multiplicity of proceedings and the risk of inconsistent judgments.

Hence, this dispute might have been better resolved had the Namibian High Court fashioned a principle similar to that accepted by the South African Supreme Court of Appeal in *Bid Industrial Holdings (Pty) Ltd v Strang*.[79] There, it was accepted that, where attachment was not possible, a South African court would have jurisdiction if (1) the defendant (or, if applicable on the facts of *Joseph & Snyman*, a third party) was served with process while in South Africa and (2) there was sufficient connection between the suit and the area of jurisdiction of the court concerned so that disposal of the case by the court would be appropriate and convenient.

The full ramifications of the *Bid Industrial* judgment are still being worked out by the courts[80] and it is unclear whether the sufficient connection test would have been met on the facts in *Joseph & Snyman* case.[81] On the assumption that it would have been satisfied, service of process on the third parties within the jurisdiction could have, at least potentially, been effected, while there were adequate connecting factors between the suit (the fact that it was otherwise between two Namibian companies, concerning a contract related, in some sense, to land in Namibia, which was to be performed in Namibia) and the Namibian court for it to have taken jurisdiction. The Namibian courts will no doubt be astute to take into account the *Bid Industrial* principle in future when considering the development of the jurisprudence in this area of the law.

---

[78] [2015] NAHCMD 161 paras [17]–[18], where Miller AJ relied on *Spier Estate v Die Bergkelder Bpk* 1988 (1) SA 94 (C) and *SOS Kinderdorf International v Effie Lentin Architects* 1992 NR 390 (Levy J, Hannah and Muller AJJ) 401I–J, where Levy J, giving the judgment of the Full Bench of the High Court stated: 'In terms of our law, a court will not have jurisdiction against a peregrine defendant unless the plaintiff, even though he may be an incola, attaches the property of the defendant either to confirm or to found jurisdiction.' This judgment was an appeal from 1990 NR 300.

[79] 2008 (3) SA 355 (SCA). This case, and its implications for the constitutionality of arrest of the *peregrinus* defendant to found jurisdiction, is fully discussed in the chapter on the Republic of South Africa.

[80] For a full treatment of these issues, see the relevant section of the chapter on the Republic of South Africa.

[81] The judgment does not refer to any reason proffered by the defendant for its failure to attach the property of the third parties, though one may surmise that the reason was that there was no such property within the jurisdiction to attach such that the potential requirement in *Bid Industrial* would, in any event, be satisfied.

7.1.2.4 *Miscellaneous bases of jurisdiction*

The bases referred to above do not quite cover all the bases that have been found to be valid jurisdictional connecting factors in Namibia. Hence, a plaintiff bringing a *condictio indebiti* – alleging that the defendant has been unjustly enriched at the expense of the plaintiff – may rely on the fact that the enrichment occurred within the jurisdiction of the court as a legitimate *ratio* (and so as part of his attempt to found or confirm the jurisdiction of that court).

The reasoning of the High Court of Namibia in *Cabinet of the Transitional Government of South West Africa v Dagnin*[82] supports this view. The substantive dispute arose out of a fatal plane accident. The crash, which was alleged to have been caused by the pilot Dagnin's negligence, killed both the pilot and an inspector of the Department of Transport. Pursuant to the Workmen's Compensation Act 1941,[83] the plaintiff, as the head of the Department of Transport, compensated the dependants of the inspector. Then, pursuant to section 8(1)(b) of the Act, the plaintiff sought to recover that compensation from the dead pilot's estate. The case was brought against the defendant because the defendant, as sole heir, had received over R100,000 after the first full and final liquidation and distribution of the estate. The defendant, who was a *peregrinus* resident in South Africa, contended that the Namibian court did not have jurisdiction to deal with the plaintiff's claim.

The question for the court was whether the events which occurred prior to the receipt of moneys by the defendant from his dead father's estate were part of the plaintiff's claim and therefore part of the *res gestae.*

Levy J[84] affirmed the view that the essence of the *condictio indebiti* was enrichment. Hence, he went on to find that the 'defendant could not have been enriched unless and until he received the moneys concerned from [the pilot's] estate'. On this premise, the judge concluded[85] that the 'cause of action arose when and where the defendant received such moneys'. Given that the 'essential factor to found the *condictio indebiti*'[86] was that payment of the moneys concerned had to take place within the jurisdiction, and given that the plaintiff had failed to allege this, the court upheld the defendant's plea that it had no jurisdiction and dismissed the suit.

The decision in *Dagnin's* case does not, however, answer the question whether a Namibian court would follow the path which seems to have been taken by

[82] 1990 NR 14.
[83] Act 30 of 1941.
[84] Ibid 19F.
[85] Ibid 19G.
[86] Ibid 19I.

the South African courts,[87] which have held that, leaving unjust enrichment situations aside, a cause of action framed neither in contractual nor delictal terms can constitute a legitimate *ratio jurisdictionis*. This approach is supported by the decision of the South African High Court in *Ongevallekommissaris v Unie en Nasionale Verekeringsmaatskappy Bpk*.[88] Here, an accident (which fell within the definition of that term, as set out in the Workmen's Compensation Act 1941) happened within the court's area of jurisdiction. The Commissioner compensated the injured party and sought to recover that sum pursuant to section 8 of the Motor Vehicle Insurance Act 1942.[89] Hofmeyr J described the basis of jurisdiction in that case as being a *ratio res gestae*. However, in *Dagnin's* case, Levy J, taking the view that the South African authority was not relevant to the *condictio indebiti* and so not relevant to the matter which he had to decide, did not express a view on its correctness.[90]

Where the plaintiff is able to show the existence of one (or more) of the above *rationes*, attachment (presuming that the plaintiff is then able to satisfy the requirements for persuading the court to grant attachment) serves the purpose of confirming or strengthening the jurisdiction which the court already has.[91]

7.1.2.5 *Submission to the jurisdiction*

Two circumstances must be distinguished under the title submission to the jurisdiction. First, where submission is alleged in extant proceedings in Namibia. Second, where the defendant has agreed (usually by contractual provision) to submit to the jurisdiction of the court in advance of a dispute arising.

7.1.2.5.1 Submission by participating in existing proceedings

There is a lack of reported authority in Namibia on the question of what conduct amounts to a submission in existing proceedings. It is plain, however, that where a respondent has instructed lawyers to oppose an application made by the plaintiff, that amounts to submission by participation.[92]

Given the proximity of the relationship between the law of Namibia and South African law, it may be helpful to set out the circumstances in which, as a matter of South African law, a party has been held to have submitted to the court's

---

87 See, in this respect, Forsyth *Private International Law* 5 ed (2012) 214 and the authorities therein cited.

88 1969 (3) SA 438 (O). The judgment is reported only in Afrikaans, a language with which the authors are not conversant.

89 Act 29 of 1942, as amended by Act 27 of 1952.

90 1990 NR 14 at 441B–C.

91 *Slabber v Blanco* 1991 NR 404 (HC) (Muller AJ), 409J–410A, citing, with approval, Herbstein and Van Winsen *The Civil Practice of the Superior Courts in South Africa* 3 ed (1979) 785.

92 *Höfelein v Bruni* [2018] NAHCMD 328 (Masuku J).

jurisdiction by participating in existing proceedings. As a matter of South African law, the enquiry will be directed at whether the acts of the party (usually the defendant) amounted to a submission to the jurisdiction or not and the onus will be on the plaintiff to show that the relevant acts did amount to a submission. In the following cases the defendant's actions have been held to evidence submission:[93] (1) pleading to the merits; (2) filing a counterclaim (reconvention); (3) requesting a postponement or agreeing to a postponement without objection; (4) demanding security; (5) appointing an agent authorised to be sued; (6) attending an enquiry into his financial position and agreeing to pay a judgment debt in instalments; (7) accepting appointment as an executor or executrix; (8) delay in taking an objection to the jurisdiction of the court before trial; (9) submission made orally to the court by counsel acting for the defendant.[94]

As a matter of South African law, the following acts have been held not to constitute submission:[95] (1) the entry of an appearance to defend: 'a defendant is entitled to take this step in order to plead want of jurisdiction but his failure to take any further steps may imply consent'; (2) the failure to enter an appearance to defend; (3) the appointment of an agent under a general power of attorney; (4) a submission to arbitration in another country did not constitute submission to the courts of that country; (5) a letter (enclosing an affidavit) from an attorney acting for the defendant but not the attorney of record.

If a party submits to the jurisdiction of the court by appearing or taking a step in proceedings, the question then arises whether that appearance (and so submission) can undo the effects of an attachment order. In *Bourgwells Ltd (Owners of MFV OFELIA) v Shepalov*,[96] the plaintiff, a company registered in the United Kingdom and the owner of the vessel, sought an order attaching the *peregrini* defendants' right, title and interest in a judgment which the defendants had obtained against it. This was done so as to confirm the court's jurisdiction for an action which the plaintiff intended to bring against the defendants for damage done to the vessel while the defendants had been on board.

For present purposes, interest lies in the defendants' purported consent to the jurisdiction after the attachment order had been made. On the facts, the rule *nisi* (which the plaintiff wished to make final at the hearing) and the relevant attachment order had been obtained on 28 November 1997 and executed by service on the defendants' attorneys on 1 December 1997. On 20 January 1998,

[93] Pistorius *Pollak on Jurisdiction* 2 ed (1993) 11, authorities at fns 35–41 and 45.

[94] *Agro-Grip (Pty) Ltd v Ayal* 1999 (3) SA 126 (W) 128F–G.

[95] Pistorius *Pollak on Jurisdiction* 2 ed (1993) 10, authorities at fns 25–9.

[96] 1998 NR 307 (Hannah J). Hannah J's conclusion on the fact was reversed on appeal, heard by the Full Bench of the High Court: [1999] NAHC 10 (Teek, JP; Mtambanengwe and Gibson JJ). The Full Bench of the High Court did not impugn the test which Hannah J laid down in that case; they only disagreed with the answers which he had reached.

the defendants' attorneys delivered a letter to the plaintiff's attorneys, stating that the defendants consented to the jurisdiction of the court. In the circumstances, the defendants submitted that the attachment should be discharged.

Hannah J dismissed the defendants' submission, agreeing with the view[97] that 'where an attachment has taken place, there is no basis for denying the *incola* (plaintiff) any benefit conferred thereby merely because the *peregrinus, ex post facto* and unilaterally submits to the jurisdiction of the Court'. Hannah J was happy to extend this principle to the attachment of property at the instance of a *peregrinus* plaintiff.[98]

Thus, where the order of attachment has already been executed, the fact that submission takes place thereafter should not, as the judge set out, deprive the plaintiff of the security of his attachment.[99]

7.1.2.5.2 Submission by agreement

7.1.2.5.2.1 *Jurisdiction clauses*

Often, parties wishing to submit to the jurisdiction employ a jurisdiction clause in favour of a particular country's courts when writing their contract.

The High Court of South West Africa first had the opportunity to consider the effect of such clauses in *Brecher v Brecher.*[100] In this case, the plaintiff issued a summons against his wife seeking to set aside a decree of judicial separation which had been granted by the Witwatersrand Local Division (a court in the Republic of South Africa). The court, *mero motu*, raised the question whether it had jurisdiction to set aside the decree in question.[101] It decided that it did not have such jurisdiction.

---

[97] 1998 NR 307, 313G–H, expressed in *Elscint (Pty) Ltd v Mobile Medical Scanners (Pty) Ltd* 1986 (4) SA 552 (W) (Goldstone J) 557E.

[98] Agreeing with the approach in *Blue Continent Products (Pty) Ltd v Foroya Banki PF* 1993 (4) SA 563 (C) 574D (Farlam AJ).

[99] Frimpong Oppong *Private International Law in Commonwealth Africa* (2013) 73, states: 'where a *ratio jurisdictionis* exists, submission or consent to jurisdiction may render unnecessary the need for attachment, but consent to jurisdiction by a *peregrinus* after an order of attachment has been executed is too late', citing *Bourgwells.* It is submitted that while the decision self-evidently vouches the second half of that statement, *Bourgwells* may not provide authority for the first half. Hannah J engaged with South African authorities in order to make good the proposition that *ex post facto* submission/consent could not lead to the discharge of an attachment order; he did not engage with any authorities (and was not required, on the facts, to so engage) for any other purpose. Be that as it may, other cases, such as *Joseph & Snyman v Freedom Square* [2015] NAHCMD 161, are capable of supporting the first half of Frimpong Oppong's statement.

[100] 1947 (3) SA 225 (SWA) (Brebner AJ).

[101] Ibid 227.

In his judgment, Brebner AJ observed[102] that the

> 'doctrine of prorogation of jurisdiction cannot apply where the court has no jurisdiction over the subject matter of the suit. A defendant may waive either expressly or by conduct a privilege personal to himself but the consent of the parties cannot confer jurisdiction over the subject matter of a suit by agreement.'

The answer to the question whether parties can vest the court with jurisdiction by submission alone therefore depends on whether the suit is (1) between an *incola* and a *peregrinus* or (2) between two *peregrini.*

In situation (1), where the *peregrinus* defendant submits to the jurisdiction, attachment is unnecessary.[103] Moreover, the consent, once given, cannot be withdrawn. That this is the position appears from the decision of the High Court of Namibia in *Joseph & Snyman v Freedom Square.*[104] There, the *incola* applicant (who was the defendant in the substantive proceedings) sought to join third parties, who were *peregrini*, resident in the Republic of South Africa, to the action. While the court concluded that this could not be done (because there was (1) no consent to the jurisdiction by the third parties on the facts and (2) no attachment of the third parties' property in the jurisdiction), Miller AJ did endorse counsel's submission to the above effect.[105]

The position is a little more complex in situation (2).

In *Slabber v Blanco,*[106] the *peregrinus* plaintiff, who was a Cape Town attorney, launched an urgent application in the High Court of Namibia against *peregrini* (Spanish) defendants. By his application, the plaintiff sought to arrest the first three defendants and to attach vessels (then lying at anchor in Namibia) belonging to the fourth to sixth defendants, either to found or to confirm the court's jurisdiction in the case. The substantive action arose out of the alleged non-payment of legal fees by the defendants to the plaintiff in relation to work

---

[102] Ibid 228–9.

[103] *Van Wyk v Matrix Mining (Pty) Ltd* [2020] NAHCNLD 109 (January J), at para [33], citing *Cinemark (Pty) Ltd v Transkei Hotel* 1984 (2) SA 332 (W) (Goldstone J).

[104] [2015] NAHCMD 161 (HC) (Miller AJ) para [14].

[105] Ibid. 'I agree with counsel for the defendant that if a peregrinus consented to the jurisdiction of this court, such consent cannot be withdrawn and as a further consequence renders an attachment unnecessary'; in support of this conclusion, Miller AJ cited the decision of the Witwatersrand Local Division in *Cinemark (Pty) Ltd v Transkei Hotel* 1984 (2) SA 332 (W). In the *Cinemark* case, the plaintiff was an *incola*, while the defendant was a *peregrinus*. The contract between the parties contained a jurisdiction clause in favour of the Witwatersrand court. Goldstone J, at 333F–H, relying on the decisions in *Centner NO v Griffin NO* 1960 (4) SA 798 (W) (Roper) AJ at 799C and *Du Preez v Philip-King* 1963 (1) SA 801 (W) (Vieyra AJ) 803A, agreed that, in such circumstances, submission to the jurisdiction by a *peregrinus* defendant is sufficient to give the court jurisdiction without an attachment of property in order to found that jurisdiction. See now *Hay Management Consultants (Pty) v P3 Management Consultants (Pty) Ltd* 2005 (2) SA 522 (SCA), which confirms the position in the Republic of South Africa.

[106] 1991 NR 404 (Muller AJ).

done by him for the defendants in criminal proceedings. The question for the court was whether it could grant the relief sought.

Muller AJ dismissed the application. He initially considered whether the mere attachment of property would be sufficient to give the court jurisdiction and answered this question in the negative: mere attachment cannot found jurisdiction when the parties to the proceedings are all *peregrini*.[107] This corresponds with the position which has been set out above. However, Muller AJ then went further, deciding[108] that, where both parties to the proceedings are *peregrini*, the defendant's submission to the jurisdiction of the court is not sufficient to confer jurisdiction upon the court. In effect, therefore, the *peregrinus* defendant's submission to the jurisdiction of the Namibian court is meaningless until the *peregrinus* plaintiff shows that the cause of action (in the sense described above) arose within the court's jurisdiction.

While not referred to in the *Slabber* decision, the position adopted by Muller AJ reflected the position which Du Toit AJ had adopted in *Argos Fishing v Friopesca SA*[109] where both parties were *peregrini*. The case was concerned with the enforcement, at common law, of a default judgment given by a court in England, but as part of his assessment of whether the English court had international jurisdiction, Du Toit AJ stated:[110]

> 'If I were, for instance to apply the principles of our law in testing whether the English court had jurisdiction in this case, the answer would be a simple 'no'. Consent by peregrine parties to the jurisdiction of our court is not by itself sufficient to found jurisdiction. Some other ground of jurisdiction must exist.'

The High Court has recently confirmed that, as a matter of Namibian law, it is still the case that where 'both plaintiff and respondent are *peregrini*, consent will not automatically confer jurisdiction unless one of the usual rationes *jurisdictionis* is present'.[111]

It is submitted that the position at which the Namibian courts have arrived is needlessly complicated and open to question as a matter of principle.[112] In an

---

[107] Ibid 409I–410A, citing Herbstein and Van Winsen *The Civil Practice of the Superior Courts in South Africa* 3 ed (1979) 785.

[108] Ibid 410B, citing: *Towers v Paisley* 1963 (1) SA 92 (E); *Greater Services (Pty) Ltd v Du Toit* 1975 (1) SA 260 (C) 216G; *Herms Versekeringsmaatskappy v Dartnell* 1980 (4) SA 279 (W) 280A–E; *Veneta Mineraria Spa v Carolina Colleries (Pty) Ltd* 1985 (3) SA 633 (D), confirmed on appeal and reported as *Veneta Mineraria Spa v Carolina Collieries (Pty) Ltd (in Liquidation)* 1987 (4) SA 883 (A); Herbstein and Vin Winsen (op cit) 782.

[109] 1991 NR 106.

[110] Ibid 111I, citing in support *Veneta Mineraria Spa v Carolina Collieries (Pty) Ltd (in Liquidation)* 1987 (4) SA 883 (A).

[111] *Van Wyk* [2020] NAHCNLD 109, at para [34].

[112] Indeed, the harshness of the law in Republic of South Africa has been somewhat ameliorated subsequently by the decision in *Hay Management Consultants (Pty) Ltd v P3 Management Consultants (Pty) Ltd* 2005 (2) SA 522 (SCA).

action involving two *peregrini*, the better view is that mere submission should, again as a matter of principle, confer jurisdiction upon the court.

The considerations (including, inter alia, that parties should be held to their bargains and that there is no valid reason why parties should not, in advance, be able to determine conclusively the forum in which their dispute is to be heard), which led the court in *Argos Fishing* to confirm that the English court had jurisdiction[113] to deliver a judgment, are equally applicable when answering the question whether a Namibian court should itself have jurisdiction. Hence, and by way of illustration only, the principle that parties should be held to their bargains is universal, rather than territorial, it is submitted.[114] Thus, and in summary, if the Namibian High Court is willing to accept that submission, by itself, is sufficient to confer jurisdiction on a foreign court, then it is difficult to see why the same court is unwilling to accept, as a matter of pure principle, that mere submission should not be sufficient to confer jurisdiction upon itself.

Moreover, from a broader commercial point of view, the requirement that a plaintiff still needs to attach the property of a *peregrinus* defendant, even if both parties have a choice of court clause in favour of the courts of Namibia, makes little sense. The requirement adds another level of complexity to proceedings and, to the extent that there was any chance to begin with that parties might choose to settle their disputes in the courts of Namibia, such chance, it is submitted, rapidly diminishes, given the existence of the need to satisfy this requirement. If Namibian courts want to attract international actors, removal of the requirement to attach the *peregrinus* defendant's property where he has already submitted to the jurisdiction would go some way to increasing the likelihood of achieving that objective.[115]

It is, by way of comparison, instructive to note the approach which the Namibian courts have taken when confronted with jurisdiction clauses purporting to confer jurisdiction on the courts of another country. In *Olympic Fruit BV v Nagrapex Holdings (Pty) Ltd*,[116] for instance, the parties entered into a marketing agreement, under which the plaintiff (incorporated and registered in the Netherlands) was appointed as the sole marketing agent for the defendant (a Namibian company). The agreement contained an exclusive jurisdiction clause

---

[113] There, of course, in the international sense but the comparison is still a valid one.

[114] Indeed, the requirement that, in the case of *peregrini* defendants, attachment is required, in addition to submission, is liable to frustrate the bargain which the parties have made, where attachment is impossible. It renders redundant the jurisdiction/choice of court clause/submission by way of agreement which the parties have put in place.

[115] All the more so in the light of the weakening of the doctrine of effectiveness. For a fuller exposition of this, see Forsyth *Private International Law* 5 ed (2012) 231 and the discussion of this point in the chapter on the Republic of South Africa.

[116] [2011] NAHC 343 (HC) (Corbett JA).

in favour of 'any competent court in Rotterdam, The Netherlands'. Both parties 'irrevocably submitted to the exclusive jurisdiction' of this court.

The plaintiff, alleging breach of contract by the defendant, instituted proceedings in Namibia, seeking an interim interdict to force the defendant to comply with its obligations, pending the outcome of substantive proceedings which the plaintiff wished to bring against the defendant.[117] The defendant opposed the application in reliance upon the jurisdiction clause.

The Namibian High Court decided that the exclusive jurisdiction clause did not oust its jurisdiction; rather, it had discretion whether or not to give effect to the jurisdiction clause in favour of the courts of Rotterdam.[118] In going on to answer the question whether the Namibian court should itself hear the case or stay the action, Corbett AJ[119] stated that he 'inclined to the view that the decisive determinant of the jurisdictional issue lies in whether or not the Rotterdam Court could give effective relief to the [plaintiff]'. Hence his conclusion[120] that:

> 'The uncertain factor of the [plaintiff] being able to obtain effective relief in the Rotterdam Court weighs heavily. There is firstly the reservation as to whether an expeditious remedy avails the [plaintiff] should it approach the Rotterdam Courts; and secondly, more compellingly even if such relief were to be granted in the Netherlands, relief *pendente lite* being interim relief would not be effective relief since any such foreign order could not be enforced by this Court. For these reasons, I conclude that this Court does have jurisdiction to entertain this application, and I exercise my discretion to hear this matter.'

With respect, the approach of the judge appears to be correct. The domestic court retains discretion as to whether to hear the case or impose a stay in favour of the chosen court. The presence of a foreign jurisdiction clause in a contract does not oust the jurisdiction of the domestic court. Had effective relief been available in the courts of the Netherlands, it would seem that this would have been determinative and that a stay would have been granted.

In addition to considering jurisdiction clauses in and of themselves, the High Court of Namibia has also had occasion to consider certain other contractual provisions which might, in principle, be used to found an argument that a party had submitted to the jurisdiction of the court.

In *Namibia Bunker Services v ETS Katanga Futur*,[121] the defendant put forward two reasons why it should be considered to have submitted to the jurisdiction, both of which were based on the contract into which the parties had entered.

---

[117] The plaintiff's urgency was based on the fact that the court in Rotterdam would not be able to give them sufficient relief prior to the start of grape harvesting season, which was imminent.

[118] [2011] NAHC 343 para [11]. In order to vouch that conclusion, Corbett AJ para [9], cited and agreed with the judgment in *Butler v Banimar Shipping Co SA* 1978 (4) SA 753 (SE) (Howie AJ) 761G–762C and, presumably, with the authorities therein cited.

[119] [2011] NAHC 343 para [9].

[120] Ibid para [13].

[121] [2014] NAHCMD 197.

The first reason[122] was that the agreement between the parties contained an arbitration clause by which the parties agreed to arbitrate in Namibia. Originally, the defendant had put this forward as an objection *in limine* to the attachment application brought against it, but this objection was withdrawn.[123] Perhaps because the objection was withdrawn,[124] Van Niekerk J did not comment on the contention that the presence of such a clause in the contract was akin to submission to the jurisdiction by way of agreement. Suffice to say, however, that the contention was not accepted.

The second reason was the presence of a choice of law clause in the contract, viz that the contract would be governed by the laws of Namibia. Again, Van Niekerk J[125] was not prepared, in the absence of cited authority on the point, to accept that the 'inclusion of a choice of law provision in an agreement in itself constitutes submission to jurisdiction'.

7.1.2.5.2.2 Domicilium citandi et executandi *clauses*

By including a *domicilium citandi et executandi* clause in their contract, a party may nominate an address to which formal notices in relation to the contract (such as a demand for payment or a threat to cancel) or the service of process in litigation arising out of the contract can be served. There is nothing to suggest that the law in Namibia on *domicilium citandi et executandi* clauses differs from the law of South Africa on the subject. In consequence, the use of such a clause (nominating an address for service, as described above, in Namibia) may, in particular where the defendant is a *peregrinus*, indicate submission to the jurisdiction of the Namibian courts.[126]

7.1.2.6 *The jurisdictional significance of arrest of the person*

Section 25 of the High Court Act[127] prohibits attachment of an *incola*'s person (otherwise known as arrest) to found jurisdiction of the High Court.

It would appear that, aside from the necessary differences,[128] the test which the plaintiff is required to satisfy when seeking attachment of the *peregrinus*

---

[122] Ibid para [36].

[123] Ibid para [42].

[124] The judgment is not clear as to why the objection was withdrawn; the matter is not addressed.

[125] [2014] NAHCMD 197 para [37].

[126] See, by way of comparison, the decision of the South African Supreme Court in *Hay Management Consultants (Pty) Ltd v P3 Management Consultants (Pty) Ltd* 2005 (2) SA 522 (SCA), *per* Heher JA (Scott, Cameron and Conradie JJA and Patel AJA agreeing) para [15]; where the clause was regarded as 'a significant factor' as was the choice of South African law as the proper law (para [14]).

[127] Act 16 of 1990.

[128] By way of illustration, the plaintiff does not need to show that the defendant belongs to himself, in the way that the plaintiff would have to show that property the subject of attachment belongs to the defendant. The plaintiff will, however, still have to show that the defendant is within the jurisdiction.

defendant's property to found jurisdiction is the same test which the plaintiff has to satisfy in order to secure arrest of the *peregrinus* defendant's person.

The arrest of a *peregrinus* defendant to establish jurisdiction over that defendant has now been found to be unconstitutional in the Republic of South Africa.[129] It is an open question whether the Namibian court will uphold the constitutionality of arrest of the person for this purpose if subject to challenge.

Parallels may be drawn between the relevant entrenched constitutional rights which were at issue in the South African case of *Bid Industrial Holdings (Pty) Ltd v Strang*[130] and those entrenched in, for instance, articles 7 and 10 of the Namibian Constitution. Parallels may also be drawn between the general limitation clause which is present in each country's constitution.[131]

Drawing these parallels, there is a considerable cross-over between the rights protected by the South African Constitution (and which were found to have been infringed in *Bid Industrial*) and the rights which are protected by the Namibian Constitution.

It is submitted that: first, given the decision in *Bid Industrial* that section 30bis of the South African Magistrates' Courts Act[132] that provides for 'attachment of the person' is unconstitutional;[133] second, the magistrate's court Act in Namibia[134] is drafted in the same terms as its South African counterpart (both Acts being identical); and third, in view of the deep affinity of Namibian law with that of the Republic of South Africa and the willingness of Namibian courts to refer to and rely on decisions of South African courts, the constitutionality of jurisdictional arrest in Namibia must be open to very serious doubt.

7.2 Enforcement of Foreign Judgments

As the Supreme Court of Namibia has recently reiterated, a 'foreign judgment has no direct operation of its own force in Namibia. By virtue of the principle of territorial sovereignty, it is only of effect in the jurisdiction in which it was issued'.[135] There are two regimes which govern the enforcement of foreign

---

[129] *Bid Industrial Holdings (Pty) Ltd v Strang* 2008 (3) SA 355 (SCA; Howie P, Nugent, Ponnan, Maya JAA and Malan JA).

[130] Ibid. See further in this respect s 12(1) of the Constitution of the Republic of South Africa, 1996.

[131] Section 36 of the South African Constitution; art 22 of the Namibian Constitution.

[132] Act 32 of 1944, as amended.

[133] See Sibanda 'Jurisdictional arrest of a foreign peregrinus now unconstitutional in South Africa: *Bid Industrial Holdings v. Strang*' (2008) 4 *Journal of Private International Law* 329. The author states, at 345: 'In particular, section 30bis of the Magistrates' Courts Act ... will be affected. Although Section 30bis does not refer to the word "arrest", it remains unconstitutional in light of the decision and reasoning in *Bid* ... should s 30bis be challenged, it is likely to get the chop.'

[134] Act 32 of 1944, as amended.

[135] *Miller NO v Prosperity Africa Holdings (Pty) Ltd* 2019 (4) NR 905 (SC) (Shivute CJ, Hoff JA and Frank AJA), at para [1].

judgments in Namibia. The first is the common-law regime. The second is that set out in the Enforcement of Foreign Civil Judgments Act 1994.[136]

7.2.1 Enforcement at common law

The founding statute of Namibia (previously South West Africa) is the Administration of Justice Proclamation (SWA), 1919,[137] section 1(1) of which provides:

> 'The Roman Dutch Law as existing and applied in the Province of the Cape of Good Hope at the date of the coming into effect of this Proclamation[138] shall, from and after the said date, be the Common Law of the Protectorate and all laws within the Protectorate in conflict therewith shall, to the extent of such conflict and subject to the provisions of this Section, be repealed.'

In *R v Goseb*,[139] the High Court of South West Africa set out the correct meaning of the Proclamation. The court was required to determine whether, as a result of the Proclamation, the South West African court was bound by the decision of the Cape Court in *R v Fortuin*.[140] In that case, the Cape Court had decided that *furtum usus* was not a crime in the Cape of Good Hope; the High Court of South West Africa had to decide whether *furtum usus* should be a crime in South West Africa.

Claassen JP was clear in his view that the provisions of the Administration of Justice Proclamation should 'receive a wide, reasonable and above all a practical interpretation'.[141] Claassen JP then went on[142] to set out the following list of factors which had to be taken into consideration when determining the true meaning of the Proclamation:

> '*(a)* The object of the Proclamation was to create a common law for South West Africa which was already a living, active system in the Cape of Good Hope.
>
> *(b)* There was created a High Court equal in status with the Provincial Division of the Cape of Good Hope (see sec. 3(4)) with the same rights of interpreting and applying the common law.
>
> *(c)* The Court was not in any way made subservient to the Cape Provincial Division, nor was a right of appeal given to that Court, nor was it stated specifically that this Court shall be bound by the decisions of the Courts of that province.

---

[136] Act 28 of 1994. This repealed the Reciprocal Enforcement of Civil Judgments Act 1966, which ha previously been in operation.

[137] 12 December 1919 (Proclamation 21 of 1919).

[138] Section 16 of the Administration of Justice Proclamation (SWA), 1919 provides, as far as is relev for present purposes: 'This Proclamation... shall come into force and effect on the first day of January 19

[139] 1956 (2) SA 696 (SWA) (Claassen JP and Hofmeyr J).

[140] 1 BAC 290.

[141] 1956 (2) SA 696 (SWA) 697.

[142] Ibid 698–9.

(d) On the 1st day of January, 1920, there were in existence in the Union the various Provincial and Local Divisions of the Supreme Court of South Africa with a common Appellate Division. That implied that there was a common law of South Africa which was fundamentally or was intended in due course to be the same for all Provinces, except in so far as this common law had been modified by local statutes. This was illustrated by a case such as Conradie v Rossouw 1919 A.D. 279, and many other cases.

(e) The common law of the Cape of Good Hope was on the 1st day of January 1920 not something separate and distinct from the common law of the rest of the Union but part and parcel of it. In my opinion, it was in effect the South African Law as existing and applied in the Cape of Good Hope that was introduced into this Territory on the first of January 1920. This view finds support, in my opinion, in the Privy Council case of Gideon Nkambule & Others v. The King 1950 A.C. 379.

(f) In my opinion sub-sec. (4) of sec. 3 quoted earlier meant no more than this Court being equal in status with the Cape Provincial Division was free to follow one of its decisions and should in fact always endeavour to do so but was, just as that Division itself, free to depart therefrom, if convinced that it was clearly wrong.

(g) I am of the opinion that this Court is not bound to follow a decision of the Cape Provincial Court if convinced that it is clearly wrong. For example, supposing that Conradie v. Roussouw had come on appeal from this Court to the Appellate Division and that case had been decided here in conformity with the eventual Appellate Division's decision in that case, would that Court have ruled that this Court should not have followed the decision of Mtembu v. Webster 21 S.C. 323? Certainly not! ...

...

(i) It was clearly, in my opinion, also not the intention of the Legislature that the law should have remained static here in terms of the law as existing and applied in the Cape of Good Hope as at the 1st of January 1920. It is clear on the authorities that a decision given by the Cape Provincial Division say in 1925 here reversing another decision earlier than 1920 could validly be followed here. This follows clearly from such decisions as Surmon v. Surmon 1926 A.D. 47; Rex v. Burgess 1927 T.P.D. 14. See also Gardiner & Landsdown at p. 365 and Gideon Nkambule v. The King 1950 A.C. 379.'

...t out these principles, Claassen JP concluded:[143]

... opinion it is to be inferred from sec. 1(1) of the Proclamation that it was the ...n of the Legislature to introduce into this Territory the law of the Union of ...ica, as existing and applied in the Cape of Good Hope, which law has for its ...ure the principles of the Roman Dutch Law. Where those principles have ...d in the Cape of Good Hope differently from the rest of the Union, this ...) the best of its ability endeavour to interpret and apply those principles as it considers the Appellate Division will interpret and apply them in a case coming before it on appeal from a decision of a Court in the Cape of Good Hope. Just as the Appellate Division will take into consideration changes introduced into the common law by statute law binding in that Province so this Court will similarly have to take such statute law into consideration as was decided in *Tittel's* case 1921 S.W.A. 58. See also the case of *Krueger v. Hoge* 1954 (4) S.A. 248 (S.W.A.).'[144]

An assessment of the term 'common law' in post-independence Namibia must be conducted in the light of both article 66 and article 140 of the Constitution.[145] Article 66 states:

'(1) Both the customary law and the common law of Namibia in force on the date of Independence shall remain valid to the extent to which such customary or common law does not conflict with this Constitution or any other statutory law.

(2) Subject to the terms of this Constitution, any part of such common law or customary law may be repealed or modified by Act of Parliament, and the application thereof may be confined to particular parts of Namibia or to particular periods.'

Article 140(1) provides:

'Subject to the provisions of this Constitution, all laws which were in force immediately before the date of Independence shall remain in force until repealed or amended by Act of Parliament or until they are declared unconstitutional by a competent court.'

Construing these provisions, the Supreme Court of Namibia[146] has set out the post-independence position as follows:

'In terms of article 78(2) of the Constitution [Namibian] courts are stated to be:

"independent and subject only to this Constitution and the law".

The expression "the law" of course includes, inter alia, both the statute law and the common law. By virtue of article 140(1) read with article 66(1) of the Constitution, the provisions of s. 1(1) of [the Proclamation] continue to remain in force until repealed or amended by Act of Parliament or until declared unconstitutional by a competent court. Consequently, the Roman-Dutch law as existing and applied in the Province of the Cape of Good Hope (as that expression has been explained in *Goseb* [1956 (2) SA 696 (SWA)] and *Binga* [*v Administrator-General, South West Africa and Others* 1984 (3) SA 949 (SWA)] continues to apply in Namibia, with the important qualification, however, that it is for the courts of Namibia to interpret and pronounce on the content and development of

---

[144] Claassen JP's conclusion, expressed at 1956 (2) SA 696 (SWA) 700, was referred to with approval by the Supreme Court of Namibia in *Hangue v The State* [2015] NASC 33 (SC) (Shivute CJ, Maritz JA and Chomba AJA), *per* Maritz JA, giving the judgment the court, para [17].

[145] Article 1(5) provides that the Constitution 'shall be the Supreme Law of Namibia'.

[146] *S v Redondo* 1992 NR 133 (SC) (Berker CJ; Mahomed and Ackermann AJA) 145G, *per* Ackermann AJA, giving the judgment of the court. This was approved by the Supreme Court in *Hangue v The State* [2015] NASC 33 (SC) (Shivute CJ, Maritz JA and Chomba AJA), *per* Maritz JA, giving the judgment of the court, para [17]. In *Hangue*, at para [17], Maritz JA stated: 'The common law so in force "on the date of Independence", became the common law of Namibia in terms of Art 66(1) of the Constitution and, to the extent that it did not conflict with the Constitution or any other statutory law, continued to be of force and effect.'

> such common law in Namibia, which courts are no longer bound by the decisions of the Appellate Division of the Supreme Court of South Africa.'

That said, Namibian courts still cite, and are still influenced by, South African jurisprudence.

At the outset, it is important to be clear on the meaning of both 'recognition' and 'enforcement' in this context. As such, and in basic terms, where a Namibian court recognises the foreign judgment, the Namibian court affords that judgment the effect which the foreign court intended it to have. Hence, a judgment creditor may rely on a recognised foreign judgment in his favour to reduce a debt which he allegedly owes in Namibia to the judgment debtor.

Enforcement of a foreign judgment, on the other hand, in this context would see the judgment creditor engage Namibian domestic law to enforce the foreign judgment as if it were, in fact, the judgment of a Namibian court.

As mentioned above, a foreign judgment is not directly enforceable at common law. Instead, the foreign judgment constitutes 'a cause of action that will be enforced by Namibian courts if certain requirements are met'.[147]

Enforcement by action is typically pursued by means of provisional sentence.[148] Hence in *Westdeutsche Landesbank Girozentrale (Landesbausparkasse) v Horsch*,[149] Levy J (as recorded in the headnote) stated:

> 'The exigencies of international trade and commerce require that final foreign judgments be recognised as far as is reasonably possible in our Courts, and that effect be given thereto. To assist a judgment creditor who has obtained such a foreign judgment, our Courts grant such judgment creditor the right to invoke the extraordinary remedy of provisional sentence, that is he has the right to obtain a provisional judgment speedily, and without resorting to the more expensive and dilatory machinery of an illiquid action.
>
> However, because this is an extraordinary remedy, the Court is strict about the compliance with certain prerequisites. These prerequisites include annexation to the summons of a certified copy of such judgment and, where the judgment is in a foreign language, a due and proper translation thereof. All foreign documentation must be duly authenticated in terms of the Rules of Court. It is essential to prove that the foreign judgment is final and enforceable according to the foreign court concerned and that is has been handed down by a court of competent jurisdiction.'[150]

---

[147] *Standic BV v Petroholland Holding (Pty)* [2020] NAHCMD 197 (Ueitele J) at para [52].

[148] Enforcement of a foreign judgment at common law may present certain difficulties to a *peregrinus* foreign judgment creditor who is seeking to enforce the foreign judgment against the *peregrinus* judgment debtor. As has been explained above, in order for the Namibian court to have jurisdiction, the judgment creditor must be able to point to a *ratio jurisdictionis*, which condition he may find difficult to satisfy in the context of actions seeking to enforce a foreign judgment. See further: Frimpong Oppong 'Recognition and enforcement of foreign judgments in Commonwealth African countries' (2014) XV *Yearbook of Private International Law* 365, 370–1.

[149] 1993 (2) SA 342 (NM) 343B–D.

[150] For more information on the prerequisites to be met by a party wanting to enforce a foreign judgment at common law, albeit in the context of the rules of court which the High Court Rules replaced, see *Standic* [2020] NAHCMD 197.

The Namibian High Court has recently confirmed[151] that the principles governing the enforcement of a foreign judgment at common law in Namibia are the same as those set out in the Republic of South Africa.[152] These principles are set out below.

(1) The foreign court must have had international jurisdiction (or competence) to give judgment in proceedings

There are a number of ways in which a foreign court may have international jurisdiction.

(1) The defendant was resident in the foreign court's area of jurisdiction at the time of the commencement of the action in the foreign court.
(2) Jurisdiction of the foreign court derived from the defendant's submission thereto, either by agreement or by conduct.

In *Argos Fishing*,[153] Du Toit AJ confirmed the general proposition that in order to recognise and enforce the judgment of the foreign court, it had to be shown that the foreign court[154] had jurisdiction in the international sense over the defendant.

The plaintiff judgment creditor was a company incorporated under the laws of the Falkland Islands. It entered into a joint venture fishing agreement and a charterparty with the defendant judgment debtor, a Spanish company.[155] Both the joint venture agreement and the charterparty contained a clause conferring (non-exclusive) jurisdiction on the English High Court. The plaintiff alleged that, pursuant to the terms of the agreements, sums had become due and owing by the defendant, which sums the defendant had not yet paid. On the strength of the jurisdiction clause, the plaintiff sued the defendant in England, obtaining a default judgment, which judgment it then tried to enforce in Namibia.[156]

Having commenced his judgment by recognising the need for the English court to have international jurisdiction, Du Toit AJ held that the question whether the English court did have international jurisdiction had to be 'decided

[151] *Standic* [2020] NAHCMD 197 at para [52].

[152] *Jones v Krok* 1995 (1) SA 677 (AD) (Corbett CJ, Van Heerden, Cumleben and Nienaber JJA and Olivier AJA).

[153] 1991 NR 106.

[154] As noted above, in this case the judgment creditor sought to enforce a default judgment from the English High Court. For the more general proposition set out above, Du Toit AJ relied on the decision of the South African Court in *Reiss Engineering Co Ltd v Insamcor (Pty) Ltd* 1983 (1) SA 1033 (W) 1036E.

[155] From this it will be seen that, from a Namibian perspective, both parties were *peregrini* of Namibia. The court also noted that both parties, absent the jurisdiction clause in both the joint venture agreement and the charterparty, had no connection with England either.

[156] The plaintiff wished to enforce the English judgment in Namibia because the defendant had assets within the jurisdiction (two vessels at anchor in Luderitz Bay, having been arrested pursuant to the provisions of the Sea Fisheries Act 1973 (Act 58 of 1973), pending criminal proceedings instituted for an alleged contravention of that Act).

in light of the principles of our law on the jurisdiction of foreign courts', going on to acknowledge that such principles may differ not only from the principles of the foreign court but also the local court being asked to enforce judgment.[157]

The issue which occupied the court was whether the mere consent (in the form of the jurisdiction clause) of parties who otherwise had nothing to do with the jurisdiction in which the proceedings were heard could confer international jurisdiction upon the foreign court. Du Toit AJ held that such consent could confer international jurisdiction on the English court.

In order to reach this conclusion, Du Toit AJ relied on the following 'general considerations':[158] (1) litigants ought to be bound by their contracts; (2) with modern communications there seemed no reason why parties should not in advance select their forum to settle disputes in relation to a contract; (3) parties of different nationalities might find it convenient to choose the courts of a neutral foreign country; (4) international commerce might find it convenient to select certain jurisdictions above others for the settlement of disputes for reasons of costs, impartiality, accessibility, language and the speed with which a result could be expected and (5) if the court which the parties have chosen accepts jurisdiction, why should that acceptance be questioned by a different court.

Du Toit AJ[159] noted the existence of reasons why the mere consent of parties should not be sufficient to confer upon foreign courts international jurisdiction. He set these out as follows:

> 'The first, as reflected in the *Veneta Mineraria*[160] case is that a court only has jurisdiction if it has the power to give effect to its judgment. This is known as the doctrine or principle of effectiveness. Now this in our law is achieved in some cases, for instance, by the attachment of property to found jurisdiction.
>
> Yet the value of the property need bear no relation to the amount in dispute. It is difficult to see how the principle of effectiveness is satisfied in such circumstances, which raises a question as to the fundamental usefulness of the application of that principle in this context.
>
> Secondly, it has been said that a court should not permit foreigners to burden its roll by allowing matters to be enrolled which have no real connection with the country of the selected forum.

[157] To illustrate this point, Du Toit AJ made clear that, if the question were to be decided by reference to the principles of jurisdiction as applied by the Namibian courts, the answer would have to be in the negative: the mere consent of peregrine parties to the jurisdiction was not, of itself, sufficient to confer jurisdiction on a Namibian court.

[158] 1991 NR 106 at 112I.

[159] Ibid 113B et seq.

[160] *Veneta Mineraria Spa v Carolina Collieries (Pty) Ltd (in liquidation)* 1987 (4) SA 883 (A). For a full treatment of this case, the reader is referred to the relevant discussion in the chapter on the Republic of South Africa.

> This seems to me to be a somewhat narrow view. If it is based on economic grounds, then there are means of skinning the cat other than by adapting the law of the jurisdiction. If it is based on considerations such as that the court is for its *incolae* only, then that would seem to be at variance with the view that it is a court's task to disperse justice to all who come before it.'

It is submitted that, in reaching the conclusion he did, Du Toit AJ was correct, both as a matter of principle and as a matter of authority.[161] From a principled point of view, the 'narrow view' cited would have unduly restricted the ability of the Namibian courts to deal with meritorious cases. Moreover, from an economic standpoint, such view would have unduly fettered the ability of the court to deal with international business, thereby hindering the court (in both Namibia and South Africa) in attracting transnational litigation. There did not, and does not, seem to be a warrant for that: why, after all, should the court question the jurisdiction of the court pronouncing judgment when both parties to proceedings have chosen that court to hear the case?

(3) The defendant was present in the jurisdiction of the foreign court at the time of commencement of the action.

(4) The defendant was domiciled within the foreign court's jurisdiction at the time of the commencement of the action.

(2) That the judgment given by the foreign court was final and conclusive and has not become superannuated

In order to be capable of recognition and enforcement, a judgment must be final and conclusive in its effect.[162] Trek J, giving the judgment of the High Court in *Bekker No v Kotze*,[163] explained: 'It is logical that this Court cannot enforce a foreign judgment unless it is final because a provisional order or judgment can be confirmed or discharged on the return date.'[164]

In *Bekker*, Trek J rejected the application. As pointed out above, the judge acknowledged, in the light of the '*exigencies*' of international trade, the need to ensure that foreign judgments could be recognised and given effect to in Namibia in as speedy a manner as possible, hence why Namibian law allowed the plaintiff to utilise the process of provisional sentence. However, in light of the exceptional

---

161 See further the substantive discussion of the *Argos Fishing* case in the chapter on the Republic of South Africa and further below.

162 The judgment creditor has to prove that the foreign judgment is final and enforceable in the eyes of the foreign court which gave it: *Westdeutsche Landesbank Girozentrale (Landesbausparkasse) v Horsch* 1993 (2) SA 342 (NM).

163 1994 NR 345.

164 See, to similar effect, the decision of the High Court in *Standic* [2020] NAHCMD 197 at paras [54] and [55], where Ueitele J held that a preliminary or interlocutory order of the Rotterdam District Court was not final and conclusive.

nature of the remedy of provisional sentence, Namibian courts strictly enforced the requirements with which the plaintiff had to comply. Hence, inter alia, the plaintiff had (and has) to annex to the summons a certified copy of the foreign judgment and, where that judgment was (and is) in a foreign language, a due and proper translation of that document[165] in compliance with the Rules of Court.

Applying these principles to the facts of the case, Trek J found that, while a copy of a German document had been provided, there was nothing to show that it was a judgment of a court of competent jurisdiction. More fundamentally, in the present context, while the plaintiff had provided a translation of the German document, there was nothing on the document to show that it was translated either by a sworn translator of this court or by a person qualified to translate from the German into English. In the absence of any authentication of these documents, the plaintiff could not make good its case.

The approach which Trek J took in the *Bekker* case can be traced back to the seminal decision of the High Court of Namibia in *Argos Fishing*. There, the High Court was asked to provide answers to two questions, viz: (1) whether the foreign court had international jurisdiction and (2) whether the judgment so produced was a 'final' judgment. Both of these points have been discussed above.

When looking at the High Court's answer to the second question identified above, it was stated that the plaintiff had to take the blame for failing to produce sufficient evidence so as to satisfy the court as to the finality of the foreign judgment. In the absence of clear evidence as to 'the rules of English law on the subject of rescinding a default judgment', Du Toit AJ did not consider himself 'in a position to evaluate finality under English law'.[166] As a result, doubtless following the view that in the absence of proof of the content of foreign law the judge is entitled to assume that the foreign law mirrors the *lex fori*, Du Toit AJ applied Namibian law and decided, pursuant to that, that the default judgment did not 'have the quality of finality which I consider the law requires'.[167]

It would be unfortunate to extrapolate from *Argos Fishing* any wider or general principle that default judgments are not enforceable at all. There is, as Kahn[168] has argued, a 'danger in being too sympathetic to defendants against whom a foreign default judgment has been delivered'. It is submitted that extrapolating any general principle from *Argos Fishing* would indeed make the law 'too sympathetic to defendants'.

---

[165] Trek J further explained that, in order to qualify for certification, the judgment had to be stamped and signed by a sworn translator of the court, in compliance with the rules of court.

[166] 1991 NR 106, 114B–C.

[167] Ibid 115A.

[168] (1991) *Annual Survey of South African Law* 590 at 593.

This view receives support from the South African case of *Blanchard, Krasner & French v Morgan Evans*.[169] There, the plaintiff sought, by way of provisional sentence, to enforce a default judgment which it had obtained against the defendant in the Superior Court of the State of California for the sum of $169,251.74 with costs.

Malan J concluded that the application should be granted. In reaching this conclusion, the judge distinguished the decision of Du Toit AJ in *Argos Fishing*,[170] on which the defendant had relied to support his argument that the judgment from the Californian court was not 'final' or 'final and conclusive'. Malan J concluded that, in *Argos Fishing*, the question of finality 'was dealt with only "scantily" in the papers and Du Toit AJ said that he was not in a position to evaluate "finality" under English law'. From this, it is apparent that the decision in *Argos Fishing* was heavily dependent upon the (unsatisfactory) state of the evidence adduced by the plaintiff. It is prudent, therefore, not to derive any general principle concerning the finality or otherwise of foreign default judgments from the decision in *Argos Fishing*.

It is submitted that the appropriate approach is that set out by Malan J in *Blanchard* itself. There, the judge approved Hahlo's[171] view:

> 'No judgment is ever final in the sense that it cannot be rescinded in any circumstances. In all Western European legal systems a judgment that is no longer subject to appeal may nevertheless be set aside, usually by the court that granted it, if the loser can show that his adversary has obtained his victory by fraud, perjury or forgery ... yet it has never been argued that the possibility of a reopening on this ground interferes with the finality of the judgment. South African law, following English law, goes even further in holding that the possibility of an appeal does not necessarily prevent a judgment from being final. Against this background, it appears quite arbitrary to say that the possibility of rescission of a default judgment precludes it from being final, however remote the prospects of success may in fact be. It is suggested that common-sense tests rather than rigid rules ought to be applied in examining whether a foreign judgment is or is not final.'

This view is also supported by Forsyth,[172] who makes the point that default judgments should be considered final and conclusive because, if this is not done, 'default judgments, even when granted by an internationally competent court, will often be worthless outside the territory of that court.' Hahlo's view is defensible from a principled standpoint as well, that, in instances where the judgment debtor in the foreign court is not subject to any time limit in which he or she must make an application to set aside default judgment, 'only an application by the defendant to have the judgment set aside can, when dismissed, transmute the judgment into an internationally enforceable one. This is "in effect... saying

[169] 2004 (4) SA 427 (W).

[170] Ibid 434G–435B para [8].

[171] 'The finality of foreign default judgments' (1969) 86 *SALJ* 354 at 357–8.

[172] *Private International Law* 5 ed (2012) 460.

that the clearer the plaintiff's case the more useless his judgment would be".'[173] Such a state of affairs has no logic to commend it.

(3) Recognition and enforcement of the foreign judgment not contrary to public policy in Namibia

As a matter of principle, it seems likely that a judgment creditor seeking to have a judgment from a foreign country recognised and enforced pursuant to the common law could be met by the judgment debtor's claim that it would be contrary to Namibian public policy to enforce the judgment in question.

It appears that there is no reported authority where this defence has been considered by the courts in Namibia.

It is worth considering the way in which a public policy defence to recognition/enforcement could develop. Frimpong Oppong[174] suggests:

> 'A likely area for the successful invocation of public policy relates to foreign judgments given in breach of jurisdiction agreements ... Because of negative perceptions about laws and judicial systems in Africa and imbalances in negotiating positions, parties to international contracts seldom choose African courts as their preferred forum for dispute settlement. Even in the rare cases where such choices are made, they are often challenged in foreign courts in the event of a dispute. It is important that parties are held to their bargain. An African court should decline to enforce a foreign judgment given in breach of an agreement that has selected the enforcing State as the choice of forum.'

It is submitted that this view is correct.

(4) The judgment was not obtained by fraudulent means

As a matter of principle, it seems likely that a judgment creditor seeking to have a judgment from a foreign country recognised and enforced pursuant to the common law could be met by a judgment debtor's claim that it would be contrary to Namibian law to enforce the judgment in question where that judgment has been obtained by fraudulent means.

It appears that there is no reported authority where this defence has been considered by the courts in Namibia.

However, the law of the Cape of Good Hope, which, as a result of the Administration of Justice Proclamation was applied in Namibia, suggests that such a requirement likely exists. According to the law of the Cape (and, generally, now, the law of South Africa),[175] where a defendant could show that the foreign

---

[173] Ibid, citing *Boyle v Victoria Yukon Trading Co* (1902) 9 BCR 213 at 223, *per* Hunter CJ.

[174] *Private International Law in Commonwealth Africa* (2013) 346.

[175] As to which, see the detailed treatment of the issue in the chapter on the Republic of South Africa.

judgment had been obtained by fraudulent means, such judgment would not be enforced in the Cape courts.[176]

In this context, the defendant is specifically required to show that the foreign judgment was obtained by fraud that has not already been the subject of judicial determination in the foreign court or, if it has, that there is evidence not available at the time of that determination to show that the plaintiff obtained the judgment by fraud.[177]

(5) The judgment does not involve the enforcement of a penal or revenue law of the foreign state

As a matter of principle, it seems likely that a Namibian court would not enforce a foreign judgment in respect of a foreign penal or revenue law.

It appears that there is no reported authority where this defence has been considered by the courts in Namibia.

7.2.2 Enforcement pursuant to statute

7.2.2.1 *The regime for enforcement pursuant to statute*

The preamble to the Enforcement of Foreign Civil Judgments Act 1994 ('the 1994 Act') states that the 1994 Act is one to 'provide that civil judgments granted in designated countries may be enforced in magistrate's courts[178] in Namibia'.

---

[176] *Goodman v Goodman* (1903) 20 SC 376 (De Villiers CJ, Kotzé J).

[177] Forsyth refers to intrinsic and extrinsic fraud; it is the latter which may provide grounds for non-recognition and enforcement (*Private International Law* 5 ed (2012) 463). The formulation in the text is slightly different in intended meaning: the questions such as perjury or forgery or suppression of material documents which Forsyth allocates to extrinsic fraud are all matters which might (depending on the facts of the case) be raised before the foreign court and adjudicated upon. In such circumstances, it would be as unfair to the plaintiff to permit relitigation of such issues, as it is accepted that it is unfair to permit relitigation of issues which are the subject of the judgment which it is sought to enforce. Clearly, if the defendant relies on evidence not reasonably available at the time the foreign court adjudicated on such issues, then the picture changes. But absent such evidence, a defendant ought not to be permitted to contest, for example, the truthfulness of evidence given abroad any more than he is allowed to contest liability under a contract forming the subject-matter of the foreign judgment. This is, more or less, the position in Canada (*Union of India v Bumper Development Corp* [1995] 7 WWR 80); Australia (*Keele v Findley* (1991) 21 NSWLR 444 (NSWSC); and in English domestic law (where the discoverability with reasonable diligence principle applies: *Chodiev v Stein* [2015] EWHC 1428 (Comm), *per* Burton J para [14]). (The English conflict rules on this subject are, by general assent, less than satisfactory as, in contradistinction to English domestic law, foreign judgments are impeachable for fraud even where the evidence of fraud is that which was relied on unsuccessfully in the foreign court: *Owens Bank Ltd v Bracco* [1992] 2 AC 443 (HL(E)). However, more recent authority suggests that relitigation of matters litigated abroad may be an abuse of the process of the English court such that the claim of fraud may be liable to be struck out: *Owens Bank Ltd v Etoile Commerciale SA* [1995] 1 WLR 44 (PC) and *Altimo Holdings and Investment Ltd v Kyrgyz Mobil Tel Ltd* [2012] 1 WLR 1804 (PC).)

[178] In terms of s 10 of the 1994 Act, '[a]ny power to make rules under section 25 of the Magistrates' Courts Act 1944 (Act 32 of 1944) shall be deemed to include the power to make rules prescribing any matter which

It should be noted that the 1994 Act provides for the enforcement of foreign civil judgments from designated countries in 'magistrate's courts' in Namibia. This may seem odd: one might well expect the enforcement of foreign civil judgments to be a matter with which the High Court of Namibia should concern itself. In this respect, the language of the Namibian statute exactly reflects the South African Enforcement of Foreign Civil Judgments Act 1988.[179]

The 1994 Act identifies the Namibian magistrate's court as the appropriate court in which to seek enforcement of foreign judgments from 'designated countries'. This might give rise to potential difficulties. Frimpong Oppong[180] points out that 'there are monetary and territorial limits on the jurisdiction of a Magistrate's Court'; the High Court's financial and territorial jurisdiction is not so limited, by contrast. Hence 'it is unclear from the Act whether a foreign judgment for a sum exceeding that which is within the jurisdiction of the Magistrate's Court can nonetheless be enforced by the court'.[181]

However, looked at in the round, there is nothing in the 1994 Act which demonstrates that the legislature intended to cap a party's ability to enforce a foreign judgment from a designated country once that judgment exceeds the financial jurisdiction of the magistrate's court.

It is also the case that section 4 of the 1994 Act provides that a judgment registered in the magistrate's court 'shall have the same effect as a civil judgment of the court at which such judgment has been so registered'. The act of registration is a purely administrative one; no limits on the registering court's jurisdiction would be relevant or applicable here because the magistrate's court is designated as the registering court pursuant to the 1994 Act. Section 4(1) of the 1994 Act deems the registered judgment to have the same effect as any judgment of the magistrate's court rendered within the jurisdiction of that court (which jurisdiction has, after all, been conferred directly upon it by the 1994 Act and which jurisdiction, as a result, is free from territorial and financial constraints).

The language of the 1994 Act does give rise to one further difficulty. It has been submitted above that the 1994 Act does not envisage a dual regime by which foreign judgments from 'designated countries' up to a certain limit (which

---

may in terms of this Act be prescribed or which is necessary or expedient to be prescribed to give effect to the provisions of this Act'. To date, it does not appear that any such specific rules have been made.

[179] Act 32 of 1988. The degree of crossover between the two Acts is not all that surprising. The only country which satisfies the definition of 'designated country' in s 1 of the South African Act is Namibia; the only country which satisfies the definition of 'designated country' in s 1 of the Namibian Act is the Republic of South Africa.

[180] Frimpong Oppong 'Recognition and enforcement of foreign judgments in Commonwealth African countries' (2014) XV *Yearbook of Private International Law* 365 at 370, fn 95. The limits about which he speaks are set out in ss 26–30 of the Magistrates' Courts Act.

[181] Oppong op cit.

limit coincides with the financial jurisdiction of the magistrate's court) can be enforced in the magistrate's court, but judgments for a quantum beyond this limit must be enforced in the High Court. However, even if that submission is correct, such that all judgments from 'designated countries' are enforceable in the magistrate's court, it may well be the case that judgments which a party seeks to have recognised and enforced pursuant to the provisions of the common law might have to be so recognised and enforced in a different court, that is, the High Court.

Of course, parties seeking to enforce a judgment from a foreign court pursuant to the common law appear to be at liberty to seek such enforcement in the magistrate's court. However, the magistrate's court's jurisdiction to hear such applications is not, in this instance, conferred upon it by the 1994 Act – the party seeking to have the foreign judgment recognised and enforced (pursuant to the common law) is, *ex hypothesi*, armed with a judgment from a non-designated country. Hence, it is plausible to argue that in this situation the territorial and jurisdictional limits on the magistrate's court, which limits do not seem to apply when the magistrate's court exercises jurisdiction pursuant to the 1994 Act, would now be in place. If this is correct, then a more complicated dualistic common-law regime would be in operation: the magistrate's court would be the appropriate court in which to seek recognition and enforcement of foreign judgments under the common law, so long as the quantum of such judgments remained equal to or below the financial limitation on the magistrate's court's jurisdiction, whereas, once the quantum of the judgment exceeded that financial limit, a party would be forced to seek recognition and enforcement in the High Court (the jurisdiction of which is not subject to the same financial limits).

The regime[182] envisaged in the previous paragraph appears to be unnecessarily complex. It may simply be the case that, contrary to the position under the 1994 Act, parties wishing to have a judgment from a foreign (non-designated) country recognised and enforced pursuant to the common law should simply seek to do that in the High Court and not the magistrate's court (which submission is supported by the fact that the identified cases dealing with recognition and

[182] It should be noted that according to s 9 of the 1994 Act, nothing therein prevents 'any court in Namibia from recognising, for the purposes of any claim, defence or counterclaim, any judgment (other than a judgment the registration of which has been set aside under s 5) granted by a court of competent jurisdiction outside Namibia in any civil matter, as conclusive of any matter of law or of fact decided in such judgment if such judgment could, before the commencement of this Act, have been so recognised by such court'. In the context of s 9 of the South African Enforcement of Foreign Civil Judgments Act 1988, the wording of which is an exact replica of s 9 of the 1994 Act Forsyth (*Private International Law* 5 ed 439 fn 144) has written that it 'leaves open the possibility that *enforcement* at common law may be prevented by the [South African] Act. However, no words of the Act suggest the creation of an exclusive avenue for enforcement' (emphasis in the original). For a fuller discussion of this in the context of South African law, which is, in all likelihood, a mirror image of Namibian law in this context, see the further discussion provided by Forsyth here.

enforcement pursuant to the common law are High Court cases). By contrast, parties armed with a judgment from a 'designated country' (ie a judgment from a court in the Republic of South Africa) must seek enforcement of the same in the magistrate's court. If that is the position, it does throw into sharper relief the apparent oddity with the language of the 1994 Act.

7.2.2.2 *Procedure for registration*

Section 3 of the 1994 Act provides:

> '(1) Whenever a certified copy[183] of a judgment granted against any person by any court in a designated country is lodged with a clerk of the court in Namibia, such clerk of the court shall register such judgment in the prescribed manner in respect of—
>
> *(a)* the balance of the amount payable in terms of such judgment, including the taxed costs awarded by the court of the designated country;
>
> *(b)* the interest, if any, which by law or by order of the court of the designated country concerned is due on the amount payable in terms of such judgment up to the time of such registration; or
>
> *(c)* the reasonable costs of and incidental to such registration, including the costs of obtaining a certified copy of the judgment.'[184]

Once the certified copy of the judgment has been so registered, the clerk of the court 'shall forthwith issue a notice directed to the judgment debtor concerned, informing him or her of such registration'.[185] This notice shall be 'served on the judgment debtor by the Messenger of the Court in the manner prescribed for the service of process'.[186]

---

[183] In terms of s 1 of the 1994 Act (the definitional section), 'certified copy' means 'a copy certified by the proper officer of the court of a designated country to be a true copy'. Section 7(2) of the 1994 Act provides that a document 'purporting to be a copy of a judgment of a court in a designated country, and purporting to be certified as a true copy of an original judgment of that court by someone styled in that document to be a registrar or a clerk of such court, shall be admissible in evidence in any proceedings under any of the provisions of this Act, and shall be prima facie proof of the contents of such document'. Section 7(3) of the 1994 Act adds that: 'Any document admissible under subsection (2), or any document which would have been admissible under any other law if made or attested within Namibia, need not be authenticated and shall be admissible as if such document has been made or attested within Namibia.'

[184] In terms of s 3(5) of the 1994 Act, the sums set out at s 1(a) and (c) shall, 'subject to section 2(1) of the Prescribed Rate of Interest Act 1975, bear interest from the date of registration of the judgment in terms of (1) until the date of payment of such amounts, calculated at the rate prescribed under section 1(2) of that Act or at the rate determined by the court of the designated country which granted such judgment, whichever is the lower'. Section 2(1) of that Prescribed Rate of Interest Act provides: 'Every judgment debt which, but for the provisions of this subsection, would not bear any interest after the date of the judgment or order by virtue of which it is due, shall bear interest from the day on which such judgment debt is payable, unless that judgment or order provides otherwise.'

[185] Section 3(2) of the 1994 Act.

[186] Section 3(3) of the 1994 Act. Presumably, this is a reference to the way in which process is meant to be served pursuant to rr 8 and 9 of the Rules of the High Court of Namibia, referred to above. A 'messenger of the court' is defined in s 14 of the Magistrates' Courts Act 1944.

It is important to note the mandatory language of the 1994 Act here. The clerk of the registering court does not have discretion as to whether to register the judgment of the designated country or not: he or she must register that judgment.

As has been hinted at above, the definition of 'designated country' under the 1994 Act is quite narrow. Section 1 states that '"designated country" means a country declared as a designated country under section 2(a)'; section 2(a) provides that the Minister of Justice may, by notice in the *Gazette* either:

> '*(a)* for the purposes of this Act declare as a designated country, any country with which Namibia has in terms of the Namibian Constitution entered into an agreement providing for the reciprocal enforcement of foreign civil judgments; and
>
> *(b)* withdraw any such declaration.'

To date, the only country which has been so designated is the Republic of South Africa.[187] Judgments emanating from courts in other countries must be recognised and enforced in Namibia using the common law.

Only 'final' judgments may be enforced under the 1994 Act.[188] The question as to what constitutes a 'final judgment' has received some attention in the context of the common-law regime for the recognition and enforcement of foreign judgments (which regime is outlined below). It is submitted that caution should be exercised before either (1) drawing any general principle from that case law or (especially) (2) applying any general principle which may be drawn from that case law to the 1994 Act.

In *Argos Fishing*,[189] the Namibian High Court was asked to recognise and enforce an English default judgment. Du Toit AJ dismissed the application, holding that, on the facts, insufficient evidence as to the finality of the default judgment as a matter of English law had been adduced by the applicant, such that the judge could not be sure that the default judgment was, in fact, final. The judge also concluded that, under Namibian law, the default judgment, of which the defendants to the application had 'at best six or eight days' notice' would not be considered final. Accordingly, Du Toit AJ held that, as a matter of common law,

---

[187] As detailed in the *Government Gazette* of the Republic of Namibia 1095 of 15 June 1995.

[188] Section 1 of the 1994 Act defines 'judgment' in the following way: 'Any final judgment or order for the payment of money, granted or made before or after the commencement of this Act by any court in any civil proceedings or in respect of compensation or damages to any aggrieved party in any criminal proceedings and which is enforceable by execution in the country in which it was granted or made, but does not include any judgment or order granted or made by any court on appeal from a judgment or order of a court other than a court as defined in this Act, or for the payment of any tax or charge of a like nature or of any fine or other penalty or for the periodical payment of sums of money towards the maintenance of any person.' Section 7(1) of the 1994 Act provides: 'A judgment shall be deemed to be a final judgment notwithstanding that an appeal against such judgment is pending in a court of the designated country or that the time prescribed by the law of such country for appealing against such judgment has not expired.'

[189] *Argos Fishing v Friopesca SA* 1991 NR 106, 1991 (3) SA 255.

the English judgment sought to be enforced in this case, did not meet the 'finality' threshold at common law: a judgment 'not susceptible to being set aside by the very court from which it emanates' (which this default judgment was not).[190]

It is submitted that it is questionable whether the decision in *Argos Fishing* is helpful on the interpretation of the word 'judgment' in the 1994 Act, principally because the judge in the Namibian High Court was not being asked to interpret the words of the 1994 Act (which had not yet come into being in any event).[191]

On the other hand, it is arguable that the 1994 Act defines only the word 'judgment' but not the word 'final'. To this extent, therefore, it is arguable that the 1994 Act relies on the definition given to the word 'final' by the common law. The principle which underpins that argument – that it is unnecessarily complex to have a definition of finality which varies depending on whether one is using the common law or the 1994 Act – is a sound one. The better view, therefore, is that the 1994 Act does rely on the common law's definition of 'final' and hence the definition of 'judgment' in the 1994 Act subsumes the definition of '*final*' provided by the common law.

However, it is submitted that the conclusion in *Argos Fishing* was inevitably heavily dependent on the facts of the case: Du Toit AJ should not be taken to have formulated any overarching general principle about the finality of foreign default judgments. In any event, it is submitted that the approach to 'finality' by Malan J in *Blanchard, Krasner and French v Evans*[192] is clearer.[193]

A default judgment can, in principle, satisfy the definition of 'judgment' which is provided in section 1 of the 1994 Act.[194] While a party against whom a default judgment has been given might well be given a right, by the procedural law of the foreign court, to apply to set aside the default judgment, which right may or may not be subject to a time limit. That a default judgment is liable to be set aside upon application does not make it any less final, it is submitted. Section 7 of the 1994 Act supports this view, providing that a judgment shall be deemed to be final even though an 'appeal against such judgment is pending in a court of the designated country or that the time prescribed by the law of such a country for appealing against such judgment has not expired'. Hence, one could easily

[190] 1991 NR 106 at 114B. The conclusion reached in this case has been labelled 'disappointing' by Forsyth: 'Submission as a ground of international competence and the finality of foreign default judgments' (1992) 109 *SALJ* 1 at 5.

[191] And, for that reason, it is plausible to argue that a judge should simply construe the words of the 1994 Act itself, as they appear therein.

[192] 2004 (4) SA 427 (WLD), in which *Argos Fishing* was cited and distinguished.

[193] The reasons for this submission appear in the discussion of the common-law regime for the recognition and enforcement of foreign judgments, as set out above.

[194] The correct treatment of default judgments for the purposes of registration/recognition and enforcement is set out in the context of the discussion of the common-law regime.

analogise between the position of a judgment given in (say) the English High Court which is subject to an appeal and the position of a default judgment given in the English High Court, in respect of which the judgment debtor has made an application to have it set aside. Both judgments remain in force until they are set aside and both are at least liable to be set aside, in the sense that they may be set aside if the appeal or application is decided in favour of the judgment debtor. In the light of this, there seems little reason to distinguish between the finality of a default judgment and a substantive judgment under the 1994 Act.

This conclusion does not leave the judgment debtor with insufficient protection under the 1994 Act. In *Argos Fishing*, the Namibian High Court was concerned somewhat by its 'doubt as to whether the English summons in fact came to the notice of a responsible person in the administration of Friopesca'.[195] This concern, which 'exercised'[196] the judge's mind, at least played some part in the conclusion which the High Court reached.

It is submitted that Du Toit AJ was correct to state that 'such considerations may strictly speaking not fall under the heading of finality'.[197] Properly analysed, such considerations may be described as 'jurisdiction or procedural fairness principles', relevant to the question whether the foreign court had jurisdiction, in the international sense, to give judgment in the case or whether the judgment so given was undermined by procedural impropriety, rather than concerning the finality of the judgment so given by the foreign court. Treating them in the manner in which they should have been treated would not have been to the detriment of the judgment debtor, in the authors' view.

To prove the point, the judgment debtor may seek to set aside the registered foreign judgment, which application may be made for a myriad reasons, including that the

> 'judgment debtor did not receive notice of the proceedings in which the judgment was granted, as prescribed by the law of the designated country, or, if no such notice is prescribed, that he or she did not receive reasonable notice of the said proceedings to enable him or her to defend the proceedings, and did not appear'.[198]

Hence, even if the foreign court of the 'designated country' is found to have jurisdiction in the international sense, such that the judgment creditor is entitled to register the foreign judgment pursuant to the 1994 Act, the judgment debtor in the position of Friopesca (the judgment debtor in *Argos Fishing*) could still seek to set such registration aside. Indeed:

---

195 1991 NR 106 at 114A.

196 Ibid.

197 Ibid.

198 Section 5(1)(c) of the 1994 Act. On setting aside the registered judgment generally, see s 5 of the 1994 Act.

> 'A judgment registered in terms of section 3(1) shall not be executed before the expiration of 21 days after service in accordance with section 3(3) of the notice referred to in section 3(2) or until an application in terms of section 5 has been finally disposed of.'[199]

Accordingly, the 1994 Act specifically ensures that the judgment debtor cannot be prejudiced by the judgment creditor's immediate attempts to enforce a registered judgment.

Properly understood, therefore, the provisions of the 1994 Act undermine Du Toit AJ's concerns, at least as expressed in the context of *Argos Fishing*. It is submitted that it appears to be unnecessary to distort the clear definition of 'judgment'[200] so as to exclude automatically default judgments from falling within it, so as to protect the respondent judgment debtor in a Namibian court in such a situation. The 1994 Act contains the machinery with which the judgment debtor can protect himself.

Where 'a judgment has been registered in terms of section 3(1), such judgment shall have the same effect as a civil judgment of the court at which such judgment has been so registered'.[201] Execution on the strength of a judgment so registered shall not take place before the expiration of 21 days after service of the requisite notice or until an application made pursuant to section 5 of the 1994 Act has been disposed of finally.[202]

Section 3(2) of the 1994 Act requires the clerk of the court registering the foreign judgment to issue a notice directed to the judgment debtor, informing him of the registration of that judgment. Such notice operates as an 'interdict against the judgment debtor on whom it was served, and against any person having knowledge of such notice, not to remove or dispose of any assets of the judgment debtor if such removal or disposal would prejudice the execution of the judgment'.[203]

7.2.2.3 *Setting aside registration*

The High Court has held that the 1994 Act 'creates its own statutory regime in terms of which foreign judgments, which have been registered in accordance with the provisions of [the 1994 Act] can be set aside'.[204]

As has been mentioned, a judgment debtor has the right, pursuant to section 5 of the 1994 Act, to seek to set aside the registration of a foreign civil judgment.

---

199 Section 4(2) of the 1994 Act.

200 Defined in s 1 of the 1994 Act.

201 Section 4(1) of the 1994 Act.

202 Section 4(2) of the 1994 Act.

203 Section 8 of the 1994 Act.

204 *Maritz v Magistrate for the District of Karasburg* [2019] NAHCMD 220 (Geier J) at para [18]. As such, the 1994 Act does not empower the designated court to grant declaratory relief: ibid para [20].

In order to do this, the judgment debtor must make an application to the court at which the judgment has been registered, in the prescribed form and manner within 21 days after service of the notice informing him or her of the fact that the judgment has been so registered.[205] It is worth noting that the fact a judgment has been registered contrary to the provisions of the 1994 Act does 'not render such registration null and void, per se, but merely renders it liable to be set aside' on the judgment debtor's application.[206]

The court to which the judgment debtor has made his application shall set aside the registered judgment if it is satisfied that one of the grounds contained in section 5(1) of the 1994 Act have been made out. These grounds are as follows:

(a) the judgment was registered in contravention of any of the provisions of the 1994 Act;[207]

(b) the court of the designated country concerned had no jurisdiction in the circumstances of the case;

Whether a court of the designated country had jurisdiction or not is a question of Namibian private international law. That the court of the designated country had jurisdiction pursuant to the terms of its own domestic law is not determinative of the outcome. This can be demonstrated by the fact that in section 7(4) and (5) of the 1994 Act, the Namibian legislator has deemed that, in certain specified circumstances, the foreign court will or will not (as the case may be) have jurisdiction for the purposes of this Act.

The circumstances in which the foreign court will be deemed to have had jurisdiction to give judgment are set out in section 7(4) of the 1994 Act:

- Section 7(4)(a)(i):

  > 'if the judgment debtor was the plaintiff or plaintiff in reconvention in the proceedings or submitted to the jurisdiction of the court by which the judgment was granted by voluntarily appearing in the proceedings for any purpose other than protecting or obtaining the release of property seized or threatened with seizure in the proceedings or contesting the jurisdiction of such court';

- Section 7(4)(a)(ii):

  > 'if the judgment debtor was a defendant in the proceedings before such court and had, before the commencement of the proceedings, in writing agreed, in respect of the subject matter of the proceedings, to submit to the jurisdiction of any court of the designated country';

---

205 See s 5(1) and (2) of the 1994 Act. By way of an aside, if, upon any such application by the judgment debtor, the court at which the judgment is registered is satisfied that an appeal against the judgment is pending in a court of competent jurisdiction or that the plaintiff is entitled and intends to appeal against the judgment of a court of competent jurisdiction, it may on such conditions and for such period as it may deem appropriate suspend the execution of the judgment: s 6 of the 1994 Act.

206 *Maritz* [2019] NAHCMD 220 at para [20].

207 Section 5(1)(a) of the 1994 Act.

- Section 7(4)(a)(iii):

  'if the judgment debtor was a defendant in the proceedings before such court and, at the institution of the proceedings, resident in or being a juristic person, had its registered office or principal place of business in, such designated country or at any time had an office or place of business in such designated country through or at which the transaction to which the proceedings relate, was effected';

- Section 7(4)(b):

  'if, in any action relating to immovable property, the property was at the institution of the proceedings situate in the designated country in which the proceedings were instituted'; or

- Section 7(4)(c):

  'if, in any proceedings other than proceedings referred to in [s. 7(4)(a) or 7(4)(b)] the jurisdiction of the court by which the judgment was granted is recognised by the law of Namibia'.

The circumstances envisaged by section 7(4) of the 1994 Act, as set out above, are expressly stated to be subject to section 7(5). Hence, it is necessary to look next at the provisions set out in section 7(5) itself.

The circumstances in which a foreign court will be deemed not to have had jurisdiction are as follows:

- Section 7(5)(a): 'in proceedings relating to immovable property situated outside such designated country';
- Section 7(5)(b): 'except in cases referred to in subparagraphs (i) and (ii) of subsection (4)(a), in proceedings instituted in contravention of an agreement under which the dispute in question was to be settled otherwise than by proceedings in the court of such designated country'; or
- Section 7(5)(c): 'in proceedings in which the person against whom the judgment was granted was under the rules of public international law entitled to immunity from jurisdiction of the courts of such designated country and did not submit to such jurisdiction'.

(c) the judgment debtor did not receive notice of the proceedings in which the judgment was granted;

Pursuant to section 5(1)(c), where the judgment debtor can show that he or she 'did not receive notice of the proceedings in which the judgment was granted, as prescribed by the law of the designated country, or, if no such notice is so prescribed, that he or she did not receive reasonable notice of the said proceedings to enable him or her to defend the proceedings, and did not appear', the court at which the judgment is registered shall set aside that registration.

(d) the judgment debtor shows that the judgment was obtained by fraud;[208]

(e) the enforcement of the judgment would be contrary to public policy in Namibia;[209]

(f) the certified copy of the judgment lodged in terms of section 3 was so lodged at the request of a person other than the judgment creditor;[210]

(g) the matter in dispute in the proceedings had, prior to the date of the judgment, been the subject of a final judgment by a court of competent jurisdiction in civil proceedings before such court;[211]

(h) the judgment has been set aside by a court of competent jurisdiction;[212]

(i) the judgment has become prescribed under either the laws of Namibia or of the designated country concerned;[213]

(j) the judgment has been wholly satisfied;[214]

(k) the judgment has been partly satisfied, to the extent in which it has been so satisfied;[215]

(l) the judgment is a judgment or order which in terms of any law may not be recognised or enforced in Namibia.[216]

7.3 Interim Remedies

7.3.1 Jurisdiction to grant interim remedies

Section 2 of the High Court Act 1990 states that the High Court shall 'have jurisdiction to hear and determine all matters which may be conferred upon it by this Act or the Namibian Constitution or any other law'.

In this regard, the Constitution provides:

(1) the 'Supreme Court and the High Court shall have the inherent jurisdiction which vested in the Supreme Court of South-West Africa immediately prior to the date of Independence, including the power to regulate their own procedures and to make court rules for that purpose' (article 78(4)); and

[208] Section 5(1)(d) of the 1994 Act.
[209] Section 5(1)(e) of the 1994 Act.
[210] Section 5(1)(f) of the 1994 Act.
[211] Section 5(1)(g) of the 1994 Act.
[212] Section 5(1)(h) of the 1994 Act.
[213] Section 5(1)(i) of the 1994 Act.
[214] Section 5(1)(j) of the 1994 Act.
[215] Section 5(1)(k) of the 1994 Act.
[216] Section 5(1)(l) of the 1994 Act.

(2) the 'High Court shall have original jurisdiction to hear and adjudicate upon all civil disputes and criminal prosecutions, including cases which involve the interpretation, implementation and upholding of this Constitution and the fundamental rights and freedoms guaranteed thereunder' (article 80(2)).

The Namibian court has, therefore, inherent jurisdiction to make orders of the types available prior to independence, including orders designed to regulate its own procedure. As with the position in the Republic of South Africa, the power to grant interdictal relief is not statute based but is derived from the court's inherent jurisdiction:[217]

> 'A superior court, differing in this respect from an inferior court, has inherent jurisdiction to make orders, unlimited as to amount, in respect of matters which come before them, and such inherent jurisdiction is limited only to that extent that restraints are imposed upon it, sometimes by the common law but more often by statute.'

7.3.2 Procedure for application

Every application must be brought on notice of motion supported by an affidavit as to the facts on which the plaintiff relies for relief.[218] Where an application initiates new proceedings (rather than forming part of an existing cause or matter), that application commences with the issue of a notice of motion (addressed to the person where relief is claimed against that person or where it is necessary to give that person notice of the application)[219] signed by the registrar, date stamped with the official stamp and uniquely numbered for identification purposes.[220]

When such an application is brought, it must conclude with the form of order prayed for, be verified on oath or by affirmation by or on behalf of the plaintiff[221] and, save where it is an *ex parte* application (as to which, see below), be brought on notice of motion on Form 17.[222] It is incumbent on the plaintiff (ie for these purposes the party making the application) in that notice to: (1) appoint an address within a flexible radius of the court on which he will accept notice and

---

[217] Prest *The Law and Practice of Interdicts* (1996) 266.

[218] Where the application is made in connection with the estate of a person deceased or alleged to be a prodigal or under any legal disability, mental or otherwise, the special procedure – involving submitting the application to the master for his or her consideration – set out in r 65(7) applies. That procedure, with such modifications as are required, also applies with respect to applications for appointment of administrators or trustees under deeds or contracts relating to trust funds or to the administration of trusts set out by testamentary disposition: r 65(8).

[219] Rule 65(2).

[220] Rule 65(1).

[221] Rule 65(3).

[222] Rule 65(4). True copies of the notice of motion on Form 17 and all annexures thereto must be served, either before or after the application is issued by the registrar, on every part to whom notice of the application is to be given.

service of documents in the proceedings; (2) set out a day not less than five days after service on the defendant to the application, on or before which date the defendant is required to notify the plaintiff in writing whether the defendant intends to oppose the application;[223] and (3) state that, where no notification is given, the application will be set down for hearing on a stated day not being less than seven days after service of the notice on the defendant.

In order to bring an application, the party has to have a direct and substantial interest in the relief prayed for. This must appear from the application and founding affidavit thereto. The interest in question must not be too remotely connected to the relief claimed and it should not be of an abstract or academic nature.[224]

A plaintiff will not be barred from bringing an application on the principle that he has come to court with 'unclean hands', at least in the absence of any evidence showing that the plaintiff had acted dishonestly or fraudulently.[225] Hence, where the unlawful occupiers of land sought, by way of interdict, to prevent the owner of the land from demolishing the occupiers' houses, the Supreme Court upheld their right to make the application, irrespective of the fact that their occupation was unlawful.[226]

A defendant who wishes to oppose the grant of the order sought by way of application must: (1) give the plaintiff notice in writing (within the time stated in the notice on motion) that he intends to oppose the application and provide an address, within a flexible radius of the court, at which he will accept notice and service of documents;[227] (2) within 14 days of so notifying the plaintiff, deliver the answering affidavit, along with any other relevant documents;[228] and (3) if he

---

[223] Where the Government is the defendant to the application, the time limit may not be less than 15 days: r 65(5)(b). Generally, where the defendant (Government or otherwise) fails to notify the plaintiff, by the date mentioned for that purpose, of their intention to oppose the application, the plaintiff must inform the registrar, who must place the matter on the residual court roll: r 65(6).

[224] *MWEB v Telecom* 2012 (1) NR 331 (a decision of the Full Bench of the High Court: Damaseb JP, Mainga and Muller JJ), Muller J (with whom Mainga J and Damaseb JP concurred) para [11]. The constitutional aspects of the judgment were appealed to the Supreme Court ([2011] NASC 8) but the 'urgency' issue was authoritatively determined in the High Court. In the High Court, Muller J cited *United Watch & Diamond Co (Pty) Ltd v Disa Hotels Ltd* 1972 (4) SA 409 (C) 415F–H, where it was held that 'what is required is that a [plaintiff] should have a legal interest in the subject matter of the action which could be prejudicially affected by the judgment of the court'. See further *Cabinet of Transitional Government for the Territory of South West Africa v Eins* 1988 (3) SA 369 (A) 388A–B.

[225] *Minister of Mines and Energy v Black Range Mining (Pty) Ltd* 2011 (1) NR 31 (Strydom, Chomba and Damaseb AJA); *Shaanika v Windhoek City Police* 2013 (4) NR 1106 (Maritz and Mainga JA; O'Regan AJA) para [27]. Both are decisions of the Supreme Court of Namibia.

[226] *Shaanika v Windhoek City Police* 2013 (4) NR 1106.

[227] Rule 66(1)(a).

[228] Rule 66(1)(b). Where the defendant is the Government, the time limit may not be less than 21 days. The days in between 16 December and 15 January, both inclusive, are not counted in computing the time allowed for the delivery of a notice of intention to oppose. See further: r 70(5).

intends to raise a question of law only, deliver notice of that intention within the 14-day[229] period, in which that question is set out.[230]

In addition, a party to an application proceeding may bring a counter-application or join any party to the same extent as would be competent if the party wishing to bring the counter-application or join such party were a defendant in an action and the other parties to the application were parties to such action.[231]

The plaintiff may, within 14 days of service of the answering affidavit and relevant documentation, deliver a replying affidavit.[232] However, in this respect, it must be noted that, generally speaking, a plaintiff must make out his case in his founding papers (ie his affidavit and other documents). It is usually impermissible, therefore, to set out a skeleton case in the founding affidavit and seek to bolster or fortify this in the replying affidavit.[233] If the plaintiff does provide such scant material in his founding affidavit, he runs the risk that the application will be dismissed and cannot complain if this is done.[234] While the court does, however, retain a real discretion whether or not to dismiss the application on this basis, such discretion will only be used sparingly and in appropriate circumstances.[235]

Where the defendant neither delivers an affidavit nor a notice that he intends to raise a question of law within the appropriate period, the plaintiff must, within four days of expiry of the appropriate period, give notice to the registrar to place the application before a judge in residual court for determination.

On the premise that both parties deliver their respective affidavits and relevant documentation on time (or pleadings are otherwise considered closed), the registrar must allocate the file to a managing judge and provide the managing judge with all the documents filed of record.[236] In all cases other than in urgent applications, once the application has been placed before him or her, the managing

---

229 Or 21 days where the defendant is the Government.

230 Rule 66(1)(c).

231 Rule 69(1). In this instance, r 40 – dealing with joinder of parties and causes of action – and r 48 – dealing with counterclaims – apply with the appropriate modifications.

232 Rule 66(2).

233 *Transnamib Ltd v Imcor Zinc (Pty) Ltd (Moly-Copper Mining and Exploration Corp (SWA) Ltd* 1994 NR 11 (HC) (Frank J) 15I–16B. Compare with *Matador Enterprises (Pty) Ltd v The Namibian Agronomic Board* 2010 (1) NR 212 (HC) (Maritz J) 223G–I and the authorities therein cited.

234 *Transnamib Ltd v Imcor Zinc (Pty) Ltd (Moly-Copper Mining and Exploration Corp (SWA) Ltd* 1994 NR 11 (HC) 15I–16B. Frank J went on to say that the 'court may in its discretion allow deviations from the normal procedures but it must be borne in mind that the normal procedures developed as they did because they would almost invariably be consonant with the best interests of the administration of justice'. One might think this even more imperative given the recent restatement (in 2014) of the Rules of the High Court. For safety's sake, parties should comply with the rules, as interpreted by the courts.

235 *Matador Enterprises (Pty) Ltd v The Namibian Agronomic Board* 2010 (1) NR 212 (HC).

236 Rule 66(4). In this instance, r 21(2), dealing with docket-allocation, applies with appropriate modifications in this context.

judge must give directions through the registrar to all parties in respect of the date determined by the judge for the holding of a case management conference.[237]

It may be the case that the application cannot properly be decided on the affidavits. In this instance, the court may dismiss the application or make any order the court considers suitable or proper with the view to ensuring a just and expeditious decision.[238] After hearing the application, the court may make no order, except an order for costs, if any, but may grant leave to the plaintiff to renew the application on the same papers, supplemented by such further affidavits as the case may require or allow.[239]

The Rules of the High Court are clear, however, that, in the case of interlocutory and other applications incidental to pending proceedings, a degree of flexibility may be exercised. Thus, such applications may be brought on notice supported by such affidavits as the case may require.[240]

7.3.2.1 *Urgency*

Urgent applications are allocated to and must be heard by the duty judge at 09:00 on a court day, save where a legal practitioner certifies in a certificate of urgency that the matter is so urgent that it should be heard at any time or on any other day.[241] However, those advising clients should be aware of the need to ensure that an urgent application is not improperly made (and that the certificate of urgency procedure is not abused): where the application is dismissed for lack of urgency, the judge may make a special order of costs against the plaintiff where he is satisfied that the matter is not so urgent that it could not be heard on a court day.[242]

In these circumstances, it is important for both parties and clients to understand how the courts have defined urgency. The Full Bench of the High Court concluded, when considering the previous version of the Rules of the High Court, that a plaintiff had to show 'good cause' as to why the times provided in what are now rules 65(4) and 66(1) and 66(2) 'should be abridged' and why the plaintiff could not 'be afforded substantial redress at the hearing in due course'.[243]

---

[237] Rule 71(1). The case management conference is governed by r 25. The reader is referred to r 71(2)–(11) for both the pre- and post-case management procedure to be followed by parties in the context of an application.

[238] Rule 67(1). In particular, the court may, pursuant to r 67(1)(a), direct that oral evidence be heard on specific matters in issue between the parties with a view to resolving any dispute of fact or, pursuant to r 67(1)(b), refer the matter to trial with the appropriate directions as to pleadings, definition of issues or any other relevant matter.

[239] Rule 67(2).

[240] Rule 70(1).

[241] Rule 73(1).

[242] Rule 73(2).

[243] *MWEB v Telecom* 2012 (1) NR 331 (HC) (Damaseb JP, Mainga J and Muller J) at para [21], citing *IL & B Marcow Caterers (Pty) Ltd v Greatermans SA Ltd; Aroma Inn (Pty) Ltd v Hypermarkets (Pty) Ltd* 1981 (4)

Where the plaintiff has 'created the urgency either mala fides or through his or her culpable remissness or inaction', a court is unlikely to find that the threshold requirement for 'urgency' has been met.[244] A party's being dilatory in making the application in order to score an advantage over an opponent would exemplify such conduct.[245] In sum, when an application is brought on a basis of urgency, institution of the proceedings should take place 'as soon as reasonably possible after the cause thereof has arisen'.[246]

The court's lack of sympathy will be all the more apparent when the relief sought is essentially of a final nature and no or very little opportunity has been afforded to the defendant to present properly his or her defence.[247]

The assessment of whether the urgency threshold has been passed is an inherently fact-specific one. Indeed, the courts have commonly recognised that there are 'varying degrees of urgency',[248] such that what is considered urgent in one set of circumstances may not be considered urgent in other circumstances. To that end, the courts have fashioned a (non-exhaustive) list of factors which can be employed when deciding how urgent the application is. Such factors include: the urgent or otherwise nature of the application being made (eg a claim of spoliation is inherently urgent);[249] the logistics of putting together the application; what constitutes a reasonable time to take all reasonable steps preceding an application,

---

SA 108 (C) 110H–111A. See, in the context of the present rules, *Stocks & Stocks Leisure (Namibia) (Pty) Ltd v Swakopmund Station Hotel (Pty) Ltd t/a the Swakopmund Station Hotel and Entertainment Centre* 2020 (4) NR 1117 (HC: Ndauendapo, Ueitele and Masuku JJ) at para [14].

244 *Bergmann v Commercial Bank of Namibia Ltd* 2001 NR 48 (HC: Maritz J) 49I–49J, cited with approval in *MWEB v Telecom*, supra fn 262, at para [23].

245 *Bergmann v Commercial Bank of Namibia Ltd* 2001 NR 48 at 50A.

246 Ibid 49H–50A, approving *Twentieth Century Fox Films Corp v Anthony Black Films (Pty) Ltd* 1982 (3) SA 582 (W) and *Schweizer-Renecke Vleis Maatskappy (Edms) Bpk v Minister Van Landbou en Andere* 1971 (1) PH F11 (T). That said, 'as soon as possible' is a heavily context-specific term. An application made (say) two or three weeks after the cause has arisen because the legal firms had shut for the Christmas break when the cause so arose might meet the definition: *Shoprite Namibia v Paulo* 2010 (2) NR 475 (LC) (Hoff J).

247 *Bergmann v Commercial Bank of Namibia* 2001 NR 48 at 49J–50A. See, to similar effect, the judgment of the Namibian Supreme Court in *Beukes v Kubitzausboerdery (Pty) Ltd* 2020 (3) NR 662 (SC) (Smuts and Hoff JJA and Frank AJA) at para [10].

248 *Olympic Fruit BV v Nagrapex Holdings (Pty) Ltd* [2011] NAHC 343 (HC) (Corbett AJ) para [40], citing *Luna Meubelvervaardigers (Edms) Bpk v Makin* 1977 (4) SA 135 (W). This, in turn, was cited with approval in, amongst others, *Clear Channel Independent Advertising Namibia (Pty) Ltd v TransNamib Holdings Ltd* 2006 (1) NR 121 (HC) and *Bergmann v Commercial Bank Namibia Ltd* 2001 NR 48. In this respect, legal practitioners should be aware that where a defendant agrees to a timetable for the filing of pleadings, the defendant will be unable to say that they are prejudiced by truncated timelines set by the plaintiff, save where the defendant attacks the factual basis of the alleged urgency: *Beukes v Kubitzausboerdery* 2020 (3) NR 662 (SC) at paras [22]–[26].

249 *Three Musketeers Properties (Pty) Ltd v Ongopolo Mining and Processing Ltd* case no (P) A 298/2006 (unreported) 30 November 2006 (Smuts AJ) para [29]. The substantive decision of Smuts AJ was upheld on appeal to the Supreme Court: [2008] NASC 15. An application for a stay of execution on an arbitrator's award is also an inherently urgent application, so long as execution is reasonably imminent and the plaintiff is not guilty of any blameworthy conduct in not bringing the application timeously: *Hardap Regional Council*

such as the need to take advice; attempts to negotiate; obtaining copies of relevant documents and obtaining and preparing affidavits[250] (where all are satisfactorily explained);[251] and the court's own convenience.[252]

In the same way, the courts have set out certain factors which cannot demonstrate that the application is urgent. Hence, the mere fact that irreparable damage may be suffered is not enough to make out a case of urgency.[253] Similarly, the court has to accept for the purpose of the issue of urgency that the plaintiff has a strong case – it does not need to consider the merits of that case to determine the issue of urgency.[254] The courts have further found that the mere existence of negotiations between the parties will not *ipso facto* justify delay in bringing an application.[255]

Where the application is struck off the roll for lack of urgency[256] and the plaintiff wishes to continue to prosecute the application on its merits, he must set down the application in the normal course as an opposed motion, to which the rules of court apply.[257]

Any evidence filed in support of an urgent application must set out explicitly: (1) the circumstances which the plaintiff avers render the matter urgent and (2) the reasons why the plaintiff claims he could not be afforded substantial redress at a hearing in due course.[258]

---

v Sankwasa James Sankwasa case no (LC) 15/2009 (unreported) 28 May 2009 (Parker J) para [4], cited with approval in *Shoprite Namibia v Paulo* 2010 (2) NR 475 (Hoff J) para [24].

250 In *Three Musketeers Properties (Pty) Ltd v Ongopolo Mining and Processing Ltd* case no (P) A 298/2006 (unreported) 30 November 2006 (Smuts AJ) para [29], Smuts AJ showed more leniency than he might have done when he concluded that 'in considering the time taken to prepare the necessary papers, allowances should be made for differences between practitioners practising as attorneys and advocates' and, less surprisingly, that 'a party cannot be expected to act over hastily, particularly in complex matters'.

251 Ibid. The need for each factor to be 'satisfactorily explained' reconciles this authority with *Bergmann*, it is submitted. Smuts AJ certainly thought what he was saying was compatible with *Bergmann* (which was cited to him). The passage in question from Smuts AJ's judgment was subsequently cited with approval in *Shoprite Namibia v Paulo* 2010 (2) NR 475 (LC) (Hoff J) para [23].

252 *MWEB v Telecom* 2012 (1) NR 331 para [37], citing *Makhuva v Lukoto Bus Service (Pty) Ltd* 1987 (3) SA 376 (V) 391H.

253 *MWEB v Telecom* 2012 (1) NR 331 para [18].

254 Ibid para [31], citing *Bandle Investments (Pty) Ltd v Registrar of Deeds* 2001 (2) SA 203 (SE). Some confusion may have arisen in this context because of the decision of the High Court in *Clear Channel Independent Advertising v Transnamib Holdings* 2006 (1) NR 121 (Muller AJ) (which was not referred to in *MWEB*). At points in the *Clear Channel* judgment, it is submitted that Muller AJ risks confusing the test for urgency and the test for whether the plaintiff has demonstrated, to the appropriate standard, what he has to demonstrate in order to obtain interdictory relief. Plainly it is the case that, in determining the former issue, the court can look at the facts in issue between the parties (ie where the plaintiff says that he was not aware of some fact, thereby necessitating that they delay in bringing the application, and where the defendant says that the plaintiff was aware of that fact). The way that the matter is put in *MWEB* para [18] is conceptually clearer but can be criticised on the basis that no absolute distinction between merits and urgency can always be maintained: for example, see the facts of *Olympic Fruit*.

255 *Bergmann v Commercial Bank of Namibia* 2001 NR 48.

256 Or condonation for non-compliance with the rules of court is refused.

257 Rule 73(5).

258 Rule 73(4). See further *Olympic Fruit BV v Nagrapex Holdings (Pty) Ltd* [2011] NAHC 343 (Corbett AJ) para [40].

Given the exigencies of the situation, when confronted with an urgent application, the court may dispense with the forms and service provided in the Rules of the High Court; it may dispose of the application at such time and place and in such manner and in accordance with such procedure which must, as far as practicable, be in keeping with the Rules of the High Court[259] or be as the court considers fair and appropriate.[260]

The degree of procedural latitude which is afforded a party making an urgent application should not be taken too far: a party still needs to make out its case for the relief sought, irrespective of whether the application is urgent or not. Hence, if a party decides to bring an application on an urgent basis, that party cannot complain if another party takes the point that the plaintiff has not made out its case.[261] Similarly, save in cases where it would defeat the object of the application or, due to the degree of urgency or other exigencies of the case, it is impracticable or unreasonable, a plaintiff should

> 'effect service of an urgent application as soon as reasonably possible on a respondent and afford him or her, within reason, time to oppose the application. It is required of any applicant to act fairly and not to delay the application to snatch a procedural advantage over his or her adversary.'[262]

7.3.2.2 Ex parte *applications*

Of course, certain applications (such as those for the attachment of property to found jurisdiction) could easily be stymied by a potential defendant if the plaintiff were required to give them notice in advance. The Rules of the High Court therefore allow applications to be brought on an *ex parte* basis. Where a plaintiff wishes to bring an *ex parte* application, he must file the notice and supporting affidavit with the registrar; this must then be set down in the motion court before 12:00 on the day but one before the day on which it is to be heard.[263] In that notice to the registrar, the plaintiff has to set out: (1) the form of the order sought; (2) specify the affidavit filed in support; and (3) request, using Form 18, the registrar to place the matter on the roll for hearing.[264]

The *ex parte* application and any relief sought in that application commences with issue of the notice of motion, signed by the registrar, date stamped with the official stamp and uniquely numbered for identification purposes.[265] Any person

---

[259] *Bergmann v Commercial Bank of Namibia Ltd* 2001 NR 48 at 50I–51B.

[260] Rule 73(3).

[261] *Transnamib Ltd v Imcor Zinc (Pty) Ltd (Moly-Copper Mining and Exploration Corp (SWA) Ltd* 1994 NR 11 at 16D–16E.

[262] *Bergmann v Commercial Bank of Namibia Ltd* 2001 NR 48 at 51A–51B.

[263] Rule 72(1).

[264] Rule 72(2).

[265] Rule 72(3).

who has an interest which may be affected by a decision on an *ex parte* application may deliver notice of an application by him or her for leave to oppose, supported by an affidavit setting out the nature of that interest and the grounds on which he or she desires to be heard, after which the registrar must docket-allocate the matter to a managing judge who must set it down for hearing.[266]

In addition to complying with the relevant procedural requirements which have been set out in the previous two paragraphs, the plaintiff, given the nature of an *ex parte* application, must establish a case for urgency and is subject to a duty to put before the court all of the relevant information.[267] This duty has variously been described as one of the utmost good faith,[268] a duty of 'full and frank disclosure'[269] and one to 'lay all the relevant facts before the court, so that it may have full knowledge of the circumstances of the case before making its order'.[270] Hence, where material facts which might have influenced the decision of the court whether or not to make the order sought have not been disclosed, the court has discretion to set aside the order on grounds of non-disclosure.[271] While the discretion is real, it must be exercised judicially; hence, it has been said that, depending on the specific circumstances of the case, the court may be 'left with no discretion at all but to act against the party who has failed to uphold its duty to disclose'.[272]

When deciding whether, in the exercise of its discretion, to discharge the rule *nisi*, the court will have regard to the following (non-exhaustive) list of factors: (1) the extent to which the rule has been breached, (2) the reasons for the non-disclosure, (3) the extent to which the court might have been influenced by proper disclosure, (4) the consequences, from the point of doing justice between the parties, of denying relief to the plaintiff on the *ex parte* order, and (5) the interest of innocent third parties such as minor children, for whom protection was sought in the *ex parte* application.[273]

---

[266] Rule 72(4).

[267] *Van Wyk v Matrix Mining (Pty) Ltd* [2020] NAHCNLD 109 (January J) at para [17].

[268] *Commercial Bank of Namibia v Myburgh* 1996 NR 330 (HC) (Hannah J) 336C–E, cited with approval in *Doeseb v Kheibeb* 2004 NR 81 (HC) (Makhanya J) 87J–88C. See further *Ken Investments Close Corp v Rouwans Investments CC* [2016] NAHCMD 51 (HC) (Parker AJ) para [5].

[269] *Prosecutor-General v Lameck* 2010 (1) NR 156 (HC) (Damaseb JP and Parker J) para [24], citing *Schlesinger v Schlesinger* 1979 (4) SA 342 (W) 349A.

[270] *Estate Logie v Priest* 1926 AD 312 at 323, cited with approval in *Doeseb* at 88C–D. See also *Knouwds No v Josea* 2007 (2) NR 792 (HC) (Damaseb JP) para [18].

[271] *Commercial Bank of Namibia* 1996 NR 330 (HC) 336D, citing *De Jager v Heilbron* 1947 (2) SA 415 (W) 419.

[272] *Doeseb v Kheibeb* 2004 NR 81 (HC) 88G–H, citing in support *Schlesinger v Schlesinger* 1979 (4) SA 342 (W) 349B–C. This embodies a general theme, viz that an order which has been granted *ex parte*, where the plaintiff has failed in its duty of utmost good faith, should usually be discharged: *Jacobs v Van Zyl* [2015] NAHCMD 254 (HC) (Parker J) para [9]; *Ken Investments Close* [2016] NAHCMD 51 (HC) (Parker AJ) para [5].

[273] *Jacobs v Van Zyl* [2015] NAHCMD 254 (HC) (Parker J) para [5], repeated in *Ken Investments Close* [2016] NAHCMD 51 (HC) (Parker AJ) para [5].

When faced with an *ex parte* application, the court may grant or dismiss the application or may adjourn the hearing on such terms as to the filing of further affidavits as the court considers suitable or proper.[274] The court may also give the plaintiff leave to renew the application on the same papers supplemented by such further affidavits as the case or the court may require.[275]

Where the court grants the *ex parte* order, the party against whom the order is so granted may anticipate the return date on delivery of not less than 24 hours' notice.[276]

7.3.3 Interim interdicts

When a plaintiff asks the court to grant relief by way of an interim (or, as it is sometimes called, temporary) interdict, the plaintiff is asking the court to exercise its discretion in his favour: the court is not obliged to grant the relief which is sought.[277]

The requirements which a plaintiff has to satisfy before a court will grant interim relief are well established, though they have not always been set out consistently in the case law.[278] From that case law,[279] in order to obtain interim relief, the plaintiff must show:

(1) he has a clear right or a *prima facie* established right, though such right is open to some doubt;
(2) where he can only show a *prima facie* case, he has a well-grounded apprehension that he will suffer irreparable harm if the interim relief is not granted and he ultimately succeeds in establishing the right;
(3) he does not have any other satisfactory remedy; and
(4) the balance of convenience favours granting interim relief.

It has also been said that, in addition to the above, the plaintiff must show that a defendant has committed a wrongful act, in order to entitle him or her to relief.[280]

---

[274] Rule 72(5).

[275] Rule 72(6).

[276] Rule 72(7).

[277] *Sheehama v Inspector General, Namibian Police* 2006 (1) NR 106 (HC) 117, cited with approval in *Nakanyala v Inspector General Namibia* 2012 NR (1) 200 para [37]. The court has a wide discretion in this respect.

[278] Namibian courts, in this respect, sometimes prefer to cite South African authorities, rather than previous Namibian authorities, for certain propositions.

[279] *Maswahu v Katima Mulilo Town Council* [2015] NAHCMD 284 (HC) (Masuku AJ); *Alpine Caterers Namibia (Pty) Ltd v Owen* 1991 NR 310 (HC) (Frank J) 313E–H; *Clear Channel Independent Advertising (Pty) Ltd v Transnamib Holdings* 2006 (1) NR 121 (HC) (Muller AJ) paras [15] and [16]; *Olympic Fruit BV v Nagrapex (Pty) Ltd* [2011] NAHC 343; *Nakanyala v Inspector General Namibia* 2012 NR (1) 200 para [36].

[280] *Schultz v Butt* 1986 (3) SA 667 (A) 678, cited with approval in *Labour Supply Chain Namibia v Awaseb* 2010 (1) NR 332 para [8].

It is submitted that the better view is that the plaintiff must show that the defendant either has infringed the plaintiff's right or will infringe the plaintiff's right unless restrained by way of interdict; otherwise the formulation is too narrow.

In this respect, the range of rights for which a plaintiff may seek protection is not set in stone. Recently, Namibian courts have confirmed that interdictal protection extends to the right to confidential information regarding one's business and goodwill against loss of business and income.[281]

As stated above, the court retains discretion whether to grant the relief sought or not. In the light of this, it has been said that the requisites listed above 'are not judged in isolation since they interact'.[282] Each requirement will be examined briefly in turn.

(a) *prima facie* case

A plaintiff seeking interim relief from a court need not prove the existence of the right on a balance of probabilities.[283] The proper approach to this issue was set out in *Clear Channel Advertising (Pty) Ltd v Transnamib Holdings*,[284] where Muller AJ stated as follows:

> 'The consideration at this time in respect of interdictory relief has been set out in *Gool v Minister of Justice* 1955 (2) SA 682 (C) at 688 D–E. This approach is based on the views expressed by Clayden J, in *Webster v Mitchell* 1948 (1) SA 1186 (W). With reference to what was said in the case of *Webster v Mitchell* Ogilvie Thompson J (as he then was) said the following in *Gool's* case:
>
> "In *Webster v Mitchell*, supra, the head-note of which reads as follows:
>
> 'In an application for a temporary interdict the applicant's rights need not be shown by a balance of probabilities; it is sufficient if such right is prima facie established, though open to some doubt. The proper manner of approach is to take the facts as set out by the applicant together with any facts set out by the respondent which applicant cannot dispute and to consider whether, having regard to the inherent probabilities, the applicant could on those facts obtain final relief at the trial. The facts set up in contradiction by the respondent should then be considered, and if serious doubt is thrown upon the case of the applicant he could not succeed.'"
>
> With the greatest respect, I am of the opinion that the criteria prescribed in this statement for the first branch of inquiry thus outlined is somewhat too favourably expressed towards the [plaintiff] for an interdict. In my view the criteria on the [plaintiff's] own averred or admitted facts is: should (not could) the [plaintiff] on those facts obtain final relief at the trial. Subject to that qualification, I respectfully agree that the approach outlined by *Webster v Mitchell*, supra, is the correct approach for ordinary interdict applications.'

---

281 *Labour Supply Chain Namibia (Pty) Ltd v Awaseb* 2010 (1) NR 322 (HC) at 325 (Parker J) para [7].

282 *Alpine Caterers Namibia (Pty) Ltd v Owen* 1991 NR 310 at 313E–H.

283 *Clear Channel, per* Muller AJ para [16], citing *Gool v Minister of Justice* 1955 (2) SA 682 (C) 688d–e.

284 2006 (1) NR 121 (Muller AJ) paras [15] and [16].

It is not clear whether the court in *Gool* intended to amend the evidential and substantive tests or simply the substantive test. It is likely just the latter.

With respect to the other requirements which the plaintiff must satisfy (which are listed below), it appears to be the case that 'the stronger the right which the plaintiff proves, the less important those other matters become'.[285]

(b) well-grounded apprehension of irreparable harm

The plaintiff must prove this by way of evidence. It is not enough simply to allege that the plaintiff will suffer irreparable harm: the plaintiff must tender sufficient evidence to the court to make out his or her case.[286]

In this regard 'irreparable' does not mean literally incapable of repair but simply very difficult to repair and includes any prejudice suffered by the plaintiff as a result of the infringement of his rights.[287] Irreparable harm may comprise the prevention of the plaintiff from exercising his right at all, loss of money or the incurring of expenditure where sums are unlikely to be recovered.

(c) no other satisfactory remedy exists

The mere existence of another potential remedy to which the plaintiff would be entitled does not automatically negative the plaintiff's chances of obtaining interim interdictal relief. The question is whether the alternative remedy is satisfactory or not.

The Namibian courts have had reason to consider the existence of potential claims for damages for breach of contract when plaintiffs have sought to obtain interim relief to restrain any potential breach. The courts have shown a clear desire to protect the right of the plaintiff to performance of the obligation in question, as enshrined in the contract – ie they have not concluded that the mere existence of a claim for damages destroys the foundation of the application for relief. To force the plaintiff to be satisfied to a claim in damages would be to withhold from him a right which he bargained for when he entered into the service agreement, allowing the defendant simply to negate the right.[288]

---

[285] *Alpine Caterers Namibia (Pty) Ltd v Owen* 1991 NR 310 at 313H–I.

[286] For an example of the court looking at whether a plaintiff would suffer irreparable harm, see: *Alpine Caterers* at 313B–313F.

[287] Herbstein and Van Winsen *The Civil Practice of the High Courts of South Africa* 5 ed (2009) 1464 (in the context of the test for a final order); *Bamford v Minister of Community Development and State Auxiliary Services* 1981 (3) SA 1054 (C), where Watermeyer JP granted an urgent interim interdict restraining the respondent from interfering with the applicant's access to certain land on which residences were being constructed and which was alleged to be part of a public park.

[288] *Alpine Caterers* 313I–J. The strongest statement of the law in this respect can be found in the decision of the High Court in *Channel Life Namibia Ltd v Finance and Education (Pty)* Ltd case no (P) A 215.04 (unreported) 11 April 2005. It is cited with approval in *Olympic Fruit BV v Nagrapex (Pty) Ltd* [2011] NAHC 343 para [33].

(d) balance of convenience test is satisfied

The Namibian courts have not set out in any great detail how the balance of convenience test is to be conducted. It appears to be the case that the factors which the court has already taken into account up to this point in assessing the plaintiff's application (as set out above) are the same factors of which the court takes account when weighing the balance of convenience.[289]

7.3.4 Freezing orders/Anti-dissipation interdicts

The High Court of Namibia has accepted since at least 1990 that it may grant an order prior to judgment in the substantive proceedings to restrain the defendant (alleged) debtor from disposing of his assets so as to defeat the plaintiff's claim.[290]

The High Court of Namibia made such orders prior to the consideration of this type of application by courts in South Africa.[291] It is submitted that, given the close affinity between the legal systems of the two countries, the courts of Namibia will likely follow the test set out in the South African decision in *Knox D'Arcy v Jamieson* when determining whether or not to grant this type of relief.[292]

While fuller treatment is given to the way in which South African courts approach the grant of such relief in the chapter on the Republic of South Africa, it will be sufficient for present purposes to set out the nature of the test which is employed by the courts in that jurisdiction. Hence, EM Grosskopf JA (giving the judgment of the South African court) stated:[293]

> 'The question which arises from this approach is whether a [plaintiff] need show a particular state of mind on the part of the [defendant], ie that he is getting rid of the funds, or is likely to do so, with the intention of defeating the claims of creditors. Having regard to the purpose of this type of interdict, the answer must be, I consider, yes, except possibly

---

In *Channel Life*, Van Niekerk J said (at p 44 of the transcript): 'The rule that a decree of specific performance would not be granted where the [plaintiff] could be compensated adequately by an award of damages is an impermissible curtailment of the Court's discretion. This rule was based on English authority and derived purely from Chancery practice. The English rules regulating their Courts discretion to decree specific performance being predicated upon the remedy being available by way of equitable relief only are in conflict with the principle of our law and the indiscriminate application of English case law [and has since been deprecated in this jurisdiction].'

289 *Alpine Caterers* 314F–I; *Maswahu v Katima Mulilo Town Council* [2015] NAHCMD 284 para [28].

290 *De Roeck v Campbell* 1990 NR 126 (Levy J) 134E–H and the authorities therein cited. Those authorities also considered situations in which the defendant was about to leave the court's jurisdiction and where the debtor was specifically trying to dispose of money so as to defeat the interests of his creditors.

291 See *Knox D'Arcy v Jamieson* (283/95) [1996] ZASCA 58; 1996 (4) SA 348 (A); [1996] 3 All SA 669 (A) (EM Grosskopf, Nestadt, FH Grosskopf, Harms and Scott JJA).

292 That submission is strengthened by the fact that Namibian courts (ranging from the Supreme Court in *Northbank Diamonds Ltd v FTK Holland BV* [2002] NASC 2 to the High Court in *Olympic Fruit v Negrapex Holdings* have endorsed the *Knox D'Arcy* judgment.

293 *Knox D'Arcy Ltd v Jamieson* 1996 (4) SA 348 at 372G–I.

> in exceptional cases. As I have said, the effect of the interdict is to prevent the [defendant] from freely dealing with his own property to which the [plaintiff] lays no claim. Justice may require this restriction in cases where the [defendant] is shown to be acting *mala fide* with the intent of preventing execution in respect of the [plaintiff's] claim. However, there would not normally be any justification to compel a [defendant] to regulate his bona fide expenditure so as to retain funds in his patrimony for the payment of claims (particularly disputed ones) against him. I am not, of course, at the moment dealing with special situations which might arise, for instance, by contract or under the law of insolvency.'

And:[294]

> 'The purpose of the interdict is not to be a substitute for the claim for damages but to reinforce it - to render it more effective. And the question whether the claim is a satisfactory remedy in the absence of an interdict would normally answer itself. Except where the [defendant] is a Croesus, a claim for damages buttressed by an interdict of this sort is always more satisfactory for the plaintiff/applicant than one standing on its own feet. The question of an alternative remedy accordingly does not arise in this sort of case. The interdict with which we are dealing is sui generis. It is either available or it is not. No other remedy can really take its place (except, possibly, in certain circumstances attachments or arrests).'

The remedy is *sui generis* and is not an alternative to some other remedy. The plaintiff must therefore show that the defendant is about to dissipate or is dissipating his assets with a view to defeating the plaintiff's claim in the event the plaintiff succeeds.[295]

In the specific context of the Namibian legal system, the need to ensure that adequate safeguards are in place for the respondent is clear. Indeed, article 16 of the Namibian Constitution provides that the right to own property is a fundamental human right. Further, as the High Court has stated:[296]

> 'Ownership includes the right to possess one's property, the right to dispose of it and even the right to destroy it. If anyone else lays claim to such property or to interfere with any one of those rights which are comprehended by ownership, the onus is on such a person to justify his claim.'

Finally, in relation to this type of relief, the High Court, when considering what type of property may be caught by such an order, has explained:[297]

> 'Where, for instance, there is pending litigation concerning a particular chattel and the plaintiff has reasonable grounds for believing that the defendant will dispose of the chattel in order to defeat the plaintiff's claim, the plaintiff can apply to the court for an interim

---

[294] Ibid 1996 (4) SA 348 at 373B–E.

[295] As a matter of the law of the Republic of South Africa, a practical and common-sense approach is to be taken to the evidence: *Lagoon Beach Hotel (Pty) Ltd v Lehane* 2016 (3) SA 143 (SCA) (Navsa, Cachalia, Leach, Tshiqi and Willis JJA), *per* Leach JA, giving the judgment of the court, at para [15].

[296] *De Roeck v Campbell* 1990 NR 126 at 133F–G. This passage was cited with approval in *The Medical Association of Namibia v The Minister of Health and Social Services* [2013] NAHCMD 362 (HC) (Ueitele J) para [50].

[297] Ibid 133J–134C, citing *Stern and Ruskin NO v Appleson* 1951 (3) SA 800 (W) 803.

interdict to attach the chattel or to restrain the defendant from dealing with that chattel to the plaintiff's detriment. In such circumstances, even money, which is a fungible, can be interdicted and attached, but this can only be done where the money sought to be attached is identifiable with or earmarked as a particular fund to which the plaintiff claims to be entitled.'

7.3.5 Search and seize orders

It appears that the search and seize order[298] is as much part of Namibian Law as it is part of English and South African law.[299] The High Court has described the remedy thus:[300]

> 'An *Anton Piller* order inter alia authorises entry into and inspection of a party's premises for the purpose of finding and preserving evidence, usually in an action to be instituted, and which the applicant has a reasonable suspicion exists but which the Respondent is trying to withhold or conceal. Depending on the facts placed before a court, the court concerned may be reluctant to grant such an order lest the [plaintiff] be engaged on a fishing expedition. On the other hand there is substantially less chance of a fishing expedition, where the order is granted ... after the commencement of proceedings, and after the defendant has persistently failed to make a full and proper discovery.'

From the above, the better view is that the High Court of Namibia's attitude to *Anton Piller* orders is reflective of that of the South African courts. Accordingly, the reader is referred, for a fuller discussion of the relevant principles, to the chapter on the Republic of South Africa.

7.3.6 Third-party disclosure orders

There appears to be no reported authority handed down since Namibia obtained independence in which a Namibian court has made an order requiring a third party to give information or documents prior to the commencement of proceedings.

---

[298] Sometimes referred to as an *Anton Piller* order, after the name of one of the English cases in which it was first made: *Anton Piller KG v Manufacturing Processes Ltd* [1976] 1 All ER 779 (CA) (Lord Denning MR; Ormrod and Shaw LJJ).

[299] *South African Sugar Association v Namibia Sugar Distributors (Pty)* Ltd [2000] NAHC 17 (HC) (Levy AJ, 24 May 2000). In support of this proposition, the judge cited three unreported Namibian decisions: *Ex parte Shadrack Mivilina* January 1990; *Ex parte Ruben Nowaseb* 22 June 1991; and *Blackwood Hodge (SA Pty) Ltd v Earthquip Plant Shares and Repairs (Pty) Ltd* February 1994. Levy AJ also cited the leading cases (at the time) in the Republic of South Africa, viz: *Shoba v Officer Commanding, Temporary Police Camp, Wagendrift Dam; Maphanga v Officer Commanding, SA Police Murder & Robbery Unit, Pietermaritzburg* 1995 (4) SA 1 (A) and *Universal City Studios Inc v Network Video (Pty) Ltd* 1986 (2) SA 734 (A). As a matter of South African law, it has been confirmed that the principles set out in *Shoba* are the settled principles on which a search and seize order is made: *Viziya Corp v Collaborit Holdings (Pty) Ltd* 2019 (3) SA 173 (SCA) (Wallis, Saldulker, Mathopo and Van der Merwe JJA and Rogers AJA, *per* Mathopo, giving the judgment of the court, at para [22]).

[300] *South African Sugar Association* above at 4 and 5 of the transcript.

The position which the South African courts have adopted is set out below. Given the close affinity between Namibian and South African jurisprudence, it is to be supposed that the Namibian courts will adopt the same or substantially the same approach as that which has been adopted in South Africa.

In *Kinekor Films (Pty) Ltd v B A Adami Films (Pty) Ltd*,[301] allowing the plaintiff's appeal, the court made an order compelling the defendant to disclose the identity of the source of the films in its possession, of which the plaintiff was the copyright owner, with a view to the plaintiff bringing proceedings against those persons. Giving the judgment of the full bench of the Eastern Cape Division, Eksteen J held[302] that it was:

> 'clear that the person or persons from whom the [respondent] had obtained the infringing copies of the films were, in the same way, infringing the [plaintiff's] copyright by supplying such films to the respondent, and that the [plaintiff] would therefore, *prima facie*, have a cause of action against such suppliers. Such an action however cannot be brought unless the [plaintiff] knows who the person or persons are who are acting in breach of its copyright. It says that it does not know who these persons are, and the obvious place to seek this information is from the [defendant] who must be aware of their identity. To deny the [plaintiff] the relief it seeks would in my view not be in the interests of justice but would rather afford an unwarranted protection of the infringers of the [plaintiff's] copyright in the pursuit of their illegal activity.'

In *Roamer Watch Co SA v African Textile Distributors*,[303] Cilliers AJ drew a distinction[304] between two types of disclosure cases: first, those where

> 'the [plaintiff] seeks to proceed against an unincorporated body or the officials of an unincorporated or incorporated body, and seeks disclosure of the names of the appropriate persons to cite from another person who is possessed of this information by virtue of his being an official of that body or standing in some other similar relation to that body';

and second,[305] those where the plaintiff 'is concerned to obtain the name of a party whom he is unable to identify and against whom he may have a cause of action'. In the latter situation, the plaintiff is seeking discovery of the name from a party who may have sound commercial or other reasons for being reluctant to disclose it. Cilliers AJ stated[306] that in the second case the plaintiff would need to indicate at least the following in the papers filed for hearing:

(1) A *bona fide* belief in his right of action against the party whose name he seeks to be disclosed and that he has reasonable grounds for believing that

[301] 1976 (4) SA 935 (E) (Eksteen, Kannemeyer and De Wet JJ).

[302] Ibid 939G–J.

[303] 1980 (2) SA 254 (W).

[304] Ibid 281F–G.

[305] Ibid 281H–I.

[306] Ibid 282A–D.

he has such a claim against such party. Here the strength of the plaintiff's case against the unknown alleged wrongdoer is relevant to the exercise of the court's discretion.

(2) There is no other complete remedy. Another appropriate remedy may consist either of an adequate claim against a party who is known to him in respect of the same damages which the plaintiff claims to have suffered, or in another procedural remedy to establish the same information which he seeks from the respondent.

(3) The defendant is able to supply such information.

In *Cerebos Food Corp v Diverse Foods SA (Pty) Ltd*,[307] giving the judgment of the full bench of the Transvaal Provincial Division, Van Dijkhorst J held:[308] 'Neither in the Roman law nor the Roman-Dutch law nor in our law as laid down by the Appellate Division is there any authority for an order that a defendant disclose the names or particulars of sources and retail outlets.'

However, the court in the *Cerebos Food* case also held[309] that South African courts had no jurisdiction to make *Anton Piller* orders (defined by the court as[310] 'orders for the attachment of documents and other things can be granted where no right is claimed to them except that they should be preserved and produced as evidence in an intended Court action'). However, the Appellate Division in the Appellate Division in *Shoba v Officer Commanding, Temporary Police Camp, Wagendrift Dam; Maphanga v Officer Commanding, SA Police Murder & Robbery Unit, Pietermaritzburg*,[311] subsequently held this decision to have been wrong. The authority of the *Cerebos Food* case on ancillary orders and disclosure orders must therefore be doubted.[312]

---

[307] 1984 (4) SA 149 (T) (Boshoff JP and Van Dijkhorst and O'Donovan JJ).

[308] Ibid 168A–B.

[309] See the passages at 170H–I and 173E–F.

[310] Ibid 168B–C.

[311] 1995 (4) SA 1 (A) (Corbett CJ, EM Grosskopf, Nestadt, and Steyn JJA and Nicholas AJA).

[312] In addition, the decision in *Roamer Watch Co SA v African Textile Distributors* 1980 (2) SA 254 (W) appears not to have been cited to the court in *Cerebos Food*. Further the Appellate Division assumed, without deciding the question, that a court may order a non-party to furnish information required by the applicant for the purpose of litigation: *Krygkor Pensioenfonds v Smith* 1993 (3) SA 459 (A), where a divorcee was entitled to part of her former husband's pension; he refused to pay her and she applied, inter alia, for an order requiring the pension fund to inform her as to her husband's pension. The Appellate Division held (at 462A–B): 'The Appellate Division had authoritatively affirmed that it was entitled to adapt its procedures in the interests of justice; that it could be accepted for the purposes of the present case (without so deciding) that a Court in appropriate circumstances had the jurisdiction to order a party against whom an applicant had no cause of action and who was not a party or intended party to litigation with the applicant, to supply the required information.' This goes further than previous authority in this area by extending the range of disclosure from the identity of a wrongdoer to 'information' generally. Referring to both documents and information, Wunsh J in *Eiser v Vuna Health Care (Pty) Ltd* 1998 (3) SA 139 (W) stated (at 148A–B): 'Our Courts have an inherent jurisdiction to come to the assistance of a litigant who, before proceedings are instituted, requires

The South African authorities dealing with third-party disclosure orders so far predate the enactment of section 32 of the Constitution of the Republic of South Africa, 1996. Section 32 now appears to confirm that courts in the Republic of South Africa have jurisdiction to make third-party disclosure orders, a conclusion with which the South African High Court has agreed.[313] That said, the Constitution of Namibia does not contain a provision directly corresponding to section 32 of the South African Constitution. Even so, section 13(1) of the Namibian Constitution, entitled 'Privacy', provides:

> 'No persons shall be subject to interference with the privacy of their ... correspondence or communications save as in accordance with law and as is necessary in a democratic society ... for the protection of the rights or freedoms of others.'

It would seem, therefore, that the Namibian Constitution does not prohibit the making of a third-party disclosure order and may be taken to sanction such an order in circumstances where it is necessary for the protection of the rights of others, such as where a party is unable to vindicate his rights without information from a third party. As a result, the better view is that the court has power to make an order requiring a third party to disclose the identity of a wrongdoer.

7.3.7 Anti-suit interdicts (injunctions)

An anti-suit interdict (injunction) is an order restraining the injunction defendant from either commencing or continuing proceedings outside Namibia in breach of a legal or equitable right on the part of the injunction plaintiff not to pursue litigation outside Namibia or, conversely, restraining the injunction defendant from commencing or continuing proceedings inside Namibia in breach of a legal or equitable right on the part of the injunction plaintiff to have the dispute between the parties litigated in a jurisdiction other than Namibia.[314]

There is no reported judicial authority in Namibia on whether or not an anti-suit interdict is a remedy available to the courts in Namibia. That said, the courts

---

information from a third party, which is sparingly exercised (*Krygkor Pensioenfonds v Smith* 1993 (3) SA 459 (A)) and there are a few instances where a would-be opponent has been ordered to disclose documents before the institution of proceedings as in *Durban and District African Football Association v Dhludhla & Others* 1961 (3) SA 892 (D).'

[313] *Nampak Glass (Pty) Ltd v Vodacom (Pty) Ltd* 2019 (1) SA 257 (GJ) (Unterhalter J).

[314] In similar vein, an anti-anti-suit injunction is an order restraining the injunction defendant from commencing or continuing proceedings to restrain the injunction plaintiff from applying to restrain the injunction defendant from commencing or continuing proceedings. The leading works on this topic are: Raphael *The Anti-Suit Injunction* 2 ed (2019) and Briggs *Civil Jurisdiction and Judgments* 7 ed (2021) ch 28. It is also conceptually possible to obtain similar relief in the context of arbitration but such relief is outside the scope of this work.

of Ghana,[315] Nigeria[316] and, crucially, for present purposes, the Republic of South Africa[317] have concluded that this form of relief is available in those jurisdictions. Given the affinity which exists between the legal systems in place in Namibia and the Republic of South Africa, it is likely that the Namibia courts will be guided by the approach which the South African courts take with respect to this relief.[318]

7.3.8 *Mandament van spolie*

The fundamental principle of the remedy of *mandament van spolie* is that no one is allowed to take the law into their own hands:[319] it is not concerned with the protection of rights 'in the widest sense' and so does not bring about the ultimate determination of the competing proprietary or possessor claims of the litigants to the thing in question. Instead, the relief is concerned with the restoration of factual possession of a movable or an immovable thing, and, to that extent, constitutes a final determination of the litigants' immediate right to possess the things in question for the time being.[320]

This form of relief is granted by the Namibian courts. In order to obtain said relief, the plaintiff must prove – on the balance of probabilities[321] – that: (1) his possession is of such a kind that it warrants the protection afforded by the remedy and (2) he was unlawfully dispossessed. Where the plaintiff satisfies both requirements, the court will summarily restore the *status quo ante* and will do so as a preliminary to any enquiry or investigation into the merits of the dispute.

The logical consequence of the first requirement is that the plaintiff must have been in possession of the thing in question when the spoliation occurred.[322] It has been held that the remedy is apt to protect 'incorporeal rights'.[323] Hence, where two people shared access to a feeder road and the defendant then erected a gate

---

[315] *Quantum Oil Terminals Ltd v International Finance Corp* Suit No: Misc/00228/17 (unreported) 8 January 2018 and 23 February 2018 (H Ct) (Asiedu J).

[316] *United Bank for Africa Plc v Coker* (1996) 4 NWLR 239 (CA) (Muhammad, Ayoola and Pats-Acholonu JJCA).

[317] *Vedanta Resources Holdings Ltd v ZCCM Investment Holdings plc* 2019 JDR 1425 (GJ) (Adams J).

[318] For further guidance on the principles which a South African court would apply when asked to grant an anti-suit interdict, the reader is referred to the relevant section of the chapter on the Republic of South Africa.

[319] *Tjerije v Kaanjuka* 1994 NR 17 (HC) (Hannah J).

[320] *Kock t/a Ndhovu Safari Lodge v Walter t/a Mahangu Safari Lodge* 2011 (1) NR 10 (SC) (Maritz JA, Chomba and Langa AJA) para [5]; *Kuiiri v Kandjoze* 2009 (2) NR 447 (SC) (Maritz JA; Mtambanengwe and Chomba AJA) 462B–D citing *Nienaber v Stuckey* 1946 AD 1049 at 1053.

[321] *Kuiiri v Kandjoze* 2009 (2) NR 447 (SC) 462D.

[322] Ibid 462E of the transcript. In *Fischer v Seelenbinder* 2021 (1) NR 35 (SC) (Shivute CJ and Frank and Nkanbinde AJJA) para [22] confirmed that one who has a precarious right of possession is entitled to seek a spoliation order where they have been unlawfully despoiled of possession.

[323] *Kock t/a Ndhovu Safari Lodge v Walter t/a Mahangu Safari Lodge* 2011 (1) NR 10 (SC).

which barred the applicant's access to the road, the Supreme Court found that such a '*servitudal right*' could be protected using this remedy.[324]

In order to be worthy of protection, possession itself must have been sufficiently stable and durable to constitute peaceful and undisturbed possession.[325] Thus, it has been held that where two people enter into a contract pursuant to which the first person is to carry out certain renovations to the second person's property and the first person is then barred from accessing the property without having been fully paid, the first person is entitled to the remedy where they have the *ius possessionis* (acquired when they occupied the property) and the *ius possidendi* (acquired when the building renovation agreement was concluded).[326] Similarly, where a person was locked out of an office which he used for the purposes of deriving a personal benefit, that was deemed sufficient possession for the purposes of the *mandament van spolie* order.[327]

With respect to the second requirement identified above, whether (regarding immovable property) the possessor's physical absence from an immovable thing or the nature and extent of the use, occupation or control thereof by another party justifies the inference that he has been dispossessed is a question of fact.[328] Where, of course, a possessor abandons the thing, possession is lost; the extent of the person's use and occupation of the thing are factors to be taken into account to determine that person's physical or mental control of the thing itself. Accordingly, the Supreme Court has recently held that possession may be lost through a period of six years of continuous absence or non-beneficial use of immovable property because the only reasonable inference to be drawn from such conduct was an intention to abandon the property in question, thereby precluding the granting of a spoliation order.[329]

---

[324] Ibid para [6]. The Supreme Court also held that it was not necessary for the plaintiff to prove the servitudal right for the institution of a spoliation order, since that would amount to an investigation of the merits of the case, citing in support *Bon Quelle (Edms) Bpk v Munisipaliteit van Otavi* 1989 (1) SA 508 (A). In *Kock*, the Supreme Court also determined that, where a co-possessor unlawfully takes over exclusive control of the thing in question, the applicant may seek a spoliation order: see para [5], citing *Du Rand v Du Randt* 1995 (1) SA 401 (O). The Supreme Court of Appeal in the Republic of South Africa has recently considered matters similar in *Blendrite v Moonisami* 2021 (5) SA 61 (SCA) (Navsa, Mocumie and Dlodlo JJA and Gorven and Ledwaba AJJA).

[325] *Kuiiri v Kandjoze* 2009 (2) NR 447 (SC) 463A.

[326] *Nufesha Investments v Namibia Rights and Responsibilities Inc* 2013 (3) NR 787 (HC) para [24].

[327] *Fischer v Seelenbinder* 2021 (1) NR 35 (SC) para [26]. In *Chen Zheng Hong v Gu Kingxin* [2020] LSCA 44 (SC) (Mosito P, Chinhengo and Van Der Westhuizen AJJA), the Court of Appeal in Lesotho reached a similar conclusion on similar facts.

[328] *Kuiiri v Kandjoze* 2009 (2) NR 447 (SC) 464F–465A and 472B. That said, it does appear to have been established as a general proposition that the mere letting of an immovable thing, without more, does not justify the inference that the lessor/possessor has lost possession thereof, on which proposition all members of the court in *Kuiiri* agreed.

[329] *Koch v Koch* 2019 NASC 591 (Hoff JA and Mokgoro and Nkabinde AJJA) para [20].

The plaintiff should be aware that, where his or her application to the court seeks more than simply a spoliation order, he may well force the court to investigate the issues relevant to the further relief claimed. In such circumstances, if the defence to the application furnishes justification for the defendant's possession, the court will not order restoration of the *status quo ante*.[330] That said, there is no reason why a claim for an interdict restraining the defendant from unlawfully disturbing future possession after restoration of the thing despoiled can be said to disqualify the spoliatus from invoking the remedy.[331]

If the answer to the question whether the plaintiff who asks for more than a spoliation order from the court has in so doing provided the defendant with a defence depends on the facts of any one case, it is clear that the defendant, who has dispossessed the applicant by taking something from his land, will not gain the court's favour by arguing that restoration by taking something back onto that land is impossible, such that the remedy should not be granted. Such an argument provides the defendant with no defence to the application.[332]

As has been stated above, the object of the remedy is to reverse immediately the consequences of the interference in order to restore the *status quo ante*. Whether the defendant must simply give back possession or give back possession in a specific location will depend on the facts. It appears that the former situation (merely giving back possession) represents the general rule[333] but that, in exceptional circumstances where only giving back possession at a specific location would truly reverse the consequences of the interference, the court may make an order requiring that to be done.[334]

7.3.9 Arrest of individuals *tanquam suspectus de fuga*

> 'Arrest *tanquam suspectus de fuga* owes its origin to Roman law. It was introduced in South Africa as part of Roman-Dutch law and was first reported as a part of the rules of court from as early as 1842. The procedure existed at common law as well as in a codified form

---

[330] *Tjerije v Kaanjuka* 1994 NR 17 (HC) (Hannah J) at 20G–J, citing in support *Minister of Agriculture and Agricultural Development v Segopolo* 1992 (3) SA 967 (T) 971B. The mere inclusion of a prayer for an interdict does not however necessarily go beyond a claim for spoliatory relief.

[331] *Tjerije v Kaanjuka* at 21D–F. However, Hannah J did place emphasis on the word '*unlawfully*' because the position may be otherwise if the interdict were to go beyond that.

[332] Ibid 24B–C, citing *Ntshwaqela v Chairman, Western Cape Regional Services Council* 1988 (3) SA 218 (C) 226F.

[333] *Tjerije v Kaanjuka* 23E–F.

[334] Ibid 23E–G, citing *Mbangi v Dobsonville City Council* 1991 (2) SA 330 (W) (Fleming J) 336E. On the facts of *Tjerije*, where the plaintiff had been dispossessed of his cattle at Otjondorozu, Hannah J felt that, if the remedy did not extend to compelling the defendant to return the cattle at that location, the object of the remedy would be frustrated. He did concede, however, that the position 'may, of course, be different where the spoliatus freely accepts the restoration of possession' (at 24A). Given that this was not the case on the facts before him, the judge left the point open.

> in various rules of court. *Arrest tanquam suspectus de fuga* is ordered when a creditor on reasonable grounds suspects that a debtor, whose liability has not yet been acknowledged or proven in a court of law, is about to flee the country in order to prevent the adjudication of the dispute in this country. Only a court of law is, in terms of the common law as well as section 30(1) and (3) of the Act read with rule 56 of the magistrate's courts Rules and section 19 of the Supreme Court Act read with rule 9 of the Uniform Rules of Court, entrusted with the authority to order arrest *tanquam suspectus de fuga*.'[335]

As the above makes clear, arrest *tanquam suspectus de fuga* is a common-law remedy, with which the Namibian courts are familiar.[336] A plaintiff may apply to a Namibian court to grant an order for the arrest of the defendant *tanquam suspectus de fuga*, at least in principle.

It is an open question, however, how a court faced with such application would proceed. Prior to their amendment in 2014, the Rules of the High Court of Namibia[337] set out in terms[338] what procedure the plaintiff had to follow in order to apply for an order of arrest *tanquam suspectus de fuga*. After their amendment in 2014, the High Court Rules no longer contain any equivalent provisions. Taken by itself, the absence of a provision from the High Court rules setting out the process by which a plaintiff must make an application for arrest *tanquam suspectus de fuga* does not mean that such relief is no longer available. The remedy is, after all, one available at common law and so must still be available (at least in principle), irrespective of whether or not rules of court specifically instruct a plaintiff how to make such an application.

There are, however, other factors besides the drafting of the High Court Rules which a Namibian court would have to consider when asked to grant the relief under consideration. Chief among these factors is the decision of the South African Constitutional Court in *Malachi v Cape Dance Academy International (Pty) Ltd*.[339] The decision is important for two reasons: (1) the South African Constitutional Court there considered the constitutionality of sections 30 and 31 of the Magistrates' Courts Act 1944,[340] which Act (as amended) also applies in Namibia; and (2) it is a decision of the Constitutional Court of South Africa and so is likely to be highly persuasive in Namibia.

---

[335] *Malachi v Cape Dance Academy International (Pty) Ltd* 2010 (6) SA 1 (CC), *per* Mogoeng J para [17] (giving the judgment of the court: Ngcobo CJ, Moseneke DCJ, Cameron, Froneman, Jafta, Khampepe, Nkabinde, Skweyiya, Van der Westhuizen and Yacoob JJ).

[336] See, by way of example: *Beukes v CIC Holdings SA* [2005] NASC 5 (O'Linn, Chomba and Mtambanengwe AJA); *Wylie v Villinger* [2013] NAHCMD (HC) (Ueitele J); and *Prosecutor General v Uuyuni* [2013] NAHCMD 67 (Geier J).

[337] Published as GN 59 of 1990.

[338] At r 9.

[339] 2010 (6) SA 1 (CC) (Ngcobo CJ, Moseneke DCJ, Cameron, Froneman, Jafta, Khampepe, Nkabinde, Skweyiya, Van der Westhuizen, Yacoob and Mogoeng JJ).

[340] Act 32 of 1944.

In *Malachi*, the Constitutional Court of South Africa abolished arrest *tanquam suspectus de fuga* in that jurisdiction. Mogoeng J (giving the judgment of the court) stated:

> '[32] The object of the arrest "is to ensure that [the potential debtor] remains within the jurisdiction of the court until the court has given judgment in the matter". As soon as judgment is given, a debtor would, however, be free to catch the next flight to any foreign destination even if this is done to evade payment and no realisable asset exists in the country, from the proceeds of which payment may be effected. Arrest does not, therefore, ensure the satisfaction of the judgment debt. Admittedly, the unfairly exerted pressure of incarceration may at times force the arrestee to pay the debt or provide security. But, that does not detract from the fact that the arrest does not necessarily render the judgment any more executable or beneficial to the creditor than would have been the case had the debtor left the country. It simply limits the fundamental right to freedom of the person for no just reason.
>
> [33] The order for the arrest of persons *tanquam suspectus de fuga* under the impugned provisions is ordinarily made at the time when their civil liability has not yet been established. Their debt is only alleged on affidavit, often in an urgent application brought ex parte. The potential debtor is often only afforded the opportunity to resist the severe curtailment of the right to freedom, by the order, on the return date. Potentially the detention may endure for as long as the action is pending. The effect of this deprivation was more aptly captured in *Segal v Diners Club South Africa* where we are warned that
>
> > "[i]f the debtor has been wrongly deprived of his freedom it cannot be put right in the subsequent suit. The harm is irreparable." Nothing can undo the degrading effect of incarceration, particularly if the order were obtained ex parte. This is the position in which the plaintiff in this matter found herself for 16 days.
>
> [34] Since there is no legal basis for the imprisonment of someone who has been found civilly liable, it is inconceivable that any legal justification can ever exist for putting behind bars a person whose civil liability is yet to, or will possibly never, be proven. Although an order for arrest is granted by a court, the intervention of the judicial process cannot legitimise the deprivation of freedom, since the arrest may stem from a debt which has itself not been established through the judicial process. I therefore conclude that there is no just cause for the arrest in terms of the impugned provisions.'

Of course, while a Namibian court would not be bound to follow the decision in *Malachi*, given that the provisions of the Constitution of the Republic of South Africa, 1996 which were at issue in *Malachi*[341] correspond broadly to certain provisions of the Constitution of Namibia,[342] a Namibian court may legitimately have regard to the decision in *Malachi* when determining the constitutionality, and so the future availability and scope of, arrest *tanquam suspectus de fuga* in Namibia.

[341] That is to say, s 12(1). Above, under the sub-heading 'The jurisdictional significance of arrest of the person,' the authors have discussed certain other similarities between the Constitution of the Republic of South Africa, 1996 and the Constitution of Namibia.

[342] Arts 7 and 10.

Chapter 8

NIGERIA

8.1 Jurisdiction

The bases on which a Nigerian court may assume jurisdiction over a cause or matter are statutory in origin.

The fundamental means by which a Nigerian court is seised of jurisdiction over a defendant at the suit of a plaintiff is by service of process on the defendant.[1]

The Federal High Court (Civil Procedure) Rules 2019 ('the High Court Rules')[2] distinguish between service within and service outside the jurisdiction.

8.1.1 Service where the defendant is within the jurisdiction

Order 6A makes provision for service within the jurisdiction.[3] The default rule is that a defendant must be served personally with any originating process.[4] Provision is also made for substituted service in specified circumstances.[5] Order 6A contains further provisions addressing particular instances of service such as service on partnerships,[6] service on corporations and companies[7] and service on the local agent of a principal who is outside the jurisdiction.[8]

---

[1] On the fundamental importance of the service of process, see *Ezim v Menakaya* [2017] NGSC 21 (12 May 2017) (Sup Ct) (Ogunbiyi, Bage, Eko and Kekere-Ekun JJSC).

[2] The High Court Rules were made pursuant to s 254 of the Constitution. The current iteration of the High Court Rules came into force on 10 May 2019 and replaced the 2009 version. For the avoidance of doubt, in this work, the authors only address the rules of the Federal High Court. Nigeria is a federal state, with the consequence that there are separate high courts for each of the states within the federation. Those high courts each have their own civil procedure rules. It would be impractical to deal with each such set of rules in this chapter. For a more detailed treatment of the rules of various high courts, the reader is referred to Okoli and Oppong *Private International Law in Nigeria* (2020).

[3] Where a party wishes to serve process on a defendant who is outside the relevant territorial jurisdiction of a specific state high court, that party will need to comply with the Sheriffs and Civil Process Act 1945 (Cap S6 of the Laws of the Federation of Nigeria, 2004).

[4] Order 6A, r 2.

[5] Order 6A, r 5.

[6] Order 6A, r 7.

[7] Order 6A, r 8. It is worth pointing out that ss 78–84 of the Companies and Allied Matters Act 2020 (Act 3 of 2020) make reference to 'foreign companies' (that is, companies incorporated elsewhere than in Nigeria: s 868). Section 78 provides that a foreign company 'which before or after the commencement of this Act was incorporated outside Nigeria, and [which has] the intention of carrying on business in Nigeria, shall take all steps necessary to obtain incorporation as a separate entity in Nigeria but until so incorporated, the foreign company shall not carry on business in Nigeria or exercise any of the powers of a registered company and shall not have a place of business or an address for service of documents or processes in Nigeria for any purpose other than the receipt of notices and other documents, as matters preliminary to incorporation under this Act'. Those foreign companies which are exempt are treated as 'unregistered companies' for the purposes of the 2020 Act: s 82. Section 104 provides that 'court process shall be served on a company in the manner provided by the rules of court'. In consequence, it would appear that the 2020 Act does not put in place a separate service regime for foreign companies, unlike, say, the Ghanaian Companies Act 2019 does. On the question whether a foreign company has capacity to sue in Nigeria, see the recent decision of the Supreme Court in *BCE Consulting Engineers v Nigerian National Petroleum Corpn* (2021) All FWLR 359.

[8] Order 6A, r 12: 'Where service is to be made upon a person residing out of, but carrying on business within the jurisdiction in his own name or under the name of a firm through an authorized agent, and the

8.1.2 Service where the defendant is outside the jurisdiction

Order 6B makes provision for service outside the jurisdiction and Order 6B, rule 13, prescribes an exhaustive set of grounds on which the Nigerian court may assume jurisdiction over a person present outside the jurisdiction.

Order 6B, rule 13[9] provides:

> 'Service out of jurisdiction of a writ of summons or notice of a writ of summons[10] may be allowed by the Court or a Judge in Chambers whenever—
>
> *(a)* the whole subject matter of the action is land situate within the jurisdiction with or without rents or profits; or
>
> *(b)* any act, deed, will contract, obligation, or liability affecting land or hereditament situate within the jurisdiction, is sought to be construed, rectified, set aside or enforced in the action; or
>
> *(c)* any relief is sought against any person domiciled, or ordinarily resident, within the jurisdiction; or
>
> *(d)* the action is one brought against the defendant to enforce, rescind, dissolve, annul or otherwise effect a contract or to recover damages or other relief for or in respect of a breach of a contract—
>
> (i) made within the jurisdiction, or
>
> (ii) made by or through an agent trading or residing within the jurisdiction on behalf of a principal trading or residing out of the jurisdiction, or

proceeding is limited to a cause of action which arose within the jurisdiction, the Writ or other document may be served by giving it to the agent, and the service shall be equivalent to personal service.'

[9] The rule of the English Rules of the Supreme Court regulating service out of the jurisdiction prior to 1999 (when the Civil Procedure Rules came into effect) was O XI. Under the Rules of the Supreme Court 1883 and the Rules of the Supreme Court 1965, which superseded the 1883 Rules, O XI, r 1 provided for service out of the jurisdiction. Order 6B, r 13 is materially identical to O XI of the Rules of the Supreme Court 1883.

[10] The High Court Rules do not set out the circumstances in which a plaintiff should seek service of a writ of summons, as opposed to a *notice* of a writ of summons, on a defendant out of the jurisdiction, although the Rules contemplate and provide for this distinction (see rr 14(1), 15 and 18(1)). Certain others of the jurisdictions with which this work is concerned make this distinction and guidance may be sought from the rules in place in those other jurisdictions. Hence, in Zambia, for example, a Zambian citizen must be served with a summons, whereas all other persons must be served with notice of the summons. Similarly, in Uganda, a Commonwealth citizen or resident or British protected person must be served with a summons, whereas anyone else must be served with notice of the summons. The reasons for this are rooted in English legal history: a summons is a command from the Sovereign and it was thought discourteous to serve such a command on a person not resident in the United Kingdom and not a British subject, thus a notice of the summons was served instead (see *Nanjibhai Prabhudas and Co Ltd v Standard Bank Ltd* [1968] EA 670 (CA) (Sir Charles Newbold P, Sir Clement de Lestang V-P and Law JA), *per* Sir Charles Newbold P at 683C–E); the origin of the rule is s 19 of the English Common Law Procedure Act 1852; after the repeal of the 1852 Act, the rule was incorporated into the Rules of the Supreme Court; *Westman v Aktiebolaget Exmans Mekaniska Snickarefabrick* (1876) 1 Ex D 237.

(iii) by its terms or by implication to be governed by the law in force in the jurisdiction or is brought against the defendant in respect of a breach committed within the jurisdiction of a contract wherever made, even though the breach was preceded or accompanied by a breach out of the jurisdiction which rendered impossible the performance of the part of the contract which ought to have been performed within the jurisdiction;

(e) the action is founded on tort or other civil wrong committed within the jurisdiction; or

(f) any injunction is sought as to anything to be done within the jurisdiction or any nuisance within the jurisdiction is sought to be prevented or removed, whether damages are or are not also sought in respect of it; or

(g) any person out of jurisdiction is a necessary or proper party to an action properly brought against some other party within the jurisdiction; or

(h) the action is by a mortgagee or mortgagor in relation to a mortgage of property situate within the jurisdiction and seeks any of the following reliefs:

(i) sale,

(ii) foreclosure,

(iii) delivery of possession by the mortgagor,

(iv) redemption,

(v) reconveyance, or

(iv) delivery of possession by the mortgagee, but does not seek, unless and except so far as permissible under paragraph *(d)* of this rule, any personal judgment or order for payment of any money due under the mortgage; or

(i) the action is one brought under the Civil Aviation Act or any regulation made in pursuance of the Act or any law relating to carriage by air.'[11]

8.1.2.1 *Procedure*

Order 6B, rule 14(1) provides,

> 'An application for leave to serve a writ or notice on a defendant out of the jurisdiction shall be supported by — (a) an affidavit and a written address; or (b) or any other evidence stating — (i) that in the belief of the deponent the plaintiff has a good cause of action, (ii) the place or country the defendant is or may be found, and (iii) the grounds upon which the application is made.'

[11] It is to be noted that no provision is made for a court to permit service of the writ or notice of the writ on a defendant who is outside the jurisdiction if the action is one to enforce a foreign judgment; Frimpong Oppong 'Recognition and enforcement of foreign judgments in Commonwealth African countries' (2014) XV *Yearbook of Private International Law* 365, 371–2. By way of comparison, see the English Civil Procedure Rules, PD6B, para 3.1(10) (amended by UK SI 1181 of 1983 so as to include this additional ground for service out of the jurisdiction).

Rule 14(2) provides that the court shall not grant leave unless it is made sufficiently to appear that 'the cause is a proper one for service out of the jurisdiction under these Rules'.

The proper test for the court to apply to the evidence produced is whether there remains a strong argument that the grounds have been satisfied: a *prima facie* case against the defendant is not sufficient but neither is it necessary to satisfy the court beyond reasonable doubt that the grounds have been established.[12]

Once the plaintiff has satisfied the court to the required standard that he is within one or more of the relevant gateways under Order 6B, rule 13, the court has power to grant the plaintiff leave to serve the defendant out of the jurisdiction. Whether the court exercises this power is a matter of discretion. The discretion must be exercised with great care. In *Nwabueze v Okoye*,[13] the Supreme Court held,[14] following the principles laid down in the English courts with respect to the (then) materially identical English rules:

> 'Leave to issue a writ which is to be served out of the jurisdiction is not granted as a matter of course under the English Rules. For the discretion to grant the leave sought is exercised judicially and with great care ... And as Chief FRA Williams S.A.N. points out to us in his arguments in this appeal the question which is the forum convenience [sic] for the trial is one of the matters to be considered by the court in the exercise of this discretion. Other matters are (1) the question of comparative cost and convenience (see *Logan v. Bank of England* [1906] 1 KB 141 CA) and (2) the fact, if it exists, that proceedings in respect of the same subject-matter are already pending elsewhere ... So the application for leave to issue a writ which is to be served out of the jurisdiction is not a mere formality.'

Given that the framework within which the Nigerian courts consider the grant of leave to serve out of the jurisdiction is materially similar to the English framework, and in the light of the fact that there is an affinity between the Nigerian and English rules on service of process outside the jurisdiction, it may be of some assistance to note that the English equivalents of Nigerian Order 6B, rules 13 and 14, have been the subject of judicial consideration at the highest level in England.

In *Seaconsar Far East Ltd v Bank Markazi Jomhouri Islami Iran*,[15] the House of Lords considered the interaction of Order XI, rules 1(1) and 4, of the Rules of the Supreme Court (the equivalent to Order 6B, rules 13 and 14). Lord Goff (with whom the other Lords agreed) reviewed the authorities on the question what a plaintiff under Order XI was required to show on an application for leave

---

[12] *Cold Containers (Nigeria) Ltd v Collis Cold Containers Ltd* [1977] 1 ALR Comm 97, [1977] NCLR 97; *Barsoum v Clemency International Ltd* (1999) 12 NWLR 516 (CA) (Lagos Division; Oguntade, Pats-Acholonu and Aderemi JJCA). See also: Frimpong Oppong *Private International Law in Commonwealth Africa* (2013) 59.

[13] [1988] 4 NWLR 664 (Sup Ct) (Obaseki, Uwais, Karibi-Whyte, Agbaje and Wali JJSC).

[14] At 685E–G, *per* Agbaje JSC, giving the judgment of the Supreme Court.

[15] [1994] 1 AC 438 (HL (E)) (Lords Templeman, Griffiths, Goff, Browne-Wilkinson and Mustill).

to serve a writ out of the jurisdiction and found that the plaintiff was required to show, first, that the cause of action deposed to in the evidence in support of the application fell within the provisions of rule 1(1) and, second, that on the merits of the case there was a serious question to be tried. On the question of the standard to which these issues were required to be shown, Lord Goff stated:[16]

> 'A judge faced with a question of leave to serve proceedings out of the jurisdiction under Order 11 will in practice have to consider both (1) whether jurisdiction has been sufficiently established, on the criterion of the good arguable case laid down in Korner's case, under one of the paragraphs of rule 1(1), and (2) whether there is a serious issue to be tried, so as to enable him to exercise his discretion to grant leave, before he goes on to consider the exercise of that discretion, with particular reference to the issue of forum conveniens.'

The first of these matters was held to correspond to the requirement in Order XI, rule 4, that 'no such leave shall be granted unless it shall be made sufficiently to appear to the Court or Judge that the case is a proper one for service out of the jurisdiction under this Order'[17] and the second was a threshold requirement for the merits of the plaintiff's claim.[18]

Thus, considering the English authorities, it is suggested that, analytically, it would be helpful to determine applications for leave to serve process out of the jurisdiction by applying the following, four-component approach.[19]

(1) *The formal requirements.* Has the plaintiff produced evidence satisfying the formal requirements of Order 6B, rule 14 (or English Order XI, rule 4)? This requires the plaintiff in his affidavit in support of the application to set out: (a) the belief of the deponent that the plaintiff has a good cause of action; (b) the place or country the defendant is or probably may be found; and (c) the grounds on which the application is made.

---

[16] At 456H–457B. See also the decision of the Privy Council in *Altimo Holdings and Investment Ltd v Kyrgyz Mobil Tel Ltd* [2012] 1 WLR 1804 (Lord Phillips PSC and Lords Mance, Collins, Kerr and Clarke JJSC), *per* Lord Collins at para [71], confirming this statement of principle.

[17] *Seaconsar* at 451A–B, 452A–B, 453D–G.

[18] *Seaconsar* at 452D–E, 455A–C, 456G–H. Notwithstanding the separate treatment of the English O XI, r 4, in *Seaconsar* and the earlier authorities referred to therein, it is unclear whether the amendment in 1883 of O XI, r 3 (under the Rules of Court contained in Sch 1 to the Supreme Court of Judicature Act 1875) by the introduction of an expanded O XI, r 4, in the 1883 Rules of Court, was intended to produce this result. At the time the leading textbook on the Rules took the view that the amendment to include the wording 'no such leave shall be granted unless it shall be made sufficiently to appear to the Court or Judge that the case is a proper one for service out of the jurisdiction under this Order' was merely an amplification of the previous rule (see Wynne Baxter *Judicature Acts and Rules 1873–1883* 5 ed (1883) 176–7).

[19] As summarised in the English *Supreme Court Practice 1965* (1999 ed) 93–4, paras 11/1/9–11/1/12. The commentary referred to in the *Supreme Court Practice* refers to three elements; in the text above the present authors include four elements, the additional element being the formal requirements of English r 4 and Ghanaian r 2.

(2) *The sufficiency requirement.* Under the English Order XI, rule 4, it was held in the *Seaconsar* case that the words 'and no such leave shall be granted unless it shall be made sufficiently to appear to the Court or Judge that the case is a proper one for service out of the jurisdiction under this Order' introduced a sufficiency requirement (or, in other words, a degree of proof requirement) such that the plaintiff must show that there is a good arguable case[20] that the case falls within one of the gateways under Order XI, rule 1(1).

(3) *The merits requirement.* The plaintiff must demonstrate that there is a serious issue to be tried on the merits of the claim upon which the claimant relies. Lord Goff in *Seaconsar* stated[21] as follows:

> 'The court cannot resolve disputed questions of fact on affidavit evidence; and it is consistent with the statement of the law by Lord Davey that if, at the end of the day, there remains a substantial question of fact or law or both, arising on the facts disclosed by the affidavits, which the plaintiff bona fide desires to try, the court should, as a rule, allow the service of the writ. If this approach is correct, the standard of proof in respect of the cause of action can broadly be stated to be whether, on the affidavit evidence before the court, there is a serious question to be tried.'

(4) *The court's discretion.* Once the above matters are established by the plaintiff, the court will proceed to consider the exercise of its discretion to allow service out of the jurisdiction. The court's discretion is exercised cautiously. As was stated by Pearson J in *Société Générale de Paris v Dreyfus Brothers*:[22]

---

[20] In *Canada Trust v Stolzenberg (No 2)* [2002] 1 AC 1 (HL(E)) (Lords Steyn, Hoffmann, Cooke, Hope and Hobhouse), *per* Lord Steyn (with whom the other Lords agreed) 13F, the House of Lords appeared to approve passages from the judgment of Waller LJ in the Court of Appeal in the same case ([1998] 1 WLR 547) including the following (at 555F–G): 'It is also right to remember that the "good arguable case" test, although obviously applicable to the ex parte stage, becomes of most significance at the inter partes stage where two arguments are being weighed in the interlocutory context which, as I have stressed, must not become a "trial". "Good arguable case" reflects in that context that one side has a much better argument on the material available. It is the concept which the phrase reflects on which it is important to concentrate, i.e. of the court being satisfied or as satisfied as it can be having regard to the limitations which an interlocutory process imposes that factors exist which allow the court to take jurisdiction.' In *Goldman Sachs International v Novo Banco SA* [2018] 1 WLR 3683 (Lords Mance, Sumption and Hodge, Lady Black and Lord Lloyd-Jones), the UK Supreme Court further clarified the correct understanding of the test in the *Canada Trust* case. Lord Sumption (with whom all the other members of the court agreed and in reliance on his own judgment in *Brownlie v Four Seasons Holdings Inc* [2018] 1 WLR 192) stated at para [9]: 'For the purpose of determining an issue about jurisdiction, the traditional test has been whether the claimant had "the better of the argument" on the facts going to jurisdiction. In *Brownlie v Four Seasons Holdings Inc* [2018] 1 WLR 192, para 7, this court reformulated the effect of that test as follows: "(i) that the claimant must supply a plausible evidential basis for the application of a relevant jurisdictional gateway; (ii) that if there is an issue of fact about it, or some other reason for doubting whether it applies, the court must take a view on the material available if it can reliably do so; but (iii) the nature of the issue and the limitations of the material available at the interlocutory stage may be such that no reliable assessment can be made, in which case there is a good arguable case for the application of the gateway if there is a plausible (albeit contested) evidential basis for it."'

[21] *Seaconsar* 452C–D.

[22] (1885) 29 Ch D 239 at 242–3; cited with approval by Lord Goff in *Seaconsar* at 455D.

> 'But of course it becomes a very serious question, and ought always to be considered a very serious question, whether or not, even in a case like that, it is necessary for the jurisdiction of the Court to be invoked, and whether this Court ought to put a foreigner, who owes no allegiance here, to the inconvenience and annoyance of being brought to contest his rights in this country, and I for one say, most distinctly, that I think this Court ought to be exceedingly careful before it allows a writ to be served out of the jurisdiction.'

Turning back to Nigerian law, Order 6B, rules 15–25 contain ancillary provisions regarding such matters as the time within which a defendant must enter an appearance after service of process on him,[23] the procedure to be adopted for service where a convention governs the means of service[24] and substituted service of process for service outside the jurisdiction.[25]

The question what are the consequences of a failure to obtain leave to serve out of the jurisdiction where the writ has been issued *and* served out of the jurisdiction has been considered in a number of decisions concerning domestic cases of service out of the jurisdiction of a particular state of the Federation of Nigeria although not, it appears, in the context of a case of issuing a writ for service outside Nigeria itself. It is submitted that an authoritative decision of the Supreme Court is required to resolve the ambiguity in this area.[26]

8.1.2.2 *Bases for service out of the jurisdiction*

The bases on which the court may grant permission which are of particular significance for present purposes are discussed below.

(1) Relief is sought against any person domiciled, or ordinarily resident, within the jurisdiction

The term 'person' in Order 6B, rule 13(c), includes any natural or legal person.[27]

There is little Nigerian judicial authority on the meaning of the term 'domicile' for the purposes of the application of Order 6B, rule 13(c). It is likely, given the willingness of the Nigerian courts to look to English law for the meaning of terms inherited from colonial times, that the Nigerian courts will adopt the jurisprudence applicable in English law regarding the term 'domicile' for the

[23] Rule 15.

[24] Rule 18.

[25] Rule 24.

[26] See Okoli and Oppong *Private International Law in Nigeria* (2020) and, in particular, the discussion of this question at 75–8.

[27] Section 18(1) of the Interpretation Act 1964 (Act 1 of 1964). The correct domestic citation of this provision is 'Interpretation Act [chapter 123 of the Laws of the Federation of Nigeria 2004]'. In this regard, the reader is referred to the 'Note on the citation of statutory material in this work', which appears at the end of the 'List of Statutory Material Cited' at the beginning of this work.

purposes of determining jurisdiction over a person.[28] Under the English Rules of the Supreme Court upon which Order 6B, rule 13, of the High Court Rules is based,[29] 'domicile' was defined as follows:[30]

> 'In general the domicile of a person is in the country in which he has his permanent home (see Dicey, *Conflict of Law*, 7th ed., Chap. 6), the country in which his habitation is fixed without any present intention of removing (*Re Craignish*, [1892] 3 Ch. 180, C.A.; *Huntly v. Gaskell*, [1906] A.C. 56; *Casdagli v. C.*, [1919] A.C. 145). No person can at any time be without a domicile or have more than one domicile. The domicile of origin remains until a new domicile of choice has been adopted (*Bell v. Kennedy* (1868), L.R. 1 Sc. App. 307, H.L.; *Udny v. Udny* (1869), ibid, 441, H.L., *Winans v. A.-G.*, [1904] A.C. 287, H.L.).'

The Nigerian courts will have jurisdiction on the basis of residency 'within the jurisdiction'. This must be taken to mean that the defendant should be resident in Nigeria rather than the state forming part of the Federation of Nigeria before whose courts the application for leave to serve out of the jurisdiction is made. In *First National Bank of Nigeria plc v Abraham*,[31] the plaintiff bank had advanced loan facilities to the defendant which the bank sought to recover in the High Court of Lagos State. At the time the loans were made the defendant was resident in England, but when proceedings were issued against him he had relocated his business to Nigeria and was resident there. The defendant objected to the jurisdiction of the court on the grounds that the loan agreement had been made in London at the bank's London branch under the laws of England. The High Court and Court of Appeal found in the defendant's favour. The Supreme Court allowed the bank's appeal and held that the Nigerian courts had jurisdiction over the claim on the grounds, inter alia, that the defendant was at the time of the issuing of proceedings resident in Nigeria and that the obligation of the debtor under the loan facility was to repay the creditor bank and that the place of performance by the debtor of this obligation was Nigeria.[32]

Nigerian courts will assume jurisdiction over a legal person where it is resident or carrying on business in Nigeria.[33] The Court of Appeal considered

---

[28] See generally on the meaning of 'domicile', *Dicey, Morris and Collins on the Conflict of Laws* 15 ed (2012) vol 1, rule 34, para 6R-001.

[29] The rule of the English Rules of the Supreme Court regulating service out of the jurisdiction prior to 1999 (when the Civil Procedure Rules came into effect) was O XI. Under the Rules of the Supreme Court 1883 and the Rules of the Supreme Court 1965, which superseded the 1883 Rules, O XI, r 1 provided for service out of the jurisdiction where the defendant was domiciled or ordinarily resident within the jurisdiction.

[30] Rules of the Supreme Court 1883 (1961 ed) 144.

[31] [2008] 18 NWLR 172 (Sup Ct) (Katsina-Alu, Mukhtar, Mohammed, Tabai and Aderemi JJSC).

[32] Aderemi JSC (giving the judgment of the court) 190D–F and 192C–F. It appears from the report that the court recognised residence and place of performance as separate bases for the assumption of jurisdiction.

[33] Though, where the legal person is a foreign company, the reader is referred to the discussion of the consequences of the Companies and Allied Matters Act 2020, *supra* fn 7.

the residency of a legal person in *University of Nigeria v Orazulike Trading Co Ltd*,[34] where an issue arose regarding the residency of the University of Nigeria. Uwaifo JCA (giving the judgment of the court)[35] stated:[36]

> 'Since the University is a corporate body, it is perhaps necessary to determine its residence from the test applied to corporations. It has been held that the residence of a company is the place of its central management and control. This is normally the place where the board of directors functions or the place of business of the managing director or that of the parent company: see *Unit Construction Co. Ltd v. Bullock* [1960] AC 351, HL. The issue as to where the place of control is, is one of fact: see *Union Corpn v. IRC* [1952] 1 All ER 646 at 657 CA.'

In *Ezebube v Thomas Alpin and Co Ltd*,[37] the plaintiff brought a claim against the defendant in Sapele, Delta State, for a sum owing to the plaintiff. The defendant had its head office outside the jurisdiction in Onitsha, in Anambra State, but did have an office within the jurisdiction at which business was occasionally carried out. The defendant objected to the jurisdiction on the basis, inter alia, that it was resident outside the jurisdiction. Idigbe CJ rejected the defendant's contention, stating:[38]

> 'It seems to me, therefore, that by the expression "carries on business" the legislature intends that there should be much more than casual exercise by the company in its dealings with its customers remote and away from its headquarters or head office. *There must be something to show that the company really carries on, or intends to carry on, business in that area.* The defendants, having lodged a protest as to the jurisdiction of the court, the court ought to be satisfied that the venue of the action was within the district and this ought to be on some satisfactory evidence that the defendants "at the time of commencing the action" carried on business within the district ... the unqualified statement of the defendants' witness, Erefisi, who is branch manager of the company's office at Warri [also, like Sapele, in Delta State], that – "[the defendant] carries out its business normally in this country, including Warri and Sapele" was sufficient basis for the view that the action was justiciable within Sapele ....' (emphasis provided)[39]

---

[34] [1989] 5 NWLR 19 (CA) (Enugu Division; Macaulay, Oguntade and Uwaifo JJCA).

[35] And relying on a decision of Blackburn J in *R v The Mayor of Exeter, Wescomb's case* (1868) 4 LRQB 110 at 113 (Queen's Bench Division, English High Court).

[36] Ibid 26F–H.

[37] [1966] (2) ALR Comm 97 (H Ct Midwestern Nigeria; a domestic case).

[38] Ibid 100:35–101:10.

[39] In *Citec Internation Estates Ltd v Edicomisa International Inc and Ass* [2017] NGSC 13 (Sup Ct), the decision in *Ezebube* was not cited by the court. However, Eko JSC, giving the leading judgment of the court, approved the following statement from the judgment of the Court of Appeal in those proceedings, viz: 'To carry on business means to conduct, prosecute or continue a particular vocation or business as a continuous operation as permanent occupation. The repetition of acts may be sufficient. It also means to hold oneself out to others as engaged in the selling of goods or services.' On the face of it, this statement would appear to be consistent with the italicised part of the judgment from *Ezebube*'s case in the main text above.

The position is, therefore, that a company may be resident, inter alia, by having its place of incorporation in the jurisdiction, or by having its central management and control within the jurisdiction, or by carrying on business within the jurisdiction.

The question arises whether a company can be found to be carrying on business within the jurisdiction where, although it has no presence within the jurisdiction, it transacts business through an agent. The Supreme Court of Nigeria, in *In re Gresham Life Assurance Society (Nigeria) Ltd*,[40] considered a winding up petition by a company which, while registered in Nigeria, had its place of incorporation outside Nigeria, in London. The company had no established place of business in Nigeria and carried on business through the agency of another insurance company at a place of business occupied by that company. The petition was dismissed at first instance by George J[41] because the petitioner had no established place of business in Nigeria, such that the relevant provisions of the Companies Decree did not apply.

On appeal the petitioner contended that it had an established place of business in Nigeria at its agent's place of business because by means of its agent, it carried on business there. Elias CJ stated:[42]

> 'a clear distinction is to be drawn between a foreign company transacting business by agents and such a company transacting business through agents in Nigeria. In the latter case, a Nigerian court has no jurisdiction to entertain a winding-up petition by such a company. The present is such a case.'

A foreign company doing business *through* agents in the jurisdiction and not *by* those agents is not resident within the jurisdiction since the agent has no concern with the management of the foreign company but receives only the customary agent's commission and is not in fact an entity which operates as the principal's creature, but rather as a business which will represent the principal among its other interests.[43]

---

[40] [1973] (1) ALR Comm 215 (Sup Ct, the equivalent, today, of the Court of Appeal) (Elias CJ, Fatayi-Williams and Ibekwe JJSC).

[41] [1970] (2) ALR Comm 78.

[42] [1973] (1) ALR Comm 215, 225:23–9.

[43] Elias CJ cited an English authority, *The Lalandia* [1933] P 56 at 66–7 (*per* Langton J): 'Now taking these various tests, the test of making or selling contracts and the test of Lord Wrenbury in the Okura case of whether the defendants are acting "by" a person or "through" a person, and the value to be attached to whether the rent is paid by the foreign corporation or whether the agent in this country has the right or not to make any independent contract and has any discretion of his own—applying all these various tests as best I can to the present case, it seems to me that Escombe, McGrath and Co. fall upon the side of the line of *agents who carry on their own business and not the business of the foreign Corpn* ... I have to make up my mind *whether the foreign Corpn is really here, in the sense that it has somebody doing its business here who is not doing primarily his own business*, and I think Escombe, McGrath and Co. on the evidence are primarily doing their own business and only in a secondary sense doing the business of the East Asiatic Company' (emphasis provided).

An example of a case where the court reached a different conclusion is *Spiropoulos and Co Ltd v Nigerian Rubber Co Ltd and Thomas Barlow and Bros*[44] where the plaintiff rubber producer brought proceedings, inter alia, for breach of contract against the second defendants who were a firm of rubber merchants based in England and which had no office in Nigeria and the first defendant, which was a Nigerian company and the second defendants' agent in Nigeria. The first defendant accepted and carried out the second defendants' instructions in relation to their business interests and saw to the execution of the agreements the second defendants had made with the plaintiff. The first defendant passed the contracts negotiated by the second defendants to the plaintiff; it made pre-shipment advances of money to the plaintiff and sued for money over-paid; it monitored the plaintiff's performance of the rubber sales contract with the second defendants; it looked after the second defendants' interests and had no interests of its own save in the affairs between the second defendants and the plaintiff in which it was engaged.

The second defendant objected to the jurisdiction of the court on the ground that it was not resident in Nigeria. Ekeruche J referred to the facts as set out above and dismissed the second defendant's objection stating:[45]

> 'The evidence also shows that the first defendant, in the affairs between the plaintiff and the second defendants in which it was engaged, had no business interest of its own and that the whole business was the business of the second defendants. In my view it is clear that the second defendants were carrying on business within the jurisdiction of this court and that the first defendant was not just an agent *simpliciter* but a servant of the second defendants, accepting instructions in relation to their business interests in this jurisdiction.'

The application of the test is heavily fact dependent.

(2) The action is one brought against the defendant to enforce ... or otherwise effect a contract or to recover damages or other relief for or in respect of a breach of a contract–

(a) made within the jurisdiction, or

(b) made by or through an agent trading or residing within the jurisdiction on behalf of a principal trading or residing out of the jurisdiction, or

(c) by its terms or by implication to be governed by the law in force in the jurisdiction or is brought against the defendant in respect of a breach committed within the jurisdiction of a contract wherever made, even though the breach was preceded or accompanied by a breach out of the jurisdiction which rendered impossible the performance of the part of the contract which ought to have been performed within the jurisdiction.

---

44 [1970] (2) ALR Comm 94 (H Ct of Mid-Western State).

45 Ibid 108:39–109:8.

It is likely that, in the apparent absence of Nigerian authority on the construction and application of Order 6B, rule 13(d), a Nigerian court will be guided by the academic and judicial authorities on the construction and application of the (former) equivalent provision in the English Rules of the Supreme Court.[46]

A concise statement of that law is as follows[47] (and should be adapted substituting 'Nigeria' for 'England'):

'(i) **Where a contract is made in England**

11-181

If the parties enter into negotiations by correspondence from different countries, the contract is made where the letter of acceptance is posted. But in commercial transactions today communication by telephone, telex, fax and electronic mail is much more common than by post. It is now well established, following the decision of the Court of Appeal in *Entores v Miles Far East Corpn* (which was approved by the House of Lords [*Brinkibon Ltd v Stahag Stahl und Stahlwarenhandelsgesellschaft mbH* [1983] 2 AC 34]) that if the parties use "instantaneous" means of communication such as telephone, fax or electronic mail, the contract is made where the acceptance is communicated to the offeror. It has been held that if a contract made in England contains a submission to arbitration in a foreign country, an action in England at common law to enforce the foreign arbitration award is within this part of the clause. The contract must actually be made in England as that phrase is understood in English law. It is not sufficient if it merely says that it shall be deemed to be so made, though this may be sufficient to make it one which is governed by English law. A contract may be made in England within the meaning of this clause although it was preceded by a less formal agreement made abroad, or if it was originally made in England, but amended abroad.

(ii) **Where a contract is made by or through an agent trading or residing in England**

11-182

The clause says "by or through" an agent, not "by" an agent. Hence the case is within the clause, although the agent has no authority to make contracts on behalf of his foreign principal, but only has authority to obtain orders and transmit them to his principal for acceptance or rejection. This part of the clause is designed to bring within Rule 34 foreigners who transact business in England by or through agents, and consequently it does not apply where the agent's principal is the claimant. Hence a claimant cannot invoke clause (6)(ii) [Order 6B, rule 13(d)(ii)] where the contract was made by or through his agent.

[46] Order XI, r 1(e) and 1(d) respectively: Rules of the Supreme Court 1883 (1960 ed) and 1965.

[47] *Dicey, Morris and Collins on the Conflict of Laws* 15 ed (2012) vol 1, rule 34, paras 11-181–11-187.

> **11-183**
>
> If proceedings are brought by consignees of a cargo against foreign ship-owners under the bills of lading, the case is not within this part of the clause if the charterparty (but not the bills of lading) was made by or through agents of the shipowners in England, even though it refers to the bills of lading and was made by charterers acting on behalf of the consignees. It may be otherwise, however, if the charterers are identical with the consignees...
>
> (iii) **Where a contract is governed by English law**
>
> **11-186**
>
> ...
>
> **11-187**
>
> Although the fact that a contract is governed by English law is an important factor in the exercise of the discretion under this head in favour of the English forum, it is not conclusive. This head of jurisdiction was described as exorbitant in *Amin Rasheed Shipping Corp v Kuwait Insurance Co*, where the House of Lords held that in the circumstances it was not appropriate for the English court to determine a dispute involving a marine insurance policy governed by English law when the Kuwaiti courts were the forum conveniens. Until that decision it was generally thought that the fact that a contract was governed by English law was in itself sufficient to justify leave. But now the claimant has a heavier burden. In *Amin Rasheed* Lord Diplock suggested that, in order to justify leave under this head, the plaintiff had to show that justice could not be obtained by him in the foreign court, or could only be obtained at excessive cost, delay or inconvenience. But it was subsequently held that Lord Diplock was merely giving examples, and was not providing an exhaustive list, of the relevant factors. The court has to consider all factors, and the fact that English law is the applicable law may be of great importance, or it may be of little consequence as seen in the context of the whole case. Thus if there is likely to be no dispute on matters of law or construction, or if the law of the foreign forum is substantially the same as English law, the fact that English law is the applicable law will be of little weight. But where an issue of English public policy arises in relation to a contract which is (or may be) governed by English law, it is desirable that it should be decided by the English court; conversely, where the foreign court may apply its own public policy to defeat a claim based on a contract governed by English law, that too is a reason for the English court taking jurisdiction. If the claimant has alternative remedies in contract and tort upon the same facts, he can choose his remedy.'

The place of the performance of a contract for the purposes of service out of the jurisdiction was considered by the Court of Appeal in *Nahman v Allan Wolowicz*,[48] where the plaintiff sought to recover a sum of money denominated in Naira which he had advanced to the first defendant as a 'friendly loan'. The plaintiff sought and obtained leave to serve the first defendant outside the jurisdiction (as in England). The first defendant contended that the court had no jurisdiction

[48] [1993] 3 NWLR 443 (CA) (Lagos Division; Kalgo, Tobi and Unaezonu JJCA).

because the promissory note on which the plaintiff sued had been executed in England at a time when both parties maintained addresses in England. The first defendant's contention was rejected at first instance. In dismissing his appeal, the court held[49] that by agreeing to pay the debt in Naira there was a clear intention to give the Nigerian court jurisdiction to entertain the matter and that because the debt was to be repaid in Naira there was an implied intention to perform the contract in Nigeria.[50]

(3) The action is founded on tort or other civil wrong committed within the jurisdiction

There is a paucity of authority in Nigeria on the construction and application of Order 6B, rule 13(e). As with the construction and application of Order 6B, rule 13(d), it is likely that, in the apparent absence of Nigerian authority on the subject, a Nigerian court will be guided by the academic and judicial authorities on the construction and application of the (former) equivalent provision in the English Rules of the Supreme Court.[51]

A statement of the law is as follows:[52]

> **'11-212**
>
> ... As both the Privy Council [in *Distillers Co (Bio-chemicals) Ltd v. Thompson* [1971] AC 458] and the Supreme Court of Canada [*Moran v. Pyle National (Canada) Ltd* (1973) 43 D.L.R. (3d) 239] have pointed out, the competing theories for the determination of the place of a tort have been that (i) all ingredients of the cause of action must have occurred within the jurisdiction, or (ii) the last ingredient, the event which completes a cause of action, must have occurred within the jurisdiction, or (iii) the act which the defendant committed must have occurred within the jurisdiction.
>
> **11-213**
>
> In *Distillers Co Ltd v Thompson* the Privy Council adopted the test of the place where in substance the act or omission occurred which gave the plaintiff his cause of action. So that where the essence of the complaint was failure to warn the consumer of the dangers of a product (rather than the faulty manufacture of the product) the cause of action was held to have arisen at the place where the failure to warn occurred; and the torts of negligent and fraudulent misrepresentation, where the negligent or fraudulent statement was communicated from one country to another, were held to have been committed where the statement was received and acted upon. Prior to the adoption of that test, but consistently with it, it had been held that the tort of defamation was committed where the defamatory statements were published and not where they were posted or uttered.'

---

49 Kalgo JCA 455D and 456A–C.

50 The same principle applies to domestic jurisdictional disputes: *Misr (Nig) Ltd v Yesuf Ibrahim* (H Ct, Kano State), suit No K/65/70, unreported (referred to in *Barsasi v B Visinoni Ltd* [1973] (1) ALR Comm 373, *per* Wheeler J 376).

51 Order XI, r 1(ee) and 1(f) respectively: Rules of the Supreme Court 1883 (1960 ed) and 1965.

52 *Dicey, Morris and Collins on the Conflict of Laws* 15 ed (2012) vol 1, r 34, paras 11-212–11-213.

In *Unipetrol Nigeria Ltd v Prima Tankers Ltd*,[53] the court assumed jurisdiction over a tort (conversion) that had been committed in Nigerian territorial waters: a ship loaded with fuel oil owned by the plaintiff charterers had absconded on the orders of the owners. (In this case a jurisdiction clause in the charterparty was disregarded, inter alia, because the action was one brought in tort.)

8.1.2.3 *Submission to the jurisdiction*

Two circumstances must be distinguished under this title: first, where submission is alleged in extant proceedings in Nigeria; second, where the defendant has agreed (usually by contractual provision) to submit to the jurisdiction of the court in advance of a dispute arising.

8.1.2.3.1 Submission by appearance

It is well established in Nigeria that an appearance entered by a party solely to contest the jurisdiction of the court is not a voluntary submission to the jurisdiction of the court.[54]

In *Barsasi v B Visinoni Ltd*[55] a defendant, having been served with the writ of summons, subsequently attended by counsel on the return day for the summons, denied the claim and asked for pleadings, which the court ordered; filed an application for the transfer of the proceedings to the High Court of a different state in the federation; and filed an application for a default judgment to be set aside, which application was granted. It was held[56] that the defendant had submitted to the jurisdiction of the court.

After entering a conditional appearance in accordance with the High Court Rules, the defendant must promptly raise the objection on which he relies, failing which the court should treat the appearance as unconditional and the court must at all times ensure that a conditional appearance is entered for a genuine reason and not merely to delay the proceedings.[57]

---

[53] [1986] 5 NWLR 532 (CA) (Lagos Division; Ademola, Mohammed and Kolawole JJCA).

[54] *Holman Bros (Nig) Ltd v Kigo (Nig) Ltd* [1980] 8-11 SC 43 (Sup Ct) (Udoma, Idigbe, Obaseki, Eso and Uwais JJSC), *per* Udomo JSC (with whom the other members of the court agreed) 70:22–71:29; see O 29 of the High Court Rules concerning the entering of a conditional appearance for the purposes, inter alia, of disputing the jurisdiction of the court. For more recent authority, set against the background of an arbitration agreement, concerning the question as to when a party may be deemed to have taken a step in proceedings and so submitted to the jurisdiction of the court, see *The Vessel MT Sea Tiger v Accord Ship Management Ltd* (2020) 14 NWLR 418 (Garba, Ikyegh and Abubakar JJCA).

[55] [1973] (1) ALR Comm 373 (H Ct) (Wheeler J).

[56] Ibid 381:4–6.

[57] *Akhigbe v Paulosa (Nig) Ltd* [2006] 12 NWLR 373 (CA) (Abuja Division; (Muhammad, Odili and Rhodes-Vivour JJCA), *per* Rhodes-Vivour JCA (giving the judgment of the court) 383C–F.

8.1.2.3.2 Submission by agreement

8.1.2.3.2.1 *Jurisdiction clauses*

Notwithstanding a historic reluctance to enforce in Nigeria jurisdiction clauses obliging the parties to the agreement to bring proceedings elsewhere than Nigeria,[58] the courts now have regard to jurisdiction clauses and the Supreme Court has, as set out below, provided clear indications to the effect that courts should endeavour to give effect to jurisdiction clauses.[59] Of course, a jurisdiction clause binds only those who are party to the agreement in question.[60]

There are two Supreme Court cases which have had a significant impact in shaping the law in this area. First, in *Sonnar (Nig) Ltd v Partenreedri MS Nordwind, Owners of the ship MV Nordwind*,[61] the plaintiffs were Nigerian companies and brought proceedings in Nigeria against, inter alios, the first defendant carrier, a German company, for breach of contract arising from the non-delivery of rice. The bill of lading contained a jurisdiction clause which provided that any dispute arising under the bill of lading 'shall be decided in the country where the "carrier" has his principal place of business and the law of such county shall apply'. The first defendant applied to stay the Nigerian proceedings in favour of the German courts. Under German law, the plaintiffs' remedy was, by the time of the determination of the appeal, time-barred. Allowing the plaintiff's appeal, Eso JSC (delivering the judgment of the court) applied[62] the principles set out by

---

[58] *Ventujol v Compagnie Francaise de L'Afrique Occidentale* [1949] 19 NLR 32 (Sup Ct, at the time the equivalent of the Court of Appeal); *Allied Trading Co Ltd v China Ocean Shipping Line* [1980] (1) ALR Comm 146 (H Ct, Lagos). The basis for this antipathy was the view that such clauses ousted the jurisdiction of the court. The better analysis is that the jurisdiction clause does not oust the jurisdiction of the court but simply invites the court (on the basis of respect for contractual autonomy) not to exercise the jurisdiction that it would otherwise undoubtedly have. On this, see Okoli and Oppong *Private International Law in Nigeria* (2020) 106.

[59] Indeed, as the Court of Appeal has observed, where a party commences proceedings in Nigeria apparently in breach of a jurisdiction clause in favour of a foreign court, that is, on the face of it, an abuse of process: *Conoil plc v Vitol SA* (2012) 2 NWLR 50 (Galinje, Bada and Nwodo JJCA). That said, as Okoli and Oppong *Private International Law in Nigeria* (2020) point out (at 118), there are at least three Nigerian statutes which limit the effect of foreign jurisdiction clauses, namely: the Civil Aviation (Repeal and Reamendment) Act 2006 (Act 6 of 2006), the Admiralty Jurisdiction Act 1991 (Cap A5 of the Laws of the Federation of Nigeria, 2004) and the United Nations Convention on the Carriage of Goods by Sea (Ratification and Enforcement) Act 2005 (Act 19 of 2005).

[60] *Unipetrol Nigeria Ltd v Prima Tankers Ltd* [1986] 5 NWLR 532 (CA) (Lagos Division; Ademola, Mohammed and Kolawole JJCA).

[61] [1987] 4 NWLR 520 (Sup Ct) (Bello, Eso, Nnamani, Uwais, Kawu, Oputa and Belgore JJSC).

[62] Ibid 538C–539E.

Brandon J in *The Eleftheria*[63] and emphasised that[64] a matter to be considered by a court entertaining an application for a stay in favour of the courts nominated in a jurisdiction clause 'where the granting of a stay would spell injustice to the plaintiff as – where the action is already time-barred in the foreign court and the grant of a stay would amount to permanently denying the plaintiff any redress'.

Second, in *Nika Fishing Co Ltd v Lavina Corpn*,[65] the Supreme Court considered a bill of lading which contained a jurisdiction clause which provided, 'Any dispute rising under this bill of lading shall be decided in the country where the carrier has his principal place of business and the law of such country shall apply.' The country where the carrier had his principal place of business was Argentina. The plaintiff brought proceedings in Nigeria and the defendant applied for an order that the suit be dismissed for lack of jurisdiction. The defendant's application was dismissed at first instance and the appeal from that decision was dismissed by the Court of Appeal. Applying the principles set out previously in the *Sonnar* case, the Supreme Court allowed the defendant's appeal. Mohammed JSC (giving the leading judgment of the court) stated:[66]

> 'It is observed that this court in *Sonnar (Nig.) Ltd v. Norwind* case [sic] referred to above, while applying the Brandon Tests, was confronted with a situation which exceeded a mere balance of convenience. It was a total loss of action by the plaintiffs, if effect were given to the principle of *Pacta sunt servanda*, having regard to the peculiar circumstances of the case where the action filed in the Federal High Court here in Nigeria was already time barred in the foreign German Court agreed by the parties in the bill of lading.
>
> In the present case, however, where the [plaintiff] respondent brought its action at the trial court in clear breach of the agreement to refer any dispute to a foreign court in Argentina and the [defendant] appellant had reacted by filing an application for stay of proceedings, as the [plaintiff] respondent's suit was within the jurisdiction of that court, the court has a discretion whether or not to grant the application. The law requires such discretion to be exercised by granting a stay unless strong cause for not doing so is shown. The burden

[63] [1970] P 94; [1969] 1 Lloyd's Rep 237 (QBD, Comm Ct). Although, over a year *prior* to the decision in *The Eleftheria*, the High Court in Lagos in *Adesanya v Palm Line Ltd* [1967] (2) ALR Comm 133, had reached a similar conclusion on the enforceability of a jurisdiction clause in favour of England. Adefarasin J stated (at 137:9–21): 'What I must apply my mind to is whether, in the peculiar circumstances of this case, I ought to exercise my discretion in favour of the defendants notwithstanding that the parties had by their own act chosen a foreign tribunal. The plaintiff is domiciled in this country. His claim arose here, the damage for which he has sued was discovered here and it was here ... that the consignment of damaged potatoes was surveyed. The evidence which the plaintiff would lead is to be found in this country. The only evidence that may be found in England, and that on behalf of the defendants, is the evidence of the condition in which the consignment left Liverpool ... In the circumstances of this case, I cannot possibly say that the parties have made their bargain and must abide by it.' The judge proceeded to balance the hardship to the parties of proceeding in Nigeria and England and found that Nigeria was by far the more convenient forum for both parties and refused to stay the proceedings in Nigeria.

[64] Ibid 539C.

[65] [2008] 16 NWLR 509 (Sup Ct) (Tobi, Oguntade, Mohammed, Tabai and Ogebe JJSC).

[66] Ibid 534F–535B.

> of showing such strong cause lies on the door steps of the respondent as the plaintiff. The question is whether that burden has been discharged ...'.

The court found that it had not been discharged:[67] 'Thus, in the absence of strong cause shown by the respondent for the trial court not to grant the appellant's application for a stay, the law requires the court to exercise its discretion in favour of the appellant [here, the defendant] by granting the stay.'

As is apparent from the above, the Nigerian Supreme Court's jurisprudence has been influenced by the judgment of Brandon J (as he then was) in *Owners of cargo lately laden on board the ship or vessel Eleftheria v The Eleftheria (Owners), The Eleftheria*.[68] To lend some context, therefore, to the decisions of the Nigerian Supreme Court, it is worth dwelling for a moment on the facts of, and Brandon J's judgment in, *The Eleftheria*. In that case, the jurisdiction clause provided: 'Any dispute arising under this bill of lading shall be decided in the country where the carrier has his principal place of business [Greece].' The owners of cargo on board the *Eleftheria* commenced proceedings in England and the shipowners applied for a stay of those proceedings. In staying the proceedings in favour of the Greek courts Brandon J set out the principles on the basis of which a stay may be granted:[69]

> '(1) Where plaintiffs sue in England in breach of an agreement to refer disputes to a foreign court, and the defendants apply for a stay, the English court, assuming the claim to be otherwise within its jurisdiction, is not bound to grant a stay but has a discretion whether to do so or not. (2) The discretion should be exercised by granting a stay unless strong cause for not doing so is shown. (3) The burden of proving such strong cause is on the plaintiffs. (4) In exercising its discretion the court should take into account all the circumstances of the particular case. (5) In particular, but without prejudice to (4), the following matters, where they arise, may properly be regarded:—(a) In what country the evidence on the issues of fact is situated, or more readily available, and the effect of that on the relative convenience and expense of trial as between the English and foreign courts, (b) Whether the law of the foreign court applies and, if so, whether it differs from English law in any material respects, (c) With what country either party is connected, and how closely, (d) Whether the defendants genuinely desire trial in the foreign country, or are only seeking procedural advantages, (e) Whether the plaintiffs would be prejudiced by having to sue in the foreign court because they would: (i) be deprived of security for their claim; (ii) be unable to enforce any judgment obtained; (iii) be faced with a time-bar not applicable in England; or (iv) for political, racial, religious or other reasons be unlikely to get a fair trial.'

---

67 Ibid 536F–G.

68 [1970] P 94; [1969] 1 Lloyd's Rep 237 (QBD, Comm Ct).

69 [1970] P 94 at 99G–100C.

Having considered the decisions of the Nigerian Supreme Court and the English authority which helped to provide some context to those decisions, it may be said with justification that the decisions of lower courts, and, in particular, the Court of Appeal have been somewhat inconsistent regarding what evidence is required to be shown to demonstrate the requisite strong cause for not granting a stay.[70] Most recent authority has, however, emphasised that the court has a real discretion as to whether to grant a stay and is not mechanically bound to enforce the jurisdiction clause.[71] Obviously, therefore, whether the Nigerian court grants a stay is very much a fact-sensitive question.

8.1.2.3.2.2 *Application for service out of the jurisdiction based on a jurisdiction clause*

One question that arises is the statutory basis on which a Nigerian court may assume jurisdiction over a cause where the plaintiff in Nigeria applies for service on the putative defendant out of the jurisdiction based on a jurisdiction clause in an agreement.[72]

In the English Rules of the Supreme Court,[73] Order XI, rule 1(1)(d)(i)–(iv), the sub-rule governing service out of the jurisdiction in cases concerned with contract contains an additional sub-sub-paragraph to the equivalent provisions in the High Court Rules, namely Order 6B, rule 13(d)(i)–(iii). That additional sub-sub-rule provides as follows: 'The claim is made to enforce ... a contract which ... (iv) contains a term to the effect that the High Court shall have jurisdiction to hear and determine any action in respect of the contract.' This additional provision was included in the English rules in order to reverse the decision of the Court of Appeal in *British Wagon Co Ltd v Gray*.[74]

---

[70] C Okoli 'Analysis of Choice of Court Agreements in Nigeria in the Year 2020' (2021) 21 *Dutch Journal of Private International Law* 292 and the authorities therein cited.

[71] *BUPA Insurance v Chakraverti* (2021) LPELR-55940 (CA). This decision, once again, demonstrates a difference of emphasis as between Nigerian law and the current approach in England. While the English court is not bound to grant a stay, it does adopt an approach which accords greater respect to the jurisdiction clause: *Donohue v Armco Inc* [2002] 1 All ER 749 (HL (E)) (Lords Bingham, Mackay, Nicholls, Hobhouse and Scott), where Lord Bingham, at 754G–J, held: 'Where the dispute is between two contracting parties, A and B, and A sues in a non-contractual forum, and A's claims fall within the scope of the exclusive jurisdiction clause in their contract, and the interests of other parties are not involved, effect will in all probability be given to the clause.'

[72] In *Sonnar (Nig) Ltd v Nordwind*, the German first defendant was served with the Nigerian originating process outside the jurisdiction in Germany. The basis on which leave was granted for service does not appear from the report; however, as non-delivery of the consignment of rice occurred by the dockside in Lagos, it is reasonable to surmise that the ground may have been a breach within the jurisdiction of a contract entered into outside the jurisdiction within the meaning of O 6B, r 13(d)(iii). Cases where the *only* basis for jurisdiction is the jurisdiction clause may be rare.

[73] Rules of the Supreme Court 1965 (the successor provision to O XI, r 2(a), of the Rules of the Supreme Court 1883 (1960 ed), introduced by amendment in 1920).

[74] [1896] 1 QB 35.

Where the defendant is not present within the jurisdiction and where no other provision of the High Court Rules, Order 6B, rule 13 is applicable to the case, the question is whether the Nigerian court has power to order service out of the jurisdiction solely on the basis that the agreement between the parties contains a jurisdiction clause in favour of the Nigerian courts. It would seem not and in such a case there would be no basis on which the Nigerian court could validly make an order for service of the defendant out of the jurisdiction.

8.1.2.4 Lis alibi pendens

The approach of the Nigerian courts to concurrent proceedings concerning the same subject-matter and parties within and outside the jurisdiction was set out by George J in *Jammal v Abdalla Hashem*.[75] There, the defendant to proceedings in Nigeria applied for those proceedings to be stayed on the grounds that the plaintiff had commenced proceedings in respect of the same subject-matter in Belgium. The proceedings in Belgium had been brought not against the defendant to the Nigerian proceedings but instead against a third party. George J cited, with apparent approval, a number of English authorities to the effect that the court has power to stay proceedings before it where the defendant shows:[76] '(i) the plaintiff cannot obtain any procedural advantage from the action in the foreign court, and (ii) the [defendant] applicant is being unnecessarily vexed by the two concurrent actions.' The defendant must show the combination of no juridical advantage and vexation/oppression. George J dismissed the defendant's application on the grounds that he had failed to discharge the burden on him and that the Belgium proceedings concerned a different defendant (an unrelated corporate entity).

8.1.2.5 Forum non conveniens

The Supreme Court in both the *Nordwind* and *Nika Fishing* cases made plain that the doctrine of *forum non conveniens* is a part of Nigerian private international law (in the context of whether effect should be given to a jurisdiction clause).

More generally, where a defendant has been served outside the jurisdiction, the defendant may make an application for the court to dismiss proceedings in Nigeria in favour of a more convenient forum. In *Adel Kamel Barsoum v Clemessy International*,[77] the plaintiff was granted leave to serve the defendant French companies in France in respect of commission the plaintiff contended was due to him on contracts executed by the defendants in Nigeria. The contract sum was payable in Switzerland. The defendants contended that Nigeria was not

---

75 [1975] 2 ALR Comm 141 (H Ct, Lagos State).

76 Ibid 147:1–4, quoting from the headnote to *Ionian Bank Ltd v Couvreur* [1969] 1 WLR 781.

77 [1999] 12 NWLR 516 (CA) (Lagos Division; Oguntade, Pats-Acholonu and Aderemi JJCA).

the *forum conveniens* on the grounds that the contract had not been entered into within the jurisdiction and it was not to be performed within the jurisdiction. At first instance the court held that France was the more convenient forum for the resolution of the claim. The Court of Appeal dismissed the plaintiff's appeal and quoted from the opinion of Lord Goff in *Seaconsar Far East Ltd v Bank Markazi Jomhouri Islami Iran*:[78]

> 'The applicable standard was laid down in Ord. 11, r. 4(2), which required no more than that it should be made sufficiently to appear to the court that the case was a proper one for service out of the jurisdiction, a requirement which was inconsistent with a standard of proof "which in effect amounted to a trial of the action or a premature expression of opinion on its merits:"
>
> > ... having regard to the view formed in *Korner's* case [1951] A.C. 869, I am of the opinion that what has to be sufficiently shown by the plaintiff for the purpose of establishing jurisdiction is, in the case of, for example, sub-paragraph (i), not merely that, if the contract existed, it was made within the jurisdiction, but that (1) there was a contract, and (2) such contract was made within the jurisdiction. Likewise, under sub-paragraphs (ii), (iii) and (iv), the existence of the relevant contract has to be sufficiently proved.'

The court was unable to identify the place where the contract was entered into, as all the correspondence was in French but found the fee was collectible in Switzerland. The court further found that the evidence did not show that the contract had been entered into in Nigeria. For these reasons the court dismissed the appeal.

In *Resolution Trust Corp v FOB Investment and Property Ltd*,[79] the Court of Appeal dismissed the plaintiff's appeal from the finding of the court below that the Nigerian court was not a convenient forum. The court considered the following factors to be of significance:[80] the defendants were domiciled in the USA; the business of the plaintiff and one of the defendants was in the USA; the former employer of one of the defendants was based in the USA and had no contacts with Nigeria; the investments subject of the claim were investments to be made into the USA; the alleged breach of duty occurred in the USA; the law governing the affairs of the parties was US federal law; and the documents necessary to resolve the dispute were located in the USA. Given these factors, Chukwuma-Eneh JCA (giving the judgment of the court) concluded:[81]

> 'there can be no difficulty whatsoever in acknowledging and indeed concluding that the proper forum for trial of the instant matters is the United States where the contract ought to be performed and is the residence of all the defendants ... In sum, under the applicable

[78] The report records the reference as [1993] 3 WLR 756 (HL (E)) at 761–2; the reference to the citation from Lord Goff's opinion in *Seaconsar* as quoted above is to the official reports is as follows: [1994] 1 AC 438, HL at 453D–E and 454H–455A.

[79] [2001] 6 NWLR 246 (CA) (Lagos Division; Oguntade, Chukwuma-Eneh and Sanusi JJCA).

[80] Ibid 263D–F.

[81] Ibid 263F–H.

provisions ... neither the Lagos State High Court as well as the court below nor any court in Nigeria is a convenient forum ie a proper venue to hear and determine the suit.'

8.2 Enforcement of Foreign Judgments

As with other common-law jurisdictions, two regimes fall to be considered under this section: enforcement at common law; and enforcement pursuant to statute.

8.2.1 Enforcement at common law

While there does appear to be judicial and academic authority for the proposition that a foreign judgment may be recognised and enforced at common law in Nigeria,[82] enforcement at common law is, seemingly, no longer used by the profession in Nigeria. Little more can therefore be said about the enforcement of foreign judgments in Nigeria at common law.[83]

8.2.2 Enforcement pursuant to statute

It is difficult to disagree with the proposition that the state of the case law in Nigeria on the applicability of the statutory schemes is 'rather incoherent'.[84]

8.2.2.1 *The regimes for enforcement pursuant to statute*

The overarching statutory regime for enforcement of foreign judgments comprises two pieces of legislation: the Reciprocal Enforcement of Foreign Judgments Ordinance 1922[85] ('the 1922 Ordinance') and the Foreign Judgments (Reciprocal Enforcement) Act 1961[86] ('the 1961 Act'). Three points on this regime may conveniently be made at this stage.

---

[82] *Alfred C Toepfer Inc v Edokpolor* (1965) NCLR 89 and *Wilbros West Africa Inc v Mcdonnel Contract Mining Ltd* (2015) All FWLR 310; see also M Adigun 'Enforcing ECOWAS Judgments in Nigeria through the Common Law Rule on the Enforcement of Foreign Judgments' (2019) 15 *JIPL* 130 at 135–6.

[83] For a more detailed treatment of enforcement of foreign judgments in Nigeria at common law, see Okoli and Oppong *Private International Law in Nigeria* (2020) ch 17.

[84] Olawoyin 'Enforcement of Foreign Judgments in Nigeria: Statutory Dualism and Disharmony of Law' (2014) 10 *JIPL* 129, 140. It must also be remembered that O 6B, r 13 does not allow a Nigerian court to permit service of the writ on a defendant who is present outside the jurisdiction where the action is one to enforce a foreign judgment; Frimpong Oppong 'Recognition and enforcement of foreign judgments in Commonwealth African countries' (2014) XV *Yearbook of Private International Law* 365, 372.

[85] Enacted by way of LN 8 of 1922. It may be cited as Cap 175 of the Laws of Nigeria and Lagos, 1958. Indeed, depending on the source, this Ordinance is sometimes referred to as the Reciprocal Enforcement of Foreign Judgments Act 1958 (due to its inclusion in the Laws of the Federation of Nigeria and Lagos, 1958). For the avoidance of confusion, here it is referred to by its original title.

[86] Enacted by way of LN 56 of 1961 (now Cap 35 of the Laws of the Federation of Nigeria, 2004).

First, as will become apparent below, the 1922 Ordinance is a 'copy-out' of the applicable provisions of the United Kingdom Administration of Justice Act 1920 and the 1961 Act is a 'transposition' of the United Kingdom Foreign Judgments (Reciprocal Enforcement) Act 1933. It is to be expected therefore that a Nigerian court will have regard to (although not, of course, be bound by) decisions of the English courts, in particular, and the commentary by academics, on the interpretation of these Acts of the United Kingdom Parliament.[87]

Second, while the 1961 Act came into force on 1 February 1961, at no time since then has the Minister of Justice ordered that Part I of the 1961 Act extend to any country. As things stand, therefore, the 1961 Act is on the statute book, but no order bringing the provisions of Part I of the Act into effect, in relation to the judgments given in the superior courts of a foreign country, has been made.

Third, notwithstanding that no order has been made by the minister under section 3(1) of the 1961 Act, there is judicial support in Nigeria for the view that some of the 1961 Act nonetheless operates concurrently with the 1922 Ordinance.[88]

8.2.2.1.1 The 1922 Ordinance

The principal provisions of the 1922 Ordinance are referred to below.

Section 2 provides that the 1922 Ordinance applies to any judgments[89] or orders in any civil proceedings providing for the payment of a sum of money, and includes awards in arbitration proceedings if these can, under the law in force where they are made, be enforced in the same manner as judgments.[90]

8.2.2.1.1.1 *Procedure for registration*

Section 3(1) of the Ordinance provides that where a judgment has been obtained from the High Court in England or Ireland or the Court of Session in Scotland,

[87] The relevant parts of *Dicey, Morris and Collins on the Conflict of Laws* 15 ed (2012) on the application of the 1920 and 1933 Acts are as follows: 1920 Act – r 53, paras 14R-173–14-181; 1933 Act – r 54, paras 14R-183–14-195.

[88] Okoli and Oppong *Private International Law in Nigeria* (2020) 361 submit that the 'relationship between the 1922 Ordinance and the [1961] Act remains ambiguous'. For other academic perspectives, see G Bamodu 'The Enforcement of Foreign Money Judgments in Nigeria: a case of Unnecessary Judicial Pragmatism?' (2012) 12 *Oxford University Commonwealth Law Journal* 1, 13 and HA Olaniyan 'The Commonwealth Model and Conundrum in the Enforcement of Foreign Judgment Regime in Nigeria' (2013) 40 *Commonwealth Law Bulletin* 76, 83.

[89] It has been held by the Court of Appeal in England that the 1920 Act does not permit registration of a judgment given by a court in one state in an action to enforce a judgment given by a court in another state: *Strategic Technologies Pte Ltd v Procurement Bureau of the Republic of China Ministry of National Defence* [2020] EWCA Civ 1604 (David Richards, Males and Elisabeth Laing LJJ). It is likely that a court in Nigeria would reach the same conclusion.

[90] The equivalent of s 12(1) of the 1920 Act.

the judgment creditor may apply to the High Court in Nigeria at any time within 12 months after the date of the judgment to have the judgment registered and on such an application the court may 'if in all the circumstances of the case it thinks it just and convenient that the judgment should be enforced in Nigeria' order the judgment to be registered.[91]

Section 3(2)[92] provides that no judgment shall be registered if:

(a) the original court acted without jurisdiction;

(b) the judgment debtor[93] was neither (i) carrying on business[94] nor ordinarily resident within the jurisdiction; (ii) did not voluntarily appear or otherwise submit or agree to the jurisdiction of the court;[95]

(c) the defendant was not duly served with the proceedings and did not appear notwithstanding that he was ordinarily resident or carrying on business within the jurisdiction or had agreed to submit to the jurisdiction of the court;

(d) the judgment was obtained by fraud;[96]

---

[91] The equivalent of s 9(1) of the 1920 Act.

[92] The equivalent of s 9(2) of the 1920 Act.

[93] Being a legal or natural person.

[94] It has been held by an English court that a New Zealand insurance company did not carry on business in Ghana merely because it maintained agents there with limited powers: *Sfeir and Co v National Insurance Co of New Zealand Ltd* [1964] 1 Lloyd's Rep 330 (QB).

[95] In *Grosvenor Casinos Ltd v Halaoui* [2009] 10 NWLR 309 (Sup Ct) (Tobi, Oguntade, Mohammed, Ogbuagu and Ogebe JJSC), the court dismissed an appeal from the non-registration of an English judgment where although the defendant had been served out of the jurisdiction in Nigeria, he had merely ignored the proceedings. Oguntade JSC stated (at 338D–F): 'I have no doubt that it is inimical to the interest of trade and commerce if judgments in foreign countries cannot be readily enforced in Nigeria. It is particularly alarming that when in a case like this, a person ordinarily resident in Nigeria obtains a credit in England and in satisfaction issues a cheque which is later dishonoured, the judgment obtained against him cannot be enforced in Nigeria. Under section 3(2)(b) above, the judgment of a court in England cannot be enforced in Nigeria on the ground that a defendant has not submitted to the jurisdiction of the English court. There is an urgent need to reform our law on the matter. It is an open invitation to fraud and improper conduct.' In *Conoil plc v Vitol SA* [2012] 2 NWLR 50 (CA) (Abuja Division; Galinje, Bada and Nwodo JJCA), the plaintiff sued the defendant for damages for breach of contract in the English High Court. The defendant refused to participate in the proceedings. The plaintiff obtained judgment and sought to register and to enforce the judgment in Nigeria. The Court of Appeal dismissed the defendant's appeal on the basis that the contract contained an exclusive jurisdiction clause in favour of the English courts (p 55 of the report) and the defendant had therefore agreed to submit to the jurisdiction within s 3(2)(b) of the 1922 Ordinance.

[96] Fraud is determined by reference to the common-law principles on fraud: *Owens Bank Ltd v Bracco* [1992] 2 AC 443 (HL(E)), where it was held that s 9(2) of the 1920 Act was to be construed as having adopted the approach of the common-law courts to the finality of a foreign judgment; that, accordingly, there was no requirement, as there was in the case of an action to set aside an English judgment on the ground of fraud, that the fraud should be established by fresh evidence that had not been available to the defendant at trial and could not with reasonable diligence have been discovered by him before judgment had been delivered. This decision in effect permits a defendant to relitigate matters already disposed of before the foreign court. It is a decision which the Nigerian courts are, of course, not bound to follow.

(*e*) the judgment debtor satisfies the court that an appeal is pending or that he is entitled and intends to appeal against the judgment;

(*f*) the judgment was in respect of a cause of action which for reasons of public policy or for some other similar reasons could not have been entertained by the Nigerian court.[97]

Section 3(3)[98] provides that once registered, the judgment is of the same force and effect as if it had been originally obtained in Nigeria.

Section 5[99] provides that where the Governor-General is satisfied that reciprocal provisions have been made in any other Commonwealth country, he may declare that the 1920 Act extends to the judgments obtained in the superior courts of that jurisdiction. The 1920 Act has been extended[100] to the following jurisdictions: Gambia, Ghana, Sierra Leone,[101] Newfoundland, New South Wales, the State of Victoria, Barbados, Bermuda, British Guiana, Gibraltar, Grenada, Jamaica, Leeward Islands, St Lucia, St Vincent and Trinidad and Tobago.

Section 6[102] provides that the Chief Justice of the High Court may make rules of court for regulating the practice and procedure of proceedings under the Ordinance.

The Ordinance contains no provisions dealing with recognition of foreign judgments (as opposed to their enforcement). In the ordinary course the recognition of a foreign judgment would be addressed by a reference to common-law principles.[103] However, due to the desuetude in Nigeria of the common law on the enforcement of judgments, it is a moot point whether these principles would apply to the recognition of a foreign judgment.[104]

---

[97] In *Total Nigeria plc v Ajayi* [2004] 3 NWLR 270, public policy was explained as follows (at 294B): 'that policy of the law of not sanctioning an act which is against the public interest in the sense that it is injurious to the public welfare or public good'.

[98] The equivalent of s 9(3) of the 1920 Act.

[99] The equivalent of s 14 of the 1920 Act.

[100] The Laws of the Federation of Nigeria and Lagos (subsidiary legislation) vol IX, p 2084 (cited in Olaniyan 'The Commonwealth Model and Conundrum in the Enforcement of Foreign Judgment Regime in Nigeria' (2013) 40 *Commonwealth Law Bulletin* 76, 83 at fn 24).

[101] Here the extension was to the Supreme Court of the Gold Coast Colony, the Colony and Protectorate of Sierra Leone, the Courts and the Chief Commissioners of Ashanti and the Northern Territories of the Gold Coast and the Supreme Court of the Colony of Gambia. There is a (possibly sterile) debate as to whether these are the predecessor countries of the ones referred to above.

[102] The equivalent of s 11 of the 1920 Act.

[103] *Dicey, Morris and Collins on the Conflict of Laws* 15 ed (2012) vol 1, r 53, para 14-180.

[104] Once registered, the judgment is enforceable throughout Nigeria: *Goodchild v Onwuka* [1961] 1 All NLR 163 (H Ct).

8.2.2.1.1.2 *Setting aside registration*

Section 6 provides that the rules of court made thereunder shall provide for: (1) service on the judgment debtor of notice of registration of a judgment under the Ordinance; (2) for enabling the registering court on an application by the judgment debtor to set aside the registration of a judgment under the Ordinance on such terms as the court thinks fit; and (3) for suspending the execution of a judgment registered under the Ordinance until the expiration of the period during which the judgment debtor may apply to have the registration set aside.

Rule 6 of the rules of court provides that the order giving leave to register the judgment shall state the time within which the judgment debtor is entitled to apply to set aside registration. Rule 9 provides that notice in writing of the registration of the judgment must be served on the judgment debtor within a reasonable time after such registration. The notice of registration shall contain full particulars of the judgment registered.[105]

Rule 12 of the rules of court provides that the judgment debtor

> 'at any time within the time limited by the order giving leave to register after service on him of the notice of the registration of the judgment may apply by petition to a judge to set aside the registration or to suspend execution on the judgment and the judge on such application, if satisfied that the case comes within one of the cases in which under Section 3(2) of the Ordinance no judgment can be registered *or that it is not just and convenient* that the judgment be enforced in Nigeria *or for other sufficient reason* may order that the registration be set aside or execution on the judgment suspended either unconditionally or on such terms as he thinks fit and either altogether or until such time as he shall direct' (emphasis provided).

Rule 12 therefore confers a very broad discretion on the court whether to set aside the registration.

8.2.2.1.2 The 1961 Act

As noted above, although the Act came into force on 1 February 1961, at no time since then has the Minister of Justice exercised his powers under section 3 to order that Part I of the 1961 Act extend to any country. Any detailed treatment of the provisions of the Act is therefore premature. However, a brief summary of the principal provisions of the Act is set out below.

The Act makes provision for a system of registration of foreign judgments, the purpose of which is to domesticate the foreign judgment and render it enforceable in Nigeria as if it were a judgment of the Nigerian court.[106]

---

[105] Rule 10 of the rules of court made pursuant to s 6 of the 1922 Ordinance.

[106] Section 4(2). As noted above, the provisions of the 1961 Act correspond very closely to legislation of the United Kingdom on which the 1961 Act was based (the Foreign Judgments (Reciprocal Enforcement)

8.2.2.1.2.1 *Procedure for registration*

The procedure for registration is as follows:[107] a judgment creditor under the foreign judgment may apply to a superior court in Nigeria[108] for registration of the judgment; the procedure for registration is prescribed by the procedure rules of the appropriate court – in the case of the Federal High Court these are the rules made pursuant to section 5 of the Act; an application for registration 'may' be made within six years of the date of either the foreign judgment itself or the determination of any appeal or review proceedings in respect of the foreign judgment.[109]

Section 4(1)[110] makes the registration of the foreign judgment mandatory: 'The court shall, subject to proof of the prescribed matters and to other provisions of this Act, order the judgment to be registered.' These prescribed matters are set out in section 3(2)[111] of the Act. In consequence, the foreign judgment must be: (1) final and conclusive; (2) a money judgment not being a sum in respect of taxes or a fine or other penalty; and (3) given after the coming into force of an order extending Part I of the Act to the jurisdiction of the foreign court.

Act 1933). It is to be expected that a Nigerian court will, if the opportunity ever presents itself, refer to judicial and academic authorities on the construction of these provisions of the 1933 Act when deciding questions on the construction of corresponding provisions of the 1961 Act. In particular, reference should be made to: *Dicey, Morris and Collins on the Conflict of Laws* 15 ed (2012) vol 1, paras 14R183–14-195; Briggs *Civil Jurisdiction and Judgments* 7 ed (2021) paras 35.01-35.10.

[107] Section 4.

[108] This will be either the high court of a state or the Federal Capital Territory Abuja or the Federal High Court.

[109] Section 4(1). The six-year period is derived from s 2(1) of the Foreign Judgments (Reciprocal Enforcement) Act 1933. The terms of s 4(1) are not mandatory and appear to provide the court with discretion to permit registration outside the six-year period. In the 1933 Act the language used in relation to the six-year period is permissive ('may apply ... within six years'): Briggs *Civil Jurisdiction and Judgments* 7 ed (2021) para 35.10. As noted elsewhere in this volume, in *Harman v Leaf* 1954 (2) SA 270 (SR), a decision under earlier Zimbabwe legislation for the reciprocal enforcement of foreign judgments which contained a one-year limit on registration subject to a discretion in the court to extend that time, dismissing an application for registration two years out of time, Beadle J held the applicant had failed to provide sufficient evidence that 'he has not in any way been dilatory in pressing for registration of his judgment' and dismissed the application. It may be that the extension of the registration period from one year to six years imposes an even greater burden on an applicant seeking to persuade the court that time should be extended.

[110] The equivalent to s 2(1) of the 1933 Act.

[111] The equivalent to s 1(2) of the 1933 Act.

8.2.2.1.2.2 *Setting aside registration*

Section 6(1)(a)[112] of the Act provides that in certain prescribed circumstances the court *must* set aside registration of the foreign judgment.[113] These circumstances are that:

(1) the judgment is not a judgment to which Part I of the Act applies or was registered in contravention of any previous provisions of the Act; or

(2) the courts of the country of the original court had no jurisdiction in the circumstances of the case; or

(3) the judgment debtor, being the defendant in the proceedings in the original court, did not (notwithstanding that process may have been duly served on him in accordance with the law of the country of the original court) receive notice of those proceedings in sufficient time to enable him to defend the proceedings and did not appear; or

(4) the judgment was obtained by fraud;[114] or

(5) the enforcement of the judgment would be contrary to public policy in Nigeria;[115] or

(6) the rights under the judgment are not vested in the person by whom the application for registration was made.

Under section 6(1)(b)[116] the judgment *may* be set aside if the court is satisfied that the matter in dispute in the proceedings in the original court had previously been the subject of a final conclusive judgment by a court having jurisdiction in the matter.

---

[112] The equivalent to s 4(1)(a) of the 1933 Act.

[113] The exclusionary provisions of the 1933 Act were based on the common law: 'The grounds of jurisdiction in the 1933 Act were deliberately framed so as to reproduce the rules of the common law as closely as possible', *Dicey, Morris and Collins on the Conflict of Laws* 15 ed (2012) vol 1, para 14-190.

[114] The equivalent to s 4(1)(a)(iv) of the 1933 Act. The rules relating to setting aside a foreign judgment obtained by fraud are comprehensively set out in *Dicey, Morris and Collins on the Conflict of Laws* 15 ed (2012) vol 1, r 50, paras 14R-137–14-145; the position in English law (*Owens Bank Ltd v Bracco* [1992] 2 AC 443 (HL) see above) has not been followed in certain Commonwealth jurisdictions (eg Canada in *Beals v Saldanha* [2003] 3 SCR 416, (2003) 234 DLR (4th) 1; and New South Wales in *Keele v Findley* (1991) 21 NSWLR 444 (NSWSC); but in *Close v Arnot* (unreported) 21 November 1997 (NSW), the Common Law Division distinguished *Keele v Findley* and applied the traditional English standard of fraud in respect of a foreign judgment in a case where the defendant had, for good reason, allowed foreign proceedings to go undefended).

[115] The equivalent to s 4(1)(a)(v) of the 1933 Act. In *Dicey, Morris and Collins on the Conflict of Laws* 15 ed (2012) vol 1, para 14-191, it is stated of the equivalent provisions of the 1933 Act: 'The provisions with regard to fraud and public policy are the same as the common law rules. In particular, the common law rule that a foreign judgment can be impeached for fraud even though no newly discovered evidence is produced, and even though the fraud was alleged in the foreign proceedings, applies to enforcement and recognition under the 1933 Act. In *Owens Bank Ltd v Bracco* [1992] 2 AC 443, the House of Lords held that the fraud exception in the 1920 Act was subject to the same rule, and indicated (obiter) that the same must be so under the 1933 Act.' The relevant rule is at r 51, paras 14R-152–14-158.

[116] The equivalent to s 4(1)(b) of the 1933 Act.

The question whether the foreign court had jurisdiction is determined exhaustively[117] by the deeming provisions of section 6(2)(a).[118] The foreign court is deemed to have had jurisdiction in the case of a judgment in an action *in personam*:

(1) if the judgment debtor, being a defendant in the original court, submitted to the jurisdiction of that court by voluntarily appearing in the proceedings otherwise than for the purpose of protecting, or obtaining the release of property seized, or threatened with seizure, in the proceedings or of contesting the jurisdiction of that court; or

(2) if the judgment debtor was plaintiff in, or counter-claimed in, the proceedings in the original court; or

(3) if the judgment debtor, being a defendant in the original court, had before the commencement of the proceedings agreed, in respect of the subject-matter of the proceedings, to submit to the jurisdiction of that court or of the courts of the country of that court; or

(4) if the judgment debtor, being a defendant in the original court, was at the time when the proceedings were instituted resident in, or being a body corporate had its principal place of business in, the country of that court; or

(5) if the judgment debtor, being a defendant in the original court, had an office or place of business in the country of that court and the proceedings in that court were in respect of a transaction effected through or at that office or place.

Section 6(2)(b)[119] relates to property and provides that the foreign court has jurisdiction in proceedings relating to movable or immovable property if that property was situated in the foreign country when proceedings were commenced.

Section 6(2)(c)[120] provides that in any other case the foreign court will be deemed to have had jurisdiction if the jurisdiction of the foreign court is recognised under the law of Nigeria.

---

[117] *Société Co-opérative Sidmetal v Titan International Ltd* [1966] 1 QB 828; *Sharps Commercials Ltd v Gas Turbines Ltd* [1956] NZLR 819 (a decision on the identically worded New Zealand Act).

[118] The equivalent to s 4(2)(a) of the 1933 Act.

[119] The equivalent to s 4(2)(b) of the 1933 Act.

[120] The equivalent to s 4(2)(c) of the 1933 Act. It remains undecided whether this provision would entitle a court to recognise a basis for the jurisdiction of the foreign court not expressly provided for in the Act but available at common law, such as the presence of the defendant in the jurisdiction of the foreign court at the time of the commencement of proceedings. The discussion of this provision in *Dicey, Morris and Collins on the Conflict of Laws* 15 ed (2012) vol 1, para 14-190, suggests that this is not the case. In *Société Co-opérative Sidmetal v Titan International Ltd* [1966] 1 QB 828, Widgery J held (at 850C–D) that an action *in personam* not within s 4(2)(a) was also excluded from s 4(2)(c), 'It seems to me that an action in personam does not fall within subsection (2) unless it satisfies one or other of the conditions in paragraph (a). As I read the section, no action in personam could fall within paragraph (c) at all because all such actions are excluded by the terms of paragraph (c).'

Section 6(3) provides that the courts of the country of the original court shall not be deemed to have had jurisdiction if the subject-matter of the proceedings was immovable property outside the jurisdiction of the original court, or the original proceedings were brought in breach of an arbitration clause, or the defendant was immune from suit under the rules of public international law.

8.2.2.1.3 The relationship between the 1922 Ordinance and the 1961 Act

There exists some quite complex case law at Supreme Court level in Nigeria dealing with the interaction between the 1922 Ordinance and the 1961 Act.[121] The principal cause of controversy is whether the 1961 Act provides an alternative basis for registration notwithstanding that Part I of that Act has yet to be extended to the superior courts of any country.

In *Macaulay v RZB of Austria*,[122] the defendant to the Nigerian enforcement proceedings was the defendant to proceedings commenced in England by the plaintiff in the Nigerian proceedings. The plaintiff obtained judgment from the English High Court on 19 December 1995. On 28 August 1997, the plaintiff applied *ex parte* to the High Court in Lagos for registration of the judgment. The High Court granted leave on 8 September 1997. On 22 October 1997 the defendant applied to set aside registration of the judgment on the grounds, inter alia, that registration had been effected outside the 12-month time period provided for by section 3(1) of the 1922 Ordinance. The defendant failed at first instance and in the Court of Appeal. The Supreme Court allowed the defendant's appeal (Kalgo JSC giving the leading judgment), holding that registration had taken place outside the 12-month limit set by section 3(1) of the 1922 Ordinance.

However Kalgo JSC proceeded to set out the terms of section 10(a) of the 1961 Act as follows:

> 'A judgment given *before the commencement of an order under section 3 of this Act applying Part I of this Act* to the foreign country where the judgment was given may be registered *within twelve months from the date of the judgment* or such longer period as may be allowed by a superior court in Nigeria.' (emphasis in the original)

And to state (obiter)[123] in relation to the provisions of section 10(a):

> 'By this provision [section 10(a) of the 1961 Act], irrespective, regardless or in spite of any other provision in the [1961] Act, any judgment of a foreign country including the United Kingdom to which Part I of that Act was not extended can only be registered within 12 months from the date of the judgment or any longer period allowed by the

---

[121] See generally, Olawoyin 'Enforcement of foreign judgments in Nigeria: Statutory dualism and disharmony of law' (2014) 10 *JIPL* 129; Olaniyan 'The Commonwealth model and the conundrum in the enforcement of foreign judgment regime in Nigeria' (2014) 40 *Commonwealth Law Bulletin* 76.

[122] [2003] 18 NWLR 282 (Sup Ct) (Kutigi, Katsina-Alu, Kalgo, Uwaifo and Tobi JJSC).

[123] Ibid 298H–299B.

> court registering the judgment since the provisions of Part I of the said Act had not been extended to it. Section 4 of the 1990 Act which speaks of registering a judgment within 6 years after the date of judgment only applies to the countries where Part I of the said Act was extended, that is to say, when the Minister made an order under the 1990 Act; and in this case it was not.'

This statement has been interpreted as meaning that a 12-month period applied under the 1922 Ordinance and also that a 12-month period applied to the English judgment by virtue of the provisions of section 10(a) of the 1961 Act, notwithstanding that Part I of the 1961 Act had not been brought into force in relation to the superior courts of the United Kingdom.

The next Supreme Court decision of relevance is *Marine and General Assurance Co plc v Overseas Union Insurance Ltd*,[124] where the plaintiffs obtained judgment against the defendant in England on 25 May 1990. On 16 May 1994 the plaintiffs filed a petition in the High Court in Lagos seeking registration of the English judgment. The defendant opposed the application for registration. The High Court dismissed the petition on the basis that the 12-month period provided for by the 1922 Ordinance had expired. The Court of Appeal reversed this decision and allowed registration. The defendant appealed to the Supreme Court which allowed the appeal on the bases that the 1922 Ordinance provided for a 12-month period for registration and also that the 1961 Act provided for a 12-month period for registration, which period applied to the case;[125] the latter finding was made notwithstanding that the court accepted and found that Part I of the 1961 Act had not come into effect.[126]

The court also held that until Part I of the 1961 Act is brought into force in relation to a particular jurisdiction, the provisions of section 4 of the Act prohibiting registration of a foreign judgment in a foreign currency did not apply and that the registration of the English judgment in that case in pounds sterling was lawful.

In *VAB Petroleum Inc v Momah*,[127] the plaintiff had obtained judgment in the English High Court against the defendant in a sum in excess of $3 million. The plaintiff sought to register the judgment in Nigeria. Reversing the judge at first instance, the Court of Appeal held the judgment should not be registered. The Supreme Court held, in material part: (1) applying section 6(2)(a)(iv) of the 1961 Act,[128] the defendant was a defendant before the English court and was resident in England at the time proceedings were commenced; (2) applying

---

124 [2006] 4 NWLR 622 (Sup Ct) (Onu, Katsina-Alu, Tobi, Oguntade and Mohammed JJSC).

125 Ibid 646D–G, *per* Mohammed JSC giving the leading judgment of the court.

126 Ibid 646A–D, *per* Mohammed JSC.

127 [2013] 14 NWLR 284 (Sup Ct) (Muhammad, Fabiyi, Peter Odili, Ariwoola and Aka'Ahs JJSC).

128 Ibid 312A–H, *per* Muhammad JSC (delivering the leading judgment of the court): 'But, what is the criteria [sic] of determining jurisdiction of a foreign court, here in Nigeria? I think by the provision of

section 10(a) of the 1961 Act,[129] the judgment had been registered outside the period of 12 months set down by that provision and therefore registration should be set aside.[130]

The position regarding enforcement of judgment pursuant to statute would appear, therefore, to be as follows: the 1922 Ordinance remains in force; the 1922 Ordinance applies to those jurisdictions to which it was extended by proclamation prior to the commencement of the 1961 Act; as and when the minister designates a country pursuant to section 3 of the 1961 Act, the provisions of that Act will apply to a judgment emanating from that jurisdiction; in order to determine whether the foreign court had jurisdiction for the purposes of enforcement of a judgment emanating from that court, section 6 of the 1961 Act is applicable; as regards the time within which a foreign judgment must be registered, the courts have applied section 10(a) of the 1961 Act rather than the relevant provisions of the 1922 Ordinance.

8.3 Interim Remedies

8.3.1 Jurisdiction to grant interim remedies

The jurisdiction of the Federal High Court to grant injunctions is statutory: 'The court may grant an injunction or appoint a receiver by an interlocutory order in all cases in which it appears to the court to be just or convenient so to do.'[131]

In order for a Nigerian court to make an interim or interlocutory order in a cause, it is necessary that the court has jurisdiction over the substantive dispute between the parties.[132]

---

section 6 of the Foreign Judgment (Reciprocal Enforcements) [sic] Cap 152 of the LFN 1990, one can be able with certainty to determine where a foreign court's jurisdiction lies.'

[129] Ibid 332G–333H, *per* Muhammad JSC.

[130] The decision in *VAB Petroleum* has been the subject of academic criticism: Olawoyin 'Enforcement of Foreign Judgments in Nigeria: Statutory Dualism and Disharmony of Law' (2014) 10 *JIPL* 129, 139–40. See also Olaniyan 'The Commonwealth model and the conundrum in the enforcement of foreign judgment regime in Nigeria' (2014) 40 *Commonwealth Law Bulletin* 76 at 87.

[131] Section 13(1) of the Federal High Court Act 1990 (enacted on 13 April 1973, now Cap 12 of the Laws of the Federation of Nigeria, 2004). The Court of Appeal is similarly empowered: s 16 of the Court of Appeal Act 1976 (enacted on 1 October 1976, now CAP C36 of the Laws of the Federation of Nigeria, 2004).

[132] *Government of Cross River State v Assam* [2008] 5 NWLR 658 (CA) (Calabar Division; Ngwuta, Omokri and Owoade JJCA), *per* Ngwuta JCA (giving the judgment of the court) 671H; *Soludo v Osigbo* [2009] 18 NWLR 290 (Sup Ct) (Oguntade, Tabai, Muhammad, Fabiyi and Adekeye JJSC) *per* Oguntade JSC at 295H–296A.

8.3.2 Procedure for application

The rules governing interlocutory applications in the Federal High Court are set out in Orders 26, 28 and 30.

Order 26A is entitled 'Interlocutory Applications – Motions Generally' and provides: interlocutory applications may be made at any stage of an action;[133] where an application is authorised by the High Court Rules to be made to the court or to a judge in chambers it shall be made by motion;[134] every motion must be supported by affidavit evidence setting out the facts on which the applicant relies and the motion shall be filed along with a written address;[135] and motions must be on notice to the other party or parties except in a case of emergency.[136]

Order 26B is entitled 'Ex Parte Motions'. Rule 6(1) provides that a motion *ex parte* must be supported by an affidavit which, in addition to the requirements set out in Order 26A, must state 'sufficient facts why a delay in granting the order sought may lead to irreparable damage, loss, injury or serious mischief' to the plaintiff.

The requirement for 'urgency' was considered by the Supreme Court in *Kotoye v Central Bank of Nigeria*,[137] where Nnaemeka-Agu JSC (delivering the leading judgment) stated:[138]

> 'The *rationale* of an order made on such an application is that delay to be caused by proceeding in the ordinary way by putting the other side on notice would or might cause such an irretrievable or serious mischief. Such injunctions are for cases of real urgency. The emphasis is on "real."
>
> What is contemplated by the law is urgency between the *happening* of the event which is sought to be restrained by injunction and *the date the application could be heard* if taken after due notice to the other side. So, if an incident which forms the basis of an application occurred long enough for the applicant to have given due notice of the application to the other side if he had acted promptly but he delays so much in bringing the application until there is not enough time to put the other side on notice, then there is a case of self-induced urgency, and not one of real urgency within the meaning of the law. This self-induced urgency will not warrant the granting of the application *ex parte*.' (emphasis in original)

---

133 Order 26, r 1.

134 Order 26, r 2.

135 Order 26, r 3. Order 27 contains detailed provisions regarding the use of affidavit evidence.

136 Order 26, r 5. Rule 5(2) provides: '... the Court may, if satisfied that to delay the motion till after notice is given to the parties affected would entail irreparable damage or serious mischief to the party moving, make an order *ex parte* upon such terms as to costs or otherwise and subject to rule 12 of this Order, and upon such undertakings, as the justice of the case demands.' It is submitted that the reference to r 12 ought, in fact, to be a reference to r 10.

137 [1989] 1 NWLR 419 (Sup Ct) (Nnamani, Karibi-Whyte, Agbaje, Nnaemeka-Agu and Craig JJSC).

138 Ibid 440D–F. Applied in *Universal Trust Bank Ltd v Dolmetsch Pharmacy* [2007] 16 NWLR 520 (Sup Ct) (Tobi, Oguntade, Mukhtar, Onnoghen and Chukwuma-Eneh JJSC), *per* Onnoghen JSC at 540D: 'It is now settled law that the time relevant in determining urgency justifying the grant of ex parte interim order of injunction [sic] is the time between the happening of the event which is sought to be restrained and the date the application for an injunction could be heard if taken after due notice to the other side.'

Order 26B, rule 9, provides that where an order is made on an *ex parte* motion, any person affected by it may, within seven days after service of it or within such further time as the court may allow, apply to the court by motion to vary or discharge it. In *Universal Trust Bank Ltd v Dolmetsch Pharmacy*,[139] Onnoghen JSC (giving the lead judgment) stated:[140]

> 'The grounds on which the court will set aside, vary or discharge an order of interim injunction made *ex parte* include the following:
>
> (i) if the plaintiff has not used his administrative powers that might have resolved the difficulty;
>
> (ii) if default has been made in giving security for costs;
>
> (iii) if the affidavit has not been filed when the injunction was moved for;
>
> (iv) if it was granted on a suppression or misrepresentation of material facts;
>
> (v) if it was irregularly granted;
>
> (vi) if the plaintiff failed to attend to be cross examined;
>
> (vii) if there had been delay in complying with an undertaking to amend the writ by adding a party as plaintiff;
>
> (viii) if there is non-disclosure of material facts.
>
> It is no excuse for the plaintiff or a party to say that he was not aware of the importance of the facts which have been suppressed or not brought to the attention of the Court. The law is that the court will deal strictly with a party applying *ex parte* and who had misrepresented or suppressed material facts.'[141]

In *Gallaher Ltd v British American Tobacco (Nigeria) Ltd*,[142] the Court of Appeal gave more guidance on the principles governing non-disclosure on an *ex parte* application.[143] The materiality of a fact for the purposes of disclosure on an *ex parte* application is fixed by reference to whether the court would have felt it necessary to consider it prior to reaching a conclusion on the application and not by reference to whether the fact would have been determinative of the application.

> 'There is no dispute between the parties as to the well settled principle of law that suppression or non disclosure of relevant and material facts as well as misrepresentation of facts in an ex-parte application is a ground for the discharge of any order obtained ex-parte. The contention is on what amounts to concealment, suppression, non-disclosure or misrepresentation of material facts so as to lead to the discharge of an ex-parte order. Primarily, in an ex-parte application, the duty of the Plaintiff does not stop at ensuring that he does not mislead the court by expressly or impliedly making representations that are untrue, but it stretches to his obligation of disclosing to the court all matters which

[139] [2007] 16 NWLR 520 (Sup Ct) (Tobi, Oguntade, Mukhtar, Onnoghen and Chukwuma-Eneh JJSC).

[140] Ibid 542B.

[141] In *Gallaher Ltd v British American Tobacco (Nigeria) Ltd* (2014) LPELR 24333 (CA) these grounds were held not to be exhaustive.

[142] (2014) LPELR 24333 (CA).

[143] Ibid 39A.

> are within his knowledge or would have been discovered if proper reasonable enquiries were made; and which are material to the proceedings at hand and tilts in favour of an absent party. See: *Akuma Industries Limited v. Ayman Enterprises Limited* [1999] 13 NWLR (Pt. 633) 65; *R Benkay (Nig.) Ltd v. Cadbury Nig. Ltd* [2006] 6 NWLR (Pt. 976) 338. A matter is deemed material for the purposes of ex-parte application when it is relevant to the existence of power to grant ex-parte injunction or if it is one of those circumstances that the court takes into account in exercising its discretion. *It does not have to be shown that the undisclosed matter in question is such that would have if established, been decisive, in one way or the other, against the party who failed to make proper disclosure. Once the undisclosed fact is relevant and of such a nature that it would have been regarded by the court as of weight in the exercise of its discretion, then the undisclosed fact is deemed material.* See: *Attorney General v. Liverpool Corpn* (1850) 40 E.R. 342 at 356; *R. v. Kensington Income Tax Commissioners* [1917] 1 K. B 486 at 504; *R Benkay Nig. Ltd v. Cadbury Nig. Ltd* [2006] 6 NWLR (Pt. 976) 338. Apparent therefore is the fact that, a material fact is not dependent on the court reaching a conclusion that had the undisclosed fact been disclosed, it would not have made the ex-parte order. Rather, a material fact is judged on the basis of whether, the non-disclosed fact is such that the court would have felt compelled to consider before taking a decision in the application for interim injunction.' (emphasis provided)

The plaintiff's duty is to the court:[144]

> 'The law places a duty on a [plaintiff] applying for ex-parte interim injunction order and/or Anton Piller Order, being equitable remedies; to disclose all matters not only within his knowledge; but knowledge he would have acquired by reasonable proper enquiries which are relevant to the proceedings; and which tend to be in favour of the absent party. This duty is a duty an ex-parte [plaintiff] owes the court.'

Order 26C contains provisions empowering the court to make orders to show cause (or orders *nisi*, as they are referred to in Roman-Dutch law jurisdictions). The order to show cause must specify a return day when cause is to be shown[145] on which the court may discharge the order or make it absolute or may modify the terms of the order.[146]

Order 28 is entitled 'Interlocutory Injunctions and Interim Preservation of Property'. Rule 1 provides that an application for an injunction may be made before, during or after the trial of the action; an application should be made by motion on notice or summons but an urgent application may be made *ex parte* on affidavit. In an urgent case, the application may be made before the issue of process. Rule 2 provides, inter alia, the court may make an order for 'the detention, custody or preservation of any property which is the subject matter of the action or as to which any question may arise for the inspection of any such property in the possession of a party to the action'.

144 Ibid 43A.

145 Order 26C, r 11.

146 Order 26C, r 15.

8.3.3 Interlocutory injunctions generally

In *Kotoye v Central Bank of Nigeria*,[147] the Supreme Court drew a distinction between interim injunctions and interlocutory injunctions. The former term describes orders made to preserve the status quo until a named date or until an application on notice can be heard. An interim injunction may be made during the course of the hearing of an application for an interlocutory injunction (which distinguishes them from *ex parte* injunctions, which are themselves a form of interim injunction).[148] An interlocutory injunction is an injunction ordered after a hearing *inter partes* in order to keep matters in *statu quo* until the determination of the suit.

The Supreme Court also set out the matters to be decided by the court on an application for an interlocutory injunction. Nnaemeka-Agu JSC stated:[149]

> 'On the hearing of the application for an interlocutory injunction, the court, after avoiding all controversial issues of fact, has to decide a number of important issues, including:
>
> (i) the strength of the [plaintiff's] case. A long time ago, the plaintiff was required to show a strong prima facie case that he was entitled to relief (see *Harman Pictures N. V v. Osborne* [1967] 1 W.L.R. 723). However since the decision of the House of Lords in *American Cyanamid Co. V. Ethicon Ltd.* [1975] A.C. 396, at pp. 407~09 it has been held that what the [plaintiff] needs to show is only a real possibility, not a probability, of success at the trial - that there is a serious question to be tried. This is now an accepted principle in this country. See *Obeya Memorial Specialist Hospital Ayi - Onyema Family Ltd. v. Attorney-General of the Federation and Anor.* [1987] 3 N.W.L.R. (Pt.60) 325, at p.340. It does appear, too, from the decision in *Cory V. Reindeer S. S. Co.* (1915) 31 T.L.R. 530 that once the plaintiff satisfies this requisite standard in this respect, the order will still be made even though the Defendant has a technical defence.
>
> (ii) Once the [plaintiff] gets over the initial hurdle of showing that there is a serious question to be tried, he must succeed in showing that the balance of convenience is on his side, that is that more justice will result in granting the application than in refusing it. The onus of proving that the balance of convenience is on his side is that of the [plaintiff]: See *Missini and Ors. v. Balogun* [1968] 1 All N.L.R. 318.
>
> (iii) The [plaintiff], to succeed, even if he has shown that he has a good case and that the balance of convenience is on his side must furthermore show that damages cannot be an adequate compensation for his damage, if he succeeds at the end of the day.

[147] [1989] 1 NWLR 419 (Sup Ct) (Nnamani, Karibi-Whyte, Agbaje, Nnaemeka-Agu and Craig JJSC).

[148] All *ex parte* injunctions are interim injunctions; not all interim injunctions are *ex parte* injunctions. The distinction between interim injunctions and interlocutory injunctions was reiterated by the Court of Appeal (Kaduna Division) in *Nigerian Industrial Development Bank v Olaloni Industries Ltd* [1995] 9 NWLR 338 (Abdullahi, Okunola and Opene JJCA), *per* Abudullahi JCA at 346C–D; and in *Olowu v Building Stock Ltd* [2004] 4 NWLR 445 (CA) (Lagos Division; Onalaja, Galadima and Chukwuma-Eneh JJCA), *per* Onalaja JCA at 457E–458H.

[149] [1989] 1 NWLR 419, 441C–442A.

(iv) Conduct of the parties - has also, quite often, been a relevant factor in the consideration of whether or not to grant an application for interlocutory injunction, as with permanent injunction. For an example, a plaintiff who is also in substantial breach of contract cannot himself get an order of interlocutory injunction against a Defendant alleged to be in breach. See on this *Jackson v. Hamlyin* [1953] 1 W.L.R. 713. Also delay in bringing the application will defeat it because such a delay postulates that there is no urgency in the matter and destroys the very basis for a prompt relief by way of interlocutory injunction.

It can be seen from the nature of the above issues that they are such that they cannot, and ought not, be decided without hearing both sides to the contest.'

The applicable test for the granting of an interlocutory injunction considers, therefore: (1) the strength of the plaintiff's case, which must show a serious question to be tried; (2) whether the balance of convenience favours the plaintiff; (3) whether damages are not an adequate remedy; and (4) the conduct of the parties, in particular any delay in seeking redress on the part of the plaintiff.[150]

8.3.4 Freezing orders

A Nigerian court is able to grant a freezing injunction by way of court order (sometimes called a *Mareva* injunction).[151] In *Sotuminu v Ocean Steamship (Nig) Ltd*,[152] in the course of proceedings, the plaintiff made an application for an injunction restraining the sixth and seventh defendants from releasing certain monies to the first defendant. Dismissing the plaintiff's appeal from decisions both at first instance and in the Court of Appeal, the Supreme Court held that *Mareva* relief was available to litigants in Nigeria. Uwais JSC (delivering the leading judgment) considered the appeal on the basis the general principles applicable to the granting of interlocutory injunctions. Applying the principles set out in *American Cyanamid v Ethicon Ltd*,[153] following the Supreme Court's decisions in *John Holt Nigeria Ltd v Holt African Workers Union of Nigeria and Cameroons*[154] and *Kotoye v Central Bank of Nigeria*,[155] the judge held that the plaintiff had not

[150] The decision in *Kotoye* has since been applied in many cases; see, for example, *7-Up Bottling Co Ltd v Abiola and Sons Nigeria Ltd* [1995] 3 NWLR 257 (Sup Ct) (Uwais, Belgore, Wali, Kutigi, Ogundare, Adio and Iguh JJSC), *per* Adio JSC (giving the leading judgment) 276F.

[151] After the title of an English authority in which such orders were first approved at appellate level: *Mareva Compania Navierra SA v International Bulkcarriers SA* [1975] 2 Lloyd's Rep 509 (CA) (Lord Denning MR, Ormrod and Roskill LJJ). While Nigerian courts are able to grant a freezing injunction, it is still a moot point as to whether they can grant a worldwide freezing injunction, as well as one which operates only on the domestic plane.

[152] [1992] 5 NWLR 1 (Sup Ct) (Uwais, Kawu, Nnaemeka-Agu, Wali and Omo JJSC).

[153] [1975] AC 396, HL.

[154] [1963] 2 SCNLR 383 (Sup Ct).

[155] [1989] 1 NWLR 419 (Sup Ct).

demonstrated that there was any risk that the monies in dispute would be paid over to the first defendant or removed from the jurisdiction. Nnaemeka-Agu SCJ gave a separate judgment in which he stated the rules governing the granting of *Mareva* injunctions:[156]

> 'Now, all the decided cases on the point show that the Courts are ever conscious of the fact that because of its very nature, Mareva injunctions could be open to abuses. So they have evolved some rules and principles which are designed to guard against such abuses. By these rules, before a Mareva injunction could be granted the [plaintiff] must show:-
>
> (i) that he has a cause of action against the defendant which is justiciable in England: See-*Siskina (Owners of Cargo lately laden on board) v. Distas Compania S.A.* [1979] A.C. 210;
>
> (ii) that there is a real and imminent risk of the defendant removing his assets from jurisdiction and thereby rendering nugatory any judgment which the plaintiff may obtain: See -*Barclay-Johnson v. Ynill* [1980] 1 WLR 1259. at p.1264; also - *Rahman (Prince Abdul) him Turki al Sudiary v. Abu - Taha* [1980] 1 WLR 1268, at p.1272;
>
> (iii) that the [plaintiff] has made a full disclosure of all material facts relevant to the application: see - *Negocios Del Mar SA. v. Doric Shipping Corp. SA. (The Assios)* [1979] 1 Lloyd's Rep. 331;
>
> (iv) that he has given full particulars of the assets within the jurisdiction;
>
> (v) that the balance of convenience is on the side of the [plaintiff]; and
>
> (vi) that he is prepared to give an undertaking as to damages. If he fails to satisfy the Court in any of these preconditions for a grant of a Mareva injunction, it ought not to be granted.'

In *Adeyemi Durojaiye v Continental Feeders (Nig) Ltd*,[157] Aderemi JCA cited with approval[158] the judgment of Nnaemeka-Agu SCJ in the *Sotuminu* case and set out what an affidavit in support of a *Mareva* injunction must show:[159]

> 'The question then is, what must such an affidavit show to support the exercise of the court's discretion in granting the application? I think that from the plethora of judicial authorities an affidavit in support of such an application, must show the following:
>
> (1) there must be an action by the plaintiff pending against the defendant within jurisdiction,
>
> (2) the existence of an arguable case by the plaintiff,
>
> (3) the plaintiff must show that the defendant has assets within jurisdiction and must furnish the particulars of the assets,

---

[156] Ibid 26E–H. In *Haladu v Access Bank* [2021] 13 NWLR 434 (CA) (Lagos Division; Georgewill, Oziakpono and Ojo JJCA) the Court of Appeal held that these are 'pre-conditions' which must be met such that 'it follows that an applicant who seeks an order of *Mareva* Injunction must place sufficient materials before the court upon which it can exercise its discretion'.

[157] [2001] 10 NWLR 657 (CA) (Lagos Division; Oguntade, Galadima and Aderemi JJCA).

[158] Ibid 664C–F.

[159] Ibid 664H–665C.

(4) grounds for believing that the defendant is the owner of the assets must be seen through the affidavit,

(5) that there is real likelihood of the defendant removing the assets from within the jurisdiction thus, rendering any judgment which the plaintiff may obtain nugatory,

(6) the affidavit must show that the balance of convenience is on the side of the plaintiff; and

(7) the plaintiff must be ready to give an undertaking as to damages.

See (1) Practice Note [1983] 1 A.E.R. (1) 9 and (2) *Sotuminu v. Ocean Steamship (Nig.) Ltd*, [1992] 5 NWLR (pt. 239) 1.'

The decision in the *Sotuminu* case has since been followed and applied by the Supreme Court in *AIC Ltd v Nigerian National Petroleum Corpn.*[160]

8.3.5 Search and seize orders

Courts in Nigeria may grant an application for a search and seize order[161] (sometimes called an *Anton Piller* order).[162] Indeed, Order 26B, rule 6(2) makes specific provision for such relief, in the following terms:[163]

'(2) In an application for Anton Piller order [sic], the applicant shall in addition show:

(*a*) that he has a strong prima facie case,

(*b*) that he may suffer serious damages,

(*c*) that the defendant has incriminating documents and that there is a real possibility that the defendant may destroy such material before the discovery process.'

---

[160] [2005] 11 NWLR 563 (Sup Ct) (Uwais CJN, Kutigi, Onu, Ejiwunmi and Edozie JJSC), *per* Edozie JSC (giving the leading judgment) 595F–H.

[161] See, by way of example, the decisions of the Supreme Court in *Ayman Industries v Akuma Ltd* [2003] 13 NWLR 22 and the Court of Appeal in *British American Tobacco Nigeria Ltd v International Tobacco Co plc (*2012) LCN/5437(CA) (Abdullahi, Agube and Mbaba JJCA) and *TM Lewin Nigeria Ltd v Smartmark Ltd* (2018) LCN/10700 (CA) (Ogakwu, Obaseki-Adejumo and Tukur JJCA).

[162] After the title of the English authority in which such orders were first approved at appellate level: *Anton Piller KG v Manufacturing Processes Ltd* [1976] 1 All ER 779 (CA) (Lord Denning MR; Ormrod and Shaw LJJ).

[163] This, statutory, formulation of the test for the making of an *Anton Piller* order would appear to be a little less stringent than the prior Nigerian case law. In *Ferodo Ltd v Unibros Stores* [1980] FSR 489 (H Ct, Lagos), Anyaegbunam CJ adopted the formulation laid down by Ormrod LJ in *Anton Piller KG v Manufacturing Processes Ltd* [1976] Ch 55 (CA) (Lord Denning MR, Ormrod and Shaw LJJ) where he stated (at 62A–B): 'There are three essential pre-conditions for the making of such an order, in my judgment. First, there must be an *extremely strong* prima facie case. Secondly, the damage, potential or actual, must be *very serious* for the applicant. Thirdly, there must be clear evidence that the defendants have in their possession incriminating documents or things, and that there is a real possibility that they may destroy such material before any application inter partes can be made' (emphasis provided). In the statutory formulation, the adjectival qualifications to pre-conditions (i) and (ii) have been removed (a 'strong prima facie case' and not an 'extremely strong' one; and the damage must be 'serious' rather than 'very serious').

8.3.6 Third-party disclosure orders

There is no authority on the question whether a Nigerian court may, apart from the established post-issuing of proceedings and pre-trial procedures whereby a third party may be served with a witness summons requiring his attendance at court in order to give evidence and/or to produce documents,[164] order a person not a party to the proceedings to give disclosure. Such a power is available to the English courts in the form of a *Norwich Pharmacal* order[165] whereby an innocent third party caught up in a tort may be ordered to disclose the name or other identity of the tortfeasor.

In *Norwich Pharmacal Co v Customs and Excise Comrs*, the House of Lords[166] set out the following principle:

> 'That if through no fault of his own a person gets mixed up in the tortious acts of others so as to facilitate their wrong-doing he may incur no personal liability but he comes under a duty to assist the person who has been wronged by giving him full information and disclosing the identity of the wrongdoers... [It does not matter] whether he became so mixed up by voluntary action on his part or because it was his duty to do what he did. It may be that if this causes him expense the person seeking the information ought to reimburse him. But justice requires that he should co-operate in righting the wrong if he unwittingly facilitated its perpetration.'

More recent authority[167] has clarified the conditions which the plaintiff must satisfy in order to obtain such relief:

> 'The three conditions to be satisfied for the court to exercise the power to order *Norwich Pharmacal* relief are:
>
> i) a wrong must have been carried out, or arguably carried out, by an ultimate wrongdoer;
>
> ii) there must be the need for an order to enable action to be brought against the ultimate wrongdoer; and
>
> iii) the person against whom the order is sought must: (a) be mixed up in so as to have facilitated the wrongdoing; and (b) be able or likely to be able to provide the information necessary to enable the ultimate wrongdoer to be sued.'

If the plaintiff satisfies all those conditions, the English court will then go on to exercise its discretion. In doing so, it must keep in mind the proper scope of *Norwich Pharmacal* relief: the jurisdiction cannot be used for wide-ranging discovery or the gathering of evidence, but is strictly confined to necessary information.[168]

---

[164] Federal High Court Rules 2009, O 20, rr 8 and 15.

[165] *Norwich Pharmacal Co v Customs and Excise Comrs* [1974] AC 133 (HL(E)) (Lords Reid and Morris, Viscount Dilhorne and Lords Cross and Kilbrandon).

[166] Ibid 175, *per* Lord Reid.

[167] *Ramilos Trading Ltd v Valentin Mikhaylovich Buyanovsky* [2016] EWHC 3175 (Comm) (H Ct) (Flaux J), citing para [11], *Mitsui v Nexen Petroleum* [2005] EWHC 625 (Ch), [2005] 3 All ER 511 (H Ct) at [21] (Lightman J).

[168] *Ramilos Trading Ltd v Valentin Mikhaylovich Buyanovsky* [2016] EWHC 3175 (Comm) (H Ct) (Flaux J) para [46].

8.3.7 Anti-suit injunctions

An anti-suit injunction is an order restraining the injunction defendant from either commencing or continuing proceedings outside Nigeria in breach of a legal or equitable right on the part of the injunction plaintiff not to pursue litigation outside Nigeria or, conversely, restraining the injunction defendant from commencing or continuing proceedings inside Nigeria in breach of a legal or equitable right on the part of the injunction plaintiff to have the dispute between the parties litigated in a jurisdiction other than Nigeria.[169]

In *United Bank of Africa plc v Coker*,[170] the Court of Appeal determined that, in principle, a Nigerian court could grant an anti-suit injunction. In that case, the plaintiff commenced proceedings in Nigeria for unlawful dismissal, unfair dismissal and defamation. Thereafter, the defendant commenced proceedings in New York, seeking damages arising out of the plaintiff's alleged fraud. The plaintiff, at first instance, obtained an anti-suit injunction preventing the defendant from pursuing the action in New York. On appeal, the Court of Appeal discharged the injunction and concluded that, although the Nigerian court had the power to grant this type of injunction, this was not an appropriate case in which to do so.

The effect of the judgment in *Coker* is to confine the grant of an anti-suit injunction to cases where exceptional circumstances exist. The primary difficulty with the case is not the result which the Court of Appeal reached but, rather, the absence of any clarification as to when the necessary 'exceptional circumstances' might exist which would then justify the grant of relief.[171]

It is respectfully submitted that the Court of Appeal in *Coker* was correct to accept that it could, in principle, grant an anti-suit injunction. Indeed, as noted at section 8.3.1 above, the jurisdiction of the High Court to grant injunctions is statutory and may be exercised in all cases where it is 'just and convenient' to do so. The Court of Appeal's conclusion in *Coker* is also in harmony with

---

[169] In similar vein, an anti-anti-suit injunction is an order restraining the injunction defendant from commencing or continuing proceedings to restrain the injunction plaintiff from applying to restrain the injunction defendant from commencing or continuing proceedings. The leading works on this topic are: Raphael *The Anti-Suit Injunction* 2 ed (2019) and Briggs *Civil Jurisdiction and Judgments* 7 ed (2021), ch 28. It is also conceptually possible to obtain similar relief in the context of arbitration. Nigerian courts have accepted, for international but not domestic arbitrations, that they have the power to grant such relief: *Shell Petroleum Development Co Nigeria Ltd v Crestar Integrated Natural Resources Ltd* (2016) 9 NWLR 300 (Ikyegh, Abubakar and Obaseki-Adejumo JJCA) and *Zenith Global Merchant Ltd v Zhongfu International Investment (Nig) FZE* (2017) All FWLR 1837 (Akinyemi J). A detailed treatment of such relief is, however, outside the scope of this work.

[170] (1996) 4 NWLR 239 (CA) (Lagos Division; Muhammad, Ayoola and Pats-Acholonu JJCA).

[171] The Court of Appeal was more forthcoming as to the factors which would not convince it to grant the sought injunction: (1996) 4 NWLR 251.

the acceptance by Ghanaian[172] and South African[173] courts that they may grant similar relief.

Even so, and in the expectation that Nigerian courts will have the opportunity in the future to consider further the circumstances in which anti-suit relief may be granted, it may be of assistance to set out the principles which English courts have formulated and which English courts apply when asked to grant anti-suit relief. After all, the statutory basis upon which Nigerian courts may grant an anti-suit injunction is identical to that upon which their English counterparts exercise that jurisdiction. In addition, English jurisprudence, as Frimpong Oppong has pointed out[174] has proved to be of persuasive value to the South African court[175] when developing this type of relief and, similarly, has been oft-cited by Nigerian courts in the development of anti-arbitration injunctions. It is to be anticipated, therefore, that a Nigerian court before which an application is brought for an anti-suit injunction may well pay close attention to English authorities in setting out the principles upon which an anti-suit injunction may be granted in Nigeria. Set out below, in summary, are the principles of English law governing the grant of an anti-suit injunction, which, it will be noted, are different to the principles on which an English court would grant an interim injunction.[176]

The Nigerian court must have personal jurisdiction over the injunction defendant. The court may be seised either by service on the defendant within the jurisdiction or service out of the jurisdiction with the leave of the court.[177]

The injunction plaintiff must assert a cause of action for relief. Usually, the injunction plaintiff will contend that the injunction defendant is committing a wrong by bringing or proposing to bring proceedings in a foreign court. This will require the plaintiff to characterise the conduct of the defendant as the breach of a legal or equitable right.

---

[172] *Quantum Oil Terminals Ltd v International Finance Corp* Suit No: Misc/00228/17 (unreported) 8 January 2018 and 23 February 2018 (H Ct) (Asiedu J).

[173] *Vedanta Resources Holdings Ltd v ZCCM Investment Holdings plc* 2019 JDR 1425 (GJ) (Adams J), paras [52]–[58].

[174] R Frimpong Oppong 'Reforming Private International Law in African Countries: Looking Inward and Outward' in Jan L Neels and Eesa A. Fredericks (eds) *Commercial Private International Law in Southern Africa – Comparative and International Perspectives. Essays in Honour of Professor Christopher F Forsyth QC* (forthcoming, on file with the authors).

[175] In *Vedanta Resources Holdings Ltd v ZCCM Investment Holdings plc* 2019 JDR 1425 (GJ), Adams J cited with approval the decision of the English Court of Appeal in *Aggeliki Charis Compania Maritime SA v Pagnan SpA, The Angelic Grace* [1995] 1 Lloyd's Rep 87 (Leggatt, Millett and Neill LJJ) and the English Supreme Court in *AES Ust-Kamenogorsk Hydropower Plant LLP v Ust-Kamenogorsk Hydropower Plant JSC* [2013] UKSC 35, [2013] 1 WLR 1889 (Lords Neuberger, Mance, Clarke, Sumption and Toulson JJSC).

[176] Where there are suggestions in *Shell Petroleum Development Co Nigeria Ltd v Crestar Integrated Natural Resources Ltd* (2016) 9 NWLR 300 that the principles governing each type of relief ought to be the same, it is respectfully suggested that these suggestions ought not be persisted with in the future.

[177] The substantive law and procedure for which in Nigeria has been set out above.

A legal right may, and often will, be based on a right not to be sued in a foreign jurisdiction arising out of an exclusive jurisdiction clause in favour of the courts of Nigeria. An equitable right may be the right not to be sued in a foreign jurisdiction and may be the corollary of an equitable wrong which is that it is oppressive and vexatious and therefore unconscionable for the injunction defendant to commence or continue proceedings against the injunction plaintiff in a foreign jurisdiction.

The prime example of a cause of action based on a legal right not to be sued in a foreign jurisdiction is where the parties have agreed expressly that the courts of Nigeria should have exclusive jurisdiction over disputes arising out of the contract (which can be a substantive contract or a settlement agreement) between them.[178] In such a case proof of the underlying cause of action is likely to be a sufficient condition for the grant of the relief and that good reason would need to be shown why the discretion to order an injunction should not be exercised.[179]

The principal example of a cause of action based on an equitable wrong is where proceedings brought abroad by the defendant are oppressive and vexatious. An example of such conduct is illustrated by the decision of the Privy Council in *SNI Aerospatiale v Lee Kui Jak*,[180] where a resident of Brunei had been killed in a helicopter crash and his widow (and her brother-in-law, as co-administrator of his estate), the respondent plaintiffs in the appeal to the Privy Council, had commenced proceedings in Brunei and had subsequently been persuaded to sue in Texas instead. The appellant defendant applied for an anti-suit injunction restraining the plaintiffs from proceeding against it in Texas. The Privy Council allowed the defendant's appeal, held that an injunction ought to be granted restraining the respondents from proceeding in Texas and remitted the matter to the Brunei courts.

Transposing the findings of the Privy Council to Nigeria, it was held that an anti-suit injunction would be granted if: (1) pursuit of the foreign proceedings is vexatious or oppressive; (2) Nigeria is the natural forum for the resolution of the dispute; and (3) the injunction does not deprive the defendant of advantages in the foreign jurisdiction of which it would be unjust to deprive him.[181]

---

[178] The contract may be a substantive contract or a settlement agreement and the dispute resolution provisions may be exclusively in favour of the courts of Nigeria: *British Airways Board v Laker Airways Ltd* [1985] AC 58 (HL (E)) (Lords Diplock, Fraser, Scarman, Roskill and Brightman), *per* Lord Diplock at p 81C–E.

[179] *The Angelic Grace* [1995] 1 Lloyd's Rep 87 (CA) (Neill, Leggatt and Millett LJJ), *per* Millett LJ at p 96, col 2, and Neill LJ at p 97, col 1; *Donohue v Armco Inc* [2000] 1 Lloyd's Rep 579 (CA) (Stuart-Smith, Brooke and Sedley LJJ), where it was stated that 'strong reasons' (*per* Stuart-Smith LJ at para 35) or 'strong cause' (*per* Brooke LJ at paras 59 and 60) would be required to deny an injunction.

[180] [1987] AC 871 (PC (Brunei)) (Lords Keith, Griffiths, MacKay and Goff and Sir John Megaw).

[181] Lord Goff (giving the opinion of the Privy Council) p 896F–H. That the court to which the application is made should be the natural forum for the resolution of the dispute was repeated by the House of Lords in

Other examples of equitable wrongs which may attract an anti-suit injunction are: undermining the jurisdiction of the Nigerian court;[182] vexatious conduct by relying on foreign procedural laws;[183] wrongfully undermining a Nigerian judgment;[184] or enforcement of a foreign judgment wrongfully obtained.[185]

8.3.8 Other interlocutory relief

8.3.8.1 *Interim attachment of property*

Order 30 is entitled 'Interim Attachment of Property'; rule 1 provides:

> 'Where –
>
> *(a)* the defendant in any suit with intent to obstruct or delay the execution of any decree that may be passed against him, is about to dispose of his property, or any part thereof, or to remove any such property from jurisdiction [sic]; or
>
> *(b)* in any suit founded on contract or detinue in which the cause of action arose within the jurisdiction –
>
> (i) the defendant is absent from the jurisdiction, or there is a probable cause to believe that he is concealing himself to evade service; and
>
> (ii) the defendant is beneficially entitled to any property in the jurisdiction in the custody or under the control of any other person in the jurisdiction, or such person is indebted to the defendant,
>
> the Plaintiff may apply to the Court either at the time of the institution of the suit or at any time thereafter until final judgment, to call upon the defendant to furnish sufficient security to fulfil any law that may be made against him in the suit, and on his failing to give security, or pending the giving of such security, to direct that any property movable or immovable belonging to the defendant shall be attached until further order of the Court.'

The applicant (the likely plaintiff in substantive proceedings) for an attachment must specify the property to be attached and give an estimate of its value and declare[186] 'to the best of his information and belief the defendant is about to dispose of or remove his property with such intent as aforesaid'.

Airbus Industrie GIE v Patel [1999] 1 AC 119 (HL (E)) (Lords Goff, Slynn, Steyn, Clyde and Hutton), *per* Lord Goff (with whom the other Lords agreed) pp 138G–H and 140H–141B.

[182] For example, by commencing bankruptcy proceedings outside the jurisdiction when such proceedings are in progress in Nigeria: *SNI Aerospatiale v Lee Kui Jak* [1987] AC 871, *per* Lord Goff at pp 892G–893B.

[183] By seeking to depose witnesses in the USA where those witnesses would be subject to cross-examination in proceedings in Nigeria, for example: *Omega Group Holdings Ltd v Kozeny* [2002] CLC 132.

[184] By commencing proceedings outside the jurisdiction for declaratory relief designed to frustrate the enforcement of a Nigerian judgment in that jurisdiction: *Masri v Consolidated Contractors International (UK) Ltd (No 3)* [2009] QB 503 (CA).

[185] Where the foreign judgment was obtained through fraud and perjury: *Ellerman Lines Ltd v Read* [1928] 2 KB 144 (CA), *per* Scrutton LJ at pp 152–3.

[186] Order 30, r 2.

As Okoli and Oppong have pointed out,[187] there is no Nigerian authority on interim attachment of property. In those circumstances, those authors' suggestion that 'Nigerian courts can draw useful comparative insights from' Ghanaian case law[188] is one which the Nigerian courts should take up, it is respectfully submitted.

Even in the absence of authority, it is apparent that the provisions of Order 30, rule 1 are of significance. Rule 1(a) traverses similar ground to that of a *Mareva* injunction: the plaintiff must show that the defendant is about to dispose of some or all of his property or move property outside the jurisdiction in order to frustrate any judgment the plaintiff might ultimately obtain. A difference between Order 30, rule 1 and an application for a *Mareva* injunction is that Order 30, rule 1, empowers the court to order a defendant to 'furnish sufficient security to fulfil any decree' the plaintiff may obtain. Thus, the plaintiff's claim would appear to be secured under Order 30, rule 1, unlike the successful applicant for a *Mareva* injunction who does not obtain security for his claim. However, Order 30, rule 5, provides an important qualification to the security obtained by the plaintiff:

> 'The attachment shall not affect the right of any person not a party to the suit, and in the event of any claim being preferred to the property attached before judgment, such claim shall be investigated in the manner prescribed for the investigation of claims to property attached in execution of a law.'

8.3.8.2 *Arrest of an absconding defendant*

Finally, Order 45 provides for the arrest of a defendant in certain circumstances:

> '**Arrest of Absconding Defendant**
>
> **Defendant leaving jurisdiction or removing property.**
>
> 1. If in any suit the defendant is about to leave Nigeria or has disposed of or removed his property from the country or is about to do so, the plaintiff or applicant may make an application to the Court that security be taken for the appearance of the defendant to answer to satisfy any Judgment that may be passed against him in the suit.
>
> **Warrant to arrest.**
>
> 2. (1) Where the judge after making such investigation as he may consider necessary is of opinion that there is probable cause for believing that the defendant is about to leave Nigeria or has disposed of or removed his property or any part of it out of the country while the suit is pending and consequently the execution of any Judgment which may be made against him is likely to be obstructed or delayed; the judge

[187] Okoli and Oppong *Private International Law in Nigeria* (2020) 444–5.

[188] And, in particular, *General Development Co Ltd v Rad Forest Products Ltd* [1999–2000] 2 GLR 178 (CA) (Benin, Ansah and Amonoo-Monney JJA), in which the Ghanaian Court of Appeal considered the appropriate construction of similarly worded Ghanaian provisions.

shall issue a warrant to bring the defendant before him, that he may show cause why he should not give good and sufficient recognizance for his appearance.

(2) The defendant shall be brought to Court within two days of the execution of the warrant.

Bail for appearance or satisfaction.

3. Where the defendant fails to show cause, the judge shall order him to give recognizance for his appearance at any time when called upon while the suit is pending, until execution or satisfaction of any judgment that may be passed against him in the suit, or to give recognizance for the satisfaction of such judgment; and the surety or sureties shall undertake in default of such appearance or satisfaction, to pay any sum of money that may be adjudged against the defendant in the suit, with cost.

Deposit in lieu of bail.

4. (1) Where a defendant offers to deposit a sum of money in lieu of recognizance for his appearance, sufficient to answer the claim against him, with cost of the suit the judge may accept such deposit and direct that the deposit be paid into an interest yielding account in a bank.

(2) Where a defendant offers security other than money in lieu of bail for his appearance, sufficient to answer the claim against him, the judge may accept such security and make such order as he may deem fit in the circumstance.

Committal in default of security.

5. (1) Where the defendant fails to furnish security or offer a sufficient deposit the judge may commit him into custody until the decision of the suit or if judgment has been given against the defendant until execution of the judgment.

(2) Committal to custody under this rule shall not exceed a period of six months at a time.

(3) The judge may at any time upon reasonable cause being shown and upon such terms as to security or otherwise as may seem just, release the defendant.

Costs of subsistence of person arrested.

6. The expenses incurred for the subsistence in prison of the person so arrested shall be paid by the plaintiff or applicant in the action in advance, and the amount so disbursed may be recovered by the plaintiff or applicant in the suit, unless the judge shall otherwise order. The judge may release the person so imprisoned on failure by the plaintiff to pay the subsistence money, or in case of serious illness order his removal to hospital.'

Chapter 9

REPUBLIC OF SOUTH AFRICA

9.1 Jurisdiction

The civil jurisdiction of the High Court of the Republic of South Africa in matters which concern private international law is dealt with below in two parts. We consider first, the doctrine of effectiveness and, second, the principles governing civil jurisdiction. This approach has been adopted because the supposed centrality of the doctrine of effectiveness to the jurisdiction of the South African courts lends itself to this treatment and also because of recent developments which suggest that the place of the doctrine of effectiveness in South African law is changing.

9.1.1 The doctrine of effectiveness

Historically the doctrine of effectiveness has occupied a central position in the South African law of jurisdiction.

> 'The doctrine of effectiveness is the most important general principle underlying the jurisdiction of the High Court in the majority of cases. The basic idea behind this doctrine is that you should not waste a court's time by bringing a particular matter before it is clear from the outset that the court's judgment will not be effective.'[1]

[1] Peté et al *Civil Procedure* 2 ed (2011) 71 para 3.2. See also Pollak *The South African Law of Jurisdiction* 1 ed (1937) (referred to as *Pollak on Jurisdiction*) 15–18; Pistorius *Pollak on Jurisdiction* 2 ed (1993) 3–7; Schulze *On Jurisdiction and the Recognition and Enforcement of Foreign Money Judgments* (2005) 12–13 para 2.4.2.

In *Thermo Radiant Oven Sales (Pty) Ltd v Nelspruit Bakeries (Pty) Ltd*,[2] Potgieter JA stated:[3] 'Save for the principle of voluntary submission to jurisdiction and possibly in the case of the exclusive competency of the Court of domicile in an action affecting status, the basic principle of jurisdiction in our law is that of effectiveness.'

In *Ewing McDonald & Co Ltd v M&M Products Co*,[4] Nienaber AJA stated:

> 'The doctrine of effectiveness lies at the root of jurisdiction. A judgment would not be effective if it should yield an empty result. The result would be empty if judgment is obtained against a foreign peregrinus[5] who is absent from the jurisdiction and who owns no assets in it.'

The vitality of the doctrine of effectiveness to the South African law of jurisdiction is of importance because it informs the future development of South African law in this area. Recent developments suggest that effectiveness may be losing the doctrinal centrality it once possessed.

In *Bid Industrial Holdings (Pty) Ltd v Strang*,[6] the Supreme Court of Appeal considered the question whether the arrest of the defendant to found or confirm jurisdiction was constitutional. The respondents to the appeal were citizens of Australia and resident and domiciled in Australia. The appellant was a South African company with its registered office in Johannesburg. The appellant intended to sue the respondents in the Johannesburg High Court for damages in delict and applied for an order for the respondents' arrest. The judge at first instance dismissed the application on the ground that the appellant had failed to establish a *prima facie* case. On appeal the respondents contended that jurisdictional arrest was unconstitutional.[7] Two main questions fell to be decided. First, did jurisdictional arrest breach the relevant provisions of the Constitution? Second, if so, could it satisfy the requirements of section 36 of the Constitution?

Howie P, giving the judgment of the court, held[8] that jurisdictional arrest profoundly infringed the respondents' entrenched right to freedom and security of the person (as set out in section 12 of the Constitution). Howie P also found[9] concomitant breaches of the rights to equality, human dignity, freedom of movement and a fair trial.

---

2 1969 (2) SA 295 (A) (Steyn CJ, Ogilvie Thompson, Botha, Potgieter and Jansen JJA).

3 Ibid 307A; Steyn CJ concurring.

4 1991 (1) SA 252 (A) (Van Heerden and Smalberger JJA; Nienaber, Nicholas and Friedman AJJA).

5 The meaning of this term, and of the associated term '*incola*', is set out under the sub-heading '*Incolae* and *Peregrini*' below.

6 2008 (3) SA 355 (SCA) (Howie P, Nugent, Ponnan, Maya JJA and Malan AJA).

7 The right to equality before the law (s 9(1) of the Constitution), the guarantee against unfair discrimination (s 9(3)), the right to human dignity (s 10), the right to freedom and security of the person (s 12), the right to freedom of movement (s 21) and the right to a fair civil trial (s 34).

8 2008 (3) SA 355 (SCA) paras [32]–[42].

9 Ibid para [43].

An infringement having been found, section 36 of the Constitution then required the court to consider whether, taking into account the factors set out at section 36(1)(a)–(e), the common-law rule permitting jurisdictional arrest was 'reasonable and justifiable in an open and democratic society based on human dignity, equality and freedom'. Howie P described[10] the governmental limitation on the constitutional rights engaged as being 'to favour resident plaintiffs, in line with the common law, by seeking to enable them to establish jurisdiction which would not otherwise exist and so as to avoid the trouble and expense of suing abroad'. Assuming such a limitation to be constitutionally permissible, Howie P found[11] that it was not reasonable and justifiable to achieve such a purpose by subjecting foreign defendants to arrest and detention. Howie P stated that there were less restrictive ways of establishing jurisdiction than the defendant's arrest: the attachment of the defendant's property, for example.

He then considered the position where attachment of the defendant's property was not possible and posed the question whether jurisdiction could be established absent arrest or attachment and stated:[12] 'if the common law is to be developed by abolishing jurisdictional arrest, that development must necessarily involve providing practical expedients for cases where jurisdiction is sought to be established and there can be neither arrest nor attachment.' The rationale of arrest and attachment (assisting a resident plaintiff) still applied in the absence of those means of establishing jurisdiction. The question whether jurisdiction could be established in the absence of arrest or attachment had not been the subject of judicial authority in South Africa and it was a question 'that must now be resolved by reference to the court's obligations and powers under the Constitution'.[13]

In formulating what he described as 'a substitute practice', Howie P noted that the Supreme Court of Appeal had previously accepted[14] that, for the purposes of investing a court with international jurisdiction when considering enforcement of a foreign judgment in South Africa, the defendant's mere physical presence in the foreign court's territorial jurisdiction was sufficient. Further, in a number of important passages which bear full citation, Howie P stated:[15]

> '[55] Obviously the jurisdictional principles we are concerned with here have originated because courts have always sought to avoid having to try cases when their judgments will, or at least could, prove hollow because of the absence of any possibility of meaningful execution in the plaintiff's jurisdiction. It seems to me that, firstly, one

---

[10] Ibid para [45].

[11] Ibid.

[12] Ibid para [48].

[13] Ibid para [49].

[14] *Richman v Ben-Tovim* 2007 (2) SA 283 (SCA) (Zulman, Cameron, Brand and Maya JJA; Theron AJ), paras [7]–[9].

[15] 2008 (3) SA 355 (SCA) paras [55]–[57].

has to apply reasonable and practical expedients in moving away, where necessary, from historical practices that cannot achieve what they were intended to. Secondly, the responsibility for achieving effectiveness, absent attachment, is essentially that of the parties, and more especially the plaintiff. Economic considerations will dictate whether a South African judgment has prospects of successful enforcement abroad and thus influence a plaintiff in deciding whether to attach and sue here or to sue there (leaving aside, of course, other costs considerations). And if the plaintiff decides in favour of suing here it is open to the defendant to contest, among other things, whether the South African court is the *forum conveniens* and whether there are sufficient links between the suit and this country to render litigation appropriate here rather than in the court of the defendant's domicile.

[56] In my view it would suffice to empower the court to take cognisance of the suit if the defendant were served with the summons while in South Africa and, in addition, there were an adequate connection between the suit and the area of jurisdiction of the South African court concerned from the point of view of the appropriateness and convenience of its being decided by that court. Appropriateness and convenience are elastic concepts which can be developed case by case. Obviously the strongest connection would be provided by the cause of action arising within that jurisdiction.

[57] As to the principle of effectiveness, despite its having been described as "the basic principle of jurisdiction in our law" it is clear that the importance and significance of attachment has been so eroded that the value of attached property has sometimes been "trifling". However, as I have said, effectiveness is largely for the plaintiff to assess and to act accordingly.'

Howie P then held:[16]

'[59] For all these reasons the common-law rule that arrest is mandatory to found or confirm jurisdiction cannot pass the limitations test set by s 36(1). It is contrary to the spirit, purport and objects of the Bill of Rights. The common law must be, and is hereby, developed by abolition of the rule and the adoption in its stead, where attachment is not possible, of the practice according to which a South African High Court will have jurisdiction if the summons is served on the defendant while in South Africa and there is sufficient connection between the suit and the area of jurisdiction of the court concerned so that disposal of the case by that court is appropriate and convenient. It goes without saying that the new practice could itself be subject to development with time.'

It is submitted that this finding, that jurisdiction can be established in South Africa by personal service combined with a sufficient connection between the action and the area of jurisdiction of the court concerned, is a necessary part of the reasoning of the Supreme Court of Appeal in reaching the conclusion that the abolition of jurisdictional arrest was justified because less restrictive means

[16] Ibid para [59].

existed to establish jurisdiction.[17] This finding, therefore, forms part of the *ratio* of the case. Indeed, the court expressed itself in terms consistent only with this finding being central to its reasoning.[18]

The result would appear to be that, certainly in the case of a foreign (*peregrinus*) defendant being sued by a local (*incola*) plaintiff, a division of the High Court will have jurisdiction over the suit if 'the summons is served on the defendant while in South Africa and there is sufficient connection between the suit and the area of jurisdiction of the court concerned so that disposal of the case by that court is appropriate and convenient'.

In the context of establishing jurisdiction through service of process, *Bid Industrial* has since been referred to in three judgments of the Supreme Court of Appeal.

In *Carmel Trading Co Ltd v The Commissioner for the South African Revenue Service*,[19] the High Court (Preller J) had varied a preservation and anti-dissipation order made in respect of an executive jet situated at Le Bourget Airport near Paris, France, authorising and ordering the sheriff to sell the jet and keep the proceeds in trust, pending the conclusion of the Commissioner's action against various parties alleged to have had substantial tax liabilities to the Revenue. The Supreme Court of Appeal rejected an appeal against this order. In giving the judgment of the court,[20] Harms ADP addressed an argument advanced by the defendant that, because there had been no attachment of the jet, the court could not accept that the order of the court below could be executed and therefore that the doctrine of effectiveness was not satisfied such that the order ought not to have been made. Harms ADP stated[21] that the answer to this argument was to be found in the dictum of Howie P in *Bid Industrial*[22] that 'the responsibility for achieving effectiveness, absent attachment, is essentially that of the parties, and more especially the plaintiff'. While it is going too far to regard this as following the entirety of the reasoning in *Bid Industrial*, it certainly amounts to an approval of a component of that reasoning.[23]

---

[17] Being the practice referred to in para [59] of the judgment set out above.

[18] 'The common law must be, and is hereby, developed by abolition of the rule and the adoption in its stead ... of the practice ...'.

[19] 2008 (2) SA 433 (SCA) (Harms ADP, Scott, Mthiyane and Nugent JJA and Mhlantla AJA).

[20] Six days after the decision in *Bid Industrial*, Nugent JA was the only Judge of Appeal common to both panels.

[21] Ibid para [18].

[22] 2008 (3) SA 355 (SCA) para [55].

[23] The court may also have a statutory basis for forfeiting property outside the jurisdiction without an attachment of that property and, therefore, the non-satisfaction of the doctrine of effectiveness: see the Prevention of Organised Crime Act 1998 (Act 121 of 1998), s 48; considered in the *National Director of Public Prosecutions v Bobroff* [2021] ZASCA 56 (21 May 2021), where the court confirmed that such an order could be made. The authors are grateful to John Oxenham of Primerio International for drawing this to their attention.

In *Barrows v Benning*,[24] the respondent/plaintiff issued proceedings in the North Gauteng High Court, Pretoria, against the appellant/defendant for breach of an agreement to procure 5% of the issued shares in a company incorporated in Mauritius and transfer those shares to the plaintiff. The *incola* plaintiff's claim was for delivery of the shares or for payment of their value. The defendant, a *peregrinus* of South Africa who was resident in the United Kingdom, had been served with proceedings whilst temporarily within the jurisdiction. At first instance the court held that it had jurisdiction to entertain the claim. On appeal, in the course of argument, the plaintiff proposed an amendment regarding the scope of the relief sought which rendered the appeal and the proceedings below redundant and an order was made on the appeal which provided for the costs of the appeal and the setting aside of the order of the court of first instance. For present purposes, it is of interest that the Supreme Court of Appeal, in a very brief judgment delivered by Snyders JA, expressly endorsed[25] a concession made by the defendant that 'in view of the decision in *BID Industrial* ... that if the [plaintiff] only claimed a monetary order of payment of the value of the shares, the court below would undoubtedly have had jurisdiction to determine the matter'.

The Supreme Court of Appeal also stated:[26]

> 'Jurisdiction is the power of a court to adjudicate upon, determine and dispose of a matter. It is a territorial power that derives from the creation of courts of law by a sovereign authority with power only within the territory of that sovereign. A court has jurisdiction when, within its territory, it has sufficient authority over a defendant to be able to enforce its orders. Put in different words the court must have the power not only to take cognisance of a suit, but also to give effect to its judgment. These rules come from the Roman law, were taken over by Roman-Dutch law and adopted into our law. Even in the most recent cases on jurisdiction this Court applied the doctrine of effectiveness as a criterion for the existence of jurisdiction.'

In support of the proposition in the final sentence, the court cited three of its earlier decisions identifying the paragraphs of those judgments relied upon: *Metlika Trading Ltd v The Commissioner for the South African Revenue Service*,[27] *Gallo Africa Ltd v Sting Music (Pty) Ltd*,[28] and *BID Industrial*.[29]

The *Metlika Trading* case was concerned with the granting of an interim interdict where the court had (or was about to have) personal jurisdiction over the defendant; it is not a case concerning the existence of jurisdiction over the defendants. Further, the statement by the court, that 'If the court a quo was not

[24] [2012] ZASCA 10 (Mthiyane DP, Brand, Cloete, Snyders and Majiedt JJA).

[25] Ibid para [4].

[26] Ibid para [3].

[27] 2005 (3) SA 1 (SCA) (Streicher, Cameron and Conradie JJA and Patel and Ponnan AJJA) para [36].

[28] 2010 (6) SA 329 (SCA) (Harms DP, Nugent, Lewis, Ponnan and Cachalia JJA) paras [6] and [10].

[29] 2008 (3) SA 355 (SCA) paras [24], [39], [41], [55], [56] and [57].

able to enforce compliance with the order which it granted it had no jurisdiction to grant it', should in context be understood as referring to the principle that a court will not make an order if there is no point in doing so, the so-called principle of futility.[30] On the facts of the *Metlika Trading* case there was a point in making the order because the relevant defendant was subject to the court's personal jurisdiction and the order could, on the application of the plaintiff, be enforced against the officers of that defendant.

In *Gallo Africa*[31] the English Court of Appeal decision on which the court relied in supporting its conclusion that the South African courts did not have jurisdiction to adjudicate on disputes involving infringements of foreign copyright laws[32] was reversed by the UK Supreme Court subsequent to the decision in *Gallo Africa*.[33] Further, as the defendants in *Gallo Africa* were all subject to the personal jurisdiction of the South African court, there would appear to be no reason why (once the question of justiciability was disposed of) an order of the South African court could not have been enforced against the defendants or any of them. In *Gallo Africa* it was not effectiveness as regards enforcement of an order that was at issue, it was the justiciability in South Africa of the disputes raising foreign copyright laws.

The paragraphs in *Bid Industrial* referred to by the Supreme Court of Appeal[34] in *Barrows v Benning* as supporting the proposition that 'even in the most recent cases on jurisdiction this Court applied the doctrine of effectiveness as a criterion for the existence of jurisdiction' are paragraphs [24], [39], [41], [55], [56] and [57] of Howie P's judgment.

However, these paragraphs do not provide unqualified support for the proposition for which they were cited in *Barrows v Benning*. Paragraph [24] of Howie P's judgment states:

> 'a court has jurisdiction over a matter if it has the power not only if [sic, 'of'] taking cognisance of the suit but also of giving effect to its judgment'. However, it does not follow that if a court does not have the power to give effect to its judgment that it does not have jurisdiction. Further, Howie P proceeded to state that the court was 'not concerned with the question of jurisdictional effectiveness as such.'

---

[30] Spry *Equitable Remedies* 8 ed (2010) 493–4; Witzleb 'Equity does not act in vain: An analysis of futility arguments in claims for injunctions' (2010) 32(3) *Sydney Law Review* 503; *Mosley v News Group Newspapers Ltd* [2008] EWHC 687 (QB); *HM Revenue & Customs v Cozens* [2011] EWHC 2782 (Ch) paras [40]–[45]; *Humane Society International Inc v Kyodo Senpaku Kaisha Ltd* (2006) 154 FCR 425.

[31] 2010 (6) SA 329 (SCA) (Harms DP, Nugent, Lewis, Ponnan and Cachalia JJA).

[32] *Lucas Film Ltd v Ainsworth* [2009] EWCA Civ 1328, [2010] Ch 503 (Rix, Jacob and Patten LJJ).

[33] *Lucasfilm Limited v Ainsworth* (Lord Phillips PSC, Lord Walker, Baroness Hale and Lord Mance JJSC and Lord Collins).

[34] None of the panel in *Barrows v Benning* was a member of the panel on the appeal in *Bid Industrial.*

Paragraph [39] contains observations on the inability of a deprivation of liberty to obtain effectiveness in the context of a broader discussion of whether 'just cause' existed for the practice of arrest to found or confirm jurisdiction.

Paragraph [41] reiterates that arrest does not serve to attain jurisdictional effectiveness and then states; 'as to the function of arrest to enable the court to take cognisance of the suit, that could be appropriately achieved if the defendant were in this country when served with the summons and there were, in addition, significant factual links between the suit and South Africa'; this is a statement of principle for which the underpinning of the doctrine of effectiveness is unnecessary.

Paragraphs [55]–[57] of Howie P's judgment set out the reasoning behind the adoption of the presence plus the appropriateness/convenience principle at paragraph [59] of the judgment. Indeed at paragraphs [55]–[57] (quoted above), various statements appear which are at odds with the doctrine of effectiveness as the underpinning of the modern law of jurisdiction. For example, at paragraph [57] Howie P stated:

> '[57] As to the principle of effectiveness, despite its having been described as "the basic principle of jurisdiction in our law" it is clear that the importance and significance of attachment has been so eroded that the value of attached property has sometimes been "trifling". However, as I have said, effectiveness is largely for the plaintiff to assess and act accordingly.'

Thus, in *Bid Industrial*, far from endorsing the doctrine of effectiveness for jurisdictional purposes, the Supreme Court of Appeal characterised it as 'eroded' and proceeded to formulate a basis for the assumption of jurisdiction which took no account of the doctrine as traditionally understood and applied.

The authorities relied on by the court in *Barrows v Benning* as support for the proposition that '[e]ven in the most recent cases on jurisdiction this Court applied the doctrine of effectiveness as a criterion for the existence of jurisdiction' do not, it is submitted, provide that support.

More recently, in *Zhongji Development Construction Engineering Co Ltd v Kamoto Copper Co SARL*,[35] the appellant/claimant, a Chinese company, had entered into a contract for the supply and construction of piling and civil works at the mining site in the Democratic Republic of the Congo of DRC Copper & Cobalt Project SARL ('DRC'), a Congolese company. That contract contained an arbitration clause. About a year later, the respondent/defendant, Kamoto Copper Company SARL, another Congolese company, took over the rights and obligations of DRC. The claimant then claimed payment from the defendant. Relying on the arbitration clause in the contract, the claimant sought a declaratory order that

[35] 2015 (1) SA 345 (SCA) (Mpati P, Mbha, Willis JJA and Gorven and Mathopo AJJA).

the defendant was bound by the arbitration clause in the main agreement. The High Court dismissed the application, as did the Supreme Court of Appeal on the basis that the subject of the application for the declaration was one properly for the arbitration tribunal.

For present purposes, interest lies in the judgment of Willis JA (giving the judgment of the majority of the court: Mpati P and Mbha JA and Mathopo AJA)[36] where he stated:[37]

> 'As this court made clear in *Bid Industrial Holdings (Pty) v Strang* the effectiveness of its orders remains an important consideration when a court is making a decision as to whether jurisdiction is present, even though, nowadays, a generally more relaxed approach is taken on the issue.'

In support of that proposition, Willis JA relied on[38] paragraphs [38]–[59] of the *Bid Industrial* case and cited paragraph [36] of the *Metlika Trading* case. It is submitted that these remarks further demonstrate that the principle of effectiveness no longer plays the central role which it once did in the South African law of jurisdiction.[39]

In *Holloway v PADI EMEA Ltd*,[40] the court held that the effect of *Bid Industrial* was to import into South African law the principles set out in the decision of the House of Lords in *Spiliada Maritime Corp v Cansulex Ltd*.[41] In *Holloway*, the applicants were South African *incolae* and the respondent was a foreign *peregrinus*, being a company registered in England. The applicant applied for an order pursuant to rule 53(1)(b) of the High Court Rules that the respondent produce the full record, documents and evidence of an inquiry undertaken by the respondent in England into the applicants' responsibility for a diving fatality which had occurred in Durban at the conclusion of which the respondent had determined that the applicants had been negligent and had expelled them from the PADI organisation. The respondent had no formal presence in South Africa, save for a regional manager resident in Gauteng who was employed by the respondent under an employment contract governed by English law.

In making the order sought by the applicants Victor J, on the issue of jurisdiction, stated:[42] 'The question of appropriateness and convenience was clearly a factor to be taken into account and in this regard the Spiliada decision of the House of Lords that [sic] principle was introduced into our jurisprudence

---

[36] Gorven AJA also gave a judgment, with which Mtapi P and Mbha JA and Mathopo AJA also agreed, which relied on different reasoning.

[37] Ibid para [37] 356F–I.

[38] 2008 (3) SA 355 (SCA) 364G.

[39] To this end, see *Vedanta Resources Holdings Ltd v ZCCM Investment Holdings plc* 2019 JDR 1425 (GJ) (Adams J) paras [30]–[35].

[40] 2020 (5) SA 172 (GJ).

[41] [1987] AC 460 (HL (E)) (Lords Keith, Templeman, Griffiths, McKay and Goff).

[42] At para 14.

in the Strang case'. The judge then quoted from an academic source setting out the *Spiliada* principles and concluded, 'Now this was fully adopted into our law and of course has its origin in the doctrine of the natural forum'.

9.1.1.1 *Conclusions on the doctrine of effectiveness*

It must now be open to doubt whether the doctrine of effectiveness as traditionally articulated continues to underpin the modern South African law of jurisdiction and, consequently, whether it retains any significant role in the future development of that law. This view is taken for the reasons set out below.

A limb of the traditional application of the doctrine comprising founding or confirmation of jurisdiction by arrest has been abolished by the Supreme Court of Appeal.

It is accepted[43] that a party may confer jurisdiction on the South African courts by submission to the jurisdiction regardless of whether that party has assets within the jurisdiction against which any judgment obtained by the plaintiff might be enforced. Indeed, where an *incola* sues a foreign *peregrinus* for a judgment sounding in money and the *peregrinus* has submitted to the jurisdiction, attachment of the defendant's property is neither necessary nor permissible.[44]

In the case of attachment of property to found or confirm jurisdiction, it has been accepted for many years that even property worth only a trifling sum may suffice to found or confirm jurisdiction notwithstanding that the effectiveness of any judgment secured thereby may be only notional.

Pollak on Jurisdiction[45] states:

> 'According to South African law the attachment of property of trifling value is sufficient to found jurisdiction in an action in which a large sum of money is claimed, and it may therefore happen that the South African state cannot make the judgment effective against the defendant.'

The second edition of *Pollak on Jurisdiction*, edited by Pistorius,[46] states:

> 'Accordingly, although it has been said that effectiveness underlies the rule that a South African court will not entertain an action against a peregrinus unless there has been an arrest of his person or an attachment of his property, it is now accepted that there need be no correlation between the value of the property attached and the amount or nature of the judgment sought. It does not matter that the property is of a trifling nature, nor that after its attachment it has lost all or most of its value.'

---

[43] *American Flag plc v Great African T-Shirt Corp CC* 2000 (1) SA 356 (W) 377F; confirmed in *Hay Management Consultants (Pty) Ltd v P3 Management Consultants (Pty) Ltd* 2005 (2) SA 522 (SCA) paras [16]–[24].

[44] Ibid. Submission to the jurisdiction is dealt with in greater detail below.

[45] 1 ed (1937) 28.

[46] 2 ed (1993) 5.

Herbstein and Van Winsen[47] states:

> 'Although the main object of the attachment is to found or confirm jurisdiction, a further object of the attachment is to furnish an asset against which execution can be levied to satisfy the judgment which may be given so that the court's sentence will not be rendered nugatory or, as it has been called, a *brutum fulmen.* It has been suggested that this form of jurisdiction is anomalous and in conflict with the doctrine of effectiveness, since in order to found jurisdiction it is not necessary to attach so much property as will enable the judgment creditor to obtain complete satisfaction of a judgment in his or her favour.'

In *Thermo Radiant Oven Sales (Pty) Ltd v Nelspruit Bakeries (Pty) Ltd*,[48] Ogilvie Thompson JA (with whom Botha and Jansen JJA agreed) stated:[49]

> 'while I agree that, both historically and logically, the procedure of attachment to found or confirm jurisdiction is - as my Brother Potgieter's judgment makes clear - closely correlated with the principle of effectiveness, it appears to me to be indisputable that this latter principle has been considerably eroded by the long-established practice of our courts as exemplified in decisions like *Ex parte Smith*, 1912 C.P.D. 45, and *McKinery Construction Co. Ltd. v. Aktiebolagat Tratalja*, 1922 C.P.D. 24 (and cf. *Central African Airways Corporation v. Vickers Armstrong Ltd.*, 1956 (2) S.A. 492 (F.C.) ...) to permit the attachment, to found or confirm jurisdiction, of property whose value bears no realistic relationship to the amount of the claim advanced in the proposed litigation.'

In the same case, Potgieter JA (with whom Steyn CJ agreed) stated:[50]

> 'the practice in our Courts is to authorize property of trifling value to be attached to found jurisdiction even though the claim far exceeds that value ... What is clear, however, is that, in our practice, the property to be attached must have some saleable value. I can see no reason why the property to be attached must have some value if the purpose be not to provide the plaintiff with something that he can levy execution on if he obtains a judgment in his favour so that the Court's judgment is not completely nugatory. It is true that, if the value of the property attached is less than the amount of the judgment, the Court's order cannot be completely effective. Jurisdiction is however a somewhat abstract notion and I do not think that the word "effectiveness" should be taken too literally. It should, I consider, not be equated with a guarantee that in every case the judgment of the Court would be satisfied completely.'

And Potgieter JA further stated:[51]

> 'It appears to me that the only reason why our Courts still require an attachment to found jurisdiction is to enable the Court to given a judgment which has some effect even though ultimately the judgment may in many cases only be partially satisfied and the "effectiveness" of the judgment fictional to the extent that it is not satisfied.'

---

47 *The Civil Practice of the High Courts of South Africa* 5 ed (2009) 97.

48 1969 (2) SA 295 (A) (Steyn CJ, Ogilvie Thompson, Botha, Jansen and Potgieter JAA).

49 Ibid 300G–301A.

50 Ibid 309D and referring to the same authorities as were referred to by Ogilvie Thompson JA in the passage quoted above.

51 Ibid 310B.

The authorities cited by both Ogilvie Thompson JA and Potgieter JA relating to the value of property to be attached are instructive and are set out below.

In *Ex parte Smith, In re Estate of Main*,[52] the residuary heir to the estate of the deceased applied to the High Court of Griqualand West Local Division for leave to sue by edictal citation the executor of that estate for, inter alia, an account and for leave to attach *ad fundandam jurisdictionem* certain shares which were the property of the estate and which were in the hands of the Master (the shares being the property of the executor as trustee). The executor was domiciled outside the jurisdiction in the Transvaal. At first instance (before Lange J) it was found that the executor had taken steps to sell the shares but could not obtain an offer for them and on that basis the application for edictal citation was refused on the ground that the property which was the subject of the attachment application was 'worthless' and that therefore, 'There was no property to attach.' The Court of Appeal allowed the heir's appeal. Maasdorp JP, giving the judgment of the court, stated that at first instance the judge had found that the shares 'were practically valueless' (the judge had in fact made no such adjectival qualification to the worthlessness of the shares). Maasdorp JP further stated:[53]

> 'As a matter of fact, I think that it does not appear quite clear upon the record that these shares are now, or were, at the time that the application was made, wholly valueless. What the position would be if they were so I am not now prepared to say, because we know that it is a rule of the Court to attach property of the most trifling value for the purpose of establishing jurisdiction. In the authorities we find that even a letter which happened to arrive within the jurisdiction for defendant [sic] could be attached for the purpose of founding jurisdiction. These shares were certainly not regarded as utterly valueless at the time the account was rendered, because the executor stated that he still had the shares in his possession and that they had been offered for sale on the stock Exchange, but no offer had been made for them. He then proceeded to state that the shares would be sold as soon as possible. He therefore then contemplated that he would make another effort to sell them. That attempt seems to have been afterwards made and failed, and the position is that the shares are still there. They may not be of much value, but there is not evidence before the Court that they are now, or at the time of the application were, utterly valueless. Even if they are of mere trifling value their attachment would be sufficient to found jurisdiction.'

From the findings of the court at first instance and from the statements made in the Court of Appeal regarding the executor's attempts to dispose of the shares, it seems that there was no market for the shares and that, on the basis that markets fix prices and if there is no market there is no price, the shares were indeed valueless. The Court of Appeal appears to have been prepared to go so far as to find that the physical manifestation of the shares themselves, the certificates (one

[52] 1912 CPD 45 (Maasdorp JP and Searle and Fawkes JJ).

[53] Ibid 49.

assumes) was sufficient to found the jurisdiction of the court ('even a letter which happened to arrive within the jurisdiction for [a] defendant could be attached for the purpose of founding jurisdiction': although no authority was cited for this proposition). *Ex parte Smith* is authority not merely for the proposition that it is sufficient that an asset of 'trifling value' be attached to found the jurisdiction, but also it would seem to be authority for the proposition that an asset as trivial as a mere piece of paper is an asset capable of attachment to found the jurisdiction.

In *McKinery Construction Co Ltd v Aktiebolagat Tratalja*,[54] a *peregrinus* defendant was sued by an *incola* plaintiff for damages in the sum of approximately £3,000. The defendant entered an appearance and made a claim in reconvention in the sum of approximately £4,000. The plaintiff applied for security for the amount and the costs of its claim against the defendant. Although the plaintiff's application itself did not concern an attachment to found or confirm the jurisdiction, on the facts it appears that the plaintiff had, prior to commencing proceedings, applied for and been granted an attachment of certain timber owned by the defendant. That order was subsequently varied on the application of a preferential creditor of the defendant to the effect that a sum of only £10 remained attached to found the jurisdiction. In the course of his judgment granting the plaintiff security for both the amount of his claim and the costs of it, Van Zyl J observed:[55] 'It, however, often happens that the property attached *ad fundandam jurisdictionem* is wholly inadequate to satisfy the amount of the plaintiff's claim and costs.' In the absence of security for the plaintiff's claim being granted:

> 'Any judgment obtained by the plaintiff against the defendant might prove an empty letter, because owing to the defendant company being outside the jurisdiction of the Court there might not be anything beyond the £10 under attachment out of which the amount of the judgment and costs could be satisfied.'

The judge also described[56] the value of the property attached in the case as 'negligible' (amounting to 0.33% of the plaintiff's claim).

In *Central African Airways Corp v Vickers-Armstrong Ltd*,[57] the High Court of Southern Rhodesia on the application of the appellant/plaintiff refused to attach a debt owed by the appellant to the respondent/defendant in order to found the jurisdiction for the purposes of an action which the plaintiff proposed to bring against the defendant for damages arising out of the loss over Tanganyika of an aircraft bought from the defendant by the plaintiff and the deaths of its passengers and crew, which claims had been assigned to the plaintiff. The plaintiff was an *incola* of Southern Rhodesia and the defendant was a *peregrinus* of that jurisdiction.

---

[54] 1922 CPD 24.

[55] Ibid 27.

[56] Ibid.

[57] 1956 (2) SA 492 (Federal Supreme Court, Salisbury; Tredgold CJ and Lewey and Clayden FJJ).

It appears from the report that the debt owed by the plaintiff to the defendant which the plaintiff sought to attach was in the sum of approximately £400 and the total claim advanced by the plaintiff was in the sum of approximately £200,000. Allowing the appeal, Clayden FJ, giving the judgment of the court, stated:[58]

> 'It is settled Roman Dutch law that the Court, at the instance of an incola, will attach property of a *peregrinus* if the property is in its area of jurisdiction in order to found jurisdiction in the Court in a claim for money by the *incola* against the *peregrinus*, even if there is no other ground to exercise jurisdiction.'

Thus, the jurisdiction of the court over the defendant was founded by the attachment of a debt owed by the plaintiff to the defendant being the equivalent of 0.2% of the appellant's claim.

It is not clear what useful purpose is served by the continued adherence to a doctrine of effectiveness (from which personal arrest is now excluded) which in its application to claims against a foreign *peregrinus* requires the attachment of property to found or confirm the jurisdiction so as 'to enable the Court to give a judgment which has some effect'[59] and at the same time permits such attachment to be of property which may be essentially worthless such that the judgment of the court will be of no effect.

This is *a fortiori* the case when one considers that it is tolerably clear from the decision in *Bid Industrial* that if the foreign *peregrinus* has no property available for attachment within the jurisdiction, the plaintiff may make use of the presence basis of jurisdiction laid down in that case. This much appears from the judgment of Howie P, who stated:[60]

> 'if attachment is not possible because the defendant has no property here, there are alternative possibilities. Before considering their legal competence it is important to note that the [defendants] did not argue that if arrest were unconstitutional and attachment not possible, no jurisdiction could be established. Why that is important is because if arrest were held unconstitutional and it were further to be held that in this case, and cases like it, jurisdiction can competently be established without arrest, the necessary corollary would be that it can also be established without attachment despite the need for attachment not having been in issue and despite attachment, generally, not being unconstitutional.'

An extension of the personal service within the jurisdiction basis of jurisdiction would accord with Howie P's dictum that 'the responsibility for achieving effectiveness, absent attachment, is essentially that of the parties, and more especially the plaintiff'[61] because it would give the plaintiff the choice whether

---

[58] Ibid 492.

[59] *Thermo Radiant Oven Sales (Pty) Ltd v Nelspruit Bakeries (Pty) Ltd* 1969 (2) SA 295 (A) *per* Potgieter JA at 310B.

[60] *Bid Industrial Holdings (Pty) Ltd v Strang* 2008 (3) SA 355 (SCA) para [47].

[61] Ibid para [55].

to go to the expense of attaching property which may not be of sufficient value to justify that expense.

It would also recognise the procedural realities of attachment where it is the plaintiff who must make an application for attachment of the property of the *peregrinus* defendant, generally prior to the issuing of the summons instituting the claim against the *peregrinus*.[62] No investigation or enquiry is undertaken by the court as to whether the *peregrinus* defendant has or has not attachable assets within the jurisdiction nor is any statement by the plaintiff to that effect required as a matter of procedural law. Accordingly, a plaintiff not minded to make an application to attach low-value assets present within the jurisdiction need not do so and may proceed to establish the court's jurisdiction by way of personal service in accordance with the procedure contemplated in Howie P's judgment in *Bid Industrial*,[63] regardless of whether there are assets within the jurisdiction.

Further, as stated by Forsyth:[64]

> 'Suppose two defendants, both peregrines and both present within the jurisdiction, and a single plaintiff, an *incola*. The one defendant has no property within the jurisdiction that may be attached. Since this defendant is present (and like all defendants is no longer subject to arrest) the question will be whether there is "adequate connection". But the other defendant has property that may be attached (with the plaintiff showing a *prima facie* case etc) in order for jurisdiction to be established. It is difficult to see why these two cases should be distinguished so starkly. Surely if such a case were to arise the court might be tempted to extend the "presence approach" to the doctrine of attachment?'

Forsyth proceeds[65] to argue that adoption of the presence approach would require the development of a system of principles governing the adequacy of the connection between the dispute and South Africa (as contemplated by Howie P in *Bid Industrial*: paragraphs 55 and 56) and also for governing those cases where service outside the jurisdiction is appropriate.[66] Forsyth concludes:[67]

> 'The adoption of an English-style law of jurisdiction where presence of the defendant is tempered by a sophisticated doctrine of *forum non conveniens* would have profound consequences on the law of jurisdiction in Southern Africa (for one may anticipate that the other Roman-Dutch jurisdiction would follow suit). It would on balance assist in the emergence of the South African courts as a natural venue for international commercial litigation.'

---

62 Herbstein and Van Winsen *The Civil Practice of the High Courts of South Africa* 5 ed (2009) 120–2.

63 *Bid Industrial Holdings (Pty) Ltd v Strang* 2008 (3) SA 355 (SCA) para [47].

64 *Private International Law* 5 ed (2012) 204.

65 Ibid 204–5.

66 See *Holloway v PADI EMEA Ltd* 2020 (5) SA 172 (GJ), where the judge held that the principles of *forum non conveniens* had been imported into South African law by the decision in *Bid Industrial*.

67 Ibid 205.

9.1.1.2 Forum non conveniens

When referencing the English law of *forum non conveniens* it may be helpful to summarise the principles applicable. These were authoritatively laid down by the House of Lords in *Spiliada Maritime Corp v Cansulex Ltd*.[68] There, a Liberian-owned and flagged vessel had been chartered to carry a cargo of sulphur from Vancouver to Indian ports. The shipowner contended that the cargo had been loaded when wet and that the vessel had suffered damage by corrosion as a result. The shipowner obtained leave *ex parte* to serve proceedings on the shippers outside the jurisdiction in Vancouver on the basis that the action was one to recover damages for breach of a contract governed by English law.[69] The defendant applied for the order to be set aside. The House of Lords allowed the shipowner's appeal from the decision of the Court of Appeal, which had itself allowed the defendant's appeal from the judge at first instance. Lord Goff gave the lead opinion of the House of Lords (Lord Templeman gave a brief opinion and concurred; the other Lords concurred in Lord Goff's opinion).

Lord Goff considered first the position where the jurisdiction of the English court had been established by the plaintiff as of right (that is, where the plaintiff had effected personal service on the defendant within the jurisdiction) and the court was called upon to consider an application by the defendant to stay the proceedings:[70]

> 'In my opinion, having regard to the authorities (including in particular the Scottish authorities), the law can at present be summarised as follows.
>
> *(a)* The basic principle is that a stay will only be granted on the ground of forum non conveniens where the court is satisfied that there is some other available forum, having competent jurisdiction, which is the appropriate forum for the trial of the action, i.e. in which the case may be tried more suitably for the interests of all the parties and the ends of justice.
>
> *(b)* As Lord Kinnear's formulation of the principle indicates, in general the burden of proof rests on the defendant to persuade the court to exercise its discretion to grant a stay (see, e.g., the *Société du Gaz* case, 1926 S.C.(H.L.) 13, 21, *per* Lord Sumner; and Anton, *Private International Law* (1967) p. 150). It is however of importance to remember that each party will seek to establish the existence of certain matters which will assist him in persuading the court to exercise its discretion in his favour, and that in respect of any such matter the evidential burden will rest on the party who asserts its existence. Furthermore, if the court is satisfied that there is another

[68] [1987] AC 460 (HL (E)) (Lords Keith, Templeman, Griffiths, Mackay and Goff).

[69] One of the provisions of the Rules of the Supreme Court then in force ('gateways') pursuant to which the court could grant leave to serve out of the jurisdiction (RSC O 11, r 1(1)(f)(iii); now CPR Pt 6.37 and 6BPD.3.1(6)). For a brief summary of the history of the English court's power to authorise service out of the jurisdiction see *Lenders v Anderson* (1883) 12 QBD 50, *per* Huddleston B at 56–7.

[70] [1987] AC 460 (HL (E)) 476B–478E.

available forum which is prima facie the appropriate forum for the trial of the action, the burden will then shift to the plaintiff to show that there are special circumstances by reason of which justice requires that the trial should nevertheless take place in this country (see (f), below).

(c) The question being whether there is some other forum which is the appropriate forum for the trial of the action, it is pertinent to ask whether the fact that the plaintiff has, ex hypothesi, founded jurisdiction as of right in accordance with the law of this country, of itself gives the plaintiff an advantage in the sense that the English court will not lightly disturb jurisdiction so established ... In my opinion, the burden resting on the defendant is not just to show that England is not the natural or appropriate forum for the trial, but to establish that there is another available forum which is clearly or distinctly more appropriate than the English forum. In this way, proper regard is paid to the fact that jurisdiction has been founded in England as of right (see *MacShannon's* case [1978] A.C. 795, *per* Lord Salmon); and there is the further advantage that, on a subject where comity is of importance, it appears that there will be a broad consensus among major common law jurisdictions ...

(d) Since the question is whether there exists some other forum which is clearly more appropriate for the trial of the action, the court will look first to see what factors there are which point in the direction of another forum ... I respectfully consider that it may be more desirable, now that the English and Scottish principles are regarded as being the same, to adopt the expression used by my noble and learned friend, Lord Keith of Kinkel, in *The Abidin Daver* [1984] A.C. 398, 415, when he referred to the 'natural forum' as being "that with which the action had the most real and substantial connection." So it is for connecting factors in this sense that the court must first look; and these will include not only factors affecting convenience or expense (such as availability of witnesses), but also other factors such as the law governing the relevant transaction (as to which see *Credit Chimique v. James Scott Engineering Group Ltd.*, 1982 S.L.T. 131), and the places where the parties respectively reside or carry on business.

(e) If the court concludes at that stage that there is no other available forum which is clearly more appropriate for the trial of the action, it will ordinarily refuse a stay; see, e.g., the decision of the Court of Appeal in *European Asian Bank A.G. v. Punjab and Sind Bank* [1982] 2 Lloyd's Rep. 356. It is difficult to imagine circumstances where, in such a case, a stay may be granted.

(f) If however the court concludes at that stage that there is some other available forum which prima facie is clearly more appropriate for the trial of the action, it will ordinarily grant a stay unless there are circumstances by reason of which justice requires that a stay should nevertheless not be granted. In this inquiry, the court will consider all the circumstances of the case, including circumstances which go beyond those taken into account when considering connecting factors with other jurisdictions. One such factor can be the fact, if established objectively by cogent evidence, that the plaintiff will not obtain justice in the foreign jurisdiction; see the *The Abidin Daver* [1984] A.C. 398, 411, *per* Lord Diplock, a passage which now makes plain that, on this inquiry, the burden of proof shifts to the plaintiff. How far other advantages to the plaintiff in proceeding in this country may be relevant in this connection, I shall have to consider at a later stage.'

Lord Goff then considered the position where the principle is applied in cases where the court has granted leave to serve outside the jurisdiction and the defendant is seeking to set aside that grant of leave:[71]

> 'It seems to me inevitable that the question in both groups of cases must be, at bottom, that expressed by Lord Kinnear in *Sim v. Robinow*, 19 R. 665, 668, viz. to identify the forum in which the case can be suitably tried for the interests of all the parties and for the ends of justice.'

And:[72]

> 'The effect is, not merely that the burden of proof rests on the plaintiff to persuade the court that England is the appropriate forum for the trial of the action, but that he has to show that this is clearly so. In other words, the burden is, quite simply, the obverse of that applicable where a stay is sought of proceedings started in this country as of right.'

The leading English texts in this area have summarised the *Spiliada* test in the following ways. In *Dicey, Morris and Collins on the Conflict of Laws*,[73] it is stated:

> '(2) Subject to the provisions of Council Regulation (EC) 44/2001 and the Lugano Convention on jurisdiction and the enforcement of judgments in civil and commercial matters ... an English court has power to order a stay of proceedings on the basis that England is an inappropriate forum (*forum non conveniens*) if:
>
> *(a)* the defendant shows there to be another court with competent jurisdiction which is clearly or distinctly more appropriate than England for the trial of the action, and
>
> *(b)* it is not unjust that the claimant be deprived of the right to trial in England.
>
> (3) In considering whether to assume jurisdiction in any of the cases mentioned in Rule 34 (service out of the jurisdiction with the permission of the court) [the cases mentioned in CPR 6BPD.3.1(6)] the court will generally require the claimant to show England to be the most appropriate forum for the trial of the claim.'

By way of a further explanatory note, Briggs[74] states:

> **'4.407 ii. First limb of the *Spiliada* enquiry**
>
> The first limb of the *Spiliada* enquiry has three parts: it requires the defendant to demonstrate that there is another court, which has or will accept that it has jurisdiction over the defendant in relation to the claim, and that this court is clearly more appropriate than England for the trial of the action ...
>
> **4.409 iii. Second limb of the *Spiliada* enquiry**
>
> If the defendant is able to show that the *forum conveniens* is elsewhere, it will be presumed that the interests of justice will favour a stay of the English proceedings. This presumption

---

71 Ibid 480G.

72 Ibid 481D.

73 15 ed (2012) vol 1, r 38, p 533.

74 *Private International Law in English Courts* (2014) 336–40.

may be rebutted by the claimant if he is able to satisfy the court that, under the second limb of the test, it would be so unjust to leave him to his remedies before that foreign court that the stay should not be ordered at all ...

4.413 iv. Conclusion of the *Spiliada* enquiry

In the end, the two limbs of the exercise required by the *Spiliada* enquiry are only signposts to what the interests of justice require. They are not boundary marks. There will be cases, even if they are few in number, in which the court should conclude that even though the two limbs of the test suggest that there should or should not be a stay of proceedings, the interests of justice, in the individual case, point to the opposite conclusion ... The proper question to ask is not where the natural forum for the claim is in an abstract sense, but whether the interests of justice favour telling his particular claimant that he will have to go and pursue his claim against this particular defendant in another court. It is obviously proper that the court retain this overall discretion, for the *Spiliada* test has to apply to large commercial disputes, as well as those advanced by small claimants against more powerful corporations, as well as those claimants who would use their money and power to bully those who advance the cause of freedom of speech. A test which is applicable to all such cases must, if it is to be successful, offer the court an overall discretion which is capable of responding to the interests of justice in the individual case. *Spiliada* was designed to do just that, and it still does it.'

9.1.1.3 *Constitutional law implications for the attachment of property*

Further, there may be constitutional law implications for the attachment of property.[75] In *Bid Industrial*, the Court of Appeal was not called upon to decide any question relating to the constitutionality of attachment of property. Howie P alluded to the point stating:[76] 'Attachment ordinarily involves no infringement of constitutional rights (absent, for example, seizure of the means by which the defendant's livelihood is earned). But, more importantly, the property attached will, unless entirely worthless, obviously provide some measure of security or some prospect of successful execution.'

As Forsyth[77] has observed:

'The SCA is surely right that attachment does not raise the acute constitutional issues that arrest does. But this does not mean that attachment will be upheld in all cases. Section 14 of the Constitution outlaws "the seizure of private possessions" and the question will often be whether s. 36(1) saves any apparent breach. As noted above attachment is instituted in order to benefit *incolae* and ensuring that peregrines pay their debts. This purpose smacks of discrimination against peregrines and is arguably not "justifiable in an open and democratic society based on freedom and equality". On the other hand, ensuring that any judgment is effective (and that property is preserved until trial) seems both reasonable and democratically justifiable.'

---

[75] Attachment of property and the jurisdictional significance thereof is dealt with in more detail below.

[76] *Bid Industrial Holdings (Pty) Ltd v Strang* 2008 (3) SA 355 (SCA) para [38].

[77] *Private International Law* 5 ed (2012) 197–8.

In a footnote to this passage Forsyth refers to the decision of the Court of Justice of the European Union (as it is now called) in *Mund & Fester v Hatrex International Transport*,[78] on the anti-discrimination provisions of the Treaty of Rome (25 March 1957; 'the EC Treaty'; article 7). This decision is referred to further below together with a decision of the English Court of Appeal on the prohibition of discrimination provisions of the European Convention for the Protection of Human Rights and Fundamental Freedoms ('the ECHR'; the relevant article being article 14). First, however, it is convenient to set out the three anti-discrimination provisions under discussion.

Section 9 of the Constitution[79] provides:

> '(1) Everyone is equal before the law and has the right to equal protection and benefit of the law.
>
> (2) Equality includes the full and equal enjoyment of all rights and freedoms ...
>
> (3) The state [including the courts: section 8(1)] may not unfairly discriminate directly or indirectly against anyone on one or more grounds, including race, gender, sex, pregnancy, marital status, ethnic or social origin, colour, sexual orientation, age, disability, religion, conscience, belief, culture, language and birth.
>
> (4) ...
>
> (5) ...'.

The EC Treaty, article 7 provided (the provision is now article 6 of the updated Treaty):[80] 'Within the scope of this Treaty, and without prejudice to any special provisions contained therein, any discrimination on grounds of nationality shall be prohibited.' The ECHR, article 14 provides: 'The enjoyment of the rights and freedoms set forth in this Convention shall be secured without discrimination on any ground such as sex, race, colour, language, religion, political or other opinion, national or social origin, association with a national minority, property, birth or other status.' Plainly differences exist between the wordings of these prohibitions on discrimination. Section 9(3) of the Constitution is perhaps more proximate to article 14 of the ECHR than to article 7 of the EC Treaty. Nonetheless, the purpose of these provisions is to combat discrimination on various grounds.[81]

---

[78] (1994) C-398/92, [1993] ECR 1–467.

[79] Constitution of the Republic of South Africa, 1996.

[80] C326/13. Article 6(3) of the Treaty on the European Union provides: 'Fundamental rights, as guaranteed by the European Convention for the Protection of Human Rights and Fundamental Freedoms and as they result from the constitutional traditions common to the Member States, shall constitute general principles of the Union's law.'

[81] In *Nasser v United Bank of Kuwait* [2002] 1 WLR 1868 (CA), Mance LJ stated of arts 7 and 14 (para [55]), 'Although the precise phraseology of article 14 of the Convention is different to that of article 6 [7] of the Treaty (which speaks simply of "nationality"), I do not think that the two articles can sensibly be distinguished as regards the protection that they may afford in respect of orders against foreign residents for

In *Mund & Fester v Hatrex International Transport*, the defendant company (registered in the Netherlands) had transported goods from Turkey to Germany where they were discovered to be damaged. Paragraph 917(1) of the German Code of Civil Procedure provided: 'An order for the seizure of assets shall be made when it is feared that enforcement of the judgment would otherwise be made impossible or substantially more difficult' in the absence of such an order. Paragraph 917(2) provided: 'The fact that judgment is to be enforced abroad shall be considered sufficient grounds for a seizure order.' The plaintiff obtained an order seizing the defendant's truck. The European Court of Justice found that the provisions of paragraph 917 were indirectly discriminatory (because they applied to German nationals too, albeit rarely) and were not objectively justified as regards the nationals of member states.

In *Nasser v United Bank of Kuwait*,[82] the English Court of Appeal considered the question whether the operation of the English Civil Procedure Rules ('the CPR') in relation to the provision of security for costs by a non-resident plaintiff to the defendant was in breach of the obligations of the court pursuant to the Human Rights Act 1998 to act compatibly with the ECHR. The appeal concerned a resident of the United States (the Court of Appeal having previously, in *Fitzgerald v Williams*,[83] held that orders for security for costs could not be made against persons domiciled and resident in another EU member state). The CPR prohibited the making of an order for security for costs against persons domiciled and resident in another EU member state and thus raised a potential issue of discrimination.[84] The court considered the application of article 14 of the ECHR and held:[85]

> 'It would be both discriminatory and unjustifiable if the mere fact of residence outside any Brussels/Lugano member state could justify the exercise of discretion to make orders for security for costs with the purpose or effect of protecting defendants ... against risks to which they would equally be subject, and in relation to which they would have no protection, if the claim ... were being brought by a resident of a Brussels or Lugano state.'

Thus *Mund & Fester v Hatrex International Transport* and *Nasser v United Bank of Kuwait* provide two examples of instances where courts have treated a requirement that one category of person is liable to give security or have their property seized, whereas another category of person is not so liable, as discriminatory when based on the nationality or residence of the first category.

---

security for costs.' It might be thought the same approach recommends itself to the application of s 9(3) of the Constitution to the property of foreign *peregrini*.

[82] [2001] EWCA Civ 556, [2002] 1 WLR 1868 (Mance and Simon Brown LJJ).

[83] [1996] QB 657 (Sir Thomas Bingham MR; Waite and Otton LJJ).

[84] *Nasser v United Bank of Kuwait* [2002] 1 WLR 1868, *per* Mance LJ (with whom Simon Brown LJ agreed) para [51].

[85] Ibid para [58].

It cannot be ruled out that a South African court would take a different view of the common law of attachment of the property of a foreign *peregrinus* to found or confirm jurisdiction (in particular where this is prohibited in respect of a domestic *peregrinus*: section 28 of the Superior Courts Act 2013).

It is now recognised by statute that the distribution of jurisdiction between the various divisions of the High Court within South Africa can be determined using notions of convenience: section 27(1)(b) of the Superior Courts Act 2013.[86]

9.1.2 Commencing proceedings where the defendant is within the jurisdiction

The Uniform Rules of Court[87] regulate the conduct of proceedings in the High Court and its Divisions ('the High Court Rules').

The issuing of court documents in the High Court is effected by fixing revenue stamps in the appropriate sum to the top right-hand corner of the relevant court document and sending it to the court having jurisdiction over the matter. The Registrar's office of the relevant Division of the High Court to which the document is sent then date stamps and cancels the revenue stamps and signs the document. In the case of originating process a case number is allocated and a court file opened.[88]

Service of 'any process' issued out of the High Court is regulated by rule 4 of the High Court Rules and is, subject to a number of exceptions, effected by way of personal service[89] through the person of the sheriff.[90] Service should be undertaken as near as possible between the hours of 07:00 and 19:00 and is impermissible on Sundays save with the leave of the court. The sheriff must serve process, inter alia: by delivering a copy to the person to be served personally; by leaving a copy at the place of residence or business of the person with the person apparently in charge of the premises at the time of delivery being a person apparently not less than 16 years of age; by delivering a copy at the place of employment of the person to some person apparently not less than 16 years of age and apparently in authority over him; in the case of a company, by delivering a copy to a responsible employee at its registered office or principal place of

[86] Act 10 of 2013.

[87] Made by the Chief Justice with the approval of the State President pursuant to s 43(2)(a) of the Supreme Court Act 1959 (Act 59 of 1959) with effect from 15 January 1965 and amended on various dates up to 8 May 2009 (with effect from 15 June 2009).

[88] Peté et al *Civil Procedure* 2 ed (2011).

[89] Personal service is the usual method of service and other methods should be used only where the defendant is elusive or untraceable: *O'Donoghue v Human* 1969 (4) SA 35 (E).

[90] High Court Rules, r 4(1)(a). Sections 5 and 6 of the Sheriffs Act 1986 provide that acting sheriffs and deputy-sheriffs may be appointed to assist the sheriff.

business within the court's jurisdiction; by delivering a copy to any authorised agent; in the case of a partnership, firm or voluntary association, by leaving a copy at the place of business of such partnership, firm or voluntary association with the person apparently in charge of the premises at the time of delivery being a person apparently not less than 16 years of age.

Service is proved by the return of service of the sheriff or where service was not effected by the sheriff, by an affidavit of the person who effected service.[91]

If any of these means of personal service are not possible the court may, on the application of the person seeking service, give directions.[92]

9.1.3 Commencing proceedings where the defendant is outside the jurisdiction

Rule 4(3) makes provision for service of process outside South Africa. Service may be effected by any person who is authorised under the law of such country to serve process or documents. The person serving the relevant documents must be certified as authorised under the law of the relevant country by, inter alios, the head of any South African diplomatic or consular mission.[93]

Documents may also be served by certain South African diplomatic personnel or certain persons employed by a South African mission if local law permits that person to serve documents or if there is no law prohibiting such service and the local authorities have not interposed any objection to it.[94]

Documents for service outside South Africa must be accompanied by a sworn translation[95] and must be delivered to the registrar together with the relevant revenue stamps, after the defacement of which the registrar delivers the documents to the Director-General of Foreign Affairs.[96]

Service of documents outside South Africa is proved by a certificate of the person effecting service containing the information set out in rule 4(7)(a) or (b) as applicable.

Service of civil process received from a state, territory or court outside South Africa is transmitted to the registrar of the local court of the person to be served and the registrar must give to the sheriff two copies of such process to be served

---

[91] High Court Rules, r 4(6).

[92] High Court Rules, r 4(2).

[93] High Court Rules, r 4(3)(a). Service in countries specified in r 4(4) may be effected by an attorney, solicitor, notary public or other legal practitioner in the particular country. These countries are: Australia, Botswana, Finland, France, Hong Kong, Lesotho, Malawi, New Zealand, Spain, Swaziland, the UK and Zimbabwe.

[94] High Court Rules, r 4(3)(b).

[95] High Court Rules, r 4(5)(a).

[96] High Court Rules, r 4(5)(b) and (c).

and two copies of a translation of such process. Service is then effected by delivering a copy of the process and of the translation to the person to be served in accordance with rule 4.

Rule 5 concerns edictal citation and provides that no process or document whereby proceedings are instituted shall be served outside South Africa save by leave of the court.[97] Leave is obtained by application to the court setting out the nature and extent of the claim, the grounds on which it is based and on which the court is said to have jurisdiction over the claim and the manner of service outside South Africa which the court is asked to authorise. The court may order such method of service as it sees fit and shall order the time within which notice of intention to defend is to be given by the person to be served.[98] A person seeking leave to serve outside South Africa a document other than one by which proceedings are instituted may make an application as above or request leave at any hearing at which the court is dealing with the matter (in which case no papers need to be filed and the court may act on such information as is given from the bar).[99]

Proceedings in the High Court may be commenced by action (meaning a proceeding commenced by summons or by writ) or by application.

9.1.3.1 Incolae *and* peregrini

South African law distinguishes between *incolae* and *peregrini.* Herbstein and Van Winsen[100] states:

> '(1) an *incola* is a person who is either domiciled (in the technical sense) or resident within the area of the jurisdiction of the court, provided that the residence is of some permanent or settled nature; and (2) a *peregrinus* is a person who is neither domiciled nor resident ... within the area of the jurisdiction of the court.'

An *incola* is such only in respect of the territorial area over which the court exercises jurisdiction and not in respect of the Republic of South Africa as a whole. Thus the terminology, local and foreign *peregrini*, to denote a *peregrinus* of a particular court in South Africa who is at the same time an *incola* of the Republic on the one hand and a person who is not an *incola* of the Republic on the other.[101]

---

[97] High Court Rules, r 5(1).

[98] High Court Rules, r 5(2).

[99] High Court Rules, r 5(3).

[100] *The Civil Practice of the High Courts of South Africa* 5 ed (2009) 69.

[101] The concepts of domicile and residence are explored in greater depth below, under the heading '*Ratio domicilii (actor sequitur forum rei)*'.

9.1.3.2 *The bases for jurisdiction*

9.1.3.2.1 Personal service combined with adequate jurisdictional connecting factors

This basis for the assumption of jurisdiction is, of course, that set out by the Supreme Court of Appeal in *Bid Industrial*:

> 'A South African High Court will have jurisdiction if the summons is served on the defendant while in South Africa and there is sufficient connection between the suit and the area of jurisdiction of the court concerned so that disposal of the case by that court is appropriate and convenient.'[102]

In addition to the Supreme Court of Appeal decisions in which *Bid Industrial* has been considered, there are a number of first instance decisions which merit reference.

In *Multi-Links Telecommunications Ltd v Africa Prepaid Services Nigeria Ltd*,[103] the court considered, inter alia, an application by a defendant Nigerian company ('APSN') for a stay on jurisdictional grounds of the proceedings brought against it by the plaintiffs, Telkom SA ('Telkom') and Multi-links ('MLT'). The former was an *incola* of the court and the latter a foreign *peregrinus*. The remaining defendants were all *incolae* of South Africa. The plaintiffs had attempted to attach property belonging to APSN but it was accepted that no valid attachment had been effected. Fabricius J stated:[104] 'In the absence of submission, both Telkom (an incola) and MLT (a foreign peregrinus) require, as a general rule, such attachment to found or confirm this court's jurisdiction, regardless of any connection between the cause and the territorial jurisdiction of this court.'

The judge summarised the decision in *Bid Industrial* and proceeded to refer to two previous cases, both decided after *Bid Industrial*. The first of these was *Zokufa v Compuscan (Credit Bureau)*[105] which concerned an application for interim relief where the plaintiff was an *incola* of the court and the defendant a local *peregrinus*. Fabricius J summarised[106] the findings of the court in *Zokufa* as being:

> 'If the requirements for the grant of an interdict were satisfied by facts within the territorial jurisdiction of the high court, the high court would possess jurisdiction to hear the matter ... On the basis of that decision it assumed jurisdiction, and it seems that this was ultimately done because there was a sufficient connection between the suit and the area of jurisdiction of the court concerned, so that disposal of the case for that court was appropriate and convenient.'

---

[102] Howie P at para [59].

[103] 2014 (3) SA 265 (GP) (Fabricius J).

[104] Ibid para [8], citing Harms JA in *Tsung v Industrial Development Corp of SA Ltd* 2006 (4) SA 177 (SCA) where he stated (para 3): '[I]f the defendant is a *peregrinus* ... an attachment or arrest is essential for the exercise of jurisdiction: A recognised *ratio jurisdictionis* by itself will not do.'

[105] 2011 (1) SA 272 (ECM).

[106] 2014 (3) SA 265 (GP) para [13].

The second was *Fleet Africa (Pty) Ltd v Cargill Cotton Genus Ltd*,[107] where the plaintiff brought proceedings against the defendant for breach of a contract of carriage. The plaintiff was an *incola* of the Gauteng High Court and the defendant a foreign *peregrinus* with its registered office in Zambia. The court there found that the contract was concluded in Zambia and its (alleged) breach occurred there also. It was held that notwithstanding that the defendant was a foreign *peregrinus* it had a substantial place of business in Johannesburg and its African operations were at all material times managed from South Africa. For these reasons the defendant resided, for the purposes of section 19(1) of the Supreme Court Act 1959 (now section 21(1) of the Superior Courts Act 2013), within the area of jurisdiction of the South Gauteng local division. Fabricius J stated[108] that the judge in *Fleet Africa*, Willis J, agreed with the view of Kuny AJ in *Tsichlas v Touch Media (Pty) Ltd*,[109] that

> 'when it came to jurisdiction, the test was really whether the defendant had a sufficient "presence" to justify the court having jurisdiction. Willis J was of the view that the *Strang* decision had adopted a similar view, and said that it seemed clear to him that the Supreme Court of Appeal had, since that decision, adopted a more relaxed view as to jurisdiction, and that considerations of appropriateness and convenience had to prevail.'

In the *Multi-Links* case, Fabricius J proceeded[110] to dismiss APSN's application for a stay or dismissal on the grounds of jurisdiction on the basis that the plaintiffs had raised a triable issue on the facts and that the question of jurisdiction should finally be decided by the trial court. However, in doing so the judge held:[111]

> 'In the context of the interpretation of s 19(1) of the Supreme Court Act, and the meaning of "causes arising", it seems to me that one must determine the forum most suitable for the ends of justice, and because [sic] pursuit of the litigation in that forum is most likely to secure those ends. The appropriate or natural forum is that with which the action has the most real and substantial connection. In that context then, the court would look to all the connecting factors, including all the background facts, convenience, experts, the law governing the relevant transaction or action, the place where the parties reside or carry on business, etc.'

It would seem therefore that the *Bid Industrial* case has been applied at first instance as a discrete basis for the assumption of jurisdiction by the High Court.

---

107 [2010] JOL 26331 (GSJ) (Willis J).
108 2014 (3) SA 265 (GP) para [16].
109 2004 (2) SA 112 (W).
110 2014 (3) SA 265 (GP) para [23].
111 Ibid.

9.1.3.2.2 The jurisdictional significance of attachment

By way of introduction and overview, where a plaintiff intends to bring proceedings against a *peregrinus*[112] it is a requirement in order to render the *peregrinus* amenable to the jurisdiction that the plaintiff attaches some property[113] owned by that *peregrinus*. Without such an attachment, the court will not assume jurisdiction over the *peregrinus* (subject to what has been set out above in relation to the *Bid Industrial* decision).

The rationale[114] for the requirement that an attachment be obtained prior to the court assuming jurisdiction over a *peregrinus* was originally:

> 'to avoid the costs which citizens would have to incur if they had to pursue the foreigner to the court of his domicile and was conceived primarily for the benefit of the *incola* ... Originally the purpose of the arrest or attachment was a kind of compulsion to which the foreigner was subjected so that he could be induced to pay his creditor rather than endure the worry of arrest or the retention of his property.'[115]

Subsequently, the requirement has been reinterpreted as being a facet of the doctrine of effectiveness such that an attachment of property serves to ensure that the court's judgment will not be entirely without effect.[116]

Attachment of property *ad fundandam* or *ad confirmandam jurisdictionem* provides security for the plaintiff's claim against the respondent/defendant: 'Once the asset has been attached, the asset is under the control of the sheriff, and nothing can be done to affect the rights of the plaintiff to the property.'[117]

If a debt is attached, settlement of that debt should be made to the sheriff and not to the creditor whose debt has been attached.[118]

Where property has been attached, the defendant is entitled to have the property released on the provision of security sufficient for the plaintiff's claim (being the amount claimed plus interest and costs).[119]

---

[112] Here, as above, the term foreign *peregrinus* is used to refer to a person who is neither resident nor domiciled in the Republic of South Africa. A person who is resident or domiciled within South Africa but not within the area of jurisdiction of the court seised of the proceedings is referred to here as a local *peregrinus*. A person who is resident or domiciled within the area of jurisdiction of the court seised of the proceedings is referred to here as an *incola*.

[113] Attachments of the person being no longer lawful pursuant to the decision of the Supreme Court of Appeal in *Bid Industrial Holdings (Pty) Ltd v Strang* 2008 (3) SA 355 (SCA).

[114] See, for example, Herbstein and Van Winsen *The Civil Practice of the High Courts of South Africa* 5 ed (2009) 97–8.

[115] *Thermo Radiant Oven Sales (Pty) Ltd v Nelspruit Bakeries (Pty) Ltd* 1969 (2) SA 295 (A), *per* Potgieter JA at 305G–H.

[116] As Potgieter JA acknowledged in *Thermo Radiant Oven Sales (Pty) Ltd v Nelspruit Bakeries (Pty) Ltd* 1969 (2) SA 295 (A) 309D–H, the practice in the Republic of South Africa is to authorise property of trifling value to be attached to found the jurisdiction notwithstanding that the claim far exceeds that value. (See generally the discussion on the doctrine of effectiveness above.)

[117] Pistorius *Pollak on Jurisdiction* 2 ed (1993) 85.

[118] Ibid.

[119] Ibid 85–6.

The provision of security is not limited to the value of the goods attached[120] and may be such sum as is a fair and reasonable amount in the circumstances of the case, taking into account the nature of the claim and counterclaim, if any.[121]

Once the attachment is executed, the property attached is in the custody of the court and under Roman-Dutch law; the court's officer is liable for negligence if he does not take proper care of the property.[122]

9.1.3.2.2.1 *The property to be attached must be within the Republic of South Africa*

It has been noted above that section 21(3) of the Superior Courts Act 2013 provides: 'Subject to section 28 and the powers granted under section 4 of the Admiralty Jurisdiction Regulation Act, 1983 (Act No 105 of 1983), any Division may issue an order for attachment of property to confirm jurisdiction' and that section 21(3) appears to have been intended broadly to correspond to the amended section 19(1)(c) of the Supreme Court Act 1959.[123]

A drafting peculiarity of section 21(3) is that it is not expressly confined to property situated within the Republic of South Africa (unlike the provisions of section 19(1)(c), which were so expressly limited).[124]

It is likely that a court would read into section 21(3) a limitation to the effect that the provision concerns only property situated within the Republic of South Africa, there being no indication from the terms of the sub-section that the legislature intended to effect such a fundamental change as to enable the courts to attach property outside of the Republic.

Property within the area of jurisdiction of one court within the Republic of South Africa can be made the subject of an order of attachment made by a court having jurisdiction over a different area within the Republic of South Africa.[125]

---

[120] *Yorigami Maritime Construction Co Ltd v Nissho-Iwai Co Ltd* 1977 (4) SA 682 (C) *per* Friedman J at 699B–D.

[121] *Banks v Henshaw* 1962 (3) SA 464 (N) *per* Miller J at 466H–467D (a defamation case; in cases involving liquidated demands it may well be that the court will require security reflecting the full amount of the plaintiff's claim and costs: at 466H). It may be that a defendant is better off providing security as this entails a broader consideration of the merits than does the initial application.

[122] Pistorius *Pollak on Jurisdiction* 2 ed (1993) 86.

[123] Hurter 'Civil and constitutional procedure and jurisdiction' 2013 *ASSAL* 102 at 104.

[124] Section 19(1)(c)(i) provided that the High Court may 'issue an order for attachment of property ... to confirm jurisdiction ... where the property ... is ... within the Republic' and (ii) 'where ... the property ... is outside its area of jurisdiction, issue an order for attachment ... regardless of where in the Republic the property ... is...'.

[125] Forsyth *Private International Law* 5 ed (2012) 201–2. See further, ss 19 and 26 of the Supreme Court Act 1959 and ss 21(3) and 42(2) of the Superior Courts Act 2013.

9.1.3.2.2.2 *The property attachable to found or confirm the jurisdiction*

A plaintiff for an attachment must satisfy the court on the balance of probabilities that the property belongs to the *peregrinus* defendant;[126] pledged property may be attached.[127]

The property attachable to found or confirm jurisdiction may be of any value including (as has been discussed above) merely nominal or trifling value.[128]

Where the value of the property attached exceeds the value of the claim itself, the court may order attachment of a part of the property only reflecting the value of the claim, if that is possible, or it may permit the *peregrinus* defendant to provide security against release of the attached property.[129]

Pursuant to the general principle of the continuation of jurisdiction that 'provided a court has jurisdiction at the time of commencement of an action, it will not matter whether the original ground for assuming jurisdiction subsequently ceases to exist'[130] and this will be the case where property attached to found or confirm jurisdiction later ceases to exist.[131]

---

[126] *Lendalease Finance (Pty) Ltd v Corporacion De Mercadeo Agricola* 1976 (4) SA 464 (A) (Rumpff CJ, Jansen and Corbett JJA, Viljoen and Miller AJJA), *per* Corbett JA at 489B–C: 'It is clear law that an applicant seeking the attachment of his debtor's property *ad fundandam jurisdictionem* must satisfy the Court, on a balance of probabilities, that the property to be attached belongs to the debtor. The onus is upon the applicant to do so. The Court will not order the attachment of the property of another for the purpose of founding jurisdiction because to do so would be futile and of no effect.' Followed in *MY Summit One*: *Farocean Marine (Pty) Ltd v Malacca Holdings Ltd* 2005 (1) SA 428 (SCA) (Marais, Scott, Farlam and Cloete JJA and Patel AJA), *per* Scott JA at 435H, a case in which the applicant contended that it had a case against one of two defendants (435I para [11]): 'If an applicant can show on a balance of probabilities that property is owned by one or other of two defendants and that he has a prima facie case against whichever one is found to be the owner, a court might possibly be justified in granting an order for the attachment of the property.'

[127] Pistorius *Pollak on Jurisdiction* 2 ed (1993) 84; Forsyth *Private International Law* 5 ed (2012) 200; Herbstein and Van Winsen *The Civil Practice of the High Courts of South Africa* 5 ed (2009) 118.

[128] Herbstein and Van Winsen *The Civil Practice of the High Courts of South Africa* 5 ed (2009) 114; *Thermo Radiant Oven Sales (Pty) Ltd v Nelspruit Bakeries (Pty) Ltd* 1969 (2) SA 295 (A), *per* Potgieter JA at 309D–F.

[129] *Deane v Kaffrarian Steam Mill Co Ltd* (1907) 28 NLR 418 (Dove Wilson ACJ, Broome J and Gardiner AJ), attachment reduced from £100 to £25 in respect of a claim valued at £18 15s; *Ex parte Daitz & Co* 1921 WLD 77 (Mason J), attachment discharged in respect of the 'clear value' of unencumbered property in excess of the amount claimed; *Ex parte Ivan Pedersen Ltd* 1929 WLD 109 (Gey Van Pittius J), £25,000 claimed by the respondent from the applicant in English proceedings, similar sum claimed by the applicant in proceedings in the Transvaal, the applicant had authorised the payment into court in England of £15,000, the court in South Africa permitted attachment of £10,000 of the respondent's property; *Rosenstrauch v Korbf* 1931 GWL 102 (Blaine J), applicant suing on a £9,500 judgment given by the Commercial Court in Antwerp, applicant attaching the respondent's diamond mining operation in Kimberley, held that the respondent's rough and polished diamonds should be excluded from the attachment because the applicant was not entitled to be absolutely secured for his claim.

[130] Forsyth *Private International Law* 5 ed (2012) 195.

[131] *Thermo Radiant Oven Sales (Pty) Ltd v Nelspruit Bakeries (Pty) Ltd* 1969 (2) SA 295 (A) *per* Ogilvie Thompson JA at 301E–G and Potgieter JA at 310D–G.

However, if the assets to be attached cease to exist prior to the institution of the proceedings but after the order granting the attachment, the attachment ought to be set aside.[132]

Immovable property belonging to a *peregrinus* defendant is susceptible to attachment to found jurisdiction. However, it has been held that, given the property to be attached is situated within the court's area of jurisdiction and that court will therefore have jurisdiction over the *peregrinus* defendant, it is not necessary to attach the property as well as seek leave to sue by edictal citation.[133] Property transferred to the plaintiff as security for the defendant's debt cannot be the subject of an attachment to found jurisdiction in an action to recover that debt.[134]

Movable property belonging to the *peregrinus* defendant may be attached to found or confirm jurisdiction, whether it is in his possession or in the possession of an agent.[135] The interest of a pledgor *peregrinus* defendant in pledged property may be attached,[136] subject to the prior claim of the pledgee.[137] Similarly, goods subject to a lien may be attached,[138] as may goods already subject to a judicial attachment.[139] It appears that an order for attachment of a defendant's movable property may be widely drafted so as to authorise attachment of all movable property belonging to the defendant situated at a particular address within the jurisdiction of the court.[140] Documents of title subject to a lien asserted by a number of different *incolae* may be the subject of an attachment.[141]

---

[132] Ibid *per* Potgieter JA at 310E–F.

[133] Herbstein and Van Winsen *The Civil Practice of the High Courts of South Africa* 5 ed (2009) 115 and the cases cited at fns 148 and 149.

[134] *Mosenthal & Co v Braun* (1889) 5 HCG 434.

[135] Herbstein and Van Winsen *The Civil Practice of the High Courts of South Africa* 5 ed (2009) 115.

[136] *Mercantile Bank of India Ltd v Davis* 1947 (2) SA 723 (C) *per* Ogilvie Thompson AJ at 736; Herbstein and Van Winsen *The Civil Practice of the High Courts of South Africa* 5 ed (2009) 118.

[137] *Ex parte liquidator 'Owl' syndicate* (1908) 18 CTR 465; *Ex parte Southern Land Ltd* 1921 CPD 150; *London Bank of Australia v Paarl Roller Flour Mills Ltd* 1921 CPD 354; *Ex parte Daitz & Co* 1921 WLD 77.

[138] *Hymore Agencies Durban (Pty) Ltd v Gin Nih Weaving Factory* 1959 (1) SA 180 (N), *per* Henochsberg J at 182.

[139] *Ex parte Gregory* 1956 (1) SA 215 (S Rhodesia), *per* Quènet J at 216, where immovable property situated in Salisbury worth £2,700 and owned by an English woman was subject to a prior attachment in respect of a debt of £1,200; the plaintiff was granted an attachment *ad fundandam jurisdictionem* in respect of an alleged debt of £276 13s.

[140] *Dabelstein v Hildebrandt* 1996 (3) SA 42 (C) (Friedman JP, Farlam J), *per* Farlam J at 70C–H: 'I can see nothing wrong, however, where a respondent is known to be in the Court's area of jurisdiction, where he or she has, on the probabilities, at least personal effects in his or her possession, for the attachment order to direct the attachment of all movable property belonging to him or her, in his or her or another's possession at a specified address. Clearly the Sheriff must satisfy to himself (or herself), before effecting an attachment, that the property being attached belongs to the respondent. If he (or she) does not do so, then he (or she) will be proceeding at his (or her) peril. It would be impracticable to require an applicant for an attachment to confirm jurisdiction in circumstances where the respondent is in the jurisdiction and in possession of at least personal effects to have to find out precisely what property the respondent has which can be attached.'

[141] *Ex parte Daitz & Co* 1921 WLD 77.

Incorporeal property belonging to the *peregrinus* defendant may be attached as long as it is within the area of the attaching court's jurisdiction,[142] for example, a notarial bond held by the *peregrinus*,[143] an inheritance due to a *peregrinus*,[144] an interest in an estate,[145] a life insurance policy ceded to the *peregrinus* and held by the plaintiff,[146] dividends due to the *peregrinus* from an insolvent estate of which he was a creditor,[147] shares held by him,[148] or an interest in a partnership business.[149] A debt owing to a *peregrinus* by an *incola* debtor may be attached to found jurisdiction.[150] The interest of a *peregrinus* in a debt due to it from the plaintiff for the attachment may itself be attached.[151] However, in such a case:

> 'it is implicit in the prospective incola plaintiff's action that the prospective peregrine defendant's claim which is sought to be attached does not exist at all, the court should ... decline to permit the plaintiff incola thus to approbate and reprobate and should, in my judgment, decline to authorize the attachment'.[152]

A *peregrinus* defendant's right to recover costs against a party may provide property which is susceptible to attachment,[153] even in circumstances where the right to recover costs is against the plaintiff for an attachment in respect of an earlier unmeritorious application by that plaintiff against that defendant for an attachment of property.[154]

The point in time at which the issue of ownership of the relevant property is assessed is at the time the application is considered by the court.[155]

---

142 Pistorius *Pollak on Jurisdiction* 2 ed (1993) 84.

143 *Ex parte Greentree* 1914 JWR 392.

144 *Barkhuysen v Van Huysten* (1880) 1 SC 26.

145 *Ex parte Hugo* (1909) 19 CTR 433.

146 *Abrey v Bourne* (1892) 6 EDC 227.

147 *Standard Bank & Liquidator Cape of Good Hope Bank v Arnholtz* (1891) 6 EDC 128.

148 *Trubshawe v Lippert* (1887) 8 NLR 165.

149 *McBride & Thomson v Vause* (1889) 3 SAR 3.

150 *Talacchi NO v Volkskas Bpk: In re Talacchi NO v Banco di Roma* 1971 (1) SA 289 (T), where it was held (*per* Bliss AJ at 293B) that no notice of the application need be given to the third-party debtor; *Araxos (East London) (Pty) Ltd v Contara Lines Ltd* 1979 (1) SA 1027 (E).

151 *Central African Airways Corp v Vickers-Armstrong Ltd* 1956 (2) SA 492 (FC); *Thermo Radiant Oven Sales (Pty) Ltd v Nelspruit Bakeries (Pty) Ltd* 1969 (2) SA 295 (A) (Steyn CJ, Ogilvie Thompson, Botha, Potgieter and Jansen JJA), *per* Ogilvie Thompson JA (Botha and Jansen JJA agreeing) 300F–G.

152 *Thermo Radiant Oven Sales (Pty) Ltd v Nelspruit Bakeries (Pty) Ltd* 1969 (2) SA 295 (A), *per* Ogilvie Thompson JA at 302A–E. Similarly, attachment of a claim in restitution may be refused where the existence of the claim depends on the outcome of the litigation in which the attachment is sought: *Ex parte Usko Ltd: In re Usko Ltd v Cortinovis SpA* 1998 (4) SA 976 (W), *per* Wunsh J at 978I–979C.

153 *Longman Distillers Ltd v Drop Inn Group of Liquor Supermarkets (Pty) Ltd* 1990 (2) SA 906 (A) (Corbett CJ, EM Grosskopf and Kumleben JJA and Nicholas and Goldstone AJJA), *per* Nicholas AJA at 914A–F.

154 *Longman Distillers Ltd v Drop Inn Group of Liquor Supermarkets (Pty) Ltd* 1990 (2) SA 906 (A); *Drive Control Services (Pty) Ltd v Troycom System (Pty) Ltd* 2000 (2) SA 722 (W); in both cases the costs order had been made in previous proceedings between the same parties.

155 *Numill Marketing CC v Sitra Wood Products Pte Ltd* 1994 (3) SA 460 (C), where the question was (at 464F) 'what the crucial moment of time is for requiring proof that first respondent is the owner of the

Although the authorities are not consistent it appears that a sum of money owed by the plaintiff to the defendant may comprise property, in the form of a debt, which is attachable on the application of the debtor/plaintiff.[156]

9.1.3.2.2.3 *Attachment in aid of foreign proceedings*

It appears that an attachment of property in the Republic of South Africa may be made where the claim is to be pursued in a foreign country.

In *Kibe v Mphoko*[157] the plaintiff and defendant were both foreign *peregrini* and at the time of the application to the Orange Free State Provincial Division ('OFS') proceedings had been commenced by the defendant against the plaintiff in Basutoland (modern-day Lesotho). The plaintiff sought an order prohibiting the defendant from withdrawing sums standing to her credit in a bank account in the OFS. It was contended that the OFS did not have jurisdiction to grant the interdict because both plaintiff and defendant were foreign *peregrini* and the cause of action arose outside the jurisdiction of the OFS. De Wet AJ rejected this contention and held:[158]

> 'Our Courts have held that, where the defendant is a *peregrinus*, the Court has jurisdiction if, in the case of a mandatory interdict, the act is to be carried out within such area, or in the case of a prohibitory interdict, if the act against which an interdict is claimed is about to be done in such area ... Where the defendant is a *peregrinus* it is however clear that in the absence of any attachment of respondent's person or property, no order for the payment of costs should be made against him.'

In *Meihuizen (Pty) Ltd v Transportes Maritimos de Portugal LDA*,[159] the Supreme Court of Appeal considered section 5(3)(a) of the Admiralty Jurisdiction Regulation Act 1983.[160] Section 5(3)(a) provides, inter alia, for the attachment of property within South Africa in support of proceedings outside South Africa:

---

property within the Court's area of jurisdiction. Is it the moment at which the application was issued out of the Registrar's office, or when the case was in fact brought before a Judge for purpose of granting a rule *nisi* or the moment of the interim attachment, or when the hearing of the rule *nisi* takes place?' Olivier J held (p 466H) that the crucial moment was generally 'when the Judge, hearing an application for attachment *ad fundandam et confirmandam jurisdictionem* is requested to issue such an order'.

[156] Such an attachment was refused in *Verster & Co v Cooke & Co* 1912 CPD 123 (Fawkes J), but granted in *Ex parte Ivan Pedersen Ltd* 1929 WLD 109 and *Central African Airways Corp v Vickers-Armstrong Ltd* 1956 (2) SA 492 (FC). The *Verster* case was not followed in *Araxos (East London) (Pty) Ltd v Contara Lines Ltd* 1979 (1) SA 1027 (E), *per* Solomon J at 1030F–G.

[157] 1958 (1) SA 364 (O).

[158] Ibid 367A–C. In so doing, De Wet AJA declined to follow the decision of Benjamin J in the Cape Provincial Division in *Hacklaender v Standard Bank* 1923 CPD 271, itself not following two earlier decisions of that Division in *Ex parte Schoeman* 1918 CPD 122 and *Ex parte Kirsten* 1921 CPD 608.

[159] 2005 (1) SA 36 (SCA) (Marais, Scott and Farlam JJA and Jones and Ponnan AJJA).

[160] Act 105 of 1983.

> 'A court may in the exercise of its admiralty jurisdiction order the arrest of any property for the purpose of providing security for a claim which is or may be the subject of any arbitration or any proceedings contemplated, pending or proceeding, either in the Republic or elsewhere, and whether or not it is subject to the law of the Republic, if the person seeking the arrest has a claim enforceable by an action *in personam* against the owner of the property concerned or an action *in rem* against such property or which would be so enforceable but for any such arbitration or proceedings.'

The plaintiff attached sums in a bank account standing to the credit of an agent of the defendant. The SCA allowed the agent's appeal against the attachment as granted but reimposed the attachment on different terms over different property. The original order made by Nel J provided, inter alia, that the sums in the bank account should be attached to found or confirm jurisdiction or, alternatively, should stand as security for the plaintiff's claim to be brought against the defendant in Lisbon. Marais JA, giving the judgment of the court, discharged the order that the property should stand as security for the plaintiff's claim to be brought against the defendant in Lisbon stating[161] that section 5(3)(a) conferred a discretion to make such an order but that there was no evidence to support the contention that such an order was necessary in the circumstances of the case. It would appear therefore that had there been such evidence the court would have been entitled, in the exercise of its discretion under section 5(3)(a), to make an order attaching goods in support of proceedings in Lisbon.

9.1.3.2.2.4 *Procedure*

An application for an attachment of property *ad fundandam* or *ad confirmandam jurisdictionem* is made by notice of motion supported by affidavit evidence and must be made prior to the issuing of the summons by which the proceedings are commenced.

The application is usually made *ex parte*. However, if the defendant is in South Africa at the time of the application and 'there is no danger of notice defeating the purpose of the application, then notice should be given'.[162]

The supporting affidavit must set out:[163]

(1) the name, address and occupation of the proposed plaintiff;

(2) the name, address and occupation of the proposed defendant;

(3) sufficient detail as to the amount and the nature of the claim to enable the court to assess whether there is a *prima facie* case; in this context the term *prima facie* case bears the meaning set out by Smalberger JA giving

[161] Ibid 45H.

[162] Herbstein and Van Winsen *The Civil Practice of the High Courts of South Africa* 5 ed (2009) 120.

[163] Ibid 122.

the judgment of the Supreme Court of Appeal in *Simon NO v Air Operations of Europe AB*:[164]

> 'All that remained for the appellant to establish was that he had a *prima facie* cause of action against ING Aviation. The requirement of a *prima facie* cause of action is satisfied if a plaintiff shows that there is evidence which, if accepted, will establish a cause of action. The mere fact that such evidence is contradicted will not disentitle the plaintiff to relief – not even if the probabilities are against him. It is only where it is quite clear that the plaintiff has no action, or cannot succeed, that an attachment should be refused';[165]

(4) facts relevant to the court's jurisdiction which indicate why the attachment is necessary and whether it is to found or confirm jurisdiction;

(5) details of the property sought to be attached, its value and situation; and

(6) facts indicating the proposed defendant is the owner of the property.

Herbstein and Van Winsen[166] does not refer to any requirement that the plaintiff give full and frank disclosure on the application, although it is likely that thus is a requirement if the application is made *ex parte*.

Where the defendant is not in South Africa at the time of the application, the attachment application should be combined with an application for leave to sue the defendant by edictal citation.

If made *ex parte* the order made is an order *nisi* and on the return date the defendant is required to show cause why the order should not be confirmed.

A writ of attachment may be discharged if: the defendant submitted to the jurisdiction prior to the execution of the writ; the defendant shows the plaintiff has no *prima facie* case; the property attached does not belong to the defendant; the defendant shows that he is an *incola* of the court in which the plaintiff sues or a local *peregrinus*; or if it can be established on the return day that there is no basis on which the court can assume jurisdiction.[167]

9.1.3.2.2.5 *Wrongful attachment*

Securing an attachment by means of a process which is void is an intentional interference with the property rights of the person whose property is attached and this may amount to an actionable delict.[168]

---

164 1999 (1) SA 217 (SCA) (Smalberger, Howie, Plewman and Streicher JJA and Ngoepe AJA) 228C–E.

165 Also, *MT Tigr: Owner of the MT Tigr v Transnet Ltd T/a Portnet (Bouygues Offshore SA Intervening)* 1998 (3) SA 861 (SCA) (Scott JA), *per* Scott JA at 868C 'an applicant need show no more than that there is evidence which, if accepted, will establish a cause of action'.

166 *The Civil Practice of the High Courts of South Africa* 5 ed (2009).

167 Ibid 124.

168 Pistorius *Pollak on Jurisdiction* 2 ed (1993) 87.

If the process is valid and there is no *animus injuriandi* then the process provides a defence for any claim for wrongful attachment. But if there was no reasonable and probable cause for the attachment this is a factor from which *animus injuriandi* may be inferred. Pistorius states[169] that if there was

> 'suppression of information with regard to the facts, thus enabling a plaintiff to obtain an attachment which might otherwise not have obtained, or the object of the attachment was, not to proceed with the action, but to force the defendant to settle because the property had been attached, that might well provide the relevant animus injuriandi'.

and that the Roman-Dutch authorities regard an unjust attachment or one made frivolously and unjustly as an *injuria*.

9.1.3.2.2.6 *Where the plaintiff and the defendant are both* incolae

Attachments of property belonging to persons resident or domiciled within the Republic of South Africa are prohibited by statute.[170]

9.1.3.2.2.7 *Where the plaintiff is an* incola *and the defendant is a foreign* peregrinus

Where the plaintiff is an *incola* and the defendant is a foreign *peregrinus*, the plaintiff's attachment of the defendant's property will found the jurisdiction of the court. This is so even if the cause of action on which the plaintiff relies has no connection with the area over which the court to be seised of proceedings exercises jurisdiction, aside from the attachment itself.[171]

In these circumstances, the *incola* plaintiff has a distinct home advantage: the only basis on which the court assumes jurisdiction is the presence of some property belonging to the *peregrinus* defendant either within its jurisdiction or (since 1998)[172] elsewhere within the Republic of South Africa – there is no need for the *incola* plaintiff to show that the cause of action on which reliance is placed arose within the jurisdiction of the court which the plaintiff seeks to seise of the proceedings.

---

[169] Ibid.

[170] Section 28 of the Superior Courts Act 2013 (re-enacting s 28 of the Supreme Court Act 1959 and s 5 of the Administration of Justice Act 1912). The better view is that provision extends to domiciliaries as well as residents, exempting both from attachment of their property: Herbstein and Van Winsen *The Civil Practice of the High Courts of South Africa* 5 ed (2009) 103–5; Forsyth *Private International Law* 5 ed (2012) 229.

[171] *Ewing McDonald & Co Ltd v M & M Products Co* 1991 (1) SA 252 (A), *per* Nienaber AJA at 258D–G. See also *Kudu Granite Holdings Ltd v Caterna Ltd* 2007 (6) SA 615 (W) (Snyders J).

[172] See s 6 of the Judicial Matters Second Amendment Act 1998 (Act 122 of 1998). The effect of this statutory provision is explained in more detail below.

This home advantage is afforded *only* to an *incola* of the court concerned and not to a resident or domiciliary of another division of the High Court within the Republic of South Africa.

If there is no attachable property within the jurisdiction of the court concerned or elsewhere within the Republic of South Africa, then self-evidently no attachment is possible and the court will not have jurisdiction over the foreign *peregrinus* defendant (and this is regardless of where the cause of action relied upon arose).[173]

It may be the case that, instead of founding the jurisdiction of the court, attachment of property actually confirms the jurisdiction of the court. An attachment will confirm the jurisdiction of the court if the plaintiff is an *incola* and the defendant is a *peregrinus* and the cause of action on which the plaintiff seeks to rely in obtaining an attachment is one which is local to the area over which the court to be seised of the proceedings exercises jurisdiction.

Both Forsyth[174] and the editors of Herbstein and Van Winsen[175] treat separately cases, on the one hand, involving an *incola* plaintiff where the cause of action arises within the area of the court's jurisdiction and, on the other hand, cases where the cause of action arises outside the area of the court's jurisdiction. The commentators state that, in both sets of cases, an attachment of property is mandatory. Perhaps a better way of putting the position of an *incola* plaintiff is provided by Pistorius where he states:[176] 'The plaintiff an *incola*, the defendant a foreign *peregrinus* ... attachment is essential. It is not necessary that there should be any other foundation for jurisdiction other than the arrest or attachment.' Following this approach, while the *incola* plaintiff must attach the property of the defendant in order to found the jurisdiction of the court, there is no need for him to apply to attach that property so as to confirm jurisdiction in these circumstances (though of course he may so apply if he chooses to do so).[177]

9.1.3.2.2.8 *Where the plaintiff and the defendant are both* peregrini

Previously, where (1) the plaintiff was either a local *peregrinus* or a foreign *peregrinus* and (2) the defendant was a foreign *peregrinus* and (3) the cause of action upon which the plaintiff relied arose within the jurisdiction of the court which the

---

[173] And it is also subject to the applicability of the alternative basis for jurisdiction set out in the *Bid Industrial* case.

[174] *Private International Law* 5 ed (2012) 223.

[175] *The Civil Practice of the High Courts of South Africa* 5 ed (2009) 101.

[176] *Pollak on Jurisdiction* 2 ed (1993) 83; an approach supported by Nienaber AJA in *Ewing McDonald & Co Ltd v M & M Products Co* 1991 (1) SA 252 (A) 258D–G, where he stated: 'Since a recognised *ratio jurisdictionis* by itself will not do it is immaterial whether such arrest or attachment is one *ad fundandam jurisdictionem* (where there is no other recognised ground of jurisdiction) or *ad confirmandam jurisdictionem* (where there is).'

[177] Which will affect the preparation of the application and the evidence in support of it.

plaintiff sought to seise of the proceedings, then (4) the plaintiff had to attach the defendant's property to confirm the jurisdiction of that court.[178]

Where, by contrast, (1) the plaintiff was either a local *peregrinus* or a foreign *peregrinus* and (2) the defendant was a foreign *peregrinus* but (3) the cause of action did not arise within the area of jurisdiction of the court which the plaintiff sought to seise of the proceedings, then (4) an attachment to confirm the jurisdiction was not available and the court would not have jurisdiction over the defendant.[179]

Forsyth has stated[180] that this rule was very unfair for local and foreign *peregrini* in that it led to a situation where a local *peregrinus* was unable to seise a South African court of the proceedings because, although the foreign *peregrinus* defendant had property attachable in South Africa, the location of that property and the location of the cause of action did not coincide, thus no local division of the High Court had jurisdiction to hear the claim. In *Siemens Ltd v Offshore Marine Engineering Ltd*,[181] Hoexter JA referred[182] to this problem: 'I venture to suggest that the unfortunate plight of a South African litigant in the sort of situation exemplified by the facts of the instant case is a matter which should engage the attention of the Legislature.'

The legislature took up Hoexter JA's invitation by enacting section 6 of the Judicial Matters Second Amendment Act 1998,[183] which added a sub-paragraph (c) to section 19(1) of the Supreme Court Act 1959. The inserted section 19(1)(c) provided (in material part):

---

[178] Derived from *Ewing McDonald & Co Ltd v M & M Products Co* 1991 (1) SA 252 (A), *per* Nienaber AJA 258J–259B, proposition (c); *Siemens Ltd v Offshore Marine Engineering Ltd* 1993 (3) SA 913 (AD) (Hoexter, Vivier, Eksteen and Grosskopf JJA and Van Coller AJA), a case concerning a local *peregrinus* plaintiff and a foreign *peregrinus* defendant but in which Hoexter JA expressly approved (at 929G–H) Nienaber AJA's proposition (c). In the *Siemens* case the plaintiff was an *incola* of the Witwatersrand Local Division and brought proceedings against the foreign *peregrinus* (English) company in the Eastern Cape Division for attachment of property situated within the area of that division. The plaintiff's application for an attachment was refused on the basis that it was a local *peregrinus* and thus was unable to attach property *ad fundandam jurisdictionem* and the cause of action had not arisen within the area of the Eastern Cape Division. A foreign *peregrinus* plaintiff will be obliged to give security for the costs of the defendant. A foreign *peregrinus* defendant is not so obliged even if he brings a claim in reconvention: *Sandock Austral Ltd v Exploitation Industrielle et Commerciale-Bretic* 1974 (2) SA 280 (D).

[179] Also derived from *Ewing McDonald & Co Ltd v M & M Products Co* 1991 (1) SA 252 (A), *per* Nienaber AJA 258J–259B, proposition (c).

[180] *Private International Law* 5 ed (2012) 226. A question arises as to how far this state of affairs complied with s 30 of the Constitution of the Republic of South Africa, 1996 which concerned the rules for the Supreme Court of Appeal and the High Court. Section 30(2) provides that the access provisions contained in s 29(3) apply to the rules of court made pursuant to s 30(1). It will rarely be in the interests of justice for a court to decline jurisdiction over a claim where the plaintiff has no remedy available in any other relevant forum.

[181] 1993 (3) SA 913 (AD) (Hoexter, Vivier, Eksteen, F H Grosskopf JJA and Van Coller, AJA).

[182] Ibid 929F–G.

[183] Act 122 of 1998.

'... any High Court may—

(i) issue an order for attachment of property ... to confirm jurisdiction ... where the property ... is outside its area of jurisdiction but within the Republic: Provided that the cause of action arose within its area of jurisdiction; and

(ii) where the plaintiff is resident or domiciled within the area of jurisdiction, but the cause of action arose outside its area of jurisdiction and the property ... concerned is outside its area of jurisdiction, issue an order for attachment of property ... to found jurisdiction regardless of where in the Republic the property ... is situated.'

This provision empowers the court: (1) to make an order of attachment *ad confirmandam jurisdictionem* where the property to be attached is outside the area of jurisdiction of that court but within South Africa as long as the cause of action arose within that court's area of jurisdiction (in practice on the application of a local or foreign *peregrinus* plaintiff); and (2) to make an order of attachment *ad fundandam jurisdictionem* where the property to be attached is outside the area of jurisdiction of that court but within South Africa and the cause of action arose outside that court's area of jurisdiction, as long as the plaintiff is an *incola* of that court.

In the first instance, the requirement of a coincidence of cause of action and property is removed in cases where attachment is sought to confirm the jurisdiction. In the second instance, the former requirement that there is property within the area of jurisdiction of the court to which application is made is removed for an *incola* of that court.

The Superior Courts Act 2013 repealed the 1959 Act in its entirety.[184]

Section 21(3) of the 2013 Act provides: 'Subject to section 28 and the powers granted under section 4 of the Admiralty Jurisdiction Regulation Act, 1983 (Act 105 of 1983), any Division may issue an order for attachment of property to confirm jurisdiction.' Section 28 of the 2013 Act prohibits the attachment of the property of a person domiciled or resident in South Africa to found jurisdiction.

Section 21(3) appears to have been intended broadly to correspond to the amended section 19(1)(c) of the 1959 Act.[185]

However, the drafting of this sub-section is not altogether satisfactory and a number of observations may be made regarding its meaning and effect:

(1) Section 21(3) makes provision for the making of an order for attachment of property to confirm jurisdiction regardless of the location of that property. However, unlike section 19(1)(c) of the 1959 Act, the power to make such an order is not subject to the express proviso that the cause of action should have arisen within the area of jurisdiction of the court which it is sought

[184] Section 55(1)(a) and Sch 1, item 1.

[185] Hurter 'Civil and constitutional procedure and jurisdiction' 2013 *ASSAL* 102 at 104.

to seise with the proceedings. There is the prospect therefore that an application may be made to a court for an attachment to confirm that court's jurisdiction where the property is not situated and the cause of action did not arise within that court's area of jurisdiction. In such circumstances, it is likely that a court would require the plaintiff to demonstrate that the cause of action arose within its area of jurisdiction because this was the position at common law prior to the amendment to the 1959 Act. However, a court would also regard itself as being at liberty to attach property within the Republic of South Africa which is not situated within its area of jurisdiction because the words 'any Division may issue an order for attachment of property to confirm jurisdiction', must be taken to refer to property outside that Division's area of jurisdiction otherwise they would be unnecessary (a Division of the High Court had the power to attach property within its area of jurisdiction prior to the passing of the 2013 Act).

(2) The sub-section does not make provision for the making of an order to *found* the jurisdiction; in terms the sub-section is concerned only with confirmation of the jurisdiction. The prospect arises, therefore, that the power vested in the courts by section 19(1)(c)(ii) to make an order attaching property to found the jurisdiction regardless of where the property is situated or where the cause of action arose is repealed and the position regarding attachments to found the jurisdiction is that of the common law prior to the amendment of the 1959 Act, that is, an *incola* plaintiff may found jurisdiction by attaching property of a foreign *peregrinus* within the area of jurisdiction of the court which the plaintiff seeks to seise of the proceedings.

(3) Section 21(3) is not expressly confined to property situated within the Republic of South Africa (unlike the provisions of section 19(1)(c), which were so expressly limited). It is likely that a court would read into section 21(3) a limitation to the effect that the provision concerns only property situated within the Republic of South Africa, there being no indication from the terms of the sub-section that the legislature intended to effect such a fundamental change as to enable the courts to attach property outside of the Republic.

Location of the cause of action

The question whether a cause of action arose within the area of jurisdiction of the court which the plaintiff seeks to seise with proceedings is discussed below under the heading *Rationes jurisdictionis*.

No discretion

Once a plaintiff has satisfied the court that the requirements for an attachment have been met, then the court has no discretion to refuse an attachment.[186]

Attachment in claims relating to immovable property

Some early authority suggests that attachment of immovable property within the area of jurisdiction of the court which the plaintiff seeks to seise of the proceedings is necessary.[187] More recent authority suggests that attachment of immovable property where the action is one to compel transfer of property within the area of the court's jurisdiction is unnecessary.[188]

Miscellaneous claims

Interdict. In cases where an interdict is sought against *peregrini* the court will have jurisdiction to grant a mandatory or prohibitory interdict if the act to be compelled or prohibited respectively is to be carried out within the area of jurisdiction of the court that the plaintiff seeks to seise with proceedings. This is the case regardless of where the cause of action arose, whether the parties (or one of them) are *peregrini* or not and whether an attachment has been obtained.[189]

In *Kibe v Mphoko*[190] the plaintiff and defendant were both foreign *peregrini* and at the time of the application to the OFS proceedings had been commenced by the defendant against the plaintiff in Basutoland (modern-day Lesotho). The plaintiff sought an order prohibiting the defendant from withdrawing sums standing to her credit in a bank account in the OFS. It was contended that the OFS did not have jurisdiction to grant the interdict because both plaintiff and defendant were foreign *peregrini* and the cause of action arose outside the jurisdiction of the OFS. De Wet AJ rejected this contention and held:[191]

> 'Our Courts have held that, where the defendant is a *peregrinus*, the Court has jurisdiction if, in the case of a mandatory interdict, the act is to be carried out within such area, or in the case of a prohibitory interdict, if the act against which an interdict is claimed is about to be done in such area ... Where the defendant is a *peregrinus* it is however clear that in the absence of any attachment of respondent's person or property, no order for the payment of costs should be made against him.'

---

[186] Herbstein and Van Winsen *The Civil Practice of the High Courts of South Africa* 5 ed (2009) 101; *Simon NO v Air Operations of Europe AB* 1999 (1) SA 217 (SCA) (Smalberger, Howie, Plewman and Streicher JJA and Ngoepe AJA), *per* Smalberger JA at 228F.

[187] Herbstein and Van Winsen *The Civil Practice of the High Courts of South Africa* 5 ed (2009) 106–7.

[188] *Jackaman v Arkell* 1953 (3) SA 31 (T), *per* Roper J at 35; *Manna v Lotter* 2007 (4) SA 315 (C), *per* Griesel J at 320 para [10].

[189] Herbstein and Van Winsen *The Civil Practice of the High Courts of South Africa* 5 ed (2009) 107.

[190] 1958 (1) SA 364 (O) (De Wet AJ).

[191] Ibid 367A–C. In so doing, De Wet AJ declined to follow the decision of Benjamin J in the Cape Provincial Division in *Hacklaender v Standard Bank* 1923 CPD 271, itself not following two earlier decisions of that Division in *Ex parte Schoeman* 1918 CPD 122 and *Ex parte Kirsten* 1921 CPD 608.

However, in *Zokufa v Compuscan (Credit Bureau)*,[192] the Eastern Cape High Court refused to follow *Kibe*. Accordingly, the position now appears to be:[193]

(1) if the defendant is an *incola*, the court may assume jurisdiction to grant an interdict (whether mandatory or prohibitory) no matter if the act in question is to be performed or restrained outside the court's area;

(2) secondly, if the defendant is a *peregrinus*, the doctrine of effectiveness dictates that the acts to be performed or restrained be within the court's area. Judgments of the local courts can be carried out anywhere in the country, so it ought to make no difference whether the act in question is to be performed or restrained outside the court's area but within South Africa or that the defendant is local peregrine of the division concerned.[194]

It has been thought that the courts do not have jurisdiction to grant mandatory or prohibitory interdicts in respect of acts to be compelled or prohibited outside the Republic.[195] However, in *Holloway v PADI EMEA Ltd*[196] an English company was ordered to produce the full record, documents and evidence of an inquiry it had undertaken in England into the applicants' conduct in South Africa.

Eviction. An attachment is not necessary for the purposes of a claim for ejectment because the court within the area of which the property is situated has exclusive jurisdiction over the claim and the court's order can be enforced even where the defendant is a *peregrinus*.[197]

Contempt of court. An attachment will not be ordered to render a contemnor amenable to the court's jurisdiction.[198]

Enforcement of arbitration awards. Although as a matter of the Roman-Dutch common law an attachment may not be granted at the instance of a *peregrinus* plaintiff against a *peregrinus* defendant where the cause of action did not arise within such area of jurisdiction, such an attachment may be granted where the application is made in support of the recognition of a foreign arbitration award.[199]

---

[192] 2011 (1) SA 272 (ECM), *per* Alkema J para [47].

[193] Forsyth *Private International Law* 5 ed (2012) 249.

[194] In *Ex parte Hay Management Consultants (Pty) Ltd* 2000 (3) SA 501 (W), Wunsh J at 507G–J, dealing with the court's ability to grant an interdict to restrain a defendant *peregrinus* from committing acts outside of South Africa, stated: 'A South African court has no control over the defendant, nor over the cessation of the acts in question and cannot entertain an application for an interdict against it ... The lack of jurisdiction cannot be cured by an attachment. Even if the defendant did consent to the jurisdiction of the Court in the agreement, its submission would not extend to an interdict to restrain it from committing delicts.'

[195] Pistorius *Pollak on Jurisdiction* 2 ed (1993) 119–20. But see below, this principle has been the subject of some erosion.

[196] 2020 (5) SA 172 (GJ).

[197] Herbstein and Van Winsen *The Civil Practice of the High Courts of South Africa* 5 ed (2009) 108; *Sandton Square Finance (Pty) Ltd v Biagi, Bertola and Vasco* 1997 (1) SA 258 (W), *per* Farber AJ at 261F.

[198] Herbstein and Van Winsen *The Civil Practice of the High Courts of South Africa* 5 ed (2009) 108; *Di Bona v Di Bona* 1993 (2) SA 682 (C), *per* Rose Innes J at 692B–D and 696E–F.

[199] *Balkan Energy Ltd v The Government of the Republic of Ghana* 2017 (5) SA 428 (GJ) (S Kuny AJ) at paras 12 and 16, following *Laconian Maritime Enterprises Ltd v Agromar Lineas Ltd* 1984 (3) SA 233 (D).

9.1.3.3 Rationes jurisdictiones

In *Einwald v The German West African Co*,[200] De Villiers CJ stated:

> 'What then are the grounds upon which the jurisdiction of this Court can be exercised, in respect of any contract over any defendant without his consent, express or implied? The grounds are threefold; *viz* by virtue of the defendant's domicile being here, by virtue of the contract either having been entered into here or having to be performed here, and by virtue of the subject matter in an action *in rem* being situated in this Colony.'

Added to these are the place of the delict and cases which concern property. The principal connecting factors for jurisdictional purposes which result are: *ratio domicilii* (*actor sequitur forum rei*); *ratio contractus*; *ratio delicti commissi*; and *ratio rei sitae*.[201]

9.1.3.3.1 *Ratio domicilii* (*actor sequitur forum rei*)

Ratio domicilii expresses the principle of Roman law that the fundamental basis of jurisdiction is that a plaintiff should sue a defendant at the defendant's place of domicile or, as has become the case, residence (*actor sequitur forum rei*).

Residence and domicile are significant connecting factors in claims sounding in money. In *Bisonboard Ltd v K Braun Woodworking Machinery (Pty) Ltd*,[202] Hoexter JA[203] stated:

> 'Provided that the defendant is an *incola* of the court's area of jurisdiction, the court will be prepared to hear the case ... Accordingly, if the defendant is either domiciled or resident in the area, this will be a sufficient jurisdictional connecting factor. Neither of these requirements predicates the actual physical presence of the defendant within the court's area. If the defendant is present, he may be brought to court by summons in the ordinary manner; if he is absent, then, subject to the Rules of Court, summons may be effected by edictal citation or substituted service, as the case may be. Domicile and residence suggest no more than a notional connection with the court's area. Absence is relevant only in regard to the procedural matter of service.'

---

[200] (1887) 5 SC 86 (De Villiers CJ) p 91 of the report.

[201] Different authors treat the organisation of this subject in different ways. Peté et al *Civil Procedure* 2 ed (2011) (at 70ff), discuss the subject under the headings *ratione domicilii*, *ratione res gestae*, *ratione rei sitae* and then claims relating to property and claims sounding in money. In Schulze *On Jurisdiction and the Recognition and Enforcement of Foreign Money Judgments* (2005), the discussion (at 1–15) revolves around domicile and the bases for assumption of jurisdiction over *incolae* and *peregrini*. In Kelbrick *Civil Procedure in South Africa* 2 ed (2012), the subject is analysed (at 42–3; paras 84–6) in terms of claims in money and property. Forsyth *Private International Law* 5 ed (2012), discusses (at 205–6) residence and domicile, the various *rationes jurisdictionis* and then claims in money or property. Herbstein and Van Winsen *The Civil Practice of the High Courts of South Africa* 5 ed (2009), discusses (at 67–81) the subject under the topic headings claims in money, property (and status). Pistorius *Pollak on Jurisdiction* 2 ed (1993), arranges the discussion under the topic headings money claims and property claims. There are merits in all of these approaches.

[202] 1991 (1) SA 482 (A) (Hoexter, Botha and Milne JJA and Goldstone and Nicholas AJJA).

[203] Ibid 488B of the report, quoting Forsyth *Private International Law* 2 ed (1990) 175–6.

9.1.3.3.1.1 *Residence of individuals*

Section 21(1) of the Superior Courts Act 2013 is entitled, 'Persons over whom and matters in relation to which Divisions have jurisdiction', and provides, inter alia:

> '(1) A Division has jurisdiction over all persons residing or being in, and in relation to all causes arising ... within, its area of jurisdiction and all other matters of which it may according to law take cognisance, and has the power—
>
> *(a)* ...
>
> *(b)* ...
>
> *(c)* in its discretion, and at the instance of any interested person, to enquire into and determine any existing, future or contingent right or obligation, notwithstanding that such person cannot claim any relief consequential upon the determination.
>
> (2) A Division also has jurisdiction over any person residing or being outside its area of jurisdiction ... if the said person resides or is within the area of jurisdiction of any other Division.
>
> (3) Subject to section 28 and the powers granted under section 4 of the Admiralty Jurisdiction Regulation Act, 1983 (Act 105 of 1983), any Division may issue an order for attachment of property to confirm jurisdiction.'

Section 1 of the 2013 Act (and its predecessors) does not define 'residence' for the purposes of the legislation. The courts have refused to equate 'residence' with 'being' (in the sense of presence) and historically have not considered their jurisdiction as dependent on mere physical presence.[204]

No comprehensive definition of residence has been given by the South African courts

> 'probably because it is impossible to frame a definition which is wide enough to cover all the cases in which a person has been held to be resident in a territory and yet is not so wide as to enable cases in which it has been held that a person is not resident in a territory to be included'.[205]

Bristowe J, in *Robinson v Commissioner of Taxes*,[206] stated that residence was: not the same as domicile (a person can be domiciled in a country where he has never set foot; and, by contrast, a domicile of choice requires an intention to stay indefinitely whereas residence does not); not necessarily permanent; and not necessarily exclusive,

---

[204] *Bisonboard Ltd v K Braun Woodworking Machinery (Pty) Ltd* 1991 (1) SA 482 (A), *per* Hoexter JA, approving a passage in the second edition (1990) of Forsyth *Private International Law*, which now appears at 205 of the fifth edition (2012). Query the effect of the *Bid Industrial* case on this proposition however.

[205] Pistorius *Pollak on Jurisdiction* 2 ed (1993) 54–5.

[206] 1917 TPD 542 at 547.

> 'Perhaps the best general description of what is imported by residence is that it means a man's home or one of his homes for the time being; though exactly what period or what circumstances constitute home is a point on which it is impossible to lay down any clearly defined rule.'

If someone establishes himself or herself in a location and lives there at intervals then he or she will be resident at that location regardless of how many further locations that person has established himself or herself.

Various judicial views of what amounts to residence are:[207] a person resides 'where he lives or where his home is';[208] 'Residence in a place in the ordinary sense means having one's home or place of abode there';[209] 'It has never been laid down what degree of permanence is required in residence; but at all events it ought to be shown that the person ... had some interest in the place ... in the sense that there was some good reason for regarding it as his ordinary place of habitation ...';[210] 'A "resident" means something more than a visitor. A "resident" of a country is a man who has his home in that country';[211] 'When it is said of an individual that he resides at a place it is obviously meant that it is his home, his place of abode, the place where he generally sleeps after the work of the day is done';[212] 'To reside in a place means to have your home in that place, and that implies an intention to live in the place for some time';[213] 'some good reason for regarding it as his place of ordinary habitation'.[214]

Whether an individual is resident at a particular place depends on all the facts. In *Becker v Forster*,[215] physical presence in a magisterial area for about six weeks was held to be residence in that area, although the person intended to and did in fact leave the area a few days after the expiry of that period. Physical presence for a week was held not to be residence.[216]

Residence probably does not require an *animus residendi*: for example, persons incapable of forming intent can nonetheless reside at a particular place. However, it may well be that a person's intentions towards and generally his mental state

[207] Pistorius *Pollak on Jurisdiction* 2 ed (1993) 55 fn 5.

[208] *TW Beckett & Co Ltd v Kroomer Ltd* 1912 WLD 53, 59 (Bristowe J; reversed on appeal on the question of the place of residence of a company, 1912 AD 324).

[209] *Schlimmer v Executrix in Estate of Rising* 1904 TH 108 (Bristowe J) 112–13.

[210] *Hogsett v Buys* 1913 CPD 200, 205.

[211] *Ismael v R* 1908 TS 1088, 1096.

[212] *Beedle & Co v Bowley* (1895) 12 SC 401, 403.

[213] *Lewis v Tosseau* 1913 TPD 338, 341.

[214] *Ex parte Minister of Native Affairs* 1941 AD (De Wet CJ; Waterman, Tindall, Centlivres and Feetham JJA) 53, 58.

[215] 1913 CPD 962.

[216] *Lewis v Tosseau* 1913 TPD 338, 341.

regarding a particular place may be relevant to establishing whether that place is his residence for jurisdictional purposes.[217]

It has been held that a person can be resident at more than one place at one time. In *Maritz v Erasmus*,[218] the defendant was found to be resident at his farms in the district of Sutherland and the district of Beaufort. He was at his farm in Sutherland when he was served with a summons issued out the Sutherland magistrate's court. It was held that the defendant was resident in the district of Sutherland and therefore that the court had jurisdiction over him. However, it seems that for the purposes of determining the jurisdiction of the court a person can only be resident at any given time at the place where he is physically present, regardless of how many residences he has.[219]

If the defendant is resident and physically present within the area over which the court exercises territorial jurisdiction, the court has jurisdiction to entertain an action for a judgment sounding in money against him. Pistorius states[220] that it must follow that if a defendant is an *incola* by reason of domicile or residence then, as where the jurisdiction of the court to entertain a claim for a judgment sounding in money is based on the domicile of the defendant within the area of the court, if the defendant is resident it does not matter: (1) that the defendant is not physically present in the jurisdiction at the time the action is commenced;[221]

---

[217] See the facts of the *Mayne v Main* 2001 (2) SA 1239 (SCA) (Smalberger ADCJ, Nienaber, Farlam and Mpati JJA and Mthiyane AJA), where it was found that the respondent's romantic attachment with a resident of Johannesburg informed the finding of the respondent's own residence in Johannesburg.

[218] 1914 CPD 120.

[219] *Ngadi v Temba* (1905) 22 SC 574 (*per* Buchanan AJA at 576, 'It is possible for a person to reside in more than one district ... but if he is to be summoned in one or the other district, he must be residing in that district for the time being.') Both Pistorius and Forsyth criticise this decision (Pistorius *Pollak on Jurisdiction* 2 ed (1993) 56; Forsyth *Private International Law* 5 ed (2012) 206, fn 277), the former characterising it as illogical: 'Where a person is known to keep two residences, his absence from one of them (probably because he is in the other) is less likely to denote a change of residence than is the absence of a person from his only known residence. If he has two residences then his temporary absence from one does not mean that he no longer resides there but has chosen to reside in the other. Why should a plaintiff be prejudiced by the defendant's arrangements?' Forsyth points out that residence in more than one place was recognised in *Ex parte Minister of Native Affairs* 1941 AD 53 at 58 and *Sandton Square Finance (Pty) Ltd v Biagi, Bertola and Vasco* 1997 (1) SA 258 (W) 261B, but that in *Mayne v Main* 2001 (2) SA 1239 (SCA) it was held (at 1243F) that for jurisdictional purposes 'a person can only be residing in one place at any given moment'. However, it appears from the relevant paragraph of the judgment of Smalberger ADCJ in the *Mayne* case (para [4]) that this point was conceded by counsel for both of the parties and thus not argued and it appears from the listing of authorities (at 1242) that the passage from Pistorius *Pollak on Jurisdiction* 2 ed (1993), set out above, was not referred to the court by counsel for either party. Further, the SCA overturned the decision of the judge at first instance that the respondent was not resident in Johannesburg and found (at 1250B para [30]) that other than residence in Johannesburg on the evidence, 'No acceptable alternative place suggests itself where he might have been residing at the time [the summons was served].' Thus the finding at para [4] of the judgment was not necessary to the decision and should be regarded as obiter.

[220] *Pollak on Jurisdiction* 2 ed (1993) 56–7.

[221] *Goedhals & Du Toit v Pienaar* 1908 EDC 157. The defendant can be brought to court by service on him of process elsewhere in the Republic of South Africa or outside the jurisdiction by edictal citation.

(2) that the defendant changes his residence after proceedings have been commenced; (3) that the cause of action arise outside the area of jurisdiction; or (4) what the nature of the cause of action is.

9.1.3.3.1.2 *Domicile of individuals*

An individual's domicile will frequently determine which court has jurisdiction over him. In the Republic of South Africa, the law relating to domicile is governed by the common law and by the Domicile Act of 1992.[222] The 1992 Act came into force in August 1992 and it is necessary to apply the common law to determine an individual's domicile prior to 1 August 1992.[223]

Domicile is not defined by the 1992 Act and the common law does not provide a received definition. Forsyth[224] favours the definition proposed by Barry JP in *Mason v Mason*,[225] 'Domicile means the place or country which is considered by law to be a person's permanent home.' This understanding equates with that which obtains in English law:[226]

> '**Permanent home**. The notion which lies at the root of the concept of domicile is that of permanent home. "By domicile we mean home, the permanent home; and if you do not understand your permanent home I am afraid that no illustration drawn from foreign writers or foreign languages will very much help you to do it." A person may be said to have his home in a country if he resides in it without any intention of at present removing from it permanently or for an indefinite period. But a person does not cease to have his home in a country merely because he is temporarily resident elsewhere; and a person who has formed the intention of leaving a country does not cease to have his home in it until he acts according to that intention.'

The common law recognises three types of domicile: domicile of origin, domicile of choice and domicile of dependence. The 1992 Act recognises only two types: domicile of choice and assigned domicile.

Domicile is determined by the *lex fori*.[227]

---

[222] Act 3 of 1992.

[223] Although the 1992 Act purports to apply to 'Every person' (s 1(1)) and the term 'person' is defined by s 2 of the Interpretation Act 1957 (Act 33 of 1957) as including any company, as a matter of construction the application of the 1992 Act must be taken as being confined to individuals (because, for example, the Act refers to acquisition of a domicile of choice after the age of 18 years).

[224] *Private International Law* 5 ed (2012) 131.

[225] (1885) 4 EDC 330.

[226] *Dicey, Morris and Collins on the Conflict of Laws* 15 ed (2012) vol 1, r 4(1), p 132 para 6–004, quoting from the opinion of Lord Cranworth in *Whicker v Hume* (1858) 7 HLC 124 at 160.

[227] Forsyth *Private International Law* 5 ed (2012) 135; Pistorius *Pollak on Jurisdiction* 2 ed (1993) 52 and the authorities at fn 12; *Dicey, Morris and Collins on the Conflict of Laws* 15 ed (2012) vol 1, r 8, p 139.

9.1.3.3.1.3 *Common law*

Domicile of origin. The general rule is that every person receives at birth a domicile of origin. A legitimate child takes the domicile of his father, if living, at the time of the child's birth and that of the child's mother if illegitimate.[228]

If the father dies prior to the birth of his child, the child takes the domicile of origin of the mother.[229]

A legitimate child born after the divorce of its parents takes the domicile of its father unless sole guardianship has been awarded to its mother or some other person.[230]

The domicile of origin of a foundling is probably determined by the country in which it is found.[231]

Historically, the question whether a domicile of origin endures has excited debate. One view is that a person's domicile of origin recrudesces at any point in his life where a domicile of choice is abandoned without a dove-tailing further domicile of choice being acquired (the revival approach). The rival view is that any given domicile persists until replaced by another; thus, a domicile of choice persists until replaced by another domicile of choice (the persistence approach). As a matter of English law a domicile of origin will revive in the event that a person loses his domicile of choice and does, not at the same instant, replace it with a new domicile of choice.[232] In the Republic of South Africa there is only one judicial decision where the revival approach forms part of the *ratio decidendi* of the decision, *Ex parte Donnelly.*[233] However, this approach has been much criticised as potentially leading to a person being domiciled in a country with which he has no connection and which may lead to entirely unintended and undesired consequences (in terms of the laws of succession or status).[234]

---

[228] Whether and, if so, how this distinction is to be maintained in the light of the equality and anti-discrimination provisions of the Constitution is moot (s 9 of the Constitution). Further, this rule appears to apply also to adopted children where the domiciles of either or both of its biological parents may be difficult to determine: Forsyth *Private International Law* 5 ed (2012) 154. Generally, see too *Dicey, Morris and Collins on the Conflict of Laws* 15 ed (2012) vol 1, r 9, p 140.

[229] Forsyth *Private International Law* 5 ed (2012) 155.

[230] Ibid 155 and fn 145.

[231] Ibid 154–5.

[232] *Dicey, Morris and Collins on the Conflict of Laws* 15 ed (2012) vol 1, rule 13(2), p 161. *Udny v Udny* (1869) LR 1 Sc & Div 441.

[233] 1915 WLD 29.

[234] *Dicey, Morris and Collins on the Conflict of Laws* 15 ed (2012) vol 1, r 13(2), p 162, para 6–076. Forsyth *Private International Law* 5 ed (2012) 155–8 and the striking example of *Re Jones' Estate* 192 Iowa 78, 182 NW 227 (1921), cited by Forsyth at 156.

It is difficult to disagree with Forsyth's[235] conclusion in this regard that, 'The fact is that both the doctrine of revival and the doctrine of persistence may in certain circumstances lead to artificial results' and that the persistence approach 'would generally produce the results more in accord with the factual realities'. The 1992 Act itself provides for the persistence approach (section 3) and it is also the approach now adopted in New Zealand and Australia.[236] It is to be expected that if the question arises again for judicial determination in South Africa the courts are highly likely to be persuaded by Forsyth's submission on the question.

It also appears that notwithstanding that the issue is in principle decided on the balance of probabilities, the question whether a domicile of origin has been replaced by a domicile of choice is more difficult to establish than either whether a domicile of choice has been discarded or whether a domicile of choice has been replaced by a further domicile of choice.[237]

In order to discard a domicile of origin it is necessary to establish the facts of lawful[238] presence in another country[239] and an intention to remain there indefinitely or permanently.[240]

Retention of an intention to return to a previous domicile (*animus revertendi*) or, alternatively, the absence of an intention to remain indefinitely or permanently in another country (*animus manendi*) will result in the domicile of origin persisting (or recrudescing, in the case of a failure to acquire a further domicile of choice).

Domicile of choice. A domicile of choice is acquired by a person with capacity to acquire it by a combination of presence in the relevant country (or jurisdiction) and an intention to remain there indefinitely (*animus manendi*).[241] Presence and intention must coincide.

---

[235] *Private International Law* 5 ed (2012) 156. Forsyth advances the entirely credible theory (at 155) that: 'The reasons for the adoption of the doctrine of revival of the domicile of origin in English law are, it is submitted, relatively clear. It is no coincidence that the doctrine was established in the middle of the nineteenth-century. At that time the British Empire was growing and there was a clear need to maintain all those far-flung Englishmen within the blanket of the common law. The natural expectations of Englishmen out serving the Empire was that their affairs would continue to be governed by English law and, to this end, the doctrine of the revival of the domicile of origin and its tenaciousness was fashioned consciously or unconsciously by the late nineteenth-century English judges.'

[236] New Zealand: Domicile Act 1976, s 11; Australia: Domicile Act 1982, s 7 (which extends to all Australian states and territories (s 3(2)).

[237] *Dicey, Morris and Collins on the Conflict of Laws* 15 ed (2012) vol 1, r 9, p 141, para 6–031; Forsyth *Private International Law* 5 ed (2012) 158–60, for the historic reasons noted earlier; *Johnson v Johnson* 1931 AD 391.

[238] A requirement of South African law (Forsyth *Private International Law* 5 ed (2012) 158) but no longer a requirement of English law, either as regards acquisition of a domicile of choice in England or another country (*Mark v Mark* [2005] UKHL 42, [2006] 1 AC 98).

[239] Or, more accurately, jurisdiction, because a domicile of choice can be acquired in a state of a federal system.

[240] Forsyth *Private International Law* 5 ed (2012) 158.

[241] Ibid 138; *Dicey, Morris and Collins on the Conflict of Laws* 15 ed (2012) vol 1, r 10, p 142.

Although some writers refer to a requirement of residence in the country of choice,[242] the requirement is more accurately described as lawful[243] presence.[244] Such presence can be for any period of time, however brief, so long as it is accompanied by the relevant intention.[245]

As regards the intention required to acquire a domicile of choice, two types present themselves:[246] first, 'an intention to reside in a country for an indefinite period, ie until and unless something, the happening of which is uncertain, occurs to induce the person to leave'; second, 'an intention to reside forever'. The first test is a less stringent test than the second. It is stated by Forsyth[247] that in *Johnson v Johnson*,[248] the Appellate Division adopted the second of these tests because De Villiers CJ[249] adopted the test of *animus manendi* set out by Westlake: 'The intention necessary for acquiring a domicile of choice excludes all contemplation of any event on the occurrence of which the residence would cease.'

In *Johnson v Johnson* there were proceedings in South Africa and Sweden concerned with the breakdown of the parties' relationship and the distribution of matrimonial property, which issue it was agreed would be governed by the law of the matrimonial domicile. Both parties had Swedish domiciles of origin. However, the parties had been married in New Jersey. Swedish law was more generous to Mrs Johnson than the law of New Jersey. Mr Johnson contended that, prior to their marriage in June 1892, he had acquired a domicile of choice in New Jersey, having arrived there in November 1890 from Sweden (a period of approximately 18 months).

The test formulated and applied by De Villiers CJ[250] was as follows: 'Has it been proved with perfect clearness and satisfaction to myself that Johnson at the date of the marriage had formed a fixed and deliberate intention to abandon his Swedish domicile and settle in the State of New Jersey', which omits that part of the Westlake formulation which forbids any contemplation of contingent events on the occurrence of which the residence would cease.

---

[242] See, for example, *Dicey, Morris and Collins on the Conflict of Laws* 15 ed (2012) vol 1, r 10.

[243] As mentioned above, a requirement of South African law (Forsyth *Private International Law* 5 ed (2012) 158) but no longer a requirement of English law, either with regard to acquisition of a domicile of choice in England or another country (*Mark v Mark* [2005] UKHL 42, [2006] 1 AC 98).

[244] Forsyth *Private International Law* 5 ed (2012) 139, (i).

[245] *Dicey, Morris and Collins on the Conflict of Laws* 15 ed (2012) vol 1, para 6–036; Forsyth *Private International Law* 5 ed (2012) 140.

[246] Formulated by Pollak as intention types three and four in 'Domicile' (1933) 50 *SALJ* 449, 465; quoted by Forsyth *Private International Law* 5 ed (2012) 141.

[247] *Private International Law* 5 ed (2012) 142–3.

[248] 1931 AD 391 (De Villiers CJ, Curlewis, Roos and Stratford JJA).

[249] With whom Curlewis and Roos JJA agreed.

[250] 1931 AD 391 at 399.

On the facts, De Villiers CJ found[251] that there was 'ample evidence' that Mr Johnson was 'not a man whose word can be unreservedly accepted'. The judge considered Mr Johnson's evidence that by July 1890 he had made up his mind to make his permanent home in America and stated:[252] 'I have difficulty in believing that at that time he had made up his mind to make his permanent home in America.' The judge found,[253] applying the test he had articulated, that by June 1892 Mr Johnson had not made New Jersey his permanent home.

Johnson v Johnson would seem therefore to be authority for the proposition that a person seeking to show that he has shed a domicile of origin and acquired a domicile of choice must demonstrate that at the time of his presence in the relevant jurisdiction he had chosen to make that jurisdiction his permanent home. Even assuming that De Villiers CJ intended to endorse the Westlake formulation, the judge proceeded to articulate his own formulation and apply that to the facts. The ratio of the case is that Mr Johnson had failed to show that he intended to make New Jersey his permanent home.

The account of *Johnson v Johnson* set out above is, it is submitted, consistent with the judgment of the Appellate Division in *Ley v Ley's executors.*[254] Ley's case concerned a Cornish stonemason who was attracted to South Africa by the relatively higher wages offered there for his trade. After her husband's death in Pretoria, Mrs Ley commenced proceedings in the Transvaal Provincial Division seeking, inter alia, orders that at the date of their marriage in England in 1905 Mr Ley was domiciled in the Colony of the Cape of Good Hope or in the Transvaal and that the marriage was in community of property. The executors contended that in 1905 Mr Ley was domiciled in England (where there was no such community of property). The Appeal Court reversed the decision of Clayden J at first instance and held that Mr Ley had acquired a domicile of choice in the Cape by the time he was married in 1905.

The judge at first instance had construed *Johnson v Johnson* to set out as the test for the mental element of the acquisition of a domicile of choice the Westlake formulation and had then applied that formulation in such a way as to require a party contending that a domicile of choice had been acquired to show not just that the person in question had decided to live permanently in a country, but also to show that that person 'had reasonably excluded as his home in the new land some other of the then constituent colonies'.[255]

---

[251] Ibid 405.

[252] Ibid.

[253] 1931 AD 391 at 406 and 407.

[254] 1951 (3) SA 186 (A) (Centlivres CJ, Schreiner and De Villiers AJA).

[255] Ibid 190G.

Centlivres CJ (with whom the other members of the court agreed) stated:[256] 'It is important to observe that what appears to have been of decisive importance to the learned trial judge was the adoption by this Court in *Johnson's* case of the rule laid down by Westlake.' The Chief Justice then proceeded to quote the rule laid down by Westlake and then to quote from *Winans v A-G*,[257] relied on by Westlake and *Johnson v Johnson*. The selection by Centlivres CJ of the passages to quote from these two authorities is instructive.

From *Winans*, Centlivres CJ[258] quoted Lord Macnaughten as follows:

> 'On the whole I am unable to come to the conclusion that Mr Winans ever formed a fixed and settled purpose of abandoning his American domicile (which was his domicile of origin) and finally settling in England. I think up to the very last he had an expectation or hope of returning to America.'

From *Johnson v Johnson*, Centlivres CJ quoted[259] the following passage: '[whether Mr Johnson] had formed a fixed and deliberate intention to abandon his Swedish domicile and settle in the State of New Jersey'. Neither of these passages feature that part of the Westlake formulation which forbids any contemplation of contingent events on the occurrence of which the residence would cease.

Centlivres CJ then stated:[260]

> 'Both in *Johnson's* case and in *Winans'* case the finding that it had not been proved that the *de cujus* had ever intended to abandon his domicile of origin was, of course, decisive. In the instant case, however, it is clear on all the evidence that at no time after leaving England for South Africa in January, 1903, did Ley contemplate returning to England for the purpose of remaining there. When he left England in 1903 he intended to abandon his English domicile irrevocably and to settle in South Africa and the only question is whether he in fact acquired a domicile of choice in the Cape Colony.'

The answer to that question was given by the Chief Justice in two parts. First:[261]

> 'It seems to me that on a preponderance of probabilities it has been proved that Ley's headquarters were Cape Town and that he had at the time of his marriage acquired a domicile of choice in the Cape Colony, unless it is doubtful whether he had yet made up his mind to settle there.'

Thus the first part of the answer was that Mr Ley had intended to settle in Cape Town, unless there was something which suggested he had not so intended.

---

256 Ibid 193 A–B.

257 [1904] AC 287 (Earl of Halsbury LC and Lords Macnaghten and Lindley).

258 *Ley v Ley's executors* 1951 (3) SA 186 (A) 193D.

259 Ibid 193E.

260 Ibid 193F.

261 Ibid 194A.

The Chief Justice provided the second part of the answer when commenting on *Bell v Kennedy*[262] as follows:[263]

> 'The House of Lords held that the onus of proving that Bell had acquired a domicile of choice in Scotland in or before September, 1838, had not been discharged, the main ground being that his letters showed that he had not yet made up his mind as to whether he would make his home in Scotland. In the present case, however, the preponderance of probabilities seems to me to prove that Ley did intend to settle in the Cape Colony.'

Centlivres CJ approached the question whether Mr Ley had acquired a domicile of choice in the Cape by posing the question whether Mr Ley had intended to settle in the Cape and, on the evidence, answering it in the affirmative (the same question posed by De Villiers CJ in *Johnson v Johnson*).

Centlivres CJ identified the fault in the approach of Clayden J as being the elevation of questions of evidence into ones of principle. The judge at first instance had directed himself that it had to be shown that Mr Ley 'had reasonably excluded as his home in the new land some other of the then constituent colonies'. Centlivres CJ stated[264] that the relevant enquiry was into the state of mind of the person alleged to have acquired a domicile of choice, which is essentially a factual enquiry:

> 'Any doubt *actually* present to his mind as to whether he will move or not will according to Westlake's statement exclude the intention to settle permanently, but the possibility that, if the idea of a move in the future had been suggested to him, he might not at once have scouted it does not amount to contemplation of an event on which the residence would cease. It is only the former that has to be disproved by the person alleging a change in domicile' (emphasis provided).

Thus, where (and only where) there is evidence that, as a matter of fact, the relevant person entertained doubt as to his move to the new country, must the party alleging a change in domicile negative that evidence if he wishes to succeed on the issue. If there is no evidence of doubt, then the evidential burden does not shift and the party alleging a change in domicile does not have to negative that evidence (because there is none to negative) if he wishes to succeed on the issue. Evidence of a possibility is not sufficient to shift the evidential burden on the main issue of intention (as it would not be on any other issue of fact in proceedings). However, evidence of doubt as to the existence of the main issue of intention clearly is sufficient to shift the evidential burden.

It is submitted therefore that both *Johnson v Johnson* and the *Ley* case propound functionally the same test for the abandonment of a domicile of origin and the

[262] (1866–69) LR 1 Sc & Div App Cas 307 (Lord Cranworth and Lords Chelmsford, Westbury and Colonsay).

[263] *Ley v Ley's executors* 1951 (3) SA 186 (A) 194E.

[264] Ibid 195A–E.

acquisition of a domicile of choice: the party alleging a change of domicile must show that the individual concerned intended to abandon his domicile of origin and to settle in the new country. This formulation is equivalent to the first less stringent test referred to above.

The requirements of a domicile of choice are, therefore: the fact of physical presence in the country, combined with the coincidental intention to reside or settle in that country indefinitely or permanently.

On the matter of evidence, the onus is on the person contending for a domicile of choice; the possibility that the residence was not, would not or will not be indefinite is not sufficient to shift the evidential burden from the person opposing the contended-for domicile of choice back to the person advocating it; the existence of an event which in the future will terminate the residence may defeat the claim that the individual acquired a domicile of choice (because, *ex hypothesi*, the residence will not be indefinite).[265]

9.1.3.3.1.4 *Limitations of choice of domicile*

In the case of those who are present in a country under compulsion, such as prisoners or members of the armed forces, or not by their personal choice, such as members of the diplomatic corps or employees transferred abroad, the common law previously imposed restrictions on their capacity to acquire a domicile of choice.

---

[265] Although, even here, if the evidence supports the relevant *animus manendi* a domicile will be acquired: a series of Botswana cases on the acquisition of a domicile of choice by employees on short-term contracts suggests that this is the case: *Kenyon v Kenyon & Jenkins* [1974] (1) BLR 2 and *Dance v Dance* [1976] (2) BLR 43 (CA). In the *Kenyon* case the plaintiff sued for divorce in the Botswana High Court, which would only have jurisdiction over the suit if the plaintiff was domiciled in Botswana. The plaintiff moved to Botswana in 1971 and issued proceedings in 1973. He was on a ten-year employment contract and his residency permit was due to expire in 1974, with no guarantee that it would be renewed. Aguda CJ held that the plaintiff had not acquired a domicile of choice in Botswana but stated that neither the fact that his employment contract was fixed term nor that his permit required renewal were of themselves conclusive (the judge found that the plaintiff had lied to him and, on that basis, found that he could not rely on his statements of intention to reside permanently). In the *Dance* case the plaintiff/appellant contending for the acquisition of a domicile of choice in Botswana had been posted to Botswana from Kenya on a contract renewable every second year, which the plaintiff said would go on indefinitely, there being no reason his employment should terminate; the plaintiff also stated that he would apply for another job in Botswana if his present contract was not renewed 'in the suppositional event of his declining a request by his directors to return to Kenya'. This evidence was accepted and the Court of Appeal (Maisels P and Milne and Doyle JJA) held that he acquired a domicile of choice in Botswana. See also *Joosab v Salaam* 1940 TPD 177 (Greenberg JP), where a domicile of choice was acquired by a person who had resided in the Republic of South Africa since December 1933 on a temporary residence permit, which had been renewed from time to time. Greenberg JP followed the English Court of Appeal decision in *Boldrini v Boldrini & Martini* [1932] P 9, in holding that the fact that a person *may* be deported does not prevent the acquisition of a domicile of choice. On the facts it was found that it was likely that he would be allowed to remain permanently.

Forsyth[266] states that the modern trend is towards removing such restrictions and that the question as regards these categories of person is likely to centre around the evidential basis for asserting that they satisfy the legal test.

In the absence of modern judicial authority on the point, the position today is likely to be that prisoners,[267] members of the armed forces,[268] members of the diplomatic corps[269] and those working under fixed-term contracts or who are required to move at the direction of their employer,[270] can all acquire a domicile of choice (provided the applicable test is met).

This is also the case with immigrants to the Republic of South Africa and those who move to the country to enjoy an environment more conducive to their health.[271]

Deportees and those unlawfully resident in South Africa cannot acquire a domicile of choice there. The relevant residency must be lawful.[272]

9.1.3.3.1.5 *Domicile of dependence*

The domicile of a dependent person is generally the same as and changes with that of the person on whom the person is dependent. Three categories of person have been included in this type of domicile: married women; children; and the mentally incapacitated.

Married women.[273] A woman, on marriage, takes the domicile of her husband.[274] On the dissolution of the marriage by divorce or death, the domicile of dependence persists until a new domicile is acquired. If the marriage is void, then the woman does not take her husband's domicile, but retains whatever domicile she had at the time of the void marriage. Where the marriage is voidable, the woman will take her husband's domicile until such time as a decree is granted voiding the marriage. There would appear to be no exceptions to the unity of matrimonial domicile principle.

---

266 *Private International Law* 5 ed (2012) 146–52.

267 Ibid 146(a).

268 Ibid 147(b).

269 *Naville v Naville* 1957 (1) SA 280 (C).

270 Forsyth *Private International Law* 5 ed (2012) 148(c).

271 Ibid 151–2.

272 *Essop v Commissioner of Immigration* 1932 AD 223, *per* Stratford JA at 228–9; Forsyth *Private International Law* 5 ed (2012) 149(d); contrast the position in England, *Mark v Mark* [2005] UKHL 42, [2006] 1 AC 98. Likewise, fugitives from justice cannot acquire a domicile of choice in the country to which they have fled: *Bekker NO v Kotzé* 1996 (4) SA 1293 (Namibia High Court, *per* Strydom JP at 1296H). (It does not appear whether the respondent, who claimed to be a Namibian citizen, possessed a Namibian domicile of origin and it does not appear to have been argued that, if he did, this revived upon him fleeing South Africa.)

273 Forsyth *Private International Law* 5 ed (2012) 161.

274 See now the Domicile Act 1992.

Minors.[275] A minor takes as his or her domicile of dependence the domicile of his or her father if legitimate or his or her mother if illegitimate.[276]

Professor Kahn has proposed two exceptions to this general rule: first, where a father, without emancipating the child, grants to the child the capacity to acquire his or her own domicile; second, the child takes the father's domicile only when the child's interests are not affected or prejudiced by the change.[277]

Minority can end in a number of ways. A child attains the age of majority at 18 years[278] and can acquire a domicile thereafter. Minority can also terminate by marriage (in which case the domicile of the girl is the husband's domicile), by a grant of *venia aetatis* or tacit emancipation.

The preponderance of academic authority is in favour of the domicile of a child following the domicile of the person with custody of a child in the event of the father's custody having been terminated by death or court order.[279]

The question what domicile does a child have, in the event of the mother's remarriage after the death of the father or the grant of custody to the mother, has not yet been resolved. Forsyth's[280] view that, considering the theoretical choices, 'perhaps it would not be too bad if the child does follow its stepfather's domicile; after all at least then it will share that domicile with its mother' has much to recommend it.

The mentally incapacitated. It is generally accepted that the incapacitated minor will take the domicile of his natural guardian on whom he is dependent and that he will continue to follow that domicile after attaining majority at 21 years.[281] In the absence of a guardian it seems that the incapacitated person's curator will confer the domicile of the incapacitated person. Mentally incapacitated married women will continue to take the husband's domicile as it changes.[282]

When an independent person becomes incapacitated he will retain the domicile he last had when having capacity.[283]

---

[275] Forsyth *Private International Law* 5 ed (2012) 162.

[276] This general rule may not apply in two possible cases mentioned by Forsyth: where the minor does not accompany the father when the father changes his domicile; and where the minor has sufficient understanding to acquire his or her own domicile. Forsyth expresses doubt whether the first of these forms part of South African law.

[277] Forsyth *Private International Law* 5 ed (2012) 163.

[278] Children's Act 38 of 2005, s 17 (brought into force on 1 July 2007; enacting s 28(3) of the Constitution).

[279] Forsyth *Private International Law* 5 ed (2012) 164.

[280] Ibid 165.

[281] Ibid.

[282] Ibid 165 and fn 215.

[283] Ibid 165 and fn 216; similar to the position in England, *Dicey, Morris and Collins on the Conflict of Laws* 15 ed (2012) vol 1, p 173, r 16.

9.1.3.3.1.6 *Domicile under the Domicile Act 1992*

The 1992 Act refers to only two types of domicile: domicile of choice; and assigned domicile. The domicile of choice may be acquired by anyone satisfying the statutory requirements, whereas the assigned domicile is a domicile assigned to those who have not or cannot acquire a domicile of choice.

Section 1 of the Act deals with the domicile of choice. Section 1 fixes the ability to acquire a domicile of choice to the age of majority and sets out what is required to be established in order to acquire such a domicile in fact.

Section 1(1) provides that every person who is over the age of 18 years and every person under the age of 18 years who by law has the status of a major shall be competent to acquire a domicile of choice. An exception to this is provided for those who do not have the mental capacity to make a rational choice. (Thus, sub-section (1) removes the disability of a married woman to acquire a domicile of choice.)

Section 1(2) provides that a domicile of choice may be acquired by a combination of: (a) lawful presence; (b) at a particular place; (c) with an intention, (i) to settle there, (ii) for an indefinite period. The possible requirement under the common law of an intention to settle permanently is therefore removed (assuming it existed). It seems that lawful presence need not be in pursuance of the relevant intention but that they need only coincide.[284]

Section 2 of the 1992 Act assigns a domicile to those persons who are not capable of acquiring a domicile of choice pursuant to section 1. Such persons fall into two groups: minors and those incapable of making a rational choice.

Section 2(1) provides that a person not capable of acquiring a domicile of choice shall be domiciled at the place with which he is most closely connected. Thus the concept of closest connection replaces the domicile of dependence for minors and those incapable of making a rational choice. This closest connection is not defined in the 1992 Act, but Forsyth notes that the Law Commission considered that the concept allowed domicile to be 'determined objectively with reference to all the circumstances surrounding' the relevant person.[285]

In the case of minors, section 2(2) contains a presumption that if 'in the normal course of events, a child has his home with his parents or with one of them, it shall be presumed, unless the contrary is shown, that the parental home concerned is the child's domicile'. The term 'parents' is defined in sub-section 2(3) as including 'the adoptive parents of a child and the parents of a child who are not married to each other'.

---

[284] Forsyth *Private International Law* 5 ed (2012) 140.

[285] Ibid 153.

Section 3 makes provision for the succession of domicile and abolishes the domicile of origin.

Section 3(1) provides that 'no person shall lose his domicile until he has acquired another domicile whether by choice or by operation of law'. This contemplates a series of choices where a prior domicile of choice is not replaced until a further choice is made. The domicile of choice persists until the acquisition of another (or until one is assigned).

Section 3(2) provides that a person's domicile of origin shall not revive except in so far as it happens to be the same as a domicile of choice or an assigned domicile.

Section 4 excludes the operation of *renvoi* from questions where, according to the rules of South African private international law, a question is to be referred to the law of a party's domicile where that domicile is outside of the Republic of South Africa. A South African court will apply only the internal or domestic law of the relevant jurisdiction and not the private international law rules of that jurisdiction.[286]

Section 5 provides that the acquisition or loss of a domicile shall be determined on a balance of probabilities.

Sections 6 and 7 make consequential amendments to the Divorce Act 1979.

Section 8(2) provides that the 1992 Act is not retrospective with regard to a person's domicile and any rights, obligations or liabilities accrued thereby prior to the commencement of the Act (1 August 1992).

9.1.3.3.1.7 *Residence of a partnership*

Pollak on Jurisdiction[287] observes that, notwithstanding the position at common law that a partnership is simply an association of individuals lacking in separate legal personality, the High Court Rules, by permitting a partnership to be sued in its own name[288] and to be served at the premises of the partnership have, for commercial convenience, invested partnerships for limited purposes with a separate personality (what has been referred to as a '*juristic ghost*').[289]

---

[286] But see Forsyth's persuasive criticism of this provision in *Private International Law* 5 ed (2012) 91–4, citing *Neilson v Overseas Projects Corp of Victoria Ltd* [2005] HCA 54 and the policy of advancing the uniformity of judicial decision-making in support.

[287] Pistorius 2 ed (1993) 70.

[288] The High Court Rules, r 14(2).

[289] *Strydom v Protea Eiendomsagente* 1979 (2) SA 206 (T), *per* Nestadt J at 209F.

In *Pollak on Jurisdiction*,[290] Pistorius expresses the view:

> 'In some of the early cases under the common law it was held that the members of a partnership could not be sued in the court exercising jurisdiction over a particular area merely because the partnership carried on business in that area. Artificial as it may be to ascribe the term "residence" to the place where a partnership carries on business, it is submitted that, as in the case of companies, the principal place of business of a partnership constitutes a sufficient connecting factor with the court concerned to permit it to exercise jurisdiction over the partnership.'

This passage was quoted by Streicher JA in the *Metlika Trading* case:[291]

> 'In these circumstances, the court in whose area of jurisdiction the principal place of business of a partnership is should be the most convenient forum as far as the partnership is concerned and should in general be the court whose judgments against the partnership could most effectively be enforced.'

However, Streicher JA expressly stated that it was not necessary to decide the point as to whether the court at first instance had jurisdiction on this basis because the court had jurisdiction over the two partners in the relevant partnership in any event. The passage from his judgment quote above is, therefore, obiter.[292]

Forsyth[293] has characterised the submission by Pistorius as 'bold'. Forsyth states that partners must be sued as individuals and:

> 'since the action is against each individual partner, each partner must be amenable to the jurisdiction of the court before it will be prepared to hear the case against that partner: Pollak 90. Hence if all the partners are *incolae*, the court will have jurisdiction; if all the partners are peregrines, attachment will be necessary ... It is irrelevant whether the partnership carries on business in the court's area, since this will not suffice to give the court jurisdiction.'

Forsyth further states:

> 'If some of the partners are *incolae* and others peregrines, the court will have jurisdiction over the peregrine partners only if there has been attachment. On the other hand, if all or any of the partners are *incolae* of the Republic but peregrines of the forum, then the court may assume jurisdiction provided only that the contract was entered into in its area, or was to be performed there, or the cause of action arose within its area.'

However, it is submitted that the approach taken by Pistorius and quoted with apparent approval by Streicher JA is manifestly the most convenient one.[294]

---

[290] Pistorius 2 ed (1993) 70.

[291] *Metlika Trading Ltd v Commissioner, South African Revenue Service* 2005 (3) SA 1 (SCA) 13C, with apparent approval.

[292] In this regard Peté et al *Civil Procedure* 2 ed (2011) para 2.4.1(c), pp 61–2, overstate the position: the SCA did not *hold* that if the principal place of business of a partnership is located within the area of jurisdiction of a particular court that should be sufficient to confer jurisdiction on that court. The observations were obiter.

[293] *Private International Law* 5 ed (2012) 222 fn 400.

[294] On the basis that the common-law nature of a partnership has not been changed by r 14(2), Pistorius states in relation to a claim sounding in money (at 70–1): (1) if all the partners are *incolae* of the relevant

9.1.3.3.1.8 *Residence of a firm*

Rule 14(2) also permits a firm to be sued in its own name. However, a firm is no more than 'a business ... carried on by the sole proprietor thereof under a name other than his own' (rule 14(1); the sole proprietor may be a legal person). A firm is thus not separate in identity from its proprietor and, if sued in the name of the firm, may be sued where the proprietor resides but not where the principal place of business of the firm is located, unless other grounds exist to confer jurisdiction on the local court of that place.

9.1.3.3.1.9 *Residence of associations*

An association is defined by rule 14(1) as 'any unincorporated body of persons, not being a partnership'. Rule 14(2) provides that such a body can sue and be sued in its own name.

Pistorius submits[295] that in claims sounding in money: (1) the common-law principles governing jurisdiction in the case of an association which has acquired a separate legal personality such that it can acquire rights apart from the rights of those individuals constituting it and by its enjoying perpetual succession (ie, the association continues, notwithstanding changes in its membership)[296] apply to actions against an association (whether *universitas personarum* or not), such that an association may be sued in the area of a court where the cause of action arose or the contract was concluded; and (2) by analogy with partnerships, an association may sue where the association has a principal place of business or a place where its principal functions are carried out.

9.1.3.3.1.10 *Residence of domestic corporations*

In *Bisonboard Ltd v K Braun Woodworking Machinery (Pty) Ltd*,[297] the Appellate Division considered the jurisdiction of the Witwatersrand Local Division over a company which was incorporated under South African law, had its registered office in Johannesburg and its principal place of business in the Transkei (which at

---

court's area of jurisdiction then proceedings against the partnership may be brought there regardless of where the principal place of business of the partnership is located; (2) if all the partners are local *peregrini* and the principal place of business is not within the court's area of jurisdiction then an action against the partnership may be brought there only if the cause of action arose or the contract was concluded within the area of that court's jurisdiction; (3) if the partners are all foreign *peregrini* and the partnership carries on business within South Africa, then partnership property needs to be attached to found or confirm the jurisdiction before an action against the partnership can proceed.

[295] *Pollak on Jurisdiction* 2 ed (1993) 72.

[296] Such an association being termed a *universitas personarum* (such status being acquired by virtue of the terms of its constitution, statutory or contractual).

[297] 1991 (1) SA 482 (A) (Hoexter, Botha and Milne JJA and Goldstone and Nicholas AJJA).

the time was an independent state).[298] Hoexter JA[299] reviewed earlier authorities and held that a South African company resides at its principal place of business:[300]

> 'it is convenient to acknowledge, in general terms, that it was held in each of them that a company resides at the place where its general administration is located, ie at the seat of its central management and control, from where the general superintendence of its affairs takes place, and where, consequently, it is said that it carries on its real or principal business. For the sake of brevity I shall refer to this as the company's "place of central control".'

However, he also held that a company might reside where its registered office is and for this reason determined that proceedings should continue in the WLD:

> 'Since "residence" is a concept based on the habits of a natural man, the notion of a company's "residence", as has already been pointed out, is necessarily a somewhat abstruse and nebulus one. Insofar as the law requires the concept to be assigned to a corporation, however, it seems to me that the idea of the registered office of a domestic South African company as its "home" represents a juristic abstraction which is by no means unsound in principle.'

This decision therefore opens up the prospect of a company having more than one residence.

A local division will have jurisdiction over a domestic company in a claim sounding in money if that company's central management or principal place of business or where it is registered (or where the cause of action arose or the contract was concluded) is within that court's area of jurisdiction.

A branch office within a particular territorial area of the High Court is not sufficient for jurisdictional purposes however.[301]

9.1.3.3.1.11 *Domicile of domestic corporations*

Prior to the *Bisonboard* case it had been thought that a corporation was domiciled in its place of incorporation.[302] In the context of South Africa this meant that the corporation was domiciled in South Africa and thus the concept of domicile

[298] According to South African law.

[299] 1991 (1) SA 482 (A) 496A–B. Botha JA and Goldstone AJA agreed with Hoexter JA's judgment.

[300] Confirmed and applied in *PMG Motors Kyalami (Pty) Ltd v Firstrand Bank Ltd, Wesbank Division* 2015 (2) SA 634 (SCA) (Lewis, Ponnan and Willis JJA and Mathopo and Gorven AJJA), *per* Gorven AJA giving the judgment of the court at para 9. The court also confirmed that a company retained its place of residence notwithstanding that it was in liquidation (at paras 11–13).

[301] *Kruger NO v Boland Bank Bpk* 1991 (4) SA 107 (T) (*per* Roos J), where the Transvaal Local Division lacked jurisdiction over a bank with its registered office in the Cape in respect of facts arising out of its branch in Pietermaritzburg, Natal (notwithstanding that it had a branch in Pretoria). Contrast the position of a branch of a foreign company (see below).

[302] A passage from Forsyth *Private International Law* 2 ed (1990) 167 to this effect was approved by Hoexter JA in *Bisonboard* at 501I–502A, 'That in the conflict of laws a company incorporated in South Africa with its registered office somewhere within the Republic will have a South African domicile is manifest.'

played no useful role in allocating jurisdiction between the various local divisions of the High Court.

However, Hoexter JA considered[303] that domicile could play a useful role and stated:

> 'But it seems to me, with respect, to be far from obvious that in the situation where domicile is being invoked as a connecting factor to establish jurisdiction such a company cannot have a domicile territorially narrower and more circumscribed than a national domicile. Whatever may be the position in other legal systems, I see no ground, in the light of the peculiar judicial structure of South Africa, for excluding what may conveniently be described as 'provincial' domicile.'

Hoexter JA stated[304] that the concept of domicile lends itself to exemplification rather than definition but that for the purposes of the case he found a useful statement in the judgment of Chitty J in *In re Craignesh, Craignesh v Hewitt*[305] 'that place is properly the domicil of a person in which his habitation is fixed without any present intention of removing therefrom'. He held that in the circumstances of the case, the defendant's domicile was in the area of jurisdiction of the WLD by reason of its registered office being situated there.[306]

Nicholas AJA dissented on the question whether a company's residence was at its place of incorporation (preferring instead the principal place of business), but agreed[307] that the WLD was the defendant's domicile.[308]

9.1.3.3.1.12 *Residence of foreign corporations*

Companies not incorporated in South Africa (referred to as 'external' companies in various statutory provisions,[309] but referred to here as foreign companies) may be resident in South Africa (and thus exempt from the attachment of property by virtue of the provisions of section 28 of the Superior Courts Act 2013).

---

303 1991 (1) SA 482 (A) 502A–B.

304 Ibid 502J–503A.

305 [1892] 3 Ch 180.

306 Although Hoexter JA, at 503D–F, left open the possibility that a company's domicile might not coincide with the place of its registered office.

307 1991 (1) SA 482 (A) 507C and 508A. Milne JA agreed with Nicholas AJA.

308 Although this was subject to the qualification that the company's principal place of business, if it was within South Africa, would be the company's domicile for the purposes of conferring jurisdiction on a local division of the High Court. On the facts of *Bisonboard* the defendant's principal place of business was outside South Africa and this led Nicholas AJA to state (at 507D): 'Where it does not have its principal place of business in the Republic, then, for want of anything better, it must be said to be domiciled in the area in which it is regarded as being present', which he found to be the place of incorporation.

309 Section 1 of the Companies Act 1973 (Act 61 of 1973); ss 1 and 23(2) of the Companies Act 2008 (Act 71 of 2008).

In *Appleby (Pty) Ltd v Dundas Ltd*,[310] the defendant company was registered in England, had its head office in England and had a branch office in Johannesburg at which it carried on business. The branch had concluded contracts with the plaintiff at Port Elizabeth, where the plaintiff had its registered office and where it carried on business. The plaintiff sued in the Eastern Districts Local Division. The defendant contended that the EDLD had no jurisdiction because it was domiciled and resided in England where it was incorporated and also because there had been no attachment of its property within the EDLD. The plaintiff needed to establish two points in order to succeed on the jurisdiction issue: first, that the contracts were concluded at Port Elizabeth; and, second, that the defendant resided within the Union. Hoexter J found for the plaintiff on both issues. On the second issue Hoexter J stated:[311]

> 'In my opinion a defendant resides in the Union within the meaning of sec. 5 of Act 27 of 1912 if he is sufficiently resident to make him amenable to the jurisdiction of one or other of the Divisions of the Supreme Court. The main objects of Act 27 of 1912 appear to be (1) to make a defendant who is, by virtue of his residence, amenable to the jurisdiction of any one Division of the Supreme Court, amenable also to the jurisdiction of any other Division which is competent to adjudicate upon the cause of action against the defendant, e.g. *ratione contractus*, and (2) to prohibit the arrest *ad fundandam jurisdictionem* of such a defendant or his property. (See e.g. *Brooks v Maquassi Halls Ltd.* (1914 CPD 371), and *Wright v Stuttaford & Co.* (1929, E.D.L. 10).)
>
> It follows that if the defendant is amenable, in the present case, to the jurisdiction of the Witwatersrand Local Division by reason of the fact that it carries on business at its branch office at Johannesburg, then it resides in the Union within the meaning of sec. 5 of Act 27 of 1912.
>
> In my opinion it is so amenable in respect of any cause of action arising out of the business carried on at its Johannesburg branch.'

[310] 1948 (2) SA 905 (EDLD) (Hoexter J).

[311] Ibid 909–10. Section 5 of the Administration of Justice Act 27 of 1912 referred to in the quoted passage, is the equivalent of s 28 of the Superior Courts Act 2013 in prohibiting the attachment of a defendant's property where the defendant is resident in South Africa. (Section 3 of the 1912 Act provided for service of a summons issued out of what would not be any local division in any part of the Union, as it was then, on a defendant who is resident in the Union.)

Having reviewed the authorities[312] Hoexter J concluded:[313]

> 'The defendant, by virtue of the business which it carries on at its branch in Johannesburg, is sufficiently resident in the Union to make it amenable, in respect of any cause of action arising out of such business, to the jurisdiction of any Division of the Supreme Court which is competent to adjudicate upon that cause of action.'

Thus it is clear that, unlike domestic cases, where the defendant is a foreign corporation, something less than residence in the domestic sense of a principal place of business is sufficient to establish jurisdiction where the cause of action arises out of that business. *A fortiori* where the foreign corporation has a principal place of business in South Africa it will be resident for jurisdictional purposes.[314]

In *ISM Inter Ltd v Maraldo*,[315] the plaintiff had obtained an order in the Transvaal Local Division for the attachment of the defendant's property *ad fundandam jurisdictionem*. The defendant was a company incorporated and registered in Switzerland. The defendant contended that it was an *incola* of the Transvaal by virtue of its having carried on business in the Transvaal as a distributor of coffee machines and a water-saving device.[316] The cause of action on which the defendant was sued was wholly unrelated to these activities and concerned a contract with the defendant whereby the plaintiff was to sell the defendant's services as a labour recruitment bureau to a third party. The plaintiff claimed commission in respect of the sale. The plaintiff contended that, even if the defendant carried on business

---

[312] *Wallis v The Gordon Diamond Mining Co Ltd* 6 HCG 43, where the defendant was a foreign company, registered in England and with its head office in England, and it was held by Solomon J that, because it carried on mining operations in Griqualand West, it was sufficiently resident there to be amenable to the jurisdiction of the High Court of Griqualand West in respect of causes of action arising out of contracts concluded in the course of its business in Griqualand West. In *Swift v National Bank of SA* 1923 OPD 24, De Villiers JP stated (at 27) that the *Wallis* decision 'thus recognises the doctrine of a limited or partial domicil (or rather residence) in the case of a juristic person which carries on some part of its business in a country other than that in which it has its true domicil, i.e., in which it has its principal place of business'. As Hoexter J makes plain, this limited departure is made for reasons of commercial convenience: 'The principle is founded largely on commercial convenience a point which is stressed in most of the decided cases. So, for instance, Gutsche, J, in the case of *Ochs v Kolmanskop Diamond Mines Ltd.* (1921, SWA 8), gave the following reasons for accepting it: "If it were held otherwise great inconveniences would arise and commercial dealings might, in consequence, become restricted. There might be companies whose head offices are in Berlin, but whose business is carried out in this country. It might not be in the best interests of such companies themselves, and it would be a hardship on those who had dealings with such companies, if the latter could not be sued in respect of transactions that arose wholly in this jurisdiction, until their property had been attached *ad fundandam jurisdictionem* and leave be granted to sue by edictal citation."'

[313] 1948 (2) SA 905 (EDLD) 912.

[314] With the consequence that, in both cases, the defendant will be exempt from attachment by reason of s 28 of the Superior Courts Act 2013.

[315] 1983 (4) SA 112 (T) (Fleming J).

[316] The defendant also contended that it had a registered office in the Transvaal. However, under the then companies legislation, the Companies Act 1973, s 322, all external companies were required to have registered offices in South Africa. However, it had long been held that this requirement was mainly procedural in nature and did not amount to residence: *Grimshaw v Mica Mines* 1912 TPD 450.

in the Transvaal, it was nevertheless not an *incola*. The plaintiff conceded that a foreign company, which had its main place of business in a foreign country, could simultaneously be resident within South Africa if it carried on business there, but such business would be recognised only in relation to a dispute arising out of the local business activities of that company.

Flemming J found that the defendant was not resident in South Africa. The judge then stated:[317]

> 'The underlying thought seems to be, seen from the negative formulation, that jurisdiction will not exist in regard to a transaction which has nothing to do with the local operations. A positive formulation is more difficult. The dominant idea, initially at least, appears to be that a transaction concluded locally may give rise to a dispute and that a Court should have jurisdiction (and regard the defendant as an *incola pro tanto*) in regard to such a dispute. It is obvious that if the negative and positive approach were to apply in the words in which I have couched them, there may be cases where the transactions are not completely unrelated, but on the other hand do not come within the terms of the positive formulation.'

The result appears to be that the courts will entertain a departure from the domestic principal place of business test of residence to permit a foreign corporation to be resident for jurisdictional purposes where: (1) the foreign corporation's place of business in South Africa does not amount to its principal place of business; (2) the dispute concerns the corporation's business in South Africa; and (3) the cause of action arises before the Local Division seised of the matter.

In this connection, Pistorius has formulated four propositions relating to the circumstances in which a local division of the High Court will have jurisdiction over a foreign corporation for a claim sounding in money:[318]

(1) If the foreign corporation has its principal place of business within the area of the local division then it is resident within that area and the court has jurisdiction without the necessity of an attachment of property *ad fundandam jurisdictionis.*[319]

(2) If the foreign corporation has its principal place of business outside South Africa but carries on business within the area of the local division, that court has jurisdiction if a recognised *ratio jurisdictionis* exists within the area and if the claim arises out of or is connected with the business of the corporation which is being carried on in that area. In this case it is not necessary (or permissible in terms of section 28 of the Superior Courts Act 2013) to attach the corporation's property.

[317] 1983 (4) SA 112 (T) 117F.

[318] Pistorius *Pollak on Jurisdiction* 2 ed (1993) 77–8.

[319] In the circumstances, attachment would in any event be impermissible: s 28 of the Superior Courts Act 2013.

(3) If the foreign corporation has its principal place of business outside South Africa but carries on business within the area of the local division but no recognised *ratio jurisdictionis* exists within the area and the claim does not arise out of or is not connected with the business of the corporation which is being carried on in that area, the court has jurisdiction only if property within the area of that court has been attached.[320]

(4) If the foreign corporation (not being an external company as defined by the relevant legislation) has its principal place of business outside South Africa and does not carry on business within the area of the local division, it will be amenable to the jurisdiction of the court only if its property has been attached to found jurisdiction (the plaintiff must be an *incola* of that court).

It is submitted that propositions (2) and (3) are too widely stated. There is no need for the foreign corporation's carrying on of business to be within the local court's area of jurisdiction.[321]

In proposition (3) the formulation that there should be no recognised *ratio jurisdictionis* is surplusage: it is sufficient to state that there should be no connection between the claim and the defendant's business.[322]

As regards proposition (4), it is unclear why it should make a difference if the foreign corporation is, technically, an external company or not. In the absence of registration, foreign corporations are nonetheless recognised in local law.[323]

As stated above, a foreign corporation's residence for jurisdictional purposes is established where: (1) the foreign corporation's place of business in South Africa does not amount to its principal place of business; (2) the dispute concerns the corporation's business in South Africa; and (3) the cause of action arises before the local division seised of the matter.[324]

---

[320] Pistorius states that the distinction between (2) and (3) is dubious (at 78): 'It was suggested in the first edition of this book that it would be more in accord with the common law rules of jurisdiction if it were held that attachment of the property of a foreign company whose principal place of business is not within the Republic is always necessary. If its principal place of business is not within the Republic of South Africa, a foreign company ought not to be regarded as residing in the area where it carried on business as it does.' Pistorius suggests that an attachment is required for (3) and not (2) because the courts have accepted that the fact of a relationship between the claim and the business carried on within the area of jurisdiction of the court concerned constituted an additional jurisdictional connecting factor.

[321] *Appleby (Pty) Ltd v Dundas Ltd* 1948 (2) SA 905 (EDLD).

[322] If there is no claim – no cause of action – there can be no connection in any event.

[323] *Wiseman v Ace Table Soccer (Pty) Ltd* 1991 (4) SA 171 (W), *per* Claassen AJ at 176G.

[324] Attachment to found jurisdiction would, therefore, appear to be impermissible: s 28 Superior Courts Act 2013.

9.1.3.3.1.13 *Domicile of foreign corporations*

There is little judicial or academic authority on the question where a foreign corporation is domiciled. As has been noted in the *Bisonboard* case,[325] in the context of domestic corporations, Hoexter JA stated[326] that in relation to the concept of domicile, for the purposes of the case, he found a useful statement in the judgment of Chitty J in *In re Craignesh, Craignesh v Hewitt*[327] 'that place is properly the domicil of a person in which his habitation is fixed without any present intention of removing therefrom' and held that in the circumstances of the case, the defendant's domicile was in the area of jurisdiction of the WLD by reason of its registered office being situated there.

By parity of reasoning, it would seem that the domicile of a foreign corporation is at the place where its registered office is located and that this will, usually by definition, be abroad.

9.1.3.3.1.14 *The government*

Forsyth[328] notes with apparent approval that Pistorius submits[329] that the central government should be treated as if it were a domestic company and its place of business and residence (and, presumably, its domicile also) is deemed to be Pretoria and a claim against the government should be brought there. But where a cause of action arose or where a contract was entered into or was to be performed within the area of another local division, then that court will have jurisdiction.

9.1.3.3.2 *Ratio contractus*

Where: (1) the contract was concluded (the *locus contractus*); (2) the contract is to be performed in whole or in part (the *locus solutionis*); and (3) the contract was breached in the manner relied upon by the plaintiff; a court may, *ratio contractus*, exercise jurisdiction.

There is a difference of opinion among academic authorities as to whether (3) above is an independent *ratio jurisdictionis*.

---

325 1991 (1) SA 482 (A).

326 Ibid 502J–503A.

327 [1892] 3 Ch 180.

328 *Private International Law* 5 ed (2012) 212.

329 *Pollak on Jurisdiction* 2 ed (1993) 80–1; *Minister of Law and Order v Patterson* 1984 (2) SA 739 (A) (Rabie CJ, Corbett, Kotzé, Trengove and Viljoen JJA) at 756C–E, *per* Rabie CJ: 'The considerations which move the Courts to restrict, for jurisdictional purposes, the "residence" or "place of business" of a trading corporation to the place where the central management of such corporation is exercised apply with equal, and even greater, force to the case of the State, considering its vast and country-wide activities. In the case of the State that place is Pretoria, which is, according to s 23 of the Republic of South Africa Constitution Act 32 of 1961, "the seat of Government of the Republic".'

In his discussion of the criterion by which the ground of jurisdiction is to be determined, Forsyth[330] cites Pollak's suggestion that a ground of jurisdiction is defined by reference to 'the act of the defendant which gives the plaintiff his cause for complaint', and states that this formulation is too widely drawn. In Forsyth's view, Pollak's suggestion omits to consider cases where a contract has been entered into and is to be performed outside the area of the court's jurisdiction, but where the breach of a contract occurred within the area of the court's jurisdiction. This set of circumstances is not sufficient to found the jurisdiction of the court, according to Forsyth.[331]

Peté et al[332] state that a contractual cause of action sufficient to ground jurisdiction arises 'where the contract was breached in the manner relied upon by the plaintiff' in the area of the court's jurisdiction, citing *Minesa Energy (Pty) Ltd v Stinnes International AG*[333] in support of that proposition.

Pistorius[334] states that the *rationes jurisdictionis* embracing contract comprise: the formation of a contract within the area of the jurisdiction of the relevant court; the performance of whole or part of a contract within that area, regardless of where the contract was formed; and: 'A third alternative, which is often treated as falling within the jurisdiction conferred upon a court as the forum contractus, is if the breach of contract upon which the claim is founded occurred within the area over which the court exercises jurisdiction.'[335] In *Frank Wright (Pty) Ltd*,[336] Searle J held[337] that the local *peregrinus* plaintiff could not attach *ad confirmandam jurisdictionem* certain cork tiles belonging to the foreign (Portuguese) *peregrinus* defendant and located in Cape Province because the breach of contract in question occurred either in Portugal or in the Transvaal, but in any event not in the Cape: 'The breach in respect of which the defendant is sued must be a breach of a duty which he was bound to perform within the jurisdiction.'

As a matter of judicial authority the issue whether a breach of contract within the jurisdiction amounts to a *ratio jurisdictionis* does not seem to have been the subject of an adverse decision and there is support for such a position in the *Minesa*

---

[330] *Private International Law* 5 ed (2012) 215.

[331] Ibid. Forsyth cites, at 215 fn 347, the following authority in support of his view: *Einwald v German West African Co* (1887) 5 SC 86; *Ex parte Jackson* (1896) 13 SC 13; *Kopelowitz v West* 1954 (4) SA 296 (W); and *Roberts Construction Co Ltd v Willcox Bros (Pty) Ltd* 1962 (4) SA 326 (A).

[332] *Civil Procedure* 2 ed (2011) 76.

[333] 1988 (3) SA 903 (D) (Bristowe J).

[334] *Pollak on Jurisdiction* 2 ed (1993) 63.

[335] Citing (at fn 39) *Taboryski v Schweizer and Apirion NO* 1917 WLD 152 (*per* Ward J at 158 and 159); *Walker v Taylor* 1934 WLD 101 (*per* De Waal JP, following *Taboryski*, at 112–13) and *Frank Wright (Pty) Ltd v Corticas BCM Ltd* 1948 (4) SA 456 (C).

[336] 1948 (4) SA 456 (C) (Searle J).

[337] Ibid 463, citing in support *Taboryski v Schweizer and Apirion NO* 1917 WLD 152 and *Walker v Taylor* 1934 WLD 101.

Energy case (see below). The preferable view would seem to be that a breach of contract within the jurisdiction is sufficient to amount to a *ratio jurisdictionis.* This is because it is generally accepted that the *locus solutionis* provides a *ratio jurisdictionis* and, as a matter of commercial reality, the *locus solutionis* will usually only be relevant to a dispute if performance is not delivered in accordance with the contract, ie there has been a breach of contract, and not where performance has been delivered in accordance with the contract.

Turning to the authorities cited by Forsyth, it is submitted that these authorities are distinguishable. In *Einwald v German West African Co*,[338] a contract for the provision of the services of an expedition guide was made between the plaintiff and the defendant in Germany where both parties were resident and domiciled. The agreement was that the parties would travel to Table Bay in the Cape Colony and the plaintiff would be paid £5 for his travelling expenses. At the Cape the expedition would proceed to Walwich Bay, within the Cape Colony, where the plaintiff was to receive a salary. From there the expedition would proceed to Ovampoland and then to the Zambezi. On arrival at Table Bay the plaintiff was dismissed without payment. The plaintiff sought to attach the expedition's goods to found jurisdiction. Dismissing the application De Villiers CJ held[339] that the expedition started in Hamburg:

> 'The fact that the starting point in Africa is Walwich Bay, which is within the Colony, does not justify the Court in holding that the contract is to be performed within the jurisdiction. The same remark applies to the circumstances, that a portion of the plaintiff's travelling expenses was to be paid upon arrival of the expedition in Cape Town ... The alleged breach of contract consists, not in refusing to pay the small sum payable in Cape Town, but in dismissing the plaintiff altogether, and preventing him from joining the expedition in the interior.'

Having found that no performance was due to be rendered within the jurisdiction, it is difficult to envisage how the judge could have found that a breach of an obligation had occurred within the jurisdiction. The court appears to have held that the breach of contract was in preventing the plaintiff joining the expedition where the expedition was due to commence, in the interior and outside the jurisdiction.

In *Ex parte Jackson*,[340] De Villiers CJ, with whom the other members of the court agreed, dismissed an application for an attachment brought by an English plaintiff for breach of a contract of service made in England. The terms of the contract were that the plaintiff would travel to Table Bay, Cape Colony, and from there by train to Johannesburg in the service of the defendant. From the

---

338 (1887) 5 SC 86.

339 Ibid 89.

340 (1896) 13 SC 13 (De Villiers CJ, Buchanan and Maasdorp JJ).

report it appears that the plaintiff embarked for the Cape on 18 January 1896, was dismissed from the defendant's service on 28 January and then arrived in the Cape on 4 February. So it seems that any breach of contract took place prior to the plaintiff's arrival in the jurisdiction. However, counsel for the plaintiff contended that the contract was to date from the time of arrival in Cape Town and that part of the contract was therefore to be performed in the Cape (while at the same time contending that the plaintiff had been dismissed from service on the voyage). De Villiers CJ rejected this contention and followed his decision in *Einwald* holding that the contract was one to be performed in Johannesburg and that 'it was not contemplated that more than a couple of days service would be performed in the Colony'. As in *Einwald*, the court appears to have concluded that the performance of the parties' obligations was to take place outside the jurisdiction (subject to a *de minimis* couple of days in the Cape) and therefore that non-performance, or breach, of those obligations was also a matter occurring or to occur outside the jurisdiction.

In *Kopelowitz v West*,[341] the plaintiff sought an order that certain sums standing to the credit of a man called Marx in a bank were the plaintiff's property. The plaintiff had been sold Russian squirrel pelts for £1,297, 10s, by a man called West. That contract had been concluded in the Cape and the plaintiff had paid by cheque. West had proceeded to Johannesburg and had sold more of the pelts to a man called Lewis. The plaintiff's cheque had been endorsed to West's nominee Marx and deposited in Marx's bank account. Unfortunately, West had not obtained an import licence and the government confiscated the pelts in the possession of both the plaintiff and Lewis. The plaintiff's application to attach the balance of the sums in Marx's account was rejected, inter alia, because there was no *ratio jurisdictionis* to underpin such an attachment. Murray J held[342] that no part of the contract between the plaintiff and West fell to be performed in the area of the jurisdiction of the Witwatersrand Local Division and thus there was no basis for the attachment sought. Here there was no possibility of a breach of contract within the jurisdiction.

Returning to *Minesa Energy (Pty) Ltd v Stinnes International AG*, Bristowe J[343] held that a breach of contract within the jurisdiction of the court would provide a ground of jurisdiction:

> 'Pollak *The South African Law of Jurisdiction* at 80 where the following passage occurs: "In an action based upon failure to perform a contract, it is not sufficient that any portion of the contract is to be performed within the area to which the Court belongs. It is necessary that the defendant should have been bound to perform that portion of the

---

[341] 1954 (4) SA 296 (W) (Murray J).

[342] Ibid 301E.

[343] 1988 (3) SA 903 (D) 904G.

> contract, in respect of which he is being sued, within such area. In other words it is necessary that the breach, upon which the plaintiff bases his claim, should have occurred within the area to which the Court belongs. There is no doubt that such a Court would have jurisdiction. See *Roberts Construction Co Ltd v Willcox Bros (Pty) Ltd* 1962 (4) SA 326 (A) at 337A–B."'

Bristow J continued:[344]

> 'I note that amongst the authorities upon which Pollack relies for his proposition are two Natal cases. They are *City Timber Mills v Nagdee* 1916 NPD 255 *and Van der Linden v Eppel* 1922 NPD 57. These are both decisions of the Full Bench of this Division and it seems to me that they do indeed furnish support for Pollak's view. In particular this is so in the passage occurring in the judgment of Broome J in the *City Timber Mills* case at 258 - 9: "The only performance which is referred to in the declaration is the delivery of the goods said to have been effected in Pietermaritzburg, but in regard to the performance of that portion of the contract which is sought to be enforced, namely payment of the price, the declaration and the summons are silent, as are also the particulars. There is no statement that the whole of the contract was to be performed in Natal, nor the performance of that portion which the plaintiff seeks to enforce, had to take place in this province." It is to be noted also that Dove-Wilson JP expressly agreed with Broome J that the declaration, to which exception had been taken, was bad for the reasons stated by Broome J.'

From this survey, it is apparent that the balance of judicial authority supports the formulation set out above of the circumstances in which, *ratio contractus*, a court may exercise jurisdiction.[345] The occurrence of any of these circumstances within the jurisdiction of a particular court will provide that court with a *causa jurisdictionis*.

9.1.3.3.3 *Ratio delicti commissi*

A court may have jurisdiction by reason of a *ratio delicti commissi* in the event that a delict was committed or occurred within its area of jurisdiction.

Usually the answer to the question whether a *ratio delicti commissi* exists will be self-evident: the *locus delicti* of a car accident caused by negligent driving will be the place where the accident occurred and the court having jurisdiction over the area within which the accident occurred will have jurisdiction by virtue of the *ratio delicti commissi*.

However, the place of a delict will not always be so easily ascertainable. In *Thomas v BMW South Africa (Pty) Ltd*,[346] the plaintiff was injured in a car accident in the Cape while driving a BMW 535i. The plaintiff alleged that the vehicle

---

[344] Ibid 905G.

[345] In other words, the authorities support the correctness of the conclusion that a court in the place where contract was breached in the manner relied upon by the plaintiff may exercise jurisdiction *ratio contractus*.

[346] 1996 (2) SA 106 (C) (Van Reenen J).

suddenly and unexpectedly accelerated, went out of control, left the road and crashed into a fence at the side of the road and that the cause of this surge of acceleration was the malfunctioning of the vehicle's cruise-control system. The defendant was the manufacturer/distributor of new BMW motor vehicles in South Africa and had its registered office and principal place of business in Gauteng. The plaintiff commenced proceedings in the Cape Provincial Division claiming damages for personal injuries. The defendant raised a jurisdictional objection. In support of the CPD having jurisdiction, the plaintiff contended that: (1) the cruise-control system of his motor vehicle malfunctioned; and (2) the ensuing collision took place; and (3) he sustained injuries; and (4) the defendant through its dealership in Cape Town supplied a vehicle with a defective cruise-control system all within the CPD's area of jurisdiction. The defendant contended that for the court to have jurisdiction, all the elements of the plaintiff's cause of action – in the sense of every fact which is material to be proved to entitle the plaintiff to succeed in his claim – had to take place within its area of jurisdiction.

Rejecting the defendant's contention and dismissing the defendant's objection to the jurisdiction, Van Reenen J held:[347]

> 'the most apparent solution appears to be to devise qualitative and quantitative criteria to determine, with reference to the elements of the delict in question - to the extent that it is possible to break a delict up into metaphysical components - the court which is the most closely associated with the delict, the *locus* whereof has to be determined. Such criteria, however, should accord with the principles of our common law regarding jurisdiction, be consonant with developments in our case law and accommodate the demands of modern society. Bearing all this in mind, the *locus* of a delict for jurisdictional purposes, in my view, should be determined with reference to the materiality of and the number of the ingredients thereof which have occurred in a court's area of jurisdiction.'

The court found[348] that the damage had occurred and[349] that the duty of care owed by the defendant to the plaintiff was owed within the area of jurisdiction of the CPD.

In the context of defamation, it seems that the *ratio delicti commissi* will be established by the publication of the defamatory statement within the area of the court's jurisdiction. In *Tsichlas v Touch Line Media*,[350] the first plaintiff was the club secretary of the second plaintiff's football club and the defendant was the owner and publisher of a football magazine and internet website. The first plaintiff sought various forms of interdictal relief and commenced proceedings in the Witwatersrand Local Division for defamation against the defendant arising out of material which had been published in its magazine. The defendant had

[347] Ibid 125E.
[348] Ibid 126D.
[349] Ibid 126I.
[350] 2004 (2) SA 112 (W) (Kuny AJ).

a place of business within the area of jurisdiction of the WLD but its principal place of business was in Cape Town. On that basis, inter alia, the defendant denied that the WLD had jurisdiction to entertain the claim. The plaintiff relied for jurisdiction, inter alia, on the fact that the cause of action had arisen within the area of jurisdiction of the WLD because the plaintiff's attorney had accessed the defendant's website within its area of jurisdiction.

Kuny AJ held:[351]

> 'I am of the view that the statements were published of and concerning the plaintiff within the area of jurisdiction of this Court. Once they had been accessed by, and thereby published to, the attorney, there was, in my view, "publication" as a requisite element of defamation.'

9.1.3.3.4 *Ratio rei sitae*

The location of movable or immovable property within the area of jurisdiction of the court will confer on that court a *ratio rei sitae*.

9.1.3.3.4.1 *Immovable property*

Title

The *forum rei sitae* has exclusive jurisdiction over claims involving the title to immovable property and thus only the local division in which the property is situated has jurisdiction to determine title.[352]

Transfer

In respect of actions seeking an order for the transfer of immovable property the *forum rei sitae* will have jurisdiction not least because the officials of that forum will be able to effect a transfer of the relevant property to the plaintiff: 'The court of the area in which the property is situate can certainly control the transfer of, or any interference with the property through the Registrar of Deeds of that area, and by other means.'[353]

The *forum rei sitae* will also be competent in an action *in personam* (for breach of a contract of sale, for example) for the transfer of immovable property, even though none of the grounds of jurisdiction in actions in which a judgment sounding in money is claimed present and the court may in addition to ordering

[351] Ibid 120A.

[352] Pistorius *Pollak on Jurisdiction* 2 ed (1993) 89–90; Forsyth *Private International Law* 5 ed (2012) 235–6.

[353] *Sonia (Pty) Ltd v Wheeler* 1958 (1) SA 555 (A) (Fagan CJ, De Beer and Malan JJA, Reynolds and Price AJJA), *per* Price AJA at 562A–B.

the transfer of the property, give judgment for a claim in money or for an order for costs:[354]

> 'Any judgment in respect of the money claim given by the Eastern Districts Court, which has jurisdiction to cancel the contract, can be enforced both by attachment of the property under a writ issued from that Court and by a writ issued in any of the other Provinces by means of the machinery provided by sec. 112 of the South Africa Act. If the Eastern Districts Court has jurisdiction to decree cancellation of the contract of sale, every consideration of convenience and common sense would suggest that it may exercise jurisdiction in respect of any consequential claims, such as a claim for return of the purchase price and costs. It would be monstrous if the plaintiff were entitled to sue in the Eastern Districts Court for cancellation of the sale, but the law obliges him to sue in some other Province where the defendant is domiciled for any consequential money claims, especially where the Eastern Districts Court is quite able to give an effective judgment which it can enforce in respect of the money claims.'

The *forum domicilii* is also competent to hear actions concerning the transfer of immovable property where a local division which has jurisdiction over the defendant on a basis recognised under the common law can compel him to execute a deed transferring the property to the plaintiff.[355] In *Hugo v Wessels*,[356] as part of a divorce settlement, the OFS had ordered the plaintiff husband to pay R25,000 to the defendant wife to purchase a property and had ordered the defendant to transfer that property into the names of her three sons. The property which the defendant bought was situated in the Transvaal. The defendant did not register the property in the names of her three sons as ordered. The plaintiff bought an action in the OFS for an order that the defendant cause the property to be registered in the names of her sons or, failing that, an order that the Registrar of the OFS sign the documents on her behalf. These documents could be used to effect a transfer of the property in the Transvaal to the sons. The Appellate Division held that the fact that the divorce settlement was concluded in the Orange Free State and was incorporated into an order of the OFS was sufficient to vest the OFS with jurisdiction.

These principles are thought also to apply to the partition of immovable property.[357]

Declarations

Declarations that immovable property is subject to or free from a real right are subject to the (probably) exclusive jurisdiction of the *forum rei sitae* on the

---

[354] Ibid 563F–564D.

[355] Pistorius *Pollak on Jurisdiction* 2 ed (1993) 92.

[356] 1987 (3) SA 837 (A) (Hoexter, Botha, Grosskopf, Smalberger AJJ and Kumleben AJA).

[357] Pistorius *Pollak on Jurisdiction* 2 ed (1993) 93; Forsyth *Private International Law* 5 ed (2012) 237–8.

same basis as that court has exclusive jurisdiction over matters relating to title of immovable property.[358]

Possession of immovables

The *forum rei sitae* has exclusive jurisdiction over questions relating to the possession of immovable property, as its officers will be able to give the plaintiff possession and this is so whether the defendant is an *incola* or *peregrinus* (of either sort).[359]

Rescission of a contract for the transfer of immovables

A claim asking the court to rescind a contract for the transfer of immovables may be entertained by the *forum rei sitae*, as any order made will be effective. In *Sonia (Pty) Ltd v Wheeler*,[360] Price AJA, 'on grounds of principle, convenience and common sense', held:[361]

> 'A claim to rescind a contract for the sale of immovable property can be effectively dealt with by the Courts of the State in which the property is situate. Such State has complete control over the property and can therefore effectively release a person from his obligation to transfer or to take transfer of the property. It follows that in an action in which a judgment rescinding a contract to transfer immovable property is claimed it is a sufficient basis for jurisdiction that the property is situate within the State in whose Court the action is brought.'

Power over the defendant is not necessary and it does not matter whether the defendant is an *incola* or a *peregrinus*.

The *forum rei sitae* does not have exclusive jurisdiction, however. *Hugo v Wessels* establishes that if the court has jurisdiction over the defendant in an *in personam* claim, the court should have jurisdiction to order rescission of the contract.[362]

Declaration that immovable property is executable

If a debt has been secured by a mortgage over immovable property, the plaintiff is entitled not only to judgment for the amount of the debt but also to an order declaring the mortgaged property executable. The *forum rei sitae* clearly has jurisdiction to make such an order, since the court can order its own sheriff to attach the property and to sell it in execution. Pistorius states that for this reason the *forum rei sitae* has exclusive jurisdiction, because a sheriff cannot attach

---

358 Forsyth *Private International Law* 5 ed (2012) 237; Pistorius *Pollak on Jurisdiction* 2 ed (1993) 93–4.

359 Ibid; Pistorius *Pollak on Jurisdiction* 2 ed (1993) 94.

360 1958 (1) SA 555 (A) (Price AJA).

361 Ibid 561G–H, quoting from *Pollak on Jurisdiction* 1 ed (1937) 111, but misattributing the quote to *Palm v Simpson* (1848) 3 M 565.

362 Forsyth *Private International Law* 5 ed (2012) 238; Pistorius *Pollak on Jurisdiction* 2 ed (1993) 96–7.

property outside the area for which he is sheriff and a court cannot order the sheriff of a different area to attach and sell property in that area.[363]

Forsyth agrees with this statement in so far as it concerns immovable property outside South Africa. As regards immovable property within South Africa it would now seem that a court other than the *forum rei sitae* may make a declaration as to the executability of immovable property because such an order is simply 'part of the procedure by which the execution of a judgment debt is obtained and does not constitute an exercise of jurisdiction over such property by the court from which it issues'.[364]

Application for leave to sell or mortgage immovable property

If immovable property is owned by a minor, the child's parent or guardian has no authority to alienate or mortgage the property without an order of the court.[365] The court of the child's domicile is the court which must grant such leave and the *forum rei sitae* will not entertain such an application until that authority has been granted.

Where the court of the child's domicile is overseas and the property is situated within South Africa, an application probably must be made to the *forum rei sitae* for a further order authorising such sale or mortgage, before the Registrar of Deeds in the relevant area will act on the order of the domiciliary court.[366]

Where the child is domiciled in South Africa, however, and the property is situated in the area of another division of the High Court then the order of the division of the High Court of the child's domicile 'shall be given effect to by the registrar of such other province without the necessity of having such order confirmed by the court of the province in which the property is situate'.[367]

Appointment of a curator bonis[368] *in respect of immovable property*

Both the *forum rei sitae* and the *forum domicilii* have jurisdiction to appoint a *curator bonis* of immovable property if appropriate.

Further, pursuant to sections 56 and 58 of the Mental Health Act 1973,[369] any division of the High Court in which the patient happens to be will have jurisdiction to make such an appointment.

---

363 *Pollak on Jurisdiction* 2 ed (1993) 97.

364 *Ivoral Properties (Pty) Ltd v Sheriff, Cape Town* 2005 (6) SA 96 (C) (Van Reenen J) 114C–D.

365 Forsyth *Private International Law* 5 ed (2012) 238; Pistorius *Pollak on Jurisdiction* 2 ed (1993) 97–8.

366 *Ex parte Fell* 1934 (2) PH M 32 (C), where the minor was an English domiciliary and an order authorising the sale of his property in the Cape was made by the Chancery Court. The order was confirmed by the CPD.

367 Deeds Registries Act 1937 (Act 47 of 1937), s 97(2) (as inserted by Act 43 of 1957).

368 A guardian or trustee appointed to take care of property in certain cases; as for the benefit of creditors.

369 Act 18 of 1973.

9.1.3.3.4.2 *Movable property*

In the absence of judicial authority dealing with movable property, Pistorius sets out four principles which are applicable to movables.[370]

First, like immovables, movable property is subject to the control of the authority of the area in which it is located. Unlike immovables, however, movable property may be taken away from that area by or on the instructions of the owner or otherwise. This suggests that the power to deal with movable property may lie not only in the courts of the *rei sitae*, but also in the courts of the place which has power over the person who, as owner, controls the movables.

Second, the principle of effectiveness applies to a judgment by any court enjoying authority over a defendant because the judgment of that court will be executable elsewhere in South Africa and this extends to judgments concerning title to movables.

Third, if any claim relating to movable property is brought *in personam* then (following *Hugo v Wessels*) the court which has power over the defendant should be able to give judgment against him in regard to that property and that judgment will be enforceable.

Fourth, it would seem that the only situation in which a South African court must defer to the *forum rei sitae* is where the property is situated outside South Africa.

Title to movables

The *forum rei sitae* will have jurisdiction to decide questions of title to movable property.[371] A division of the High Court may decide such questions in relation to movable property within its area of jurisdiction. It does not matter whether the defendant is an *incola* or a *peregrinus* or whether he is present in that area. If the defendant is a *peregrinus*, attachment of the property is unnecessary.[372]

Pistorius states[373] that the *forum sitae rei* does not have exclusive jurisdiction to determine title to movables within South Africa and that the *forum domicilii* has jurisdiction to determine such questions. If the property were situated in South Africa, then a judgment rendered by such a court would satisfy the principle of effectiveness.

---

[370] *Pollak on Jurisdiction* 2 ed (1993) 100–1.

[371] Forsyth *Private International Law* 5 ed (2012) 241; Pistorius *Pollak on Jurisdiction* 2 ed (1993) 101.

[372] *Jackaman v Arkell* 1953 (3) SA 31 (T) 35; Forsyth points out, however, that attachment may be granted in order to secure property for execution of the judgment (at 242 fn 521).

[373] *Pollak on Jurisdiction* 2 ed (1993) 102–3, citing Voet *Commentarius ad Pandectas* 5.1.77.

Claims for the delivery of movables

The *forum rei sitae* has control over the movable property, the possession of which is in dispute and therefore can render an effective judgment and has jurisdiction over such a dispute.[374] Any division of the High Court being the *forum rei sitae* has jurisdiction in such a dispute and this is so, regardless of whether the defendant is an *incola, peregrinus* or present within the jurisdiction.[375]

Both Pistorius and Forsyth state that the *forum rei sitae* does not have exclusive jurisdiction and that the *forum domicilii* is sometimes considered an alternative because the principle of effectiveness is thought to be satisfied thereby. Where the property is situated in South Africa, but not in the area of the *forum domicilii*, a judgment relating to that property will nonetheless be effective elsewhere in South Africa.

The *forum domicilii* does not have jurisdiction in respect of property located outside South Africa, even though the defendant is an *incola* of the court seised of the matter.[376]

Declaration regarding rights over movables

The *forum rei sitae* will have jurisdiction over disputes as to the existence of real rights in movables, such as pledges, liens, hypothecs[377] and possibly leases.[378]

In *Norden v Solomon*,[379] the Supreme Court of the Cape was held to have jurisdiction to make a declaration that the plaintiff was entitled to a tacit hypothec over movable property of the defendant situated in the court's jurisdiction, notwithstanding that the defendant was a *peregrinus*.[380]

Where the real right in the movable is not registered, so that registers and the officials to operate them are not involved, Forsyth states that the case for the *forum rei sitae* is weak and other courts having jurisdiction over the defendant may entertain the claim.

---

[374] Forsyth *Private International Law* 5 ed (2012) 242; Pistorius *Pollak on Jurisdiction* 2 ed (1993) 102–3.

[375] Pistorius cites *Brown v McDonald* 1911 EDL 423, where the defendant was a local *peregrinus* not physically present within the area of jurisdiction of the court. It was held that as the property was within the area of jurisdiction of the court, the court had jurisdiction to grant an interdict to restrain alienation of the property, pending an action to be brought in a 'competent court'.

[376] Both Pistorius and Forsyth cite *Lenders & Co Ltd v Lourenço Marques Wharf Co Ltd* 1904 TH 176, where it was held that there was no jurisdiction in the Transvaal High Court to entertain an action relating to movables in Mozambique, notwithstanding that the defendant was a Transvaal company with its head office on the Witwatersrand.

[377] A right established over a debtor's property that remains in the debtor's possession.

[378] Forsyth *Private International Law* 5 ed (2012) 242; Pistorius *Pollak on Jurisdiction* 2 ed (1993) 104.

[379] (1847) 2 M 377.

[380] Cited by Pistorius at 104.

Appointment of a curator bonis[381] *in respect of movable property*

The position in relation to the appointment of a *curator bonis* over immovable property applies *mutatis mutandis* in relation to such an appointment over movable property.[382]

9.1.3.3.4.3 *Incorporeal property*

Incorporeal property has no physical location and for jurisdictional purposes a locality is assigned to it by operation of law. Pistorius states:[383] 'In attributing a situs to incorporeal property the general principle adopted by the law is that an incorporeal is situated where it can be dealt with effectively.'

Ordinary debts

The *situs* of a debtor's obligation to pay money is the area where the debtor is an *incola*. It is in that location that the debtor will be subject to the jurisdiction of the court and is presumed to have sufficient assets to satisfy the debt.[384]

Money deposited in an account with a bank is a debt owed by the bank to the customer, the *situs* of which is the branch of the bank where the account is kept.[385]

Debts secured by a mortgage bond

If the debtor is an *incola* of the area where the mortgaged property is located then the *situs* of the debt is there.

If the debtor is not an *incola* of the same area where the mortgaged property is located then the *situs* of the debt will depend on the nature of the dispute. Forsyth states[386] that if the right in dispute concerns the bond as an acknowledgement of the debt due to the creditor, the *situs* will be where the debtor is an *incola*, but if the dispute concerns the creditor's right to the registered security then the *situs* will be where the mortgaged property is located, as the court of that area will have control over the relevant register.

---

[381] A guardian or trustee appointed to take care of property in certain cases; as for the benefit of creditors.

[382] Forsyth *Private International Law* 5 ed (2012) 242; Pistorius *Pollak on Jurisdiction* 2 ed (1993) 104, Pistorius pointing out that *Ex parte Hodgins* 1951 (1) SA 286 (O) and *Ex parte Berry* 1961 (4) SA 79 (D), the authorities he cites under immovable property, in fact concerned movable property.

[383] Pistorius *Pollak on Jurisdiction* 2 ed (1993) 105. Pistorius further states that the *situs* of incorporeal property has been considered most often in relation to the attachment of property because a court can only attach property within the area of its jurisdiction.

[384] Forsyth *Private International Law* 5 ed (2012) 243–4. In the event that the debtor has two residences, Forsyth states that the debt will be located at the place where it is primarily payable (at 244 fn 545).

[385] Ibid 244 fn 545.

[386] Ibid 244; Pistorius expresses the same view at 107, citing *Lief NO v Dettman* 1964 (2) SA 252 (A).

As regards a notarial bond over movables, Pistorius states that in so far as the secured rights are concerned there are two possibilities: first, as the rights are in respect of movables with which the debtor can deal, the court of which he is an *incola* has jurisdiction; or, second, as the rights are registered and can only be transferred and formally extinguished through the relevant register in the Deeds Office, the *situs* is the area where that office is situated. Pistorius favours the latter view but that this does not mean that the *forum rei sitae* has exclusive jurisdiction.

Negotiable instruments

The *situs* of a debt evidenced by a negotiable instrument is where that underlying debt is located.[387]

Shares

The question here is whether the *situs* of a share is the area in which the share certificate is found or the area in which the registered office of the company is situated. The *situs* of a share has been held to be the place where the registered office of the company is located.[388]

The *forum rei sitae*, however, does not have exclusive jurisdiction. A court with jurisdiction (on some other recognised basis) over the defendant himself may compel him to deliver the relevant share certificates and to sign the requisite share transfer form to enable the transfer to be registered at the company's registered office.[389]

Intellectual property rights

The general rule is that these are situated where they can be effectively transferred. In the case of patents and trademarks, this will be where they are registered.

In *Rembrandt Fabrikante en Handelaars (Edms) Bpk v Gulf Oil Corp*,[390] a trade mark was held to be situated at the place where the Register of Trade Marks was kept and the *forum rei sitae* had jurisdiction. *Rembrandt* was followed and approved in *Ewing McDonald & Co Ltd v M & M Products Co*,[391] in which the Witwatersrand Local Division did not have jurisdiction to attach trade marks, the *situs* of which was within the area of jurisdiction of the Transvaal Provincial Division.

---

387 Forsyth *Private International Law* 5 ed (2012) 244; Pistorius *Pollak on Jurisdiction* 2 ed (1993) 108–9.

388 Forsyth *Private International Law* 5 ed (2012) 244–5; Pistorius *Pollak on Jurisdiction* 2 ed (1993) 109; *The Treasury v Consolidated Mines Selection Co Ltd* 1918 TPD 13.

389 Pistorius on the authority of *Hugo v Wessels* 1987 (3) SA 837.

390 1963 (3) SA 341 (A) (Steyn CJ; Van Blerk, Botha, Holmes JAA and Hoexter AJA).

391 1991 (1) SA 252 (A).

Pistorius raises the question whether the *forum rei sitae* has exclusive jurisdiction.[392] In *Mobbs Ltd v Sargent Ltd*,[393] the court held that it had jurisdiction to order the defendant company, which was an *incola* of the Eastern Districts, to take steps to procure the cancellation of a design of which it was the registered proprietor. Pistorius states:[394]

> 'The decision is in accordance with that in Hugo v. Wessels and it is submitted that if the action in regard to the right in question is brought in personam and the court has power to order the defendant to take steps to cause some act to be effected in the relevant register, then such court will have jurisdiction to deal with the matter.'

Copyright does not generally require formalities to subsist and Pistorius states that the *situs* of copyright is where the owner is an *incola*.

9.1.3.3.5 *Ratione causa continentia*

The *causa continentia* rule is one that permits a court to assume jurisdiction in a case in which, but for the application of the rule, it might not have jurisdiction over the entirety of the dispute or over a particular defendant. The application of the rule is intended to avoid 'a multiplicity of proceedings and the possibility of conflicting judgments on the same cause and allows for the more convenient disposition of cases'.[395] Pistorius states[396] that in order for the rule to apply 'it must be established that there is no other forum which has jurisdiction in respect of all the defendants on other recognised grounds of jurisdiction'.

In *Roberts Construction Co Ltd v Willcox Bros (Pty) Ltd*,[397] the plaintiff brought proceedings against the defendant for breach of contract and fraudulent misrepresentation relating to the sale of a bridge spanning the Orange River. The contract was entered into in Johannesburg and any misrepresentation was also made there. Part of the bridge was situated in the Cape Province and a part of the bridge was situated in the Orange Free State. Both the plaintiff and the defendant were *incolae* of South Africa, but *peregrini* of the Orange Free State Provincial Division ('OFS') where the plaintiff commenced proceedings. The defendant challenged the jurisdiction of the OFS to entertain the action. The only jurisdictional link with the OFS was that a part of the bridge was situated within its jurisdiction. The defendant appealed the decision of the court at first instance dismissing the challenge to the jurisdiction. Dismissing the appeal,

---

392 *Pollak on Jurisdiction* 2 ed (1993) 110.

393 1936 EDL 356.

394 Although where the action is *in rem*, relating to the title to the patent, trade mark or design, the true defendant is the registrar and the *forum rei sitae* will have exclusive jurisdiction (Pistorius at 110 fn 38).

395 Pistorius *Pollak on Jurisdiction* 2 ed (1993) 25.

396 Ibid 26.

397 1962 (4) SA 326 (A) (Steyn CJ; Beyers, Rumpff, Botha and Van Winsen AJJ).

Steyn CJ concluded that the *causae continentia* doctrine applied and on that ground the OFS had jurisdiction.

The *causae continentia* doctrine has found statutory expression in the form of section 21(2) of the Superior Courts Act 2013:[398]

> 'A Division also has jurisdiction over any person residing or being outside its area of jurisdiction who is joined as a party to any cause in relation to which such court has jurisdiction or who in terms of a third party notice becomes a party to such cause, if the said person resides or is within the area of jurisdiction of any other Division.'

Thus, as regards an *incola* of South Africa whom a plaintiff wishes to join to proceedings in a court in respect of which he is a local *peregrinus*, section 21(2) provides the means of bringing such a party into proceedings without the need to rely on the *causae continentia* doctrine. However, the doctrine continues to be of relevance in cases with a foreign element.

In *Berger v Aiken*,[399] a testator devised certain sums on trusts to members of his family (the Jaffe, Kapelus and Bloom families). The Kapelus family comprised two branches: C and P. The three children of C (C1–3) were resident in Maryland, USA, and in Israel. The children of P were thought to have been killed in Lithuania in the course of World War II. In 1952 the trustees (it is to be surmised) applied for and were granted an order presuming the children of P to have died and declaring the sole beneficiaries of the Kapelus family share of the trusts to be C1–3. Distributions were made to C1–3 thereafter. In 1961 it was brought to the attention of the trustees that P had survived the war. P applied to the court for orders, inter alia: that the trustees be indicted from further distributing sums to C1–3; and authorising the sheriff to attach proposed payments to C1–3 to found jurisdiction in proceedings which P intended to bring (1) to amend the 1952 order and (2) to seek restitution of sums paid to C1–3, since 1952 by which P alleged C1–3 had been unjustly enriched (*condictio indebiti*).

Boshoff J stated[400] that both sets of potential parties (excluding the trustees) were *peregrini* of South Africa and that attachment would not itself therefore found jurisdiction; the court would entertain the action only if in addition it had jurisdiction under the common law. It was submitted that the court did have jurisdiction under the common law because the action *condictio indebiti* was so closely connected and interwoven with the application to amend the 1952 order that considerations of convenience and expense made it desirable that all proceedings should be brought in one court. The judge referred to the

---

[398] Re-enacting s 19 of the Supreme Court Act 1959 as amended by s 2 of Act 41 of 1970. The reason for this provision is 'to avoid a multiplicity of actions with all the inconvenience and expense that that involves': *Majola v Santam Insurance Co Ltd* 1976 (1) SA 874 (SE), *per* Eksteen J at 877C–D.

[399] 1964 (2) SA 396 (W).

[400] Ibid 399H.

Roberts Construction case and stated that there the contractual obligations and misrepresentation were in respect of all the girders of the bridge spanning the Orange River and that[401] 'it was decided that as the claim in respect of both sides of the border was nothing but the same case', the court had jurisdiction over the contract claim. Further,

> 'As regards the alternative claim [in misrepresentation] it was decided that the two claims together really constituted one case in that the alternative claim began where the main claim ended, and that in a real sense it was only a continuation of the same case and could not be separated from the main claim and instituted before another Court without inconvenience and obstruction.'

However, in the instant case, the court refused to assume jurisdiction over the action *condictio indebiti* on the basis that although the amendment to the 1952 order was necessary in order to enable P to enforce their rights as beneficiaries under the trusts, it was a step which had to be taken quite independently of an action *condictio indebiti* against C1–3:

> 'I do not think that the two claims really constitute one case in the sense that the one begins where the other ends and that in a real sense the one is only a continuation of the other and cannot be separated without inconvenience and obstruction.'

There was not therefore such an inherent connection between the two claims as to constitute a *causae continentia* so as to vest the court with jurisdiction over the restitution claim.

The judge went on to state:[402]

> 'Moreover, I do not think that the *continentia* rule would apply as a ground for jurisdiction in view of the fact that this Court, the Israeli Court and the Court of the United States do not function in the framework of the same system of legal administration. The two claims are entirely separate and the fact the trusts are South African trusts to which South African law must be applied, does not I think affect the matter at all.'

This, notwithstanding that the court accepted that it could have given an effective judgment because the trustees were *incolae* of South Africa (although this does not expressly appear from the report, it must have been the case).

It is difficult to disagree with the finding that the application to amend or vary the 1952 order to which the trustees would have been party was not the same case as the intended substantive *condictio indebiti* action against C1–3 (in the sense used in the *Roberts Construction* case, the contract and misrepresentation claims being one case).

However, it is also difficult to see the policy considerations at work in requiring beneficiaries of South African trusts governed by South African law (with South

---

401 Ibid 402A.

402 Ibid 403F.

African trustees) to pursue claims concerning trust assets in Maryland, USA and Israel, where both sets of claims could have been pursued in the Republic of South Africa and an effective judgment rendered in one jurisdiction.

In *New York Shipping Co Ltd v EMMI Equipment Ltd*,[403] the plaintiff brought proceedings against a number of defendants on promissory notes, payable at Windhoek, of which the first defendant was the maker, the second defendant was payee and had signed as an indorser in Johannesburg and further defendants who had signed as co-principal debtors and sureties. Of these defendants, only the first and the fourth were within the jurisdiction of the court. An objection to the jurisdiction was taken by the other five defendants on the basis that they, together with the plaintiff, were *peregrini* of the court, being *incolae* of Johannesburg. Further, these defendants contended that the notes were signed in Johannesburg, the transactions between themselves and the plaintiff concluded in Johannesburg, and all moneys involved in the underlying transactions were paid in Johannesburg. The court found that there was no *ratione rei gestae* applicable to the five objecting defendants (because the *locus solutionis* was not Namibia). The court also found[404] that the defendants had, by lodging affidavits opposing a provisional sentence application, submitted to the jurisdiction of the court.[405]

Muller J referred to the *Roberts Construction* case where he stated that the Chief Justice had referred to 'examples of *causae continentia* mentioned by the authorities ... where several debtors, jointly liable for the same debt, are within different areas of jurisdiction', but that they should nevertheless be amenable to the jurisdiction of a single court. The judge held in emphatic terms that the *causae continentia* rule applied to the instant case and dismissed the objections to the jurisdiction:

> 'Why then must there be a multiplicity of actions with, as pointed out in the *Roberts Construction Co.* case, the possibility of conflicting judgments, when this Court can conveniently dispose of the matter in one judgment to which effect can be given in South-West Africa as well as in the Republic of South Africa.'[406]

The significance of the case for present purposes is that the judge distinguished *Towers v Paisley*[407] by holding: 'the *causae continentia* rule could not apply in the circumstances of that case'.[408] This could be taken to indicate that the judge was finding that the rule did not apply in cases where both plaintiff and defendant were *peregrini*. However, in context, it is more likely that the judge meant the

---

[403] 1968 (1) SA 355 (South West Africa Division (Namibia): Muller J).

[404] Ibid 363D.

[405] And so distinguishing *Towers v Paisley* 1963 (1) SA 92 (E).

[406] 1968 (1) SA 355 (SWA) 365A.

[407] 1962 (1) SA 92 (E), where Jennett JP refused to grant an interdict in the absence of a *ratio jurisdictionis* linking the cause to the area of the court where both plaintiff and defendant were *peregrini* and the defendant had submitted but where the acts sought to be restrained were outside the jurisdiction.

[408] At 365B.

causae continentia rule did not apply in *Towers v Paisley* because that case did not concern a multiplicity of proceedings or parties and thus the rule did not apply. In other words, the *New York Shipping* case does not appear to support the domestic restriction placed upon the *causae continentia* rule in *Berger v Aiken*. Indeed, given the very general terms in which the judge expressed his agreement with the rationale behind the rule, the case might be taken as support for a broader application of the rule than the court in *Berger v Aiken* was prepared to accept.

It is difficult to disagree with Forsyth[409] that 'it would be a pity if the rule were so parochially conceived even where considerations of convenience make it clear that a court should be prepared to extend its jurisdiction more broadly'.[410]

Recently the Supreme Court of Appeal in *Permanent Secretary, Department of Welfare, Eastern Cape v Ngxuza*,[411] considered the application of the *causae continentia* rule to class action proceedings concerning the suspension or cancellation of disability grants by the Eastern Cape provincial government. In an attempt to eradicate abuse and fraud in the claiming and payment of grants, the government had decided to cancel or suspend all such payments pending the reapplication for grants by grantees. The numbers affected by this decision amounted to tens of thousands of Eastern Cape residents. The three plaintiffs, assisted by the Legal Resources Centre (an NGO), brought the class action so as to represent all grantees and sought directions to that effect. The application was granted at first instance and the government appealed on the ground, inter alia, that the Eastern Cape Division, Grahamstown, where the proceedings had been commenced, did not have jurisdiction over all of the individual potential class members. The basis for this contention was that although the court had jurisdiction over the three plaintiffs who had started the proceedings because their payments had been made within the jurisdiction of the court and that such intra-jurisdictional receipt of a payment created a *ratio jurisdictionis*, the same was not the case for potential class members who were not resident within the court's area of jurisdiction. These non-residents of the local division's area would usually have to bring proceedings in the Ciskei High Court because the seat of the provincial government, at Bisho, lay within that court's jurisdiction, or in another division of the Eastern Cape within the territorial jurisdiction of which the relevant class-member had been paid (at the time, the Umtata local division).

---

409 *Private International Law* 5 ed (2012) 195.

410 In fn 196 to this text Forsyth states: 'The English courts will extend their jurisdiction over persons abroad, on similar grounds.' The relevant English rule is CPR 6.36 and 6BPD para 3.1(3) which makes provision for the joining of any 'necessary or proper party' into a claim by a claimant against a defendant over which the court has jurisdiction. As Forsyth makes clear, this provision does not extend to further connected claims in respect of which the English court is not already seised.

411 2001 (4) SA 1184 (SCA) (Hefer ACJ, Harms, Streicher, Cameron and Mpati JJA).

Dismissing the appeal, the court rejected this argument. Cameron JA, with whom the other members of the court agreed, cited the *Roberts Construction* case and stated:[412]

> 'The Court expressly left open the further development and application of the doctrine of cohesion of causes. The present seems to me a matter amply justifying its further evolution. The Eastern Cape Division has jurisdiction over the original plaintiffs and over members of the class entitled to payment of their pensions within its domain. That, in my view, is sufficient to give it jurisdiction over the whole class, who, subject to satisfactory "opt out" procedures, will accordingly be bound by its judgment.'

In *Multi-Links Telecommunications Ltd v Africa Prepaid Services Nigeria Ltd*,[413] Fabricius J, referring to the decision in *Ngxuca*, stated:[414]

> 'Where one court has jurisdiction over a part of a cause, considerations of convenience, justice and good sense justify its exercising its jurisdiction over the whole cause. In the present case it is common cause that no other court has jurisdiction over all the defendants. The causae upon which Telkom and Multi-Links' cases are founded largely occurred in this court's area of jurisdiction involved parties that are resident therein, and the facts giving rise to the action are intertwined.'

The judge held,[415] however, that the issue was one which should ultimately be dealt with by the trial judge.

Miscellaneous bases of jurisdiction

The bases referred to above do not quite cover the entirety of the bases that have been found to be valid jurisdictional connecting factors. A claim in unjust enrichment has been held to be a valid connecting factor,[416] as have claims based on a subrogated claim for compensation under the Motor Vehicle Insurance Act[417] and a challenge to an administrative decision taken by a statutory body.[418]

---

412 Ibid para [22].

413 2014 (3) SA 265 (GP). The facts of this case have been referred to above in connection with the *Bid Industrial* case.

414 Ibid para [21].

415 Ibid para [23].

416 *Cape Explosive Works Ltd v SA Oil & Fat Industries Ltd* 1921 CPD 244.

417 *Ongevallekommissaris v Unie en Nasionale Versekeringsmaatskappy* 1969 (3) SA 438 (O) (Hofmeyr J) – the headnote reads: 'Where an accident as defined in the Workmen's Compensation Act, 30 of 1941, occurred within the jurisdiction of the Court, and the Workmen's Compensation Commissioner has paid compensation to the injured persons, then the Court has jurisdiction in respect of the Commissioner's claim for recovery, in terms of section 8 of the Act, against the insurer liable therefor under the Motor Vehicle Insurance Act, 29 of 1942.' The Motor Vehicle Insurance Act may be cited as Act 29 of 1942.

418 *Estate Agents Board v Lek* 1979 (3) SA 1048 (A), where the respondent to the appeal was an estate agent who had been refused a fidelity fund certificate, a precondition to trade, by the Estate Agents Board, a body established by the Estate Agents Act 112 of 1976. The 1976 Act also provided for an appeal to the court against a decision to withhold such a certificate. The Board's place of business and residence was Johannesburg. The respondent appealed to the Cape of Good Hope Provincial Division, which allowed the

These non-contract and delict cases are sometimes referred to as providing a *ratio res gestae*.[419]

A further basis for assuming jurisdiction over a dispute, where actions which have occurred outside South Africa have effects within South Africa, was recognised in principle in *Achugo v Absa Bank Ltd*,[420] where the applicant brought an application for relief in respect of an alleged infringement of section 27 of the Constitution, sub-section (1)(b) of which accords to everyone the right to have access to sufficient food. The first and second respondents had infringed commodities futures trading laws in the USA and had been penalised by the relevant regulator. The infringements comprised certain prearranged non-competitive trades in corn and soya beans. The applicant alleged that this conduct had or may have created a risk to his family and most South African families that the price of food, especially maize meal, would be compromised. The judge described the issue before him as whether the courts, 'enjoy jurisdiction to consider a violation of the Bill of Rights in respect of conduct that took place outside the territory of South Africa that has effects within its borders'.[421] The judge found that the courts did have jurisdiction.[422]

9.1.3.4 *Submission to the jurisdiction*

South African law recognises submission to the jurisdiction as a basis for the assumption of jurisdiction over a dispute in certain circumstances.

In the past it was considered that the assumption of jurisdiction on the basis of submission was not always reconcilable with the doctrine of effectiveness[423] or that submission was an exception to the doctrine of effectiveness.[424] It has however been held more recently that 'that is only true ... insofar as it is an exception to the rule that a court must be able to give effect to its *own* judgment' (emphasis in original) and that there is 'no difference in principle between

appeal and set aside the Board's order. The Board appealed arguing, inter alia, that the CPD did not have jurisdiction because its place of business or residence was in Johannesburg and that accordingly only the Transvaal Provincial Division or the Witwatersrand Local Division had jurisdiction to entertain the appeal. The Appellate Division held, inter alia, that (1) the respondent resided in Cape Town, within the jurisdiction of the court of first instance; (2) the decision of the Board, taken in Johannesburg, adversely affected the respondent's legal capacity or right to practise in Cape Town as an estate agent; and (3) every consideration of convenience and common sense indicated that the court below was an appropriate court to grant the declaratory relief that the respondent claimed.

[419] See, for example, Peté et al *Civil Procedure* 2 ed (2011) p 76 and fn 399.

[420] 2020 (1) SA 533 (GJ) (Unterhalter J).

[421] Para 19.

[422] Paras 21–24.

[423] *Pollak on Jurisdiction* 1 ed (1937) 19.

[424] *Thermo Radiant Oven Sales (Pty) Ltd v Nelspruit Bakeries (Pty) Ltd* 1969 (2) SA 295 (A), *per* Potgieter JA (at 307A; Steyn CJ concurring).

bilateral and unilateral submissions' because 'both types of submission render a judgment given on the strength thereof internationally enforceable'.[425]

Generally, submission may take one of two forms. First, unilateral submission, whereby a party against whom proceedings have been commenced takes a step in the proceedings, which as a matter of South African law renders him amenable to the jurisdiction of the South African courts. Second, consensual submission, whereby the parties agree, prior to or subsequent to a dispute arising, to submit to the jurisdiction of the South African courts.

9.1.3.4.1 Submission by participating in existing proceedings

In the case of unilateral consent, the questions will be directed at whether the acts of the party (usually the defendant) amounted to a submission to the jurisdiction or not and the onus will be on the plaintiff to show that the relevant acts did amount to a submission.[426] In the following cases the defendant's actions were held to evidence submission:[427] (1) pleading to the merits; (2) filing a counterclaim; (3) requesting a postponement or agreeing to a postponement without objection; (4) demanding security; (5) appointing an agent authorised to be sued; (6) attending an enquiry into his financial position and agreeing to pay a judgment debt in instalments; (7) accepting appointment as an executor or executrix; (8) delay in taking an objection to the jurisdiction of the court before trial; (9) submission made orally to the court by counsel acting for the defendant.[428]

A case where the plaintiff may be found to have submitted to the jurisdiction is where the plaintiff brings a claim and the defendant responds with a claim in reconvention, over which claim in reconvention the court would not ordinarily have had jurisdiction over the plaintiff.[429]

The following acts have been held not to constitute submission:[430] (1) the entry of an appearance to defend: 'A defendant is entitled to take this step in order to plead want of jurisdiction but his failure to take any further steps may imply

---

[425] *Jamieson v Sabingo* 2002 (4) SA 49 (SCA), *per* Farlam JA (with whom Nienaber, Navsa and Mthiyane JJA and Lewis AJA agreed) para [26].

[426] *Du Preez v Philip-King* 1963 (1) SA 801 (W) 803.

[427] Pistorius *Pollak on Jurisdiction* 2 ed (1993) 11, authorities at fns 35–41 and 45.

[428] *Agro-Grip (Pty) Ltd v Ayal* 1999 (3) SA 126 (W) 128F–G.

[429] Pistorius *Pollak on Jurisdiction* 2 ed (1993) 65–7; *Mediterranean Shipping Co v Speedwell Shipping Co Ltd* 1986 (4) SA 329 (D), *per* Van Heerden J at 333H: 'The court in which a plaintiff brings his action also has jurisdiction to entertain a defendant's counterclaim even should the action be withdrawn'; *Birkett v Birkett* 1953 (4) SA 445 (T), *per* Dowling J at 451H: 'There is the further fact that not only has applicant expressly submitted to the jurisdiction of this Court, but in seeking the jurisdiction of this Court he has thereby submitted himself to the jurisdiction of the Court in respect of any counterclaim, adjudication upon which is not dependent on the domicile of the applicant.' Where the defendant claims in reconvention (as noted above) he will have submitted: Pistorius *Pollak on Jurisdiction* 2 ed (1993) 11, authorities at fn 36.

[430] Pistorius *Pollak on Jurisdiction* 2 ed (1993) 10, authorities at fns 25–9.

consent'; (2) the failure to enter an appearance to defend; (3) the appointment of an agent under a general power of attorney; (4) a submission to arbitration in another country did not constitute submission to the courts of that country; (5) a letter (enclosing an affidavit) from an attorney acting for the defendant, but not the attorney of record.

9.1.3.4.2 Submission by agreement

9.1.3.4.2.1 *Jurisdiction clauses*

Questions may arise regarding, for example, the scope of the parties' consent, whether the dispute falls within the terms of the relevant jurisdiction clause and whether the agreement in which the jurisdiction clause appears is valid.

By way of general comment on the approach which the courts should, in principle, take to construction of, and effect given to, jurisdiction agreements, the authors submit that, in the modern world, it is commercially sensible for parties to be able to litigate disputes in the forum upon which they agree, purely on the basis of that agreement. There is no policy argument which militates against that approach, in the authors' view.[431]

However, the South African courts have, in certain circumstances, limited the effect to be given to a jurisdiction clause between parties. In *Veneta Mineraria Spa v Carolina Collieries (Pty) Ltd*,[432] the court was faced with a dispute between a foreign *peregrinus* plaintiff and a local *peregrinus* defendant. The contract between the parties contained a jurisdiction clause conferring jurisdiction on the courts of Durban and Coast Local Division. It was held that the mere submission to the jurisdiction by the foreign *peregrinus* defendant was not enough to confer jurisdiction on the court.[433] By contrast, where the defendant is a foreign *peregrinus* and the plaintiff is an *incola*, the defendant's submission by way of agreement, will, without more, confer jurisdiction upon the court.[434]

As things presently stand, the burden will be on the defendant to show why an agreement containing a jurisdiction clause in favour of the South African

[431] Forsyth *Private International Law* 5 ed (2012) 230–1. It is noted, at this point, that there are alternative regimes in different legal systems which are designed to ensure the effectiveness of jurisdiction clauses. One such regime is contained within the Hague Convention on Choice of Court Agreements (signed on 30 June 2005: see, in the context of European Union law, Council Decision 2014/887/EU). The Hague Convention is not considered in any depth here because the Republic of South Africa has not acceded to it.

[432] 1987 (4) SA 883 (A).

[433] Ibid 894A–B, *per* Viljoen JA: 'By prorogation a defendant subjects his person to the jurisdiction of the Court, but that is not enough. One or more of the traditional grounds of jurisdiction must also be present.' See further, Forsyth *Private International Law* 5 ed (2012) 232.

[434] *Hay Management Consultants (Pty) Ltd v P3 Management Consultants (Pty) Ltd* 2005 (2) SA 522 (SCA), approving the decision in *American Flag plc v Great African T-Shirt Corp* 2000 (1) SA 356 (W).

courts, or an agreement that by implication amounts to a submission to the South African courts, should not be enforced.[435]

In English law the court has a discretion to stay proceedings brought in England in apparent breach of a jurisdiction clause[436] and the same obtains in the Republic of South Africa. In *Foize Africa (Pty) Ltd v Foize Beheer BV*,[437] the appellant/plaintiff was a South African company which had entered into a software licensing agreement in Johannesburg with a company incorporated in the Netherlands, the third respondent/third defendant in the appeal. The agreement contained a Dutch choice of law clause, a non-exclusive jurisdiction clause in favour of the Dutch courts and an arbitration clause providing for arbitration in the Netherlands with the seat of the arbitration being Amsterdam. The relationship between the parties broke down and the plaintiff commenced proceedings in the North Gauteng High Court seeking, inter alia, interim relief. The third defendant contended that the court did not have jurisdiction to entertain the proceedings. At first instance, the court held that it did not have

---

[435] Forsyth *Private International Law* 5 ed (2012) 218. In English law, the question is dealt with as follows (*Dicey, Morris and Collins on the Conflict of Laws* 15 ed (2012) vol 1, r 39, p 612, para 12–114): 'where the English court is called on to exercise jurisdiction in circumstances in which the material jurisdictional facts are not agreed, the party who wishes to invoke the jurisdiction will be required to have the better of the argument that the facts which support its invocation of the jurisdiction are satisfied. It is likely that the same principle applies in mirror image when a party challenges the exercise of jurisdiction by pointing to an agreement providing for the jurisdiction of the courts of a foreign country. If the court is required to decide who, on the material before it, has the better of the argument on the facts and matters relevant to the existence and exercise of jurisdiction, the question of who has the burden of proof will be the ordinary one, that the party who seeks to establish a fact bears the burden of establishing it.' See too Briggs *Agreements on Jurisdiction and Choice of Law* (2008); and Briggs *Private International Law in English Courts* (2014) paras 4.421–4.429.

[436] *Owners of cargo lately laden on board the ship or vessel Eleftheria v The Eleftheria (Owners), The Eleftheria*, [1970] P 94, where the relevant jurisdiction clause provided: 'Any dispute arising under this bill of lading shall be decided in the country where the carrier has his principal place of business [Greece].' English proceedings were commenced by the owners of cargo on board the *Eleftheria* and the owners applied for a stay of proceedings. In staying the proceedings in favour of the Greek courts, Brandon J set out the principles on the basis of which a stay may be granted: '(1) Where plaintiffs sue in England in breach of an agreement to refer disputes to a foreign court, and the defendants apply for a stay, the English court, assuming the claim to be otherwise within its jurisdiction, is not bound to grant a stay but has a discretion whether to do so or not. (2) The discretion should be exercised by granting a stay unless strong cause for not doing so is shown. (3) The burden of proving such strong cause is on the plaintiffs. (4) In exercising its discretion the court should take into account all the circumstances of the particular case. (5) In particular, but without prejudice to (4), the following matters, where they arise, may properly be regarded:—(a) In what country the evidence on the issues of fact is situated, or more readily available, and the effect of that on the relative convenience and expense of trial as between the English and foreign courts, (b) Whether the law of the foreign court applies and, if so, whether it differs from English law in any material respects, (c) With what country either party is connected, and how closely, (d) Whether the defendants genuinely desire trial in the foreign country, or are only seeking procedural advantages, (e) Whether the plaintiffs would be prejudiced by having to sue in the foreign court because they would: (i) be deprived of security for their claim; (ii) be unable to enforce any judgment obtained; (iii) be faced with a time-bar not applicable in England; or (iv) for political, racial, religious or other reasons be unlikely to get a fair trial.'

[437] 2013 (3) SA 91 (SCA) (Mthiyane DP, Cloete, Heher, Shongwe and Leach JJA), *per* Leach JA, giving the judgment of the court, at para [21].

jurisdiction to entertain the proceedings. This decision was reversed on appeal where the Supreme Court of Appeal granted the interim relief sought and held that the court did have jurisdiction to entertain the proceedings, that the court had a discretion whether to enforce a foreign jurisdiction or arbitration clause and that 'no hard and fast rule can be laid down as to the stage when a court should exercise its discretion to enforce a foreign jurisdiction or arbitration clause'.[438]

The Supreme Court of Appeal considered the factors to be taken into account in the exercise of the court's discretion and adopted those set out by Brandon J (as he was then) in *Owners of cargo lately laden on board the ship or vessel Eleftheria v The Eleftheria (Owners), The Eleftheria.*[439] The court also set out a number of further factors which the court may take into account:[440]

'*(a)* Flowing from the sanctity of contracts, it has often been said that a decision not to enforce either an arbitration or foreign jurisdiction clause should only be made where there is a very strong case made out for the parties not to be bound by their agreement.

(b) It is desirable if at all possible to avoid a multiplicity of actions in different courts with the associated potential complication of conflicting decisions. In the present case this may well be a weighty factor bearing in mind that there is no reason why the appellant's claims in respect of all but the first and third respondents cannot be determined in the high court and only those two respondents may seek to invoke clause 10 to have their dispute with the appellant determined elsewhere.

(c) Moreover, a single action has the undoubted advantage of saving time, expense and costs when compared to a multiplicity of actions. This too may be a weighty factor as the appellant's claims that are capable of being determined in the high court against most of the respondents will involve the same factual matrix and the same witnesses as in the foreign proceedings against the first and third respondents.

(d) When considering the issue of costs, it should also be remembered, certainly if the cost of litigation in England is any barometer, that the cost of litigation in Europe may well be astronomical when compared to the cost of litigation in this country. Sight must also not be lost of the likely fees and charges of the arbitrators should an arbitration take place.

(e) If the dispute involves questions of law rather than of fact, arbitration may well prove to be both inconvenient and impractical. Consequently regard should be had to whether the dispute is readily capable of being dealt with by way of arbitration. If not, it would count heavily against the enforcement of an arbitration clause.'

---

[438] Ibid 100G–I, para [26]. Leach JA had previously stated (99F–G, para [21]): 'It can now be regarded as well settled that a foreign jurisdiction or arbitration clause does not exclude the court's jurisdiction. Parties to a contract cannot exclude the jurisdiction of a court by their own agreement, and where a party wishes to invoke the protection of a foreign jurisdiction or arbitration clause, it should do so by way of a special or dilatory plea seeking a stay of the proceedings. That having been done, the court will then be called on to exercise its discretion whether or not to enforce the clause in question.'

[439] [1970] P 94 at 99G–100C.

[440] Leach JA at 101F–102D, para [28].

It is likely that a South African court may now grant an anti-suit interdict (injunction) to restrain the commencement or continuance of proceedings brought in a foreign court in apparent breach of a jurisdiction clause in favour of the South African courts, because the act interdicted would take place outside the jurisdiction.[441]

(Or an interdict to prohibit a foreign party applying to a foreign court for an anti-suit interdict/injunction against a litigant in proceedings in South Africa.)

As held in the *Foize Africa* case, the presence of an arbitration clause in an agreement does not oust the jurisdiction of the South African courts and may be overridden by them where justice demands it.[442] Indeed, a party seeking to bring proceedings in the teeth of an arbitration clause may be restrained by interdict from doing so.[443]

9.1.3.4.2.2 Domicilium citandi et executandi *clauses*

The use of a *domicilium citandi et executandi* clause[444] in an agreement may, in particular where the defendant is a foreign *peregrinus*, indicate submission.[445]

9.1.3.4.3 The effect of submission

It would appear that in many cases submission, whether consensual or unilateral, is not sufficient to found jurisdiction in the South African courts. The answer to the question when is submission without more sufficient to found jurisdiction seems to depend on the status of the plaintiff and, more particularly, the defendant. In summary, submission without more is sufficient to found jurisdiction where the plaintiff is an *incola* of the local court and the defendant is a foreign *peregrinus* (and, probably, a local *peregrinus*). In all other cases,[446] submission by itself is not sufficient to found jurisdiction and a *ratio jurisdictionis* is required.

---

[441] *Vedanta Resources Holdings Ltd v ZCCM Investment Holdings plc* 2019 JDR 1425 (GJ) (Adams J), where the court, albeit considering whether to grant an anti-suit interdict to restrain the breach of an arbitration clause, confirmed that it could grant such an interdict.

[442] *Yorigami Maritime Construction Co Ltd v Nissho-Iwai Co Ltd* 1977 (4) SA 682 (C), *per* Friedman J at 692H, 694A; approved in *Foize Africa (Pty) Ltd v Foize Beheer BV* 2013 (3) SA 91 (SCA).

[443] *Vedanta Resources Holdings Ltd v ZCCM Investment Holdings plc* 2019 JDR 1425 (GJ) (Adams J).

[444] An address where formal notices in relation to the contract (such as a demand for payment or a threat to cancel) or a summons in litigation arising out of the contract can be served.

[445] *Hay Management Consultants (Pty) Ltd v P3 Management Consultants (Pty) Ltd* 2005 (2) SA 522 (SCA), *per* Heher JA (Scott, Cameron and Conradie JJ and Patel AJA agreeing) para [15]; where the clause was regarded as 'a significant factor', as was the choice of South African law as the proper law (para [14]). Leaving a summons fixed to the grass outside a *domicilium citandi et executandi* premises is not sufficient to effect service: *Absa Bank Ltd v Mare* 2021 (2) SA 151 (GP), Meyer J (Misa J and Moosa AJ concurring) para 27.

[446] If the defendant is an *incola* then obviously issues of submission do not arise as *actor sequitur forum rei* applies.

Thus, a local *peregrinus* seeking to bring proceedings against a foreign *peregrinus* on the basis of a fully negotiated jurisdiction clause will be unable to proceed in the absence of a *ratio jurisdictionis.* Similarly, a foreign *peregrinus* seeking to bring proceedings against a local *peregrinus* on the basis of such a clause will be unable to proceed. The same is the case for a foreign *peregrinus* seeking to bring proceedings against a foreign *peregrinus* or (probably) a local *peregrinus* seeking to bring proceedings against another local *peregrinus.*

Of this apparent hostility to *peregrini* invoking the jurisdiction of the South African courts Forsyth, in a passage which merits full quotation, refers to a 'fundamental issue of policy' and states:[447]

> 'If the principle of effectiveness that underlies much of the law of jurisdiction is given an absolute meaning - so that only if the court controls the person or property of the defendant will it have jurisdiction - then the fact that a defendant has submitted to the jurisdiction of a court which would not otherwise be able to exercise jurisdiction over him, should be of little consequence: the mere consent of a defendant contains no absolute guarantee that the court's judgment will be effective and so cannot fulfil the need for the attachment which would otherwise be required. However, as we have seen, today the doctrine of effectiveness is artificial and conceptual rather than realistic. Moreover, submission is widely recognized in legal systems across the world as a ground on [sic "of"] international competence justifying the enforcement of the judgment of a foreign court to which the defendant has submitted. Thus, on the whole, a judgment based on submission will be effective. It is submitted that effectiveness in this slightly attenuated sense should suffice to justify the exercise of jurisdiction on the grounds of submission. The fact is that most other legal systems - and in particular the legal systems of South Africa's trading partners - give wide recognition to and encourage submission as a ground of jurisdiction. And this is widely welcomed by the parties to international contracts who frequently submit their disputes to resolution by courts with which they have but little connection. This is for good and obvious reasons - convenience, speed, judicial reputation, expense, neutrality ... It is to the benefit of international commerce that this should be so. The South African court should as a matter of policy encourage submission. As economic development in Southern and Central Africa proceeds, why should the local courts not develop an international role akin to that of the Commercial Court in London. The judicial policy should not be "Peregrines go home" but "Peregrines welcome". Thus peregrines should not find that, if they have submitted to the jurisdiction of the South African courts, their property is still at risk of being seized to found or confirm jurisdiction. That is a brake on inward investment. Moreover, there should be no bar on the submission to the South African courts of disputes where neither party is an *incola* and there may be no obvious link with South Africa. Such use of the South African courts is a tribute to them and it encourages international trade and commerce to the general benefit.'

[447] *Private International Law* 5 ed (2012) 230–1.

The modern statement of the law restricting access to the South African courts by submitting parties is found in *Veneta Mineraria Spa v Carolina Collieries (Pty) Ltd (in liquidation)*,[448] in which a foreign *peregrinus* plaintiff (an Italian company) brought proceedings in the Durban Local Division against a local *peregrinus* defendant (which had its head office in Johannesburg, Transvaal) for damages for breach of contract. The defendant denied the allegations and counterclaimed. There was a written consent to the jurisdiction (although it does not appear from the report whether this consent arose from a contractual term or arose subsequently). The judge at first instance dismissed the claim and counterclaim, inter alia, on the basis that the court lacked jurisdiction.

On appeal by the plaintiff, Viljoen JA, with whom the other members of the court agreed, distinguished between 'the so-called grounds of jurisdiction by virtue of which a court would normally *ipso jure* have jurisdiction and jurisdiction which is conferred on a court'.[449] Into the former category fell the *rationes jurisdictiones*: the defendant's domicile or residence; the place of the making, performance or breach of an agreement; the place of the delict. Into the second category fell: attachment of goods or arrest of the person *ad fundandam jurisdictionem*; consent to the jurisdiction; and transfer of proceedings from one domestic court to another, pursuant to section 9 of the Supreme Court Act 1959[450] on the grounds of convenience where the transferee court lacked jurisdiction absent the transfer. The judge then stated:[451]

> 'The crisp point to be decided is whether a consent to the jurisdiction can stand alone as conferring jurisdiction on a court or whether it serves merely to supply, complementarily to some *causa jurisdictionis*, an element to the jurisdiction which would, but for such consent, be defective.'

The judge framed the 'crucial question': 'What jurisdiction does a Supreme Court in SA law possess? A court can only be said to have jurisdiction in a matter if it has power not only of taking cognisance of the suit but also of giving effect to its judgment.'[452]

Referring to the judgment of Innes ACJ in *The Owners Master and Crew of the SS 'Humber' v The Owners and Master of the SS 'Answald'*,[453] Viljoen JA held:[454]

> 'This dictum again emphasises the principle that in addition to the machinery of arrest (which, in the case of a local *peregrinus*, is dispensed with by law) something more is required before a court can take cognisance of a matter in its area of jurisdiction. By prorogation a defendant subjects his person to the jurisdiction of the court, but that is not enough. One or more of the traditional grounds of jurisdiction must also be present.'

---

448 1987 (4) SA 883 (A) (Viljoen, Smalberger and Vivier JJA; Boshoff and Steyn AJJA).

449 Ibid 887A–B.

450 Now s 27(1) of the Superior Courts Act 2013.

451 1987 (4) SA 883 (A) 888C–E.

452 Ibid 893E–F, citing *Steytler NO v Fitzgerald* 1911 AD 295 at 346/7.

453 1912 AD 546 at 554.

454 1987 (4) SA 883 (A) 894A–B.

This passage from the judgment of Viljoen JA, subsequently referred to as 'the *Veneta* dictum',[455] was not welcomed by commentators[456] and its effect has since been cut back by subsequent decisions. As Forsyth[457] has forcefully pointed out:

> 'Since *Veneta Mineraria Spa* makes it clear that one of the traditional grounds must always be present, the role of submission is reduced to providing a substitute for attachment *ad confirmandam*. There is no substitute for attachment *ad fundandam* with the result that if the cause of action did not arise locally, two peregrines cannot agree that their disputes should be settled in the local courts. The point may be stressed: submission is not a *ratio jurisdictionis*, it is a substitute for attachment *ad confirmandam*.'[458]

The *Veneta* dictum was followed in *Briscoe v Marais*,[459] in which the plaintiff was an *incola* (unlike *Veneta*) and the defendant a *peregrinus*. Streicher J stated that the Appellate Division in Veneta 'did not, however, restrict its decision to cases where the plaintiff was a peregrinus of the Court' and, quoting the *Veneta* dictum, held that consent could not confer jurisdiction on the court absent a *ratione jurisdictionem*.

However, Streicher J appears not to have been referred to *Centner NO v Griffin NO*[460] where Roper AJ stated:

> 'It is I think clear that in our modern practice submission to the jurisdiction by a *peregrinus* is sufficient to give the Court jurisdiction without an attachment of property *ad fundandam jurisdictionem* (*King and Son v. Jamel* 8 NLR 129; *Kopelowitz v. Auerbach* 24 SC 567; Pollak *SA Law of Jurisdiction* at 85; cf Dicey 7th ed at 17 *et seq*.'

Similarly, Streicher J was not referred to *Cinemark (Pty) Ltd v Transkei Hotel*[461] where *Centner* was relied on by Goldstone J when he allowed an application by an *incola* of the court for leave to sue by edictal citation a *peregrinus* of South Africa

---

455 Forsyth *Private International Law* 5 ed (2012) 233. *Hay Management Consultants (Pty) Ltd v P3 Management Consultants (Pty) Ltd* 2005 (2) SA 522 (SCA), *per* Heher JA at para [19].

456 Forsyth *Private International Law* 5 ed (2012) 230 fn 448; Schulze *On Jurisdiction and the Recognition and Enforcement of Foreign Money Judgments* (2005) para 2.4.2, pp 13–15.

457 *Private International Law* 5 ed (2012) 232.

458 Section 30 of the Superior Courts Act 2013 concerns the rules for the Supreme Court of Appeal and the High Court. Section 30(2) provides that the access provisions contained in s 29(3) apply to the rules of court made pursuant to s 30(1). It will rarely be in the interests of justice for a court to decline jurisdiction over a claim where the plaintiff has no remedy available in any other relevant forum. The application of s 29(3) to High Court proceedings raises the question whether the High Court is now obliged to accept jurisdiction in cases where no other forum is practically available for the determination of the plaintiff's rights and where, in the absence of the High Court assuming jurisdiction, the plaintiff would be left without any recourse to a court, which possibility gains support from s 34. For comparative purposes, the view of English law in similar circumstances is set out in the speech of Lord Diplock in *British Airways Board v Laker Airways Ltd* [1985] AC 58 (Lords Diplock, Fraser, Scarman, Roskill and Brightman).

459 1992 (2) SA 413 (W) (Streicher J).

460 1960 (4) SA 798 (W) 799C.

461 1984 (2) SA 332 (WLD) (Goldstone J).

where the parties had consented to the jurisdiction of the court without the need for an attachment *ad fundandam jurisdictionem*.

In *American Flag plc v Great African T-Shirt Corp CC*,[462] the full bench of the Witwatersrand High Court distinguished *Veneta* on the ground that in *Veneta* the parties were both *peregrini*. There, the court held that where the plaintiff was an *incola* and the defendant a *peregrinus*, submission was sufficient without more to found jurisdiction and that attachment was neither necessary nor permissible. The court also held that *Briscoe v Marais* had been wrongly decided.

Subsequently, in *Hay Management Consultants (Pty) Ltd v P3 Management Consultants (Pty) Ltd*,[463] the Supreme Court of Appeal affirmed the decision in *American Flag*.

In summary, therefore: (1) the court has jurisdiction over a dispute between an *incola* plaintiff and a local or foreign *peregrinus* defendant solely on the basis of a consensual submission by the parties or a unilateral submission by the defendant; (2) in all other cases of submission,[464] in order for the court to have jurisdiction over the dispute, there must be a *ratio jurisdictionis*, absent which the court does not have jurisdiction.[465]

The effect of a submission to the jurisdiction on the requirement for an attachment of property

Where the plaintiff is an *incola* and the *peregrinus* defendant has submitted to the jurisdiction of the court, an attachment of the defendant's property, either to found or confirm jurisdiction, is neither necessary nor permissible.[466] The position of a submitting *peregrinus* defendant is thus assimilated to that of an *incola* of the Republic of South Africa.[467]

---

[462] 2000 (1) SA 356 (W) (Wunsh, Navsa and Snyders JJ).

[463] 2005 (2) SA 522 (SCA) paras [16]–[24].

[464] Apart from an *incola* being sued in his local court.

[465] In this regard the following passage in Peté et al *Civil Procedure* 2 ed (2011) 84 para 3.5.1(b) requires some elaboration: 'As discussed in the previous section, when dealing with a claim sounding in money against a foreign *peregrinus*, an *attachment ad confirmandam* or *ad fundandam jurisdictionem* is usually required. The principle of consent to jurisdiction is of relevance in these cases because, should the foreign *peregrinus* defendant consent to jurisdiction, such consent renders attachment impermissible.' This is undoubtedly the case where the plaintiff is an *incola*. But it is not the case where the plaintiff is a local or foreign *peregrinus* where a *ratio jurisdictionis* is required (thus Forsyth's observation quoted above that the *Veneta* dictum has rendered submission in this scenario merely an alternative to an attachment *ad confirmandam jurisdictionem*).

[466] *American Flag plc v Great African T-Shirt Corp CC* 2000 (1) SA 356 (W), *per* Wunsh J at 377F; *Hay Management Consultants (Pty) Ltd v P3 Management Consultants (Pty) Ltd* 2005 (2) SA 522 (SCA) (Scott, Cameron, Conradie and Heher JJA and Patel AJA), *per* Heher JA (giving the judgment of the court) 530 para [26]: 'I am satisfied that *American Flag plc* correctly reflects the law in actions for money between a plaintiff *incola* of the court and a *peregrinus* when the defendant has submitted to the jurisdiction.'

[467] Section 28 of the Superior Courts Act 2013.

Where, however, the plaintiff is also a *peregrinus* (local or otherwise), it seems that in addition to a recognised *ratio jurisdictionis* an attachment *ad confirmandam jurisdictionem* is required. Submission is a substitute for such attachment; hence where the defendant is a *peregrinus*, his submission and the existence of a *ratio jurisdictionis* will confer jurisdiction upon the court; his submission by itself is not enough.[468]

Timing of the submission

Where the plaintiff is an *incola*, a submission to the jurisdiction by a *peregrinus* defendant will render an attachment impermissible if the submission is made prior to the application for an attachment being made by the plaintiff.

If the submission is made after the order for an attachment is made, but before it is executed, then the *peregrinus* defendant is likely to secure the discharge of the order.[469]

If, however, the submission is made after the attachment is executed, the *peregrinus* defendant will not be entitled to its discharge.[470]

9.1.3.5 *The jurisdictional significance of arrest of the person*

As a result of the decision of the Supreme Court of Appeal in *Bid Industrial Holdings (Pty) Ltd v Strang*,[471] arrest of the person to found or confirm the jurisdiction of the court has been found to be unconstitutional. Accordingly, it no longer forms part of the law of the Republic of South Africa.[472]

9.2 Enforcement of Foreign Judgments

Under South African law a foreign money judgment and a foreign judgment in respect of property[473] may be enforced in the Republic of South Africa, either at

---

[468] *Veneta Mineraria Spa v Carolina Collieries (Pty) Ltd* 1987 (4) SA 883 (A); *Tsung v Industrial Development Corp of SA Ltd* 2006 (4) SA 177 (SCA) (Harms, Farlam, Cameron and Jafta JJA and Cachalia AJA), *per* Harms JA (giving the judgment of the court) 181E–F para [6]; Forsyth *Private International Law* 5 ed (2012) 230–3.

[469] *Jamieson v Sabingo* 2002 (4) SA 49 (SCA) (Nienaber, Farlam, Navsa and Mthiyane JJA and Lewis AJA), *per* Farlam JA (giving the judgment of the court) 59E–I paras [30] and [31]: it was not suggested that the submission was not voluntary and that any judgment given on the strength of it would not be internationally recognised, in which case other considerations might have applied (*Blue Continent Products (Pty) Ltd v Foroya Banki PF* 1993 (4) SA 563 (C) (Friedman JP and Farlam JA), *per* Farlam JA at 574F–G; submission post-attachment may not be considered voluntary).

[470] *Tsung v Industrial Development Corp of SA Ltd* 2006 (4) SA 177 (SCA) (Harms, Farlam, Cameron and Jafta JJA and Cachalia AJA), *per* Harms JA (giving the judgment of the court) 185A–E para [13].

[471] 2008 (3) SA 355 (SCA) (Howie P, Nugent, Ponnan, Maya JJA and Malan AJA). We discuss this decision at length above, under the heading 'The doctrine of effectiveness'.

[472] See further: Forsyth *Private International Law* 5 ed (2012) 196–8.

[473] Matrimonial matters are excluded from the discussion.

common law or under the statutory regime set out in the Enforcement of Foreign Civil Judgments Act 1988.[474]

Recognition of a foreign judgment means that the domestic South African court before which the question of the effect of a foreign judgment arises accords that judgment the effect that the foreign court intended it to have. For example, a foreign judgment creditor may plead *res judicata* as a defence to an action brought by the foreign judgment debtor on the cause that was the subject of the foreign judgment.[475] Similarly, a foreign judgment creditor may raise the judgment debt as a counterclaim in diminution or extinction of a claim brought in the Republic of South Africa by the foreign judgment debtor.

Enforcement of the foreign judgment involves the foreign judgment creditor engaging the domestic machinery of enforcement of a domestic judgment for the purpose of enforcing the foreign judgment of which he is the beneficiary.

The regime for the recognition and enforcement of foreign judgments is to be found in the common-law principles governing the area and also in statutory provision. Under the common law a foreign judgment is not directly enforceable and is enforceable by action only.

9.2.1 Jurisdiction to enforce a foreign judgment

A consequence of this is that the local court before which the plaintiff seeks to enforce the foreign judgment must itself have jurisdiction to entertain the enforcement action. Both Forsyth[476] and Pistorius[477] state that as a foreign judgment will usually sound in money, the rules on assumption of jurisdiction in money claims apply. Both writers agree that the presence of executable property within the jurisdiction of a local division in South Africa will not be sufficient to permit that court to assert jurisdiction over the claim on the foreign judgment unless the property is attachable *ad fundandam jurisdictionem* (if the plaintiff is an *incola* of that court) or *ad confirmandam jurisdictionem*, if the plaintiff is a local *peregrinus* or a foreign *peregrinus* and there is a recognised *ratio jurisdictionis* available.[478]

---

[474] Act 32 of 1988.

[475] In the text the terms 'foreign judgment creditor' and 'foreign judgment debtor' refer to the parties subject of the foreign judgment and not to the residence of domicile of either of those parties. The foreign judgment creditor and debtor could both be *incolae* of South Africa.

[476] *Private International Law* 5 ed (2012) 474.

[477] *Pollak on Jurisdiction* 2 ed (1993) 165–8.

[478] Forsyth cites two Botswana decisions: *Paver v Roper & Roper* [1974] 1 BLR 8 (HC; Rooney ACJ) 10; and *Pretorius v Sweiger* [1979–1980] BLR 124 and 129 (HC; Edwards J) 124 and 130. Pistorius cites *Lunt v Balmoral Diamond Mining Co Ltd* (1906) 10 HCG 58, where a company was refused enforcement of a Transvaal judgment against assets of the defendant in Griqualand West where the defendant was not domiciled and where no other *ratio jurisdictionem* was available.

In the case of a foreign judgment, the availability of a recognised *ratio jurisdictionis* to support an attachment *ad confirmandam jurisdictionem* for a local *peregrinus* or a foreign *peregrinus* is unlikely and because no attachment *ad fundandam jurisdictionem* is possible, the local court will not have jurisdiction to enforce the judgment, notwithstanding the presence of the defendant's assets within its area of jurisdiction.[479]

Pistorius summarises the current position as to jurisdiction as follows:[480]

(1) Defendant is an *incola*. Here there is no difficulty; the court before which the plaintiff seeks to enforce the foreign judgment has jurisdiction on the basis of the principle *actor sequitur forum rei.*

(2) Plaintiff is an *incola* and the defendant is a foreign *peregrinus*. Attachment of the defendant's property to found (or confirm) jurisdiction will be required for the court to assume jurisdiction.

(3) Plaintiff is an *incola* and the defendant is a local *peregrinus*. Attachment of the defendant's property is not permitted and a recognised *ratio jurisdictionis* is required for the court to be properly seised. The plaintiff must proceed in the court of whose area the defendant is an *incola*, if any.

(4) Plaintiff is a local *peregrinus* or a foreign *peregrinus* and the defendant is a foreign *peregrinus*. The plaintiff must attach property belonging to the defendant and must have available a recognised *ratio jurisdictionis*.

(5) Plaintiff is a local *peregrinus* or a foreign *peregrinus* and the defendant is a local *peregrinus*. Attachment of the defendant's property is not permitted and a recognised *ratio jurisdictionis* is required for the court to be properly seised. The plaintiff must proceed in the court of whose area the defendant is an *incola*, if any.

---

[479] However, the effect of the *Bid Industrial Holdings (Pty) Ltd v Strang* 2008 (3) SA 355 (SCA) will need to be considered by the courts in this field. There, personal service by an *incola* on a *peregrinus* and a close connection with the jurisdiction of the court in question were considered sufficient to seise the court of the proceedings, where the Supreme Court of Appeal held that arrest of the person was unconstitutional and there was no property to be attached (para [59], *per* Howie P, emphasis provided): 'The common law must be, and is hereby, developed by abolition of the rule and the adoption in its stead, *where attachment is not possible*, of the practice according to which a South African High Court will have jurisdiction if the summons is served on the defendant while in South Africa and there is sufficient connection between the suit and the area of jurisdiction of the court concerned so that disposal of the case by that court is appropriate and convenient. It goes without saying that the new practice could itself be subject to development with time.' It is not clear whether, in the context of enforcement of a foreign judgment, the presence of the defendant's assets within the jurisdiction of the court might furnish such a close connection for enforcement purposes. Were it to do so, it might go some way towards ameliorating the unattractive feature of the present law identified by Forsyth (at 474): 'No country should be a haven for recalcitrant debtors adjudged as such by a court of competent jurisdiction, even if they and their creditors are peregrines.'

[480] *Pollak on Jurisdiction* 2 ed (1993) 166–8.

(6) Claim for enforcement in a claim in reconvention. If the defendant is sued in the Republic of South Africa by the plaintiff, he can set up a claim in reconvention based on a foreign judgment granted against the plaintiff.

Subject to the foreign judgment satisfying the requirements of recognition and enforcement (set out in *Jones v Krok* below), the court seised of the plaintiff's claim has jurisdiction to enforce the foreign judgment against the plaintiff.

(7) In the case of a foreign judgment sounding in money where the defendant submits to the jurisdiction of the local South African court in accordance with the rules relating to submission set out above, the defendant's submission will empower the South African court to enforce the foreign judgment against him.

9.2.2 Procedure for enforcing a foreign judgment

Enforcement by action is typically pursued by means of provisional sentence and the general approach of the South African courts to such applications was explained in *Westdeutsche Landesbank Girozentrale (Landesbausparkasse) v Horsch*,[481] by Levy J as follows:[482]

> 'The exigencies of international trade and commerce require that final foreign judgments be recognised as far as is reasonably possible in our Courts, and that effect be given thereto. To assist a judgment creditor who has obtained such a foreign judgment, our Courts grant such judgment creditor the right to invoke the extraordinary remedy of provisional sentence, that is he has the right to obtain a provisional judgment speedily, and without resorting to the more expensive and dilatory machinery of an illiquid action.
>
> However, because this is an extraordinary remedy, the Court is strict about the compliance with certain prerequisites. These prerequisites include annexation to the summons of a certified copy of such judgment and, where the judgment is in a foreign language, a due and proper translation thereof. All foreign documentation must be duly authenticated in terms of the Rules of Court. It is essential to prove that the foreign judgment is final and enforceable according to the foreign court concerned and that is [sic] has been handed down by a court of competent jurisdiction.'

[481] 1993 (2) SA 342 (NM).

[482] Ibid 343J–344A.

9.2.3 Recognition and enforcement of foreign money judgments at common law

9.2.3.1 *Principles of general application*

The Appellate Division in *Jones v Krok*[483] held that there are six conditions that need to be satisfied before a foreign judgment will be recognised or enforced.[484]

Although *Jones v Krok* itself concerned a judgment sounding in money, the same principles are applicable to a judgment relating to property. Corbett CJ (giving the judgment of the court) stated:[485]

> 'the present position in South Africa is that a foreign judgment is not directly enforceable, but constitutes a cause of action and will be enforced by our Courts provided (i) that the court which pronounced the judgment had jurisdiction to entertain the case according to the principles recognised by our law with reference to the jurisdiction of foreign courts (sometimes referred to as "international jurisdiction or competence"); (ii) that the judgment is final and conclusive in its effect and has not become superannuated; (iii) that the recognition and enforcement of the judgment by our Courts would not be contrary to public policy; (iv) that the judgment was not obtained by fraudulent means; (v) that the judgment does not involve the enforcement of a penal or revenue law of the foreign state; and (vi) that enforcement of the judgment is not precluded by the provisions of the Protection of Businesses Act 99 of 1978 as amended ... Apart from this, our Courts will not go into the merits of the case adjudicated upon by the foreign court and will not attempt to review or set aside its findings of fact or law.'

Before dealing with the relevant constituent elements of the above formulation of principle, it is necessary, first, when considering the enforcement of a foreign judgment, to consider the question of what amounts to a foreign court. Forsyth states:[486] 'The courts have generally accepted readily that foreign tribunals may be classified as courts, but the question of whether a particular tribunal is judicial or quasi-judicial may be of significance' and refers to the decision

---

[483] 1995 (1) SA 677 (A) (Corbett CJ, Van Heerden, Kumleben and Nienaber JJA and Olivier AJA).

[484] Cited with approval in *Purser v Sales* 2001 (3) SA 445 (SCA); *Purser v Sales* was itself cited with approval in *Government of the Republic of Zimbabwe v Fick* 2013 (5) SA 325 (CC) (Mogoeng CJ, Moseneke DCJ, Froneman, Jafta, Khampepe, Nkabinde, Skweyiya, Van der Westhuizen and Zondo JJ and Mhlantla AJ) *per* Mogoeng CJ at 337D, para [38]); and approved in *Richman v Ben-Tovim* 2007 (2) SA 283 (SCA), *per* Zulman JA at 285G–286A, para [5], where Zulman JA also stated (at 286B–D, para [6]) that principle (i) 'appears to telescope two components. First the principles of our law and second the jurisdiction of the foreign court according to its law. The second component is a matter of fact.' The foreign court must itself have had jurisdiction over the matter. This raises the question whether, if the foreign court did not have jurisdiction but the parties (and court) treated it as if it did, jurisdiction can be conferred by estoppel and by reference to what system of law that issue would fall to be determined. It would seem likely that this issue would be subject to the law of the foreign court rather than to that of the court entertaining the enforcement proceedings. It is unlikely that such an issue would be viewed as procedural and thus referable to the *lex fori*. Recently applied in *International Fruit Genetics LLC v Okran 28 (Pty) Ltd* [2019] ZAWCHC 37.

[485] 1995 (1) SA 677 (A) 685B–E.

[486] *Private International Law* 5 ed (2012) 472.

in *Gabelsberger v Babl*,[487] where Van Dijkhorst J treated a German court-recorded settlement, which was not and could not be made an order of the court, but which was enforceable as a judgment in Germany, as an enforceable foreign judgment.

Recently the question has arisen whether an order made by a supra-national body is one made by a court for the purposes of enforcement. In *Government of the Republic of Zimbabwe v Fick*,[488] one question for the decision of the Constitutional Court was whether an order for costs made by the Tribunal of the Southern African Development Community was enforceable. The court found that, at common law as it then stood, the order was not enforceable[489] but that the common law should be developed to render the orders of the Tribunal enforceable.[490]

Against this background, it is possible to address the respective constituent elements of the formulation of principle in *Jones v Krok*.

(1) The court which pronounced the judgment had international jurisdiction

Turning to the first of these, it appears to be generally accepted that there are three instances where a foreign court will be found to have had international jurisdiction for the purposes of recognition or enforcement of its judgment in South Africa: residence; submission; and presence.[491] There may also be a fourth instance, where the foreign court was the court of the defendant's domicile. This is more controversial but, given the state of the authorities, is included within this section.

(1) The defendant was resident within the jurisdiction of the foreign court at the time of the commencement of proceedings

Pistorius,[492] Forsyth[493] and Schulze[494] are all in agreement that the defendant's residence within the jurisdiction of the foreign court at the time of the commencement of proceedings is sufficient to confer international jurisdiction

---

487 1994 (2) SA 677 (T).

488 2013 (5) SA 325 (CC) (Mogoeng CJ, Moseneke DCJ, Froneman, Jafta, Khampepe, Nkabinde, Skweyiya, Van der Westhuizen, Zondo JJ and Mhlantla AJ).

489 Ibid *per* Mogoeng CJ (giving the majority judgment) 346A–B para [64]: 'This court is thus enjoined, not only by art 32 of the Tribunal Protocol but also by s 8(3) of the Constitution, to either apply or develop the common law in order to give effect to the farmers' right to have the costs order enforced. And since the common law as it stands does not provide for the enforcement of the Tribunal's decision, the only option available is development.'

490 Ibid *per* Mogoeng CJ at 347H–348D paras [70]–[72].

491 In relation to the first two see Pistorius *Pollak on Jurisdiction* 2 ed (1993) 162–8; Schulze *On Jurisdiction and the Recognition and Enforcement of Foreign Money Judgments* (2005) 18–26 para 3.1; Forsyth *Private International Law* 5 ed (2012) 421–8. In relation the third, the first two works mentioned above pre-date the decision of the Supreme Court of Appeal in *Richman v Ben-Tovim* 2007 (2) SA 283 (SCA). However, this was Pollak's view in *Pollak on Jurisdiction* 1 ed (1937) 219.

492 *Pollak on Jurisdiction* 2 ed (1993) 162, 'As to residence, there is no doubt that this is sufficient to establish the international competence of a court in regard to judgments sounding in money.'

493 *Private International Law* 5 ed (2012) 421–2. The author concludes that 'the position of residence must not be considered well established'.

494 *On Jurisdiction and the Recognition and Enforcement of Foreign Money Judgments* (2005) 18 para 3.1.1.

over that defendant for the purposes of recognition or enforcement of that court's judgment in South Africa.

The academic authorities cite the decision of Bresler J in *De Naamloze Vennootschap Alintex v Von Gerlach*[495] in support of the proposition. Bresler J there refused to enforce a judgment of the court of appeal of Amsterdam in the Netherlands because it was clear from the Amsterdam judgment that the defendant had no place of residence in the Netherlands and had in fact[496] never even been in the Netherlands. Citing the Privy Council's decision in *Sirdar Gurdyal Singh v The Rajah of Faridkote*,[497] Bresler J stated:[498] 'It seems that in all personal actions it is the Courts of the country in which the defendant resides which must be resorted to and not the Courts of the country where the cause of action arose.'

The question what comprises 'residence' for the purposes of this area of the law has not been the subject of judicial decision. Forsyth[499] states that 'residence requires more than a temporary or transient visit or abode, but less than the intention to settle indefinitely requires to establish domicile'. Schulze cites the Appellate Division in *Ex parte Minister of Native Affairs*[500] where Centlivres JA, giving the judgment of the court, distinguished between residence and domicile, finding[501] that the latter concept was to be distinguished from the former for the purposes of ascertaining a person's residence and further held:[502]

> 'The Courts have studiously refrained from attempting the impossible task of giving a precise or exhaustive definition of the word "resides". For as Searle J, correctly said in *Hogsett v. Buys* (1913 CPD at p. 205):- "It has never been laid down what degree of permanence is required in residence; but at all events it ought to be shown that the person sought to be brought within the jurisdiction had some interest in the place where he was served, in the sense that there was some good reason for regarding it as his place of ordinary habitation at the date of service."'

In *Zwyssig v Zwyssig*,[503] ownership of a home and presence in South Africa for six months, maintenance of a telephone line at that home and membership of a local health club were sufficient to establish residence in South Africa.

Notwithstanding the view that the concept of international jurisdiction or competence is an independent concept in South African private international law 'which is not affected by the internal jurisdiction rules of the foreign court nor

495 1958 (1) SA 13 (T).

496 Ibid 14E.

497 [1894] AC 670, PC (Earl of Selborne, Lords Watson, Hobhouse, Macnaghten, Morris and Shand and Sir Richard Couch).

498 1958 (1) SA 13 (T) 15D.

499 *Private International Law* 5 ed (2012) 422.

500 1941 AD 53 (De Wet CJ, Watermeyer, Tindall, Centlivres and Feetham JJA).

501 1958 (1) SA 13 (T) 58.

502 Ibid 59.

503 1997 (2) SA 467 (W).

by the internal jurisdiction rules of the South African courts',[504] it may well be that the search for the meaning of 'residence' in the present context need not go too far beyond the meaning of 'residence' as discussed above in the context of the domestic South African rules for the assumption of jurisdiction over defendants.

As regards corporations, Forsyth states that a foreign court will not be considered internationally competent unless the corporate defendant over which the foreign court assumed jurisdiction had a permanent business establishment within the jurisdiction of the foreign court.[505]

(2) Where the defendant has submitted to the jurisdiction of the foreign court

Again, Pistorius,[506] Forsyth[507] and Schulze[508] are all in agreement that the defendant's submission to the jurisdiction of the foreign court is sufficient to confer international jurisdiction over that defendant for the purposes of recognition or enforcement of that court's judgment in South Africa.

The basis for this head of international jurisdiction was articulated by S du Toit AJ in *Argos Fishing Co Ltd v Friopesca SA*.[509] There the plaintiff, a company incorporated under the laws of the Falkland Islands, applied to have a default judgment obtained in the English courts against the respondent, a Spanish company, recognised and enforced by the High Court of Namibia. The plaintiff and defendant had entered into a joint venture agreement pursuant to which the parties agreed to co-operate in a fishing venture in the South Atlantic and in particular in the catching of loligo squid in the Falkland Islands Conservation Zone. The plaintiff would apply for the necessary licences to catch the squid. The defendant would provide the plaintiff with three fishing vessels under the terms of a charterparty. The agreement contained a clause in the following terms: 'This agreement is subject to English law and any disputes shall be determined in the High Court of Justice in London' and the charterparty contained a similar clause. S du Toit JA held that the English court had international jurisdiction but dismissed the application to have the judgment recognised and enforced on the ground that it was not clear that the judgment was final.

As regards the effect of jurisdiction agreements, S du Toit AJ stated:[510]

---

[504] Schulze *On Jurisdiction and the Recognition and Enforcement of Foreign Money Judgments* (2005) 18 para 3.1.

[505] *Private International Law* 5 ed (2012) 422, based on the provisions of s 1E(1)(b) of the Protection of Businesses Act 1978 (Act 99 of 1978); as inserted by the Protection of Businesses Amendment Act 1987 (Act 87 of 1987).

[506] *Pollak on Jurisdiction* 2 ed (1993) 162.

[507] *Private International Law* 5 ed (2012) 422–3. The author concludes: 'It is widely recognised, by both writers and the decided cases, that submission by the defendant to the jurisdiction of the foreign court grants to that court international competence even if it would not otherwise enjoy that competence.'

[508] *On Jurisdiction and the Recognition and Enforcement of Foreign Money Judgments* (2005) 19 para 3.1.1.

[509] 1991 (3) SA 255 (Nm).

[510] Ibid 261C–G.

> 'However, I am of the view that I am free to consider the question of the international competence of the English Court in this case by reference to what I would term general considerations.
>
> It is of course desirable that litigants be bound by their bargains. Secondly, in a world of almost instant communication there seems no practical reason why parties should not in advance select their forum to settle disputes in relation to a particular contract. Thirdly, parties of different nationalities may find it convenient to choose the courts of a (neutral) third country. Fourthly, international commerce may find it convenient to select certain jurisdictions above others, for the settlement of disputes. Parties may be influenced by such matters as cost, convenience, impartiality, accessibility, language and the speed with which a result can be expected to be achieved. If contracting parties do consider such matters when they contract, why, may one ask, should their agreement not be enforced. Fifthly, if the court which the parties have chosen, accepts jurisdiction, why should that acceptance be questioned by another court.'

The *Argos Fishing* case also exemplifies the separate character of the concept of international jurisdiction for the purposes of recognition or enforcement of a foreign judgment: in that case the judgment of the English court which it was sought to be enforced in what was then South West Africa (and is now Namibia) was in respect of a matter over which the South African courts could not themselves have exercised jurisdiction.[511]

As with the head of residence above, the question arises what comprises 'submission' for the purposes of this head of international jurisdiction. Some academic authority exists for the treatment of this head of international jurisdiction in an identical manner to the law of submission in the domestic context.[512] However, Forsyth submits[513]

> 'that the law relating to what amounts to submission for the purpose of international competence is not identical to that which deals with submission to the jurisdiction of the South African court. There may consequently be cases in which the conduct in question amounts to submission to a local court, but not – *mutatis mutandis* – to submission to a foreign court; and, of course, vice versa. After all, in matters of internal competence the court will be bound by all the rules, technical or otherwise, of Roman-Dutch law but this will not be the case with international competence where a less technical and comparativist approach will be appropriate.'

This is a view with which the authors respectfully agree. In the light of it, it is necessary to address the circumstances in which, for the purposes of the

---

[511] Because both parties were *peregrini* and the cause of action did not arise within the territorial jurisdiction of the court that the plaintiff sought to seise of the matter.

[512] Forsyth cites Dr Spiro 'Jurisdiction by consent' (1967) 84 *SALJ* 295 at 306; and Silberberg *The Recognition and Enforcement of Foreign Judgments in South Africa* Pretoria Institute for Foreign and Comparative Law (1977) 13ff.

[513] *Private International Law* 5 ed (2012) 424.

enforcement of foreign judgments, a judgment debtor will be taken to have submitted to the jurisdiction of the foreign court. Two such circumstances will be discussed below: situations in which the judgment debtor may be adjudged to have submitted by way of agreement and situations in which the judgment debtor may be taken to have submitted by virtue of their conduct.

Turning, first, to submission by way of agreement, the courts have accepted that a non-exclusive jurisdiction clause will confer international competence on the foreign court that rendered the judgment that is sought to be enforced in South Africa.

A fortiori, an exclusive jurisdiction clause will confer international competence on the foreign court that rendered the judgment that is sought to be enforced in South Africa.

The question arises, however, by reference to what system of law is the validity and effect of the jurisdiction agreement to be determined. Ordinarily, this should pose no problem, as typically the choice of law and jurisdiction clause will coincide in the same legal system (as in the *Argos Fishing* case) or, if there is no choice of law clause, an exclusive jurisdiction clause in favour of a particular jurisdiction may assist the court in identifying the proper law as the same as that of that jurisdiction.[514] But this will not always be so and Forsyth gives the example of a contract containing both a jurisdiction clause in favour of the Australian courts and a choice of law clause stipulating German law as the governing law of the contract pursuant to which the jurisdiction clause would be invalid.

Forsyth proposes that, in such a case, German law as the proper law should determine the validity of the jurisdiction clause, with the result that the Australian courts would not, according to South African law, have international competence to render a judgment capable of being recognised or enforced in the Republic of South Africa.[515] This approach was followed by Cloete J in *Blanchard, Krasner & French v Evans*[516] where the judge expressly approved the approach proposed by Forsyth.

Such an approach has the merit of conforming to commercial common sense: participants in international commerce, where the content and terms of choice of law and choice of court clauses are usually the subject of negotiations, more often than not with the assistance of advice from lawyers, may be taken to have

---

514 *Qui elegit iudicem elegit ius.*

515 *Private International Law* 5 (ed) (2012) 427.

516 2002 (4) SA 144 (T) 149C–D; a case where the proper law was the law of California and the choice of jurisdiction was that of a procedure provided for by the California Code of Civil Procedure of reference to a retired judge which, because the defendant did not respond to the plaintiff's complaint, ceased to be available to the plaintiff who then sought and obtained judgment in default. Cloete J accepted expert evidence that the effect of proper law on the interpretation of the agreement was to confer jurisdiction on the Superior Court for the County of San Diego.

regard to their own interests and to be in a position to inform themselves of the ramifications of agreeing to a proper law which differs from the law administered by the courts on which jurisdiction is conferred by a jurisdiction clause. In such cases it makes sense that the substantive choice of a governing law for the contract should govern all the clauses of that contract.

Such an approach is seen in current English law. *Dicey, Morris and Collins on the Conflict of Laws* states:[517]

> 'as a matter of common law, normally a jurisdiction agreement ... is governed by the law applicable to the contract of which it forms a part. Accordingly, and as a matter of the common law principles of the conflict of laws, the law which governs the contract will also generally govern the jurisdiction agreement. This means ... that this law governs the construction and interpretation of the agreement; it will also, in principle at least, govern the original validity of the agreement.'

The question then arises, what if the proper law is itself not expressed? In these circumstances the existence of a jurisdiction clause, the validity of which is challenged, might bear upon and influence the identification of a proper law pursuant to which the challenge to the validity of the clause is made. If no proper law is expressed then the jurisdiction agreement potentially forms an important part of the calculus in identifying the proper law (*qui elegit iudicem elegit ius*).[518]

---

[517] 15 ed (2012) vol 1, 604 para 12–103. See also Briggs *Private International Law in English Courts* (2014) paras 7.12–7.15. Judicial authority for the proposition is found in *Akai Pty Ltd v People's Insurance Co Ltd* [1998] 1 Lloyd's Rep 90 (Thomas J) 98, col 2.

[518] Forsyth would apply the *qui elegit iudicem elegit ius* principle to a choice of an arbitrator, but not a choice of court (*Private International Law* 5 ed (2012) 328) on the grounds that 'in most cases' the arbitrator will be a layman and 'can hardly be expected to apply any but his own law' whereas, '[a] person who submits to a court's jurisdiction does not necessarily intend thereby that that court should abandon its choice of law process and mechanically apply the *lex fori*'. However, arbitration clauses typically do not identify the arbitrators with a system of law in the same way as a jurisdiction clause identifies a judge of a court with that jurisdiction's system of law: an arbitration clause will frequently identify the seat of the arbitration but not the arbitrators, who may not share the same nationality as the seat and may be from one or more different jurisdictions with different legal traditions. As regards jurisdiction clauses, it is submitted that while it might be the case that such a hypothetical contracting party might not *necessarily* intend that the chosen court should abandon its choice of law process, it is more likely that commercial parties choosing a particular forum in which to litigate would have in mind the domestic law of such a jurisdiction and not (experience teaches) its *outré* conflict of laws rules. (This is, however, not a view shared by other, eminent, authorities in this field (see Briggs *Private International Law in English Courts* (2014) paras 7.10 and 7.310).)

In European law the choice of a forum is accepted as influential in ascertaining an inferred choice of law: see the Giuliano and Lagarde Report (OJ 1980 C282) accompanying the EEC Convention on the law applicable to contractual obligations ('the Rome Convention') 17 col 1, where examples of matters from which a choice of law may be inferred are described, inter alia: 'In some cases the choice of a particular forum may show in no uncertain manner that the parties intend the contract to be governed by the law of that forum, but this must always be subject to the other terms of the cntract [sic] and all the circumstances of the case'; and the Rome Convention's replacement instrument, the Rome 1 Regulation (593/2008) which states at Recital (12): 'An agreement between the parties to confer on one or more courts or tribunals of a Member State exclusive jurisdiction to determine disputes under the contract should be one of the factors to be taken into account in determining whether a choice of law has been clearly demonstrated.' Under the

In such a case a system of law is needed to provide an assessment of the validity of the jurisdiction clause in advance of the identification of the proper law. The *lex fori* would provide such an assessment, after which the proper law might be identified using the usual criteria.[519]

Thus the law by reference to which the validity of a jurisdiction clause is to be assessed might more accurately be described as the law governing the jurisdiction agreement rather than the proper law of the contract (although in cases of an express choice of law, surely the majority of cases, they will usually be the same).[520]

Forsyth distinguishes between three types of submission by agreement.[521] First, express submission; second, tacit submission; and, third, implied submission.

Express submission has been discussed above. As long as the express agreement to submit is lawful under the proper law of the instrument in which that agreement appears, then it is effective.

Tacit submission arises where the parties agree to submit but do not record that agreement in their contract. Here such an agreement, albeit tacit, is nonetheless effective. Whether such a tacit agreement exists is a question of the parties' intention. In *Standard Bank Ltd v Butlin*,[522] Didcott J held:

> 'When it comes to undertakings, decisions, commitments and the like which have legal force, contractual or otherwise, our law does not ordinarily differentiate between those made expressly and others reached impliedly or tacitly. There are exceptions, of course. A statute's insistence on formality may disqualify the tacit from recognition in particular instances, and the implied too, once at any rate the implication's material goes beyond the language used on the occasion in question. In general, however, the intention of the person concerned is what counts, whether such be gleaned from his words, inferred from

---

Rome Convention, the English courts have held that a jurisdiction clause in favour of the English court was to be treated as an inferred choice of English law: *Marubeni Hong Kong and South China Ltd v Mongolian Government* [2002] 2 All ER (Comm) 873.

This reflects the position at common law in England: Cheshire, North and Fawcett, *Private International Law* 15 ed (2017) 720.

[519] *Dicey, Morris and Collins on the Conflict of Laws* states (para 12–103): 'It has been held, and appears to be correct, that this preliminary assessment has to be undertaken by reference to English domestic law principles. But it should follow that once the law governing the contract has been identified by these means, it is that law which must be used to make the definitive assessment whether the jurisdiction agreement in question is in fact one of the terms of the contract.'

[520] This contention gains support from art 3(d) of the Hague Convention on Choice of Court Agreements, which provides: 'An exclusive choice of court agreement that forms part of a contract shall be treated as an agreement independent of the other terms of the contract. The validity of the exclusive choice of court agreement cannot be contested solely on the ground that the contract is not valid.' There is hence a division between the contract and the jurisdiction agreement.

[521] *Private International Law* 5 ed (2012) 428.

[522] 1981 (4) SA 158 (D) 161E–H. In this passage Didcott J seems to have used the terms 'tacit' and 'implied' synonymously; the 'or' at the end of the first and last sentences of the passage above would appear to have been meant conjunctively.

> his conduct, or gathered from both. Mere details these are. They furnish the evidence of his intention. But their significance goes no deeper. Sometimes, according to the rules of evidence, the words employed, if any, are all that may be taken into account. But that does not affect the principle now under discussion. As far as such goes, I can see no reason why submissions to jurisdiction should be put into a compartment of their own. Usually, to be sure, they have important consequences. So, however, do numerous consents given impliedly or tacitly, yet altogether effectively.'

Thus the enquiry for the court will be whether the party intended to submit to the jurisdiction of the foreign court and this enquiry will be answered by applying the tools of construction used by the court in ascertaining intent in other contexts.

Implied submission occurs by operation of law where certain facts are present. Forsyth gives the example of registering a partnership in a foreign country leading to the foreign law deeming the partners to have submitted to the foreign forum. Forsyth submits that this type of submission is not sufficient for the purposes of recognising the foreign judgment. Forsyth notes that implied submission is not sufficient under English law.[523] This, however, is no longer correct.[524]

Regardless of the English position, the position in the Republic of South Africa may be exemplified by the decision in *Standard Bank Ltd v Butlin*. There,

---

[523] *Private International* Law 5 ed (2012) 428, citing *Vogel v Kohnstamm Ltd* [1973] 1 QB 133; *Sirdar Gurdyal Singh v Rajah of Faridkote* [1894] AC 670 (PC) and *Emanuel v Symon* [1908] 1 KB 302 (CA). In *Vogel*, which was a case concerning a contract, Ashworth J used the term 'implied' agreement in the sense of a term being implied into an agreement where the parties had not themselves intended its implication. In the *Faridkote* case (a misfeasance claim), Lord Selbourne rejected (obiter) the proposition that consent to the jurisdiction of the *forum loci contractus* was generally to be implied into contracts. In *Emanuel*, Kennedy LJ stated that a term consenting to the jurisdiction was not to be implied 'from the mere fact of entering into a contract in a foreign country'. These decisions are perhaps better categorised as decisions regarding what Forsyth describes as 'express/tacit' submission (which is how Lord Collins characterised them (at para [56]) in the *Vizcaya* decision: as to which, see below. In each case no express agreement to submit was found and an implied (or 'tacit') submission was held to be insufficient.

[524] The Privy Council has found that submission to the jurisdiction may be implied. In *Vizcaya Partners Ltd v Pickard* [2016] UKPC 5, [2016] Bus LR 413 (Lords Neuberger, Mance, Clarke, Sumption and Collins). Lord Collins, giving the judgment of Privy Council, stated, at para [32]: 'There has been a division of authority on the question whether at common law an agreement or consent to submit to the jurisdiction of the foreign court can be implied or inferred, and, if so, how the implication or inference can arise', and that, accordingly (at para [55]), it was necessary to consider 'the question as a matter of principle and authority'. His Lordship, in setting out the view that such submission could be implicit, stated, at para [56], that the 'real question is whether the judgment debtor consented in advance to the jurisdiction of the foreign court'. Having identified the question, Lord Collins then went on to give guidance as to how that question might be answered, depending on whether the term at issue was implied as a matter of fact or as a matter of law: see paras [57]–[61]. The question whether a judgment debtor submitted to the foreign jurisdiction is a question referable, in the context of a contract, to the proper law of that contract. If, by the proper law of the contract, a term falls to be implied into the contract, either as a matter of fact or as a matter of law, to the effect that in either case the judgment debtor submitted to the jurisdiction of the foreign court, then that court will have had international jurisdiction. Thus tacit or implied submission are now both recognised in English law (certainly in the context of contractual submission).

Didcott J rejected[525] the contention that a *domicilium citandi et executandi* clause amounted to a submission to the jurisdiction of the Rhodesian court, finding that its function was merely to designate a place for service.[526]

Having then considered the circumstances in which a judgment debtor may be taken to have submitted to the jurisdiction of the foreign court by way of agreement, it is necessary to address the second above-mentioned situation, viz where the judgment debtor may be taken to have submitted by virtue of their conduct. In *Du Preez v Philip-King*,[527] the court considered whether a foreign *peregrinus* sued in South Africa had submitted to the jurisdiction. The defendant was sued for damages arising out of a collision. He entered an appearance and by letter requested particulars of the damages claimed. After service of the declaration, the defendant filed a request for particulars. He then filed a plea on the merits and a special plea in which he pleaded that the court had no jurisdiction because it was alleged that the defendant was neither domiciled nor resident in the Republic of South Africa, but was domiciled and resident in England. Vieyra AJ stated:[528]

> 'A submission may be in consequence of an agreement between the parties to that effect ... But it may also arise consequent upon unilateral conduct following upon citation before a tribunal not ordinarily competent to give judgment against a particular defendant ... The difficulty is, of course, to determine in each case whether the conduct of the defendant is tantamount to a submission to jurisdiction. It seems to me that although a submission of this sort is a unilateral act only and therefore does not have to fulfil all the requirements of a waiver, nevertheless just as in waiver at least all the elements of an acquiescence must be present.To constitute acquiescence the conduct which is the subject matter of the enquiry must be of such a nature that the Court must be able to say that it is consistent only with acquiescence.'

The judge held that the defendant had not submitted to the jurisdiction by reason of the actions he had taken in relation to the proceedings (the plea to the merits was qualified by reference to his objection to the jurisdiction), none of

---

[525] 1981 (4) SA 158 (D) 165C–E, the judge did so, having concluded that as a matter of intent, the clause could not have been intended by the eventual defendant to the proceedings in Rhodesia to have conferred jurisdiction by submission on the Rhodesian court because, at the time he entered into the agreement containing the clause, he was already amenable to the jurisdiction. Conversely, in *Beverley Building Society v De Courcy* 1964 (4) SA 264 (SR), Maisels J held (270B–E and 273A) that a *domicilium citandi et executandi* clause was of significance in finding there had been a tacit submission, because at the time the agreement containing the clause had been entered into the defendant had not been amenable to the foreign court's jurisdiction and that this, combined with other factors, led to the conclusion that the defendant had tacitly consented to the jurisdiction.

[526] However, authorities such as *Hay Management Consultants (Pty) Ltd v P3 Management Consultants (Pty) Ltd* 2005 (2) SA 522 (SCA) indicate that the existence of such a clause in a contract may well be used in support of the contention that a party has submitted itself to the jurisdiction of the South African courts.

[527] 1963 (1) SA 801 (W).

[528] Ibid 803A–C.

which individually or cumulatively were consistent only with submission to the jurisdiction.

It is likely (but not certain)[529] therefore that the same test will be used where the international competence of the foreign court is being considered in the context of a contention that the defendant in the foreign proceedings submitted by conduct.

Section 1E(1)(a) of the Protection of Businesses Act 1978 provides that an appearance before the foreign court, whether conditionally or otherwise, does not amount to submission where that appearance was entered for one of the following purposes:

> '(i) to contest the jurisdiction of that court;
>
> (ii) to apply for the dismissal of the action in question or for the setting aside of the writ or summons in those proceedings on the ground that the court did not have the required jurisdiction;
>
> (iii) to protect or to obtain the release of any property attached for the purpose of such proceedings, or threatened with attachment in those proceedings;
>
> (iv) to apply to the court not to exercise its jurisdiction, if it was a case where that court had a discretion to decide whether or not to exercise its jurisdiction;
>
> (v) to apply to such court for the dismissal of, or a stay of, the proceedings on the ground that the matter should be referred to arbitration or to a court in another country for a decision;
>
> (vi) to institute review proceedings in connection with, or to lodge an appeal against, any order made in the proceedings mentioned in paragraphs (i) to (v).'

Section 1E(2) provides that an appearance to contest the merits is not a submission if

> 'in terms of the law governing such court and the proceedings conducted therein, such person was not entitled to contest the jurisdiction of the court unless he entered such appearance or took such step, as the case may be, in order to defend the action on the merits'.

An appearance that is made to contest the merits without any qualification will be treated as a submission to the jurisdiction of the foreign court.[530]

[529] For example, the consequences in the foreign jurisdiction of taking a particular step in proceedings may differ from those of taking the same step in South African proceedings.

[530] Forsyth *Private International Law* 5 ed (2012) 426; *Purser v Sales* 2001 (3) SA 445 (SCA) (Hefer ADCJ, Marais and Zulman JJA and Mpati and Mthiyane AJJA), where, inter alia, the making of an application by the judgment debtor in the foreign court to have the claim of the judgment creditor dismissed for want of prosecution was held to amount to a submission.

Pistorius states further[531] that the following actions have been deemed to evidence submission: filing a counterclaim;[532] requesting a postponement or agreeing to a postponement without objection; demanding security; appointing an agent authorised to be sued; attending an enquiry into his financial position and agreeing to pay a judgment debt in instalments; and accepting appointment as an executor or executrix.

(3) Where the defendant is present within the jurisdiction of the foreign court at the time proceedings were commenced and served

It had been thought that the defendant's presence within the foreign jurisdiction at the time of the commencement and service of proceedings without more did not confer international jurisdiction on the foreign court.[533]

However, the Supreme Court of Appeal in *Richman v Ben-Tovim*[534] overturned this orthodoxy and held that presence could confer international jurisdiction on a foreign court. The appellant/plaintiff sought provisional sentence on a default judgment granted against the respondent/defendant by the High Court in England in respect of legal fees and disbursements incurred by the plaintiff on behalf of the defendant. The defendant was at the time of the commencement and service of proceedings on him in London neither resident nor domiciled in England and was present there temporarily (possibly even only transiently)[535] for the purposes of his business. The judge at first instance, Van Zyl J, held that the judgment was not enforceable because the English court lacked international jurisdiction. The plaintiff's case on appeal was:[536]

> 'there is international competence in South African law if a defendant is merely physically present in the jurisdiction of the foreign court at the time action is instituted and process served, and that in the present case the English court was also the *locus contractus* as well as the *locus solutionis*'.

Allowing the appeal, Zulman JA quoted[537] from the judgment of Van Dijkhorst in *Reiss Engineering Co Ltd v Insamcor (Pty) Ltd*,[538] in which the judge himself quoted from *Pollak on Jurisdiction*,[539] to the effect that international jurisdiction would be established by presence at the time of commencement of the action

---

531 *Pollak on Jurisdiction* 2 ed (1993) 162–3 and 11.

532 Forsyth *Private International Law* 5 ed (2012) 426 fn 63.

533 Pistorius *Pollak on Jurisdiction* 2 ed (1993) 164; Schulze *On Jurisdiction and the Recognition and Enforcement of Foreign Money Judgments* (2005) 22 para 3.1.5.

534 2007 (2) SA 283 (SCA) (Zulman, Cameron, Brand and Maya JJA and Theron AJA).

535 Ibid 285C–D para [3].

536 Ibid 285D–E.

537 Ibid 286D–H para [7].

538 1983 (1) SA 1033 (W).

539 Pollak 1 ed (1937).

(service of the proceedings) and proceeded to hold that presence was sufficient. The judge noted that the *Reiss* case had been approved and applied in *Jones v Krok*,[540] *Erskine v Chinatex Oriental Trading Co*[541] and *Blanchard, Krasner & French v Evans*.[542] Zulman JA then distinguished[543] the Supreme Court of Appeal decision in *Purser v Sales*,[544] which it was contended conflicted with the *Reiss* case in this regard. Having reviewed other academic texts Zulman JA held:[545]

> 'There are compelling reasons why, as submitted by the plaintiff's counsel, in this modern age, traditional grounds of international competence should be extended, within reason, to cater for itinerant international businessmen. In addition it is now well established that the exigencies of international trade and commerce require "that final foreign judgments be recognised as far as is reasonably possible in our courts, and that effect be given thereto". This Court (albeit in a slightly different context) said in *Mayne v Main* that a "common-sense" and "realistic approach" should be adopted in assessing jurisdictional requirements because of
>
> > "modern-day conditions and attitudes and the tendency towards a more itinerant lifestyle, particularly among business people. And because not to do so might allow certain persons habitually to avoid the jurisdictional nets of the courts and thereby escape legal accountability for their wrongful actions."
>
> In my view, and having regard to all of the above factors, the view expressed by Pollak, quoted with approval by Van Dijkhorst J in *Reiss*, should be followed.'

The judgment of the SCA in *Richman v Ben-Tovim* has been criticised.[546] However, the question whether an individual's presence is a sufficient ground for international jurisdiction may be taken to have been settled.

It is unclear whether the same principle applies to a corporation. Under English law a corporation is 'present' in the area of jurisdiction of a foreign court for the purposes of international jurisdiction if

> 'either (i) it has established and maintained at its own expense (whether as owner or lessee) a fixed place of business of its own in the other country and for more than a minimal period of time has carried on its own business at or from such premises by its servants or agents (a "branch office" case), or (ii) a representative of the overseas corporation has for more than a minimal period of time been carrying on the overseas corporation's business in the other country at or from some fixed place of business'.[547]

---

540 1995 (1) SA 677 (A) 685G.

541 2001 (1) SA 817 (C) 820J–821B.

542 2001 (4) SA 86 (W) 89H–90A.

543 2007 (2) SA 283 (SCA) 287A–F paras [7]-[8].

544 2001 (3) SA 445 (SCA).

545 2007 (2) SA 283 (SCA) 289A–E para [9].

546 See Forsyth *Private International Law* 5 ed (2012) 429–30.

547 *Adams v Cape Industries plc* [1990] 2 WLR 657 (CA) (Slade, Mustill and Ralph Gibson LJJ) *per* Slade LJ (giving the judgment of the court) 747A–H.

As Forsyth has pointed out, this test amounts to a residency test rather than a presence test.[548]

(4) Where the foreign court which gave the judgment was the court of the defendant's domicile

As a matter of judicial authority, in *Purser v Sales*,[549] Mpati AJA approved, obiter,[550] the proposition that domicile was sufficient to confer international jurisdiction. The relevant passage in the *Purser* case was cited by Kuny AJ with apparent approval in *Balkan Energy Ltd v Government of Ghana*.[551]

However, most recent academic authority[552] favours the view that domicile is not a basis of international jurisdiction. This is because the rules relating to the acquisition and loss of domicile are considered to be technical and artificial and inapt to render a person amenable to the jurisdiction of a foreign court with which that person has no physical, residential or other substantive connection.[553]

Cases where there is not international jurisdiction of competence

In the following cases, it would appear that the foreign court does not have international jurisdiction of competence.

(1) *Where the defendant was at the time of commencement of proceedings a national of the foreign state whose courts rendered the judgment.* It is generally accepted that nationality is not a sufficient basis for international jurisdiction.[554]

(2) *Where the foreign court attached the defendant's property to found jurisdiction.* It is generally accepted that attachment by the foreign court is not a sufficient basis for international jurisdiction.[555]

---

548 *Private International Law* 5 ed (2012) 431.

549 2001 (3) SA 445 (SCA) (Hefer ADCJ, Marais and Zulman JJA and Mpati and Mthiyane AJJA).

550 At 450J–451B, para [12].

551 2017 (5) SA 428 (GJ) 434A-C, para [14].

552 Forsyth *Private International Law* 5 ed (2012) 431–3; Schulze *On Jurisdiction and the Recognition and Enforcement of Foreign Money Judgments* (2005) 22–3 para 3.1.6.

553 There is, however, the alternative view that since the coming into force of the Domicile Act 1992, s 1(2) provides for the acquisition of a domicile of choice which is acquired when a person is 'lawfully present at a particular place and has the intention to settle there for an indefinite period'; s 3(1) provides that '[n]o person shall lose his domicile until he has acquired another domicile, whether by choice or by operation of law' and s 3(2) abolishes the revival of a person's domicile of origin. Thus, it may well be that the modern South African approach to domicile renders that concept sufficiently certain and adequately connected to a person's place of residence or his home as to render it usable as a basis for ascribing international jurisdiction to a foreign court in the area of jurisdiction of which that person is found to have settled for an indefinite period at the time proceedings commenced.

554 Pistorius *Pollak on Jurisdiction* 2 ed (1993) 165; Schulze *On Jurisdiction and the Recognition and Enforcement of Foreign Money Judgments* (2005) 23 para 3.1.7; Forsyth *Private International Law* 5 ed (2012) 433–4; *Foord v Foord* 1924 WLD 81, *per* Mason JP 87–8.

555 Pistorius *Pollak on Jurisdiction* 2 ed (1993) 164; Schulze *On Jurisdiction and the Recognition and Enforcement of Foreign Money Judgments* (2005) 23 para 3.1.8; Forsyth *Private International Law* 5 ed (2012) 434; *Acutt Blaine*

(3) *Where the cause of action arose within the jurisdiction of the foreign court.* The preponderance of academic and judicial authority support the view that the cause of action arising within the area of jurisdiction of the foreign court is not sufficient to give that court international jurisdiction.[556]

(4) *Where the defendant is a fugitive from justice.* There is a decision of the Rhodesia Appellate Division dating from 1973[557] to the effect that international jurisdiction can be conferred by a combination of presence and the cause of action arising within the jurisdiction of the foreign court and that where the defendant is absent from the foreign jurisdiction through his own wrong, the enforcing court may fulfill fictionally the requirement of presence and permit the judgment to be enforced.

It is to be noted that this decision has not proved popular amongst commentators. Forsyth[558] concludes: 'Sufficient has now been said of this judgment to indicate why it should not be relied upon for any purpose.' Schulz[559] states: 'Since the Steinberg decision is so patently incorrect, one can only agree ... that it can confidently be predicted that it would not be followed by South Africa courts in similar circumstances.'

(2) The judgment is final and conclusive in its effect and has not become superannuated

In order to be capable of recognition and enforceable, a judgment must be final and conclusive in its effect. South African law has followed English law as regards the meaning of this requirement.[560]

& Co v Colonial Marine Assurance Co (1882) 1 SC 402; *Mendelssohn v Mendelssohn's Executor* 1908 TH 190; mere possession of property *a fortiori* does not confer international jurisdiction.

[556] Pistorius *Pollak on Jurisdiction* 2 ed (1993) 164–5; Schulze *On Jurisdiction and the Recognition and Enforcement of Foreign Money Judgments* (2005) 24 para 3.1.9; Forsyth *Private International Law* 5 ed (2012) 434–5; *Borough of Finsbury Permanent Investment Building Society v Vogel* (1910) 31 NL 402 (Dove Wilson AJP, Broome and Hathorn JJ); *Supercat Incorporated v Two Oceans Marine CC* 2001 (4) SA 27 (C), *per* Conradie J at 31A–D where the judge stated that the only contrary judicial decision, that of Shearer J in *Duarte v Lissack* 1973 (3) SA 615 (D), was *per incuriam* and of no persuasive value.

[557] *Steinberg v Cosmopolitan National Bank of Chicago* 1973 (4) SA 564 (RA) (Beadle CJ, Macdonald JP and Lewis JA), *per* Beadle CJ (at 576A–B): 'The case should be approached, therefore, on the assumption that the defendant was in America at the relevant time and duly served with process there. If the defendant is not permitted to raise this defence the practical result is that it can be assumed against him that he was in America when the proceedings started and duly served with process there', even though the defendant was not in America at the relevant time and was not, therefore, duly served with process there.

[558] *Private International Law* 5 ed (2012) 437.

[559] *On Jurisdiction and the Recognition and Enforcement of Foreign Money Judgments* (2005) 25 para 3.1.10.

[560] *Greathead v Greathead* 1946 TPD 404, *per* Ramsbottom J at 407–8, referred to with apparent approval by Corbett CJ in *Jones v Krok* 1995 (1) SA 677 (A) (Corbett CJ, Van Heerden, Kumleben and Nienaber JJA and Olivier AJA) 689B–H and 692H–J (South African law will look to other systems of law in this area, for reasons of comity). The principles are similar to those adopted in Canadian jurisdictions, Australia, the USA and Scotland (Corbett CJ at 689–91).

The judgment must be unalterable by the particular court which pronounced it (although the mode of payment under the judgment may be alterable).[561]

A judgment which is final on the merits of the claim will be regarded as a final judgment notwithstanding that the judgment contains an error as to the quantum awarded against a defendant which the foreign court could have remedied by a variation of the part of the order dealing with quantum.[562]

The fact that a judgment may be appealed does not affect its finality.

A judgment in respect of which an appeal is being (or is about to be) pursued, is nonetheless a final judgment.[563]

However, where the judgment is subject to an appeal, the general principles the courts apply are as follows:[564]

> '(1) The fact that the judgment is subject to appeal or even that an appeal is pending in the foreign jurisdiction does not affect the finality of the judgment, provided that in all other respects it is final and conclusive.
>
> (2) Where, however, it is shown that the judgment is subject to such an appeal or that such an appeal is pending, the Court in this country which is asked to enforce the judgment enjoys a discretion and in the exercise thereof may, instead of giving judgment in favour of the plaintiff, stay the proceedings pending the final determination of the appeal or appeals in the foreign jurisdiction.
>
> (3) Although the onus of proving that a foreign judgment is final and conclusive rests upon the party seeking to enforce it ... it seems to me that, where this onus has been discharged, it is up to the defendant to place before the Court the facts relating to the impending appeal and such other relevant facts as may persuade the Court to exercise its discretion in favour of granting a stay of proceedings.
>
> (4) In exercising this discretion the Court may take into account all relevant circumstances, including (but not confined to) whether an appeal is actually pending, the consequences to the defendant if judgment be given in favour of [the] plaintiff and thereafter (possibly after the judgment has been satisfied) the appeal succeeds in

---

561 *C Hoare & Co v Runewitsch* 1997 (1) SA 338 (W).

562 In *Elan Boulevard Pty Ltd v FNYN Investments (Pty) Ltd* 2019 (3) SA 441 (SCA) (Ponnan, Dambuza, Mocumie and Schippers JJS and Mothle AJA), the judgment creditor sought to enforce a judgment from the Supreme Court of Queensland, Australia, against judgment debtors two of whom had guaranteed in different amounts the obligations of the third judgment debtor. The judge had erroneously ordered both guarantors to pay the full amount of the third judgment debtor's obligations. It was not in dispute that this was an error nor was it in dispute what the correct sums guaranteed were and the court allowed the judgment creditor's appeal from the decision of Gauteng Division refusing enforcement and ordered enforcement of the correct sums against each guarantor (*per* Ponnan JA, giving the judgment of the court, at paras 13–14).

563 *Rosenstrauch v Korbf* 1931 GWLD 102, *per* Blaine AJ: 'If the judgment was final in the Tribunal of Commerce [in Antwerp], and there is nothing before me to suggest that it was not, then it is none the less so because it is subject to appeal'; cited with approval by Corbett CJ in *Jones v Krok* 1995 (1) SA 677 (A) (Corbett CJ, Van Heerden, Kumleben and Nienaber JJA and Olivier AJA) 691B–E.

564 *Jones v Krok* 1995 (1) SA 677 (A) (Corbett CJ, Van Heerden, Kumleben and Nienaber JJA and Olivier AJA), *per* Corbett CJ at 692B–G.

> the foreign jurisdiction and whether the defendant is pursuing the right of appeal genuinely and with due diligence. As a rule, however, the Court will refuse to assess the merits and demerits of the appeal and its prospects of success in the foreign Court.'

As regards default judgments, where typically (though not always) the foreign court will not have engaged with the merits of the plaintiff's case and where the foreign court may have power to discharge or rescind the default judgment, it seems that the requirement of finality is satisfied where the possibility of discharge or rescission is remote. In *Blanchard, Krasner & French v Morgan Evans*,[565] Malan J approved[566] the following statement of the law: 'It is suggested that common-sense tests rather than rigid rules ought to be applied in examining whether a foreign judgment is or is not final', and held that nothing had been shown in that case to persuade him that a postponement of the enforcement of a judgment for costs of the Superior Court of the state of California, San Diego, should be given to the defendant to investigate or bring proceedings for rescission of that judgment.

The judgment must not have become superannuated.[567]

(3) The recognition and enforcement of the judgment by the courts would not be contrary to public policy.

A judgment rendered contrary to natural justice will not be recognised or enforced as being contrary to public policy. Here, natural justice bears its usual meaning: the defendant must have had notice of the proceedings and an opportunity to present his case before an impartial tribunal.

Forsyth states that the courts 'do not take a technical approach to natural justice, but do what their notions of fairness seem to require in the circumstances'.[568]

In *Rubie v Haines*,[569] a judgment pronounced by the King's Bench Division was enforced, notwithstanding the defendant's contention that the proceedings had been conducted in a manner contrary to natural justice by reason of his request for an adjournment having been refused (a decision which had itself been upheld by the English Court of Appeal).

---

565 2004 (4) SA 427 (W).

566 Ibid 434G–435B. Malan J also distinguished the decision of Du Toit AJ in *Argos Fishing Co Ltd v Friopesca SA* 1991 (3) SA 255 (Nm), on the basis that Du Toit AJ expressly stated that on the evidence he was not in a position to assess the finality of an English default judgment. Forsyth prefers the Malan J approach to that of Du Toit AJ: *Private International Law* 5 ed (2012) 460.

567 That is, unenforceable in the foreign jurisdiction by reason of effluxion of time: *National Milling Co Ltd v Mohamed* 1966 (3) SA 22 (R), *per* Goldin J at 23H.

568 *Private International Law* 5 ed (2012) 461.

569 1948 (4) SA 998 (W).

In *Steinberg v Cosmopolitan National Bank of Chicago*,[570] the Rhodesian Appellate Division refused to enforce a judgment of a circuit court of the state of Illinois, USA, in proceedings where the plaintiff had relied on a *cognovit* clause in its surety agreement with the defendant, the effect of which was to authorise 'any attorney of any court of record to appear' for him and consent to judgment 'without any process'. It was common ground that the defendant had not been given notice of the proceedings in Illinois.

In *Lissack v Duarte*,[571] the defendant had hired a car in Lourenço Marques, Mozambique, and then damaged it in Swaziland. The plaintiff commenced proceedings against the defendant in the Lourenço Marques courts. The defendant received various documents from the court, including a summons in translation and replied by letter to the effect that he did not understand the documents received by him, he did not know the plaintiff and was unaware of the allegations made against him. Reversing the decision of Shearer J, the court refused to enforce the judgment rendered by the Mozambique court. Leon J stated:[572] 'Where judgment is granted in a country against an absent foreigner the enquiry as to a possible failure of natural justice is to be answered by reference to all the circumstances of the case.' The court held that insufficient information had been given to the defendant to enable him to defend the proceedings: 'In the light of the information which he had been given and the defendant's response thereto, fundamental principles of fairness required the Lourenço Marques Court to apprise the defendant of the correct procedure after his letter had been received.'

In *Corona v Zimbabwe Iron & Steel Co Ltd*,[573] the plaintiff/respondent had commenced proceedings in the Zimbabwe High Court against a company for breach of a contract for the sale of vehicles. The plaintiff then commenced separate proceedings in the same court against the defendant/appellant on the same cause of action on the basis that he had acted in an individual capacity. The plaintiff had obtained judgment in default from the Zimbabwe High Court against the company and had then obtained judgment in default against the defendant. In the Transkei Appellate Division, Goldin JA, giving the judgment of the court, allowed the defendant's appeal and refused to enforce the judgment on the basis that 'it is clearly contrary to natural justice for a litigant who obtains judgment against one defendant, to seek judgment against another for the same sum and one [sic] the same grounds as happened here', without elaborating on why this means of proceeding engaged issues of natural justice in the first place

[570] 1973 (3) SA 885 (Rhodesia AD) (Macdonald ACJ, Lewis AJP and Goldin AJA).

[571] 1974 (4) SA 560 (N) (Fannin, Leon and Hoexter JJ).

[572] Ibid 565F–G.

[573] 1985 (2) SA 423 (TkA) (Goldin, James and Davies JJA).

or why the defendant ought not to have raised any such issues before the court in Zimbabwe.[574]

It is contrary to public policy to enforce at common law a foreign judgment that contains a multiple or punitive element. However, whether a foreign judgment contains a multiple or punitive element will depend on the facts of each case. In *Jones v Krok*,[575] Kirk-Cohen J held: (1) it is the policy of South African law and practice that for a breach of contract the injured party is entitled to no more than compensation for the damage actually suffered, irrespective of reprehensible behaviour on the part of the defendant or the flagrancy of the breach;[576] (2) the mere fact that awards are made by a foreign court on a basis not recognised in South Africa does not mean that they are necessarily contrary to public policy and whether a judgment or award is contrary to public policy depends largely on the facts of each case;[577] and (3) in principle it would be wrong to refuse to enforce a foreign judgment of punitive damages merely because it is unknown in South Africa and it cannot be said that this principle is necessarily unconscionable.[578]

In *Danielson v Human*, [579] the court enforced a judgment rendered by the US District Court for the Western District of North Carolina that contained a treble damages award. The expert evidence of US federal law (relating to the Racketeer Influenced and Corrupt Organisations Act, 'RICO') before the court was that the award of treble damages was designed to compensate the plaintiff in the US proceedings for unquantifiable losses and that the RICO legislation did not authorise the award of punitive damages.

Also under the rubric 'public policy' are such instances as the non-enforceability of a judgment based on a grossly usurious contract.[580]

(4) The judgment was not obtained by fraudulent means

Here the defendant must show that the foreign judgment was obtained by fraud that has not already been the subject of judicial determination in the foreign court or, if it has, that there is evidence which was not available at the time of that determination to show that the plaintiff obtained the judgment by fraud.[581]

---

[574] This is a decision criticised by Forsyth (*Private International Law* 5 ed (2012) 462–3).

[575] 1996 (1) SA 504 (T), the decision which followed on from the decision of the Appellate Division in *Jones v Krok* 1995 (1) SA 677 (A), referred to above.

[576] At 516G.

[577] At 515H.

[578] At 516E.

[579] 2017 (1) SA 141 (WCC) (Cloete J).

[580] *Taylor v Holland* (1886) 2 SAR 78.

[581] Forsyth refers to intrinsic and extrinsic fraud. It is the latter which may provide grounds for non-recognition and enforcement (*Private International Law* 5 ed (2012) 463). The formulation in the text is slightly different in intended meaning: the questions such as perjury or forgery or suppression of material documents which Forsyth allocates to extrinsic fraud are all matters which might be raised before the foreign court and

In *Goodman v Goodman*,[582] the plaintiff sought to enforce a judgment on three promissory notes against his brother. The defendant's evidence was that the promissory notes had been procured by him, the defendant, for the plaintiff to advance to a partnership in which the defendant was one of two partners so that the defendant's funding of the partnership could be concealed from his co-partner. The court declined to enforce the judgment at the provisional sentence stage and required the plaintiff to proceed to the principal case. The court found[583] that if the defendant's statements were true then it would be fraud on the part of the plaintiff to seek to enforce the foreign judgment against the person who was really entitled to the benefit of the judgment.

In *Joffe v Salmon*,[584] Innes CJ cited with approval a passage from the headnote to *The Bank of Australia v Nias*:[585]

> 'A foreign judgment is examinable, and is only prima facie evidence of debt here, so far as to show that the foreign court had not jurisdiction on the subject-matter of the suit, or that the defendant was never served with process, or that the judgment was fraudulently obtained; but is conclusive upon the defendant so far as to prevent him from alleging that the promises upon which it is founded were never made, or were obtained by fraud of the plaintiff. Any pleas which might have been pleaded to the original action cannot be pleaded to the action upon the judgment.'

(5) The judgment does not involve the enforcement of a penal or revenue law of the foreign state

Foreign penal and revenue laws cannot be enforced by way of a foreign judgment.

---

adjudicated upon. In such circumstances, it would be as unfair to the plaintiff to permit relitigation of such issues, as it is accepted it is unfair to permit relitigation of the issues, the subject of the judgment which it is sought to enforce. Clearly, if the defendant relies on evidence not reasonably available at the time the foreign court adjudicated on such issues, then the picture changes. But absent such evidence, a defendant ought not to be permitted to contest, for example, the truthfulness of evidence given abroad, any more than he is allowed to contest liability under a contract forming the subject-matter of the foreign judgment. This is, more or less, the position in Canada (*Union of India v Bumper Development Corp* [1995] 7 WWR 80); Australia (*Keele v Findley* (1991) 21 NSWLR 444 (NSWSC); and in English domestic law (where the discoverability with reasonable diligence principle applied: *Chodiev v Stein* [2015] EWHC 1428 (Comm), *per* Burton J para [14]). (The English conflict rules on this subject are, by general assent, less than satisfactory as, in contradistinction to English domestic law, foreign judgments are impeachable for fraud, even where the evidence of fraud is that which was relied on unsuccessfully in the foreign court: *Owens Bank Ltd v Bracco* [1992] 2 AC 443 (HL(E)). However, more recent authority suggests that relitigation of matters litigated abroad may be an abuse of the process of the English court, such that the claim of fraud may be liable to be struck out: *Owens Bank Ltd v Etoile Commerciale SA* [1995] 1 WLR 44 (PC) and *Altimo Holdings and Investment Ltd v Kyrgyz Mobil Tel Ltd* [2012] 1 WLR 1804 (PC).)

582 (1903) 20 SC 376 (De Villiers CJ, Kotzé J).

583 Ibid 377, *per* De Villiers CJ.

584 (1904) TS 317 (Innes CJ and Solomon J).

585 (1851) 20 LJQB 284 (judgment of Lord Campbell CJ) 284, col 2.

(6) Enforcement of the judgment is not precluded by the provisions of the Protection of Businesses Act 99 of 1978 as amended.

The 1978 Act prohibits the enforcement of a foreign judgment in two circumstances: first, where the foreign judgment provides for the payment of 'multiple or punitive damages';[586] and, second, where the foreign judgment relates to personal injury resulting from the consumption or use of or exposure to any natural resource of the Republic of South Africa, unless the same liability would have arisen under South African law.[587]

9.2.3.2 *Specific principles regarding judgments in respect of property*

In cases of judgments in respect of property, it is accepted that the *forum rei sitae* has international jurisdiction to render a judgment in relation to property.[588]

9.2.3.2.1 Immovable property

It appears that the *forum rei sitae* has exclusive international jurisdiction to render a judgment in relation to immovable property.[589] Further, Pistorius states that if the foreign judgment relates to immovable property situated outside the Republic of South Africa, no South African court could enforce that judgment because South African courts have no jurisdiction to entertain actions relating to immovable property outside the jurisdiction.[590]

---

586 Section 1A. It is not clear whether non-multiple or non-punitive parts of such a judgment award would be unenforceable or whether the compensatory constituent of a multiple or punitive award would nonetheless be enforceable. On similarly worded legislation in England, recent authority is to the effect that where the foreign judgment is given in respect of a number of causes of action and the multiplication of damages has been applied in respect of some but not others of them, the inoffensive part of the judgment is severable and enforceable: *Lewis v Eliades* [2004] 1 WLR 692 (CA) (where separate damages awards were made for breach of fiduciary duty, fraud and violation of RICO). The Court of Appeal in *Lewis v Eliades* left open the question whether the compensatory constituent of a multiple damages award would be recoverable. However, at first instance Nelson J had held that the basic compensatory award for violation of RICO was enforceable before the option to multiply had been exercised by the claimant. As a condition of enforcing this part of the judgment, Nelson J required undertakings from the claimant not to enforce against the defendants any claim for multiple damages (see generally, Kellman 'Enforcement of judgments and blocking statutes: *Lewis v Eliades*' (2004) 53 *ICLQ* 1025). For the position at common law in South Africa, see *Danielson v Human* 2017 (1) SA 141 (WCC), above.

587 Section 1D.

588 Forsyth *Private International Law* 5 ed (2012) 455.

589 Ibid 456.

590 *Pollak on Jurisdiction* 2 ed (1993) 169; a South African court would, however, recognise such a judgment if its effects required recognition; *Rosa's Heirs v Inhambane Estates* 1905 TH 11; *Rood's Trustees v Scott and De Villiers* 1910 TS 47.

However, a judgment in respect of a claim sounding in money arising out of rescission of a contract of sale of immovable property (damages or the return of the purchase price) will be capable of being enforced in South Africa.[591]

9.2.3.2.2 Movable property

Pistorius states that for the purposes of the recognition of a foreign judgment relating to movables, the *forum rei sitae* at the time of the commencement of the action has exclusive international jurisdiction to pronounce a judgment relating to that property.[592]

A judgment of the *forum rei sitae* relating to movable property will be enforced in the Republic of South Africa if the property subject of the judgment is brought into South Africa.

If the foreign judgment is for delivery of property with an alternative of damages, then enforcement of the latter will be treated as an action sounding in money and it will be necessary for the purposes of enforcement to establish the presence of one of the grounds of jurisdiction in actions in which a judgment sounding in money is claimed.[593]

9.2.4 Enforcement pursuant to statute

9.2.4.1 *The regime for enforcement pursuant to statute*

The Enforcement of Foreign Civil Judgments Act 1988 provides for a means of enforcement by the registration of a foreign judgment from the courts of a designated country.[594]

9.2.4.2 *Procedure for registration*

Registration is undertaken by the clerk of the magistrate's court of the district where the judgment debtor resides, carries on business or is employed or owns any movable or immovable property or, in the case of a legal person, where it has its registered office or principal place of business or, in the case of a partnership, where it has its business premises or any member of it resides.[595] Upon registration, the clerk of the court must issue a notice to the judgment debtor informing him of the registration of the judgment.[596]

---

[591] Pistorius *Pollak on Jurisdiction* 2 ed (1993) 169; *Estate Cassim v Cassim* 1915 NPD 14; *Eloff v Grobler's Executor* 1934 CPD 10 at 24.

[592] *Pollak on Jurisdiction* 2 ed (1993) 169–70.

[593] Ibid 170.

[594] Section 3; to date only Namibia has been thus designated.

[595] Section 1. The jurisdiction limit of the magistrate's court of R100,000.

[596] Section 3(2).

Execution of a registered judgment is delayed for a period of 21 days after service of such a notice on the judgment debtor.[597]

Pursuant to section 5, the registration shall be set aside if the court is satisfied of any of the matters set out therein. These grounds for setting aside broadly correspond to the common-law grounds for resisting enforcement, but include a provision for setting aside if the judgment has become the subject of a period of prescription pursuant to the laws of the Republic of South Africa or the country from which the judgment originated.[598]

Various presumptions are contained in section 7, including presumptions that the foreign court is deemed to have international jurisdiction where the defendant was, for example, resident within the jurisdiction of that court at the time of the commencement of proceedings[599] or submitted to the jurisdiction by agreement or by voluntarily appearing.[600] The section also contains presumptions that the foreign court does not have jurisdiction where the proceedings concerned immovable property outside the country in question.[601]

9.2.4.3 *Setting aside registration*

Section 5 of the Enforcement of Foreign Civil Judgments Act sets out a series of circumstances in which a court shall set aside the registration of a judgment which has taken place pursuant to section 3. Accordingly, section 5 provides that, on the application of a judgment debtor,[602] the registration of the judgment shall be set aside if the court at which the judgment is registered is satisfied:

'*(a)* that the judgment was registered in contravention of any provision of this Act;

(b) that the court of the designated country concerned had no jurisdiction in the circumstances of the case;

(c) that the judgment debtor did not receive notice of the proceedings in which the judgment was given, as prescribed by the law of the designated country, or, if no such notice is so prescribed, that he did not receive reasonable notice of the said proceedings to enable him to defend the proceedings, and did not appear;

(d) that the judgment was obtained by fraud;[603]

(e) that the enforcement of the judgment would be contrary to public policy in the Republic;

---

[597] Section 4(2).

[598] Section 5(1)(i).

[599] Section 7(4)(a)(iii).

[600] Section 7(4)(a)(i) and (ii).

[601] Section 7(5)(a).

[602] Section 5(2) provides that the application shall be brought within 21 days after service of the notice referred to in s 3(2). The court hearing the application may at any time postpone the hearing of the application to such date as it may determine: s 5(3).

[603] See *supra* fn 582 and the text associated therewith.

(*f*) that the certified copy of the judgment lodged in terms of section 3 was so lodged at the request of a person other than the judgment creditor;

(*g*) that the matter in dispute in the proceedings had, prior to the date of the judgment, been the subject of a final judgment in civil proceedings by a court of competent jurisdiction;

(*h*) that the judgment has been set aside by a court of competent jurisdiction;

(*i*) that the judgment has become prescribed under either the laws of the Republic or the designated country concerned;

(*j*) that the judgment has been wholly satisfied;

(*k*) that the judgment has been partly satisfied, to the extent in which it has been so satisfied;

(*l*) that the judgment is a judgment or order which in terms of any law may not be recognized or enforced in the Republic.'

9.3 Interim Remedies

9.3.1 Jurisdiction to grant interim remedies

Section 173 of the Constitution of the Republic of South Africa, 1996 provides that the Constitutional Court, the Supreme Court of Appeal and the High Court 'each has the inherent power to protect and regulate their own process, and to develop the common law, taking into account the interests of justice'.

The power of the superior courts of South Africa to grant interdictal relief is not statute based but is derived from the court's inherent jurisdiction:[604]

> 'A superior court, differing in this respect from an inferior court, has inherent jurisdiction to make orders, unlimited as to amount, in respect of matters which come before them, and such inherent jurisdiction is limited only to that extent that restraints are imposed upon it, sometimes by the common law but more often by statute.'

As long ago as 1962, De Vos Hugo J observed in *Mtshali v Mtambo*:[605] 'There is a singular dearth of authority in the form of decided cases dealing with jurisdiction in the interdict procedure. None in point has been cited to me and my own researches have failed to reveal any such case.'[606]

In particular, it seems still to be an open question whether and to what extent the jurisdictional requirements for a court to entertain an action sounding in money or one concerning movables are imported into this area of law, thereby

---

[604] Prest *The Law and Practice of Interdicts* (1996) 266.

[605] 1962 (3) SA 469 (GW) 473C-D.

[606] A state of affairs still being lamented in 2011 (see *Zokufa v Compuscan (Credit Bureau)* 2011 (1) SA 272 (ECM) (*per* Alkema J at 276D para [21]).

requiring a plaintiff to establish jurisdiction over the substantive cause of action, as well as satisfying the requirements for the grant of an interim interdict.[607]

The principles applicable to the grant of an interim interdict vary depending on whether the relief sought is mandatory (requiring an act to be done) or prohibitory (restraining an act from being done) and whether the parties to the application are *incolae* or *peregrini* or a mix of both. A feature of this area of law is that considerations of effectiveness loom large.

The principles may be stated as follows:[608]

(1) The defendant is an *incola* and the act to be performed or restrained will occur within the area of jurisdiction of the court to which the application is made

The court will have jurisdiction because the defendant is an *incola* of the court and because the act that is the subject of the application is to occur within the jurisdiction. Thus, on general principles the court will have jurisdiction over the

---

[607] For example, in England the position was that a court had no jurisdiction to grant interim relief unless the court had jurisdiction over the substantive cause of action in respect of which such relief was sought: *Siskina (owners of cargo lately on board) v Distos Compania Naviera SA (The Siskina)* [1979] AC 210. This position was as a result of the jurisdiction of the courts to grant injunctive relief being statutory and the courts considering that an extension of that jurisdiction to embrace injunctive relief where the court did not have jurisdiction over the substantive claim was a matter for the legislature and not the courts (*per* Bridge LJ, giving a dissenting judgment in the Court of Appeal at 243, 'We are neither midwives nor rainmakers'; for any reader interested in the art of elevating the recitation of mundane facts into high prose, the judgment of Lord Denning MR in *The Siskina* (at 225) is essential reading). The position in England was remedied by the legislature by way of s 25 of the Civil Jurisdiction and Judgments Act 1982.

An area of debate in this field is whether the application for an interim interdict itself gives the court jurisdiction to consider the application (by analogy with an application for an attachment to found or confirm the jurisdiction, the court will have jurisdiction to hear and determine the application) or whether something more is required and, if so, what. The preponderance of authority is in favour of the latter view that the application for an interdict per se does not give the court jurisdiction to hear and determine the application, but that the court must consider various other factors to determine the question of jurisdiction. In favour of the former view is the judgment of De Vos Hugo J in *Mtshali v Mtambo* 1962 (3) SA 469 (GW) 473H: 'There is obviously ample justification for the rule that an interdict founds jurisdiction and that no exception to the Court's jurisdiction can be taken in such proceedings. The interdict procedure is an extraordinary remedy devised for matters which do not admit of delay – *periculum in mora* – and in which the power of the Court should be summarily interposed to prevent and, if necessary, to discontinue, the perpetration of unlawful acts forthwith and for good pending action. The administration of justice would be seriously hampered, if not frustrated, if a Court does not have such power within its own area of jurisdiction.' (A correction to the official report of this decision needs to be made at 473H where the passage reading, 'The administration of justice would be seriously hampered, if not frustrated, if a Court does have such power within its own area of jurisdiction', should read, 'The administration of justice would be seriously hampered, if not frustrated, if a Court does *not* have such power within its own area of jurisdiction' (corrected in the passage quoted by Prest at 266–7).

[608] Following, with modifications, the categorisation, though not necessarily the content, of Pistorius in *Pollak on Jurisdiction* 2 ed (1993) 117–20. Throughout, plaintiff and defendant are used to denote applicant and respondent, respectively.

defendant (*actor sequitur forum rei*) and will be in a position to give an effective judgment because the location of the act and the residence of the defendant coincide, rendering enforcement easier.

(2) The defendant is an *incola* and the act to be performed or restrained will not occur within the area of jurisdiction of the court to which the application is made but will occur in the Republic of South Africa

The court will have jurisdiction if the defendant is an *incola* and the act to be performed or restrained will occur within the Republic of South Africa, rather than the area of jurisdiction of the court to which the application is made. On general principles, the court will have jurisdiction over the defendant (*actor sequitur forum rei*) and will be in a position to give an effective judgment because effect can be given to its judgment pursuant to section 42 of the Superior Courts Act 2013.[609]

(3) The defendant is an *incola* and the act to be performed will not occur within the Republic of South Africa

Where the defendant is an *incola* and the application brought is to compel the doing of an act outside the Republic of South Africa, it was previously thought that the court did not have jurisdiction to make the order sought.[610]

---

[609] Sub-section (2) provides: 'The civil process of a Division runs throughout the Republic and may be served or executed within the jurisdiction of any Division' (following the wording of s 26 of the Supreme Court Act 1959).

[610] Pistorius *Pollak on Jurisdiction* 2 ed (1993) 118. In *Lenders & Co Ltd v Lourenco Marques Wharf Co Ltd* 1904 TH 176, Smith J refused an application by a foreign *peregrinus* (an English company) to require an *incola* defendant to deliver to the plaintiff or allow the plaintiff to take certain timber belonging to the plaintiff and in the possession of the defendant at Delagoa Bay in Mozambique. The defendant asserted a lien over the timber for unpaid charges. The judge held (at 178) that it was 'clear that this Court has not, and cannot have, any direct jurisdiction over property situated' outside the Republic of South Africa because a judgment requiring delivery of the timber to the plaintiff could not be enforced by the officers of the South African court at Delagoa Bay. The plaintiff was left to pursue its remedies in Mozambique.

In *Minister of Agriculture v Grobler* 1918 TPD 483, the defendant had seized cattle belonging to the plaintiff which he had brought across the border into the Republic of South Africa from Botswana unlawfully. The defendant then removed the cattle from South Africa and offered them for sale in Botswana. The plaintiff sought an order restraining the government from selling the cattle and requiring the government to deliver the cattle to him. At first instance, the judge made an order restraining the government from selling the cattle, but refused to make an order requiring the government to deliver the cattle to the plaintiff. On the cross-appeal by the plaintiff (the government's appeal was dismissed) Wessels J held (at 488) that although it was clear that the plaintiff was entitled to possession of the cattle, 'I am not prepared, however, to give an order on the Government to hand over the cattle in Bechuanaland. It is a very thorny question whether this Court has jurisdiction to give such an order.' Mason J was more equivocal (at 489): 'I am not prepared to express a definite opinion one way or the other as to whether this Court has jurisdiction to make a specific mandatory order with reference to property in another country. There is considerable authority, to my mind, in favour of such a proposition. On the other hand, there is the definite decision of Sir William Smith to the contrary.' Bristowe J concurred in both judgments.

It is now clear that where the defendant is an *incola*, a court has jurisdiction to make such an order to compel the doing of an act outside the Republic of South Africa or in respect of movable property situated outside South Africa.

In *Melamed NO v Munnikhuis*,[611] the court ordered the defendant to perform outside the jurisdiction a contractual undertaking she had given in the Republic of South Africa. The case concerned a Jersey-registered trust subject to Jersey law having a Panamanian corporate trustee. An undertaking had been given by the defendant to procure the resignation of the corporate trustee, but had not been performed. In proceedings for the enforcement of the undertaking, the court found[612] that the undertaking had been given as part of a contract concluded in the Republic of South Africa between the parties who were subject to the jurisdiction of the court and held[613] that it had jurisdiction to make the order sought:

> 'While the effect of the order sought will undoubtedly impact upon the rights of a party to the trust deed this Court cannot, it seems to me, deny the remedy sought on that ground alone. Where, for instance, it is clear that a party has undertaken to fulfil a specific obligation in circumstances where performance is required in a foreign jurisdiction and there is no dispute that the obligation is capable of fulfilment, the only question, it seems to me, is whether this Court has original jurisdiction in respect of the obligation contracted for. If it does, then the order which it makes is one for the fulfilment of the obligation.'

The judge also approached the question from the point of view of effectiveness:[614]

> 'The same conclusion may be derived in a different way. The doctrine of effectiveness ... If the facts before the Court demonstrate that the order which it proposes to make will be effective notwithstanding that the order is to be performed beyond its jurisdiction, then there is no reason why the Court should not make the order if it is based upon a contract upon which the Court manifestly does have jurisdiction.'

In *Metlika Trading Ltd v Commissioner, South African Revenue Service*,[615] the Supreme Court of Appeal considered the jurisdiction of the High Court to grant an interdict against an *incola* defendant where the act in question related to a movable and was to be performed outside the jurisdiction. The Transvaal Provincial Division had ordered the third appellant to take all necessary steps to procure the return of an aircraft registered to it to the Republic of South Africa. Streicher JA, giving the judgment of the court, stated:[616] 'If the court *a quo* was not able to enforce

---

[611] 1996 (4) SA 126 (W), *per* Van Schalkwyk J.

[612] Ibid 131B–E.

[613] Ibid 131E–F.

[614] Ibid 131G–I.

[615] 2005 (3) SA 1 (SCA) (Streicher, Cameron and Conradie JJA and Patel and Ponnan AJJA).

[616] Ibid para [36], in which, at line 5, the terms 'respondents' and 'appellants' appear to have been transposed: the passage should refer to the appellants' submission that the court *a quo* could not give effect to its order and therefore lacked jurisdiction to make it (see para [35]).

compliance with the order which it granted it had no jurisdiction to grant it.' Streicher JA concluded:[617]

> 'In the light of the aforegoing I agree with Forsyth's view that if the defendant is an *incola*, the court may assume jurisdiction to grant an interdict (whether mandatory or prohibitory) *in personam* no matter if the act in question is to be performed or restrained outside the court's area of jurisdiction. The authority to the contrary is not persuasive and should, to the extent not consistent with this judgment, be considered to have been overruled.'

Although the *Metlika Trading* case concerned an aircraft and not immovable property, it is likely that the South African court has jurisdiction to make a mandatory order in respect of immovable property where the defendant is an *incola*. There are two reasons for this: (1) the passage from Forsyth,[618] which was approved by the court in *Metlika* was, and is,[619] not confined to movable property and the court itself did not so confine its finding; and (2) in *Hugo v Wessels*,[620] the Appellate Division held that exclusive jurisdiction does not necessarily vest in the *forum sitae* in the case of transfers of immovable property: the fact that the divorce settlement was concluded in the Orange Free State and incorporated into an order of the OFS was sufficient to vest that court with jurisdiction.

(4) The defendant is an *incola* and the act to be restrained will not occur within the Republic of South Africa

Where the defendant is an *incola* and the application brought is to restrain the doing of an act or in relation to movable or immovable property outside the Republic of South Africa, the court will have jurisdiction to make the order sought. This had been authoritatively determined even prior to the decision of the Supreme Court of Appeal in the *Metlika Trading* case by Neser J in *CM Asbestos Co v King Chrysotyle Asbestos Mines*.[621]

---

617 2005 (3) SA 1 (SCA) para [49], having referred to Forsyth *Private International Law* 4 ed (2003) 233 and recent decisions of the English court.

618 *Private International Law* 4 ed (2003) 233.

619 *Private International Law* 5 ed (2012) 249.

620 1987 3 SA 837 (A).

621 1953 (3) SA 431 (W) 435B–H. An action involving the transfer of certain base metal claims located in the Transvaal where the parties were all *incolae* of the Witwatersrand Local Division. It was accepted by the parties that the claim concerned immovable property: see 434D–G and 432H.

(5) The defendant is a local or foreign *peregrinus* and the act to be performed or restrained will occur within the area of jurisdiction of the court to which the application is made

Here, the court has jurisdiction to make an order requiring or restraining an act to be performed because the act that is the subject of the application is to occur within the jurisdiction. Thus, the principle of effectiveness is satisfied because the court will be in a position to control the acts within its jurisdiction.[622]

In *Leyland v Chetwynd*,[623] the plaintiff and defendant were both *peregrini* and the court assumed jurisdiction over the matter on the basis that the subject of the mandatory interdict, the defendant's children, were within the jurisdiction of the court (the court enforced an English custody order transferring custody from the defendant to the plaintiff).

In *Ex parte Schoeman*,[624] the plaintiff and defendant were both *peregrini*; the plaintiff had a foreign judgment against the defendant and sought an interim interdict in the Cape (pending commencement of proceedings in either the Transvaal or the Cape), restraining the defendant from dissipating an inheritance due in favour of his wife (with whom he was in community of property) and the executors of the estate from paying out the inheritance. The court made the order sought apparently on the basis that the estate from which the payment was to be made was administered in the Cape Province.

In *Brown v McDonald*,[625] the plaintiff and defendants were local *peregrini* (resident in Natal). The defendant owed the plaintiff certain sums on a notarial bond registered in Natal which pledged to him a racing stallion called 'Elope'. The horse had been removed by the defendant to a farm owned by a third party within the jurisdiction of the court. The court granted a rule *nisi*, calling upon the third party and a named auctioneer to show cause why they should not be restrained from parting with Elope or alienating him in any way, pending an action to be brought in a competent court by the plaintiff against the defendant. The rule was to operate as an interim interdict.

In *Ex parte Kirsten*,[626] both plaintiff and defendant were *peregrini* of the court, being resident in the SW Africa Protectorate and engaged in proceedings there concerning a contract concluded in the Protectorate in relation to immovable property situated there. The court granted an order restraining a bank in the Cape from parting with funds belonging to a party to those proceedings (here the order was made against the bank).

---

622 Pistorius *Pollak on Jurisdiction* 2 ed (1993) 118–19; Forsyth *Private International Law* 5 ed (2012) 249.
623 (1901) 18 SC 239 (Buchanan ACJ and Jones and Maasdorp JJ).
624 1918 CPD 122 (Gardiner J).
625 1911 EDL 423 (Kotze JP, Graham J and Sampson AJ).
626 1921 CPD 608 (Gardiner J).

In *Kibe v Mphoko*,[627] where both the plaintiff and the defendant were *peregrini* resident in Basutoland (Lesotho) and engaged in litigation there, the court made an order restraining the *peregrinus* defendant from operating and drawing from a bank account within the jurisdiction of the court. The judge stated:[628]

> 'Our Courts have held that, where the defendant is a *peregrinus*, the Court has jurisdiction if, in the case of a mandatory interdict, the act is to be carried out within such area, or in the case of a prohibitory interdict, of the act against which an interdict is claimed is about to be done in such area ... Where the defendant is a *peregrinus* it is however clear that in the absence of any attachment of the respondent's ... property, no order for the payment of costs should be made against him. (See *Wells v. Dean-Willcocks* 1924 CPD 89).'[629]

(6) The defendant is a local *peregrinus* and the act to be performed or restrained will occur in the Republic of South Africa, but will not occur within the area of jurisdiction of the court to which the application is made

Where the defendant is a local *peregrinus* and the application is for an order requiring or restraining an act to be performed outside its area of jurisdiction, but within the Republic of South Africa, there appear to be two views of what the position is in law.

The first view is that the court has jurisdiction to grant an order in these circumstances. Forsyth[630] states:

> 'Because judgments of the local courts can be carried out anywhere in the country, it should make no difference whether the act in question is to be performed or restrained outside the court's area but within South Africa, or that the defendant is [a] local peregrine of the division concerned.'

In support of this, Forsyth cites *Pollak on Jurisdiction*,[631] and the decision of Alkema J in *Zokufa v Compuscan (Credit Bureau)*.[632] In *Zokufa* the plaintiff applied to the Eastern Cape High Court at Mthatha for a final interdict that the defendant, a credit provider based in Stellenbosch, comply with its obligations under the National Credit Act 2005[633] to make available to the plaintiff the credit record

---

[627] 1958 (1) SA 364 (O) (De Wet AJ).

[628] Ibid 367A–C.

[629] See also *Kramarski v Kramarski* 1906 TS 937; *Brown v McDonald* 1911 EDL 423; *Ex parte Winter* 1948 (3) SA 377 (W). But see *Zokufa v Compuscan (Credit Bureau)* 2011 (1) SA 272 (ECM), where Alkem J declined to follow this approach (paras [39]–[42] and [53]–[62]).

[630] *Private International Law* 5 ed (2012) 249.

[631] Pollak 1 ed (1937) 130. The most relevant passage on this page of Pollak is as follows: 'A South African court therefore has no jurisdiction to grant a mandatory interdict which is to be carried out outside the Union. But what is the position if the act, though it is to be done in the Union, is to be done outside the area to which the court belongs? In such a case it is possible that the court has jurisdiction to grant the mandatory interdict, provided that the defendant or respondent is an *incola* of the area to which the court belongs.' This passage does not seem to lend support to the proposition advanced by Forsyth. This passage from Pollak supports the position as stated at *(c)* above.

[632] 2011 (1) SA 272 (ECM).

[633] Act 34 of 2005.

and other related information in the possession of the defendant. The plaintiff was an *incola* of the court and the defendant was a local *peregrinus*. The judge held that the defendant was in breach of its statutory obligation to issue the plaintiff with a report and that the location of the defendant's obligation to do so was Stellenbosch and that the defendant was obliged to comply with the relevant provisions of the Act at its place of business in Stellenbosch.[634] The court also found that the order sought by the plaintiff did not require the defendant to do anything outside of its domicile or place of business and that the steps it was required to take were to be taken in Stellenbosch.[635] The court made the order sought by the plaintiff.[636]

The second view is that which Pistorius[637] puts forward:

> 'Thus even where the defendant is a peregrine of the area over which the court exercises jurisdiction but an *incola* of the Republic as a whole, and the unlawful act is not required to be performed or prohibited within that area, the court has no jurisdiction to grant an interdict.'

In support of this proposition, Pistorius cites *Ex parte Goldstein*[638] in which the defendant was a local *peregrinus* domiciled in Johannesburg and the plaintiff applied to the Cape court for an order restraining the defendant from parting with certain cash and promissory notes situated in Johannesburg. Gardiner J refused the application on the basis that the court had no jurisdiction in a case where the defendant and the property concerned were outside the area of jurisdiction of the court. Pistorius also refers to *Towers v Paisley*,[639] where both plaintiff and defendant were local *peregrini*. The plaintiff sought an order from the circuit court for the district of Port Elizabeth restraining the defendant from breaching a restraint of trade clause in a contract. The contract had been concluded and the breach of the restraint of trade clause was occurring outside the jurisdiction of the court. The defendant had, however, submitted to the jurisdiction of the

634 2011 (1) SA 272 (ECM) 286I para [85] and 286A para [87].

635 Ibid 291G–I.

636 As appears below, the court held that it had jurisdiction to make the order sought because the requirements for the granting of a final interdict were satisfied by facts occurring within the jurisdiction.

637 *Pollak on Jurisdiction* 2 ed (1993) 119.

638 1916 CPD 483. It was argued in *Ex parte Goldstein* that an interdict granted by the court in the Cape would satisfy the principle of effectiveness because s 6 of the Administration of Justice Act 1912 made provision for the execution of an order for a writ of arrest where the person was within the Republic of South Africa, but outside the jurisdiction of the court making the order and thus (so the argument ran) the court could make an effective order because it could enforce it through an order for arrest of the defendant for contempt which would be enforceable in Johannesburg. The court rejected this argument on the basis that s 6 had not enlarged the jurisdiction of the courts but had been intended simply to facilitate the enforcement throughout the Republic of South Africa of the orders of municipal courts otherwise properly seised of a matter. The Appellate Division in *Ewing McDonald & Co Ltd v M & M Products Co* 1991 (1) SA 252 (A) reached the same conclusion (at 259D–264D), citing *Ex parte Goldstein* with approval.

639 1963 (1) SA 92 (E).

court. The court held that it did not have jurisdiction over the matter in the absence of a *ratione jurisdictionis* (such as *ratione rei sitae, rei gestae* or *contractus*). Neither *Ex parte Goldstein* nor *Towers v Paisley* appear to have been cited to the court in *Zokufa*.

It may be that these two positions can be reconciled by modifying the proposition stated by Pistorius to accommodate cases where the underlying cause of action on the basis of which the interdict is sought is relevantly connected to the area of jurisdiction of the court from which the interdict is sought.[640] This was the case in *Zokufa* (where the judge found[641] that the facts satisfying the test for the grant of a final interdict were within the jurisdiction of the court) and was not the case in either *Ex parte Goldstein* or *Towers v Paisley*.

A court may, therefore, grant an interdict against a local *peregrinus* where the application is for an order requiring or restraining an act to be performed outside its area of jurisdiction but within South Africa and the basis on which the interdict is sought is relevantly connected to the area of jurisdiction of the court from which the interdict is sought.

(7) The defendant is a local *peregrinus* and the act to be performed or restrained will not occur in South Africa

The question then arises whether the court has jurisdiction to grant an interdict against a local *peregrinus* where the application is for an order requiring or restraining an act to be performed outside its area of jurisdiction and outside South Africa.

There appears to be no judicial authority directly on this point. However, for the following reasons, it is submitted that the court does have jurisdiction to make an order against a local *peregrinus* concerning acts to be performed or restrained outside the jurisdiction in circumstances where the basis on which the interdict is sought is relevantly connected to the area of jurisdiction of the court from which the interdict is sought.

First, the court has jurisdiction to make such an order in respect of a partnership where the sole partners are an *incola* and a foreign *peregrinus* and the interdict is addressed not only to the *incola* but also to the foreign *peregrinus*.[642] It must follow

---

[640] Indeed, Pistorius hints at such a position in *Pollak on Jurisdiction* 2 ed (1993) 119 fn 35 where he states in his commentary on *Towers v Paisley*: 'It is suggested that the submission [of the defendant] could have been considered a sufficient connecting factor but it does, nevertheless, seem that the position may be different if the interdict flows from a contract which was concluded within the area of jurisdiction of the court or from a cause of action which arises in that area.'

[641] 2011 (1) SA 272 (ECM) para [110].

[642] The *Metlika Trading* case (2005 (3) SA 1 (SCA)), where the partners in the enjoined partnership were HAS and Carmel (an *incola* and a foreign *peregrinus* respectively). The order made at first instance by Hartzenberg J expressly enjoined not only HAS but also Carmel from committing certain acts and also

that there is nothing in theory to prevent a court making such an order against a local *peregrinus* where precedent exists for such an order having been made against a foreign *peregrinus*.

Second, an order requiring a party to undertake an act outside the Republic of South Africa does not interfere with the sovereignty of a foreign court because it is an order *in personam* against persons subject to the court's jurisdiction and is lawful.[643]

Third, such an order will be effective against a local *peregrinus* by reason of the scope and execution of process provisions of section 42 of the Superior Courts Act 2013.[644]

Fourth, as in the *Zokufa* case,[645] if there are sufficient relevant connecting facts between the dispute and the area of jurisdiction of the local court, this should serve to assuage concerns regarding any extension of the jurisdiction of a local court beyond its territory.

Fifth, as was stated by the Supreme Court of Appeal in the *Metlika Trading* case,[646] there is a public interest in ensuring that wrongdoers are not able to take advantage of their wrongs by reason of placing their assets outside the jurisdiction. The court there cited a number of English authorities concerning *Mareva* injunctions to the effect that as a matter of principle in order to safeguard the enforceability of its own judgment, the court had power to order a defendant to bring within the jurisdiction assets located abroad in a jurisdiction where the English court's judgment would not be enforceable.[647]

(8) The defendant is a foreign *peregrinus* and the act to be performed or restrained will not occur within the area of jurisdiction of the court to which the application is made

Pistorius states[648] that where the defendant is a foreign *peregrinus*, and the application is for an order requiring or restraining an act to be performed outside its area of jurisdiction, the court has no jurisdiction to make the order.[649]

---

ordered HAS and Carmel to perform certain acts outside the jurisdiction (see the terms of the order at 9I–10B (paras 1.1 and 1.3 of the order) and 11A–B (para 2.4 of the order)). The order made was worded as being against 'the partnership', but that entity comprised solely HAS and Carmel and the order must be taken as directed at them jointly and severally, as the only partners (at 9A-C, para [15]; this must be case regardless of the provisions of r 14 of the High Court Rules enabling a partnership to be sued in its own name because, ultimately, the partnership can only act through its member partners).

643 The *Metlika Trading* case, *per* Streicher JA at 20A para [52].

644 The position in the *Zokufa* case where the enjoined party was a local *peregrinus*.

645 2011 (1) SA 272 (ECM).

646 2005 (3) SA 1 (SCA).

647 Ibid 17E–18H paras [44]–[46].

648 *Pollak on Jurisdiction* 2 ed (1993) 119–20.

649 In support of his contention, Pistorius cites, at 120 fn 36, the decision in *Trustees Assigned Estate of Epstein v Manchester Assurance Co* (1903) 24 NLR 41 (Bale CJ, Finnemore and Beaumont JJ). In this case, the

However, this view may need to be qualified in view of the decision in the *Metlika Trading* case where, as noted above, an interdict was ordered, inter alios, against a foreign *peregrinus* to do acts abroad (procure the return of the Falcon aircraft).[650]

(9) Is an attachment necessary?

In cases involving foreign *peregrini* defendants the question arises whether an attachment is necessary to found/confirm the jurisdiction of the court.

In *Mali v Mali*,[651] Smalberger J referred to the obiter statement of De Wet AJ in *Kibe v Mphoko* to the effect that, in the absence of an attachment of the defendant's property, no order for costs should be made against her and, dismissing the plaintiff's application for costs, stated:[652]

> 'Reliance for the latter proposition was placed on the decision in *Wells v. Dean-Wilcocks* 1924 CPD 89 where Gardiner J held at 93 that:
>
> > "In the absence, however, of any attachment of the respondent's person or property, I am not satisfied that I have jurisdiction to make an order for costs against him."

---

plaintiff applied to the Natal court for an order requiring the defendant to comply with certain arbitration provisions in an insurance policy, the court refused to make the order on the basis that the policy had been entered into in the Cape in respect of goods situated in a warehouse there, the defendant was a *peregrinus* of South Africa and no property had been attached in Natal – save for the presence of the plaintiff, the case was entirely unconnected with Natal; *South Atlantic Islands Development Corp v Buchan* 1971 (1) SA 234 (C) (Van Zijl and Diemont JJ and Tebbutt AJ), the *incola* plaintiff applied for an order that the court restrain the *peregrini* owner and master of a fishing vessel then docked at Cape Town from sailing within the territorial waters of Tristan da Cunha in breach of the plaintiff's fishing rights within those territorial waters. Diemont J, giving the judgment of the court stated (at 239H–240A): 'The crisp question which must be asked is whether the Cape Provincial Division of the Supreme Court of South Africa has the power to stop a fisherman from fishing in the Atlantic Ocean in the waters of a remote British Colony situated half way between South Africa and South America. Prima facie it would seem most unlikely that this Court has such power.' Basing the decision on the principle of effectiveness the court held (at 340D–F) that 'the Court is concerned with the effectiveness or otherwise of its judgment. Where the relief asked for is such that it will not be enforceable, the judgment becomes illusory and the Court should not undermine its authority by giving such a judgment. This no doubt is why it has been repeatedly stated that the principle of effectiveness is the basis of jurisdiction' and 'The principle has been stated in many ways. Dicey, for example, in *The Conflict of Laws* at p. 20 says: "The Courts of any country have jurisdiction over (i.e., have a right to adjudicate upon) any matter with regard to which they can give an effective judgment, and have no jurisdiction over (i.e., have no right to adjudicate upon) any matter with regard to which they cannot give an effective judgment." The merit of this statement is that Dicey stresses the point that it is power to give an effective judgment and not merely power over the defendant which is the test of jurisdiction. In other words the fact that the respondent in this case may be temporarily resident within the jurisdiction of this Court is of no consequence - the question is whether this Court can enforce an order against him if and when he starts fishing in the waters of Tristan da Cunha. Seen in that light it seems to me that there can be little doubt that this Court will be powerless to enforce its judgment if Buchan chooses to ignore the interdict. It would be idle for the Court to make the rule final.'

[650] See also, *Holloway v PADI EMEA Ltd* 2020 (5) SA 172 (GJ), where an English company was ordered to produce the full record, documents and evidence of an inquiry it had undertaken in England into the applicants' conduct in South Africa.

[651] 1982 (4) SA 569 (SE).

[652] Ibid 570C–H.

> No reasons were given by Gardiner J for his expressed lack of satisfaction on the point in issue. See also Pollak *The South African Law of Jurisdiction* at 132.
>
> In *Kibe's* case no order for costs was asked for. To this extent, therefore, the remarks concerning costs were *obiter*. While the plaintiff in *Kibe's* case was a *peregrinus*, the position in principle would be no different in the case of an *incola*.
>
> Counsel for the plaintiff was not able to refer me to any other cases in point. Nor have I been able to find any.
>
> To the best of my knowledge the correctness of the decision in *Kibe's* case has not been called into question. It is in keeping with the common law principle that jurisdiction depends upon the power of the Court to give an effective judgment (*Steytler NO v Fitzgerald* 1911 AD 295 at 346; *Thermo Radiant Oven Sales (Pty) Ltd v Nelspruit Bakeries (Pty) Ltd* 1969 (2) SA 295 (AD)). This principle is the basis of the rule that the Court will not entertain an action against a *peregrinus* unless either his person or property has been attached (Herbstein and Van Winsen *The Civil Practice of the Superior Court in South Africa* 3rd ed at 29 and authorities there quoted). There appears to be no logical reason why this principle should not also extend to apply to an order for costs. No order for costs against a peregrine defendant can be effective without prior attachment of his person or property, and where there has been no such attachment no order for costs would be appropriate.'

Thus, if an order for costs is sought against a *peregrinus* defendant in interim interdict proceedings (an application which will itself be rare), an attachment of the defendant's property will be necessary for the court to have jurisdiction to entertain that part of the application.

Is an attachment of property necessary when the plaintiff applies for an interdict itself however? Forsyth[653] submits that 'provided the other necessary requirements are fulfilled, attachment would be required for the court to assume jurisdiction over a *peregrinus*'. Pistorius states:[654]

> 'In none of the decisions which have been given since [the 1st edition, 1937], has the need for attachment, either *ad confirmandam* or *ad fundandam jurisdictionem* been considered ... it is suggested that, on common law principles, attachment might be required when the defendant is a *peregrinus* of South Africa.'

As things stand, however, there is a body of authority in which interdicts have been granted against *peregrini* defendants without the court expressing a need for an attachment of the defendant's property to found or confirm jurisdiction. Further, in those cases where attachment has been raised and considered it has been in the context of a claim by the plaintiff for costs which the court has characterised as a money claim and applied the rule that an attachment is necessary to found/confirm jurisdiction only for that sort of claim.

---

[653] *Private International Law* 5 ed (2012) 249.

[654] *Pollak on Jurisdiction* 2 ed (1993) 119 and 120, where he refers to p 88 of the work (authored by Adv DJ Shaw QC, whose view this is).

In the *Metlika Trading* case,[655] the Supreme Court of Appeal upheld an order made by the Transvaal Provincial Division that an attachment of certain assets of a party to the proceedings was necessary to confer jurisdiction on the court. That party was a company registered in Mauritius and was the subject of certain of the interdictory orders made by the court at first instance.[656] At the time the attachment was ordered, the only substantive relief claimed against the *peregrinus* company was interdictory relief.

Thus it would seem that an attachment of the assets of a *peregrinus* defendant is required in interim interdict proceedings in order to found or confirm[657] the jurisdiction of the court and that if an attachment is effected, the court will have jurisdiction over a *peregrinus* defendant in respect of acts to be performed and/or prohibited outside South Africa.

(10) Are there any other jurisdictional requirements?

In *Melamed NO v Munnikhuis*,[658] the court suggested that, in addition to the defendant being an *incola* of the court, what was required for a mandatory interdict was jurisdiction over the substantive cause of action (in that case the contract and its breach).[659]

In *Zokufa v Compuscan (Credit Bureau)*,[660] the court considered the requirements for a final mandatory interdict relating to the production of a report on the plaintiff's credit rating by the defendant credit bureau. The court noted[661] that various tests for jurisdiction in the case of an application for an interdict had been referred to in the judicial authorities:

> 'However, the distinction between *Kibe* (supra) and *Mtshali* (supra), and between the various tests for jurisdiction, such as the cause of action, the location of the pending unlawful act or omission to act, or the location of the facts supporting the requirements for an interdict, seems not to be made in any of the reported judgments. The prevailing position in our case law today appears to be that if any of the aforesaid tests can be successfully applied to the facts, then the court will have jurisdiction in interdict proceedings.'

[655] 2005 (3) SA 1 (SCA).

[656] At 13H–I para [29]: 'Carmel is a company registered in Mauritius. An attachment of its assets was, therefore, required in order to confer jurisdiction on the Court *a quo* or to confirm its jurisdiction over the company. Such attachment was performed in terms of a provisional order granted by de Vos J, which was confirmed by Hartzenberg J.'

[657] The court in *Metlika* was unclear which.

[658] 1996 (4) SA 125 (W), *per* Van Schalkwyk J.

[659] Ibid 131E–F: 'While the effect of the order sought will undoubtedly impact upon the rights of a party to the trust deed this Court cannot, it seems to me, deny the remedy sought on that ground alone. Where, for instance, it is clear that a party has undertaken to fulfil a specific obligation in circumstances where performance is required in a foreign jurisdiction and there is no dispute that the obligation is capable of fulfilment, the only question, it seems to me, is whether this Court has original jurisdiction in respect of the obligation contracted for. If it does, then the order which it makes is one for the fulfillment of the obligation.'

[660] 2011 (1) SA 272 (ECM).

[661] Ibid 281G–I para [54].

The court opined that the academic authorities had fared no better:[662] 'Not surprisingly, and perhaps by reason of the aforesaid, the position is no different in the legal writings on the subject. Our legal writers likewise appear to apply the aforesaid three tests indiscriminately and arbitrarily.'

The court held that the correct test to apply in the case of an application for an interdict was[663]

> 'that if the requirements for the grant of an interdict are satisfied by facts within the territorial jurisdiction of a High Court, the court will possess jurisdiction to decide the matter. For the reasons more fully discussed above I respectfully agree with this approach, and I intend to follow it in this case.'

The relevant requirements for the grant of an interdict are those set out in *Setlogelo v Setlogelo*.[664]

However, as Forsyth points out,[665] this is an incomplete statement because there may be cases in which the *Setlogelo* requirements are satisfied, but where the defendant is a *peregrinus* without assets to be attached to found/confirm jurisdiction and the court will not have jurisdiction.

At present it seems that jurisdiction to grant an interdict exists if any of the following requirements are satisfied, at the time the application is made: the relevant cause of action accrued within the jurisdiction of the court; the act to be performed or prohibited is to occur or has occurred within the jurisdiction of the court; the facts supporting the granting of an interdict occurred within the jurisdiction of the court.

9.3.2 Procedure for application[666]

Save where proceedings by way of petition are prescribed by law, every application for interim relief shall be brought on notice of motion, supported by an affidavit as to the facts upon which the plaintiff relies for relief.[667] When relief is claimed against any person, or where it is necessary or proper to give any person notice of such application, the notice of motion shall be addressed to both the registrar and such person; otherwise it shall be addressed to the registrar only.[668] Every petition shall conclude with the form of order prayed and be verified upon oath by or on behalf of the petitioner.[669]

---

662 Ibid 281I–J para [55].

663 Ibid 282H–I para [61.

664 1914 AD 221.

665 *Private International Law* 5 ed (2012) 249 fn 580.

666 Peté et al *Civil Procedure* 2 ed (2011) 120–2 and 136–9; Herbstein and Van Winsen *The Civil Practice of the High Courts of South Africa* 5 ed (2009) 1478–80.

667 High Court Rules, r 6(1).

668 High Court Rules, r 6(2).

669 High Court Rules, r 6(3).

An application for interim relief may also be brought *ex parte* in appropriate circumstances such as where the nature of the relief sought is such that giving notice to the defendant may defeat the purpose of the application (such as an anti-dissipation interdict) or where immediate relief is essential because the harm against which the order is sought is imminent. In this regard, the Supreme Court of Appeal has stated, 'The ex parte litigant's duty of the utmost good faith requires not only complete and fair disclosure; it imposes a more fundamental obligation to give notice to the other side unless, objectively, the absence of notice is justified.'[670]

An *ex parte* application is brought in the High Court[671] by means of a notice of motion following the requirements of High Court Form 2 which sets out the basic format for the notice of motion in an *ex parte* application as follows: (1) the identity of the application; (2) the date and time when the application will be made; (3) the terms of the order the court will be asked to make; (4) that the application is supported by affidavit evidence attached to the notice of motion; and (5) the name and address of the plaintiff's attorney. The form also contains an instruction to the Registrar to set the matter down for hearing; a notice of set-down is therefore incorporated into the application itself.

On an *ex parte* application, the court may make a final order when the court is satisfied that the rights of no other person are affected by the order or, more usually, the court will conclude that the rights of other persons are affected and will issue a rule *nisi*. A rule *nisi* is a peremptory order calling upon the named defendants and any other interested parties[672] to show cause (give reasons) why the order should not be made a final order at hearing on the return day and the court will usually be invited to order that the rule should act immediately as an interim order pending the return day. The effect was stated as follows in a recent Constitutional Court decision:[673]

> '[28] Our common law has recognised both the great importance of the *audi* rule as well as the need for flexibility, in circumstances where a rigid application of the rule would defeat the very rights sought to be enforced or protected. In such circumstances, the court issues a rule *nisi* calling on the interested parties to appear in court on a certain fixed date to advance reasons why the rule should not be

[670] *Recycling and Economic Development Initiative of South Africa v The Minister of Environmental Affairs* 2019 (3) SA 251 (SCA) (Cachalia, Saldulker, Van der Merwe and Molemela JJA and Rogers AJA) *per* Cachalia JA (giving the judgment of the court) at para 84.

[671] High Court Rules, r 6.6(4).

[672] In *Brown v McDonald* 1911 EDL 423, for example, the rule *nisi* was addressed to the farmer on whose farm the race horse, Elope, was present and to an auctioneer, neither of whom were intended parties to the plaintiff's proceedings.

[673] *National Director of Public Prosecutions v Mohamed NO* 2003 (4) SA 1 (CC) (Chaskalson CJ, Langa DCJ, Ackermann, Goldstone, Madala, Mokgoro, Moseneke, Ngcobo, O'Regan and Yacoob JJ), *per* Ackermann J, giving the judgment of the court, at 12H–13F paras [28]–[29].

made final, and at the same time orders that the rule *nisi* should act immediately as a temporary order, pending the return day. This practice has been recognised by the South African courts for over a century:

> "The term 'rule *nisi*' is derived from English law and practice, and the rule may be defined as an order by a court issued at the instance of the plaintiff and calling upon another party to show cause before the court on a particular day why the relief applied for should not be granted. Our common law knew the temporary interdict and, as Van Zyl points out, a 'curious mixture of our practice with the practice of England' took place and the practice arose of asking the court for a rule returnable on a certain day, but in the meantime to operate as a temporary interdict." [Erasmus]

[29] The flexibility and utility of the rule *nisi* acting at the same time as an interim order, has been recognised by the courts and it has been applied to modern problems in commercial suits. I would endorse the following passages from the judgment of Corbett JA, writing for a unanimous Appellate Division in the *Safcor* case [*Safcor Forwarding (Johannesburg) (Pty) Ltd v. National Transport Commission* 1982 (3) SA 654 (A)]:

> "The Uniform Rules of Court do not provide substantively for the granting of a rule *nisi* by the Court. Nevertheless, the practice, in certain circumstances, of doing so is firmly embedded in our procedural law (see, generally, Van Zyl *The Judicial Practice in South Africa* 2nd ed at 355ff, 370 - 1; Herbstein and Van Winsen *The Civil Practice of the Superior Courts in South Africa* 3rd ed at 89 - 90). This is recognised by implication in the Rules (see, eg, Rule 6(8) and Rule 6(13)). The procedure of a rule *nisi* is usually resorted to in matters of urgency and where the plaintiff seeks interim relief in order adequately to protect his immediate interests. It is a useful procedure and one to be encouraged rather than disparaged in circumstances where the plaintiff can show, prima facie, that his rights have been infringed and that he will suffer real loss or disadvantage if he is compelled to rely solely on the normal procedures for bringing disputes to Court by way of notice of motion or summons.'"

Ex parte applications carry with them an obligation of utmost good faith including a duty of full and frank disclosure on the part of the plaintiff.[674] All facts and law relevant to the application, whether they are for or against the plaintiff's case, must be brought to the attention of the court hearing the application. A breach

[674] In *Schlesinger v Schlesinger* 1979 (4) SA 342 (W), Le Roux J, at 349A–B, extracted the following principles applicable to the utmost good faith rule from the relevant authorities: '(1) [I]n *ex parte* applications all material facts must be disclosed which might influence a Court in coming to a decision; (2) the non-disclosure or suppression of facts need not be wilful or *mala fide* to incur the penalty of rescission [ie of the order obtained *ex parte*]; and (3) the Court, apprised of the true facts, has a discretion to set aside the former order or to preserve it.' In *Recycling and Economic Development Initiative of South Africa v The Minister of Environmental Affairs* 2019 (3) SA 251 (SCA) (Cachalia, Saldulker, Van der Merwe and Molemela JJA and Rogers AJA) the court discharged *ex parte* orders on the basis of, inter alia, the Minister's failure to give full and frank disclosure to the court at first instance (at paras 80–91, Cachalia JA giving the judgment of the court).

of this duty will not necessarily lead to the dismissal of the application when the default is brought to the attention of the court, but may do so.[675]

9.3.2.1 *Urgency*

An application for an interlocutory order, such as an interdict, may be brought on as a matter of urgency, in which case, depending on the degree of urgency, a progressive deviation from the rules of court will be permitted.[676]

The plaintiff must inform the court of the reasons why the application is urgent and why he cannot wait in order to obtain relief by making the application in the normal way.[677] The court will assess the urgency of the situation and may allow a departure from the rules of court to the extent that it is justified.[678]

Deviation from the rules may also justify a departure from the usual rules of evidence such that hearsay evidence may be adduced in support of the application, but as a precondition for the admission into evidence of such statements they must be accompanied by a statement of 'information and belief' identifying the source of the evidence, so as to enable the defendant to the application to check its accuracy and to conduct independent investigations of his own including, if so advised, verification of the statement from the source itself, and also a statement that the deponent believes the hearsay statements to be true.[679]

---

[675] Plaintiffs' attorneys should be astute to ensure reasonable and sufficient enquiries are made (including, but not limited to, of their clients) to secure compliance with the requirement of utmost good faith. If, after the rule is made but prior to the return day, matters emerge which would have adversely affected the position at the time the rule was made, these should be brought to the court's attention forthwith and not wait until the return day. In *MV Rizcun Trader v Manley Appledore Shipping Ltd* 2000 (3) SA 776 (C), Van Reenen J stated (at 799D–F): 'The next question to be decided is whether this Court, having been apprised of the real facts, should, in the exercise of its discretion, set aside the arrest order or keep it intact. Margo J in *Cometal-Mometal SARL v Corlana Enterprises (Pty) Ltd* 1981 (2) SA 412 (W) 414G–H listed certain factors that should be taken into account by a court in the exercise of its discretion whether to grant or deny relief to a litigant who has breached the *uberrima fides* rule. Those factors are the extent to which the rule has been breached; the reasons for the non-disclosure; the extent to which a Court might have been influenced by a proper disclosure; the consequences, from the point of doing justice between the parties, of denying relief to the applicant on the *ex parte* order; and the interests of innocent third parties.' In that case the judge found that there had been a 'flagrant' abuse of the good faith rule and set aside the rule *nisi* that had been issued.

[676] Urgency must not, obviously, be self-created through dilatoriness on the part of the applicant: *Nelson Mandela Metropolitan Municipality v Greyvenouw CC* 2004 (2) SA 81 (SE) (Plaskett AJ) 93–4, paras [33]–[34].

[677] In KwaZulu-Natal, the Registrar of the High Court requires an advocate to attach a certificate of urgency to the papers before they are enrolled for hearing.

[678] The High Court Rules, rule 6(12) provides: '(a) In urgent application the court or a judge may dispense with the forms and service provided for in these rules and may dispose of such matter at such time and place and in such manner and in accordance with such procedure (which shall as far as practicable be in terms of these rules) as to it seems meet. (b) In every affidavit or petition filed in support of any application under paragraph (a) of this sub-rule, the applicant shall set forth explicitly the circumstances which he avers render the matter urgent and the reasons why he claims that he could not be afforded substantial redress at a hearing in due course.'

[679] *Southern Pride Foods (Pty) Ltd v Mohidien* 1982 (3) SA 1068 (C), *per* Odes AJ at 1071D–1072C.

9.3.3 Interim interdicts

9.3.3.1 *The test for an interim interdict*

The requirements for an interim interdict appear not to be controversial.[680] In *LF Boshoff Investments (Pty) Ltd v Cape Town Municipality*,[681] Corbett J stated the requirements as follows:[682]

> 'Be that as it may, counsel for both parties addressed argument to the Court on the question as to whether the requisites for the grant of a temporary interdict pending determination of the main action had been established by the Company and I shall now consider this question.
>
> Briefly these requisites are that the plaintiff for such temporary relief must show–
>
> *(a)* that the right which is the subject-matter of the main action and which he seeks to protect by means of interim relief is clear or, if not clear, is prima facie established, though open to some doubt;
>
> *(b)* that, if the right is only *prima facie* established, there is a well grounded apprehension of irreparable harm to the plaintiff if the interim relief is not granted and he ultimately succeeds in establishing his right;
>
> *(c)* that the balance of convenience favours the granting of interim relief; and
>
> *(d)* that the plaintiff has no other satisfactory remedy.'

9.3.3.2 Prima facie *case*

The requirement of a clear right or a right *prima facie* established though open to some doubt,[683] and the interrelationship between this requirement and the other requirements was considered by Holmes J in *Olympic Passenger Service (Pty) Ltd v Ramlagan*,[684] where he stated:[685]

> 'It thus appears that where the plaintiff's right is clear, and the other requisites are present, no difficulty presents itself about granting an interdict. At the other end of the scale, where his prospects of ultimate success are nil, obviously the Court will refuse an interdict. Between those two extremes fall the intermediate cases in which, on the papers as a whole,

---

[680] See Prest *The Law and Practice of Interdicts* (1996) 49–51; Peté et al *Civil Procedure* 2 ed (2011) 409; Herbstein and Van Winsen *The Civil Practice of the High Courts of South Africa* 5 ed (2009) 1456–7.

[681] 1969 (2) SA 256 (C). See also *Setlogelo v Setlogelo* 1914 AD 221, *per* Innes JA at 227; *City of Tshwane Metropolitan Municipality v Afriforum* 2016 (6) SA 279 (CC) (Mogoeng CJ, Moseneke DCJ, Bosielo AJ, Cameron J, Froneman J, Jafta J, Khampepe J, Madlanga J, Mhlantla J, Nkabinde J and Zondo J), *per* Mogoeng CJ (giving the judgment of the court) para 49.

[682] Ibid 267A–E.

[683] In *Annex Distribution (Pty) Ltd v Bank of Baroda* 2018 (1) SA 562 (GP) (Fabricius J), an attempt to introduce into practice an 'interim-interim interdict' (an interim interdict pending the hearing of the application for an interim interdict) requiring the applicant to show only a triable issue and not a right *prima facie* established, was rejected by the court.

[684] 1957 (2) SA 382 (D).

[685] Ibid 383C–G.

> the plaintiffs' prospects of ultimate success may range all the way from strong to weak. The expression "*prima facie* established though open to some doubt" seems to me a brilliantly apt classification of these cases. In such cases, upon proof of a well grounded apprehension of irreparable harm, and there being no adequate ordinary remedy, the Court may grant an interdict - it has a discretion, to be exercised judicially upon a consideration of all the facts. Usually this will resolve itself into a nice consideration of the prospects of success and the balance of convenience - the stronger the prospects of success, the less need for such balance to favour the plaintiff: the weaker the prospects of success, the greater the need for the balance of convenience to favour him. I need hardly add that by balance of convenience is meant the prejudice to the plaintiff if the interdict be refused, weighed against the prejudice to the defendant if it be granted.
>
> I have not overlooked the many Provincial decisions dealing with interdicts. Unfortunately they are disconcertingly inharmonious. Perhaps therefore I may be forgiven for respectfully refraining from garnishing the judgment with copious extracts from other decisions - a practice which sometimes serves only to burden the annotations and confuse the weary searcher after simple legal principles.'

At one extreme are the clear cases and at the other are the hopeless cases. In the former, an interim interdict will usually be granted; in the latter, an interdict will be refused.

The majority of applications will fall into the intermediate group of cases where the plaintiff establishes a *prima facie* right that is open to some doubt. The means by which this requirement is assessed has been the subject of various formulations, of which the most commonly cited is that of Clayden J in *Webster v Mitchell*,[686] where he stated:[687]

> 'The use of the phrase "*prima facie* established though open to some doubt" indicates I think that more is required than merely to look at the allegations of the plaintiff, but something short of a weighing up of the probabilities of conflicting versions is required. The proper manner of approach I consider is to take the facts as set out by the plaintiff, together with any facts set out by the defendant which the plaintiff cannot dispute, and to consider whether, having regard to the inherent probabilities, the plaintiff could on those facts obtain final relief at a trial. The facts set up in contradiction by the defendant should then be considered. If serious doubt is thrown on the case of the plaintiff he could not succeed in obtaining temporary relief, for his right, *prima facie* established, may only be open to 'some doubt'. But if there is mere contradiction, or unconvincing explanation, the matter should be left to trial and the right be protected in the meanwhile, subject of course to the respective prejudice in the grant or refusal of interim relief. Although the grant of a temporary interdict interferes with a right which is apparently possessed by the defendant, the position of the defendant is protected because, although the plaintiff sets up a case which *prima facie* establishes that the defendant has not the right apparently exercised

[686] 1948 (1) SA 1186 (W). Affirmed as being the correct test in *Simon NO v Air Operations of Europe AB* 1999 (1) SA 217 (SCA) (Smalberger, Howie, Plewman and Streicher JJA, Ngoepe AJA) 228F–H.

[687] Ibid 1189–90.

> by him, the test whether or not temporary relief is to be granted is the harm which will be done. And in a proper case it might well be that no relief would be granted to the plaintiff except on conditions which would compensate the defendant for interference with his right, should the plaintiff fail to show at the trial that he was entitled to interfere.'

Thus, after consideration of the evidence concerning the existence and nature of the right in the manner set out by Clayden J, the court assesses whether the right, protection of which is claimed in the application, is a *prima facie* right though open to some doubt. If the right is open to serious doubt, this will not be sufficient to justify the grant of an interim interdict.

A question that has arisen concerns the disposability of issues of fact or law relating to the *prima facie* right at an interlocutory stage. There is authority[688] for the view that factual issues should be remitted to trial, but that issues of law may properly be dealt with in advance of trial such that the question whether, as a matter of law, the plaintiff has a legal right should be resolved at an interlocutory stage. The better view is that legal (and factual) issues ought not to be resolved at the interlocutory stage unless they are straightforward and whether this is so, is a question for the judge concerned:

> 'If a legal issue could be disposed of at an interlocutory stage it would be sensible to do so. The problem, however, is that no hard and fast rule can be formulated to distinguish between difficult and not so difficult questions of law. A question of law, which at first blush, seems to be difficult, might not be so difficult depending on the expertise of the particular judge. The converse could also apply. It is submitted that the decision whether to dispose of a legal issue at the interlocutory stage should be left to the discretion of the judge concerned in particular where situations of urgency require prompt decision. In those situations the English test for the first requirement, namely whether there is a serious question to be tried, seems to be the most apposite.'[689]

9.3.3.3 *Apprehension of irreparable harm*

Once this assessment has been undertaken, the court will then consider both the evidence of irreparable harm to the plaintiff and the contention that there is no adequate ordinary remedy available to the plaintiff. If these requirements are satisfied then the court has a discretion to grant an interim interdict. This discretion is to be exercised judicially in the light of all the facts.

---

[688] *Fourie v Olivier* 1971 (3) SA 274 (T), *per* Viljoen J at 284–5; *Ex parte St Clair Lynn* 1980 (3) SA 163 (W), *per* Coetzee J at 164.

[689] Herbstein and Van Winsen *The Civil Practice of the High Courts of South Africa* 5 ed (2009) 1463. The English test referred to being that set down by the House of Lords in *American Cyanamid Co v Ethicon Ltd* [1975] 1 All ER 504. See also *Johannesburg Municipal Pension Fund v City of Johannesburg* 2005 (6) SA 273 (W), *per* Malan at 282–3.

In this regard 'irreparable' does not mean literally incapable of repair, but simply very difficult to repair and includes any prejudice suffered by the plaintiff as a result of the infringement of his rights.[690] Irreparable harm may comprise the prevention of the plaintiff from exercising his right at all, loss of money or the incurring of expenditure where sums are unlikely to be recovered.

It is not enough for the plaintiff simply to allege irreparable loss; the facts deposed to by the plaintiff must show that there is an actual or well-grounded apprehension of irreparable loss if no interdict is granted.

9.3.3.4 *No adequate ordinary remedy*

The alternative remedy, the absence of which must be established by the plaintiff, must: (1) be adequate in the circumstances; (2) be ordinary and reasonable; (3) be a legal remedy; and (4) grant similar protection.[691]

A question arises whether the absence of an alternative remedy is an essential requirement of the grant of an interim interdict or whether it is a matter to be taken into account in the exercise of the court's discretion. Herbstein and Van Winsen[692] categorises it as a matter to be taken into account in the exercise of the court's discretion. This is a view shared by Prest:[693]

> 'It has been held, correctly it is submitted, that the discretion of the court, apart from the position relating to the grant of interlocutory interdicts, where considerations of prejudice and convenience are of importance, is bound up with the question whether the rights of the party complaining can be protected by any other ordinary remedy. It is noticeable that in Van der Linden's exposition of the requisites, a discretion comes into play only in the case of his subsidiary rule relating to irreparable harm which applies to interlocutory relief.'

---

690 Herbstein and Van Winsen *The Civil Practice of the High Courts of South Africa* 5 ed (2009) 1464 (in the context of the test for a final order); *Bamford v Minister of Community Development and State Auxiliary Services* 1981 (3) SA 1054 (C), where Watermeyer JP granted an urgent interim interdict restraining the respondent from interfering with the applicant's access to certain land on which residences were being constructed and which was alleged to be part of a public park.

691 Herbstein and Van Winsen *The Civil Practice of the High Courts of South Africa* 5 ed (2009) 1467–8; *Minister of Law and Order v Committee of the Church Summit* 1994 (3) SA 89 (BG), *per* Friedman AJP at 99F–H: 'Concerning the alternative remedy, the courts have determined that it must be adequate in the circumstances, be ordinary and reasonable, be a legal remedy and also grant similar protection to a party. See *Free State Gold Areas Ltd v Merriespruit (Orange Free State) Gold Mining Co Ltd* 1961 (2) SA 505 (W) 524–5; *Martin v Kiesbeampte, Newcastle Afdeling* 1958 (2) SA 649 (D) 654; *Cape Town Municipality v Abdulla* 1974 (4) SA 428 (C) 440. Generally [a plaintiff] will not obtain an interdict if he can be awarded adequate compensation or amends by way of damages. The enquiry on this essential is whether an interdict is the only relief or remedy to help the [plaintiff], or is there a satisfactory alternative remedy. Furthermore, the circumstances relating to each case will indicate whether the award of damages is an adequate alternative remedy. The Court maintains a discretion. It is a factor in the general discretion of the Court.'

692 *The Civil Practice of the High Courts of South Africa* 5 ed (2009) 1468.

693 *The Law and Practice of Interdicts* (1996) 48 and 77.

In *Candid Electronics (Pty) Ltd v Merchandise Buying Syndicate (Pty) Ltd*,[694] Cooper J stated:[695] 'The grant or refusal of an interdict is a matter within the discretion of the Court hearing the application and depends on the facts peculiar to each individual case and the right the plaintiff is seeking to enforce or protect' and, 'The rule that an interdict may not be granted when the plaintiff can obtain adequate redress by an award of damages is objectionable as it is an impermissible curtailment of the Court's discretion.'

The remedy that is usually proposed as an alternative to an interdict is damages. Damages will not be considered an adequate alternative remedy when: there is a continuing violation of the plaintiff's rights;[696] damages will be difficult or impossible to assess;[697] the plaintiff is not likely to be able to recover damages from the defendant because, for example, he is a man of straw;[698] or the award of damages will otherwise be worthless.[699]

9.3.3.5 *Discretion – the balance of convenience*

On the question of the exercise of the discretion,[700] Holmes J stated[701] that this would usually resolve itself into a consideration of the prospects of success and the balance of convenience (being the balance of prejudice to the plaintiff and defendant if the relief sought is refused or granted). The stronger the merits of the case in favour of the plaintiff, the more likely the balance of convenience is to tilt in his favour.[702] In *Knox D'Arcy Ltd v Jamieson*,[703] EM Grosskopf JA stated:[704]

---

694 1992 (2) SA 459 (C). Prest (at 78) quotes Sachs LJ in *Evans Marshall & Co Ltd v Bertola SA* [1973] 1 All ER 992 (CA) 1005d: 'The standard question in relation to the grant of an injunction, are damages an adequate remedy? might perhaps, in the light of the authorities of recent years, be re-written: is it just, in all the circumstances, that plaintiff should be confined to his remedy in damages?'. EM Grosskopf JA, in *Knox D'Arcy Ltd v Jamieson* 1996 (4) SA 348 (A) 362B–C (giving the judgment of the court), took the view that the availability of alternative remedies fell to be considered as a factor in the exercise of the court's discretion.

695 1992 (2) SA 459 (C) 464G and 465A, respectively.

696 *Wynberg Municipality v Dreyer* 1920 AD 439; *Buitendach v West Rand Proprietary Mines Ltd* 1925 TPD 886; *Rivas v Premier (Transvaal) Diamond Mining Co Ltd* 1929 WLD 1.

697 *Charney v Truebig* 1920 SWA 46.

698 *Aetiology Today CC v Van Aswegen* 1992 (1) SA 807 (W), *per* Cloete AJ at 815G–H: 'Even although an injury may be capable of pecuniary evaluation and compensation, a Court will generally grant an interdict if the respondent is a man of straw or if damages would be difficult to assess. In addition, the conduct of the respondents is likely to continue.'

699 *Boiler Efficiency Services CC v Coalcor (Cape) (Pty) Ltd* 1989 (3) SA 460 (C), *per* Howie J at 475G: 'The value of a damages award in several years' time is of questionable adequacy in these inflationary times when in law one cannot obtain pre-judgment interest on the damages.'

700 See Prest *The Law and Practice of Interdicts* (1996) 67–77.

701 *Olympic Passenger Service (Pty) Ltd v Ramlagan* 1957 (2) SA 382 (D) 383G.

702 Peté et al *Civil Procedure* 2 ed (2011) 411 para 7.3; Prest *The Law and Practice of Interdicts* (1996) 79; Herbstein and Van Winsen *The Civil Practice of the High Courts of South Africa* 5 ed (2009) 1472.

703 1996 (4) SA 348 (A) (EM Grosskopf, Nestadt, FH Grosskopf, Harms and Scott JJA).

704 Ibid 362B–C.

> 'The Courts have not defined the considerations which may be taken into account in exercising the so-called discretion, save for mentioning the obvious examples such as the strength or weakness of the plaintiff's right, the balance of convenience, the nature of the prejudice which may be suffered by the plaintiff and the availability of other remedies. Whilst this list is not exclusive, it does indicate what the relevant features are in an application of this sort. I find it difficult to imagine that considerations which are entirely unrelated to these features could be accorded weight in granting or refusing an application for an interim interdict.'

In an appropriate case the potential prejudice to third parties can be considered when the court exercises its discretion.[705]

The court may make an order that the plaintiff provide security for any damage the defendant may suffer as a result of the making of the order[706] or may require an undertaking to that effect from the plaintiff.[707]

A refusal by a plaintiff for an interdict to offer an undertaking to compensate the defendant for any loss he suffers as a result of the making of the order may contribute to the balance of convenience being found to favour the defendant.[708]

The refusal or discharge of an interim interdict is appealable because it cannot be reversed on the same facts and as such it is final.[709] On appeal, the court is not confined to deciding whether the court below exercised its discretion properly. The term 'discretion' is not used in a strict sense, but in a looser sense that the court is entitled to have regard to a number of disparate and incommensurable features in reaching a decision.[710] In *Knox D'Arcy Ltd v Jamieson*,[711] EM Grosskopf JA described the approach of the Appellate Court to appeals from the discharge or refusal of an interim interdict as follows:[712]

---

705 *Roberts v Chairman, Local Road Transportation Board, Cape Town* 1979 (4) SA 604 (C) (Watermeyer AJP and Friedman J), *per* Friedman J at 608D where in the context of an application for the immediate enforcement of an order concerning the unlawfulness of fare rises on the buses, the judge took into account the prejudice to the general public in not requiring the order to be complied with.

706 *Hillman Bros (West Rand) (Pty) Ltd v Van den Heuvel* 1937 WLD 41, *per* Greenberg J at 46, where he imposed a condition on an interim interdict restraining the respondent from receiving certain sums of money from contractors that if the applicant failed to prove its allegations then it would be liable to the respondent for any damages suffered by the respondent by reason of the interdict being granted in an amount larger than that which the applicant was entitled to have secured. See Prest *The Law and Practice of Interdicts* (1996) 80 and 156–60.

707 *Cronshaw v Fidelity Guards Holdings (Pty) Ltd* 1996 (3) SA 686 (A) (EM Grosskopf, FH Grosskopf, Harms and Schutz JJA and Plewman AJA) 690H–J.

708 *Hix Networking Technologies v System Publishers (Pty) Ltd* 1997 (1) SA 391 (A) (Corbett CJ, EM Grosskopf, Harms, Schutz and Plewman JJA,), *per* Plewman JA (giving the judgment of the court) 403F: 'In the present case the appellant's refusal to offer an undertaking would, in my view, have ensured that the balance of convenience favoured the respondents.'

709 EM Grosskopf JA in *Knox D'Arcy Ltd v Jamieson* 1996 (4) SA 348 (A) 358A–B and generally 358B–360D. The *grant* of an interim interdict is not appealable.

710 Herbstein and Van Winsen *The Civil Practice of the High Courts of South Africa* 5 ed (2009) 1482.

711 1996 (4) SA 348 (A).

712 Ibid 360D–361B.

> 'In assessing the petitioners' prospects of success on appeal it is necessary to consider how a Court would approach such an appeal. On behalf of the respondents it was argued that a Court of first instance always has a discretion to refuse an interim interdict, even if the requisites have been established. Consequently, so it was contended, an Appeal Court would only be entitled to interfere if it came to the conclusion that the lower Court had not exercised a judicial discretion. The issue is not, it was said, whether the lower Court had arrived at the correct decision, but whether it had exercised its discretion properly.
>
> The Appeal Court is not entitled to interfere because in its opinion it would have come to a different conclusion. This would be substituting its discretion for that of the Court *a quo*.
>
> This argument was not seriously contested by the petitioners, but I do not think it should pass unchallenged.
>
> That a Court has a discretion whether or not to grant a temporary interdict has often been said. We were, however, not referred to any case in which an appeal in respect of an interim interdict was dealt with on the basis that the Appeal Court could not interfere except on the restricted grounds suggested by the respondents. As far as the Appellate Division is concerned, the authority which I have been able to find goes the other way. Thus, in *Messina (Transvaal) Development Co Ltd v South African Railways and Harbours* 1929 AD 195 at 215-16 Curlewis JA said:
>
>> "In an application for an interim interdict pending action, the Court has a large discretion in granting or withholding an interdict. Where there is merely a possibility, not a practical certainty, of interference or injury, as in the present case, the Court will be reluctant to grant an interdict, especially if the party seeking the interdict will have other means of redress and will not suffer irreparable damage. And the Court is entitled to and must regard the possible consequences, both to the [plaintiff] and to the [respondent], which will ensue if an interdict be granted or withheld."
>
> It is significant that, despite emphasising the discretionary nature of the relief claimed, the learned Judge did not, in the result, decide the case on the limited basis contended for in the present case. In fact he did not even consider the question whether the trial Judge had properly and judicially exercised a discretion. Curlewis JA decided the matter according to his own views of the merits of the application and came to the conclusion that "no sufficient case for an interdict has been made out" (at 216).'

It would seem therefore that an appeal against the refusal or discharge of an interim interdict is in the nature of a rehearing before the appeal court.

On the state of the judicial authorities, it is unclear whether a court has power to grant an interim interdict pending an appeal against that same court's decision to refuse or discharge an interdict. The editors of Herbstein and Van Winsen *The Civil Practice of the High Courts of South Africa* consider that the courts have such a power[713] and there is a majority decision in the Appeal Division in the context of licensing (cited by Herbstein and Van Winsen) which is to the same effect.[714]

---

[713] 5 ed (2009) 1485.

[714] *Airoadexpress v LRTB, Durban* 1986 (2) SA 663 (A) (Kotzé, Miller, Joubert, Van Heerden and Grosskopf JJA), *per* Kotzé JA (Grosskopf and Joubert JJA agreeing) 676B–D: 'I cannot accept that, if it can be shown in a case of this kind that the appellant must inevitably succeed in the appeal, interim relief pending the

9.3.4 Freezing orders/Anti-dissipation interdicts

A freezing order[715] is a special type of interdict which may be granted where the defendant[716] is believed to be arranging his affairs in such a way as to ensure that by the time the plaintiff is in a position to execute any judgment he may obtain, there will be no assets or insufficient assets on which to execute the judgment. The principles on the basis of which a freezing order will be granted were settled in *Knox D'Arcy Ltd v Jamieson*;[717] EM Grosskopf JA (giving the judgment of the court) stated:[718]

> 'The question which arises from this approach is whether a plaintiff need show a particular state of mind on the part of the defendant, ie that he is getting rid of the funds, or is likely to do so, with the intention of defeating the claims of creditors. Having regard to the purpose of this type of interdict, the answer must be, I consider, yes, except possibly in exceptional cases. As I have said, the effect of the interdict is to prevent the defendant from freely dealing with his own property to which the plaintiff lays no claim. Justice may require this restriction in cases where the defendant is shown to be acting *mala fide* with the intent of preventing execution in respect of the plaintiff's claim. However, there would not normally be any justification to compel a defendant to regulate his *bona fide* expenditure so as to retain funds in his patrimony for the payment of claims (particularly disputed ones) against him. I am not, of course, at the moment dealing with special situations which might arise, for instance, by contract or under the law of insolvency.'

And:[719]

> 'The purpose of the interdict is not to be a substitute for the claim for damages but to reinforce it - to render it more effective. And the question whether the claim is a satisfactory remedy in the absence of an interdict would normally answer itself. Except where the defendant is a Croesus, a claim for damages buttressed by an interdict of this

---

determination thereof can lawfully be withheld solely by reason of an order which cannot conceivably be sustained. I am of the view further that in principle the same approach should prevail where a strong *prima facie* case is established that the permits applied for were wrongly refused. In my view the principle applied in the *De Fraetas* type of case should be extended to a case like the present. The decision in that case is based on the existence of a "general power" or, put differently, an inherent jurisdiction to grant *pendente lite* relief to avoid injustice and hardship. An inherent power of this kind is a salutary power which should be jealously preserved and even extended where exceptional circumstances are present and where, but for the exercise of such power, a litigant would be remediless, as is the case here.'

715 Peté et al *Civil Procedure* 2 ed (2011) 417–19; Herbstein and Van Winsen *The Civil Practice of the High Courts of South Africa* 5 ed (2009) 1488–94. (Prest *The Law and Practice of Interdicts* (1996) 160–2 addresses the position prior to the decision of the Appellate Division in *Knox D'Arcy Ltd v Jamieson* 1996 (4) SA 348 (A).) No settled and generally accepted nomenclature exists to describe this sort of interdict. Terms such as '*Mareva* interdict', 'anti-dissipation interdict', '*Knox D'Arcy* interdict', 'anti-dissipatory interdict', and 'interdict *in securitatem debiti*' have all been used. 'Freezing order' is the term used as it describes briefly what the order is intended to do.

716 The terminology of defendant/plaintiff is used to describe respondent/applicant.

717 1996 (4) SA 348 (A) (EM Grosskopf, Nestadt, FH Grosskopf, Harms and Scott JJA).

718 Ibid 372G–I.

719 Ibid 373B–E.

> sort is always more satisfactory for the plaintiff/applicant than one standing on its own feet. The question of an alternative remedy accordingly does not arise in this sort of case. The interdict with which we are dealing is *sui generis*. It is either available or it is not. No other remedy can really take its place (except, possibly, in certain circumstances attachments or arrests).'

The remedy is *sui generis* and is not an alternative to some other remedy. The plaintiff must therefore show that the defendant is dissipating his assets with a view to defeating the plaintiff's claim in the event the plaintiff succeeds.[720]

Although EM Grosskopf JA left open the possibility of a *bona fide* transaction amounting to dissipation, the cases where this is capable of proof will be rare, as he appeared to confirm when endorsing a statement in the English Court of Appeal in *Polly Peck International plc v Nadir (No 2)*,[721] to the effect that a freezing order is not intended to alter a defendant's ordinary conduct:[722]

> 'The contention is that the respondents' [defendants'] business set-up was such that profits were earned by the Netherlands company. This resulted in money earned in this country being sent overseas, which rendered it likely that there would be no assets to attach in South Africa if a judgment were to be obtained against the respondents. As I stated above, there may be exceptional circumstances in which even a *bona fide* disposition of assets may be interdicted, but in my view this is not that sort of case. First, this was not the petitioners' case on the papers. There they pinned their colours to the mast of the intentional secreting of assets. But, in any event, the facts of this case do not require that the respondents should be interdicted from dealing with their own assets. The respondents have a corporate structure which results in money leaving this country. They adopted this structure for good business reasons and, on the assumption underlying this contention, are using it in good faith for that purpose. No authority in our law has been quoted in support of the petitioners' contention that an interdict may be granted in a case like this, nor could I find any. In English law, which, it would seem, inspired the application in the present case, a *Mareva* injunction would not be available in a case like the present. As was stated in *Polly Peck International plc v Nadir and Others* (No 2) [1992] 4 All ER 769 (CA) at 785*g-h*:
>
> > "It is not the purpose of a Mareva injunction to prevent a defendant acting as he would have acted in the absence of a claim against him."'

The burden of proof is on the plaintiff to make out the requirements of the order and the standard of proof would seem to be the establishing of a *prima facie* case that the requirements are made out.[723]

---

[720] A practical and common-sense approach is to be taken to the evidence: *Lagoon Beach Hotel (Pty) Ltd v Lehane* 2016 (3) SA 143 (SCA) (Navsa, Cachalia, Leach, Tshiqi and Willis JJA), *per* Leach JA (giving he judgment of the court) para [15].

[721] [1992] 4 All ER 769.

[722] Ibid 377A–E.

[723] *Knox D'Arcy Ltd v Jamieson* 1996 (4) SA 348 (A) 373E–H. Although EM Grosskopf JA also seems to have considered (at 378J–379B) that the balance of convenience approach might be applied to this type of application.

A freezing order does not give the plaintiff any priority over the frozen assets in preference to other creditors in insolvency.[724]

The grant of a freezing order is draconian and the procedure for obtaining it should reflect that fact. An order may be granted *ex parte* and at a hearing *in camera* but 'this should happen only in very clear cases where justice cannot be served otherwise than by depriving the defendant of his right to be heard. In the nature of things such cases would be exceptional.'[725] Clearly any application brought *ex parte* at a hearing *in camera* will need to be supported by evidence explaining why such a way of proceeding is justified.

EM Grosskopf JA approved[726] the following statement by Stegmann J in the court below:

> 'The exercise of such powers must be attended with due caution; with all practical safeguards against abuse; and with a careful attempt to visualise the ways in which the order may prove to be needlessly oppressive to the intended defendant. Consideration must also be given to the manner in which the order may interfere with the rights and obligations of third parties, such as banks or other debtors of the intended defendant, or other custodians of the intended defendant's assets. Both the oppressiveness of the order to the intended defendant and its interference with the rights and obligations of third parties must be kept to the minimum ...'.

Ancillary orders to a freezing order may include orders for the disclosure of facts and documents to ensure the interdict is effective and workable.[727]

A cross-undertaking as to damages will usually be required as a condition for the making of the order whereby the plaintiff undertakes to pay the defendant all such damages as may be caused by the order in the event that the plaintiff fails to establish his case at trial.[728]

The order will also usually exclude sums such as are reasonably necessary to enable the defendant to carry on his business, to live and to defend the proceedings.[729]

---

[724] Ibid 372A–C.

[725] Ibid 379I.

[726] Ibid 380A–B.

[727] *Knox D'Arcy Ltd v Jamieson* 1994 (3) SA 700 (W), *per* Stegmann J at 709C–E and 710C–E where the judge held that he had power to order disclosure of the defendants' assets within the Republic of South Africa and worldwide, but ordered only the former disclosure.

[728] For example, the plaintiff in *Knox D'Arcy Ltd v Jamieson* 1994 (3) SA 700 (W), offered such an undertaking (710A–B).

[729] *Knox D'Arcy Ltd v Jamieson* 1994 (3) SA 700 (W), *per* Stegmann J at 711A–C. Whether this concession to a defendant's expenditure extends to proprietary claims is as yet undecided. In England the approach is as follows: 'Difficulties can arise where the injunction is of a proprietary nature (so that the assertion is that the frozen monies belong to the [plaintiff]), and the defendant wishes to draw on these funds for its legal costs or to enable it to honour pre-existing contractual obligations. In such a case, four questions fall to be asked (1) has the [plaintiff] an arguable proprietary claim to the money? (2) if yes, does the defendant have arguable grounds for denying that claim? (3) if yes, has the defendant demonstrated that, without the release

As with other interim interdicts, the plaintiff has a duty of full and frank disclosure on any application made in the absence of the defendant.[730]

It is also good practice to make a note of the *ex parte* hearing and serve that note on the defendant, together with the issued notice of motion and order.[731]

9.3.5 *Res litigiosa* orders

The court has power to make an order preserving property which is the subject of the litigation itself. In *Pepkor Holdings Ltd v AJVH Holdings (Pty) Ltd*,[732] an appeal was allowed against orders made by the Western Cape Division restraining dealing with certain shares. Schippers JA, giving the judgment of the Supreme Court of Appeal, stated:[733]

> '*Res litigiosa* is property which is the subject of litigation. A plaintiff may in principle apply to preserve *res litigiosa, pendente lite*. The requirements are those for an ordinary interim interdict. As a general principle, there are two additional features: the first is that the property which is the subject of the interim interdict is the subject of the action; and the second, that the action and the interim application are between the same parties.'

The stage at which property becomes *res litigiosa* is, in the case of a real action (*in rem*), at the time the defendant is informed of the issue of a summons against him or her regarding that property.[734] In an action *in personam* the relevant property only becomes *res litigiosa* after close of pleadings: 'The doctrine of *res litigiosa* only

---

of the funds in issue, it cannot effectively defend the proceedings? (4) if yes, where does the balance of justice lie? (*Independent Trustee Services Ltd v GP Noble Trustees Ltd* [2009] EWHC 161 (Ch), January 26, 2009, unrep (Lewison J.) [para 6])', (notes to the English Civil Procedure Rules 1998, at Pt 25, para 25.1.25.6).

[730] The notes to the English Civil Procedure Rules 1998 state (at Pt 25, para 25.3.5): 'The [plaintiff] must disclose fully to the court all matters relevant to the application, including all matters, whether of fact or of law, which are, or may be, adverse to it' (Chancery Guide para 5.22, see vol 2, para 1A-35). In *Memory Corp Plc v Sidhu (No 2)* [2000] 1 WLR 1443 (CA) Mummery LJ (at 1460A–B) stated that 'there is a high duty to make full, fair and accurate disclosure of material information to the court and to draw the court's attention to significant factual, legal and procedural aspects of the case'.

[731] The provision of a note of the *ex parte* hearing is a requirement of English civil procedure. The notes to the English Civil Procedure Rules 1998 state (at Pt 25, para 25.3.10): '[Plaintiffs] without notice for relief are under a duty to provide full notes of the hearing with all expedition to any party that would be affected by the relief sought; a failure to do so may result in an award of indemnity costs in favour of the party affected (*Interoute Telecommunications (UK) Ltd v Fashion Gossip Ltd* The Times, November 10, 1999 (Lightman J.)) ... Counsel and solicitors have responsibility for taking full notes of what was said at the hearing and they should not expect that a transcript of the hearing would be available or would suffice if it were (*Cinpres Gas Injection Ltd v Melea Ltd* [2005] EWHC 3180 (Pat), December 14, 2005, unrep (Pumfrey J.) (setting aside interim injunction made without notice restraining threats against witnesses)).'

[732] 2021 (5) SA 115 (SCA) (Cachalia, Zondi, Movumie and Schippers JJA and Goosen AJA). See also Prest *The Law and Practice of Interdicts* (1996) 161, where this form of relief is alluded to obliquely but not separately discussed.

[733] At para 19.

[734] *Pepkor* at para 22 and not, as previously held, on service of the summons on the defendant: *Opera House (Grand Parade) Restaurant (Pty) Ltd v Cape Town City Council* 1986 (2) SA 656 (C), *per* Berman J at p 661C.

applies where there is a *lis* between the plaintiff enforcing a right to or ownership of property and the possessor thereof'.[735]

The defendant may deal with the property the subject of an interim interdict *res litigiosa* but only if such dealing will not prejudice the plaintiff's alleged rights.[736]

In *Pepkor* the orders made at first instance were discharged for three reasons: first, the shares in respect of which the orders were made were not *litigiosa* in relation to the companies owning those shares; second, the orders restrained dealing with the shares when the shares were not the subject of the main action; and, third, the main action was not one *in rem*, but instead was an action *in personam* in which the relevant property only became *res litigiosa* after close of pleadings, but the plaintiffs had wrongly applied for the interim interdict prior to that time.

9.3.6 Search and seize orders

A search and seize order[737] is an interdict the object of which is to ensure that vital evidence is preserved for use in a subsequent trial. It is generally (if not always) obtained *ex parte* at a hearing *in camera*. The application will usually be brought on as an urgent application in anticipation of the vital evidence being destroyed by the prospective defendant to the proceedings. The plaintiff engaging in such a procedure will need to show that there is a 'real possibility that the evidence will be lost to him if the defendant gets wind of the application'.[738]

The remedy was described by the Appellate Division in *Shoba v Officer Commanding, Temporary Police Camp, Wagendrift Dam; Maphanga v Officer Commanding, SA Police Murder & Robbery Unit, Pietermaritzburg*.[739] Corbett CJ (giving the judgment of the court) held:[740]

---

[735] *Pepkor* at para 25.

[736] *Opera House (Grand Parade) Restaurant (Pty) Ltd v Cape Town City Council* 1986 (2) SA 656 (C), *per* Berman J at p 661D-I, citing *Coronel v Gordon Estate and Gold Mining Co* 1902 TS 95 and *Blue-Cliff Investments (Pty) Ltd v Griessel* 1971 (3) SA 93 (C).

[737] Peté et al *Civil Procedure* 2 ed (2011) 415–17; Herbstein and Van Winsen *The Civil Practice of the High Courts of South Africa* 5 ed (2009) 1495–1515; Prest *The Law and Practice of Interdicts* (1996) 172–98. This type of relief is sometimes referred to as an *Anton Piller* order, after the name of one of the English cases in which it was first made: *Anton Piller KG v Manufacturing Processes Ltd* [1976] 1 All ER 779 (CA).

[738] *Universal City Studios Inc v Network Video (Pty) Ltd* 1986 (2) SA 734 (A), *per* Corbett JA (as he then was) 755E; approved by the Constitutional Court in *National Director of Public Prosecutions v Mohamed NO* 2003 (4) SA 1 (CC) (Chaskalson CJ, Langa DCJ, Ackermann, Goldstone, Madala, Mokgoro, Moseneke, Ngcobo, O'Regan and Yacoob JJ), *per* Ackermann J (giving the judgment of the court) 14E–15A, para [31].

[739] 1995 (4) SA 1 (A) (Corbett CJ, E M Grosskopf, Nestadt, and Steyn JJA and Nicholas AJA).

[740] Ibid 15F–J, following the acceptance of the practice obiter in *Universal City Studios Inc v Network Video (Pty) Ltd* 1986 (2) SA 734 (A), *per* Corbett JA (as he then was) 755A–C. The principles set out in *Shoba* are the settled principles on which a search and seize order is made: *Viziya Corp v Collaborit Holdings (Pty) Ltd* 2019

> 'At this point it is necessary to give a decision in regard to what was left open in both the *Universal City Studios* case *supra* and *Jafta's* case *supra*, viz whether an *Anton Piller* order directed at the preservation of evidence should be accepted as part of our practice. In my view, it should; and I would define what an applicant for such an order, obtained *in camera* and without notice to the respondent, must *prima facie* establish, as the following:
>
> (1) That he, the applicant, has a cause of action against the respondent which he intends to pursue;
>
> (2) that the respondent has in his possession specific (and specified) documents or things which constitute vital evidence in substantiation of the applicant's cause of action (but in respect of which the applicant cannot claim a real or personal right); and
>
> (3) that there is a real and well-founded apprehension that this evidence may be hidden or destroyed or in some manner be spirited away by the time the case comes to trial or to the stage of discovery.'[741]

As regards the requirement that the evidence at which the order is directed should be 'vital evidence', Corbett CJ stated:[742]

> 'I have used the words "vital evidence" in the sense of being evidence of great importance to the plaintiff's case. In the case of *Ex parte Matshini and Others* 1986 (3) SA 605 (E) it was held that in order to obtain an *Anton Piller* order the applicant would have to show that the evidence was "essential" or "absolutely necessary" in order for him to prove his claim and that its non-availability at the trial would result in the administration of justice being defeated (at 613A-C). As I suggested in *Jafta's* case (at 294A), this poses too stringent a test.'

The search order jurisdiction is confined to applications for the preservation of evidence and does not extend further into the enforcement of proprietary or possessory claims.[743]

---

(3) SA 173 (SCA) (Wallis, Saldulker, Mathopo and Van der Merwe JJA and Rogers AJA, *per* Mathopo, giving the judgment of the court, at para 22.

[741] Applying these principles to the facts, Corbett CJ held (at 21F–H): 'As to the factual merits, it seems to me that the applicant established (i) a strong *prima facie* case of having been assaulted and tortured while in police custody; (ii) that he intended to pursue against the second respondent a civil action arising from such assault and torture; (iii) that, if it existed, the torture apparatus would be vital evidence in such a civil action; and that there was a real and well-founded apprehension that such apparatus, if it existed, would be hidden or destroyed before the matter came to trial. This was hardly in dispute. In my opinion, the Court *a quo* should, therefore, have granted an *Anton Piller* order in this case.'

[742] Ibid 15J–16B.

[743] *Memory Institute SA CC t/a SA Memory Institute v Hansen* 2004 (2) SA 630 (SCA) (Harms, Schutz, Cameron, Conradie and Heher JJA), Harms JA (giving the judgment of the court) said of the introduction of the search order jurisdiction (at 633C–D, para [2]): 'In this country the seed fell initially on rocky ground guarded by prophets of old but eventually took root and the plant grew and prospered. What is permitted and what not for the grant of these orders, considering the number of reported judgments on the matter, should also be common knowledge. Regrettably it is not' and (at 630E–F, para [30]): '*Anton Piller* orders are for the preservation of evidence and are not a substitute for possessory or proprietary claims. They require built-in protection measures such as the appointment of an independent attorney to supervise the execution of the order.'

In *Roamer Watch Co SA v African Textile Distributors*,[744] Cilliers AJ suggested[745] guidelines for search order applications:

'*(a)* The applicant should make out a clear case against the party against whom the order is sought. I would not necessarily go so far as Ormrod LJ, who stated that "an extremely strong *prima facie* case" should be made out by the applicant, but the respondent should not be exposed to attachment and removal of his documents, information and goods, on grounds which are speculative or fail clearly to make out a case for relief against the respondent. In particular, the applicant's case should not be entirely dependent on such evidence as may or may not be found in the respondent's possession: that would amount to a mere "fishing expedition". The strength of the case made out by the applicant would certainly be a relevant consideration when the Court weighs, on the one hand, the prejudice which the respondent may suffer in regard to the loss of his legitimate trade secrets, the disruption of his business, or the adverse influence which an attachment or removal may have on his trading reputation, and, on the other hand, the need of the applicant to obtain evidence which may otherwise be lost to him ...

(b) The remedy of attachment and, where appropriate, removal of documents, information, articles and the like, must be the only practicable means of protecting the applicant's rights and of doing justice between the parties; if the applicant can obtain the same evidence in some other way without undue hardship, the procedure of attachment without notice should not be permitted.'

A strong *prima facie* case is required at the *ex parte* stage of the application.[746] For example, if the evidence might be available through the use of the *subpoena duces tecum* procedure then a search order will be inappropriate.[747]

'*(c)* The evidence provided by the documents, information, articles and the like to be attached must be material to the applicant's case; the incriminatory value of such evidence must not be a mere makeweight when considered together with the applicant's other available evidence.'

The evidence must be '*vital evidence*' and not a mere makeweight.[748]

'*(d)* There must be clear evidence that the respondent has such incriminating documents, information, articles and the like in his possession, or that, at least, there are good grounds for believing that this is the case.

(e) The applicant must fully set out cogent reasons for believing that there is a real danger that the documents, information, articles and the like, will be removed or destroyed and the ends of justice will be defeated, if the respondent were given notice of the proceedings against him.

---

[744] 1980 (2) SA 254 (W).

[745] Ibid 272C–275A.

[746] *Friedshelf 1509 (Pty) Ltd v Kalianji* 2015 (4) SA 163 (GJ), *per* Strathern AJ at para 50.

[747] *Sun World International Inc v Unifruco Ltd* 1998 (3) SA 151 (C), *per* Van Reenen J at 169F–H.

[748] See Corbett CJ's formulation of the approach in the *Shoba* case, above.

> *(f)* The Court always retains a discretion whether or not to grant this extraordinary relief *ex parte*, and the importance and value of the applicant's interests to be protected will always have to be weighed against the prejudice the respondent may suffer as result of an *ex parte* order for attachment and, where appropriate, removal being granted and carried out.'

The plaintiff may proceed *ex parte* and apply for the hearing to be *in camera* but he will need to show that there is a 'real possibility that the evidence will be lost to him if the respondent gets wind of the application'.[749]

The order made will usually be in rule *nisi* form, together with an interim preservation and seizure order pending the return day of the rule.[750]

Where the hearing is to be held *in camera* there is some difference in view as to whether counsel must provide a certificate certifying the suitability of the matter for the *in camera* procedure.[751]

> '*(g)* The order should go no further than is strictly necessary for the preservation of the evidence sought to be preserved: it should not, as far as it may be practicable, afford an applicant the substantive relief which he may be entitled to obtain at a later stage after the respondent has had a proper opportunity of being heard. To ensure, as far as practicable, this object, a number of safeguards may be built into the order. These could include the following:'

(1) The applicant should identify as best he can the documents or other information and articles which he seeks to have attached and/or removed.

(2) In appropriate cases the judge should spell out the object for which each part of the order is granted in order to reduce the scope for misunderstanding of the nature and scope of the order.

(3) The order should provide that the order is to be carried out by the deputy sheriff. Neither the attorney acting on behalf of the applicant nor the applicant should accompany the deputy sheriff.[752] An additional safeguard may be the appointment of an independent supervising attorney.[753]

---

749 *Universal City Studios Inc v Network Video (Pty) Ltd* 1986 (2) SA 734 (A), *per* Corbett JA (as he then was) 755E; approved by the Constitutional Court in *National Director of Public Prosecutions v Mohamed NO* 2003 (4) SA 1 (CC) (Chaskalson CJ, Langa DCJ, Ackermann, Goldstone, Madala, Mokgoro, Moseneke, Ngcobo, O'Regan and Yacoob JJ), *per* Ackermann J (giving the judgment of the court) 14E–15A, para [31].

750 *National Director of Public Prosecutions v Mohamed NO* 2003 (4) SA 1 (CC) (Chaskalson CJ, Langa DCJ, Ackermann, Goldstone, Madala, Mokgoro, Moseneke, Ngcobo, O'Regan and Yacoob JJ), *per* Ackermann J (giving the judgment of the court) 13F–15C, paras [30]–[32].

751 *Universal City Studios Inc v Network Video (Pty) Ltd* 1986 (2) SA 734 (A), *per* Corbett JA (as he then was) 755E; however, in *Workforce Group Holdings v Young* [2003] 3 All SA 235 (O) at 243–4, Ebrahim J granted a search order without such a certificate as he considered that the applicant had established the substance of the contents of the certificate in its absence. The editors of Herbstein and Van Winsen *The Civil Practice of the High Courts of South Africa* 5 ed (2009), at 1507–8, consider that this is the better view and it is difficult to disagree with their reasoning.

752 *Memory Institute SA CC t/a SA Memory Institute v Hansen* 2004 (2) SA 630 (SCA) (Harms, Schutz, Cameron, Conradie and Heher JJA), *per* Harms JA (giving the judgment of the court) 633F para [3].

753 Ibid, *per* Harms JA said of the introduction of the search order jurisdiction (at 633E–F, para [3]): '*Anton Piller* orders are for the preservation of evidence and are not a substitute for possessory or proprietary claims.

(4) The applicant should not be permitted to inspect the documents, information and articles and copying or photographing of the material should not generally be permitted.[754]

(5) The applicant will be required to give a cross-undertaking as to damages and should be required to fortify it by way of a guarantee if his financial position does not appear to be sufficient to meet any reasonable damages award under the undertaking.

The defendant may anticipate the return date and apply on notice to discharge the order.[755]

On the return date, the standard of proof the plaintiff must meet is the usual civil standard, proof on the balance of probabilities.[756]

9.3.7 Third-party disclosure orders

In *Kinekor Films (Pty) Ltd v B A Adami Films (Pty) Ltd*,[757] allowing the plaintiff's appeal, the court made an order compelling the defendant to disclose the identity of the source of the films in its possession, of which the plaintiff was the copyright owner, with a view to the plaintiff bringing proceedings against those persons.

They require built-in protection measures such as the appointment of an independent attorney to supervise the execution of the order.'

754 *Kebble v Wellesley-Hood* 2004 (5) SA 274 (W) *per* Schwartzman J at 280G–H, para [9.3] (and authorities there cited): 'When a non-proprietary right is asserted, all that the applicant is entitled to is an order that will preserve evidence that would otherwise be lost. After attachment, such an applicant is not entitled to look at or copy such evidence, nor is it entitled to use such evidence to frame a cause of action or support a cause of action', not following the decision of Wunsh J in *Eiser v Vuna Health Care (Pty) Ltd* 1998 (3) SA 139 (W). The decision of Schwartzman J is plainly correct in principle.

755 *Lourenco v Ferela (Pty) Ltd (No 1)* 1998 (3) SA 281 (T), *per* Southwood J at 289H–290A: 'In the present case the order does not contain a provision that the respondents are entitled to apply on notice to vary or discharge the order: it is simply in the form of a rule *nisi*. This indicates clearly that the respondents are entitled to show cause on the return day why the rule should not be made final. That would obviously include showing that the order should not have been granted at the outset because there was no proper case made out for that order on the papers. The fact that the order does not expressly provide for the respondents to anticipate the return date or provide that they are entitled to apply on notice to discharge the order cannot be an obstacle to the Court entertaining an application on either basis. *Anton Piller* relief is of such a drastic nature that the Court should not adopt an unduly strict or technical approach when a respondent seeks to be heard.'

756 *Sun World International Inc v Unifruco Ltd* 1998 (3) SA 151 (C), *per* Van Reenen J at 162H–163B. In *The Reclamation Group (Pty) Ltd v Smit* 2004 (1) SA 215 (SE), Froneman J stated (at 221B–C): 'Such a general and undifferentiated approach would not, in my judgment, be appropriate.' However, he did not elaborate on what approach to the standard of proof, other than the usual standard of proof on a contested notice of motion, would be appropriate. It may be that the judge had in mind the fact that by the return date the order will have been executed and the documents seized. However, the plaintiff must still establish his right to the order or risk both being unable to use the (*ex hypothesi*) 'vital' evidence at trial and paying the defendant's costs of the application. It is difficult to posit any alternative standard of proof to the balance of probabilities at this stage so as to do justice to the defendant's evidence, as well as the plaintiff's.

757 1976 (4) SA 935 (E; Eksteen, Kannemeyer and De Wet JJ).

Giving the judgment of the full bench of the Eastern Cape Division, Eksteen J held[758] that it was:

> 'clear that the person or persons from whom the respondent had obtained the infringing copies of the films were, in the same way, infringing the appellant's copyright by supplying such films to the respondent, and that the appellant would therefore, *prima facie*, have a cause of action against such suppliers. Such an action however cannot be brought unless the appellant knows who the person or persons are who are acting in breach of its copyright. It says that it does not know who these persons are, and the obvious place to seek this information is from the respondent who must be aware of their identity. To deny the appellant the relief it seeks would in my view not be in the interests of justice but would rather afford an unwarranted protection of the infringers of the appellant's copyright in the pursuit of their illegal activity.'

In *Roamer Watch Co SA v African Textile Distributors*,[759] Cilliers AJ drew a distinction[760] between two types of disclosure cases: first, those where

> 'the applicant seeks to proceed against an unincorporated body or the officials of an unincorporated or incorporated body, and seeks disclosure of the names of the appropriate persons to cite from another person who is possessed of this information by virtue of his being an official of that body or standing in some other similar relation to that body'.

And, second,[761] those where the plaintiff is concerned to obtain the name of a party whom he is unable to identify and against whom he may have a cause of action'. In the latter situation, the plaintiff is seeking discovery of the name from a party who may have sound commercial or other reasons for being reluctant to disclose it. Cilliers AJ stated that in the second case the plaintiff would need to indicate at least the following in the papers filed for hearing:

(1) A *bona fide* belief in his right of action against the party whose name he seeks to be disclosed and that he has reasonable grounds for believing that he has such a claim against such party. Here the strength of the plaintiff's case against the unknown alleged wrongdoer is relevant to the exercise of the court's discretion.

(2) There is no other complete remedy. Another appropriate remedy may consist either of an adequate claim against a party who is known to him in respect of the same damages which the plaintiff claims to have suffered, or in another procedural remedy to establish the same information which he seeks from the respondent.

(3) The respondent is able to supply such information.

---

758 Ibid 939G–J.

759 1980 (2) SA 254 (W).

760 Ibid 281F–G.

761 Ibid 281H–I.

In *Cerebos Food Corp v Diverse Foods SA (Pty) Ltd*,[762] giving the judgment of the full bench of the Transvaal Provincial Division, Van Dijkhorst J held:[763] 'Neither in the Roman law nor the Roman-Dutch law nor in our law as laid down by the Appellate Division is there any authority for an order that a defendant disclose the names or particulars of sources and retail outlets.'

However, the court in the *Cerebos Food* case also held[764] that South African courts had no jurisdiction to make *Anton Piller* orders (defined by the court as[765] 'orders for the attachment of documents and other things can be granted where no right is claimed to them except that they should be preserved and produced as evidence in an intended Court action'). In view of the fact that this decision has been held to be wrong by the Appellate Division (in the *Shoba* case), the authority of the *Cerebos Food* case on ancillary orders and disclosure orders must be doubted.[766]

The better view is that the court has power to make an order requiring a third party to disclose the identity of a wrongdoer.

Further, these decisions all pre-date the Constitution 1996, section 32(1) of which provides in broad terms for a right to access to information:

---

[762] 1984 (4) SA 149 (T) (Boshoff JP and Van Dijkhorst and O'Donovan JJ).

[763] Ibid 168A–B. But the court also held that South African courts had no jurisdiction to make *Anton Piller* orders (defined by the court as, 'Orders for the attachment of documents and other things can be granted where no right is claimed to them except that they should be preserved and produced as evidence in an intended Court action': 168B–C); see the passages at 170H–I and 173E–F. Given that this view has been held to be wrong by the Appellate Division (in the *Shoba* case), the authority of the *Cerebos Food* case on ancillary orders and disclosure orders must be doubted.

[764] Ibid; see the passages at 170H–I and 173E–F.

[765] Ibid 168B–C of the report.

[766] In addition, the decision in *Roamer Watch Co SA v African Textile Distributors* 1980 (2) SA 254 (W) appears not to have been cited to the court in *Cerebos Food*. Further, the Appellate Division assumed, without deciding the question, that a court may order a non-party to furnish information required by the applicant for the purpose of litigation: *Krygkor Pensioenfonds v Smith* 1993 (3) SA 459 (A), where a divorcee was entitled to part of her former husband's pension; he refused to pay her and she applied, inter alia, for an order requiring the pension fund to inform her as to her husband's pension. The Appellate Division held (at 462A–B, Headnote): 'The Appellate Division had authoritatively affirmed that it was entitled to adapt its procedures in the interests of justice; that it could be accepted for the purposes of the present case (without so deciding) that a Court in appropriate circumstances had the jurisdiction to order a party against whom an applicant had no cause of action and who was not a party or intended party to litigation with the applicant, to supply the required information.' This goes further than previous authority in this area by extending the range of disclosure from the identity of a wrongdoer to 'information' generally. Referring to both documents and information, Wunsh J in *Eiser v Vuna Health Care (Pty) Ltd* 1998 (3) SA 139 (W), stated (at 148A–B): 'Our Courts have an inherent jurisdiction to come to the assistance of a litigant who, before proceedings are instituted, requires information from a third party, which is sparingly exercised (*Krygkor Pensioenfonds v. Smith* 1993 (3) SA 459 (A)) and there are a few instances where a would-be opponent has been ordered to disclose documents before the institution of proceedings as in *Durban and District African Football Association v. Dhludhla & Others* 1961 (3) SA 892 (D).'

'(1) *Everyone has the right of access to—*

(a) any information held by the state; and

(b) *any information that is held by another person and that is required for the exercise or protection of any rights*' (emphasis provided).

It is significant that section 32(1)(b) confers on a private person as regards another private person a right to obtain information held by the latter, if required by the former to vindicate or protect a right of the former. The nature of the right is not prescribed but the language used by section 32 is apt to cover private law rights. Section 32 does not make it a condition of its application that the possessor of the information required by a person seeking to exercise or protect a right is a party to litigation or even that litigation should be a pre-condition for the exercise of the section 32(1)(b) right of access against the other person in possession of such information. This provision supports the view expressed above that the court has jurisdiction to make a third-party disclosure order.

Thus, it would appear that the South African courts have power to order a third party to identify a wrongdoer and produce information and documents prior to the commencement of proceedings.[767]

This was confirmed by the Gauteng Local Division in *Nampak Glass (Pty) Ltd v Vodacom (Pty) Ltd*,[768] where the court held that Norwich Pharmacal relief should be recognised and that doing so was 'an appropriate development of our law and the requirements of English law, suitably adapted, serve well enough to provide an effective remedy'.[769]

9.3.8 Anti-suit interdicts (injunctions)

An anti-suit interdict (injunction) is an order restraining the injunction defendant from either commencing or continuing proceedings outside the Republic of South Africa in breach of a legal or equitable right on the part of the injunction plaintiff not to pursue litigation outside South Africa or, conversely, restraining the injunction defendant from commencing or continuing proceedings inside South Africa in breach of a legal or equitable right on the part of the injunction

[767] See also, *Holloway v PADI EMEA Ltd* 2020 (5) SA 172 (GJ), where an English company was ordered to produce the full record, documents and evidence of an inquiry it had undertaken in England into the applicants' conduct in South Africa. In this case, the applicant sought production pursuant to r 53(1)(b) of the High Court Rules at a stage where review proceedings had not commenced.

[768] 2019 (1) SA 257 (GJ), Unterhalter J.

[769] At para 20. In practice this form of order, requiring disclosure of identity or information to assist a prospective plaintiff, had been made by the courts: *BL v FL* 2015 (4) SA 271 (FB), Tsatsi AG, where an order was made against a husband's pension administrator requiring disclosure of financial information so that his former wife could ascertain whether the husband had complied with the court order dealing with their divorce which had made provision for 50% of the husband's pension to be paid to her.

plaintiff to have the dispute between the parties litigated in a jurisdiction other than the Republic.[770]

Recently, the South African High Court has confirmed that it can grant an anti-suit interdict.[771] The applicant and the respondent were parties to a shareholders' agreement, which contained an arbitration clause, pursuant to which disputes arising would be resolved by way of arbitration in Johannesburg. In apparent breach of the arbitration clause, the respondent had commenced winding-up proceedings in the High Court of Zambia; the applicant sought to restrain the respondent from taking further steps in those Zambian proceedings and intended to commence arbitral proceedings in Johannesburg.

In a seminal ruling, the High Court, relying heavily on the decision of the English Supreme Court in *AES Ust-Kamenogorsk Hydropower Plant LLP v Ust-Kamenogorsk Hydropower Plant JSC*[772] and the English Court of Appeal ruling in *The Angelic Grace*[773] held that there is 'no good reason for diffidence in granting an interdict to restrain foreign proceedings on the clear and simple ground that the [respondent] has promised not to bring them'. Adams J also made clear that an anti-suit interdict

> 'does not direct the foreign court to do something or restrain from doing anything which it has no power to do. Rather it acts *in personam*, enjoining the party who seeks to litigate elsewhere from doing so, in order to enforce the contractual undertaking [here, to arbitrate] that that party has given. In acting in this way, it does not presume to tell a foreign court what it must or must not do.'

In the circumstances, Adams J granted the relief which the applicant sought.

It is respectfully submitted that the South African High Court was correct to modernise the principles governing the grant of anti-suit interdicts in South African law. That said, having found that the court could grant an anti-suit interdict, Adams J went on to apply the traditional domestic test governing the grant of an interim interdict, as set out in section 9.3.3.1 above, to determine whether to grant an anti-suit interdict. In circumstances where the South African High Court relied so heavily on English jurisprudence to reach the conclusion it

---

[770] In similar vein, an anti-anti-suit injunction is an order restraining the injunction defendant from commencing or continuing proceedings to restrain the injunction plaintiff from applying to restrain the injunction defendant from commencing or continuing proceedings. The leadings works on this topic are: Raphael *The Anti-Suit Injunction* 2 ed (2019) and Briggs *Civil Jurisdiction and Judgments* 7 ed (2021), ch 28. It is also conceptually possible to obtain similar relief in the context of arbitration, but such relief is outside the scope of this book.

[771] *Vedanta Resources Holdings Ltd v ZCCM Investment Holdings plc* 2019 JDR 1425 (GJ) (Adams J), paras [52]–[58].

[772] [2013] UKSC 35, [2013] 1 WLR 1889 (Lords Neuberger, Mance, Clarke, Sumption and Toulson JJSC).

[773] *Aggeliki Charis Compania Maritime SA v Pagnan SpA, The Angelic Grace* [1995] 1 Lloyd's Rep 87 (Leggatt, Millett and Neill LJJ).

did in *Vedanta*, and in the expectation that the future cases might require courts to reconsider the application of domestic interim interdict principles to anti-suit interdict applications, it may be of assistance to set out the principles which English courts have formulated and which English courts apply when asked to grant anti-suit relief (there, of course, in the form of an anti-suit injunction). These principles are therefore summarised below.

The South African court must have personal jurisdiction over the injunction defendant. The basis on which a South African court may have such personal jurisdiction has been set out extensively above.

The injunction plaintiff must assert a cause of action for relief. Usually, the injunction plaintiff will contend that the injunction defendant is committing a wrong by bringing or proposing to bring proceedings in a foreign court. This will require the plaintiff to characterise the conduct of the defendant as the breach of a legal or equitable right.

A legal right may, and often will, be based on a right not to be sued in a foreign jurisdiction arising out of an exclusive jurisdiction clause in favour of the courts of South Africa. An equitable right may be the right not to be sued in a foreign jurisdiction and may be the corollary of an equitable wrong which is that it is oppressive and vexatious and therefore unconscionable for the injunction defendant to commence or continue proceedings against the injunction plaintiff in a foreign jurisdiction.

The prime example of a cause of action based on a legal right not to be sued in a foreign jurisdiction is where the parties have agreed expressly that the courts of South Africa should have exclusive jurisdiction over disputes arising out of the contract (which can be a substantive contract or a settlement agreement) between them.[774] In such a case proof of the underlying cause of action is likely to be a sufficient condition for the grant of the relief and that good reason would need to be shown why the discretion to order an interdict should not be exercised.[775]

The principal example of a cause of action based on an equitable wrong is where proceedings brought abroad by the defendant are oppressive and vexatious. An example of such conduct is illustrated by the decision of the Privy Council in *SNI Aerospatiale v Lee Kui Jak*,[776] where a resident of Brunei had been killed

[774] The contract may be a substantive contract or a settlement agreement and the dispute resolution provisions may be exclusively in favour of the courts of South Africa or may be in favour of arbitration: *British Airways Board v Laker Airways Ltd* [1985] AC 58 (HL (E)) (Lords Diplock, Fraser, Scarman, Roskill and Brightman), *per* Lord Diplock at p 81C–E and, in South Africa, see, on this last point *Vedanta Resources Holdings Ltd v ZCCM Investment Holdings plc* 2019 JDR 1425 (GJ).

[775] *The Angelic Grace* [1995] 1 Lloyd's Rep 87 (CA) (Neill, Leggatt and Millett LJJ), *per* Millett LJ at p 96, col 2, and Neill LJ at p 97, col 1; *Donohue v Armco Inc* [2000] 1 Lloyd's Rep 579 (CA) (Stuart-Smith, Brooke and Sedley LJJ), where it was stated that 'strong reasons' (*per* Stuart-Smith LJ at para 35) or 'strong cause' (*per* Brooke LJ at paras 59 and 60) would be required to deny an injunction.

[776] [1987] AC 871 (PC (Brunei)) (Lords Keith, Griffiths, MacKay and Goff and Sir John Megaw).

in a helicopter crash and his widow (and her brother-in-law, as co-administrator of his estate), the respondent plaintiffs in the appeal to the Privy Council, had commenced proceedings in Brunei and had subsequently been persuaded to sue in Texas instead. The appellant defendant applied for an anti-suit injunction restraining the plaintiffs from proceeding against it in Texas. The Privy Council allowed the defendant's appeal, held that an injunction ought to be granted restraining the respondents from proceeding in Texas and remitted the matter to the Brunei courts.

Transposing the findings of the Privy Council to South Africa, it was held that an anti-suit interdict would be granted if: (1) pursuit of the foreign proceedings is vexatious or oppressive; (2) South Africa is the natural forum for the resolution of the dispute; and (3) the interdict does not deprive the defendant of advantages in the foreign jurisdiction of which it would be unjust to deprive him.[777]

Other examples of equitable wrongs which may attract an anti-suit interdict are: undermining the jurisdiction of the South African court;[778] vexatious conduct by relying on foreign procedural laws;[779] wrongfully undermining a South African judgment;[780] or enforcement of a foreign judgment wrongfully obtained.[781]

9.3.9 *Mandament van spolie*

A spoliation order[782] is an order whereby a person who has unlawfully deprived another person of possession of a thing is ordered to restore that person to possession of that thing. The remedy is a summary remedy and the person who dispossessed another cannot defend the application by contending that the person who was dispossessed was not entitled to be in possession of the thing in the first place.

The court will restore possession before deciding upon entitlement to possession and the competing claims to entitlement to possession.

---

[777] Lord Goff (giving the opinion of the Privy Council) p 896F–H. That the court to which the application is made should be the natural forum for the resolution of the dispute was repeated by the House of Lords in *Airbus Industrie GIE v Patel* [1999] 1 AC 119 (HL (E)) (Lords Goff, Slynn, Steyn, Clyde and Hutton), *per* Lord Goff (with whom the other Lords agreed) pp 138G-H and 140H-141B.

[778] For example, by commencing bankruptcy proceedings outside the jurisdiction when such proceedings are in progress in South Africa: *SNI Aerospatiale v Lee Kui Jak* [1987] AC 871, *per* Lord Goff at pp 892G–893B.

[779] By seeking to depose witnesses in the US where those witnesses would be subject to cross-examination in proceedings in South Africa, for example: *Omega Group Holdings Ltd v Kozeny* [2002] CLC 132.

[780] By commencing proceedings outside the jurisdiction for declaratory relief designed to frustrate the enforcement of a South African judgment in that jurisdiction: *Masri v Consolidated Contractors International (UK) Ltd (No 3)* [2009] QB 503 (CA).

[781] Where the foreign judgment was obtained through fraud and perjury: *Ellerman Lines Ltd v Read* [1928] 2 KB 144 (CA), *per* Scrutton LJ at pp 152–3.

[782] Peté et al *Civil Procedure* 2 ed (2011) 423–5. See generally, *Blendrite v Moonisami* 2021 (5) SA 61 (SCA) (Navsa, Mocumie and Dlodlo JJA and Gorven and Ledwaba AJJA), *per* Gorven AJA, giving the judgment of the court, at paras 5–7, citing Innes CJ in *Nino Bonino v De Lange* 1906 TS 120 at 122.

The object is to prevent people taking the law into their own hands by taking possession of things in advance of the legal rights to the thing being determined by a court.

The application for a spoliation order is usually made *ex parte* and the plaintiff needs to prove on the balance of probabilities that: (1) he was in peaceful and undisturbed possession of the thing;[783] and (2) he was forcibly dispossessed of that thing.

The remedy is available not only for movable and immovable property, but also for incorporeal property where the possession of the property is characterised as quasi-possession or juridical possession, for example, servitudes.[784] The right to draw water from a particular source has been held to be a servitude in respect of the purported termination of which spoliatory relief is available.[785]

The use of certain supplies of services to property which are incidental to the possession of immovable property is also recognised as incorporeal property capable of quasi-possession and spoliatory relief, for example, the deprivation of a supply of water or electricity where it has been received as an incident of occupation of the property.[786]

It is a defence to an application for a spoliation order to show that the property is no longer in the hands of the respondent. In *Monteiro v Diedricks*,[787] the respondent had left his motor vehicle with a garage for routine maintenance. When the car was ready for collection, the garage sent a text to the registered owner of the

---

[783] The plaintiff need not show that he was entitled to possession nor that his possession was lawful. He need only show that he was in de facto possession: *Zulu v Minister of Works KwaZulu* 1992 (1) SA 181 (D), *per* Thirion J at 187E–H: 'The *mandament van spolie* is a possessory remedy by which a person who has been illicitly deprived of his possession is restored to his possession before the merits of the dispute regarding the lawfulness of his possession are enquired into. An applicant for a spoliation order has to prove that he had possession ... *mandament van spolie* is not concerned with the protection or restoration of rights at all. Its aim is to restore the factual possession of which the *spoliatus* has been unlawfully deprived. The question of the lawfulness of the *spoliatus'* possession is not enquired into at all.' In that case, a Zulu prince failed to succeed in obtaining a spoliation order in respect of a supply of water to his property that had been cut off by the water company. (Although incorporeal rights may be the subject of a spoliation order: *Nienaber v Stuckey* 1946 AD 1049 (Greenberg and Schreiner JJA and Davis AJA), *per* Greenberg JA at 1055–1056 – giving the example of servitutal rights of way, where the holder does not have exclusive possession of the land, but can obtain relief against dispossession by spoliation.)

[784] *Blendrite v Moonisami* 2021 (5) SA 61 (SCA) (Navsa, Mocumie and Dlodlo JJA and Gorven and Ledwaba AJJA), *per* Gorven AJA (giving the judgment of the court) paras 10–12.

[785] *Bon Quelle (Edms) Bpk v Munisipaliteit van Otavi* 1989 (1) SA 508 (A). Cited with approval in *Blendrite*.

[786] *Blendrite*, at para 16; also *Eskom Holdings Soc Ltd v Masinda* 2019 (5) SA 386 (SCA) (Leach, Wallis and Mocumie JJA and Mokgohloa and Weiner AJJA), *per* Leach JA (giving the judgment of the court) para 22 fn 17 of *Blendrite*. Also, *Makeshift 1190 (Pty) Ltd v Colleen Cilliers* 2020 (5) SA 538 (WCC) (Rogers and Cloete JJ) *per* Rogers J, (giving the judgment of the court) paras 46–50. *Bill v Waterfall Estate Home Owners Association NPC* 2020 (6) SA 145 (GJ), *per* Southwood AJ at paras 50–52, 91 and 133 (withdrawal of biometric access to the Estate restrained by spoliation order).

[787] 2021 (3) SA 482 (SCA) (Dambuza, Schippers, and Plasket JJA and Goosen and Mabindla-Boqwana AJJA).

vehicle, a company called Street Talk Trading 178 (Pty) Ltd, with which the respondent was in dispute. The company collected the vehicle from the garage. Subsequent to this the respondent made an application against the garage for a spoliation order. The order was granted at first instance but the garage's appeal was allowed by the Supreme Court of Appeal. The decision was a split decision with the majority[788] holding that the order was not available because the garage no longer had possession of the vehicle at the time the application was made and the minority[789] disagreeing with this reasoning on the facts but allowing the appeal on other grounds.

Correspondence terminating agreements pursuant to which permission had been granted to enter upon leased land do not amount to spoliation.[790]

In *Outdoor Network Ltd v The Passenger Rail Agency of South Africa*,[791] the court considered an application for a final interdict to restrain threatened spoliation. The plaintiffs were lessees of land from the defendants for the purpose of placing advertising billboards on that land. The defendants terminated the leases and threatened to remove the plaintiff's structures. The plaintiffs claimed that they had a right to possession that was at immediate risk of being interfered with. Boruchowitz J rejected the application, finding that the plaintiffs did not satisfy the criteria for a final interdict set out in *Setlogelo v Setlogelo*[792] and in the course of doing so stated:[793]

> '23 Where the *mandament van spolie* is relied on, the possession which must be proved is not possession in the juridical sense; it is enough if the holding by the [plaintiff] is with the intention of securing some benefit for himself. The lawfulness or injustice of the possession is irrelevant. Thus, even a thief or robber is entitled to avail himself of the *mandament*. Also, a lessee who is deprived of the use of and enjoyment of premises is entitled to invoke the *mandament* to have the use and enjoyment restored to him even though he is not a possessor in the juristic sense.
>
> 24 If mere factual possession, irrespective of how it was obtained, was sufficient to establish a clear right, even a thief or *mala fide* possessor would be entitled to obtain a final interdict. There can be no justification for the protection by means of an interdict of illicitly or illegally obtained possession.
>
> 25 The *mandament van spolie* cannot be invoked to prohibit a threatened spoliation; it is only available to a de facto possessor who has been despoiled ...'.

---

[788] Dambuza and Plasket JJA and Goosen AJA, Goosen AJA giving the judgment of the majority. Plasket JA, unusually, giving a separate judgment addressing the points relied on by the minority judges.

[789] Schippers JA and Mabindla-Boqwana AJA.

[790] *Bisschoff v Welbeplan Boerdery (Pty) Ltd* 2021 (5) SA 54 (SCA) (Dlodo, Wallis, Dambuza and Schippers JJA and Mabindla-Boqwana AJA).

[791] Case no 2013/26064 (unreported) 30 May 2014 (Gauteng Local Division).

[792] 1914 AD 221.

[793] Case no 2013/26064 (unreported) 30 May 2014 (Gauteng Local Division) paras [23]–[25]. The dictum in para [25] was applied in *Jigger Properties CC v Maynard NO* 2017 (4) SA 569 (KZP) (Jappie JP, Van Zÿl and Seegobin JJ), *per* Seegobin J at 578A–D para [24].

The plaintiffs could not show a clear right that was about to be infringed and thus did not satisfy the first criterion in the *Setlogelo* case. Neither could the plaintiffs show that they had been dispossessed and thus a spoliation order was not available to them.

9.3.10 Arrest of individuals *tanquam suspectus de fuga*

Rule 9 of the High Court Rules empowers the court, on the application of the plaintiff, to arrest a defendant where the plaintiff believes that the defendant is about to depart or is making preparations to depart from the Republic of South Africa.

In *Malachi v Cape Dance Academy International (Pty) Ltd*,[794] the Constitutional Court considered an equivalent provision to rule 9 of the High Court Rules in the Magistrates' Courts Act 1944,[795] which made provision for the arrest of a defendant *tanquam suspectus de fuga*. The plaintiff, a Ms Tatiana Malachi, was a citizen of the Republic of Moldova who had been recruited from Moldova and employed by Cape Dance Academy International (Pty) Ltd and (the inauspiciously named) House of Rasputin Properties (Pty) Ltd as an exotic dancer. On her arrival in the Republic of South Africa, the plaintiff was required to surrender her passport to her employers. When she subsequently asked for its return she was informed that it was being held as security for the money her employers alleged they had spent on her travel, visa and accommodation. The plaintiff grew dissatisfied with her conditions of employment and enlisted the assistance of the Consul General of Russia to secure an air ticket home. Her employers learned of her intended departure and obtained an order of arrest *tanquam suspectus de fuga* from the Cape Town Magistrate's Court on an application by which they alleged that she owed them approximately R100,000. The plaintiff was arrested and detained at Pollsmoor Correctional Facility for a period of 16 days. On an application to the High Court for her release, the High Court ordered her release and held that the relevant provisions of the Magistrates' Courts Act were inconsistent with the Constitution.

Giving the judgment of the court, Mogoeng J reviewed[796] the history of arrest *tanquam suspectus de fuga* and characterised[797] this form of arrest as one the intention of which 'is to stop an alleged debtor from fleeing this country with the intention of preventing the adjudication of the dispute within it'. The judge found, however,[798] that as soon as judgment is given

794 2010 (6) SA 1 (CC) (Ngcobo CJ, Moseneke DCJ and Cameron, Froneman, Jafta, Khampepe, Nkabinde, Skweyiya, Van der Westhuizen and Yacoob JJ).

795 Act 32 of 1944.

796 2010 (6) SA 1 (CC) paras [17]–[18].

797 Ibid para [21].

798 Ibid para [32].

> 'the debtor would be free to catch the next flight to any foreign destination even if this is done to evade payment and no realisable asset exists in the country, from the proceeds of which payment may be effected. Arrest does not, therefore, ensure the satisfaction of the judgment debt.'

The judge stated[799] that there was no legal basis for the imprisonment of a defendant who has been found civilly liable (referring to the legislation of the 1970s by which civil imprisonment for debt had been abolished and which was considered in the judgment of Sachs J in *Coetzee v Government of South Africa*)[800] and concluded that, 'It is inconceivable that any legal justification can ever exist for putting behind bars a person whose civil liability is yet to, or will possibly never be, proven.'

The judge proceeded to find that the limitation on freedom represented by an order of arrest *tanquam suspectus de fuga* was not justifiable in terms of section 36 of the Constitution. In doing so, he found that: the provisions struck at debtors who could not pay, as well as those who could, but refused to, pay and were thus overbroad;[801] the arrest *tanquam suspectus de fuga* had historically been regarded as an extraordinary remedy and a high financial threshold for a claim had been applied to it which had, over the decades, become devalued to the point where the threshold for an order was R40 'probably the cost of two small chickens';[802] and comparable jurisdictions had done away with arrest and detention that aims to prevent flight or to recover debts.[803]

---

799 Ibid para [34].

800 1995 (4) SA 631 (CC).

801 Ibid para [38], as with those in the *Coetzee* case.

802 Ibid para [41].

803 The judge, in fns 11 and 56, cited various examples of this, including a supposed power of arrest to prevent a defendant fleeing the jurisdiction available to the English courts and a supposed power in the English court to grant security (attachment) for the plaintiff's claim in the form of a *Mareva* injunction. In so concluding, the judge relied on Aird 'The Scottish arrestment and the English freezing order' (2002) 51 *ICLQ* 155. However, it appears that the judge may not have had the article properly explained to him or may have been misled by the article itself in that: (1) there is no existing power of arrest in the English court; the examples cited by Aird are of the making of passport orders where the defendant's passport is retained by the court (or the plaintiff's solicitors) but the defendant is neither arrested nor imprisoned or otherwise detained; and (2) the *Mareva* injunction does not provide security for the plaintiff's claim in the sense used in the article at 157: 'security effective even against the insolvency of the [defendant]', but instead merely preserves assets pending judgment – if another creditor seeks enforcement of a debt prior to the plaintiff obtaining judgment and that debt exhausts the sums subject to the *Mareva* injunction, the plaintiff can do nothing about it.

It would now seem inconceivable that a court when presented with the issue would find otherwise than that rule 9 of the High Court Rules is unconstitutional.[804]

[804] In Peté et al *Civil Procedure* 2 ed (2011) 388, the editors state: 'Notionally at least such arrests are still permissible, although given the Constitutional Court's confirmation of the High Court's finding of constitutional invalidity in respect of common law arrests and arrests under s. 30 of the Magistrates' Courts Act, any litigant who chooses to pursue an application for an arrest *tanquam suspectus de fuga* under rule 9 of the Uniform Rules does so at considerable risk.' It might be added that it is at the very least arguable that advice suggesting that such an application should be made would be professionally negligent.

Chapter 10

SIERRA LEONE

10.1 Jurisdiction

The bases on which a court in Sierra Leone may assume jurisdiction over a cause or matter are statutory in origin.

The fundamental means by which a court in Sierra Leone is seised of jurisdiction over a defendant at the suit of the plaintiff is by service of process on the defendant.

The High Court Rules 2007 ('the High Court Rules')[1] distinguish between service within and service outside the jurisdiction.

10.1.1 Service where the defendant is within the jurisdiction

Civil proceedings may be commenced by the filing of a writ, originating summons, originating motion or petition.[2] The plaintiff in any action should consider the High Court Rules closely before commencing proceedings: certain claims can only be commenced using a particular type of originating process.[3]

Where the plaintiff uses a writ to commence process, he should be clear whether he wishes to serve the writ within or outside the jurisdiction. In domestic cases, the writ must be issued out of the Master's Office or a District Registry and must be signed and sealed by the Master or District Registrar; at this point, the writ is deemed to be issued (and every writ of summons shall bear the date of issue).[4]

Order 10 deals with service of originating process within the jurisdiction. The default rule is that an originating process must be 'served personally by delivering to the person to be served a copy of the document duly certified by the Master as being a true copy of the original process filed, without exhibiting the original of the document'.[5] In circumstances where the defendant, by his solicitor, undertakes in writing to accept service, it is unnecessary to serve originating

[1] Constitutional Instrument 25 of 2007. The High Court Rules were made by the Rules of Court Committee in the exercise of the powers conferred on it by s 145(2) of the Constitution of Sierra Leone, 1991 (Act 6 of 1991).

[2] Order 5, r 1. The High Court Rules then go on to give further guidance pertaining to each specific form of originating process; hence: for writs, see O 6; for originating summonses, see O 7; for originating motions, see O 8 and for petitions, see O 9.

[3] See, for example, O 5, r 2, which provides that, save where an enactment or the High Court Rules themselves indicate otherwise, claims for 'relief or remedy for any tort other than trespass to land', claims 'based on an allegation of fraud' and claims for 'any breach of duty [irrespective of whether the duty is contractual or tortious] where the damages claimed consist of or include damages for the death of any person or for any personal injuries or damage to any property' are expressly required to be begun by writ. A plaintiff should note that no process (here taken to include a writ, judgment, notice, order, petition, originating or other summons or warrant) shall be served or executed within the jurisdiction on a Sunday except, in case of urgency, with the leave of the Court: O 58, r 10.

[4] Order 6, r 7.

[5] Order 10, r 2(1). Order 10, r 2(2) provides that: 'Where personal service of document is hindered by violence or threats or other acts of obstruction of that person or of any other person with or under that person it shall be sufficient service to leave it as near that person as may be practicable.' The rules regarding process and other documents, the service of which does not have to be effected by way of personal service, are contained in O 58, r 5.

process on the defendant;[6] where the defendant's solicitor undertakes in writing to accept service of a writ on behalf of his client, the writ shall be deemed to have been duly served on the defendant when served on the solicitor.[7] Detailed provision is also made for substituted service in specified circumstances.[8] Order 10 also contains provisions addressing particular instances of service, including: service on a local agent,[9] service using a contractually agreed method[10] and service of a writ in certain actions for the possession of land.[11]

Of course, Order 10 also makes provision for the service of process on a body corporate.[12] Such provision as Order 10 that makes for service of process on a body corporate is supplemented by Order 58.[13]

---

[6] Order 10, r 3(1). See further, O 58, r 6.

[7] Order 10, r 3(2). Where the defendant's solicitor omits to give an address for service 'all writs, notices, pleadings, orders, summonses, warrants and other documents, proceedings and written communications in respect of which personal service is not requisite may be served by filing them with the Master': Order 58, r 7.

[8] Order 10, r 5. See further, O 58, r 4: '(1) If, in the case of any document which by virtue of any provision of these Rules is required to be served personally or is a document to which rule 1 of Order 10, applies, it appears to the Court that it is impracticable for any reason to serve that document in the manner prescribed, the Court may make an order for substituted service of that document. (3) [sic] Substituted service of a document, in relation to which an order is made under this rule, is effected by taking such steps as the Court may direct to bring the document to the notice of the person to be served.'

[9] Order 10, r 8: '(1) Where a contract has been entered into within Sierra Leone by or through an agent residing or carrying on business within Sierra Leone on behalf of a principal residing or carrying on business outside Sierra Leone, a writ of summons in an action relating to or arising out of the contract may, by leave of the Court or a judge given before the determination of the agent's authority or his business relations with the principal, be served on the agent. (2) Notice of the order giving the leave and a copy of the notice and of the writ of summons shall be sent by prepaid registered post to the defendant at his address outside Sierra Leone. (3) Nothing in this rule shall invalidate or affect any other mode of service in force at the time this rule comes into operation.'

[10] Order 10, r 9: '(1) Where — (a) a contract contains a term to the effect that the Court shall have jurisdiction to hear and determine any action in respect of the contract or apart from such term, the Court has jurisdiction to hear and determine such action; and (b) the contract provides that in the event of any action in respect of the contract being commenced, the process by which it is commenced may be served on the defendant or any other person on behalf of the defendant as may be specified in the contract or in such manner or at such place, whether in or outside Sierra Leone as may be specified, then, if action in respect of the contract is commenced and the writ is served in accordance with the contract, the writ shall, subject to Order 11, be deemed to have been duly served on the defendant.'

[11] Order 10, r 10: 'Where a writ is indorsed with a claim for the possession of land, the Court may — (a) if satisfied on *an ex parte* application that no person appears to be in possession of the land and that service cannot be otherwise effected on any defendant, authorise service on that defendant to be effected by affixing a copy of the writ to some conspicuous part of the land; (b) if satisfied on such an application that no person appears to be in possession of the land and that service could not otherwise have been effected on any defendant, order that service already effected by affixing a copy of the writ to some conspicuous part of the land shall be treated as good service on that defendant.'

[12] By way of example: see O 10, r 4(2)(c).

[13] By way of example: see O 58, r 3. In addition, the Sierra Leone Companies Act 2009 (Act 5 of 2009), s 514 provides that a document may be served on a company by leaving it at or sending it by post to the registered office of the company in Sierra Leone.

It should be noted that the Companies Act 2009[14] has created an alternative regime for, inter alia, service of process on what Part XVIII of the 2009 Act refers to as 'companies incorporated outside Sierra Leone [which carry] on business within Sierra Leone'. Part XVIII applies to all companies incorporated outside Sierra Leone which, after the commencement of the Act, establish a place of business within Sierra Leone; and to all companies incorporated outside Sierra Leone which have, before the commencement of the Act, established a place of business within Sierra Leone and continue to have an established place of business within Sierra Leone after the commencement of the 2009 Act.[15]

Section 493(d) defines a place of business as a

> 'branch, management, shares, transfer or registration office, factory, mine or other fixed place of business but does not include an agency unless the agent has, and habitually exercises, a general authority to negotiate and conclude contracts on behalf of the company or maintains a stock of merchandise belonging to that company from which he regularly fills orders on its behalf'.

However, a company shall not be deemed to have a place of business in Sierra Leone merely because it carries on business dealings in Sierra Leone through a *bona fide* broker or general commission agent acting in his business as such. Similarly, the fact that a company has a subsidiary which is registered, resident or carrying on business in Sierra Leone whether through a place of business or otherwise shall not itself constitute the place of business of that subsidiary.

Section 485 imposes an obligation on companies to which Part XVIII of the Act applies, within the relevant period of time,[16] to deliver to the Corporate Affairs Commission, inter alia, the full address of the registered or principal office of the company and their principal place of business in Sierra Leone and the names and addresses of one or more persons resident in Sierra Leone authorised to accept on behalf of the company service of process and any notices required to be served on the company.

Process shall be 'sufficiently served if addressed to any person whose name has been delivered to the Commission under [Part XVIII] and left at or sent by post to the address which has been so delivered'.[17]

Where a company defaults in delivering to the Commission the name and address of a person resident in Sierra Leone who is authorised to accept on behalf of the company service of process or notices; or if at any time all the persons whose names and addresses have been so delivered are dead or have ceased to

---

[14] Act 5 of 2009.

[15] Section 484(a) and (b).

[16] Within three months from the commencement of the Act or within one month from the establishment of the place of business.

[17] Section 488 of the 2009 Act.

reside, or refuse to accept service on behalf of the company, or for any reason cannot be served, a document may be served on the company by leaving it at or sending it by post to the principal place of business established by the company in Sierra Leone.[18]

10.1.2 Service where the defendant is outside the jurisdiction

Order 11 makes provision for service of process out of the jurisdiction.[19] However, service out of the jurisdiction of a writ of summons or notice of a writ of summons[20] may only be effected by leave of the court[21] in certain, defined, circumstances.

Order 11, rule 1 prescribes an exclusive[22] set of grounds on which the Sierra Leone court may assume jurisdiction over a person present outside the jurisdiction:[23]

> '(1) Service out of the jurisdiction of a writ of summons or notice of a writ of summons may be effected with leave of the Court in cases where—
>
> *(a)* a relief is sought against a person domiciled in Sierra Leone;
>
> *(b)* an injunction is sought ordering the defendant to do or refrain from doing anything within Sierra Leone (whether or not damages are claimed in respect of a failure to do or the doing of that thing);
>
> *(c)* the claim is brought against a person duly served in Sierra Leone or out of it and a person out of Sierra Leone is a necessary or proper party to the action;

---

[18] Ibid.

[19] Order 11, r 7 sets out in terms the processes or notices of the processes which a judge may allow to be served out of the jurisdiction.

[20] The circumstances in which the writ/notice of the writ is to be served are explained in O 11, r 5: 'When the defendant is a non-citizen notice of the writ, and not the writ itself, shall be served.' The reasons for this are rooted in English legal history: a summons is a command from the sovereign and it was thought discourteous to serve such a command on a person not resident in the United Kingdom and not a British subject; thus, a notice of the summons was served instead (see *Nanjibhai Prabhudas & Co Ltd v Standard Bank Ltd* [1968] EA 670 (CA) (Sir Charles Newbold P, Sir Clement de Lestang V-P and Law JA), *per* Sir Charles Newbold P at 683C–E; the origin of the rule is s 19 of the English Common Law Procedure Act 1852; after the repeal of the 1852 Act, the rule was incorporated into the Rules of the Supreme Court; *Westman v Aktiebolaget Ekmans Mekaniska Snickarefabrick* (1876) 1 Ex. D. 237). Where leave is given to serve a notice of a writ of summons out of the jurisdiction, the notice shall be served in a manner in which writs of summons are served: O 11, r 6.

[21] Order 6, r 8.

[22] Save for O 11, r 2, which deals with probate actions with which we are not presently concerned. See too O 56, r 4(1) which deals with admiralty actions.

[23] The rule of the English Rules of the Supreme Court regulating service out of the jurisdiction prior to 1999 (when the English Civil Procedure Rules came into effect) was O XI. Under the Rules of the Supreme Court 1883 and the Rules of the Supreme Court 1965, which superseded the 1883 Rules, O XI, r 1, provided for service out of the jurisdiction. The terms of the Sierra Leone O 11, r 1 are, for the most part, materially identical to the Rules of the Supreme Court 1965.

(d) the claim is brought to enforce, rescind, dissolve or otherwise affect a contract, being (in either case) a contract which—

(i) was made in Sierra Leone;

(ii) was made by or through an agent trading or residing outside Sierra Leone;

(iii) is by its terms or by implication governed by Sierra Leone law;

(e) the claim is brought in respect of a breach committed in Sierra Leone of a contract made in Sierra Leone and irrespective of the fact, if such is the case that the breach was preceded or accompanied by a breach committed outside Sierra Leone that rendered impossible the performance of so much of the contract as ought to have been performed in Sierra Leone;

(f) the claim is founded on a tort and the damage was sustained or resulted from an act committed in Sierra Leone;

(g) the whole subject matter of the action is land situate in Sierra Leone (with or without rents or profits) or the perpetuation of testimony relating to land so situate;

(h) the claim is brought to construe, rectify, set aside or enforce an act, deed, will, contract, obligation or liability affecting land situate in Sierra Leone;

(i) the claim is made for a debt secured on immovable property or is made to assert, declare or determine proprietary or possessory rights, or rights of security in or over movable property or to obtain authority to dispose of movable property in Sierra Leone;

(j) the claim is brought to execute the trust of a written instrument, being trust that ought to be executed according to Sierra Leone law and of which the person to be served with the writ is a trustee or for any relief or remedy which might be obtained in such action;

(k) the claim is made for the administration of the estate of a person who died domiciled in Sierra Leone or for any relief or remedy which might be obtained in such action;

(l) if the action begun by the writ is by a mortgagee[24] of immovable property situated within Sierra Leone and seeks the sale of the property, foreclosure of the mortgage or delivery by the mortgagor of possession of the property but not an order for payment of any moneys due under the mortgage;

(m) if the action is by a mortgagor of immovable property situate within Sierra Leone and seeks redemption of the mortgage or delivery by the mortgagee of possession of the property but not a personal judgment; or

(n) if the action begun by the writ is in respect of a contract which contains a term to the effect that the Court shall have jurisdiction to hear and determine any action in respect of the contract.'[25]

---

[24] Order 11, r 2 provides as follows: 'In this rule— "mortgage" includes a charge or lien; "mortgagee" means a person entitled to or interested in a mortgage; "mortgagor" means a person entitled to or interested in the property subject to a mortgage; "writ" means writ of summons or notice of writ of summons.'

[25] It will be noted that there is no provision made for the court to permit service of the writ on a defendant who is out of the jurisdiction if the action is one to enforce a foreign judgment; Frimpong Oppong

10.1.2.1 *Procedure*

Order 11, rule 3 sets out the procedure which a plaintiff seeking the court's leave to serve process on a defendant out of the jurisdiction must follow. The plaintiff must make an application to court. This application must be supported by an affidavit, stating:

(a) the grounds on which the application is made;

(b) that in the deponent's belief the plaintiff has a good cause of action;

(c) in what place or country the defendant is or probably may be found; and

(d) where the application is made under rule 1(1)(c) (ie the claim is brought against a person duly served in Sierra Leone or out of it and a person out of Sierra Leone is a necessary or proper party to the action), the grounds for the deponent's belief that there is between the plaintiff and the person on whom a writ has been served a real issue which the plaintiff may reasonably ask the Court to try.

Order 11, rule 3(2) provides: 'No leave shall be granted unless it is made sufficiently to appear to the Court that the case is a proper one for service out of the jurisdiction under this Order.' The meaning and effect of this provision is examined further below.

Where the Sierra Leone court does give leave to effect service, the court's order must 'limit a time after the service ... within which the defendant is to enter an appearance and the time shall depend on the place or country where or within which the writ is to be served'.[26]

The framework within which the courts in Sierra Leone consider the grant of leave to serve out of the jurisdiction is derived from earlier English rules of court.[27]

In view of this affinity with earlier English rules of court and, indeed, in view of the affinity which the law of Sierra Leone has with the law of England generally, it is likely that when considering the matters referred to in this section, a court in Sierra Leone may derive some assistance from the English authorities.

Set out below, therefore, is guidance which is drawn from the English authorities in which the equivalent rules have been considered.

'Recognition and enforcement of foreign judgments in Commonwealth African countries' (2014) XV *Yearbook of Private International Law* 365, 372.

[26] Order 11, r 4.

[27] The rule of the English Rules of the Supreme Court regulating service out of the jurisdiction prior to 1999 (when the English Civil Procedure Rules came into effect) was O XI. Under the Rules of the Supreme Court 1883 and the Rules of the Supreme Court 1965, which superseded the 1883 Rules, O XI, r 1, provided for service out of the jurisdiction.

The English equivalents of Sierra Leone's Order 11, rules 1 and 3, have been the subject of judicial consideration at the highest level in England. In *Seaconsar Far East Ltd v Bank Markazi Jomhouri Islami Iran*,[28] the House of Lords considered the interaction of Order XI, rules 1(1) and 4, of the Rules of the Supreme Court (the equivalent to Order 11, rules 1(1) and 3(2) of the Sierra Leone High Court Rules). Lord Goff (with whom the other Lords agreed) reviewed the authorities on the question what a plaintiff under Order XI was required to show on an application for leave to serve a writ out of the jurisdiction and found that the plaintiff was required to show, first, that the cause of action deposed to in the evidence in support of the application fell within the provisions of rule 1(1) and, second, that on the merits of the case there was a serious question to be tried. On the question of the standard to which these issues were required to be shown, Lord Goff stated:[29]

> 'A judge faced with a question of leave to serve proceedings out of the jurisdiction under Order 11 will in practice have to consider both (1) whether jurisdiction has been sufficiently established, on the criterion of the good arguable case laid down in *Korner's* case, under one of the paragraphs of rule 1(1), and (2) whether there is a serious issue to be tried, so as to enable him to exercise his discretion to grant leave, before he goes on to consider the exercise of that discretion, with particular reference to the issue of forum conveniens.'

The first of these matters was held to correspond to the requirement in Order XI, rule 4, that 'no such leave shall be granted unless it shall be made sufficiently to appear to the Court or Judge that the case is a proper one for service out of the jurisdiction under this Order'[30] and the second was a threshold requirement for the merits of the plaintiff's claim.[31]

Thus, considering the English authorities, it is suggested that, analytically, it would be helpful to determine applications for leave to serve process out of the jurisdiction by applying the following, four-component approach.[32]

---

[28] [1994] 1 AC 438 (HL(E)) (Lords Templeman, Griffiths, Goff, Browne-Wilkinson and Mustill).

[29] Ibid 456H–457B. See also the decision of the Privy Council in *Altimo Holdings and Investment Ltd v Kyrgyz Mobil Tel Ltd* [2012] 1 WLR 1804 (Lord Phillips PSC and Lords Mance, Collins, Kerr, and Clarke JJSC), *per* Lord Collins para [71], confirming this statement of principle.

[30] *Seaconsar* 451A–B, 452A–B, 453D–G.

[31] Ibid 452D–E, 455A–C, 456G–H. Notwithstanding the separate treatment of the English O XI, r 4, in *Seaconsar* and the earlier authorities referred to therein, it is unclear whether the amendment in 1883 of O XI, r 3 (under the Rules of Court contained in Sch 1 to the Supreme Court of Judicature Act 1875) by the introduction of an expanded O XI, r 4, in the 1883 Rules of Court, was intended to produce this result. At the time the leading textbook on the Rules took the view that the amendment to include the wording 'no such leave shall be granted unless it shall be made sufficiently to appear to the Court or Judge that the case is a proper one for service out of the jurisdiction under this Order' was merely an amplification of the previous rule (see Wynne Baxter *Judicature Acts & Rules 1873–1883* 5 ed (1883) 176–7).

[32] As summarised in the *English Supreme Court Practice 1965* (1999 ed) 93–4, paras 11/1/9–11/1/12. The commentary referred to in the Supreme Court Practice refers to three elements; in the text above, the

(1) *The formal requirements.* Has the plaintiff produced evidence satisfying the formal requirements of Order 11, rule 3(1)? This requires the plaintiff in Sierra Leone to set out in his affidavit in support of the application to serve out: (a) the grounds on which the application is made; (b) that in the deponent's belief, the plaintiff has a good cause of action; (c) in what place or country the defendant is or probably may be found; and (d) where the application is made under rule 1(1)(c) the grounds for the deponent's belief that there is between the plaintiff and the person on whom a writ has been served a real issue which the plaintiff may reasonably ask the court to try.

(2) *The sufficiency requirement.* Under the English Order XI, rule 4 (Order 11, rule 3(2) of the Sierra Leone High Court Rules), it was held in the *Seaconsar* case that the words 'and no such leave shall be granted unless it shall be made sufficiently to appear to the Court or Judge that the case is a proper one for service out of the jurisdiction under this Order' introduced a sufficiency requirement (or, in other words, a degree of proof requirement) such that the plaintiff must show that there is a good arguable case[33] that the case falls within one of the gateways under Order XI, rule 1(1).

present authors include four elements, the additional element being the formal requirements of English r 4 and Sierra Leone's O 11, r 3.

[33] In *Canada Trust v Stolzenberg (No 2)* [2002] 1 AC 1 (HL(E)) (Lords Steyn, Hoffmann, Cooke, Hope and Hobhouse), *per* Lord Steyn (with whom the other Lords agreed) 13F, the House of Lords appeared to approve passages from the judgment of Waller LJ in the Court of Appeal in the same case ([1998] 1 WLR 547) including the following (at 555F–G): 'It is also right to remember that the "good arguable case" test, although obviously applicable to the ex parte stage, becomes of most significance at the inter partes stage where two arguments are being weighed in the interlocutory context which, as I have stressed, must not become a "trial". "Good arguable case" reflects in that context that one side has a much better argument on the material available. It is the concept which the phrase reflects on which it is important to concentrate, i.e. of the court being satisfied or as satisfied as it can be having regard to the limitations which an interlocutory process imposes that factors exist which allow the court to take jurisdiction.' In *Goldman Sachs International v Novo Banco SA* [2018] 1 WLR 3683 (Lords Mance, Sumption and Hodge, Lady Black and Lord Lloyd-Jones), the UK Supreme Court further clarified the correct understanding of the test in the *Canada Trust* case. Lord Sumption (with whom all the other members of the court agreed and in reliance on his own judgment in *Brownlie v Four Seasons Holdings Incorporated* [2018] 1 WLR 192) stated at para [9]: 'For the purpose of determining an issue about jurisdiction, the traditional test has been whether the claimant had "the better of the argument" on the facts going to jurisdiction. In *Brownlie v Four Seasons Holdings Inc* [2018] 1 WLR 192, para 7, this court reformulated the effect of that test as follows: "(i) that the claimant must supply a plausible evidential basis for the application of a relevant jurisdictional gateway; (ii) that if there is an issue of fact about it, or some other reason for doubting whether it applies, the court must take a view on the material available if it can reliably do so; but (iii) the nature of the issue and the limitations of the material available at the interlocutory stage may be such that no reliable assessment can be made, in which case there is a good arguable case for the application of the gateway if there is a plausible (albeit contested) evidential basis for it.".'

(3) *The merits requirement.* The plaintiff must demonstrate that there is a serious issue to be tried on the merits of the claim upon which the claimant relies. Lord Goff in *Seaconsar* stated[34] as follows:

> 'The court cannot resolve disputed questions of fact on affidavit evidence; and it is consistent with the statement of the law by Lord Davey that if, at the end of the day, there remains a substantial question of fact or law or both, arising on the facts disclosed by the affidavits, which the plaintiff bona fide desires to try, the court should, as a rule, allow the service of the writ. If this approach is correct, the standard of proof in respect of the cause of action can broadly be stated to be whether, on the affidavit evidence before the court, there is a serious question to be tried.'

(4) *The court's discretion.* Once the above matters are established by the plaintiff, the court will proceed to consider the exercise of its discretion to allow service out of the jurisdiction. The court's discretion is exercised cautiously. As was stated by Pearson J in *Société Générale de Paris v Dreyfus Brothers*:[35]

> 'But of course it becomes a very serious question, and ought always to be considered a very serious question, whether or not, even in a case like that, it is necessary for the jurisdiction of the Court to be invoked, and whether this Court ought to put a foreigner, who owes no allegiance here, to the inconvenience and annoyance of being brought to contest his rights in this country, and I for one say, most distinctly, that I think this Court ought to be exceedingly careful before it allows a writ to be served out of the jurisdiction.'

The exercise of the court's discretion is dealt with under the sub-heading '*Forum non conveniens*' below.

10.1.2.2 *Bases for service out of the jurisdiction*

Given the material identity between Order 11, rule 1, of the High Court Rules and Order XI, rule 1 of the English Rules of the Supreme Court, it is to be expected that English authority will provide persuasive guidance to the meaning of Order 11, rule 1, of the High Court Rules. That guidance is set out, where appropriate, below.

(1) Relief is sought against any person domiciled in Sierra Leone

The term 'person' in Order 11, rule 1 includes any company or association or body of persons, corporate or unincorporated, as well as an individual.[36] Such a person must be domiciled in Sierra Leone: that the person is ordinarily resident there will not be sufficient.

---

[34] *Seaconsar* 452C–D.

[35] (1885) 29 Ch D 239 at 242–3; cited with approval by Lord Goff in *Seaconsar* at 455D.

[36] Section 4(1) of the Interpretation Act 1971 (Act 8 of 1971).

As noted above, Order 11 of the High Court Rules is based on Order XI of the English Rules of the Supreme Court, which regulated service out of the jurisdiction in England prior to 1999 (when the Rules of the Supreme Court were replaced by the Civil Procedure Rules). As originally drafted, the English Order XI, rule 1(1) entitled the English court to grant leave to a plaintiff to serve out on a defendant who was 'domiciled or ordinarily resident in England'. In 1983, Order XI, rule 1(1) was amended such that the court could grant the plaintiff leave to serve out of the jurisdiction where 'a claim [was] made for a remedy against a person domiciled within the jurisdiction'.

There is no reported authority in Sierra Leone on the meaning of the term 'domicile' for the purposes of the application of Order 11, rule 1(1)(a). It is likely, given the similarities between the English provisions and Order 11, rule 1(1)(a) itself, and the general willingness of courts in Sierra Leone to look to English law for the meaning of terms inherited from colonial times, that the courts in Sierra Leone will adopt the jurisprudence applicable in English law regarding the term 'domicile' for the purposes of determining jurisdiction over a person.[37] Under the English Rules of the Supreme Court, 'domicile' was defined as follows:[38]

> 'In general the domicile of a person is in the country in which he has his permanent home (see Dicey, *Conflict of Law*, 7th ed., Chap. 6), the country in which his habitation is fixed without any present intention of removing (Re *Craignish*, [1892] 3 Ch. 180, C.A.; *Huntly v. Gaskell*, [1906] A.C. 56; *Casdagli v. C.*, [1919] A.C. 145). No person can at any time be without a domicile or have more than one domicile. The domicile of origin remains until a new domicile of choice has been adopted (*Bell v. Kennedy* (1868), L.R. 1 Sc. App. 307, H.L.; *Udny v. Udny* (1869), ibid, 441, H.L., *Winans v. A.-G.*, [1904] A.C. 287, H.L.).'

The question of where a company or corporation can be said to have its 'domicile' does not appear to have come before the Sierra Leone courts. However, again considering the similarities which exist between the English Rules of the Supreme Court (and now the English Civil Procedure Rules) and Order 11 of the High Court Rules, it is likely that a court in Sierra Leone would have regard to the English authorities. As such, it may be useful for a Sierra Leone court to be cognisant of the traditional definition of the 'domicile' of a legal person under the early English Rules of the Supreme Court:[39]

> 'A corporation is domiciled where it is registered, if the law requires it to be registered, and if it does not it is domiciled in the country by whose law it is incorporated (Dicey, *Conflict of Laws*, 7th ed., p. 477). A corporation is "resident" and "ordinarily resident" where its central management and control is exercised ...'.

[37] See generally on the meaning of 'domicile', *Dicey, Morris and Collins on the Conflict of Laws* 15 ed (2012) vol 1, r 34, para 6R-001.

[38] Rules of the Supreme Court 1883 (1960 ed) 144.

[39] Ibid 145.

(2) *The claim is brought to enforce, rescind, dissolve or otherwise affect a contract, being (in either case) a contract which –*

(i) was made in Sierra Leone;

(ii) was made by or through an agent trading or residing outside Sierra Leone;

(iii) is by its terms or by implication governed by Sierra Leone law; or

The claim is brought in respect of a breach committed in Sierra Leone of a contract made in Sierra Leone and irrespective of the fact, if such is the case that the breach was preceded or accompanied by a breach committed outside Sierra Leone that rendered impossible the performance of so much of the contract as ought to have been performed in Sierra Leone.

With respect to Order 11, rule 1(1)(d), it is likely that, in the apparent absence of authority in Sierra Leone on the construction and application of this provision, a Sierra Leone court will be guided by the academic and judicial authorities on the construction and application of the (former) equivalent provision in the English Rules of the Supreme Court.[40] Where relevant, that guidance is set out below.

With respect to Order 11, rule 1(1)(d)(i), a concise statement of the law is as follows[41] (and should be adapted substituting 'Sierra Leone' for 'England'):

'(i) **Where a contract is made in England**

11-181

If the parties enter into negotiations by correspondence from different countries, the contract is made where the letter of acceptance is posted. But in commercial transactions today communication by telephone, telex, fax and electronic mail is much more common than by post. It is now well established, following the decision of the Court of Appeal in *Entores v. Miles Far East Corp* (which was approved by the House of Lords [*Brinkibon Ltd v. Stahag Stahl und Stahlwarenhandelsgesellschaft mbH* [1983] 2 AC 34]) that if the parties use "instantaneous" means of communication such as telephone, fax or electronic mail, the contract is made where the acceptance is communicated to the offeror. It has been held that if a contract made in England contains a submission to arbitration in a foreign country, an action in England at common law to enforce the foreign arbitration award is within this part of the clause. The contract must actually be made in England as that phrase is understood in English law. It is not sufficient if it merely says that it shall be deemed to be so made, though this may be sufficient to make it one which is governed by English law. A contract may be made in England within the meaning of this clause although it was preceded by a less formal agreement made abroad, or if it was originally made in England, but amended abroad.'

---

[40] Order XI, r 1(e) respectively: Rules of the Supreme Court 1883 (1960 ed) and O XI, r 1(d) and (e) of the Rules of the Supreme Court 1965.

[41] *Dicey, Morris and Collins on the Conflict of Laws* 15 ed (2012) vol 1, r 34, para 11-181.

With respect to Order 11, rule 1(1)(d)(ii), the authors submit that this provision is, on its face, difficult to understand. It confers upon a Sierra Leone court discretion to permit service of process out of the jurisdiction where the claim is brought to enforce, rescind, dissolve or otherwise affect a contract which was made by or through an agent trading or residing *outside* Sierra Leone.

The difficulty stems from the fact that, again on its face, Order 11, rule 1(1)(d)(ii) seemingly confers upon the Sierra Leone court the power to grant leave to serve process out of the jurisdiction of a claim 'brought to enforce, rescind, dissolve or otherwise affect' any contract entered into anywhere by anyone. In short, and in contrast to the remainder of the provisions set out in Order 11, rule 1, as drafted, rule 1(1)(d)(ii) obviates the need for the claim in question to have anything to do with Sierra Leone at all.

Such a rule seemingly arrogates to the Sierra Leone court a jurisdiction of such exorbitance in contract as to render that jurisdiction unique.[42] It may also be said, with force, that the arrogation of such jurisdiction would likely be considered internationally unacceptable. In this latter respect, it is worth pointing out that the language used in Order 11, rule 1(1)(d)(ii) of the High

---

[42] All the more so in the light of the likely origin of O 11. Section 24 of the Courts Act 1945 (Act 7 of 1945; published as Cap 7 of the Laws of Sierra Leone 1960), conferred upon the Rules Committee the power to make rules of court. The Rules Committee, in the exercise of that power, produced the Supreme Court Rules (originally published as PN 251 of 1947) and which, as amended, are as set out at p 125 of Vol VI of the Laws of Sierra Leone. The Supreme Court Rules were amended by PN 41 of 1969 (entitled the 'Supreme Court (Amendment) Rules'). In 1971, Sierra Leone adopted a new Constitution (Act 6 of 1971, as amended by Act 7 of 1971; 19 April 1971), s 66(1) of which altered the existing division of the court system (Supreme Court, Court of Appeal and then appeal to the Privy Council) so as to establish a High Court, Court of Appeal and a Supreme Court (to which appeals from the Court of Appeal would be made), each exercising power in accordance with the 1971 Constitution (and this division is also found in ss 101–12 of the 1978 Constitution (Act 12 of 1978) and ss 121–34 of the Constitution of Sierra Leone 1991). In consequence of the change brought about by the 1971 Constitution, s 95(1) of the 1971 Constitution itself provided that 'existing law and enactments shall ... have effect after the entry into force of this Constitution as if they had been made in pursuance of this Constitution and shall be read and construed with such modifications, adaptations, qualifications and exceptions as may be necessary to bring them into conformity with this Constitution'. Accordingly, from the date of the enactment of the 1971 Constitution onwards, the Supreme Court Rules had to be construed as applying to the High Court and, from that date onwards (it seems), were referred to as 'High Court Rules'. This explains the title to PN 20 of 1984 – 'High Court (Amendment) Rules' – which amended the substance of what had previously been known as the Supreme Court Rules (but which, as has just been explained, had seemingly now become known as 'High Court Rules'). The 2007 High Court Rules 'revoked' (O 62, r 4) and replaced the 'High Court Rules' which had previously been in place. In doing so, the drafting of O 11, r 1(1) of the 2007 High Court Rules (seemingly deliberately) departs from the drafting of the 'High Court Rules' previously in place. Order VIII, r1(1)(e) of the 'High Court Rules' previously in place, mirroring the English procedural rules, contained a provision materially identical to O 11, r 1(1)(e) of the 2007 High Court Rules but records no trace of any power as broad as that seemingly conferred by O 11, r 1(1)(d)(ii) of the 2007 High Court Rules. Against this background, it must be assumed that the change effected by O 11, r 1(1)(d)(ii) of the 2007 High Court Rules is a deliberate one, such that O 11, r 1(1)(d)(ii) of the 2007 High Court Rules really does intend to confer upon the Sierra Leone court a uniquely wide jurisdiction to permit service of process on a defendant out of the jurisdiction when a case concerns matters to which it applies.

Court Rules is materially different to that used in other jurisdictions in Africa which share a similar legal heritage to that of Sierra Leone. Hence, and by way of example only, corresponding rules in Ghana[43] and Nigeria[44] provide that courts in those countries may grant permission to serve process on a defendant out of the jurisdiction where the action is brought against a defendant to:

> 'enforce, rescind, dissolve, annul or otherwise affect a contract, or to recover damages or obtain other relief in respect of the breach of a contract which was *made by or through an agent trading or residing within the jurisdiction on behalf of a principal trading or residing out of the jurisdiction*'[45] (emphasis provided).

That said, while these points demonstrate the difficulties generated by the wording of Order 11, rule 1(1)(d)(ii) of the High Court Rules, it is still the case that the provision has been drafted using the words that have been set out above. Given that the legislator has used those words, a judge in Sierra Leone could, the authors submit, scarcely legitimately interpret 'outside' to mean 'within' while remaining faithful to the judicial function as an interpreter of the law. Accordingly, whatever the difficulties which emerge in the light of the wording of Order 11, rule 1(1)(d)(ii), until such time as the Rules of Court Committee[46] makes an amendment to the High Court Rules to obviate those difficulties, the conclusion to which one is driven is that the jurisdiction of the Sierra Leone court to permit service out when the claim is brought to enforce, rescind, dissolve or otherwise affect a contract is extraordinarily wide.

From this, one further point might be said to follow. Given the exorbitant nature of the jurisdiction conferred upon a court in Sierra Leone by Order 11, rule 1(1)(d)(ii), it would be legitimate to expect that court to consider carefully the question whether the case is a proper one for service out. While the court is required to do this,[47] it is likely that, at least when dealing with applications made pursuant to Order 11, rule 1(1)(d)(ii), the Sierra Leone court would consider this question at a very early stage when deciding whether to give permission to serve process out of the jurisdiction in such circumstances.

With respect to Order 11, rule 1(1)(d)(iii), a concise statement of the law is as follows[48] (and should be adapted substituting 'Sierra Leone' for 'England'):

---

[43] Order 8, r 3(1)(f)(ii) of the High Court (Civil Procedure) Rules 2004.

[44] Order 6B, r 13(d)(ii) of the Federal High Court (Civil Procedure) Rules 2009.

[45] By way of comparison, in terms of Practice Direction 6B, para 3.1(6)(b), a court may permit service out of the jurisdiction where a claim is made in respect of a contract where the contract was made by or through an agent trading or residing within the jurisdiction. On the wording of the English rule, see *Dicey, Morris and Collins on the Conflict of Laws* 15 ed (2012) vol 1, r 34, paras 11-182–11-183.

[46] Exercising the powers conferred upon it by s 145 of the Constitution of Sierra Leone.

[47] Order 11, r 3(2). The doctrine of *forum non conveniens* and its application in Sierra Leone is dealt with in greater depth further below.

[48] *Dicey, Morris and Collins on the Conflict of Laws* 15 ed (2012) vol 1, r 34, paras 11-186 and 11-187.

'(iii) **Where a contract is governed by English law**

11-187

Although the fact that a contract is governed by English law is an important factor in the exercise of the discretion under this head in favour of the English forum, it is not conclusive. This head of jurisdiction was described as exorbitant in *Amin Rasheed Shipping Corp v. Kuwait Insurance Co*, where the House of Lords held that in the circumstances it was not appropriate for the English court to determine a dispute involving a marine insurance policy governed by English law when the Kuwaiti courts were the forum conveniens. Until that decision it was generally thought that the fact that a contract was governed by English law was in itself sufficient to justify leave. But now the plaintiff has a heavier burden. In *Amin Rasheed* Lord Diplock suggested that, in order to justify leave under this head, the plaintiff had to show that justice could not be obtained by him in the foreign court, or could only be obtained at excessive cost, delay or inconvenience. But it was subsequently held that Lord Diplock was merely giving examples, and was not providing an exhaustive list, of the relevant factors. The court has to consider all factors, and the fact that English law is the applicable law may be of great importance, or it may be of little consequence as seen in the context of the whole case. Thus if there is likely to be no dispute on matters of law or construction, or if the law of the foreign forum is substantially the same as English law, the fact that English law is the applicable law will be of little weight. But where an issue of English public policy arises in relation to a contract which is (or may be) governed by English law, it is desirable that it should be decided by the English court; conversely, where the foreign court may apply its own public policy to defeat a claim based on a contract governed by English law, that too is a reason for the English court taking jurisdiction. If the plaintiff has alternative remedies in contract and tort upon the same facts, he can choose his remedy.'

With respect to Order 11, rule 1(1)(e), it has been held[49] that the general rule that a debtor must follow his creditor and pay where his creditor resides is applicable to a contract whereby one party promises to sell the other party's goods abroad and remit the proceeds of sale to him. Accordingly, in the absence of a definite agreement by the parties as to the mode of payment, when the creditor's country of residence is Sierra Leone, remittance should be made there, bringing the contract within the jurisdiction of the Sierra Leone courts.

(3) The claim is founded on a tort and the damage was sustained or resulted from an act committed in Sierra Leone

Order 11, rule 1(1)(f) is identical to Order XI, rule 1(1)(f) of the English Rules of the Supreme Court.[50] In the absence of authority in Sierra Leone on the correct construction of, and interpretation to be given to, this provision, it is likely that a

[49] *Aboud v Mandi* [1920–36] ALR SL 240 (Tew CJ) 242, lines 11–31.

[50] Rules of the Supreme Court 1965 (1999 ed).

court in Sierra Leone will have regard to English judicial and academic authority when determining when an action is 'founded on a tort'.

A statement of the law is as follows:[51]

> 'In *Metall und Rohstoff AG v. Donaldson Lufkin & Jenrette Inc* the Court of Appeal posed the question of what law is to be applied in resolving whether the claim is "founded on a tort" ... and answered it in part by citing a statement in the eleventh edition of this work that the question concerned the interpretation of a connecting factor, which would always be answered in accordance with the English rules of the conflict of laws. Accordingly, relying exclusively on principles of English law, the Court of Appeal decided that claims based on constructive trust, or procuring a breach of trust, were not claims based on tort...
>
> **11- 216**
>
> In the second part of the formula, "an act committed within the jurisdiction" also extends to negligent omissions such as a failure to give adequate warning about the dangers of a product. In the *Metall und Rohstoff* case it was held that, it is not necessary that all of the damage be sustained within the jurisdiction, or that all of the acts be committed within the jurisdiction. Some significant damage must have occurred in England; or the damage (wherever sustained) must result from substantial and efficacious acts committed within the jurisdiction, irrespective of whether or not other substantial and efficacious acts have been committed elsewhere.'

10.1.2.3 *Submission to the jurisdiction*

Two circumstances must be distinguished under the title 'Submission to the jurisdiction'. First, where submission is alleged in extant proceedings in Sierra Leone. Second, where the defendant has agreed (usually by contractual provision) to submit to the jurisdiction of the court in advance of a dispute arising.

10.1.2.3.1 Submission by appearance

The question of when a party will be taken, by his action, to have submitted to the jurisdiction of the Sierra Leone court has not received a great deal of judicial attention. The answer, such as it is, must be derived from oblique comments in a selection of cases.

At the outset, a party who wishes to dispute on any ground the jurisdiction of the Sierra Leone court should, within the time limited for service of a defence, apply to the court for the relevant order under Order 12, rule 16.[52] In

---

[51] *Dicey, Morris and Collins on the Conflict of Laws* 15 ed (2012) vol 1, r 34, paras 11-215 and 11-216.

[52] The party wishing to dispute the jurisdiction of the court may apply, inter alia, for: (1) an order setting aside the process or service of process on him; (2) an order declaring that the process has not been duly served on him; (3) the discharge of any order giving leave to serve process on him out of the jurisdiction; and (4) the discharge of any order extending the validity of the process for the purpose of service.

circumstances where a party is not allowed to enter a conditional appearance,[53] it would seem logical that a party making an application to the court for an order pursuant to Order 12, rule 16 could not, by so doing, be taken to have submitted to the jurisdiction of the court.

In contrast, a party who enters an appearance and files a defence (and, potentially, counterclaim[54]) to claims made against him is likely to be taken to have submitted to the jurisdiction.[55] Similarly, a party who wishes to set aside a judgment which has been properly entered against him (ie a judgment which is not infected by a procedural error) and who has filed a proposed defence for that purpose will likely be found to have submitted to the jurisdiction.[56]

10.1.2.3.2 Submission by agreement

10.1.2.3.2.1 *Jurisdiction clauses*

The courts in Sierra Leone have, on several occasions, had to grapple with the question of whether to give effect to a jurisdiction or arbitration clause. First, in *AP Mollier v Hadson-Taylor & Co*,[57] the Court of Appeal, relying on *Spiliada Maritime Corp v Cansulex Ltd*[58] provided some general guidance. However, more recently, the High Court in *Leone Mining Co v Euro African Import and Export Co*[59] restated and set out at greater length the principles by which a court ought to be guided when determining whether to enforce a jurisdiction or arbitration clause.

In this case, the plaintiff and the defendants had entered into two contracts in Barcelona: one contract was for a joint venture; the other was a loan agreement.

[53] Order 12, r 14. Though it does not always appear to have been the case that a party was forbidden from entering a conditional appearance: *Leone Mining Co v Euro African Import and Export Co* [2007] SLHC 14 (H Ct) (Edwards J). Given its procedural history and the timing of the judgment hand down, the case was governed by the (English) Supreme Court Rules 1960 (which previously had effect in Sierra Leone and which the High Court Rules replaced). Under the Supreme Court Rules 1960, a party was not prevented from entering a conditional appearance: conditional appearance was not mentioned at all in O 9 thereof. In those circumstances, O 12, r 14 of the High Court Rules would appear to mark a deliberate change from the old practice: now a party is not entitled to enter a conditional appearance in a case governed by the High Court Rules.

[54] *Timis Mining Corp (SL) Ltd v Dawnus (SL) Ltd* [2015] SLHC 58 (H Ct) (Koroma J). In this case, the defendant applicant sought a stay of proceedings. The defendant applicant was an English company which, as it said, had entered into a non-exclusive jurisdiction agreement for the courts of England with the plaintiff respondent. The defendant applicant had filed a counterclaim but the judge did not appear to conclude that, in so doing, the defendant applicant had submitted to the jurisdiction (such that the application for a stay ought to fail). Instead, the judge appeared to treat the filing of the counterclaim as a matter to be weighed in the balance as part of his *forum non conveniens* analysis.

[55] *Samco Ltd v Novel Commodities* [2008] SLHC 2 (H Ct) (Edwards J).

[56] Ibid.

[57] Civ App 10/88 (unreported).

[58] [1987] AC 460 (HL(E)) (Lords Keith, Templeman, Griffiths, Mackay and Goff).

[59] [2007] SLHC 14 (H Ct) (Edwards J).

The joint venture agreement contained a clause stating that the 'parties expressly submit any disputes that may arise concerning the interpretation, fulfilment or breach of this agreement to legal arbitration by the Barcelona Arbitration Tribunal, the award of which they undertake to abide by'. The loan agreement contained a clause providing that the parties submit any disputes 'concerning the fulfilment, interpretation or breach' of it exclusively to the courts in Barcelona. The plaintiff then brought proceedings in Sierra Leone, by which it claimed that the defendants had not made payment of sums due under the contracts. The defendants entered a conditional appearance[60] and sought a stay of proceedings in Sierra Leone,[61] relying on the clause contained in the loan agreement.

Edwards J found for the defendants and granted the stay. Having referred to various English authorities[62] he set out the following list of principles which should guide a Sierra Leone court when deciding whether to give effect to a jurisdiction clause or not:[63]

> '1. Where plaintiffs sue in Sierra Leone in breach of an agreement to refer disputes to a foreign tribunal or court and the defendants apply for a stay of proceedings, the Sierra Leone High Court, assuming the claim to be otherwise within its jurisdiction, is not bound to grant a stay but has discretion whether to do so or not;
>
> 2. The discretion could be exercised to grant the stay or refuse the stay;
>
> 3. The discretion to grant the stay would only be exercised in favour of the defendant only where the defendant can show not merely that Sierra Leone was not the natural or appropriate forum for the trial but there was another available forum which was clearly or distinctly more appropriate than the Sierra Leone High Court.'

Edwards J then proceeded to provide further guidance as to the factors which the Sierra Leone High Court would take into account when deciding whether it was more appropriate to have the case heard in a forum other than Sierra Leone:[64]

> 'A) [The court must] look for the forum with which the action had the most real and substantial connection in terms of:
>
> a) In what country the evidence on the issues of fact is situated, or more readily available, and the effect of that on the relative convenience and expense of the trial as between the Sierra Leone and foreign court;

[60] A decision under the Supreme Court Rules 1960. Conditional appearance is no longer permitted under the High Court Rules: O 12, r 14.

[61] Initially, the defendant had argued that the court in Sierra Leone did not have jurisdiction to try the matter, based on the wording of the joint venture agreement. That application was dismissed and the defendant then changed its legal representation, at which point it put forward the argument based on the wording of the loan agreement.

[62] Including *Cargo lately laden on board the ship or vessel Fehmarn v The Fehmarn (Owners), The Fehmarn* [1958] 1 WLR 159 (CA) (Lord Denning, Hodson and Morris LJJ); *Aratra Potato Co Ltd v Egyptian Navigation Co (The El Amria)* [1981] 2 Lloyd's Rep 119 (CA(E)) (Stephenson and Brandon LJJ and Sir Stanley Rees); and *Spiliada Maritime Corp v Cansulex Ltd* [1987] AC 460 (HL(E)) (Lords Keith, Templeman, Griffiths, Mackay and Goff).

[63] [2007] SLHC 14 at p 2 of the transcript.

[64] Ibid 2–3 of the transcript.

b) Whether the law [of the foreign forum] govern[s] the relevant transaction and, if so, whether it differs from [Sierra Leone law] in any material respects;

c) With what country either party is connected and how closely, in effect what country or places the parties reside or carry on business;

d) Whether the defendants genuinely desire trial in the foreign country or are only seeking procedural advantages.

B) Where the defendant[s] can show by affidavit evidence that [its] chosen forum is that to which the action has the most real and substantial connection, [it] would have established a prima-facie case for a stay of proceedings.

C) Even so, the plaintiff might be able to get the courts to refuse the stay if [it] can prove (the plaintiff is under obligation or has the burden to prove) that there are circumstances militating against a stay for example if the plaintiff would not obtain justice in the foreign tribunal in terms of:

i. being deprived of security for their claim;

ii. be[ing] unable to enforce any judgment obtained;

iii. be[ing] faced with a time bar not applicable in Sierra Leone; [or]

iv. for political, racial, religious or other reasons be[ing] likely to get a fair trial.'

Applying these principles to the facts of the case, Edwards J decided,[65] on the basis that the parties were Spanish, the second defendant was domiciled in Spain, there were no experts in Spanish commercial law in Sierra Leone and that all of the parties' witnesses of fact were in Spain or Belgium, that the defendants had established a *prima facie* case that the stay should be granted. The plaintiff was unable to show the court any circumstances which militated against the stay. Edwards J found for the defendants.

In several subsequent cases, the High Court has followed the approach set down in the *Leone Mining* case,[66] even where, as in *Lidon BVC v Golden Century*,[67]

---

[65] Ibid 6 of the transcript.

[66] See, eg *Transmarine Shipping and Trading Co v The Owners and/or Persons interested in the vessels 'F/V Kawa'* [2007] SLHC 22 (H Ct) (Edwards J). Here, the High Court was not, principally at any rate, concerned with the proper construction, or application, of the jurisdiction clause. The principal issue in the case was whether the plaintiff had a contractual cause of action against the defendant, which question the court answered in the negative. In those circumstances, it is difficult to see why the court paid any heed to the defendant's argument that it was entitled to rely on the exclusive jurisdiction clause (for the courts of Piraeus): the court ultimately came to the conclusion that there was no contract between the plaintiff and the defendant. In those circumstances, it is difficult to see the basis upon which the defendant sought to obtain comfort from a jurisdiction clause in a contract to which it was not a party. Be that as it may, the defendant's argument with respect to the exclusive jurisdiction clause itself failed to convince. The defendant did not allege that Greece was the *forum conveniens*; rather that the plaintiff should never have instituted proceedings in Sierra Leone, given the presence of the exclusive jurisdiction clause in favour of the Greek courts. The High Court rejected this submission: parties cannot oust the jurisdiction of the Sierra Leone courts by a private stipulation in the form of an exclusive jurisdiction clause. See further: *Technoscavi v Civil Engineering Co* [2007] SLHC 40 (H Ct) (Roberts J) and *Samco Ltd v Novel Commodities* [2008] SLHC 2 (H Ct) (Edwards J).

[67] [2018] SLHC 1266 (H Ct) (Koroma J). This is not an easy case to understand. The plaintiffs were companies incorporated in the BVI and Russia; the first defendant was a German company, the second

Leone Mining is not referred to explicitly. While the approach in *Leone Mining* may be criticised[68] on the basis that, at least in principle, it unduly broadens the circumstances in which a Sierra Leone court may refuse to uphold a jurisdiction or arbitration clause, it must be stressed that the practical decision which a court reaches in the application of these principles depends very much on the factual matrix of individual cases.[69]

10.1.2.3.2.2 *Application for service out of the jurisdiction based on a jurisdiction clause*

In the English Rules of the Supreme Court,[70] Order XI, rule 1(1)(d)(i)–(iv), the sub-rule governing service out of the jurisdiction in cases concerned with contract provides as follows: 'The claim is made to enforce ... a contract which ... (iv) contains a term to the effect that the High Court shall have jurisdiction to hear and determine any action in respect of the contract.' This additional provision was included in the English rules in order to reverse the decision of the Court of Appeal in *British Wagon Co Ltd v Gray.*[71]

---

defendant was a representative thereof and the third to fifth defendants were companies incorporated in Sierra Leone. The agreement between the first plaintiff and the first defendant contained a clause by which disputes arising out of such agreement ought to be determined by way of arbitration under ICC rules. The agreement between the second plaintiff and the first defendant contained a jurisdiction clause in favour of the courts of Russia. The agreement between the second plaintiff and the third defendant also contained a jurisdiction clause in favour of the courts of Russia. The judge determined, at [20], that the various arbitration and jurisdiction clauses should be upheld, but the reasoning in support of that conclusion is difficult to understand. It is not, for instance, clear on what basis the court had jurisdiction over the first and second defendants; it is not clear whether permission was sought to serve the first and second defendants out of the jurisdiction; and it is not clear whether the first and second defendants made any application to the court (eg to argue that the court had no jurisdiction or to argue that proceedings ought to be stayed) which required the court to consider whether the arbitration or jurisdiction clauses ought to be upheld. What the case does, however, show is a willingness to hold parties to their contractual bargain and so prevent plaintiffs bringing proceedings in Sierra Leone in the teeth of arbitration or jurisdiction clauses which demonstrate a promise to the contrary. See also: *Timis Mining Corp (SL) Ltd v Dawnus (SL) Ltd* [2015] SLHC 58 (H Ct), where the court was faced with an application by the defendant to stay its proceedings. The defendant relied on the fact that the parties had entered into a non-exclusive jurisdiction clause in favour of the courts of England and Wales. The application was refused.

[68] Kennedy 'Approaches to jurisdiction clauses in Anglophone African common law countries: principle and policy' (2019) 27 *African Journal of International and Comparative* Law 378, 395.

[69] See *Samco Ltd v Novel Commodities SA* [2008] SLHC 2 (H Ct). In this case, the defendant sought to set aside a judgment which had already been entered on the basis that Sierra Leone had not been the *forum conveniens*. Unsurprisingly, this argument was rejected. Edwards J applied (p 8 et seq of the transcript) the principles from *Leone Mining* to determine which forum had the most 'real and substantial connection with the dispute' and determined this to be Sierra Leone.

[70] Rules of the Supreme Court 1965 (the successor provision to O XI, r 2(a), of the Rules of the Supreme Court 1883 (1960 ed), introduced by amendment in 1920).

[71] [1896] 1 QB 35.

Order 11, rule 1(1)(n) of the High Court Rules contains the equivalent provision, viz: 'if the action begun by the writ is in respect of a contract which contains a term to the effect that the court shall have jurisdiction to hear and determine any action in respect of the contract'.

Where the defendant is not present within the jurisdiction and where the agreement between the parties contains a jurisdiction clause in favour of the Sierra Leone courts, an order may be made for service of the defendant out of the jurisdiction.

10.1.2.4 Lis alibi pendens

There seems to be little authority from the Sierra Leone courts on the question of concurrent proceedings concerning the same subject-matter and parties within and outside the jurisdiction.

The Sierra Leone courts may well look to the approach adopted by the English courts in this regard. In *de Dampierre v de Dampierre*,[72] the House of Lords held that where a stay of English proceedings is sought on the basis that there are parallel proceedings in another jurisdiction, the principles of *forum non conveniens* enunciated in *Spiliada Maritime Corp v Cansulex Ltd*[73] apply. Thus in *de Dampierre*, a case concerning parallel divorce proceedings in France and England, the court considered the connections between the parties and the two jurisdictions and the appropriateness of proceedings in France rather than England and concluded that the English proceedings should be stayed:[74]

> 'Here it is beyond dispute that there are very strong factors connecting the case with France, whereas now there are practically none connecting the case with England. Neither party suggests that New York is the appropriate forum. It follows that prima facie the courts of France clearly provide the appropriate jurisdiction for the resolution of the dispute, so that a stay should be granted unless justice requires otherwise. In considering the question, the [judge at first instance] ... did indeed invoke the authority of one of the earlier authorities on the inherent jurisdiction, relying as he did on the much-quoted dictum of Lord Diplock in *MacShannon v. Rockware Glass Ltd.* [1978] A.C. 975, 812. He recognised the undoubted "Frenchness" of the marriage and the spouses, but considered that the wife's absence from what he described as the "harsh" French regime and her presence in the more "benevolent" regime which prevails here, plainly afforded a juridical advantage to her and that, following Lord Diplock's approach, this must outweigh the "Frenchness" of the marriage of the spouses and point to the conclusion that England was the more appropriate jurisdiction for the dissolution of the marriage.'

[72] [1988] AC 92 (HL (E)) (Lords Keith, Brandon, Templeman, Ackner and Goff).

[73] [1987] AC 460 (HL (E)).

[74] Ibid 109E–H *per* Lord Goff.

And:[75]

> 'The weight to be given to what has been called a "legitimate personal or juridical advantage" was considered by your Lordships' House in the *Spiliada* case [1987] A.C. 460, 482-484. The conclusion there reached was that, having regard to the underlying principle, the court should not, as a general rule, be deterred from granting a stay of proceedings simply because the plaintiff in this country will be deprived of such an advantage, provided that the court is satisfied that substantial justice will be done in the appropriate forum overseas. Reference was made, in particular, to cases concerning discovery where, as is well known, there is a spectrum of systems of discovery applicable in various jurisdictions; and the opinion was expressed that, generally speaking, injustice cannot be said to be done if a party is compelled to accept one of these well recognised systems of discovery in another forum. If I follow that approach in the circumstances of the present case, I find that French matrimonial law contains provisions for "compensation" which, unlike our own, place emphasis upon the question whether the breakdown of the marriage was due to the exclusive fault of one of the parties, providing (subject to an important exception) that a party so at fault is deprived of the right to an award of compensation. Such an approach is no longer acceptable in this country, though it bears a close resemblance to the principles applicable here not so very long ago. But it is evidently still acceptable in a highly civilised country with which this country has very close ties of friendship, not least nowadays through our common membership of the European Community; and I find it impossible to conclude that, objectively speaking, justice would not be done if the wife was compelled to pursue her remedy for financial provision under such a regime in the courts of a country which provide, most plainly, the natural forum for the resolution of this matrimonial dispute.'

Thus what is required is a balancing of the various factors in the case to ascertain in which jurisdiction the case is most appropriately decided.

10.1.2.5 Forum non conveniens

The court will not grant leave to serve process on a defendant who is out of the jurisdiction unless it is made sufficiently to appear to the court that the case is a proper one for service out of the jurisdiction under Order 11.[76] Order 11, rule 3(2) seemingly enshrines and gives effect to the principle of *forum conveniens*.

As noted at section 10.1.2.3.2.1 above, the Sierra Leone High Court has provided some guidance on the proper application of the *forum non conveniens* doctrine, largely[77] when faced with applications for a stay in circumstances where proceedings have been commenced in Sierra Leone in breach of a jurisdiction clause contained in a contract into which the parties have entered.[78]

---

[75] Ibid 110B–F.

[76] Order 11, r 3(2).

[77] But not exclusively: *Lidon BVC v Golden Century* [2018] SLHC 1266 (H Ct).

[78] See, by way of example, *Leone Mining Co v Euro African Import and Export Co* [2007] SLHC 14 (H Ct) (Edwards J). See, further, the authorities cited *supra* fns 62 and 63.

Indeed, as the above discussion demonstrated, the Sierra Leone High Court has referred[79] to the principles which English courts formulated and to which English courts continue to have regard when confronted with the question whether a case is a proper one for service out of the jurisdiction, or whether, leave to issue and serve out of the jurisdiction having been granted, the court ought to stay the English proceedings in favour of a different forum.

In case it may be of assistance, therefore, to provide a summary of those principles, they may be summarised as follows. Historically, the English courts seemed always to have held that a major factor in the exercise of the discretion to grant leave to serve out of the jurisdiction or stay proceedings already served out of the jurisdiction was whether the English proceedings were vexatious and oppressive. The expression 'vexatious and oppressive' bore a wide meaning and extended to considerations related to the comparative convenience of proceedings in England as opposed to a particular foreign forum. For example, in *Logan v Bank of Scotland (No 2)*,[80] the Court of Appeal granted an application staying proceedings served as of right in England in favour of Scotland. Sir Gorell Barnes P stated:[81]

> 'Now, it is true that the Courts of this country have not gone so far as to express themselves upon the question of convenience in terms similar to those used in the Scotch cases, though, as I have already noticed, it may be doubted whether there is any substantial difference between the two. Yet it seems to me clear that the inconvenience of trying a case in a particular tribunal may be such as practically to work a serious injustice upon a defendant and be vexatious. This would probably not be so if the difference of trying in one country rather than in another were merely measured by some extra expense; but where the difficulty for the defendant of trying in the country in which the action is brought is such that it is impracticable to properly try the case by reason of the difficulty of procuring the attendance of busy men as witnesses, and keeping them during trial, and of having to deal with masses of books, documents, and papers which are not in the country where the action is brought, and of dealing with law foreign to the tribunal, it appears to me that a case of vexation in some circumstances may be made out if the plaintiff chooses to sue in that country rather than in that where everybody is and where all the witnesses and material for the trial are.'

In *Spiliada Maritime Corp v Cansulex Ltd*,[82] the House of Lords decided:[83]

> 'The basic principle is that a stay will only be granted on the ground of forum non conveniens where the court is satisfied that there is some other available forum, having competent jurisdiction, which is the appropriate forum for the trial of the action, i.e. in which the case may be tried more suitably for the interests of all the parties and the ends of justice.'

[79] By way of illustration, see the *Leone Mining* case: [2007] SLHC 14 (H Ct) (Edwards J).

[80] [1906] 1 KB 141 (CA) (Sir Gorell Barnes, President, Collins MR, and Romer LJ).

[81] Ibid 151–2. This was a decision under the 1883 Rules of the Supreme Court.

[82] [1987] AC 460 (Lords Keith, Templeman, Griffiths, Mackay and Goff).

[83] Ibid 476C, *per* Lord Goff, with whom the other Lords of Appeal agreed (Lord Templeman delivering a concurring opinion). A decision under the 1965 Rules of the Supreme Court.

The English courts will, therefore, refuse leave to issue and serve a writ out of the jurisdiction or (in a case where leave has been granted but the defendant disputes the jurisdiction of the court) will stay English proceedings if England is not the *forum conveniens*.[84]

It would be open to the courts in Sierra Leone to take the view that considerations of convenience are appropriate to take into account when considering whether to grant leave to issue and serve out of the jurisdiction (or whether to grant a stay of proceedings already commenced).

10.2 Enforcement of Foreign Judgments

Under Sierra Leone law, foreign judgments may be enforced either using the common law or the Foreign Judgments (Reciprocal Enforcement) Act 1935[85] ('the Act').

10.2.1 Enforcement at common law

There is an absence of reported authority on the circumstances, if any, in which a judgment creditor may seek to enforce a foreign judgment in his favour pursuant to the common law in Sierra Leone.[86] However, it is difficult to see why an action to enforce a foreign judgment at common law may not be brought in Sierra Leone.[87]

---

[84] See, generally, *Dicey, Morris and Collins on the Conflict of Laws* 15 ed (2012) vol 1, r 38(2) and (3), para 12-007 et seq; r 38 states the modern English law as follows, inter alia: '(2) ... an English court has power to order a stay of proceedings on the basis that England is an inappropriate forum (forum non conveniens) if: (a) the defendant shows there to be another court with competent jurisdiction which is clearly or distinctly more appropriate than England for the trial of the action, and (b) it is not unjust that the plaintiff be deprived of the right to trial in England. (3) In considering whether to assume jurisdiction in any of the cases mentioned in Rule 34 (service out of the jurisdiction with the permission of the court) the court will generally require the plaintiff to show England to be the most appropriate forum for the trial of the claim.' See further *Vedanta Resources plc v Lungowe* [2020] AC 1045 (SC) (Lady Hale, Lords Wilson and Hodge, Lady Black and Lord Briggs) [66]–[70].

[85] Act 11 of 1935. The Act refers to itself as an Ordinance, reflecting the history of its drafting. However, more modern sources, including the High Court Rules (eg O 45, r 1) refer to the 'Foreign Judgments (Reciprocal Enforcement) Act', which terminology has also been employed here.

[86] The only proposition which can be stated with some certainty is that where a Sierra Leone court is faced with a judgment from a foreign country to which the Sierra Leone Foreign Judgments (Reciprocal Enforcement) Act extends (as to which, see s 3 of the Act), and to which Part 1 of the Act applies, no proceedings for recovery of a sum payable under the foreign judgment, other than by way of registration of the foreign judgment, shall be entertained by any court in Sierra Leone (see s 8 of the Act).

[87] In support of this view, it may be said that the Act is closely modelled on the United Kingdom Foreign Judgments (Reciprocal Enforcement) Act 1933, which does not prevent a judgment creditor from seeking to enforce pursuant to the common law where, say, the judgment creditor wishes to enforce a judgment from a country not falling within its scope or the scope of some other international convention or treaty to

Section 74 of the Courts Act 1965[88] provides:

> 'Subject to the provisions of the Constitution and any other enactment, the common law, the doctrines of equity, and the statutes of general application in force in England on the 1st day of January, 1880, shall be in force in Sierra Leone.'[89]

By 1880 the basic English law principles of enforcement at common law had been settled and it is to be expected that a Sierra Leone court will have regard to developments in the English common law that have occurred since that time.[90]

These principles are conveniently set out in *Dicey, Morris and Collins on the Conflict of Laws*:[91]

> 'Rule 42
>
> (1) Subject to the Exceptions hereinafter mentioned and to Rule 62 (international conventions), a foreign judgment *in personam* given by the court of a foreign country with jurisdiction to give that judgment in accordance with the principles set out in Rules 43 to 46, and which is not impeachable under any of Rules 49 to 54, may be enforced by a claim or counterclaim for the amount due under it if the judgment is
>
> *(a)* for a debt, or definite sum of money (not being a sum payable in respect of taxes or other charges of a like nature or in respect of a fine or other penalty); and
>
> *(b)* final and conclusive,
>
> but not otherwise.
>
> Provided that a foreign judgment may be final and conclusive, though it is subject to an appeal, and though an appeal against it is actually pending in the foreign country where it was given.
>
> (2) A foreign judgment given by the court of a foreign country with jurisdiction to give that judgment in accordance with the principles set out in Rules 43 to 46, which is not impeachable under any of Rules 49 to 54 and which is final and conclusive on the merits, is entitled to recognition at common law and may be relied on in proceedings in England.

---

which the United Kingdom is a signatory. In the light of the similarities in drafting, it is unlikely that it was the legislator's intention to remove from a foreign judgment creditor in Sierra Leone the ability to enforce a foreign judgment in his favour where that foreign judgment does not fall within the material scope of the Act.

[88] Act 31 of 1965.

[89] See also s 170(2) of the Constitution of Sierra Leone 1991, which provides: 'The common law of Sierra Leone shall comprise the rules of law generally known as the common law, the rules of law generally known as the doctrines of equity, and the rules of customary law including those determined by the Superior Court of Judicature.'

[90] That the courts in Sierra Leone are cognisant of the developments in the English common law since 1880 is demonstrated by, inter alia, the following authorities: *S v Kamara* [2006] SLCA 6 (CA) (Muria, Stronge and Kamanda JAA) (citing *Campbell v Mirror Group Newspapers* [2004] UKHL 22) and *Richards v Jalloh* [2009] SLHC 10 (HC) (Edwards J) (citing *Hollington v Hewthorn* [1943] KB 587).

[91] 15 ed (2012) vol 1, para 14R-020.

> (3) No proceedings may be brought by a person on a cause of action in respect of a judgment which has been given in his favour in proceedings between the same parties or their privies in a court in another part of the United Kingdom or in a court in an overseas country unless that judgment is not enforceable according to clause (1), or not entitled to recognition according to clause (2), of this Rule.'

In order for its judgment to be enforceable the foreign court must have possessed international competence to determine the cause. As a matter of common law a foreign court will have been internationally competent in the following cases:[92] (1) if the person against whom the judgment was given was, at the time the proceedings were instituted, present in the foreign country; or (2) if the person against whom the judgment was given was claimant, or counterclaimed, in the proceedings in the foreign court; or (3) if the person against whom the judgment was given, submitted to the jurisdiction of that court by voluntarily appearing in the proceedings; or (4) if the person against whom the judgment was given, had before the commencement of the proceedings agreed, in respect of the subject-matter of the proceedings, to submit to the jurisdiction of that court or of the courts of that country.

Among the established defences to an action at common law on a foreign judgment are the following: (1) where the foreign judgment was procured by either (a) fraud on the part of the party in whose favour the judgment is given, or (b) fraud on the part of the court pronouncing the judgment;[93] (2) the enforcement or recognition of the foreign judgment would be contrary to public policy;[94] and (3) where the proceedings in which the foreign judgment was obtained were contrary to the rules of natural justice.[95]

If a court in Sierra Leone were to apply these principles, the authors submit that an action to enforce a foreign judgment at common law would be available to a foreign judgment creditor.[96]

---

[92] *Dicey, Morris and Collins on the Conflict of Laws* 15 ed (2012) vol 1, r 43, para 14R-054.

[93] Ibid vol 1, r 50, para 14R-137.

[94] Ibid vol 1, r 51, para 14R-152.

[95] Ibid vol 1, r 52, para 14R-162.

[96] Frimpong Oppong certainly assumes that such an action is available to a judgment creditor: 'Recognition and enforcement of foreign judgments in Commonwealth African countries' (2014) XV *Yearbook of Private International Law* 365, 369. However, it must be noted that, if a foreign judgment may be enforced pursuant to the common law in Sierra Leone, O 11, r 1, of the High Court Rules does not allow a court in Sierra Leone to permit service of the writ on a defendant who is present outside the jurisdiction where the action is one to enforce a foreign judgment; Frimpong Oppong 'Recognition and enforcement of foreign judgments in Commonwealth African countries' (2014) XV *Yearbook of Private International Law* 365, 372.

10.2.2 Enforcement pursuant to statute

10.2.2.1 *The regime for enforcement pursuant to statute*

As has been noted above, the statutory regime for the enforcement of foreign judgments in Sierra Leone is found in the Foreign Judgments (Reciprocal Enforcement) Act 1935.[97] The High Court Rules contain provisions designed to give effect to the Act.[98]

The overall scheme and particular parts of the Act are recognisable as having been derived from the United Kingdom Foreign Judgments (Reciprocal Enforcement) Act 1933. Indeed, it does not appear that the Act has been amended since it was enacted in its original form, such that it is, in certain respects, out of line with both the High Court Rules and the legal system currently in operation in Sierra Leone.[99] In those circumstances, the Act would benefit from significant amendment and revision. As it is, given the Act's origin, a court in Sierra Leone may refer to judicial and academic authorities on the construction of these provisions of the 1933 Act.[100]

The Act applies to jurisdictions to which it has been extended by Order:[101] Gambia and Ghana,[102] Nigeria[103] and the United Kingdom. That said, section 11 entitles the 'Governor' (which, it is submitted, should now be read as 'President'), by Order, to direct that no proceedings shall be entertained in any court in Sierra

---

[97] The preamble states the Act's purpose as follows: 'To make provision for the enforcement in Sierra Leone of judgments given in foreign countries which accord reciprocal treatment to judgments given in Sierra Leone for facilitating the enforcement in foreign countries of judgments given in Sierra Leone and for other purposes in connection with the matters aforesaid.'

[98] Section 5 of the Act provides that the 'power to make rules of court ... shall, subject to the provisions of this section, include power to make rules for the following purposes: a) for making provisions with respect to the giving of security for costs by persons applying for registration of judgments; b) for prescribing the matters to be proved on an application for the registration of a judgment and for regulating the mode of proving those matters; c) for providing for the service on the judgment debtor of a notice of the registration of a judgment; d) for making provision with respect to the fixing of the period within which an application may be made to have the registration of the judgment set aside and with respect to the extension of the period so fixed; e) for prescribing the method by which any question arising under this [Act] whether a foreign judgment can be enforced by execution in the country of the original court, or what interest is payable under a foreign judgment under the law of the original court, is to be determined and f) for prescribing any matter which under this Part of this [Act] is to be prescribed.'

[99] Where such misalignment occurs, it is brought to the reader's attention in the main text.

[100] In particular, reference should be made to: *Dicey, Morris and Collins on the Conflict of Laws* 15 ed (2012) vol 1, paras 14R183–14-195; A Briggs *Civil Jurisdiction and Judgments* 7 ed (2021) paras 35.01-35.10.

[101] Section 3(1). This refers to the 'Governor in Council', a term which ceased to be useful when Sierra Leone became an independent state on 27 April 1961. It stands to reason that the power to make such an order must now lie with the President, as the head of state.

[102] Foreign Judgments (Reciprocal Enforcement) (Gambia and Ghana) Order in Council (PN 56 of 1945).

[103] Foreign Judgments (Reciprocal Enforcement) (Federation of Nigeria) Order in Council (PN 39 of 1957).

Leone for the recovery of any sum alleged to be payable under a judgment given in a court of a foreign country, where it appears to him:

> 'the treatment in respect of the recognition and enforcement accorded by the courts of any foreign country to judgments given in the superior courts of Sierra Leone is substantially less favourable than that accorded by the courts of Sierra Leone to judgments of the superior courts of that country'.

10.2.2.2 *Procedure for registration*

A brief summary of the principal provisions of the Act is set out below. Pursuant to section 4(1) of the Act, a judgment creditor[104] under a judgment[105] to which Part I of the Act applies[106] may make an application to the Supreme Court[107] at any time within six years after the date of the judgment or, where there have been proceedings by way of appeal against the judgment, after the date of the last judgment given in those proceedings, to have the judgment registered in the Supreme Court. On any such application, the court shall, subject to proof of prescribed matters and save as otherwise provided, order the judgment to be registered, except where, at the date of application, the judgment has been wholly

---

[104] Defined in s 2 to mean the 'person in whose favour the judgment was given and includes any person in which the rights under the judgment have become vested by succession or assignment or otherwise'.

[105] Defined in s 2 to mean 'a judgment or order given or made by a court in any civil proceedings, or a judgment or order given or made by a court in any criminal proceedings for the payment of a sum of money in respect of compensation or damages to an injured party and includes an award in proceedings on an arbitration, if the award has in pursuance of the law in the place where it was made become enforceable in the same manner as a judgment given by a court of that place. Any such award shall, where necessary, be deemed to be the judgment of a superior court.' Were a court in Sierra Leone to be persuaded by the reasoning of the English Court of Appeal in *Strategic Technologies Pte Ltd v Procurement Bureau of the Republic of China Ministry of National Defence* [2020] EWCA Civ 1604 (David Richards, Males and Elisabeth Laing LJJ), it would likely conclude that the definition of 'foreign judgment' does not extend to a judgment granted by the court of a jurisdiction to which the Act does apply which judgment is itself based on a judgment granted by the courts of a jurisdiction to which the Act does not apply.

[106] Section 3(2) provides: 'A judgment of a superior court of a foreign country to which this Part of this [Act] applies, other than a judgment of such a court given on appeal from a court which is not a superior court, shall be a judgment to which this Part of this [Act] applies if – a) it is final and conclusive as between the parties thereto; and b) there is payable thereunder a sum of money, not being a sum payable in respect of taxes or other charges of a like nature or in respect of a fine or other penalty; and c) it is given after the coming into operation of the Order directing that this Part of this [Act] shall extend to that foreign country.' Section 3(3) goes on to provide that: 'For the purposes of this section, a judgment shall be deemed to be final and conclusive notwithstanding that an appeal may be pending against it, or that it may still be subject to appeal, in the country of the original court.'

[107] This is an example of a situation in which the language of the Act and the language of the High Court Rules are out of sync with one another. Order 45, r 2 states: 'An application under subsection (1) of section 4 of the Act for leave to have a judgment obtained in a superior court in a country to which the Act has been or shall hereinafter be extended, *registered in the High Court* shall be made by originating summons ex parte' (emphasis added). In those circumstances, it is submitted that a court in Sierra Leone would read 'Supreme Court' in the Act to mean 'High Court' (as per the High Court Rules).

satisfied or the judgment could not be enforced by execution in the country of the original court.

An application under section 4(1) of the Act shall be made by originating summons *ex parte*.[108] The application shall be supported by an affidavit of fact exhibiting either the judgment or a verified, certified or otherwise duly authenticated copy of it. The deponent should state that, to the best of his belief, the judgment creditor is entitled to enforce the judgment and the judgment does not fall within any of the cases set out in section 4(1) of the Act in which a judgment cannot properly be ordered to be registered.[109] The affidavit must also state, so far as the deponent can: the full name, title, trade or business and usual or last known place of residence or business of the judgment creditor and the judgment debtor.[110] The court may order the judgment creditor to give security for the costs of the application for registration and any of the proceedings which may be brought to set aside the registration.[111]

Subject to the provisions of the Act which deal with the setting aside of registration of the foreign judgment (which are dealt with below), a registered judgment:

'*(a)* shall, for the purposes of execution, be of the same force and effect; and
(b) proceedings may be taken on a registered judgment; and
(c) the sum for which a judgment is registered shall carry interest; and
(d) the registering court shall have the same control over the execution of a registered judgment';

as if the judgment had been a judgment ordinarily given in the registering court and entered on the date of registration.[112] However, this is subject to the proviso that execution on the judgment so registered shall not issue so long as it is competent for any party to make an application to have the registration of the judgment set aside, or, where such an application is made, until after the application has been finally determined.[113]

10.2.2.3 *Setting aside registration*

Where the court makes an order giving leave to register the judgment, that order shall state the time within which the judgment debtor is to be entitled to apply

[108] Order 45, r 2.
[109] Order 45, r 3(1).
[110] Order 45, r 3(2). The affidavit must also deal with all other matters which it is required to deal with in s 4(2), (3), (4), (5) and (6) of the Act.
[111] Order 45, r 5.
[112] Section 4(2) of the Act; O 13.
[113] Ibid.

to set aside the registration.[114] Further, notice in writing of the registration of the judgment, together with the order granting leave to register the judgment, shall be served on the judgment debtor within seven days after registration.[115] Such notice[116] shall, unless a judge orders otherwise, be served on the judgment debtor by personal service, though the judge retains a discretion, at any stage of the proceedings, to authorise or direct some other mode of service (with power to order substituted service or service out of the jurisdiction or both).

Section 6 of the Act provides that a party against whom a registered judgment may be enforced may make an application asking the court to set aside the registration of the judgment in question. As noted above, this application may be made at any time within the time limited by the order giving leave to register after service on him of the notice of the registration of the judgment.[117] Such application must be made by summons to a judge to set aside the registration or to suspend execution on the judgment.[118]

Section 6 of the Act distinguishes between cases where the court, when faced with such an application, 'shall' (ie must) set aside the registered judgment and those where the court 'may' do so.[119]

Those cases in which the court 'shall' set aside registration of the foreign judgment are detailed, in section 6(1)(a), as follows:

'(i) the judgment is not a judgment to which Part 1 of the Act applies or was registered in contravention of the Act's provisions;

(ii) the courts of the country of the original court had no jurisdiction in the circumstances of the case;

(iii) the judgment debtor, being the defendant in the proceedings in the original court, did not (notwithstanding that process may have been duly served on him in accordance with the law of the country of the original court) receive notice of those proceedings in sufficient time to enable him to defend the proceedings and did not appear;

---

114 Order 45, r 6(1). Order 45, r 6(2) provides that, where the judgment debtor is resident in Freetown, the time referred to in O 45, r 6(1) shall ordinarily be eight days after service of the notice of registration and where the judgment debtor is resident out of Freetown shall be 21 days thereafter.

115 Order 45, r 9(1).

116 Which, pursuant to O 45, r 10 shall 'contain full particulars of the judgment registered and of the order for such registration and shall state the name and address of the judgment creditor or of his solicitor or agent on whom and at which service of any summons issued by the judgment debtor may be served.'

117 Order 45, r 11(1). However, O 45, r 11(2) states that the 'judge on good and sufficient cause shown may allow the application to be made at any time after the expiration of the time mentioned' in O 45, r 11(1).

118 Order 45, r 11(1). The summons is an ordinary summons intituled in the manner set out in O 45, r 4; O 45, r 12.

119 Where the case falls into one of these categories, or where the judge decides that it is not just or convenient that the judgment should be enforced in Sierra Leone or for some other reason decides that the registration should be set aside, the judge can order that the registration be so set aside or execution on the judgment be suspended, either unconditionally or on such terms as he thinks fit and either altogether or until such time as he shall direct: O 45, r 11(1).

(iv) where the judgment was obtained by fraud;[120]

(v) the enforcement of the judgment would be contrary to public policy in Sierra Leone;[121] or

(vi) the rights under the judgment are not vested in the person by whom the application for registration was made.'

The court may set aside a registered judgment where it is

> 'satisfied that the matter in dispute in the proceedings in the original court had previously to the date of the judgment in the original court been the subject of a final and conclusive judgment by a court having jurisdiction in the matter'.[122]

The Act[123] provides that the original court will be deemed to have had jurisdiction in the following circumstances:

'*(a)* in the case of a judgment given *in personam*:[124]

(i) if the judgment debtor, being a defendant in the original court, submitted to the jurisdiction of that court by voluntarily appearing in the proceedings otherwise than for the purpose of protecting, or obtaining the release of,

---

120 The equivalent to s 6(1)(a)(iv) of the 1933 Act. The rules related to setting aside a foreign judgment obtained by fraud are comprehensively set out in *Dicey, Morris and Collins on the Conflict of Laws* 15 ed (2012) vol 1, r 50, paras 14R-137–14-145. In *The Conflict of Laws*, para 14-191, it is stated of the fraud provisions of the 1933 Act: 'The provisions with regard to fraud and public policy are the same as the common law rules. In particular, the common law rule that a foreign judgment can be impeached for fraud even though no newly discovered evidence is produced, and even though the fraud was alleged in the foreign proceedings, applies to enforcement and recognition under the 1933 Act. In *Owens Bank Ltd v. Bracco* [[1992] 2 AC 443 (HL (E))] the House of Lords held that the fraud exception in the 1920 Act was subject to the same rule, and indicated (obiter) that the same must be so under the 1933 Act.' *Owens Bank* has not been followed in certain Commonwealth jurisdictions (eg Canada in *Beals v Saldanha* [2003] 3 SCR 416, (2003) 234 DLR (4th) 1; and New South Wales in *Keele v Findley* (1991) 21 NSWLR 444 (NSWSC); but in *Close v Arnot* (unreported) 21 November 1997 (NSW), the Common Law Division distinguished *Keele v Findley* and applied the traditional English standard of fraud in respect of a foreign judgment in a case where the defendant had, for good reason, allowed foreign proceedings to go undefended. A court in Sierra Leone would not be bound by the *Owens Bank* decision.

121 The equivalent to s 4(1)(a)(v) of the 1933 Act. The relevant rule in *The Conflict of Laws* is at r 51, paras 14R-152–14-158.

122 Section 6(1)(b) of the Act. See also *Lewis & Peat Produce Ltd v Pellizzari* [2001] SLCA 8 (CA) (Thompson, Stronge and Cowan JJA). Here, the Court of Appeal considered the question whether a garnishee order made in proceedings which, at their heart, sought to enforce a judgment which the plaintiff had obtained before the English High Court could count as a 'final order'. The garnishee order was made in the following terms: 'Unless sufficient cause can be shown to the contrary by the [3rd garnishee] the rent of $120,000 be made by the [3rd garnishee] to the plaintiff [the judgment creditor] in default of execution might be issued.' In reliance on the English Court of Appeal decision in *Bozson v Altrincham Urban District Council* [1903] 1 KB 547 (Earl of Halsbury LC; Lord Alverstone CJ and Sir H F Jeune P), Tolla Thompson JA, on behalf of the court, adopted (p 7 of the transcript) this test for deciding whether the judgment or order was final: 'Does the judgment or order as made finally dispose of the rights of the parties.' On this basis, the Court of Appeal concluded that the garnishee order was not a final one.

123 Section 6(2).

124 Section 2(2) provides that this expression 'shall not be deemed to include any matrimonial cause or any proceedings in connection with any of the following matters, that is to say: matrimonial matters, administration of the estates of deceased persons, bankruptcy, winding up of companies, lunacy or guardianship of infants'.

property seized, or threatened with seizure, in the proceedings or of contesting the jurisdiction of that court; or

(ii) if the judgment debtor was plaintiff in, or counterclaimed in, the proceedings in the original court; or

(iii) if the judgment debtor, being a defendant in the original court, had before the commencement of the proceedings agreed, in respect of the subject matter of the proceedings, to submit to the jurisdiction of that court or the courts of the country of that court; or

(iv) if the judgment debtor, being a defendant in the original court, was at the time when proceedings were instituted resident in, or being a body corporate had its principal place of business in, the country of that court; or

(v) if the judgment debtor, being a defendant in the original court, had an office or a place of business in the country or that court and the proceedings in that court were in respect of a transaction effected through or at that office or place;

(b) in the case of a judgment given in an action of which the subject matter was immovable property or in an action *in rem* of which the subject matter was movable property, if the property in question was at the time of the proceedings in the original court situate in the country of that court; or

(c) in the case of a judgment given in an action other than such action as is mentioned in *(a)* or *(b)* above, if the jurisdiction of the original court is recognised by the law of the registering court.'

However, the above cited list is subject to the following exceptions, viz circumstances in which the original court shall not be deemed to have had jurisdiction:[125]

'*(a)* if the subject matter of the proceedings was immovable property outside the country of the original court; or

(b) except in cases mentioned in sections 6(2)(a)(i), (ii), (iii) and 6(2)(c), if the bringing of the proceedings in the original court was contrary to an agreement under which the dispute in question was to be settled otherwise than by proceedings in the courts of the country of that court; or

(c) if the judgment debtor, being a defendant in the original proceedings, was a person who under the rules of public international law was entitled to immunity from jurisdiction of the courts of the country of the original court and did not submit to the jurisdiction of that court.'

In addition, where the judgment debtor, in an application to set aside the registration of a judgment, satisfies the court in Sierra Leone that he is either currently appealing, or entitled and intending to appeal against the judgment (which has been registered), the court may either set aside the registration or adjourn the application to set aside the registration until the expiration of such period as appears to the court to be reasonably sufficient to enable the applicant

[125] As set out in s 6(3).

to take the necessary steps to have the appeal disposed of by the competent tribunal.[126] Where the court makes an order on this basis, or solely for the reason that, at the time the application for registration was made, the judgment was not enforceable by execution in the country of the original court, that does not prejudice a further application to register the judgment in the Sierra Leone court being made when the appeal has been disposed of or the judgment becomes enforceable in the original court.[127]

It would appear that where Part 1 of the Act applies to a foreign judgment, no proceedings for recovery of a sum payable under that judgment, other than proceedings by way of registration of the judgment, shall be entertained by a court in Sierra Leone.[128] In these circumstances, the judgment creditor does not have a choice between enforcement via the common law and enforcement via the statutory route: his only option is the latter.

The Act[129] also provides that a judgment to which Part 1 of the Act applies shall be recognised in any court in Sierra Leone as conclusive between the parties thereto in all proceedings founded on the 'same cause of action and may be relied on by way of defence or counter-claim in any such proceedings', irrespective of whether the judgment has been registered or not. This provision, however, does not apply where:[130]

> '*(a)* the judgment has been registered and the registration was set aside on some ground other than that:
>
> (i) a sum of money was not payable under the judgment; or
>
> (ii) that the judgment had been wholly or partly satisfied; or
>
> (iii) that at the date of the application the judgment could not be enforced by execution in the country of the original court; or
>
> *(b)* where the judgment has not been registered, it is shown that if the judgment had been registered the registration thereof would have been set aside on an application for that purpose on some ground other than that specified in *(a)* above.'

Finally, where a judgment under which a sum of money is payable, and the sum of money is not in respect of a tax, or other such charge, or a fine or penalty, has been entered in the High Court and the judgment creditor wishes to enforce the judgment in a country to which Part 1 of the Act applies, the judgment creditor may apply for a certified copy of the judgment.[131]

---

126 Section 7(1).

127 Section 7(2). Similarly, pursuant to s 7(3), where registration of a judgment is set aside solely because the judgment had, at the date of registration, been partly satisfied but had been registered for the whole sum payable under the judgment, the Sierra Leone court shall, on the application of the judgment creditor, order judgment to be registered for the balance remaining payable at that date.

128 Section 8.

129 Section 10.

130 Section 10(2).

131 Section 12. The application shall be made by way of originating summons made *ex parte* supported by an affidavit made by the judgment creditor or by his solicitor: O 45, r 15.

10.3 Interim Remedies

10.3.1 Jurisdiction to grant interim remedies

The jurisdiction of the High Court to grant injunctions is statutory:[132]

> 'The Court may grant an injunction by an interlocutory order in all cases in which it appears to the Court to be just or convenient to do so, and the order may be made either unconditionally or upon such terms and conditions as the Court considers just.'[133]

10.3.2 Procedure for application

Order 8 of the High Court Rules details how applications made by way of motion should proceed.[134] Except where an application by motion may properly be made *ex parte*, no motion shall be made without previous notice to the parties affected thereby, but the court, if satisfied that the delay caused by proceeding in this ordinary way would or might entail irreparable or serious mischief, may make an order *ex parte* on such terms as to costs or otherwise, and subject to such undertaking, if any, as it thinks just.[135] Unless the court gives leave to the contrary, there should be at least two clear days between the service of notice of a motion and the date of the hearing.[136]

The notice of motion itself must be in the appropriate form[137] and it must include a concise statement of the relief or remedy required.[138]

---

[132] Order 35, r 1(1) of the High Court Rules. The High Court Rules are made by the Rules Committee pursuant to the powers conferred upon them by s 145(2) of the Constitution, which itself is an Act of Parliament.

[133] See: *Jabbie v Sierra Leone People's Party* [2011] SLSC 02 (Sup Ct) (UH Tejan-Jalloh CJ; S Bash-Taqi, PO Hamilton, VAD Wright and MET Thompson JJSC). The Supreme Court here made reference, at pp 3 and 4 of the ruling, to the usual terminology employed in this area of the law. UH Tejan-Jalloh CJ stated that: 'It is usual for an interim injunction to be granted pending the granting of an interlocutory injunction, which seeks to restrain the defendant until the final determination of the matter. However, it is equally not unusual for an interim injunction to be granted pending the determination of the substantive matter ... The phrase "interim injunction" has gained currency and is now being used as an equivalent for an "interlocutory injunction".' As such, it appears that the terms 'interlocutory injunction' and 'interim injunction' are used interchangeably (unlike in Nigeria, where there is an apparently rigid distinction between the two: *Kotoye v Central Bank of Nigeria* [1989] 1 NWLR 419 (Sup Ct, Nigeria) (Nnamani, Karibi-Whyte, Agbaje, Nnaemeka-Agu and Craig JJSC). In the main text, the term 'interlocutory' is used to describe all pre-trial injunctions (*ex parte* or *inter partes*).

[134] Order 38 makes similar provision for how applications in chambers should proceed.

[135] Order 8, r 3(1). Any party affected by such order may apply to the court to set it aside.

[136] Order 8, r 3(2).

[137] Order 8, r 4(1).

[138] Order 8, r 4(2).

10.3.3 Interlocutory injunctions generally

The rules governing interlocutory applications for injunctive relief in the High Court are contained in Order 35. Order 35, rule 1(1), which confers 'wide discretionary powers on the court',[139] provides:

> 'The Court may grant an injunction by an interlocutory order in all cases in which it appears to the Court to be just or convenient to do so and the order may be made either conditionally or upon such terms and conditions as the Court considers just.'

An application shall be made by notice of motion and shall be supported by an affidavit.[140] Parties who wish to facilitate the 'speedy preparation and perfection of the order' are encouraged to file a draft of the order sought with their application.[141]

Where the plaintiff seeks an interlocutory injunction,[142] it shall be a precondition to the making of such an order that the plaintiff give an undertaking to the defendant to pay any damages which the defendant may suffer as a result of the grant of the application if it turns out that in the end the plaintiff was not entitled to the order.[143] Where the plaintiff gives the undertaking, the court shall, at the end of the proceedings in which the undertaking was given, assess the damages, if any, which the defendant has suffered and which the plaintiff is liable to pay and shall give such judgment as the circumstances require.[144]

A defendant who desires to oppose the application shall file an affidavit in opposition.[145]

Where an order granting interlocutory injunctive relief in response to an application made by notice of motion is made by the court, unless an application it made to the court to extend the validity of that order, it shall lapse after the expiration of seven days from its being made unless the court otherwise directs.[146]

A party to a cause or matter may apply for the grant of an injunction before or after the trial of the cause or matter whether or not a claim for the injunction was included in that party's writ, counterclaim or third-party notice.[147]

The High Court Rules permit a plaintiff to make an application for interlocutory injunctive relief before the issue or process by which the action

[139] *Sesay v Lahood* [2019] SLHC 39 (H Ct) [9] (Mansaray J).

[140] Order 35, r 1(4).

[141] Order 35, r 1(5).

[142] Or an interim order for the detention, custody or preservation of any property which is the subject-matter of the cause or matter. As to these other types of interim order, see further below, under the heading 'Other interlocutory relief'.

[143] Order 35, r 9(1) and (2).

[144] Order 35, r 9(3).

[145] Order 35, r 1(6).

[146] Order 35, r 1(10).

[147] Order 35, r 1(2)

is to be begun where the case is urgent.[148] In an urgent case, the plaintiff may make an *ex parte* application supported by an affidavit.[149] Where, in response to this type of application, an order is made, that order shall not remain in force for more than seven days.[150] Upon an application by a party affected by an order which has been granted in response to an *ex parte* application, the court may set aside the order made on such terms as it thinks fit.

The Sierra Leone Supreme Court has confirmed on several occasions[151] that courts should be guided by the principles set out by the House of Lords in *American Cyanamid & Co v Ethicon Ltd.*[152] In *Jabbie v Sierra Leone People's Party*,[153] for example, Tejan-Jalloh CJ stated:[154]

> 'The purpose of an interim or interlocutory injunction, therefore, is to preserve the status quo until the substantive matter is tried and determined. This application seeks to do just that – a temporary relief to maintain the status quo until the trial and the determination of the action.
>
> The principle under which the Court will exercise its undoubted discretion to grant such relief is well established in the celebrated case of [*American Cyanamid*] – 'The Court must be satisfied that there is a serious not a frivolous issue for trial.
>
> The court should also consider the balance of convenience as the nature of the injury on the one hand, which the defendant will suffer, if the injunction is granted and turns out that the defendant was right and the injury which the plaintiff, on the other hand, will sustain, if the injunction was refused and it turns out that he was right.[155]
>
> There is no onus [on] the plaintiff to make out a prima facie case before an interlocutory injunction is granted.'

---

148 Order 35, r 1(3).

149 Order 35, r 1(7). Order 35, r 1(8) goes on to provide: 'An application so made shall not be granted unless the applicant gives sufficient reasons for making it *ex parte* and specifies some irreparable damage or mischief which will be caused to the plaintiff if he proceeds in the ordinary manner.' The inconsistently employed terminology has the potential to confuse: the High Court Rules must, in this regard, proceed on the premise that it is the plaintiff who is seeking interlocutory injunctive relief.

150 Order 35, r 1(9).

151 *Jabbie v Sierra Leone People's Party* [2011] SLSC 02 (Sup Ct) (Tejan-Jalloh CJ; Bash-Taqi, Hamilton, Wright and Thompson JJSC); *PC Sheriff II v Attorney General* [2011] SLSC 05 (Sup Ct) (Tejan-Jalloh CJ; Bash-Taqi, Hamilton, Wright and Thompson JJSC); and *Kamara & Kamara v 2 others* [2011] SLSC 07 (Sup Ct) (Tejan-Jalloh CJ; Bash-Taqi, Hamilton, Wright and Thompson JJSC). The Court of Appeal has recently applied this approach in *Alusine Bangura v SLPP Chairman & Leader* [2017] SLCA 1181 (Flynn, Sesay and Halloway JJA).

152 [1975] AC 396 (HL (E)) (Lord Diplock, Viscount Dilhorne and Lords Cross, Salmon and Edmund-Davies).

153 [2011] SLSC 02 (Tejan-Jalloh CJ; Bash-Taqi, Hamilton, Wright and Thompson JJSC).

154 Ibid 8.

155 In *Kamara*, at p 2 of the ruling, Tejan Jalloh CJ provided the following further guidance: 'An interlocutory injunction is an equitable relief which is normally granted at the discretion of the court. Generally, it is granted where an irreparable injury would otherwise be caused to the applicant. Such irreparable injury must be substantial and [one] which could never be "adequately remedied or atoned for by damages". See Halsbury['s] *Laws of England* 2nd edition, volume 18.'

In *American Cyanamid*, Lord Diplock gave the leading judgment (with which the other Lords agreed). The speech of Lord Diplock is generally taken as establishing a test comprising two elements:

(1) 'The court ... must be satisfied that the claim is not frivolous or vexatious; in other words, that there is a serious issue to be tried';[156]

'... unless the material available to the court at the hearing of the application for an interlocutory injunction fails to disclose that the plaintiff has any real prospect of succeeding in his claim for a permanent injunction at the trial, the court should go on to consider whether the balance of convenience lies in favour of granting or refusing the interlocutory relief that is sought';[157]

(2) On the balance of convenience:[158]

'... the governing principle is that the court should first consider whether, if the plaintiff were to succeed at the trial in establishing his right to a permanent injunction, he would be adequately compensated by an award of damages for the loss he would have sustained as a result of the defendant's continuing to do what was sought to be enjoined between the time of the application and the time of the trial. If damages in the measure recoverable at common law would be adequate remedy and the defendant would be in a financial position to pay them, no interlocutory injunction should normally be granted, however strong the plaintiff's claim appeared to be at that stage. If, on the other hand, damages would not provide an adequate remedy for the plaintiff in the event of his succeeding at the trial, the court should then consider whether, on the contrary hypothesis that the defendant were to succeed at the trial in establishing his right to do that which was sought to be enjoined, he would be adequately compensated under the plaintiff's undertaking as to damages for the loss he would have sustained by being prevented from doing so between the time of the application and the time of the trial. If damages in the measure recoverable under such an undertaking would be an adequate remedy and the plaintiff would be in a financial position to pay them, there would be no reason upon this ground to refuse an interlocutory injunction.

It is where there is doubt as to the adequacy of the respective remedies in damages available to either party or to both, that the question of balance of convenience arises. It would be unwise to attempt even to list all the various matters which may need to be taken into consideration in deciding where the balance lies, let alone to suggest the relative weight to be attached to them. These will vary from case to case.

Where other factors appear to be evenly balanced it is a counsel of prudence to take such measures as are calculated to preserve the status quo.'

These, then, are the principles which a court in Sierra Leone will follow in considering whether to grant an interlocutory injunction.[159]

---

[156] [1975] AC 396 (HL (E)) 407G.

[157] Ibid 408A–B.

[158] Ibid 408B–G.

[159] As demonstrated recently by the decision in *Sesay v Lahood* [2019] SLHC 39 at [9] and *Augustine Marrah v Sierra Leone Bar Association* [2019] SLHC 3 (H Ct) (King J, 28 May 2019).

10.3.4 Freezing orders

Although judicial authority directly in point is sparse, it seems that a freezing injunction by way of court order (sometimes called a *Mareva* injunction)[160] is a remedy available in Sierra Leone.[161]

It is likely that the court in Sierra Leone, when considering whether to make such an order, would take cognisance of the guidelines set out by the English Court of Appeal in *Mareva Compania Naviera v International Bulk Carriers SA*,[162] where Lord Denning[163] stated:

> 'In my opinion that principle applies to a creditor who has a right to be paid the debt owing to him, even before he has established his right by getting judgment for it. If it appears that the debt is due and owing, and there is a danger that the debtor may dispose of his assets so as to defeat it before judgment, the court has jurisdiction in a proper case to grant an interlocutory judgment so as to prevent him disposing of those assets.'

In *Third Chandris Shipping Corp v Unimarine SA*,[164] Lord Denning MR[165] provided further guidance:

> 'The guidelines
>
> In endeavouring to set out some guidelines, I have had recourse to the practice of many other countries which have been put before us. They have been most helpful. These are the points which those who apply for it should bear in mind. (i) The Plaintiff should make full and frank disclosure of all matters in his knowledge which are material for the judge to know... (ii) The Plaintiff should give particulars of his claim against the Defendant, stating the ground of his claim and the amount thereof, and fairly stating the points made against it by the Defendant. (iii) The Plaintiff should give some grounds for believing that the Defendants have assets here ...The existence of a bank account in England is enough, whether it is in overdraft or not. (iv) The Plaintiff should give some grounds for believing that there is a risk of the assets being removed before the judgment or award is satisfied. The mere fact that the Defendant is abroad is not by itself sufficient. No one would wish any reputable foreign company to be plagued with a *Mareva* injunction simply because it has agreed to London arbitration. But there are some foreign companies whose structure invites comment. We often see in this court a corporation which is registered in a country where the company law is so loose that nothing is known about it, where it does no work

---

[160] After the title of the English authority in which such orders were first approved at appellate level: *Mareva Compania Naviera SA v International Bulkcarriers SA* [1975] 2 Lloyd's Rep 509 (CA) (Lord Denning MR, Ormrod and Roskill LJJ).

[161] See *Conteh v The Vessels F/V Nangbeto, F/V Amou, F/V Amoulome, F/V Kawa and F/V Frosty and The Owners and All Interested in These Vessels* [2007] SLHC 1 (H Ct) (Edwards J). At p 12 of the transcript, Edwards J refers to 'mareva injunctions'. The Sierra Leone court may make an order where it is 'just or convenient' to do so (O 35, r 1(1)) which is the same basis on which the English courts have jurisdiction to make freezing orders.

[162] [1980] 1 All ER 213 (CA) (Lord Denning MR, Roskill and Ormrod LJJ).

[163] Ibid 215b.

[164] [1979] 2 All ER 972 (CA) (Lord Denning MR, Lawton and Cumming-Bruce LJJ).

[165] Ibid 984g–985d.

> and has no officers and no assets. Nothing can be found out about the membership, or its control, or its assets, or the charge on them. Judgment cannot be enforced against it. There is no reciprocal enforcement of judgments. It is nothing more than a name grasped from the air, as elusive as the Cheshire cat. In such cases the very fact of incorporation there gives some ground for believing there is a risk that, if judgment or an award is obtained, it may go unsatisfied. Such registration of such companies may carry many advantages to the individuals who control them but they may suffer the disadvantage of having a *Mareva* injunction granted against them. The giving of security for a debt is a small price to pay for the convenience of such a registration. Security would certainly be required in New York. So also it may be in London. Other grounds may be shown for believing there is a risk. But some such should be shown. (v) The Plaintiffs must, of course, give an undertaking in damages, in case they fail in their claim or the injunction turns out to be unjustified. In a suitable case this should be supported by a bond or security: and the injunction only granted on it being given, or undertaken to be given.'

10.3.5 Search and seize orders

There is no reported authority in Sierra Leone on the question whether a court will grant an order requiring one party to admit another party to premises in order that the second party be entitled to search for documents or other movable property and to take away such documents and movable property and retain them for the time being. An English court may grant such an order.[166] It remains to be seen whether, following English authorities (which courts in Sierra Leone are apt to do), this form of relief is developed in Sierra Leone in due course. It is submitted that it is likely, should the opportunity present itself, a Sierra Leone court would recognise this form of relief.[167]

In England, this form of relief is usually referred to as an *Anton Piller* order. Such relief was available at common law[168] and is granted in cases in which the preconditions set out by Ormrod LJ in the *Anton Piller* case itself have been satisfied. Those pre-conditions are as follows:[169]

> 'There are three essential pre-conditions for the making of such an order, in my judgment. First, there must be an extremely strong prima facie case. Secondly, the damage, potential or actual, must be very serious for the [plaintiff]. Thirdly, there must be clear evidence that the defendants have in their possession incriminating documents or things, and that there is a real possibility that they may destroy such material before any application inter partes can be made.'

---

[166] *Anton Piller KG v Manufacturing Processes Ltd* [1976] 1 Ch 65 (CA) (Lord Denning MR, Ormrod and Shaw LJJ).

[167] The Sierra Leone court may make an order where it is 'just or convenient' to do so (O 35, r 1(1)) which is the same basis on which the English courts have jurisdiction to make *Anton Piller* orders.

[168] The English court's powers to make such orders is now on a statutory basis.

[169] At 62A.

10.3.6 Third-party disclosure orders

There is no authority on the question whether a Sierra Leone court may, apart from the established post-issuing of proceedings and pre-trial procedures whereby a third party may be served with a witness summons requiring his attendance at court in order to give evidence and/or to produce documents,[170] order a person not a party to the proceedings to give disclosure. Such a power is available to the English courts in the form of a *Norwich Pharmacal* order[171] whereby an innocent third party caught up in a tort may be ordered to disclose the name or other identity of the tortfeasor.

The statutory basis on which a Sierra Leone court may grant injunctions is very similar to the basis an English court may grant injunctions[172] and it is submitted that it is likely, if invited to do so, a Sierra Leone court would have regard to the English authorities on the making on third-party disclosure orders and would consider itself empowered to make such an order.

In *Norwich Pharmacal Co v Customs and Excise Comrs*, the English House of Lords[173] set out the following principle:

> 'That if through no fault of his own a person gets mixed up in the tortious acts of others so as to facilitate their wrong-doing he may incur no personal liability but he comes under a duty to assist the person who has been wronged by giving him full information and disclosing the identity of the wrongdoers... [It does not matter] whether he became so mixed up by voluntary action on his part or because it was his duty to do what he did. It may be that if this causes him expense the person seeking the information ought to reimburse him. But justice requires that he should co-operate in righting the wrong if he unwittingly facilitated its perpetration.'

More recent authority[174] has clarified the conditions which the plaintiff must satisfy in order to obtain such relief:

> 'The three conditions to be satisfied for the court to exercise the power to order *Norwich Pharmacal* relief are:
>
> i) a wrong must have been carried out, or arguably carried out, by an ultimate wrongdoer;
>
> ii) there must be the need for an order to enable action to be brought against the ultimate wrongdoer; and

[170] Federal High Court Rules 2009, O 20, rr 8 and 15.

[171] *Norwich Pharmacal Co v Customs & Excise Comrs* [1974] AC 133 (HL(E)) (Lords Reid and Morris, Viscount Dilhorne and Lords Cross and Kilbrandon).

[172] The Sierra Leone court may make an order where it is 'just or convenient' to do so (O 35, r 1(1)) which is the same basis on which the English courts have jurisdiction to make third party disclosure orders.

[173] Ibid 175, *per* Lord Reid.

[174] *Ramilos Trading Ltd v Valentin Mikhaylovich Buyanovsky* [2016] EWHC 3175 (Comm) (H Ct) (Flaux J), citing, para [11], *Mitsui v Nexen Petroleum* [2005] EWHC 625 (Ch); [2005] 3 All ER 511 at [21] (H Ct) (Lightman J).

iii) the person against whom the order is sought must: (a) be mixed up in so as to have facilitated the wrongdoing; and (b) be able or likely to be able to provide the information necessary to enable the ultimate wrongdoer to be sued.'

If the plaintiff satisfies all of those conditions, the English court will then go on to exercise its discretion. In doing so, it must keep in mind the proper scope of *Norwich Pharmacal* relief: the jurisdiction cannot be used for wide-ranging discovery or the gathering of evidence, but is strictly confined to necessary information.[175]

10.3.7 Anti-suit injunctions

An anti-suit injunction is an order restraining the injunction defendant from either commencing or continuing proceedings outside Sierra Leone in breach of a legal or equitable right on the part of the injunction plaintiff not to pursue litigation outside Sierra Leone or, conversely, restraining the injunction defendant from commencing or continuing proceedings inside Sierra Leone in breach of a legal or equitable right on the part of the injunction plaintiff to have the dispute between the parties litigated in a jurisdiction other than Sierra Leone.[176]

There is no reported judicial authority in Sierra Leone on whether or not an anti-suit injunction is a remedy available to the courts in Sierra Leone.[177] However, as noted at section 10.3.1 above, the jurisdiction of the High Court to grant injunctions is statutory and may be exercised in all cases where it is 'just and convenient' to do so.

This is the same identical basis to that upon which English courts exercise the jurisdiction to make anti-suit injunctions and, given the affinity of Sierra Leone's law with English law in this regard,[178] it is to be anticipated that a court in Sierra Leone before which an application is brought for an anti-suit injunction will

---

[175] *Ramilos Trading Ltd v Valentin Mikhaylovich Buyanovsky* [2016] EWHC 3175 (Comm) (H Ct) (Flaux J) para [46].

[176] In similar vein, an anti-anti-suit injunction is an order restraining the injunction defendant from commencing or continuing proceedings to restrain the injunction plaintiff from applying to restrain the injunction defendant from commencing or continuing proceedings. The leading works on this topic are: Raphael *The Anti-Suit Injunction* 2 ed (2019) and Briggs *Civil Jurisdiction and Judgments* 7 ed (2021), ch 28. It is also conceptually possible to obtain similar relief in the context of arbitration but such relief is outside the scope of this work.

[177] That said, in *Timis Mining Corp (SL) Ltd v Dawnus (SL) Ltd* [2016] SLHC 1 (H Ct) (Koroma J) the court did refer, but without comment, to proceedings in England in which an anti-suit injunction had been sought and refused.

[178] It is worth noting that the High Court of South Africa in *Vedanta Resources Holdings Ltd v ZCCM Investment Holdings plc* 2019 JDR 1425 (GJ) paras [11], [54] and [56] (Adams J) and the High Court of Nigeria in *Zenith Global Merchant Ltd v Zhongfu International Investment (Nig) FZE* (2017) All FWLR 1837, 1924 (Akinyemi J) have also referred to English principles in a similar context.

have regard to the English authorities in setting out the principles upon which an anti-suit injunction may be granted in Sierra Leone. Set out below, in summary, are the principles of English law governing the grant of an anti-suit injunction.

The court must have personal jurisdiction over the injunction defendant. The court may be seised either by service on the defendant within the jurisdiction or service out of the jurisdiction with the leave of the court.[179]

The injunction plaintiff must assert a cause of action for relief. Usually, the injunction plaintiff will contend that the injunction defendant is committing a wrong by bringing or proposing to bring proceedings in a foreign court. This will require the plaintiff to characterise the conduct of the defendant as the breach of a legal or equitable right.

A legal right may, and often will, be based on a right not to be sued in a foreign jurisdiction arising out of an exclusive jurisdiction clause in favour of the courts of Sierra Leone. An equitable right may be the right not to be sued in a foreign jurisdiction and may be the corollary of an equitable wrong which is that it is oppressive and vexatious and therefore unconscionable for the injunction defendant to commence or continue proceedings against the injunction plaintiff in a foreign jurisdiction.

The prime example of a cause of action based on a legal right not to be sued in a foreign jurisdiction is where the parties have agreed expressly that the courts of Sierra Leone should have exclusive jurisdiction over disputes arising out of the contract (which can be a substantive contract or a settlement agreement) between them.[180] In such a case proof of the underlying cause of action is likely to be a sufficient condition for the grant of the relief and that good reason would need to be shown why the discretion to order an injunction should not be exercised.[181]

The principal example of a cause of action based on an equitable wrong is where proceedings brought abroad by the defendant are oppressive and vexatious. An example of such conduct is illustrated by the decision of the Privy Council in *SNI Aerospatiale v Lee Kui Jak*,[182] where a resident of Brunei had been killed in a helicopter crash and his widow (and her brother-in-law, as co-administrator of his estate), the respondent plaintiffs in the appeal to the Privy Council, had

[179] The substantive law and procedure for which in Sierra Leone has been set out above.

[180] The contract may be a substantive contract or a settlement agreement and the dispute resolution provisions may be exclusively in favour of the courts of Sierra Leone or may be in favour of arbitration: *British Airways Board v Laker Airways Ltd* [1985] AC 58 (HL (E)) (Lords Diplock, Fraser, Scarman, Roskill and Brightman), *per* Lord Diplock at p 81C–E.

[181] *The Angelic Grace* [1995] 1 Lloyd's Rep 87 (CA) (Neill, Leggatt and Millett LJJ), *per* Millett LJ at p 96, col 2, and Neill LJ at p 97, col 1; *Donohue v Armco Inc* [2000] 1 Lloyd's Rep 579 (CA) (Stuart-Smith, Brooke and Sedley LJJ), where it was stated that 'strong reasons' (*per* Stuart-Smith LJ at para 35) or 'strong cause' (*per* Brooke LJ at paras 59 and 60) would be required to deny an injunction.

[182] [1987] AC 871 (PC (Brunei)) (Lords Keith, Griffiths, MacKay and Goff and Sir John Megaw).

commenced proceedings in Brunei and had subsequently been persuaded to sue in Texas instead. The appellant defendant applied for an anti-suit injunction restraining the plaintiffs from proceeding against it in Texas. The Privy Council allowed the defendant's appeal, held that an injunction ought to be granted restraining the respondents from proceeding in Texas and remitted the matter to the Brunei courts.

Transposing the findings of the Privy Council to Sierra Leone, it was held that an anti-suit injunction would be granted if: (1) pursuit of the foreign proceedings is vexatious or oppressive; (2) Sierra Leone is the natural forum for the resolution of the dispute; and (3) the injunction does not deprive the defendant of advantages in the foreign jurisdiction of which it would be unjust to deprive him.[183]

Other examples of equitable wrongs which may attract an anti-suit injunction are: undermining the jurisdiction of the Sierra Leone court;[184] vexatious conduct by relying on foreign procedural laws;[185] wrongfully undermining a Sierra Leone judgment;[186] or enforcement of a foreign judgment wrongfully obtained.[187]

10.3.8 Other interlocutory relief

10.3.8.1 *Interim preservation of property*

Order 35, rule 2 provides as follows:

> '(1) On the application of any party to a cause or matter, the Court may make an order for the detention, custody or preservation of any property which is the subject matter of the cause or matter, or as to which any question may arise in the action or for the inspection of such property in the possession of a party to the cause or matter.
>
> (2) To enable any order made under subrule (1) to be carried out, the court may by order authorise any person to enter upon any land or building in the possession of any party to the cause or matter.

[183] Lord Goff (giving the opinion of the Privy Council) p 896F–H. That the court to which the application is made should be the natural forum for the resolution of the dispute was repeated by the House of Lords in *Airbus Industrie GIE v Patel* [1999] 1 AC 119 (HL (E)) (Lords Goff, Slynn, Steyn, Clyde and Hutton), *per* Lord Goff (with whom the other Lords agreed) pp 138G–H and 140H–141B.

[184] For example, by commencing bankruptcy proceedings outside the jurisdiction when such proceedings are in progress in Sierra Leone: *SNI Aerospatiale v Lee Kui Jak* [1987] AC 871, *per* Lord Goff at pp 892G–893B.

[185] By seeking to depose witnesses in the USA where those witnesses would be subject to cross-examination in proceedings in Sierra Leone, for example: *Omega Group Holdings Ltd v Kozeny* [2002] CLC 132.

[186] By commencing proceedings outside the jurisdiction for declaratory relief designed to frustrate the enforcement of a Sierra Leone judgment in that jurisdiction: *Masri v Consolidated Contractors International (UK) Ltd (No 3)* [2009] QB 503 (CA).

[187] Where the foreign judgment was obtained through fraud and perjury: *Ellerman Lines Ltd v Read* [1928] 2 KB 144 (CA), *per* Scrutton LJ at pp 152–3.

(3) Where the right of any party to a specific fund is in dispute, the court may, on the application of a party to the cause or matter, order the fund to be paid into court or otherwise secured.

(4) An order under this rule may be made on such terms, if any, as the court thinks just.

(5) Unless the court otherwise directs, an application by a defendant for such an order may not be made before he enters an appearance to the writ or other originating process by which the cause or matter was begun.'

In *Harold G Slone v Arcadia Mining Co*,[188] the substantive proceedings were concerned with the winding up of a mining company. In the interim proceedings, the plaintiff applicant sought an order for the preservation of several items, asking the court to direct that such items be kept in safe custody by the police, the bailiffs of the High Court or such other persons as the High Court may direct, pending the hearing and determination of the petition.

In granting the order, Edwards J stated:[189]

> 'In *Chaplin v. Barnet* (1912) 28 TLR 256 it was held that the power of the court to order the detention custody and preservation of property the subject of proceedings extends to every case where the court see [sic] that as between the parties there is something which ought to be done for the security of the property.
>
> In this instant matter it comes out clearly from the totality of facts that something ought be done [sic] for the security of the property, the assets of Arcadia Mining Company as listed in the face of the motion and in the petition. Also in the case of [*New Orleans Steamship Co v. London & Provincial Marine and General Insurance* [1909] KB 943] it was held that the court will not be deterred from making an order because a party against whom the order is sought has a proprietary interest.
>
> In the instant case the application itself and the way it is couched excepting the arguments gives the impression that it is made against the [defendants] and that they too have proprietary interest. This however could in no way deter the court from making an order as long as it is to protect the property.'

There is little other authority on the correct interpretation of, or procedure to be invoked when using, Order 35, rule 2. Given that (1) Order 35, rule 2 mirrors Order XXIX, rule 2 of the English Rules of the Supreme Court 1965 and (2) the Sierra Leone courts are have regard to English authorities on matters where Sierra Leone law is derived from earlier English law, it is likely that the Sierra Leone courts will rely on English judicial and academic authorities if required further to interpret or engage with Order 35, rule 2. In those circumstances, it is submitted that a court in Sierra Leone might find useful the following statement

[188] [2007] SLHC 16 (H Ct) (Edwards J).

[189] Ibid 4 of the transcript.

of principle,[190] which statement has been based on, and takes account of, the authorities cited in the commentary to Order XXIX, rule 2 of the English Rules of the Supreme Court:

'*(a)* As decided in Garrard v. Edge & Sons (1889) 58 LJ Ch 397, CA, the order must be made against the person in possession or custody of the property in dispute. See also Wilder v Wilder and Charters (No 2) (1912) 56 SJ 571, CA.

(b) The property must be the subject-matter of the suit. Thus in Scott v Mercantile Accident Insurance Co (1892) 8 TLR 431 the lower court made an order that certain jewellery should remain in the custody of the police. An appeal against this order was allowed because it was admitted on the evidence that the property was not the subject-matter of the action, but that only a question might arise about it in the cause or matter.

(c) It was held in Leney & Sons, Ltd v. Callingham & Thompson [1908] KB 79 at 84, CA, per Farwell LJ that:

"... the question of the exercise of the judicial discretion was always based, and is still based, upon this, that there is property in dispute to some interest in which the plaintiff shows a prima facie title; and preservation is ensured until the rights of the parties can be finally determined."

(d) The case of Chaplin v. Barnett (1912) 28 TLR 256, CA decides that the order will be granted so long as there is something which ought to be done to ensure the security of the property.

(e) An order will be made in order to preserve the subject-matter of the suit from destruction: see Strelley v. Pearson (1880) 15 Ch D 113 where the court granted an order restraining the defendant from ceasing to pump water of a mine for the sole purpose of preventing the mine from destruction.

(f) The court will also grant an order in court to preserve the subject-matter from depreciation physically or in value. So if it is established that it is necessary to do so the court will grant it; hence an order was made in the case of Steamship New Orleans Co v. London and Provincial Marine and General Insurance Co [1909] 1 KB 943, CA that a ship lying in a port in Singapore be brought to England for preservation there. However an order may not be made if it will cause undue hardship in carrying it out or will serve no useful purpose.

These grounds are by no means exhaustive; other grounds may unfold due to a particular case under consideration.'

---

[190] The statement of principle is taken from the decision of the Ghanaian Court of Appeal in *General Development Co Ltd v Rad Forest Products Ltd* [1999–2000] 2 GLR 178 (CA) 182–3, *per* Bendin JA. There the Court of Appeal addressed O 25, r 2 of the equivalent Ghanaian High Court Rules, which is in the same terms as O 35, r 2 of the High Court Rules.

10.3.8.2 *Arrest of absconding defendant*

The Debtors Act[191] and Order 54 confer jurisdiction to arrest a party to an action and to impose bail conditions.[192] Order 54 itself provides:

'1. (1) A plaintiff may at the institution of an action or at any time before final judgment, make an application[193] *ex parte* supported by an affidavit to the court for an order for security to be taken for the appearance of the defendant to answer any judgment that may be given against him in the action where the amount involved in the action exceeds Le 20,000 and

(a) the defendant has disposed of or removed all or part of his property from the country; or

(b) the defendant is about to leave the country.

2. Where the court is satisfied that the provisions in paragraph *(a)* or *(b)* of subrule (1) have been substantiated and that the execution of any judgment in the action against the defendant is likely to be obstructed or delayed, it may issue a warrant to bring the defendant immediately before the court or a judge to show cause why the defendant should not give good and sufficient bail for his appearance[194]...

3. Where the defendant fails to show cause, the court shall order him to give bail for his appearance at any time while the action is pending until the execution or satisfaction of any judgment that may be given against him in the action, and the surety shall undertake to pay any money that may be adjudged to be paid by the defendant in the action in default of his appearance.

4. A deposit of money or other valuable property by the defendant sufficient to satisfy the claim and costs of the action may be accepted by the court in lieu of bail.

5. Where the defendant fails to furnish security or to provide sufficient security, he may –

(a) be committed to custody until the determination of the action; or

(b) if the judgment is against the defendant, until the executions [sic] of the order if the court so orders,

but the court may at any time release the defendant upon reasonable cause being shown and upon such terms as security or other relevant matters.

---

191 Act 7 of 1883, published as Cap 24 of the Laws of Sierra Leone 1960

192 *Sukiasyan v Hayraptyan* [2012] SLHC 20 (H Ct) (Browne-Marke J).

193 Order 56, r 7(1) provides that the application may be made to any court where the defendant may be found and that court may issue the warrant to detain and bring the defendant before the court and may make such further orders as it considers just in the circumstances. Where that warrant is issued by a court other than the court before which the action is pending, that court shall, upon the request of either party to the action, transmit the application and the evidence to the court before which the action is pending: O 54, r 7(2). The transferring court shall take sufficient security for the appearance of the defendant in that court or send the defendant to the court before which the action is pending in the custody of an officer of the court: O 54, r 7(3).

194 Order 54, r 1(3) goes on to provide that the 'defendant may, at any time after arrest, apply to the court to rescind or vary the order'.

6. The money deposited, the security and all proceedings relating to them shall be subject to the order and control of the court ...

8. (1) The expenses incurred for keeping the arrested person in custody shall be of such sum as shall be determined by the court and shall be paid by the plaintiff in advance to the prison authority.

(2) Any amount expended under subrule (1) may be recovered by the plaintiff in the action unless the court otherwise orders.

(3) The court may order the release of the person in custody if the plaintiff fails to pay the subsistence expenses or in the case of serious illness, order the removal of the person to a hospital.'

In *Sukiasyan v Hayraptyan*,[195] the High Court provided helpful guidance as to the correct construction to be given to, and the correct application of, the applicable rules. That guidance may be summarised as follows:

(1) Before the court can request the defendant to put up bail or provide security, the plaintiff must satisfy the court that the plaintiff has a cause of action against the defendant[196] and that the defendant has removed, or has disposed of his property or the defendant is about to leave Sierra Leone.

(2) Sections 4 and 5 of the Debtors Act, and Order 54, are aimed at persons, citizens and residents alike of Sierra Leone, as well as non-citizens and non-residents of Sierra Leone, who intend to leave Sierra Leone, while a claim is pending against them, and by so doing will thereby frustrate any attempt to execute judgment against them.

(3) The court's power to order a defendant to provide security cannot be used by the plaintiff to obtain a tactical advantage over the defendant.

On the facts of the case, and weighing particularly point (3), the court determined that the defendant should deposit his passport with the court registrar and ought not leave Sierra Leone without the express permission of the court.

While the decision in *Sukiasyan v Hayraptyan* appears to demonstrate that the Sierra Leone court has no doubt as to the constitutionality of provisions allowing for the arrest of a debtor to secure his appearance, there is greater doubt in other common-law jurisdictions in Africa.[197]

It may be the case, therefore, that a court in Sierra Leone in due course might be required to examine the constitutionality of Order 54 in light of section 17 of the Constitution, which provides, so far as is material, as follows:

---

[195] [2012] SLHC 20 (H Ct). Both parties were citizens of the Republic of Armenia.

[196] Presumably, for a sum in the relevant amount.

[197] See, for example, in Ghana: Brobbey JSC *Enforcement of Judgment and Orders by Justice of the Supreme Court.*

'(1) No person shall be deprived of his personal liberty except as may be authorised by law in any of the following cases, that is to say —

a. in consequence of his unfitness to plead to a criminal charge; or

b. in the execution of a sentence or order of a Court whether in Sierra Leone or elsewhere in respect of a criminal offence of which he has been convicted; or

c. in the execution of an order of the High Court or the Court of Appeal or the Supreme Court or such other court as may be prescribed by Parliament on the grounds of his contempt of any such court or of another court or tribunal or commission of inquiry as the case may be; or

d. in the execution of an Order of a court made in order to secure the fulfilment of any obligation imposed on him by law; or

e. for the purpose of bringing him before a court or tribunal, as the case may be, in execution of the order of a court; or

f. upon reasonable suspicion of his having committed or of being about to commit a criminal offence; or

g. in the case of a person who has not attained the age of twenty-one years, for the purpose of his education or welfare; or

h. for the purpose of preventing the spread of an infectious or contagious disease; or

i. in the case of a person who is, or is reasonably suspected to be, of unsound mind, addicted to drugs or alcohol, or a vagrant, for the purpose of his care or treatment or the protection of the community; or

j. for the purpose of preventing the unlawful entry of that person into Sierra Leone, or for the purpose of effecting the expulsion, extradition or other lawful removal of that person from Sierra Leone or the taking of proceedings thereto.'

The savings prescribed by section 17(1)a–j appear inapt to cover the case of a person arrested in a civil cause in the circumstances prescribed by the rules set out above. There are grounds, therefore, to think that the arrest of a defendant, absconding or otherwise, is contrary to the Constitution and so unlawful.

Chapter 11

ESWATINI[1]

[1] In the first edition of this work, this chapter was entitled "Swaziland". The jurisdiction changed its name to Eswatini in April 2018, too late for amendments to be made to the first edition. This change is reflected in the change of title for this chapter. Further, the authors now refer to Eswatini or the courts of Eswatini throughout this chapter. However, where the authors refer to legislation or the names of cases, the authors have kept these in their original state, which is why the chapter still contains references to 'Swaziland' or 'Swazi'.

11.1 Jurisdiction

The High Court Rules 1969 ('the High Court Rules')[2] do not contain specific provision for an application for an order for the arrest of an individual or attachment of an individual's property *ad fundandam jurisdictionem* or *ad confirmandam jurisdictionem*. The court's power to make such orders arises at common law.[3]

11.1.1 Commencing proceedings where the defendant is within the jurisdiction

Actions are generally commenced through the office of the Registrar by summons addressed to the defendant and signed by the plaintiff or his attorney and by the court registrar who issued it.[4] The defendant then has the time stated on the summons not being less than ten days or, in the case of a combined summons (one annexing a statement of claim), 21 days to give notice of intention to defend.[5]

Service on the defendant of 'any process of the court' must be effected by the sheriff or deputy sheriff (or in the case of an application by an attorney or

[2] Legal Notices 3 and 27 of 1969. The High Court Rules were made pursuant to s 10 of the High Court Act 1954 (Act 20 of 1954).

[3] See the Zimbabwe authorities, *Mackay v Hepker* [1941] SRLR 33 (HC) *per* Hudson J at 35–6 and the judgment of Beck J in *African Distillers Ltd v Zietkiewicz* 1980 ZLR 135 (HC) 136F–H.

[4] Rule 17.

[5] Rules 17(1) and 19(1); exclusive of the day of service of the summons. The document in which the plaintiff's claim is set out (save where he has served a combined summons) is referred to as a declaration which is served within 14 days of the delivery of the defendant's notice of intention to defend (r 20(1)). The defendant's answer to the plaintiff's declaration is referred to as the defendant's plea (r 22(1)). The defendant may at the same time advance any claim he has against the plaintiff by way of a claim in reconvention (r 24(1)). The defendant must serve the plea within 21 days of replication, which itself is to be filed within 14 days after the service of the plea (r 25(1)). The plaintiff's answer to any claim in reconvention is the plaintiff's plea to the claim in reconvention (r 25(1)). The defendant may within 14 days respond to the plaintiff's plea in reconvention by means of a defendant's replication to the plea in reconvention (r 25(4)).

an employee of the attorney).[6] If the sheriff or his deputy has failed to effect service within 21 days of receipt of the process, the Registrar may authorise any other person to effect service.[7] Service must be effected by one of the methods set out by rule 4(2) (inter alia: personal service, by leaving a copy at the place of residence of business of the person to be served, by delivering a copy to the person's place of employment, in the case of a corporation by delivering a copy to a 'responsible person' at its registered office or a responsible employee at its principal place of business). Personal service is a requirement where the process or application concerns the liberty of the party to be served.[8]

11.1.2 Commencing proceedings where the defendant is outside the jurisdiction

Where the plaintiff seeks to issue proceedings against a defendant who is resident outside the jurisdiction, the leave of the court is required.[9] An application for leave is made pursuant to rule 5 of the High Court Rules which provides that all applications (other than oral applications in the course of a hearing)[10] shall be made by application pursuant to rule 6, which requires a notice of motion and supporting evidence by way of affidavit to be filed. An application may be made *ex parte* and the rule requiring filing of the application the day prior to the hearing may be dispensed with in an urgent case.[11]

On such an application the court may make such order as to the manner of service as seems 'meet' and shall make an order regarding the time within which the notice of intention to defend or any other step is to be taken by the defendant.[12]

11.1.2.1 Incolae *and* peregrini

Eswatini law differentiates between those persons who are *incolae* and those who are *peregrini*. In order to distinguish between *incolae* and *peregrini*, the courts have, at least when dealing with individuals, fashioned a test which is based on the residence of the defendant.[13] In other words, where a defendant is resident within

---

[6] Rule 4(1).

[7] Ibid.

[8] Rule 4(2)(j).

[9] Rule 5(1).

[10] Rule 5(2).

[11] Rule 6(4).

[12] Rule 5(2).

[13] In some of the earlier authorities, such as *Standard Bank of Swaziland v Cassamo* [1979–1981] SWLR 247 (Nathan CJ), the courts took the view that a *peregrinus* 'is a person who is neither domiciled nor permanently resident within the area of jurisdiction of the court'. However, more recent authorities, such as *Kiwanuka*

the jurisdiction and such person is considered to be an *incola*, the Eswatini courts will, without more, exercise jurisdiction over him.[14] Whether an individual is considered to be resident within the jurisdiction will depend on whether he has 'some real interest there which gives his presence some permanence'.[15]

The approach which the court adopts in order to determine whether a corporate defendant is an *incola* or a peregrine is less clear. In *Terblanche Transport (Pty) Ltd v Dlamini*,[16] the defendant was considered to be a *peregrinus* by virtue of the fact that it had neither its principal (indeed any) place of business nor a registered office in Eswatini. The Eswatini court's consideration of these particular factors means that it appears to be conducting a similar exercise to that carried out by the courts in the Republic of South Africa when assessing whether a corporate defendant is a *peregrinus* or not.[17]

11.1.2.2 *The jurisdictional significance of attachment*

11.1.2.2.1 Where the plaintiff and the defendant are both *incolae*

Where both the parties to a dispute are *incolae*, no jurisdictional problems arise. The dispute is a purely domestic one over which the court has jurisdiction.

11.1.2.2.2 Where the plaintiff is an *incola* and the defendant is a *peregrinus*

Given the close affinity between the law of Eswatini and the law of the Republic of South Africa, it appears that, in the circumstances currently under consideration, the Eswatini court simply follows the approach which the South African courts have taken when dealing with this issue, as demonstrated by the case of *Mbhilibhi (Pty) Ltd v Esor Construction (Pty) Ltd*.[18]

---

v Muwanga [1999] SZHC 63 (HC), *per* Masuku J and *Diamond v Shilubane NO* (535/13) [2013] SZHC 178 (Ota J) para [3] seem to put the focus on residence, albeit that neither of those more recent authorities make reference to *Cassamo*.

[14] The position of the peregrine defendant is dealt with below.

[15] *Kiwanuka v Muwanga* [1999] SZHC 63 (HC), *per* Masuku J. Hence, the judge intimated that being a traveller in Eswatini would not meet this test.

[16] [2005] SZHC 45 (Annandale ACJ) para [42].

[17] It should be noted, however, that the courts in the Republic of South Africa appear to use a nuanced approach, which allows them to deal with a domestic company slightly differently to how they deal with a foreign company. While the reader is referred to the relevant discussion in the chapter on South Africa for a fuller treatment of this issue, briefly put, when a South African court considers the residence of a domestic company for jurisdictional purposes, it will have jurisdiction over that defendant domestic company where the company's central management or principal place of business or place of registration is within that court's jurisdiction: *Bisonboard Ltd v K Braun Woodworking Machinery (Pty) Ltd* 1991 (1) SA 482 (A) (Hoexter, Botha and Milne JJA and Goldstone and Nicholas AJJA). By contrast, where the defendant is a foreign corporation, something less than residence in the domestic sense of a principal place of business is sufficient to establish jurisdiction where the cause of action arises out of that business: *Appleby (Pty) Ltd v Dundas Ltd* 1948 (2) SA 905 (EDLD) (Hoexter J).

[18] [2021] SZHC 13 (HC) (Dlamini J).

A court in Eswatini,[19] therefore, seems to apply the following principle: 'The plaintiff an incola, the defendant a peregrinus. Attachment is essential. It is not necessary that there should be any other foundation for jurisdiction other than the attachment.'[20]

That attachment is essential in such circumstances has been confirmed by the Supreme Court in *Dludlu v Coal Power Africa (Pty) Ltd*.[21] In that case, the Supreme Court was asked to determine whether it

> 'could pierce the corporate veil of a company resident, and carrying on its real and principal business in South Africa, and direct that there should be an equal division and distribution of funds accruing to the company from sales to customers in this jurisdiction but where it has not been alleged or proved that the sale agreements were concluded in this jurisdiction, on account of a dispute between its members which clearly did not arise in this jurisdiction'.[22]

This question was answered in the negative: it appears that there was no property to attach so as to found[23] jurisdiction in Eswatini in this case.

11.1.2.2.3 Where the plaintiff and the defendant are both *peregrini*

A court in Eswatini is prepared to attach the assets of a *peregrinus* defendant at the request of a *peregrinus* plaintiff, but only where the court has jurisdiction in the suit apart from the attachment, ie where a *ratio jurisdictionis* exists.[24] This is the effect of the decision in *De Hart NO v Kleynhans*,[25] where Elyan CJ stated:[26]

> 'Before considering whether the interdict sought should be granted I would like as to attachment *ad fundandam jurisdictionem*, to say that whilst jurisdiction cannot be founded by mere attachment, even where a Court has jurisdiction upon one or other of the common law grounds, it is still necessary for a peregrine plaintiff to attach the property or person of a peregrine defendant to confirm or strengthen the jurisdiction already possessed by the Court. Or in other words the Courts will attach the person or property of a *peregrinus* at the instance of another *peregrinus* provided the Court has jurisdiction in the suit apart from the attachment.'

---

19 For a fuller treatment of the issue currently under consideration, the reader is referred to the relevant discussion in the chapter on the Republic of South Africa.

20 Pistorius *Pollak on Jurisdiction* 2 ed (1993) 83.

21 [2018] SZSC 64 (SC) (Maphalala CJ, Matsebula AJA and Manzini AJA) paras [24] and [25].

22 Ibid para [23].

23 The Supreme Court was clear, at para [26], that an order for attachment *ad confirmandam jurisdictionem* was improper here.

24 This requirement creates certain difficulties for a *peregrinus* foreign judgment creditor who is seeking to enforce the foreign judgment against a *peregrinus* judgment debtor. See further below under the heading 'Enforcement of Foreign Judgments' and Frimpong Oppong 'Recognition and enforcement of foreign judgments in Commonwealth African countries' (2014) XV *Yearbook of Private International Law* 365, 370. All the same, the plaintiff will succeed where he can demonstrate that there is evidence which, if accepted, will establish a cause of action: *Standard Bank of Swaziland v Cassamo* [1979–1981] SWLR 247 (6 May 1981; Nathan CJ).

25 [1963–1969] SWLR 373 (HC) (14 October 1968).

26 Ibid 376.

In this case, the court's common-law jurisdiction was established by the proprietary claim (*jurisdictionem rei sitae*) that the plaintiff asserted over a bank account within the jurisdiction. Such jurisdiction having been established, an interim remedy[27] was granted on the basis that, at the conclusion of the proceedings taking place abroad (in the Orange Free State) and the granting of judgment in favour of the plaintiff in those proceedings, the plaintiff would then wish to enforce the judgment in Eswatini. Elyan CJ characterised the application as one *pendent lite* the proceedings in the Orange Free State.[28]

11.1.2.3 Rationes jurisdictiones

There is no suggestion that the law in Eswatini differs from the law in the Republic of South Africa on the acceptable *rationes jurisdictiones*. While more in-depth treatment is afforded the *rationes jurisdictiones* in the chapter on South Africa,[29] the basic position may be summarised by reference to the judgment of the Supreme Court of the Cape in *Einwald v The German West African Co.*[30] There, De Villiers CJ stated:[31]

> 'What then are the grounds upon which the jurisdiction of this Court can be exercised, in respect of any contract over any defendant without his consent, express or implied? The grounds are threefold: *viz* by virtue of the defendant's domicile being here, by virtue of the contract either having been entered into here or having to be performed here, and by virtue of the subject-matter in an action *in rem* being situated in this Colony.'

Added to these are the place of the delict and cases which concern property. The principal connecting factors for jurisdictional purposes which result are: *ratio domicilii* (*actor sequitur forum rei*); *ratio contractus*; *ratio delictus*; and *ratio rei sitae*.[32] To this list may also be added *ratio causa continentia*.

---

[27] Which concept is explored in more detail below under the heading 'Interim Remedies'.

[28] In confirming the rule *nisi* the judge relied on the South African authority *Kibe v Mphoko* 1958 (1) SA 364 (OFS PD), where an interdict was granted to a *peregrinus* preventing a defendant *peregrinus* drawing on his bank account within the jurisdiction of the court, pending an action which had been instituted in Lesotho.

[29] To which the reader is referred.

[30] (1887) 5 SC 86 (De Villiers CJ).

[31] Ibid 91.

[32] Different authors treat the organisation of this subject in different ways. Peté et al *Civil Procedure* 2 ed (2011) (at 70ff) discuss the subject under the headings *ratione domicilii, ratione res gestae, ratione rei sitae* and then claims relating to property and claims sounding in money. In Schulze *On Jurisdiction and the Recognition and Enforcement of Foreign Money Judgments* (2005) the discussion (at 1–15) revolves around domicile and the bases for assumption of jurisdiction over *incolae* and *peregrini*. In Kelbrick *Civil Procedure in South Africa* 2 ed (2012), the subject is analysed (at 42–3; paras 84–6) in terms of claims in money and property. Forsyth *Private International Law* 5 ed (2012) discusses (at 205–6) residence and domicile, the various *rationes jurisdictionis* and then claims in money or property. Herbstein and Van Winsen *The Civil Practice of the High Courts of South Africa* 5 ed (2009) discusses (at 67–81) the subject under the topic headings claims in money, property (and status). Pistorius *Pollak on Jurisdiction* 2 ed (1993) arranges the discussion under the topic headings money claims and property claims. There are merits in all of these approaches.

11.1.2.3.1 *Ratio domicilii* (*actor sequitur forum rei*)

Ratio domicilii expresses the principle of Roman law that the fundamental basis of jurisdiction is that a plaintiff should sue a defendant at the defendant's place of domicile or, as has become the case, residence (*actor sequitur forum rei*). There is nothing to suggest that the Eswatini courts would treat this issue any differently to the courts in the Republic of South Africa.[33]

11.1.2.3.2 *Ratio contractus*

There is nothing to suggest that the Eswatini courts would treat this issue any differently to the courts in the Republic of South Africa. Accordingly, a court where: (1) the contract was concluded (the *locus contractus*); (2) the contract is to be performed in whole or in part (the *locus solutionis*); or (3) the contract was breached in the manner relied upon by the plaintiff in Eswatini may, *ratio contractus*, exercise jurisdiction.[34]

11.1.2.3.3 *Ratio delicti commissi*

A court may have jurisdiction by reason of a *ratio delicti commissi* in the event that a delict was committed or occurred within its area of jurisdiction. Again, there is nothing to suggest that the Eswatini courts treat this issue any differently to the courts in the Republic of South Africa.[35]

11.1.2.3.4 *Ratio rei sitae*

The location of movable or immovable property within the area of jurisdiction of a court will confer on that court jurisdiction by reason of a *ratio rei sitae*: it is the court of the place where the property is situated. Again, there is nothing to suggest that the Eswatini courts treat this issue any differently to the courts in the Republic of South Africa.[36]

---

[33] Accordingly, for a more detailed treatment of this issue, the reader is referred to the corresponding discussion in the chapter on the Republic of South Africa.

[34] Given that there is nothing to suggest that the courts in Eswatini treat this issue any differently to the courts in the Republic of South Africa, the reader is referred to the corresponding discussion in the chapter on South Africa for a more detailed treatment of this issue.

[35] Accordingly, for a more detailed treatment of this issue, the reader is referred to the corresponding discussion in the chapter on the Republic of South Africa.

[36] Accordingly, for a more detailed treatment of this issue, the reader is referred to the corresponding discussion in the chapter on the Republic of South Africa.

11.1.2.3.5 *Ratio causa continentia*

There is nothing to suggest that the courts in Eswatini treat the *causa continentia* doctrine differently to the courts in the Republic of South Africa. Accordingly, the *causa continentia* rule is one that permits a court to assume jurisdiction in a case in which, but for the application of the rule, it might not have jurisdiction over the entirety of the dispute or over a particular defendant. The application of the rule is intended to avoid a 'multiplicity of proceedings and the possibility of conflicting judgments on the same cause and allows for the more convenient disposition of cases'.[37] Pistorius states[38] that in order to apply 'it must be established that there is no other forum which has jurisdiction in respect of all the defendants on other recognised grounds of jurisdiction'.[39]

11.1.2.4 *Submission to the jurisdiction*

Eswatini law recognises submission to the jurisdiction as a basis for the assumption of jurisdiction over a dispute in certain circumstances.

Generally, submission may take one of two forms. First, unilateral submission, whereby a party against whom proceedings have been commenced takes a step in the proceedings which as a matter of Eswatini law renders him amenable to the jurisdiction of the Eswatini courts. Second, consensual submission, whereby the parties agree, prior to or subsequent to a dispute arising, to submit to the jurisdiction of the Eswatini courts.

11.1.2.4.1 Submission by participating in existing proceedings

There is authority in Eswatini to the effect that a *peregrinus* defendant who submits to the jurisdiction of the court does so only in respect of his person and that this is insufficient to found jurisdiction. As a result, in order for the Eswatini court to have jurisdiction over the claim the plaintiff must demonstrate a *ratio jurisdictionis* as well. In *AG Thomas (Pty) Ltd v Grinaker Lta (Ltd)*,[40] the applicant (the plaintiff in the intended proceedings) applied to attach a debt owed by then government of Eswatini to the peregrine respondents in order to found or confirm jurisdiction. The respondents had in correspondence purported to consent to the jurisdiction of the Eswatini court (with a view to avoiding the plaintiff applying successfully to attach their assets within the jurisdiction). On the plaintiff's application to

[37] Pistorius *Pollak on Jurisdiction* 2 ed (1993) 25.

[38] Ibid 26.

[39] Given that there is nothing to suggest that the courts in Eswatini treat this issue any differently to the courts in the Republic of South Africa, the reader is referred to the corresponding discussion in the chapter on South Africa for a more detailed treatment of this issue.

[40] [2005] SZHC 4 (HC) (28 January 2005).

attach the debt owed by the government to the respondents, it was contended by the respondents that their submission was only in respect of the person and not the cause of action and that because the contract pursuant to which the plaintiff intended to bring proceedings contained an arbitration clause, the court did not have jurisdiction over the cause of action and therefore lacked jurisdiction over the claim. Attachment of the respondent's assets by itself was insufficient to found jurisdiction, notwithstanding the respondents' submission.

Maphalala J agreed with the respondent's contention and held[41] that a peregrine respondent's consent to the jurisdiction is insufficient in the absence of one or more of the accepted *rationes jurisdictiones*. In reaching this conclusion the judge relied on the South African authorities *Sonia (Pty) Ltd v Wheeler*[42] and *Veneta Mineraria SPA v Carolina Collieries (Pty) Ltd*.[43] However, the South African Supreme Court of Appeal in *Hay Management Consultants (Pty) Ltd v P3 Management Consultants (Pty) Ltd*[44] considered the decision in the *Veneta Mineraria* case. In *Hay Management Consultants*, the court held[45] that where the plaintiff is an *incola* and the *peregrinus* defendant submitted to the jurisdiction of the court there was no need for any *ratio jurisdictiones* or further ground for jurisdiction: the defendant's submission, without more, conferred jurisdiction upon the court. It is of note, for present purposes, that although *Hay Management Consultants* was decided before the judgment of Maphalala J in the *AG Thomas* case, it was not referred to by the judge or, it would seem, counsel (possibly because it was reported after the judgment was given).

It would appear that the Eswatini High Court has recently moved away from the approach in the *AG Thomas* case and towards the approach adopted by the South African Supreme Court of Appeal in the *Hay Management* case. In *Shell South Africa Energy (Pty) Ltd v Mthethwa*[46] the plaintiff *peregrinus*, a South African company, by combined summons sought two sums of money from the *incola* defendant. The defendant then filed a counterclaim. While there was no doubt that the court had jurisdiction to hear the claim, a question arose as to whether the court had jurisdiction to hear the counterclaim by the *incola* defendant (the plaintiff on the counterclaim).

---

[41] Ibid para [17].

[42] 1958 (1) SA 555 (A).

[43] 1987 (4) SA 883 (A). The Appellate Division in the *Veneta Mineraria* case was faced with a contract which contained a jurisdiction clause conferring jurisdiction on the courts of the Durban and Coast Local Division of the High Court of South Africa (where the plaintiff had begun the action). Accordingly, it is a case about submission by agreement, though nothing turns on this for present purposes.

[44] 2005 (2) SA 522 (SCA) (Scott, Cameron, Conradie and Heher JJA and Patel AJA; judgment dated 30 November 2004, but reported after the decision in *AG Thomas (Pty) Ltd v Grinaker Lta (Ltd)* [2005] SZHC 4 (HC) (28 January 2005)).

[45] 2005 (2) SA 522 (SCA) paras [21]–[23].

[46] [2017] SZHC 57 (HC) (Mabuza PJ).

In answering this question, Mabuza PJ held:[47]

> 'This Court would not have jurisdiction in respect of the counterclaim if it had not been brought as part of the litigation initiated by the Plaintiff. This is because the Plaintiff (the Defendant in the counterclaim) does not reside within the jurisdiction of the [Eswatini] High Court, nor do any of the factors which might give the Court jurisdiction exist (the *rationes jurisdictionis*). The Court may have jurisdiction if the Defendant is domiciled in its jurisdiction (*ratio domicilii*); or the place of concluding or performing the contract is within its jurisdiction (*ratio contractus*); or the breach and cause of action arises within its jurisdiction (*ratio res gestae*), See *Erasmus, Superior Court Practice, 2nd Ed at A2-103ff.* In this case each of these factors occurs in South Africa. This court would not therefore ordinarily have jurisdiction over Defendant's counterclaim. But the counterclaim is a response to a claim by the Plaintiff in which the [Eswatini] High Court does have jurisdiction. In bringing the claim in [Eswatini] the Plaintiff has submitted to the jurisdiction of this Honourable Court. Accordingly, but for the fact that the Plaintiff submitted to the Court's jurisdiction by bringing the main claim, this Court would have no jurisdiction to consider the counterclaim. But, since there has been such submission to jurisdiction, the Court indeed has jurisdiction.'[48]

In reaching this decision, Mabuza PJ did not refer to *AG Thomas* or the decision in the *Hay Management* case. In those circumstances, the most that can be said is that the High Court in Eswatini appears, substantively, to have adopted the approach followed by courts in the Republic of South Africa (that is, submission by a *peregrinus* defendant faced with a claim brought by an *incola* plaintiff will alone confer jurisdiction on the court), albeit without referring either to existing Eswatini authority or the most recent South African authority governing the defendant's submission to the jurisdiction.

Once an attachment of property to confirm the jurisdiction of the court has been executed (if it is required), the subsequent unilateral submission of the defendant to the jurisdiction of the court cannot result in the discharge of the attachment. In *SMADCO Investments (Pty) Ltd v Inyoni Boerdery Vervoer*,[49] the plaintiff, an *incola* of Eswatini, had obtained an order attaching certain properties of the defendant, a peregrine. After the attachment was executed against the properties, the defendant unilaterally submitted to the jurisdiction of the court and provided a letter of guarantee from a South African bank guaranteeing payment of any judgment debt obtained by the plaintiff against the defendant. The defendant then applied to discharge the attachment.

---

[47] At para [11].

[48] For which proposition, the judge cited *Mediterranean Shipping Co v Speedwell Shipping Co* 1986 (4) SA 329 (D) 333D–334C and *MV Rizcun Trader v Manley Appledore Shipping Ltd* 2000 (3) SA 776 (C) 803H–804B.

[49] [2012] SZHC 243 (HC).

In dismissing the defendant's application, Ota J, relying on the decisions of the South African Supreme Court of Appeal in *Jamieson v Sabingo*[50] and *Tsung v Industrial Development Corp of South Africa Ltd*,[51] stated:[52] 'Though the primary purpose of an attachment is to found or confirm jurisdiction, it's [sic] further object is to furnish an asset upon which to execute the judgment debt.' Hence, where a peregrine has unilaterally submitted to the jurisdiction prior to attachment of his property (or person)

> 'the necessity for the attachment will be rendered nugatory ... because submission to jurisdiction has a better effect in that it makes the judgment of the court internationally enforceable against the peregrinus and binds all his possessions, but an attachment of property alone without consent to jurisdiction, makes the judgment binding only on the property attached'.[53]

However, returning to the case before him, the judge concluded that once the attachment has been executed then unilateral submission is not a ground for setting aside the attachment, save in exceptional circumstances.[54] Accordingly, it is very important to be cognisant of the time at which the *peregrinus* defendant submits to the jurisdiction of the court, vis-a-vis execution of the order of attachment.

A defendant may by application apply for the attachment to be discharged or the sum set for security for the plaintiff's claim reduced:

> 'In such an application a court ought to be at large to look at all the circumstances of the case, such as the amount of the claim, the likelihood of the plaintiff succeeding, the financial position of the defendant, the ease or otherwise of executing on a judgment in the country of domicile of the defendant, the hardship to the defendant if the attachment remains and similar considerations. The Court can then decide if the attachment is to remain unaltered or if it is to be reduced, set aside, or substituted with some other form of attachment or security.'[55]

---

[50] [2003] 3 All SA 392 (A); 2002 (4) SA 49 (SCA).

[51] 2006 (4) SA 177 (SCA).

[52] Ibid para [9].

[53] Ibid para [10].

[54] Ibid para [19]. Unilateral submission could not be a ground for setting aside attachment because such consent does not 'secure realisation of effectiveness of the judgment'. The judge's conclusion that the attachment, even when executed, could be set aside in exceptional circumstances was based on a concession of counsel (recorded at para [4]). The judgment makes clear that none of the factors emphasised by the defendant were sufficiently exceptional as to meet the test; no indication was given, however, of what might amount to such an 'exceptional circumstance'.

[55] Hartzenberg J in *Bettencourt v Kom* 1994 (2) SA 513 (TPD) 517D–F, quoted by Ota J para [15]. In *Banks v Henshaw* 1962 (3) SA 464 (N), Miller J reduced the amount which the defendant had been required to pay as security for his release from personal jurisdictional attachment from R7,000 to R3,000, taking into account the defendant's claim in reconvention and the possible inflation of the plaintiff's claim in damages for defamation.

11.1.2.4.2 Submission by agreement

11.1.2.4.2.1 *Jurisdiction clauses*

Eswatini courts will give effect to jurisdiction clauses in an agreement between the parties to proceedings. In *Barlows Central Finance Corp (Pty) Ltd v Joncon (Pty) Ltd*,[56] the plaintiff obtained a rule *nisi* against the defendant which, inter alia, declared certain sale agreements cancelled, required the defendant to deliver up various plant to the plaintiff and directed the defendant to make certain payments to the plaintiff. The defendant disputed the jurisdiction of the court to make the orders sought on the basis that the sale agreements between the parties[57] contained a South African choice of law clause and a clause which provided:

> 'The Buyer [defendant] hereby consents to the jurisdiction of the Magistrate's Court ... Notwithstanding the aforegoing the Seller [plaintiff] shall be entitled to institute all or any Proceedings against the Buyer connected with this agreement in any division of the Supreme Court of South Africa having jurisdiction.'

Relying on decisions of the English courts in *Evans Marshall v Bertola SA*[58] and *Mackender v Feldia AG*,[59] Masuku J approached the question whether the jurisdiction clause bound the parties to bring proceedings in the Republic of South Africa on the basis that it did but that the court could decide not to give effect to the clause in special circumstances: 'It is clear therefore that the Court will only allow a breach of the *pacta sunt servanda* principle in cases where there are strong and special reasons.' The judge decided that the jurisdiction clause could be disregarded because: first, there was a close connection between the court and the substance of the case, including the fact that the defendant was an *incola* of the court; second, the plaintiff was a peregrine and had surrendered the advantages of bringing proceedings in its own home jurisdiction of South Africa; third, the law of the Republic of South Africa and Eswatini was very similar; and, fourth, the judge was of the view that the defendant did not *bona fide* desire a trial in South Africa and did not seriously intend litigating there.

The court cannot be criticised for the conclusion it reached on the facts. However, it is important to note that the court failed to distinguish between exclusive, non-exclusive and hybrid jurisdiction clauses. In both of the English cases relied on by the judge, the court was concerned with an exclusive jurisdiction clause, that is, a clause by which the parties agreed to bring proceedings relating to a dispute under the contract in a particular jurisdiction and no other.[60]

---

[56] [1999] SZHC 57 (HC) (28 December 1999).

[57] The report is unclear as to how many sale agreements were in issue and whether they all contained the same clause.

[58] [1973] 1 WLR 349 (CA); [1973] 1 All ER 992 (CA).

[59] [1967] 2 QB 590 (HC (Comm)) (Diplock J).

[60] Generally, it will be more difficult to persuade a court to disregard an exclusive jurisdiction clause than a non-exclusive jurisdiction clause.

It is generally understood that a non-exclusive jurisdiction clause is one that 'records the parties' agreement, or the absence of objection, to the jurisdiction of courts of a particular country without requiring proceedings to be brought there'.[61] In *Barlows Central Finance*, the jurisdiction clause gave one party, the seller/plaintiff, the right to bring proceedings in the Republic of South Africa, but did not oblige it to do so. In the event, the plaintiff decided to waive its right to do so. Accordingly, the only question the court needed to consider was whether, on ordinary grounds, it had jurisdiction over the defendant. Because the defendant was an *incola* of the court, the court had jurisdiction without more.

The *Barlows Central Finance* case does, however, demonstrate a willingness to recognise and enforce jurisdiction clauses in appropriate cases.

11.1.2.4.2.2 Domicilium citandi et executandi *clauses*

By including a *domicilium citandi et executandi* clause in their contract, a party may nominate an address to which formal notices in relation to the contract (such as a demand for payment or a threat to cancel) or the service of process in litigation arising out of the contract can be served.[62] There is nothing to suggest that the law in Eswatini on *domicilium citandi et executandi* clauses differs from the law of the Republic of South Africa on the subject. In consequence, the use of such a clause (nominating an address for service, as described above, in Eswatini) may, in particular where the defendant is a *peregrinus*, indicate submission to the jurisdiction of the Eswatini courts.[63]

11.1.2.5 *The jurisdictional significance of arrest of the person*

In *Standard Bank of Swaziland Ltd v Cassamo*,[64] the plaintiff, a bank located in Eswatini and therefore an *incola*, had applied[65] for and had been granted a rule *nisi* calling upon the defendant to show cause why the deputy sheriff should not arrest him in order to 'found and confirm jurisdiction' in an action to be instituted by the plaintiff. The defendant was a Portuguese national resident in Maputo, Mozambique, who had drawn against a cheque deposited with the plaintiff, which cheque was subsequently dishonoured. Nathan CJ confirmed the rule *nisi* and ordered the arrest of the defendant to found or confirm jurisdiction

---

[61] *Dicey, Morris and Collins on the Conflict of Laws* 15 ed (2012) vol 1, para 12-105.

[62] See, by way of example, *Dorbyl Vehicle Trading and Finance Co (Pty) Ltd v Sciolla (NULL)* [1996] SZHC 22 (Dunn J).

[63] See, by way of comparison, the decision of the South African Supreme Court in *Hay Management Consultants (Pty) Ltd v P3 Management Consultants (Pty) Ltd* 2005 (2) SA 522 (SCA) *per* Heher JA (Scott, Cameron and Conradie JJA and Patel AJA agreeing) para [15]; where the clause was regarded as 'a significant factor', as was the choice of South African law as the proper law (para [14]).

[64] [1979–1981] SWLR 247 (Nathan CJ).

[65] Ibid 248B–E, where the judge pointed out that the application for attachment in such circumstances should be made *ex parte*.

over him and ordered the defendant to pay the costs of the application. The judge stated[66] that the defendant could obtain his release from arrest by payment of security for the plaintiff's claim and costs in an amount to be determined by the Registrar of the High Court.

The Eswatini courts have not yet directly addressed the question whether the provisions of the Eswatini Constitution[67] affect the Roman-Dutch common law relating to the arrest of a *peregrinus* in order to found jurisdiction.[68] It remains to be seen whether the courts will take the same view as the Supreme Court of Appeal in South Africa that constitutional provisions of this sort preclude the common-law right to arrest the person of a *peregrinus* in order to found or confirm the jurisdiction of the court.[69]

11.2 Enforcement of Foreign Judgments

A foreign judgment may be enforced in Eswatini by ordinary action at common law[70] or, pursuant to the Reciprocal Enforcement of Judgments Proclamation 1922[71] (sometimes referred to as the Reciprocal Enforcement of Judgments Act) and the Reciprocal Enforcement of Judgments Rules of Court 1923.[72]

---

[66] Ibid 248E and 251B–C.

[67] Which acquired force as a result of the Constitution of the Kingdom of Swaziland Act 2005 (Act 1 of 2005). For present purposes, the most relevant provision of the Constitution is s 16, which provides that a person shall not be deprived of his personal liberty except as authorised by law. The two specific exceptions to the general principle which are of relevance here are 'in execution of the order of a court made to secure the fulfilment of any obligation imposed on that person by law' (ground (c)) and 'for the purpose of bringing that person before a court in the execution of the order of a court' (ground (d)). Section 26, 'Protection of freedom of movement', would not seem to provide protection from jurisdictional arrest for a *peregrinus* defendant. Although s 26(1) provides: 'A person shall not be deprived of the freedom of movement ...', sub-s (2) excepts from this any 'lawful detention of that person' and sub-s (3)(g) excepts 'the imposition of restrictions on the right of any person to leave Eswatini that are reasonably required in order to secure the fulfilment of any obligation imposed on that person by law'. The former exception at least would appear to cover jurisdictional arrest.

[68] In *SMADCO Investments (Pty) Ltd v Inyoni Boerdery Vervoer* [2012] SZHC 243 Ota J, in the context of his assessment of whether a *peregrinus* could successfully set aside an order of attachment which had been made against him by submitting to the jurisdiction post execution, mentioned, at para [17] the process of arresting a defendant in order to found/confirm the jurisdiction of the court. While only a passing reference, nothing in that judgment suggested that the process was unconstitutional.

[69] *Bid Industrial Holdings (Pty) Ltd v Strang* 2008 (3) SA 355 (SCA).

[70] *USA Distillers (Proprietary) Ltd v Improchem (Proprietary) Ltd* [2020] SZSC 51 (SC) (Dlamini and Matsebula JJA and Manzini AJA). This is also the position in the Republic of South Africa: Forsyth *Private International Law* 5 ed (2012) 473; *Jones v Krok* 1995 (1) SA 677 (AD) (Corbett CJ, Van Heeren, Kumbleben, Nienaber and Oliver JJA) *per* Corbett JA (giving the judgment of the court) 685B–D.

[71] Proclamation 4 of 1922 as amended by Proclamation 68 of 1922 (which erroneously refers to an amendment to s 5 of Proclamation 4 of 1922 when the amendment is to s 6). By a High Commissioner's Notice (97 of 1922, entitled 'Reciprocal Enforcement of Judgments') the Proclamation was extended to Basutoland (Botswana), Bechuanaland Protectorate (Lesotho), Southern Rhodesia (Zimbabwe), Northern Rhodesia (Zambia), Zanzibar Protectorate, Nyasaland Protectorate (Malawi), Colony and Protectorate of Kenya, New Zealand, Western Australia, Tanganyika Territory (Tanzania), Uganda, New South Wales, Victoria, Territory of North Australia and Territory of Central Australia.

[72] High Commissioner's Notice 52 of 1923. These Rules are cited in the footnotes which follow as 'REJ Rule/REJ r ...'.

11.2.1 Enforcement at common law

As the Supreme Court of Eswatini clarified in *USA Distillers (Proprietary) Ltd v Improchem (Proprietary) Ltd*,[73] the basic law of Eswatini is to be found in the General Law and Administration Proclamation 1907[74] ('the 1907 Proclamation') and the Constitution of Eswatini 2005[75] ('the Constitution').

The 1907 Proclamation provides, inter alia:

> '3 (1) The Roman-Dutch common law, save in so far as the same has heretofore or may from time to time hereafter be modified by statute, shall be law in [Eswatini].
>
> (2) Save and except in so far as the same have been repealed or amended the statutes in force in the Transvaal on the fifteenth day of October, 1904, and the statutory regulations thereunder shall *mutatis mutandis*, and as far as they may be applicable, be in force in [Eswatini].
>
> (3) Where under any such statute aforesaid any power or authority is at the date of this Proclamation exercisable in the Transvaal by the Governor or the Governor in Council, such power and authority shall in the application of such law to [Eswatini] be exercised by the High Commissioner.'

Thus, as at 22 February 1907 (the date of the Proclamation), the law applicable to Eswatini was the 'Roman-Dutch common law'. The 1907 Proclamation remained in force as at the date of Eswatini's independence on 6 September 1968.

At independence, therefore, the law of Eswatini was the 'Roman-Dutch common law' as provided for by the 1907 Proclamation.

The Constitution of Eswatini confirms the continuing applicability of Roman-Dutch common law in Eswatini:

> '252 (1) Subject to the provisions of this Constitution or any other written law, the principles and rules that formed, immediately before the 6th September, 1968 (Independence Day), the principles and rules of the Roman Dutch Common Law as applicable to [Eswatini] since 22 February 1907 are confirmed and shall be applied and enforced as the common law of [Eswatini] except where and to the extent that those principles or rules are inconsistent with this Constitution or a statute.'

Accordingly, the common law currently in force in Eswatini is the 'Roman-Dutch common law' as provided for by the 1907 Proclamation, except where and to the extent that the principles of that law are inconsistent with the Constitution or a statute.[76]

---

[73] [2020] SZSC 51 (SC) para [24].

[74] Proclamation 4 of 1907, dated 22 February 1907; superseding the corresponding provisions of the General Administration Proclamation (Proclamation 11 of 1905).

[75] Which acquired force as a result of the Constitution of the Kingdom of Swaziland Act 2005 (Act 1 of 2005).

[76] See *Umcebo Mining (Pty) Ltd v USA Distillers (Pty) Ltd* [2017] SZHC 202 (HC, Maphalala PJ, Mamba and Dlamini JJ; 06 October 2017).

In the *USA Distillers*[77] the Supreme Court was asked to recognise a judgment of the High Court of South Africa in Eswatini. The Supreme Court confirmed that the passage of the Reciprocal Enforcement of Judgments Act 1922[78] did not remove the ability at common law to have recognised and enforced a judgment from a country, like the Republic of South Africa, to which the 1922 Act did not apply.[79]

Further, the Supreme Court held that the following requirements had to be satisfied in order for a foreign judgment to be recognised and enforced under the common law: first, the foreign court had international jurisdiction (or competence) to decide the case; second, that the judgment rendered was final and conclusive and had not become superannuated; and third, the recognition and enforcement of the foreign judgment must not be against public policy.[80] On the facts of the case, the Supreme Court determined that the aforementioned requirements were so satisfied. The plaintiff in an action to enforce a foreign judgment by ordinary action may seek provisional sentence[81] in the action or summary judgment or may proceed to prove the case at trial.

Given the Eswatini Supreme Court's reliance in *USA Distillers*[82] on the decision in *Jones v Krok*,[83] it may be worth pointing out that in the latter case Corbett CJ provided the following guidance on the question of the finality of a judgment in the context of an appeal against the foreign judgment:[84]

> '(1) The fact that the judgment is subject to appeal or even that an appeal is pending in the foreign jurisdiction does not affect the finality of the judgment, provided that in all other respects it is final and conclusive.
>
> (2) Where, however, it is shown that the judgment is subject to such an appeal or that such an appeal is pending, the Court in this country which is asked to enforce the judgment enjoys a discretion and in the exercise thereof may, instead of giving judgment in favour of the plaintiff, stay the proceedings pending the final determination of the appeal or appeals in the foreign jurisdiction.
>
> (3) Although the onus of proving that a foreign judgment is final and conclusive rests upon the party seeking to enforce it ... it seems to me that, where this onus has been

---

[77] [2020] SZSC 51 (SC).

[78] Number 4 of 1922 as amended by Proclamation 68 of 1922.

[79] [2020] SZSC 51 (SC) para [4], relying on *Economa (Pty) Ltd v Hudson* [1994] SZHC 40 (HC; 17 June 1994) (Dunn J) and the decision of the Appellate Division of the South African Supreme Court in *Jones v Krok* 1995 (1) SA 677 (AD) (Corbett CJ, Van Heerden, Cumleben and Nienaber JJA and Olivier AJA). The Supreme Court in *USA Distillers* also, at para [45], disapproved of the decision in *Mamba v Mamba* [2011] SZHC 40 (HC) (Ota J), which had been to the contrary effect.

[80] [2020] SZSC 51 (SC) paras [30] and [44].

[81] *Jones v Krok* 1995 (1) SA 677 (AD), *per* Corbett CJ at 685F.

[82] [2020] SZSC 51 (SC).

[83] 1995 (1) SA 677 (AD), *per* Corbett CJ at 689B–693C.

[84] Ibid 692B–G.

discharged, it is up to the defendant to place before the Court the facts relating to the impending appeal and such other relevant facts as may persuade the Court to exercise its discretion in favour of granting a stay of proceedings.

(4) In exercising this discretion the Court may take into account all relevant circumstances, including (but not confined to) whether an appeal is actually pending, the consequences to the defendant if judgment be given in favour of plaintiff and thereafter (possibly after the judgment has been satisfied) the appeal succeeds in the foreign jurisdiction and whether the defendant is pursuing the right of appeal genuinely and with due diligence. As a rule, however, the Court will refuse to assess the merits and demerits of the appeal and its prospects of success in the foreign Court.'

The plaintiff in an action to enforce a foreign judgment by ordinary action may seek provisional sentence[85] in the action or summary judgment or may proceed to prove the case at trial.

11.2.2 Enforcement pursuant to statute

11.2.2.1 *The regime for enforcement pursuant to statute*

The 1922 Proclamation makes provision for a system of registration of foreign judgments,[86] the purpose of which is to domesticate the foreign judgment and render it enforceable in Eswatini as if it were a judgment of the Eswatini court.[87]

11.2.2.2 *Procedure for registration*

Where a judgment has been obtained in the courts of a territory to which the Proclamation applies,[88] the judgment creditor may apply to the Eswatini court to

---

[85] *Jones v Krok* 1995 (1) SA 677 (AD), *per* Corbett CJ at 685F.

[86] Section 3.

[87] Section 3(3). The provisions of the 1922 Proclamation correspond very closely to legislation of the United Kingdom (Administration of Justice Act 1920) on which the 1922 Proclamation was based. In particular, ss 2, 3, 4, 5 and 6 are effectively transpositions of, respectively, ss 12(1), 9, 10, 11 and 14 of the Administration of Justice Act 1920. It is to be expected that a court in Eswatini will refer to judicial and academic authorities on the construction of these provisions of the 1920 Act when deciding questions on the construction of corresponding provisions of the 1922 Proclamation. The House of Lords has held that the provisions of the 1920 Act 'have to be construed with reference to the common law as understood in 1920': *Owens Bank Ltd v Bracco* [1992] 2 AC 443 (HL (E)), *per* Lord Bridge (giving the leading speech with which Lords Griffiths, Ackner, Goff and Browne-Wilkinson agreed) 488E–F. Lord Bridge also set out a brief legislative history of the 1920 Act at 488B–E. See also: *Dicey, Morris and Collins on the Conflict of Laws* 15 ed (2012) vol 1, paras 14R-173–14-181; Briggs *Civil Jurisdiction and Judgments* 7 ed (2021) paras 35.01–35-10.

[88] By a High Commissioner's Notice (97 of 1922, entitled 'Reciprocal Enforcement of Judgments') the Proclamation was extended to Basutoland (Botswana), Bechuanaland Protectorate (Lesotho), Southern Rhodesia (Zimbabwe), Northern Rhodesia (Zambia), Zanzibar Protectorate, Nyasaland Protectorate (Malawi), Colony and Protectorate of Kenya, New Zealand, Western Australia, Tanganyika Territory (Tanzania), Uganda, New South Wales, Victoria, Territory of North Australia and Territory of Central Australia. See further *USA Distillers* [2020] SZSC 51 (SC) para [19].

have that judgment registered.[89] The application must be made within 12 months of the date of the judgment or such longer period as the court may allow. The court may then order the judgment to be registered with the consequence that it may then be enforced as if it were a judgment of the Eswatini court. The Eswatini court may only allow registration if 'in all the circumstances ... it is just and convenient'[90] to do so. Registration is, therefore, ultimately a matter of discretion.

Section 3(2) of the Proclamation provides for a number of defences to registration:

(1) The original court acted without jurisdiction.[91] For the purposes of the 1922 Proclamation, the foreign court has international jurisdiction for the purposes of the registration of its judgments if the judgment debtor was ordinarily resident or carrying on business within the jurisdiction of that court.[92] In *Sfeir & Co v National Insurance Co of New Zealand*,[93] it was held that a New Zealand insurance company was not carrying on business in Ghana by reason only of retaining agents in Ghana having authority limited to bind the company by settlements of claims arising in Ghana under its policies issued elsewhere: the business carried on by the agents was the agents' own and not the company's.[94]

(2) The judgment debtor did not voluntarily appear and neither submitted nor agreed to the jurisdiction of the foreign court where the foreign court did not otherwise have jurisdiction.[95]

(3) The judgment debtor was not duly served with the process of the foreign court. There is some judicial authority under the corresponding provisions of the 1920 Act that '*duly served*' means served in accordance with the law of the foreign court whose document it was.[96]

(4) The judgment of the foreign court was obtained by fraud.[97] Fraud here bears a broad meaning reflecting the common law as it was in 1920.

[89] Considered in *Mamba v Mamba* [2011] SZHC 43 (HC), where Ota J refused to apply the Proclamation to a judgment of the Circuit Court of Montgomery County, Maryland, USA, concerning matrimonial matters. (The judge accepted that the courts of the husband's domicile at the time proceedings are commenced have exclusive jurisdiction over the matrimonial proceedings. The position is different in cases where the allegation is that the marriage is a nullity; here, the courts of the plaintiff's domicile will have jurisdiction, regardless of the domicile of the husband: *Magagula v Chibesakunda* [2013] SZHC 28 (HC) (Mamba J).

[90] Section 3(1).

[91] Section 3(2)(a).

[92] Presence within the foreign jurisdiction is not sufficient to give the foreign court international jurisdiction over the defendant for the purposes of the 1922 Proclamation.

[93] [1964] 1 Lloyd's Rep 330 (QB).

[94] Ibid 339, col 1, *per* Mocatta J.

[95] Section 3(2)(b).

[96] *Sfeir & Co v National Insurance Co of New Zealand* [1964] 1 Lloyd's Rep 330, *per* Mocatta J at 341, col 1.

[97] Section 3(2)(d).

A judgment debtor may set aside the registration of a foreign judgment if he can persuade the court that the judgment was obtained by fraud. It is irrelevant in this context that the foreign court has already considered and determined against the judgment debtor the same questions of fact on which the judgment debtor seeks to rely in the Eswatini court in order to set aside the registration of the foreign judgment. There is no requirement that the facts relied on as establishing fraud should not have been discoverable with the exercise of reasonable diligence at the time the proceedings in the foreign court took place. However undesirable it may seem, the position is clear under the 1920 Act and therefore under the 1922 Proclamation: a judgment debtor may effectively relitigate before the Eswatini court issues of fraud already determined against him in the foreign court by the very judgment which the judgment creditor seeks to enforce in Eswatini.[98]

(5) The judgment debtor satisfies the court that an appeal is pending or that he is entitled to appeal the foreign judgment and intends to do so. No doubt the court could place conditions on the setting aside of the registration of the foreign judgment, such that any appeal was prosecuted expeditiously.

(6) The foreign judgment was in respect of a cause of action that for reasons of public policy or some similar reason could not have been entertained by the Eswatini court.

(7) The judgment debtor satisfies the court that for some other reason it is not just and convenient to register the judgment or that it is just and convenient to set aside registration.

The procedure for registration of a foreign judgment under the 1922 Proclamation is set out in the Reciprocal Enforcement of Judgments Rules of Court.[99] An application is made for registration; an order granting leave to register may then be made; written notice of registration must then be served on the judgment debtor advising him of his right to seek to set aside the order granting leave and of the time within which such an application must be made.

---

[98] *Owens Bank Ltd v Bracco* [1992] 2 AC 443 (HL (E)), *per* Lord Bridge at 489B–H. The rules relating setting aside a foreign judgment obtained by fraud are comprehensively set out in *Dicey, Morris and Collins on the Conflict of Laws* 15 ed (2012) vol 1, rule 50, paras 14R-137–14-145; the position in English law has not been followed in certain Commonwealth jurisdictions (eg Canada in *Beals v Saldanha* [2003] 3 SCR 416, (2003) 234 DLR (4th) 1; and New South Wales in *Keele v Findley* (1991) 21 NSWLR 444 (NSWSC); but in *Close v Arnot* (unreported) 21 November 1997 (NSW), the Common Law Division distinguished *Keele v Findley* and applied the traditional English standard of fraud in respect of a foreign judgment in a case where the defendant had, for good reason, allowed foreign proceedings to go undefended.

[99] High Commissioner's Notice 52 of 1923 ('REJ').

The application may be made *ex parte* or by summons and, if made *ex parte*, the court may direct that a summons be issued.[100] The application must be supported by an affidavit setting out the facts regarding the judgment, exhibiting the judgment or a verified or otherwise authenticated copy and stating that, to the best of the deponent's information and belief, the judgment creditor is entitled to enforce the judgment and that the judgment does not fall within any of the cases to which section 3(2) refers (that there is no defence to the registration).[101]

An order giving leave to register the judgment must state the time period within which the judgment debtor may apply to set aside the registration (at least 14 days, depending on the distance of the judgment debtor's ordinary residence from Mbabane).[102] If the application was by summons the order must be served on the judgment debtor but, if the application was *ex parte*, service of the order is not required.[103]

Notice in writing of registration of the judgment must be served on the judgment debtor within a reasonable time after the registration and such notice must state that the judgment debtor is entitled to apply to set aside registration and must also state the number of days for applying to set aside registration, limited by the order giving leave to register the judgment.[104]

11.2.2.3 *Setting aside registration*

The judgment debtor may apply by summons for registration to be set aside and the court may order that the registration be set aside unconditionally or on terms if the court is satisfied that the case falls within one of the cases under section 3(2) of the 1922 Proclamation; or it is not just and convenient to register the judgment; or 'for any other sufficient reasons'.[105]

11.3 Interim Remedies

11.3.1 Jurisdiction to grant interim remedies

According to section 151(1)(a) of the Eswatini Constitution,[106] the High Court has 'unlimited original jurisdiction in civil and criminal matters as the High Court possesses at the date of commencement of this Constitution'. Section 140(2) provides:

---

[100] REJ r 1.
[101] REJ r 2.
[102] REJ r 6.
[103] REJ r 5.
[104] REJ r 9.
[105] REJ r 12.
[106] Constitution of the Kingdom of Swaziland Act 2005 (1 of 2005).

> 'In the exercise of the judicial power under this Constitution or any other law, the superior courts may, in relation to any matter within their jurisdiction, issue such orders or directions as may be necessary to ensure the enforcement of any judgement, decree or order of those courts.'

Section 2(1) of the High Court Act 1954 provides: 'The High Court shall within the limits of and subject to this or any other law possess and exercise all the jurisdiction, power and authority vested in the Supreme Court of South Africa.' As noted in the chapter on the Republic of South Africa, the power of the South African superior courts to grant interdictal relief is not statute based, but is derived from the court's inherent jurisdiction.[107] It may be supposed, therefore, that the basis for the Eswatini courts to grant interdictal relief is similarly part of the court's inherent jurisdiction.

The discussion below sets out the various types of interim remedy which the High Court may, as a result, grant in Eswatini, focusing, in particular, on the grant of: interim interdicts, freezing orders/anti-dissipation interdicts and search and seizure orders.

11.3.2 Procedure for application

Rule 6 of the High Court Rules provides that, save where proceedings by way of petition are prescribed by law, every application shall be brought on notice of motion, supported by an affidavit or affidavits as to the facts upon which the application relies for relief.[108] Applications may be made *inter partes* on notice, *ex parte* without notice on an urgent basis.

Inter partes applications are made on notice. Where such an application is made, it must be brought on notice of motion as near as may be in accordance with Form 3 of the First Schedule to the High Court Rules and true copies of the notice, the supporting affidavit or affidavits and all annexures thereto shall be served upon every party to whom notice thereof is to be given.[109]

---

[107] Prest *The Law and Practice of Interdicts* (1996) 266.

[108] Rule 6(1).

[109] Rule 6(9). The plaintiff must also comply with the provisions set out in r 6(10). Rule 6(11)–(18) set out the process by which any defendant may oppose the application and the further procedure with which a plaintiff must comply where the defendant wishes so to oppose the application. Where the plaintiff makes an interlocutory or other application incidental to pending proceedings, that may be brought on notice supported by such affidavits as the case may require and set down at a time assigned by the registrar or as directed by a judge: r 6(24).

11.3.2.1 *Urgency*

An application for interim relief may also be made *ex parte*[110] on an urgent basis.[111] Where the plaintiff makes an urgent application, the court or the judge may dispense with the forms and service for which the High Court Rules otherwise provide and, instead, dispose of the matter at such a time and place and in such manner and in accordance with such procedure (which, so far as practicable, will be in the terms of the High Court Rules) as to the court or judge, as the case may be, seems fit.[112] When making an urgent application, the plaintiff must set out explicitly the circumstances which he avers renders the matter urgent and the reasons why he claims that he could not be afforded substantial redress at a hearing in due course.[113]

11.3.3 Interim interdicts

In *Dlamini v Prince Chief GasawNgwane*[114] the Supreme Court of Eswatini reaffirmed the conditions to be satisfied for the granting of an interim interdict. Relying on the South African decisions in *Setlogelo v Setlogelo*[115] and *Eriksen Motors Ltd v Protea Motors*[116] and citing with approval the Eswatini case of *Dlamini v Okonda*,[117] the Supreme Court endorsed the following summary:

> 'A [plaintiff] who seeks an interim interdict should establish the following essential requirements: firstly, a right which is though *prima facie* established is open to some doubt, namely that he has a *prima facie* right. Secondly, a well grounded apprehension of irreparable injury if the interim relief is not granted. Thirdly, that the balance of convenience favours the grant of an interim interdict. Fourthly, that there is no other satisfactory remedy.'

To provide an example of how the courts in Eswatini apply this test, reference may be made to *Steffanutti Stocks (Pty) Ltd v Government of the Kingdom of Swaziland*.[118] Here, the plaintiff, a peregrine (South African) company, sought to challenge the tender process of a road and bridge building contract and the award by the

---

[110] Rule 6(4). Any person who has an interest which may be affected by a decision on an application being brought *ex parte* may deliver notice of an application by him for leave to oppose, supported by an affidavit setting forth the nature of such interest and the ground upon which he desires to be heard, whereupon the Registrar shall set such application down for hearing at the same time as the application brought *ex parte*: r 6(7). See further in this respect, r 6(8).

[111] Rule 6(25).

[112] Rule 6(25)(a).

[113] Rule 6(25)(b). As to the importance of complying with the rules governing urgent applications, see *Mavimbela v Ingemba Investments (Pty) Ltd* [2017] SZHC 56 (HC, Maphanga J; 08 March 2017).

[114] [2019] SZSC 40 (SC) (Maphalala CJ, Matsebula and Currie AJJA) para [29].

[115] 1914 AD 221.

[116] 1973 (3) SA 685 (AD).

[117] [2013] SZHC 167 (HC) (Maphalala J).

[118] [2013] SZHC 160 (HC) (Mabuza J).

government of the contract to a competitor, a company incorporated outside the jurisdiction but with its principal place of business in Eswatini (the third defendant). The tender process was commenced in April 2012 by way of an advertisement in the press. The plaintiff submitted its tender in July 2012. The contract was awarded to the third defendant in late September 2012 and the plaintiff was notified of the reasons for this decision in late November 2012. The tender documentation provided for a right of appeal against the decision and the plaintiff notified the government of its intention to appeal in early December 2012. Also in early December 2012 the government signed the construction contract with the third defendant. In late February 2013 the plaintiff, having received no reply to its notification in early December 2012, wrote again to the government. The government and the plaintiff then entered into correspondence, culminating in the issuing of the application for an interim interdict in April 2013 seeking an order restraining the award or commencement of the contract pending the determination of the plaintiff's appeal.

Mabuza J considered the requirements for an interim interdict: (1) although the plaintiff had a *prima facie* right to appeal the award of the contract to the third defendant, that right had to be exercised within 90 days of the plaintiff being notified that it had not been awarded the contract, which period had expired by the time the plaintiff made the application, with the consequence that 'the *prima facie* right has been effectively incapacitated';[119] (2) because the third defendant had already commenced works, the balance of convenience favoured not making the order sought;[120] and (3) damages were an adequate remedy in any event.[121]

11.3.4 Freezing orders/Anti-dissipation interdicts

A court in Eswatini will have jurisdiction in respect of an application for interim relief in the form of a freezing order or an anti-dissipation interdict where that order is sought in respect of assets within the jurisdiction, even though the plaintiff and defendant are *peregrini* and the proceedings between the plaintiff and defendant are progressing outside the jurisdiction.[122]

The Eswatini courts will make freezing orders/anti-dissipation interdicts in appropriate cases and will do so on an urgent application brought *ex parte* if

[119] Ibid paras [30]–[34].

[120] Ibid paras [37]–[39].

[121] Ibid para [40].

[122] This is the effect of the decision of the High Court in *De Hart NO v Kleynhans* [1963–1969] SWLR 373 (HC) (14 October 1968).

certain conditions are met. In *HP Enterprises (Pty) Ltd t/a Heather's Fashions v Nedbank (Swaziland) Ltd*,[123] Sapire CJ stated:

> 'A litigant seeking to invoke the urgency procedures must make specific allegations of fact, which demonstrate that the observance of the normal procedures and time limits prescribed by the Rules will result in irreparable loss or irreversible deterioration to his prejudice in the situation giving rise to the litigation. The facts alleged must not be contrived, but must give rise to a reasonable fear that if immediate relief is not afforded, irreparable harm will follow.'

A plaintiff (ie the applicant for a freezing order) must show, in addition[124] to the other requirements for an interim interdict, a risk of dissipation on the part of the defendant. In *First National Bank Swaziland Ltd v Hlatshwayo*,[125] the plaintiff applied for an order directing the defendant to pay into an interest-bearing account the proceeds of sale of a property. The plaintiff alleged that the defendant had, while employed by the plaintiff, misappropriated sums from it. Maphalala J considered the requirements for an anti-dissipation interdict and stated:[126]

> 'It also appears to be trite law that in such interdicts the [plaintiff] is obliged to prove all the requirements in interdict generally and further for the [plaintiff] to show that the [defendant] was "**arranging his affairs in such a way as to ensure that he will be without assets within the country by the time when the** [plaintiff] **is in a position to execute**".' (emphasis in original)

The judge found that the plaintiff had failed to demonstrate that there was a risk of dissipation and dismissed the application.

It appears not to have been argued that the evidence of the defendant's misappropriation of funds was sufficient to demonstrate dishonesty and for that reason presented a risk of dissipation. In *Spintex Swaziland (Pty) Ltd v Motsa*,[127] Mamba J accepted that evidence of fraud on the part of the defendant was a factor to be taken into account in determining whether or not there is a real risk of dissipation. Similarly, in *Taft v Taft*[128] the defendant's history of default in the payment of maintenance and other financial obligations owed to his former wife and their child, combined with evidence that the defendant had already divested himself of significant assets within the jurisdiction, taken together were held by Annandale ACJ to present a risk of dissipation justifying the making of an anti-dissipation interdict.

---

[123] [1999] SZHC 115 (HC) (Sapire CJ), cited by Annandale ACJ in *Taft v Taft* [2006] SZHC 141 (HC) para [14].

[124] As to which, see *Sifundzany Primary v Priscilla* [2021] SZHC 44 (Langwenya J).

[125] [2005] SZHC 63 (HC).

[126] Ibid para [7], citing *Knox D'Arcy Ltd v Jamieson* 1994 (3) SA 700 (W).

[127] [2013] SZHC 97 (HC).

[128] [2006] SZHC 141 (HC).

There is some doubt as to whether a plaintiff must show not only that the defendant is dissipating his assets but that he is doing so with the intention of defeating the plaintiff's claim. The doubt emerges from the contradictions which are present in the case law on the subject. It is submitted that, as a matter of principle, the plaintiff should be required to demonstrate that the defendant is dissipating his assets with the intention of defeating the plaintiff's claim. It is further submitted that, as a matter of practice, the High Court in *Fakudze v Sukke Ontime Investment*[129] has reaffirmed the plaintiff's need to demonstrate intention on the part of the defendant. Indeed, the High Court referred to the South African Court of Appeal decision in *Knox D'Arcy Ltd v Jamieson*,[130] in which EM Grosskopf JA, giving the judgment of the Court,[131] stated:[132]

> 'The question which arises from this approach is whether a [plaintiff] need show a particular state of mind on the part of the [defendant], ie that he is getting rid of the funds, or is likely to do so, with the intention of defeating the claims of creditors. Having regard to the purpose of this type of interdict, the answer must be, I consider, yes, except possibly in exceptional cases. As I have said, the effect of the interdict is to prevent the [defendant] from freely dealing with his own property to which the [plaintiff] lays no claim. Justice may require this restriction in cases where the [defendant] is shown to be acting *mala fide* with the intent of preventing execution in respect of the [plaintiff's] claim. However, there would not normally be any justification to compel a [defendant] to regulate his *bona fide* expenditure so as to retain funds in his patrimony for the payment of claims (particularly disputed ones) against him. I am not, of course, at the moment dealing with special situations which might arise, for instance, by contract or under the law of insolvency.'

In consequence, it follows, as a matter of principle, that the defendant's expenditure on normal personal and business expenses or in the ordinary course of business does not represent dissipation of assets for the purposes of obtaining an anti-dissipation interdict.

It is in this connection that the aforementioned contradictions have arisen in the case law. By way of example, the decision of Ota J in *Nedbank Swaziland Ltd v Dlamini*,[133] is, it is submitted, incorrect. In that case, Ota J considered whether a pension payment should continue to be made to the defendant, a former employee of the plaintiff who had defrauded it of substantial sums of money. The defendant's evidence was that he would use the pension payments to maintain his family. Relying on the South African authority *Msunduzi Municipality v Natal*

---

[129] [2020] SZHC 60 (HC) (Dlamini J) paras [24] and [25].

[130] 1996 (4) SA 348 (A).

[131] EM Grosskopf, Nestadt, FH Grosskopf, Harms and Scott JJA.

[132] 1996 (4) SA 348 (A) 372G–I.

[133] [2012] SZHC 158 (HC).

Joint Municipal Pension/Provident Fund,[134] the judge referred to the evidence that the defendant had little or no other assets to satisfy a judgment debt and stated:[135]

> 'This coupled with the 1st [defendant's] averments that it [sic] is unemployed, has no other source of income and will depend solely on the Pension benefits to sustain himself and his dependents, show clearly the irreparable harm anticipated by the [plaintiff]. When one considers how long it takes for Court cases to be concluded, it becomes very apparent in these circumstances, that the Pension benefits may be dissipated leaving the [plaintiff's] victory nugatory. It is the judicial consensus as clearly demonstrated by the case of [Msunduzi Municipality] that if a [plaintiff] for an interdict against dissipation of assets fears that the [defendants] would not be able to preserve their assets pending resolution of the dispute in the main action and it is evident that they have little or no assets to satisfy the judgment debt if it goes against them, the [plaintiff's] fear of being left with a hollow judgment is well grounded.'

This passage appears to suggest that all that need be shown on an application for a freezing order/anti-dissipation interdict is a risk of dissipation, regardless of the intention accompanying the dissipation. However, the *Msunduzi Municipality* case itself referred to the South African Court of Appeal decision in *Knox D'Arcy Ltd v Jamieson*,[136] which case, properly considered, points to the contrary conclusion. In point of fact, therefore, the absence of a proprietary or vindicatory claim against the assets which it is sought to freeze, evidence that the defendant is paying ordinary expenses is not relevant evidence of dissipation for the purposes of obtaining an anti-dissipation interdict (even where such an interdict is granted, the defendant is entitled to pay ordinary expenses out of the sums frozen). The suggestion by Ota J in *Nedbank Swaziland Ltd v Dlamini* that the defendant could be prevented from making such payments is questionable. However, the approach of Ota J has received subsequent judicial support.

In *Swazi Spa Holdings Ltd v Standard Bank Swaziland Ltd*,[137] Hlophe J stated:[138] 'It is in law not essential that the [plaintiff] presents proof that the [defendant] intends to frustrate an anticipated judgment by dissipating the assets, but it is enough if the conduct of the [defendant] is likely to have that effect.' The judge had, in the previous paragraph of his judgment, referred to the decision of Stegmann J at first instance in *Knox D'Arcy Ltd v Jamieson*,[139] where the judge set out the requirements for an anti-dissipation interdict as including the requirement that a defendant should be shown to 'have an intention to defeat the plaintiff's claim, or to render it hollow, by secreting his assets in any of a number of ways

[134] 2007 (1) SA 142 (N).
[135] [2012] SZHC 158 (HC) para [62].
[136] 1996 (4) SA 348 (A).
[137] [2012] SZHC 185 (HC).
[138] Ibid para [27].
[139] 1994 (3) SA 700 (W) 706B–E.

(for example, by apparently or actually disposing of them or by removing them beyond the jurisdiction of the Court)'.

The passage from *Swazi Spa Holdings* was cited with apparent approval by Mamba J in *Spintex Swaziland (Pty) Ltd v Motsa*,[140] where the judge made no reference to a need to demonstrate an intention to dissipate in order to defeat the plaintiff's claim.

The line of case law which stands for the proposition that it is unnecessary to show an intention on the part of the defendant to dissipate his assets so as to defeat the plaintiff's claim marks an undesirable departure from what the Eswatini court considered the appropriate principles were. It is submitted that this line of authority is incorrect and the conclusion reached in *Fakudze v Sukke Ontime Investment*[141] is correct and ought be followed instead.

In keeping with other Roman-Dutch jurisdictions, failure to make full and frank disclosure on an *ex parte* application for an anti-dissipation interdict may lead to the rule *nisi* obtained on such an application being discharged.[142]

However, it would appear that the practice in Eswatini is not to require a cross-undertaking from the plaintiff that, if it transpires the interdict ought not to have been granted, the plaintiff is obliged to indemnify the defendant for any damage suffered by the defendant as a result of the interdict (assuming an enquiry as to damages is ordered by the court and that the enquiry finds that the defendant in fact suffered compensatable loss).[143]

It also appears that disclosure orders may be made as part of the rule *nisi* and/ or interdict and that these orders, requiring the addressee to disclose the amount of the potential defendant's assets, may be directed not only at the potential defendant, but also at the party holding the potential defendant's assets, for example, a bank.[144]

Notwithstanding that a bank is a third party to the plaintiff's intended proceedings, it seems that the practice is that no order for the plaintiff to meet the third party's reasonable costs of complying with the order is made.[145]

The property that is sought to be frozen should be proportionate to the sum claimed by the plaintiff. In *Cargo Carriers Swaziland (Pty) Ltd v USA Distillers (Pty) Ltd*,[146] the plaintiff obtained a rule *nisi*, the effect of which was to freeze plant

---

140 [2013] SZHC 97 (HC) (30 April 2013).

141 [2020] SZHC 60 (HC).

142 As was the case in *Cargo Carriers Swaziland (Pty) Ltd v USA Distillers (Pty) Ltd* [2003] SZHC 120 (HC), *per* Maphalala J at 9–11.

143 See, for example, *Swazi Spa Holdings Ltd v Standard Bank Swaziland Ltd* [2012] SZHC 185 (HC) and *Spintex Swaziland (Pty) Ltd v Motsa* [2013] SZHC 97 (HC).

144 In *Swazi Spa Holdings Ltd v Standard Bank Swaziland Ltd* [2012] SZHC 185 (HC), disclosure orders were made against two banks at which the potential defendant maintained accounts; similar orders were made against banks in *Spintex Swaziland (Pty) Ltd v Motsa* [2013] SZHC 97 (HC).

145 *Swazi Spa Holdings Ltd v Standard Bank Swaziland Ltd* [2012] SZHC 185 (HC).

146 [2003] SZHC 120 (HC).

worth E140 million owned by the defendant and located within the jurisdiction in respect of the plaintiff's claim, which was worth E1 million. Maphalala J cited the South African decision in *Pohlman v Van Schalkwyk*,[147] where Froneman J stated[148] the following:

> 'The courts have devised at least three different and complementary safeguards. The first is to be found in the substantive requirements that must be met before any order is granted. These I have already referred to in dealing with the facts of this case. These requirements ensure the interest that a [plaintiff] seeks to protect is worthy of protection (there must be a proper cause of action) and that these interests are really under threat (real apprehension of harm and the like) [and] the second kind of safeguard is aligned with these aims, namely to ensure that the methods by which the [plaintiff's] interests are protected are not disproportionate to the interest being protected.'

Maphalala J held[149] that the plaintiff's rule *nisi* was disproportionate to the claim and discharged it on, inter alia, that ground.

11.3.5 Search and seize orders

In *Green v Swaziland Royal Insurance Corp*,[150] Maphalala J considered an application by a former employee of a company for an *Anton Piller* order against his former employer's employee liability insurers for seizure of the policy of employee liability insurance. The judge held[151] that an *Anton Piller* order 'is available only to preserve specific evidence for trial and not for the purpose of founding a cause of action'. Maphalala J cited[152] with apparent approval the decision of the South African Court of Appeal in *Universal City Studios Inc v Network Video (Pty) Ltd*,[153] where Corbett JA stated:[154]

> 'In a case where the [plaintiff] can establish *prima facie* that he has a cause of action against the [defendant] which he intends to pursue, that the [defendant] has in his possession specific documents or things which constitute vital evidence in substantiation of the [plaintiff's] cause of action (but in respect of which the [plaintiff] can claim no real or personal right), that there is a real and well-founded apprehension that this evidence may be hidden or destroyed or in some manner spirited away by the time the case comes to trial, or at any rate to the stage of discovery, and the [plaintiff] asks the Court to make an order designed to preserve the evidence in some way, is the Court obliged to adopt a *non possumus* attitude? Especially if there is no feasible alternative? I am inclined to think not.

147 2001 (1) SA 690 (EC).
148 Ibid 698G–I.
149 [2003] SZHC 120 (HC) p 11 of the transcript.
150 [2012] SZHC 78 (HC).
151 Ibid para [43].
152 Ibid para [44].
153 1986 (2) SA 734 (A) (Corbett, Kotzé, Miller and Botha JJA and Galgut AJA).
154 Ibid 755A–E.

> It would certainly expose a grave defect in our system of justice if it were to be found that in circumstances such as these the Court were powerless to act. Fortunately I am not persuaded that it would be. An order whereby the evidence was in some way recorded, eg by copying documents or photographing things or even by placing them temporarily, ie *pendente lite*, in the custody of a third party would not, in my view, be beyond the inherent powers of the Court. Nor do I perceive any difficulty in permitting such an order to be applied for *ex parte* and without notice and in camera, provided that the [plaintiff] can show the real possibility that the evidence will be lost to him if the [defendant] gets wind of the application.'

Maphalala J also cited[155] with apparent approval a subsequent decision of the South African Court of Appeal in *Shoba v Officer Commanding, Temporary Police Camp, Wagendrift Dam; Maphanga v Officer Commanding, SA Police Murder & Robbery Unit, Pietermaritzburg*,[156] where Corbett CJ, giving the judgment of the court, stated:[157]

> 'It is necessary to give a decision in regard to what was left open in both the *Universal City Studios* case supra and *Jafta's* case supra, viz whether an Anton Piller order directed at the preservation of evidence should be accepted as part of our practice. In my view, it should; and I would define what a [plaintiff] for such an order, obtained in camera and without notice to the respondent, must prima facie establish, as the following:
>
> (1) That he, the [plaintiff], has a cause of action against the [defendant] which he intends to pursue;
>
> (2) that the [defendant] has in his possession specific (and specified) documents or things which constitute vital evidence in substantiation of plaintiff's cause of action (but in respect of which [plaintiff] cannot claim a real or personal right); and
>
> (3) that there is a real and well-founded apprehension that this evidence may be hidden or destroyed or in some manner be spirited away by the time the case comes to trial or to the stage of discovery ...
>
> The Court to which application is made for such an Anton Piller order has a discretion whether to grant the remedy or not and, if it does, upon what terms. In exercising this discretion the Court will pay regard, inter alia, to the cogency of the prima facie case established with reference to the matters listed (1), (2) and (3) above; the potential harm that will be suffered by the [defendant] if the remedy is granted as compared with, or balanced against, the potential harm to the [plaintiff] if the remedy is withheld; and whether the terms of the order sought are no more onerous than is necessary to protect the interests of the [plaintiff].'[158]

---

155 [2012] SZHC 78 (HC) (28 March 2012) para [46].

156 1995 (4) SA 1 (A) (Corbett CJ, EM Grosskopf, Nestadt and MT Steyn JJA and Nicholas AJA).

157 Ibid 15F–16C.

158 Section 22 of the Constitution provides that a person 'shall not be subjected — (a) to the search of the person or the property of that person; (b) to the entry by others on the premises of that person; [or] (c) to the search of the private communications of that person, except with the free consent of that person first obtained'. The question arises whether this prohibits the granting of intrusive relief such as *Anton Piller* (search and seize order) relief. In *Green v Swaziland Royal Insurance Corp* [2012] SZHC 78 (HC), Maphalala J recorded (para [25]) that the second defendant (the former employer) argued that the order authorising the

It would seem therefore that the judicial view in Eswatini is that the South African approach to the making of an *Anton Piller* interdict is to be followed in Eswatini.[159]

If this is correct then, following South African practice, the order must contain a cross-undertaking as to damages fortified in appropriate cases with the payment into court of security.

An aspect of English practice which should be considered is whether any *Anton Piller* order made should provide for the deputy sheriff to be accompanied not by the plaintiff's lawyer but by an independent lawyer appointed by the court to ensure fairness in the process and to take custody of the relevant evidence.

11.3.6 Third-party disclosure orders

There appears to be no reported judicial authority in which an Eswatini court has made an order requiring a third party to give information or documents prior to the commencement of proceedings.

The position in the Republic of South Africa is as set out below and it is to be supposed that this will be influential in the future development of Eswatini law.

In *Kinekor Films (Pty) Ltd v BA Adami Films (Pty) Ltd*,[160] allowing the plaintiff's appeal, the court made an order compelling the defendant to disclose the identity of the source of the films in its possession of which the plaintiff was the copyright owner, with a view to the plaintiff bringing proceedings against those persons. Giving the judgment of the full bench of the Eastern Cape Division, Eksteen J held[161] that it was:

> 'clear that the person or persons from whom the defendant had obtained the infringing copies of the films were, in the same way, infringing the [plaintiff's] copyright by supplying such films to the [defendant], and that the [plaintiff] would therefore, *prima facie*, have a cause of action against such suppliers. Such an action however cannot be brought unless

sheriff to search for and seize the policy was a violation of its constitutional right to privacy and property enshrined in s 22 of the Constitution. In dismissing the application the judge noted (para [48]) that in Eswatini, 'This remedy has been subjected to severe criticism over the years on the basis that it violates section 22 of the Constitution which seeks to protect the right to privacy …'. The judge, having set out s 22, continued (para [50]), 'However, the constitutionality of the *Anton Piller* order is not in issue, and it is not a basis upon which the application is opposed', notwithstanding the judge having earlier set out the argument of the second defendant that the application was opposed on precisely that basis. Presently, therefore, the question of the constitutionality of the *Anton Piller* order in Eswatini is unresolved as a matter of judicial authority. However, it appears that the grant of such orders has been considered, notwithstanding s 22 having been raised as a defence. Until the matter is addressed by a court, the position appears to be that the Eswatini courts are prepared to entertain applications for *Anton Piller* orders and to make them in appropriate cases where the requirements are otherwise satisfied.

[159] See also *Fakudze v Sukke Ontime Investment* [2020] SZHC 60 (HC) (Dlamini J).

[160] 1976 (4) SA 935 (E; Eksteen, Kannemeyer and De Wet JJ).

[161] Ibid 939G–J.

> the [plaintiff] knows who the person or persons are who are acting in breach of its copyright. It says that it does not know who these persons are, and the obvious place to seek this information is from the defendant who must be aware of their identity. To deny the [plaintiff] the relief it seeks would in my view not be in the interests of justice but would rather afford an unwarranted protection of the infringers of the [plaintiff's] copyright in the pursuit of their illegal activity.'

In *Roamer Watch Co SA v African Textile Distributors*,[162] Cilliers AJ drew a distinction[163] between two types of disclosure cases: first, those where

> 'the [plaintiff] seeks to proceed against an unincorporated body or the officials of an unincorporated or incorporated body, and seeks disclosure of the names of the appropriate persons to cite from another person who is possessed of this information by virtue of his being an official of that body or standing in some other similar relation to that body'

and second,[164] those where the plaintiff 'is concerned to obtain the name of a party whom he is unable to identify and against whom he may have a cause of action'. In the latter situation, the plaintiff is seeking discovery of the name from a party who may have sound commercial or other reasons for being reluctant to disclose it. Cilliers AJ stated[165] that in the second case the plaintiff would need to indicate at least the following in the papers filed for hearing:

(1) A *bona fide* belief in his right of action against the party whose name he seeks to be disclosed and that he has reasonable grounds for believing that he has such a claim against such party. Here the strength of the plaintiff's case against the unknown alleged wrongdoer is relevant to the exercise of the court's discretion.

(2) There is no other complete remedy. Another appropriate remedy may consist either of an adequate claim against a party who is known to him in respect of the same damages which the plaintiff claims to have suffered, or in another procedural remedy to establish the same information which he seeks from the respondent to the application.

(3) The respondent is able to supply such information.

In *Cerebos Food Corp v Diverse Foods SA (Pty) Ltd*,[166] giving the judgment of the full bench of the Transvaal Provincial Division, Van Dijkhorst J held:[167] 'Neither in the Roman law nor the Roman-Dutch law nor in our law as laid down by the Appellate Division is there any authority for an order that a defendant disclose the names or particulars of sources and retail outlets.'

---

[162] 1980 (2) SA 254 (W).

[163] Ibid 281F–G.

[164] Ibid 281H–I.

[165] Ibid 282A–D.

[166] 1984 (4) SA 149 (T) (Boshoff JP and Van Dijkhorst and O'Donovan JJ).

[167] Ibid 168A–B.

However, the court in the *Cerebos Food* case also held[168] that South African courts had no jurisdiction to make *Anton Piller* orders (defined by the court as[169] 'orders for the attachment of documents and other things can be granted where no right is claimed to them except that they should be preserved and produced as evidence in an intended Court action'). In view of the fact that this decision has been held to be wrong by the Appellate Division (the *Shoba* case),[170] the authority of the *Cerebos Food* case on ancillary orders and disclosure orders must be doubted.[171]

The better view is that the court has power to make an order requiring a third party to disclose the identity of a wrongdoer.[172]

11.3.7 Anti-suit interdicts (injunctions)

An anti-suit interdict (injunction) is an order restraining the injunction defendant from either commencing or continuing proceedings outside Eswatini in breach of a legal or equitable right on the part of the injunction plaintiff not to pursue litigation outside Eswatini or, conversely, restraining the injunction defendant from commencing or continuing proceedings inside Eswatini in breach of a legal or equitable right on the part of the injunction plaintiff to have the dispute between the parties litigated in a jurisdiction other than Eswatini.[173]

---

[168] Ibid; see the passages at 170H–I and 173E–F

[169] Ibid 168B–C.

[170] 1995 (4) SA 1 (A) (Corbett CJ, EM Grosskopf, Nestadt and MT Steyn JJA and Nicholas AJA).

[171] In addition, the decision in *Roamer Watch Co SA v African Textile Distributors* 1980 (2) SA 254 (W) appears not to have been cited to the court in *Cerebos Food*. Further, the Appellate Division assumed, without deciding the question, that a court may order a non-party to furnish information required by the plaintiff for the purpose of litigation: *Krygkor Pensioenfonds v Smith* 1993 (3) SA 459 (A), where a divorcee was entitled to part of her former husband's pension; he refused to pay her and she applied, inter alia, for an order requiring the pension fund to inform her as to her husband's pension. The Appellate Division held (at 462A–B): 'The Appellate Division had authoritatively affirmed that it was entitled to adapt its procedures in the interests of justice; that it could be accepted for the purposes of the present case (without so deciding) that a Court in appropriate circumstances had the jurisdiction to order a party against whom a [plaintiff] had no cause of action and who was not a party or intended party to litigation with the [plaintiff], to supply the required information.' This goes further than previous authority in this area by extending the range of disclosure from the identity of a wrongdoer to 'information' generally. Referring to both documents and information, Wunsh J in *Eiser v Vuna Health Care (Pty) Ltd* 1998 (3) SA 139 (W), stated (at 148A–B): 'Our Courts have an inherent jurisdiction to come to the assistance of a litigant who, before proceedings are instituted, requires information from a third party, which is sparingly exercised (*Krygkor Pensioenfonds v Smith* 1993 (3) SA 459 (A)) and there are a few instances where a would-be opponent has been ordered to disclose documents before the institution of proceedings as in *Durban and District African Football Association v Dhludhla* 1961 (3) SA 892 (D).'

[172] The authorities cited in this section predate the enactment of s 32 of the Constitution of the Republic of South Africa, 1996, which provision confirms that courts in the Republic of South Africa have the jurisdiction to make third-party disclosure orders: *Nampak Glass (Pty) Ltd v Vodacom (Pty) Ltd* 2019 (1) SA 257 (GJ), Unterhalter J.

[173] In similar vein, an anti-anti-suit injunction is an order restraining the injunction defendant from commencing or continuing proceedings to restrain the injunction plaintiff from applying to restrain the

There is no reported judicial authority in Eswatini on whether or not an anti-suit interdict is a remedy available to the courts in Eswatini. That said, the courts of Ghana,[174] Nigeria[175] and, crucially, for present purposes, the Republic of South Africa[176] have concluded that this form of relief is available in those jurisdictions. Given the affinity which exists between the legal systems in place in Eswatini and the Republic of South Africa, it is likely that the Eswatini courts will be guided by the approach which the South African courts take with respect to this relief.[177]

11.3.8 *Mandament van spolie*

The protection from dispossession available in the Republic of South Africa is similarly available under Eswatini law. The principles to which a court in Eswatini will seek to give effect when asked to grant such relief are set out below.

In *Shiba v Myeni NO*,[178] Annandale J considered the rationale for allowing a plaintiff to make an application for a spoliation order:[179]

> 'The rationale behind a spoliation order is to prevent people from taking the law into their own hands ... avoiding dispossession of another without lawful authority. If it does so occur, restoration of possession will be ordered summarily by the courts, *status quo ante*, before any inquiry is held into the merits of the dispute, in accordance with the maxim *spoliatus ante omnia restituendus est.* Therefore, and in the ordinary course, the courts will not entertain allegations pertaining to the lawfulness or otherwise of the [plaintiff's] possession, nor delve into the question of ownership, or claimed damages or counterclaims or claims for the value of the despoiled property.'

The Eswatini Supreme Court in *The Regional Administrator, Lubombo Region v Matsenjwa*[180] has confirmed the conditions which the plaintiff must satisfy in order to obtain a spoliation order. Hence, a plaintiff must show that: (1) he was in peaceful and undisturbed possession of the property; and (2) the defendant

---

injunction defendant from commencing or continuing proceedings. The leading works on this topic are: Raphael *The Anti-Suit Injunction* 2 ed (2019) and Briggs *Civil Jurisdiction and Judgments* 7 ed (2021) ch 28. It is also conceptually possible to obtain similar relief in the context of arbitration but such relief is outside the scope of this work.

[174] *Quantum Oil Terminals Ltd v International Finance Corp* (H Ct) (Asiedu J, Suit No: Misc/00228/17).

[175] *United Bank for Africa Plc v Coker* (1996) 4 NWLR 239 (CA) (Muhammad, Ayoola and Pats-Acholonu JJCA).

[176] *Vedanta Resources Holdings Ltd v ZCCM Investment Holdings plc* 2019 JDR 1425 (GJ) (Adams J).

[177] For further guidance on the principles which a South African court would apply when asked to grant an anti-suit interdict, the reader is referred to the relevant section of the chapter on the Republic of South Africa.

[178] [2009] SZHC 266 (HC).

[179] Ibid para [10].

[180] [2016] SZSC 13 (SC, Maphalala CJ; Dr Odoki JA and Nxumalo AJA), *per* Maphalala CJ at para [10], endorsing the Supreme Court's previous decision in *Gibson Ndlovu v Siboniso Dlamini* [2011] SZSC 36.

deprived him of the possession of that property forcibly or wrongfully against his consent.[181]

In *Maseko v Thwala*,[182] the Court of Appeal (now Supreme Court) clarified the type of possession which will attract the protection of the law: 'It is well established law that all that a person despoiled has to prove is that he had possession of the kind that warrants protection and that he was illegally ousted from such possession.' The burden of proof in showing a lack of consent is on the plaintiff for the order.

As has been mentioned above, where the plaintiff satisfies the conditions necessary for the court to grant a spoilation order, the court will order that possession be restored to the plaintiff. In consequence, where the property has been destroyed, such that restoration of possession is no longer available, the plaintiff will be unable to obtain an order for spoilation.[183]

A spoliation order is usually final and is not contingent on the outcome of any other proceedings. The focus of the order is on possession;[184] it is a possessory remedy separate from ownership.[185]

A defendant to spoliation proceedings may have defences available to him: the defence of denial;[186] the impossibility of restoration; the spoliation was a response to a spoliation by the plaintiff suffered by the spoliator/defendant the instant before; and in exceptional cases the court may deviate from the usual path and determine the underlying dispute if it is in the interests of justice to do so.[187] It is worth noting that the defendant is required to set out with sufficient

[181] It is apparent from the decision of the Court of Appeal (now Supreme Court) in *Maseko v Thwala* [2005] SZSC 17 (Browde, Steyn and Back JJA; 11 November 2005) that the test can be traced back to the decision of the Supreme Court of the Transvaal in *Nino Bonino v de Lange* 1906 TS 120 (Innes CJ, Smith and Mason JJ).

[182] [2005] SZSC 17 (11 November 2005), *per* Browde JA at para [8].

[183] *Hlatshwayo v Dlamini* [2019] SZHC 25 (HC; 20 February 2019) (Dlamini J) para [43], following the decision of the South African Supreme Court in *Tswelopele Non-Profit Organisation v City of Tshwane Metropolitan Municipality* 2007 (6) SA 511 (SCA: Scott, Cameron, Nugent and Maya JJA and Snyders AJA).

[184] As made clear by the Supreme Court of Eswatini in *Gina v Simelane* [2019] SZSC 53 (SC) (Maphalal CJ, Matsebula and Currie AJA) para [16]. In *Siteki Town Council v Swaziland Commercial Amadoda Road Transportation Council* [2012] SZSC 62 (SC) (Ramodibedi CJ and Dr Twum and Ota JJA), the Supreme Court had made a similar point when refusing to uphold a spoliation order granted to users of a bus rank where it was never claimed by the users of the bus rank that they ever had possession of the rank. The extent of their rights was to have access to the rank on payment of a permit fee. This was not possession for the purposes of a spoliation order.

[185] *Shiba v Myeni NO* [2009] SZHC 266 (HC) (17 December 2009) para [11].

[186] In *Zwane v Zwane* [2021] SZHC 82 (HC) (Maphanga J) para [47], explained that a defendant might deny that the plaintiff was in peaceful and undisturbed possession of the thing at the time of the alleged deprivation or deny that he had committed an act of spoilation.

[187] Ibid para [15]; *Shiba* was an unusual case where the ownership of cattle had been in dispute and subject to litigation as long ago as 1999. Annandale J clearly formed the view that a departure from established principle was the lesser of two evils.

particularity the basis for the defence on which they rely. As such, the defendant "must respond to the material matters raised in the [plaintiff's] founding affidavit in relation to the events or circumstances so alleged".[188]

11.3.9 Arrest of individuals *tanquam suspectus de fuga*

Rule 9 contains provisions governing the issue of a writ of arrest against an individual *suspectus tanquam de fuga*.[189] The writ of arrest should be in the form set out in Form 5 of Schedule 1 to the High Court Rules. The writ must be delivered to the registrar of the High Court for signature and must be accompanied by an affidavit which must contain:[190] (1) a true description of the person making the affidavit setting out his place of residence and a statement of the sum due to the plaintiff and the cause of the claim and where it was incurred and its value; (2) an allegation that the plaintiff has no or no sufficient security for his demand; and (3) a statement of the deponent's belief that the defendant is about to depart or is making preparations to depart from Eswatini and the grounds for that belief.

Rule 9 makes further provision for the mechanics of the writ of arrest *suspectus tanquam de fuga*, including: the release of the defendant if he pays the sum or delivers the thing referred to in the writ of arrest or if a bond or other security is given for the sums claimed;[191] the person arrested may anticipate the return day and apply to discharge the writ of arrest on notice to the plaintiff.[192]

It should be noted, however, that in *Malachi v Cape Dance Academy International (Pty) Ltd*,[193] the Constitutional Court of South Africa abolished arrest *tanquam suspectus de fuga* in the Republic of South Africa. Mogoeng J (giving the judgment of the court) stated:

> '[32] The object of the arrest "is to ensure that [the potential debtor] remains within the jurisdiction of the court until the court has given judgment in the matter." As soon as judgment is given, a debtor would, however, be free to catch the next flight to any foreign destination even if this is done to evade payment and no realisable asset exists in the country, from the proceeds of which payment may be effected. Arrest does not, therefore, ensure the satisfaction of the judgment debt. Admittedly, the unfairly exerted pressure of incarceration may at times force the arrestee to pay the debt or provide security. But, that does not detract from the fact that the arrest does not necessarily render the judgment any more executable or beneficial to the creditor than would have been the case had the debtor left the country. It simply limits the fundamental right to freedom of the person for no just reason.

---

188 *Zwane v Zwane* [2021] SZHC 82 (HC) para [48].

189 Rule 9(5).

190 Rule 9(3)–(5).

191 Rule 9(10).

192 Rule 9(14).

193 2010 (6) SA 1 (CC) (Ngcobo CJ, Moseneke DCJ, Cameron, Froneman, Jafta, Khampepe, Nkabinde, Skweyiya, Van der Westhuizen, Yacoob and Mogoeng JJ).

> [33] The order for the arrest of persons *tanquam suspectus de fuga* under the impugned provisions is ordinarily made at the time when their civil liability has not yet been established. Their debt is only alleged on affidavit, often in an urgent application brought *ex parte*. The potential debtor is often only afforded the opportunity to resist the severe curtailment of the right to freedom, by the order, on the return date. Potentially the detention may endure for as long as the action is pending. The effect of this deprivation was more aptly captured in *Segal v Diners Club South Africa* where we are warned that "[i]f the debtor has been wrongly deprived of his freedom it cannot be put right in the subsequent suit. The harm is irreparable." Nothing can undo the degrading effect of incarceration, particularly if the order were obtained *ex parte*. This is the position in which the plaintiff in this matter found herself for 16 days.
>
> [34] Since there is no legal basis for the imprisonment of someone who has been found civilly liable, it is inconceivable that any legal justification can ever exist for putting behind bars a person whose civil liability is yet to, or will possibly never, be proven. Although an order for arrest is granted by a court, the intervention of the judicial process cannot legitimise the deprivation of freedom, since the arrest may stem from a debt which has itself not been established through the judicial process. I therefore conclude that there is no just cause for the arrest in terms of the impugned provisions.'

It would appear that, since the judgment in *Malachi*, the Eswatini courts have not yet had the opportunity to consider or clarify authoritatively the present state of the law. Indeed, the Industrial Court in Eswatini is the only court, it seems, to have considered the ambit and effect of arrest *suspectus tanquam de fuga*. In *Stawu v Unitrans Swaziland Ltd*,[194] that court held that the 'main objective [of such arrest] is to attach a debtor's assets to found jurisdiction'. With respect, this is at odds with what the Constitutional Court of South Africa of Africa held in *Malachi* and seems to confuse the purpose of arrest *suspectus tanquam de fuga* with general principles of attachment so as to found or confirm jurisdiction. It cannot, for those reasons, be seen as an authoritative judgment.

In case it should prove helpful to the courts in Eswatini when they come to consider properly the ambit and effect of arrest *suspectus tanquam de fuga*, the authors offer some observations on the decision of the South African Constitutional Court in *Malachi*. First, that case turned on section 12(1) of the Constitution of South Africa, 1996, which concerns the right to liberty. The equivalent provisions in the Constitution of Eswatini are contained in section 16:

[194] [2013] SZIC 12/2018 (IC) (Nsibande JP; Manana and Dlamini NMC) para [6].

> '16 (1) *A person shall not be deprived of personal liberty save as may be authorised by law in any of the following cases—*
>
> *(a)* ...
>
> *(b)* ...
>
> *(c)* in execution of the order of a court made to secure the fulfilment of any obligation imposed on that person by law;
>
> *(d)* for the purpose of bringing that person before a court in execution of the order of a court;
>
> *(e)–(j)* ...'.

Second, these provisions are inapt to cover the arrest of a defendant *tanquam suspectus de fuga*: such an arrest is not made in fulfilment of an obligation imposed by law; and while an order for arrest is undoubtedly effective in bringing a person before the court in execution of an order for arrest *tanquam suspectus de fuga*, the language of section 16(1)(d) contemplates arrest for the purpose of execution of some other order other than the order for arrest, the sub-section does not, it is submitted, endorse the institution of arrest *tanquam suspectus de fuga* itself.

Third, in the absence of an authoritative judgment from an Eswatini court on this subject, and in the light of the persuasive nature of South African authorities in the courts in Eswatini, it is to be anticipated[195] that the courts in Eswatini will have regard to and adopt the reasoning of Mogoeng J, as set out above, when they come to review arrest *suspectus tanquam de fuga* in due course.

---

[195] Because of the affinity between Eswatini constitutional and private law and that of the Republic of South Africa, it is to be expected that the decisions of the Supreme Court of Appeal of the Republic of South Africa will be given weight by the courts in Eswatini when the latter come to give an authoritative judgment on the subject.

Chapter 12

TANZANIA

12.1 Introduction

At the outset, it is necessary to make certain clarificatory points, so as to explain: (1) the relationship between the High Court in Tanzania and the High Court in Zanzibar and the relevant procedures of each and (2) the relationship between the Civil Procedure Code Act 1966 in Tanzania[1] (hereafter, the 'Code'), the First Schedule to which contains the Tanzanian Civil Procedure Rules (hereafter, the 'Civil Procedure Rules') and the Tanzanian High Court (Commercial Division) Procedure Rules 2012 (hereafter, the 'High Court (Commercial Division) Rules').

[1] Act 49 of 1966, GN 410 of 1966. The Act is expressed to be 'an Act to replace the Indian Code of Civil Procedure, 1908'. Domestically, Acts have been organised into chapters in the most recent revision of the Laws of Tanzania (2019 edition). Accordingly, this may now be cited as Cap 33 of the Laws of Tanzania, 2019. In this regard, the reader is referred to the 'Note on the citation of statutory material in this work', which appears at the end of the 'List of Statutory Material Cited' at the beginning of this work.

12.1.1 The relationship between the High Court in Tanzania and the High Court in Zanzibar

Article 1 of the Constitution of the United Republic of Tanzania[2] provides that 'Tanzania is one State and is a sovereign United Republic'. The territory of the 'United Republic consists of the whole of the area of mainland Tanzania and the whole of the area of Tanzania Zanzibar, and includes the territorial waters'.[3]

As such, in the main text, references to the 'United Republic' should be taken to include both 'mainland Tanzania' (hereafter, 'Tanzania') and Tanzania Zanzibar (hereafter, 'Zanzibar').

The Constitution makes provision for the existence of a High Court of Tanzania[4] and, in accordance with the law applicable in Zanzibar, a High Court of Zanzibar or courts subordinate to it.[5] Subject to the provisions of the Constitution of the United Republic, where any law enacted by Parliament in the United Republic applicable to both Tanzania and Zanzibar, vests power in the High Court of Tanzania, then the High Court of Zanzibar may exercise that power concurrently with the High Court of Tanzania.[6]

The procedure to be employed when litigating in the High Court of Tanzania is derived from a series of separate sources. While those sources are similar in content and origin to the sources from which the relevant procedure to be employed when litigating in the High Court of Zanzibar is derived, the relevant procedure is not all the same: one must look in different places to discover the appropriate procedure to be employed in each court.

As such, the procedural rules to be employed in the High Court of Tanzania are derived from a combination of the Code, the Civil Procedure Rules and

[2] Ratified in 1977 and given effect to by Act 1 of 1977. The Civil Procedure Rules mentioned in the main text were made pursuant to s 80 of the Civil Procedure Code; the High Court (Commercial Division) Rules mentioned in the main text may be cited as GN 250 of 2012 and were made pursuant to s 4 of the Judicature and Application of Laws Act (Act 7 of 1922, now Cap 358 of the Laws of Tanzania, 2019). The revised version of the Act consists of the Indian Acts (Application) Act 1920 (Act 7 of 1920) and the Judicature and Application of Laws Act.

[3] Article 2(1) of the Constitution of the United Republic of Tanzania.

[4] Article 108(1) describes this as the 'High Court of the United Republic'. However, to avoid confusion of nomenclature, this will be referred to as the 'High Court of Tanzania' in the main text. Such an approach receives support from art 108(2), which provides: 'Where this Constitution or any other law does not expressly provide that any specified matter shall first be heard by a court specified for that purpose, then the High Court shall have jurisdiction to hear every matter of such type. Similarly, the High Court shall have jurisdiction to deal with any matter which, according to legal traditions obtaining in Tanzania, is ordinarily dealt with by a High Court ...'.

[5] Article 114. Further, art 115(1) provides that, subject to art 83, which is concerned with the validity of appointments and elections of Members of Parliament, and art 116, which is concerned with the day-to-day running of the Court of Appeal, 'the jurisdiction of the High Court of Zanzibar shall be as specified in the laws applicable in Zanzibar'.

[6] Article 115(2) of the Constitution of the United Republic.

(at least when litigating in the Commercial Division of the High Court), the High Court (Commercial Division) Rules.[7]

By contrast, the procedural rules to be employed in the High Court of Zanzibar are derived from a combination of the Zanzibar Civil Procedure Decree 1908[8] (hereafter, the 'Zanzibar Code'), the second schedule to which contains the Zanzibar Civil Procedure Rules and (at least when litigating in the Commercial Division of the High Court of Zanzibar) the rules contained in the Establishment of Zanzibar Commercial Court Act 2013.[9]

12.1.2 The relationship between the applicable court rules in Tanzania[10]

The Civil Procedure Code and (by extension) the Civil Procedure Rules, save as provided by express provisions of any written law, shall apply to all proceedings in the High Court Tanzania.[11]

The Civil Procedure Rules provide that no suit shall be instituted in the Commercial Division of the High Court concerning a commercial matter which is pending before another court or tribunal of competent jurisdiction or which falls within the competency of a lower court.[12] The Civil Procedure Rules further provide that it shall not be mandatory for a commercial case to be instituted in the Commercial Division of the High Court.[13]

In the Commercial Division of the High Court, preliminary matters, including the decision whether or not the suit concerns a commercial case, shall be determined by a judge and such suit shall not come up for mention except for the judge to make a rescheduling order in respect of that case.[14]

It is unfortunate that the Code does not provide a definition of the words 'commercial case'.

---

[7] The High Court (Commercial Division) Rules may be found in GN 250 of 2012.

[8] Decree 17 of 1917, effective 1 January 1917.

[9] Act 9 of 2013.

[10] A similar relationship exists between the Zanzibar Code, the Zanzibar Civil Procedure Rules and the rules contained in the Establishment of Zanzibar Commercial Court Act.

[11] Section 22 of the Code; O IV, r 1(1) of the Civil Procedure Rules.

[12] Order IV, r 1(3) of the Civil Procedure Rules.

[13] Order IV, r 1(4). However, it is not wholly clear how this provision interacts with r 5(2) of the High Court (Commercial Division) Rules. That latter provision uses mandatory language which might be taken to indicate that, where the conditions therein set out are satisfied, the court must exercise its jurisdiction – ie that a case must be brought in the Commercial Division. Alternatively, it may be construed as meaning that the Commercial Division of the High Court has jurisdiction in the circumstances therein mentioned and, if asked to exercise it, shall do so. See further fn 16 below.

[14] Order IV, r 1(5) of the Civil Procedure Rules.

However, the High Court (Commercial Division) Rules,[15] which apply unless expressly provided otherwise to all commercial cases before the Commercial Division of the High Court of Tanzania, do provide assistance as to the meaning of 'commercial case'.[16]

Rule 3 provides as follows:

> '"Commercial case" means a civil case involving a matter considered by the [Commercial Division of the High Court of Tanzania] to be of commercial significance, including any claim or application arising out of a transaction of trade or commerce but not limited to: –
>
> *(a)* the formation of a business or commercial organisation;
>
> *(b)* the management of a business or commercial organisation;
>
> *(c)* the contractual relationship of a business or commercial organisation with other bodies or person[s] outside the business or commercial organisation;
>
> *(d)* the liability of a business or commercial organisation or official of the business or commercial organisation arising out of its commercial or business activities;
>
> *(e)* the liabilities of a business or commercial person arising out of that person's business or commercial activities;
>
> *(f)* banking and financial services;
>
> *(g)* the restructuring or payment of commercial debts by or to business or commercial organisation or person;
>
> *(h)* the enforcement of [an] arbitral award;
>
> *(i)* the enforcement of awards of a regional court or tribunal of competent jurisdiction made in accordance with a Treaty or Mutual Assistance arrangement[17] to which the United Republic of Tanzania is a signatory and which forms part of the law of the United Republic;
>
> *(k)* admiralty proceedings; and
>
> *(l)* arbitration proceedings.'

It would appear that, where they apply, the High Court (Commercial Division) Rules act as an adjunct to, rather than a replacement for, the Civil Procedure Rules. This is apparent from the drafting of the High Court (Commercial Division) Rules, which stress that, in the case of any *lacuna* therein, the provisions

---

[15] Made pursuant to s 4 of the Judicature and Application of Laws Act 1961, which provides that 'subject to the provisions of any other written law, the Chief Justice may make rules for regulating the practice and procedure of the High Court and all other courts established in Tanzania'. The revised version of the Act appears as Cap 358 of the Laws of Tanzania, 2019. The revised version of the Act consists of the Indian Acts (Application) Act 1920 and the Judicature and Application of Laws Act.

[16] Rule 2(1) and r 3. Rule 5(1) provides that there 'shall be a Commercial Division of the High Court of Tanzania vested with both original and appellate jurisdiction over commercial cases'. Further, r 5(2) confirms that the Commercial Division of the High Court 'shall have and exercise original jurisdiction in a commercial case in which the value of the claim shall be at least one hundred million shillings in a case of proceedings for recovery of possession of immovable property and at least seventy million shillings in proceedings where the subject matter is capable of being estimated at a money value'.

[17] The expression 'Treaty' and the expression 'Mutual Assistance arrangement' are left undefined.

of the Code (and so the provisions of the Civil Procedure Rules) will apply.[18] That said, where the Code (and so the Civil Procedure Rules) differ from the High Court (Commercial Division) Rules, litigants in the Commercial Division of the High Court should comply with the High Court (Commercial Division) Rules.

Accordingly, in what follows, the provisions of the Code (and so the Civil Procedure Rules) will be set out first. Where there are material differences between those provisions and the provisions contained in the Commercial Division Procedure Rules, these are highlighted.

12.2 Jurisdiction

The bases on which a court in Tanzania may assume jurisdiction over a cause or matter are statutory in origin.

The fundamental means by which a court in Tanzania is seised of jurisdiction over a defendant at the suit of the plaintiff is by service of process on the defendant.

The Civil Procedure Rules[19] distinguish between (1) service of a summons within Tanzania, (2) service of a summons in Zanzibar, (3) service of a summons in Kenya, Uganda, Malawi or Zambia and (4) service of a summons in some other country.

12.2.1 Tanzanian law on service where the defendant is within the jurisdiction

Civil proceedings are begun by the institution of suit. The general rule[20] is that every suit shall be instituted by presenting a plaint to the court or such officer as it appoints in that behalf and, where the suit is instituted against the government, delivering a copy of the plaint to the Attorney-General.

---

[18] Rule 2(2) of the High Court (Commercial Division) Rules.

[19] Order V, rr 9–33. The Zanzibar Civil Procedure Code contains equivalent provisions. It distinguishes between (1) service of a summons within Zanzibar, (2) service of a summons in Kenya, Uganda, Nyasaland (modern-day Malawi) and Tanganyika (modern-day Tanzania) and (3) service of a summons in some other country. In the main text, comparisons will be made with Zanzibar where pertinent.

[20] Civil Procedure Rules, O IV, r 1. Rule 10 of the High Court (Commercial Division) Rules provides that, save as otherwise required by law, proceedings in the Commercial Division of the High Court shall be instituted by plaint or originating summons. Rule 10(2) of the High Court (Commercial Division) Rules provides that proceedings where the sole or principal question at issue is/is likely to be one of the construction of any written law or of any instrument made under any written law, or deed, contract or any other document or in which there is unlikely to be any substantial dispute of fact unless the plaintiff intends in those proceedings to obtain judgment under O XIV of the Code or for any other reason considers the proceedings more appropriate to be instituted by a plaint may be instituted by way of originating summons. Where the plaintiff does institute proceedings by way of originating summons in the Commercial Division of the High Court, the originating summons must contain the particulars set out in r 11 of the High Court (Commercial Division) Rules. For comparison, see r 10 of the rules contained in the Establishment of Zanzibar Commercial Court Act.

The plaint should comply with the rules contained in Order VI (which is headed 'Pleading Generally') and Order VIII (which is headed 'Written Statement, Set-Off and Counterclaim').[21]

When a suit has been duly instituted, a summons may be 'issued to' to the defendant at the time when the suit is assigned to a specific judge.[22] By that summons, the defendant may be required to appear and answer the claim on a day to be specified (a 'summons to appear')[23] or if the suit is instituted in a court other than the High Court and the court so determines, to file a written statement of defence to the claim (a 'summons to file a defence').[24] However, no summons is to be issued when the defendant has appeared at the presentation of the plaint, the defendant has proved his identity to the satisfaction of the court and has admitted the plaintiff's claim.[25]

Every summons shall be signed by the judge or magistrate or such officer as may be appointed by the Chief Justice in that behalf and shall be sealed with the seal of the court.[26] Every summons must be accompanied by a copy of the plaint

---

[21] Order IV, r 1(2) of the Civil Procedure Rules (and in the Commercial Division of the High Court: r 19 of the High Court (Commercial Division) Procedure Rules). It is unclear whether the wording of O IV, r 1(2) is incorrect or not. Order VIII, which is headed 'Written Statement, Set-Off and Counterclaim', deals with matters with which the defendant, rather than the plaintiff, is likely to be concerned. It would make more sense to stipulate that the plaint must comply with the rules set out in O VII, which is headed 'Plaint', and provides, inter alia, that the plaint shall contain certain particulars, eg the name of the court in which the suit is brought: O VII, r 1(a). This view is strengthened by reference to r 12(1) of the High Court (Commercial Division) Rules, which provides that: 'Notwithstanding the provisions of rule 1 of O VII of the [Civil Procedure Rules], the plaintiff shall file, along with the plaint, the full address, including e-mail, fax and telephone number of a plaintiff and defendant or their advocates to the extent known to the plaintiff.' For comparison, see O IV of the Zanzibar Civil Procedure Rules.

[22] Order V, r 1 of the Civil Procedure Rules. It should be noted that it is more common to speak of 'service of documents' on the defendant, rather than the 'issue' to him of such documents. In any event, according to O IV, r 3, a judge of the High Court who is in charge of the High Court or a magistrate in charge of a District Court shall within four days after the institution of a suit cause it to be assigned to a specific judge or magistrate. This rule is modified when dealing with a commercial case before the Commercial Division of the High Court, in that, within a maximum of one day after the institution of a suit, it shall be assigned manually or electronically to a specific judge: r 14 of the High Court (Commercial Division) Rules.

[23] Order V, r 1(a) of the Civil Procedure Rules. For comparison, see O V, r 1 of the Zanzibar Civil Procedure Rules.

[24] Order V, r 1(b) of the Civil Procedure Rules.

[25] Order V, r 1 of the Civil Procedure Rules. This also goes on to provide: 'No summons shall be issued under this rule to the Attorney-General (i) except on the application of the plaintiff made not less than fourteen days after the suit has been duly instituted; and (ii) unless the court is satisfied that a request made by the Attorney-General for a further and better statement of the nature of the claim, or for further and better particulars of any matter stated in the plaint, has been complied with or that no such request has been made.' For comparison, see O V, r 1(1) of the Zanzibar Civil Procedure Rules.

[26] Order V, r 2 of the Civil Procedure Rules. Pursuant to r 16 of the High Court (Commercial Division) Rules, in the Commercial Division of the High Court a summons shall be signed manually or electronically by a judge.

and copies of other documents as may be prescribed by the Chief Justice for the information of the defendant regarding the future conduct of the suit.[27]

Where the court sees reason to require the personal appearance of the defendant, the summons shall order him to appear in person in court on the day therein specified.[28] The power of the court to require the personal appearance of a party 'shall not be effected by the issue of a summons to file a defence but where in any such case the court sees fit to require such personal appearance, it may issue a separate summons to that effect'.[29] In circumstances where the court does not require the personal appearance of the defendant, the defendant in respect of whom a summons to appear is issued may appear either in person or by an advocate instructed and able to answer all material questions relating to the suit or by an advocate accompanied by some person able to answer all such questions or, where the Attorney-General is the defendant, by a public officer duly authorised by him in that behalf.[30]

Where the defendant resides within the jurisdiction of the court in which the suit is instituted, or where an agent is resident within that jurisdiction who is empowered to accept service of the summons, the summons shall, unless the court otherwise directs, be delivered or sent to the proper officer[31] to be served by him or one of his subordinates.[32]

Service of the summons shall be made within 21 days after it has been received by delivering or tendering a copy thereof signed by the judge, magistrate or such other officer as the Chief Justice may appoint in this behalf and sealed with the seal of the court.[33] Wherever it is practicable, service shall be made on the

---

[27] Order V, r 3 of the Civil Procedure Rules. By O V, r 4, a 'summons to appear issued by a court other than the High Court shall direct that the defendant shall produce on the day fixed for his appearance: (a) all documents in his possession or power upon which he intends to rely in supporting his case; and (b) all witnesses upon whose evidence he intends to rely in support of his case'. For comparison, see O V, r 7 of the Zanzibar Civil Procedure Rules.

[28] Order V, r 7(1) of the Civil Procedure Rules.

[29] Order V, r 7(3) of the Civil Procedure Rules. That said, it would appear that a fetter is placed on the court's power to order a defendant to appear in person, viz that the person must either reside within the local limits of the court's ordinary jurisdiction or live without such limits but at a place less than 50 miles away, or, where there is a railway or steamer communication or other established public conveyance for five-sixths of the distance between the place where he resides and the place where the court is situate, less than 200 miles distance from the court-house: O V, r 8. For comparison, see O V, r 4 of the Zanzibar Civil Procedure Rules.

[30] Order V, r 5 of the Civil Procedure Rules.

[31] Order V, r 9(2) provides that the proper officer may be an officer of the court other than that in which the suit is instituted and, where he is such an officer, the summons may be sent to him by post or in such other manner as the court may direct.

[32] Order V, r 9(1) of the Civil Procedure Rules.

[33] Order V, r 10 of the Civil Procedure Rules. Order V then goes on to particularise the rules of service as they apply in specific situations. As such, r 15 sets out the circumstances in which service may be made on any adult member of the defendant's family; r 17 (read with r 19), the procedure which is to be used when the defendant cannot be found; r 20 the procedure for substituted service (though in a commercial case in the

defendant in person, unless he has an agent empowered to accept service, in which case service on such agent shall be sufficient.[34]

Where the serving officer delivers or tenders a copy of the summons to the defendant personally or to an agent or other person on his behalf, he shall require the person to whom the copy is so delivered or tendered to sign an acknowledgement of service endorsed on the original summons. However, where the defendant (or such other person) refuses to sign the acknowledgment, the serving officer shall leave a copy thereof with him and return the original to the court, together with an affidavit stating that the person upon whom the summons was served refused to sign the acknowledgement, that he left a copy of the summons with the person and the name and address of the person (if any) by whom the person on whom the summons was served was identified.[35]

A party wishing to serve a summons on a company in Tanzania may do so in accordance with the Civil Procedure Rules. Hence, service may be effected, inter alia, on the secretary or on any director or other principal officer of the company[36] or by leaving it or sending it by post addressed to the company at the registered office, or if there is no registered office then at the place where the corporation carries on business.[37]

It should be noted that Part XII of the Companies Act 2002[38] has created an alternative regime for service of process on 'foreign companies', that is:

> 'companies incorporated outside Tanzania which, after the appointed day, establish a place of business within Tanzania and companies incorporated outside Tanzania which have, before the appointed day, establish a place of business within Tanzania and continue to have a place of business within Tanzania on and after the appointed day'

Commercial Division of the High Court, one must consider r 17 of the High Court (Commercial Division) Rules) and r 21 service by post. On this last point, see O V, r 30, which sets out when service by post may be deemed to have been duly effected. It is necessary to be aware, however, that r 12(2) of the Commercial Division Procedure Rules provides that: 'Without prejudice to the modes of service of summons provided by the [Commercial Division Procedure Rules] or any other law, the email address and fax provided, may be used by the Court and the parties for effecting services and other necessary communication throughout the course of the suit.' For comparison, see O V, r 10 of the Zanzibar Civil Procedure Rules, which omits the reference to 'twenty-one days'). Order V of the Zanzibar Civil Procedure Rules likewise particularises the rules of service as they apply in specific situations.

[34] Order V, r 12 of the Civil Procedure Rules. For comparison, see O V, r 12 of the Zanzibar Civil Procedure Rules.

[35] Order V, r 16 of the Civil Procedure Rules. Order V, r 18 goes on to provide that the serving officer shall 'within fourteen days of service in all the cases in which the summons has been served under rule 16, endorse or annex or cause to be endorsed or annexed, on or to the original summons, a return stating the time when and the manner in which the summons was served, and the name and address of the person (if any) identifying the person served and witnessing the delivery or tender of the summons'. For comparison, see O V, rr 16–19 of the Zanzibar Civil Procedure Rules.

[36] Order XXVIII, r 2(a) of the Civil Procedure Rules.

[37] Order XXVIII, r 2(b) of the Civil Procedure Rules.

[38] Act 12 of 2002 (Cap 212 of the Laws of Tanzania 2019).

so long as they are not a company incorporated outside Tanzania which is registered under Part XII of the Building Societies Ordinance. [39]

Section 433(2) clarifies that a 'foreign company' shall not be deemed to have a place of business in Tanzania solely on account of its doing business through an agent in Tanzania at the place of business of the agent'. That said, the 2002 Act provides only an inclusive definition of 'place of business', saying that 'it includes a share transfer or share registration office'.[40]

Section 434 imposes an obligation on foreign companies which, after the appointed day, establish a place of business within Tanzania, within 30 days of the establishment of the place of business, to deliver to the registrar for registration, inter alia, the names of and addresses of one or more persons resident in Tanzania who are authorised to accept service of process on behalf of the company and the full address of the registered or principal office of the company and the full address of the place of business in Tanzania.[41]

Section 440 then provides that process required to be served on a foreign company shall be 'sufficiently served if addressed to any person whose name has been delivered to the Registrar' in accordance with the obligations described above. Where a company fails to provide to the Registrar the information described above or where the persons whose names and addresses have been delivered to the registrar are dead or cease to reside in Tanzania or refuse to accept service on behalf of the company or cannot be served, process may be served on the company 'by leaving it at or sending it by registered post to any place of business established by the company in Tanzania'.[42]

12.2.2 Tanzanian law on service of a summons in Zanzibar

Where the defendant resides within the jurisdiction of the High Court of Zanzibar, the original and a copy of the summons may be sent by the court by which it is issued either by one of its officers or by post to the High Court of Zanzibar or to any court subordinate thereto within whose jurisdiction the defendant resides for service on the defendant.[43] By Order V, rule 23 of the Civil Procedure Rules, the High Court of Zanzibar shall, upon receipt of the original and a copy of the summons, proceed as if the summons had been issued by such court and shall then within 14 days of completing such proceeding return the summons to the court of issue, together with the record (if any) of its proceedings with regard thereto.

---

[39] Section 433(1) of the Companies Act 2002. By comparison with, say, s 493(d) of the Sierra Leone Companies Act 2009, this definition is quite sparse.

[40] Section 443(c).

[41] Section 434(1)(d) and (e).

[42] Section 440.

[43] Order V, r 22(2) of the Civil Procedure Rules.

12.2.3 Tanzanian law on service where the defendant is outside the jurisdiction

12.2.3.1 *Service of a summons in Kenya, Uganda, Malawi or Zambia*[44]

Order V, rule 28 of the Civil Procedure Rules makes provision for service of the summons on a defendant who is believed to reside in Kenya, Uganda, Malawi or Zambia and has no known agent in Tanzania empowered to accept service. In these circumstances, the summons may be served:

(1) where the plaintiff has furnished the postal address of the defendant, by post;[45]

(2) in any other case, through the courts of the country in which the defendant is believed to reside;[46] or

(3) by leave of the court, by the plaintiff or his agent.

Where the summons is to be served under sub-paragraph (2) above, the court may send the original and a copy of the summons for service direct to any court having civil jurisdiction in the place where the defendant is believed to reside.[47]

At this juncture, it should be noted that, where the defendant is believed to reside in Kenya, Uganda, Malawi or Zambia and has no known agent in Tanzania empowered to accept service, the Civil Procedure Rules do not appear to require the plaintiff to make an application to the court to sanction either service being effected by way of post or through the courts of the country in which the defendant is believed to reside. In this respect, the provisions of Order V, rule 28 appear to be different to those of Order V, rule 29, which govern service on a defendant who is believed to be resident outside the jurisdiction elsewhere than in Kenya, Uganda, Malawi or Zambia.

12.2.3.2 *Service of a summons in some other country*[48]

Order V, rule 29 of the Civil Procedure Rules has application where the defendant is believed to reside outside Tanzania, elsewhere than in Kenya, Uganda, Malawi or Zambia and has no known agent in Tanzania empowered to accept service. In these circumstances:

---

[44] Order V, r 28 of the Zanzibar Civil Procedure Rules contains equivalent provisions. It, however, makes special provision for service of a summons on a defendant in Kenya, Uganda, Nyasaland (modern-day Malawi) and Tanganyika (modern-day Tanzania).

[45] See ss 82 and 83 of the Interpretation of Laws Act.

[46] By O V, r 33(3) of the Civil Procedure Rules, a 'summons shall not be sent for service through the courts of any other country unless there has been deposited with the court or secured a sum sufficient in the opinion of the court to cover the expenses of service'.

[47] Order V, r 33(2) of the Civil Procedure Rules.

[48] Order V, r 29 of the Zanzibar Civil Procedure Rules contains equivalent provisions.

> '[T]he court may, on the application of the plaintiff, order that service of the summons may be effected:
>
> *(a)* by post;
>
> *(b)* by the plaintiff or his agent; or
>
> *(c)* through the courts of the country in which the defendant is believed to reside.'[49]

Hence, Order V, rule 29 of the Civil Procedure Rules requires the plaintiff to make an application to the court whenever the plaintiff wishes to serve the summons on the defendant out of the jurisdiction and, in this respect, is different to Order V, rule 28.

Order V, rule 33(1) of the Civil Procedure Rules provides as follows:

> 'Where the court of a resident magistrate or a district court has ordered the service of a summons to be effected through the courts of any country, other than Kenya, Uganda, Malawi or Zambia, in which the defendant is believed to reside, it shall remit to the Registrar of the High Court at Dar es Salaam, and where the High Court has so ordered, the Registrar shall issue a summons together with two copies thereof and two copies of a translation thereof in the language of the country in which the summons is to be served, if that language is other than English, and the Registrar shall thereupon send those documents together with a certificate as to the sum of money deposited or secured to cover the expenses of service, to the Principal Secretary to the Ministry for the time being responsible for legal affairs—
>
> *(a)* where leave has been given for service to be effected in a country with which a convention has been made by the United Republic concerning the service of civil processes, for transmission to the representative of the United Republic in that country or as the convention may otherwise provide; or
>
> *(b)* for transmission to the Government of the country in which leave has been given for service to be effected through the courts of that country.'[50]

Irrespective of the country (so long as it is not Tanzania) in which the defendant is believed to be resident, service through the courts of that country may be deemed to have been duly effected if the summons is returned by any such court with an endorsement that it has been served.[51]

---

[49] Order V, r 29 of the Civil Procedure Rules.

[50] It is submitted that the language employed here creates difficulty. It is not wholly clear into which 'conventions' the United Republic has entered. It is also unclear whether, if the United Republic has entered into any conventions, those conventions differ from those mentioned in O V, r 32(a) of the Zanzibar Civil Procedure Rules. If they are different, then such difference produces further difficulty for, strictly speaking, an act – such as entering into a service convention – of Zanzibar is not an act of the United Republic. That said, and in any event, by O V, r 33(3) of the Civil Procedure Rules, a 'summons shall not be sent for service through the courts of any other country unless there has been deposited with the court or secured a sum sufficient in the opinion of the court to cover the expenses of service'.

[51] Order V, r 32 of the Civil Procedure Rules.

The Tanzanian Civil Procedure Rules appear to be unique among the Anglophone African jurisdictions – certainly when compared with those of neighbouring jurisdictions such as Kenya, Uganda, Malawi and Zambia – in that they do not set out the grounds upon which the Tanzanian court may grant leave to the plaintiff to serve a summons on a defendant believed to be resident in a foreign jurisdiction.[52] However, where a plaintiff wishes to serve a summons on a defendant who is believed to reside in Kenya, Uganda, Malawi or Zambia and has no known agent in Tanzania empowered to accept service, the summons may be served according to Order V, rule 28 without the leave of the court.[53]

12.2.3.3 *Service out of the jurisdiction: A comparison with the position in Zanzibar*

As noted above, in Tanzania the Civil Procedure Rules omit to provide any explanation of the grounds upon which the court will grant leave to serve the summons out of the jurisdiction. Such an omission is made all the more puzzling in the light of the Zanzibar Civil Procedure Rules. As noted above, articles 114[54] and 116(1)[55] of the Constitution of the United Republic confirms that the Zanzibar High Court has different procedural rules to the High Court of Tanzania.

Order V, rule 27[56] of the Zanzibar Civil Procedure Rules provides as follows:

> 'Service of a summons on a defendant outside Zanzibar may be allowed by the court whenever:
>
> *(a)* the whole subject matter of the action is land situated in Zanzibar (with or without rent and profits); or
>
> *(b)* any act, deed, will, contract, obligation or liability affecting land or hereditaments situate within the jurisdiction, is sought to be construed, rectified, set aside or enforced in, the suit; or

[52] It is also not clear whether, as part of its considerations, the Tanzania High Court must take account of the principle of *forum conveniens.*

[53] Save in the case where service of the defendant is sought by the plaintiff or his agent (r 28(c)).

[54] '... it is hereby declared that the provisions contained in this Chapter do not prevent the continuance or establishment, in accordance with the law applicable in Zanzibar of the High Court of Zanzibar or courts subordinate to it'.

[55] 'Subject to the provisions of sub-article (2) [which provides that the Chief Justice of Tanzania shall from time to time consult with the Chief Justice of Zanzibar over the administration of the business of the Court of Appeal] the Chief Justice [of Tanzania] shall have no power over any matter concerning the structure and administration of the day-to-day business of the courts established in accordance with the Constitution of Zanzibar, 1984, or any law of Tanzania Zanzibar.'

[56] The rule of the English Rules of the Supreme Court regulating service out of the jurisdiction prior to 1999 (when the English Civil Procedure Rules came into effect) was O XI. Under the Rules of the Supreme Court 1883 and the Rules of the Supreme Court 1965, which superseded the 1883 Rules, O XI, r 1, provided for service out of the jurisdiction. The terms of the Zanzibar O V, r 27, are materially identical to the Rules of the Supreme Court 1883 (1960 ed). Thus, it is to be expected that the Zanzibar courts will have regard to English authority when interpreting the meaning of O V, r 27.

(c) any relief is sought against any person domiciled or ordinarily resident in Zanzibar; or

(d) the action is for the administration of the personal estate of any deceased person, who at the time of his death was domiciled in Zanzibar or for the execution (as to property situate in Zanzibar) of the trusts of any written instrument, of which the person to be served is a trustee, which ought to be executed according to the law of Zanzibar; or

(e) the action is one brought to enforce, rescind, dissolve, annul or otherwise affect a contract or to recover damages or other relief for or in respect of the breach of a contract—

i. made in Zanzibar,

ii. made by or through an agent trading or residing in Zanzibar on behalf of a principal trading or residing out of Zanzibar, or

iii. by its terms or by implication is to be governed by Zanzibar law,

or is one brought in respect of a breach committed in Zanzibar of a contract wherever made, even though such breach was preceded or accompanied by a breach out of Zanzibar which rendered impossible the performance of the part of the contract which ought to have been performed in Zanzibar; or

(f) the action is founded on a tort committed in Zanzibar; or

(g) any injunction is sought as to anything to be done in Zanzibar or any nuisance in Zanzibar is sought to be prevented or removed, whether damages are or not also sought in respect thereof; or

(h) any person out of Zanzibar is a necessary or proper party to any action properly brought against some other person duly served in Zanzibar.'[57]

Order V, Rule 28 of the Zanzibar Civil Procedure Rules supplements the above by stating:

> 'Where leave is asked from the court or a judge to serve a writ, under [Rule 27], in Kenya, Uganda, [Malawi] or Tanzania, if it shall appear that there may be a concurrent remedy in the place of the defendant's residence the court shall have regard to the comparative cost and convenience of proceedings in Zanzibar or in the place where the defendant resides.'

12.2.3.3.1 Procedure under the law of Zanzibar for service out of the jurisdiction

The defendant's characteristics inform what it is that the plaintiff must serve upon him. Hence, if the defendant is British or a citizen of Zanzibar, they should be served with the summons itself. By contrast, where the defendant is not a

[57] It should be noted that the Zanzibar Civil Procedure Rules fail to make provision for a court to permit service of the writ on a defendant who is present out of the jurisdiction if the action is one to enforce a foreign judgment. By way of comparison, see the English Civil Procedure Rules, PD6B, para 3.1(10).

British or a Zanzibar citizen and is not 'in Her Majesty's dominions or in any British Protectorate or Territory administered by or on behalf of Her Majesty's Government under any Trust, notice of the summons and not the summons itself is to be served upon him'.[58]

In order to obtain leave of the court in Zanzibar to serve the summons or notice thereof on the defendant outside of Zanzibar, the plaintiff must make an application in accordance with Order V, rule 30 of the Zanzibar Civil Procedure Rules. This provides:

> 'Every application for leave to serve such summons or notice of summons on a defendant out of Zanzibar shall be supported by affidavit or other evidence, stating that in the belief of the deponent the plaintiff has a good cause of action, and showing in what place and country such defendant is or probably may be found, and whether such defendant is a British or Zanzibar subject or not, and the grounds on which the application is made; and no such leave shall be granted unless it shall be made sufficiently to appear to the court that the case is a proper one for service out of Zanzibar under this order.'[59]

In all cases the court retains discretion whether to grant leave to serve the defendant outside the jurisdiction. Given the framework within which the Zanzibar courts consider whether to grant such leave, it would be unsurprising were a Zanzibar court to look for guidance on, inter alia, the structure of that discretion in the English authorities and that guidance is, where appropriate, set out below.

Indeed, given the similarities which exist between the rules in Zanzibar and in England governing the service of process out of the jurisdiction it should be noted that the English equivalents of Zanzibar Order V, rules 27 and 30, have been the subject of judicial consideration at the highest level in England.

In *Seaconsar Far East Ltd v Bank Markazi Jomhouri Islami Iran*,[60] the House of Lords considered the interaction of Order XI, rules 1(1) and 4, of the Rules of the Supreme Court (the equivalent to Order V, rules 27 and 30). Lord Goff (with whom the other Lords agreed) reviewed the authorities on the question what a plaintiff under Order XI was required to show on an application for leave to serve a writ out of the jurisdiction and found that the plaintiff was required

[58] Order V, r 29 of the Zanzibar Civil Procedure Rules. The reasons for this are rooted in English legal history: a summons is a command from the sovereign and it was thought discourteous to serve such a command on a person not resident in the United Kingdom and not a British subject; thus, notice of the summons was served instead (see *Nanjibhai Prabhudas and Co Ltd v Standard Bank Ltd* [1968] EA 670 (CA) (Sir Charles Newbold P, Sir Clement de Lestang V-P and Law JA), *per* Sir Charles Newbold P at 683C–E; the origin of the rule is s 19 of the English Common Law Procedure Act 1852. After the repeal of the 1852 Act, the rule was incorporated into the Rules of the Supreme Court: *Westman v Aktiebolaget Ekmans Mekaniska Snickarefabrick* (1876) 1 Ex D 237. It is submitted that, in O V, r 29 itself, the language of 'Her Majesty's Dominions' is now out of date. It is, in England, more common to speak about 'nations within the Commonwealth'.

[59] The exercise of the court's discretion is considered below under the heading '*Forum non conveniens*'.

[60] [1994] 1 AC 438 (HL(E)) (Lords Templeman, Griffiths, Goff, Browne-Wilkinson and Mustill).

to show, first, that the cause of action deposed to in the evidence in support of the application fell within the provisions of rule 1(1) and, second, that on the merits of the case, there was a serious question to be tried. On the question of the standard to which these issues were required to be shown, Lord Goff stated:[61]

> 'A judge faced with a question of leave to serve proceedings out of the jurisdiction under Order 11 will in practice have to consider both (1) whether jurisdiction has been sufficiently established, on the criterion of the good arguable case laid down in *Korner's* case, under one of the paragraphs of rule 1(1), and (2) whether there is a serious issue to be tried, so as to enable him to exercise his discretion to grant leave, before he goes on to consider the exercise of that discretion, with particular reference to the issue of forum conveniens.'

The first of these matters was held to correspond to the requirement in Order XI, rule 4, that 'no such leave shall be granted unless it shall be made sufficiently to appear to the Court or Judge that the case is a proper one for service out of the jurisdiction under this Order'[62] and the second was a threshold requirement for the merits of the plaintiff's claim.[63]

Thus, considering the English authorities, it is suggested that, analytically, it would be helpful to determine applications for leave to serve process out of the jurisdiction by applying the following, four-component approach.[64]

(1) *The formal requirements.* Has the plaintiff produced evidence satisfying the formal requirements of Order V, rule 30 (or English Order XI, rule 4)? In Zanzibar, this requires the plaintiff in his affidavit in support of the application to set out: (a) the belief of the deponent that the plaintiff has a good cause of action; (b) in what place and country such defendant is or probably may be found; (c) whether such defendant is a British or Zanzibar subject or not; and (d) the grounds on which the application is made.

---

[61] Ibid 456H–457B. See also the decision of the Privy Council in *Altimo Holdings and Investment Ltd v Kyrgyz Mobil Tel Ltd* [2012] 1 WLR 1804 (Lords Phillips PSC, Mance, Collins, Kerr and Clarke JJSC), *per* Lord Collins at para [71], confirming this statement of principle.

[62] *Seaconsar* 451A-B, 452A–B, 453D–G.

[63] *Seaconsar* 452D–E, 455A–C, 456G–H. Notwithstanding the separate treatment of the English O XI, r 4, in *Seaconsar* and the earlier authorities referred to therein, it is unclear whether the amendment in 1883 of O XI, r 3 (under the Rules of Court contained in Sch 1 to the Supreme Court of Judicature Act 1875) by the introduction of an expanded O XI, r 4, in the 1883 Rules of Court, was intended to produce this result. At the time the leading textbook on the Rules took the view that the amendment to include the wording, 'No such leave shall be granted unless it shall be made sufficiently to appear to the Court or Judge that the case is a proper one for service out of the jurisdiction under this Order', was merely an amplification of the previous rule (see Wynne Baxter *Judicature Acts and Rules 1873–1883* 5 ed (1883) 176–7).

[64] As summarised in the English *Supreme Court Practice 1965* (1999 ed) 93–4 paras 11/1/9–11/1/12. The commentary referred to in the *Supreme Court Practice* refers to three elements; in the text above the present authors include four elements, the additional element being the formal requirements of English rule 4 and Zanzibar rule 30.

(2) *The sufficiency requirement.* Under the English Order XI, rule 4, it was held in the *Seaconsar* case that the words 'and no such leave shall be granted unless it shall be made sufficiently to appear to the Court or Judge that the case is a proper one for service out of the jurisdiction under this Order' introduced a sufficiency requirement (or, in other words, a degree of proof requirement) such that the plaintiff must show that there is a good arguable case[65] that the case falls within one of the gateways under Order XI, rule 1(1).

(3) *The merits requirement.* The plaintiff must demonstrate that there is a serious issue to be tried on the merits of the claim upon which the claimant relies. Lord Goff in *Seaconsar* stated[66] as follows:

> 'The court cannot resolve disputed questions of fact on affidavit evidence; and it is consistent with the statement of the law by Lord Davey that if, at the end of the day, there remains a substantial question of fact or law or both, arising on the facts disclosed by the affidavits, which the plaintiff bona fide desires to try, the court should, as a rule, allow the service of the writ. If this approach is correct, the standard of proof in respect of the cause of action can broadly be stated to be whether, on the affidavit evidence before the court, there is a serious question to be tried.'

(4) *The court's discretion.* Once the above matters are established by the plaintiff, the court will proceed to consider the exercise of its discretion to allow service out of the jurisdiction. The court's discretion is exercised cautiously. As was stated by Pearson J in *Société Générale de Paris v Dreyfus Brothers:*[67]

---

[65] In *Canada Trust v Stolzenberg (No 2)* [2002] 1 AC 1 (HL(E)) (Lords Steyn, Hoffmann, Cooke, Hope and Hobhouse), *per* Lord Steyn (with whom the other Lords agreed) 13F, the House of Lords appeared to approve passages from the judgment of Waller LJ in the Court of Appeal in the same case ([1998] 1 WLR 547) including the following (at 555F–G): 'It is also right to remember that the "good arguable case" test, although obviously applicable to the ex parte stage, becomes of most significance at the inter partes stage where two arguments are being weighed in the interlocutory context which, as I have stressed, must not become a "trial". "Good arguable case" reflects in that context that one side has a much better argument on the material available. It is the concept which the phrase reflects on which it is important to concentrate, i.e. of the court being satisfied or as satisfied as it can be having regard to the limitations which an interlocutory process imposes that factors exist which allow the court to take jurisdiction.' In *Goldman Sachs International v Novo Banco SA* [2018] 1 WLR 3683 (Lords Mance, Sumption and Hodge, Lady Black and Lord Lloyd-Jones), the UK Supreme Court further clarified the correct understanding of the test in the *Canada Trust* case. Lord Sumption (with whom all the other members of the court agreed and in reliance on his own judgment in *Brownlie v Four Seasons Holdings Incorporated* [2018] 1 WLR 192) stated at para [9]: 'For the purpose of determining an issue about jurisdiction, the traditional test has been whether the claimant had "the better of the argument" on the facts going to jurisdiction. In *Brownlie v Four Seasons Holdings Inc* [2018] 1 WLR 192, para 7, this court reformulated the effect of that test as follows: "(i) that the claimant must supply a plausible evidential basis for the application of a relevant jurisdictional gateway; (ii) that if there is an issue of fact about it, or some other reason for doubting whether it applies, the court must take a view on the material available if it can reliably do so; but (iii) the nature of the issue and the limitations of the material available at the interlocutory stage may be such that no reliable assessment can be made, in which case there is a good arguable case for the application of the gateway if there is a plausible (albeit contested) evidential basis for it.'

[66] *Seaconsar* 452C–D.

[67] (1885) 29 Ch D 239 at 242–3; cited with approval by Lord Goff in *Seaconsar* at 455D.

> 'But of course it becomes a very serious question, and ought always to be considered a very serious question, whether or not, even in a case like that, it is necessary for the jurisdiction of the Court to be invoked, and whether this Court ought to put a foreigner, who owes no allegiance here, to the inconvenience and annoyance of being brought to contest his rights in this country, and I for one say, most distinctly, that I think this Court ought to be exceedingly careful before it allows a writ to be served out of the jurisdiction.'

Returning to the law of Zanzibar, where the court does make an order granting leave to effect service of a summons or notice of a summons out of Zanzibar,[68] the order shall limit a time after such service within which the defendant is to file a written statement, such time to depend on the place or country where or within which the service is to be effected.[69]

12.2.3.3.2 Bases on which the court may grant leave to serve out of Zanzibar

In the absence of authority on the point in Tanzania, it is appropriate to consider the bases upon which a Zanzibar court may grant leave to serve out of the jurisdiction.

(1) Relief is sought against a person domiciled or ordinarily resident in Zanzibar

It appears that the term 'person' in Order V, rule 27(c) of the Zanzibar Civil Procedure Rules, includes any natural or legal person.[70]

There is little judicial authority in Zanzibar[71] on the meaning of the term 'domicile' for the purposes of the application of Order V, rule 27(c). It is likely, given the close relationship between the Zanzibar legal system and those of, inter alia, Kenya and Uganda (which in turn look to English law for the meaning of terms inherited from colonial times), that the Zanzibar courts will adopt the jurisprudence applicable in English law regarding the term 'domicile' for the

[68] And where such an order giving leave is made, service may be effected in any of the ways set out in O V, r 32 of the Zanzibar Civil Procedure Rules. Likewise, any other order, notice or summons shall be deemed to be duly served upon a person resident out of Zanzibar if served in the manner prescribed for service of a summons on a defendant resident out of Zanzibar.

[69] Order V, r 31 of the Zanzibar Civil Procedure Rules.

[70] Section 4 of the Interpretation of Laws Act. This Act was passed by the Tanzanian Parliament and in terms of s 2(1) is said to 'apply to Mainland Tanzania as well as to Tanzania Zanzibar in relation to all laws which apply throughout the United Republic'. Of course, the Zanzibar Civil Procedure Rules do not apply throughout the United Republic: they only apply in Zanzibar (given that the Civil Procedure Rules apply in Mainland Tanzania). That said, in the absence of an Interpretation Act applicable to Zanzibar only, it appears likely that the term 'person', as set out in the Zanzibar Civil Procedure Rules, would be given the same definition as provided in the Interpretation of Laws Act.

[71] Or Tanzania.

purposes of determining jurisdiction over a person.[72] Under the English Rules of the Supreme Court upon which Order V, rule 27 of the Zanzibar Civil Procedure Rules appears to have been based,[73] 'domicile' was defined as follows:[74]

> 'In general the domicile of a person is in the country in which he has his permanent home (see Dicey, *Conflict of Law*, 7th ed., Chap. 6), the country in which his habitation is fixed without any present intention of removing (Re *Craignish*, [1892] 3 Ch. 180, C.A.; *Huntly v. Gaskell*, [1906] A.C. 56; *Casdagli v. C.*, [1919] A.C. 145). No person can at any time be without a domicile or have more than one domicile. The domicile of origin remains until a new domicile of choice has been adopted (*Bell v. Kennedy* (1868), L.R. 1 Sc. App. 307, H.L.; *Udny v. Udny* (1869), ibid, 441, H.L., *Winans v. A.-G.*, [1904] A.C. 287, H.L.).'

The Zanzibar courts have jurisdiction on the basis of ordinary residence within Zanzibar. Whether a person is ordinarily resident in Zanzibar is likely to be a question of fact to be determined in all the circumstances of the case.[75]

As regards the domicile and ordinary residence of a company, these concepts do not appear to have been the subject of judicial analysis in the Zanzibar courts. As a guide to the meaning of these terms the Zanzibar courts may look to the traditional definition of the 'domicile' and 'residence' of a legal person under the English Rules of the Supreme Court[76] (from which Order V, rule 27 of the Zanzibar Civil Procedure Rules appears to be derived):

> 'A corporation is domiciled where it is registered, if the law requires it to be registered, and if it does not it is domiciled in the country by whose law it is incorporated (Dicey, *Conflict of Laws*, 7th ed., p. 477). A corporation is "resident" and "ordinarily resident" where its central management and control is exercised ...'.

(2) The action is one brought to enforce, rescind, dissolve, annul or otherwise affect a contract or to recover damages or other relief for or in respect of the breach of a contract:

(a) made in Zanzibar; or

(b) made by or through an agent trading or residing in Zanzibar on behalf of a principal trading or residing out of Zanzibar; or

---

[72] See generally on the meaning of 'domicile', *Dicey, Morris and Collins on the Conflict of Laws* 15 ed (2012) vol 1, r 34, para 6R-001.

[73] The English Rules of the Supreme Court regulating service out of the jurisdiction prior to 1999 (when the Civil Procedure Rules came into effect) was O XI. Under the Rules of the Supreme Court 1883 and the Rules of the Supreme Court 1965, which superseded the 1883 Rules, O XI, r 1 provided for service out of the jurisdiction where the defendant was domiciled or ordinarily resident within the jurisdiction.

[74] The Rules of the Supreme Court 1883 (1960 ed) 144.

[75] In *Donnebaum v Mikolaschek* [1964] EA 645, Rudd J found that the defendant had ceased to be ordinarily resident in Kenya a matter of two days prior to the commencement of proceedings, thereby depriving the Kenyan courts of jurisdiction in the case. It is submitted that a Zanzibar court is likely to consider this case to be highly persuasive, if not strictly binding.

[76] *Rules of the Supreme Court 1883* (1960 ed) 145.

(c) by its terms or by implication to be governed by Zanzibar law

or is brought in respect of a breach committed in Zanzibar of a contract, wherever made, even though such breach was preceded or accompanied by a breach out of Zanzibar which rendered impossible the performance of the part of the contract which ought to have been performed in Zanzibar.

The place where a contract was made was considered by the Court of Appeal of East Africa in *Karachi Gas Co Ltd v Issaq*,[77] in which correspondence written in both Kenya and Pakistan was concluded for the sale by the plaintiff, a Kenyan resident, to the defendant, a company incorporated in Pakistan, of 100,000 feet of pipes f.o.b.[78] Mombasa, Kenya. The plaintiff was also to arrange for the relevant export permit and the defendant was to arrange for the relevant import licences. After certain delays the defendant repudiated the contract by refusing to accept delivery of the pipes f.o.b. Mombasa. The plaintiff commenced proceedings in Kenya and obtained an order granting him leave to serve the defendant outside the jurisdiction in Pakistan. The defendant applied to have that order set aside, inter alia, on the basis that the court had no jurisdiction because the proper law of the contract was Pakistan law and not Kenyan law.

On the question where the contract was made, the majority of the court[79] applied 'the postal rule'[80] and held that the contract had been made in Kenya as this was the country from which the plaintiff had posted his acceptance of the defendant's counter-offer.[81]

The court also held[82] that the proper law of the contract (or that part of it relevant for the purposes of the appeal)[83] was Kenyan law because, inter alia: the contract had been made in Kenya; the goods which were the subject of the contract were in Kenya at the time the contract was made; delivery of those goods was to be made in Kenya; the language of the contract was English; and the terms were terms familiar in English contracts of sale.

---

[77] [1965] EA 42 (CA) (Newbold Ag. V-P and Spry and Duffus JJA). It is submitted that a Zanzibar court is likely to find this authority highly persuasive, if not binding. Cited and followed in *Nairobi Projector Services Ltd v Kabuleeta* [2006] eKLR 55 (HC) (Visram J).

[78] Free (or freight) on board, ie, the plaintiff's obligations were to deliver the pipes to the ship's railing; the defendant was to arrange for marine freight, insurance and unloading.

[79] Duffus JA at 49H–I and Spry JA at 55G–I.

[80] The rule of English conflict of laws that a contract is made in the country where the acceptance is *posted*; in cases of instantaneous communications, telex, fax, email, etc, the contract is made in the country where the communication is *received* (*Entores Ltd v Miles Far East Corp* [1955] 2 QB 327 (CA) (Denning, Birkett and Parker LJJ)).

[81] A further example of the fact that a contract was made in Kenya provided the court with jurisdiction is *African Mercantile Co Ltd v Patel* (1927–28) 11 KLR 69 (HC) (Stephens J), where the defendant was in India, but the contract had been made in Kenya.

[82] As *per* Newbold ag. V-P at 54A–D and Spry JA at 56A–57C, applying the 'system of law with which the transaction has its closest and most real connection' test.

[83] As *per* Duffus JA at 49I–50A.

Finally, the court found that there had been a breach of the contract in Kenya because the defendant refused to accept delivery of the goods f.o.b. Mombasa, where both the plaintiff's and defendant's obligations regarding delivery and acceptance were due to be performed.[84]

It is likely that, in the absence of further reported authority in Zanzibar or Tanzania (or Kenya) on the construction and application of Order V, rule 27(1)(e), a Zanzibar court will have regard to the academic and judicial authorities on the construction and application of the (former) equivalent provision in the English Rules of the Supreme Court.[85]

A concise statement of the law is as follows:[86]

'(i) **Where a contract is made in England**

11–181

If the parties enter into negotiations by correspondence from different countries, the contract is made where the letter of acceptance is posted. But in commercial transactions today communication by telephone, telex, fax and electronic mail is much more common than by post. It is now well established, following the decision of the Court of Appeal in *Entores v Miles Far East Corp* (which was approved by the House of Lords [*Brinkibon Ltd v. Stahag Stahl und Stahlwarenhandelsgesellschaft mbH* [1983] 2 AC 34]) that if the parties use "instantaneous" means of communication such as telephone, fax or electronic mail, the contract is made where the acceptance is communicated to the offeror. It has been held that if a contract made in England contains a submission to arbitration in a foreign country, an action in England at common law to enforce the foreign arbitration award is within this part of the clause. The contract must actually be made in England as that phrase is understood in English law. It is not sufficient if it merely says that it shall be deemed to be so made, though this may be sufficient to make it one which is governed by English law. A contract may be made in England within the meaning of this clause although it was preceded by a less formal agreement made abroad, or if it was originally made in England, but amended abroad.

(ii) **Where a contract is made by or through an agent trading or residing in England**

11–182

The clause says "by or through" an agent, not "by" an agent. Hence the case is within the clause, although the agent has no authority to make contracts on behalf of his foreign principal, but only has authority to obtain orders and transmit them to his principal for acceptance or rejection. This part of the clause is designed to bring within Rule 34

[84] As regards the place of performance, in *Kenya School of Flying v ACE INA UK Ltd* [2005] eKLR 55 (HC) (Waweru J), it was held, inter alia, that an insurance policy placed and issued in London was due to be performed in England and not Kenya were an insured event had occurred. (A contract case and not a tort case – for which it is cited in Frimpong Oppong *Private International Law in Commonwealth Africa* (2013) 55 fn 36.)

[85] Order XI, r 1(e), *Rules of the Supreme Court 1883* (1960 ed).

[86] *Dicey, Morris and Collins on the Conflict of Laws* 15 ed (2012) vol 1, 34, paras 11–181–11–187.

foreigners who transact business in England by or through agents, and consequently it does not apply where the agent's principal is the claimant. Hence a claimant cannot invoke clause (6)(ii) [Order V, rule 27(e)(ii)] where the contract was made by or through his agent.

11–183

If proceedings are brought by consignees of a cargo against foreign ship-owners under the bills of lading, the case is not within this part of the clause if the charterparty (but not the bills of lading) was made by or through agents of the shipowners in England, even though it refers to the bills of lading and was made by charterers acting on behalf of the consignees. It may be otherwise, however, if the charterers are identical with the consignees...

(iii) **Where a contract is governed by English law**

11–186

...

11–187

Although the fact that a contract is governed by English law is an important factor in the exercise of the discretion under this head in favour of the English forum, it is not conclusive. This head of jurisdiction was described as exorbitant in *Amin Rasheed Shipping Corp v Kuwait Insurance Co*, where the House of Lords held that in the circumstances it was not appropriate for the English court to determine a dispute involving a marine insurance policy governed by English law when the Kuwaiti courts were the *forum conveniens*. Until that decision it was generally thought that the fact that a contract was governed by English law was in itself sufficient to justify leave. But now the claimant has a heavier burden. In *Amin Rasheed* Lord Diplock suggested that, in order to justify leave under this head, the plaintiff had to show that justice could not be obtained by him in the foreign court, or could only be obtained at excessive cost, delay or inconvenience. But it was subsequently held that Lord Diplock was merely giving examples, and was not providing an exhaustive list, of the relevant factors. The court has to consider all factors, and the fact that English law is the applicable law may be of great importance, or it may be of little consequence as seen in the context of the whole case. Thus if there is likely to be no dispute on matters of law or construction, or if the law of the foreign forum is substantially the same as English law, the fact that English law is the applicable law will be of little weight. But where an issue of English public policy arises in relation to a contract which is (or may be) governed by English law, it is desirable that it should be decided by the English court; conversely, where the foreign court may apply its own public policy to defeat a claim based on a contract governed by English law, that too is a reason for the English court taking jurisdiction. If the claimant has alternative remedies in contract and tort upon the same facts, he can choose his remedy.'

(3) The action is founded on a tort committed in Zanzibar

There is little judicial authority on the meaning and application of Order V, rule 27(f) of the Zanzibar Civil Procedure Rules and, as with the construction and application of Order V, rule 27(e), it is likely that a Zanzibar court will have regard to the academic and judicial authorities on the construction and application of the (former) equivalent provision in the English Rules of the Supreme Court on the question when is a tort committed within Zanzibar.[87]

A statement of the law is as follows:[88]

> **'11–212**
>
> ... As both the Privy Council [in *Distillers Co (Bio-chemicals) Ltd v. Thompson* [1971] AC 458] and the Supreme Court of Canada [*Moran v. Pyle National (Canada) Ltd* (1973) 43 D.L.R. (3d) 239] have pointed out, the competing theories for the determination of the place of a tort have been that (i) all ingredients of the cause of action must have occurred within the jurisdiction, or (ii) the last ingredient, the event which completes a cause of action, must have occurred within the jurisdiction, or (iii) the act which the defendant committed must have occurred within the jurisdiction.
>
> **11–213**
>
> In *Distillers Co Ltd v Thompson* the Privy Council adopted the test of the place where in substance the act or omission occurred which gave the plaintiff his cause of action. So that where the essence of the complaint was failure to warn the consumer of the dangers of a product (rather than the faulty manufacture of the product) the cause of action was held to have arisen at the place where the failure to warn occurred; and the torts of negligent and fraudulent misrepresentation, where the negligent or fraudulent statement was communicated from one country to another, were held to have been committed where the statement was received and acted upon. Prior to the adoption of that test, but consistently with it, it had been held that the tort of defamation was committed where the defamatory statements were published and not where they were posted or uttered.'

12.2.3.4 *Tanzania: Submission to the jurisdiction*[89]

Two circumstances need to be distinguished under this title: first, where submission is alleged in extant proceedings in Tanzania; second, where the defendant has agreed (usually by contractual provision) to submit to the jurisdiction of the court in advance of a dispute arising.

12.2.3.4.1 Submission by appearance

The question of when a party will be taken, by his action, to have submitted to the jurisdiction of the Tanzanian court has received some judicial consideration, principally in cases concerned with the correct scope and application of an arbitration agreement into which the parties have entered.[90]

---

[87] Order XI, r 1(ee) and 1(f) respectively: *Rules of the Supreme Court 1883* (1960 ed).

[88] *Dicey, Morris and Collins on the Conflict of Laws* 15 ed (2012) vol 1, r 34, paras 11–212–11–213.

[89] There appears to be very little authority on the question of when a party will be deemed to have submitted to the jurisdiction in Zanzibar. Accordingly, this section deals with the law as applied in Tanzania only. For reasons already mentioned, it is submitted that the Zanzibar court would likely follow the approach adopted by the Tanzanian court on this issue.

[90] It is submitted that, in this context, cases which consider the correct interpretation of the Arbitration Act 1931 (Act 26 of 1931, now Cap 15 of the Laws of Tanzania, 2019) and reach a conclusion on the question

In *Motokov v Auto Garage*,[91] the plaintiff sued the first defendant on bills of exchange. The defendant alleged that he had been induced to enter into the contract as a result of the plaintiff's fraudulent misrepresentations. The defendant also counterclaimed for breach of contract. The plaintiff filed a request for better particulars and obtained an order on it. Two years later, the plaintiff sought an order staying the counterclaim on the basis that the issues raised therein ought to be referred to arbitration in Czechoslovakia, according to the relevant clause of the contract. So far as relevant for present purposes, the defendant alleged that the plaintiff had 'taken a step in proceedings', such that the plaintiff could no longer ask for a stay.

In reaching the decision not to grant the stay, Georges CJ stated[92] that, while difficult to define, any 'application to a court for an order in respect of the proceedings can be described as a step in the proceedings'. Georges CJ then went on to agree[93] with the plaintiff's argument that the request for better particulars had been made in respect of the defence and not the counterclaim, such that the plaintiff had taken the 'step in relation to the defence and not in relation to the counterclaim and consequently that the jurisdiction of the court to order a stay had not been ousted'. However, Georges CJ ultimately refused[94] to grant the stay on the basis that 'the defence and the counterclaim are so inextricably mixed that it is obviously more convenient to have both of them decided together in one set of proceedings ... despite the availability of arbitration'.

It is submitted that the judgment in *Motokov* is correct in that it requires the court to consider the specific step which the party has taken and the specific

whether a party may be taken to have submitted (by way of appearance) to court proceedings may act as a guide in working out when a party will be taken to have submitted (by way of appearance) in a pure litigation context. However, a clear health warning is necessary: the Arbitration Act 1931 (apparently unlike the Civil Procedure Rules) contains an express mechanism by which parties can challenge, in a fashion, the (existence or exercise of the) court's jurisdiction. Hence, s 6 of the Arbitration Act 1931 provides: 'Where a party to a submission to which this Part applies, or a person claiming under him, commences a legal proceedings against any other party to the submission or any person claiming under him in respect of any matter agreed to be referred, a party to the legal proceedings may, at any time after appearance and before filing a written statement or taking any other steps in the proceedings apply to the court to stay the proceedings; and the court, if satisfied that there is no sufficient reason why the matter should not be referred in accordance with the submission and that the applicant was, at the time when the proceedings were commenced, and still remains, ready and willing to do all things necessary for the proper conduct of the arbitration, may make an order staying the proceedings.' No equivalent provision appears in the Code or the Civil Procedure Rules.

[91] [1970] EA 249 (High Court of Tanzania) (Georges CJ).

[92] Ibid 252. At 253, Georges CJ went on to cite the decision of the English High Court in *Austin and Whiteley Ltd v Bowley and Sons* (1913) 108 LT 921, where Ridley J stated: 'What is intended by a step in proceedings is some step which indicates an intention on the part of a party to the proceedings that he desires that the action should proceed and has no desire that the matter should be referred to arbitration.'

[93] [1970] EA 249 at 252.

[94] Ibid 253I–254A.

reason why the party has taken that step[95] in deciding whether the party can be said to have submitted (by way of appearance in proceedings) to the jurisdiction of the court.

Subsequent cases have confirmed that the approach in *Motokov* should be followed in Tanzania. That said, what amounts to taking a step in proceedings is a question of fact, doubtless to be answered sensitively in each case. Examining the authorities, these have variously held that a party will be deemed to have taken a 'step in proceedings'[96] when: acquiescing without protest in an order giving time to file a written statement of defence;[97] in making applications for extensions of time to file said written statement of defence and filing; and, in response to a plaintiff's plaint and application for an interim injunction, filing a counter affidavit contesting the application for the issuance of the injunction.[98]

It is not apparent from the Code how a party challenges the jurisdiction of the court.[99] That said, by analogy with the procedure set out in section 6 of the Arbitration Act, it may be the case that, when the defendant appears to answer the summons (and without filing a written statement or such other documentation to which reference has been made above), he should, making it clear that he does not submit to the jurisdiction of the court, make an application to the court for an order declaring that the court has no jurisdiction in the substantive matter.

12.2.3.4.2 Submission by agreement

12.2.3.4.2.1 *Jurisdiction clauses*

Where parties agree to submit their disputes to a foreign arbitrator, the courts in Tanzania will endeavour to give effect to that agreement. Where made, such agreement does not amount to the improper ouster of the jurisdiction of the Tanzanian court and the clause is not invalid for that reason.[100] It is submitted that the Tanzanian court is likely to follow the same approach when confronted

[95] Compare, for example, the decision of the English Court of Appeal in *Murthy v Sivajothi* [1999] 1 WLR 467 (Evans, Morritt and Chadwick LJJ).

[96] In the specific context of the Arbitration Act 1931.

[97] *Kassam Ahmed v Mohamed Dewshi and Sons* [1973] LRT 42 (High Court of Tanzania) (Onyiuke J).

[98] *Transnet v Spoornet*, Commercial Case 55 of 2006 (Commercial Division of the High Court of Tanzania). For critical commentary of the decision in this case, and a general critique of the Tanzanian court's approach to arbitration clauses in general, see Mkumbukwa 'Is the Commercial Court jealous of arbitration?' (2009) *Tanzania Lawyer Journal* 3(2) 3 at 138.

[99] See, by way of contrast, r 11(1) of the English Civil Procedure Rules, which provides that a defendant who wishes to dispute the jurisdiction of the court must make an application to that effect, having first filed an acknowledgment of service.

[100] *Motokov v Auto Garage* [1970] EA 249 (HC) (Georges CJ) at 251, citing *Norske Atlas Insurance Co v London General Insurance Co Ltd* (1927) 43 TLR 541 (English High Court) (Mackinnon J).

with a contractual clause whereby which parties agree to submit their disputes to the jurisdiction of a foreign court.[101]

The Tanzanian court has discretion whether to give effect to the arbitration clause or jurisdiction clause.[102] It would appear that the Tanzanian court will lean in favour of upholding the arbitration clause or jurisdiction clause even in the face of a party's arguing that the substantive contract containing that clause has been affected by fraud or misrepresentation. When faced with precisely those arguments, Nsekela J stated:[103]

> '"Any dispute" should not be read as excluding disputes involving fraud or misrepresentation. It is not the function of the court to rewrite and insert provisions to which the parties could have agreed to deal with in a situation which might arise. Although not particularly relevant to the issue at hand, in the case of *Harbour Assurance Co. (UK) v. Kansa General International Assurance Co. Ltd [1993] 3 All ER 897*, Hoffmann LJ stated at page 915 as follows:
>
> > "It is necessary to bear in mind the powerful commercial reasons for upholding arbitration clauses unless it is clear that this would offend the policy of the illegality rule. These are, first, the desirability of giving effect to the right of the parties to choose a tribunal to resolve their disputes and secondly, the practical advantages of one stop adjudication, or, in other words, the inconvenience of having one issue resolved by the court and then, contingently on the outcome of that decision, further issues to be decided by the arbitrator."'[104]

In deciding whether or not to give effect to the arbitration clause or jurisdiction clause, the Tanzanian court appears to have a broad discretion[105] as to what factors to take into account.

Given the affinity between the Tanzanian and Kenyan legal traditions, a Tanzanian court is likely to be influenced by the approach adopted by the Kenyan courts when deciding whether to uphold a jurisdiction clause or not.

---

[101] After all, this is the approach which is adopted by English and Kenyan courts to this matter. Tanzanian courts have been influenced by English and Kenyan authorities when making decisions concerning clauses submitting disputes to foreign arbitration.

[102] *Shamji v Treasury Registrar* [2002] TZHC 12 (HC) (Nsekela J). Here, the court was asked to construe an arbitration clause in a wholly domestic setting. There is no indication that the principles adopted and applied by the High Court would have been different had the case arisen in a cross-border context.

[103] Ibid.

[104] As a matter of English law on this subject, see the decision of the House of Lords in *Fiona Trust and Holding Corp v Privalov* [2007] UKHL 40 (Lord Hoffmann, Lord Hope, Lord Scott, Lord Walker and Lord Brown), where Lord Hoffmann, giving the leading speech, returned to a similar theme.

[105] *Shamji v Treasury Registrar* [2002] TZHC 12, where Nsekela J, in deciding whether to uphold an arbitration clause, stated that: 'I am fully aware that there are no hard and fast rules as to how judicial discretion should be exercised.'

In summary, the Kenyan Court of Appeal has twice[106] concluded that the principles formulated by the English courts should provide the guide for the Kenyan courts when deciding whether to uphold a jurisdiction clause or not. Those principles were set out by Brandon J in *Owners of cargo lately laden on board the ship or vessel Eleftheria v The Eleftheria (Owners), The Eleftheria*,[107] where he considered earlier authorities and set out a statement of the principles applicable to an application for a stay of proceedings where there was a jurisdiction clause relied on by the party seeking the stay. Brandon J's statement of those principles has since been accepted as the authoritative statement in this area (not merely in England, but in other common-law jurisdictions, such as Canada and Nigeria).[108]

In *The Eleftheria* the jurisdiction clause provided: 'Any dispute arising under this bill of lading shall be decided in the country where the carrier has his principal place of business [Greece].' The owners of cargo on board the *Eleftheria* commenced proceedings in England and the shipowners applied for a stay of those proceedings. In staying the proceedings in favour of the Greek courts, Brandon J set out the principles on the basis of which a stay may be granted:[109]

> '(1) Where plaintiffs sue in England in breach of an agreement to refer disputes to a foreign court, and the defendants apply for a stay, the English court, assuming the claim to be otherwise within its jurisdiction, is not bound to grant a stay but has a discretion whether to do so or not. (2) The discretion should be exercised by granting a stay unless strong cause for not doing so is shown. (3) The burden of proving such strong cause is on the plaintiffs. (4) In exercising its discretion the court should take into account all the circumstances of the particular case. (5) In particular, but without prejudice to (4), the following matters, where they arise, may properly be regarded:—(a) In what country the evidence on the issues of fact is situated, or more readily available, and the effect of that on the relative convenience and expense of trial as between the English and foreign courts, (b) Whether the law of the foreign court applies and, if so, whether it differs from English law in any material respects, (c) With what country either party is connected, and how closely, (d) Whether the defendants genuinely desire trial in the foreign country, or are only seeking procedural advantages, (e) Whether the plaintiffs would be prejudiced by having to sue in the foreign court because they would: (i) be deprived of security for their claim; (ii) be unable to enforce any judgment obtained; (iii) be faced with a time-bar not applicable in England; or (iv) for political, racial, religious or other reasons be unlikely to get a fair trial.'

---

[106] First in *Ronning v Société Navale Chargeurs Delmas Vieljeux, The François Vieljeux* [1987] Revue de Droit Uniforme 537, [1976–85] 1 EA 513, [1982–88] 1 KAR 398 (CA) (Hancox JA and Nyarangi and Chesoni Ag JJA) and then again in *United India Insurance Co Ltd v East African Underwriters (Kenya) Ltd* [1982–88] 1 KAR 639 (CA) (Madan, Kneller and Hancox JJA).

[107] [1970] P 94; [1969] 1 Lloyd's Rep 237 (QBD, Comm Ct).

[108] *Aratra Potato Co Ltd v Egyptian Navigation Co (The El Amria)* [1981] 2 Lloyd's Rep 119 (CA, Eng); *Anraj Fish Products Industries Ltd v Hyundai Merchant Marine Co Ltd* [2000] ILPr 717 (Fed Ct, Can); *Nika Fishing Co Ltd v Lavina Corp* [2008] 16 NWLR 509 (Sup Ct, Nigeria).

[109] [1970] P 94 at 99G–100C.

12.2.3.4.2.2 *Application for service out of the jurisdiction based on a jurisdiction clause*

As has been noted above,[110] there is an absence of authority in Tanzania as to the grounds upon which the court will grant leave to serve the summons out of the jurisdiction. While Order V, rule 27 of the Zanzibar Civil Procedure Rules does set out the bases upon which courts in Zanzibar can grant leave to serve process outside that jurisdiction, it does not appear to permit service out solely on the ground that the parties have agreed to submit to the jurisdiction of the Zanzibar courts. Accordingly, in the absence of reported authority, it is presently unclear as to whether a party, wishing to sue in Zanzibar,[111] may successfully persuade the court to permit service out of the jurisdiction purely because of the existence of a jurisdiction clause/jurisdiction agreement between the parties.

12.2.3.5 Lis alibi pendens

An explanatory note to section 8 of the Code provides: 'The pendency of a suit in a foreign court does not preclude the courts in Tanzania from trying a suit founded on the same cause of action.'

It appears that this provision has seldom been referred to by the Tanzanian courts.[112] Of course, while a Tanzanian court is not precluded from hearing such a suit, section 8 of the Code does not state that the Tanzanian court must go on to hear the suit in any event.[113] In those circumstances, when determining whether to hear the suit or not, the Tanzanian court may have regard to the approach which English courts have taken on the matter, especially given that the Kenyan courts may well take the same approach.

In *de Dampierre v de Dampierre*,[114] the House of Lords held that where a stay of English proceedings is sought on the basis that there are parallel proceedings in another jurisdiction, the principles of *forum non conveniens* enunciated in *Spiliada Maritime Corp v Cansulex Ltd*[115] apply. Thus in *de Dampierre*, a case concerning parallel divorce proceedings in France and England, the court considered the connections between the parties and the two jurisdictions and the appropriateness of proceedings in France rather than England and concluded that the English proceedings should be stayed:[116]

---

[110] See the main text underneath the sub-heading 'Tanzanian law on service outside the jurisdiction'.

[111] Or Tanzania.

[112] See Frimpong Oppong *Private International Law in Commonwealth Africa* 103 fn 62.

[113] See, to like effect, s 10 of the Civil Procedure Code of Myanmar and the commentary thereon in Briggs *Private International Law In Myanmar* (2015) 30.

[114] [1988] AC 92 (HL (E)) (Lords Keith, Brandon, Templeman, Ackner and Goff).

[115] [1987] AC 460 (HL (E)).

[116] Ibid 109E–H *per* Lord Goff.

> 'Here it is beyond dispute that there are very strong factors connecting the case with France, whereas now there are practically none connecting the case with England. Neither party suggests that New York is the appropriate forum. It follows that *prima facie* the courts of France clearly provide the appropriate jurisdiction for the resolution of the dispute, so that a stay should be granted unless justice requires otherwise. In considering the question, the [judge at first instance] ... did indeed invoke the authority of one of the earlier authorities on the inherent jurisdiction, relying as he did on the much-quoted dictum of Lord Diplock in *MacShannon v. Rockware Glass Ltd.* [1978] A.C. 975, 812. He recognised the undoubted "Frenchness" of the marriage and the spouses, but considered that the wife's absence from what he described as the "harsh" French regime and her presence in the more "benevolent" regime which prevails here, plainly afforded a juridical advantage to her and that, following Lord Diplock's approach, this must outweigh the "Frenchness" of the marriage of the spouses and point to the conclusion that England was the more appropriate jurisdiction for the dissolution of the marriage.'

And:[117]

> 'The weight to be given to what has been called a "legitimate personal or juridical advantage" was considered by your Lordships' House in the *Spiliada* case [1987] A.C. 460, 482–484. The conclusion there reached was that, having regard to the underlying principle, the court should not, as a general rule, be deterred from granting a stay of proceedings simply because the plaintiff in this country will be deprived of such an advantage, provided that the court is satisfied that substantial justice will be done in the appropriate forum overseas. Reference was made, in particular, to cases concerning discovery where, as is well known, there is a spectrum of systems of discovery applicable in various jurisdictions; and the opinion was expressed that, generally speaking, injustice cannot be said to be done if a party is compelled to accept one of these well recognised systems of discovery in another forum. If I follow that approach in the circumstances of the present case, I find that French matrimonial law contains provisions for "compensation" which, unlike our own, place emphasis upon the question whether the breakdown of the marriage was due to the exclusive fault of one of the parties, providing (subject to an important exception) that a party so at fault is deprived of the right to an award of compensation. Such an approach is no longer acceptable in this country, though it bears a close resemblance to the principles applicable here not so very long ago. But it is evidently still acceptable in a highly civilised country with which this country has very close ties of friendship, not least nowadays through our common membership of the European Community; and I find it impossible to conclude that, objectively speaking, justice would not be done if the wife was compelled to pursue her remedy for financial provision under such a regime in the courts of a country which provide, most plainly, the natural forum for the resolution of this matrimonial dispute.'

Thus what is required is a balancing of the various factors in the case to ascertain in which jurisdiction the case is most appropriately decided.

---

[117] Ibid 110B–F *per* Lord Goff.

12.2.3.6 Forum non conveniens[118]

Historically, the English courts seemed always to have held that a major factor in the exercise of the discretion to grant leave to serve out of the jurisdiction or stay proceedings already served out of the jurisdiction was whether the English proceedings were vexatious and oppressive. The expression 'vexatious and oppressive' bore a wide meaning and extended to considerations related to the comparative convenience of proceedings in England as opposed to a particular foreign forum. For example, in *Logan v Bank of Scotland (No 2)*,[119] the Court of Appeal granted an application staying proceedings served as of right in England in favour of Scotland. Sir Gorell Barnes P stated:[120]

> 'Now, it is true that the Courts of this country have not gone so far as to express themselves upon the question of convenience in terms similar to those used in the Scotch cases, though, as I have already noticed, it may be doubted whether there is any substantial difference between the two. Yet it seems to me clear that the inconvenience of trying a case in a particular tribunal may be such as practically to work a serious injustice upon a defendant and be vexatious. This would probably not be so if the difference of trying in one country rather than in another were merely measured by some extra expense; but where the difficulty for the defendant of trying in the country in which the action is brought is such that it is impracticable to properly try the case by reason of the difficulty of procuring the attendance of busy men as witnesses, and keeping them during trial, and of having to deal with masses of books, documents, and papers which are not in the country where the action is brought, and of dealing with law foreign to the tribunal, it appears to me that a case of vexation in some circumstances may be made out if the plaintiff chooses to sue in that country rather than in that where everybody is and where all the witnesses and material for the trial are.'

In *Spiliada Maritime Corp v Cansulex Ltd*[121] the House of Lords decided:[122]

> 'The basic principle is that a stay will only be granted on the ground of forum non conveniens where the court is satisfied that there is some other available forum, having

[118] There is some indication that the principle is also known to the courts of Tanzania, despite the fact that it is not mentioned in the Civil Procedure Rules. For instance, in *Willow Investment v Ntumba* [1997] TLR 47 (HC), Mapigano J at 49A–B, refers to the requirement that a 'proper nexus [exist] between litigants and Tanzania' for the court to have jurisdiction over the matter. This type of language might be thought to refer to the principle currently under consideration. That the principle is known to the courts in Tanzania is also apparent from comments made about a Tanzanian judgment by the English Court of Appeal in *Standard Chartered (Hong Kong) Ltd v Independent Power Tanzania* [2016] EWCA Civ 411 (Longmore, Black and Hamblen LJJ). At para [15] Longmore LJ stated that the claimant to the English proceedings had argued that Tanzania was not the correct forum, which argument was dismissed by the Tanzanian High Court. It has not, however, proved possible to obtain the relevant judgment of the Tanzanian court.

[119] [1906] 1 KB 141 (CA) (Sir Gorell Barnes, President, Collins MR, and Romer LJ).

[120] Ibid 151–2. This was a decision under the 1883 Rules of the Supreme Court.

[121] [1987] AC 460 (Lords Keith, Templeman, Griffiths, Mackay and Goff).

[122] Ibid 476C, *per* Lord Goff, with whom the other Lords of Appeal agreed (Lord Templeman delivering a concurring opinion). A decision under the 1965 Rules of the Supreme Court.

> competent jurisdiction, which is the appropriate forum for the trial of the action, i.e. in which the case may be tried more suitably for the interests of all the parties and the ends of justice.'

The English courts will, therefore, refuse leave to serve a writ out of the jurisdiction or (in a case where leave has been granted but the defendant enters a conditional appearance) will stay English proceedings if England is not the *forum conveniens*.[123]

It would be open to the Zanzibar High Court to take the view that considerations of convenience are appropriate to take into account when considering whether to grant leave to serve out of the jurisdiction (or whether to grant a stay of proceedings already commenced).

12.3 Enforcement of foreign judgments

It is necessary to deal separately with the enforcement of foreign judgments in Tanzania and in Zanzibar.

12.3.1 Tanzania

Under Tanzanian law, foreign judgments may be enforced either using the common law[124] or the statutory regime in force there.

12.3.1.1 *Enforcement at common law*

That a judgment creditor may seek to enforce a foreign judgment in his favour pursuant to the common law in Tanzania would appear to have been confirmed by the High Court[125] but still remains a controversial issue for some commentators.[126]

---

[123] See, generally, *Dicey, Morris and Collins on the Conflict of Laws* 15 ed (2012) vol 1, r 38(2) and (3), para 12–007 et seq; r 38 states the modern English law as follows, inter alia: '(2) … an English court has power to order a stay of proceedings on the basis that England is an inappropriate forum (forum non conveniens) if: (a) the defendant shows there to be another court with competent jurisdiction which is clearly or distinctly more appropriate than England for the trial of the action, and (b) it is not unjust that the claimant be deprived of the right to trial in England. (3) In considering whether to assume jurisdiction in any of the cases mentioned in Rule 34 (service out of the jurisdiction with the permission of the court) the court will generally require the claimant to show England to be the most appropriate forum for the trial of the claim.'

[124] In Tanzania, the theoretical basis on which a foreign judgment is enforceable is the doctrine of obligation: see Frimpong Oppong 'Recognition and Enforcement of Foreign Judgments in Commonwealth African Countries' (2014) XV *Yearbook of Private International Law* 365, 368, citing *Willow Investment v Mbomba Ntumba* [1996] TLR 377.

[125] *Willow Investment v Mbomba Ntumba* [1996] TLR 377 (HC) (Mapigano J).

[126] See, for example, the differing views expressed by, on the one hand, Kapinga, author of the relevant chapter on Tanzania in LW Newman (ed) *Enforcement of Money Judgments* (2017) and, on the other hand,

Where a judgment does not fall within the scope of the statutory regime currently in operation in Tanzania, the provisions of that statutory regime[127] do not apply where the judgment creditor seeks to enforce that judgment in Tanzania.[128]

In *Willow Investment v Mbomba Ntumba*,[129] the judgment creditor of a judgment obtained in Zaire, successfully registered that judgment in Tanzania, using the Reciprocal Enforcement of Foreign Judgments Act 1935. Pursuant to that registration, further orders attaching, and ultimately granting permission to sell, property were made. The applicant sought a review of those further orders, on the basis that the initial registration of the judgment was improper: Zaire was not a country to which the legislation extended (or extends), hence there was no mechanism by which that judgment could have been registered and/or enforced in Tanzania.

While agreeing that the Reciprocal Enforcement of Foreign Judgments Act was inapplicable, Mapigano J held[130] that this did not imply that the court lacked power to enforce the judgment given in Zaire. Instead:[131]

> 'The jurisdiction of this court to enforce judgments given in foreign countries emanates from statutory law, common law and treaties. In the absence of any such written law and treaty in relation to Zaire, judgments given in that country are, I think, enforceable at common law in Tanzania on what has come to be known as the doctrine of obligation.

Frimpong Oppong 'Recognition and Enforcement of Foreign Judgments in Commonwealth African Countries' (2014) XV *Yearbook of Private International Law* 354 fn 7 and associated text. The controversy would seem to remain in the jurisprudence of the Tanzanian courts as well: see *Koroso v AG of Kenya* [2011] TZHCCOMD 2012 (Juma J), where Juma J stated: 'Foreign judgments ... are enforced in Tanzania by virtue of the conditions prescribed under the [relevant Act]. These foreign judgments are enforced in Tanzania if they were delivered by courts of foreign countries which have reciprocal arrangements with Tanzania to enforce their respective judgments'. On the face of it, these remarks do not appear to leave any room available for enforcement at common law. However, it is submitted that the judge did not, in fact, intend to say anything contrary to the judgment in *Willow Investment*, given that he cites the case without disapproval.

[127] And, specifically, s 8 of the Reciprocal Enforcement of Foreign Judgments Act 1935 (O 12 of 1935, now Cap 8 of the Laws of Tanzania, 2019). This provides: 'No proceedings for the recovery of a sum payable under a foreign judgment, being a judgment to which this Part applies, other than proceedings by way of registration of the judgment, shall be entertained by any court in Mainland Tanzania.'

[128] *Shah Devsi Vardhaman v TCN Haridas* [1958] EA 527 (HC) (Spry ag J), a judgment on s 13 of the then operative Code of Civil Procedure, which was drafted in identical terms to s 8 of the Reciprocal Enforcement of Foreign Judgments Act). See further *Willow Investment v Mbomba Ntumba* [1996] TLR 377.

[129] [1996] TLR 377.

[130] Ibid 380.

[131] Section 11 of the Code provides that: 'A foreign judgment shall be conclusive as to any matter thereby directly adjudicated upon between the same parties or between parties under whom they or any of them claim litigating under the same title except: (a) where it has not been pronounced by a court of competent jurisdiction; (b) where it has not been given on the merits of the case; (c) where it appears on the face of the proceedings to be founded on an incorrect view of international law or a refusal to recognise the law of Tanzania in cases in which such law is applicable; (d) where the proceedings in which the judgment was obtained are opposed to natural justice; (e) where it has been obtained by fraud; (f) where it sustains a claim founded on a breach of any law in force in Tanzania.'

> In accordance with that doctrine, where a foreign court of competent jurisdiction has adjudicated a certain sum to be due from one person to another, the liability to pay that sum becomes a legal obligation which is recognised and enforceable in Tanzania. The foreign judgment is strictly not enforceable as such, but is to be regarded as creating a simple contract debt enforceable by an action of debt. Once the judgment is proved, the burden would lie on the judgment debtor to show cause why he should not perform the obligation. This is consistent with Section 11 of the [Code].'

Mapigano J, perhaps mindful of procedural concerns, continued:[132]

> 'It follows that a judgment creditor who seeks to enforce a foreign judgment at common law cannot do so by direct execution of the judgment. Enforcement must be sought by bringing an action on the debt. The procedure obtaining in England would serve as a model. The evidence would be on an affidavit and the defendant should be given proper opportunity of showing cause why the foreign judgment should not be recognized or enforced. If a decree is ultimately passed in favour of the plaintiff, he may proceed to execute it in Tanzania in the manner provided by the [Code].'[133]

This is clear authority for the proposition that, where a judgment creditor has obtained in his favour a judgment from a country to which the statutory regime does not apply, the judgment creditor may still seek to enforce that judgment pursuant to the common law.[134]

While, in principle, the creditor of a foreign judgment may be able to enforce that judgment in Tanzania pursuant to the common law, there are certain jurisdictional difficulties which he will have to overcome in order so to enforce that foreign judgment. It will be recalled that the Civil Procedure Rules fail to provide any guidance as to the grounds (if any) upon which the Tanzanian court may grant leave to the plaintiff to serve a summons on a defendant believed to be resident in a foreign jurisdiction.[135] In consequence, the basis upon which a foreign

---

[132] [1996] TLR 377 at 380I–381B.

[133] Having set out the principles, the judge then applied them to the facts of the case. He held, at [1996] TLR 377, 381B-C, that the 'enforcement of the judgment was bad altogether', on the basis that certain irregularities attended the registration of the judgment which rendered the registration invalid.

[134] Kapinga in LW Newman (ed) *Enforcement of Money Judgments* (2017) writes that: 'If there is no treaty which provides for the enforcement of judgments in Tanzania from the country of origin, then no court in Tanzania is permitted to entertain any proceedings for the recovery of money payable under a judgment given in the country of origin.' However, the author cites no authority for that proposition and specifically fails to refer to the decision in *Willow Investment*. It is certainly the case that a judgment creditor wishing to enforce a foreign judgment at common law will face jurisdictional difficulties, which difficulties are explained in the main text. Yet, to admit that there are difficulties in the judgment creditor's way is a very different thing than arguing that the court is not permitted to entertain proceedings for the enforcement of a foreign judgment at common law in Tanzania. Accordingly, Kapinga puts the matter far too high: what he says does not accurately reflect Mapigano J's judgment reported at [1996] TLR 377, the present authors submit.

[135] Frimpong Oppong 'Recognition and enforcement of foreign judgments in Commonwealth African countries' (2014) XV *Yearbook of Private International Law* 365, 371–2. By way of comparison, see the English Civil Procedure Rules, PD6B, para 3.1(10).

judgment creditor may convince the Tanzanian court to assume jurisdiction over the action by which he seeks to enforce the foreign judgment is unclear.

That this is so emerges from the further decision of the High Court in *Willow Investment v Ntumba*.[136] This was a continuation of matters which had initially come before the High Court the previous year.[137] Having had the process by which a judgment creditor of a foreign judgment could seek to enforce that foreign judgment in Tanzania pursuant to the common law explained in the previous round of litigation, the judgment creditor followed that guidance and sought to enforce the judgment of the court in Zaire at common law. Judgment was then entered in favour of the judgment creditor in Tanzania in the sum as specified by the judgment of the court in Zaire.

The judgment debtor sought a review of the order that had been made in favour of the judgment creditor. It sought that review, inter alia, on the basis that the Tanzanian High Court 'did not have jurisdiction to entertain the suit'[138] which the judgment creditor had brought. Finding in favour of the judgment debtor, Mapigano J held:[139]

> 'The parties in this case ... are both foreigners, and it matters for little that [the judgment creditor] is owned by Tanzanians. It is true that there is nothing in the evidence that was presented by [the judgment creditor] which shows why it has not executed the decree in Zaire. Surely the High Court of Tanzania cannot and should not pretend to be an international judicial tribunal to which foreign litigants, all and sundry, can resort to. As [counsel for the judgment debtor] put it, there must be a proper nexus between litigants and Tanzania.'

While Mapigano J clearly held that nothing in this (second) judgment called into question anything said in the previous judgment,[140] what Mapigano J decided in the second judgment makes it more difficult to enforce, pursuant to the common law, a foreign judgment in Tanzania. The proper nexus between litigants and Tanzania will not, it seems, simply be achieved by the judgment debtor's having assets in the jurisdiction.[141]

---

[136] [1997] TLR 47 (HC) (Mapigano J).

[137] Supra fn 139. Part of Mapigano J's judgment in that earlier case has been set out in the main text above.

[138] [1997] TLR 47, 48E–F.

[139] Ibid 49A–B.

[140] Ibid 49F–H, which reinforces what has been *said* supra fn 144, the authors submit.

[141] As has been discussed above, the Civil Procedure Rules posit no basis or bases upon which a Tanzanian court can grant leave to serve process out of the jurisdiction. Generally, therefore, it would be beneficial for a rule or rules positing those bases to be drafted. Specifically, however, given the difficulties which currently stand in the way of a creditor of a foreign judgment who wishes to enforce that judgment in Tanzania pursuant to the common law, the authors see merit in the suggestion that, if a rule or rule positing the bases upon which a Tanzanian court can grant leave to serve out is drafted, it should make specific provision dealing with an action to enforce a foreign judgment: see Frimpong Oppong 'Recognition and enforcement of foreign judgments in Commonwealth African countries' (2014) XV *Yearbook of Private International Law* 365, 372.

12.3.1.2 *Enforcement pursuant to statute*[142]

12.3.1.2.1 The regimes for enforcement pursuant to statute

The statutory regime for the enforcement of foreign judgments in Tanzania is found in: (1) the Reciprocal Enforcement of Foreign Judgments Act 1935[143] (hereafter the 'Reciprocal Enforcement Act') and the Reciprocal Enforcement of Foreign Judgments (Extension of Part II) Order,[144] (2) the Reciprocal Enforcement of Foreign Judgments Rules (hereafter the 'Reciprocal Enforcement Rules')[145] and (3) the Judgments Extension Act 1921.[146]

The overall scheme, and particular parts of the Reciprocal Enforcement Act, are recognisable as having been derived from the United Kingdom Foreign Judgments (Reciprocal Enforcement) Act 1933.

[142] If the Tanzanian statutes which currently contain the statutory regimes pursuant to which a party may enforce a judgment of a foreign court are considered to be 'Mutual Assistance arrangements' for the purposes of r 5 of the High Court (Commercial Division) Rules, it may be best practice to seek enforcement of such judgments in the Commercial Division of the High Court. The relationship between the statutory regime and the High Court (Commercial Division) Rules is yet to be worked out.

[143] Order 12 of 1935, now Cap 8 of the Laws of Tanzania, 2019.

[144] Government Notices 8 and 9 of 1936.

[145] As contained in GN 15 of 1936. This was made pursuant to s 5 of the Reciprocal Enforcement Act. Section 5(1) provides that the High Court may, with the approval of the President, make rules '(a) with respect to the giving of security for costs by persons applying for the registration of judgments; (b) prescribing the matters to be proved on an application for the registration of a judgment and for regulating the mode of proving those matters; (c) for the service on the judgment debtor of a notice of the registration of a judgment; (d) prescribing the period within which an application may be made to have the registration of the judgment set aside and with respect to the extension of the period so prescribed; (e) prescribing the method by which any question arising under this Act whether a foreign judgment can be enforced by execution in the country of the original court, or what interest is payable under a foreign judgment under the law of the original court, is to be determined; and (f) for prescribing any matter which under this Part may be prescribed.' Such rules of court as are made have effect subject to any provisions contained in orders made by the President under s 3 of the Act as are declared by those orders to be necessary for giving effect to agreements made between the United Republic and foreign countries in relation to matters with respect to which there is power to make rules of court for the purposes of Part II of the Act.

[146] Ordinance 13 of 1921, now Cap 7 of the Laws of Tanzania, 2019.

12.3.1.2.1.1 *The Reciprocal Enforcement of Foreign Judgments Act and Reciprocal Enforcement of Foreign Judgments (Extension of Part II) Order*

The Reciprocal Enforcement Act applies to judgments[147] given by a superior court in jurisdictions to which it has been extended by Order:[148] Lesotho, Botswana, Sri Lanka, Mauritius, New South Wales, Zambia, the Seychelles, Somalia, Zimbabwe, the Kingdom of Eswatini and the United Kingdom.[149] Section 11 entitles the President, by the making of rules, to bring it about that no proceedings shall be entertained in any court in Tanzania for the recovery of any sum alleged to be payable under a judgment given in a court of a country to which those rules apply.[150] The President may do this if it appears

> 'that the treatment in respect of recognition and enforcement accorded by the courts of any foreign country to judgments given in the superior courts of ... Tanzania is substantially less favourable than that accorded by the courts of ... Tanzania to judgments of the superior courts of that country'.[151]

Procedure for registration

A brief summary of the principal provisions of the Reciprocal Enforcement Act is set out as follows.

[147] Section 1 of the Reciprocal Enforcement Act states that judgment 'means a judgment or order given or made by a court in civil proceedings, or a judgment or order given or made by a court in any criminal proceedings, for the payment of a sum of money in respect of compensation or damages to an injured party'. Were Tanzanian courts to apply English authority by way of analogy when construing s 1 of the Reciprocal Enforcement Act, they would likely conclude that it does not permit registration of a judgment given by a court in one state in an action to enforce a judgment given by a court in another state: *Strategic Technologies Pte Ltd v Procurement Bureau of the Republic of China Ministry of National Defence* [2020] EWCA Civ 1604 (David Richards, Males and Elisabeth Laing LJJ).

[148] Section 3(1) of the Reciprocal Enforcement Act. The power to make such an order is vested in the President. Section 3(1)(b) directs that 'such courts of that foreign country as are specified in the order shall be deemed to be superior courts of that country for the purposes of this Part'.

[149] The Reciprocal Enforcement of Foreign Judgments (Extension of Part II) Order (GN 8 and 9 of 1936). The courts of the relevant jurisdictions to which the Reciprocal Enforcement Act has been extended are also contained in the order. Frimpong Oppong 'Recognition and Enforcement of Foreign Judgments in Commonwealth African Countries' (2014) XV *Yearbook of Private International Law* 378 fn 141 wrongly states that the order extends Part I of the Reciprocal Enforcement Act (it extends Part II). Similarly, LW Newman (ed) *Enforcement of Money Judgments* (1999) vol 2, TAN-16 inaccurately reproduces the relevant provisions of the Act and inaccurately states that it is Part I of the Act which is extended. It would appear that there is still some confusion in Tanzania as to the jurisdictions to which the Reciprocal Enforcement Act has been extended. By way of example, in *Koroso v AG of Kenya* [2011] TZHCCOMD 2012 (Juma J), the judge, having not had his attention called to the relevant provisions, wrongly assumed or proceeded from the premise that the Act had been extended to judgments handed down by a Kenyan court. It would appear that the Judgments Extension Act 1921 was the applicable legislation on the facts.

[150] Section 11(2) of the Reciprocal Enforcement Act.

[151] Section 11(1) of the Reciprocal Enforcement Act.

Pursuant to section 4(1) of the Reciprocal Enforcement Act, a judgment creditor[152] under a judgment[153] to which Part II of the Act applies[154] may make an application to the High Court at any time within six years after the date of the judgment, or, where there have been proceedings by way of appeal against the judgment, within six years after the date of the last judgment given in those proceedings, to have the judgment registered in the High Court. On any such application, the court shall, subject to proof of the prescribed matters and to the other provisions of the Reciprocal Enforcement Act, order the judgment to be registered except where, at the date of the application, the judgment has been wholly satisfied or could not be enforced by execution in the country of the original court.[155]

Rule 2 of the Reciprocal Enforcement Rules provides that an application made pursuant to section 4 of the Reciprocal Enforcement Act to have a foreign judgment to which Part II of that Act applies registered in the High Court may be made *ex parte* to a judge in chambers. Pursuant to rule 3(1), the application for registration shall be supported by an affidavit of the facts:

'*(a)* exhibiting certified copy of the judgment issued by the original court and authenticated by its seal and a translation of the judgment certified by a notary public or authenticated by affidavit;[156]

(b) stating that to the best of the information and belief of the deponent—

(i) that the applicant is entitled to enforce the judgment;

(ii) as the case may require, either at the date of application the judgment has not been satisfied or, if the judgment has been satisfied in part, what the amount is in respect of which it remains unsatisfied;

---

[152] Defined in s 2(1) thereof to mean 'the person in whose favour judgment was given and includes any person in whom the rights under the judgment have become vested by succession or assignment or otherwise'.

[153] *Supra* fn 157.

[154] Section 3(2) provides: 'A judgment of a superior court of a foreign country to which this Part extends, other than a judgment of such a court given on appeal from a court which is not a superior court, shall be a judgment to which this Part applies if — (a) it is final and conclusive as between the parties thereto; and (b) there is payable thereunder a sum of money, not being a sum payable in respect of taxes or other charges of a like nature or in respect of a fine or other penalty; and (c) it is given after the coming into operation of the order directing that this Part shall extend to that foreign country.' Section 3(3) goes on to provide that: 'For the purposes of this section, a judgment shall be deemed to be final and conclusive notwithstanding that an appeal may be pending against it, or that it may still be subject to appeal, in the courts of the country of the original court.'

[155] Rule 13 of the Reciprocal Enforcement Rules provides that: 'If, whether under the [Reciprocal Enforcement Act] or these Rules, any question arises whether a foreign judgment can be enforced by execution in the country of the original court, or what interest is payable under the foreign judgment under the law of that country, that question shall be determined in accordance with such provisions, if any, in that behalf, as are contained in the order of the President extending the Act to that country.'

[156] In this respect, s 12 of the Code provides that: 'A court shall presume, upon the production of any document purporting to be a certified copy of a foreign judgment, that such judgment was pronounced by a court of competent jurisdiction, unless the contrary appears on the record; but such presumption may be displaced by proving want of jurisdiction.'

(iii) that at the date of the application the judgment can be enforced by execution in the country of the original court;

(iv) that, if the judgment were registered, the registration would not be, or liable to be, set aside under s 6 of the [Reciprocal Enforcement] Act.

(c) Specifying the amount of the interest, if any, which under the law of the country of the original court has become due under the judgment up to the time of registration,

And shall be accompanied by such other evidence with respect to matters referred to in (b)(iii) or (c) as may be required having regard to the provisions contained in the Order of the President extending the Act to the country of the original court.'[157]

Save as otherwise provided by any relevant order of the President, a judge may, in respect of an application for registration made to him, order the judgment creditor to find security for the costs of an application and of any proceedings which may thereafter be brought to set aside the registration.[158]

Subject to the provisions of the Reciprocal Enforcement Act which deal with the setting aside of registration of the foreign judgment, a registered judgment:

(1) shall, for the purposes of its execution, be of the same force and effect;

(2) proceedings may be taken on a registered judgment;

(3) the sum for which a judgment is registered shall carry interest; and

(4) the registering court shall have the same control over the execution of a registered judgment,

as if the judgment had been a judgment originally given in the registering court and entered on the date of registration.[159] However, this is subject to the proviso that execution on the judgment so registered shall not issue so long as, under Part II of the Reciprocal Enforcement Act and the Reciprocal Enforcement Rules, it is competent for any party to make an application to have the registration of the judgment set aside or, where such application is made, until after the application has been finally determined.[160]

---

[157] Pursuant to s 2(1) of the Reciprocal Enforcement Act, 'original court' in relation to any judgment means the court by which judgment was given. Where the sum payable under the judgment is expressed in a currency other than the currency of the United Republic, the affidavit must comply with r 3(2). The affidavit must, in all cases, state the full name, title, trade or business and the usual or last known place of abode or business of the judgment creditor and the judgment debtor respectively, so far as known to the deponent: r 3(3). Where a judgment is in respect of different matters and some, but not all, of the provisions of the judgment are such that, if those provisions had been contained in separate judgments, those judgments could properly have been registered, the affidavit shall state the provisions in respect of which it is sought to register the judgment: r 3(4). In all cases, the affidavit shall be titled in accordance with r 5.

[158] Rule 4 of the Reciprocal Enforcement Rules.

[159] Section 4(2) of the Reciprocal Enforcement Act.

[160] Section 4(3) of the Reciprocal Enforcement Act then details how the judgment should be registered where the sum payable thereunder is expressed in a currency other than that of the United Republic. Section 4(4) deals with registration where the judgment of the original court has been partly satisfied on the

In addition to the sum of money payable under the judgment of the original court, including any interest which by the law of the country of the original court becomes due under the judgment up to the time of registration, the judgment shall be registered for the reasonable costs of and incidental to registration, including the costs of obtaining a certified copy of the judgment from the original court.[161]

Setting aside registration

Where the High Court makes an order granting leave to register a judgment, that order shall be drawn up by, or on behalf of, the judgment creditor.[162] Such order shall state the period within which an application may be made to set aside the registration and shall contain a notification that execution of the judgment will not issue until after the expiration of that period.[163] A judge may, on an application made at any time while it remains competent for any party to apply to have the registration set aside, grant an extension of the period (either as originally fixed or subsequently extended) during which an application to have the judgment set aside may be made.[164]

Section 6 of the Reciprocal Enforcement Act provides that a party against whom a registered judgment may be enforced may make an application asking the court to set aside the registration of the same.[165] Such application shall be made to a judge in chambers by summons supported by affidavit.[166] On any such application, the judge may direct that an issue between the judgment creditor and the judgment debtor shall be stated and tried and may give such directions in relation to the trial of the issue as may be necessary.[167]

---

date of the application for registration thereof. Section 4(5) is effective where it appears to the registering court that the judgment sought to be enforced is in respect of different matters and that some, but not all, of the provisions of the judgment are such that, if those provisions had been contained in separate judgments, those judgments could properly have been registered.

[161] Section 4(6) of the Reciprocal Enforcement Act.

[162] Rule 6(1) of the Reciprocal Enforcement Rules. Notice in writing of the registration of a judgment shall be served on the judgment debtor. Rule 8 of the Reciprocal Enforcement Rules. Where the judgment debtor is within the jurisdiction, such notice shall be served by way of personal service as in the case of a summons, unless some other mode of service is ordered by a judge: r 8(1). Where the judgment debtor is out of the jurisdiction, such notice shall be served in accordance with the rules applicable to the service of a summons out of the jurisdiction, unless some other mode of service is ordered by a judge. Any such notice of registration must comply with r 8(2) of the Reciprocal Enforcement Rules. The person serving the notice must ensure that they endorse the notice or a copy of its duplicate in accordance with r 9 of the Reciprocal Enforcement Rules.

[163] Rule 6(3) of the Reciprocal Enforcement Rules. Execution of a registered judgment shall not issue until after the end of this period: r 11(1).

[164] Rule 6(4) of the Reciprocal Enforcement Rules.

[165] Where such application is made, execution shall not issue until the application has been disposed of: r 11(2) of the Reciprocal Enforcement Rules.

[166] Rule 10(1) of the Reciprocal Enforcement Rules. Such affidavit shall be entitled in the manner set out in r 5: r 10(2).

[167] Rule 10(3) of the Reciprocal Enforcement Rules.

Section 6 of the Reciprocal Enforcement Act distinguishes between cases where the court, when faced with such application 'shall' (ie must) set aside the registered judgment and those where it 'may' do so.

Those cases in which the court 'shall' set aside registration of the foreign judgment are detailed in section 6(1)(a) as follows:[168]

(1) the judgment is not a judgment to which Part II of the Act applies or the judgment was registered in contravention of the Act's provisions;

(2) the courts of the country of the original court had no jurisdiction in the circumstances of the case;[169]

(3) the judgment debtor, being the defendant in the proceedings in the original court, did not (notwithstanding that process may have been duly served on him in accordance with the law of the country of the original court) receive notice of those proceedings in sufficient time to enable him to defend the proceedings and did not appear;

(4) the judgment was obtained by fraud;[170] or

(5) the enforcement of the judgment would be contrary to public policy in the country of the registering court.[171]

---

[168] There is a degree of crossover between s 6(1)(a) of the Reciprocal Enforcement Act and s 11 of the Code, which provides: 'A foreign judgment shall be conclusive as to any matter thereby directly adjudicated upon between the same parties or between parties under whom they or any of them claim litigating under the same title except — (a) where it has not been pronounced by a court of competent jurisdiction; (b) where it has not been given on the merits of the case; (c) where it appears on the face of the proceedings to be founded on an incorrect view of international law or a refusal to recognise the law of Tanzania in cases in which such law is applicable; (d) where proceedings in which the judgment was obtained are opposed to natural justice; (e) where it has been obtained by fraud; (f) where it sustains a claim founded on a breach of any law in force in Tanzania.'

[169] See *FX Oliso-Emosingoit v The Secretary General of the East African Community* [1982] TLR 155 (High Court) (Biron J). The case is criticised by Frimpong Oppong 'Recognition and enforcement of foreign judgments in Commonwealth African countries' (2014) XV *Yearbook of Private International Law* 379 fn 144.

[170] The equivalent to s 6(1)(a)(iv) of the 1933 Act. The rules related to setting aside a foreign judgment obtained by fraud are comprehensively set out in *Dicey, Morris and Collins on the Conflict of Laws* 15 ed (2012) vol 1, r 50, paras 14R-137–14–145. In *The Conflict of Laws* para 14–191, it is stated of the fraud provisions of the 1933 Act: 'The provisions with regard to fraud and public policy are the same as the common law rules. In particular, the common law rule that a foreign judgment can be impeached for fraud even though no newly discovered evidence is produced, and even though the fraud was alleged in the foreign proceedings, applies to enforcement and recognition under the 1933 Act. In *Owens Bank Ltd v. Bracco* [[1992] 2 AC 443] the House of Lords held that the fraud exception in the 1920 Act was subject to the same rule, and indicated (obiter) that the same must be so under the 1933 Act.' *Owens Bank* has not been followed in certain Commonwealth jurisdictions (eg Canada in *Beals v Saldanha* [2003] 3 SCR 416, (2003) 234 DLR (4th) 1; and New South Wales in *Keele v Findley* (1991) 21 NSWLR 444 (NSWSC); but in *Close v Arnot* (unreported) 21 November 1997 (NSW), the Common Law Division distinguished *Keele v Findley* and applied the traditional English standard of fraud in respect of a foreign judgment in a case where the defendant had, for good reason, allowed foreign proceedings to go undefended). A Tanzanian court would not be bound by the *Owens Bank* decision.

[171] *FX Oliso-Emosingoit v The Secretary General of the East African Community* [1982] TLR 155 (HC) (Biron J).

The court '*may*' set aside a registered judgment where it is 'satisfied that the matter in dispute in the proceedings in the original court had prior to the date of the judgment in the original court, been the subject of a final and conclusive judgment by a court having jurisdiction in the matter'.[172]

The Reciprocal Enforcement Act[173] provides that the original court will be deemed to have had jurisdiction in the following circumstances:

(1) in the case of a judgment given in an action *in personam*:

  (a) if the judgment debtor, being a defendant in the original court, submitted to the jurisdiction of that court by voluntarily appearing in the proceedings otherwise than for the purposes of protecting, or obtaining the release of, property seized or threatened with seizure, in the proceedings or of contesting the jurisdiction of that court; or

  (b) if the judgment debtor was plaintiff or counterclaimed in the proceedings in the original court; or

  (c) if the judgment debtor, being a defendant in the original court, had before the commencement of the proceedings agreed, in respect of the subject-matter of the proceedings, to submit to the jurisdiction of that court or of the courts of the country of that court; or

  (d) if the judgment debtor, being a defendant in the original court, was at the time when the proceedings were instituted resident, or being a body corporate had its principal place of business in the country of that court; or

  (e) if the judgment debtor, being a defendant in the original court, had an office or place of business in the country of that court and the proceedings in that court were in respect of a transaction effected or at that office or place;

(2) in the case of a judgment given in an action of which the subject-matter was immovable property or in an action *in rem* of which the subject-matter was movable property, if the property in question was at the time of the proceedings in the original court situate in the country of that court;

(3) in the case of a judgment given in an action other than is mentioned in (1) or (2) above, if the jurisdiction of the original court is recognised by the law of the registering court.

---

[172] Section 6(1)(b) of the Reciprocal Enforcement Act.

[173] Section 6(2).

However, the deeming provisions of section 6 set out above are subject to the following exceptions, circumstances in which the original court shall be deemed not to have had jurisdiction:[174]

(1) if the subject-matter of the proceedings was immovable property outside the country of the original court; or
(2) except in cases mentioned in section 6(2)(a)(i), (ii), (iii) and (2)(c), if the institution of the proceedings in the original court was contrary to an agreement under which the dispute in question was to be settled otherwise than by proceedings in the courts of the country of that court; or
(3) if the judgment debtor, being a defendant in the original proceedings, was a person who under the rules of public international law was entitled to immunity from jurisdiction of the courts of the country of the original court and did not submit to the jurisdiction of that court.

In addition, where the judgment debtor, in an application to set aside the registration of a judgment, satisfies the court in Tanzania that he is either currently appealing, or entitled and intending to appeal against the judgment (which has been registered), the court may either set aside the registration or adjourn the application to set aside the registration until the expiration of such period as appears to the court to be reasonably sufficient to enable the applicant to take the necessary steps to have the appeal disposed of by the competent tribunal.[175] Where the court makes an order on this basis, or solely for the reason that, at the time the application for registration was made, the judgment was not enforceable by execution in the country of the original court, that does not prejudice a further application to register the judgment in the Tanzanian High Court being made when the appeal has been disposed of or the judgment becomes enforceable in the original court.[176]

As noted above, section 8 of the Reciprocal Enforcement Act provides that, where Part II of the Act applies, no proceedings for the recovery of a sum payable under a foreign judgment, other than proceedings by way of registration of the judgment, shall be entertained by any court in Tanzania.

The Reciprocal Enforcement Act[177] also provides that a judgment to which Part II thereof applies, or would have applied if a sum of money had been payable thereunder, shall be recognised in any court in Tanzania as conclusive between

---

[174] As set out in s 6(3) of the Reciprocal Enforcement Act.

[175] Section 7(1) of the Reciprocal Enforcement Act.

[176] Section 7(2) of the Reciprocal Enforcement Act. Similarly, pursuant to s 7(3), where registration of a judgment is set aside solely because the judgment had, at the date of registration, been partly satisfied but had been registered for the whole sum payable under the judgment, the Tanzanian court shall, on the application of the judgment creditor, order judgment to be registered for the balance remaining payable at that date.

[177] Section 10.

the parties thereto in all proceedings founded on the 'same cause of action and may be relied on by way of defence or counter-claim in any such proceedings', irrespective of whether the judgment has been registered or not.

This provision, however, does not apply where:[178]

(1) the judgment has been registered and the registration was set aside on some ground other than that:
   (a) a sum of money was not payable under the judgment; or
   (b) that the judgment had been wholly or partly satisfied; or
   (c) that at the date of the application the judgment could not be enforced by execution in the country of the original court; or
(2) where the judgment has not been registered, it is shown (whether it could have been registered or not) that if the judgment had been registered, the registration thereof would have been set aside on an application for that purpose on some ground other than that specified in (1) above.

12.3.1.2.1.2 *The Judgments Extension Act 1921*[179]

Before leaving this topic, it is necessary to note the provisions of the Judgments Extension Act 1921, which provide for a special regime in respect of decrees for any debt, damages or costs obtained or entered up in the High Courts of Kenya, Uganda, Malawi or Zanzibar or any court subordinate to any of those courts. Where it is desired that the decree shall be executed upon the person or property of the defendant in Tanzania, the decree may be transferred to the High Court of Tanzania (or any court subordinate thereto) for execution and such transfer and execution shall be governed by the provisions of the Code[180] in the same manner as if the decree had been obtained or entered up in one court and were transferred to another court within the jurisdiction of the High Court. After the transfer, all proceedings shall be had and taken as if the decree had been a decree originally obtained in the High Court or a subordinate court, and all reasonable costs and charges with regard to the transfer and execution of the decree shall be recovered in like manner as if they were part of the original judgment.[181]

Section 3 of the Judgments Extension Act provides as follows:[182]

---

[178] Section 10(2) of the Reciprocal Enforcement Act.

[179] Ordinance 13 of 1921, *supra* fn 156.

[180] Section 2 of the Judgments Extension Act.

[181] Ibid.

[182] It would appear that, with respect to the civil arrest of a defendant, a similar regime is in place in Uganda – see s 3 of the Judgments Extension Act 1908 and the relevant part of the chapter on Uganda. In Malawi, s 3 of the Nyasaland Judgments Extension Ordinance 1912, as amended, allows a judge sitting in the High Court in that country to 'execute a warrant for the arrest of the defendant where the warrant has been issued in' Kenya, Uganda, Tanzania or Zanzibar (and see further the discussion of this Ordinance in

'(1) Where any warrant issued by the High Court of Kenya, Uganda, Malawi or Zanzibar or by any court subordinate to any such court for the arrest of a defendant in a civil case either before or after judgment, a judge of the High Court or a magistrate of a subordinate court shall have power:

(a) to indorse and execute the warrant; or

(b) to issue, before such endorsement, a provisional warrant for the arrest of the defendant, upon receipt of a telegraphic or other information and in such circumstances as would in his opinion justify the issue of a warrant in a civil case within the jurisdiction:

Provided that a person arrested under a provisional warrant shall be discharged unless the original warrant is produced and endorsed within such reasonable time as may in the circumstances seem requisite:

Provided also that no such warrant shall be endorsed or executed and no provisional warrant shall be issued unless the warrant or information from the court desiring the arrest is accompanied by an intimation that such court indemnifies the High Court or subordinate court against all costs, charges and expenses to be incurred by the High Court or the subordinate court.

(2) The provisions of the [Code] for the arrest of defendants before and after judgment shall apply in the same manner as if the suit had been originally instituted in the High Court or a subordinate court and all reasonable costs and expenses with regard to proceedings for arrest shall be recoverable in a like manner as if they had been incurred in the court in which the suit had actually been instituted.'[183]

12.3.2 Zanzibar

12.3.2.1 *Enforcement at common law*

There is an absence of reported authority on the circumstances, if any, in which a judgment creditor may seek to enforce a foreign judgment in his favour pursuant to the common law in Zanzibar. Given, however, that the statutory regime in

the relevant part of the chapter on Malawi). In Zanzibar, s 3 of the Judgments Extension Decree 1908, as amended by s 2 of the Judgments Extension (Amendment) Decree 1921, allows a judge, inter alia, to indorse or execute a warrant issued by the High Court of the Colony and Protectorate of Kenya, or of 'Nyasaland' (Malawi) or of the 'Tanganyika Territory' (Tanzania) or of Uganda. In Kenya, there is no equivalent regime in place. There, enforcement of a foreign judgment pursuant to statute is governed by the Foreign Judgments (Reciprocal Enforcement) Act 1984. That Act does not make reference to 'warrants of arrest' and, in any event, only applies to jurisdictions to which it has been extended by order; it has not yet been extended to any one of Uganda, Malawi, Tanzania or Zanzibar.

[183] In terms of s 4 of the Judgments Extension Act: 'A judge of the High Court or a magistrate of a subordinate court requesting the arrest of a defendant under any law similar to this Act by any court in Kenya, Uganda, Malawi or Zanzibar shall, before communicating with a court of any of those countries, take security from the plaintiff in such sum as shall be sufficient to cover all the costs, charges and expenses to be incurred by the court to which the application is made and shall indemnify that court against those costs, charges and expenses.'

place in Zanzibar (as contained in the Judgments Extension Decree 1908[184] and the British Judgments Decree 1921)[185] shares several features with that in force in Tanzania, it is submitted that the courts of Zanzibar are likely to have regard to the principles which can be derived from Tanzanian law (which principles have been set out above).

In the light of both these shared features and the principles that can be derived from Tanzanian law, it is unlikely that it was the legislator's intention to remove a judgment creditor's ability to enforce a foreign judgment in his favour at common law in circumstances where that foreign judgment does not fall within the material scope of the statutory regime in place.

However, beyond these rather general propositions, it is not possible to go.

12.3.2.2 *Enforcement pursuant to statute*[186]

12.3.2.2.1 The regimes for enforcement pursuant to statute

The statutory regimes for the enforcement of foreign judgments in Zanzibar are contained in the Judgments Extension Decree 1908 and the British Judgments Decree 1921 (the '1921 Decree') and the Rules of Procedure (Registration of British Judgments) 1923 (hereafter the 'Registration Rules').[187]

---

[184] Decree 11 of 1908, as amended by the Judgments Extension (Amendment) Decree.

[185] Decree 25 of 1921.

[186] If the Zanzibar statutes which currently make up the statutory regimes pursuant to which a party may enforce a judgment of a foreign court are considered to be 'Mutual Assistance' arrangements for the purposes of r 5 of the rules contained in the Establishment of Zanzibar Commercial Court Act, it may be best practice to seek enforcement of such judgments in the Commercial Division of the High Court. The relationship between the statutory regime and the High Court (Commercial Division) Rules is yet to be worked out. However, r 5 talks of 'Mutual Assistance' arrangements to which the 'United Republic of Tanzania is a signatory'. Phrasing the rule thus creates some difficulty, given that the statutes which comprise the regime for the enforcement of foreign judgments in Tanzania give effect to reciprocal arrangements with more countries than does the statutory regime in place in Zanzibar.

[187] Government Notice 29 of 1923. The Registration Rules were made pursuant to s 3(4) of the Decree ('Rules of court shall provide — (a) for service on the judgment debtor of notice of the registration of a judgment under this section; (b) for enabling the registering court on an application by the judgment debtor to set aside the registration of a judgment under this section under such terms as the court thinks fit; and (c) for suspending the execution of a judgment registered under this section until the expiration of the period during which the judgment debtor may apply to have the registration set aside'. Section 4 of the Decree also provides: 'Provision may be made by the Rules of court for regulating the practice and procedure (including scales of fees and evidence) in respect of proceedings of any kind under this Decree.' It appears that the Registration Rules should have been added as O XXA to the Zanzibar Civil Procedure Rules. No such addition is found within the Zanzibar Civil Procedure Rules themselves.

12.3.2.2.1.1 *The British Judgments Decree 1921*

As originally drafted, the 1921 Decree applied to judgments[188] obtained in the 'Superior Court'[189] in England, Scotland or Ireland. The 1921 Decree[190] also provides:

> '(1) When the British Resident[191] is satisfied that any reciprocal provisions have been made by the legislature in any part of His Majesty's Dominions outside England, Scotland and Ireland for the enforcement within that part of His Majesty's Dominions of any judgment obtained in [His Britannic Majesty's Court for Zanzibar][192] the British Resident may by notice in the Gazette order that this Decree shall extend to judgments obtained in a superior court of that part of His Majesty's Dominions in like manner as it extends to judgments obtained in a superior court of the United Kingdom, and on any such order being made this Decree shall extend accordingly.
>
> (2) For the purposes of this section, the expression "part of His Majesty's Dominions[193] outside England, Scotland and Ireland" shall be deemed to include any territory which is under His Majesty's protection or in respect of which a mandate is being exercised by the Government of any part of His Majesty's Dominions.
>
> (3) Any order under this section may be varied or revoked by any subsequent order.'

The 1921 Decree was later extended, by Order of the British Resident, to judgments obtained in the Superior Court of the Somaliland Protectorate,[194] the Court of the Resident Commissioner of Basutoland (modern-day Lesotho), the Courts of the Assistant Commissioners or magistrates in the Bechuanaland Protectorate (modern-day Botswana) and the Special Court of Swaziland (modern-day Eswatini)[195] and the Supreme Court of New South Wales.[196]

---

[188] Section 2 of the Decree provides that 'judgment' means 'any judgment or order given or made by a court in any civil proceedings, whether before or after the passing of this Decree whereby any sum of money is made payable, and includes an award in proceedings on an arbitration if the award has, in pursuance of the law in force in the place where it was made, become enforceable in the same manner given by a court in that place'.

[189] Which expression is left undefined by the 1921 Decree.

[190] In terms of s 5.

[191] It is submitted that this should now be read as 'President of Zanzibar'. The fact that the decree is so old means that now might well be an appropriate time to reconsider the objectives, substance and drafting of the provisions therein contained.

[192] It is submitted that this should now be read as 'High Court of Zanzibar'.

[193] Such language is out of date. Now, it would be more natural to talk in terms of 'Members of the Commonwealth'.

[194] Government Notice 145 of 1924.

[195] All by GN 34 of 1925.

[196] Government Notice 17 of 1926.

Procedure for registration

Pursuant to section 3(1) of the 1921 Decree, a judgment creditor[197] under a judgment obtained in the superior court in England, Scotland or Ireland, may apply to His Britannic Majesty's Court for Zanzibar, at any time within 12 months after the date of judgment, or such longer period as may be allowed, to have the judgment registered in that court and, on such application, the court may, if in all the circumstances of the case it thinks it is just and convenient that the judgment should be enforced in Zanzibar, and subject to the provisions of section 3 of the Decree, order the judgment to be registered accordingly.

Any application made under section 3 shall be made *ex parte* or by summons[198] to a judge.[199] If the application is made *ex parte*, the judge to whom it is made may direct a summons to be issued.[200] The application shall be supported by an affidavit[201] of facts exhibiting the judgment or a certified copy thereof and stating that to the best of the information and belief of the deponent the judgment creditor is entitled to enforce the judgment and the judgment does not fall within any of the cases listed in section 3(2) of the 1921 Decree in which a judgment cannot properly be ordered to be registered.[202] The affidavit must also, so far as the deponent can, give the full name, title, trade or business and usual or last-known place of abode or business of the judgment creditor and the judgment debtor[203] respectively.

The court[204] 'shall' (ie must) not register[205] a foreign judgment if:

---

[197] Section 2 provides that 'judgment creditor' means 'the person by whom the judgment was obtained, and includes the successors and assigns of that person'.

[198] Which is to be an originating summons and (unless otherwise ordered by a judge) shall be served in the same manner as an ordinary summons is required to be served.

[199] Rule 1 of the Registration Rules.

[200] Rule 2 of the Registration Rules. The rule itself actually makes reference to an application made under s 2 of the Decree. However, this cannot be right, given that s 2 of the Decree is a definitional section. The relevant rule must mean s 3.

[201] Intituled in accordance with r 3 of the Registration Rules.

[202] Rule 2 of the Registration Rules.

[203] Section 2 of the 1921 Decree provides that 'judgment debtor' means 'the person against whom the judgment was given, and includes any person against whom the judgment is enforceable in the place where it was given'.

[204] Pursuant to s 3(2) of the 1921 Decree.

[205] This is materially different to the corresponding provision in the Reciprocal Enforcement Act in Tanzania. There, similar factors to those about to be discussed provide reasons for the court to set aside a foreign judgment which has already been registered. Here, by contrast, such factors provide reasons for the court not to register the judgment in the first place (though it would also appear that, pursuant to the Registration Rules, the judgment debtor also has the chance to apply to set aside the judgment so registered if of the view that it should not have been so registered – see below). For a Tanzanian court applying an approach more in keeping with the provisions of the Decree, see *FX Oliso-Emosingoit v The Secretary General of the East-African Community* [1982] TLR 155 (High Court) (Biron J).

(1) the original court[206] acted without jurisdiction;[207] or

(2) the judgment debtor being a person who was neither carrying on business nor ordinarily resident within the jurisdiction of the original court, did not voluntarily appear or otherwise submit or agree to submit to the jurisdiction of that court; or

(3) the judgment debtor, being the defendant in the proceedings, was not duly served with the process of the original court and did not appear, notwithstanding that he was ordinarily resident or was carrying on business within the jurisdiction of that court or agree to submit to the jurisdiction of that court; or

(4) the judgment was obtained by fraud;[208] or

(5) the judgment debtor satisfies the registering court that either an appeal is pending or that he is entitled to and intends to appeal against the judgment; or

(6) the judgment was in respect of a cause of action which for reasons of public policy or for some other similar reason could not have been entertained by the registering court.[209]

Where the Zanzibar court makes an order[210] giving leave to register the judgment, notice[211] in writing of the registration of the judgment must be served

---

[206] Section 2 of the 1921 Decree provides that 'original court' means 'the court by which the judgment was given'.

[207] Section 9 of the Zanzibar Civil Procedure Decree 2008 provides: 'The court shall presume, upon the production of any document purporting to be a certified copy of a foreign judgment, that such judgment was pronounced by a court of competent jurisdiction, unless the contrary appears on the record; but such presumption may be displaced by proving want of jurisdiction.'

[208] *Supra* fn 180.

[209] There is a degree of crossover between s 3(2) of the 1921 Decree and s 8 of the Zanzibar Civil Procedure Code which provides: 'A foreign judgment shall be conclusive as to any matter thereby directly adjudicated upon between the same parties or between the parties under whom they or any of them claim litigating under the same title except — (a) where it has not been pronounced by a court of competent jurisdiction; (b) where it has not been given on the merits of the case; (c) where it appears on the face of proceedings to be founded on an incorrect view of international law or a refusal to recognise the law of Zanzibar in a case where such law is applicable; (d) where proceedings in which the judgment was obtained are opposed to natural justice; (e) where it has been obtained by fraud; (f) where it sustains a claim founded on a breach of any law in force in Zanzibar.'

[210] Which order shall state the time within which the judgment debtor is to be entitled to apply to set aside the registration. Such time shall be in the discretion of the judge making the order and shall depend on the distance from the town of Zanzibar of the place where the judgment debtor resides and the postal facilities between the town of Zanzibar and that place: r 6 of the Registration Rules.

[211] Notice of the registration shall contain full particulars of the judgment registered and of the order for such registration and shall state the name and address of the judgment creditor or of his solicitor or agent on whom and at which service of any summons issued by the judgment debtor may be served: r 10 of the Registration Rules. The person serving the notice must comply with r 11. The notice shall state that the defendant is entitled, if he has grounds for doing so, to apply to set aside the registration and shall also state

on the judgment debtor within a reasonable time after such registration.[212] In the absence of an order by the judge for the method of service of that notice, it shall be served on the judgment debtor by personal service (though there is power to order substituted service or service out of the jurisdiction or both) and the judge may at any stage in the proceedings authorise or direct some other mode of service to be employed.[213]

Where the Zanzibar court makes an order giving leave to register the judgment:

(1) the judgment shall, as from the date of registration, be of the same force and effect and proceedings may be taken thereon, as if it had been a judgment originally obtained or entered up on the date of registration in Zanzibar;

(2) the Zanzibar court shall have the same control and jurisdiction over the judgment as it has over similar judgments given by itself, but in so far only as relates to execution under section 3 of the Decree; and

(3) the reasonable costs of and incidental to the registration of the judgment (including the costs of obtaining a certified copy thereof from the original court and of the application for registration) shall be recoverable under the judgment.[214]

Setting aside registration

That said, the judgment debtor may at any time within the time limited by the order[215] giving leave to register after service on him of the notice of the registration of the judgment apply by ordinary summons[216] to a judge to set aside the registration or to suspend the execution of judgment.[217] On such application, the judge, if satisfied that the case comes within one of the cases set out in section 3(2) of the 1921 Decree or that it is not just and convenient that the judgment should be enforced in Zanzibar or for other sufficient reasons may order that the registration be set aside or execution on the judgment suspended either unconditionally or on such terms as he thinks fit either altogether or until such time as he shall direct.[218]

---

the number of days for applying to set aside the registration limited by the order for giving leave to register: r 10.

[212] Rule 9 of the Registration Rules.

[213] Ibid.

[214] Section 3(3) of the 1921 Decree.

[215] Though the judge may allow an application to be made after such time has expired: r 12 of the Registration Rules.

[216] Rule 13 of the Registration Rules. Such summons should be intituled in accordance with r 3 of the Registration Rules.

[217] Rule 12 of the Registration Rules.

[218] Ibid.

No execution shall issue on a judgment registered under the 1921 Decree until after the expiration of the time limited by the order giving leave to register after service on the judgment debtor of notice of the registration thereof, provided that the judge who makes the order for such registration or a judge at chambers may at any time order that execution shall be suspended for a longer time.[219] That said, the court may, upon application of the judgment creditor, order the arrest or attachment of the person or property of the judgment debtor before registration of the judgment or expiration of the time so limited and the provisions of Order XLIII of the Zanzibar Civil Procedure Code apply accordingly.[220]

In a similar fashion, no execution shall be issued on a judgment registered under the 1921 Decree until such evidence of service of the notice of registration has been produced before the proper officer as would be required in the case of proof of service of a summons in a suit.[221]

12.3.2.2.1.2 *The Judgments Extension Decree 1908*

Before leaving this topic, it is necessary to note the provisions of the Judgments Extension Decree, which provide for a special regime in respect of decrees for any debt, damages or costs obtained or entered up in the High Courts of Kenya, Uganda, Malawi or Tanzania or any court subordinate to any of those courts.[222] Where it is desired that the decree shall be executed upon the person or property of the defendant in Tanzania, the decree may be transferred to the High Court of Tanzania (or any court subordinate thereto) for execution and such transfer and execution should[223] be governed by the provisions of the Zanzibar Code in

[219] Rule 14(1) of the Registration Rules.

[220] Rule 14(2) of the Registration Rules, which actually refers to O XXXVIII of the Zanzibar Civil Procedure Rules. It is submitted that this must be read as a reference to O XLIII thereof and this Order is discussed in detail below.

[221] Rule 15 of the Registration Rules.

[222] It would appear that, with respect to the civil arrest of a defendant, a similar regime is in place in Uganda: see s 3 of the Judgments Extension Act 1908 and the relevant part of the chapter on Uganda. In Malawi, s 3 of the Nyasaland Judgments Extension Ordinance 1912, as amended, allows a judge sitting in the High Court in that country to 'execute a warrant for the arrest of the defendant where the warrant has been issued in' Kenya, Uganda, Tanzania or Zanzibar (and see further the discussion of this Ordinance in the relevant part of the chapter on Malawi). In Tanzania, s 3 of the Judgments Extension Act 1921 allows a judge, inter alia, to indorse or execute a warrant issued by the High Court of the High Court of Kenya, or of Malawi or of Zanzibar or of Uganda. In Kenya, there is no equivalent regime in place. There, enforcement of a foreign judgment pursuant to statute is governed by the Foreign Judgments (Reciprocal Enforcement) Act 1984. That Act does not make reference to 'warrants of arrest' and, in any event, only applies to jurisdictions to which it has been extended by Order; it has not yet been extended to any one of Uganda, Malawi, Tanzania or Zanzibar.

[223] Section 1 of the Judgments Extension Decree, as amended, provides that transfers shall be conducted in accordance with the provisions of Ch XIX of the Indian Code of Civil Procedure. In the light of developments since the drafting of the Judgments Extension Decree, as amended, it is submitted that it is now more appropriate for the transfer to be governed by the Zanzibar Code.

the same manner as if the decree had been obtained or entered up in one court and were transferred to another court within the jurisdiction of the High Court. After the transfer, all proceedings shall be had and taken as if the decree had been a decree originally obtained in the High Court or a subordinate court, and all reasonable costs and charges with regard to the transfer and execution of the decree shall be recovered in like manner as if they were part of the original judgment.[224]

Section 2 of the Judgments Extension Decree[225] provides as follows:

> '(1) Where any warrant issued by the [High Court of Kenya] or of [Tanzania] or [Malawi] or Uganda or by any court subordinate to any such High Court for the arrest of a defendant in a civil case either before or after judgment, Our Town Magistrate, or any of Our officers appointed to hold a District Court or the Judge, Assistant Judge ... shall have power:
>
> (a) to indorse and execute such warrant; or
>
> (b) to issue, before such indorsement, a provisional warrant for the arrest of the defendant, upon receipt of such telegraphic or other information and in such circumstances as would in his opinion justify the issue of a warrant in a civil case within the jurisdiction:
>
> Provided that a person arrested under a provisional warrant shall be discharged unless the original warrant is produced and indorsed within such reasonable time as may in the circumstances seem requisite:
>
> Provided also that no such warrant shall be indorsed or executed and no provisional warrant shall be issued unless the warrant or information from the court desiring the arrest is accompanied by an intimation that such court indemnifies the [High Court] against all costs, charges and expenses to be incurred by the High Court or the subordinate court.
>
> Provided also that [the provisions of the Zanzibar Code] for the arrest of debtors before and after judgment shall apply in the same manner as if the suit had been originally instituted in the [High Court] and all reasonable costs and expenses with regard to proceedings for arrest shall be recoverable in a like manner as if they had been incurred in the court in which the suit had actually been instituted.'[226]

---

[224] Ibid.

[225] As amended.

[226] In terms of s 4 of the Judgments Extension Act: 'A judge of the High Court or a magistrate of a subordinate court requesting the arrest of a defendant under any law similar to this Act by any court in Kenya, Uganda, Malawi or Zanzibar shall, before communicating with a court of any of those countries, take security from the plaintiff in such sum as shall be sufficient to cover all the costs, charges and expenses to be incurred by the court to which the application is made and shall indemnify that court against those costs, charges and expense.'

Section 3 of the Judgments Extension Decree[227] provides that a decree for any debt, damages or costs obtained or entered up in the

> 'Supreme Court of the Kenya Colony and Protectorate, the High Court of Uganda, Nyasaland or Tanzania, or in any court subordinate to any such courts, where it is desired that such decree shall be executed upon the person or property of the defendant in our dominions, such decree may be transferred to our court for Zanzibar and Pemba, or to any of the courts subordinate thereto, or [His Britannic Majesty's Court for Zanzibar] any courts subordinate thereto for execution'.

12.4 Interim remedies

12.4.1 Jurisdiction to grant interim remedies

The Tanzanian High Court (and, save where otherwise indicated, the Zanzibar High Court also)[228] has the power to grant a temporary injunction, make a declaratory order or make an interlocutory order.[229]

12.4.2 Procedure for application

Order XXXVII (which is headed 'Temporary Injunctions, Declaratory Orders and Interlocutory Orders') sets out how a plaintiff should apply for the interim remedies which are specified therein. The specific procedure which a plaintiff should employ when making an application for such relief is considered in greater detail under the relevant sub-headings below.

---

[227] The drafting of which is extremely similar to s 3 of the Judgments Extension Act. In His Britannic Majesty's Court for Zanzibar (ie High Court of Zanzibar), the Provisions of the Zanzibar Civil Procedure Decree for the transfer and execution of decrees shall apply in the same manner as if such decree had been obtained or entered up in one of the courts and were transferred for execution to another court within the jurisdiction of the High Court. Section 4 of the Judgments Extension Decree is drafted in the same terms as the Judgments Extension Act, save the replacement of the word 'Zanzibar' (as found in the Judgments Extension Act) with the word 'Tanzania' for the purposes of the Judgments Extension Decree. Pursuant to s 5 of the Judgments Extension Decree, a judge of His Britannic Majesty's Court for Zanzibar (ie the High Court of Zanzibar), before communicating with a court in Kenya, Uganda, Nyasaland or Tanzania with a view to the arrest of a defendant under any law or ordinance in force therein similar in terms to the Judgments Extension Decree, must take security from the plaintiff in such sum as shall be sufficient to cover all the costs, charges and expenses to be incurred by the court to which the application is made and shall indemnify such court against all such costs, charges and expenses.

[228] Given that there is no material difference, in this respect, between the code and the Zanzibar Civil Procedure Code.

[229] Order XXXVII of the Civil Procedure Rules. The equivalent provision in the Zanzibar Civil Procedure Rules is O XLIV.

12.4.3 Interlocutory injunctions generally[230]

Where in any suit it is proved by affidavit or otherwise either:

(1) any property in dispute in that suit is in danger of being wasted, damaged or alienated by any party to the suit or that the property will suffer loss of value by reason of its continued use by any party to the suit or that it will be wrongly sold in execution of a decree; or

(2) that the defendant threatens, or intends to remove or dispose of his property with a view to defraud his creditors,[231]

the court may by order grant a temporary injunction[232] to restrain such act.[233] However, the court is not bound to make such an order; it may 'make such other order for the purpose of staying and preventing the wasting, damaging, alienation, sale, loss in value, removal or disposition of property as the court thinks fit, until the disposal of the suit or until further orders'.[234]

Additionally, where a plaintiff brings a suit seeking to restrain a defendant from committing a breach of contract or other injury of any kind, irrespective of whether compensation is claimed in that suit or not, the plaintiff may, at any time after the commencement of the suit and either before or after judgment, apply to the court for a temporary injunction to restrain the defendant from committing the breach of contract or injury complained of or any breach of contract or injury of a like kind arising out of the same contract or relating to the same property or right.[235]

---

[230] In Tanzania, such an injunction appears to be referred to as a 'temporary injunction'. For ease of exposition and consistency, the authors refer to these as 'interlocutory injunctions'. A temporary injunction cannot be issued against a stranger to the suit in question: *National Bank of Commerce v Education and Office Stationery* [1995] TLR 272 (CA of the United Republic) (Omar, Mnzavas and Lubuva JAA). Similarly, therefore, an order for a temporary injunction cannot be made in a proceeding which is not, *stricto sensu*, a suit: *Calico Textile Industries v Zenon Investments* (Misc. Civil Case 10 of 1998) (HC) (Mackanja J; 16 June 1998).

[231] As to which, see the text set out under the sub-heading 'Freezing orders' below.

[232] And where such injunction is directed to a corporation, it is binding not only on the corporation itself but also on all members and officers of the corporation whose personal action it seeks to restrain: O XXXVII, r 6 of the Civil Procedure Rules. Order XLIV, r 5 of the Zanzibar Civil Procedure Rules, the equivalent provision, has been drafted in identical terms.

[233] Order XXXVII, r 1 of the Civil Procedure Rules. The equivalent provision in the Zanzibar Civil Procedure Rules is O XLIV, r 1.

[234] Order XXXVII, r 1 of the Civil Procedure Rules, though it is subject to the proviso that an order granting a temporary injunction shall not be made against the government, but the court may in lieu thereof make an order declaratory of the rights of the parties. Order XLIV of the Zanzibar Civil Procedure Rules contains no such proviso.

[235] Order XXXVII, r 2(1) of the Civil Procedure Rules. This is subject to the proviso that no application shall be made for a temporary injunction where the defendant is the Attorney-General but, in such case, the plaintiff may apply to the court for an order declaratory of the rights of the parties. The equivalent provision in the Zanzibar Civil Procedure Rules is O XLIV, r 2(1), though this does not contain the said proviso.

In Tanzania, a court may require a party to provide security or to keep an account when it grants by order either of the above-mentioned injunctions,[236] which order shall be in force for a period specified by the court, though such period should not exceed six months.[237] That said, the court which has granted the injunction may, from time to time, extend such period for a further period which, in aggregate, shall not exceed one year. The court may do this upon being satisfied, on the application of the holder of such court injunction, that the applicant has diligently been taking steps to settle the matter complained of and such extension as is sought is in the interests of justice, or is necessary or desirable.[238]

Where a party disobeys or breaches the terms of an injunction restraining him from committing a breach of contract or other injury, the court granting the injunction may order the property of the person guilty of such disobedience or breach to be attached[239] and may also order such person to be detained as a civil prisoner for a term not exceeding six months, unless in the meantime it directs his release.[240]

A court faced with an application for an injunction shall direct that notice of that application be given to the opposite party, save where it appears that the object of granting the injunction would be defeated by the delay.[241] It has been held that, to justify the immediate issue of a temporary injunction on an *ex parte* basis, there must be some evidence of an immediate danger to property by sale or other disposition.[242] The onus of satisfying the court that there is a good cause for dispensing with the requirement to give notice will lie upon the plaintiff.[243]

---

[236] Order XXXVII, r 3.

[237] Ibid.

[238] See the proviso to O XXXVII, r 3. Order XLIV, r 2(2) of the Zanzibar Civil Procedure Code (the equivalent provision) does not impose a fetter on the length of time for which the injunction may last. It simply provides that: 'The court may by order grant such injunction, on such terms as to the duration of the injunction, keeping an account, giving security or otherwise as the court thinks fit.'

[239] Order XXXVII, r 2(2). Such attachment shall remain in force for no more than one year, at the end of which time, if the disobedience or breach continues, the property attached may be sold, and out of the proceeds the court may award such compensation as it thinks fit, and shall pay the balance, if any, to the party entitled thereto: O XXXVII, r 2(3) of the Civil Procedure Rules. Order XLIV, r 2(4) of the Zanzibar Civil Procedure Code has been drafted in identical terms.

[240] Order XXXVII, r 2(2) of the Civil Procedure Rules. Order XLIV, r 2(3) of the Zanzibar Civil Procedure Rules, the equivalent provision, omits all references to the defendant's being made a civil prisoner as a result of the disobedience or breach. What has been said above in this respect is repeated.

[241] Order XXXVII, r 3 of the Civil Procedure Rules. Order XLIV, r 3 of the Zanzibar Civil Procedure Rules has been drafted in materially similar terms.

[242] *Noor Mohamed Jan Mohamed v Kassamali Virji Madhani* (1953) 20 EACA 8 (East African Court of Appeal) (Sir Newnham Worley VP).

[243] Ibid 11. That O XXXVII, r 3 of the Civil Procedure Rules is mandatory and that the relevant onus is on the plaintiff has been confirmed several times subsequently: *Devan v Bhadreasa* [1972] EA 23 (East African Court of Appeal) (Law AGV-P; Lutta and Mustafa JAA); *Golcher v G Manager MCM* (1987) TLR 78 (HC) (Maina J); *Knitwear Ltd v Shamshu Esmail* [1989] TLR 48 (HC) (Mapigano J).

The principles by which the High Court of Tanzania will be guided when deciding whether to grant a temporary injunction were set out in *Attilo v Mbowe*,[244] where the plaintiff argued that the temporary injunction which had already been granted in his favour should continue until trial. Georges CJ described the conditions which must be satisfied before the court will grant a temporary injunction in the following terms:

> '1) there must be a serious question to be tried on the facts alleged and a probability that the plaintiff will be entitled to the relief prayed;
>
> 2) [it must be shown] that the court's interference is necessary to protect the plaintiff from the kind of injury which may be irreparable before his legal right is established. With respect to this condition, the court must be satisfied that the damage which the plaintiff will suffer will be such that mere money compensation will not be adequate. A temporary injunction will normally be granted only if the whole point of the perpetual injunction claimed would be defeated if the temporary injunction is not granted. On the other hand, it could be argued that granting the injunction may amount virtually to deciding the issue now against the defendant since he will be deprived of the possession which he claims to have been lawfully given to him under a valid contract. If this can be the effect of an injunction it should not normally be granted...; [and]
>
> 3) that on balance there will be greater hardship and mischief suffered by the plaintiff from the withholding of the injunction than will be suffered by the defendant from the granting of it ... The primary consideration there is the maintenance of the status quo pending the determination of the action. The status quo, in my view, is the status quo at the date of filing the action.'[245]

These principles bear a passing resemblance to those set out by the English House of Lords in *American Cyanamid and Co v Ethicon Ltd*,[246] though Georges CJ's formulation still maintains a more explicit focus on the merits of the case than the approach of Lord Diplock, who gave the leading speech in *American Cyanamid* (with which the other Law Lords agreed).

The speech of Lord Diplock is generally taken as establishing a test comprising two elements:

> (1) 'The court ... must be satisfied that the claim is not frivolous or vexatious; in other words, that there is a serious issue to be tried';[247]
>
> '... unless the material available to the court at the hearing of the application for an interlocutory injunction fails to disclose that the plaintiff has any real prospect of succeeding in his claim for a permanent injunction at the trial, the court should go on to consider whether the balance of convenience lies in favour of granting or refusing the interlocutory relief that is sought';[248]

---

[244] (1969) HCD 284 (HC) (Georges CJ).

[245] That these conditions still govern the grant of a temporary injunction in Tanzania is apparent from *Gineke v Gineke* [2006] TZHC 15 (HC) (Orivo J).

[246] [1975] AC 396 (HL (E)) (Lords Diplock, Dilhorne, Cross, Salmon and Edmund-Davies).

[247] Ibid 407G.

[248] Ibid 408A–B.

(2) On the balance of convenience:[249]

'... the governing principle is that the court should first consider whether, if the plaintiff were to succeed at the trial in establishing his right to a permanent injunction, he would be adequately compensated by an award of damages for the loss he would have sustained as a result of the defendant's continuing to do what was sought to be enjoined between the time of the application and the time of the trial. If damages in the measure recoverable at common law would be adequate remedy and the defendant would be in a financial position to pay them, no interlocutory injunction should normally be granted, however strong the plaintiff's claim appeared to be at that stage. If, on the other hand, damages would not provide an adequate remedy for the plaintiff in the event of his succeeding at the trial, the court should then consider whether, on the contrary hypothesis that the defendant were to succeed at the trial in establishing his right to do that which was sought to be enjoined, he would be adequately compensated under the plaintiff's undertaking as to damages for the loss he would have sustained by being prevented from doing so between the time of the application and the time of the trial. If damages in the measure recoverable under such an undertaking would be an adequate remedy and the plaintiff would be in a financial position to pay them, there would be no reason upon this ground to refuse an interlocutory injunction.

It is where there is doubt as to the adequacy of the respective remedies in damages available to either party or to both, that the question of balance of convenience arises. It would be unwise to attempt even to list all the various matters which may need to be taken into consideration in deciding where the balance lies, let alone to suggest the relative weight to be attached to them. These will vary from case to case.

Where other factors appear to be evenly balanced it is a counsel of prudence to take such measures as are calculated to preserve the status quo.'

Where the English and Tanzanian formulations differ, of course, the Tanzanian High Court will follow the formulation set out in *Attilio*.

A party who is dissatisfied with the grant of an order for an injunction may make an application to the court to discharge, vary or set aside that order.[250]

Dealing with a related type of relief, Order XXXVII, rule 8 of the Civil Procedure Rules provides as follows:

'(1) The court may, on the application of any party to a suit, and on such terms as it thinks fit—

(a) make an order for the detention, preservation or inspection of any property which is the subject matter of such suit, or as to which any question may arise therein;

---

[249] 408B–G.

[250] Order XXXVII, r 4 of the Civil Procedure Rules. Order XLIV, r 4 of the Zanzibar Civil Procedure Rules has been drafted in identical terms.

(*b*) for all or any of the purposes aforesaid authorize any person to enter upon or into any land or building in the possession of any other party to such suit; and

(*c*) for all or any of the purposes aforesaid authorise any samples to be taken, or any observation to be made or experiment to be tried, which may seem necessary or expedient for the purpose of obtaining full information or evidence.

(2) The provisions as to execution of process shall apply, *mutatis mutandis*, to persons authorised to enter under this rule.'[251]

There is little other authority on the correct interpretation of, or procedure to be invoked when using, Order XXXVII, rule 8 of the Civil Procedure Rules. However, given that (1) Order XXXVII, rule 8 mirrors Order XXIX, rule 2 of the English Rules of the Supreme Court 1965; (2) the Tanzanian courts take account of English authorities; and (3) the Tanzanian legal system has a close relationship with other legal systems in which English authority carries persuasive weight, Tanzanian courts may well rely on English judicial and academic authorities if required further to interpret or engage with Order XXXVII, rule 8. In those circumstances, a court in Tanzania might find useful the following statement of principle by the Ghanaian Court of Appeal,[252] which statement is based on, and takes account of, the authorities cited in the commentary to Order XXIX, rule 2 of the English Rules of the Supreme Court:

'(*a*) As decided in Garrard v. Edge and Sons (1889) 58 LJ Ch 397, CA, the order must be made against the person in possession or custody of the property in dispute. See also Wilder v. Wilder and Charters (No 2) (1912) 56 SJ 571, CA.

(*b*) The property must be the subject-matter of the suit. Thus in Scott v Mercantile Accident Insurance Co (1892) 8 TLR 431 the lower court made an order that certain jewellery should remain in the custody of the police. An appeal against this order was allowed because it was admitted on the evidence that the property was not the subject-matter of the action, but that only a question might arise about it in the cause or matter.

(*c*) It was held in Leney and Sons, Ltd v. Callingham and Thompson [1908] KB 79 at 84, CA, *per* Farwell LJ that:

> "... the question of the exercise of the judicial discretion was always based, and is still based, upon this, that there is property in dispute to some interest in which the plaintiff shows a prima facie title; and preservation is ensured until the rights of the parties can be finally determined."

---

[251] Order XLIV, r 7 of the Zanzibar Civil Procedure Rules, the equivalent provision, is drafted in identical terms. However, O XLIV, r 8 of the Zanzibar Civil Procedure Rules then goes on to provide that: '(1) an application by the plaintiff for an order under rule 7 may be made after notice to the defendant at any time after the institution of the suit [and] (2) an application by the defendant for a like order may be made after notice to the plaintiff at any time after appearance.' Order XXXVII, r 8 of the Civil Procedure Rules is not subject to the same provision: O XXXVII, r 9 of the Civil Procedure Rules. The reason for the discrepancy is not immediately obvious.

[252] *General Development Co Ltd v Rad Forest Products Ltd* [1999–2000] 2 GLR 178 (CA) 182–3, *per* Bendin JA. It is submitted that this statement of principle would also be instructive for a court in Zanzibar, when called upon to interpret the equivalent provision of the Zanzibar Civil Procedure Code.

(d) The case of Chaplin v. Barnett (1912) 28 TLR 256, CA decides that the order will be granted so long as there is something which ought to be done to ensure the security of the property.

(e) An order will be made in order to preserve the subject-matter of the suit from destruction: see Strelley v. Pearson (1880) 15 Ch D 113 where the court granted an order restraining the defendant from ceasing to pump water of a mine for the sole purpose of preventing the mine from destruction.

(f) The court will also grant an order in court to preserve the subject-matter from depreciation physically or in value. So if it is established that it is necessary to do so the court will grant it; hence an order was made in the case of Steamship New Orleans Co v London and Provincial Marine and General Insurance Co [1909] 1 KB 943, CA that a ship lying in a port in Singapore be brought to England for preservation there. However an order may not be made if it will cause undue hardship in carrying it out or will serve no useful purpose.

These grounds are by no means exhaustive; other grounds may unfold due to a particular case under consideration.'

12.4.4 Freezing orders

There is a lack of reported authority in Tanzania[253] on the availability of, and conditions which must be satisfied for the grant of, a freezing injunction which the court may grant by order (sometimes referred to as a *Mareva*[254] injunction). This is an injunction which operates *in personam* and freezes the defendant's assets (usually) before trial of the substantive action (although the relief is also available post-judgment). Such injunction may also be known as a 'freezing order'.

It is submitted that Order XXXVII, rule 1(b) of the Civil Procedure Rules[255] would be the correct basis upon which to make an application for *Mareva* relief. It is important, at this point, to be clear as to the proper basis upon which an application for such relief could be made so as to avoid the confusion which has bedevilled the Kenyan jurisprudence[256] on this issue (all the more so, given the strength of the ties between the Tanzanian and Kenyan legal systems).[257] As such, and as demonstrated further below, one must be clear that Order XXXVI, rule 6 of the Civil Procedure Code[258] deals with security for the plaintiff's claim

[253] Or Zanzibar.

[254] After the title of the English authority in which such orders were first approved at appellate level: *Mareva Compania Naviera SA v International Bulkcarriers SA* [1975] 2 Lloyd's Rep 509 (CA) (Lord Denning MR, Ormrod and Roskill LJJ).

[255] Order XLIV, r 1(b) of the Zanzibar Civil Procedure Rules is the equivalent provision and is drafted in identical terms.

[256] As to which, see the relevant section of the chapter on Kenya.

[257] For a full discussion of the Kenyan jurisprudence on this issue, see the relevant section in the chapter on Kenya.

[258] See the text set out heading 'Attachment', and the sub-heading 'Tanzania' below.

and is a proprietary remedy; Order XXXVII, rule 1(b) does not purport to grant the plaintiff security and operates solely *in personam* over the defendant.

The Kenyan courts have demonstrated a willingness to adopt the principles of English practice regarding the grant of *Mareva* relief.[259] It is submitted that the Tanzanian[260] courts would likely be influenced by the Kenyan approach. Hence, in *International Air Transport Association v Akarim Agencies Co Ltd*,[261] the Kenyan court adopted the statement of the conditions for the grant of a *Mareva* injunction set out in the English textbook, *Goode on Commercial Law*:[262]

> 'The grant of a freezing injunction is governed by principles quite distinct from those laid down for ordinary interim injunctions… Before granting a freezing injunction the court will usually require to be satisfied that;
>
> *(a)* The claimant has "a good arguable case" based on a pre-existing cause of action;
>
> *(b)* The claim is one over which the court has jurisdiction;
>
> *(c)* The defendant appears to have assets within the jurisdiction;
>
> *(d)* There is a real risk that those assets will be removed from the jurisdiction or otherwise dissipated if the injunction is not granted; and
>
> *(e)* There is a balance of convenience in favour of granting the injunction;
>
> *(f)* The Court can also order disclosure of documents or the administration of requests for further information to assist the claimant in ascertaining the location of the defendant's assets.'

The judge in the *International Air Transport Association* case then confirmed[263] that the test for 'arguable case' 'has been assigned a meaning within the context of freezing order [sic] and has been adopted with approval by many courts in Kenya'. That meaning is that set out by Mustill J in *The Niedersachsen*:[264] 'A case which is more than barely capable of serious argument, and yet not necessarily one which the Judge believes to have a better than 50 *per* cent. chance of success.'

12.4.5 Search and seize orders

There does not appear to be any reported authority in Tanzania,[265] at least in a purely civil context, on the question whether a court will grant an order requiring one party to admit another party to premises in order that the second

---

[259] See *Kanduyi Holdings Ltd v Balm Kenya Foundation* [2013] eKLR (HC) (Gikonyo J); *Cleopatra Kama Mugyenyi v Aispan* [2016] eKLR (Employment and Labour Relations Ct) (Nelson J).

[260] And, by extension, Zanzibar.

[261] [2014] eKLR (HC) (Gikonyo J; orders stayed pending an appeal).

[262] 4 ed (2010) 1287 para [31] of the judgment.

[263] Paragraph [32], quoting inaccurately the passage from *The Niedersachsen* relied on.

[264] [1983] 2 Lloyd's Rep 600 at 605, col 1.

[265] Or Zanzibar.

party be entitled to search for documents or other movable property and to take away such documents and movable property and retain them for the time being. An English court may grant such an order[266] and a search and seize order may be referred to as an *Anton Piller* order, after the leading case authority.

Order XXXVII, rule 8 is inapposite to cover an application for *Anton Piller*-type relief, inter alia, because it is confined to cases where the property in question is the subject of the dispute in the suit or as regards which a question arises in the suit and observations, samples or experiments are needed for the purpose of the suit. An *Anton Piller* order may be granted where the risk is of the destruction of evidence.

Certain statutory provisions in place in Tanzania give the impression that, in specific contexts, Tanzanian law is familiar with the concept of *Anton Piller* relief. Hence, regulation 18(4) of the Tanzanian Merchandise Marks Regulations 2008[267] provides:

> 'Subject to an *ex parte* search order obtained from the District Court upon application, the Chief Inspector or the right holder or the applicant may enter and search the premises suspected to contain counterfeit goods, and may co-opt the assistance of a court broker and the police or private security firm.'

However, the Merchandise Marks Act 1963 itself is concerned with the imposition of criminal liability upon those who commit offences thereunder defined. In the scenario envisaged by regulation 18(4), the court's *imprimatur* is being given to those who wish to search for 'counterfeit goods', ostensibly for the same purposes as those set out in the Act. As a result, the order which a district court may make in those circumstances is of a different character to the order conventionally understood as *Anton Piller* relief.[268]

That is not to say that the Tanzanian court does not have jurisdiction to grant *Anton Piller* relief. Section 95 of the Code provides that nothing in the Code itself 'shall be deemed to limit or otherwise affect the inherent power of the court to

[266] *Anton Piller KG v Manufacturing Processes Ltd* [1976] 1 All ER 779 (CA) (Lord Denning MR; Ormrod and Shaw LJJ). This case decided, for the first time at appellate level, that a court could grant such an order.

[267] Government Notice 89 of 2008. The Regulations were made pursuant to the Merchandise Marks Act 1963 (Act 20 of 1963, now Cap 85 of the Laws of Tanzania, 2019).

[268] As such, Mrema (*Recent Legislative Changes in Trademark Law in Tanzania*, available at: www.mkono.com/pdf/Inta%20paper%202009-Final%20doc.pdf) may not be correct to label the order of which reg 18(4) makes mention as an '*Anton Piller*' Order (para 3.2.8). While a 'right holder' may be the beneficiary of the court's orders, so may a chief inspector (one who has been appointed by a minister and so is clothed with the state's stamp of approval). In order to assess fully whether Tanzanian courts are familiar with *Anton Piller* relief, at least as that term would be understood by an English lawyer, it is necessary to consider their grant outwith the context of the Merchandise Marks Act. Moreover, even if the order referred to in reg 18(4) is properly referred to an *Anton Piller* order, there is no indication therein given as to the conditions which must be satisfied before the applicant will be entitled to that relief. It is submitted that, if the Tanzanian court is entitled to grant such relief, such grant will be in accordance with the principles set out by the English Court of Appeal in *Anton Piller* itself.

make such orders as may be necessary for the ends of justice or to prevent abuse of the process of the court'. This power referred to in this provision is of sufficient amplitude to support the making of an order granting *Anton Piller* relief.[269]

12.4.6 Third-party disclosure orders

There is no authority on the question whether a Tanzanian[270] court may, apart from the established post-issuing of proceedings and pre-trial procedures whereby a third party may be served with a witness summons requiring his attendance at court in order to give evidence and/or to produce documents,[271] order a person not a party to the proceedings to give disclosure. Such a power is available to the English courts in the form of a *Norwich Pharmacal* order,[272] whereby an innocent third party caught up in a tort may be ordered to disclose the name or other identity of the tortfeasor.

Pursuant to section 95 of the Code, the authors consider that the Tanzanian courts have power to make such an order. As mentioned above, section 95 is of considerable breadth and supports making an order, such as a *Norwich Pharmacal* order, 'necessary for the ends of justice', which was the justification relied on by the House of Lords in the *Norwich Pharmacal* case itself.

In *Norwich Pharmacal Co v Customs and Excise Commrs*, the English House of Lords[273] set out the following principle:

> 'That if through no fault of his own a person gets mixed up in the tortious acts of others so as to facilitate their wrong-doing he may incur no personal liability but he comes under a duty to assist the person who has been wronged by giving him full information and disclosing the identity of the wrongdoers ... [It does not matter] whether he became so mixed up by voluntary action on his part or because it was his duty to do what he did.

---

[269] Section 129 of the Zanzibar Civil Procedure Code is drafted in very similar terms. Both s 95 of the Code and s 129 of the Zanzibar Civil Procedure Code are drafted in identical terms to s 151 of the Code of Civil Procedure in India. As to how that provision has been interpreted, see Paul and Srivastava *Mulla: The Code of Civil Procedure* 16 ed (2001) 1421 et seq; s 151 of the Indian Code provides, 'Nothing in this Code shall be deemed to limit or otherwise affect the inherent power of the Court to make such orders as may be necessary for the ends of justice or to prevent abuse of the process of the Court.' The editors of *Mulla* state (at 1423) that 'the power under this section relates to matters of procedure. If the ordinary rules of procedure result in injustice, and there is no other remedy, [they] can be broken in order to achieve the ends of justice.' Section 151 was considered by the Privy Council in *Sabitri v Savi* (1921) 48 IA 76, AIR 1921 PC 80, where the board confirmed that, 'in terms of the section the inherent powers saved are such as are used to secure the ends of justice'. Section 151 has been employed to issue an injunction in cases not falling under the relevant provisions of O 39 (temporary injunctions; *Monoharlal v Seth Hiralal* AIR 1962 SC 527).

[270] Or Zanzibar.

[271] Order V, r 1 and r 4 of the Civil Procedure Rules. Order V, r 1 and r 7 of the Zanzibar Civil Procedure are the equivalent provisions.

[272] *Norwich Pharmacal Co v Customs and Excise Comrs* [1974] AC 133 (HL(E)) (Lords Reid and Morris, Viscount Dilhorne, Lords Cross and Kilbrandon).

[273] Ibid 175, *per* Lord Reid.

It may be that if this causes him expense the person seeking the information ought to reimburse him. But justice requires that he should co-operate in righting the wrong if he unwittingly facilitated its perpetration.'

More recent authority[274] has clarified the conditions which the plaintiff must satisfy in order to obtain such relief:

'The three conditions to be satisfied for the court to exercise the power to order *Norwich Pharmacal* relief are:

i) a wrong must have been carried out, or arguably carried out, by an ultimate wrongdoer;

ii) there must be the need for an order to enable action to be brought against the ultimate wrongdoer; and

iii) the person against whom the order is sought must: (a) be mixed up in so as to have facilitated the wrongdoing; and (b) be able or likely to be able to provide the information necessary to enable the ultimate wrongdoer to be sued.'

If the plaintiff satisfies all of those conditions, the English court will then go on to exercise its discretion. In doing so, it must keep in mind the proper scope of *Norwich Pharmacal* relief: the jurisdiction cannot be used for wide-ranging discovery or the gathering of evidence, but is strictly confined to necessary information.[275]

12.4.7 Anti-suit injunctions

An anti-suit injunction is an order restraining the injunction defendant from either commencing or continuing proceedings outside Tanzania[276] in breach of a legal or equitable right on the part of the injunction plaintiff not to pursue litigation outside Tanzania or, conversely, restraining the injunction defendant from commencing or continuing proceedings inside Tanzania in breach of a legal or equitable right on the part of the injunction plaintiff to have the dispute between the parties litigated in a jurisdiction other than Tanzania.[277]

---

[274] *Ramilos Trading Limited v Valentin Mikhaylovich Buyanovsky* [2016] EWHC 3175 (Comm) (HC) (Flaux J), citing, at para [11], *Mitsui v Nexen Petroleum* [2005] EWHC 625 (Ch); [2005] 3 All ER 511 (HC) at [21] (Lightman J).

[275] *Ramilos Trading Ltd v Valentin Mikhaylovich Buyanovsky* [2016] EWHC 3175 (Comm) (HC) (Flaux J) para [46].

[276] Or Zanzibar.

[277] In similar vein, an anti-anti-suit injunction is an order restraining the injunction defendant from commencing or continuing proceedings to restrain the injunction plaintiff from applying to restrain the injunction defendant from commencing or continuing proceedings. The leading works on this topic are: Raphael *The Anti-Suit Injunction* 2 ed (2019) and Briggs *Civil Jurisdiction and Judgments* 7 ed (2021), ch 28. It is also conceptually possible to obtain similar relief in the context of arbitration but such relief is outside the scope of this work.

There is no reported judicial authority in Tanzania on whether or not an anti-suit injunction is a remedy available to the courts in Tanzania. However, as noted at section 12.4.5 above, section 95 of the Code provides that nothing in the Code itself 'shall be deemed to limit or otherwise affect the inherent power of the court to make such orders as may be necessary for the ends of justice or to prevent abuse of the process of the court'. This power referred to in this provision is of sufficient amplitude to support the making of an order granting anti-suit relief.

It may be instructive to note that the courts of Nigeria[278] and the Republic of South Africa[279] have determined that they have the ability to grant anti-suit injunctions or similar injunctions in the context of arbitration. In developing such relief, those courts have been influenced by the development of English law on the subject. In consequence, therefore, and in case it may be of some assistance, set out below, in summary, are the principles of English law governing the grant of an anti-suit injunction.

The court must have personal jurisdiction over the injunction defendant. The court may be seised either by service on the defendant within the jurisdiction or service out of the jurisdiction with the leave of the court.[280]

The injunction plaintiff must assert a cause of action for relief. Usually, the injunction plaintiff will contend that the injunction defendant is committing a wrong by bringing or proposing to bring proceedings in a foreign court. This will require the plaintiff to characterise the conduct of the defendant as the breach of a legal or equitable right.

A legal right may, and often will, be based on a right not to be sued in a foreign jurisdiction arising out of an exclusive jurisdiction clause in favour of the courts of Tanzania. An equitable right may be the right not to be sued in a foreign jurisdiction and may be the corollary of an equitable wrong which is that it is oppressive and vexatious and therefore unconscionable for the injunction defendant to commence or continue proceedings against the injunction plaintiff in a foreign jurisdiction.

The prime example of a cause of action based on a legal right not to be sued in a foreign jurisdiction is where the parties have agreed expressly that the courts of Tanzania should have exclusive jurisdiction over disputes arising out of the contract (which can be a substantive contract or a settlement agreement) between them.[281] In such a case proof of the underlying cause of action is likely to be a

[278] *United Bank of Africa Plc v Coker* (1996) 4 NWLR 239. In the arbitral context, see *Zenith Global Merchant Ltd v Zhongfu International Investment (Nig) FZE* (2017) All FWLR 1837 (Akinyemi J).

[279] *Vedanta Resources Holdings Ltd v ZCCM Investment Holdings plc* 2019 JDR 1425 (GJ).

[280] The substantive law and procedure for which in Sierra Leone has been set out above.

[281] The contract may be a substantive contract or a settlement agreement and the dispute resolution provisions may be exclusively in favour of the courts of Sierra Leone or may be in favour of arbitration:

sufficient condition for the grant of the relief and that good reason would need to be shown why the discretion to order an injunction should not be exercised.[282]

The principal example of a cause of action based on an equitable wrong is where proceedings brought abroad by the defendant are oppressive and vexatious. An example of such conduct is illustrated by the decision of the Privy Council in *SNI Aerospatiale v Lee Kui Jak*,[283] where a resident of Brunei had been killed in a helicopter crash and his widow (and her brother-in-law, as co-administrator of his estate), the respondent plaintiffs in the appeal to the Privy Council, had commenced proceedings in Brunei and had subsequently been persuaded to sue in Texas instead. The appellant defendant applied for an anti-suit injunction restraining the plaintiffs from proceeding against it in Texas. The Privy Council allowed the defendant's appeal, held that an injunction ought to be granted restraining the respondents from proceeding in Texas and remitted the matter to the Brunei courts.

Transposing the findings of the Privy Council to Tanzania, it was held that an anti-suit injunction would be granted if: (1) pursuit of the foreign proceedings is vexatious or oppressive; (2) Tanzania is the natural forum for the resolution of the dispute; and (3) the injunction does not deprive the defendant of advantages in the foreign jurisdiction of which it would be unjust to deprive him.[284]

Other examples of equitable wrongs which may attract an anti-suit injunction are: undermining the jurisdiction of the court in Tanzania;[285] vexatious conduct by relying on foreign procedural laws;[286] wrongfully undermining a Tanzanian judgment;[287] or enforcement of a foreign judgment wrongfully obtained.[288]

British Airways Board v Laker Airways Ltd [1985] AC 58 (HL (E)) (Lords Diplock, Fraser, Scarman, Roskill and Brightman), *per* Lord Diplock at 81C–E.

[282] *The Angelic Grace* [1995] 1 Lloyd's Rep 87 (CA) (Neill, Leggatt and Millett LJJ), *per* Millett LJ at 96, col 2, and Neill LJ at 97, col 1; *Donohue v Armco Inc* [2000] 1 Lloyd's Rep 579 (CA) (Stuart-Smith, Brooke and Sedley LJJ), where it was stated that 'strong reasons' (*per* Stuart-Smith LJ at para 35) or 'strong cause' (*per* Brooke LJ at paras 59 and 60) would be required to deny an injunction.

[283] [1987] AC 871 (PC, Brunei) (Lords Keith, Griffiths, MacKay and Goff and Sir John Megaw).

[284] Lord Goff (giving the opinion of the Privy Council) 896F–H. That the court to which the application is made should be the natural forum for the resolution of the dispute was repeated by the House of Lords in *Airbus Industrie GIE v Patel* [1999] 1 AC 119 (HL (E)) (Lords Goff, Slynn, Steyn, Clyde and Hutton), *per* Lord Goff (with whom the other Lords agreed) 138G–H and 140H–141B.

[285] For example, by commencing bankruptcy proceedings outside the jurisdiction when such proceedings are in progress in Tanzania: *SNI Aerospatiale v Lee Kui Jak* [1987] AC 871, *per* Lord Goff at 892G–893B.

[286] By seeking to depose witnesses in the USA where those witnesses would be subject to cross-examination in proceedings in Tanzania, for example: *Omega Group Holdings Ltd v Kozeny* [2002] CLC 132.

[287] By commencing proceedings outside the jurisdiction for declaratory relief designed to frustrate the enforcement of a Tanzanian judgment in that jurisdiction: *Masri v Consolidated Contractors International (UK) Ltd (No 3)* [2009] QB 503 (CA).

[288] Where the foreign judgment was obtained through fraud and perjury: *Ellerman Lines Ltd v Read* [1928] 2 KB 144 (CA), *per* Scrutton LJ at 152–3.

12.4.8 Other interlocutory relief

12.4.8.1 *Attachment of the defendant's property*

Tanzania

Order XXXVI, rule 6 of the Civil Procedure Rules, as noted above, provides as follows:

> '(1) Where, at any stage of a suit, the court is satisfied, by affidavit or otherwise, that the defendant, with intent to obstruct or delay the execution of any decree that may be passed against him—
>
> *(a)* is about to dispose of the whole or any part of his property; or
>
> *(b)* is about to remove the whole or any part of his property from the local limits of the jurisdiction of the court,
>
> the court may direct the defendant, within a time to be fixed by it, either to furnish security, in such sum as may be specified in the order, to produce and place at the disposal of the court, when required, the said property or the value of the same, or such portion thereof as may be sufficient to satisfy the decree, or to appear and show cause why he should not furnish security.
>
> (2) The plaintiff shall, unless the court otherwise directs, specify the property[289] required to be attached and estimate the value thereof.
>
> (3) The court may also in the order direct the conditional attachment of the whole or any portion of the property so specified.'

It would appear that the plaintiff's application for attachment can be made by way of a chamber summons.[290] The court must be satisfied that the defendant is acting 'with intent' and that he is about to commit the mischief about which the complaint is made.[291] The court must be so satisfied because the power to attach property should not be lightly made and without clear proof of the mischief at which the relief is aimed.[292]

Where the defendant fails to show cause why he should not furnish security, or fails to furnish the security required, within the time fixed by the court, the

[289] It would appear that such property has to be movable, as opposed to immovable property: *Abdillah Shrwa v Sheikh Mohamed Haj Ahmed* [1977] LRT N43 (CA) (Law VP). At 193, Law VP stated that: 'It is doubtful whether Rule 6 allows the attachment of immovable property as opposed to property capable of being disposed of or removed outside the jurisdiction.' This interpretation is open to doubt; a person may dispose of his land by selling it: there is no need, at least so far as r 6(1)(a) is concerned, for the property to be removed from the jurisdiction. Rule 6 is equivalent to O 38, r 5 of the Indian Code of Civil Procedure. The Indian courts have held that the 'expression "property" includes the property of every description whether movable or immovable': Paul and Srivastava *Mulla: The Code of Civil Procedure* 16 ed (2001) vol 4 at 3678.

[290] *Mtale v January Kapembwa* [1976] LRT N7 (HC) 24 (Sisya AG J).

[291] Ibid 27.

[292] Ibid.

court may order that the property specified or such portion thereof as appears sufficient to satisfy any decree which may be passed in the suit, be attached.[293]

Where an order for attachment is made before judgment, the court shall order the attachment to be withdrawn when the defendant furnishes the security required, together with security for the costs of the attachment, or when the suit is dismissed.[294]

On the other hand, where the defendant shows such cause or furnishes the required security and the property specified or any portion of it has been attached, the court shall order the attachment to be withdrawn, or make such other order as it sees fit.[295]

In circumstances where an attachment before judgment is made, that attachment shall not affect the rights, existing prior to the attachment, of persons not parties to the suit, nor bar any person holding a decree against the defendant from applying for the sale of the property under attachment in execution of such decree.[296]

Zanzibar

The equivalent provisions governing attachment of property before judgment are contained in Order XLIII, rules 5–13 of the Zanzibar Civil Procedure Rules. They are, in all material respects, the same as the rules in operation in Tanzania, save that Order XLIII, rule 5 of the Zanzibar Civil Procedure Rules also makes provision for what should happen when a subordinate court directs the provisional attachment of immovable property[297] or the produce of such property.

---

[293] Order XXXVI, r 7(1) of the Civil Procedure Code. Save as expressly otherwise provided, the attachment shall be made in the manner provided for the attachment of property in the execution of a decree: O XXXVI, r 8. That said, O XXXVI, r 13 is very clear that nothing in O XXXVI itself shall 'be deemed to authorise the plaintiff to apply for the attachment of any agricultural produce in the possession of an agriculturalist, or to empower the court to order the attachment or production of such produce'.

[294] Order XXXVI, r 10 of the Civil Procedure Code. Where property is under attachment by virtue of the provisions set out in O XXXVI and a decree is subsequently passed in favour of the plaintiff, it shall not be necessary upon an application for execution of such decree to apply for re-attachment of the property.

[295] Order XXXVI, r 7(2) of the Civil Procedure Code.

[296] Order XXXVI, r 11 of the Civil Procedure Code. Any person with an existing interest at the time of the attachment may file an objection against such attachment: *Nyanza Distributors Co Ltd v Geita General Stores* [1977] TLR N2. For what may count as an existing interest: *AD Mashoto v AH Kaunga* [1986] TLR 67 (HC) (Chipeta J). It appears that a person may, rather than file an objection, commence a fresh suit, alleging that the attachment is improper: *Kangaulu Mussa v Mpunghati Mchodo* [1984] TLR 348 (HC) (Lugakingira J).

[297] This marks a material difference between the procedure in place in Tanzania (which seems not to encompass immovable property: *Abdillah Shrwa v Sheikh Haj Ahmed* [1977] LRT N43) and that in place in Zanzibar.

Summary

The equivalent provision to Order XXXVI, rule 6 of the Civil Procedure Rules and Order XLIV, rule 5 of the Zanzibar Civil Procedure Rules, appears in the Indian Civil Procedure Rules.[298] In *Sardar Govindrao Mahadik v Devi Sahai*,[299] the Indian Supreme Court stated:[300]

> 'The sole object behind the order levying attachment before judgment is to give an assurance to the plaintiff that his decree if made would be satisfied. It is a sort of guarantee against the decree becoming infructuous for want of property available from which the plaintiff can satisfy the decree.'

This correctly states the effect of the Tanzanian and Zanzibar provisions: the object is to provide security for the plaintiff.

12.4.8.2 *Arrest of the defendant*

Tanzania

Order XXXVI, rule 1, of the Code sets out the circumstances in which a plaintiff may apply for the arrest of an absconding defendant. Hence:

> '(1) Where at any stage of a suit, other than a suit of the nature referred to in paragraphs (a) to (d) of section 14 [of the Code],[301] the court is satisfied, by affidavit or otherwise—
>
> (a) that the defendant, with intent to delay the plaintiff, or to avoid any process of the court or to obstruct or delay the execution of any decree that may be passed against him—
>
> (i) has absconded or left the local limits of the jurisdiction of the court; or
>
> (ii) is about to abscond or leave the local limits of the jurisdiction of the court; or
>
> (iii) has disposed of or removed his property or any part thereof or
>
> (b) that the defendant is about to leave Tanzania under circumstances affording reasonable probability that the plaintiff will or may thereby be obstructed or delayed in the execution of any decree that may be passed against the defendant in the suit, the court may issue a warrant to arrest the defendant and bring him before the court to show cause why he should not furnish security for his appearance:

---

[298] Order 38, r 5 thereof.

[299] [1982] 1 SCC 237, AIR 1982 SC 989, [1982] 2 SCR 186 (Indian Sup Ct). See generally, Takwani *Civil Procedure* 5 ed (2003) 224–8.

[300] [1982] 2 SCR 186 at 223C–D.

[301] That is to say: suits for the recovery of immovable property with or without rents or profits; suits for the partition of immovable property; suits for foreclosure, sale or redemption in the case of a mortgage of or a charge upon immovable property; and suits for the determination of any other right to, or interest in, immovable property.

> Provided that the defendant shall not be arrested if he pays to the officer entrusted with the execution of the warrant any sum specified in the warrant to satisfy the plaintiff's claim; and such sum shall be held in deposit by the court until the suit is disposed of or until further order of the court.'

Where a court issues a warrant of arrest under Order XXXVI, rule 1, it may, by telegram, request any district court within the area of whose jurisdiction the defendant is believed to be, to arrest him and cause him to be taken under escort to the court which issued the warrant.[302] On receipt of that telegram, the court to which it is addressed shall issue a provisional warrant in accordance with the particulars contained in the telegram and shall cause the same to be executed.[303]

Where the defendant cannot show cause, as required by Order XXXVI, rule 1 of the Civil Procedure Rules, the court shall order him either to deposit in court money or other property sufficient to answer the claim against him or to furnish security for his appearance at any time when called upon while the suit is pending and until satisfaction of any decree that may be passed against him in the suit, or make such other order as it sees fit in regard to the sum which may have been paid by the defendant under the proviso in rule 1.[304]

Where the defendant fails to comply with any such order,[305] the court may commit him as a civil prisoner until the decision of the suit or, where a decree is passed against the defendant, until the decree has been satisfied.[306] This is subject to the proviso that no person shall be detained in prison under this rule in any case for a longer period than six months or for a longer period than six weeks when the amount or value of the subject-matter of the suit does not exceed 150 shillings; where a person complies with the relevant order, he shall be detained in prison no longer.[307]

There is an absence of judicial authority in Tanzania on the correct interpretation to be given to these provisions.

---

[302] Order XXXVI, r 2(1) of the Civil Procedure Rules. The telegram so sent must comply with the provisions set out in O XXXVI, r 2(2).

[303] Order XXXVI, r 2(3) of the Civil Procedure Rules.

[304] Order XXXVI, r 3(1) of the Civil Procedure Rules. Rule 3(2) and r 4 provide for the situation in which a person stands as a surety for the appearance of the defendant.

[305] Or an order under r 4 of the Civil Procedure Rules.

[306] Order XXXVI, r 5 of the Civil Procedure Rules.

[307] Ibid.

Zanzibar

Order XLIII of the Zanzibar Civil Procedure Rules provides:

> '(1) Where at any stage of a suit, the court is satisfied by affidavit or otherwise, that—
>
> (*a*) the plaintiff has a good cause of action against the defendant to the amount of two hundred shillings or upwards; and
>
> (*b*) there is probable cause for believing that the defendant is about to quit [Zanzibar] unless he be apprehended; and
>
> (*c*) the absence of the defendant will materially prejudice the plaintiff in the prosecution of his suit,
>
> the court may issue a warrant to arrest the defendant and bring him before the court to show cause why he should not furnish security for his appearance or be committed to the civil prison in default of furnishing such security:
>
> Provided that the defendant shall not be arrested if he pays to the officer entrusted with the execution of the warrant any sum specified in the warrant as sufficient to satisfy the plaintiff's claim; and such sum shall be held in deposit by the court until the suit is deposited of or until the further order of the court.'

Where the defendant fails to show such cause, the court shall order him either to deposit in court money or other property sufficient to answer the claim against him, or to furnish security for his appearance at any time when called upon while the suit is pending and until satisfaction of any decree that may be passed against him in the suit, or make such order as it thinks fit in regard to the sum which may have been paid by the defendant under the proviso to rule 1 above.[308]

Where the defendant fails to comply with an order made under rule 2,[309] the court may commit him to civil prison until the decision of the suit, on the proviso that no person shall be so detained in prison after he has complied with the order, or in default of compliance, for any longer period than six months.[310]

There is an absence of judicial authority in Zanzibar as to the correct interpretation to be given to these provisions.

---

308 Order XLIII, r 2(1) of the Zanzibar Civil Procedure Rules. Rules 2(2) and 3 provide for the situation in which a person stands as a surety for the appearance of the defendant.

309 Or r 3 of the Zanzibar Civil Procedure Rules.

310 Order XLIII, r 4 of the Zanzibar Civil Procedure Rules.

Chapter 13

THE GAMBIA

13.1 Jurisdiction

The bases on which a court in The Gambia may assume jurisdiction over a cause or matter are statutory in origin.

The fundamental means by which a court in The Gambia is seised of jurisdiction over a defendant at the suit of a plaintiff is by service of process on the defendant.

At the outset, it is necessary to explain in a little detail the procedural rules currently in force in The Gambia. Section 55(1) of the Courts Act 1964[1] provides that the:

> 'Rules Committee[2] may at any time make Rules of Court for the High Court or for all or any subordinate court or courts for the better carrying into effect of this Act, and without prejudice to the generality of the foregoing power, for any or all of the following matters for …
>
> *(b)* regulating the pleading, practice and procedure of courts, including all matters connected with the forms to be used and the fees to be payable … [and]
>
> *(e)* regulating the procedure and practice, including fees and costs, in the High Court on and incidental to an application for sealing a probate or letters of administration under the Probates (Re-sealing) Act.'

Section 56 of the Courts Act states that, notwithstanding the provisions of section 55, the Rules of the Supreme Court 1928, the Supreme Court (Prize Court Fees) Rules, and the Order under the Prize Court Rules, 1939 shall, *mutatis mutandis*, continue in full force and effect as if they had been made in respect of the High Court of The Gambia under the provisions of the Courts Act, until or unless they are revoked and replaced or amended by rules made under the provisions of the Courts Act. Thus, the rules referred to in section 56 are the Rules of the High Court for present purposes.

There is an explanatory note to the Rules of the High Court,[3] which confirms that the rules therein set out are 'deemed to be made under section 55 of the Courts Act'.[4] Certain further revisions have been made[5] to the provisions of

---

[1] Act 13 of 1964. Now reproduced as Chapter 6:01 of The Laws of The Gambia, published in 2009 with the authority of the Government of the Gambia. In this regard, the reader is referred to the 'Note on the citation of statutory material in this work', which appears at the end of the 'List of Statutory Material Cited' at the beginning of this work.

[2] Which term is defined in s 54 of the Courts Act. The Rules Committee 'shall consist of the Chief Justice as Chairperson, the Attorney-General, and a practising member of the Bar selected by members of the Bar'.

[3] Which may be found in vol 2 of The Laws of The Gambia, 2009.

[4] The note goes on to confirm that the rules there set out were originally called 'The rules of the Supreme Court 1928' and that, in this particular revision and reprinting of the Rules of the High Court, 'the numbers of the Orders and of the rules within each Order have not been revised. They still have the same numbers as hitherto. This conforms with the usual practice when the rules of court are revised and is for the general convenience of those whose work has required them to be familiar with them and with their numbering.'

[5] See the High Court (Amendment) Rules 2009. These were made pursuant to s 55 of the Courts Act and so form part of Cap 6:01 of the Laws of The Gambia, 2009. The High Court (Amendment) Rules were made on 14 September 2009 and took effect on 1 January 2010.

the Rules of the High Court in the recent past. In those circumstances, it would appear that the Rules of the Supreme Court etc have been 'revoked and replaced or amended by rules made under the provisions of the Courts Act'. It is, in any event, tolerably clear that the Rules of the High Court located in the schedules to the Courts Act are those currently in force in The Gambia.

The Rules of the High Court distinguish between service of process within the jurisdiction and service outside the jurisdiction.

13.1.1 Service where the defendant is within the jurisdiction

The second schedule[6] to the Rules of the High Court contains rules which 'shall be applied in all civil causes, matters and proceedings to which they extend'. While previously[7] every civil suit had to be commenced by way of a writ of summons accompanied by a written statement of claim, it appears that Rules of the High Court no longer require a civil suit to be commenced using this form of originating process.[8] It is now simply the case that, save for suits which are placed on the undefended list, a civil suit commenced by way of writ of summons shall be accompanied by a statement of claim which complies with Order XXIII, affidavits of statements or testimonies of persons the plaintiff intends to call to testify during the trial and the documents the plaintiff relies on or intends to rely on in the trial of the suit.[9]

The defendant who is present[10] within the jurisdiction shall be served with a writ or other document within the time and in the manner directed by the court.[11] While there is no specific provision made in the second schedule to the Rules of the High Court for service on an individual in The Gambia, it would appear that the court might direct service to take place in accordance with any

[6] All references hereafter to 'orders' and 'rules' shall be to orders and rules contained in the second schedule to the Rules of the High Court, unless otherwise stated.

[7] As in, prior to the coming into force of the High Court (Amendment) Rules 2009.

[8] See r 3 of the High Court (Amendment) Rules 2009. That the mandatory commencement of the civil suit by way of writ of summons has been done away with does not mean that the majority of suits are now commenced using some other form of originating process. Indeed, from the language of r 3 of the High Court (Amendment) Rules, it would appear that the majority of civil suits are likely still to be commenced using a writ of summons.

[9] That said, it would appear that the High Court (Amendment) Rules 2009 have made no change to O V, r 1(1) which states that, while it is sufficient for the plaintiff to state his or her claim in the writ of summons briefly in a general form, the plaintiff may deliver to the Registrar of the High Court, at the time of making application for the writ of summons, particulars of his or her demand in any form which shall give the defendant reasonably sufficient information as to the details of his or her claim. It would also appear that O II, r 1(2), which applies when civil proceedings are brought against the State, has not been altered by the High Court (Amendment) Rules 2009.

[10] *Solo Dabo v Mohammed Abdalla Mousa* (1963–1966) GR 22 (Court of Appeal of the Gambia) (Ames P; Dove-Edwin JA, Luke Ag JA).

[11] Order VIII, r 1.

of the methods set out in Order III of the first schedule to the Courts Act.[12] As such, service may be made by any literate person[13] and, if a literate person serves a document on any party not able to understand the same, the literate person is obliged to explain to the recipient party the contents of the document.[14] The default rule is that a defendant must be served personally with any document.[15] Provision is also made for substituted service in specified circumstances.[16]

Despite the fact that the Orders and rules contained in the second schedule omit to deal with service on an individual within the jurisdiction, they do deal specifically with service on partners;[17] on a Gambian corporation or company;[18] on board ship;[19] on prisoners and lunatics[20] and on the local agent of a principal who is resident outside of, but carries on business within, the jurisdiction.[21]

Specific provision is made for service on a foreign company or corporation within the jurisdiction.[22] Hence, when the suit is against a foreign corporation or company, having an office and carrying on business within the jurisdiction, and such suit is limited to a cause of action which arose within the jurisdiction, the writ or document may be served by giving the same to the principal officer of such foreign corporation or company within the jurisdiction.

It should be noted that the Companies Act 2013 has created an alternative regime for, inter alia, service of process on what Chapter XIII of the Act refers to as 'foreign companies'. Section 584 states that Chapter XIII:

> 'applies to foreign companies, that is, companies incorporated outside The Gambia which (a) after the commencement of this Act establish a place of business within The Gambia; and (b) have, before the commencement of this Act, established a place of business within The Gambia and continue to have an established place of business within The Gambia at the commencement of this Act.'[23]

---

[12] Given that the rules in the first schedule apply to all causes, matters and proceedings: O I, r 1(1) of the first schedule to the Courts Act.

[13] Order III, r 1(1) of the first schedule to the Courts Act.

[14] Order III, r 1(2) of the first schedule to the Courts Act. Whether a certificate of service is required or not depends on the method of service employed: O III, r 2 of the first schedule to the Courts Act.

[15] Order III, r 3 of the first schedule to the Courts Act.

[16] Order III, r 5 of the first schedule to the Courts Act.

[17] Order VIII, r 2.

[18] Order VIII, r 3.

[19] Order VIII, r 5.

[20] Order VIII, r 6.

[21] Order VIII, r 7.

[22] Order VIII, r 4.

[23] Chapter XIII leaves the phrase 'place of business' undefined. Section 357 of the now repealed Companies Act 1955 (Act 9 of 1955) identified 'place of business' to include 'a share transfer or share registration office'. Section 583 of the 2013 Act, the equivalent provision, contains only the definitions of the words 'certified', 'director' and 'secretary'.

Section 585 imposes an obligation on companies to which Chapter XIII of the Act applies, within the relevant period of time,[24] to deliver to the Registrar for registration, inter alia, the full address of the registered or principal office of the company and its principal place of business in The Gambia and the names and addresses of one or more persons resident in The Gambia authorised to accept on behalf of the company service of process and any notices required to be served on the company.

Process shall be 'sufficiently served if addressed to a person whose name has been delivered to the Registrar under Section 585 of this Act and left at or sent by post to the address of the person'.[25]

Where a company defaults in delivering to the Registrar the name and address of a person resident in The Gambia who is authorised to accept on behalf of the company service of process or notices; or if at any time all the persons whose names and addresses have been so delivered are dead or have ceased to reside in The Gambia, or refuse to accept service on behalf of the company, or for any reason cannot be served, a document may be served on the company by leaving it at or sending it by post any place of business established by the company in The Gambia.[26]

13.1.2 Service where the defendant is outside the jurisdiction

A plaintiff may not use substituted service within the jurisdiction as a means to circumvent the provisions which govern service out of the jurisdiction. Hence, in *Blell v Isaac*,[27] the plaintiff, through substituted service – by publishing the writ in a newspaper circulating in The Gambia – purported to serve process on the defendant at a time when the defendant was not present within the jurisdiction. The Court of Appeal, *suo motu*, questioned the propriety of that service on the defendant. It concluded that the plaintiff should have served the process out of the jurisdiction on the defendant. In the absence of such service, the case

> 'was not actuated by the satisfaction of a condition precedent, i.e. service on the defendant and so the High Court had no competence or jurisdiction to proceed. A defect in competence is fatal to a case and renders the whole proceedings a nullity.'[28]

---

[24] Within six months from the commencement of the Act or within one month from the establishment of the place of business.

[25] Section 590(1) of the 2013 Act.

[26] Section 590(2) of the 2013 Act.

[27] [1997–2001] GR 748 (Court of Appeal of The Gambia) (Yahaya and Akamba JJA, Janneh AGJA).

[28] In reaching this decision, Yahaya JA, who delivered the judgment of the Court of Appeal, relied, at 749, on the decision of the Nigerian Supreme Court in *Adeigbe v Kusimo* [1965] All NLR 248 (Ademola CJ; Bairamian and Idigbe JJSC — the case is incorrectly referenced in the judgment of the Court of Appeal of The Gambia).

Order VIII, rule 8[29] provides:

'(1) Service outside of the jurisdiction of a writ of summons or notice of a writ of summons[30] may be allowed by the court whenever—

(a) the whole subject matter of the action is land situate within the jurisdiction (with or without rents or profits), or the perpetuation of testimony relating to land within the jurisdiction;

(b) any act, deed, will, contract, obligation or liability affecting land or hereditaments situate within the jurisdiction is sought to be construed, rectified, set aside or enforced in the action;

(c) any relief is sought against a person domiciled or ordinarily resident within the jurisdiction;

(d) the action is for the administration of the personal estate of any deceased person, who at the time of his or her death was domiciled within the jurisdiction, or for the execution (as to property situated within the jurisdiction) of the trusts of any written instrument, of which the person to be served is a trustee, which ought to be executed according to the laws of The Gambia;

(e) the action is brought to enforce, rescind, dissolve, annul or otherwise affect a contract or to recover damages or other relief for or in respect of the breach of a contract—

(i) made within the jurisdiction,

(ii) made by or through an agent trading or residing within the jurisdiction on behalf of a principal trading or residing out of the jurisdiction, or

(iii) by its terms or implication is to be governed by the laws of The Gambia,

or is one brought against a defendant in respect of a breach committed within the jurisdiction of a contract wherever made, even though such breach was preceded or accompanied by a breach out of the jurisdiction which rendered impossible the performance of the part of the contract which ought to have been performed within the jurisdiction;

---

[29] The rule of the English Rules of the Supreme Court regulating service out of the jurisdiction prior to 1999 (when the English Civil Procedure Rules came into effect) was O XI. Under the Rules of the Supreme Court 1883 and the Rules of the Supreme Court 1965, which superseded the 1883 Rules, O XI, r 1 provided for service out of the jurisdiction. Order VIII, r 8 in The Gambia, is materially identical to O XI, r 1 of the Rules of the Supreme Court 1883.

[30] The Rules of the High Court do not set out the circumstances in which notice of a summons, rather than the writ of summons itself, must be served on the defendant. In certain other Anglophone African jurisdictions which are considered in this work, the same distinction is made. The law in those other jurisdictions may be a useful source of guidance as to the proper understanding and application of the Rules of the High Court themselves. Hence, and by way of example only, in Sierra Leone a non-citizen defendant is to be served with notice of the writ and not the writ itself. The reasons for this are rooted in English legal history: a summons is a command from the sovereign and it was thought discourteous to serve such a command on a person not resident in the United Kingdom and not a British subject; thus a notice of the summons was served instead (see *Nanjibhai Prabhudas and Co Ltd v Standard Bank Ltd* [1968] EA 670 (CA) (Sir Charles Newbold P, Sir Clement de Lestang V-P and Law JA), *per* Sir Charles Newbold P at 683C–E; the origin of the rule is s 19 of the English Common Law Procedure Act 1852. After the repeal of the 1852 Act, the rule was incorporated into the Rules of the Supreme Court; *Westman v Aktiebolaget Ekmans Mekaniska Snickarefabrick* (1876) 1 Ex D 237).

(*f*) the action is founded on a tort committed within the jurisdiction;

(*g*) an injunction is sought as to anything to be done within the jurisdiction or any nuisance within the jurisdiction is sought to be prevented or removed, whether damages are or are not also sought in respect thereof;

(*h*) a person out of the jurisdiction is a necessary or proper party to an action properly brought against some other person duly served within the jurisdiction; or

(*i*) the action is by a mortgagee[31] or mortgagor[32] in relation to a mortgage[33] or personal property situate within the jurisdiction, and seeks relief of the nature or kind following, that is to say, sale, foreclosure, delivery of possession by the mortgagor, redemption, reconveyance, delivery of possession by the mortgagee, but does not seek (unless and so far as permissible under paragraph (e) of this rule) any personal judgment or order for payment of any moneys due under the mortgage.'[34]

Order VIII, rule 9 provides as follows:

> 'Every application for an order for leave to serve a writ or notice on a defendant out of the jurisdiction shall be supported by evidence by affidavit or otherwise, showing in what place or country the defendant is or probably may be found, and the grounds on which the application is made.'

13.1.2.1 *Procedure*

In order to serve a writ of summons or notice of a writ of summons on a defendant outside of the jurisdiction, the plaintiff must make an application for leave to do so.[35] Every such application shall be supported by evidence by affidavit or otherwise showing in what place or country the defendant is or probably may be found, and the grounds on which the application is made.

The framework within which the courts of The Gambia consider the grant of leave to serve out of the jurisdiction appears to be derived from earlier English rules of court[36] set out below. In view of this affinity with earlier English rules of court and, indeed, in view of the affinity which the law of The Gambia has

[31] Defined in O VIII, r 8(2) as 'a party for the time being entitled to or interested in a mortgage'.

[32] Defined in O VIII, r 8(2) as 'a party for the time being entitled to or interested in property subject to a mortgage'.

[33] Defined in O VIII, r 8(2) as 'a mortgage, charge or lien of any description'.

[34] It will be noted that there is no provision made for the court to permit service of the writ on a defendant who is present out of the jurisdiction if the action is one to enforce a foreign judgment; Frimpong Oppong 'Recognition and enforcement of foreign judgments in Commonwealth African countries' (2014) XV *Yearbook of Private International Law* 365 at 372.

[35] Order VIII, r 9.

[36] The English Rules of the Supreme Court, 1883 and, by extension, the later editions and versions of these Rules.

with the law of England generally, it is likely that when considering the matters referred to in this section, a court in The Gambia may derive some assistance from the English authorities.

Set out below, therefore, is guidance which is drawn from the English authorities in which the equivalent rules have been considered.

The English equivalents of The Gambia's Order VIII, rules 8 and 9, have been the subject of judicial consideration at the highest level in England. In *Seaconsar Far East Ltd v Bank Markazi Jomhouri Islami Iran*,[37] the House of Lords considered the interaction of Order XI, rules 1(1) and 4, of the Rules of the Supreme Court (the equivalent to Gambian Order VIII, rules 8 and 9). Lord Goff (with whom the other Lords agreed) reviewed the authorities on the question what a plaintiff under Order XI was required to show on an application for leave to serve a writ out of the jurisdiction and found that the plaintiff was required to show, first, that the cause of action deposed to in the evidence in support of the application fell within the provisions of rule 1(1) and, second, that on the merits of the case there was a serious question to be tried. On the question of the standard to which these issues were required to be shown, Lord Goff stated:[38]

> 'A judge faced with a question of leave to serve proceedings out of the jurisdiction under Order 11 will in practice have to consider both (1) whether jurisdiction has been sufficiently established, on the criterion of the good arguable case laid down in *Korner's* case, under one of the paragraphs of rule 1(1), and (2) whether there is a serious issue to be tried, so as to enable him to exercise his discretion to grant leave, before he goes on to consider the exercise of that discretion, with particular reference to the issue of forum conveniens.'

The first of these matters was held to correspond to the requirement in Order XI, rule 4, that 'no such leave shall be granted unless it shall be made sufficiently to appear to the Court or Judge that the case is a proper one for service out of the jurisdiction under this Order'[39] and the second was a threshold requirement for the merits of the plaintiff's claim.[40]

---

[37] [1994] 1 AC 438 (HL(E)) (Lords Templeman, Griffiths, Goff, Browne-Wilkinson and Mustill).

[38] Ibid 456H–457B. See also the decision of the Privy Council in *Altimo Holdings and Investment Ltd v Kyrgyz Mobil Tel Ltd* [2012] 1 WLR 1804 (Lords Phillips PSC, Mance, Collins, Kerr and Clarke JJSC), *per* Lord Collins at para [71], confirming this statement of principle.

[39] *Seaconsar* 451A–B, 452A–B, 453D–G.

[40] *Seaconsar* 452D–E, 455A–C, 456G–H. Notwithstanding the separate treatment of the English O XI, r 4, in *Seaconsar* and the earlier authorities referred to therein, it is unclear whether the amendment in 1883 of O XI, r 3 (under the Rules of Court contained in Sch 1 to the Supreme Court of Judicature Act 1875) by the introduction of an expanded O XI, r 4, in the 1883 Rules of Court, was intended to produce this result. At the time the leading textbook on the Rules took the view that the amendment to include the wording 'no such leave shall be granted unless it shall be made sufficiently to appear to the Court or Judge that the case is a proper one for service out of the jurisdiction under this Order', was merely an amplification of the previous rule (see Wynne Baxter *Judicature Acts and Rules 1873–1883* 5 ed (1883) 176–7).

Thus, considering the English authorities, it is suggested that, analytically, it would be helpful to determine applications for leave to serve process out of the jurisdiction by applying the following, four-component approach.[41]

(1) *The formal requirements.* Has the plaintiff produced evidence satisfying the formal requirements of Order XIII, rule 9 (or English Order XI, rule 4)? In The Gambia, as has been noted above, the Rules of the High Court require a plaintiff, in his affidavit or other evidence in support of the application, to set out: (a) in what place or country the defendant is or probably may be found; and (b) the grounds on which the application is made.

(2) *The sufficiency requirement.* Under the English Order XI, rule 4, it was held in the *Seaconsar* case that the words 'and no such leave shall be granted unless it shall be made sufficiently to appear to the Court or Judge that the case is a proper one for service out of the jurisdiction under this Order' (which words do not appear in the Rules of the High Court in The Gambia) introduced a sufficiency requirement (or, in other words, a degree of proof requirement) such that the plaintiff must show that there is a good arguable case[42] that the case falls within one of the gateways under Order XI, rule 1(1).

---

[41] As summarised in the *English Supreme Court Practice 1965* (1999 ed) 93–4, paras 11/1/9–11/1/12. The commentary referred to in the *Supreme Court Practice* refers to three elements; in the text above the present authors include four elements, the additional element being the formal requirements of English r 4 and The Gambia's r 9.

[42] In *Canada Trust v Stolzenberg (No 2)* [2002] 1 AC 1 (HL(E)) (Lords Steyn, Hoffmann, Cooke, Hope and Hobhouse), *per* Lord Steyn (with whom the other Lords agreed) 13F, the House of Lords appeared to approve passages from the judgment of Waller LJ in the Court of Appeal in the same case ([1998] 1 WLR 547) including the following (at 555F–G): 'It is also right to remember that the "good arguable case" test, although obviously applicable to the ex parte stage, becomes of most significance at the inter partes stage where two arguments are being weighed in the interlocutory context which, as I have stressed, must not become a "trial". "Good arguable case" reflects in that context that one side has a much better argument on the material available. It is the concept which the phrase reflects on which it is important to concentrate, i.e. of the court being satisfied or as satisfied as it can be having regard to the limitations which an interlocutory process imposes that factors exist which allow the court to take jurisdiction.' In *Goldman Sachs International v Novo Banco SA* [2018] 1 WLR 3683 (Lords Mance, Sumption and Hodge, Lady Black and Lord Lloyd-Jones), the United Kingdom Supreme Court further clarified the correct understanding of the test in the *Canada Trust* case. Lord Sumption (with whom all the other members of the court agreed and in reliance on his own judgment in *Brownlie v Four Seasons Holdings Incorporated* [2018] 1 WLR 192) stated at para [9]: 'For the purpose of determining an issue about jurisdiction, the traditional test has been whether the claimant had "the better of the argument" on the facts going to jurisdiction. In *Brownlie v Four Seasons Holdings Inc* [2018] 1 WLR 192, para 7, this court reformulated the effect of that test as follows: "(i) that the claimant must supply a plausible evidential basis for the application of a relevant jurisdictional gateway; (ii) that if there is an issue of fact about it, or some other reason for doubting whether it applies, the court must take a view on the material available if it can reliably do so; but (iii) the nature of the issue and the limitations of the material available at the interlocutory stage may be such that no reliable assessment can be made, in which case there is a good arguable case for the application of the gateway if there is a plausible (albeit contested) evidential basis for it."'

It has been noted above that Order VIII, rule 9, is the Gambian equivalent of the English Order XI, rule 4, and that rule 9 omits the wording of Order XI, rule 4, set out in the preceding sub-paragraph[43] that was held in the *Seaconsar* case to introduce a sufficiency requirement. The question arises, therefore, whether, by reason of the omission of this wording, Order VIII, rule 9, of the Gambian High Court Rules should be construed as not imposing a requirement that the plaintiff should show a good arguable case that the case falls within one of the gateways under Order VIII, rule 8.

It would seem to follow from this omission that a plaintiff under Order VIII, rule 9, must simply depose to the facts which bring the case within rule 8 and that the court must assess whether those facts are established to a degree less than a good arguable case. It is likely that this standard will be held to be a *prima facie* case.[44]

(3) *The merits requirement.* As a matter of English law, the plaintiff must demonstrate that there is a serious issue to be tried on the merits of the claim upon which the claimant relies. Lord Goff in *Seaconsar* stated[45] as follows:

> 'The court cannot resolve disputed questions of fact on affidavit evidence; and it is consistent with the statement of the law by Lord Davey that if, at the end of the day, there remains a substantial question of fact or law or both, arising on the facts disclosed by the affidavits, which the plaintiff bona fide desires to try, the court should, as a rule, allow the service of the writ. If this approach is correct, the standard of proof in respect of the cause of action can broadly be stated to be whether, on the affidavit evidence before the court, there is a serious question to be tried.'

(4) *The court's discretion.* As a matter of English law, once the above matters are established by the plaintiff, the court will proceed to consider the exercise of its discretion to allow service out of the jurisdiction. The court's discretion is exercised cautiously. As was stated by Pearson J in *Société Générale de Paris v Dreyfus Brothers*:[46]

---

[43] For the avoidance of doubt, 'and no such leave shall be granted unless it shall be made sufficiently to appear to the Court or Judge that the case is a proper one for service out of the jurisdiction under this Order'.

[44] A view supported by the notes to English O XI, r 4, in Lushington et al *The Yearly Supreme Court Practice 1900* (1900 ed), where the editors stated of the words in r 4, 'Made sufficiently to appear', that (at 172), 'The Court will not, on an application for leave, go into the merits of the case, but will grant leave if a sufficient *prima facie* case is made out' (citing *Badische Anilin und Soda Fabrik v Henry Johnson and Co* [1896] 1 Ch 25 (CA; Lindley, AL Smith and Rigby LJJ), *per* Lindley LJ at 28). In rules lacking the evaluative wording, 'made sufficiently to appear', the standard of *prima facie* case appears *a fortiori* appropriate.

[45] *Seaconsar* 452C–D.

[46] (1885) 29 Ch D 239 at 242–3; cited with approval by Lord Goff in *Seaconsar* at 455D.

> 'But of course it becomes a very serious question, and ought always to be considered a very serious question, whether or not, even in a case like that, it is necessary for the jurisdiction of the Court to be invoked, and whether this Court ought to put a foreigner, who owes no allegiance here, to the inconvenience and annoyance of being brought to contest his rights in this country, and I for one say, most distinctly, that I think this Court ought to be exceedingly careful before it allows a writ to be served out of the jurisdiction.'[47]

Turning back to the law of The Gambia, where the court grants leave to effect service out of the jurisdiction, the order giving such leave shall prescribe the mode of service and shall fix a date subsequent to such service as the return day, such date to depend on the place or country where or within which the writ (or, presumably, notice of the writ) is to be served and the court may receive an affidavit or statutory declaration of the service having been effected as *prima facie* evidence thereof.[48] Where the order directs that service is to be effected in a country outside the Commonwealth, the document for service shall be sealed with the seal of the High Court and signed by the Chief Justice.[49] In those circumstances, the document will be forwarded by the Chief Justice to the minister responsible for foreign affairs with a request for transmission for service through the proper diplomatic channel.[50]

It is very important that the processes set out in the previous paragraph are followed strictly.[51] Hence, where the Registrar of the High Court (rather than the Chief Justice) forwarded the documents to be served in a country outside the Commonwealth to the permanent secretary, rather than to the minister responsible for foreign affairs as required by Order VIII, rule 10(2), the Court of Appeal dismissed the subsequent application[52] made on the faith of this event. Instead, it ordered the Registrar of the High Court to take immediate steps to compile the 'relevant processes in this appeal, take them to the Chief justice for sealing, signature and forward [them] to the Minister [responsible for foreign affairs]'.[53]

Before any order granting leave to effect service out of the jurisdiction is made, the court may direct that the plaintiff or his legal representative file a written undertaking to be responsible for all expenses incurred in respect of effecting the

[47] The exercise of the court's discretion is dealt with in greater depth below, under the heading '*Forum non conveniens*'.

[48] Order VIII, r 10(1).

[49] Order VIII, r 10(2).

[50] Ibid.

[51] *Joseph Sarjuka Jobe v Jack Alderlifste* (2002–8) 2 GR 433 (Court of Appeal of The Gambia) (Agim PCA, sitting alone).

[52] The content of which does not appear from the report.

[53] It is submitted that the outcome in the case is not very satisfactory. It is one thing to ensure that parties comply with the Rules of the High Court; it is quite another to punish them for the failings of the court staff.

service and on receipt of the notification of the amount of such expenses to pay the same, or give security for the payment of such expenses in such other form as the Chief Justice may order.[54]

13.1.2.2 *Bases for service out of the jurisdiction*

The bases on which the court may grant permission which are of particular significance for present purposes are discussed below.

Given the material identity between the Gambian High Court Rules, Order VIII, rule 8, and Order XI, rule 1, of the English Rules of the Supreme Court 1883,[55] it would be unsurprising were a court in The Gambia to seek guidance on the interpretation of these rules in the English authorities, and that guidance is set out, where appropriate, below.

(1) Relief is sought against any person domiciled, or ordinarily resident, within the jurisdiction

The term 'person' in Order VIII, rule 8 includes any company or association or body of persons corporate or unincorporated.[56]

There is an absence of authority in The Gambia on the correct definition of 'domicile' and 'ordinary residence'. However, it is likely that, given: (1) the jurisprudential history of the legal systems of The Gambia and England; and (2) the received meaning in English law of the terms 'domicile' and 'ordinary residence', courts in The Gambia will have regard to English authority when interpreting both terms.[57]

Domicile has been authoritatively described in the following terms:[58]

> 'The notion which lies at the root of the concept of domicile is that of permanent home. "By domicile we mean home, the permanent home; and if you do not understand your permanent home I am afraid that no illustration drawn from foreign writers or foreign languages will very much help you to it." A person may be said to have his home in a country if he resides in it without any intention of at present removing from it permanently or for an indefinite period. But a person does not cease to have his home

[54] Order VIII, r 10(3).

[55] The rule of the English Rules of the Supreme Court regulating service out of the jurisdiction prior to 1999 (when the English Civil Procedure Rules came into effect) was O XI. Under the Rules of the Supreme Court 1883 and the Rules of the Supreme Court 1965, which superseded the 1883 Rules, O XI, r 1 provided for service out of the jurisdiction. As mentioned above, O VIII, r 8 in The Gambia, is materially identical to O XI, r 1 of the Rules of the Supreme Court 1883.

[56] Section 3 of the Interpretation Act 1966 (Act 10 of 1966, now Cap 4:01 of the Laws of The Gambia, 2009).

[57] See generally on the meaning of 'domicile', *Dicey, Morris and Collins on the Conflict of Laws* 15 ed (2012) vol 1, r 4, para 6–004.

[58] *Dicey, Morris and Collins on the Conflict of Laws* 15 ed (2012) vol 1, r 4, para 6R-001, quoting from *Whicker v Hume* (1858) 7 HLC 124 at 160.

in a country merely because he is temporarily resident elsewhere; and a person who has formed the intention of leaving a country does not cease to have his home in it until he acts according to that intention.'

Given the affinity between the Rules of the High Court and the English Rules of the Supreme Court,[59] it may also be of relevance to note that 'domicile' was defined in the notes to the latter as follows:[60]

> 'In general the domicile of a person is in the country in which he has his permanent home (see Dicey, *Conflict of Law*, 7th ed., Chap. 6), the country in which his habitation is fixed without any present intention of removing (Re *Craignish*, [1892] 3 Ch. 180, C.A.; *Huntly v. Gaskell*, [1906] A.C. 56; *Casdagli v. C.*, [1919] A.C. 145). No person can at any time be without a domicile or have more than one domicile. The domicile of origin remains until a new domicile of choice has been adopted (*Bell v. Kennedy* (1868), L.R. 1 Sc. App. 307, H.L.; *Udny v. Udny* (1869), ibid, 441, H.L., *Winans v. A.-G.*, [1904] A.C. 287, H.L.).'

The 'domicile' of a legal person has been described as follows:[61]

> 'A corporation is domiciled where it is registered, if the law requires it to be registered, and if it does not it is domiciled in the country by whose law it is incorporated (Dicey, *Conflict of Laws*, 7th ed., p. 477). A corporation is 'resident' and 'ordinarily resident' where its central management and control is exercised ....

The term 'ordinarily resident' has been explained as follows:[62]

> 'It has sometimes been said that "ordinary residence" means nothing more or less than "residence", but it is submitted that the better view is that the adjective does add something, an element of continuity, order, or settled purpose.'

(2) The action is one brought against the defendant to enforce ... or otherwise effect a contract or to recover damages or other relief for or in respect of a breach of a contract:

(1) made within the jurisdiction; or

(2) made by or through an agent trading or residing within the jurisdiction on behalf of a principal trading or residing out of the jurisdiction; or

(3) by its terms or by implication to be governed by the law in force in the jurisdiction;

---

[59] The rule of the English Rules of the Supreme Court regulating service out of the jurisdiction prior to 1999 (when the Civil Procedure Rules came into effect) was O XI. Under the Rules of the Supreme Court 1883 and the Rules of the Supreme Court 1965, which superseded the 1883 Rules, O XI, r 1 provided for service out of the jurisdiction where the defendant was domiciled or ordinarily resident within the jurisdiction.

[60] The Rules of the Supreme Court 1883 (1961 ed) 144. Under the Rules of the Supreme Court 1883 and the Rules of the Supreme Court 1965, which superseded the 1883 Rules, O XI, r 1 provided for service out of the jurisdiction where the defendant was domiciled or ordinarily resident within the jurisdiction.

[61] Rules of the Supreme Court 1883 (1961 ed) 145. The same meaning followed through to the 1965 Rules of the Supreme Court.

[62] *Dicey, Morris and Collins on the Conflict of Laws* 15 ed (2012) vol 1, para 6–160.

> or is brought against the defendant in respect of a breach committed within the jurisdiction of a contract wherever made, even though such breach was preceded or accompanied by a breach out of the jurisdiction which rendered impossible the performance of the part of the contract which ought to have been performed within the jurisdiction.

It is likely that, in the apparent absence of authority in The Gambia itself and in other jurisdictions in the region (principally Nigeria) on the construction and application of Order VIII, rule 8(e), a court in The Gambia will be guided by the academic and judicial authorities on the construction and application of the (former) equivalent provision in the English Rules of the Supreme Court.[63]

A concise statement of that law is as follows[64] (and should be adapted substituting 'The Gambia' for 'England'):

'**(i) Where a contract is made in England**

11–181

If the parties enter into negotiations by correspondence from different countries, the contract is made where the letter of acceptance is posted. But in commercial transactions today communication by telephone, telex, fax and electronic mail is much more common than by post. It is now well established, following the decision of the Court of Appeal in *Entores v Miles Far East Corp* (which was approved by the House of Lords [*Brinkibon Ltd v. Stahag Stahl und Stahlwarenhandelsgesellschaft mbH* [1983] 2 AC 34]) that if the parties use "instantaneous" means of communication such as telephone, fax or electronic mail, the contract is made where the acceptance is communicated to the offeror. It has been held that if a contract made in England contains a submission to arbitration in a foreign country, an action in England at common law to enforce the foreign arbitration award is within this part of the clause. The contract must actually be made in England as that phrase is understood in English law. It is not sufficient if it merely says that it shall be deemed to be so made, though this may be sufficient to make it one which is governed by English law. A contract may be made in England within the meaning of this clause although it was preceded by a less formal agreement made abroad, or if it was originally made in England, but amended abroad.

(ii) Where a contract is made by or through an agent trading or residing in England

11–182

The clause says "by or through" an agent, not "by" an agent. Hence the case is within the clause, although the agent has no authority to make contracts on behalf of his foreign principal, but only has authority to obtain orders and transmit them to his principal for acceptance or rejection. This part of the clause is designed to bring within Rule 34 foreigners who transact business in England by or through agents, and consequently

[63] Order XI, r 1(e) and 1(d) respectively: Rules of the Supreme Court 1883 (1961 ed) and 1965.

[64] *Dicey, Morris and Collins on the Conflict of Laws* 15 ed (2012) vol 1, r 34, paras 11–181–11–187.

it does not apply where the agent's principal is the claimant. Hence a claimant cannot invoke clause (6)(ii) [Order XIII, rule 8(e)(ii)] where the contract was made by or through his agent.

11–183

If proceedings are brought by consignees of a cargo against foreign ship-owners under the bills of lading, the case is not within this part of the clause if the charterparty (but not the bills of lading) was made by or through agents of the shipowners in England, even though it refers to the bills of lading and was made by charterers acting on behalf of the consignees. It may be otherwise, however, if the charterers are identical with the consignees…

(iii) Where a contract is governed by English law

11–186

…

11–187

Although the fact that a contract is governed by English law is an important factor in the exercise of the discretion under this head in favour of the English forum, it is not conclusive. This head of jurisdiction was described as exorbitant in *Amin Rasheed Shipping Corp v Kuwait Insurance Co*, where the House of Lords held that in the circumstances it was not appropriate for the English court to determine a dispute involving a marine insurance policy governed by English law when the Kuwaiti courts were the *forum conveniens*. Until that decision it was generally thought that the fact that a contract was governed by English law was in itself sufficient to justify leave. But now the claimant has a heavier burden. In *Amin Rasheed* Lord Diplock suggested that, in order to justify leave under this head, the plaintiff had to show that justice could not be obtained by him in the foreign court, or could only be obtained at excessive cost, delay or inconvenience. But it was subsequently held that Lord Diplock was merely giving examples, and was not providing an exhaustive list, of the relevant factors. The court has to consider all factors, and the fact that English law is the applicable law may be of great importance, or it may be of little consequence as seen in the context of the whole case. Thus if there is likely to be no dispute on matters of law or construction, or if the law of the foreign forum is substantially the same as English law, the fact that English law is the applicable law will be of little weight. But where an issue of English public policy arises in relation to a contract which is (or may be) governed by English law, it is desirable that it should be decided by the English court; conversely, where the foreign court may apply its own public policy to defeat a claim based on a contract governed by English law, that too is a reason for the English court taking jurisdiction. If the claimant has alternative remedies in contract and tort upon the same facts, he can choose his remedy.'

(3) The action is founded on a tort committed within the jurisdiction

There is a paucity of authority in The Gambia (and other Anglophone African jurisdictions in the region)[65] on the construction and application of Order VIII, rule 8(f). As with the construction and application of Order VIII, rule 8(e), it is likely that, in the absence of authority in The Gambia on the subject, a court in The Gambia will be guided by the academic and judicial authorities on the construction and application of the former (equivalent) provision in the English Rules of the Supreme Court.[66]

A statement of the law is as follows:[67]

> **'11–212**
>
> ... As both the Privy Council [in *Distillers Co (Bio-chemicals) Ltd v. Thompson* [1971] AC 458] and the Supreme Court of Canada [*Moran v. Pyle National (Canada) Ltd* (1973) 43 D.L.R. (3d) 239] have pointed out, the competing theories for the determination of the place of a tort have been that (i) all ingredients of the cause of action must have occurred within the jurisdiction, or (ii) the last ingredient, the event which completes a cause of action, must have occurred within the jurisdiction, or (iii) the act which the defendant committed must have occurred within the jurisdiction.
>
> **11–213**
>
> In *Distillers Co Ltd v Thompson* the Privy Council adopted the test of the place where in substance the act or omission occurred which gave the plaintiff his cause of action. So that where the essence of the complaint was failure to warn the consumer of the dangers of a product (rather than the faulty manufacture of the product) the cause of action was held to have arisen at the place where the failure to warn occurred; and the torts of negligent and fraudulent misrepresentation, where the negligent or fraudulent statement was communicated from one country to another, were held to have been committed where the statement was received and acted upon. Prior to the adoption of that test, but consistently with it, it had been held that the tort of defamation was committed where the defamatory statements were published and not where they were posted or uttered.'

13.1.2.3 *Submission to the jurisdiction*

Two circumstances must be distinguished under the title submission to the jurisdiction: first, where submission is alleged in extant proceedings in The Gambia; second, where the defendant has agreed (usually by contractual provision) to submit to the jurisdiction of the court in advance of a dispute arising.

[65] Specifically, in Nigeria, given the closeness of the ties between those legal systems.

[66] Order XI, r 1(ee) and 1(f) respectively: Rules of the Supreme Court 1883 (1961 ed) and 1965.

[67] *Dicey, Morris and Collins on the Conflict of Laws* 15 ed (2012) vol 1, r 34, paras 11–212–11–213.

13.1.2.3.1 Submission by appearance

The Rules of the High Court do not allow for the defendant to enter a conditional appearance with a view to contesting the jurisdiction of the court. In these circumstances, a defendant must be careful not to 'take a step' in proceedings[68] and so submit to the jurisdiction of the court.

Upon service of the writ of summons and other documents as are required,[69] the defendant must within not less than five days before the date fixed for the hearing notify the Registrar of the High Court that he or she intends to defend the suit and send with such notification an affidavit setting out the grounds of defence on which he or she intends to rely.[70] If the defendant does not do that, unless the court is satisfied that the defendant has a good defence to the action on the merits, or has disclosed such facts as may be deemed sufficient to entitle him or her to defend, the suit shall be heard as an undefended suit.[71]

The High Court (Amendment) Rules 2009 have introduced some additional matters which must be considered in order to convey a complete account of the law currently in force in The Gambia. It is submitted that they do not interact completely harmoniously with such of the existing Rules of the High Court as remain unaltered thereby. Hence, the requirement to notify (as set out in the previous paragraph) and[72] file a statement of defence, accompanied by affidavits or testimonies of persons the defendant intends to call during the trial and all documents which the defendant relies on or intends to rely on in the trial of the suit, might be thought to increase the risk of the defendant's being taken to have submitted to the jurisdiction of the court.

Indeed, to complicate matters a little further, where a defendant fails to file the statement of defence within the time specified, and, having obtained permission to file within a period of a further 14 days,[73] fails to comply again, he shall be deemed to have no defence to the case and the court shall proceed to determine the case on the basis of the plaintiff's statement of claim.[74]

In these circumstances, where a defendant is mandated to file a statement of defence, it would seem unfortunate to conclude that the filing of that defence amounts to a submission to the court's jurisdiction. If this is the conclusion, it presents the defendant with an invidious choice: fail to enter a defence and have the court determine the matter on the basis of the plaintiff's statement of claim or enter a defence and be deemed to have submitted to the jurisdiction of the court.

---

[68] *ESB International Ltd v Utilities Holding Corp* [1997–2001] GR 297 (Court of Appeal of The Gambia) (Chomba P; Lartey and Gelaga King JJA).

[69] As set out in the main text above.

[70] Order II, r 9.

[71] Ibid.

[72] Rule 3(2) of the High Court (Amendment) Rules 2009

[73] Rule 3(3) of the High Court (Amendment) Rules 2009.

[74] Rule 4(3)(a) of the High Court (Amendment) Rules 2009.

Rule 3(7) of the High Court (Amendment) Rules 2009 partially assuages these concerns. It provides that, after the filing of a defence and accompanying documents, and after service of the same on the plaintiff, the judge shall set a date for a pre-trial conference. At that conference, the judge shall 'hear and determine any objection to the suit on such grounds as lack of jurisdiction'. The pre-trial conference is hence held only after the filing of the written statement of defence. Questions pertaining to the jurisdiction of the court in The Gambia are therefore only answered after the written statement of defence has been filed. Consequently, in such circumstances it would seem unlikely that simply because the defendant has filed a written statement of defence, he would be deemed to have submitted to the jurisdiction of the court.

That said, it is difficult to be prescriptive about the current state of the law in The Gambia on this issue. Hence, parties should take a conservative approach towards, and a court should take a high degree of care when defining, the expression 'taking a step in proceedings'.

In *ESB International Ltd v Utilities Holding Corp*,[75] the court considered the meaning of 'taking a step in the proceedings'. Here, the plaintiffs (the respondents in the Court of Appeal) and the defendants (the appellants in the Court of Appeal) had entered into a management contract agreement. That agreement contained an arbitration clause, stipulating that any difference or dispute should be settled by arbitrators named in accordance with the rules of the International Chamber of Commerce. A dispute then arose and the plaintiffs commenced proceedings, seeking an injunction restraining the defendants from withdrawing a set sum from their bank account. In response, the defendants, without entering a conditional appearance, filed a motion, supported by affidavit, seeking the plaintiffs' action be stayed, pending a reference to arbitration.

In allowing the defendants' appeal, the Court of Appeal concluded that section 5 of the Arbitration Act[76] would be construed as referring only to

[75] [1997–2001] GR 297.

[76] Act 6 of 1955. At the time of the litigation, this was the applicable statute. Section 5 thereof provided that: 'If any party to a submission, or any person claiming through or under him, commences any legal proceedings in any court against any other party to the submission, or any other person claiming through or under him, in respect of any matter agreed to be referred, any party to such legal proceedings may at any time after appearance, and before delivering any pleadings or taking other steps in the proceedings, apply to that court to stay the proceedings, and that court if satisfied that there is no sufficient reason why the matter should not be referred in accordance with the submission, and that the applicant was at the time when the proceedings were commenced and still remains, ready and willing to do all things necessary to the proper conduct of the arbitration, may make an order staying the proceedings.' This has now been replaced by the Alternative Dispute Resolution Act 2005 (Act 6 of 2006, now Cap 6:08 of the Laws of The Gambia, 2009), s 12 of which provides: '(1) A court before which proceedings are brought in a matter which is the subject of an arbitration agreement shall, if a party so requests not later than when submitting his or her first statement on the substance of the dispute, stay those proceedings and refer the parties to arbitration; (2) A court shall not stay proceedings under subsection (1) if it finds that — (a) the agreement is null and void, inoperative or

entering an appearance before delivering any pleadings: the defendants did not have to enter a conditional appearance before they could apply for a stay of court proceedings.[77] The Court of Appeal further held that the defendants' filing an affidavit showing cause in the circumstances of the case did not amount to a defence pleading, thus did not amount to 'taking a step in the proceedings'. The defendants had not submitted to the jurisdiction of the court.[78]

It is submitted that the difficulty with this decision is the indication that filing a pleaded defence would amount to taking a step in proceedings, since this could be held to be a 'substantive' step taken by a party. Indeed, the High Court of The Gambia had previously refused a stay of court proceedings in favour of arbitral proceedings on the basis that the party making the request had taken a fresh step in the proceedings by giving notice, after the court had ordered pleadings, of an intention to file a defence and counterclaim.[79]

Notwithstanding and outside the context of arbitration, the Court of Appeal of The Gambia has held that, in the context of a matrimonial dispute, entering an appearance under protest, after service of (in that case) a petition, did not amount to a submission to the court's jurisdiction.[80] Anin P, giving the judgment of the court, stated:[81]

> 'The husband's counsel's document in fact filed was a 'memorandum of appearance under protest' and not an entry of appearance simpliciter. There is, in fact and in law, a whole world of difference between the two; and in the document actually filed, the [husband] went further therein to explain why he was entering an appearance under protest [because the husband was challenging the jurisdiction of the court]. Nothing could be more explicit or self-explanatory than that! And the primary object of a pleading was thereby served; namely the [wife] was duly put on notice; and not taken by surprise but warned of the husband's imminent preliminary or answer to the petition.'

---

incapable of being performed; or (b) there is not, in fact, any dispute between the parties with regard to the matters agreed to be referred; (3) Where proceedings referred to in subsection (1) have been brought, arbitral proceedings may nevertheless be commenced or continued, and an award may be made, while the issue is pending before the court.'

77 [1997–2001] GR 297 at 301.

78 In reaching its conclusion, the Court of Appeal relied on the decision of the English High Court in *Zalinoff v Hammond* [1898] 2 Ch 92 (Stirling J). There, Stirling J held: 'What is a "step in proceedings" which will preclude a party to an action from moving to refer the case to arbitration? In *Ives and Barker v Williams* (1894) 2 Ch 484 Lindley LJ said: "The authorities shew that a step in the proceedings means something in the nature of an application to the court, and not mere talk between solicitors' clerks, nor the writing of letters, but the taking of some step, such as taking out a summons or something of that kind, which is, in the technical sense, a step in proceedings." It seems to me that the mere filing of affidavits in defence to a motion for a receiver is not in the nature of an application to the court and, consequently, not a "step in proceedings" within the meaning of the section. By such a step is meant a substantive step taken by a party.'

79 *Sogea v Aziz Sarr T/A Janha Construction Ltd* (CS 342/92 SNO 28).

80 *Mary R Siwingwa v Nicholas R Siwingwa* [1994] GR 276 (Court of Appeal of The Gambia) (Anin P; Chomba and N'Jie JJA).

81 Ibid 287–8.

It is submitted that the state of the authorities on the issue of submission by way of appearance in The Gambia is confused and confusing. That confusion is made more apparent (and worse) by the High Court (Amendment) Rules 2009 which seemingly require the defendant, upon service of the writ, to file a written statement of defence, which, apparently, leaves the defendant with an invidious choice. It is submitted that the present law can be stated in the following propositions:

(1) In the context of arbitration, a court before which proceedings are brought in a matter which is the subject of an arbitration agreement shall, if a party so requests not later than when submitting his or her first statement on the substance of the dispute, stay those proceedings and refer the parties to arbitration;[82]

(2) A defendant who has been served with the writ and other necessary documentation will not be taken to have submitted to the jurisdiction of the court if he makes very clear (eg by filing a defence under protest) that he disputes the jurisdiction of the court.[83] That said, where the defendant does make clear that he disputes the jurisdiction of the court but defends on the merits, it is not clear whether that will amount to 'taking a step in proceedings' (though it is submitted that it cannot, reasonably, do so, given the imperative language of rule 3(2) of the High Court (Amendment) Rules 2009); and

(3) A defendant who has been served with the writ and other necessary documentation will be taken to have submitted to the jurisdiction if he files a written statement of defence on the merits of the case without challenging the jurisdiction of the court. He cannot challenge the jurisdiction of the court thereafter: it will be too late.[84]

13.1.2.3.2 Submission by agreement

13.1.2.3.2.1 *Jurisdiction clauses*

There is a lack of authority in The Gambia as to the approach which the courts will take towards clauses ostensibly requiring disputes to be settled in a foreign jurisdiction. That said, it is possible to infer the court's likely approach to such question from the approach it adopts to arbitration clauses of a similar ilk.

---

[82] Section 12 of the Alternative Dispute Resolution Act 2005 (now Cap 6:08 of the Laws of the Gambia, 2009).

[83] *Mary R Siwingwa v Nicholas R Siwingwa* [1994] GR 276 (Court of Appeal of The Gambia) (Anin P; Chomba and N'Jie JJA).

[84] *Sogea v Aziz Sarr T/A Janha Construction Ltd* (CS 342/92 SNO 28).

When faced with a clause stating that disputes should be settled by way of arbitration, a court in The Gambia will, in the exercise of its discretion, seek to uphold that clause, because, as it has been put: 'it is a *prima facie* duty of the court to act upon the agreement between the parties.'[85] In consequence, it is likely that a court in The Gambia will follow the same general approach when confronted with a contractual clause, whereby parties agree to submit their disputes to the jurisdiction of a foreign court.[86]

Given that courts in The Gambia treat as persuasive judgments of courts in Nigeria, it is likely that Gambian courts will adopt the same approach towards the enforcement of jurisdiction clauses as courts in that jurisdiction. Traditionally,[87] Nigerian courts have been content to adopt the reasoning of the English High Court, as set out in *Owners of cargo lately laden on board the ship or vessel Eleftheria v The Eleftheria (Owners), The Eleftheria.* [88] There, Brandon J considered earlier authorities and set out a statement of the principles applicable to an application for a stay of proceedings where there was a jurisdiction clause relied on by the party seeking the stay.

In *The Eleftheria* the jurisdiction clause provided: 'Any dispute arising under this bill of lading shall be decided in the country where the carrier has his principal place of business [Greece].' The owners of cargo on board the *Eleftheria* commenced proceedings in England and the shipowners applied for a stay of those proceedings. In staying the proceedings in favour of the Greek courts Brandon J set out the principles on the basis of which a stay may be granted:[89]

> '(1) Where plaintiffs sue in England in breach of an agreement to refer disputes to a foreign court, and the defendants apply for a stay, the English court, assuming the claim to be otherwise within its jurisdiction, is not bound to grant a stay but has a discretion whether to do so or not. (2) The discretion should be exercised by granting a stay unless strong cause for not doing so is shown. (3) The burden of proving such strong cause is on the plaintiffs. (4) In exercising its discretion the court should take into account all the circumstances of the particular case. (5) In particular, but without prejudice to (4), the following matters, where they arise, may properly be regarded:—(a) In what country the evidence on the issues of fact is situated, or more readily available, and the effect of that on the relative convenience and expense of trial as between the English and foreign courts, (b) Whether the law of the foreign court applies and, if so, whether it differs from

[85] *ESB International Ltd v Utilities Holding Corp* [1997–2001] GR 297 at 303, where Chomba P cited with approval the decision of the English Court of Appeal in Chancery in *Willesford v Watson* (1873) 8 Ch App 473 (Lord Selborne, LC, Sir W. M. James and Sir G. Mellish, LJJ).

[86] This is the approach adopted by Nigerian courts and courts in The Gambia are apt to consider Nigerian jurisprudence as being highly persuasive.

[87] *Nika Fishing Co Ltd v Lavina Corp* [2008] 16 NWLR 509 (Sup Ct) (Tobi, Oguntade, Mohammed, Tabai and Ogebe JJSC). For a more in-depth treatment of this decision, see the relevant section of the chapter on Nigeria.

[88] [1970] P 94; [1969] 1 Lloyd's Rep 237 (QBD, Comm Ct).

[89] [1970] P 94 at 99G–100C.

> English law in any material respects, (c) With what country either party is connected, and how closely, (d) Whether the defendants genuinely desire trial in the foreign country, or are only seeking procedural advantages, (e) Whether the plaintiffs would be prejudiced by having to sue in the foreign court because they would: (i) be deprived of security for their claim; (ii) be unable to enforce any judgment obtained; (iii) be faced with a time-bar not applicable in England; or (iv) for political, racial, religious or other reasons be unlikely to get a fair trial.'

It is likely that *The Eleftheria*, as applied by the courts in Nigeria, will be regarded as the authoritative approach to adopt by courts in The Gambia when confronted with a jurisdiction clause that is controversial in its application to the facts.[90]

13.1.2.3.2.2 *Application for service out of the jurisdiction based on a jurisdiction clause*

One question that arises is the statutory basis on which a court in The Gambia may assume jurisdiction over a cause where a plaintiff in The Gambia applies for service on the defendant out of the jurisdiction based on a jurisdiction clause in an agreement.

In the English Rules of the Supreme Court,[91] Order XI, rule 1(1)(d)(i)–(iv), the sub-rule governing service out of the jurisdiction in cases concerned with contract contains an additional sub-sub-paragraph to the equivalent provisions in the Rules of the High Court, Order VIII, rule 8(e)(i)–(iii). That additional sub-sub-rule provides as follows: 'The claim is made to enforce ... a contract which ... (iv) contains a term to the effect that the High Court shall have jurisdiction to hear and determine any action in respect of the contract.' This additional provision was included in the English rules in order to reverse the decision of the Court of Appeal in *British Wagon Co Ltd v Gray*.[92]

Where the defendant is not present within the jurisdiction and where no other provision of Order VIII, rule 8 is applicable to the case, the question is whether a court in The Gambia has power to order service out of the jurisdiction solely on the basis that the agreement between the parties contains a jurisdiction clause in favour of the courts in The Gambia. It would seem not and in such a case there

---

[90] Adopting such an approach, of course, would demonstrate a divergence between the law of The Gambia (and the law of Nigeria) and the law of England on this point. English law now adopts an approach which accords greater respect to the jurisdiction clause: *Donohue v Armco Inc* [2002] 1 All ER 749 (HL (E)) (Lords Bingham, Mackay, Nicholls, Hobhouse and Scott), where Lord Bingham, at 754G–J, held: 'Where the dispute is between two contracting parties, A and B, and A sues in a non-contractual forum, and A's claims fall within the scope of the exclusive jurisdiction clause in their contract, and the interests of other parties are not involved, effect will in all probability be given to the clause.'

[91] Rules of the Supreme Court 1965 (the successor provision to O XI, r 2(a), of the Rules of the Supreme Court 1883 (1961 ed), introduced by amendment in 1920).

[92] [1896] 1 QB 35 (English Court of Appeal) (Lord Esher MR; Lopes and Kay LJJ).

would be no basis on which a court in The Gambia could validly make an order for service of the defendant out of the jurisdiction.

13.1.2.4 Lis alibi pendens

The approach of the courts in The Gambia to concurrent proceedings concerning the same subject-matter and parties within and outside the jurisdiction is not clear. It is likely, however, that a court in The Gambia, following English or Nigerian[93] principles, would conclude that the court has power to stay proceedings before it where the defendant shows:[94] '(i) the plaintiff cannot obtain any procedural advantage from the action in the foreign court, and (ii) the applicant [ie the defendant] is being unnecessarily vexed by the two concurrent actions.' The defendant must show the combination of no juridical advantage and vexation/oppression.

13.1.2.5 Forum non conveniens

Neither the grounds contained in Order XVIII, rule 8, nor the evidence which the plaintiff has to adduce in support of his application (as set out in Order VIII, rule 9), provide that, in order to obtain leave to serve the defendant out of the jurisdiction, the plaintiff must show, or the court must be satisfied, that The Gambia is the appropriate place in which to bring the action. In short, the Rules of the High Court seemingly do not contain a reference to the principle of *forum conveniens*.

That said, it is clear that a court in The Gambia has a discretion as to whether to grant leave to serve process on a defendant outside of the jurisdiction or not. It may well be that, as part of that discretion, a court could consider whether The Gambia is itself the appropriate forum in which to litigate. In any event, it seems likely that a party who has been served with process outside the jurisdiction may apply to a court in The Gambia to stay proceedings on the basis that The Gambia is not the appropriate forum for the resolution of the dispute between the parties and that some other forum is the more appropriate one.

If a court in The Gambia adopted any part of the approach which has been set out in the previous paragraph, it is likely, given the history of the legal system in The Gambia, that it would have cognisance of the principles to be derived from English case law, which may be summarised as follows.

---

[93] *Jammal v Abdalla Hashem* [1975] 2 ALR Comm 141 (High Court (Lagos State)) (George J). That a court in The Gambia would do this is made more likely by the decision in *Bourgi v Withams H/V* (2002–2008) 2 GR 38 (Court of Appeal of The Gambia) (Agim PCA; Yeboah JA and Dordzie AGJA).

[94] *Jammal v Abdalla Hashem* [1975] 2 ALR Comm 141 at 147:1–4, quoting from the headnote to *Ionian Bank Ltd v Couvreur* [1969] 1 WLR 781.

Historically, the English courts seemed always to have held that a major factor in the exercise of the discretion to grant leave to serve out of the jurisdiction or stay proceedings already served out of the jurisdiction was whether the English proceedings were vexatious and oppressive. The expression 'vexatious and oppressive' bore a wide meaning and extended to considerations related to the comparative convenience of proceedings in England as opposed to a particular foreign forum. For example, in *Logan v Bank of Scotland (No 2)*,[95] the Court of Appeal granted an application staying proceedings served as of right in England in favour of Scotland. Sir Gorell Barnes P stated:[96]

> 'Now, it is true that the Courts of this country have not gone so far as to express themselves upon the question of convenience in terms similar to those used in the Scotch cases, though, as I have already noticed, it may be doubted whether there is any substantial difference between the two. Yet it seems to me clear that the inconvenience of trying a case in a particular tribunal may be such as practically to work a serious injustice upon a defendant and be vexatious. This would probably not be so if the difference of trying in one country rather than in another were merely measured by some extra expense; but where the difficulty for the defendant of trying in the country in which the action is brought is such that it is impracticable to properly try the case by reason of the difficulty of procuring the attendance of busy men as witnesses, and keeping them during trial, and of having to deal with masses of books, documents, and papers which are not in the country where the action is brought, and of dealing with law foreign to the tribunal, it appears to me that a case of vexation in some circumstances may be made out if the plaintiff chooses to sue in that country rather than in that where everybody is and where all the witnesses and material for the trial are.'

In *Spiliada Maritime Corp v Cansulex Ltd*,[97] the House of Lords decided:[98]

> 'The basic principle is that a stay will only be granted on the ground of forum non conveniens where the court is satisfied that there is some other available forum, having competent jurisdiction, which is the appropriate forum for the trial of the action, i.e. in which the case may be tried more suitably for the interests of all the parties and the ends of justice.'

The English courts will, therefore, refuse leave to serve a writ out of the jurisdiction or (in a case where leave has been granted but the defendant enters a conditional appearance) will stay English proceedings if England is not the *forum conveniens*.[99]

---

[95] [1906] 1 KB 141 (CA) (Sir Gorell Barnes, President, Collins MR, and Romer LJ).

[96] Ibid 151–2. This was a decision under the Rules of the Supreme Court 1883.

[97] [1987] AC 460 (Lords Keith, Templeman, Griffiths, Mackay and Goff).

[98] Ibid 476C, *per* Lord Goff, with whom the other Lords of Appeal agreed (Lord Templeman delivering a concurring opinion). A decision under the 1965 Rules of the Supreme Court.

[99] See, generally, *Dicey, Morris and Collins on the Conflict of Laws* 15 ed (2012) vol 1, r 38(2)–(3), para 12–007 et seq; r 38 states the modern English law as follows, inter alia: '(2) ... an English court has power to order a stay of proceedings on the basis that England is an inappropriate forum (forum non conveniens) if:

Given that the discretion when considering whether to grant leave to serve out of the jurisdiction is not fettered in this respect, it may well be open to a court in The Gambia to take the view that it is appropriate to take into account considerations of convenience (though probably better labelled as 'propriety') when determining whether to grant leave to serve out of the jurisdiction (or whether to grant a stay of proceedings already commenced).[100]

13.2 Enforcement of foreign judgments

It is unclear whether a foreign judgment may be enforced at common law in The Gambia. By contrast, there is no doubt that a foreign judgment may be enforced pursuant to statutory regimes currently in force in that jurisdiction.

13.2.1 Enforcement at common law

There is a tension between such authority as exists in The Gambia and the views of commentators as to whether or not a judgment creditor of a foreign judgment may enforce such a judgment at common law in The Gambia.[101]

In *Bourgi v Withams*,[102] the plaintiff (the appellant before the Court of Appeal), a Gambian company, had entered into a contract for the sale of goods with the defendants (the respondents before the Court of Appeal), which were incorporated in the Netherlands. Despite the plaintiff's payment, the first defendant suspended delivery of the goods on account of the plaintiff's alleged non-compliance with the terms of the contract.

The contract stipulated that the general trade conditions deposited at the Chamber of Commerce in Eindhoven would govern the parties' relationship. The contract also contained an exclusive jurisdiction clause in favour of the Rotterdam courts.

(a) the defendant shows there to be another court with competent jurisdiction which is clearly or distinctly more appropriate than England for the trial of the action, and (b) it is not unjust that the claimant be deprived of the right to trial in England. (3) In considering whether to assume jurisdiction in any of the cases mentioned in Rule 34 (service out of the jurisdiction with the permission of the court) the court will generally require the claimant to show England to be the most appropriate forum for the trial of the claim.'

[100] That *forum conveniens* principles, or principles akin thereto, are known to the courts of The Gambia is made clear by reference to *Bourgi v Withams H/V* (2002–8) 2 GR 38 at 43 (Court of Appeal of The Gambia) (Agim PCA; Yeboah JA and Dordzie AGJA).

[101] If a judgment creditor of a foreign judgment may enforce that foreign judgment at common law in The Gambia, it must be remembered that O VIII, r 8 of the Rules of the High Court does not allow a court in The Gambia to permit service of the writ on a defendant who is present outside the jurisdiction where the action is one to enforce a foreign judgment; Frimpong Oppong 'Recognition and enforcement of foreign judgments in Commonwealth African countries' (2014) XV *Yearbook of Private International Law* 365 at 371–2.

[102] (2002–8) 2 GR 38 (Court of Appeal of The Gambia) (Agim PCA; Yeboah JA and Dordzie AGJA).

The plaintiff first brought proceedings in the courts of Rotterdam, where it lost. The Rotterdam court decided that the plaintiff was in default of its contractual obligations, such that the first defendant was entitled to suspend performance of the agreement. Undeterred, the plaintiff then brought proceedings in The Gambia. The High Court declined to hear the matter, concluding that it had no jurisdiction to do so. The Court of Appeal[103] upheld that conclusion, Agim PCA stated:

> 'The court [below] was right to have reached the conclusion that since it is not in dispute that the Holland judgment [sic] is in respect of the same subject matter, issues as well as parties, the present suit is not maintainable and the court lacks jurisdiction to entertain it. The common law rule as to the conclusiveness of foreign judgments applies in The Gambia by virtue of s. 7(1) of the 1997 Constitution[104] which makes the common law part of the Laws of The Gambia. The common law rule is preserved and given effect by s. 9 of the Foreign Judgments Reciprocal Enforcement Act[105]...
>
> The Rotterdam court judgment is clearly a judgment to which Part 1 of the Foreign Judgments Reciprocal Enforcement Act applies as it is a judgment given in the superior court of a foreign country. The effect of s. 9 is to accord such judgment recognition as conclusive between the parties in The Gambia even though it cannot be registered under the Act since there is no arrangement for the reciprocal enforcement of judgments in superior courts between The Gambia and Netherlands and no sum of money was payable under such judgment. The section does not operate to enable the registration of a foreign judgment that has not fulfilled the requirements for registration under a law. It only enables an unregistered foreign judgment to be recognised for the purpose of preventing a retrial of the same cause of action between the same parties in The Gambia. It effectively grounds the plea of estoppel *per rem judicatem*.'

Agim PCA then held[106] that the rule on the conclusiveness of foreign judgments may only be invoked successfully if the parties and cause of action are the same in all proceedings, the judgment already given is final and conclusive between the parties on the merits and the judgment was given by a court of competent jurisdiction. Given that those criteria were met in the instant case, the rule applied.

---

[103] Ibid 41.

[104] Which provides that: 'In addition to this Constitution, the laws of The Gambia consist of ... (d) the common law and principles of equity.'

[105] Act 6 of 1936 (now Cap 8:06 of the Laws of Gambia, 2009). Section 9 provides, as far as relevant: '(1) Subject to the provisions of this section, a judgment to which Part 1 of this Act applies or would have applied if a sum of money has been payable thereunder, whether it can be registered or not, and whether, if it can be registered, it is registered or not, shall be recognised in any court in The Gambia as conclusive between the parties thereto in all proceedings founded on the same cause of action and may be relied upon by way of a defence or counterclaim in any such proceedings.'

[106] (2002) 2 GR 38 at 42.

There are two difficulties with the judgment. The first is that it is not clear that the Foreign Judgments Reciprocal Enforcement Act, and particularly section 9 thereof, works in the way that the Court of Appeal considered it to work in this case.[107] The second and, for present purposes, more important difficulty is that it is not clear what the Court of Appeal considered was the proper interaction between the statutory regime and the judgment creditor's (potential) ability to enforce a judgment at common law.

One reading of the above judgment is that, where a judgment cannot be registered, and so enforced, pursuant to the statutory regime, it cannot be enforced at all. Certainly, no mention is made of any potential enforcement pursuant to the common law, where registration (and so enforcement) pursuant to the statutory regime is unavailable to the judgment creditor. If it is correct that the judgment creditor may only use the statutory regime to enforce a foreign judgment (because there is no common-law regime available), this would make the law of The Gambia the same as the law of Nigeria on this question.[108]

However, it is submitted, that the better view is that the Court of Appeal in *Bourgi* was not required to consider the enforcement of a foreign judgment pursuant to the common law and their remarks, however cryptic, do not support the proposition that there is no right at common law to enforce a foreign judgment. Indeed, the express reference in Agim PCA's judgment to the preservation of the common law by the 1997 Constitution of The Gambia suggests that the court considered that the common law survived the enactment of the Foreign Judgments Reciprocal Enforcement Act 1936.

Two reasons may be cited in support of the view set out in the previous paragraph. Firstly, the statutory regime, as a whole, in force in The Gambia is merely a transposition of the statutory regime that was in force (and still in force) in England,[109] and the English statutory regime has not abrogated a judgment creditor's right to seek enforcement, at common law, of a foreign judgment to which the statutory regime does not apply. Secondly, Frimpong Oppong[110] states:

> 'A judgment creditor cannot go into direct execution in the territory of another sovereign and independent state. He or she can only do that after the judgment has been recognised by the courts of that state … In [The] Gambia … the judgment creditor has to bring an action of debt on the foreign judgment. A foreign judgment creates a new cause of action on which the judgment-creditor is entitled to sue.'

---

[107] As to which, see further below, under the sub-heading 'Foreign Judgments Reciprocal Enforcement Act 1936'.

[108] Olawoyin 'Enforcement of Foreign Judgments in Nigeria: Statutory Dualism and Disharmony of Law' (2014) 10 *JIPL* 129 at 132; Olaniyan 'The Commonwealth Model and the Conundrum in the Enforcement of Foreign Judgments Regime in Nigeria' (2014) 40 *Commonwealth Law Bulletin* 76 at 88, where the author speculates 'whether the Nigerian bar and bench have [consigned] the common law procedure to history'.

[109] As set out in the Administration of Justice Act 1920 and the Foreign Judgments (Reciprocal Enforcement) Act 1933.

[110] *Private International Law in Commonwealth Africa* 317, though the author does not cite any authority in The Gambia to support the point.

That is apt to explain enforcement at common law.

It is submitted that, if the enforcement of a foreign judgment pursuant to the common law is permissible in The Gambia, attempts at such enforcement are likely to be governed by principles similar to, or the same as, those espoused by the courts of England.

By 1894[111] the basic English law principles of enforcement at common law had been settled and it is to be expected that a court in The Gambia will have regard to developments in the English common law that have occurred since that time.

These principles are conveniently set out in *Dicey, Morris and Collins on the Conflict of Laws*:[112]

> '***Rule 42***
>
> (1) Subject to the Exceptions hereinafter mentioned and to Rule 62 (international conventions), a foreign judgment in personam given by the court of a foreign country with jurisdiction to give that judgment in accordance with the principles set out in Rules 43 to 46, and which is not impeachable under any of Rules 49 to 54, may be enforced by a claim or counterclaim for the amount due under it if the judgment is
>
> *(a)* for a debt, or definite sum of money (not being a sum payable in respect of taxes or other charges of a like nature or in respect of a fine or other penalty); and
>
> *(b)* final and conclusive,
>
> but not otherwise.
>
> Provided that a foreign judgment may be final and conclusive, though it is subject to an appeal, and though an appeal against it is actually pending in the foreign country where it was given.
>
> (2) A foreign judgment given by the court of a foreign country with jurisdiction to give that judgment in accordance with the principles set out in Rules 43 to 46, which is not impeachable under any of Rules 49 to 54 and which is final and conclusive on the merits, is entitled to recognition at common law and may be relied on in proceedings in England.

---

[111] English law was received into The Gambia by The Gambia Protectorate Order in Council 1893 (made on 23 November 1893) and The Gambia Protectorate Ordinance 1894 (made on 27 December 1894). The Gambia Protectorate Order in Council 1946 (SI 2085 of 1946) revoked the 1893 Order in Council but provided (in s 3(2)): 'The continued operation of any law in force in the Protectorate immediately before the appointed day shall not be affected by reason only of the revocation of the said Order in Council.' The Gambia Independence Order (SI 135 of 1965) provided (in s 4(1)): 'The existing laws shall, as from the commencement of this Order, be construed with such modifications, adaptations qualifications and exceptions as may be necessary to bring them into conformity with the Gambia Independence Act 1964 and this Order', thereby ensuring that English common-law principles are still applicable in The Gambia. Section 7(d) of the 1997 Constitution preserves this position. It provides: 'The laws of The Gambia consist of the common law and principles of equity.'

[112] 15 ed (2012) vol 1, para 14R-020.

(3) No proceedings may be brought by a person on a cause of action in respect of a judgment which has been given in his favour in proceedings between the same parties or their privies in a court in another part of the United Kingdom or in a court in an overseas country unless that judgment is not enforceable according to clause (1), or not entitled to recognition according to clause (2), of this Rule.'

In order for its judgment to be enforceable, the foreign court must have possessed international jurisdiction to determine the cause. As a matter of common law, a foreign court will have such international jurisdiction in the following cases:[113] (1) if the person against whom the judgment was given was, at the time the proceedings were instituted, present in the foreign country; or (2) if the person against whom the judgment was given was claimant, or counterclaimed, in the proceedings in the foreign court; or (3) if the person against whom the judgment was given submitted to the jurisdiction of that court by voluntarily appearing in the proceedings; or (4) if the person against whom the judgment was given had before the commencement of the proceedings agreed, in respect of the subject-matter of the proceedings, to submit to the jurisdiction of that court or of the courts of that country.

Among the established defences to an action at common law on a foreign judgment are the following: (1) where the foreign judgment was procured by fraud either: (a) fraud on the part of the party in whose favour the judgment is given, or (b) fraud on the part of the court pronouncing the judgment;[114] (2) the enforcement or recognition of the foreign judgment would be contrary to public policy;[115] and (3) where the proceedings in which the foreign judgment was obtained were contrary to the rules of natural justice.[116]

13.2.2 Enforcement pursuant to statute

13.2.2.1 *The regimes for enforcement pursuant to statute*

The statutory regimes in force in The Gambia are contained in the Reciprocal Enforcement of Foreign Judgments Act 1922[117] ('the 1922 Act') (and the rules of court made pursuant thereto)[118] and the Foreign Judgments Reciprocal Enforcement Act 1936[119] ('the 1936 Act'). As has been noted above, the statutory regimes in force in The Gambia are recognisable as having been derived from the equivalent English statutory provisions.[120]

---

[113] *Dicey, Morris and Collins on the Conflict of Laws* 15 ed (2012) vol 1, r 43, para 14R-054.

[114] *Dicey, Morris and Collins on the Conflict of Laws* 15 ed (2012) vol 1, r 50, para 14R-137.

[115] Ibid r 51, para 14R-152.

[116] Ibid r 52, para 14R-162.

[117] Act 12 of 1922 (now Cap 8:05 of the Laws of The Gambia, 2009).

[118] Reciprocal Enforcement of Judgments Rules 1924 (r 2 of 1924, LN 54 of 1963).

[119] Act 6 of 1936 (now Cap 8:06 of the Laws of The Gambia, 2009).

[120] That is to say, the Administration of Justice Act 1920 and the Foreign Judgments (Reciprocal Enforcement) Act 1933.

13.2.2.1.1 Reciprocal Enforcement of Foreign Judgments Act 1922

The 1922 Act applies to a judgment[121] which has been obtained in the High Court in England or Northern Ireland, or in the Court of Session in Scotland.[122] Section 6(1) of the 1922 Act provides that the 1922 Act itself may be extended, by way of ministerial order published in the *Gazette*, to 'judgments obtained in a superior court' in any other part of the Commonwealth.[123]

To date, the 1922 Act has been extended to judgments from the Supreme Court of Sierra Leone[124] and the Supreme Court of New South Wales.[125] The 1922 Act has also apparently been extended to judgments obtained in the High Court and the Court of Appeal of the State of Tasmania,[126] the High Court and Court of Appeal of the Australian Capital Territory and Northern Territory.[127] These later extensions to the statutory regime, as a whole, in force in The Gambia, should have been made pursuant to the 1936 Act, which was ostensibly in operation at the time at which the said extensions were made and it is unclear why this was not done.[128]

---

[121] Defined in s 2 of the 1922 Act as meaning 'any judgment or order given or made by a court in any civil proceedings, whether before or after the passing of this Act, whereby any sum of money is made payable, and includes an award in proceedings on an arbitration if the award has, in pursuance of the law in force in the place where it was made, become enforceable in the same manner as a judgment given by a court in that place'.

[122] Section 3(1) of the 1922 Act.

[123] The minister may do this where 'satisfied that reciprocal provisions have been made by the legislature of any part of the Commonwealth outside the UK for the enforcement within that part of the Commonwealth of judgments obtained in the High Court of The Gambia'. The expression 'part of the Commonwealth outside the UK' is defined in s 6(2) as being deemed to 'include any territory which is under Her Majesty's protection or in respect of which a mandate is being exercised by the Government of any part of the Commonwealth'. That said, there should be no further extensions of the 1922 Act. Such further extensions of the statutory regime in The Gambia should be made pursuant to s 3 of the 1936 Act, as to which see further below.

[124] By way of ministerial order made on 30 January 1924. It is submitted that this must now refer to the High Court of Sierra Leone.

[125] By way of ministerial order made on 26 January 1926.

[126] Reciprocal Enforcement of Judgments (State of Tasmania) Order 1975, deemed to come into operation on the first day of January 1972 (LN 6 of 1975).

[127] Reciprocal Enforcement of Judgments (Australian Capital Territory and Northern Territory) Order 1975, deemed to come into operation on the fifth day of September 1973 (LN 12 of 1975).

[128] Section 8 of the 1936 Act regulates its interaction with the 1922 Act. Section 8(1) of the 1936 Act provides that Part 1 of the said 1936 Act 'shall apply to the Commonwealth outside The Gambia and to judgments obtained in the courts of the Commonwealth as it applies to foreign countries and judgments obtained in the courts of foreign countries, and the [1922 Act] shall cease to have effect except in relation to those parts of the Commonwealth to which it extends at the date of coming into operation of this Act'. It is unclear why extensions were made to the 1922 Act after 31 March 1936 (the date of commencement of the 1936 Act). It is arguable that these extensions were *ultra vires* the minister who made them.

13.2.2.1.1.1 *The procedure for registration*

A judgment creditor[129] of a judgment emanating from a court in a country to which the 1922 Act applies[130] may apply to the High Court of The Gambia, at any time within 12 months after the date of the judgment, or such longer period as may be allowed by the High Court, to have the judgment registered thereat.[131] On any such application, the High Court may, if in all the circumstances of the case it thinks it is just and convenient that the judgment should be enforced in The Gambia, order the judgment to be registered accordingly.[132]

Any such application from the judgment creditor must be made *ex parte* or by originating[133] summons to the Chief Justice.[134] The application shall be supported by an affidavit of the facts, exhibiting the judgment or verified or certified or otherwise authenticated copy thereof.[135] The affidavit must state that, to the best of the information and belief of the deponent, the judgment creditor is entitled to enforce the judgment and the judgment does not fall within any of the cases in which under section 3(2) a judgment cannot properly be ordered to be registered.[136]

Section 3(2) of the 1922 Act provides that a judgment shall not be ordered to be registered if:

(a) the original court acted without jurisdiction;

(b) the judgment debtor, being a person who was neither carrying on business nor ordinarily resident within the jurisdiction of the original court[137] did not voluntarily appear or otherwise submit or agree to submit to the jurisdiction of that court;

---

[129] Defined in s 2 of the 1922 Act as meaning 'the person by whom the judgment was obtained, and includes the successors and assigns of that person'.

[130] It has been held by the Court of Appeal in England that the Administration of Justice Act 1920 does not permit registration of a judgment given by a court in one state in an action to enforce a judgment given by a court in another state: *Strategic Technologies Pte Ltd v Procurement Bureau of the Republic of China Ministry of National Defence* [2020] EWCA Civ 1604 (David Richards, Males and Elisabeth Laing LJJ).

[131] Section 3 of the 1922 Act.

[132] Ibid.

[133] Rule 5 of the Reciprocal Enforcement of Judgments Rules, made pursuant to s 5 of the 1922 Act.

[134] Rule 2 of the Reciprocal Enforcement of Judgments Rules. Where the application is made *ex parte*, the Chief Justice may direct a summons to be issued. The summons and the affidavit must be entitled in accordance with r 4 of the Reciprocal Enforcement of Judgments Rules.

[135] Rule 3 of the Reciprocal Enforcement of Judgments Rules.

[136] Ibid. The affidavit must also, so far as the deponent can, give the full name, title, trade or business and usual or last known place of abode or business of the judgment creditor and the judgment debtor ('the person against whom the judgment was given and includes any person against whom the judgment is enforceable in any place where it was given': s 2 of the 1922 Act) respectively.

[137] Defined by s 2 of the 1922 Act as 'the court by which the judgment was given'.

(c) the judgment debtor, being the defendant in the proceedings, was not duly served with the process of the original court and did not appear, notwithstanding that he or she was ordinarily resident or was carrying on business within the jurisdiction of that court, or agree to submit to the jurisdiction of that court;

(d) the judgment was obtained by fraud;[138]

(e) the judgment debtor satisfies the High Court of The Gambia that either an appeal is pending, or that he or she is entitled and intends to appeal against the judgment; or

(f) the judgment was in respect of a cause of action which for reasons of public policy or for some other similar reason could not have been entertained by the High Court.

If the High Court of The Gambia gives leave to register the foreign judgment, such order shall be drawn up by or on behalf of the judgment creditor.[139] Where the judgment is registered under section 3 of the 1922 Act, the judgment shall, as from the date of registration, be of the same force and effect, and proceedings may be taken thereon, as if it had been a judgment ordinarily obtained or entered upon the date of registration in the High Court of The Gambia.[140] The High Court shall have the same control and jurisdiction over the judgment as it has over similar judgments given by itself, but in so far only as relates to execution under section 3 of the 1922 Act.[141]

13.2.2.1.1.2 *Setting aside registration*

Where the court grants leave to register a foreign judgment pursuant to section 3 of the 1922 Act, that order shall state the time within which the judgment debtor

[138] A comparison may be drawn between this provision and s 6(1)(a)(iv) of the English 1933 Act. In *Dicey, Morris and Collins on the Conflict of Laws* para 14–191, it is stated of the fraud provisions of the English 1933 Act: 'The provisions with regard to fraud and public policy are the same as the common law rules. In particular, the common law rule that a foreign judgment can be impeached for fraud even though no newly discovered evidence is produced, and even though the fraud was alleged in the foreign proceedings, applies to enforcement and recognition under the 1933 Act. In *Owens Bank Ltd v Bracco* [[1992] 2 AC 443] the House of Lords held that the fraud exception in the 1920 Act was subject to the same rule, and indicated (obiter) that the same must be so under the 1933 Act.' *Owens Bank* has not been followed in certain Commonwealth jurisdictions (eg Canada in *Beals v Saldanha* [2003] 3 SCR 416, (2003) 234 DLR (4th) 1; and New South Wales in *Keele v Findley* (1991) 21 NSWLR 444 (NSWSC); but in *Close v Arnot* (unreported) 21 November 1997 (NSW), the Common Law Division distinguished *Keele v Findley* and applied the traditional English standard of fraud in respect of a foreign judgment in a case where the defendant had, for good reason, allowed foreign proceedings to go undefended). A court in The Gambia would not, of course, be bound by the judgment of the English House of Lords.

[139] Rule 6 of the Reciprocal Enforcement of Judgments Rules.

[140] Section 3(3)(a) of the 1922 Act.

[141] Section 3(3)(b) of the 1922 Act.

is to be entitled to set aside the registration.[142] The judgment debtor must also be served, within a reasonable time after the registration of the foreign judgment, with a notice in writing of its being registered.[143] That notice shall contain full particulars of the judgment registered and the order for such registration and shall state that the judgment debtor is entitled, if he has grounds for doing so, to apply to set aside the registration and the number of days within which he must make that application.[144]

No execution shall issue on the judgment registered under the 1922 Act until after the expiration of the time limited by the order giving leave to register after service on the judgment debtor of notice of registration thereof.[145]

13.2.2.1.2 Foreign Judgments Reciprocal Enforcement Act 1936

As has been noted above, the second part of the statutory regime in operation in The Gambia is to be found in the 1936 Act.[146]

13.2.2.1.2.1 *The procedure for registration*

Pursuant to section 4(1) of the 1936 Act, a judgment creditor[147] under a judgment[148] to which Part I of the Act applies[149] may make an application to the High Court

[142] Rule 7 of the Reciprocal Enforcement of Judgments Rules. Where the judgment debtor is, or is ordinarily resident, within the city of Banjul or the Kanifing Municipality, the time shall usually be 14 days and where the judgment debtor is, or is ordinarily, resident in the Regions, the time shall ordinarily be the same as is limited for entering appearance after service in the Regions of a writ of summons or notice thereof. It is submitted that this rule now needs to be redrafted to make it cohere with the Rules of the High Court.

[143] Rule 10 of the Reciprocal Enforcement of Judgments Rules. In the absence of any order by the Chief Justice, the notice may be served on the judgment debtor by personal service as in the case of a writ of summons, though the Chief Justice may at any stage of the proceedings authorise or direct some other mode of service, and if he or she does, the service shall be affected in accordance with the authority or direction.

[144] Rule 11 of the Reciprocal Enforcement of Judgments Rules. Such application must be made in accordance with r 13 of the Reciprocal Enforcement of Judgments Rules.

[145] Rule 14 of the Reciprocal Enforcement of Judgments Rules.

[146] The 1936 Act does not contain a provision allowing rules of court to be made pursuant thereto. By way of contrast, see s 5 of the 1922 Act. There is no indication whether the rules made pursuant to the 1922 Act should apply to, inter alia, the making of an application under, say, s 4(1) of the 1936 Act.

[147] Defined in s 2 to mean the 'person in whose favour the judgment was given and includes any person in whom the rights under the judgment have become vested by succession or assignment or otherwise'.

[148] Defined in s 2 to mean 'a judgment or order given or made by a court in any civil proceedings, or a judgment or order given or made by a court in any criminal proceedings for the payment of a sum of money in respect of compensation or damages to an injured person'. Given the similarity in language between this provision and s 2 of the 1922 Act, it is likely that, were a court in The Gambia persuaded to adopt the approach of the English Court of Appeal in *Strategic Technologies PTE Ltd v Procurement Bureau of the Republic of China Ministry of National Defence* [2020] EWCA Civ 1604 when interpreting s 2 of the 1922 Act, it would adopt the same approach when interpreting s 2 of the 1936 Act.

[149] Section 3(2) provides: 'A judgment of a superior court of a foreign country to which this Part of this [Act] extends, other than a judgment of such a court given on appeal from a court which is not a superior court, shall be a judgment to which this Part of this [Act] applies if — a) it is final and conclusive as between

of The Gambia at any time within six years after the date of the judgment or, where there have been proceedings by way of appeal against the judgment, after the date of the last judgment given in those proceedings, to have the judgment registered in the High Court. On any such application, the court shall, subject to proof of prescribed matters and save as otherwise provided, order the judgment to be registered, except where, at the date of application, the judgment has been wholly satisfied or the judgment could not be enforced by execution in the country of the original court.

Pursuant to section 3(1) of the 1936 Act, the minister may, by order published in the *Gazette*, direct that Part 1 of the Act shall extend to judgments given in the superior courts of foreign countries.[150] The minister has exercised this power so as to extend the 1936 Act only to the Federal Republic of Nigeria.[151]

Subject to the provisions of the 1936 Act which deal with the setting aside of registration of the foreign judgment (which are dealt with below), a registered judgment:

(1) shall, for the purposes of execution, be of the same force and effect; and

(2) proceedings may be taken on a registered judgment; and

(3) the sum for which a judgment is registered shall carry interest; and

(4) the registering court shall have the same control over the execution of a registered judgment;

as if the judgment had been a judgment ordinarily given in the registering court and entered on the date of registration.[152] However, execution on the judgment so registered shall not issue so long as it is competent for any party to make an application to have the registration of the judgment set aside, or, where such an application is made, until after the application has been finally determined.[153]

---

the parties thereto; and b) there is payable thereunder a sum of money, not being a sum payable in respect of taxes or other charges of a like nature or in respect of a fine or other penalty; and c) it is given after the coming into operation of the Order directing that this Part of this [Act] shall extend to that foreign country'. Section 3(3) goes on to provide that: 'For the purposes of this section, a judgment shall be deemed to be final and conclusive notwithstanding that an appeal may be pending against it, or that it may still be subject to appeal, in the country of the original court.'

[150] Section 10(1) of the 1936 Act allows the minister, by order, to declare that no proceedings shall be entertained in any court in The Gambia for the recovery of any sum alleged to be payable under a judgment given in a country where the treatment by that country in respect of recognition and enforcement of judgments given in The Gambia is substantially less favourable than that accorded by the High Court in The Gambia to judgments of the superior courts of that country.

[151] Achieved by way of the Foreign Judgments Reciprocal Enforcement (Nigeria) Order (Order 11 of 1956). For the purposes of the 1936 Act, this Order provides that the Supreme Court of Nigeria, the High Court of Western Nigeria, the High Court of Northern Nigeria, the High Court of Eastern Nigeria and the High Court of Lagos are superior courts.

[152] Section 4(3) of the 1936 Act.

[153] Section 4(4) of the 1936 Act. Section 4(5) deals with the situation where the sum payable under the judgment to be registered is expressed in a different currency to that of The Gambia; s 4(6) deals with the

13.2.2.1.2.2 *Setting aside registration*

Section 5 of the Act provides that a party against whom a registered judgment may be enforced may make an application asking the court to set aside the registration of the same. Section 5 then distinguishes between cases where the court, when faced with such an application, 'shall' (ie must) set aside the registered judgment and those where the court 'may' do so.

Those cases in which the court 'shall' set aside registration of the foreign judgment are detailed in section 5(1)(a) of the 1936 Act, as follows:

(1) the judgment is not a judgment to which Part 1 of the Act applies or was registered in contravention of the Act's provisions;

(2) the courts of the country of the original court had no jurisdiction in the circumstances of the case;

(3) the judgment debtor, being the defendant in the proceedings in the original court, did not (notwithstanding that process may have been duly served on him in accordance with the law of the country of the original court) receive notice of those proceedings in sufficient time to enable him to defend the proceedings and did not appear;

(4) the judgment was obtained by fraud;[154]

(5) the enforcement of the judgment would be contrary to public policy in The Gambia; or

(6) the rights under the judgment are not vested in the person by whom the application for registration was made.

The court may set aside a registered judgment where it is

> 'satisfied that the matter in dispute in the proceedings in the original court has previously to the date of the judgment in the original court been the subject of a final and conclusive judgment by a court having jurisdiction in the matter.'[155]

The 1936 Act[156] provides that the original court will be deemed to have had jurisdiction in the following circumstances:

---

situation where, at the date of the application for registration, the judgment has been partly satisfied and s 4(7) deals with the situation where the judgment is in respect of different matters, not all of which are capable of being properly registered.

[154] The equivalent to s 6(1)(a)(iv) of the 1933 Act. See further *Dicey, Morris and Collins on the Conflict of Laws* 15 ed (2012) vol 1, r 50, paras 14R-137–14–145.

[155] Section 5(1)(b) of the 1936 Act.

[156] Section 5(2) of the 1936 Act.

(1) in the case of a judgment given *in personam*:[157]

(a) if the judgment debtor, being a defendant in the original court, submitted to the jurisdiction of that court by voluntarily appearing in the proceedings otherwise than for the purpose of protecting or obtaining the release of property seized, or threatened with seizure, in the proceedings or of contesting the jurisdiction of that court; or

(b) if the judgment debtor was plaintiff in, or counterclaimed in, the proceedings in the original court; or

(c) if the judgment debtor, being a defendant in the original court, had before the commencement of the proceedings agreed, in respect of the subject-matter of the proceedings, to submit to the jurisdiction of that court or the courts of the country of that court; or

(d) if the judgment debtor, being a defendant in the original court, was at the time when proceedings were instituted, resident in, or being a body corporate had its principal place of business in, the country of that court; or

(e) if the judgment debtor, being a defendant in the original court, had an office or a place of business in the country or that court and the proceedings in that court were in respect of a transaction effected through or at that office or place.

(2) in the case of a judgment given in an action of which the subject-matter was immovable property or in an action *in rem* of which the subject-matter was movable property, if the property in question was at the time of the proceedings in the original court situate in the country of that court; or

(3) in the case of a judgment given in an action other than such action as is mentioned in (1) or (2) above, if the jurisdiction of the original court is recognised by the law of the registering court.

The foreign court shall be deemed not to have had jurisdiction in the following circumstances:[158]

(1) if the subject-matter of the proceedings was immovable property outside the country of the original court; or

(2) except in cases mentioned in section 5(2)(a)(i), (ii), (iii) and (2)(c), if the bringing of the proceedings in the original court was contrary to an

[157] Section 2(2) provides that this expression 'shall not be deemed to include any matrimonial cause or any proceedings in connection with matrimonial matters, administration of the estates of deceased persons, bankruptcy, winding up of companies, lunacy or guardianship of infants'.

[158] As set out in s 5(3) of the 1936 Act.

agreement under which the dispute in question was to be settled otherwise than by proceedings in the courts of the country of that court; or

(3) if the judgment debtor, being a defendant in the original proceedings, was a person who under the rules of public international law was entitled to immunity from jurisdiction of the courts of the country of the original court and did not submit to the jurisdiction of that court.

In addition, where the judgment debtor, in an application to set aside the registration of a judgment, satisfies the court in The Gambia that an appeal is pending, or that he is entitled to and intends to appeal against the judgment (which has been registered), the court may either set aside the registration or adjourn the application to set aside the registration until the expiration of such period as appears to the court to be reasonably sufficient to enable the applicant to take the necessary steps to have the appeal disposed of by the competent tribunal.[159] Where the court makes an order on this basis, or solely for the reason that, at the time the application for registration was made, the judgment was not enforceable by execution in the country of the original court, that does not prejudice a further application to register the judgment in a court in The Gambia being made when the appeal has been disposed of or the judgment becomes enforceable in the original court.[160]

It would appear that where Part 1 of the 1936 Act applies to a foreign judgment, no proceedings for recovery of a sum payable under that judgment, other than proceedings by way of registration of the judgment, shall be entertained by a court in The Gambia.[161] In these circumstances, the judgment creditor does not have a choice between enforcement via the common law (presuming such method of enforcement exists) and enforcement via the statutory route: the only option is the latter one.

Section 9 of the 1936 Act has been mentioned above. It provides that a judgment to which Part 1 of the Act applies shall be recognised in any court in The Gambia as conclusive between the parties thereto in all proceedings founded on the 'same cause of action and may be relied on by way of defence or counter-claim in any such proceedings', irrespective of whether the judgment has been registered or not. It is submitted that, in *Bourgi v Withams*,[162] the Court of Appeal of the Gambia paid insufficient regard to the wording of sections 2 and 3 of the

---

[159] Section 6(1) of the 1936 Act.

[160] Section 6(2) of the 1936 Act. Similarly, pursuant to s 6(3), where registration of a judgment is set aside solely because the judgment had, at the date of registration, been partly satisfied but had been registered for the whole sum payable under the judgment, a court in The Gambia shall, on the application of the judgment creditor, order judgment to be registered for the balance remaining payable at that date.

[161] Section 7 of the 1936 Act.

[162] (2002–2008) 2 GR 38 (Court of Appeal of The Gambia) (Agim PCA; Yeboah JA and Dordzie AGJA) 41.

1936 Act when deciding that the 1936 Act (and so section 9 thereof) applied in that case. The 1936 Act does not apply to judgments given by courts in every foreign country. It applies only to judgments given in courts in countries to which it has been extended (that is, Nigeria).

That point notwithstanding, there is no doubt that section 9 of the 1936 Act does not apply where:[163]

(1) the judgment has been registered and the registration was set aside on some ground other than that:
   (a) a sum of money was not payable under the judgment; or
   (b) the judgment had been wholly or partly satisfied; or
   (c) at the date of the application the judgment could not be enforced by execution in the country of the original court; or
(2) where the judgment has not been registered, it is shown that if the judgment had been registered, the registration thereof would have been set aside on an application for that purpose on some ground other than that specified in (1) above.[164]

13.2.2.2 *The relationship between the regimes*

Section 8 of the 1936 Act regulates the relationship between the 1922 and the 1936 Acts. It provides as follows:

> '(1) [Part 1 of the 1936 Act] shall apply to the Commonwealth outside The Gambia and to judgments obtained in the courts of the Commonwealth as it applies to foreign countries and judgments obtained in the courts of foreign countries, and the [1922 Act] shall cease to have effect except in relation to those parts of the Commonwealth to which it extends at the date of coming into operation of this Act.
>
> (2) When the Minister has made an order under section 3 of [the 1936 Act] extending Part 1 [of the 1936 Act] to any part of the Commonwealth to which the [1922 Act] extends,[165] as aforesaid –
>
> *(a)* the said [1922 Act] shall cease to have effect in relation to that part of the Commonwealth; and
>
> *(b)* the said Part 1 shall, in relation to that part of the Commonwealth, have effect as if –
>
> (i) the expression "judgment" included an award in proceedings on an arbitration if the award has, in pursuance of the law in force in the place where it was made, become enforceable in the same manner as a judgment given by a court in that place;

[163] Section 9(2) of the 1936 Act.

[164] That said, nothing in s 9(2) shall be taken to prevent any court in The Gambia recognising any judgment as conclusive of any matter of law or fact decided therein if that judgment would have been so recognised before the passing of the 1936 Act: s 9(3).

[165] Which, as has been noted, has not yet happened.

(ii) the fact that a judgment was given before the coming into operation of the Order did not prevent it from being a judgment to which the said Part 1 applies, but at the time limited for the registration of a judgment were, in the case of a judgment so given, twelve months from the date of the judgment or such longer period as may be allowed by the court;

(iii) any judgment registered in the court under the said [1922 Act] under the said Part 1 and anything done in relation thereto under the said [1922 Act] or any rules of court or other provisions applicable to the said Act had been done under the said Part 1 of the corresponding rules of court or other provisions applicable to the said Part 1.'

Hence, section 8 of the 1936 Act deals with the extension of the provisions of Part 1 thereof to Commonwealth jurisdictions. Section 8 would appear to contemplate a two-stage approach. First, and as set out in section 8(1), on the date upon which the 1936 Act came into operation, the 1922 Act immediately ceased to have effect except in relation to those parts of the Commonwealth to which the 1922 Act already extended on that date. Second, and as set out in section 8(2), the minister may make an order under section 3 of the 1936 Act extending the 1936 Act to any part of the Commonwealth to which the 1922 Act continues (in the light of section 8(1)) to extend. Upon the making of such an order, the 1936 Act envisages (at section 8(2)(a)) that the 1922 Act shall cease to have effect in relation to the part of the Commonwealth to which the Order relates and Part 1 of the 1936 Act itself shall, in accordance with the provisions of section 8(2)(b), have effect in relation to that part of the Commonwealth instead.

On 31 March 1936, the date of commencement of the 1936 Act, the 1922 Act extended to England, Scotland or Northern Ireland, Sierra Leone and New South Wales. Since 31 March 1936, the Minister has made a ministerial order, as contemplated in section 8(2) of the 1936 Act, in respect of the Federal Republic of Nigeria only. Section 8(1) of the 1936 Act would therefore apparently indicate that a judgment creditor of an English, Scottish, Northern Irish, Sierra Leone or New South Wales judgment must still use the regime set out in the 1922 Act, rather than the 1936, to enforce that judgment in The Gambia.

The position of a judgment creditor of a judgment of a court in Tasmania, the Australian Capital Territory or Northern Territory is less clear. The orders extending the 1922 Act to these territories were made after the date of commencement of the 1936 Act. Hence, on a strict application of section 8(1) of the 1936 Act, and in spite of the aforementioned orders apparently extending the 1922 Act, it would appear that a judgment creditor of a judgment from a court in Tasmania, the Australian Capital Territory or Northern Territory ought to use the regime set out in the 1936 Act, rather than the 1922 Act, to enforce that judgment in The Gambia. If that is the position, however, it only serves to heighten the oddity of the minister seeking, by order, to extend the 1922 Act after the commencement of the 1936 Act itself.

13.3 Interim remedies

13.3.1 Jurisdiction to grant interim remedies

The jurisdiction of the court to grant interim relief is statutory:[166]

> The High Court shall have the jurisdiction and powers provided by the Constitution and all the jurisdiction, powers and authorities which were vested in or capable of being exercised by Her Majesty's High Court of Justice in England immediately before the eighteenth day of February, 1965.

13.3.2 Procedure for application

Unless otherwise provided for by the Rules of the High Court, an application for interlocutory relief to a judge in court shall be made by motion.[167] Unless the court orders otherwise, a motion shall not be entertained until the party moving has filed a motion paper or made a verbal application to the Registrar of the High Court, distinctly stating the terms of the order sought.[168] There shall, unless the court gives special leave to the contrary, be at least two clear days between the service of a notice of motion and the day named in the notice for hearing the motion.[169]

A plaintiff may make a motion *ex parte* and without notice.[170] That said, interlocutory relief sought on an *ex parte* basis may only be granted for extremely urgent reasons: the power must be exercised judiciously.[171] Where an *ex parte* motion is moved, the party moving shall apply for either an immediate absolute order of the court or an order that the other party appear on a certain day and show cause why an order should not be made in the terms of the motion paper.[172] Where an *ex parte* motion is made, Order XXV, rule 9 provides that the plaintiff may support the motion by argument on the facts put in evidence, but that only the plaintiff may be heard at that point in time.

---

166 Section 3 of Courts Act 1964. .

167 Order XXV, r 1. Order XXVI sets out the procedure to be used when an application is made to a judge in chambers.

168 Order XXV, r 2. All of the affidavits on which the person moving intends to apply must be filed with the motion paper: O XXV, r 4.

169 Order XXV, r 17. Notice of motion may, without leave of the court, be served on any person, notwithstanding that such person is not an officer of the court.

170 Order XXV, r 7.

171 *Felix Thomas v Annette Ibkendanz* (2002–2008) 2 GR 306 at 309 (Court of Appeal of The Gambia) (Agim and Dordzie JJCA and Anin-Yeboah AGJCA), relying on the decision of the Nigerian Supreme Court in *Kotoye v Central Bank of Nigeria* [1989] 1 NWLR 419 (Nnamani, Karibi-Whyte, Agbaje, Nnaemeka-Agu and Craig JJSC).

172 Order XXV, r 9 of the Rules of the High Court.

Where an *ex parte* motion is made, the court may refuse to make the order sought, or may grant an order to show cause why the order should not be made, or may allow the motion to be made on notice to the parties to be thereby affected.[173]

Where an order is made on an *ex parte* motion, a party affected by it may, within seven days of service of it, or within such further time as the court shall allow, apply to the court by motion to vary or discharge it; and the court, on notice to the party obtaining the order, either may refuse to vary or discharge it, or may vary or discharge it with or without imposing terms as to costs or security, or otherwise, as seems just.[174]

Order XIV, rule 1 provides that the court, when making any order to hold bail, or of sale, or of injunction or attachment may impose such terms and conditions as the court shall deem just and, in particular, it may require the person applying for such order to enter into such security as the court considers requisite for his being answerable in any damages that may accrue through such order or warrant.

Where, in any case where the order set out in Order XIV, rule 1 is made, it appears that the plaintiff's application for any of the orders set out in the previous paragraph was made on insufficient grounds, or the suit in which any such application was made is dismissed and it appears to the court that there was no probable ground for instituting it, the defendant may apply, within six months from the termination of the suit, for redress.[175] On the defendant's application, the court may award against the plaintiff such amount not exceeding the sum of 2,000 dalasis, as it may deem reasonable compensation to the defendant for any loss, injury or expense which he has suffered by reason of the arrest, attachment, order of sale or injunction.[176]

13.3.3 Interlocutory[177] injunctions generally

Order XII, rule 4 of the Rules of the High Court provides that, where the plaintiff, in his substantive suit, seeks to restrain the defendant from committing a breach of contract or other injury, whether or not the plaintiff also seeks damages, he

---

173 Order XXV, r 10 of the Rules of the High Court.

174 Order XXV, r 11. The importance of complying with this rule is demonstrated by *Lindell v Kombo Beach Hotel* [1997–2001] GR 750 (Court of Appeal of The Gambia) (Yahaya and Akamba JJA and Janneh AGJA).

175 Order XIV, r 2 of the Rules of the High Court.

176 Ibid. This is, however, subject to the principle of double recoverability, which is set out in O XIV, r 3.

177 It would appear that in The Gambia, the expressions 'interim' and 'interlocutory' may be used interchangeably: *United Democratic Party v Attorney General (No 1)* [1997–2001] GR 789 (Supreme Court of The Gambia) (Jallow JSC, sitting as a single justice of the Supreme Court). In this respect, the law of The Gambia is different to the law of Nigeria, where there is a (rigid, apparently) distinction between the terms: *Kotoye v Central Bank of Nigeria* [1989] 1 NWLR 419 (Nigerian Sup Ct) (Nnamani, Karibi-Whyte, Agbaje, Nnaemeka-Agu and Craig JJSC). In the main text, the term 'interlocutory' is used to describe all pre-trial injunctions (*ex parte* or *inter partes*).

may seek, and the court may grant, at any time after the commencement of the suit and either before or after judgment, an injunction to restrain the defendant from the repetition or continuation of the breach of contract or wrongful conduct of which the plaintiff complains.[178]

The procedure for making an application for an interlocutory injunction is set out in Order XXV of the Rules of the High Court. Such application shall, unless otherwise authorised (either by the Rules of the High Court or by the judge in the High Court), be made by way of motion.[179] The plaintiff shall file with the motion all affidavits on which he intends to rely.[180]

When making an order pursuant to Order XII, rule 4, the court may also grant an injunction to prevent the defendant committing any breach of contract or injury of a like kind arising out of the same contract, or relating to the same property or right, and such injunction may be granted by the court on such terms as to the duration of the injunction, keeping an account, giving security or otherwise, as to what the court shall seem reasonable and just. Of course, an injunction may be discharged or varied or set aside by the court on application made to it by any party which is dissatisfied with such order.

The Supreme Court of The Gambia has set out the test to be applied when deciding whether to grant an interlocutory injunction of the type just identified. Hence, in *United Democratic Party v Attorney General (No 1)*,[181] where the plaintiffs sought an order suspending the chairman of the Independent Electoral Commission pending the determination of substantive proceedings, Jallow JSC stated[182] as follows:

> 'The basic requirement for the exercise of the court's discretion in granting an interlocutory or interim injunction is that the court should be satisfied that the [plaintiff] has a cause of action recognised at law and that it is just and convenient to grant interlocutory relief...
>
> An interlocutory or interim injunction is primarily granted in an appropriate case as *per* Lord Wilberforce in *Hoffman v La Roche* [1974] 2 All ER 1128 in order to "prevent a litigant, who must necessarily suffer the law's delay, from losing by that delay the fruit of his litigation". It is a discretionary remedy but the discretion: "is not one to be exercised according to the fancy of whoever is to exercise the jurisdiction of equity, but is a discretion to be exercised according to the rules which have been established by a long series of decisions". The House of Lords in *American Cyanamid* [*v Ethicon Ltd*][183] laid down a series of guiding tests or principles for the exercise of the discretion. These tests

---

[178] Order XII, r 4 of the Rules of the High Court.

[179] Order XXV, r 1 of the Rules of the High Court.

[180] Order XXV, r 4 of the Rules of the High Court.

[181] [1997–2001] GR 789 (Supreme Court of The Gambia) (Jallow JSC, sitting as a single justice of the Supreme Court).

[182] Ibid 804.

[183] [1975] AC 396 (HL (E)) (Lords Diplock, Dilhorne, Cross, Salman and Edmund-Davies).

> and principles were not meant to be exhaustive. The basic requirement is that the court should be satisfied that the [plaintiff] has a cause of action recognised at law and that it is just and convenient to grant interlocutory relief. Each case needs to be examined in light of its particular circumstances. There may be special factors which need to be taken into account, particularly where the defendant against whom the interim injunction is sought is a public body or authority with statutory responsibilities to discharge.'

It is clear, therefore, that, when deciding whether to grant an interlocutory injunction, a court in The Gambia will have regard to principles of English law. Lord Diplock's speech in *American Cyanamid* is generally taken as establishing a test comprising two elements:

(1) 'The court … must be satisfied that the claim is not frivolous or vexatious; in other words, that there is a serious issue to be tried':[184]

'unless the material available to the court at the hearing of the application for an interlocutory injunction fails to disclose that the plaintiff has any real prospect of succeeding in his claim for a permanent injunction at the trial, the court should go on to consider whether the balance of convenience lies in favour of granting or refusing the interlocutory relief that is sought';[185]

(2) On the balance of convenience:[186]

'the governing principle is that the court should first consider whether, if the plaintiff were to succeed at the trial in establishing his right to a permanent injunction, he would be adequately compensated by an award of damages for the loss he would have sustained as a result of the defendant's continuing to do what was sought to be enjoined between the time of the application and the time of the trial. If damages in the measure recoverable at common law would be adequate remedy and the defendant would be in a financial position to pay them, no interlocutory injunction should normally be granted, however strong the plaintiff's claim appeared to be at that stage. If, on the other hand, damages would not provide an adequate remedy for the plaintiff in the event of his succeeding at the trial, the court should then consider whether, on the contrary hypothesis that the defendant were to succeed at the trial in establishing his right to do that which was sought to be enjoined, he would be adequately compensated under the plaintiff's undertaking as to damages for the loss he would have sustained by being prevented from doing so between the time of the application and the time of the trial. If damages in the measure recoverable under such an undertaking would be an adequate remedy and the plaintiff would be in a financial position to pay them, there would be no reason upon this ground to refuse an interlocutory injunction.

It is where there is doubt as to the adequacy of the respective remedies in damages available to either party or to both, that the question of balance of convenience arises. It would be unwise to attempt even to list all the various matters which may

---

[184] Ibid 407G.

[185] Ibid 408A–B.

[186] Ibid 408B–G.

> need to be taken into consideration in deciding where the balance lies, let alone to suggest the relative weight to be attached to them. These will vary from case to case.
>
> Where other factors appear to be evenly balanced it is a counsel of prudence to take such measures as are calculated to preserve the status quo.'

13.3.4 Freezing orders

There is no reported authority on the question of whether a court may grant a freezing injunction by way of court order (previously called a *Mareva* injunction),[187] by which the plaintiff can prevent the defendant from dealing with his assets. Such an injunction operates *in personam* against the defendant, rather than *in rem* against his assets.

The English Court of Appeal has set down the following guidance on when a *Mareva* injunction should be granted. Hence, in *Mareva Compania Naviera v International Bulk Carriers SA*,[188] Lord Denning[189] stated:

> 'In my opinion that principle applies to a creditor who has a right to be paid the debt owing to him, even before he has established his right by getting judgment for it. If it appears that the debt is due and owing, and there is a danger that the debtor may dispose of his assets so as to defeat it before judgment, the court has jurisdiction in a proper case to grant an interlocutory judgment so as to prevent him disposing of those assets.'

In *Third Chandris Shipping Corp v Unimarine SA*,[190] Lord Denning MR[191] provided this further guidance:

> **'The guidelines**
>
> In endeavouring to set out some guidelines, I have had recourse to the practice of many other countries which have been put before us. They have been most helpful. These are the points which those who apply for it should bear in mind. (i) The Plaintiff should make full and frank disclosure of all matters in his knowledge which are material for the judge to know… (ii) The Plaintiff should give particulars of his claim against the Defendant, stating the ground of his claim and the amount thereof, and fairly stating the points made against it by the Defendant. (iii) The Plaintiff should give some grounds for believing that the Defendants have assets here… The existence of a bank account in England is enough, whether it is in overdraft or not. (iv) The Plaintiff should give some grounds for believing that there is a risk of the assets being removed before the judgment or award is satisfied. The mere fact that the Defendant is abroad is not by itself sufficient. No one would wish

---

187 After the title of the English authority in which such orders were first approved at appellate level: *Mareva Compania Naviera SA v International Bulkcarriers SA* [1975] 2 Lloyd's Rep 509, CA (Lord Denning MR, Ormrod and Roskill LJJ).

188 [1980] 1 All ER 213, CA (Lord Denning MR, Roskill and Ormrod LJJ).

189 Ibid 215b.

190 [1979] 2 All ER 972 (CA) (Lord Denning MR, Lawton and Cumming-Bruce LJJ).

191 Ibid 984g–985d.

> any reputable foreign company to be plagued with a *Mareva* injunction simply because it has agreed to London arbitration. But there are some foreign companies whose structure invites comment. We often see in this court a corporation which is registered in a country where the company law is so loose that nothing is known about it, where it does no work and has no officers and no assets. Nothing can be found out about the membership, or its control, or its assets, or the charge on them. Judgment cannot be enforced against it. There is no reciprocal enforcement of judgments. It is nothing more than a name grasped from the air, as elusive as the Cheshire cat. In such cases the very fact of incorporation there gives some ground for believing there is a risk that, if judgment or an award is obtained, it may go unsatisfied. Such registration of such companies may carry many advantages to the individuals who control them but they may suffer the disadvantage of having a *Mareva* injunction granted against them. The giving of security for a debt is a small price to pay for the convenience of such a registration. Security would certainly be required in New York. So also it may be in London. Other grounds may be shown for believing there is a risk. But some such should be shown. (v) The Plaintiffs must, of course, give an undertaking in damages, in case they fail in their claim or the injunction turns out to be unjustified. In a suitable case this should be supported by a bond or security: and the injunction only granted on it being given, or undertaken to be given.'

Despite appearances, Order XLVIII, which deals with 'proceedings by foreign attachment', is of no assistance here. Rule 1 of Order XLVIII provides that 'proceedings by foreign attachment may be taken as hereinafter prescribed in all suits founded on contract or for detinue or trover, provided that the cause of action arose within the jurisdiction'. It is of no assistance because, pursuant to the procedure set out in the remainder of the rules in Order XLVIII, the court may 'issue a writ of general attachment against all property, movable and immovable, of the defendant within the jurisdiction, or such part thereof or property specified as may be sufficient to answer the amount of the plaintiff's claim'.[192] Given that the remedy is concerned with attachment of property, rather than an *in personam* order made against the defendant, this does not amount to the grant of *Mareva* style relief.

It remains to be seen whether the courts in The Gambia will develop *Mareva* relief in due course.

13.3.5 Search and seize orders

There is no reported authority in The Gambia on the question of whether a court may grant an order requiring one party to admit another party to premises in order that the second party be entitled to search for documents or other movable property and to take away such documents and movable property and retain

[192] Order XLVIII, r 2 of the Rules of the High Court.

them for the time being. An English court may grant such an order[193] (and, following the first decision at appellate level in England granting such relief, this order may sometimes be referred to as an '*Anton Piller*' order). It remains to be seen whether, following English authorities (which courts in The Gambia are apt to do), this form of relief is developed in The Gambia in due course.

In England, *Anton Piller* relief at common law may be granted in cases in which the pre-conditions set out by Ormrod LJ in the *Anton Piller* case itself have been applied. Those pre-conditions are as follows:[194]

> 'There are three essential pre-conditions for the making of such an order, in my judgment. First, there must be an extremely strong prima facie case. Secondly, the damage, potential or actual, must be very serious for the applicant. Thirdly, there must be clear evidence that the defendants have in their possession incriminating documents or things, and that there is a real possibility that they may destroy such material before any application inter partes can be made.'

13.3.6 Third-party disclosure orders

There is no reported authority on the question whether a court in The Gambia may, apart from the established post-issuing of proceedings and pre-trial procedures whereby a third party may be served with a witness summons requiring his attendance at court in order to give evidence and/or to produce documents,[195] order a person not a party to the proceedings to give disclosure. Such a power is available to the English courts in the form of a *Norwich Pharmacal* order[196] whereby an innocent third party caught up in a tort may be ordered to disclose the name or other identity of the tortfeasor.

In *Norwich Pharmacal Co v Customs* and *Excise Comrs*, the English House of Lords[197] set out the following principle:

> 'That if through no fault of his own a person gets mixed up in the tortious acts of others so as to facilitate their wrong-doing he may incur no personal liability but he comes under a duty to assist the person who has been wronged by giving him full information and disclosing the identity of the wrongdoers ... [It does not matter] whether he became so mixed up by voluntary action on his part or because it was his duty to do what he did. It may be that if this causes him expense the person seeking the information ought to reimburse him. But justice requires that he should co-operate in righting the wrong if he unwittingly facilitated its perpetration.'

---

193 *Anton Piller KG v Manufacturing Processes Ltd* [1976] 1 All ER 779 (CA) (Lord Denning MR; Ormrod and Shaw LJJ).

194 *Anton Piller KG v Manufacturing Processes Ltd* [1976] Ch 55 (CA) (Lord Denning MR, Ormrod and Shaw LJJ), *per* Ormrod LJ at 62A.

195 Order XX, rr 8 and 9 of the Rules of the High Court.

196 *Norwich Pharmacal Co v Customs and Excise Comrs* [1974] AC 133 (HL(E)).

197 Ibid 175, *per* Lord Reid.

More recent authority[198] has clarified the conditions which the plaintiff must satisfy in order to obtain such relief:

> 'The three conditions to be satisfied for the court to exercise the power to order *Norwich Pharmacal* relief are:
>
> i) a wrong must have been carried out, or arguably carried out, by an ultimate wrongdoer;
>
> ii) there must be the need for an order to enable action to be brought against the ultimate wrongdoer; and
>
> iii) the person against whom the order is sought must: (a) be mixed up in so as to have facilitated the wrongdoing; and (b) be able or likely to be able to provide the information necessary to enable the ultimate wrongdoer to be sued.'

If the plaintiff satisfies all of those conditions, the English court will then go on to exercise its discretion. In doing so, it must keep in mind the proper scope of *Norwich Pharmacal* relief: the jurisdiction cannot be used for wide-ranging discovery or the gathering of evidence, but is strictly confined to necessary information.[199]

13.3.7 Anti-suit injunctions

An anti-suit injunction is an order restraining the injunction defendant from either commencing or continuing proceedings outside The Gambia in breach of a legal or equitable right on the part of the injunction plaintiff not to pursue litigation outside The Gambia or, conversely, restraining the injunction defendant from commencing or continuing proceedings inside The Gambia in breach of a legal or equitable right on the part of the injunction plaintiff to have the dispute between the parties litigated in a jurisdiction other than The Gambia.[200]

There is no reported judicial authority in The Gambia on whether or not an anti-suit injunction is a remedy available to the courts in The Gambia.

---

[198] *Ramilos Trading Ltd v Valentin Mikhaylovich Buyanovsky* [2016] EWHC 3175 (Comm) (H Ct) (Flaux J), citing, at para [11], *Mitsui v Nexen Petroleum* [2005] EWHC 625 (Ch); [2005] 3 All ER 511 (H Ct) para [21] (Lightman J).

[199] *Ramilos Trading Ltd v Valentin Mikhaylovich Buyanovsky* [2016] EWHC 3175 (Comm) (H Ct) (Flaux J) para [46].

[200] In similar vein, an anti-anti-suit injunction is an order restraining the injunction defendant from commencing or continuing proceedings to restrain the injunction plaintiff from applying to restrain the injunction defendant from commencing or continuing proceedings. The leading works on this topic are: Raphael *The Anti-Suit Injunction* 2 ed (2019) and Briggs *Civil Jurisdiction and Judgments* 7 ed (2021) ch 28. It is also conceptually possible to obtain similar relief in the context of arbitration but such relief is outside the scope of this work.

However, as noted at section 13.3.1 above, the jurisdiction of High Court to grant injunctions is statutory. That jurisdiction may be exercised in all cases where it is 'just and convenient' to do so.[201]

Given that the jurisdictional basis on which a court in The Gambia may grant an interim injunction is identical to that upon which an English court may grant that relief, and given the affinity of The Gambia's law with English law in this regard,[202] it is to be anticipated that a court in The Gambia before which an application is brought for an anti-suit injunction will have regard to the English authorities in setting out the principles upon which an anti-suit injunction may be granted in The Gambia. Set out below, in summary, are the principles of English law governing the grant of an anti-suit injunction.

The court must have personal jurisdiction over the injunction defendant. The court may be seised either by service on the defendant within the jurisdiction or service out of the jurisdiction with the leave of the court.[203]

The injunction plaintiff must assert a cause of action for relief. Usually, the injunction plaintiff will contend that the injunction defendant is committing a wrong by bringing or proposing to bring proceedings in a foreign court. This will require the plaintiff to characterise the conduct of the defendant as the breach of a legal or equitable right.

A legal right may, and often will, be based on a right not to be sued in a foreign jurisdiction arising out of an exclusive jurisdiction clause in favour of the courts of The Gambia. An equitable right may be the right not to be sued in a foreign jurisdiction and may be the corollary of an equitable wrong which is that it is oppressive and vexatious and therefore unconscionable for the injunction defendant to commence or continue proceedings against the injunction plaintiff in a foreign jurisdiction.

The prime example of a cause of action based on a legal right not to be sued in a foreign jurisdiction is where the parties have agreed expressly that the courts of The Gambia should have exclusive jurisdiction over disputes arising out of the contract (which can be a substantive contract or a settlement agreement) between them.[204] In such a case proof of the underlying cause of action is likely to be a

---

[201] Section 3 of the Courts Act 1964 provides that the High Court 'shall have the jurisdiction and powers provided by the Constitution and all the jurisdiction, powers and authorities which were vested in or capable of being exercised by Her Majesty's High Court of Justice in England immediately before the eighteenth day of February, 1965'. There is no doubt that, on that date, the English High Court had the power to grant an injunction where it was 'just and convenient' to do so: *Fourie v Le Roux* [2007] 1 WLR 320 (HL(E)) (Lords Bingham, Hope, Scott, Rodger and Carswell), *per* Lord Scott at [25].

[202] It is worth noting that the High Court of South Africa in *Vedanta Resources Holdings Ltd v ZCCM Investment Holdings plc* 2019 JDR 1425 (GJ) paras [11], [54] and [56] (Adams J) and the High Court of Nigeria in *Zenith Global Merchant Ltd v Zhongfu International Investment (Nig) FZE* (2017) All FWLR 1837 at 1924 (Akinyemi J) have also referred to English principles in a similar context.

[203] The substantive law and procedure for which in The Gambia has been set out above.

[204] The contract may be a substantive contract or a settlement agreement and the dispute resolution provisions may be exclusively in favour of the courts of The Gambia or may be in favour of arbitration:

sufficient condition for the grant of the relief and that good reason would need to be shown why the discretion to order an injunction should not be exercised.[205]

The principal example of a cause of action based on an equitable wrong is where proceedings brought abroad by the defendant are oppressive and vexatious. An example of such conduct is illustrated by the decision of the Privy Council in *SNI Aerospatiale v Lee Kui Jak*,[206] where a resident of Brunei had been killed in a helicopter crash and his widow (and her brother-in-law, as co-administrator of his estate), the respondent plaintiffs in the appeal to the Privy Council, had commenced proceedings in Brunei and had subsequently been persuaded to sue in Texas instead. The appellant defendant applied for an anti-suit injunction restraining the plaintiffs from proceeding against it in Texas. The Privy Council allowed the defendant's appeal, held that an injunction ought to be granted restraining the respondents from proceeding in Texas and remitted the matter to the Brunei courts.

Transposing the findings of the Privy Council to The Gambia, it was held that an anti-suit injunction would be granted if: (1) pursuit of the foreign proceedings is vexatious or oppressive; (2) The Gambia is the natural forum for the resolution of the dispute; and (3) the injunction does not deprive the defendant of advantages in the foreign jurisdiction of which it would be unjust to deprive him.[207]

Other examples of equitable wrongs which may attract an anti-suit injunction are: undermining the jurisdiction of a court of The Gambia;[208] vexatious conduct by relying on foreign procedural laws;[209] wrongfully undermining a judgment of a court of The Gambia;[210] or enforcement of a foreign judgment wrongfully obtained.[211]

British Airways Board v Laker Airways Ltd [1985] AC 58 (HL (E)) (Lords Diplock, Fraser, Scarman, Roskill and Brightman), *per* Lord Diplock at p 81C–E.

[205] *The Angelic Grace* [1995] 1 Lloyd's Rep 87 (CA) (Neill, Leggatt and Millett LJJ), *per* Millett LJ at p 96, col 2, and Neill LJ at p 97, col 1; *Donohue v Armco Inc* [2000] 1 Lloyd's Rep 579 (CA) (Stuart-Smith, Brooke and Sedley LJJ), where it was stated that 'strong reasons' (*per* Stuart-Smith LJ at para 35) or 'strong cause' (*per* Brooke LJ at paras 59 and 60) would be required to deny an injunction.

[206] [1987] AC 871 (PC (Brunei)) (Lords Keith, Griffiths, MacKay and Goff and Sir John Megaw).

[207] Lord Goff (giving the opinion of the Privy Council) p 896F–H. That the court to which the application is made should be the natural forum for the resolution of the dispute was repeated by the House of Lords in *Airbus Industrie GIE v Patel* [1999] 1 AC 119 (HL (E)) (Lords Goff, Slynn, Steyn, Clyde and Hutton), *per* Lord Goff (with whom the other Lords agreed) 138G-H and 140H-141B.

[208] For example, by commencing bankruptcy proceedings outside the jurisdiction when such proceedings are in progress in The Gambia: *SNI Aerospatiale v Lee Kui Jak* [1987] AC 871, *per* Lord Goff at 892G–893B.

[209] By seeking to depose witnesses in the US where those witnesses would be subject to cross-examination in proceedings in The Gambia; for example: *Omega Group Holdings Ltd v Kozeny* [2002] CLC 132.

[210] By commencing proceedings outside the jurisdiction for declaratory relief designed to frustrate the enforcement of a judgment of a court in The Gambia in that jurisdiction: *Masri v Consolidated Contractors International (UK) Ltd (No 3)* [2009] QB 503 (CA).

[211] Where the foreign judgment was obtained through fraud and perjury: *Ellerman Lines Ltd v Read* [1928] 2 KB 144 (CA), *per* Scrutton LJ at 152–3.

13.3.8 Other interlocutory relief

13.3.8.1 *Interim attachment of property*

Order XI, rule 1 of the Rules of the High Court provides that, in a suit for an amount or value of 200 dalasis[212] or more, where the defendant, with the intent to obstruct or delay the execution of any decree that may be passed against him or her, is about to dispose of his or her property, or any part thereof, or remove such property from the jurisdiction of the court, the plaintiff may apply to the court, either at the institution of the suit or any time thereafter, for relief. In the circumstances, the plaintiff may require the defendant to

> 'furnish security to fulfil any decree that may be made against him or her in the suit, and on his or her failing to give such security, [the court may] direct that any property movable or immovable belonging to the defendant shall be attached until further order of the court.'

For reasons already set out above when considering Order XLVIII (with which Order XI has a natural affinity), Order XI cannot accurately be described as *Mareva* relief.

An application for the interim attachment of property shall contain a specification of the property required to be attached and the plaintiff's estimated value of the same.[213] In that affidavit, the plaintiff shall declare that to the best of his or her information and belief, the defendant is about to dispose of or remove his or her property with the requisite intent.

Where the court is satisfied that the defendant is about to dispose of or remove his or her property with the necessary intent, the court may order the defendant, within a time fixed by the court, either to furnish security in such sum as may be specified in the order and place this at the disposal of the court or to appear and show cause as to why he or she should not furnish security.[214] If the defendant cannot show such cause, the court may then direct the attachment of the property specified in the application.[215]

13.3.8.2 *Arrest of absconding defendant*

Order X, rule 1 provides that, in a suit for an amount for the value of 200 dalasis or upwards, where the defendant is about to leave the jurisdiction of the court or has disposed of or removed his property, or any part thereof, from the jurisdiction,

---

212 Approximately US$4.00.

213 Order XI, r 2 of the Rules of the High Court.

214 Order XI, r 3 of the Rules of the High Court.

215 Order XI, r 4(1). Where property is attached, such attachment shall not affect the rights of persons not parties to the suit: O XI, r 5 of the Rules of the High Court. See further: *Breckwoldt v Khushal (London) Ltd* (1963–1966) 1 GR (CS) 1 (Court of Appeal of The Gambia) (Ames P; Dove-Edwin and Marcus-Jones JJA.).

the plaintiff may, either at the institution of the suit or at any time thereafter until final judgment, apply to the court that security be taken for the appearance of the defendant to answer any judgment that may be passed against him in the suit.

Unlike when the plaintiff is seeking an interim attachment of the defendant's property, the plaintiff does not need to show any intention on the part of the defendant when seeking his arrest. Instead, where the court is of the opinion that there is probable cause[216] for believing that the defendant is about to leave the jurisdiction of the court, or that he has disposed or removed his property from the jurisdiction and that, in consequence, the execution or any order or decree which may be made is likely to be frustrated or delayed, the court may issue a warrant to bring the defendant before the court.[217] The defendant, when before the court, will be required to show cause why he should not give good and sufficient bail for his appearance.[218]

---

[216] There is an absence of authority on the meaning of the words 'probable cause'. The question has arisen whether the order might be made simply on the basis that the defendant is not a national of The Gambia. In *Banjul Oxygen Ltd v Aki Allen* [1987] Judgments and Orders of The Gambia Court of Appeal 118 (Livesey Luke, Ag P; Anin JA and Olayinka Ayoola CJ) 125, Olayinka Ayoola CJ, giving the judgment of the Court of Appeal, stated: 'The fact of the defendant not being a Gambian is not by itself a sufficient ground for making an order in the plaintiff's favour [under this Order].' *Banjul Oxygen* has since been referred to with approval in *Barry (No 2) v Seow Guan Co* [1997–2001] GR 354 (Court of Appeal of The Gambia) (Chomba P, Lartey and Gelaga King JJA).

[217] Order X, r 2 of the Rules of the High Court. The defendant's appearance before the court is not a mere technicality: *Banjul Oxygen Ltd v Aki Allen* [1987] Judgments and Orders of The Gambia Court of Appeal 118.

[218] Order X, r 2 of the Rules of the High Court. If the defendant fails to show good cause, the court shall order him to give bail for his or her appearance at any time when called on while the suit is pending and, until execution or satisfaction of any decree that may be passed against him in the suit: O X, r 3 of the Rules of the High Court. Where the defendant neither furnishes security nor offers sufficient deposit, he may be committed to custody until the decision of the suit, or, if judgment is given against the defendant, until execution of the decree: r 5(1). The expenses incurred for the subsistence in prison of the defendant shall be paid by the plaintiff in advance: r 6.

Chapter 14

UGANDA

14.1 Jurisdiction

The bases on which a Ugandan court may assume jurisdiction over a cause or matter are statutory in origin.

Section 139(1) of the Constitution of the Republic of Uganda provides:

> '**139. Jurisdiction of the High Court**.
>
> (1) The High Court shall, subject to the provisions of this Constitution, have unlimited original jurisdiction in all matters and such appellate and other jurisdiction as may be conferred on it by this Constitution or other law.'

The fundamental means by which a Ugandan court is seised of jurisdiction over a defendant at the suit of a plaintiff is by service of process on the defendant.

Order IV, rule 1 of the Civil Procedure Rules 2014[1] ('the CPR') provides that suits in Uganda are commenced by the plaintiff presenting a plaint to the court. The plaint must comply with the requirements of Orders VI and VII,[2] so far as applicable.

Once a plaint has been presented to the court a summons may be issued to the defendant[3] '(a) ordering him or her to file a defence within a time to be specified in the summons; or (b) ordering him or her to appear and answer the claim on a day to be specified in the summons'. The summons must be served within 21 days.[4] The summons must be accompanied by[5] 'a copy of the plaint, a brief summary of the evidence to be adduced, a list of witnesses, a list of documents and a list of authorities to be relied on'.

The CPR then distinguishes between service within and service outside the jurisdiction.

---

[1] Promulgated by statutory instrument, SI 71/1, 1 May 2014. Now amended by the Civil Procedure (Amendment) Rules 2019, SI 33 of 2019. The Civil Procedure Rules 2014 replaced the Civil Procedure Rules 1964, SI 71/1, 31 January 1964. Where the 2014 Rules appear materially identical to the 1964 Rules, authorities interpreting the 1964 Rules ought to be followed when considering questions of the construction of the 2014 Rules.

[2] Order VII, r 1, provides, 'The plaint shall contain the following particulars— (a) the name of the court in which the suit is brought; (b) the name, description and place of residence of the plaintiff, and an address for service; (c) the name, description and place of residence of the defendant, so far as they can be ascertained; (d) where the plaintiff or defendant is a minor or person of unsound mind, a statement to that effect; (e) the facts constituting the cause of action and when it arose; (f) the facts showing that the court has jurisdiction; (g) the relief which the plaintiff claims; (h) where the plaintiff has allowed a setoff or relinquished a portion of his or her claim, the amount so allowed or relinquished; and (i) a statement of the value of the subject matter of the suit so far as the case admits.' A plaint may be rejected by the court on the grounds, for example, that it discloses no cause of action (r 11(a)) and, if that course is taken, the judge must record the reasons for the rejection of the plaint in an order (r 12).

[3] Order V, r 1(1).

[4] Though time may be extended on application to the court, made within 25 days after the expiration of the 21 days, showing sufficient reasons for the extension: O V, r 1(2).

[5] Order V, r 2.

14.1.1 Service where the defendant is within the jurisdiction

Order V makes provision for service within the jurisdiction.[6] The default rule is that a defendant must be served personally with any originating process and accompanying documentation.[7] Provision is also made for substituted service in specified circumstances.[8]

The CPR also make provision for particular instances of service. By way of example, Order XXIX deals specifically with service on corporations,[9] while Order XXX addresses service on partnerships.[10]

The Companies Act 2012[11] has created an alternative regime for, inter alia, service of process on what the Act refers to as 'foreign companies'. These are defined by section 251 as: 'companies incorporated outside Uganda which establish a place of business in Uganda and companies incorporated outside Uganda which have established a place of business in Uganda and continue to have a place of business in Uganda'. By section 261, the expression 'place of business' includes a share transfer or share registration office.

A foreign company which establishes a place of business within Uganda shall, within 30 days after the establishment of the place of business, deliver to the registrar for registration, inter alia, the names and postal addresses of one or more persons resident in Uganda authorised to accept on behalf of the company service

---

[6] Section 15 of the Civil Procedure Act 1929 (Act 1 of 1928), governs the distribution of jurisdiction within Uganda itself (ie in which domestic court the plaintiff should institute proceedings). See *Wigglesworth Clearing Ltd v Trago (U) Ltd* [1999] Kam LR 772 (H Ct) (Okello Ag J), where the defendant company was incorporated in Uganda and was therefore resident in Uganda for the purposes of s 15 of the 1929 Act. The correct domestic citation of the 1929 Act is 'The Civil Procedure Act [Chapter 71]' of the Laws of Uganda 2000. In this regard, the reader is referred to the 'Note on the citation of statutory material in this work', which appears at the end of the 'List of Statutory Material Cited' at the beginning of this work.

[7] Order V, r 1(2) and r 10, the latter of which provides: 'Wherever it is practicable, service shall be made on the defendant in person, unless he or she has an agent empowered to accept service, in which case service on the agent shall be sufficient.'

[8] Order V, r 18. See also *Bitamisi v Rwabuganda* [2017] UGSC 19 (Katureebe CJ, Tumwesigye, Kisaakye, Arach-Amoko and Mwangusya JJ).

[9] Order XXIX, r 2, which provides that, subject to any statutory provision regulating service of process, where the suit is against a corporation, the summons may be served on the secretary or on any director or other principle officer of the corporation; or by leaving it or sending it by post addressed to the corporation at the registered office, or if there is no registered office, then at the place where the corporation carries on business. The Companies Act 2012 (Act 1 of 2012), at s 274 provides that a document may be served on a company formed and registered under the Act or an existing or re-registered company under the Act by personally serving it on an officer of the company, by sending it by registered post to the registered postal address of the company in Uganda or by sending an email to the known electronic address or by leaving it at the registered office of the company.

[10] Order XXX, r 3.

[11] Brought into force on 1 July 2013 by SI 24 of 2013. The Companies Act 2012 repealed, by s 298, and replaced the Companies Act 1961 (formerly Cap 110 of the Laws of Uganda 2000).

of process and any notices required to be served on the company; and the full address of the registered or principal office of the company.[12]

By section 258(1), any process or notice to be served on a foreign company shall be sufficiently served if addressed to any person whose name has been delivered to the registrar (in conformity with the requirements set out in the previous paragraph) and left at or sent by registered post to the address which has been delivered to the registrar. In circumstances where: (1) a foreign company has failed to deliver to the registrar the name and address of a person resident in Uganda authorised to accept service of process or notices on behalf of the company; or (2) where, at any time, those people whose names and addresses have been delivered to the registrar are dead or have ceased to reside in Uganda or cease to accept service on behalf of the company or for any reason cannot be served, a document may be served on the foreign company by leaving it at or sending it by registered post to any place of business established by the company in Uganda.[13]

14.1.2 Service where the defendant is outside the jurisdiction

Order V, rule 22 makes provision for service of process[14] outside the jurisdiction and prescribes an exhaustive set of grounds on the basis of which the Ugandan court may assume jurisdiction over a person present outside the jurisdiction.

Order V, rule 22 provides:[15]

> **'22. In certain cases service of the summons, etc. allowed out of jurisdiction**
>
> Service out of the jurisdiction of a summons or notice of a summons may be allowed by the court whenever—
>
> *(a)* the whole subject matter of the suit is immovable property situated within the jurisdiction, (with or without rents and profits);

[12] Section 252(1).

[13] Section 258(2).

[14] It will be noted that the provisions of O V distinguish between a summons and a notice of a summons. Order V, rr 26 and 27 (which are discussed further below) explain why.

[15] Order V, r 22 is materially identical to O XI, r 1, of the English Rules of the Supreme Court 1883. Apart from minor differences in language, the main differences are: the 1883 Rules make provision for service out of the jurisdiction in cases of a claim in contract: where the contract is made within the jurisdiction; where a contract is made by or through an agent trading or residing within the jurisdiction; and where the contract is governed by English law (O XI, r 1(e)(i)–(iii)). (The 1883 Rules also contain, at r 1(h), a provision concerning actions by a mortgagee or mortgagor of personal property within the jurisdiction that is absent from the provisions of O V, r 22.) The sequence of sub-rules in O V, r 22 is also a little different: the tort basis for service out appears in the 1961 edition of the 1883 Rules as sub-r (ee) and in the Ugandan CPR as sub-r (h) (in substitution for O XI, r 1(h)). In view of this very close correspondence between the wording of O XI, r 1 of the 1883 Rules and wording of O V, r 22 of the CPR, it is to be expected that Ugandan courts will be assisted in interpreting the provisions of O V, r 22 by English judicial and academic authorities on the meaning of O XI, r 1 and its successors.

(b) any act, deed, will, contract, obligation or liability affecting immovable property situate within the jurisdiction is sought to be construed, rectified, set aside or enforced in the suit;

(c) any relief is sought against any person domiciled or ordinarily resident within the jurisdiction;

(d) the suit is for the administration of the personal estate of any deceased person, who at the time of his or her death was domiciled within the jurisdiction, or for the execution (as to property situate within the jurisdiction) of the trusts of any written instrument, of which the person to be served is a trustee, which ought to be executed according to the law of Uganda;

(e) the suit is founded on any breach or alleged breach within the jurisdiction of any contract wherever made which, according to the terms of the contract, ought to be performed within the jurisdiction;

(f) any injunction is sought as to anything to be done within the jurisdiction, or any nuisance within the jurisdiction is sought to be prevented or removed, whether damages are or are not also sought in respect thereof;

(g) any person out of the jurisdiction is a necessary or proper party to a suit properly brought against some other person duly served within the jurisdiction; or

(h) the suit is founded on a tort committed within the jurisdiction.'[16]

14.1.2.1 *Procedure*

Order V, rule 24 provides:

'24. Application to be supported by evidence.

Every application for leave to serve the summons or notice on a defendant out of the jurisdiction shall be supported by affidavit or other evidence, stating that in the belief of the deponent the plaintiff has a good cause of action, and showing in what place or country the defendant is or probably may be found, and whether the defendant is a Commonwealth citizen or British protected person or not, and the grounds on which the application is made; and no such leave shall be granted unless it is made sufficiently to appear to the court that the case is a proper one for service out of the jurisdiction under this Order.'

[16] It is to be noted that O V, r 22 does not provide for service out of the jurisdiction in order to enforce a foreign judgment against a person not domiciled or resident within the jurisdiction where a judgment creditor might wish to enforce the judgment because of the presence within the jurisdiction of assets belonging to the judgment debtor (a similar omission was remedied in the English CPR by the introduction of such a basis for service out by SI 1181 of 1983 and, for the purposes of comparison, reference may now be made to the English CPR, PD 6B, para 3.1(10)); see also, Frimpong Oppong 'Recognition and enforcement of foreign judgments in Commonwealth African countries' (2014) XV *Yearbook of Private International Law* 365 at 371–2. Further, O V, r 22 does not provide for service out of the jurisdiction, inter alia, in the following cases: where damage is sustained within the jurisdiction as a result of a tort committed outside the jurisdiction; where a contract is made within the jurisdiction; where a contract is made by or through an agent trading or residing within the jurisdiction; where the contract is governed by Ugandan law; and the contract contains a jurisdiction clause in favour of the Ugandan courts.

It is unclear as a matter of Ugandan law what standard a plaintiff who makes an application for leave to serve out of the jurisdiction must satisfy before that leave will be granted.[17] In English law the test is that of a good arguable case.[18]

It has been noted above that the Ugandan CPR provisions empowering the court to grant leave to serve outside the jurisdiction are derived from the English Rules of the Supreme Court 1883. In view of this affinity with the earlier English rules of court and, indeed, in view of the affinity which the law of Uganda has with the law of England generally, it is likely that, when considering the matters referred to in this section, a court in Uganda may derive some assistance from the English authorities.

Set out below, therefore, is guidance that is drawn from the English authorities in which the equivalent rules have been considered.

The English equivalents of Ugandan CPR Order V, rules 22 and 24, have been the subject of judicial consideration at the highest level in England. In *Seaconsar Far East Ltd v Bank Markazi Jomhouri Islami Iran*,[19] the House of Lords considered the interaction of Order XI, rules 1(1) and 4 of the Rules of the Supreme Court

[17] On identically worded provisions in the Nigerian High Court Rules, the Nigerian High Court held that the proper test for the court to apply to the evidence produced is whether there remains a strong argument that the grounds have been satisfied: a *prima facie* case against the defendant is not sufficient, but neither is it necessary to satisfy the court beyond reasonable doubt that the grounds have been established *Cold Containers (Nigeria) Ltd v Collis Cold Containers Ltd* (1977) 1 ALR Comm 97, [1977] NCLR 97; see also, Frimpong Oppong *Private International Law in Commonwealth Africa* (2013) 59. For a full treatment of the Nigerian jurisprudence, see the relevant section of the chapter on Nigeria.

[18] In *Canada Trust v Stolzenberg (No 2)* [2002] 1 AC 1 (HL(E)) (Lords Steyn, Hoffmann, Cooke, Hope and Hobhouse), *per* Lord Steyn (with whom the other Lords agreed) 13F, the House of Lords appeared to approve passages from the judgment of Waller LJ in the Court of Appeal in the same case ([1998] 1 WLR 547) including the following (at 555F–G): 'It is also right to remember that the "good arguable case" test, although obviously applicable to the ex parte stage, becomes of most significance at the inter partes stage where two arguments are being weighed in the interlocutory context which, as I have stressed, must not become a "trial". "Good arguable case" reflects in that context that one side has a much better argument on the material available. It is the concept which the phrase reflects on which it is important to concentrate, i.e. of the court being satisfied or as satisfied as it can be having regard to the limitations which an interlocutory process imposes that factors exist which allow the court to take jurisdiction.' In *Goldman Sachs International v Novo Banco SA* [2018] 1 WLR 3683 (Lords Mance, Sumption and Hodge, Lady Black and Lord Lloyd-Jones), the UK Supreme Court further clarified the correct understanding of the test in the *Canada Trust* case. Lord Sumption (with whom all the other members of the court agreed and in reliance on his own judgment in *Brownlie v Four Seasons Holdings Incorporated* [2018] 1 WLR 192) stated at para [9]: 'For the purpose of determining an issue about jurisdiction, the traditional test has been whether the claimant had "the better of the argument" on the facts going to jurisdiction. In *Brownlie v Four Seasons Holdings Inc* [2018] 1 WLR 192, para 7, this court reformulated the effect of that test as follows: "(i) that the claimant must supply a plausible evidential basis for the application of a relevant jurisdictional gateway; (ii) that if there is an issue of fact about it, or some other reason for doubting whether it applies, the court must take a view on the material available if it can reliably do so; but (iii) the nature of the issue and the limitations of the material available at the interlocutory stage may be such that no reliable assessment can be made, in which case there is a good arguable case for the application of the gateway if there is a plausible (albeit contested) evidential basis for it."'

[19] [1994] 1 AC 438 (HL(E)) (Lords Templeman, Griffiths, Goff, Browne-Wilkinson and Mustill).

(the equivalent to CPR, Order V, rules 22 and 24). Lord Goff (with whom the other Lords agreed) reviewed the authorities on the question what a plaintiff under Order XI was required to show on an application for leave to serve a writ out of the jurisdiction and found that the plaintiff was required to show, first, that the cause of action deposed to in the evidence in support of the application fell within the provisions of rule 1(1) and, second, that on the merits of the case there was a serious question to be tried. On the question of the standard to which these issues were required to be shown, Lord Goff stated:[20]

> 'A judge faced with a question of leave to serve proceedings out of the jurisdiction under Order 11 will in practice have to consider both (1) whether jurisdiction has been sufficiently established, on the criterion of the good arguable case laid down in *Korner's* case, under one of the paragraphs of rule 1(1), and (2) whether there is a serious issue to be tried, so as to enable him to exercise his discretion to grant leave, before he goes on to consider the exercise of that discretion, with particular reference to the issue of forum conveniens.'

The first of these matters was held to correspond to the requirement in Order XI, rule 4 (CPR, Order V, rule 24) that 'no such leave shall be granted unless it shall be made sufficiently to appear to the Court or Judge that the case is a proper one for service out of the jurisdiction under this Order'[21] and the second was a threshold requirement for the merits of the plaintiff's claim.[22]

Thus, considering the English authorities, it is suggested that, analytically, it would be helpful to determine applications for leave to serve process out of the jurisdiction by applying the following, four-component approach.[23]

(1) *The formal requirements.* Has the plaintiff produced evidence satisfying the formal requirements of Order V, rule 24 (or English Order XI, rule 4)? In Uganda, under the CPR, a plaintiff in his affidavit or other evidence in support of the application is required to set out: (a) the belief of the deponent

[20] Ibid 456H–457B. See also the decision of the Privy Council in *Altimo Holdings and Investment Ltd v Kyrgyz Mobil Tel Ltd* [2012] 1 WLR 1804 (Lord Phillips PSC, Lords Mance, Collins, Kerr and Clarke JJSC), *per* Lord Collins at para [71], confirming this statement of principle.

[21] *Seaconsar* at 451A–B, 452A–B, 453D–G.

[22] Ibid 452D–E, 455A–C, 456G–H. Notwithstanding the separate treatment of the English O XI, r 4, in *Seaconsar* and the earlier authorities referred to therein, it is unclear whether the amendment in 1883 of O XI, r 3 (under the Rules of Court contained in Sch 1 to the Supreme Court of Judicature Act 1875) by the introduction of an expanded O XI, r 4, in the 1883 Rules of Court, was intended to produce this result. At the time the leading textbook on the Rules took the view that the amendment to include the wording, 'No such leave shall be granted unless it shall be made sufficiently to appear to the Court or Judge that the case is a proper one for service out of the jurisdiction under this Order' was merely an amplification of the previous rule (see Wynne Baxter *Judicature Acts and Rules 1873–1883* 5 ed (1883) 176–7).

[23] As summarised in the English *Supreme Court Practice 1965* (1999 ed) 93–4, paras 11/1/9–11/1/12. The commentary referred to in the *Supreme Court Practice* refers to three elements; in the text above the present authors include four elements, the additional element being the formal requirements of English r 4 and Ugandan r 24.

that the plaintiff has a good cause of action; (b) the place or country the defendant is or probably may be found; (c) whether the defendant is a Commonwealth citizen or British protected person or not; and the grounds on which the application is made.

(2) *The sufficiency requirement.* Under the English Order XI, rule 4, it was held in the *Seaconsar* case that the words 'and no such leave shall be granted unless it shall be made sufficiently to appear to the Court or Judge that the case is a proper one for service out of the jurisdiction under this Order' introduced a sufficiency requirement (or, in other words, a degree of proof requirement) such that the plaintiff must show that there is a good arguable case that the case falls within one of the gateways under Order XI, rule 1(1). Order V, rule 24 contains the same requirement.

(3) *The merits requirement.* As a matter of English law, the plaintiff must demonstrate that there is a serious issue to be tried on the merits of the claim upon which the claimant relies. Lord Goff in *Seaconsar* stated[24] as follows:

> 'The court cannot resolve disputed questions of fact on affidavit evidence; and it is consistent with the statement of the law by Lord Davey that if, at the end of the day, there remains a substantial question of fact or law or both, arising on the facts disclosed by the affidavits, which the plaintiff bona fide desires to try, the court should, as a rule, allow the service of the writ. If this approach is correct, the standard of proof in respect of the cause of action can broadly be stated to be whether, on the affidavit evidence before the court, there is a serious question to be tried.'

(4) *The court's discretion.* As a matter of English law, once the above matters are established by the plaintiff, the court will proceed to consider the exercise of its discretion to allow service out of the jurisdiction. The court's discretion is exercised cautiously. As was stated by Pearson J in *Société Générale de Paris v Dreyfus Brothers*:[25]

> 'But of course it becomes a very serious question, and ought always to be considered a very serious question, whether or not, even in a case like that, it is necessary for the jurisdiction of the Court to be invoked, and whether this Court ought to put a foreigner, who owes no allegiance here, to the inconvenience and annoyance of being brought to contest his rights in this country, and I for one say, most distinctly, that I think this Court ought to be exceedingly careful before it allows a writ to be served out of the jurisdiction.'[26]

Turning back to the law in Uganda, once the plaintiff has satisfied the court to the required standard that he is within one or more of the relevant gateways

24 *Seaconsar* 452C–D.

25 (1885) 29 Ch D 239 at 242–3; cited with approval by Lord Goff in *Seaconsar* at 455D.

26 The exercise of the court's discretion is dealt with in greater depth below.

under Order V, rule 22, the court has power to grant the plaintiff leave to serve the defendant out of the jurisdiction. As provided in the final words of Order V, rule 24, the court must be satisfied that the cause is a proper one for service out of the jurisdiction.[27] Whether the court exercises this power is a matter of discretion. In exercising that discretion, the court will take into account the appropriateness of Uganda as a forum for the resolution of the dispute. The exercise of the court's discretion is dealt with under the sub-heading '*Forum non conveniens*' below.

Order V, rules 25–28 contain ancillary provisions concerning, inter alia, the time within which the defendant must enter an appearance after service of process on him,[28] the distinction to be drawn between service on Commonwealth citizens and British protected persons, on the one hand, and service on all other foreigners, on the other hand,[29] what ought practically to happen when leave is given to serve notice of the summons out of the jurisdiction[30] and substituted service of process for service outside the jurisdiction.[31]

Finally, the application for leave to serve outside the jurisdiction is made *ex parte* and, as is usual in such circumstances, there is a duty on the plaintiff to make full and frank disclosure of all material facts. Although no Ugandan authority is directly in point, in the Kenyan case of *Donnebaum v Mikolaschek*,[32] Farrell J held,[33] citing an English authority, *The Hagen*,[34] that there had not been full and frank disclosure on the plaintiff's (second) application to serve outside the jurisdiction and that this alone would justify the setting aside of the order granted to serve the defendant outside the jurisdiction.

---

[27] These words have been held, as a matter of English authority, to mean that the court must be satisfied that the case falls within one of the jurisdictional gateways in the rule: *Seaconsar Far East Ltd v Bank Markazi Jomhouri Islami Iran* [1994] 1 AC 438 (HL(E)) (Lords Templeman, Griffiths, Goff, Browne-Wilkinson and Mustill), *per* Lord Goff at 451A–B. In this, Lord Goff was following Lord Davey in *Chemische Fabrik vormals Sandoz v Badische Anilin und Soda Fabriks* (1904) 90 LT 733 at 735, where he said in relation to similar words under the former rule: 'The words at the end of the order do not, I think, mean more than that the court is to be satisfied that the case comes within the class of cases in which service abroad may be made under the first rule of the order.'

[28] Rule 25.

[29] Rules 26 and 27.

[30] Rule 28.

[31] Rule 28(e).

[32] [1966] EA 25 (H Ct) (Farrell J). This was the plaintiff's second attempt to seise the Kenyan court of jurisdiction. The first attempt was dismissed by Rudd J in September 1964: [1964] EA 645.

[33] Ibid 28A.

[34] [1908] P 189 CA (Lord Alverstone CJ and Farwell and Kennedy LJJ), *per* Farwell LJ at 201: 'The second point which we considered established by the cases was this, that, if on the construction of any of the sub-heads of Order XI. there was any doubt, it ought to be resolved in favour of the foreigner; and the third is that, inasmuch as the application is made *ex parte*, full and fair disclosure is necessary, as in all *ex parte* applications, and a failure to make such full and fair disclosure would justify the Court in discharging the order, even although the party might afterwards be in a position to make another application.'

14.1.2.2 *Bases for service out of the jurisdiction*

The bases on which the court may grant leave that are of particular significance for present purposes are discussed below.

(1) Relief is sought against any person domiciled, or ordinarily resident, within the jurisdiction

The term '*person*' in Order V, rule 22, includes any natural or legal person.[35]

There is little Ugandan judicial authority on the meaning of the term 'domicile' for the purposes of the application of Order V, rule 22(c). It is likely, given the willingness of the Ugandan courts to look to English law for the meaning of terms inherited from colonial times, that the Ugandan courts will adopt the jurisprudence applicable in English law regarding the term 'domicile' for the purposes of determining jurisdiction over a person.[36] Under the English Rules of the Supreme Court upon which Order V, rule 22, of the CPR appears to have been based,[37] 'domicile' was defined as follows:[38]

> 'In general the domicile of a person is in the country in which he has his permanent home (see Dicey, *Conflict of Law*, 7th ed., Chap. 6), the country in which his habitation is fixed without any present intention of removing (Re *Craignish*, [1892] 3 Ch. 180, C.A.; *Huntly v. Gaskell*, [1906] A.C. 56; *Casdagli v. C.*, [1919] A.C. 145). No person can at any time be without a domicile or have more than one domicile. The domicile of origin remains until a new domicile of choice has been adopted (*Bell v. Kennedy* (1868), L.R. 1 Sc. App. 307, H.L.; *Udny v. Udny* (1869), ibid, 441, H.L.; *Winans v. A.-G.*, [1904] A.C. 287, H.L.).'

The Ugandan courts will have jurisdiction on the basis of ordinary residence 'within the jurisdiction'. In *Wigglesworth Clearing Ltd v Trago (U) Ltd*,[39] the plaintiff Kenyan company issued proceedings against the defendant company, which had been incorporated in Uganda, for breach of a contract. The defendant objected to the jurisdiction of the Ugandan court on the basis that the contract was made and was to have been performed in Kenya. The defendant was served within the jurisdiction. The defendant contended that, because, pursuant to section 15(3) of the Civil Procedure Act 1929,[40] the cause of action arose outside the jurisdiction,

---

[35] Interpretation Act 1976 (Act 18 of 1976, Cap 3 of the Laws of Uganda 2000) s 2(uu): '"person" includes any company or association or body of persons corporate or unincorporate'.

[36] See generally on the meaning of 'domicile', *Dicey, Morris and Collins on the Conflict of Laws* 15 ed (2012) vol 1, r 34, para 6R-001.

[37] The rule of the English Rules of the Supreme Court regulating service out of the jurisdiction prior to 1999 (when the Civil Procedure Rules came into effect) was O XI. Under the Rules of the Supreme Court 1883, r 1(c) provided for service out of the jurisdiction where the defendant was domiciled or ordinarily resident within the jurisdiction.

[38] Rules of the Supreme Court 1883 (1960 ed) 144.

[39] [1999] Kam LR 772 (H Ct) (Okello Ag J).

[40] In fact the Act, as the judge pointed out in the course of his judgment, has only sub-ss (a)–(c) and explanations (1)–(3).

the court did not have jurisdiction to entertain the claim. It seems to have been agreed between the parties that section 15 of the 1929 Act was applicable to the case. The court held that section 15(a) and (b) applied and that because the defendant was a company incorporated in Uganda and carried on business there, the court had jurisdiction on the bases that the defendant resided in Uganda and carried on business there.

The position is, therefore, that a company may be resident, inter alia, by having its place of incorporation in the jurisdiction, or by having its central management and control within the jurisdiction,[41] or by carrying on business within the jurisdiction.

(2) The action is founded on any breach or alleged breach within the jurisdiction of any contract wherever made which, according to the terms of the contract, ought to be performed within the jurisdiction

As noted above, Order V, rule 22(e) is an attenuated form even of the English Rules of the Supreme Court 1883 in that it excludes as bases for the Ugandan court to assume jurisdiction over a defendant in a contractual matter the following connecting factors: (1) the contract was made within Uganda; (2) the contract was made by or through an agent trading or residing within Uganda on behalf of a principal trading or residing outside the jurisdiction; (3) the contract is by its terms or implication governed by Ugandan law; and (under the 1965 Rules of the Supreme Court) (4) the contact contains a clause conferring jurisdiction on the Uganda courts.

Under Order V, rule 22(e), the plaintiff must show that: (1) the action is based on a breach of contract; (2) the breach was within Uganda; and (3) the contract was to be performed in Uganda.

It is likely that, in the apparent absence of Ugandan authority on the construction and application of Order V, rule 22(e), a Ugandan court will be influenced by the academic and judicial authorities on the construction and application of the (former) equivalent provision in the English Rules of the Supreme Court.[42]

A concise statement of the law is as follows[43] (and should be adapted substituting 'Uganda' for 'England'):

> **'11-197**
>
> The normal form of breach is the failure of one party to perform one or more of his obligations under the contract. In such a case it is not necessary that the whole contract was to be performed in England by both the parties thereto, but it is necessary that some part of it was to be performed in England and that there has been a breach of that part.

[41] *Dicey, Morris and Collins on the Conflict of Laws* 15 ed (2012) vol 1, r 30, 11R-077, (3)(c)(ii) and (4). This form of words is the formula used by the editors to describe 'domicile'.

[42] Order XI, r 1(e): Rules of the Supreme Court 1883 (1960 ed) and 1965.

[43] *Dicey, Morris and Collins on the Conflict of Laws* 15 ed (2012) vol 1, r 34, paras 11-197–11-203.

It is not sufficient if the contract or part of it might be performed either in England or abroad; it is necessary that the contract or part of it was to be performed in England and not elsewhere. The contract need not contain an express term providing for performance in England. It is enough if the court can gather that this was the intention of the parties by construing the contract in the light of the surrounding circumstances, including the course of dealing between the parties. In most of the reported cases, the breach complained of was the failure to pay money, a matter in which it is especially difficult to determine the place of performance in the absence of an express term in the contract. "The general rule is that where no place of payment is specified, either expressly or by implication, the debtor must seek out his creditor." But this is only a general rule and, as stated, it only applies where no place of payment is expressed or implied in the contract. It certainly does not mean that a creditor can confer jurisdiction on the English court merely by taking up his residence in England after the making of the contract.

11-198

If the contract is for the sale of goods by a seller in England to a buyer abroad, it will, in the absence of a contractual term to the contrary, be easy to infer that the buyer's obligation was to pay for the goods in England. The same is the case if a principal in England sends goods to an agent abroad to be sold by him on commission. But it is otherwise if, on the true construction of the contract, the only duty of the foreign agent is to sell the goods and remit the proceeds to England from abroad in a specified manner, because it will be inferred that his duty is at an end when he makes the remittance. If a foreign principal appoints an agent in England to sell his goods on commission, it is usually inferred that the commission is payable in England. In such a case, the fact that the agent claims an account of sales does not take the case out of the clause.

11-199

The duties of the seller of goods under a c.i.f. contract are to ship the goods and deliver the shipping documents to the buyer. It is not his duty to deliver the goods to the buyer. Consequently, if the foreign seller ships goods which are found to be defective upon their arrival in England, or if he fails to ship them at all, the breach is not committed in England within the meaning of the clause.

11-200

In a contract of service, wages or salary would normally be payable where the service is to be performed, in the absence of an express or implied term in the contract. But if the servant is employed in only a nominal or consultative capacity, and is free to reside where he likes, his salary may be payable in England, if that is where he decides to live. In a contract for services, it may be possible to infer that the fee or commission is payable at the contractor's usual place of business, even if the work is to be performed abroad.

11-201

The fact that the contract provides for payment to be made in English currency has sometimes been held to yield the inference that payment was to be made in England, but this is by no means a decisive consideration. Conversely, the fact that payment is to be made in foreign currency does not necessarily mean that England was not to be the place of payment. No inference as to the place of payment can properly be drawn from the fact that the contract contains a gold clause.

11-202

If money is due under a compromise of a disputed claim, it is usually inferred that the money is payable where litigation is pending or would probably have taken place. An implied warranty of authority has been held to have been broken where the warranty was relied on.

11-203

If the contract is governed by a foreign applicable law, the applicable law of the contract will determine where money due thereunder is payable.'

(3) The action is founded on tort or other civil wrong committed within the jurisdiction.

There is a paucity of authority in Uganda on the construction and application of Order V, rule 22(h). As with the construction and application of Order V, rule 22(e), it is likely that, in the apparent absence of Ugandan authority on the subject, a Ugandan court will be influenced by the academic and judicial authorities on the construction and application of the (former) equivalent provision in the English Rules of the Supreme Court.[44]

A statement of the law is as follows:[45]

'11-212

... As both the Privy Council [in *Distillers Co (Bio-chemicals) Ltd v. Thompson* [1971] AC 458] and the Supreme Court of Canada [*Moran v. Pyle National (Canada) Ltd* (1973) 43 D.L.R. (3d) 239] have pointed out, the competing theories for the determination of the place of a tort have been that (i) all ingredients of the cause of action must have occurred within the jurisdiction, or (ii) the last ingredient, the event which completes a cause of action, must have occurred within the jurisdiction, or (iii) the act which the defendant committed must have occurred within the jurisdiction.

11-213

In *Distillers Co Ltd v Thompson* the Privy Council adopted the test of the place where in substance the act or omission occurred which gave the plaintiff his cause of action. So that where the essence of the complaint was failure to warn the consumer of the dangers of a product (rather than the faulty manufacture of the product) the cause of action was held to have arisen at the place where the failure to warn occurred; and the torts of negligent and fraudulent misrepresentation, where the negligent or fraudulent statement was communicated from one country to another, were held to have been committed where the statement was received and acted upon. Prior to the adoption of that test, but consistently with it, it had been held that the tort of defamation was committed where the defamatory statements were published and not where they were posted or uttered.'

---

[44] Order XI, r 1(ee): Rules of the Supreme Court 1883 (1960 ed) and 1965.

[45] *Dicey, Morris and Collins on the Conflict of Laws* 15 ed (2012) vol 1, r 34, paras 11-212–11-213.

14.1.2.3 *Submission to the jurisdiction*

Two circumstances must be distinguished under the title submission to the jurisdiction: first, where submission is alleged in extant proceedings in Uganda; second, where the defendant has agreed (usually by contractual provision) to submit to the jurisdiction of the court in advance of a dispute arising.

14.1.2.3.1 Submission by appearance

A defendant may appear for the limited purpose of challenging the jurisdiction of the court. If the defendant wishes to challenge the jurisdiction of the court he must first give notice of intention to defend the proceedings and then, within the time allowed for service of a defence, make an application by summons in chambers under Order IX, rule 3. If the defendant makes an application under rule 3(1) the filing of a defence by him does not amount to a submission to the jurisdiction;[46] conversely, the filing of a defence in the absence of an application under rule 3(1) will amount to a submission to the jurisdiction.[47]

The same answer will be reached where the defendant participates in proceedings despite the inclusion in the parties' contract of a jurisdiction clause[48] conferring jurisdiction on a foreign court. Hence, in *CMA CGM Uganda Ltd v M/S H Ssekatawa International Ltd*,[49] it was agreed between the plaintiff and the respondent (both incorporated and registered in Uganda) that goods would be transported by sea to Kampala. During the transit of the goods, extra costs were incurred and this led to a dispute between the parties over the exact amount of money which the plaintiff had to pay under the contract. The defendant gave instructions that the goods should not be released to the plaintiff until the alleged debt had been settled. The plaintiff therefore commenced proceedings in Uganda.[50]

---

[46] Order XI, r 3(5).

[47] Order IX, r 3(6). See further: *Tamp Engineering Consultant Ltd v Macdowell Ltd* [2016] UGCOMMC 9 (Comm Ct) (Anglin J). In this case, the defendant had filed a defence without having made an application under O IX, r 3(1), and, it appeared, was incorporated in Uganda and had entered into a contract made in Uganda and governed by Ugandan law.

[48] Jurisdiction clauses are dealt with in greater depth under the sub-sub-heading 'Jurisdiction clauses' below.

[49] [2015] UGCOMMC 59 (Comm Ct) (Anglin J).

[50] Originally, the plaintiff commenced proceedings in the High Court. The defendant then filed a defence and applied for a temporary injunction to be granted pending the disposal of the main suit. The matter came before Kirabwire J, who dismissed the application and directed the main suit be transferred to the Chief Magistrate for trial. The Chief Magistrate determined that the Ugandan court did not have jurisdiction to hear the matter. This decision was then appealed to the High Court (Commercial Division).

The bill of lading provided:

> 'Actions against the carrier under the contact of carriage evidenced by this Bill of Lading **shall** be brought before "Tribunal de Commerce de Marseille" and **no other court shall have jurisdiction** with regard to any such action. **Actions against the Merchant under the contract of carriage** evidenced by this Bill of Lading **may** be brought before the "Tribunal de Commerce de Marseille" **or, in carriers' discretion, in another court of competent jurisdiction**.' (emphasis in original)

Reversing[51] the decision of the Chief Magistrate of Mengo, Anglin J held:

> 'In the present case the parties filed both the suit, and the counter claim in Ugandan Courts, although they had contracted in Japan, and agreed that the disputes against the carrier would be filed in the French Court, while disputes against the merchant could be brought in the French court or in **any other court of competent jurisdiction**.
>
> The court finds that, in the circumstances the parties voluntarily submitted to the jurisdiction of the Ugandan Courts; despite the fact that they had agreed to give the French Court exclusive jurisdiction to rule on a claim between the merchant and the carrier.' (emphasis in original)[52]

14.1.2.3.2 Submission by agreement

14.1.2.3.2.1 *Jurisdiction clauses*

Before exploring the attitude of the Ugandan courts to jurisdiction clauses, it is necessary to understand the effect of a jurisdiction agreement at common law. While certain decisions of the Ugandan courts suggest otherwise,[53] an agreement between the parties that a dispute between them will be the subject of litigation in a court outside Uganda does not oust the jurisdiction of the Ugandan court itself. As was set out in section 14.1 above, the fundamental means by which a Ugandan court is seised of jurisdiction is by service of process on the defendant; the parties' agreement cannot 'oust' that jurisdiction.[54]

---

[51] [2015] UGCOMMC 59 at p 3 of the electronic report.

[52] Later on in her judgment, at p 4 of the electronic report, Anglin J went on to state: 'The courts in Uganda had jurisdiction and the Carrier exercised its discretion to bring such a suit in Uganda and by virtue of the fact that the contract was partly performed in Uganda.' In *De Smet v Nakassanga* [2017] UGCOMMC 135 (Kaianamura J), the Commercial Division of the High Court appears to have considered, at p 2 of the electronic report, that, in *CMA CGM Uganda* the court decided it had jurisdiction because 'the contract was performed in Uganda'. It is submitted that the safer basis on which to conclude that the Ugandan court had jurisdiction in the *CMA CGM* case is the one set out in the main text above: the parties submitted to the jurisdiction of the court. See also: *Portland International (PTY) Ltd v Sembule Steel Mills Ltd* [2017] UGCOMMC 118 (Anglin J).

[53] By way of example, see: *Larco Concrete Products Ltd v Transair Ltd* [1987] HCB 40 and [1988-90] HCB 80; and *Uganda Telecom Ltd v Rodrigo Chacon t/a Andes Alpes Trading* [2008] UGCOMMC 77 (Comm Ct) (Arach-Amoko J).

[54] As demonstrated by the more recent decisions of the High Court in *Huadar Guangdong Chinese Co Ltd v Damco Logistics Uganda Ltd* [2013] UGCOMMC 195 (Comm Ct) (Izama J) and *De Smet v Nakassanga* [2017] UGCOMMC 135 (Com Ct) (Kaianamura J).

As it emerges from the jurisprudence on the subject, and as explained in more detail below, the approach of the Ugandan courts appears to be one which, in principle, aims to give effect to the parties' agreement on jurisdiction. Despite this, in practice Ugandan courts have, on several occasions, failed to hold parties to the contractual bargain struck.

Exclusive jurisdiction clauses

The most recent jurisprudence of the High Court of Uganda[55] suggests very strongly that, 'where parties have bound themselves by an exclusive jurisdiction clause, effect should ordinarily be given to that obligation unless the party suing in the non-contractual forum discharges the burden cast on him showing strong reasons for suing in that forum'.[56] In adopting this approach, the High Court has relied on the decision of the House of Lords in *Donohue v Armco*[57] and that of the Kenyan Court of Appeal in *Raytheon Aircraft Credit Corp v Air Al-Faraj Ltd*.[58]

That Ugandan courts adopt this approach ensures that they retain discretion whether to give effect to the clause or not. The language cited in the previous paragraph suggests that the Ugandan court will, more often than not, give effect to the parties' agreement on jurisdiction. In spite of this, the cases that have come before the courts seem to indicate that a defendant who wishes to rely on the jurisdiction clause when disputing the court's jurisdiction under Order IX will face a more difficult challenge than might be expected.

By way of example, in *De Smet v Nakassanga*,[59] the plaintiff brought proceedings in the High Court of Uganda, contra an exclusive jurisdiction clause in favour of the courts of Antwerp, which clause was contained in the parties' contract.

---

[55] *Huadar Guangdong Chinese Co Ltd v Damco Logistics Uganda Ltd* [2013] UGCOMMC 195 (Comm Ct) (Izama J); *De Smet v Nakassanga* [2017] UGCOMMC 135 (Com Ct) (Kaianamura J); *ICCO Cooperation v Trivision Uganda Ltd* [2018] UGCOMMC 14 (Wangutusi J); and *International Tin Association Ltd v Kerilee Investments Ltd* [2020] UGHCCD 71 (Andrew J).

[56] For a case where the court determined that the jurisdiction clause did not apply to both of the parties before it, see *Rapid Shipping and Freight Ltd v Copy Line International LLC* [2012] UGCOMMC 105 (H Ct) (Madrama J).

[57] *Donohue v Armco Ltd* [2002] 1 All ER 749 (HL (E)) (Lords Bingham, Mackay, Nicholls, Hobhouse and Scott).

[58] [2005] 2 EA 259 (Tunoi, Githinju and Onyango Otieno JJA). Slightly older Ugandan High Court authority, like *Uganda Telecom Ltd v Rodrigo Chacon t/a Andes Alpes Trading* [2008] UGCOMMC 77 (Comm Ct) (Arach-Amoko J) had adopted the approach set out by the US Supreme Court in *Bremen v Zapata Off-Shore Co* 407 US 1 (1972) (Sup Ct) (Berger CJ gave the lead opinion with which Brennan, Stewart, White, Marshall, Blackmun, Powell, and Rehnquist JJ agreed. White J, filed a concurring statement. Douglas J gave a dissenting opinion). It might well be that the approach in *Bremen* and the approach in *Donohue* yield the same result (this was certainly the view of Lord Bingham in *Donohue* [2002] 1 All ER 749, 760B–C) but what is clear is that Ugandan courts now routinely cite *Donohue* as representative of the approach which must be taken, rather than *Bremen*.

[59] [2017] UGCOMMC 135 (Com Ct) (Kaianamura J).

In dismissing the defendant's preliminary objection that the High Court did not have jurisdiction to entertain the suit, Kaianamura J held that the plaintiff had shown that it was reasonable for the Ugandan court to entertain the matter because: it would be very expensive to take witnesses to Belgium; the cost of having the matter determined in Belgium was so high as to be unreasonable; the defendant did not show why she desired to have the case tried in Belgium when it would be extremely expensive for her for it to be so tried; and the only logical conclusion was that the defendant therefore wished to avoid liability.

Similarly, in the *ICCO Cooperation*[60] case, the plaintiffs brought proceedings in Uganda despite, as the court seemed to suggest,[61] the fact that the parties had agreed to the exclusive jurisdiction of the District Court of Utrecht, in the Netherlands. In dismissing the defendant's application for an order that proceedings be dismissed, the court put significant stress on, inter alia, the following matters: the contract was drawn and executed in Uganda; the plaintiffs were from and resided in Uganda; and if the suit was heard outside Uganda, the cost of transporting, housing and feeding witnesses and the litigation costs of proceedings in the Netherlands would weigh heavily on the respondents and so would potentially deny them access to the court.

It may be – and citing with approval the approach of the Kenyan courts may hint at this – that Ugandan courts continue to pay regard to the principles set out by Brandon J (as he then was) in *Owners of cargo lately laden on board the ship or vessel Eleftheria v The Eleftheria (Owners), The Eleftheria*,[62] albeit that, as a matter of English law, the approach in *Donohue* has overtaken previous decisions on the subject. As an aside, it is worth noting that in certain other Anglophone jurisdictions in the region, including (as mentioned) Kenya,[63]

---

[60] *ICCO Cooperation v Trivision Uganda Ltd* [2018] UGCOMMC 14 (Wangutusi J);

[61] The contractual clause in question provided: 'If a dispute exists which cannot be resolved in mutual consultation ... one or more of the parties may submit the dispute to the District Court in Utrecht, the Netherlands. Dutch law shall exclusively apply to this contract...'. On its face, it is not plain that this is, in fact, an exclusive jurisdiction clause. It is submitted that, had the court spent more time on the exercise of construction, it might have found that the clause in question was a non-exclusive jurisdiction clause, such that the plaintiff's bringing proceedings in Uganda did not amount to a breach of its contractual promise/ allowing proceedings to continue in Uganda did not sit ill with the approach set out in *Donohue*.

[62] [1970] P 94; [1969] 1 Lloyd's Rep 237 (QBD: Comm Ct).

[63] *Raytheon Aircraft Credit Corp v Air Al-Faraj Ltd* [2005] 2 KLR 47 (CA) (Tunoi, Githinji and Onyango Otieno JJA). *Raytheon* was cited with approval by Anglin J in *CMA CGM Uganda Ltd v M/S H Ssekatawa International Ltd* [2015] UGCOMMC 59 (Comm Ct). While Anglin J was there concerned with a non-exclusive jurisdiction clause, she proceeded, at p 4 of the electronic report, to hold that courts should, when determining whether to give effect to a jurisdiction clause, consider the factors set out at proposition (5) in the passage cited in the main text above from Brandon J's judgment in *The Eleftheria*. In *De Smet v Nakassanga* [2017] UGCOMMC 135 (Kaianamura J), a case concerned with an exclusive jurisdiction clause in favour of the Court of Commerce in Antwerp, the Commercial Division of the High Court referred to the passage from Anglin J's judgment without any apparent disapproval.

Malawi[64] and Nigeria,[65] the courts have adopted the principles set out in *The Eleftheria*. In that case, the jurisdiction clause provided: 'Any dispute arising under this bill of lading shall be decided in the country where the carrier has his principal place of business [Greece].' The owners of cargo on board the *Eleftheria* commenced proceedings in England and the shipowners applied for a stay of those proceedings. In staying the proceedings in favour of the Greek courts, Brandon J set out the principles on the basis of which a stay may be granted:[66]

> '(4) In exercising its discretion the court should take into account all the circumstances of the particular case. (5) In particular, but without prejudice to (4), the following matters, where they arise, may properly be regarded:—(a) In what country the evidence on the issues of fact is situated, or more readily available, and the effect of that on the relative convenience and expense of trial as between the English and foreign courts, (b) Whether the law of the foreign court applies and, if so, whether it differs from English law in any material respects, (c) With what country either party is connected, and how closely, (d) Whether the defendants genuinely desire trial in the foreign country, or are only seeking procedural advantages, (e) Whether the plaintiffs would be prejudiced by having to sue in the foreign court because they would: (i) be deprived of security for their claim; (ii) be unable to enforce any judgment obtained; (iii) be faced with a time-bar not applicable in England; or (iv) for political, racial, religious or other reasons be unlikely to get a fair trial.'

If these principles do continue to operate on the mind of a Ugandan judge when faced with an application by a defendant to dismiss proceedings commenced in Uganda in the teeth of a jurisdiction clause in favour of a foreign court, it is worth repeating that the defendant will find it more difficult to rely on the jurisdiction clause than the approach in *Donohue* might be thought to suggest.

Non-exclusive jurisdiction clauses

In *Larco Concrete Products Ltd v Transair Ltd*,[67] the plaintiff and defendant, both companies incorporated under English law, had drawn up an agreement in England for the charter of one of the plaintiff's aircraft to the defendant with delivery to be made at Entebbe Airport, Kampala. The agreement contained a jurisdiction clause whereby both parties submitted to the non-exclusive jurisdiction of the English courts. The defendant took delivery of the aircraft and it then crashed in Uganda. The plaintiff commenced proceedings against the defendant in Uganda for damages for negligence and breach of contract. At first instance the defendant's application for a declaration that the court

[64] *Mirza v AMI (Malawi) Ltd* (unreported) 4 December 2007 (H Ct) (Chombo J).

[65] *Sonnar (Nig) Ltd v Partenreedri MS Nordwind, Owners of the ship MV Nordwind* [1987] 4 NWLR 520 (Sup Ct) (Bello, Eso, Nnamani, Uwais, Kawu, Oputa and Belgore JJSC) and *Nika Fishing Co Ltd v Lavina Corp* [2008] 16 NWLR 509 (Sup Ct) (Tobi, Oguntade, Mohammed, Tabai and Ogebe JJSC).

[66] [1970] P 94 at 99G–100C.

[67] [1987] HCB 40 (CA) (Civil Appeal 3 of 1987). The High Court has recently followed the approach in the *Larco* case: *Portland International (Pty) Ltd v Sembule Steel Mills Ltd* [2017] UGCOMMC 118 (Anglin J).

did not have jurisdiction was granted on the basis that the clause ousted the jurisdiction of the Ugandan court. The Court of Appeal allowed the plaintiff's appeal holding, inter alia: the non-exclusive jurisdiction clause did not shut out other jurisdictions, in particular jurisdictions in which the agreement was to be performed; considerations pointing in favour of Ugandan jurisdiction were that the final contract[68] had been made in Uganda and business was being carried out in Uganda by the defendant for gain. (Although the report is incomplete, it is also reasonable to surmise that witnesses to the maintenance of the aircraft and its operation would have been in Uganda.)

Finally, where parties provide in their agreement that the agreement should be interpreted by reference to a specified system of law, effect ought to be given to that stipulation and the contract interpreted in accordance with the canons of interpretation of that system of law.[69] Thus, the chosen system of law should be applied in construing the scope and applicability of the jurisdiction agreement to the dispute of which the court is seised.

14.1.2.3.2.2 *Application for service out of the jurisdiction based on a jurisdiction clause*

One question that arises is the statutory basis on which a Ugandan court may assume jurisdiction over a cause where the plaintiff in Uganda applies for service on the putative defendant out of the jurisdiction based on a jurisdiction clause in an agreement.

In the English Rules of the Supreme Court,[70] Order XI, rule 1(1)(d)(i)–(iv), the sub-rule governing service out of the jurisdiction in cases concerned with contract contains specific provision for service out of the jurisdiction based on a jurisdiction clause: 'The claim is made to enforce ... a contract which ...

[68] It is worth pointing out that whenever a court is asked to give effect to a jurisdiction clause (be it exclusive or non-exclusive), the mere fact that the governing law of the contract is not that of Uganda will not in itself justify a stay of proceedings in Uganda: *World Population Foundation v Uganda Youth Anti-Aids Association* [2003] Kam LR 287 (H Ct) (Tinyinondi J). A choice of law clause in favour of the law of the Netherlands did not result in the Ugandan court holding that it had no jurisdiction to entertain proceedings for breach of contract. In this case the contract was made in Uganda and concerned property in Kampala. In reaching this conclusion the judge considered and regarded as 'very persuasive indeed' the opinion of Lord Goff in *Spiliada Maritime Corp v Cansulex Ltd* [1987] AC 460 (HL (E)). The same conclusion was reached in *Eastern and Southern African Trade and Development Bank v Hasan Basajjabalaba* [2007] UGCOMMC 30 (H Ct) (Bamwine J) where the judge considered a claim on a deed of guarantee containing an English choice of law clause and involving solely Ugandan residents. The court dismissed an objection to the court's jurisdiction based on the choice of law clause.

[69] This proposition barely needs citation of authority and is a principle of considerable maturity: see Dicey *Conflict of Laws* 5 ed (1932), r 161; Morris and Cheshire 'The proper law of the contract in the conflict of laws' (1940) 56 *LQR* 320.

[70] Rules of the Supreme Court 1965 which is the successor provision to O XI, r 2(a), of the Rules of the Supreme Court 1883 (1960 ed), introduced by amendment in 1920. This amendment does not appear in the CPR in Uganda.

(iv) contains a term to the effect that the High Court shall have jurisdiction to hear and determine any action in respect of the contract.' This additional provision was included in the English rules in order to reverse the decision of the Court of Appeal in *British Wagon Co Ltd v Gray*.[71]

Where the defendant is not present within the jurisdiction and where no other provision of Order V, rule 22 of the CPR is applicable to the case, the question is whether the Ugandan court has power to order service out of the jurisdiction solely on the basis that the agreement between the parties contains a jurisdiction clause in favour of the Ugandan courts. It would seem not and in such a case there would be no other basis on which the Ugandan court could validly make an order for service of the defendant out of the jurisdiction.

14.1.2.4 Lis alibi pendens

Section 6 of the Civil Procedure Act 1929 provides:

> '**6. Stay of suit**.
>
> No court shall proceed with the trial of any suit or proceeding in which the matter in issue is also directly and substantially in issue in a previously instituted suit or proceeding between the same parties, or between parties under whom they or any of them claim, litigating under the same title, where that suit or proceeding is pending in the same or any other court having jurisdiction in Uganda to grant the relief claimed.
>
> Explanation.—The pendency of a suit in a foreign court shall not preclude a court from trying a suit in which the same matters or any of them are in issue in that suit in the foreign court.'

Ugandan law therefore provides for a domestic *lis alibi pendens* rule but excepts from its operation proceedings in foreign courts. There would appear to be no authority on the approach of the Ugandan courts to concurrent foreign proceedings concerning the same or similar subject-matter as proceedings before the Ugandan courts.

In the absence of any Ugandan authority on the subject, the Ugandan courts may well look to the approach adopted by the English courts in this regard. In *de Dampierre v de Dampierre*,[72] the House of Lords held that where a stay of English proceedings is sought on the basis that there are parallel proceedings in another jurisdiction, the principles of *forum non conveniens* enunciated in *Spiliada Maritime Corp v Cansulex Ltd*,[73] (which are dealt with more fully below), apply. Thus in *de Dampierre*, a case concerning parallel divorce proceedings in France and England, the court considered the connections between the parties and the

---

[71] [1896] 1 QB 35.

[72] [1988] AC 92 (HL(E)) (Lords Keith, Brandon, Templeman, Ackner and Goff).

[73] [1987] AC 460 (HL(E)).

two jurisdictions and the appropriateness of proceedings in France rather than in England and concluded that the English proceedings should be stayed:[74]

> 'Here it is beyond dispute that there are very strong factors connecting the case with France, whereas now there are practically none connecting the case with England. Neither party suggests that New York is the appropriate forum. It follows that *prima facie* the courts of France clearly provide the appropriate jurisdiction for the resolution of the dispute, so that a stay should be granted unless justice requires otherwise. In considering the question, the [judge at first instance] ... did indeed invoke the authority of one of the earlier authorities on the inherent jurisdiction, relying as he did on the much-quoted dictum of Lord Diplock in *MacShannon v. Rockware Glass Ltd.* [1978] A.C. 975, 812. He recognised the undoubted "Frenchness" of the marriage and the spouses, but considered that the wife's absence from what he described as the 'harsh' French regime and her presence in the more 'benevolent' regime which prevails here, plainly afforded a juridical advantage to her and that, following Lord Diplock's approach, this must outweigh the "Frenchness" of the marriage of the spouses and point to the conclusion that England was the more appropriate jurisdiction for the dissolution of the marriage.'

And:[75]

> 'The weight to be given to what has been called a 'legitimate personal or juridical advantage' was considered by your Lordships' House in the *Spiliada* case [1987] A.C. 460, 482-484. The conclusion there reached was that, having regard to the underlying principle, the court should not, as a general rule, be deterred from granting a stay of proceedings simply because the plaintiff in this country will be deprived of such an advantage, provided that the court is satisfied that substantial justice will be done in the appropriate forum overseas. Reference was made, in particular, to cases concerning discovery where, as is well known, there is a spectrum of systems of discovery applicable in various jurisdictions; and the opinion was expressed that, generally speaking, injustice cannot be said to be done if a party is compelled to accept one of these well recognised systems of discovery in another forum. If I follow that approach in the circumstances of the present case, I find that French matrimonial law contains provisions for 'compensation' which, unlike our own, place emphasis upon the question whether the breakdown of the marriage was due to the exclusive fault of one of the parties, providing (subject to an important exception) that a party so at fault is deprived of the right to an award of compensation. Such an approach is no longer acceptable in this country, though it bears a close resemblance to the principles applicable here not so very long ago. But it is evidently still acceptable in a highly civilised country with which this country has very close ties of friendship, not least nowadays through our common membership of the European Community; and I find it impossible to conclude that, objectively speaking, justice would not be done if the wife was compelled to pursue her remedy for financial provision under such a regime in the courts of a country which provide, most plainly, the natural forum for the resolution of this matrimonial dispute.'

Thus what is required is a balancing of the various factors in the case to ascertain in which jurisdiction the case is most appropriately decided.

---

[74] [1988] AC 92, *per* Lord Goff at 109E–H.

[75] Ibid *per* Lord Goff at 110B–F.

14.1.2.5 Forum non conveniens[76]

As noted at section 14.1.2.1 above, the final stage in the court's analysis when determining whether to permit service out is to consider whether, in the exercise of its discretion, the court should permit service out. In other words, the court must consider whether Uganda is the *forum conveniens.*

In *World Population Foundation v Uganda Youth Anti-Aids Association*,[77] the judge, in reaching the conclusion that a choice of law clause in favour of the Netherlands ought not to disturb the Ugandan court's jurisdiction to determine the dispute between the parties,[78] quoted from, considered and described[79] as 'very persuasive indeed' the opinion of Lord Goff in *Spiliada Maritime Corp v Cansulex Ltd.*[80]

Some years previously, the Court of Appeal had decided *SC Baxi v The Bank of India Ltd.*[81] There, the plaintiff was a Ugandan who maintained a bank account with the defendant bank at its Mumbai (formerly known as 'Bombay') branch. When the plaintiff was in Mumbai, he drew a cheque for Rs5,000 on his account. Due to an error on the part of the bank, the cheque was dishonoured and in consequence the plaintiff failed to complete on the purchase of a property. On his return to Uganda the plaintiff issued proceedings claiming damages and served them on the defendant's Kampala branch. The defendant applied to have the proceedings struck out as vexatious and oppressive.

The Court of Appeal, dismissing the plaintiff's appeal from the decision of the judge at first instance holding that the proceedings were vexatious and oppressive, cited in support of this conclusion the English decision in *Logan v Bank of Scotland (No 2)*.[82] The Court of Appeal held that the plaintiff's cause of action arose in Mumbai, the witnesses the plaintiff would need to prove damage were in Mumbai, the applicable law was Indian, the defendant's witnesses were in Mumbai together with the relevant documents and bankers' books. Law JA stated:[83]

> 'to allow the suit to proceed in Uganda would work serious injustice upon the defendant, out of all proportion to the inconvenience which the plaintiff will suffer if he has to bring his action in Bombay. I see no reason to differ from the finding that the proposed suit is vexatious and oppressive and an abuse of the process of the court.'

[76] The observations set out under this sub-heading should be read alongside the observations which have been made above on the likely exercise of its discretion by the Ugandan court.

[77] [2003] Kam LR 287 (H Ct) (Tinyinondi J).

[78] See also *Pan Africa Logistics Ltd v Sophie Shipping Logistics Ltd* [2017] UGHCCD 160 (Mugambe J), where the judge determined that, in a contract made between the parties in Kenya, but for the performance of freight, shipping and logistics businesses to be carried out both within and outside Kenya, a choice of law clause in favour of Kenya did 'not limit jurisdiction over disputes arising between the parties to the Kenyan courts'.

[79] Ibid 291.

[80] [1987] AC 460 (HL (E)).

[81] [1966] EA 130 (CA) (Sir Clement de Lestang, Spry and Law JJA).

[82] [1906] 1 KB 141 (CA) (Sir Gorell Barnes, President, Collins MR, and Romer LJ), in which Sir Gorell Barnes P approached the question of jurisdiction by assessing the relative convenience of the competing *fora*.

[83] Ibid 133F.

The reference in the judgment of Law JA to the suit being 'vexatious and oppressive' has its origin in early English judicial authority. Historically, the English courts seem always to have held that a major factor in the exercise of the discretion to grant leave to serve out of the jurisdiction or stay proceedings already served out of the jurisdiction was whether the English proceedings were vexatious and oppressive. The expression 'vexatious and oppressive' bore a wide meaning and extended to considerations related to the comparative convenience of proceedings in England as opposed to a particular foreign forum. In *Logan v Bank of Scotland (No 2),*[84] the decision referred to by Law JA, the Court of Appeal granted an application staying proceedings commenced and served as of right in England in favour of Scotland. Sir Gorell Barnes P stated:[85]

> 'Now, it is true that the Courts of this country have not gone so far as to express themselves upon the question of convenience in terms similar to those used in the Scotch cases, though, as I have already noticed, it may be doubted whether there is any substantial difference between the two. Yet it seems to me clear that the inconvenience of trying a case in a particular tribunal may be such as practically to work a serious injustice upon a defendant and be vexatious. This would probably not be so if the difference of trying in one country rather than in another were merely measured by some extra expense; but where the difficulty for the defendant of trying in the country in which the action is brought is such that it is impracticable to properly try the case by reason of the difficulty of procuring the attendance of busy men as witnesses, and keeping them during trial, and of having to deal with masses of books, documents, and papers which are not in the country where the action is brought, and of dealing with law foreign to the tribunal, it appears to me that a case of vexation in some circumstances may be made out if the plaintiff chooses to sue in that country rather than in that where everybody is and where all the witnesses and material for the trial are.'

In *Spiliada Maritime Corp v Cansulex Ltd,*[86] the House of Lords developed this approach into a doctrine of *forum non conveniens*. The lead opinion in *Spiliada* is that of Lord Goff, the relevant passages of which are quoted below:[87]

> '*(a)* The basic principle is that a stay will only be granted on the ground of forum non conveniens where the court is satisfied that there is some other available forum, having competent jurisdiction, which is the appropriate forum for the trial of the action, i.e. in which the case may be tried more suitably for the interests of all the parties and the ends of justice.

[84] [1906] 1 KB 141 (CA) (Sir Gorell Barnes, President, Collins MR, and Romer LJ).

[85] Ibid 151–2. This was a decision under the 1883 Rules of the Supreme Court.

[86] [1987] AC 460 (HL (E)) (Lords Keith, Templeman, Griffiths, Mackay and Goff).

[87] Ibid 476C–478E (with whom Lords Keith, Templeman, Griffiths and Mackay agreed). Passages quoted with approval by Tinyinondi J in *World Population Foundation v Uganda Youth Anti-Aids Association* [2003] Kam LR 287 (H Ct) 289–90.

(b) As Lord Kinnear's formulation of the principle indicates, in general the burden of proof rests on the defendant to persuade the court to exercise its discretion to grant a stay (see, e.g., the Société du Gaz case, 1926 S.C. (H.L.) 13, 21, per Lord Sumner; and Anton, Private International Law (1967) p. 150). It is however of importance to remember that each party will seek to establish the existence of certain matters which will assist him in persuading the court to exercise its discretion in his favour, and that in respect of any such matter the evidential burden will rest on the party who asserts its existence. Furthermore, if the court is satisfied that there is another available forum which is prima facie the appropriate forum for the trial of the action, the burden will then shift to the plaintiff to show that there are special circumstances by reason of which justice requires that the trial should nevertheless take place in this country (see (f), below).

(c) ... In my opinion, the burden resting on the defendant is not just to show that England is not the natural or appropriate forum for the trial, but to establish that there is another available forum which is clearly or distinctly more appropriate than the English forum. In this way, proper regard is paid to the fact that jurisdiction has been founded in England as of right (see MacShannon's case [1978] A.C. 795, per Lord Salmon); and there is the further advantage that, on a subject where comity is of importance, it appears that there will be a broad consensus among major common law jurisdictions. I may add that if, in any case, the connection of the defendant with the English forum is a fragile one (for example, if he is served with proceedings during a short visit to this country), it should be all the easier for him to prove that there is another clearly more appropriate forum for the trial overseas.

(d) Since the question is whether there exists some other forum which is clearly more appropriate for the trial of the action, the court will look first to see what factors there are which point in the direction of another forum ... I respectfully consider that it may be more desirable, now that the English and Scottish principles are regarded as being the same, to adopt the expression used by my noble and learned friend, Lord Keith of Kinkel, in The Abidin Daver [1984] A.C. 398, 415, when he referred to the "natural forum" as being 'that with which the action had the most real and substantial connection.' So it is for connecting factors in this sense that the court must first look; and these will include not only factors affecting convenience or expense (such as availability of witnesses), but also other factors such as the law governing the relevant transaction ... and the places where the parties respectively reside or carry on business.

(e) If the court concludes at that stage that there is no other available forum which is clearly more appropriate for the trial of the action, it will ordinarily refuse a stay.

(f) If however the court concludes at that stage that there is some other available forum which prima facie is clearly more appropriate for the trial of the action, it will ordinarily grant a stay unless there are circumstances by reason of which justice requires that a stay should nevertheless not be granted. In this inquiry, the court will consider all the circumstances of the case, including circumstances which go beyond those taken into account when considering connecting factors with other jurisdictions. One such factor can be the fact, if established objectively by cogent

> evidence, that the plaintiff will not obtain justice in the foreign jurisdiction; see the The Abidin Daver [1984] A.C. 398, 411, per Lord Diplock, a passage which now makes plain that, on this inquiry, the burden of proof shifts to the plaintiff ....'

It is to be expected that after the decisions in *World Population Foundation v Uganda Youth Anti-Aids Association*[88] and *SC Baxi v The Bank of India Ltd*,[89] the Ugandan courts will continue to approach the question of jurisdiction by balancing the appropriateness of one forum as against others and develop the law in much the same way as was undertaken in the *Spiliada* case and subsequently.[90]

14.2 Enforcement of foreign judgments

Foreign judgments may be enforced in Uganda pursuant to common law or statute.

14.2.1 Enforcement at common law

By the Uganda Order in Council 1911,[91] amending the Uganda Order in Council 1902,[92] it was provided, inter alia, the law to be administered in Uganda was 'the common law, the doctrines of equity and statutes of general application in force in England on the 11th August 1902'.[93]

By 1902 the common law relating to the enforcement of foreign judgments was settled. The principles applicable under the common law are conveniently set out in *Dicey, Morris and Collins on the Conflict of Laws*:[94]

> **'Rule 42**
>
> (1) Subject to the Exceptions hereinafter mentioned and to Rule 62 (international conventions), a foreign judgment in personam given by the court of a foreign country with jurisdiction to give that judgment in accordance with the principles set out in Rules 43 to 46, and which is not impeachable under any of Rules 49 to 54, may be enforced by a claim or counterclaim for the amount due under it if the judgment is
>
> *(a)* for a debt, or definite sum of money (not being a sum payable in respect of taxes or other charges of a like nature or in respect of a fine or other penalty); and

---

88 [2003] Kam LR 287 (H Ct) (Tinyinondi J).

89 [1966] EA 130 (CA).

90 See, generally, *Dicey, Morris and Collins on the Conflict of Laws* 15 ed (2012) vol 1, r 38(2) and (3) para 12-007 et seq. For more recent guidance on the subject, see further *Vedanta Resources plc v Lungowe* [2020] AC 1045 (SC) (Lady Hale, Lords Wilson and Hodge, Lady Black and Lord Briggs) [66]–[70].

91 4 March 1911, gazetted 4 July 1911.

92 11 August 1902, gazetted 31 October 1902.

93 Continuing in operation after independence: Uganda Independence Act 1962, s 1(4).

94 15 ed (2012) vol 1, para 14R-020.

(*b*) final and conclusive,

but not otherwise.

Provided that a foreign judgment may be final and conclusive, though it is subject to an appeal, and though an appeal against it is actually pending in the foreign country where it was given.

(2) A foreign judgment given by the court of a foreign country with jurisdiction to give that judgment in accordance with the principles set out in Rules 43 to 46, which is not impeachable under any of Rules 49 to 54 and which is final and conclusive on the merits, is entitled to recognition at common law and may be relied on in proceedings in England.

(3) No proceedings may be brought by a person on a cause of action in respect of a judgment which has been given in his favour in proceedings between the same parties or their privies in a court in another part of the United Kingdom or in a court in an overseas country unless that judgment is not enforceable according to clause (1), or not entitled to recognition according to clause (2), of this Rule.'[95]

In order for its judgment to be enforceable the foreign court must have possessed international competence to determine the cause.[96] As a matter of common law, a foreign court will have been internationally competent in the following cases:[97] (1) if the person against whom the judgment was given was, at the time the proceedings were instituted, present in the foreign country; or (2) if the person against whom the judgment was given was claimant, or counterclaimed, in the proceedings in the foreign court; or (3) if the person against whom the judgment was given, submitted to the jurisdiction of that court by voluntarily appearing in the proceedings;[98] or (4) if the person against whom the judgment was given, had before the commencement of the proceedings agreed, in respect of the subject-matter of the proceedings, to submit to the jurisdiction of that court or of the courts of that country.

Among the established defences to an action at common law on a foreign judgment are the following: (1) where the foreign judgment was procured by fraud either, (a) fraud on the part of the party in whose favour the judgment is given, or (b) fraud on the part of the court pronouncing the judgment;[99] (2) the

[95] It must be remembered, however, that O V, r 22 of the Rules of the CPR does not allow a court in Uganda to permit service of the writ on a defendant who is present outside the jurisdiction where the action is one to enforce a foreign judgment; Frimpong Oppong 'Recognition and enforcement of foreign judgments in Commonwealth African countries' (2014) XV *Yearbook of Private International Law* 365 at 371–2.

[96] Frimpong Oppong *Private International Law in Commonwealth Africa* (2013) 322–4 (although the authority cited for the proposition on p 324 concerns enforcement under statute and not at common law).

[97] *Dicey, Morris and Collins on the Conflict of Laws* 15 ed (2012) vol 1, r 43, para 14R-054.

[98] Frimpong Oppong 'Recognition and enforcement of foreign judgments in Commonwealth African countries' (2014) XV *Yearbook of Private International Law* 365 at 374, writing specifically about Uganda and citing the decision of the Supreme Court in *Transroad Ltd v Bank of Uganda* [1998] Kam LR 106, states: 'Particularly noteworthy ... is post-judgment conduct, which, in Uganda, has been held not to constitute submission to the jurisdiction of the foreign court.'

[99] *Dicey, Morris and Collins on the Conflict of Laws* 15 ed (2012) vol 1, r 50, para 14R-137.

enforcement or recognition of the foreign judgment would be contrary to public policy;[100] and (3) where the proceedings in which the foreign judgment was obtained were contrary to the rules of natural justice.[101]

Section 9 of the Civil Procedure Act 1929 makes provision for the circumstances in which a foreign judgment shall not be considered conclusive:

> '**9. When foreign judgment not conclusive**.
>
> A foreign judgment shall be conclusive as to any matter directly adjudicated, upon by it between the same parties or between parties under whom they or any of them claim, litigating under the same title, except—
>
> *(a)* where it has not been pronounced by a court of competent jurisdiction;
>
> *(b)* where it has not been given on the merits of the case;
>
> *(c)* where it appears on the face of the proceedings to be founded on an incorrect view of international law or a refusal to recognise the law of Uganda in cases in which that law is applicable;
>
> *(d)* where the proceedings in which the judgment was obtained are opposed to natural justice;
>
> *(e)* where it has been obtained by fraud;
>
> *(f)* where it sustains a claim founded on a breach of any law in force in Uganda.'[102]

As can be seen, these provisions correspond broadly with the statement of the common-law principles set out above.

In *Sales v Attorney-General*,[103] the court considered a judgment of the US District Court for the Southern District of New York which had been rendered against the State of Uganda and Uganda's Ambassador to the UN. (There are no statutory reciprocal enforcement arrangements between the USA and Uganda.) In deciding in favour of the plaintiff judgment creditors, the court made two significant findings. First, the court found that in Uganda the basis on which a foreign judgment is enforceable at common law is international comity. In support of this finding the judge cited the US Supreme Court decision in *Hilton v Guyot*,[104] thereby marking a departure from the theory underlying English

---

[100] Ibid r 51, para 14R-152.

[101] Ibid r 52, para 14R-162.

[102] The provisions of s 10 of the Civil Procedure Act 1929 must also be noted. Section 10 provides: 'The court shall presume, upon the production of any document purporting to be a certified copy of a foreign judgment, that that judgment was pronounced by a court of competent jurisdiction, unless the contrary appears on the record; but that presumption may be displaced by proving want of jurisdiction.' The burden of proof in showing that the foreign court was not a court of competent jurisdiction would therefore appear to fall on the judgment debtor: Frimpong Oppong 'Recognition and enforcement of foreign judgments in Commonwealth African countries' (2014) XV *Yearbook of Private International Law* 365 at 375.

[103] [2013] UGHCCD 15 (H Ct) (Mwangusya J). The defendants had appeared in the proceedings in New York and had appealed a decision of the District Court, but then abandoned the appeal.

[104] 159 US 113 (1895) 163–4.

common-law enforcement which is based on the creation by the foreign court of an obligation, enforceable by action, to pay the sum represented by the judgment debt. Notwithstanding this difference in approach, it is tolerably clear that in practice the US and English common-law principles applicable are very similar. In *Hilton v Guyot*, the principles were stated as follows:[105]

> 'In view of all the authorities upon the subject, and of the trend of judicial opinion in this country and in England, following the lead of Kent and Story, we are satisfied that, where there has been opportunity for a full and fair trial abroad before a court of competent jurisdiction, conducting the trial upon regular proceedings, after due citation or voluntary appearance of the defendant, and under a system of jurisprudence likely to secure an impartial administration of justice between the citizens of its own country and those of other countries, and there is nothing to show either prejudice in the court, or in the system of laws under which it was sitting, or fraud in procuring the judgment, or any other special reason why the comity of this nation should not allow it full effect, the merits of the case should not, in an action brought in this country upon the judgment, be tried afresh, as on a new trial or an appeal, upon the mere assertion of the party that the judgment was erroneous in law or in fact. The defendants, therefore, cannot be permitted, upon that general ground, to contest the validity or the effect of the judgment sued on.'

The second finding made by the court was that the six-year limitation period provided for in section 3(1) of the Foreign Judgments (Reciprocal Enforcement) Act 1961[106] did not apply by analogy, thereby saving the plaintiff judgment creditors' claim from being statute barred (the judgment dated back to 1993 and the enforcement proceedings in Uganda commenced in 2011, an 18-year delay).

14.2.2 Enforcement pursuant to statute

14.2.2.1 *The regimes for enforcement pursuant to statute*

The statutory regimes for enforcement of foreign judgments are found in three pieces of legislation: the Judgments Extension Act 1908 ('the 1908 Act');[107] the Reciprocal Enforcement of Judgments Act 1922 ('the 1922 Act');[108] and the Foreign Judgments (Reciprocal Enforcement) Act 1961 ('the 1961 Act').[109]

One observation on the regimes may conveniently be made at this stage: as will become apparent below, the 1922 Act is a transposition of the applicable provisions of the United Kingdom Administration of Justice Act 1920 and the 1961 Act is a transposition of the United Kingdom Foreign Judgments (Reciprocal

[105] 159 US 113 (1895), *per* Gray J delivering the opinion of the court, at 202–3.

[106] Act 4 of 1961 (Cap 9 of the Laws of Uganda 2000).

[107] Act 3 of 1908 (Cap 12 of the Laws of Uganda 2000).

[108] Act 9 of 1922 (Cap 21 of the Laws of Uganda 2000).

[109] Act 4 of 1961 (Cap 9 of the Laws of Uganda 2000).

Enforcement) Act 1933. It is to be expected therefore that a Ugandan court will have regard to (although not, of course, be bound by) decisions of the English courts, in particular, and the commentary by academics on the interpretation of these Acts of the United Kingdom Parliament.[110]

14.2.2.1.1 Judgments Extension Act 1908

The 1908 Act is a brief enactment that makes provision for the transfer and execution in Uganda of decrees (and also warrants) obtained in Kenya, Malawi or Tanzania.[111] The decrees may be from the High Courts of those countries or any subordinate tribunal. The 1908 Act does not define the term 'decree';[112] however, a definition of this term is to be found in section 2 of the Civil Procedure Act 1929:[113]

> '"decree" means the formal expression of an adjudication which, so far as regards the court expressing it, conclusively determines the rights of the parties with regard to any of the matters in controversy in the suit and may be either preliminary or final. It shall be deemed to include the rejection of a plaint or writ and the determination of any question within section 34 or 92, but shall not include—
>
> (i) any adjudication from which an appeal lies as an appeal from an order; or
>
> (ii) any order of dismissal for default;
>
> Explanation —A decree is preliminary when further proceedings have to be taken before the suit can be completely disposed of. It is final when the adjudication completely disposes of the suit. It may be partly preliminary and partly final.'

Section 1 of the 1908 Act provides:

> '... *where it is desired that the decree shall be executed upon the person or property of the defendant in Uganda*, the decree may be transferred to the High Court or to any of the courts subordinate to it (hereafter called subordinate courts) for execution, and the provisions of the Civil Procedure Act for the transfer and execution of decrees shall apply in the same manner as if the decree had been obtained or entered in one court and were transferred for execution to another court within the jurisdiction of the High Court, and all proceedings shall, and may be, had and taken as if the decree had been a decree originally obtained

---

[110] The relevant parts of *Dicey, Morris and Collins on the Conflict of Laws* 15 ed (2012) on the application of the 1920 and 1933 Acts are as follows: 1920 Act – r 53, paras 14R-173–14-181; 1933 Act – r 54, paras 14R-183–14-195.

[111] As noted in *Mitchell Cotts Freight (K) Ltd v Three Ways Shipping Services (Group) Ltd* [2004] UGCOMMC 31 (Comm Ct) (Arach-Aoko LJ).

[112] The Interpretation Act 1976 also contains no definition of the term.

[113] A definition adopted by the court in *Kamiri v Oseko* [2012] UGCOMMC 135 (Obura LJ), in which the Ugandan court was invited to grant a *Mareva* injunction in support of a Kenyan *ex parte* order for the repossession of six vehicles which had been removed from Kenya and were being used in Uganda. The court declined to do so because the Kenyan order was not a 'decree' within the meaning of s 2 of the 1929 Act, see further below.

> in the High Court or a subordinate court, and all the reasonable costs and charges with regard to the transfer and execution of the decree shall be recovered in like manner as if it were part of the original judgment.' (emphasis provided)

The Act contemplates not only civil arrest of the judgment debtor in Uganda, but also the civil arrest in Kenya, Malawi or Tanzania at the behest of the Ugandan plaintiff of a defendant present within any of those jurisdictions.[114]

In *Kamiri v Oseko*,[115] the court considered an application to 'register' under the 1908 Act an *ex parte* order made by the Chief Magistrate's Court in Nairobi that ordered the impounding of certain vehicles formerly situated in Kenya but situated by the time of the application in Uganda. The court refused enforcement under the 1908 Act on the basis that the *ex parte* order was not a decree within the meaning of section 2 of the Civil Procedure Act 1929, because it did not conclusively determine the rights of the parties for the purposes of being a decree within the meaning of section 1 of the 1908 Act. (The court made a further point that the purported judgment creditor was not the creditor itself but instead was a third-party debt collector.)

The court also stated that an application for enforcement could not be brought under both the 1908 Act and the 1961 Act because the Acts created two regimes that could not be mixed; they 'provide for two distinct procedures which can neither be mixed in one application nor used interchangeably', and that, in any event, the *ex parte* order was not a 'judgment' for the purposes of the 1961 Act.

The 1908 Act makes no provision for a limitation period applicable to applications under section 1, a feature that places those making applications for enforcement of decrees from Kenya, Malawi and Tanzania at an advantage over those making applications for registration under the 1922 and 1961 Acts.

---

[114] Section 3. It would appear that, with respect to the civil arrest of a defendant, a similar regime is in place in Malawi: s 3 of the Nyasaland Judgments Extension Ordinance 1912, as amended, allows a judge sitting in the High Court in that country to 'execute a warrant for the arrest of the defendant where the warrant has been issued in' Kenya, Uganda, Tanzania or Zanzibar (and see further the discussion of this Ordinance in the relevant part of the chapter on Malawi). In Tanzania, s 3 of the Judgments Extension Act 1921 allows a judge, inter alia, to indorse or execute a warrant issued by the High Court of the High Court of Kenya, or of Malawi or of Zanzibar or of Uganda. It is worth noting that, while the 1908 Act does not apply to Zanzibar, in Zanzibar itself, s 3 of the Judgments Extension Decree 1908, as amended by s 2 of the Judgments Extension (Amendment) Decree 1921) allows a judge, inter alia, to indorse or execute a warrant issued by the High Court of the Colony and Protectorate of Kenya, or of 'Nyasaland' (Malawi) or of the 'Tanganyika Territory' (Tanzania) or of Uganda. In Kenya, there is no equivalent regime in place. There, enforcement of a foreign judgment pursuant to statute is governed by the Foreign Judgments (Reciprocal Enforcement) Act 1984. That Act does not make reference to 'warrants of arrest' and, in any event, only applies to jurisdictions to which it has been extended by Order; it has not yet been extended to any one of Uganda, Malawi or Tanzania (or Zanzibar).

[115] [2012] UGCOMMC 135 (Comm Ct) (Obura LJ).

14.2.2.1.2 Reciprocal Enforcement of Judgments Act 1922

The principal provisions of the 1922 Act are referred to below. The 1922 Act is legislation intended to make provision for the enforcement in Uganda of judgments made in the United Kingdom and other Commonwealth countries and of the Republic of Ireland ('Ireland').[116]

In terms of section 1(1)(a), the 1922 Act applies to any judgments or orders in any civil proceedings providing for the payment of a sum of money, and includes awards in arbitration proceedings if these can, under the law in force where they are made, be enforced in the same manner as judgments and excludes an award of compensation made in criminal proceedings (unlike the 1961 Act, below, which excludes the former and includes the latter).[117]

14.2.2.1.2.1 *Procedure for registration*

Section 2(1) of the 1922 Act provides that where a judgment[118] has been obtained from the High Court in England or Ireland or the Court of Session in Scotland, the judgment creditor may apply to the High Court in Uganda at any time within 12 months after the date of the judgment to have the judgment registered and on such an application the court may, 'if in all the circumstances of the case it thinks it is just and convenient that the judgment should be enforced in

[116] It is a singularity that the version of the 1922 Act contained in the Laws of Uganda 2000 (published pursuant to the provisions of the Laws (Revised Edition) Act 1994 (commencement date 14 October 1994), s 12 of which provides: '**Revised Edition to be Authentic Text** ... the Revised Edition is, in all courts and for all purposes, the sole authentic text of the laws of Uganda', vol II, p 481 et seq, differs from the references to the section numbering of the 1922 Act contained in the reported cases. (This may be attributable to a change in the chapter numbering of the Act, although what difference that made to the section numbering is unclear.) In the text above, all references are to the official, authentic version.

[117] The equivalent of s 12(1) of the 1920 Act.

[118] Defined in s 1(1)(a) to mean 'any judgment or order given or made by a court in any civil proceedings, whether before or after the passing of this Act, by which any sum of money is made payable, and includes an award in proceedings on an arbitration if the award has, in pursuant of the law in force in the place where it was made, become enforceable in the same manner as a judgment given by a court in that place'. It has been held by the Court of Appeal in England that the 1920 Act does not permit registration of a judgment given by a court in one state in an action to enforce a judgment given by a court in another state: *Strategic Technologies Pte Ltd v Procurement Bureau of the Republic of China Ministry of National Defence* [2020] EWCA Civ 1604 (David Richards, Males and Elisabeth Laing LJJ). Given the material similarity in the definition of 'judgment' as between the English and the Ugandan legislation, it is likely that a Ugandan court may well be persuaded by this reasoning.

Uganda', order the judgment to be registered.[119] The short period within which an application for the judgment to be registered may be made should be noted.[120]

In terms of section 5[121] of the 1922 Act, where the minister is satisfied that reciprocal provisions have been made in any other Commonwealth country, he may declare that the 1922 Act extends to the judgments obtained in the superior courts of that jurisdiction. Since its enactment, the 1922 Act has been extended[122] to the following jurisdictions: Botswana, Lesotho, Mauritius, New South Wales, Seychelles, Sri Lanka and Eswatini.

---

[119] Section 2(1) is the equivalent of s 9(1) of the 1920 Act. The Ugandan Supreme Court, in *Bank of Uganda v Transroad Ltd* [1998] UGSC 7 (SC) (Wambuzi CJ, Oder, Karokora, Mulenga and Kanyeihama JJSC) held that, in order for the foreign judgment to be registered under the 1922 Act, two requirements had to be satisfied. First, under s 2(1), the court must be satisfied that in all the circumstances of the case it is just and convenient that the foreign judgment should be enforced in Uganda. Second, the foreign judgment must not be subject to any bars in s 2(2) of the Act. It is important to note that the court has discretion to decide whether or not in the circumstances of the case it is just and convenient that the judgment in question should be enforced in Uganda: *In The Matter Of An Application By Sterling Civil Engineering Ltd* [2017] UGHCCD 76 (Musota J). In this case, the High Court refused to register an order of the Commercial Court in England. By way of context to the decision of the Uganda High Court, Sterling Civil Engineering had been successful in arbitration proceedings (the seat of which was Dar es Salaam) against the government of the United Republic of Tanzania. It appears that Sterling Civil Engineering then had judgment entered in England in the terms of the arbitral award and sought, pursuant to the 1922 Act, to have that English judgment registered in Uganda. In refusing the application, Musota J held that it was 'inconvenient for and unjust to subject the government with a huge economy and the functional system of government and tax base like Tanzania to unnecessary process of enforcement of foreign judgment in another state without proper justification for the same. [Sterling Civil Engineering] has not shown this court that the Tanzanian government has refused or failed to pay the sums awarded in the arbitral award ... It is also suspicious that [Sterling Civil Engineering] seeks to register the UK Order instead of the Tanzanian Order [presumably a reference to the award of the arbitral tribunal]. To me this appeared to be an attempt to undermine the sovereignty of the United Republic of Tanzania which would cause problems in execution and is an undesirable situation in Uganda. Therefore on this basis alone I would decline to register the Foreign Order.' The remainder of the judgment contains illuminating (but necessarily obiter) comments on the proper way to enforce arbitral awards in Uganda.

[120] In *In re Sir John Bagaire* [1995] Kam LR 681 (H Ct) (Katutsi J), the judgment creditor brought proceedings on a written guarantee against the judgment debtor in the High Court in England in 1991 and secured an *ex parte* judgment against the judgment debtor the same year. In 1994 the judgment creditor applied in Uganda to register the judgment under the 1922 Act. Registration was refused on two bases: first, the application was out of time, having been made outside the 12-month limitation period in s 2(1) (the report refers to s 3(1)); and, second, the judgment debtor had not submitted to the jurisdiction of the English court and so the court did not have jurisdiction pursuant to s 2(2)(b) of the 1922 Act (the report refers to s 3(2)(b)). However, in *Transroad Ltd v Bank of Uganda* it is recorded in the judgment of Berko J at first instance, reported at [1996] 1 KALR 103, that the Supreme Court in an earlier application in those proceedings had granted an extension of time under s 2(1) of the 1922 Act so that a judgment from the English High Court made in 1990 could be registered, subject to the other provisions of the Act, by way of an application for registration dated 25 November 1994 (see p 105). It seems that the reason for this leniency was that the defendant bank had, with the complicity of various officials of the government of Uganda, 'put off' the judgment creditor by entering into negotiations and then continually promising to pay the sums due over a period of years.

[121] The equivalent of s 14 of the 1920 Act.

[122] Reciprocal Enforcement of Judgments (Extension) Order, SI 21-2.

Where a judgment creditor wishes to have a judgment emanating from the superior courts of any of these jurisdictions registered in Uganda, he must do so according to the Reciprocal Enforcement of Judgment Rules,[123] which were made pursuant to section 4[124] of the 1922 Act.

The Reciprocal Enforcement of Judgment Rules provide, inter alia: any application for registration of a judgment from the United Kingdom or Ireland must be made *ex parte* or by originating summons to a judge and, if made *ex parte*, the judge may direct an originating summons to be issued;[125] the application must be supported by an affidavit of the facts containing a statement that the judgment creditor is entitled to enforce the judgment, that the judgment does not fall within one of the cases in section 2(2) of the Act (as to which, see immediately below) and exhibiting the judgment or an authenticated copy of it;[126] the originating summons issued, if any, or directed by the judge to be issued, must be served in the same way as a summons is required to be served.[127]

As noted above, section 2(2)[128] of the 1922 Act provides that no judgment shall be registered if:

(1) the original court acted without jurisdiction;

(2) the judgment debtor[129] was neither (a) carrying on business[130] nor ordinarily resident within the jurisdiction; (b) did not voluntarily appear or otherwise submit or agree to the jurisdiction of the court;[131]

(3) the defendant was not duly served with the proceedings and did not appear notwithstanding that he was ordinarily resident or carrying on business within the jurisdiction or had agreed to submit to the jurisdiction of the court;

---

[123] Reciprocal Enforcement of Judgment Rules, SI 21-1.

[124] The equivalent of s 11 of the 1920 Act.

[125] Rules 2 and 5(1).

[126] Rule 3.

[127] Rule 5.

[128] The equivalent of s 9(2) of the 1920 Act.

[129] Being a legal or natural person.

[130] It has been held by an English court that a New Zealand insurance company did not carry on business in Ghana merely because it maintained agents there with limited powers: *Sfeir and Co v National Insurance Co of New Zealand Ltd* [1964] 1 Lloyd's Rep 330 (QB).

[131] The Supreme Court in *Transroad Ltd v Bank of Uganda* [1998] Kam LR 106 (Wambuzi CJ, Oder, Karokora, Mulenga and Kanyeihamba JJSC), held that the bank had not submitted to the jurisdiction of the English court within the meaning of s 2(2)(b) because, although the bank had made an application to the English court which had been dismissed by consent with costs, it had only done so in order to contest the jurisdiction of the court and to dispute a garnishee order *nisi* obtained by the judgment creditor and, by doing so, protect its own property. (The bank had applied to set aside the default judgment which the judgment creditor had obtained and then entered into a consent order dismissing the application to set aside the default judgment with costs, but also discharging the garnishee order *nisi* with costs.)

(4) the judgment was obtained by fraud;[132]

(5) the judgment debtor satisfies the court that an appeal is pending or that he is entitled and intends to appeal against the judgment;

(6) the judgment was in respect of a cause of action which for reasons of public policy or some other similar reasons could not have been entertained by the Ugandan court.

Section 2(3)[133] provides that once registered the judgment is of the same force and effect as if it had been originally obtained in Uganda.

The 1922 Act contains no provisions dealing with recognition of foreign judgments (as opposed to their enforcement). In the ordinary course the recognition of a foreign judgment would be addressed by a reference to common-law principles referred to above.[134]

14.2.2.1.2.2 *Setting aside registration*

The order giving leave to register the judgment must be served on the judgment debtor and shall state the time within which the judgment debtor should apply to set aside the registration of the judgment.[135] Once registered in the register of foreign judgment maintained for that purpose at the registry of the High Court, written notice of the registration of the judgment (containing various specified details of the judgment and the procedure for setting it aside) must be served on the judgment debtor.[136] The judgment debtor may then within the time set out in the order granting leave to register the judgment apply by summons to the judge to set aside registration or suspend enforcement of the judgment.[137]

---

[132] Fraud is determined by reference to the common-law principles on fraud: *Owens Bank Ltd v Bracco* [1992] 2 AC 443 (HL (E)), where it was held that s 9(2) of the 1920 Act was to be construed as having adopted the approach of the common-law courts to the finality of a foreign judgment; that, accordingly, there was no requirement, as there was in the case of an action to set aside an English judgment on the ground of fraud, that the fraud should be established by fresh evidence that had not been available to the defendant at trial and could not with reasonable diligence have been discovered by him before judgment had been delivered. This decision in effect permits a defendant to relitigate matters already disposed of before the foreign court. *Owens Bank* has not been followed in certain Commonwealth jurisdictions (eg Canada in *Beals v Saldanha* [2003] 3 SCR 416, (2003) 234 DLR 4th 1; and New South Wales in *Keele v Findley* (1991) 21 NSWLR 444 (NSWSC); but in *Close v Arnot* (unreported) 21 November 1997 (NSW), the Common Law Division distinguished *Keele v Findley* and applied the traditional English standard of fraud in respect of a foreign judgment in a case where the defendant had, for good reason, allowed foreign proceedings to go undefended. A Ugandan court would not be bound by the *Owens Bank* decision.

[133] The equivalent of s 9(3) of the 1920 Act.

[134] *Dicey, Morris and Collins on the Conflict of Laws* 15 ed (2012) vol 1, r 53, para 14-180.

[135] Rule 7 of the Reciprocal Enforcement of Judgment Rules.

[136] Rule 10. The notice must contain the particulars set out in r 11.

[137] Rule 12.

14.2.2.1.3 Foreign Judgments (Reciprocal Enforcement) Act 1961

The 1961 Act makes provision for a system of registration of foreign judgments, the purpose of which is to domesticate the foreign judgment and render it enforceable in Uganda as if it were a judgment of the Ugandan court.[138]

Section 1(1) provides that the 1961 Act extends to any judgment or order 'given or made by a court in any civil proceedings, or a judgment or order given or made by a court in any criminal proceedings for the payment of a sum of money in respect of compensation or damages to an injured party'. Unlike the 1922 Act, the 1961 Act excludes arbitration awards, but includes awards made in criminal proceedings.

14.2.2.1.3.1 *Procedure for registration*

An application for registration of a foreign judgment[139] pursuant to the 1961 Act 'may' be made within six years of the date of either the foreign judgment itself or the determination of any appeal or review proceedings in respect of the foreign judgment.[140]

---

[138] Section 3(2). As noted above, the provisions of the 1961 Act correspond very closely to legislation of the United Kingdom on which the 1961 Act was based (the Foreign Judgments (Reciprocal Enforcement) Act 1933). It is to be expected that a Ugandan court will, if the opportunity ever presents itself, refer to judicial and academic authorities on the construction of these provisions of the 1933 Act when deciding questions on the construction of corresponding provisions of the 1961 Act. In particular, reference should be made to: *Dicey, Morris and Collins on the Conflict of Laws* 15 ed (2012) vol 1, paras 14R183–14-195; A Briggs *Civil Jurisdiction and Judgments* 7 ed (2021) paras 35.01-35.10.

[139] Defined by s 1(1)(c) to mean: 'a judgment or order given or made by a court in any civil proceedings, or a judgment or order given or made by a court in any criminal proceedings for the payment of a sum of money in respect of compensation or damages to an injured party'. As noted above, the Court of Appeal in England in *Strategic Technologies Pte Ltd v Procurement Bureau of the Republic of China Ministry of National Defence* [2020] EWCA Civ 1604 (David Richards, Males and Elisabeth Laing LJJ) held that the 1920 Act does not permit registration of a foreign judgment given by a court in one state in an action to enforce a judgment given by another state. Given the material similarity in the definition of the term judgment as between the English 1920 Act, the English 1933 Act and the 1961 Act, a Ugandan court might well be persuaded by the decision in *Strategic Technologies* as applied to the 1961 Act as well.

[140] Section 3(1). The six-year period is derived from s 2(1) of the Foreign Judgments (Reciprocal Enforcement) Act 1933. The terms of s 3(1) are not mandatory and appear to provide the court with discretion to permit registration outside the six-year period. In the 1933 Act the language used in relation to the six-year period is different and has been construed as imposing a temporal limit on registration: Briggs *Civil Jurisdiction and Judgments* 7 ed (2021) para 35.10. As noted elsewhere in this volume, in *Harman v Leaf* 1954 (2) SA 270 (SR), a decision under earlier Zimbabwe legislation for the reciprocal enforcement of foreign judgments which contained a one-year limit on registration, subject to a discretion in the court to extend that time, dismissing an application for registration two years out of time, Beadle J held the plaintiff had failed to provide sufficient evidence that 'he has not in any way been dilatory in pressing for registration of his judgment' and dismissed the application. It may be that the extension of the registration period from one year to six years imposes an even greater burden on an application seeking to persuade the court that time should be extended.

Section 4[141] of the 1961 Act states that provision may be made by rules of court for regulating the practice and procedure of proceedings under the Act. Those rules are the Foreign Judgments (Reciprocal Enforcement) Rules.[142]

An application for registration may be made *ex parte* by notice of motion supported by an affidavit[143] and the affidavit must state: the judgment creditor is entitled to enforce the judgment; the judgment has not been satisfied; the judgment could be enforced by execution in the original court and registration of the judgment is not liable to be set aside under section 5 of the 1961 Act, while a certified copy of the foreign judgment must be exhibited to the affidavit.[144]

Where the court grants leave to register the judgment, that order must specify a period within which any application to set aside registration must be made.[145] If the court grants leave to register the judgment, it is entered on the register of such judgments at the High Court registry.[146] Notice of registration must be served on the judgment debtor personally, unless otherwise ordered;[147] and the judgment debtor may apply by summons supported by an affidavit to have registration of the judgment set aside.[148]

Section 3(1)[149] makes the registration of the foreign judgment mandatory: 'The court shall, subject to proof of the prescribed matters and to other provisions of this Act, order the judgment to be registered.' These prescribed matters are set out in section 2(2)[150] of the 1961 Act; the foreign judgment must: (1) be final and conclusive; (2) be a money judgment not being a sum in respect of taxes or a fine or other penalty; and (3) be given after the coming into force of an order extending Part II of the Act to the jurisdiction of the foreign court.

14.2.2.1.3.2 *Setting aside registration*

Section 5(1)(a)[151] of the 1961 Act provides that in certain prescribed circumstances the court *must* set aside registration of the foreign judgment.[152] These circumstances are that:

141 The equivalent of s 3 of the 1933 Act.

142 SI 9-1.

143 Rule 4.

144 Rule 4(3) and (4). The court may, upon the judgment creditor's application to register the foreign judgment, order that he provide security for the costs of the registration application and for any proceedings that may be brought to have the registration of the judgment set aside: r 3.

145 Rule 5(3).

146 Rule 6.

147 Rule 7. The notice must contain the particulars set out in r 8.

148 Rule 10.

149 The equivalent to s 2(1) of the 1933 Act.

150 The equivalent to s 1(2) of the 1933 Act.

151 The equivalent to s 4(1)(a) of the 1933 Act.

152 The exclusionary provisions of the 1933 Act were based on the common law: 'The grounds of jurisdiction in the 1933 Act were deliberately framed so as to reproduce the rules of the common law as closely as possible', *Dicey, Morris and Collins on the Conflict of Laws* 15 ed (2012) vol 1, para 14-190.

(i) the judgment is not a judgment to which Part II of the 1961 Act applies or was registered in contravention of any previous provisions of the 1961 Act; or

(ii) the courts of the country of the original court had no jurisdiction in the circumstances of the case; or

(iii) the judgment debtor, being the defendant in the proceedings in the original court, did not (notwithstanding that process may have been duly served on him in accordance with the law of the country of the original court) receive notice of those proceedings in sufficient time to enable him to defend the proceedings and did not appear; or

(iv) the judgment was obtained by fraud;[153] or

(v) the enforcement of the judgment would be contrary to public policy in Uganda;[154] or

(vi) the rights under the judgment are not vested in the person by whom the application for registration was made.

Under section 5(1)(b)[155] of the 1961 Act the judgment *may* be set aside if the court is satisfied that the matter in dispute in the proceedings in the original court had previously been the subject of a final conclusive judgment by a court having jurisdiction in the matter.

The question whether the foreign court had jurisdiction is determined exhaustively[156] by the deeming provisions of section 5(2)(a).[157] The foreign court

[153] The equivalent to s 4(1)(a)(iv) of the 1933 Act. The rules related to setting aside a foreign judgment obtained by fraud are comprehensively set out in *Dicey, Morris and Collins on the Conflict of Laws* 15 ed (2012) vol 1, r 50, paras 14R-137–14-145. In *The Conflict of Laws*, para 14-191, it is stated of the fraud provisions of the 1933 Act: 'The provisions with regard to fraud and public policy are the same as the common law rules. In particular, the common law rule that a foreign judgment can be impeached for fraud even though no newly discovered evidence is produced, and even though the fraud was alleged in the foreign proceedings, applies to enforcement and recognition under the 1933 Act. In *Owens Bank Ltd v Bracco* [1992] 2 AC 443 the House of Lords held that the fraud exception in the Administration of Justice Act 1920 was subject to the same rule, and indicated (obiter) that the same must be so under the 1933 Act.' *Owens Bank* has not been followed in certain Commonwealth jurisdictions (eg Canada in *Beals v Saldanha* [2003] 3 SCR 416, (2003) 234 DLR 4th 1; and New South Wales in *Keele v Findley* (1991) 21 NSWLR 444 (NSWSC)); but in *Close v Arnot* (unreported, 21 November 1997) (NSW), the Common Law Division distinguished *Keele v Findley* and applied the traditional English standard of fraud in respect of a foreign judgment in a case where the defendant had, for good reason, allowed foreign proceedings to go undefended. A Ugandan court would not be bound by the *Owens Bank* decision.

[154] The equivalent to s 4(1)(a)(v) of the 1933 Act. The relevant rule in *The Conflict of Laws* r 51, paras 14R-152–14-158.

[155] The equivalent to s 4(1)(b) of the 1933 Act.

[156] *Société Co-opérative Sidmetal v Titan International Ltd* [1966] 1 QB 828; *Sharps Commercials Ltd v Gas Turbines Ltd* [1956] NZLR 819 (a decision on the identically worded New Zealand Act).

[157] The equivalent to s 4(2)(a) of the 1933 Act.

is deemed to have had jurisdiction in the case of a judgment in an action *in personam* if:

(1) the judgment debtor, being a defendant in the original court, submitted to the jurisdiction of that court by voluntarily appearing in the proceedings otherwise than for the purpose of protecting, or obtaining the release of property seized, or threatened with seizure, in the proceedings or of contesting the jurisdiction of that court;[158] or

(2) the judgment debtor was a plaintiff in, or counter-claimed in, the proceedings in the original court; or

(3) the judgment debtor, being a defendant in the original court, had before the commencement of the proceedings agreed, in respect of the subject-matter of the proceedings, to submit to the jurisdiction of that court or of the courts of the country of that court; or

(4) the judgment debtor, being a defendant in the original court, was, at the time when the proceedings were instituted, resident in, or being a body corporate had its principal place of business in, the country of that court; or

(5) the judgment debtor, being a defendant in the original court, had an office or place of business in the country of that court and the proceedings in that court were in respect of a transaction effected through or at that office or place.

Section 5(2)(b)[159] relates to property and provides that the foreign court has jurisdiction in proceedings relating to movable or immovable property if that property was situated in the foreign country when proceedings were commenced.

Section 5(2)(c)[160] provides that in any other case the foreign court will be deemed to have had jurisdiction if the jurisdiction of the foreign court is recognised under the law of Uganda.

---

[158] A point dealt with by the Supreme Court under the similar provisions of the 1922 Act in *Transroad Ltd v Bank of Uganda* [1998] Kam LR 106 (see above).

[159] The equivalent to s 4(2)(b) of the 1933 Act.

[160] The equivalent to s 4(2)(c) of the 1933 Act. It remains undecided whether this provision would entitle a court to recognise a basis for the jurisdiction of the foreign court not expressly provided for in the Act but available at common law, such as the presence of the defendant in the jurisdiction of the foreign court at the time of the commencement of proceedings. The discussion of this provision in *Dicey, Morris and Collins on the Conflict of Laws* 15 ed (2012) vol 1, para 14-190, suggests that this is not the case; in *Société Co-opérative Sidmetal v Titan International Ltd* [1966] 1 QB 828, Widgery J held (at 850C–D) that an action *in personam* not within s 4(2)(a) was also excluded from s 4(2)(c): 'It seems to me that an action *in personam* does not fall within subsection (2) unless it satisfies one or other of the conditions in paragraph (a). As I read the section, no action *in personam* could fall within paragraph (c) at all because all such actions are excluded by the terms of paragraph (c).'

Section 5(3) provides that the courts of the country of the original court shall not be deemed to have had jurisdiction if the subject-matter of the proceedings was immovable property outside the jurisdiction of the original court, or the original proceedings were brought in breach of an arbitration clause, or the defendant was immune from suit under the rules of public international law.

Section 7 provides that a foreign judgment that is registrable under the 1961 Act must be enforced by way of proceedings under the 1961 Act and not otherwise.

14.2.2.2 *The relationship between the regimes*

Section 8 of the 1961 Act deals with the extension of the provisions of Part II thereof to other Commonwealth jurisdictions.[161] Section 8 contemplates two varieties of extension order. First, a general application order by which the minister may direct that Part II of the Act shall apply to 'the territories of the Commonwealth' and to judgments obtained in those territories. Second, after a general application order has been made, the minister may make what is referred to as a specific application order under section 2 of the 1961 Act by which Part II is extended to a specific Commonwealth territory, in which case Part II applies to arbitration awards enforceable in that territory.[162]

The effect of a general application order is to disapply the 1922 Act to the Commonwealth, save for those territories of the Commonwealth to which the 1922 Act applied before the making of the general application order.

The effect of a specific application order is to disapply the 1922 Act to the specified territory.

In 2002, the minister made a general application order extending the 1961 Act to the Commonwealth by way of the Foreign Judgments (Reciprocal Enforcement) (General Application) Order.[163] The minister also made a specific application order in respect of Grenada.[164]

At present, therefore, the somewhat untidy position may be set out as follows: (1) the 1922 Act applies to the United Kingdom, Ireland, Botswana, Lesotho, Mauritius, New South Wales, Seychelles, Sri Lanka and Eswatini; (2) the 1961 Act applies to the judgments emanating from the rest of the Commonwealth; but (3) by virtue of the decision of the High Court in *In Re Application by*

[161] Section 2 deals with the extension of Part II to foreign jurisdictions; s 2(1) provides that if the minister is satisfied that 'substantial reciprocity of treatment will be assured as respects the enforcement in that foreign country of judgments given in the superior courts of Uganda', he may extend Part II to that country.

[162] Section 8(2). On its true construction, this sub-section will apply to awards originating in that specified territory and, it is thought, not awards that happen also to be enforceable in that territory regardless of their origin. (The term 'place' in the sub-section must refer to the territory in which the award is enforceable.)

[163] SI 35 of 2002.

[164] Foreign Judgments (Reciprocal Enforcement) (Grenada) Order 2002, SI 36 of 2002.

Michael Ndichu Mburu (Receiver/Manager of Mandeeq Africa Ltd (In Receivership),[165] judgments from the High Court of Kenya (and, presumably, the High Court of Malawi or Tanzania too[166]) may be enforced either under the 1908 Act or the 1961 Act (but not both).[167]

14.3 Interim remedies

14.3.1 Jurisdiction to grant interim remedies

The jurisdiction of the High Court to grant interim relief is to be found in a number of statutory sources that are referred to below.

Ugandan legislation makes provision for the pre-judgment arrest of a defendant and the attachment of a defendant's property. Section 64 of the Civil Procedure Act 1929 provides:

> '**64. Supplemental proceedings**.
>
> (1) In order to prevent the ends of justice from being defeated, the court may, if it is so prescribed—
>
> *(a)* issue a warrant to arrest the defendant and bring him or her before the court to show cause why he or she should not give security for his or her appearance, and if the defendant fails to comply with any order for security commit him or her to prison;
>
> *(b)* direct the defendant to furnish security to produce any property belonging to him or her and to place the same at the disposal of the court or order the attachment of any property;
>
> *(c)* grant a temporary injunction and in case of disobedience commit the person guilty of it to prison and order that his or her property be attached and sold;
>
> *(d)* appoint a receiver of any property and enforce the performance of his or her duties by attaching and selling his or her property;
>
> *(e)* make such other interlocutory orders as may appear to the court to be just and convenient.'

The powers conferred on the court under section 64 include: the power to issue an arrest warrant for the defendant; the power to require the defendant to provide security for the plaintiff's claim; the power to attach the defendant's property; an apparently unlimited power to 'grant a temporary injunction'; and the power

---

[165] [2008] UGCOMMC 70 (Arach-Amoko LJ).

[166] By parity of reasoning with the judgment in *Michael Ndichu Mburu (Receiver/Manager of Mandeeq Africa Ltd (In Receivership)*.

[167] In *In Re: Application by Michael Ndichu Mburu (Receiver/Manager of Mandeeq Africa Ltd (In Receivership)*, the court did not make mention of either the 1908 Act or the decision in *Kamiri v Oseko* [2012] UGCOMMC 135 (Comm Ct) (Obura LJ). The formulation in the main text therefore represents, in the view of the authors, the best way to rationalise the decisions in these cases.

to make 'such other interlocutory orders as may appear to the court to be just and convenient'. These are powers expressed in language of great amplitude and would appear to provide a firm statutory foundation for *Mareva* injunctions and *Anton Piller* orders. Each of these orders is dealt with under the relevant headings below.

An overarching statutory power to grant injunctions restraining acts is to be found in section 38 of the Judicature Act 1996:[168]

> '**38. Injunctions**.
>
> (1) The High Court shall have power to grant an injunction to restrain any person from doing any act as may be specified by the High Court.
>
> (2) Where an injunction is granted restraining any person from acting in any office in which he or she is not entitled to act, the High Court may declare the office to be vacant.
>
> (3) Where before, at or after the hearing of any cause or matter, an application is made for an injunction to prevent a threatened or apprehended waste or trespass, an injunction may be granted, if the High Court thinks fit—
>
> (i) whether or not the person against whom the injunction is sought is in possession under any claim of title or claims a right to do the act sought to be restrained under any colour of title; and
>
> (ii) whether the estates claimed by the parties or any of the parties are legal or equitable.'

The power referred to in these sections (and those under the inherent jurisdiction of the court) has been the subject of more detailed provision in the CPR.

Orders XL and XLI of the CPR provide for the making of interlocutory orders. Although there is no authority directly in point, it is likely that in order for a Ugandan court to make an interlocutory order in a cause, it is necessary that the court has jurisdiction over the substantive dispute between the parties.[169]

---

[168] Act 13 of 1996 (Cap 13 of the Laws of Uganda 2000). Section 33 of the Judicature Act 1996 also provides: '***33. General provisions as to remedies***. The High Court shall, in the exercise of the jurisdiction vested in it by the Constitution, this Act or any written law, grant absolutely or on such terms and conditions as it thinks just, all such remedies as any of the parties to a cause or matter is entitled to in respect of any legal or equitable claim properly brought before it, so that as far as possible all matters in controversy between the parties may be completely and finally determined and all multiplicities of legal proceedings concerning any of those matters avoided.' The jurisdiction vested in the High Court pursuant to s 139 of the Constitution is 'unlimited original jurisdiction in all matters'.

[169] Such was the position in the United Kingdom prior to the passing of s 25 of the Civil Jurisdiction and Judgments Act 1982 which now empowers courts in the UK to grant relief in aid of proceedings outside the jurisdiction *(Siskina (Owners of cargo lately on board) v Distos Compania Naviera SA, The Siskina* [1979] AC 210 (HL (E)).

14.3.2 Procedure for application

In Uganda, unless the CPR expressly provides otherwise, all applications to the court shall be by motion and shall be heard in open court.[170] No motion shall be made without notice to the parties affected by the motion, save that a court may, if satisfied that the delay caused by proceeding in the ordinary way would or might entail irreparable or serious mischief, make an order *ex parte* upon such terms as to costs or otherwise, and subject to such undertaking, if any, as may seem just.[171]

Every notice of motion shall state in general terms the grounds of the application and, where any motion is grounded on evidence by affidavit, a copy of any affidavit intended to be used shall be served with the notice of motion.[172]

14.3.3 Interlocutory injunctions generally

Order XLI is entitled 'Temporary Injunctions and Interlocutory Orders', and provides for three principal types of order: (1) an order to protect property; (2) an order to restrain a breach of duty; and (3) an order that property that is the subject of the suit be preserved, detained or inspected. With regard to the first two of these orders, the application is by summons in chambers, and in the case of the third (and any other application under Order XLI) the application is by motion on notice.[173]

Rule 3 provides generally, 'The court shall in all cases, before granting an injunction, direct notice of the application for the injunction to be given to the opposite party.' This rule is somewhat ambiguous in its wording. It is thought that the proper construction of the rule is that in applications made *ex parte*, before making an order the judge must direct that the defendant be given notice of the application. (Usually, an order will be time-limited until the return day when the plaintiff will need to, in effect, reapply for the order with the defendant present. Notice of the application rather than notice of the injunction is merely a means of communicating this aspect of procedure. Obviously, the defendant will have notice of the temporary injunction because it will have been served on him.)

---

[170] Order LII, r 1.

[171] Order LII, r 2. Any party affected by such *ex parte* order may move to set that order aside. Where the court is of the opinion that sufficient notice has not been given or that any person to whom notice has not been given ought to have had the notice, the court may either dismiss the motion or application or adjourn the hearing of it in order that the notice may be given upon such terms, if any, as the court may think fit to impose: O LII, r 4.

[172] Order LI, r 3.

[173] Order XLI, r 9. All applications by summons shall be in chambers and, if supported by affidavit, a copy of any affidavit or affidavits relied upon shall be attached to each copy of the summons directed to be served.

(1) Order XLI, rule 1: An order to protect property

Rule 1 provides:

> '**1. Cases in which temporary injunction may be granted**.
>
> Where in any suit it is proved by affidavit or otherwise—
>
> *(a)* that any property in dispute in a suit is in danger of being wasted, damaged, or alienated by any party to the suit, or wrongfully sold in execution of a decree; or
>
> *(b)* that the defendant threatens or intends to remove or dispose of his or her property with a view to defraud his or her creditors,
>
> the court may by order grant a temporary injunction to restrain such act, or make such other order for the purpose of staying and preventing the wasting, damaging, alienation, sale, removal or disposition of the property as the court thinks fit until the disposal of the suit or until further orders.'

Rule 1 is concerned with two situations: (a) where the action concerns a particular property, such as possession of a vehicle, and the defendant acts in such a way as to damage that property or sell the property;[174] or (b) where the defendant has creditors and the defendant threatens or intends to remove or dispose of his property 'with a view to' defraud those creditors. The wording of rule 1(b) would not seem to support the making of a pre-judgment *Mareva* injunction because such an injunction is granted prior to the plaintiff becoming a judgment creditor and thus a creditor for the purposes of rule 1(b).

(2) Order XLI, rule 2: An order to restrain a breach of duty

Rule 2 provides:

> '**2. Injunction to restrain repetition or continuance of breach**.
>
> (1) In any suit for restraining the defendant from committing a breach of contract or other injury of any kind, whether compensation is claimed in the suit or not, the plaintiff may, at any time after the commencement of the suit, and either before or after judgment, apply to the court for a temporary injunction to restrain the defendant from committing the breach of contract or injury complained of, or any injury of a like kind arising out of the same contract or relating to the same property or right.
>
> (2) The court may by order grant such injunction on such terms as to an inquiry as to damages, the duration of the injunction, keeping an account, giving security or otherwise, as the court thinks fit.
>
> (3) In cases of disobedience, or of breach of any such terms, the court granting an injunction may order the property of the person guilty of the disobedience or breach to be attached, and may also order the person to be detained in a civil prison for a period not exceeding six months unless in the meantime the court directs his or her release.

---

[174] For an application of O XLI, r 1(a), see: *Mujogya v Bwango* [2019] UGHCCD 279 (HC) (Musene J).

(4) No attachment under this rule shall remain in force for more than one year, at the end of which time, if the disobedience or breach continues, the property attached may be sold, and out of the proceeds the court may award such compensation as it thinks fit, and shall pay the balance, if any, to the party entitled to it.'

The title to rule 2 is slightly misleading as it refers to repetition or continuance of conduct, whereas the rule itself appears concerned with restraining conduct that is threatened but has yet to occur. The rule is also drafted widely to embrace a threatened breach of contract 'or other injury of any kind'. These words are of sufficient amplitude to include torts and breaches of other duties such as fiduciary duties, duties imposed by statute and potentially trustee duties. The rule also makes express mention of an inquiry into damage suffered by the defendant as a result of the injunction, presumably under a cross-undertaking as to damages given by the plaintiff as part of the grant of the order.

The provisions of rule 2 are underpinned by section 38(1) of the Judicature Act 1996.

(3) Order XLI, rule 7: Preservation of property

Rule 7 provides:

'**7. Detention, preservation, inspection, etc. of property**.

(1) The court may, on the application of any party to a suit, and on such terms as it thinks fit—

(a) make an order for the detention, preservation or inspection of any property which is the subject matter of the suit, or as to which any question may arise in the suit;

(b) for all or any of the purposes aforesaid authorise any person to enter upon or into any land or building in the possession of any other party to the suit; and

(c) for all or any of the purposes aforesaid authorise any samples to be taken, or any observation to be made, or experiment to be tried, which may seem necessary or expedient for the purpose of obtaining full information or evidence.

(2) The provisions as to execution of process shall apply *mutatis mutandis* to persons authorised to enter under this rule.'

The scope of rule 7 is limited to actions taken in relation to 'any property which is the subject matter of the suit', for example, a cargo of maize alleged to be spoilt or a machine alleged to be defective. The power provided by rule 7 is an accessory power to assist the court and the parties in the process leading up to the trial of the proceedings. From the wording of rule 7(1)(a) it would seem that this provision may also provide some statutory support for the granting of an *Anton Piller* order (assuming statutory support is required). An application under rule 7 is by motion on notice.[175]

[175] Rule 9.

The principles on the basis of which a temporary injunction will be granted

In *Kiyimba-Kaggwa v Nasser*,[176] the plaintiff was the registered proprietor of the property subject of the proceedings. The plaintiff had been granted two leases of the property and although these had expired there was evidence that the lessor would renew the leases. The defendant contended that he had been offered a lease of the property and had proceeded to commence cultivating the land. In granting the injunction restraining the defendant's conduct, the court stated that the test previously adopted in Uganda of requiring the plaintiff to show 'a *prima facie* case with a probability of success'[177] was incorrect and that the correct test was that promulgated by Lord Diplock in the House of Lords in *American Cyanamid Co v Ethicon Ltd*,[178] that there needs to be 'a serious question to be tried'.

In *GAPCO Uganda Ltd v Kaweesa*,[179] Murangira J followed the decision in *Kiyimba-Kaggwa v Nasser* and the subsequent, but unreported, decision of the Court of Appeal in *Kiingi v Attorney General*,[180] and held that the test for the grant of an interlocutory injunction had three stages to it: (1) the plaintiff must show that there is a serious issue to be tried; (2) the plaintiff must show that he will suffer irreparable damage that will not be adequately compensated for by damages if the injunction is not made; and (3) the balance of convenience is in favour of the granting of the injunction. The judge stated,[181] following *Kiyamba-Kaggwa v Nasser*, that the requirement that the plaintiff must show irreparable injury did not mean that there must not be a physical possibility of repairing the injury, but instead means that the injury must be a substantial or material one and one that cannot adequately be compensated by damages.[182]

In view of the willingness of the Ugandan courts to rely on the decision in *American Cyanamid*[183] in this area of law, it bears citation in the original. The opinion of Lord Diplock is generally taken as establishing a test for the making of an interlocutory injunction comprising two elements:

---

176 [1985] HCB 43 (H Ct) (Odoki J).

177 The use of this wording has persisted notwithstanding that the courts accept that it means that the plaintiff must show a serious issue to be tried. It would be better were this wording explicitly replaced by 'serious issue to be tried' wording.

178 [1975] AC 396 (HL (E)) (Lord Diplock, Viscount Dilhorne and Lords Cross, Salmon and Edmund-Davies).

179 [2013] UGHCLD 47 (H Ct, Land Division) (Murangira J). Murangira J followed his decision in the *GAPCO* case a few weeks later in *Natayi v Barclays Bank of Uganda Ltd* [2013] UGHCLD 60 (H Ct) and then again in *Matovu v Nabale* [2013] UGHCLD 64.

180 (Constitutional Application 29 of 2012).

181 Ibid p 4.

182 More recently, the High Court, in *Musinguzi v Baryomunsi* [2017] UGHCCD 61 (Musota J) has reiterated the correctness of the decisions in both the *Kiyimba* case and the *GAPCO* case, describing the principles governing the grant of a temporary injunction as 'well settled'.

183 [1975] AC 396 (HL (E)) (Lord Diplock, Viscount Dilhorne and Lords Cross, Salmon and Edmund-Davies).

(1) 'The court ... must be satisfied that the claim is not frivolous or vexatious; in other words, that there is a serious issue to be tried';[184]

'... unless the material available to the court at the hearing of the application for an interlocutory injunction fails to disclose that the plaintiff has any real prospect of succeeding in his claim for a permanent injunction at the trial, the court should go on to consider whether the balance of convenience lies in favour of granting or refusing the interlocutory relief that is sought';[185]

(2) On the balance of convenience:[186]

'... the governing principle is that the court should first consider whether, if the plaintiff were to succeed at the trial in establishing his right to a permanent injunction, he would be adequately compensated by an award of damages for the loss he would have sustained as a result of the defendant's continuing to do what was sought to be enjoined between the time of the application and the time of the trial. If damages in the measure recoverable at common law would be adequate remedy and the defendant would be in a financial position to pay them, no interlocutory injunction should normally be granted, however strong the plaintiff's claim appeared to be at that stage. If, on the other hand, damages would not provide an adequate remedy for the plaintiff in the event of his succeeding at the trial, the court should then consider whether, on the contrary hypothesis that the defendant were to succeed at the trial in establishing his right to do that which was sought to be enjoined, he would be adequately compensated under the plaintiff's undertaking as to damages for the loss he would have sustained by being prevented from doing so between the time of the application and the time of the trial. If damages in the measure recoverable under such an undertaking would be an adequate remedy and the plaintiff would be in a financial position to pay them, there would be no reason upon this ground to refuse an interlocutory injunction.

It is where there is doubt as to the adequacy of the respective remedies in damages available to either party or to both, that the question of balance of convenience arises. It would be unwise to attempt even to list all the various matters which may need to be taken into consideration in deciding where the balance lies, let alone to suggest the relative weight to be attached to them. These will vary from case to case.

Where other factors appear to be evenly balanced it is a counsel of prudence to take such measures as are calculated to preserve the status quo.'

These, then, are likely to be the principles that a Ugandan court will apply in considering whether to grant an interlocutory injunction.[187]

---

[184] Ibid 407G.

[185] Ibid 408A–B.

[186] Ibid 408B–G.

[187] By way of an aside here, in circumstances where the plaintiff wishes to make the application *ex parte*, there can be little serious doubt that he will owe the court a duty to make full and frank disclosure of all facts relevant to the court's decision whether or not to make the order sought.

14.3.4 Freezing orders

A Ugandan court may make a freezing injunction by way of court order (sometimes called a *Mareva* injunction).[188]

In *Asiimwe v Air Uganda*,[189] the court cited the English Court of Appeal decision in *Mareva Compania Naviera SA v International Bulk Carriers SA*,[190] and quoted from the judgment of Lord Denning MR:[191]

> 'In my opinion that principle applies to a creditor who has a right to be paid the debt owing to him, even before he has established his right by getting judgment for it. If it appears that the debt is due and owing, and there is a danger that the debtor may dispose of his assets so as to defeat it before judgment, the court has jurisdiction in a proper case to grant an interlocutory judgment so as to prevent him disposing of those assets.'

The court proceeded to cite the English Court of Appeal decision in *Third Chandris Shipping Corp v Unimarine SA*,[192] and quoted the guidelines for the making of *Mareva* injunctions there set out by Lord Denning MR:[193]

> '**The guidelines**
>
> In endeavouring to set out some guidelines, I have had recourse to the practice of many other countries which have been put before us. They have been most helpful. These are the points which those who apply for it should bear in mind. (i) The Plaintiff should make full and frank disclosure of all matters in his knowledge which are material for the judge to know... (ii) The Plaintiff should give particulars of his claim against the Defendant, stating the ground of his claim and the amount thereof, and fairly stating the points made against it by the Defendant. (iii) The Plaintiff should give some grounds for believing that the Defendants have assets here. ...The existence of a bank account in England is enough, whether it is in overdraft or not. (iv) The Plaintiff should give some grounds for believing that there is a risk of the assets being removed before the judgment or award is satisfied. The mere fact that the Defendant is abroad is not by itself sufficient. No one would wish any reputable foreign company to be plagued with a *Mareva* injunction simply because it has agreed to London arbitration. But there are some foreign companies whose structure invites comment. We often see in this court a corporation which is registered in a country where the company law is so loose that nothing is known about it, where it does no work and has no officers and no assets. Nothing can be found out about the membership, or

---

188 That a Ugandan court has such a power has seemingly been confirmed by the Supreme Court in *Clive v Stanbic Bank* [2016] UGSC 6 (SC) (Nshimye, Mwangusya, Opio-Aweri, Mwondha and Tibatemwa-Ekirikubinza JJSC), though the Supreme Court did not discuss the principles which governed the grant of such an order. A *Mareva* order is so called after the title of the English authority in which such orders were first approved at appellate level: *Mareva Compania Naviera SA v International Bulkcarriers SA* [1975] 2 Lloyd's Rep 509 (CA) (Lord Denning MR, Ormrod and Roskill LJJ).

189 [2014] UGCOMMC 144 (H Ct (Comm)) (Madrama Izama J).

190 [1980] 1 All ER 213 (CA) (Lord Denning MR, Roskill and Ormrod LJJ).

191 Ibid 215b.

192 [1979] 2 All ER 972 (CA) (Lord Denning MR, Lawton and Cumming-Bruce LJJ).

193 Ibid 984g–985d.

> its control, or its assets, or the charges on them. Judgment cannot be enforced against it. There is no reciprocal enforcement of judgments. It is nothing more than a name grasped from the air, as elusive as the Cheshire cat. In such cases the very fact of incorporation there gives some ground for believing there is a risk that, if judgment or an award is obtained, it may go unsatisfied. Such registration of such companies may carry many advantages to the individuals who control them, but they may suffer the disadvantage of having a *Mareva* injunction granted against them. The giving of security for a debt is a small price to pay for the convenience of such a registration. Security would certainly be required in New York. So also it may be in London. Other grounds may be shown for believing there is a risk. But some such should be shown. (v) The Plaintiffs must, of course, give an undertaking in damages, in case they fail in their claim or the injunction turns out to be unjustified. In a suitable case this should be supported by a bond or security: and the injunction only granted on it being given, or undertaken to be given.'

The court in *Asiimwe v Air Uganda*, described these statements by Lord Denning MR as 'very persuasive'[194] and adopted them as representing Ugandan law.[195]

14.3.5 Search and seize orders

The circumstances in which a Ugandan court may grant an order requiring one party to admit another party to premises in order that the second party search for documents or other movable property and to take away such documents and movable property and retain them for the time being (previously referred to as an *Anton Piller* order)[196] were canvassed in *Uganda Performing Rights Society Ltd v Fred Mukubira*.[197] In this case, the Ugandan court, making an *Anton Piller* order (seemingly for the first time), cited the original English decision in which such an order had been made, *Anton Piller KG v Manufacturing Processes Ltd*,[198] and a decision of the Kenyan Commercial Court, *Microsoft Corp v Mitsumi Computer Garage Ltd*,[199] in which the *Anton Piller* decision was cited and followed.[200]

---

[194] [2014] UGCOMMC 144 at p 14 of the electronic report.

[195] Part of the court's focus was on the similarity between the statutory provision relied on by the Court of Appeal in the *Mareva* case and the statutory provision relied on by the judge in the *Assimwe* case. In the former it was a provision that empowered the court to grant an injunction 'in all cases in which it shall appear to the Court to be just and convenient' (s 45 of the Supreme Court of Judicature (Consolidation) Act 1925); in the *Assimwe* case it was a provision in materially identical terms (s 37(1) of the Judicature Act 1996; although the judge could also have referred to s 64(1)(e) of the Civil Procedure Act 1929). In both cases, the courts found that these provisions gave them power to make the order sought.

[196] After the title of the English authority in which such orders were first approved at appellate level: *Anton Piller KG v Manufacturing Processes Ltd* [1976] 1 All ER 779 (CA) (Lord Denning MR; Ormrod and Shaw LJJ).

[197] [2004] UGCOMMC 2 (H Ct) (Kiryabwire J). Loss of revenue was held to amount to serious damage for these purposes.

[198] [1976] Ch 55 (CA) (Lord Denning MR, Ormrod and Shaw LJJ).

[199] [2001] EA 127 (H Ct (Comm)) (Ringera J).

[200] Ibid 133e–g, quoting from the judgment of Ormrod LJ, which is cited in the text below.

The test adopted by the Ugandan court was that formulated by Ormrod LJ in the *Anton Piller* case (and adopted by the Kenyan court in the *Microsoft* case). Ormrod LJ stated:[201]

> 'There are three essential pre-conditions for the making of such an order, in my judgment. First, there must be an extremely strong prima facie case. Secondly, the damage, potential or actual, must be very serious for the [plaintiff]. Thirdly, there must be clear evidence that the defendants have in their possession incriminating documents or things, and that there is a real possibility that they may destroy such material before any application *inter partes* can be made.'

This now seems to represent Ugandan law on the subject. In the *Uganda Performing Rights* case the judge also set out[202] the following warning to the plaintiff:

> 'An *Anton Piller* Order is not a search warrant which entitles a holder to force his way into the Defendant's premises against his will. The Defendant by the *Anton Piller* Order is only enjoined by court to "do permit" the entry, inspection or other direction of the court. The order should be served on the [defendant] attended by counsel for the [plaintiff] who is and must strictly act as an officer of the court. The [defendant] must be given an opportunity to consider the order and if necessary consult his/her own counsel. If entry is refused, the [plaintiff] should not force his way in. The [plaintiff] however may bring the refusal to the notice of the court, if need be by an application to commit for contempt of court.'

The *Uganda Performing Rights* case was followed and applied in *Muse-Af Enterprises Co Ltd v Bilen General Trading Ltd*,[203] and in *Pastificio Lucio SPA v Semwanga*.[204]

14.3.6 Third-party disclosure orders

There is no authority on the question whether a Ugandan court may, apart from the established post-issuing of proceedings and pre-trial procedures whereby a third party may be served with a witness summons requiring his attendance at court in order to give evidence and/or to produce documents,[205] order a person not a party to the proceedings to give disclosure. Such a power is available to the English courts in the form of a *Norwich Pharmacal* order[206] whereby an innocent third party caught up in a tort may be ordered to disclose the name or other identity of the tortfeasor.

---

201 [1976] Ch 55 at 62A–B.

202 [2004] UGCOMMC 2 at p 7 of the electronic report.

203 [2013] UGCOMMC 62 (H Ct (Comm)) (Obura J).

204 [2014] UGCOMMC 25 (H Ct (Comm)) (Obura J).

205 CPR, O XVI, r 1.

206 *Norwich Pharmacal Co v Customs and Excise* [1974] AC 133 (HL (E)) (Lords Reid and Morris, Viscount Dilhorne and Lords Cross and Kilbrandon).

In *Norwich Pharmacal Co v Customs and Excise Comrs*, the English House of Lords[207] set out the following principle:

> 'That if through no fault of his own a person gets mixed up in the tortious acts of others so as to facilitate their wrong-doing he may incur no personal liability but he comes under a duty to assist the person who has been wronged by giving him full information and disclosing the identity of the wrongdoers ... [It does not matter] whether he became so mixed up by voluntary action on his part or because it was his duty to do what he did. It may be that if this causes him expense the person seeking the information ought to reimburse him. But justice requires that he should co-operate in righting the wrong if he unwittingly facilitated its perpetration.'

More recent authority[208] has clarified the conditions which the plaintiff must satisfy in order to obtain such relief:

> 'The three conditions to be satisfied for the court to exercise the power to order *Norwich Pharmacal* relief are:
>
> i) a wrong must have been carried out, or arguably carried out, by an ultimate wrongdoer;
>
> ii) there must be the need for an order to enable action to be brought against the ultimate wrongdoer; and
>
> iii) the person against whom the order is sought must: (a) be mixed up in so as to have facilitated the wrongdoing; and (b) be able or likely to be able to provide the information necessary to enable the ultimate wrongdoer to be sued.'

If the plaintiff satisfies all of those conditions, the English court will then go on to exercise its discretion. In doing so, it must keep in mind the proper scope of *Norwich Pharmacal* relief: the jurisdiction cannot be used for wide-ranging discovery or the gathering of evidence, but is strictly confined to necessary information.[209]

In view of the similarity of the wording of the powers to order interim relief conferred on both the English and Ugandan courts and the affinity between the two systems of law in this regard, it is likely that, in the event an application for a third-party disclosure order were made before a Ugandan court, that court would have regard to the English authorities in disposing of the application.

---

207 Ibid 175, *per* Lord Reid.

208 *Ramilos Trading Ltd v Valentin Mikhaylovich Buyanovsky* [2016] EWHC 3175 (Comm) (H Ct) (Flaux J), citing, at para [11], *Mitsui v Nexen Petroleum* [2005] EWHC 625 (Ch); [2005] 3 All ER 511 [21] (H Ct) (Lightman J).

209 *Ramilos Trading Ltd v Valentin Mikhaylovich Buyanovsky* [2016] EWHC 3175 (Comm) (H Ct) (Flaux J) para [46].

14.3.7 Anti-suit injunctions

An anti-suit injunction is an order restraining the injunction defendant from either commencing or continuing proceedings outside Uganda in breach of a legal or equitable right on the part of the injunction plaintiff not to pursue litigation outside Uganda or, conversely, restraining the injunction defendant from commencing or continuing proceedings inside Uganda in breach of a legal or equitable right on the part of the injunction plaintiff to have the dispute between the parties litigated in a jurisdiction other than Uganda.[210]

There is no reported judicial authority in Uganda on whether or not an anti-suit injunction is a remedy available to the courts in Uganda. However, as noted at section 14.3.1 above, the jurisdiction of the High Court to grant injunctions is statutory and, in exercising it, the court 'shall make such interlocutory orders as may appear to the court to be just and convenient'.

This is the identical basis to that upon which English courts exercise the jurisdiction to make anti-suit injunctions and, given the affinity of Uganda's law with English law in this regard,[211] it is to be anticipated that a court in Uganda before which an application is brought for an anti-suit injunction will have regard to the English authorities in setting out the principles upon which an anti-suit injunction may be granted in Uganda. Set out below, in summary, are the principles of English law governing the grant of an anti-suit injunction.

The court must have personal jurisdiction over the injunction defendant. The court may be seised either by service on the defendant within the jurisdiction or service out of the jurisdiction with the leave of the court.[212]

The injunction plaintiff must assert a cause of action for relief. Usually, the injunction plaintiff will contend that the injunction defendant is committing a wrong by bringing or proposing to bring proceedings in a foreign court. This will require the plaintiff to characterise the conduct of the defendant as the breach of a legal or equitable right.

A legal right may, and often will, be based on a right not to be sued in a foreign jurisdiction arising out of an exclusive jurisdiction clause in favour of

---

[210] In similar vein, an anti-anti-suit injunction is an order restraining the injunction defendant from commencing or continuing proceedings to restrain the injunction plaintiff from applying to restrain the injunction defendant from commencing or continuing proceedings. The leading works on this topic are: Raphael *The Anti-Suit Injunction* 2 ed (2019) and Briggs *Civil Jurisdiction and Judgments* 7 ed (2021) ch 28. It is also conceptually possible to obtain similar relief in the context of arbitration, but such relief is outside the scope of this work.

[211] It is worth noting that the High Court of South Africa in *Vedanta Resources Holdings Ltd v ZCCM Investment Holdings plc* 2019 JDR 1425 (GJ) paras [11], [54] and [56] (Adams J) and the High Court of Nigeria in *Zenith Global Merchant Ltd v Zhongfu International Investment (Nig) FZE* (2017) All FWLR 1837 at 1924 (Akinyemi J) have also referred to English principles in a similar context.

[212] The substantive law and procedure for which in Uganda has been set out above.

the courts of Uganda. An equitable right may be the right not to be sued in a foreign jurisdiction and may be the corollary of an equitable wrong, which is that it is oppressive and vexatious and therefore unconscionable for the injunction defendant to commence or continue proceedings against the injunction plaintiff in a foreign jurisdiction.

The prime example of a cause of action based on a legal right not to be sued in a foreign jurisdiction is where the parties have agreed expressly that the courts of Uganda should have exclusive jurisdiction over disputes arising out of the contract (which can be a substantive contract or a settlement agreement) between them.[213] In such a case proof of the underlying cause of action is likely to be a sufficient condition for the grant of the relief and that good reason would need to be shown why the discretion to order an injunction should not be exercised.[214]

The principal example of a cause of action based on an equitable wrong is where proceedings brought abroad by the defendant are oppressive and vexatious. An example of such conduct is illustrated by the decision of the Privy Council in *SNI Aerospatiale v Lee Kui Jak*,[215] where a resident of Brunei had been killed in a helicopter crash and his widow (and her brother-in-law, as co-administrator of his estate), the respondent plaintiffs in the appeal to the Privy Council, had commenced proceedings in Brunei and had subsequently been persuaded to sue in Texas instead. The appellant defendant applied for an anti-suit injunction restraining the plaintiffs from proceeding against it in Texas. The Privy Council allowed the defendant's appeal, held that an injunction ought to be granted restraining the respondents from proceeding in Texas and remitted the matter to the Brunei courts.

Transposing the findings of the Privy Council to Uganda, it was held that an anti-suit injunction would be granted if: (1) pursuit of the foreign proceedings is vexatious or oppressive; (2) Uganda is the natural forum for the resolution of the dispute; and (3) the injunction does not deprive the defendant of advantages in the foreign jurisdiction of which it would be unjust to deprive him.[216]

---

[213] The contract may be a substantive contract or a settlement agreement and the dispute resolution provisions may be exclusively in favour of the courts of Zambia or may be in favour of arbitration: *British Airways Board v Laker Airways Ltd* [1985] AC 58 (HL (E)) (Lords Diplock, Fraser, Scarman, Roskill and Brightman), *per* Lord Diplock at p 81C–E.

[214] *The Angelic Grace* [1995] 1 Lloyd's Rep 87 (CA) (Neill, Leggatt and Millett LJJ), *per* Millett LJ at p 96, col 2, and Neill LJ at p 97, col 1; *Donohue v Armco Inc* [2000] 1 Lloyd's Rep 579 (CA) (Stuart-Smith, Brooke and Sedley LJJ), where it was stated that 'strong reasons' (*per* Stuart-Smith LJ at para 35) or 'strong cause' (*per* Brooke LJ at paras 59 and 60) would be required to deny an injunction.

[215] [1987] AC 871 (PC (Brunei)) (Lords Keith, Griffiths, MacKay and Goff and Sir John Megaw).

[216] Lord Goff (giving the opinion of the Privy Council) p 896F–H. That the court to which the application is made should be the natural forum for the resolution of the dispute was repeated by the House of Lords in *Airbus Industrie GIE v Patel* [1999] 1 AC 119 (HL (E)) (Lords Goff, Slynn, Steyn, Clyde and Hutton), *per* Lord Goff (with whom the other Lords agreed) pp 138G-H and 140H-141B.

Other examples of equitable wrongs which may attract an anti-suit injunction are: undermining the jurisdiction of the Ugandan court;[217] vexatious conduct by relying on foreign procedural laws;[218] wrongfully undermining a Uganda judgment;[219] or enforcement of a foreign judgment wrongfully obtained.[220]

14.3.8 Other interlocutory relief

14.3.8.1 *Arrest and attachment before judgment*

As noted above, section 64 of the Civil Procedure Act 1929 makes provision for the pre-judgment arrest of a defendant and the attachment of a defendant's property. Order XL of the CPR, which supplements section 64, is entitled 'Arrest and Attachment Before Judgment', and provides that a plaintiff may apply by summons in chambers,[221] usually supported by affidavit evidence, for an order that the defendant be arrested. The court may issue a warrant for the defendant's arrest if it is satisfied:[222]

> '*(a)* that the defendant with intent to delay the plaintiff, or to avoid any process of the court, or to obstruct or delay the execution of any decree that may be passed against him or her—
>
> > (i) has absconded or left the local limits of the jurisdiction of the court;
> >
> > (ii) is about to abscond or leave the local limits of the jurisdiction of the court; or
> >
> > (iii) has disposed of or removed from the local limits of the jurisdiction of the court his or her property or any part of it; or
>
> *(b)* that the defendant is about to leave Uganda in circumstances affording a reasonable probability that the plaintiff will or may thereby be obstructed or delayed in the execution of any decree that may be passed against the defendant in the suit.'

If the court issues a warrant it will be in terms that the defendant is brought before the court to show cause why he should not be ordered to provide security.

---

[217] For example, by commencing bankruptcy proceedings outside the jurisdiction when such proceedings are in progress in Uganda: *SNI Aerospatiale v Lee Kui Jak* [1987] AC 871, *per* Lord Goff at pp 892G–893B.

[218] By seeking to depose witnesses in the US where those witnesses would be subject to cross-examination in proceedings in Uganda, for example: *Omega Group Holdings Ltd v Kozeny* [2002] CLC 132.

[219] By commencing proceedings outside the jurisdiction for declaratory relief designed to frustrate the enforcement of a Ugandan judgment in that jurisdiction: *Masri v Consolidated Contractors International (UK) Ltd (No 3)* [2009] QB 503 (CA).

[220] Where the foreign judgment was obtained through fraud and perjury: *Ellerman Lines Ltd v Read* [1928] 2 KB 144 (CA), *per* Scrutton LJ at pp 152-153.

[221] Rule 12.

[222] Rule 1. An exception is made in r 1 for actions referred to in s 12(a)–(d) of the Civil Procedure Act 1929. Those sub-sections are concerned with actions relating to immovable property '(a) for the recovery of immovable property, with or without rent or profits; (b) for the partition of immovable property; (c) for the foreclosure, sale or redemption in the case of a mortgage of, or charge upon, immovable property; (d) for the determination of any other right to or interest in immovable property'.

The defendant can avoid arrest if he pays to the officer executing the arrest warrant the amount, if any, specified in the warrant as being sufficient to satisfy the plaintiff's claim.

If the defendant fails to show cause as to why he should not be ordered to provide security, the court may order that the defendant deposit in court cash or property in an amount sufficient to satisfy the plaintiff's claim.[223] If the defendant fails to provide security as ordered, the court may detain the defendant in prison until the conclusion of the proceedings or for six months, whichever is the shorter.[224]

The plaintiff may also apply by summons in chambers for an order that the defendant's property be attached.[225] The court may direct the defendant to provide security or property sufficient to satisfy the plaintiff's claim or appear and show cause why he should not be ordered to provide security, if the plaintiff establishes the conditions in rule 5:

> '(1) Where at any stage of a suit the court is satisfied, by affidavit or otherwise, that the defendant, with intent to obstruct or delay the execution of any decree that may be passed against him or her—
>
> *(a)* is about to dispose of the whole or any part of his or her property;
>
> *(b)* is about to remove the whole or any part of his or her property from the local limits of the jurisdiction of the court; or
>
> *(c)* has quitted the jurisdiction of the court leaving in that jurisdiction property belonging to him or her ....'

The plaintiff must specify the property to be attached by the court. In the event that the defendant does not show cause why he should not provide security, the court may order the property specified by the plaintiff to be attached so as to provide security for the plaintiff's claim.[226] The attachment does not operate to exclude the rights of third parties existing prior to the attachment or those claiming under a judgment against the defendant.[227]

---

[223] Rule 2.

[224] Rule 4.

[225] It is very important to understand that the court's power to direct that the defendant's property be attached is different to, and so distinct from, the granting of a *Mareva* order. A *Mareva* order is not an attachment of the defendant's assets. Accordingly, it is submitted that the High Court's judgment in *Coil Ltd v Transtrade Services Ltd* [2016] UGHCCD 93 (Mubiru J) ought to be treated with caution. There, the court was faced with an application that the respondent defendant's vehicles be attached. Perhaps oddly, the application was brought pursuant to s 98 of the Civil Procedure Act and O XL. It may be that this misled the judge, who, despite the application being one for attachment, applied the principles governing a *Mareva* injunction. While the court reached the right result in the application, it is submitted that it is a mistake to refer to the principles governing the grant of a *Mareva* injunction in the context of applications made pursuant to O XL.

[226] Rule 6.

[227] Rule 10.

The plaintiff must show that the defendant has the relevant intention before an arrest warrant or attachment may be made. The intention is to obstruct or delay the execution of any decree obtained by the plaintiff in the ways specified in those rules. It follows that a disposal of property by the defendant where it occurs in the normal course of the defendant's business or personal life ought not to be sufficient to establish the necessary intention.

In summarising the above, it is worth heeding the guidance given by the High Court in *Makubuya Willy T/A Pollaplast v Songdoh Firms*:[228]

> 'The power to arrest the defendant before judgment in favour of the plaintiff is a drastic action and must be taken after due care, caution and circumspection. Before a court exercises such discretion, it must have reason to believe on adequate material that unless the power is exercised, there is real danger that the defendant will remove himself/herself or his/her property from the jurisdiction of the court.
>
> Similarly, an attachment before judgment practically takes away the power of alienation and such a restriction on the exercise of the undoubted rights of ownership ought not be imposed upon an individual except upon clear and convincing proof that the order is needed for the protection of the plaintiff.
>
> A man is not debarred from dealing with his property just because a suit has been filed against him. Otherwise in every case in which a suit is brought against a man if during the pendency of the proceedings he sells some of his properties that would at once be a ground to satisfy the court that he is disposing his property with intent to defraud the plaintiff.'

It may, of course, be the case that a defendant who has been arrested or whose property has been attached feels aggrieved. Such a defendant may look to section 65 of the Civil Procedure Act 1929, which, in full, provides:

> **'65. Compensation for arrest, attachment or injunction on insufficient grounds.**
>
> (1) Where, in any suit in which an arrest or attachment has been effected or a temporary injunction granted under section 64—
>
> *(a)* it appears to the court that the arrest, attachment or injunction was applied for on insufficient grounds; or
>
> *(b)* the suit of the plaintiff fails and it appears to the court that there was no reasonable or probable ground for instituting the suit,
>
> the defendant may apply to the court, and the court may, upon that application, award against the plaintiff by its order such amount, not exceeding two thousand shillings, as it deems a reasonable compensation to the defendant for the expense or injury caused to him or her; except that a court shall not award under this section an amount exceeding the limits of its pecuniary jurisdiction.
>
> (2) An order determining any such application shall bar any suit for compensation in respect of such arrest, attachment or injunction.'

---

[228] [2018] UGHCCD 93 (Ssekaana J), which has been cited with approval subsequently by the High Court in *Nobert v Monaban Co Ltd* [2021] UGHC 28 (Ojok J).

It can be seen, therefore, that section 65 provides a mechanism for compensation in two situations: (1) where the arrest or attachment was made on insufficient grounds; and/or (2) where the plaintiff's claim fails and it appears to the court that there was no reasonable or probable ground for bringing proceedings. The first situation is likely to arise either at the stage where the defendant appears to show cause why he should not be required to give security or (probably less commonly) at the conclusion of the case. The second situation will arise at the conclusion of proceedings and will involve the court assessing the grounds for the plaintiff instituting proceedings at the time the proceedings were commenced – it does not appear that the assessment is to be made with the benefit of hindsight.

Chapter 15

ZAMBIA

15.1 Jurisdiction

The bases on which the Zambian courts may assume jurisdiction over a cause or matter are statutory in origin.[1] For present purposes the relevant court is the High Court, being the sole superior court with unlimited original jurisdiction over, inter alia, civil matters.

The High Court Act 1960,[2] section 9(1) provides:

> 'The Court shall be a Superior Court of Record, and, in addition to any other jurisdiction conferred by the Constitution and by this or any other written law, shall, within the limits and subject as in this Act mentioned, possess all the jurisdiction, powers and authorities vested in the High Court of Justice in England.'

The Constitution of Zambia 1996[3] and the Constitution of Zambia (Amendment) Act 2016,[4] make provision[5] for the establishment of a High Court having unlimited original jurisdiction to hear and determine, inter alia, civil proceedings. Neither of these enactments repealed the High Court Act 1960 and the provisions of the 1960 Act, in so far as they are not inconsistent with the terms of the Constitution of Zambia (Amendment) Act 2016, continue to govern the operation and functioning of the High Court.

The substantive law administered by the High Court is contained in the statutes and subordinate legislation passed by the Zambian Parliament. In addition, substantial tracts of English law have, by statute, been imported into Zambian law. The English Law (Extent of Application) Act 1963,[6] section 2, provides:

> 'Subject to the provisions of the Constitution of Zambia and to any other written law—
>
> *(a)* the common law; and
>
> *(b)* the doctrines of equity; and

[1] The Constitution of Zambia (Amendment) Act 2016 (Act 2 of 2016) substantially reformed the structure of the Zambian Superior Courts. Part VIII of the Act makes provision for superior courts structured as follows: a Supreme Court having appellate jurisdiction over appeals from the Court of Appeal (arts 124–6); a Constitutional Court having original and final jurisdiction over questions relating, inter alia, to the interpretation and violation of the Constitution (arts 127–9); the Supreme Court and the Constitutional Court rank 'equivalently' (art 121); a Court of Appeal having appellate jurisdiction to hear appeals from, inter alia, the High Court (arts 130–2); and the High Court having unlimited original jurisdiction in, inter alia, civil matters (arts 133–5). Under the previous Constitution of 1996, the superior court structure comprised the Supreme Court and High Court.

[2] Act 41 of 1960 and Act 43 of 1961. This may now be cited as Chapter 27 of the Laws of the Republic of Zambia 1995. In this regard, the reader is referred to the 'Note on the citation of statutory material in this work', which appears at the end of the 'List of Statutory Material Cited' at the beginning of this work.

[3] Act 18 of 1996. This repealed and replaced Act 1 of 1991.

[4] Act 2 of 2016.

[5] At art 94 of the Constitution of Zambia 1996 and art 134 of the Constitution of Zambia (Amendment) Act 2016.

[6] Act 4 of 1963 (now Cap 11 of the Laws of the Republic of Zambia 1995).

> *(c)* the statutes which were in force in England on the 17th August, 1911 (being the commencement of the Northern Rhodesia Order in Council 1911); and
>
> *(d)* any statutes of later date than that mentioned in paragraph *(c)* in force in England, now applied to the Republic, or which hereafter shall be applied thereto by any Act or otherwise;
>
> shall be in force in the Republic.'

Thus, in considering whether, for example, the High Court has power to make a third-party disclosure order, the High Court not merely *may*, but is *bound* to apply English common law or equitable principles.

That this is the case was confirmed by the Supreme Court in *Mileta Pakou v Rudnap Zambia Ltd*,[7] where, in a case concerned with the enforcement of a foreign judgment not registrable under the relevant legislation, the Chief Justice (giving the judgment of the court) stated:[8]

> 'We see little point in discussing Section 10 of the High Court Act. The law which applies in this country in default of any statute is the Common Law of England and the position at Common Law can readily be ascertained by reference to any of the many reference books that are available.'[9]

Rules governing the practice and procedure of civil litigation in the High Court in Zambia have been made pursuant to the High Court Act. These are contained within the Rules Made Under the High Court Act – Chapter 3 of the 1960 Edition of the Laws ('Rules of the High Court').[10]

Despite the existence of the Rules of the High Court, Zambian courts in certain circumstances still can, and still do, have resort to rules set out in the 1999 edition of the English Supreme Court Practice 1965 ('English Rules of the Supreme Court').[11] This is authorised by what might be termed the 'lacuna principle',[12] which principle is contained within section 10 of the High Court Act 1960.[13]

---

7 [1998] ZR 233 (Sup Ct) (Ngulube CJ and Sakala and Chaila JJSC).

8 Ibid 234:21–4.

9 The reference to s 10 of the High Court Act 1960 was in order to address a submission of the plaintiff in the case. The plaintiff's counsel ought to have referred the court to s 2 of the 1963 Act and not to s 10 of the 1960 Act, which concerns practice and procedure; see further below.

10 As subsequently amended.

11 See: *In The Matter of Charles Matakala Sikuka* (1978) ZR 138 (HC) (Hadden J), 139; *Mung'omba v Machungwa* [2003] ZMSC 10 (SC) (Chirwa, Chibesakunda and Mambilima, JJSC); *The People v The Patents and Companies Registration Agency* [2018] ZMCC 250 (SC) (Chibomba, PC, Sitali, Mulembe, Mulonda and Munalula, JJSC); and *Chanda v Kaira* [2020] ZMCA 3 (CA) (Kondolo SC, Makungu and Siavwapa JJA).

12 *Indeni Petroleum Refinery Co Ltd v Kafco Oil Ltd* [2017] ZMSC 60 (Hamaundu, Malila and Mutuna JJS). Here, the Supreme Court referred to the 'lacuna acknowledged to exist in our law by … [the decision of Hadden J in] *Sikuka*'.

13 As amended by s 2 of the High Court Amendment Act 2011 (Act 7 of 2011).

Section 10 of the High Court Act, which is entitled 'Practice and procedure', provides:

> '(1) The jurisdiction vested in the Court shall, as regards practice and procedure, be exercised in the manner provided by this Act ... or such written law or by such rules, order or directions of the Court as may be made under this Act ... or such written law and in default thereof in substantial conformity with the Supreme Court Practice, 1999 (White Book) of England and, subject to subsection (2), the law and practice applicable in England in the High Court of Justice up to 31st December, 1999.
>
> (2) The Civil Court Practice, 1999 (Green Book) of England and any civil court practice rules issued in England after 31st December, 1999, shall not apply to Zambia.'

As interpreted by the courts in Zambia, where the Rules of the High Court etc do not govern the particular circumstances with which the court is confronted (in other words, where there is a 'lacuna' in, say, the Rules of the High Court), this section authorises the Zambian court to act 'in substantial conformity' with the English Rules of the Supreme Court.[14]

It is submitted that the wording of section 10 and the construction of those words by the Zambian courts are matters which are not entirely free from difficulty. After all, it is clear that the operation of the aforementioned 'lacuna principle' hinges on the existence of a lacuna. Whether Zambian courts are willing to find a lacuna depends on how widely or narrowly those courts are willing to construe, inter alia, the wording of the Rules of the High Court. To put the point another way, a Zambian judge may be faced with a choice between two opposing approaches and so may be forced to ask: is there a lacuna where the words of the Rules of the High Court do not explicitly govern the situation before the court or is there a lacuna only where the words of the Rules of the High Court, placing the widest construction on them, make no provision at all for the situation before the court.

Of course, a Zambian judge will not be required to choose which approach to adopt in all cases: in certain instances, the existence of a lacuna is clear. By way of example, the Rules of the High Court make no provision for judicial review, such that Zambian courts have regard to the English Rules of the Supreme Court to determine the procedure which ought to apply.[15] Other cases, of course, are not

---

[14] As pointed out by Ordor in her review of the first edition of this work (136(3) *SALJ* 2019 587, at 592), 'it is important that contracting and litigating parties as well as foreign counsel understand that in legal practice in Zambia, lawyers generally rely on the High Court Rules of Zambia and the White Book of England concurrently'. The authors agree that, traditionally, this has been the position, irrespective of whether, as a matter of strict law, it is correct. The authors submit, however, that the most recent jurisprudence explored in the main text below with respect to the existence of a 'lacuna' may alter the position which has traditionally been taken.

[15] *The People v The Patents and Companies Registration Agency* [2018] ZMCC 250.

so easy to determine and, in such cases, courts have not always been consistent in deciding which approach towards the task of construction to adopt.

In *Chanda v Kaira*,[16] for instance, the Court of Appeal's approach led to the conclusion that there was no lacuna in the Rules of the High Court. The plaintiff appellant had applied for leave to discontinue the action brought against the defendants. The appellant made that application pursuant to Order XXI of the English Rules of the Supreme Court; the judge at first instance granted the application to discontinue but did so on the basis of the provisions of Order XVII of the Rules of the High Court.[17] Before the Court of Appeal, the appellant argued that it was appropriate to rely on the English Rules of the Supreme Court because these were 'more elaborate than Order [XVII of the Zambian Rules of the High Court], which did not provide for parties to apply for leave to withdraw a matter without paying costs [such that Order XXI of the English Rules of the Supreme Court] filled a lacuna in that respect'. The Court of Appeal rejected this argument and found that there was no lacuna in the Rules of the High Court: while the Rules of the High Court did not 'specifically provide for leave to apply to withdraw a matter for the purposes of avoiding costs', Order XVII was sufficiently wide in its scope to ensure that a party was at liberty to provide the court with reasons as to why it should not be condemned in costs.

However, dicta and decisions in other cases, and particularly in cases before the Supreme Court, demonstrate much less reluctance on the part of Zambian judges to find the existence of a lacuna. In *New Plast Industries Ltd v Commissioner of Lands & Attorney General*,[18] the Supreme Court held that the English Rules of the Supreme Court could be resorted to if the provisions in force in Zambia were 'silent or not fully comprehensive'.[19] Similarly, in *Ticklay v Road Transport & Safety Agency & Intercape Mainliner (Zambia) Ltd*,[20] the Supreme Court pointed out that the Zambian rule on the point gave the court discretion to make an order as to costs but 'did not specifically address the issue before [the court]'; it was permissible, therefore, to resort to the English Rules of the Supreme Court.

---

[16] *Chanda v Kaira* [2020] ZMCA 3 (CA) (Kondolo SC, Makungu and Siavwapa JJA).

[17] In essence, counsel for the appellant argued that it was proper to resort to O 21 of the English Rules of the Supreme Court because the 'circumstances of [the] case required that the Appellant should not be condemned in costs, a situation which was provided for by O 21 [of the RSC] but not by O 17 [of the Zambian High Court Rules], meaning that there was a lacuna'.

[18] (2001) ZR 51 (SC) (Sakala Ag DCJ; Chirwa and Lewanika JJSC), a case concerned with the correct interpretation of ss 87 and 89 of the Lands and Deeds Registry Act 1994 (Act 13 of 1994, Cap 185 of the Laws of Zambia 1995).

[19] The respondent in *Chanda* relied on the decision in *New Plast*. With respect, the conclusion reached in *New Plast* rather supported the argument made by the appellant in *Chanda*, viz: O XVII of the Rules of the High Court was not as 'elaborate', and so not as 'comprehensive', as O XXI of the English Rules of the Supreme Court.

[20] [2016] ZMSC 16 (SC) (Hamaundu, Mutuna and Chinyama JJSC), a case concerned with the correct construction of the Zambian Supreme Court Rules (made pursuant to Cap 25 of the Laws of Zambia 1995).

It might, of course, be fairly said that neither of the cases cited in the previous paragraph were concerned with the correct construction to be placed on the Rules of the High Court and so are of limited relevance to the present discussion.[21] Even so, it is submitted that those cases do exhibit a particular judicial attitude, which judicial attitude may translate into cases which require courts to decide whether a lacuna exists in the Rules of the High Court.

That the Court of Appeal and the Supreme Court have not displayed entirely the same attitude when considering the existence of a lacuna (albeit, as mentioned above, that the Supreme Court cases have not been directly concerned with the wording of the Rules of the High Court of Zambia) is, with respect, potentially a cause of some difficulty for parties who wish to sue, and who might be sued, in Zambia. To take an example: Order X of the Rules of the High Court[22] makes no provision for service out of the jurisdiction on a constructive trustee. By contrast, Order XI[23] of the English Rules of the Supreme Court permits service out of the jurisdiction where: 'the claim is brought ... for an account or other relief against the defendant as constructive trustee, and the defendant's alleged liability arises out of acts committed, whether by him or otherwise, within the jurisdiction'. In the light of the foregoing discussion, a question – which currently cannot be answered - arises as to whether a party wishing to obtain permission to serve out of the jurisdiction in Zambia in a claim for an account against a constructive trustee[24] could argue that there was a lacuna in the Rules of the High Court and so rely, instead, on the English Rules of the Supreme Court so as to obtain that permission.

In the light of the above discussion, it may well be that section 10 ought to be repealed after entirely comprehensive domestic rules have been enacted and promulgated. That said, for as long as section 10 of the High Court Act is drafted in its present terms, the courts will have to confront the difficult question of when, exactly, the Rules of the High Court of Zambia contain a lacuna, such that the courts may apply the 'lacuna principle'.

15.1.1 Service where the defendant is within the jurisdiction

The issuing and service of proceedings within Zambia is regulated by Orders VI[25] and X of the Rules of the High Court.

---

[21] Indeed, this was the basis on which the Court of Appeal in *Chanda* distinguished the decision of the Supreme Court in *Ticklay*, despite the similarity of the rules in issue in those cases.

[22] Which is dealt with in greater depth below.

[23] At para 1(t).

[24] A claim known to the law of Zambia, it is submitted, by virtue of the English Law (Extent of Application) Act 1963 (Act 4 of 1963, now Cap 11 of the Laws of the Republic of Zambia 1995).

[25] As amended by the High Court (Amendment) Rules 2020 (SI 58 of 2020).

Proceedings in the High Court are, save as otherwise provided in the Rules of the High Court or any other written law, commenced, in writing or electronically, by writ of summons endorsed and accompanied by: a statement of claim; a list and description of documents to be relied on at trial; a list of witnesses to be called by the plaintiff at trial; and a letter of demand whose receipt shall be acknowledged by the defendant or an affidavit of service attesting to the service of the letter of demand, which shall set out the claim and the circumstances surrounding the claim in detail.[26] Where a writ of summons is not accompanied by the aforementioned document, it shall not be accepted.[27]

It is convenient to note at this stage that the Constitution of Zambia (Amendment) Act 2016 substantially reformed the structure of the High Court. Part VIII, article 133(2) of the Act established four divisions of the High Court, being the Industrial Relations Court, the Commercial Court, the Family Court and the Children's Court. The High Court Rules Committee had previously established[28] a Commercial List having its own Registrar, Registry, Presiding Judge and Rules.[29] The filing of a commercial action, as defined in the Rules, in the Commercial List Registry is mandatory.[30] Practitioners should be alert to these Rules as they represent a departure from previous practice.[31]

Once issued, the writ may be served personally by any person.[32] Provision is also made for substituted service in circumstances where it is made to appear to the court that prompt personal service cannot be effected.[33] Order X contains further provisions addressing particular instances of service such as service on

[26] O VI, r 1, as amended by the High Court (Amendment) Rules 2020.

[27] O VI, r 2, as amended by the High Court (Amendment) Rules 2020.

[28] Pursuant to ss 44 and 45 of the High Court Act 1960.

[29] The High Court (Amendment) Rules 2012 (SI 27 of 2012), r 8. These Rules introduced, inter alia, a new O LIII dealing with commercial actions as defined in O LIII, r 1. These Rules also contain important new provisions regarding electronic filing of documents.

[30] Order LIII, r 5, 'A commercial action shall be commenced and filed in the Registry' (emphasis provided).

[31] For example, the judge may order that the parties refer the dispute to mediation and, if the mediation fails because of the non-attendance of a party, the judge may order the defaulting party to be liable for all the costs of the litigation, regardless of the outcome (O LIII, r 8).

[32] Order X, r 1(1). The drafting of O X as regards the mode of service required being personal service of process is a little ambiguous. The Order refers only to personal service where such service 'is required' or non-personal service where personal service is 'not requisite', but without defining the circumstances where personal service is or is not required (see, for example, rr 1(1), 2(1), 3 and 6; only r 5 appears to define a circumstance where the defendant's advocate undertakes in writing to accept service). However, whilst O X does not make it explicit that personal service is the primary means of service and, therefore, of establishing jurisdiction over the defendant as of right, it seems reasonable to proceed on the basis that this is what O X as a whole envisages. (In this connection it is noteworthy that personal service is expressly required by the civil procedure codes of, inter alia, Kenya (O 5, r 8), Sierra Leone (O 10, r 2) and the Republic of South Africa (r 4(1)(a)).)

[33] Order X, r 3.

partnerships,[34] service on a body corporate other than a company[35] and service on the local agent of a principal who is resident outside the jurisdiction in circumstances where the principal carries on business in the jurisdiction through that agent and the suit is limited to a cause of action which arose within the jurisdiction.[36]

It should be noted the Companies Act 2017[37] broadens the circumstances in which the Zambian High Court may take jurisdiction over a claim brought against what Part XIV refers to as a 'foreign company'. A foreign company is defined[38] as: (1) a body corporate formed outside Zambia that has been registered under the Companies Act 2017; or (2) an existing[39] foreign company, subject to section 297 of the Companies Act 2017.[40]

A body corporate formed outside Zambia may register as a foreign company by lodging with the Registrar an application, which application must be accompanied by the requisite documentation.[41] If a foreign company has not set up or acquired an established place of business[42] at the time it lodges an application for registration as a foreign company, it shall do so within 28 days after the lodgement.[43] A foreign company must also appoint at least one local director.[44]

Section 305(1) sets out the methods by which a document may be served on a foreign company. A document may be so served by: leaving it at an address

---

[34] Order X, r 11(1) and (2).

[35] Order X, r 11(3).

[36] Order X, r 14. This provision was considered briefly by the High Court in *J & M Advocates v Glencore International AG* [2020] ZMHC 292 (Yangailo LJ), where the question was whether sufficient instructions had been given to an entity by the defendant to make that entity the defendant's local agent in the relevant matter. The court determined that such instructions had not been given, such that the plaintiff was required, but had failed, to serve process directly on the defendant. A Zambian court wanting to find more detailed treatment of this provision may be assisted by considering the decision of the English High Court in *The Lalandia* [1933] P 56 (HC) (Langton J) 66–7.

[37] Act 10 of 2017, Cap 388 of the Laws of the Republic of Zambia 1995.

[38] Section 3 of the Companies Act 2017.

[39] An 'existing foreign company' is defined by s 3 of the Companies Act 2017 as a 'body corporate incorporated outside Zambia which immediately before the commencement of this Act was registered as a foreign company in accordance with the repealed [Companies Act 1994]'.

[40] Section 297 simply provides that, subject to the provisions of Part XIV of the Companies Act 2017, Part XIV applies to an existing foreign company as if: 'a) it had been duly registered in accordance with this Act as a foreign company; and b) any document that, in accordance with the repealed [Companies Act 1994], was duly lodged by it with the Registrar, or duly registered by the Registrar, had been duly lodged or registered in accordance with this Act'.

[41] Section 209(1).

[42] By s 300(1), a foreign company has an 'established place of business' if it has any of the following in Zambia: (1) a branch or management office; (2) an office for the registration of transfer of shares; (3) a factory or mine; or any other fixed place of business.

[43] Section 299(5).

[44] Section 303(1). A local director is defined by s 3 as: 'a director of a foreign company who is resident in Zambia and empowered and authorised to conduct and manage the affairs, property, business and other operations of the company in Zambia'.

registered as the address of a documentary agent of the foreign company; personal service on a documentary agent of the company if the agent is an individual; leaving it at the registered office of the foreign company, if the company has no registered documentary agent or at the registered address of such an agent; personal service on a local director; leaving it at the registered office or principal place of business of the foreign company in the country of its incorporation; or by personal service on a director or secretary of the foreign company in the country of its incorporation.[45]

The Companies Act 2017 has therefore extended the circumstances in which a company may be served beyond those provided for by the Rules of the High Court. More than that, however, it would appear, by virtue of the last two mentioned situations in the previous paragraph, section 305(1)(e) and (f) provide a way around the provisions requiring leave for service of process outside the jurisdiction, which are contained in Order X, rule 15 of the Rules of the High Court.

15.1.2 Service where the defendant is outside the jurisdiction

Order X, rule 15, makes provision for service outside the territorial jurisdiction of Zambia. It provides:

> 'Service out of jurisdiction of a writ of summons, originating summons or originating notice of motion, or notice of such writ of summons, originating summons or notice of motion may be allowed by the Court or a Judge whenever—
>
> *(a)* The whole subject matter of the action is land situate within the jurisdiction (with or without rents or profits), or the perpetuation of testimony relating to land within the jurisdiction; or
>
> *(b)* Any act, deed, will, contract, obligation, or liability affecting land or hereditaments situate within the jurisdiction, is sought to be construed, rectified, set aside, or enforced in the action or matter; or
>
> *(c)* Any relief is sought against any person domiciled or ordinarily resident, within the jurisdiction; or
>
> *(d)* The action is for the administration of the personal estate of any deceased person who, at the time of his death was domiciled within the jurisdiction, or for the execution (as to property situate within the jurisdiction) of the trusts of any written instrument, or which the person to be served is a trustee, which ought to be executed according to the law of Zambia; or

[45] It is worth pointing out that nothing in s 305 derogates from the power of the court to direct how service of a document relating to legal proceedings before the court shall be effected: s 305(4).

(e) The action is one brought to enforce, rescind, dissolve, annul or otherwise affect a contract or to recover damages or other relief for or in respect of the breach of a contract—

(i) made within the jurisdiction; or

(ii) made by or through an agent trading or residing within the jurisdiction on behalf of a principal trading or residing out of the jurisdiction; or

(iii) by its terms or by implication to be governed by Zambian law;

or it is one brought in respect of a breach committed within the jurisdiction of a contract wherever made, even though such breach was preceded or accompanied by a breach out of the jurisdiction which rendered impossible the performance of the part of the contract which ought to have been performed within the jurisdiction;

(f) The action is founded on a tort committed within the jurisdiction; or

(g) Any injunction is sought as to anything to be done within the jurisdiction, or any nuisance within the jurisdiction is sought to be prevented or removed, whether damages are or are not also sought in respect thereof; or

(h) Any person out of jurisdiction is a necessary or proper party to an action properly brought against some other person duly served within the jurisdiction; or

(i) The action is by a mortgagee or mortgagor in relation to a mortgage of personal property situate within the jurisdiction and seeks relief of the nature or kind following that is to say, sale, foreclosure, delivery of possession by the mortgagor, redemption, re-conveyance, delivery of possession by the mortgagee; but does not seek (unless and except so far as permissible under paragraph *(e)*) any personal judgment or order for payment of any money due under the mortgage.'[46]

Order X, rule 15 is, in all material respects, a verbatim transposition of Order XI, rule 1 of the Rules of the Supreme Court 1883 (1960 edition), the English High Court rule regulating service out of the jurisdiction. It is to be expected that, in construing the terms of Order X, rule 15, the Zambian courts will be mindful of and have regard to the judicial and academic authorities on the construction and meaning of the equivalent English rule.

[46] It is to be noted that O X, r 15 does not provide for service out of the jurisdiction in order to enforce a foreign judgment against a person not domiciled or resident within the jurisdiction, where a judgment creditor might wish to enforce the judgment because of the presence within the jurisdiction of assets belonging to the judgment debtor (a similar omission was remedied in the English Civil Procedure Rules by the introduction of such a basis for service out by SI 1983/1181 and, for the purposes of comparison, reference may now be made to the English CPR, PD 6B, para 3.1(10)); Frimpong Oppong 'Recognition and enforcement of foreign judgments in Commonwealth African countries' (2014) XV *Yearbook of Private International Law* 365 at 371–2.

15.1.2.1 *Procedure*

Order X, rule 16 sets out the procedure for applying for leave to serve a writ (or other process) outside the jurisdiction. It provides:

> 'An application for leave to issue for service out of the jurisdiction a writ of summons, originating summons, or originating notice of motion or a concurrent writ of summons, originating summons or originating notice of motion may be made *ex parte* to the Court or a Judge on deposit of the writ, summons or notice with the Registrar together with an affidavit in support of such application. The affidavit shall state—
>
> *(a)* the grounds upon which the application is made and the facts which bring the plaintiff's case within the class in respect of which service out of the jurisdiction may be allowed;
>
> *(b)* that the deponent is advised and believes that the plaintiff has a good cause of action or right to relief;
>
> *(c)* in what place or country the defendant resides or probably may be found;
>
> *(d)* whether the defendant is a citizen of Zambia or not.'[47]

The Court of Appeal in *Pascall v ZCCM Investments Holdings plc*[48] explained that the process for which Order X, rule 16 provides has two stages: '[f]irstly, one has to issue the writ of summons out of jurisdiction (exhibiting a copy of the writ) and once leave is granted, the writ is then filed and then the plaintiff can apply to serve process out of jurisdiction'.[49]

Where a plaintiff, in breach of Order X, rule 16, fails to obtain leave at the relevant time, it may be the case that the court considers this default to be curable and not fatal. In *Leopold Walford (Zambia) Ltd v Unifreight*,[50] the Supreme Court considered an appeal from the decision of the District Registrar striking out a

[47] The significance of the distinction between a citizen of Zambia and all other persons is that in the former case, a defendant will be served with the writ of summons itself (O X, r 18), whereas all other defendants are served with notice of the summons and not the summons itself (O X, r 18 and O VII, r 4). The reasons for this are rooted in English legal history: a summons is a command from the sovereign and it was thought discourteous to serve such a command on a person not resident in the United Kingdom and not a British subject. Thus a notice of the summons was served instead (see *Nanjibhai Prabhudas & Co Ltd v Standard Bank Ltd* [1968] EA 670 (CA) (Sir Charles Newbold P, Sir Clement de Lestang V-P and Law JA), *per* Sir Charles Newbold P at 683C–E; the origin of the rule is s 19 of the English Common Law Procedure Act 1852. After the repeal of the 1852 Act, the rule was incorporated into the Rules of the Supreme Court: *Westman v Aktiebolaget Ekmans Mekaniska Snickarefabrick* (1876) 1 Ex D 237).

[48] [2019] ZMCA 1 (CA) (Chashi, Lengalenga and Siavwapa JJA).

[49] This approach has been followed by the High Court in *J & M Advocates v Glencore International AG* [2020] ZMHC 292 (Yangailo LJ). Even so, and with respect, it is not immediately apparent that O X, r 16 ought to be construed in this manner. On the face of it, O X, r 16 makes clear that what is required is an application for leave 'to issue' for service outside the jurisdiction, such that a plaintiff intending to serve outside the jurisdiction ought to be required to apply to the court for permission to issue process before doing so under the provisions of O VI.

[50] [1985] ZR 203 (SC) (Silungwe CJ, Ngulube DCJ and Muwo JSC).

writ for service outside the jurisdiction where, inter alia, leave to issue had not been sought in breach of Order X, rule 16.

Silungwe CJ (giving the judgment of the court), allowing the appeal, held[51] that this breach of a regulatory rule was not fatal but curable: the plaintiff could amend the writ and then seek the court's leave in order to serve the writ outside of the jurisdiction. In the light of the cases which have interpreted *Leopold*, it would appear to be the case that whether the default can be cured depends on the stage which the proceedings have reached and the prejudice which the default causes to the defendant.[52]

While the provisions of Order X, rule 16 are not a *verbatim* transposition of Order XI, rule 4 of the Rules of the Supreme Court 1883 (1960 edition) (the equivalent rule to rule 16), the two rules are almost identical in content. There is, however, one material difference between the provisions of rule 16 of the Zambian Rules and those of rule 4 of the English Rules: the Zambian rule omits the wording at the end of the English rule 4, 'and no such leave shall be granted unless it shall be made sufficiently to appear to the Court or Judge that the case is a proper one for service out of the jurisdiction under this Order'.[53] Instead, the Zambian rule contains the additional wording under rule 16(a), 'the grounds upon which the application is made <u>and the facts which bring the plaintiff's case within the class in respect of which service out of the jurisdiction may be allowed</u>' (the underlined words are an addition to the wording of the English rule).

This difference in wording between the two rules is significant and one which, on the face of it, was intended by the body promulgating the High Court Rules for (what became) Zambia.[54] The effect of this apparently intentional departure from the English wording Order XI, rule 4, is addressed below.

The English equivalents of Zambian Order X, rules 15 and 16, have been the subject of judicial consideration at the highest level in England. In *Seaconsar Far East Ltd v Bank Markazi Jomhouri Islami Iran*,[55] the House of Lords considered the interaction of Order XI, rules 1(1) and 4, of the Rules of the Supreme Court (the

---

[51] Ibid 205: 5–11.

[52] See *Pascall v ZCCM Investments Holdings plc* [2019] ZMCA 1 and *J & M Advocates v Glencore International AG* [2020] ZMHC 292 for instances where the plaintiff was able to cure their default and *Cavmont Bank Ltd v Shikongo* [2015] ZMHC 100 (Chashi J), where they were not.

[53] Also, for the sake of completeness, O X, r 16, refers to an application for leave to issue a writ, whereas this requirement appears earlier in the English Rules of the Supreme Court.

[54] The High Court Rules were promulgated by GN 193 of 1933, as amended between 1933 and 1995, the enabling statute for which was the High Court Ordinance 18 of 1933. The English Rules of the Supreme Court containing the wording quoted in the main text were introduced in 1883. It would have been a straightforward matter to have incorporated the entirety of the English O XI, r 4, into the Zambian O X, r 16. It seems that a conscious decision was made to omit incorporation of the final lines of the English O XI, r 4, into the Zambian O X, r 16.

[55] [1994] 1 AC 438 (HL(E)) (Lords Templeman, Griffiths, Goff, Browne-Wilkinson and Mustill).

equivalent to Order X, rules 15 and 16). Lord Goff (with whom the other Lords agreed) reviewed the authorities on the question what a plaintiff under Order XI was required to show on an application for leave to serve a writ out of the jurisdiction and found that the plaintiff was required to show, first, that the cause of action deposed to in the evidence in support of the application fell within the provisions of rule 1(1) and, second, that on the merits of the case there was a serious question to be tried. On the question of the standard to which these issues were required to be shown, Lord Goff stated:[56]

> 'A judge faced with a question of leave to serve proceedings out of the jurisdiction under Order 11 will in practice have to consider both (1) whether jurisdiction has been sufficiently established, on the criterion of the good arguable case laid down in *Korner's* case, under one of the paragraphs of rule 1(1), and (2) whether there is a serious issue to be tried, so as to enable him to exercise his discretion to grant leave, before he goes on to consider the exercise of that discretion, with particular reference to the issue of forum conveniens.'

The first of these matters was held to correspond to the requirement in Order XI, rule 4, that 'no such leave shall be granted unless it shall be made sufficiently to appear to the Court or Judge that the case is a proper one for service out of the jurisdiction under this Order'[57] and the second was a threshold requirement for the merits of the plaintiff's claim.[58]

Thus, considering the English authorities, it is suggested that, analytically, it may be helpful to determine applications for leave to serve process out of the jurisdiction by applying the following four-component approach:[59]

(1) *The formal requirements.* Has the plaintiff produced evidence satisfying the formal requirements of Order X, rule 16 (or English Order XI, rule 4)? This requires the plaintiff in his affidavit in support of the application to set out: (a) the grounds on which the application is made and the facts

---

[56] Ibid 456H–457B. See also the decision of the Privy Council in *Altimo Holdings and Investment Ltd v Kyrgyz Mobil Tel Ltd* [2012] 1 WLR 1804 (Lord Phillips PSC and Lords Mance, Collins, Kerr, and Clarke JJSC), *per* Lord Collins at para [71], confirming this statement of principle.

[57] *Seaconsar* at 451A–B, 452A–B, 453D–G.

[58] Ibid 452D–E, 455A–C, 456G–H. Notwithstanding the separate treatment of the English O XI, r 4, in *Seaconsar* and the earlier authorities referred to therein, it is unclear whether the amendment in 1883 of O XI, r 3 (under the Rules of Court contained in Sch 1 to the Supreme Court of Judicature Act 1875) by the introduction of an expanded O XI, r 4, in the 1883 Rules of Court, was intended to produce this result. At the time, the leading textbook on the Rules took the view that the amendment to include the wording, 'No such leave shall be granted unless it shall be made sufficiently to appear to the Court or Judge that the case is a proper one for service out of the jurisdiction under this Order', was merely an amplification of the previous rule (see Wynne Baxter *Judicature Acts & Rules 1873–1883* 5 ed (1883) 176–7).

[59] As summarised in the English Supreme Court Practice 1965 (1999 ed) 93–4, paras 11/1/9–11/1/12. The commentary referred to in the Supreme Court Practice refers to three elements; in the text above the present authors include four elements, the additional element being the formal requirements of English r 4 and Zambian r 16.

which bring the plaintiff's case within one of the gateways under rule 15; (b) the deponent's belief that the plaintiff has a good cause of action; (c) the place where the defendant resides or may probably be found; and (d) whether the defendant is a citizen of Zambia or not.

(2) *The sufficiency requirement.* Under the English Order XI, rule 4, it was held in the *Seaconsar* case that the words 'and no such leave shall be granted unless it shall be made sufficiently to appear to the Court or Judge that the case is a proper one for service out of the jurisdiction under this Order' introduced a sufficiency requirement (or, in other words, a degree of proof requirement) such that the plaintiff must show that there is a good arguable case[60] that the case falls within one of the gateways under Order XI, rule 1(1).

It has been noted above that Order X, rule 16, is the Zambian equivalent of the English Order XI, rule 4, and that rule 16 omits the wording of Order XI, rule 4, set out in the preceding sub-paragraph that was held in the *Seaconsar* case to introduce a sufficiency requirement. The question arises, therefore, whether, by reason of the omission of this wording, Order X, rule 16, of the Zambian High Court Rules should be construed as not imposing a requirement that the plaintiff should show a good arguable case that the case falls within one of the gateways under Order X, rule 15.

---

[60] In *Canada Trust v Stolzenberg (No 2)* [2002] 1 AC 1 (HL(E)) (Lords Steyn, Hoffmann, Cooke, Hope and Hobhouse), *per* Lord Steyn (with whom the other Lords agreed) 13F, the House of Lords appeared to approve passages from the judgment of Waller LJ in the Court of Appeal in the same case ([1998] 1 WLR 547) including the following (at 555F–G): 'It is also right to remember that the "good arguable case" test, although obviously applicable to the ex parte stage, becomes of most significance at the inter partes stage where two arguments are being weighed in the interlocutory context which, as I have stressed, must not become a "trial". "Good arguable case" reflects in that context that one side has a much better argument on the material available. It is the concept which the phrase reflects on which it is important to concentrate, i.e. of the court being satisfied or as satisfied as it can be having regard to the limitations which an interlocutory process imposes that factors exist which allow the court to take jurisdiction.' In *Goldman Sachs International v Novo Banco SA* [2018] 1 WLR 3683 (Lords Mance, Sumption and Hodge, Lady Black and Lord Lloyd-Jones), the UK Supreme Court further clarified the correct understanding of the test in the *Canada Trust* case. Lord Sumption (with whom all the other members of the court agreed and in reliance on his own judgment in *Brownlie v Four Seasons Holdings Incorporated* [2018] 1 WLR 192) stated at para [9]: 'For the purpose of determining an issue about jurisdiction, the traditional test has been whether the claimant had "the better of the argument" on the facts going to jurisdiction. In *Brownlie v Four Seasons Holdings Inc* [2018] 1 WLR 192, para 7, this court reformulated the effect of that test as follows: "(i) that the claimant must supply a plausible evidential basis for the application of a relevant jurisdictional gateway; (ii) that if there is an issue of fact about it, or some other reason for doubting whether it applies, the court must take a view on the material available if it can reliably do so; but (iii) the nature of the issue and the limitations of the material available at the interlocutory stage may be such that no reliable assessment can be made, in which case there is a good arguable case for the application of the gateway if there is a plausible (albeit contested) evidential basis for it."'

As also noted above, rule 16 contains additional wording to the wording of the English rule 4 as follows, that the plaintiff should state 'the grounds upon which the application is made <u>and the facts which bring the plaintiff's case within the class in respect of which service out of the jurisdiction may be allowed</u>' (the underlined words are an addition to the wording of the English rule). This wording does not contain any reference to an evaluative criterion such as the requirement in rule 4 of the English rules that it should be made 'sufficiently to appear' that the case is a proper one for service out. It would seem to follow, therefore, that a plaintiff under Order X, rule 16, must simply depose to the facts which bring the case within rule 15 and that the court must assess whether those facts are established to a degree less than a good arguable case. It is likely that this standard will be held to be a *prima facie* case.[61]

(3) *The merits requirement.* The plaintiff must demonstrate that there is a serious issue to be tried on the merits of the claim upon which the claimant relies. Lord Goff in *Seaconsar* stated[62] as follows:

> 'The court cannot resolve disputed questions of fact on affidavit evidence; and it is consistent with the statement of the law by Lord Davey that if, at the end of the day, there remains a substantial question of fact or law or both, arising on the facts disclosed by the affidavits, which the plaintiff bona fide desires to try, the court should, as a rule, allow the service of the writ. If this approach is correct, the standard of proof in respect of the cause of action can broadly be stated to be whether, on the affidavit evidence before the court, there is a serious question to be tried.'

(4) *The court's discretion.* Once the above matters are established by the plaintiff, the court will proceed to consider the exercise of its discretion to allow service out of the jurisdiction. The court's discretion is exercised cautiously. As was stated by Pearson J in *Société Générale de Paris v Dreyfus Brothers*:[63]

> 'But of course it becomes a very serious question, and ought always to be considered a very serious question, whether or not, even in a case like that, it is necessary for the jurisdiction of the Court to be invoked, and whether this Court ought to put a foreigner, who owes no allegiance here, to the inconvenience and annoyance of being brought to contest his rights in this country, and I for one say, most distinctly, that I think this Court ought to be exceedingly careful before it allows a writ to be served out of the jurisdiction.'

---

[61] A view supported by the notes to O XI, r 4, in Lushington et al *The Yearly Supreme Court Practice 1900* (1900 ed), where the editors stated of the words in r 4, 'Made sufficiently to appear' that (at 172), 'The Court will not, on an application for leave, go into the merits of the case, but will grant leave if a sufficient *prima facie* case is made out' (citing *Badische Anilin und Soda Fabrik v Henry Johnson & Co* [1896] 1 Ch 25 (CA) (Lindley, AL Smith and Rigby LJJ), *per* Lindley LJ at 28). In rules lacking the evaluative wording, 'made sufficiently to appear', the standard of *prima facie* case appears *a fortiori* appropriate.

[62] *Seaconsar* at 452C–D.

[63] (1885) 29 Ch D 239 at 242–3; cited with approval by Lord Goff in *Seaconsar* at 455D.

The principal consideration in the exercise of the court's discretion will be the question whether Zambia is the *forum conveniens* for the determination of the dispute. This is dealt with under the sub-heading '*Forum non conveniens*' below.

The position with regard to commercial actions has recently been modified.[64] The new Order LIII[65] provides at rule 10(1) that an 'interlocutory application' in the Commercial List (now the Commercial Division)[66] shall be made to a judge in chambers. Although the term 'interlocutory application' is not defined in the rules, it is thought that, as a matter of ordinary English usage, it must cover applications by a defendant to set aside service on him of a writ and/or discharge of the order granted leave to serve out of the jurisdiction. Order LIII, rule 10(8), provides for the documents to be filed with an interlocutory application: a skeleton argument setting out the facts, law and authorities relied on, with copies of the authorities where possible. Although not specifically provided for, it will clearly be sensible for a plaintiff also to file any affidavit evidence of fact on which reliance is sought to be placed.

Finally, in all cases where an *ex parte* application is made to issue and serve a writ out of the jurisdiction (and this will be the overwhelming majority of cases), the plaintiff has a duty to make full and frank disclosure to the court. In an English authority, *The Hagen*,[67] it was held:

> 'The second point which we considered established by the cases was this, that, if on the construction of any of the sub-heads of Order xi. there was any doubt, it ought to be resolved in favour of the foreigner; and the third is that, inasmuch as the application is made *ex parte*, full and fair disclosure is necessary, as in all *ex parte* applications, and a failure to make such full and fair disclosure would justify the Court in discharging the order, even although the party might afterwards be in a position to make another application.'

15.1.2.2 *Bases for service out of the jurisdiction*

The bases on which the court may grant permission which are of particular significance for present purposes are discussed below.

[64] The High Court (Amendment) Rules 2012 (SI 27 of 2012), provide at r 8 (new) O LIII, r 2(3), that the rules governing commercial actions shall prevail in the event of any inconsistency between them and the High Court Rules.

[65] See the High Court (Amendment) Rules 2012 (SI 27 of 2012), r 8.

[66] See art 133(2) of the Constitution of Zambia (Amendment) Act 2016 (Act 2 of 2016).

[67] [1908] P 189 (CA) (Lord Alverstone CJ and Farwell and Kennedy LJJ), *per* Farwell LJ at 201.

(1) *Relief is sought against any person domiciled, or ordinarily resident, within the jurisdiction*

The term 'person' in Order X, rule 15(c), includes any natural or legal person.[68]

As regards individuals, there is little Zambian judicial authority on the meaning of the term 'domicile' for the purposes of the application of Order X, rule 15(c). It is likely, given the willingness of the Zambian courts to look to English law for the meaning of terms inherited from English statutes and statutory instruments, that the Zambian courts will adopt the jurisprudence applicable in English law regarding the term 'domicile' for the purposes of determining jurisdiction over a person.[69] Under the English Rules of the Supreme Court upon which Order X, rule 15, of the High Court Rules 1960 is based,[70] 'domicile' was defined as follows:[71]

> 'In general the domicile of a person is in the country in which he has his permanent home (see Dicey, *Conflict of Law*, 7th ed., Chap. 6), the country in which his habitation is fixed without any present intention of removing (*Re Craignish*, [1892] 3 Ch. 180, C.A.; *Huntly v. Gaskell*, [1906] A.C. 56; *Casdagli v. C.*, [1919] A.C. 145). No person can at any time be without a domicile or have more than one domicile. The domicile of origin remains until a new domicile of choice has been adopted (*Bell v. Kennedy* (1868), L.R. 1 Sc. App. 307, H.L.; *Udny v. Udny* (1869), ibid, 441, H.L., *Winans v. A.-G.*, [1904] A.C. 287, H.L.).'

The Zambian courts will also have jurisdiction on the basis of residency 'within the jurisdiction'. The question of the location of the residence of an individual will usually pose no particular difficulties: an individual will be resident where he lives.

Zambian courts will assume jurisdiction over a legal person where it is domiciled or resident in Zambia. Under the English Rules of the Supreme Court upon which Order X, rule 15, of the High Court Rules 1960 is based,[72] the 'domicile' of a corporation is at the place where it is registered[73] and the residence

---

[68] The Interpretation and General Provisions Act 1964 (Act 60 of 1964), s 3: person 'includes any company or association or body or persons, corporate or unincorporate'.

[69] See generally on the meaning of 'domicile', *Dicey, Morris and Collins on the Conflict of Laws* 15 ed (2012) vol 1, r 34, para 6R-001.

[70] The rule of the English Rules of the Supreme Court regulating service out of the jurisdiction prior to 1999 (when the Civil Procedure Rules came into effect) was O XI. Under the Rules of the Supreme Court 1883 and the Rules of the Supreme Court 1965, which superseded the 1883 Rules, O XI, r 1 provided for service out of the jurisdiction where the defendant was domiciled or ordinarily resident within the jurisdiction.

[71] The Rules of the Supreme Court 1883 (1960 ed) 144.

[72] The rule of the English Rules of the Supreme Court regulating service out of the jurisdiction prior to 1999 (when the Civil Procedure Rules came into effect) was O XI. Under the Rules of the Supreme Court 1883 and the Rules of the Supreme Court 1965, which superseded the 1883 Rules, O XI, r 1 provided for service out of the jurisdiction where the defendant was domiciled or ordinarily resident within the jurisdiction.

[73] The Rules of the Supreme Court 1883 (1960 ed) 145.

of a company is where its central management and control is exercised (a company may, therefore, be resident for these purposes in more than one country, as was found in *Commonwealth Development Corp v Central African Power Corp*).[74, 75]

(2) The action is one brought against the defendant to enforce … or otherwise affect a contract or to recover damages or other relief for or in respect of the breach of a contract:

(i) made within the jurisdiction, or

(ii) made by or through an agent trading or residing within the jurisdiction on behalf of a principal trading or residing out of the jurisdiction, or

(iii) by its terms or by implication to be governed by the law in force in the jurisdiction or is brought against the defendant in respect of a breach committed within the jurisdiction of a contract wherever made, even though the breach was preceded or accompanied by a breach out of the jurisdiction which rendered impossible the performance of the part of the contract which ought to have been performed within the jurisdiction.

It has been held that an action to recover money paid under a mistake of fact is not an action arising in contract (or tort). In *Northern Rhodesia Tobacco Co-operative Society v Baird*,[76] a grant of leave by the Registrar to serve the defendant out of the jurisdiction in Southern Rhodesia (Zimbabwe) was set aside by the High Court where the plaintiff's claim was for repayment of a sum mistakenly paid to the defendant in respect of the sale by the plaintiff of the defendant's tobacco crop. The court held that the plaintiff's claim was not within Order X, rule 15(e), because it was not a claim arising out of a contract but was instead a claim arising out of an obligation imposed on the defendant by operation of law.

It is likely that, in the apparent absence of Zambian authority on the construction and application of Order X, rule 15(e), a Zambian court will be guided by the academic and judicial authorities on the construction and application of the (former) equivalent provision in the English Rules of the Supreme Court.[77]

A concise statement of the law is as follows[78] (and should be adapted substituting 'Zambia' for 'England'):

---

[74] [1968] ZR 70 (H Ct) Magnus J at 81:23–24, where the defendant was resident in both Zambia and Rhodesia.

[75] The Rules of the Supreme Court 1883 (1960 ed) 145. Thus the place of a company's residence will normally be the place where the board of directors operates or the place of business of the managing director or that of the parent company: *Unit Construction Co Ltd v Bullock* [1960] AC 351 (HL), *per* Lord Simmonds at 362–3. The issue as to where the place of control is, is one of fact: *Union Corp v IRC* [1952] 1 All ER 646 (CA), *per* Evershed MR at 662B–C.

[76] [1949–54] NRLR 387 (H Ct) (Woodman J).

[77] Order XI, r 1(e) and 1(d) respectively: Rules of the Supreme Court 1883 (1961 ed) and 1965.

[78] *Dicey, Morris and Collins on the Conflict of Laws* 15 ed (2012) vol 1, r 34, paras 11-181–11-187.

'(i) **Where a contract is made in England**

11-181

If the parties enter into negotiations by correspondence from different countries, the contract is made where the letter of acceptance is posted. But in commercial transactions today communication by telephone, telex, fax and electronic mail is much more common than by post. It is now well established, following the decision of the Court of Appeal in *Entores v Miles Far East Corp* (which was approved by the House of Lords [*Brinkibon Ltd v. Stahag Stahl und Stahlwarenhandelsgesellschaft mbH* [1983] 2 AC 34]) that if the parties use "instantaneous" means of communication such as telephone, fax or electronic mail, the contract is made where the acceptance is communicated to the offeror. It has been held that if a contract made in England contains a submission to arbitration in a foreign country, an action in England at common law to enforce the foreign arbitration award is within this part of the clause. The contract must actually be made in England as that phrase is understood in English law. It is not sufficient if it merely says that it shall be deemed to be so made, though this may be sufficient to make it one which is governed by English law. A contract may be made in England within the meaning of this clause although it was preceded by a less formal agreement made abroad, or if it was originally made in England, but amended abroad.

(ii) **Where a contract is made by or through an agent trading or residing in England**

11-182

The clause says "by or through" an agent, not "by" an agent. Hence the case is within the clause, although the agent has no authority to make contracts on behalf of his foreign principal, but only has authority to obtain orders and transmit them to his principal for acceptance or rejection. This part of the clause is designed to bring within Rule 34 foreigners who transact business in England by or through agents, and consequently it does not apply where the agent's principal is the claimant. Hence a claimant cannot invoke clause (6)(ii) [Order X, rule 15(e)(ii)] where the contract was made by or through his agent.

11-183

If proceedings are brought by consignees of a cargo against foreign ship-owners under the bills of lading, the case is not within this part of the clause if the charterparty (but not the bills of lading) was made by or through agents of the shipowners in England, even though it refers to the bills of lading and was made by charterers acting on behalf of the consignees. It may be otherwise, however, if the charterers are identical with the consignees...

(iii) **Where a contract is governed by English law**

11-186

...

11-187

Although the fact that a contract is governed by English law is an important factor in the exercise of the discretion under this head in favour of the English forum, it is not conclusive. This head of jurisdiction was described as exorbitant in *Amin Rasheed Shipping Corp v Kuwait Insurance Co*, where the House of Lords held that in the circumstances it was not appropriate for the English court to determine a dispute involving a marine insurance policy governed by English law when the Kuwaiti courts were the forum conveniens. Until that decision it was generally thought that the fact that a contract was governed by English law was in itself sufficient to justify leave. But now the claimant has a heavier burden. In *Amin Rasheed* Lord Diplock suggested that, in order to justify leave under this head, the plaintiff had to show that justice could not be obtained by him in the foreign court, or could only be obtained at excessive cost, delay or inconvenience. But it was subsequently held that Lord Diplock was merely giving examples, and was not providing an exhaustive list, of the relevant factors. The court has to consider all factors, and the fact that English law is the applicable law may be of great importance, or it may be of little consequence as seen in the context of the whole case. Thus if there is likely to be no dispute on matters of law or construction, or if the law of the foreign forum is substantially the same as English law, the fact that English law is the applicable law will be of little weight. But where an issue of English public policy arises in relation to a contract which is (or may be) governed by English law, it is desirable that it should be decided by the English court; conversely, where the foreign court may apply its own public policy to defeat a claim based on a contract governed by English law, that too is a reason for the English court taking jurisdiction. If the claimant has alternative remedies in contract and tort upon the same facts, he can choose his remedy.'

The place of the performance of a contract for the purposes of service out of the jurisdiction was considered by the Supreme Court in *Fratelli Fasani SPA v Zambital Ltd*,[79] where the contract was between a Zambian importer and an Italian exporter and the court at first instance had held that the Zambian court did not have jurisdiction over the claim because the contract fell to be performed in Italy and not Zambia. The Supreme Court allowed the plaintiff's appeal on the basis that the performance of the contract had to be carried out in Zambia.[80]

(3) The action is founded on tort committed within the jurisdiction

There is a paucity of authority in Zambia on the construction and application of Order X, rule 15(f). As with the construction and application of Order X, rule 15(e), it is likely that, in the apparent absence of Zambian authority on the

[79] [1983] ZR 129 (SC) (Ngulube DCJ, Gardner and Muwo JJS).

[80] The report is extremely brief and the facts on the basis of which the finding of the Supreme Court was made are not clear. Further, the Supreme Court held that both parties had, in any event, submitted to the jurisdiction. As regards this latter finding, it is unclear whether this was a contractual submission or a procedural one (see below: a contractual submission is by way of a jurisdiction clause and a procedural submission is by way of participation in proceedings).

subject, a Zambian court will be informed by the academic and judicial authorities on the construction and application of the (former) equivalent provision in the English Rules of the Supreme Court.[81]

A statement of the law is as follows:[82]

> **'11-212**
>
> ... As both the Privy Council [in *Distillers Co (Bio-chemicals) Ltd v. Thompson* [1971] AC 458] and the Supreme Court of Canada [*Moran v. Pyle National (Canada) Ltd* (1973) 43 D.L.R. (3d) 239] have pointed out, the competing theories for the determination of the place of a tort have been that (i) all ingredients of the cause of action must have occurred within the jurisdiction, or (ii) the last ingredient, the event which completes a cause of action, must have occurred within the jurisdiction, or (iii) the act which the defendant committed must have occurred within the jurisdiction.
>
> **11-213**
>
> In *Distillers Co Ltd v Thompson* the Privy Council adopted the test of the place where in substance the act or omission occurred which gave the plaintiff his cause of action. So that where the essence of the complaint was failure to warn the consumer of the dangers of a product (rather than the faulty manufacture of the product) the cause of action was held to have arisen at the place where the failure to warn occurred; and the torts of negligent and fraudulent misrepresentation, where the negligent or fraudulent statement was communicated from one country to another, were held to have been committed where the statement was received and acted upon. Prior to the adoption of that test, but consistently with it, it had been held that the tort of defamation was committed where the defamatory statements were published and not where they were posted or uttered.'

15.1.2.3 *Submission to the jurisdiction*

Two circumstances must be distinguished under the title submission to the jurisdiction. First, where submission is alleged in extant proceedings in Zambia. Second, where the defendant has agreed (usually by contractual provision) to submit to the jurisdiction of the court in advance of a dispute arising.

15.1.2.3.1 Submission by appearance

As noted above, Order XI, rule 21, provides that before appearing a defendant may, without entering a conditional appearance, take out a summons or notice of motion to set aside the service on him of the writ or notice of the writ or to discharge the order granted leave for such service. It appears, therefore, that a defendant may either enter a conditional appearance and contest the jurisdiction or take out a summons or notice of motion as envisaged by rule 21.

---

81 Order XI, r 1(ee) and 1(f) respectively: Rules of the Supreme Court 1883 (1960 ed) and 1965.

82 *Dicey, Morris and Collins on the Conflict of Laws* 15 ed (2012) vol 1, r 34, paras 11-212–11-213.

In *Commonwealth Development Corp v Central African Power Corp*,[83] the defendant appeared to defend an application for summary judgment and it was accepted by the parties and by the court that the court had jurisdiction over the defendant because this appearance was a submission to the jurisdiction.

In the context of Zambian domestic law, if a writ is irregularly issued and an application is made for that writ to be set aside, the application will be refused if the defendant has taken a 'fresh step' in the proceedings after having become aware of the irregularity. It has been held that entering an unconditional appearance is such a fresh step.[84] The same approach is likely to be followed in cases where a defendant challenges the jurisdiction of the Zambian court having entered an unconditional appearance first.

15.1.2.3.2 Submission by agreement

15.1.2.3.2.1 *Jurisdiction clauses*

It would appear that, increasingly, the courts in Zambia are faced with cases in which they are required to determine whether to give effect to jurisdiction agreements in favour of foreign courts or (more often) whether to uphold arbitration agreements. Indeed, with respect to the latter, section 10 of the Arbitration Act 2000[85] requires a court to uphold an arbitration agreement – by imposing a stay on proceedings brought in contravention of that agreement – where the dispute between the parties falls within the scope of that agreement and where the agreement is not 'null and void, inoperative or incapable of being performed'.[86]

Given that there is not, as yet, a sizeable body of case law on the subject, it is not possible to tell exactly what approach the Zambian courts will take when they are asked to uphold jurisdiction agreements in favour of foreign jurisdictions.

Even so, it is submitted that the decision of the High Court in *Construction & Industrial Maintenance Services Ltd t/a Wako Kwikform v Fair Face Enterprises*[87] provides some early guidance on the point. The plaintiff required the defendants to sign a deposit account application form. Clause 12 of that form contained an agreement that proceedings arising out of or in connection with the contract on the courts of the Republic of South Africa. Notwithstanding clause 12, the plaintiff then commenced proceedings in Zambia; the defendants applied for

[83] [1968] ZR 70 (H Ct) (Magnus J) 81:27–30.

[84] *Bellamano v Ligure Lombarda Ltd* [1976] ZR 267 (SC) (Baron DCJ, Gardner JSC and Bruce-Lyle AJSC), *per* Gardner JS (giving the judgment of the Court) 270:15–22.

[85] Act 19 of 2000.

[86] *Intermarket Banking Corp Zambia Ltd v Munkanta* [2012] ZMHC 78 (H Ct) (Mutuna J).

[87] [2020] ZMHC 233 (Bowa J).

the dismissal of the proceedings 'for want of jurisdiction'. Having construed clause 12, Bowa J concluded that the parties 'unequivocally submitted to the jurisdiction of [the courts of the Republic of South Africa]. This was a choice freely made by the parties and the court's role is to enforce the party's agreement'.[88] *Construction & Industrial Maintenance Services Ltd* therefore suggests that Zambian courts will adopt an approach which gives effect to the parties' agreements in favour of foreign jurisdictions.[89]

If Zambian courts are more frequently asked to determine whether to give effect to jurisdiction agreements in favour of foreign courts, it may be the case that they obtain guidance from the approach which courts in other African jurisdictions adopt on the same issue. By way of example, in Kenya[90] and Malawi[91] courts have adopted the principles set out by Brandon J (as he then was) in *Owners of cargo lately laden on board the ship or vessel Eleftheria v The Eleftheria (Owners), The Eleftheria.*[92] There a jurisdiction clause provided: 'Any dispute arising under this bill of lading shall be decided in the country where the carrier has his principal place of business [Greece].' The owners of cargo on board the *Eleftheria* commenced proceedings in England and the shipowners applied for a stay of those proceedings. In staying the proceedings in favour of the Greek courts Brandon J set out the principles on the basis of which a stay may be granted:[93]

---

[88] In reaching this conclusion, Bowa J adverted to the decision of the Ugandan Court of Appeal in *Larco Concrete Products Ltd v Transair Ltd* [1987] HCB 40, but found it to be inapplicable on the facts of the case before him.

[89] It is submitted that some of the language used by Bowa J in *Intermarket* is unfortunate. Service of process on the defendant founds the jurisdiction of the court. In consequence, where that has happened, the court does not 'want for jurisdiction' by virtue of the existence of a jurisdiction agreement between the parties in favour of a foreign court. Instead, the existence of a jurisdiction agreement in favour of a foreign court offers a reason why the Zambian court should not exercise the jurisdiction that it has. On this, see Kennedy, 'Approaches to jurisdiction clauses in Anglophone African common law countries: principle and policy' (2019) 27 *African Journal of International and Comparative Law* 378 at 380–1.

[90] *Raytheon Aircraft Credit Corp v Air Al-Faraj Ltd* [2005] 2 KLR 47 (CA) (Tunoi, Githinji and Onyango Otieno JJA).

[91] *Mirza v AMI (Malawi) Ltd* (unreported) 4 December 2007 (H Ct) (Chombo J).

[92] [1970] P 94; [1969] 1 Lloyd's Rep 237 (QBD, Comm Ct). (It is of interest that in Nigeria, over a year *prior* to the decision in *The Eleftheria*, the High Court in Lagos in *Adesanya v Palm Line Ltd* [1967] (2) ALR Comm 133, reached a similar conclusion on the enforceability of a jurisdiction clause in favour of England. Adefarasin J stated (at 137:9–21): 'What I must apply my mind to is whether, in the peculiar circumstances of this case, I ought to exercise my discretion in favour of the defendants notwithstanding that the parties had by their own act chosen a foreign tribunal. The plaintiff is domiciled in this country. His claim arose here, the damage for which he has sued was discovered here and it was here ... that the consignment of damaged potatoes was surveyed. The evidence which the plaintiff would lead is to be found in this country. The only evidence that may be found in England, and that on behalf of the defendants, is the evidence of the condition in which the consignment left Liverpool ... In the circumstances of this case, I cannot possibly say that the parties have made their bargain and must abide by it.' The judge proceeded to balance the hardship to the parties of proceeding in Nigeria and England and found that Nigeria was by far the more convenient forum for both parties and refused to stay the proceedings in Nigeria.)

[93] [1970] P 94 at 99G–100C.

> '(1) Where plaintiffs sue in England in breach of an agreement to refer disputes to a foreign court, and the defendants apply for a stay, the English court, assuming the claim to be otherwise within its jurisdiction, is not bound to grant a stay but has a discretion whether to do so or not. (2) The discretion should be exercised by granting a stay unless strong cause for not doing so is shown. (3) The burden of proving such strong cause is on the plaintiffs. (4) In exercising its discretion the court should take into account all the circumstances of the particular case. (5) In particular, but without prejudice to (4), the following matters, where they arise, may properly be regarded:—(a) In what country the evidence on the issues of fact is situated, or more readily available, and the effect of that on the relative convenience and expense of trial as between the English and foreign courts, (b) Whether the law of the foreign court applies and, if so, whether it differs from English law in any material respects, (c) With what country either party is connected, and how closely, (d) Whether the defendants genuinely desire trial in the foreign country, or are only seeking procedural advantages, (e) Whether the plaintiffs would be prejudiced by having to sue in the foreign court because they would: (i) be deprived of security for their claim; (ii) be unable to enforce any judgment obtained; (iii) be faced with a time-bar not applicable in England; or (iv) for political, racial, religious or other reasons be unlikely to get a fair trial.'[94]

In conformity with the doctrine of privity of contract, a jurisdiction clause will bind only those who are party to the agreement in question.

15.1.2.3.2.2 *Application for service out of the jurisdiction based on a jurisdiction clause*

One question that arises is the statutory basis on which a Zambian court may assume jurisdiction over a cause where the plaintiff in Zambia applies for service on the putative defendant out of the jurisdiction based on a jurisdiction clause in an agreement.

In the English Rules of the Supreme Court[95] Order XI, rule 1(1)(d)(i)–(iv), the sub-rule governing service out of the jurisdiction in cases concerned with contract contains an additional sub-sub-paragraph to the equivalent provisions in the Zambian High Court Rules, Order X, rule 15(e)(i)–(iii). That additional sub-sub-paragraph provides as follows: 'The claim is made to enforce ... a contract which ... (iv) contains a term to the effect that the High Court shall

[94] Were a Zambian court to adopt this approach, of course, that would demonstrate a divergence between the law of Zambia and the law of England on this point. English law now adopts an approach which accords greater respect to the jurisdiction clause: *Donohue v Armco Inc* [2002] 1 All ER 749 (HL (E)) (Lords Bingham, Mackay, Nicholls, Hobhouse and Scott), where Lord Bingham, at 754G–J, held: 'Where the dispute is between two contracting parties, A and B, and A sues in a non-contractual forum, and A's claims fall within the scope of the exclusive jurisdiction clause in their contract, and the interests of other parties are not involved, effect will in all probability be given to the clause.'

[95] Rules of the Supreme Court 1965 (the successor provision to O XI, r 2(a) of the Rules of the Supreme Court 1883 (1960 ed), introduced by amendment in 1920).

have jurisdiction to hear and determine any action in respect of the contract.' This additional provision was included in the English rules in order to reverse the decision of the Court of Appeal in *British Wagon Co Ltd v Gray*.[96]

Where the defendant is not present within the jurisdiction and where no other provision of the High Court Rules, Order X, rule 15 is applicable to the case, the question is whether the Zambian court has power to order service out of the jurisdiction solely on the basis that the agreement between the parties contains a jurisdiction clause in favour of the Zambian courts. Subject to the discussion of the 'lacuna principle' above, it would appear that the answer to the question is 'no' and in such a case there would be no basis on which the Zambian court could validly make an order for service of the defendant out of the jurisdiction.

15.1.2.4 Lis alibi pendens

In the absence of domestic authority on the question whether the court should stay proceedings in favour of another forum where parallel proceedings have been commenced, the Zambian courts may well look to the approach adopted by the English courts in this regard.[97]

In *de Dampierre v de Dampierre*,[98] the House of Lords held that where a stay of English proceedings is sought on the basis that there are parallel proceedings in another jurisdiction, the principles of *forum non conveniens* enunciated in *Spiliada Maritime Corp v Cansulex Ltd*[99] apply. Thus in *de Dampierre*, a case concerning parallel divorce proceedings in France and England, the court considered the connections between the parties and the two jurisdictions and the appropriateness of proceedings in France rather than England and concluded that the English proceedings should be stayed:[100]

> 'Here it is beyond dispute that there are very strong factors connecting the case with France, whereas now there are practically none connecting the case with England. Neither party suggests that New York is the appropriate forum. It follows that *prima facie* the courts of France clearly provide the appropriate jurisdiction for the resolution of the dispute, so that a stay should be granted unless justice requires otherwise. In considering the question, the [judge at first instance] ... did indeed invoke the authority of one of the earlier authorities on the inherent jurisdiction, relying as he did on the much-quoted dictum of Lord Diplock in *MacShannon v. Rockware Glass Ltd.* [1978] A.C. 975, 812. He recognised the undoubted "Frenchness" of the marriage and the spouses, but considered that the wife's absence from what he described as the "harsh" French regime and her presence in

[96] [1896] 1 QB 35.

[97] See s 2 of the English Law (Extent of Application) Act 1963.

[98] [1988] AC 92 (HL (E)) (Lords Keith, Brandon, Templeman, Ackner and Goff).

[99] [1987] AC 460 (HL (E)).

[100] Ibid 109E–H *per* Lord Goff.

> the more "benevolent" regime which prevails here, plainly afforded a juridical advantage to her and that, following Lord Diplock's approach, this must outweigh the "Frenchness" of the marriage of the spouses and point to the conclusion that England was the more appropriate jurisdiction for the dissolution of the marriage.'

And:[101]

> 'The weight to be given to what has been called a "legitimate personal or juridical advantage" was considered by your Lordships' House in the *Spiliada* case [1987] A.C. 460, 482-484. The conclusion there reached was that, having regard to the underlying principle, the court should not, as a general rule, be deterred from granting a stay of proceedings simply because the plaintiff in this country will be deprived of such an advantage, provided that the court is satisfied that substantial justice will be done in the appropriate forum overseas. Reference was made, in particular, to cases concerning discovery where, as is well known, there is a spectrum of systems of discovery applicable in various jurisdictions; and the opinion was expressed that, generally speaking, injustice cannot be said to be done if a party is compelled to accept one of these well recognised systems of discovery in another forum. If I follow that approach in the circumstances of the present case, I find that French matrimonial law contains provisions for "compensation" which, unlike our own, place emphasis upon the question whether the breakdown of the marriage was due to the exclusive fault of one of the parties, providing (subject to an important exception) that a party so at fault is deprived of the right to an award of compensation. Such an approach is no longer acceptable in this country, though it bears a close resemblance to the principles applicable here not so very long ago. But it is evidently still acceptable in a highly civilised country with which this country has very close ties of friendship, not least nowadays through our common membership of the European Community; and I find it impossible to conclude that, objectively speaking, justice would not be done if the wife was compelled to pursue her remedy for financial provision under such a regime in the courts of a country which provide, most plainly, the natural forum for the resolution of this matrimonial dispute.'

Thus, what is required is a balancing of the various factors in the case to ascertain in which jurisdiction the case is most appropriately decided.

15.1.2.5 Forum non conveniens

As noted at section 15.1.2.1, the final stage in the court's analysis when determining whether to permit service out is to consider whether, in the exercise of its discretion, the court should permit service out. In other words, the court must consider whether Zambia is the *forum conveniens.*

It appears that the Zambian courts consider it appropriate to take into account considerations of convenience when deciding whether to grant leave to issue and serve out of the jurisdiction (or whether to grant a stay of proceedings already commenced). That this is so clearly emerges from the decision of the High Court

[101] Ibid 110B–F *per* Lord Goff.

in *Steak Ranch Ltd v Steak Ranchers International BV*.[102] Here, the defendant made an application to stay proceedings commenced in Zambia, arguing that the matter ought to be heard in the courts of the Republic of South Africa. In short, the plaintiff and defendant had entered into a franchising agreement in South Africa which contained a choice of law clause in favour of South African law. It appears from the judgment that the place of performance of the agreement, that is the restaurant franchise, was Zambia and that the plaintiff was a company registered under the laws of Zambia and operated and controlled from Zambia, whereas the defendant was a company registered under the laws of the Netherlands and operated and controlled from that jurisdiction. The court refused the application for a stay.

In reaching that conclusion, the Zambian High Court adopted the formulation of the doctrine of *forum non conveniens* as found in English law and, in particular, in the decision of the House of Lords in *Spiliada Maritime Corp v Cansulex Ltd, The Spiliada*.[103] Applying the relevant principles, therefore, the court found that the agreement had its closest connection with Zambia and had no connection with South Africa, save for the choice of law clause, which itself left open the option for the application of Zambian law in the event that a Zambian court having jurisdiction to hear a dispute relating to the agreement refused to apply South African law.

In an effort to contextualise the approach which the High Court adopted in the *Steak Ranch* case, it is worth pointing out that, historically, the English courts seemed always to have held that a major factor in the exercise of the discretion to grant leave to serve out of the jurisdiction or stay proceedings already served out of the jurisdiction was whether the English proceedings were vexatious and oppressive. The expression 'vexatious and oppressive' bore a wide meaning and extended to considerations related to the comparative convenience of proceedings in England as opposed to a particular foreign forum. For example, in *Logan v Bank of Scotland (No 2)*,[104] the Court of Appeal granted an application staying proceedings served as of right in England in favour of Scotland. Sir Gorell Barnes P stated:[105]

> 'Now, it is true that the Courts of this country have not gone so far as to express themselves upon the question of convenience in terms similar to those used in the Scotch cases, though, as I have already noticed, it may be doubted whether there is any substantial difference between the two. Yet it seems to me clear that the inconvenience of trying a case in a particular tribunal may be such as practically to work a serious injustice upon a defendant and be vexatious. This would probably not be so if the difference of trying

[102] (2012) 2 ZR 562 (H Ct) (Mutuna J).

[103] [1987] AC 460 (HL (E)) (Lords Keith, Templeman, Griffiths, Mackay and Goff).

[104] [1906] 1 KB 141 (CA) (Sir Gorell Barnes, President, Collins MR, and Romer LJ).

[105] Ibid 151–2. This was a decision under the 1883 Rules of the Supreme Court.

in one country rather than in another were merely measured by some extra expense; but where the difficulty for the defendant of trying in the country in which the action is brought is such that it is impracticable to properly try the case by reason of the difficulty of procuring the attendance of busy men as witnesses, and keeping them during trial, and of having to deal with masses of books, documents, and papers which are not in the country where the action is brought, and of dealing with law foreign to the tribunal, it appears to me that a case of vexation in some circumstances may be made out if the plaintiff chooses to sue in that country rather than in that where everybody is and where all the witnesses and material for the trial are.'

In *Spiliada Maritime Corp v Cansulex Ltd, The Spiliada*, the House of Lords decided:[106]

> 'The basic principle is that a stay will only be granted on the ground of *forum non conveniens* where the court is satisfied that there is some other available forum, having competent jurisdiction, which is the appropriate forum for the trial of the action, i.e. in which the case may be tried more suitably for the interests of all the parties and the ends of justice.'

The English courts will, therefore, refuse leave to issue and serve a writ out of the jurisdiction or (in a case where leave has been granted but the defendant enters a conditional appearance) will stay English proceedings if England is not the *forum conveniens*.[107] It is likely that a Zambian court will have regard to these principles in considering the exercise of its discretion both to grant leave to serve a writ out of the jurisdiction and in considering any application to set aside service of a writ served outside the jurisdiction or stay proceedings where it is contended that a different jurisdiction is the appropriate jurisdiction for resolution of the dispute.

15.2 Enforcement of Foreign Judgments

Under Zambian law a foreign judgment may be enforced in Zambia either at common law or under the statutory regime set out in the Foreign Judgments (Reciprocal Enforcement) Act 1937[108] and the Service of Process and Execution of Judgments Act 1957[109] (and, arguably, under the British and Colonial Judgments Act 1922[110]).

---

[106] Ibid 476C, *per* Lord Goff, with whom the other Lords of Appeal agreed (Lord Templeman delivering a concurring opinion). A decision under the 1965 Rules of the Supreme Court.

[107] See *Dicey, Morris and Collins on the Conflict of Laws* 15 ed (2012) vol 1, r 38(3), para 12-053 et seq.

[108] Act 5 of 1937 (now Cap 76 of the Laws of the Republic of Zambia, 1995). On occasion this Act is referred to by a different year of enactment, '1959'. The reason for this seems to be that over the years the Chapter number under which Zambia's statutes are organised has changed and sometimes reference is made to 1959, the year of the passing of an amendment to the 1937 Act. Here, the orthodox reference to the year of the promulgation of the law is used and not to the year of subsequent amendments of that law.

[109] Act 4 of 1956 (now Cap 79 of the Laws of the Republic of Zambia 1995).

[110] Ordinance 8 of 1922. This does not appear in the Laws of the Republic of Zambia 1995.

15.2.1 Enforcement at common law

In *Mileta Pakou v Rudnap Zambia Ltd*,[111] the Supreme Court confirmed that English common-law principles applied to the enforcement of foreign judgments in Zambia, although the basis on which this finding was made is somewhat unsatisfactory. The court held that the Foreign Judgments (Reciprocal Enforcement) Act 1937 did not apply to the foreign judgment in issue, a judgment rendered by the Basic Court of Associated Labour in Belgrade in what was, at the time, Yugoslavia, because Yugoslavia was not one of the countries to which that Act had been extended. The court proceeded to find that enforcement proceedings could have been, but had not been, pursued by action at common law. The court stated that English common-law principles applied by reason of the operation of section 10 of the High Court Act 1960. However, section 10 of the 1960 Act refers only to the practice and procedure of the High Court and not the substantive law to be applied by the High Court.[112] The court ought to have based its decision on section 2(a) of the English Law (Extent of Application) Act 1963 which provides that the common law shall be in force in Zambia, subject to the Constitution and to any other written law. Be that is it may, it is plain that a foreign judgment may be enforced at common law in Zambia.[113]

The applicable common-law principles are as follows:

(1) A foreign judgment *in personam* given by the court of a foreign country with jurisdiction to give that judgment may be enforced by a claim or counterclaim for the amount due under it if the judgment is: (a) for a debt,

[111] [1998] ZR 233 (Sup Ct) (Ngulube CJ, Sakala and Chaila JJS). Recently, the *Mileta Pakou* case was cited with approval by the Supreme Court in *Murray & Roberts Construction Ltd v Lusaka Premier Health Ltd* [2017] ZMSC 143 (S Ct) (Malila, Kajimanga and Mutunu JJSC).

[112] As amended by s 2 of the High Court (Amendment) Act 2011 (Act 7 of 2011).

[113] See *Murray & Roberts Construction Ltd v Lusaka Premier Health Ltd* [2017] ZMSC 143 (SC) (Malila, Kajimanga and Mutunu JJSC). In this case, the Supreme Court confirmed that a judgment creditor of a judgment rendered by a court in the Republic of South Africa (a country to which the statutory regime for the enforcement of foreign judgments in Zambia has not yet been extended by order), could, in principle, seek to enforce it at common law by commencing an action on that judgment as a cause of action. It must be remembered, however, that O X, r 15 of the Rules of the High Court does not, on its face (but potentially subject to the 'lacuna principle') empower the Zambian court to permit service of the writ on a defendant who is present outside the jurisdiction where the action is one to enforce a foreign judgment; Frimpong Oppong 'Recognition and enforcement of foreign judgments in Commonwealth African countries' (2014) XV *Yearbook of Private International Law* 365 at 371–2. Frimpong Oppong, at 372, then considers what should happen if the judgment creditor is unable to satisfy this aforementioned 'jurisdictional requirement' and suggests that the judgment creditor may ignore the foreign judgment and bring a fresh action on the original cause of action. In Zambia, so Frimpong Oppong argues (citing *Mileta Pakou v Rudnap Zambia Ltd* (1998) ZR 377 at 380), the 'judgment creditor retains the right to sue on their original cause of action'. However, Frimpong Oppong acknowledges that: 'In such an action on the original cause of action, the jurisdiction of the domestic court must, however, be established. In addition, there may be questions of estoppel and limitation of action that could undermine the viability of bringing a fresh action.'

or definite sum of money (not being a sum payable in respect of taxes or other charges of a like nature or in respect of a fine or other penalty); and (b) final and conclusive, but not otherwise.[114] A foreign judgment may be final and conclusive, though it is subject to an appeal, and though an appeal against it is actually pending in the foreign country where it was given.

(2) In order for the judgment of a foreign court to be recognised and enforceable in England, the foreign court must have 'international jurisdiction' in the eyes of the common law. A court of a jurisdiction outside England has international jurisdiction, in the eyes of the common law, to give a judgment *in personam* in the following cases:[115]

- (a) If the person against whom the judgment was given was, at the time the proceedings were instituted, present in the foreign country.
- (b) If the person against whom the judgment was given was claimant, or counterclaimed, in the proceedings in the foreign court.
- (c) If the person against whom the judgment was given, submitted to the jurisdiction of that court by voluntarily appearing in the proceedings.
- (d) If the person against whom the judgment was given, had before the commencement of the proceedings agreed, in respect of the subject-matter of the proceedings, to submit to the jurisdiction of that court or of the courts of that country.[116]

The common-law rules as to when a foreign court has international jurisdiction are not exhaustive and may be the subject of development in the future. However, the following matters have been held not to give a foreign court international jurisdiction to render a judgment capable of recognition and enforcement in England: (a) possession by the defendant of property in the foreign country; (b) presence of the defendant in the foreign country at the time when the cause of action arose; (c) where the defendant is a national of the foreign country; (d) where the defendant is domiciled, but not present or resident, in the foreign country; (e) reciprocity, in either of two senses: first, that the foreign court would recognise and enforce a like judgment of the English court or, second, that the foreign court assumed jurisdiction on a basis that the English court would have assumed jurisdiction (for example, one of the heads of jurisdiction under the RSC, Order XI); (f) a real and substantial connection between

---

[114] *Dicey, Morris and Collins on the Conflict of Laws* 15 ed (2012) vol 1, r 42, paras 14-021–14-053.

[115] Ibid r 43, paras 14-055–14-081.

[116] These statements or principle were expressly approved by the Supreme Court in *Mileta Pakou v Rudnap Zambia Ltd* [1998] ZR 233.

the foreign court and the claim; (g) a judgment *in personam* of a foreign court ancillary to a divorce decree.

(3) International jurisdiction has been held not to exist in the following case: a court of a foreign country has no jurisdiction to give a judgment capable of enforcement or recognition in England against a person who under the rules of public international law was entitled to immunity from the jurisdiction of the courts of that country and did not submit to them.[117]

(4) A court of a foreign country outside the United Kingdom has international jurisdiction to give a judgment *in rem* capable of enforcement or recognition in England if the subject-matter of the proceedings where that judgment was given was immovable or movable property which was at the time of the proceedings situated in the foreign country. (The corollary is that a foreign court has no jurisdiction to render judgment in respect of title or possession of immovable property situated outside the foreign country.)[118]

(5) An English court will not recognise or enforce a foreign judgment where:
   (a) The foreign court did not have international jurisdiction on one of the bases set out above.[119]
   (b) The foreign judgment is impeachable for fraud either on the part of the party seeking to enforce the judgment or on the part of the foreign court itself.[120]
   (c) The foreign judgment is impeachable on the grounds of public policy.[121]

---

[117] *Dicey, Morris and Collins on the Conflict of Laws* 15 ed (2012) vol 1, r 45, paras 14-102–14-105.

[118] Ibid r 47, paras 14-109–14-115.

[119] Ibid r 49, paras 14-129–14-135.

[120] Fraud is determined by reference to the common-law principles on fraud: *Owens Bank Ltd v Bracco* [1992] 2 AC 443 (HL (E)) (Lords Griffiths, Bridge, Ackner, Goff and Browne-Wilkinson), where it was held that the approach of the common-law courts to the finality of a foreign judgment was that there was no requirement, as there was in the case of an action to set aside an English judgment on the ground of fraud, that the fraud should be established by fresh evidence that had not been available to the defendant at trial and could not with reasonable diligence have been discovered by him before judgment had been delivered. This decision in effect permits a defendant to relitigate matters already disposed of before the foreign court. The rules relating setting aside a foreign judgment obtained by fraud are comprehensively set out in *Dicey, Morris and Collins on the Conflict of Laws* 15 ed (2012) vol 1, r 50, paras 14-137–14-145; the position in English law (*Owens Bank Ltd v Bracco* [1992] 2 AC 443 (HL (E)), see above) has not been followed in certain Commonwealth jurisdictions (eg Canada in *Beals v Saldanha* [2003] 3 SCR 416, (2003) 234 DLR (4th) 1; and New South Wales in *Keele v Findley* (1991) 21 NSWLR 444 (NSWSC); but in *Close v Arnot* (unreported) 21 November 1997 (NSW), the Common Law Division distinguished *Keele v Findley* and applied the traditional English standard of fraud in respect of a foreign judgment in a case where the defendant had, for good reason, allowed foreign proceedings to go undefended).

[121] *Dicey, Morris and Collins on the Conflict of Laws* 15 ed (2012) vol 1, r 51, paras 14-153–14-157. For example, if the performance of a contract necessarily involves the commission of an act that is legally objectionable: *Koufou v Greenberg* [1982] ZR 30 (H Ct) (Mumba C).

(d) The foreign judgment is impeachable on the grounds that it was obtained in proceedings which offend the rules of natural justice.[122]

(6) A foreign judgment which is final and conclusive on the merits and not impeachable under any of the bases set out above is conclusive as to any matter adjudicated upon, and cannot be impeached for any error either of fact or of law (on the supposition that the proper place to raise any alleged error of fact or law is in the foreign court or on appeal from the judgment to the foreign appeal tribunal).[123]

It is to be expected that, in compliance with section 2(a) of the English Law (Extent of Application) Act 1963, a Zambian court will apply these principles to the enforcement at common law of a foreign judgment.

15.2.2 Enforcement pursuant to statute

The statutory regimes for enforcement of foreign judgments comprise three pieces of legislation: the British and Colonial Judgments Act 1922 ('the 1922 Act'), the Foreign Judgments (Reciprocal Enforcement) Act 1937 ('the 1937 Act') and the Service of Process and Execution of Judgments Act 1957 ('the 1957 Act'). Four points on these regimes may conveniently be made at this stage.

First, as will become apparent below, the 1922 Act and 1937 Act are materially *verbatim* transpositions of, respectively, the applicable provisions of the United Kingdom Administration of Justice Act 1920 and Foreign Judgments (Reciprocal Enforcement) Act 1933. It is to be expected therefore that a Zambian court will have regard to (although not, of course, be bound by) decisions of the English courts, in particular, and the commentary by academics on the interpretation of these Acts of the United Kingdom Parliament.[124]

Second, there is an issue whether the 1922 Act has been repealed such that its provisions are no longer operative.

Third, it should be noted that the 1922 Act extended to[125] Zimbabwe, Tanzania, Malawi, Lesotho, Botswana, Eswatini, Kenya, New South Wales,

---

[122] *Dicey, Morris and Collins on the Conflict of Laws* 15 ed (2012) vol 1, r 52, paras 14-163–14-167. For example, a breach of the *audi alteram partem* rule: *Contract Haulage v Kamayoyo* [1982] ZR 13 (S Ct) (Gardner Ag DCJ, Cullinan JSC and Muwo Ag JSC); *Shilling Bob Zinka v The Attorney-General* (1990–2) ZR 73 (S Ct) (Silungwe CJ, Ngulube DCJ, and Gardner, Chaila and Chirwa JJS).

[123] *Dicey, Morris and Collins on the Conflict of Laws* 15 ed (2012) vol 1, r 48, paras 14-119–14-125.

[124] The relevant parts of *Dicey, Morris and Collins on the Conflict of Laws* 15 ed (2012) on the application of the 1920 and 1933 Acts are as follows: 1920 Act – r 53, paras 14R-173–14-181; 1933 Act – r 54, paras 14R-183–14-195. See also Briggs *Civil Jurisdiction and Judgments* 7 ed (2021) paras 35.01–35.10.

[125] Using the modern names for these countries. Notwithstanding that certain of these jurisdictions are now independent and have changed their names, the legislation ought to continue to apply to them (Acts and other legislation are generally construed as 'living' or 'always speaking', such that terminology may be

Victoria, Scotland, England, Northern Ireland and the Republic of Ireland. The 1937 Act, notwithstanding that Part II of the Act has been extended pursuant to section 9(1) of the Act to 'Her Britannic Majesty's dominions',[126] has been extended only to the Gilbert and Ellice Islands[127] and to the British Solomon Islands[128] pursuant to the power in section 3 of the Act.

Fourth, the 1957 Act applies only to judgments from Malawi and Zimbabwe.

It is convenient to address the second point referred to above before discussing the application of the 1922 Act and 1937 Act, that is, whether the 1922 Act remains in force today.

The overarching scheme of the United Kingdom Foreign Judgments (Reciprocal Enforcement) Act 1933, which is mirrored by the 1937 Act, has been described as follows:[129]

> 'The 1933 Act empowers the Crown in Council to extend Pt I of that enactment to all parts of the Commonwealth outside the United Kingdom. It is provided that upon the application of the later Act in this manner the 1920 Act shall cease to have effect except in relation to such territories to which it extends at the date of such Order. The effect of this provision, which has been acted upon, is merely to prevent the further extension of the system of enforcement envisaged by the 1920 Act. Its effect is not to apply instead the scheme of the 1933 Act. For Pt I of the latter to come into operation in relation to any particular territory, a further and specific Order in Council is required.'

Thus, the promulgation of two Orders in Council is contemplated by the 1933 Act so as to bring any given Commonwealth country within the ambit of the 1933 Act. First, is an Order in Council made pursuant to section 7(1), extending Part I of the 1933 Act to all parts of the Commonwealth outside the United Kingdom. This Order has the effect of preventing the 1920 Act applying further to Commonwealth countries. Second, is a further, specific Order in Council made pursuant to section 1, bringing the Act into force in relation to a particular country.

Upon the making of the Order in Council pursuant to section 7(1), the 1920 Act ceases to have effect in relation to the Commonwealth outside the United Kingdom, with the exception of those territories to which the 1920 Act extended at the time of the making of the Order in Council pursuant to section 7(1).

---

adapted to events; for example, the term 'Northern Rhodesia' in a United Kingdom statutory instrument dated 1922 was construed as meaning 'Zambia' after independence: *Jamieson v Northern Electricity Supply Corp (Pte) Ltd* [1970] SLT 113, *per* Lord Johnston at 115).

[126] The Foreign Judgments (Reciprocal Enforcement) Order of 1958 (GN 28 of 1958).

[127] Judgments (Reciprocal Enforcement) (Gilbert and Ellice Islands Colony) Order (GN 29 of 1958); now two separate states, Kiribati and Tuvalu.

[128] Judgments (Reciprocal Enforcement) (British Solomon Islands Protectorate) Order (GN 30 of 1930); now the Solomon Islands.

[129] *Dicey, Morris and Collins on the Conflict of Laws* 15 ed (2012) vol 1, r 53, para 14-175.

The Zambian legislation mirrors this approach. On the making of a statutory order pursuant to section 9(1) of the 1937 Act (the equivalent to section 7(1) of the 1933 Act), the 1922 Act ceases to have effect 'except in relation to those parts of the said dominions [the Commonwealth] to which it extends at the commencement of the order'.

The statutory objective of replacing the 1922 Act entirely through the incorporation into the scheme of the 1937 Act of those territories to which the 1922 Act extended, required and requires the making of a further Order pursuant to section 3 of the 1937 Act in relation to each of those territories (set out above), extending Part II of the 1937 Act to those territories or any of them. Upon the making of that further Order pursuant to section 3, the 1922 Act would no longer apply to those territories.[130] The statutory objective of transferring the recognition and enforcement regime from the 1922 Act over to the 1937 Act would thereby be achieved.

However, no section 3 Order has ever been made pursuant to which any of the territories to which the 1922 Act applied had extended to it Part II of the 1937 Act.

Instead, in 1959, the 1922 Act was repealed by section 3 of the Foreign Judgments (Reciprocal Enforcement) (Amendment) Act 1959.

This state of affairs has led some commentators to conclude that judgments rendered by the courts of the territories to which the 1922 Act applied or was extended, specifically the courts of England, are no longer enforceable under statute in Zambia.[131] This approach to the legislation has also been followed by the High Court.[132] In *Attorney-General v Chiluba*,[133] the plaintiff had obtained a judgment from the English High Court and sought to register the judgment under the 1937 Act. The judgment was registered in Zambia and the judgment debtor

---

[130] This is the effect of s 9(2) of the 1937 Act.

[131] See Frimpong Oppong *Private International Law in Commonwealth Africa* (2013) 382–4; GLG (Global Legal Group) *The International Comparative Legal Guide to: Litigation & Dispute Resolution 2016* (2016), ch 51, Zambia, p 414, col 2, para 9.3, Jalasi & Linyama (of Eric Silwamba, Jalasi and Linyama, Legal Practitioners); Mandhu & Mwamulima Africa Encyclopaedia of Law *Practice and Procedure of Registering and Enforcing Foreign Judgments in Zambia* (2017) at http://lawin.co.za.

[132] This view would also seem to be shared by the Supreme Court. In *Murray & Roberts Construction Ltd v Lusaka Premier Health Ltd* [2017] ZMSC 143 (Malila, Kajimanga and Mutunu JJS), Kajimanga JS, giving the judgment of the court, stated, at pp 11 and 12 of the electronic report: 'The point should be made that in Zambia two avenues are available for enforcing a judgment awarded by a foreign court. The first avenue is to seek to register the foreign judgment pursuant to the Foreign Judgments (Reciprocal Enforcement) Act ... [or where a judgment creditor of a judgment delivered by a court to which that statutory regime does not apply] to seek to enforce it at Common Law by commencing an action founded on that judgment as a cause of action.' However, the 1922 Act was never extended to the Republic of South Africa and so could not have applied in this case in any event. The Supreme Court therefore was not considering its potential (continued) application. It would be wrong, therefore, to put too much weight on the statement of the Supreme Court in *Murray & Roberts Construction* in support of the view set out in the main text.

[133] [2010] 1 ZR 287 (H Ct).

applied for registration to be set aside. In granting the application, Hamaundu J noted that the 1922 Act had been repealed in 1959 and held that Part II of the 1937 Act had not been extended to the United Kingdom. The judge concluded that, in the absence of any other statutory provision pursuant to which judgments rendered by courts in the United Kingdom could be enforced by registration, the judgment of the English court could only be enforced at common law.

However, in the *Chiluba* case, the court was not referred to the relevant provisions of the Interpretation and General Provisions Act 1964 bearing upon the issue. Section 13 of the 1964 Act, entitled 'Repeal and substitution', provides: 'Where a written law repeals wholly or partially any former written law and substitutes provisions for the written law repealed, the repealed written law shall remain in force until the substituted provisions come into operation.'

As has been described above, the legislative scheme of the 1937 Act is to replace the scheme for registration under the 1922 Act and to do so in respect of countries already covered by the 1922 Act only when a specific second Order is made under the 1937 Act, having the effect of substituting the regime under the 1937 Act for that under the 1922 Act. To date, as regards Zimbabwe, Tanzania, Malawi, Lesotho, Botswana, Eswatini, Kenya, New South Wales, Victoria, Scotland, England, Northern Ireland and the Republic of Ireland, no such Order has been made. It is, therefore, at the very least, seriously arguable that the 1922 Act remains in force in relation to these countries and territories in accordance with section 13 of the 1964 Act until such time as an Order is made bringing the 1937 Act into effect in relation to these countries and territories or any of them.

On the basis of the reasoning set out above, the law of Zambia may be stated as follows: judgments emanating from jurisdictions covered by the regime set out in the 1922 Act remain capable of registration and enforcement in Zambia until such time as an Order is made under section 3 of the 1937 Act in respect of a particular jurisdiction. At that point, the 1922 Act will cease to apply to that jurisdiction and the 1937 Act will start to apply instead.

15.2.2.1 *The regimes for enforcement pursuant to statute*

15.2.2.1.1 British and Colonial Judgments Act 1922

The principal provisions of the 1922 Act are referred to below.

Section 2 of the 1922 Act provides that the 1922 Act applies to any judgments or orders in any civil proceedings providing for the payment of a sum of money, and includes awards in arbitration proceedings if these can, under the law in force where they are made, be enforced in the same manner as judgments.[134]

---

[134] The equivalent of s 12(1) of the United Kingdom Administration of Justice Act 1920.

15.2.2.1.1.1 *Procedure for registration*

Section 3 of the 1922 Act provides that where a judgment has been obtained from the High Court in England or Ireland[135] or the Court of Session in Scotland, the judgment creditor may apply to the High Court in Zambia at any time within 12 months after the date of the judgment to have the judgment registered and on such an application the court may 'if in all the circumstances of the case it thinks it just and convenient that the judgment should be enforced in Zambia' order the judgment to be registered.[136]

Section 4[137] of the 1922 Act provides that no judgment shall be registered if:

(1) the original court acted without jurisdiction;

(2) the judgment debtor[138] was neither (a) carrying on business[139] nor ordinarily resident within the jurisdiction; (b) did not voluntarily appear or otherwise submit or agree to the jurisdiction of the court;

(3) the defendant was not duly served with the proceedings and did not appear notwithstanding that he was ordinarily resident or carrying on business within the jurisdiction or had agreed to submit to the jurisdiction of the court;

(4) the judgment was obtained by fraud;[140]

(5) the judgment debtor satisfies the court that an appeal is pending or that he is entitled and intends to appeal against the judgment;

(6) the judgment was in respect of a cause of action which for reasons of public policy for some other similar reasons could not have been entertained by the Zambian court.

Section 5[141] provides that once registered the judgment is of the same force and effect as if it had been originally obtained in Zambia.

---

135 Now the High Court in the Republic of Ireland and the High Court in Northern Ireland.

136 The equivalent of s 9(1) of the 1920 Act.

137 The equivalent of s 9(2) of the 1920 Act.

138 Being a legal or natural person.

139 It has been held by an English court that a New Zealand insurance company did not carry on business in Ghana merely because it maintained agents there with limited powers: *Sfeir & Co v National Insurance Co of New Zealand Ltd* [1964] 1 Lloyd's Rep 330 (QB).

140 Fraud is determined by reference to the common-law principles on fraud: *Owens Bank Ltd v Bracco* [1992] 2 AC 443 (HL (E)), where it was held that s 9(2) of the 1920 Act was to be construed as having adopted the approach of the common-law courts to the finality of a foreign judgment; that, accordingly, there was no requirement, as there was in the case of an action to set aside an English judgment on the ground of fraud, that the fraud should be established by fresh evidence that had not been available to the defendant at trial and could not with reasonable diligence have been discovered by him before judgment had been delivered. This decision in effect permits a defendant to relitigate matters already disposed of before the foreign court. It is a decision which the Zambian courts are, of course, not bound to follow.

141 The equivalent of s 9(3) of the 1920 Act.

Section 9 provides that the High Court may make rules of court for regulating the practice and procedure of proceedings under the Act.

The 1922 Act contains no provisions dealing with recognition of foreign judgment (as opposed to their enforcement). In the ordinary course the recognition of a foreign judgment would be addressed by reference to common-law principles.[142]

15.2.2.1.1.2 *Setting aside registration*

The British and Colonial Judgments Rules, made pursuant to section 6 of the 1922 Act, are to provide (and do so provide) for service on the judgment debtor of notice of registration of a judgment. The British and Colonial Judgments Rules also enable the High Court, on the application of a judgment debtor (made by way of summons) to set aside registration of a judgment on such terms as the court sees fit.

15.2.2.1.2 Foreign Judgments (Reciprocal Enforcement) Act 1937

As noted above, although the 1937 Act was passed and came into force in 1937, Part II of the 1937 Act has been extended only to the Gilbert and Ellice Islands[143] and to the British Solomon Islands.[144] Any detailed treatment of the provisions of the 1937 Act is therefore likely to be of limited practical utility. However, a brief summary of the principal provisions of the 1937 Act is set out below.

The 1937 Act makes provision for a system of registration of foreign judgments, the purpose of which is to domesticate the foreign judgment and render it enforceable in Zambia as if it were a judgment of the Zambian court.[145]

15.2.2.1.2.1 *Procedure for registration*

The procedure for registration is as follows:[146] a judgment creditor under the foreign judgment may apply to High Court in Zambia for registration of the

---

[142] *Dicey, Morris and Collins on the Conflict of Laws* 15 ed (2012) vol 1, r 53, para 14-180.

[143] Today, Kiribati and Tuvalu.

[144] Today, the Solomon Islands.

[145] Section 4(2). As noted above, the provisions of the 1937 Act correspond very closely to legislation of the United Kingdom on which the 1937 Act was based (the Foreign Judgments (Reciprocal Enforcement) Act 1933). It is to be expected that a Zambian court will, if the opportunity ever presents itself, refer to judicial and academic authorities on the construction of these provisions of the 1933 Act when deciding questions on the construction of corresponding provisions of the 1937 Act. In particular, reference should be made to: *Dicey, Morris and Collins on the Conflict of Laws* 15 ed (2012) vol 1, paras 14R183–14-195; Briggs *Civil Jurisdiction and Judgments* 7 ed (2021) paras 35.01-35.10.

[146] Section 4.

judgment;[147] the procedure for registration is prescribed by rules of court made pursuant to section 5 of the Act and the High Court Act 1960; an application for registration 'may' be made within six years of the date of either the foreign judgment itself or the determination of any appeal or review proceedings in respect of the foreign judgment.[148]

Section 4(1)[149] makes the registration of the foreign judgment mandatory: 'The court shall, subject to proof of the prescribed matters and to other provisions of this Act, order the judgment to be registered.' These prescribed matters are set out in section 3(2)[150] of the 1937 Act; the foreign judgment must: (1) be final and conclusive; (2) be a money judgment not being a sum in respect of taxes or a fine or other penalty; and (3) it is given after the coming into force of an order extending Part II of the 1937 Act to the jurisdiction of the foreign court.

15.2.2.1.2.2 *Setting aside registration*

Section 6(1)(a)[151] of the 1937 Act provides that in certain prescribed circumstances the court *must* set aside registration of the foreign judgment.[152] These circumstances are that:

---

[147] Defined in s 2 to mean 'a judgment or order given or made by a court in any civil proceedings, or a judgment or order given or made by a court in any criminal proceedings for the payment of a sum of money in respect of compensation or damages to an injured party and includes an award in proceedings on an arbitration, if the award has in pursuance of the law in the place where it was made become enforceable in the same manner as a judgment given by a court of that place. Any such award shall, where necessary, be deemed to be the judgment of a superior court.' Were a court in Sierra Leone to be persuaded by the reasoning of the English Court of Appeal in *Strategic Technologies Pte Ltd v Procurement Bureau of the Republic of China Ministry of National Defence* [2020] EWCA Civ 1604 (David Richards, Males and Elisabeth Laing LJJ), it would likely conclude that the definition of 'foreign judgment' does not extend to a judgment granted by the court of a jurisdiction to which the Act does apply which judgment is itself based on a judgment granted by the courts of a jurisdiction to which the Act does not apply.

[148] Section 4(1). The six-year period is derived from s 2(1) of the Foreign Judgments (Reciprocal Enforcement) Act 1933. The terms of s 4(1) are not mandatory and appear to provide the court with discretion to permit registration outside the six-year period. However, the provision in the 1933 Act has been construed as imposing a temporal limit on registration: Briggs *Civil Jurisdiction and Judgments* 6 ed (2015) para 7.93. As noted elsewhere in this volume, in *Harman v Leaf* 1954 (2) SA 270 (SR), a decision under earlier Zimbabwe legislation for the reciprocal enforcement of foreign judgments which contained a one-year limit on registration subject to a discretion in the court to extend that time, dismissing an application for registration two years out of time Beadle J held that the plaintiff had failed to provide sufficient evidence that 'he has not in any way been dilatory in pressing for registration of his judgment'. It may be that the extension of the registration period from one year to six years imposes an even greater burden on an application seeking to persuade the court that time should be extended.

[149] The equivalent to s 2(1) of the 1933 Act.

[150] The equivalent to s 1(2) of the 1933 Act.

[151] The equivalent to s 4(1)(a) of the 1933 Act.

[152] The exclusionary provisions of the 1933 Act were based on the common law: 'The grounds of jurisdiction in the 1933 Act were deliberately framed so as to reproduce the rules of the common law as closely as possible' *Dicey, Morris and Collins on the Conflict of Laws* 15 ed (2012) vol 1, para 14-190.

(1) the judgment is not a judgment to which Part I of the 1937 Act applies or was registered in contravention of any previous provisions of the 1937 Act;[153] or

(2) the courts of the country of the original court had no jurisdiction in the circumstances of the case; or

(3) the judgment debtor, being the defendant in the proceedings in the original court, did not (notwithstanding that process may have been duly served on him in accordance with the law of the country of the original court) receive notice of those proceedings in sufficient time to enable him to defend the proceedings and did not appear; or

(4) the judgment was obtained by fraud;[154] or

(5) the enforcement of the judgment would be contrary to public policy in Zambia;[155] or

(6) the rights under the judgment are not vested in the person by whom the application for registration was made.

Under section 6(1)(b)[156] the judgment *may* be set aside if the court is satisfied that the matter in dispute in the proceedings in the original court had previously been the subject of a final conclusive judgment by a court having jurisdiction in the matter.

The question whether the foreign court had jurisdiction is determined exhaustively[157] by the deeming provisions of section 6(2)(a).[158] The foreign court is deemed to have had jurisdiction in the case of a judgment in an action *in personam*:

---

[153] By way of example, see *Beza Consulting Inc (Virginua USA) v Yadeta* [2020] ZMHC 112 (HC) (Sikazwe J).

[154] The equivalent to s 4(1)(a)(iv) of the 1933 Act. The rules relating to setting aside a foreign judgment obtained by fraud are comprehensively set out in *Dicey, Morris and Collins on the Conflict of Laws* 15 ed (2012) vol 1, r 50, paras 14R-137–14-145; the position in English law (*Owens Bank Ltd v Bracco* [1992] 2 AC 443 (HL) (see above)) has not been followed in certain Commonwealth jurisdictions (eg Canada in *Beals v Saldanha* [2003] 3 SCR 416, (2003) 234 DLR (4th) 1; and New South Wales in *Keele v Findley* (1991) 21 NSWLR 444 (NSWSC); but in *Close v Arnot* (unreported) 21 November 1997 (NSW), the Common Law Division distinguished *Keele v Findley* and applied the traditional English standard of fraud in respect of a foreign judgment in a case where the defendant had, for good reason, allowed foreign proceedings to go undefended).

[155] The equivalent to s 4(1)(a)(v) of the 1933 Act. In *Dicey, Morris and Collins on the Conflict of Laws* 15 ed (2012) vol 1, para 14-191, it is stated of the equivalent provisions of the 1933 Act: 'The provisions with regard to fraud and public policy are the same as the common law rules. In particular, the common law rule that a foreign judgment can be impeached for fraud even though no newly discovered evidence is produced, and even though the fraud was alleged in the foreign proceedings, applies to enforcement and recognition under the 1933 Act. In *Owens Bank Ltd v Bracco* [[1992] 2 AC 443 (HL (E))] the House of Lords held that the fraud exception in the 1920 Act was subject to the same rule, and indicated (obiter) that the same must be so under the 1933 Act.' The relevant rule is at r 51, paras 14R-152–14-158.

[156] The equivalent to s 4(1)(b) of the 1933 Act.

[157] *Société Co-opérative Sidmetal v Titan International Ltd* [1966] 1 QB 828; *Sharps Commercials Ltd v Gas Turbines Ltd* [1956] NZLR 819 (a decision on the identically worded New Zealand Act).

[158] The equivalent to s 4(2)(a) of the 1933 Act.

(1) if the judgment debtor, being a defendant in the original court, submitted to the jurisdiction of that court by voluntarily appearing in the proceedings otherwise than for the purpose of protecting, or obtaining the release of property seized, or threatened with seizure, in the proceedings or of contesting the jurisdiction of that court; or

(2) if the judgment debtor was plaintiff in, or counterclaimed in, the proceedings in the original court; or

(3) if the judgment debtor, being a defendant in the original court, had before the commencement of the proceedings agreed, in respect of the subject-matter of the proceedings, to submit to the jurisdiction of that court or of the courts of the country of that court; or

(4) if the judgment debtor, being a defendant in the original court, was at the time when the proceedings were instituted resident in, or being a body corporate had its principal place of business in, the country of that court; or

(5) if the judgment debtor, being a defendant in the original court, had an office or place of business in the country of that court and the proceedings in that court were in respect of a transaction effected through or at that office or place.

Section 6(2)(b)[159] relates to property and provides that the foreign court has jurisdiction in proceedings relating to movable or immovable property if that property was situated in the foreign country when proceedings were commenced.

Section 6(2)(c)[160] provides that in any other case the foreign court will be deemed to have had jurisdiction if the jurisdiction of the foreign court is recognised under the law of Zambia.

Section 6(3) provides that the courts of the country of the original court shall not be deemed to have had jurisdiction if the subject-matter of the proceedings was immovable property outside the jurisdiction of the original court, or the original proceedings were brought in breach of an arbitration clause (save in cases falling within section 6(2)(a)(i)–(iii) and 6(2)(c)), or the defendant was immune from suit under the rules of public international law.

---

159 The equivalent to s 4(2)(b) of the 1933 Act.

160 The equivalent to s 4(2)(c) of the 1933 Act. It remains undecided whether this provision would entitle a court to recognise a basis for the jurisdiction of the foreign court not expressly provided for in the Act but available at common law, such as the presence of the defendant in the jurisdiction of the foreign court at the time of the commencement of proceedings. The discussion of this provision in *Dicey, Morris and Collins on the Conflict of Laws* 15 ed (2012) vol 1, para 14-190, suggests that this is not the case; in *Société Co-opérative Sidmetal v Titan International Ltd* [1966] 1 QB 828, Widgery J held (at 850C–D) that an action *in personam* not within s 4(2)(a) was also excluded from s 4(2)(c): 'It seems to me that an action *in personam* does not fall within subsection (2) unless it satisfies one or other of the conditions in paragraph (a). As I read the section, no action *in personam* could fall within paragraph (c) at all because all such actions are excluded by the terms of paragraph (c).'

15.2.2.1.3 Service of Process and Execution of Judgments Act 1957

The Service of Process and Execution of Judgments Act 1957 applies only to Malawi and Zimbabwe.

The 1957 Act is intended to provide for the service in Zambia of civil or criminal process and the enforcement of civil judgments emanating from Nyasaland and Southern Rhodesia (modern-day Malawi and Zimbabwe, respectively). Part V concerns the enforcement of judgments.[161]

Subject to the few points made below, it seems that registration and enforcement under the 1957 Act is as of right and there is little or no room for the exercise of discretion by the court.

15.2.2.1.3.1 *Procedure for registration*

The procedure in the 1957 Act is as follows:[162] the judgment creditor may, within 12 months of the date of the original judgment, or later with the leave of the Zambian court,[163] register a certificate of the foreign judgment by the production of the certificate to the High Court of Zambia or a subordinate court of Zambia, depending on whether the judgment is from the foreign High Court or subordinate court; the judgment certificate is then registered in a 'Register of Zimbabwe and Malawi Judgments';[164] the court in Zambia must be satisfied that the registration of the certificate is 'reasonable and justifiable under the circumstances', although the 1957 Act gives no guidance as to what the court is meant to take into account in assessing whether registration is or is not reasonable and justifiable;[165] the judgment creditor must then, prior to execution, file an affidavit with the court in Malawi at which the certificate is registered, stating the amount for which execution is proposed and confirming that it is actually due and payable.[166]

15.2.2.1.3.2 *Setting aside registration*

The registering court may, on the application of the judgment debtor,[167] (1) stay proceedings on terms as to giving security and/or making an application to set aside the judgment, (2) grant other relief as the court deems fit. (The grounds on which the judgment may be set aside are not specified in the 1957 Act, however.)

---

[161] Defined by s 10 as 'any judgment or order whereunder a sum of money is payable, given or made by a court in any civil proceedings'. Part V also applies to an arbitration award if enforceable in the country in which it was made, but excludes a maintenance order for a man's wife or child or other dependants.

[162] Sections 11–15.

[163] Section 11(4).

[164] Section 11(2).

[165] Section 12(1).

[166] Section 13.

[167] Section 14.

15.3 Interim Remedies

15.3.1 Jurisdiction to grant interim remedies

The jurisdiction of the Zambian High Court to grant injunctions is statutory:[168]

> 'The court ... shall, within the limits and subject as in this Act mentioned, possess and exercise all the jurisdiction, powers and authorities vested in the High Court of Justice in England';

And:

> 'In every civil cause or matter which shall come in dependence in the Court, law and equity shall be administered concurrently, and the Court, in the exercise of the jurisdiction vested in it, shall have the power to grant, and shall grant, either absolutely or on such reasonable terms and conditions as shall seem just, all such remedies or reliefs whatsoever, interlocutory or final, to which any of the parties thereto may appear to be entitled in respect of any and every legal or equitable claim or defence properly brought forward by them respectively or which shall appear in such cause or matter, so that, as far as possible, all matters in controversy between the said parties may be completely and finally determined, and all multiplicity of legal proceedings concerning any of such matters avoided ...'.

15.3.2 Procedure for application

The rules governing interlocutory applications in the High Court are set out in Orders XXV ('Arrest of Defendant under section 10 of the Debtors Act'); XXVI ('Interim Attachment of Property'); XXVII ('Injunctions, etc.') and XXX ('Applications and Proceedings in Chambers and in Court').[169]

Order XXX, 'Applications and Proceedings in Chambers and in Court', provides that every application in chambers shall be made by summons to be supported by an affidavit. The summons must be in the prescribed form and must be served four clear days before the return date 'unless it shall be otherwise ordered'.[170] The court may order that time for service of an urgent application made *ex parte* be abridged and effected after the hearing in chambers. Further, Order III, rule 2, provides:

> 'Subject to any particular rules, the Court or a Judge may, in all causes and matters, make any interlocutory order which it or he considers necessary for doing justice, whether such order has been expressly asked by the person entitled to the benefit of the order or not.'

There is nothing in Order XXX or Order III preventing a court, in an appropriate case, from hearing and determining an application for an injunction prior to

---

168 High Court Act 1960, ss 9(1) and 13.

169 As amended by the High Court (Amendment) Rules 2020 (SI 58 of 2020).

170 Order XXX, r 3. Parties should also be aware of the new rules, set out in O XXX, r 3A, dealing with the filing of a skeleton argument etc.

the issuing of proceedings (subject to the usual undertaking to issue and serve proceedings forthwith).[171]

Rule 11 identifies the business to be disposed of in chambers, being matters such as applications for leave to amend pleadings and questions arising concerning the construction of a statute, but allows the court power to determine 'such other matters as a Judge may think fit to dispose of in chambers'.[172] All other matters should be dealt with in open court.

15.3.3 Interlocutory injunctions generally

As noted above, the English Law (Extent of Application) Act 1963 provides that in Zambia English common law and doctrines of equity are in force.[173] In view of this provision and the decisions of the Zambian courts referred to below, the law regarding interlocutory injunctions set out by the House of Lords in *American Cyanamid Co v Ethicon Ltd*,[174] will be applied in Zambia. In *American Cyanamid* Lord Diplock gave the lead opinion (with which the other Lords agreed) and it may be of benefit to set out briefly the principles established by this decision.

The opinion of Lord Diplock is generally taken as establishing a test comprising two elements:

(1) 'The court ... must be satisfied that the claim is not frivolous or vexatious; in other words, that there is a serious issue to be tried';[175]

'unless the material available to the court at the hearing of the application for an interlocutory injunction fails to disclose that the plaintiff has any real prospect of succeeding in his claim for a permanent injunction at the trial, the court should go on to consider whether the balance of convenience lies in favour of granting or refusing the interlocutory relief that is sought';[176]

(2) On the balance of convenience:[177]

'the governing principle is that the court should first consider whether, if the plaintiff were to succeed at the trial in establishing his right to a permanent injunction, he would be adequately compensated by an award of damages for the loss he would have sustained as a result of the defendant's continuing to do what was sought to be

---

[171] Pre-action remedies are therefore available in Zambia: O XXX, r 3, affords the court wide discretion to abridge time which is not limited to doing so after the commencement of proceedings; and the powers of the English High Court, preserved by ss 9(1) and 13 of the High Court Act 1960, include the power to grant relief in appropriate cases in advance of the issuing of proceedings.

[172] Order XXX, r 11(j).

[173] Section 2(a) and (b).

[174] [1975] AC 396 (HL (E)) (Lord Diplock, Viscount Dilhorne and Lords Cross, Salmon and Edmund-Davies).

[175] Ibid 407G.

[176] Ibid 408A–B.

[177] Ibid 408B–G.

> enjoined between the time of the application and the time of the trial. If damages in the measure recoverable at common law would be adequate remedy and the defendant would be in a financial position to pay them, no interlocutory injunction should normally be granted, however strong the plaintiff's claim appeared to be at that stage. If, on the other hand, damages would not provide an adequate remedy for the plaintiff in the event of his succeeding at the trial, the court should then consider whether, on the contrary hypothesis that the defendant were to succeed at the trial in establishing his right to do that which was sought to be enjoined, he would be adequately compensated under the plaintiff's undertaking as to damages for the loss he would have sustained by being prevented from doing so between the time of the application and the time of the trial. If damages in the measure recoverable under such an undertaking would be an adequate remedy and the plaintiff would be in a financial position to pay them, there would be no reason upon this ground to refuse an interlocutory injunction.
>
> It is where there is doubt as to the adequacy of the respective remedies in damages available to either party or to both, that the question of balance of convenience arises. It would be unwise to attempt even to list all the various matters which may need to be taken into consideration in deciding where the balance lies, let alone to suggest the relative weight to be attached to them. These will vary from case to case.
>
> Where other factors appear to be evenly balanced it is a counsel of prudence to take such measures as are calculated to preserve the status quo.'

The Supreme Court, in *Ubuchinga Investments Ltd v Teklemicael Menstab*,[178] affirmed a long line of authority that adopted and applied the *American Cyanamid* test. Chibesakunda Ag CJ stated:[179]

> 'Our view is that the principles established in *American Cyanamid* case were an attempt, not to create rigid rules for the Court but to act as a mere guideline for purposes of ensuring that these wide discretionary powers are exercised in the fairest and most reasonable manner and at the same time to achieve the ends of justice.
>
> Lord Diplock in *American Cyanamid v Ethicon* put it this way:–
>
>> "The Court no doubt, must be satisfied that the claim is not frivolous or vexatious. In other words, that there is a serious question to be tried ... unless the material available to the Court at the hearing of the application for an interlocutory injunction fails to disclose that the Plaintiff has any real prospects of succeeding in his claim ... the Court should go on to consider whether the balance of convenience lies in favour of granting or refusing the interlocutory relief that is sought."
>
> So in our view, the learned trial Judge made the right inquisition by following the three-stage test established in the *American Cyanamid* case namely, (i) a serious question to be tried; (ii) irreparable harm if relief denied; and (iii) balance of convenience or inconvenience.'

---

178 [2014] ZMSC 119 (Sup Ct) (Chibesakunda Ag CJ, Chibomba and Lisimba JJSC).

179 Ibid 19–20 of the transcript.

And:[180]

> 'Before we leave this subject, we would like to state that in as much as agree that the law is not static, we respectfully disagree with Mr. Robert that the *American Cyanamid* principles are only applicable to other applications for injunctions in the White book. To the contrary, the age-old *American Cyanamid* principles, approved in *Shell and BP Zambia Limited v Conidaris and Others*, are still good law. The passage referred to by the learned trial Judge in *Cambridge Nutrition Limited v BBC* should not be seen as discrediting the American Cyanamid principles but rather as merely setting out the exceptions. For instance, the guidelines were said to be inappropriate where the injunction would have the effect of disposing of the dispute between the parties thus having a final effect as was the case in *Cambridge Nutrition Limited v BBC* and *RJR Macdonald Inc v Canada AG* or as Lord Denning put it, where there were other special factors such as the urgent need to reach a conclusion.'

In the event, the Supreme Court dismissed the appeal.

Additionally, Order XXVII, 'Injunctions, etc.', makes provision for four types of interlocutory injunction, the grant of which is a matter for the exercise of the court's discretion. These orders are as follows: (1) to restrain waste or damage to property; (2) to order the sale of goods; (3) to detain, preserve or inspect property; and (4) to restrain a breach of contract or the commission of a tort.

Although these rules set out what a plaintiff for an order under Order XXVII is required to demonstrate, the rules do not themselves provide any guidance on the exercise of the court's discretion whether to make an order or not. In this context it should be noted that the Zambian courts are likely to be guided by the principles set out by the House of Lords in the *American Cyanamid* case (as to which, see above).

(1) To restrain waste or damage to property. Order XXVII, rule 1, provides that if a party to an action shows to the satisfaction of the court that 'any property which is in dispute in the suit is in danger of being wasted, damaged or alienated' by any party to the action, the court may order that party to refrain from the act complained of or make any other order the court considers just in the circumstances, including the appointment of a manager or receiver of the property. This is a remedy that is likely to be appropriate where the ownership of an asset is in dispute and that asset requires ongoing management, such as a rental property or commercial lease, and it is feared that a party to the proceedings (plaintiff or defendant or third party) is acting in such a way as to effect adversely the value of the asset.[181]

---

[180] Ibid pp 24–5 of the transcript.

[181] In *Standard Bank Ltd v Brocks* [1972] ZR 306 (H Ct) (Doyle CJ), the High Court refused an application under O XXVII, r 1, brought by a bank against an alleged debtor seeking to restrain him from drawing money from a sum standing to his credit with the Ministry of Finance. The court held (at 307:1–7) that the

(2) To order the sale of goods. Rule 2 empowers the court to make an order for the sale of 'any goods, wares or merchandise, the right to which is in dispute in the suit, which may be of a perishable nature, or likely to depreciate from keeping, or for which, or for any other just and sufficient reason it may be desirable to have sold at once'. Typically, this a remedy which will be sought in relation to goods, particularly fresh produce, landed at a port or airport, where there is a dispute as to ownership of the produce.

(3) To detain, preserve or inspect property. Rule 3 makes provision for the detention, preservation or inspection of 'any property being the subject of such suit', or all three purposes, and the court may authorise any person to enter premises or property in the possession of any party to the action for any of the three purposes or to make observations or perform experiments for the purpose of obtaining full information or evidence. The words 'property being the subject of such suit' preclude the rule from being used to support an application for *Anton Piller* relief (as to which, see below). This form of order may be used, for example, where the quality of goods delivered in purported performance of a contract is in issue and the plaintiff or defendant (depending in whose possession the goods are) wishes to take a sample of the goods for testing.

(4) To restrain a breach of contract or the commission of a tort. Rule 4 refers only to an application by the plaintiff. This form of injunction is self-explanatory and is what was formerly referred to as a *quia timet* injunction. The requirements for such an injunction were set out in a decision of the Chancery Division of the English High Court in *Fletcher v Bealey*:[182]

> 'I do not think, therefore, that I shall be very far wrong if I lay it down that there are at least two necessary ingredients for a *quia timet* action. There must, if no actual damage is proved, be proof of imminent danger, and there must also be proof that the apprehended damage will, if it comes, be very substantial. I should almost say it must be proved that it will be irreparable, because, if the danger is not proved to be so imminent that no one can doubt that, if the remedy is delayed, the damage will be suffered, I think it must be shewn that, if the damage does occur at any time, it will come in such a way and under such circumstances that it will be impossible for the Plaintiff to protect himself against it if relief is denied to him in a *quia timet* action.'

---

sum standing to his credit was not 'property in dispute' within r 1, because there was no doubt it belonged to the defendant, albeit that the plaintiff hoped it would be paid over to it if it was successful in the dispute.

[182] (1885) 28 Ch D 688, *per* Pearson J at 698.

Thus, what is required is proof: (1) of imminent danger of damage; (2) that the damage will be irreparable; (3) that the injunction is necessary to protect the plaintiff. These requirements will today be read alongside the *American Cyanamid* test (as to which, see above).

15.3.4 Freezing orders

The freezing order, made by way of injunction, is a form of anti-dissipation of assets injunction that operates *in personam*. This type of order is known to Zambian law. The basis for granting a freezing order (which may also be known as *Mareva* relief, so named after the leading English case on the subject, as to which see further below) is the English Law (Extent of Application) Act 1963 which provides that in Zambia English common law and doctrines of equity are in force.[183]

In *Costain Simamba v Admac-Carmichael Ltd*,[184] the plaintiff sought a freezing injunction to freeze the defendants' assets both within and outside the jurisdiction and to restrain them from dealing with those assets pending trial of the claim. The plaintiff was engaged by the first defendant through the agency of the second defendant to act as a debt collector to renegotiate a contract entered into between the first defendant and the Ministry of Communications and Transport for the delivery by the first defendant of certain fire tenders which had been part performed by the first defendant. The plaintiff's claim was for payment due under the contract with the defendants. In dismissing the application the court did not make any adverse observation on the terms of the order seeking to freeze the defendants' assets outside the jurisdiction.

The court cited the *Mareva* case[185] and quoted from the judgment of Lord Denning MR, concluding:

> 'Two ingredients for a *Mareva* injunction immediately stand out from that case. First, there must be a debt due and owing. Second, there must exist a danger that the debtor may dissipate or dispose of his assets so as to defeat any judgment the Court may grant in favour of the Plaintiff.'

The court found that there was no evidence that any sums were about to be paid to the defendants by the ministry or that the defendants were intending to dissipate their assets. In this regard, the court also approved a passage quoted from the judgment of Lawton LJ in *Third Chandris Shipping Corp v Unimarine SA*,[186] where it was stated:[187]

---

[183] Section 2(a) and (b).

[184] [2011] ZMHC 7 (H Ct (Comm)) (Kajimanga J).

[185] [1980] 1 All ER 213 (CA) (Lord Denning MR, Roskill and Ormrod LJJ)

[186] [1979] 2 All ER 972 (CA) (Lord Denning MR, Lawton and Cumming-Bruce LJJ).

[187] Ibid 987b–f.

> 'The mere fact that a defendant having assets within the jurisdiction of the Commercial Court is a foreigner or a foreign corporation cannot, in my judgment, by itself justify the granting of a *Mareva* Injunction.
>
> There must be facts from which the Commercial Court, like a prudent, sensible commercial man, can properly infer a danger of default if assets are removed from the jurisdiction ... What they have to do is to find out all they can about the party with whom they are dealing, including origins, business domicile, length of time in business, assets and the like, and they will probably be wary of the appearances of wealth which are not backed by known assets. In my judgment the Commercial Court should approve applications for *Mareva* injunctions in the same way. Its judges have special experience of commercial cases and they can be expected to identify likely debt dodgers as well as, probably better than, most businessmen. They should not expect to be given proof of previous defaults or specific incidents of commercial malpractice. Further they should remember that affidavits asserting belief in, or the fear of, default have no probative value unless the sources and grounds thereof are set out: see RSC Order 4, r.5 (2). In judgment an affidavit in support of a *Mareva* injunction should give enough particulars of the Plaintiff's case to enable the Court to assess its strength and should set out what enquiries have been made about the defendant's business and what information has been revealed, including that relating to its size, origins, business domicile, the location of its known assets and the circumstances in which the dispute has arisen. These facts should enable a commercial judge to infer whether there is likely to be any real risk of default.
>
> Default is most unlikely if the defendant is a long-established, well-known foreign corporation or is known to have substantial assets in countries where English judgments can easily be enforced under the Foreign Judgment (Reciprocal Enforcement) Act 1933 or otherwise. But if nothing can be found out about the defendant, that by itself may be enough to justify a *Mareva* injunction.'

It should be observed that the plaintiff's claim need not necessarily be for a debt but can be for damages.

On the application there is a duty to give full and frank disclosure, although it appears that the practice is not to require a cross-undertaking as to damages as an express condition of the making of the order.[188]

[188] *Elmar Engineering Ltd v Allegra Mining Zambia Ltd* [2011] ZMHC 26 (H Ct (Comm)) (Mutuna J). Here the order as set out by the judge (at p 2 of the transcript) and endorsed on the summons, did not contain a cross-undertaking and this attracted no adverse comment from the judge and no adverse submission by the defendant's counsel. The judge cited with apparent approval the submission of the defendant's counsel relying on English authorities confirming that the duty of full and frank disclosure applies to such applications (at p 4 of the transcript). See too, *Adriatic Transport Ltd v Fratelli Loci Srl Ltd* [2012] ZMHC 77 (H Ct (Comm)) (Mutuna J).

15.3.5 Search and seize orders

The *Anton Piller* order (named after the leading English authority on the subject, as to which, see further below) is a search and seize order that operates *in personam* as against the defendant, the object of which is to preserve evidence which will probably otherwise be destroyed by the defendant. This type of order is known to Zambian law, although examples of its use are rare. The basis for granting *Anton Piller* relief is the English Law (Extent of Application) Act 1963 which provides that in Zambia English common law and doctrines of equity are in force.[189]

In *Hot FM Ltd v Collins Kabwe Changwe*,[190] the court made an *Anton Piller* order in a copyright case which required the defendants to permit the plaintiff to enter their premises and inspect and search certain of the defendant's electronic record systems 'for the retrieval and preservation of the evidence relating to the copyright infringement complained of in these proceedings'.[191] It appears to be the practice that a cross-undertaking as to damages is not required by the court in making the order and that no independent lawyer is involved in executing the order. However, the decision was on the merits of the case at trial and the report contains no statement of the principles to be applied or practice to be followed on an application for *Anton Piller* relief; accordingly, a brief statement of those principles and practice is set out below.

The pre-conditions for the grant of *Anton Piller* relief were set out by Ormrod LJ in the *Anton Piller* case:[192]

(1) 'an extremely strong *prima facie* case';

(2) 'the damage, potential or actual, must be very serious for the plaintiff';

(3) 'clear evidence that the defendants have in their possession incriminating documents or things, and that there is a real possibility that they may destroy such material before any application *inter partes* can be made'.

And subsequent practice has imposed further conditions:

(4) The practice in England is that a court making an *Anton Piller* order will require as a condition for the making of the order an undertaking as to damages to be given by the plaintiff.[193]

(5) Again, the practice in England is that a court making an *Anton Piller* order will impose conditions on the order such as are provided for in the English Civil Procedure Rules, for example, the attendance of an independent supervising solicitor.[194]

---

[189] Section 2(a) and (b).

[190] [2012] ZMHC 87 (H Ct (Comm)) (Kajimanga J).

[191] Para (2) of the order made: p 2 of the transcript.

[192] *Anton Piller KG v Manufacturing Processes Ltd* [1976] Ch 55 (CA) (Lord Denning MR, Ormrod and Shaw LJJ), *per* Ormrod LJ at 62A.

[193] See the Kenyan authority: *Mumias Sugar Co Ltd v Option Two* [2014] eKLR (H Ct) (Gikonyo J) [27].

[194] See the English CPR, Pt 25, PD 25A, para 7.

15.3.6 Third-party disclosure orders

There is no authority on the question whether a Zambian court may, apart from the established post-issuing of proceedings and pre-trial procedures whereby a third party may be served with a witness summons requiring his attendance at court in order to give evidence and/or to produce documents, order a person not a party to the proceedings to give disclosure of information.

Such a power is available to the English courts in the limited form of a *Norwich Pharmacal* order,[195] whereby an innocent third party caught up in a tort may be ordered to disclose the name or other identity of the tortfeasor. Lord Reid stated the principle as follows:[196]

> 'if through no fault of his own a person gets mixed up in the tortious acts of others so as to facilitate their wrong-doing he may incur no personal liability but he comes under a duty to assist the person who has been wronged by giving him full information and disclosing the identity of the wrongdoers. I do not think that it matters whether he became so mixed up by voluntary action on his part or because it was his duty to do what he did. It may be that if this causes him expense the person seeking the information ought to reimburse him. But justice requires that he should co-operate in righting the wrong if he unwittingly facilitated its perpetration.'

The juridical basis for developing this form of relief would be, again, the English Law (Extent of Application) Act 1963 which provides that in Zambia English common law and doctrines of equity are in force.[197]

15.3.7 Anti-suit injunctions

An anti-suit injunction is an order restraining the injunction defendant from either commencing or continuing proceedings outside Zambia in breach of a legal or equitable right on the part of the injunction plaintiff not to pursue litigation outside Zambia or, conversely, restraining the injunction defendant from commencing or continuing proceedings inside Zambia in breach of a legal or equitable right on the part of the injunction plaintiff to have the dispute between the parties litigated in a jurisdiction other than Zambia.[198]

---

[195] *Norwich Pharmacal Co v Customs & Excise Comrs* [1974] AC 133 (HL(E)) (Lords Reid and Morris, Viscount Dilhorne and Lords Cross and Kilbrandon).

[196] Ibid 175B–C.

[197] Section 2(a) and (b).

[198] In similar vein, an anti-anti-suit injunction is an order restraining the injunction defendant from commencing or continuing proceedings to restrain the injunction plaintiff from applying to restrain the injunction defendant from commencing or continuing proceedings. The leading works on this topic are: Raphael *The Anti-Suit Injunction* 2 ed (2019) and Briggs *Civil Jurisdiction and Judgments* 7 ed (2021) ch 28. It is also conceptually possible to obtain similar relief in the context of arbitration but such relief is outside the scope of this work.

There is no reported judicial authority in Zambia on whether or not an anti-suit injunction is a remedy available to the courts in Zambia. However, as noted at section 15.3.1 above, the jurisdiction of the High Court to grant injunctions is statutory and, in exercising it, the court 'shall have the power to grant, and shall grant, either absolutely or on such reasonable terms and conditions as shall seem just, all such remedies or reliefs whatsoever, interlocutory or final, to which any of the parties thereto may appear to be entitled'.

Given, first, that the Zambian High Court shall, within the limits of and save as otherwise stated within the High Court Act 1960, possess and exercise all the jurisdiction, powers and authorities vested in the High Court of Justice in England and, second, the similarity between the statutory basis on which the Zambian High Court may grant interim relief and that on which the English High Court[199] may grant interim relief,[200] it is to be anticipated that a court in Zambia before which an application is brought for an anti-suit injunction will have regard to the English authorities in setting out the principles upon which an anti-suit injunction may be granted in Zambia. Set out below, in summary, are the principles of English law governing the grant of an anti-suit injunction.

The court must have personal jurisdiction over the injunction defendant. The court may be seised either by service on the defendant within the jurisdiction or service out of the jurisdiction with the leave of the court.[201]

The injunction plaintiff must assert a cause of action for relief. Usually, the injunction plaintiff will contend that the injunction defendant is committing a wrong by bringing or proposing to bring proceedings in a foreign court. This will require the plaintiff to characterise the conduct of the defendant as the breach of a legal or equitable right.

A legal right may, and often will, be based on a right not to be sued in a foreign jurisdiction arising out of an exclusive jurisdiction clause in favour of the courts of Zambia. An equitable right may be the right not to be sued in a foreign jurisdiction and may be the corollary of an equitable wrong which is that it is oppressive and vexatious and therefore unconscionable for the injunction defendant to commence or continue proceedings against the injunction plaintiff in a foreign jurisdiction.

The prime example of a cause of action based on a legal right not to be sued in a foreign jurisdiction is where the parties have agreed expressly that the courts

---

199 The English High Court may grant interim relief where it appears 'just and convenient' to do so: s 37 Senior Courts Act 1981.

200 It is worth noting that the High Court of South Africa in *Vedanta Resources Holdings Ltd v ZCCM Investment Holdings plc* 2019 JDR 1425 (GJ) paras [11], [54] and [56] (Adams J) and the High Court of Nigeria in *Zenith Global Merchant Ltd v Zhongfu International Investment (Nig) FZE* (2017) All FWLR 1837 at 1924 (Akinyemi J) have also referred to English principles in a similar context.

201 The substantive law and procedure for which in Zambia has been set out above.

of Zambia should have exclusive jurisdiction over disputes arising out of the contract (which can be a substantive contract or a settlement agreement) between them.[202] In such a case proof of the underlying cause of action is likely to be a sufficient condition for the grant of the relief and that good reason would need to be shown why the discretion to order an injunction should not be exercised.[203]

The principal example of a cause of action based on an equitable wrong is where proceedings brought abroad by the defendant are oppressive and vexatious. An example of such conduct is illustrated by the decision of the Privy Council in *SNI Aerospatiale v Lee Kui Jak*,[204] where a resident of Brunei had been killed in a helicopter crash and his widow (and her brother-in-law, as co-administrator of his estate), the respondent plaintiffs in the appeal to the Privy Council, had commenced proceedings in Brunei and had subsequently been persuaded to sue in Texas instead. The appellant defendant applied for an anti-suit injunction restraining the plaintiffs from proceeding against it in Texas. The Privy Council allowed the defendant's appeal, held that an injunction ought to be granted restraining the respondents from proceeding in Texas and remitted the matter to the Brunei courts.

Transposing the findings of the Privy Council to Zambia, it was held that an anti-suit injunction would be granted if: (1) pursuit of the foreign proceedings is vexatious or oppressive; (2) Zambia is the natural forum for the resolution of the dispute; and (3) the injunction does not deprive the defendant of advantages in the foreign jurisdiction of which it would be unjust to deprive him.[205]

Other examples of equitable wrongs which may attract an anti-suit injunction are: undermining the jurisdiction of the Zambian court;[206] vexatious conduct

---

[202] The contract may be a substantive contract or a settlement agreement and the dispute resolution provisions may be exclusively in favour of the courts of Zambia or may be in favour of arbitration: *British Airways Board v Laker Airways Ltd* [1985] AC 58 (HL (E)) (Lords Diplock, Fraser, Scarman, Roskill & Brightman), *per* Lord Diplock at 81C–E.

[203] *The Angelic Grace* [1995] 1 Lloyd's Rep 87 (CA) (Neill, Leggatt and Millett LJJ), *per* Millett LJ at 96, col 2, and Neill LJ at 97, col 1; *Donohue v Armco Inc* [2000] 1 Lloyd's Rep 579 (CA) (Stuart-Smith, Brooke and Sedley LJJ), where it was stated that 'strong reasons' (*per* Stuart-Smith LJ at para 35) or 'strong cause' (*per* Brooke LJ at paras 59 and 60) would be required to deny an injunction.

[204] [1987] AC 871 (PC (Brunei)) (Lords Keith, Griffiths, MacKay and Goff and Sir John Megaw).

[205] Lord Goff (giving the opinion of the Privy Council) 896F–H. That the court to which the application is made should be the natural forum for the resolution of the dispute was repeated by the House of Lords in *Airbus Industrie GIE v Patel* [1999] 1 AC 119 (HL (E)) (Lords Goff, Slynn, Steyn, Clyde & Hutton), *per* Lord Goff (with whom the other Lords agreed) 138G–H and 140H–141B.

[206] For example, by commencing bankruptcy proceedings outside the jurisdiction when such proceedings are in progress in Zambia: *SNI Aerospatiale v Lee Kui Jak* [1987] AC 871, *per* Lord Goff at 892G–893B.

by relying on foreign procedural laws;[207] wrongfully undermining a Zambian judgment;[208] or enforcement of a foreign judgment wrongfully obtained.[209]

15.3.8 Other interlocutory relief

15.3.8.1 *Arrest of the person*

Order XXV, 'Arrest of Defendant under section 10 of the Debtors Act', makes provision for the enforcement of section 10 of the Debtors Act 1938.[210] Section 10 of the 1938 Act provides:

> 'Where the plaintiff in any action before the High Court or any subordinate court proves at any time before final judgment by evidence on oath to the satisfaction of the court that he has good [sic] cause of action against the defendant to the amount of twenty kwacha or upwards, and that there is probable cause for believing that the defendant is about to quit Zambia unless he be apprehended and that—
>
> *(a)* the absence of the defendant from Zambia will materially prejudice the plaintiff in the prosecution of his action or in his obtaining satisfaction therein; or
>
> *(b)* the defendant has disposed of or removed out of Zambia his property or any part thereof and the execution or order will thereby be obstructed or delayed;
>
> Such court may, in the prescribed manner, order such defendant to be arrested and imprisoned for a period not exceeding six months unless and until he has sooner given the prescribed security not exceeding the amount claimed in the action that he will not leave Zambia without the leave of the court:
>
> Provided that—
>
> (i) the court may release the defendant at any time on such terms as may seem just and, in any event, no such defendant shall be determined in custody after the date of final judgment;
>
> (ii) any order made by a subordinate court of the second or third class shall be reported forthwith to the High Court which shall have full power, with or without argument, to reverse or vary such order.'

Order XXV contains the detailed provisions regulating the use of section 10 of the 1938 Act. In summary, the plaintiff must apply *ex parte* and on affidavit; the defendant may apply at any time to be discharged from custody and at any time

[207] By seeking to depose witnesses in the USA where those witnesses would be subject to cross-examination in proceedings in Zambia, for example: *Omega Group Holdings Ltd v Kozeny* [2002] CLC 132.

[208] By commencing proceedings outside the jurisdiction for declaratory relief designed to frustrate the enforcement of a Zambian judgment in that jurisdiction: *Masri v Consolidated Contractors International (UK) Ltd (No 3)* [2009] QB 503 (CA).

[209] Where the foreign judgment was obtained through fraud and perjury: *Ellerman Lines Ltd v Read* [1928] 2 KB 144 (CA), *per* Scrutton LJ at 152–3.

[210] Act 12 of 1938 (now Cap 77 of the Laws of the Republic of Zambia 1995).

provide security for the plaintiff's claim in order to secure his release; the plaintiff must pay the costs of the arrest and the costs of the defendant's subsistence in prison, which latter costs are fixed by the judge; such costs are costs in the cause.

On its face, the section 10/Order XXV procedure is a harsh one: it permits the arrest of a person, before judgment is entered and, potentially, before the proceedings have even got underway properly, on evidence that: (i) the plaintiff may be 'materially prejudiced' by the defendant's absence from Zambia (as to which test there is no guidance); and/or (2) that the defendant has removed his property from Zambia and that the execution of judgment will be obstructed or delayed as a result (which self-evidently it will); and (3) that the plaintiff has a 'good cause of action'.

There is no guidance in the Act or the Rules of the High Court as to what factors the court should take into account in the exercise of its discretion whether to make an order under Order XXV. Given the English Law (Extent of Application) Act 1963 which provides that in Zambia, English common law and doctrines of equity are in force,[211] it is likely that the exercise of the discretion will be regulated by the principles governing the grant of interlocutory injunctions as set out by the House of Lords in the *American Cyanamid* decision (as to which, see above).

15.3.8.2 *Interim attachment of property*

Order XXVI, 'Interim Attachment of Property', provides that in any case where the value exceeds 500 kwacha,[212] if the defendant is about to dispose of his property or part of his property or remove his property from the jurisdiction with intent to obstruct or delay the execution of any decree that may be passed against him, the plaintiff may apply to the court, 'either at the time of the institution of the suit, or at any time thereafter until final judgment', to require the defendant to give sufficient security to satisfy any decree that may be made against the defendant and, if the defendant fails to give security, to order that the defendant's property or any part of it shall be attached until further order.[213]

---

[211] Section 2(a) and (b).

[212] As amended by the High Court (Amendment) Rules 2020. The amendment is not easy to follow, however, for, by it, it was intended that the words 'five hundred thousand' be deleted from O XXVI, r 1 and be replaced with the words 'five hundred'. Problematically, however, it appears that the words 'five hundred thousand' did not form part of r 1 prior to its amendment; prior to amendment, r 1 stated: 'If the defendant, in any suit for an amount or value of *fifty thousand kwacha* or upwards' (emphasis added). Accordingly, there is some residual doubt as to whether 'five hundred' is the correct figure for the purposes of O XXVI, r 1.

[213] Order XXVI, r 1 and see generally *GDC Logistics Zambia Limited v Kanyata* [2017] ZMSC 40 (SC) (Mambilima CJ, Kaoma and Kajimanga JJSC).

The application must specify the property to be attached and the plaintiff must declare that to the best of his information and belief the defendant is about to dispose of or remove his property with the requisite intent.[214]

If the court is satisfied that the plaintiff has discharged the burden of proof on the matters prescribed in the Order, the court may make one of four orders:[215] (1) that the defendant provide security for the plaintiff's claim; (2) that the defendant produce and place at the disposal of the court the relevant property or the value of the property sufficient to meet the plaintiff's claim; (3) that the defendant should attend and show cause why he should not be ordered to provide security (an order *nisi*);[216] (4) that the property be attached until further order.

If the defendant's property is attached, it is provided that this does not affect the rights of third parties.[217]

Order XXVI makes no express provision for the giving of an undertaking as to damages by the plaintiff in the event that the defendant suffers loss as a result of an order made under this Order and the plaintiff does not recover at judgment the sum on the basis of which the Order was made or a lesser sum.[218] As a matter of practice, it would be desirable were the court to require a plaintiff to give such an undertaking so as to protect the legitimate interests of the defendant against whom, at the date of the application, no judgment has been entered.

This interlocutory remedy should be distinguished from a *Mareva* injunction. The former operates to provide security for the plaintiff's claim and is a proprietary remedy (subject, as mentioned above, to the rights of third parties), whereas the latter operates only *in personam* over the defendant.

In *National Airports Corp Ltd v Mines Air Services Ltd*,[219] the court confirmed that the time at which to make an application under Order XXVI was between issuing proceedings and final judgment and for this reason the plaintiff's application failed because a consent judgment had previously been entered against the defendant. The judge went on to consider the requirements under Order XXVI and found that there were two: first,[220] 'there must be a threat or intention on the part of the Defendant to dispose of his assets in order to obstruct or delay execution of any judgment'; and second,[221] before making the application under Order XXVI, the

[214] Order XXVI, r 2.

[215] Order XXVI, r 3.

[216] If the defendant is ordered to and fails to show cause, then the court may direct that the property specified in the application be attached: r 4.

[217] Order XXVI, r 5.

[218] Contrast the position under O XXVII, r 5.

[219] [2011] 2 ZR 180 (H Ct) (Mutuna J).

[220] Ibid 183:25–184:20.

[221] Ibid 184:21–185:2.

plaintiff must have asked the defendant to provide security and only when the defendant fails to do may the plaintiff make an application under Order XXVI.

The first requirement was held not to have been satisfied because the evidence the plaintiff relied on was that the defendant was in financial difficulties and had repainted certain of the vehicles in its fleet, neither of which amounted to evidence of intent as required.

The second requirement the judge derived from the wording of Order XXVI, rule 1, that 'the plaintiff may apply to the court or a judge ... to call upon the defendant to furnish sufficient security ...'. As a matter of ordinary English, it is difficult to read into these words a requirement that before making an application the plaintiff should call upon the defendant to provide security. It is submitted, therefore, that the High Court in *Qinhgai v Kingphar Co (Zambia) Ltd*[222] was on much firmer ground when it, without referring to the judgment in *National Airports Corp Ltd*, determined that, before the interim order for attachment could be made, the plaintiff ought to make an application to the court for the defendant to furnish security; a plaintiff was not required directly to request security from the defendant.

[222] [2020] ZHHC 244 (H Ct) (Mbewe J).

Chapter 16

ZIMBABWE

16.1 Jurisdiction

The High Court Act 1981 ('the 1981 Act')[1] makes provision for the jurisdiction, powers, practice and procedures of the High Court.

Section 13 of the 1981 Act concerns the original jurisdiction[2] of the High Court and provides: 'Subject to this Act and any other law, the High Court shall have full original civil jurisdiction over all persons and over all matters within Zimbabwe.'[3] This provision (as with similar provisions in South Africa and earlier Zimbabwe legislation) has been construed as including jurisdiction in cases where the action is founded on a contract entered into, to be performed and breached within the jurisdiction or where the action concerns property situated within the jurisdiction or a tort committed within the jurisdiction.[4]

---

[1] Act 29 of 1981. The domestic citation of this provision is 'High Court Act [chapter 7:06]'. In this regard, the reader is referred to the 'Note on the citation of statutory material in this work', which appears at the end of the 'List of Statutory Material Cited' at the beginning of this work.

[2] The High Court also has a review jurisdiction over 'all proceedings and decisions of all inferior courts of justice, tribunals and administrative authorities within Zimbabwe' (s 26 of the 1981 Act) as well as appellate civil and criminal jurisdiction where that is conferred by statute (ss 30 and 34 of the 1981 Act).

[3] With specified minor exceptions (eg an appeal from an order allowing an extension of time for appealing (s 43(2)(a) of the 1981 Act) or against a refusal of summary judgment (s 43(2)(b) of the 1981 Act)), an appeal lies as of right from any judgment (rendered in the exercise of its original or appellate jurisdiction) of the High Court in civil cases to the Supreme Court: s 43(1) of the 1981 Act. As a matter of construction, it is likely that such right extends to interlocutory orders and judgments where the liberty of the subject or the custody of minors is concerned, where an interdict is granted or refused and in the case of an order on a special case stated under any law relating to arbitration. This seems to be the intent behind the exception in respect of these cases to the provisions of s 43(2)(d) of the 1981 Act, which requires leave for an appeal from an interlocutory order or judgment. In the case of an interlocutory order or judgment, an appeal to the Supreme Court may be made with the leave of the judge making the order or giving the judgment or, if leave is refused, with the leave of a judge of the Supreme Court: s 43(2)(d) of the 1981 Act.

[4] *Mackay v Hepker* [1941] SR 33, *per* Hudson J at 35 (referring to s 2 of the High Court Act (ch 8)).

The High Court Rules 1971 ('the High Court Rules')[5] of particular relevance to questions relating to jurisdiction, the enforcement of judgments and interim remedies are referred to below.

16.1.1 Commencing proceedings where the defendant is within the jurisdiction

Actions are commenced by summons addressed to the defendant and signed by the court registrar who issued it.[6] The summons must contain the full name and residential or business address of the defendant and the full name and address for service of the plaintiff together with a statement of the nature, extent and grounds of the cause of action and the relief or remedies sought and the date of the issue of the summons.[7]

Service of the summons is effected by the sheriff or his deputy[8] and, in the case of a claim for an order affecting the liberty of a person, service of process[9] must be 'by delivery of a copy thereof to that person personally'.[10] In cases not involving the liberty of a person, service of process may be, inter alia: by way of personal delivery to the person concerned; delivery to a responsible person at the residence or place of business or employment of the person; or delivery to the person's legal practitioner.[11] Provision is also made for service by registered post where the person to be served has consented to such a method or where the registrar has directed the sheriff or his deputy that service may be effected by registered post.[12]

The defendant then has ten days, exclusive of the day of service,[13] to enter an appearance to defend.

---

5 Government Notice 1047/71. The High Court Rules were originally pursuant to s 57 of the High Court Act 1964. An equivalent power to make rules of court is conferred upon the Chief Justice and the Judge President by s 56 of the High Court Act 1981. This power may be exercised after consultation with a committee appointed by the Chief Justice.

6 Order 3, r 9, 'Every action shall be commenced by a summons ...'.

7 Order 3, r 11.

8 Order 5, r 37.

9 Defined as 'any document which is required to be served on any person in terms of these rules' (O 5, r 35(1)).

10 Order 5, r 39(1).

11 Order 5, r 39(2), which also contains provisions for service on a body corporate, a partnership and an association.

12 Order 5, r 42(2).

13 Order 3, r 17; exclusive of the day of service of the summons. The document in which the plaintiff's claim is set out in full is referred to as a declaration which is served with the summons or at any time after issue of the summons (O 17, rr 109 and 113). The defendant's answer to the plaintiff's declaration is referred to as the defendant's plea (O 18, r 116). The defendant may at the same time advance any claim he has against the plaintiff by way of a claim in reconvention, ie what English lawyers would refer to as a 'counterclaim' (O 18, r 120). The defendant has ten days from the date of the service of the declaration to serve the

16.1.2 Commencing proceedings where the defendant is outside the jurisdiction

A plaintiff who wishes to commence proceedings against a defendant who is not in Zimbabwe will need to serve process on that defendant by way of edictal citation; where the plaintiff seeks so to serve the defendant the leave of the court is required.[14] An application for leave is made pursuant to Order 32 of the High Court Rules which provides that all applications (other than oral applications in the course of a hearing) shall be made either:[15] (1) as a court application, that is, in writing to the court on notice to all interested parties; or (2) as a chamber application (subject to the qualification in respect of neighbouring countries below). A chamber application, however, shall not be made unless one of the exceptions set out in Order 32, rule 226(2)(a)–(e) is satisfied. These include urgent applications or applications where there are special circumstances which are set out in the application justifying the chamber application.

If, however, the plaintiff seeks to serve a summons in the Republic of South Africa, Namibia, Lesotho, Eswatini or Botswana, then the application must be made by way of a chamber application.[16]

In either case the application must set out: (1) the facts on which the cause of action is based; (2) the grounds on which the court has jurisdiction to entertain the claim; and (3) the manner of service which the court or judge is asked to authorise.[17]

On such an application the court may make such order as to the manner of service as seems proper and necessary and shall make an order regarding the time within which the notice of intention to defend or any other step is to be taken by the defendant.[18]

---

plea. However, a different rule applies where the plaintiff has served the declaration with the summons: in these circumstances, the defendant has an additional 10-day period (from the end of the usual 10-day period allowed) in order to enter an appearance (O 18, r 119). The plaintiff may reply to the defendant's plea by means of a replication which is to be filed 12 days after the service of the plea (O 19, r 125). The plaintiff's answer to any claim in reconvention is referred to as the 'plaintiff's plea – claim in reconvention' (O 19, r 127). The defendant may respond to the plaintiff's plea by means of a 'defendant's replication – claim in reconvention' (O 19, r 128). The plaintiff and/or defendant may respond to a replication by way of rejoinder in the applicable proceedings.

[14] Order 6, r 44(1), edictal citation.

[15] Order 32, r 226(1); all applications are made either as a 'court application' or a 'chamber application'.

[16] Order 6, r 45(1).

[17] Order 6, rr 44(3) and 45(3).

[18] Order 6, r 44(4). Order 6, r 45 contains a parallel provision regarding the manner of service (r 45(4)) but no parallel provision regarding the making of an order for the time within which the notice of intention to defend should be lodged. It is likely that this omission can be catered for under the court's inherent power to control its own procedures: see the Constitution, s 176.

16.1.2.1 Incolae *and* peregrini

As with other countries which have a Roman-Dutch legal system, a court's power to take jurisdiction over a defendant rests on the character of that defendant. To that end, it is necessary to distinguish between an *incola* and a *peregrinus*.

It would appear that the Zimbabwean courts look at a person's residence in order to determine whether that person is an *incola* or *peregrinus*. By way of example, in *African Distillers v Zietkiewicz*,[19] the plaintiff was an *incola*, a resident of Zimbabwe, who commenced proceedings for damages for breaches of a contract made and to be performed in Zimbabwe against three defendants, all residents of the Republic of South Africa. The defendants (two of the three who had entered an appearance) objected to the Zimbabwean court assuming jurisdiction over them on the basis that they were resident in South Africa and not in Zimbabwe, had no property in Zimbabwe which could be attached by the plaintiff and they had not been arrested by the plaintiff. Beck J determined[20] that, because all of the defendants were residents of South Africa, they were *peregrini* as far as the Zimbabwean court was concerned and held that the court had no jurisdiction to entertain the claim against the defendants.

In *Grobler v Boshoff*,[21] the defendant/respondent, who had previously been living in Zimbabwe for a several years, had moved to the Republic of South Africa just after proceedings had been commenced and served on her, but before the plaintiff/petitioner in the case was able serve[22] an order attaching goods belonging to the defendant remaining in Zimbabwe *ad confirmandam jurisdictionem*. The petitioner contended that, although the defendant was an *incola* at the time the summons was issued and served, she had by that time formed the intention to leave Zimbabwe for South Africa and did so very shortly afterwards and that, 'the respondent could not be regarded as an *incola* in the practical sense. An attachment is therefore necessary to confirm, if not to found, jurisdiction.'[23] The defendant submitted that she was an *incola* at the time of service of the proceedings and that, therefore, an attachment was unavailable to the plaintiff. The court held[24] that an attachment to found or confirm the jurisdiction was necessary in the case and therefore, by necessary implication, that the relevant time to assess whether the respondent to an attachment was an *incola* or a *peregrinus* was the time at which the rule *nisi* was sought to be served. It appeared not to be in issue in the case that the defendant left Zimbabwe to settle in South Africa with some (unspecified) degree of permanence.

---

[19] 1980 ZLR 135 (HC) (Beck J).

[20] Ibid 136A.

[21] 1988 (2) ZLR 447 (HC) (Muchechetere J).

[22] It is unclear from the report whether the defendant had left Zimbabwe for South Africa at the time the application was made.

[23] At 450B.

[24] At 450B–C.

From the above two cases, it appears that in Zimbabwe, as in Namibia,[25] the determining factor as to whether or not a person is a *peregrinus* is their place of residence.[26] A person's nationality is irrelevant and their domicile is not considered in either case.

16.1.2.2 *The jurisdictional significance of attachment*

It still seems to be an open question in Zimbabwean law as to the true nature of the relationship between the rules governing the attachment of property and the existence of a *ratio jurisdictionis*. Specifically, the question remains whether arrest or attachment is sufficient to found the court's jurisdiction over a claim by an *incola* against a *peregrinus* or whether a *ratio jurisdictionis* is also required in that situation in order to confirm the court's jurisdiction.

While the authors deal with the various circumstances in which attachment of property may carry significance as a matter of Zimbabwean law, it is useful, at this point, to set out a brief overview of the position. Hence, from the authorities,[27] a distinction appears to be drawn between situations where attachment of property alone suffices to found the jurisdiction of the Zimbabwean court (attachment *ad fundandam jurisdictionem*) and situations where both a *ratio jurisdictionis* (ie a cause of action accruing within the jurisdiction of the court)[28] and an attachment to confirm the jurisdiction of the court (attachment *ad confirmandam jurisdictionem*) are required. The mere existence of a *ratio jurisdictionis* will not by itself confer jurisdiction upon the Zimbabwean court.

The jurisdiction of the Zimbabwean court over a *peregrinus* defendant is dependent on whether the plaintiff can establish that the defendant has property capable of attachment within the jurisdiction to confirm or found the jurisdiction of that court.[29] This rule is underpinned by the doctrine of effectiveness, that is, unless the court's judgment is going to be effective as against the defendant, it will not entertain the action.[30]

---

[25] As to which, the reader is referred to the section in the chapter on Namibia.

[26] It is arguable that, in *Grobler v Boshoff* 1988 (2) ZLR 447, Muchechetere J's acceptance of counsel's submission could be interpreted as laying stress on 'presence': ie the respondent was not present within the jurisdiction, such that she could not be served. It is submitted that the case, properly understood, does not lay down a test of presence: the focus is rather on the fact that the respondent moved away to South Africa, so changing her place of residence.

[27] *African Distillers v Zietkiewicz* 1980 ZLR 135. However, see below in this respect.

[28] Which concept is explained further below.

[29] *Monarch Steel (1991) (Pvt) Ltd v Fourway Haulage (Pty) Ltd* 1997 (2) ZLR 342 (H) 345C; *Stanmarker Mining (Pvt) Ltd v Metallon Corp Ltd (13/03) ((Pvt))* [2004] ZWSC 117.

[30] *Chiyangwa v Nehanda Radio* 2014 (1) ZLR 798 (H) (Matanda-Moyo J). See also *African Distillers v Zietkiewicz* 1980 ZLR 135 (G) (Beck J) 136F–H and the authorities cited therein. In that passage, Beck J states that arrest (which is considered further below) and/or attachment, in certain cases, only partially or imperfectly satisfies the doctrine of effectiveness. Indeed, that doctrine has been subject to criticism, both

The High Court Rules do not contain specific provision for an application for an order for the attachment of an individual's property *ad fundandam jurisdictionem* or *ad confirmandam jurisdictionem*. The court's power to make such orders arises at common law.[31]

However, section 15 of the 1981 Act confers a discretion on the court as to whether or not to make an order for the arrest of a person or attachment of property where the conditions for assuming jurisdiction are otherwise satisfied:

> 'In any case in which the High Court may exercise jurisdiction founded on or confirmed by the arrest of any person or the attachment of any property, the High Court may permit or direct the issue of process,[32] within such period as the court may specify, for service either in or outside Zimbabwe without ordering such arrest or attachment, if the High Court is satisfied that the person or property concerned is within Zimbabwe and is capable of being arrested or attached and the jurisdiction of the High Court in the matter shall be founded or confirmed, as the case may be, by the issue of such process.'

This provision (and similarly worded earlier versions) has been construed as not discharging the plaintiff's burden of showing, at the time an application for service of process out of the jurisdiction is made (pursuant to Order 6, rule 44) or at the time of service of a *peregrinus* within the jurisdiction, that the *peregrinus* defendant has property within the jurisdiction (attachment being unavailable for residents or domiciliaries). It is a precondition for the exercise of the discretion in section 15 of the 1981 Act that the plaintiff make an application for attachment.

Only once the plaintiff has established that the court would otherwise have jurisdiction does the discretion not to order attachment become available to the court.[33] Hence, if the application for attachment would otherwise fail by reason of the absence of any property of the defendant within the jurisdiction, the court has no discretion to permit or direct the service of process in or outside the jurisdiction without such arrest or attachment. More will be said below about this provision, and the circumstances in which the court may exercise the discretion which it confers.

---

in the courts of South Africa and among academic commentators. For a full discussion of this, the reader is referred to the relevant section of the chapter on the Republic of South Africa.

31 *Mackay v Hepker* [1941] SR 33, *per* Hudson J at 35–6. See also the judgment of Beck J in *African Distillers Ltd v Zietkiewicz* 1980 ZLR 135 (HC) 136F–H.

32 The correct procedure being to proceed by way of an application for edictal citation: *Ex parte Mercer* 1969 (2) SA 207 (R), *per* Beadle CJ at 208H–209A; Practice Direction 1963 (4) SA 165 (SR).

33 *Mackay v Hepker* [1941] SR 33, *per* Hudson J at 35 (referring to s 17 of the High Court Act (ch 8)). See also the authorities referred to below.

16.1.2.2.1 Property which can be attached

It is trite that property which belongs to a defendant (that is, which he owns legally) can be attached, so long as it is within the jurisdiction.[34]

However, in *Stanmarker Mining (Pvt) Ltd v Metallon Corp Ltd*,[35] the Zimbabwe Supreme Court held that a defendant's beneficial interest in property may also be attached (there, in order to confirm the jurisdiction of the court). The claim, based on a contract entered into in Zimbabwe, was brought by an *incola* plaintiff against a *peregrinus* (South African) defendant. Sandura JA, giving the judgment of the court, held[36] that because the defendant was a *peregrinus*,

> 'the High Court did not, therefore, have the jurisdiction to entertain such an action, which sounded in money, unless the defendant was within Zimbabwe, or property belonging to the defendant was within Zimbabwe and could be attached in order to confirm the jurisdiction of the High Court'.

He held that the defendant's beneficial interest in a Zimbabwean gold mining company (called 'Independence') was property that could be attached to confirm the jurisdiction.[37]

In *Stanmarker*, Sandura JA also set out the requirements for an attachment to be granted.[38] Hence, the plaintiff must show:

(1) it has a *prima facie* cause of action against the defendant. To satisfy this requirement, 'the [plaintiff] must tender evidence which, if accepted, will establish a cause of action. The fact that such evidence is in dispute does not preclude an order for attachment being granted';

---

[34] *Ex parte Sletcher* 1947 (1) SA 549 (SR); *Ex parte Smith* 1956 (1) SA 252 (SR); *Ex parte Heald* 1952 (3) SA 740 (SR). Such property is not confined to movable assets which the defendant has within the jurisdiction; immovable property may be attached as well.

[35] [2004] ZWSC 117, 2004 (1) ZLR 45 (S) (Sandura, Cheda and Gwaunza JJA).

[36] Ibid 48F–H.

[37] In this connection Sandura JA held that the defendant exercised control over Independence and that this was 'of great commercial value' and was property that could be attached and sold in execution. With respect to the learned judge, this cannot be correct. 'Control' is merely an abstract concept that cannot be sold in execution. However, it seems that the defendant conceded that it 'had a beneficial interest in Independence'. Although the report does not record the terms of this concession, it is likely that it concerned ownership of the shares of Independence which had been transferred to a British Virgin Islands company called Pemberton, which was itself owned by the defendant. The concession by the defendant that it had a beneficial interest in Independence must have been to the effect that Pemberton held the shares in Independence on trust for the defendant.

[38] At 53B–F, citing *Numill Marketing CC v Sitra Wood Products PTE Ltd* 1994 (3) SA 460 (C), *per* Olivier J at 463F–I. In *Tembo v PCJ Motorways* [2017] ZWHHC 224 (Dube J) (albeit when hearing an application to attach property belonging to a *peregrinus* defendant in order to found jurisdiction), Dube J, at p 3 of the electronic report, stated: 'It is desirable to bring this type of application *ex parte* without affording the respondent an opportunity to defend the application. The respondent can defend the application on the return date. The basis for this approach is that a respondent may if alerted, decide to remove his property from the jurisdiction, torpedoing the application.'

(2) the defendant is a *peregrinus* of Zimbabwe; and

(3) the defendant is within the area of jurisdiction of the court (for the purposes of arrest) or that property in which the defendant has a (legal or beneficial) interest is within, or may be[39] within, that area. The part of this formulation dealing with attachment of property (rather than arrest of the person) is set out in more detail in the section immediately below.

It has been held that for the purposes of attachment to confirm the jurisdiction of the court, it is sufficient to show that the *peregrinus* defendant 'may' have property within the jurisdiction. This is the effect of *Ex Parte Vulcan Trading Co Ltd*,[40] where Tredgold CJ made an order on the application of an *incola* plaintiff for leave to sue a *peregrinus* defendant by edictal citation, that the sheriff be 'directed to attach any debts, money or other property to which the defendant may lay claim or be entitled in the hands of [named] persons'. On its face, such an order would appear to delegate to the sheriff the court's function to determine on the evidence what property is and what property is not that of the defendant.

There is also authority to the effect that the property to be attached *must* be within the jurisdiction at the time the order for the attachment is made for the order to be valid and not a nullity. Thus, where an *incola* plaintiff sought to attach the property of a *peregrinus* defendant and that property comprised haulage trucks that transited through Zimbabwe on commercial deliveries to Zambia, the High Court decided that the plaintiff had not discharged the burden of showing that, at the point in time at which the application for attachment was made, the defendant *in fact* had property within the jurisdiction.[41]

---

[39] *Ex parte Vulcan Trading Co Ltd* 1951 (1) SA 355 (S Rhodesia, Bulawayo). This requirement is debatable, however.

[40] Ibid.

[41] *Chirongoma v TDG Logistics* [2011] ZWBHC 6, 2011 (1) ZLR 98 (H), *per* Mathonsi J. This might be thought to be a harsh decision. When dealing with a business which involves the temporary and transient presence of the *peregrinus* defendant's property in the jurisdiction, it will be impossible for the plaintiff to know at the time of an application for attachment that the defendant's property is within the jurisdiction or not (unless the plaintiff is party to the defendant's business schedules – which will be rare). One wonders how else the plaintiff in the *Chirongoma* case could have confirmed the jurisdiction of the court. Mathonsi J followed the earlier Zimbabwe High Court decisions in *Clan Transport Co (Pvt) Ltd v Government of the Republic of Mozambique* 1993 (3) SA 795 (ZH), *per* Sandura JP (at 798F; another haulage case): 'It is clear from this paragraph that at any given time the respondent's vehicles may or may not be in Zimbabwe. There are, therefore, times when the respondent does not have any property in Zimbabwe which can be attached. In addition, the information given by the applicant is meagre. The identity and value of the property which is sought to be attached are not given. I cannot, therefore, exercise my discretion in the applicant's favour'; and *Monarch Steel (1991) (Pvt) Ltd v Fourway Haulage (Pty) Ltd* 1997 (2) ZLR 342 (H), *per* Malaba J at 345B–C. The decisions in *Chrongoma* and *Clan Transport* have recently been followed by the High Court in *Tembo v PCJ Motorways* [2017] ZWHHC 224 (Dube J), a case described by the judge (at p 5 of the electronic report) as being on 'all fours with the *Clan* case'.

The authorities dealing with the question what the plaintiff must show in relation to the property to be attached are divided between a test that the plaintiff must show the property *is* within the jurisdiction and a test that the property to be attached *may* be within the jurisdiction. The decisions in question are first instance decisions and thus it is necessary to have a resolutive decision on this point by the Zimbabwean Supreme Court.

In the interests of certainty, we submit that the proper test is that, at the time of the application to attach the defendant's property, the plaintiff must be in a position to provide evidence to the court of property which belongs to the defendant and such that the evidence satisfies the ordinary civil standard of proof and not evidence of property which 'may' belong to the defendant.

Against this background, the authors now go on to consider how the jurisdictional significance of attachment varies depending on the status of the plaintiff and/or the defendant.

16.1.2.2.2 Where the plaintiff and the defendant are both *incolae*

Where both the parties to a dispute are *incolae*, no jurisdictional problems arise. The dispute is a purely domestic one over which the court has jurisdiction.

16.1.2.2.3 Where the plaintiff is an *incola* and the defendant is a *peregrinus*

'Where an *incola* intends to sue a *peregrinus*, an attachment of the [defendant's] property[42] to [found] or confirm jurisdiction[43] is necessary in order to make the *peregrinus* defendant amenable to the jurisdiction of the court.'[44]

There is, it is submitted, no clear answer to the question whether an *incola* plaintiff need only attach the property of a *peregrinus* defendant to found jurisdiction, that is, whether the *incola* plaintiff must have a *ratio jurisdictionis* connecting the dispute with the jurisdiction, in order to seise the court with jurisdiction over the dispute.

---

[42] Or arrest of his person: arrest of the person to found or confirm the court's jurisdiction is dealt with below (though it should be noted that, in the Republic of South Africa, arrest of a *peregrinus* defendant to found or confirm the jurisdiction of the court has now been held to be unconstitutional: *BID Industrial Holdings (Pty) Ltd v Strang* [2007] ZASCA 144; [2007] SCA 144 (RSA); [2008] 2 All SA 373 (SCA); 2008 (3) SA 355 (SCA). This authority is discussed in more depth below).

[43] This mirrors the position adopted by the courts in the Republic of South Africa. However, strictly speaking, 'Since a recognised *ratio jurisdictionis* by itself will not do it is immaterial whether such arrest or attachment is one *ad fundandam jurisdictionem* (where there is no other recognised ground of jurisdiction) or *ad confirmandam jurisdictionem* (where there is)': *Ewing McDonald & Co Ltd v M & M Products Co* 1991 (1) SA 252 (A) 258D–G *per* Nienaber AJA.

[44] *Wenzhou Enterprises v Chen Shaoling* [2015] ZWHHC 61 (HC; Makoni J), p 3 of the electronic report. In formulating this proposition, Makoni J relied on *Huny Yuen Wong v HS 190 Cheng Liu* HH380/13 (HC); unreported (Mathonsi J) and Herbstein and Van Winsen *The Civil Practice of the High Courts of South Africa* 5 ed (2009) 96.

There is certainly authority which, when analysed, suggests that the *incola* plaintiff need only attach the property of the *peregrinus* defendant. In *Ex parte Heald*,[45] Beadle J made an order attaching certain property situated within the jurisdiction and belonging to a *peregrinus* defendant on the application of an *incola* plaintiff. The order made[46] attached the property expressly in order to *found* jurisdiction. Although the report is very brief and the order was made *ex parte*, it would seem from the form of order sought and granted that the plaintiff had no subsisting *ratio jurisdictionis* in respect of which the attachment would confirm the jurisdiction of the court.[47]

To similar effect is the decision by Quènet J in *Ex parte Gregory*,[48] where it was ordered that certain property already subject to an attachment should be attached to found jurisdiction in the *incola* plaintiff's claim in debt.[49] Again, as with *Ex parte Heald*, it would seem from the form of order sought and granted that the plaintiff had no subsisting *ratio jurisdictionis* in respect of which the attachment would confirm the jurisdiction of the court.

In *Central African Airways Corp v Vickers-Armstrong Ltd*,[50] at first instance the High Court of Southern Rhodesia, on the application of the *incola* plaintiff, had refused to attach a debt owed by the plaintiff to the *peregrinus* defendant in order to found jurisdiction for the purposes of an action which the plaintiff proposed to bring against the defendant. That action was for damages arising out of the loss over Tanganyika of an aircraft purchased from the defendant by the plaintiff and the deaths of its passengers and crew, which claims had been assigned to the plaintiff. Allowing the appeal, Clayden FJ giving the judgment of the court stated:[51]

> 'It is settled Roman Dutch law that the Court, at the instance of an *incola,* will attach property of a *peregrinus* if the property is in its area of jurisdiction in order to found jurisdiction in the Court in a claim for money by the *incola* against the *peregrinus,* even if there is no other ground to exercise jurisdiction.'[52]

---

[45] 1952 (3) SA 740 (SR).

[46] Ibid 742A.

[47] Although this may simply be an example of the terms 'founding' and 'confirming' being used interchangeably and inexactly: see the judgment of Beadle CJ in *Ex parte Mor-Tal Construction* 1962 (2) SA 664 (SR), where the order sought was for an attachment to found jurisdiction and it appears it was granted in those terms, notwithstanding that the court referred to the plaintiff's evidence as showing that the contract on which the action was based was entered into and that the debt due under the contract was due within the jurisdiction: 'There is no doubt, therefore, that the cause of action arose in this Territory and that as a result, this Court has jurisdiction, and that jurisdiction is not dependent solely on the attachment of property' (*per* Beadle CJ at 664E–F). The application and order ought to have been for confirmation of the jurisdiction.

[48] 1956 (1) SA 215 (SR).

[49] The prior attachment did not exhaust the value of the property.

[50] 1956 (2) SA 492 (FSC) (Tredgold CJ and Lewey and Clayden FJJ).

[51] Ibid 492H.

[52] This decision is still authoritative in Zimbabwe, it is submitted. On a different aspect of the case, and as mentioned (briefly) above and (in more detail) in the chapter on the Republic of South Africa in connection

In *Agriprocom P/L v Trustees (for the time being) of the Edulis Trust Zimbabwe (Pvt)*,[53] the *incola* plaintiff sought to attach certain shares owned by the *peregrinus* defendant. The plaintiff applied for an order to attach the shares to found or confirm jurisdiction. In making the order on both bases, Gowora J (as she was then) stated that the shares were capable of attachment to found or confirm jurisdiction and:[54]

> 'The attachment of the property of a *peregrinus* is necessary to found jurisdiction. In this case none of the respondents are resident within the jurisdiction. The contract between the parties was concluded in South Africa even though it was to be performed in this country. It is necessary therefore in order that this court has jurisdiction that the property of the respondents be attached.'[55]

In *Mackay v Hepker*,[56] the *incola* plaintiff applied for leave to sue the *peregrinus* defendant (resident in the Union of South Africa) by edictal citation. The defendant had injured the plaintiff in a car accident within the court's jurisdiction. The defendant was neither resident nor domiciled in Southern Rhodesia and had no property there. The plaintiff contended that section 17 of the High Court Act 1964[57] empowered the court to grant leave to sue by edictal citation where there existed a *ratio jurisdictionis* (as to which, see further below), notwithstanding that the defendant was not within the jurisdiction and had no property there. Hudson J refused the plaintiff's application on the basis that the court could not issue edictal citation 'unless accompanied either by the arrest of the defendant or the attachment of any of his goods within the Colony'.[58]

---

with the continued utility of the doctrine of effectiveness, it appears from the report that the debt owed by the plaintiff to the defendant which the plaintiff sought to attach was in the sum of approximately £400 and that the total claim advanced by the plaintiff was in the sum of approximately £200,000. Thus, the jurisdiction of the court over the defendant was founded by the attachment of a debt owed by the plaintiff to the defendant, being the equivalent of 0.2% of the plaintiff's claim.

[53] [2004] ZWHHC 149. Again, the plaintiff's argument in the case used the terms 'to found jurisdiction' and 'to confirm jurisdiction' interchangeably. The judgment itself, however, as apparent from the part quoted in the main text, states that attachment is necessary, in this instance, to found jurisdiction.

[54] Ibid p 2 of the transcript of the judgment.

[55] Gowora J's judgment appears to have been *ex tempore*. In giving judgment, the learned judge rejected the submission that the plaintiff had not established a cause of action, stating that the question whether a cause of action was disclosed was not one for determination at the attachment hearing. Notwithstanding that the decision of the Supreme Court in *Stanmarker Mining (Pvt) Ltd v Metallon Corp Ltd* [2004] ZWSC 117, 2004 (1) ZLR 45 (S) to opposite effect, was handed down six months earlier, the learned judge's attention was not directed to this decision. Thus, to that extent, the decision of Gowora J on this point must be regarded as *per incuriam*. It is a requirement of an application for an attachment that the plaintiff show a *prima facie* cause of action.

[56] [1941] SR 33.

[57] Section 17 of the High Court Act (Cap 8 of the Laws of Zimbabwe as they stood at that time) was in materially identical terms to s 15 of the High Court Act 1981.

[58] [1941] SR 33 at 35.

In *Risely v Watt*,[59] the *incola* plaintiff issued a summons for service out of the jurisdiction on the *peregrinus* defendant in Zambia. The defendant was resident in Zambia and had no property in Southern Rhodesia. Davies J held: 'I consider in the circumstances that *Mackay v Hepker* is applicable and that this Court therefore has no jurisdiction to entertain the action in the absence of an allegation that the defendant has property capable of attachment within its jurisdiction.' The judge continued:[60]

> 'There are to my mind other reasons why the Court should refuse to entertain this action. Apart from the fact that there are no effective means available of enforcing an order of the type sought by the plaintiff against the defendant, and that any order granted would be a *fulmen brutum*, on the face of the declaration the partnership business is conducted solely in Zambia and all books of accounts are kept there. I know of no means whereby a liquidator appointed by this Court could carry out his duties in Zambia, and considerations of convenience obviously dictate that the liquidation of the partnership should be conducted in Zambia.'

In *African Distillers Ltd v Zietkiewicz*,[61] an *incola* plaintiff of Zimbabwe issued proceedings against defendants who were *peregrini* of Zimbabwe (all of whom were resident in the Republic of South Africa), claiming damages for breaches of a contract with the plaintiff that was entered into and to be performed in Zimbabwe. The defendants had no property within Zimbabwe and objected to the jurisdiction of the Zimbabwean court on the basis that no order had been sought or obtained to attach their persons or their property. Beck J, addressing the contention that section 40 of the High Court Act[62] had abolished the need for an attachment entirely, stated:[63]

> 'The well settled common law, for which there is no dearth of judicial authority, is that for claims that sound in money brought by an *incola* or a *peregrinus* against a *peregrinus*, there must be an arrest of the person of the defendant *peregrinus* or an attachment of his property within the territorial jurisdiction of the Court in order to found jurisdiction, or to confirm jurisdiction in those cases where some other jurisdictional ground exists in relation to the claim – such as, for example, that it arises from a contract concluded or a delict[64] committed within the Court's territorial limits of jurisdiction. Such arrests or attachments are necessary in order to satisfy, albeit only partially and imperfectly in some cases, the doctrine of effectiveness, for the Court will not concern itself with suits in which the resulting judgment will be no more than a *brutum fulmen*.'[65]

---

[59] 1965 (2) SA 664 (SR).

[60] Ibid 669A–C.

[61] 1980 ZLR 135 (G).

[62] Cap 14; the predecessor to s 15 of the 1981 Act.

[63] Ibid 136F–H citing *Foord v Foord* 1924 WLD 81 at 87 and *Thermo Radiant Oven Sales (Pty) Ltd v Nelspruit Bakeries (Pty) Ltd* 1969 (2) SA 295 (A) 300D and 307A–311E.

[64] For a case dealing with attachment to confirm jurisdiction on the basis of a delict committed within the jurisdiction of the court, see: *Tarwireyi v Kunene* (HC 7549/06) [2008] ZWHHC 19 (Hungwe J).

[65] Seemingly cited with approval in *Tembo v PCJ Motorways* [2017] ZWHHC 224 (Dube J).

The court granted the (first and second) defendants' special plea that the court had no jurisdiction to entertain the plaintiff's claim.

The passage from the judgment of Beck J in *African Distillers* quoted above suggests that in a claim sounding in money brought by an *incola* or a *peregrinus* against a *peregrinus*, jurisdiction may be *either* founded by attachment of the defendant's property or arrest of his person *or* confirmed by attachment of the defendant's property or arrest of his person where there exists a *ratio jurisdictionis.*

However, it is submitted that there is reason to doubt the correctness of this proposition. Indeed, the two authorities cited by Beck J do not support such a broad proposition. In *Foord v Foord,*[66] the plaintiff wife was resident within the jurisdiction of the court (Transvaal) and her husband was neither resident nor had property within the jurisdiction (the husband was resident in Durban by the time proceedings were issued). Mason JP held[67] that the husband's nationality was a not a basis for jurisdiction and also observed that most Civil Law jurisprudence required the presence of the defendant or his property within the jurisdiction in order to seise the court. Mason JP did not state that a *peregrinus* plaintiff could seise the court of jurisdiction by arresting the *peregrinus* defendant or attaching property to found or confirm jurisdiction or that an *incola* plaintiff could seise the court by arresting the *peregrinus* defendant or attaching property to found jurisdiction.

The same observation may be made of the second authority cited by Beck J, *Thermo Radiant Oven Sales (Pty) Ltd v Nelspruit Bakeries (Pty) Ltd.*[68] The passages referred to by Beck J[69] are from the judgments of Ogilvie Thompson JA and Potgieter JA respectively. In the first passage Ogilvie Thompson JA cited a passage from Herbstein and Van Winsen,[70] which stated that an *incola* or *peregrinus* plaintiff was required to attach the property or person of a *peregrinus* defendant even if there existed a *ratio jurisdictionis.* In the second passage, Potgieter JA discussed attachment of property to found jurisdiction in the context[71] of an *incola* bringing proceedings.

In *Ewing McDonald & Co Ltd v M & M Products Co,*[72] Nienaber AJA set out[73] the grounds on which a division of the High Court in South Africa would assume jurisdiction in respect of a claim sounding in money. For present purposes ground (c) is of significance:[74]

---

66 1924 WLD 81.

67 Ibid 87.

68 1969 (2) SA 295 (A) (Steyn CJ; Ogilvie Thompson, Botha, Potgieter and Jansen JJA).

69 Ibid 300D and 307A–311E.

70 *Civil Practice* 2 ed (1966) 704.

71 1969 (2) SA 295 (A) 306H–307A.

72 1991 (1) SA 252 (A) (Van Heerden and Smalberger JJA; Nicholas, Friedman and Nienaber AJJA).

73 Ibid 258J.

74 It is also of significance that one of the two authorities cited by Nienaber AJA in support of ground (a) is the *Thermo Radiant* case at p 300D, cited by Beck J.

'*(c)* Where the plaintiff is a *peregrinus* (foreign or local) and the defendant is a foreign *peregrinus*: both a recognised *ratio jurisdictionis* as well as an arrest or attachment are essential. Any arrest[75] or attachment merely *ad fundandam jurisdictionem* would not be sufficient. To be sufficient the arrest or attachment must necessarily be one *ad confirmandam jurisdictionem*. (Cf POLLAK, [*The South African Law of Jurisdiction*, 1937, pages] 52, 58, 62-3; HERBSTEIN AND VAN WINSEN, [*The Civil Practice of the Superior Courts of South Africa*, 3rd edition, page 40]; MARITIME & INDUSTRIAL SERVICES LTD v MACIERTA COMPANIA NAVIERA SA 1969 (3) SA 28.'

The statements by Beck J in the *African Distillers* case in which he relied on the decision in *Thermo Radiant Oven Sales (Pty) Ltd v Nelspruit Bakeries (Pty) Ltd* appear to be out of line with the understanding of the ratio of that case as formulated in *Ewing McDonald & Co Ltd v M & M Products Co*,[76] by Nienaber AJA.

The recent decision of the High Court in *Marowa v Mabaya & Sons Transport & General Contractors CC*[77] has sought to clarify the position, though it is an open question as to how well it has achieved that aim. The plaintiff was involved in a car accident with a vehicle driven by the *peregrinus* defendant's employee. The plaintiff, having suffered injury, made an application to attach the defendant's property for the purposes of confirming the court's jurisdiction. However, the court, in dealing with the application, in reliance on the decision in *African Distillers Ltd v Zietkiewicz*,[78] stated:

'The requirements to be satisfied in an order for attachment to *found* jurisdiction are as follows:

(a) The cause of action has to have arisen in the [plaintiff's] jurisdiction.

(b) The [plaintiff] has a cause of action against the respondent.

(c) The claim sounds in money.

(d) The property the subject of the attachment is within the jurisdiction and is capable of attachment.' (emphasis added by way of italics).

On the face of it, the passage just quoted would seem to suggest that it is insufficient for a plaintiff who wishes to found the jurisdiction of the court simply to attach the defendant's property. Yet, the court was not asked to grant an application to attach so as to found jurisdiction in the *Marowa* case; it was asked to grant an application to confirm jurisdiction. In those circumstances, it is unlikely that Wamambo J meant to set out the requirements which a plaintiff had to meet in order to found jurisdiction; the judge more likely meant to set out the requirements which a plaintiff had to meet in order to confirm jurisdiction.

[75] Arrest of a *peregrinus* to found or confirm the jurisdiction of the court subsequently has been held to be unconstitutional in the Republic of South Africa: *BID Industrial Holdings (Pty) Ltd v Strang* [2007] ZASCA 144; [2007] SCA 144 (RSA); [2008] 2 All SA 373 (SCA); 2008 (3) SA 355 (SCA).

[76] 1991 (1) SA 252 (A).

[77] [2022] ZWMSVHC 5 (HC) (Wamambo J).

[78] 1980 ZLR 135.

It is submitted that, in the light of the ambiguity created by the judgment in *Marowa*, the question posed at the beginning of this section is still without clear answer in Zimbabwe. In that respect, the authors' view is that the ratio to be extracted from the *African Distillers* case should be confined to the facts of the case: a Zimbabwean court will have jurisdiction over a claim in money brought by an *incola* where there is a *ratio jurisdictionis* connecting the claim with the jurisdiction and the plaintiff arrests the *peregrinus* defendant or attaches his property so as to confirm the jurisdiction. Indeed, it may well be that this was what Wamambo J had in mind in the *Marowa* case but the judge simply expressed the point without the necessary clarity.

Be that as it may, in the light of the ambiguity, and in the light of the authority which exists (and which was not cited in *Marowa*), it seems sensible to conclude that, in Zimbabwe presently, an *incola* plaintiff may also found jurisdiction in a claim against a *peregrinus* defendant by attaching his property[79] in the absence of a *ratio jurisdictionis*. In both cases (that is to say the case of an *incola* plaintiff and a *peregrinus* defendant and a *peregrinus* plaintiff and a *peregrinus* defendant), the basis for the court's jurisdiction is attachment of the property.[80] It is submitted that only a decision of the Supreme Court can now clarify the situation.

16.1.2.2.4 Where the plaintiff and the defendant are both *peregrini*

This has been touched on above. In the authors' view, the Zimbabwean courts would follow the approach adopted by the South African Appellate Division in the *Ewing McDonald* case, which has been referred to above. Accordingly, where a plaintiff *peregrinus* sues a defendant *peregrinus* in Zimbabwe, it will be necessary for the plaintiff to show a *ratio jurisdictionis*; attachment should therefore properly be to confirm the jurisdiction of the Zimbabwean court.

16.1.2.3 *Rationes jurisdictiones*

There is no suggestion that the law in Zimbabwe differs from the law in the Republic of South Africa on the acceptable *rationes jurisdictiones*. While more in-depth treatment is afforded the *rationes jurisdictiones* in the chapter on South Africa,[81] the basic position may be summarised by reference to the judgment of the Supreme Court of the Cape in *Einwald v The German West African Co.*[82] There, De Villiers CJ stated:[83]

[79] Or person: arrest of the person to found or confirm the court's jurisdiction is dealt with below.
[80] Or the person.
[81] To which the reader is referred.
[82] (1887) 5 SC 86 (De Villiers CJ).
[83] Ibid 91.

> 'What then are the grounds upon which the jurisdiction of this Court can be exercised, in respect of any contract over any defendant without his consent, express or implied? The grounds are threefold: *viz* by virtue of the defendant's domicile being here, by virtue of the contract either having been entered into here or having to be performed here, and by virtue of the subject matter in an action *in rem* being situated in this Colony.'

Added to these are the place of the delict and cases which concern property. The principal connecting factors for jurisdictional purposes which result are: *ratio domicilii (actor sequitur forum rei)*; *ratio contractus*; *ratio delictus*; and *ratio rei sitae*.[84] To this list may also be added *ratio causa continentia*.

16.1.2.3.1 *Ratio domicilii* (*actor sequitur forum rei*)

Ratio domicilii expresses the principle of Roman law that the fundamental basis of jurisdiction is that a plaintiff should sue a defendant at the defendant's place of domicile or, as has become the case, residence (*actor sequitur forum rei*). There is nothing to suggest that the Zimbabwean courts would treat this issue any differently to the courts in the Republic of South Africa.[85]

16.1.2.3.2 *Ratio contractus*

There is nothing to suggest that the Zimbabwean courts would treat this issue any differently to the courts in the Republic of South Africa. Accordingly, a court where: (1) the contract was concluded (the *locus contractus*); (2) the contract is to be performed in whole or in part (the *locus solutionis*); and (3) the contract was breached in the manner relied upon by the plaintiff may, *ratio contractus*, exercise jurisdiction.[86]

---

[84] Different authors treat the organisation of this subject in different ways. Peté et al *Civil Procedure* 2 ed (2011) (at 70ff) discuss the subject under the headings *ratione domicilii*, *ratione res gestae*, *ratione rei sitae* and then claims relating to property and claims sounding in money. In Schulze *On Jurisdiction and the Recognition and Enforcement of Foreign Money Judgments* (2005), the discussion (at 1–15) revolves around domicile and the bases for assumption of jurisdiction over *incolae* and *peregrini*. In Kelbrick *Civil Procedure in South Africa* 2 ed (2012), the subject is analysed (at 42–3, paras 84–6) in terms of claims in money and property. Forsyth *Private International Law* 5 ed (2012) discusses (at 205–6) residence and domicile, the various *rationes jurisdictionis* and then claims in money or property. Herbstein and Van Winsen *The Civil Practice of the High Courts of South Africa* 5 ed (2009) discusses (at 67–81) the subject under the topic headings claims in money, property (and status). Pistorius *Pollak on Jurisdiction* 2 ed (1993) arranges the discussion under the topic headings money claims and property claims. There are merits in all of these approaches.

[85] Accordingly, for a more detailed treatment of this issue, the reader is referred to the corresponding discussion in the chapter on the Republic of South Africa.

[86] Given that there is nothing to suggest that the courts in Zimbabwe treat this issue any differently to the courts in the Republic of South Africa, the reader is referred to the corresponding discussion in the chapter on South Africa for a more detailed treatment of this issue.

16.1.2.3.3 *Ratio delicti commissi*

A court may have jurisdiction by reason of a *ratio delicti commissi* in the event that a delict was committed or occurred within its area of jurisdiction. Again, there is nothing to suggest that the Zimbabwean courts treat this issue any differently to the courts in the Republic of South Africa.[87]

16.1.2.3.4 *Ratio rei sitae*

The location of movable or immovable property within the area of jurisdiction of a court will confer on that court jurisdiction by reason of a *ratio rei sitae*: it is the court of the place where the property is situated. Again, there is nothing to suggest that the Zimbabwean courts treat this issue any differently to the courts in the Republic of South Africa.[88]

16.1.2.3.5 *Ratio causa continentia*

There is nothing to suggest that the courts in Zimbabwe treat the *causa continentia* doctrine differently to the courts in the Republic of South Africa. The *causa continentia* rule is one that permits a court to assume jurisdiction in a case in which, but for the application of the rule, it might not have jurisdiction over the entirety of the dispute or over a particular defendant. The application of the rule is intended to avoid a 'multiplicity of proceedings and the possibility of conflicting judgments on the same cause and allows for the more convenient disposition of cases'.[89] Pistorius states[90] that in order to apply 'it must be established that there is no other forum which has jurisdiction in respect of all the defendants on other recognised grounds of jurisdiction'.[91]

[87] Accordingly, for a more detailed treatment of this issue, the reader is referred to the corresponding discussion in the chapter on the Republic of South Africa.

[88] Accordingly, for a more detailed treatment of this issue, the reader is referred to the corresponding discussion in the chapter on the Republic of South Africa.

[89] Pistorius *Pollak on Jurisdiction* 2 ed (1993) 25.

[90] Ibid 26.

[91] Given, as the authors have said, that there is nothing to suggest that the courts in Zimbabwe treat this issue any differently to the courts in the Republic of South Africa, the reader is referred to the corresponding discussion in the chapter on South Africa for a more detailed treatment of this issue.

16.1.2.4 *A further basis for assuming jurisdiction over a* peregrinus *defendant: Where attachment of property is not possible*[92]

As has been mentioned above, it appears that attachment of a (putative) defendant's property[93] is a pre-condition for a Zimbabwean court assuming jurisdiction *ad fundandam* or *ad confirmandam* over a dispute involving a *peregrinus* defendant (in the former case apparently regardless of whether there exists a subsisting *ratio jurisdictionis*).

The question arises whether, in the circumstances where attachment of a (putative) defendant's property[94] is not possible, there is any other basis on which a Zimbabwean court may assume jurisdiction over a dispute involving a *peregrinus* defendant.

This was the situation which confronted the Supreme Court of Appeal of South Africa in *Bid Industrial Holdings (Pty) Ltd v Strang*,[95] where an *incola* plaintiff applied for an order[96] for the arrest of two individuals who were domiciled and resident in Australia. The plaintiff was unable to attach any property of the proposed defendants. The court held that jurisdictional arrest was unconstitutional.[97] The court then proceeded to consider whether it was possible to develop the common law so as to develop a constitutionally acceptable substitute practice to that of establishing jurisdiction by arrest.[98] The court found that such a substitute practice existed in permitting jurisdiction to be established by service of process on a defendant within South Africa, combined with an adequate connection between the proceedings and the jurisdictional area of the court which the plaintiff sought to seise of the proceedings. Howie P (giving the judgment of the court)[99] stated:

> '56. In my view it would suffice to empower the court to take cognisance of the suit if the defendant were served with the summons while in South Africa and, in addition, there were an adequate connection between the suit and the area of jurisdiction of the South African court concerned from the point of view of the appropriateness and convenience of its being decided by that court. Appropriateness

---

[92] This section also contains information pertinent to the issue of arrest of the defendant's person, which is dealt with below under the heading 'The jurisdictional significance of arrest of the person'. As is noted below, the alternative regime which the authors contemplate now may be applied with equal force to arrest of the defendant's person.

[93] Or arrest of his person – see further below.

[94] Or arrest of his person.

[95] 2008 (3) SA 355 (SCA). For a full treatment of this decision, and the jurisprudence which has followed it, the reader is referred to the chapter on the Republic of South Africa.

[96] It does not appear from the report whether the order was sought *ad fundandam jurisdictionem* or *ad confirmandam jurisdictionem*. Howie P dealt with the appeal on the basis that concerned both bases of jurisdiction (para [20] of Howie P's judgment).

[97] 2008 (3) SA 355 (SCA) paras [39], [41], [44]–[45] and [59]. For a fuller treatment of this authority, and the jurisprudence which has followed it, see the discussion in the chapter on the Republic of South Africa.

[98] Ibid paras [51]–[52].

[99] Howie P, Nugent, Ponnan and Maya JJA and Malan AJA.

and convenience are elastic concepts which can be developed case by case. Obviously the strongest connection would be provided by the cause of action arising within that jurisdiction.

57. As to the principle of effectiveness, despite its having been described as "the basic principle of jurisdiction in our law" it is clear that the importance and significance of attachment has been so eroded that the value of attached property has sometimes been "trifling". However, as I have said, effectiveness is largely for the plaintiff to assess and to act accordingly.

58. Therefore it seems to me that there are legally competent alternatives to requiring arrest as a jurisdictional prerequisite. Whether they can be established in the proposed litigation between the present parties it is impossible, from the record, to determine. Indeed, whether there are sufficiently close links with the area of jurisdiction concerned and whether effectiveness is likely to be achieved are matters dependent on the facts of each case. They should be canvassed in the pleadings and can, in addition, be dealt with as separated issues in terms of rule 33(4).

59. For all these reasons the common-law rule that arrest is mandatory to found or confirm jurisdiction cannot pass the limitations test set by s 36(1). It is contrary to the spirit, purport and objects of the Bill of Rights. The common law must be, and is hereby, developed by abolition of the rule and the adoption in its stead, where attachment is not possible, of the practice according to which a South African High Court will have jurisdiction if the summons is served on the defendant while in South Africa and there is sufficient connection between the suit and the area of jurisdiction of the court concerned so that disposal of the case by that court is appropriate and convenient. It goes without saying that the new practice could itself be subject to development with time.'

16.1.2.5 *Discretion to dispense with attachment of property*[100]

The provisions of section 15 of the 1981 Act, conferring on the court discretion to found or confirm jurisdiction by the issue of process[101] rather than attachment of the defendant's person or property does not relieve the plaintiff from proving that at the time of the issue of process the defendant had property within the jurisdiction,[102] such that the defendant was amenable to the jurisdiction of the court

[100] Or arrest of the person.

[101] The correct procedure is to proceed by way of an application for edictal citation: *Ex parte Mercer* 1969 (2) SA 207 (R), *per* Beadle CJ at 208H–209A; Practice Direction 1963 (4) SA 165 (SR).

[102] Or, if the plaintiff seeks to arrest the defendant, that the defendant was within the jurisdiction.

through attachment of his property.[103] Only then does the court have discretion to order that jurisdiction is founded or confirmed by the issue of process:[104]

> 'Although s 15 altered the common law rule to the extent that it gave the court a discretion not to order attachment of the property belonging to a peregrine defendant or order his arrest but to elect *in lieu* thereof to found or confirm its jurisdiction over the *peregrinus* by issue of process, it did not discharge the plaintiff from the burden of having to satisfy the court, before the issue of process, that the *peregrinus* was present within the country for arrest or had property within the country capable of attachment.'

In *Ex parte Mor-Tal Construction*,[105] Beadle CJ stated[106] that where the court has jurisdiction over a *peregrinus* defendant not solely on the basis of attachment of property, ie where there is a *ratio jurisdictionis*, the proper practice is for the court simply to give leave to sue by edictal citation without ordering any attachment of the property of the defendant, unless there is a proper case for such attachment. Beadle CJ also described the exercise of the discretion in the following terms:[107]

> 'Examples of the type of cases in which orders of attachment have been made are cases where the property which is sought to be attached is property which is the subject of the very dispute in question, or cases where it is quite clear that the only property which the respondent has within the jurisdiction is the property which is sought to be attached and there is a danger that, if it is not attached, he will make away with that property and then the Court's judgment would possibly be a *brutum fulmen*. But in every case where the Court otherwise has jurisdiction where leave is sought to attach property in addition to a request for leave to sue by edict, it is essential that the Court should be properly informed of the circumstances which make such an attachment necessary. The Court will want to know the value of the property which is sought to be attached, because, while the value of the property might be a quite irrelevant consideration in deciding whether or not the Court has jurisdiction, it is a most important consideration in deciding whether the Court in the exercise of its discretion can equitably order an attachment of the property to be made. Obviously if the property sought to be attached greatly exceeds the value of the claim, that would be a factor to be taken into account in refusing an attachment. Similarly, in reverse, if the value of the property sought to be attached was insignificant compared with the value of the claim, there again the necessity for attachment might not appear to arise.'

---

[103] Or arrest of his person. Section 15 provides: 'In any case in which the High Court may exercise jurisdiction founded on or confirmed by the arrest of any person or the attachment of any property, the High Court may permit or direct the issue of process, within such period as the court may specify, for service either in or outside Zimbabwe without ordering such arrest or attachment, if the High Court is satisfied that the person or property concerned is within Zimbabwe and is capable of being arrested or attached and the jurisdiction of the High Court in the matter shall be founded or confirmed, as the case may be, by the issue of such process.'

[104] *Monarch Steel (1991) (Pvt) Ltd v Fourway Haulage (Pty) Ltd* 1997 (2) ZLR 342 (H), *per* Malaba J at 345D–E. This was confirmed by the Supreme Court in *Stanmarker Mining (Pvt) Ltd v Metallon Corp Ltd* [2004] ZWSC 117, *per* Sandura JA.

[105] 1962 (2) SA 664 (SR).

[106] Ibid 665B–D; impliedly approving the view expressed in earlier authorities; followed in *Ex parte Mercer* 1969 (2) SA 207 (R) (Beadle CJ).

[107] Ibid 665D–H.

Ex Parte Sletcher[108] concerned a claim for specific performance brought by an *incola* plaintiff against a *peregrinus* defendant. Tredgold J stated[109] that section 17 of the High Court Act[110] conferred discretion to make an order of attachment and that in exercising that discretion in favour of attachment 'probably the clearest possible case is that in which an action is brought for specific performance on a contract for the sale of immovable property'. Tredgold J explained this in the following terms:[111]

> 'It has always been recognised that, apart from the effect of an attachment in confirming jurisdiction, one of the incidental functions of such attachment was to secure a property against which an order of Court could operate, and when the whole issue in the case is the question whether certain property should be transferred to the [plaintiff], and when there is a reasonable possibility that that right might be defeated while the matter was pending, it seems to me he has a strong case for attachment, coupled with his edict.'

The court may exercise its discretion not to require attachment of the defendant's property[112] 'where the Court has reason to conclude that the oppression inherent in such arrest or attachment is not, in all the circumstances, reasonably necessary for the purpose of rendering effective a judgment unfavourable to the peregrinus'.[113]

In *X & Y (Pvt) Ltd v Z*,[114] Davies J held[115] that the discretion will be exercised in an equitable manner, such that the court: 'is not bound to give the [plaintiff] preferential treatment; it can take into account the effect of the order upon third parties; it can have regard to the balance of convenience'. On the facts of the case the judge found that the intervening third party would not suffer irreparable harm by reason of the plaintiff's attachment and ordered that the attachments be continued.

16.1.2.6 *Submission to the jurisdiction*

Zimbabwean law recognises submission to the jurisdiction as a basis for the assumption of jurisdiction over a dispute in certain circumstances.

Generally, submission may take one of two forms. First, unilateral submission, whereby a party against whom proceedings have been commenced takes a step in the proceedings which as a matter of Zimbabwean law renders him amenable

[108] 1947 (1) SA 549 (SR), a decision on s 17 of the High Court Act (ch 8).

[109] Ibid 552.

[110] Section 17 of the High Court Act (Cap 8 of the Laws of Zimbabwe at that time) itself was in materially identical terms to s 15 of the High Court Act 1981.

[111] 1947 (1) SA 549 (SR) 552.

[112] Or arrest of his person.

[113] *African Distillers Ltd v Zietkiewicz* 1980 ZLR 135 (G), *per* Beck J at 139A. Cited with approval by Malaba J in *Monarch Steel (1991) (Pvt) Ltd v Fourway Haulage (Pty) Ltd* 1997 (2) ZLR 342 (H) 346D–F.

[114] 1974 (1) SA 195 (R).

[115] Ibid 200H.

to the jurisdiction of the Zimbabwean courts. Second, consensual submission, whereby the parties agree prior to or subsequent to a dispute arising to submit to the jurisdiction of the Zimbabwean courts.

16.1.2.6.1 Submission by participating in existing proceedings

In the case of unilateral consent, questions will be directed at whether the acts of the party (usually the defendant) amounted to a submission to the jurisdiction or not. The plaintiff must bear the onus of showing that the relevant acts amounted to a submission to the jurisdiction of the Zimbabwean court. Entering an appearance (save for the sole purpose of disputing the jurisdiction of the court) and engaging with the merits of a claim would amount to submission.[116]

16.1.2.6.2 Submission by agreement

16.1.2.6.2.1 *Jurisdiction clauses*

In *Tiiso Holdings (Pty) Ltd v Zimbabwe Iron & Steel Co Ltd*,[117] Patel J considered whether the Frankfurt court had international jurisdiction in circumstances where the parties had agreed that the Frankfurt court should have jurisdiction over all litigation arising out of the agreement between them[118] but that, at the time that court was seised, there were no assets of the defendant within the jurisdiction of that court. The defendant contended that, because the defendant was neither present nor had assets within the jurisdiction of the court, any judgment rendered by the court could not have been enforced in Germany and therefore the jurisdictional principle of effectiveness led to the conclusion that the German court was not seised. Rejecting this contention Patel J held[119] that 'a defendant's express submission to the jurisdiction of a foreign court suffices,

[116] See *Wenzhou Enterprises v Chen Shaoling* [2015] ZWHHC 61 (Makoni J), where the respondent filed a notice of opposition and heads of argument. He did not contest the court's jurisdiction in those pleadings, raising the matter for the first time on the day of the hearing itself. In these circumstances, having cited *Mashinen Grommer Gribtt & Co HG v Trisave Engineering Machinery Supplies (Pty) Ltd* 2003 (6) SA 69 (C) and *Supercat Incorporated v Two Oceans Marine CC* 2001 (4) SA 27 (C), Makoni J stated (at pp 3–4 of the electronic report): 'Looking at the circumstances of this matter it is my view that the respondent submitted to the jurisdiction of the court. In our jurisdiction we have the procedural regime where a plea of lack of jurisdiction is adjudicated upon *in limine* prior to the adjudication of the merits of the matter. If the respondent did not intend to submit to the jurisdiction of the court he would have raised the issue *in limine* in his Notice of Opposition. His conduct, *in casu*, clearly points to a person who had no intention, whatsoever, to contest the jurisdiction of the court. It came as after thought. After he had pleaded to the merits of the matter.' In the light of this, it is likely that a Zimbabwean court would follow the guidance given by the South African courts on the development and application of this principle. On this, the reader is referred to the chapter on the Republic of South Africa.

[117] [2010] ZWHHC 95, 2010 (2) ZLR 100 (H). The facts are set out above.

[118] At 107F–G.

[119] Ibid 9–10 of the transcript of the judgment.

ipso facto, and without any further jurisdictional ground, to endow that court with the requisite international competence, enabling and allowing the recognition and enforcement of its judgments under common law'. It would be peculiar if the Zimbabwean court, while recognising submission as a basis for the jurisdiction of a foreign court, denied submission to itself as a basis for its own jurisdiction.[120]

The position appears to be, therefore, that submission itself[121] is sufficient to give the Zimbabwean court jurisdiction over a matter.[122] Such submission may be express (as in *Tiiso Holdings (Pty) Ltd*)[123] or it may be implied by virtue of a *domicilium citandi et executandi* clause (to which the authors turn immediately below).

16.1.2.6.2.2 Domicilium citandi et executandi *clauses*

In *Beverley Building Society v De Courcy*,[124] Maisels J considered the effect of a *domicilium citandi et executandi* clause in a deed of suretyship between two *peregrini* defendants in respect of a mortgage of property in Southern Rhodesia. Neither of the defendants had property within the jurisdiction. The defendants each entered into the deed of suretyship in England and Scotland respectively on separate dates. Maisels J stated that the question was, notwithstanding the absence of any express provision in the deed, 'whether the plaintiff has nevertheless proved on the information presently before the Court that the defendants have, in fact, so consented or submitted'. Maisels J held[125] that on the true construction of the deed the defendants had submitted to the jurisdiction:

> 'It is accepted by the defendants in this case that their obligations had to be performed in Southern Rhodesia, that the loan was made in Southern Rhodesia, that the properties secured under the loans are situate in Southern Rhodesia, that the purpose of the loan was to develop property in Southern Rhodesia, that the bond was to be repayable without demand in Southern Rhodesia and that all payments under it were to be made at the

---

[120] However, the Zimbabwean court would, most likely (relying on the guidance given by the courts in the Republic of South Africa), recognise mere submission as conferring upon it jurisdiction in a case where the cause of action accrued in Zimbabwe.

[121] Without the need to attach property/arrest the person of the defendant within the jurisdiction: *Ex parte Adair Properties Ltd* [1967] RLR 56.

[122] The position adopted by the courts in Zimbabwe appears to be different to that adopted by the courts in the Republic of South Africa. In *Veneta Mineraria Spa v Carolina Collieries (Pty) Ltd* 1987 (4) SA 883 (A), a case between two *peregrini*, it was held that the mere submission to the jurisdiction by the *peregrinus* defendant was not enough to confer jurisdiction on the court. By contrast, where the defendant is a *peregrinus* and the plaintiff is an *incola*, the South African courts have held that the defendant's submission by way of agreement, will, without more, confer jurisdiction upon the court: *Hay Management Consultants (Pty) Ltd v P3 Management Consultants (Pty) Ltd* 2005 (2) SA 522 (SCA), approving the decision in *American Flag plc v Great African T-Shirt Corp* 2000 (1) SA 356 (W).

[123] [2010] ZWHHC 95, where the loan agreements in question contained a jurisdiction clause in favour of the courts of Frankfurt/Main. It does not appear from the report whether the clause was an exclusive or non-exclusive jurisdiction clause.

[124] 1964 (4) SA 264 (SR).

[125] Ibid 271H–272F.

office of the mortgagor in Salisbury. In all these circumstances it appears to me that it is more probable that the choice of a *domicilium citandi et executandi* in Salisbury was for the purpose and with the intention of submitting to the jurisdiction of the Southern Rhodesian Court than that this choice was made merely in order to facilitate service if the Court otherwise had jurisdiction.'

16.1.2.7 *The jurisdictional significance of arrest of the person*

At present, and in contrast to the position in the Republic of South Africa,[126] it would appear that arrest of a *peregrinus* defendant remains constitutionally valid in Zimbabwe as a means of securing[127] the jurisdiction of the Zimbabwean court. Whether this continues to be the position in the future remains to be seen. Given the close affinity between the legal systems of Zimbabwe and the Republic of South Africa, there are some grounds for saying that, in the light of the South African position, the position in Zimbabwe could be changed accordingly. However, viewing the matter jurisprudentially, the argument that, simply because the law of South Africa has taken one view, the law of Zimbabwe should take the same view, may not be as straightforward as it seems.

The constitutionality of certain actions, like the arrest of a *peregrinus* defendant so as to found or confirm the jurisdiction of the court, may legitimately differ as between states. The Constitution of the Republic of South Africa is, after all, not drafted in exactly the same terms as the current Constitution of Zimbabwe. As a result, for the present time, the authors simply note that, as a matter of Zimbabwean law, it is still constitutionally permissible to arrest a *peregrinus* defendant for jurisdictional purposes, while acknowledging that there is potential for the position to change in the light of the South African jurisprudence on the subject, should a Zimbabwean court consider the position in South Africa to be correct.

Against that background, many of the mechanics of jurisdictional arrest of a *peregrinus* defendant are the same as the mechanics of attachment of their property.[128] As has been mentioned above, both attachment and arrest are taken to satisfy[129] the doctrine of effectiveness.[130] Hence, by way of illustration, a plaintiff

[126] As to which, see *Bid Industrial Holdings (Pty) Ltd v Strang* 2008 (3) SA 355 (SCA) and the discussion of this authority, both *supra* fn 95 and the main text associated therewith and in the chapter on the Republic of South Africa

[127] The controversy apparent in the judgment of Beck J in *African Distillers Ltd v Zietkiewicz* 1980 ZLR 135 (G), which controversy has been discussed above (*supra* fn 65 et seq and the main text associated therewith), is equally applicable in the context of arrest as it is in the context of attachment. Accordingly, the neutral term 'secure' has been used here.

[128] The power to order the arrest of a person is a common-law power. The High Court Rules addressing arrest do so in the context of arrest *tanquam suspectus de fuga*: O 36, r 278 et seq.

[129] Occasionally only imperfectly – *African Distillers v Zietkiewicz* 1980 ZLR 135 (G) (Beck J) 136F–H.

[130] Which doctrine has had its critics, *supra* fn 24.

who wishes to arrest a defendant, so as to found or confirm the jurisdiction of the Zimbabwean court over him, must prove that the *peregrinus* defendant is within the jurisdiction.[131]

In a similar fashion, section 15 of the 1981 Act, as has been noted above, confers discretion on the court whether or not to make an order for the arrest of a person where the conditions for assuming jurisdiction are otherwise satisfied.

On the assumption that the arrest of a *peregrinus* defendant so as to found or confirm the jurisdiction of the Zimbabwean court remains constitutionally legitimate in Zimbabwe, there is no authority on whether the court will adopt the same approach to the exercise of the section 15 discretion in the case of the arrest of a person as it does in the case of attachment of property or whether the court will more readily exercise its discretion where the liberty of a person is at issue.

16.2 Enforcement of Foreign Judgments

A foreign judgment may be enforced in Zimbabwe by ordinary action at common law[132] or by using the procedure contained within the Civil Matters (Mutual Assistance) Act 1995 ('the 1995 Act').[133]

By way of general introduction, it would appear that only judgments which require a party to pay a sum of money may be registered under the 1995 Act. Hence, where a party seeks to enforce, say, a declaratory order or a judgment granting interim relief, such a judgment does not fit within the compass of the 1995 Act.[134]

It is more of an open question whether such a restriction remains in place when a party seeks to recognise and enforce a judgment at common law. Hence, it appears that a party may use the common law to seek enforcement of a judgment which has administrative consequences or proprietary implications, provided that the court rendering the judgment had international jurisdiction.[135]

---

[131] *Monarch Steel (1991) (Pvt) Ltd v Fourway Haulage (Pty) Ltd* 1997 (2) ZLR 342 (H).

[132] Although there appears to be no direct authority on this point in Zimbabwe, this is the position in the Republic of South Africa: Forsyth *Private International Law* 5 ed (2012) 473; *Jones v Krok* 1995 (1) SA 677 (A) (Corbett CJ, Van Heerden, Kumleben, Nienaber and Olivier JJA), *per* Corbett JA (giving the judgment of the court) 685B–D.

[133] In force on 1 April 1996 (Act 14 of 1995 and Act 22 of 2001; now Cap 8:02 of the Laws of Zimbabwe).

[134] It is likely that this explains, in part, the judgment in *Cook v Abrahams* [2021] ZWHHC 263 (HC) (Mangota J). There, the plaintiff sought to 'register' a judgment from the High Court of England. While the content of the English judgment does not emerge clearly from Mangota J's remarks, it would appear that said English judgment pronounced upon the validity of a will. If that is right, it is unfortunate that the judge continued to talk about 'registration' outwith the context of the 1995 Act, especially given that the judge applied the test to determine whether the English judgment could be enforced at common law, rather than 'registered' under the 1995 Act.

[135] See *Gramara (Private) Ltd v Government of the Republic of Zimbabwe* 2010 (1) ZLR 59 (H), a case concerned with the enforcement in Zimbabwe of a decision of the SADC Tribunal, where Patel J stated that it would be 'contrary to principle to restrict the scope of recognition proceedings by reference to the specific remedies

16.2.1 Enforcement at common law

Procedurally, where the plaintiff in the action/judgment creditor wishes to enforce a foreign judgment at common law, he may do so by: (1) using the provisional sentence procedure;[136] (2) applying for summary judgment; or (3) proceeding to prove the case at trial.

Substantively, authority[137] suggests that the enforcement of a foreign judgment by ordinary action at common law[138] in Zimbabwe is likely to be governed by largely[139] the same principles as are applied by a South African court in this context.[140]

The basis on which a foreign judgment will be enforced by the South African court was set out by Corbett CJ in *Jones v Krok*:[141]

> 'the present position in South Africa is that a foreign judgment is not directly enforceable, but constitutes a cause of action and will be enforced by our Courts provided (i) that the court which pronounced the judgment had jurisdiction to entertain the case according

---

enjoined by a given foreign court'. As Frimpong Oppong *Private International Law in Commonwealth Africa* (2013) 310 points out, it is unclear whether the comments from Patel J apply only in the context of attempts to enforce judgments from regional courts established by treaty or whether, in fact, a party may also enforce in Zimbabwe a non-monetary judgment handed down by a foreign court.

136 *Jones v Krok* 1995 (1) SA 677 (A), *per* Corbett CJ at 685F.

137 *Gramara (Private) Ltd v Government of the Republic of Zimbabwe* 2010 (1) ZLR 59 (H); *Specialist Ltd v Apex Holdings (Pty) Ltd* 2010 (1) ZLR 451, [2010] ZWHHC 84; and *Tiiso Holdings (Pty) Ltd v Zimbabwe Iron & Steel Co Ltd* 2010 (2) ZLR 100 (H) (Patel J), [2010] ZWHHC 95.

138 Enforcement at common law is not stymied or prevented by the 1995 Act. It will be remembered that s 25 of the 1995 Act provides that: 'This Act shall be regarded as additional to, and not as limiting the provisions of any other law relating to the recognition and enforcement of foreign judgments, the service of process or the taking of evidence, whether on commission or otherwise.' Indeed, where a judgment is not one 'sounding in money', a party cannot rely on the 1995 Act as a mechanism by which that judgment can be enforced. Hence, as Patel J stated in *Gramara (Private) Ltd v Government of the Republic of Zimbabwe* 2010 (1) ZLR 59 (H): 'The Act is clearly not exhaustive in the coverage of its provisions ... [it] does not purport to override or exclude the operation of any other law, including the common law, pertaining to the recognition and enforcement of foreign judgments. In effect, section 25 accords with the general rule of statutory interpretation that the common law cannot be ousted except by clear language or in express terms.'

139 In *Tiiso Holdings (Pty) Ltd v Zimbabwe Iron & Steel Co Ltd* [2010] ZWHHC 95, 2010 (2) ZLR 100 (H), Patel J added a further condition, viz that the foreign court rendering the judgment had to have observed the minimum standard of procedural justice in arriving at the judgment. This case is dealt with fully in the main body of text below.

140 In *Gramara (Private) Ltd v Government of the Republic of Zimbabwe* 2010 (1) ZLR 59 (H), Patel J referred to the statement of the principles of the common law in *Jones v Krok* and stated, 'In the present matter, counsel have not referred me to any Zimbabwean case authority on the subject, either following or deviating from the South African position, and I have been unable to readily locate any. I accordingly take the view, pursuant to the provisions of section 89 of the Constitution governing the law to be administered by our courts, that our common law position is *ad idem* with the common law of South Africa as stated in [*Jones v Krok*]'.

141 1995 (1) SA 677 (A) (Corbett CJ, Van Heerden, Kumleben, Nienaber JJA and Olivier AJA), *per* Corbett CJ (giving the judgment of the court) 685B–D. For a more in-depth analysis of the principles which a South African court would apply in this context, please refer to the discussion on this subject in the chapter on the Republic of South Africa.

> to the principles recognised by our law with reference to the jurisdiction of foreign courts (sometimes referred to as "international jurisdiction or competence"); (ii) that the judgment is final and conclusive in its effect and has not become superannuated; (iii) that the recognition and enforcement of the judgment by our Courts would not be contrary to public policy; (iv) that the judgment was not obtained by fraudulent means; [and] (v) that the judgment does not involve the enforcement of a penal or revenue law of the foreign State'.

In addition to the principles expressly stated by Corbett CJ, a Zimbabwean court will not recognise and enforce a foreign judgment where it is shown that the foreign court, when rendering the judgment, failed to observe the minimum standards of procedural justice.[142]

Notwithstanding that the Zimbabwean courts are likely to apply the principles (largely) developed in the South African courts, the authors develop further the following three principles, with reference to the authorities, by virtue of the fact that they have received the greatest amount of judicial consideration in the Zimbabwean courts.

(1) The foreign court which pronounced judgment must have had international jurisdiction

In *Tiiso Holdings*, the High Court confirmed that the mere fact that the foreign court had jurisdiction according to its own laws was not sufficient to confer upon it the necessary international jurisdiction. Having cited academic authorities,[143] Patel J held that the defendant's express submission to the foreign court was sufficient to confer upon the foreign court international jurisdiction.

In adopting this approach, Patel J was following, possibly unconsciously, given that the case was not cited to him, the decision of the General Division in *Coluflandres v Scandia Industrial Products (1)*.[144] There, the plaintiff sought to enforce, by way of provisional sentence, a judgment it had obtained in the Commercial Court in Ghent (Belgium). Greenfield J[145] agreed with the proposition that a Rhodesian (now, Zimbabwean) court would only enforce a foreign judgment if, under the rules of conflict of laws as applied by Rhodesian courts, the foreign court is regarded as having jurisdiction. While he went on[146] to accept that contractual submission could confer jurisdiction on the foreign court, he found that the plaintiff had not proved satisfactorily the existence of any such submission on the facts.

---

142 *Tiiso Holdings (Pty) Ltd v Zimbabwe Iron & Steel Co Ltd* [2010] ZWHHC 95, 2010 (2) ZLR 100 (H).

143 Pistorius *Pollak on Jurisdiction* 2 ed (1993) 162–3 and Forsyth *Private International Law* 4 ed (2003) 395.

144 1969 (2) RLR 431.

145 Ibid 442G–I.

146 Ibid 442I–443A.

Contractual submission (or submission by way of agreement) is, of course, not the only way in which a party may submit to the jurisdiction of the foreign court. As the High Court has also recognised,[147] a defendant may also legitimately submit to the foreign court by entering an appearance before it.[148]

(2) *The judgment is final and conclusive and has not been superannuated*

A party's attempt to enforce a default judgment[149] of a foreign court typically gives rise to difficulty. In *Tiiso Holdings*,[150] the judgment that the plaintiff sought to enforce was a default judgment of the Frankfurt court dated 25 July 2006. The defendant had not applied for the rescission of the judgment nor had it been appealed. The judge held that the default judgment did not satisfy the requirement that a foreign judgment should be final. The reasons for this were as follows: (1) the judge stated that there was no evidence of German law as to whether or not any period for appealing the judgment or seeking its rescission had expired;[151] and (2) the judgment itself stated that 'it is provisional or preliminary and only provisionally enforceable'. The judge found that it was clear from the record that 'the Frankfurt judgment is purely provisional in nature and, therefore, subject to change or nullification' and was not, therefore, a final judgment.[152]

---

[147] *Grauman v Pers* 1970 1 RLR 130 (Greenfield J).

[148] In *Grauman,* there was no doubt that the defendant had entered an appearance in the South African court so as to defend proceedings. That appearance conferred jurisdiction on the foreign court. However, at 133F–G, Greenfield J suggested that, where the defendant had entered an appearance to protest the jurisdiction, the outcome may have been different.

[149] A Zimbabwean court may be more willing to enforce a summary judgment from a foreign court. An attempt to enforce such a judgment was upheld in *Grauman* 1970 1 RLR 130. There, the defendant argued that the judgment was not sufficiently final and so should not be enforced. In rejecting this submission, Greenfield J referred, at 133A, to the South African Rules of Court and determined that the judgment was of sufficient finality to be capable of enforcement in Rhodesia.

[150] 2001 (2) ZLR 100 (H) (Patel J).

[151] There was no discussion of the principle that in the absence of proof of foreign law, the court acts on the presumption that it is the same as domestic law.

[152] The question whether the judgment was provisional solely pending the expiry of the two-week period during which, under German law, the privilege of *Einspruch* is available, was not discussed. Forsyth agrees with the view of Hahlo that 'it appears quite arbitrary to say that the possibility of rescission of a default judgment precludes it from being final, however remote the prospect of success may be' (*Private International Law* 5 ed (2012) 459). In *Tiiso Holdings* the proceedings in Zimbabwe were commenced three to four years after the judgment of the Frankfurt court and there was no evidence that the defendant had at any time sought to disturb the judgment. In these circumstances it must be correct to take the view that the prospects of disturbing the judgment were remote (so remote that the defendant itself had not considered it worth doing so). Forsyth's view is as follows (*Private International Law* 5 ed (2012) 460): 'there is a strong case for creating an exception to the "final and conclusive" rule in the case of default judgments. If this is not done default judgments, even when granted by an internationally competent court, will often be worthless outside the territory of that court. Moreover, in the absence of a time limit after which the default judgment cannot be set aside by the court which pronounced it, only an application by the defendant to have the judgment set aside can, when dismissed, transmute the judgment into an internationally enforceable one. This is "in effect ... saying that the clearer the plaintiff's case the more useless his judgment would be" [fn 311: *per*

However, it is a feature of many default judgments that generally they will be susceptible to attack by a defendant usually within time limits set by the local court.[153] The fact that a judgment is susceptible to attack does not mean that the attack will be made or, if made, will succeed. In a case such as *Tiiso Holdings* where three to four years had expired between the making of the default judgment and the proceedings on that judgment in the Zimbabwe High Court, during which time the defendant appeared to have done nothing whatsoever to set aside or otherwise attack the judgment (possibly for the reason that such an attempt would be bound to fail), it seems very unfair to a plaintiff in possession of an apparently valid judgment from a court possessing international jurisdiction to refuse enforcement simply because the defendant might do in the future what he has chosen not to do in the past. A more nuanced approach would be appropriate in such a case requiring the defendant to show why no steps have been taken to attack the judgment. Such a requirement would not be unduly burdensome on the defendant, as the reasons for a defendant's inaction are uniquely within that defendant's own knowledge. If the reasons relied on by the defendant are unconvincing or non-existent, then there would seem very little reason in principle to deprive a plaintiff of the benefit of an existing judgment simply because the defendant has not, but might in the future, take steps to attack that judgment.

The question of the finality of a judgment in the context of an appeal against the foreign judgment was addressed by Corbett CJ in *Jones v Krok*,[154] where he set out the following rules:[155]

> '(1) The fact that the judgment is subject to appeal or even that an appeal is pending in the foreign jurisdiction does not affect the finality of the judgment, provided that in all other respects it is final and conclusive.
>
> (2) Where, however, it is shown that the judgment is subject to such an appeal or that such an appeal is pending, the Court in this country which is asked to enforce the judgment enjoys a discretion and in the exercise thereof may, instead of giving judgment in favour of the plaintiff, stay the proceedings pending the final determination of the appeal or appeals in the foreign jurisdiction.

Hunter CJ in *Boyle v. Victoria Yukon Trading Co* (1902) 9 BCR 213 at 223]. That cannot be right.' This point is also raised in the context of the discussion on the enforcement of foreign judgments in Namibia. For a comparison between the approach to finality adopted in Zimbabwe and Namibia (which appear to be quite similar), see the decision of the Namibian High Court in *Argos Fishing v Friopesca SA* 1991 NR 106, 1991 (3) SA 255 (NM).

[153] Under the Zimbabwe High Court Rules, this period is one month after knowledge of the default judgment (O 9, r 63(1)), such knowledge being deemed within two days of the judgment (r 63(3)).

[154] 1995 (1) SA 677 (A), *per* Corbett CJ (giving the judgment of the court) 689B–693C.

[155] Ibid 692B–G. It is submitted that, on the strength of the authorities cited above, the Zimbabwean courts would also follow and apply such rules.

(3) Although the onus of proving that a foreign judgment is final and conclusive rests upon the party seeking to enforce it ... it seems to me that, where this onus has been discharged, it is up to the defendant to place before the Court the facts relating to the impending appeal and such other relevant facts as may persuade the Court to exercise its discretion in favour of granting a stay of proceedings.

(4) In exercising this discretion the Court may take into account all relevant circumstances, including (but not confined to) whether an appeal is actually pending, the consequences to the defendant if judgment be given in favour of plaintiff and thereafter (possibly after the judgment has been satisfied) the appeal succeeds in the foreign jurisdiction and whether the defendant is pursuing the right of appeal genuinely and with due diligence. As a rule, however, the Court will refuse to assess the merits and demerits of the appeal and its prospects of success in the foreign Court.'

In permitting the court discretion whether to enforce the foreign judgment where that judgment is either subject to appeal or will be so subject in the near future, the Zimbabwean common law mirrors the position adopted by the legislature in the 1995 Act.[156]

(3) Recognition and enforcement of the foreign judgment not contrary to public policy

The third principle from *Jones v Krok*, that is, the recognition and enforcement of a foreign judgment by the courts of Zimbabwe should not be contrary to public policy, has received the most judicial consideration. In *Gramara*,[157] the defendant argued that the High Court of Zimbabwe should not recognise and enforce a judgment rendered by the South African Development Community Tribunal, on the basis that it impugned the legality of the government's land reforms, the constitutionality of which had already been upheld by the Zimbabwean Supreme Court.

Patel J acceded to this argument. It was, he considered, incorrect to force a government to act in a manner manifestly incompatible with that which had been constitutionally ordained.[158] In reaching his conclusion, Patel J helpfully confirmed that notions of public policy are 'not immutable and must perforce vary with time, place and circumstance, in tandem with changing social mores. Antecedent case authorities are obviously highly persuasive but may not always be germane or decisive.'[159] An argument against the recognition and enforcement of a foreign judgment on the basis of public policy must be analysed with specific reference to the facts of the case before the court.[160]

---

[156] See further below.

[157] *Gramara (Private) Ltd v Government of the Republic of Zimbabwe* 2010 (1) ZLR 59 (H).

[158] Ibid 76B–D.

[159] Ibid 73B–C.

[160] Ibid 74C–F. In this respect, Patel J confirmed that it would generally be contrary to public policy for a state to violate its international treaty obligations within its domestic realm: hence demonstrating that

The High Court of Zimbabwe was able to consider the ambit of the public policy argument again in *Venetian Blinds Specialist Ltd v Apex Holdings (Pty) Ltd.*[161] Here, Patel J considered an action on a judgment of the Malawi Supreme Court of Appeal for an order that the judgment be recognised as binding and enforceable. The defendant contended that the judgment should not be so recognised because to do so would be contrary to public policy (and also that the judgment had been satisfied previously).

The Malawian judgment was said to be fundamentally erroneous in certain respects,[162] such that it ought not be recognised and enforced by the court. Patel J observed:

> 'the uniform approach in common law jurisdictions is to be extremely chary about delving into questions of legal or factual correctness. It is generally inappropriate to review a judgment of a foreign court of competent jurisdiction and to deny or withhold recognition, even if there is shown to be a clear misapprehension by that court of the law or facts founding its judgment.'[163]

Patel J found that the defendant had voluntarily participated in the trial and appeal before the Malawian courts and that it was not suggested that the proceedings were other than procedurally correct. The judge dismissed the defendant's contention.

However, the judge found that the plaintiff had indeed already been paid the sum representing the judgment debt and dismissed the plaintiff's claim.[164]

---

the international context can help to cast light on the relevant public policy at issue (a concept which is notoriously difficult to define in precise terms).

[161] [2010] ZWHHC 84, 2010 (1) ZLR 451 (H); on appeal, [2012] ZWSC 13.

[162] For example, the court had calculated loss of profit on a gross and not a net basis.

[163] Citing authorities from the USA, England and *Jones v Krok* 1995 (1) SA 677 (A).

[164] The Malawi judgment was given in partly in Kwachas but mainly in USD. The defendant had paid the plaintiff MK4,819,512 in February 2004 when the exchange rate was MK:USD 72.2:1 (approximately). Instead of valuing the defendant's payment to the plaintiff in February 2004 at the MK:USD rate prevailing in February 2004, the judge valued the payment by reference to the MK:USD rate prevailing when the contract was concluded in 1993, a rate (4.4788:1) vastly more beneficial to the defendant than to the plaintiff, which resulted in the plaintiff's claim being satisfied by the February 2004 payment. The reasoning supporting this approach is suspect: the judge stated (1) nothing in the judgments suggested that awards in Kwachas had devalued since the contact was entered into and (2) that no evidence of the rate of exchange on Kwacha awards had been led. However, (1) the judge had earlier found that the currency of account was the USD and thus the value of any payment in an alternative currency should have been calculated in USD at the exchange rate at the date of payment and (2) judicial notice can be taken of exchange rates or, if the judge were unwilling to do so, a short adjournment could have been granted so that the evidence could be produced. The result of this was that the plaintiff's judgment of USD848,662.50 was satisfied by a payment worth USD66,752.24 when it was tendered. The justice of this result is not self-evident. Indeed, the Supreme Court of Zimbabwe appeared to concur with this when it heard, and allowed, the appeal: *Venetian Blinds Specialists Ltd v Apex Holdings (Pvt) Ltd* (171/10) [2012] ZWSC 13 (Garwe JA; Omerjee and Gowora JAA). There, Garwe JA, giving judgment for the court, at p 2 of the transcript, concluded that the High Court did not have sufficient evidence to reach the conclusion that it did, such that the matter should be remitted to it, with the correct evidence, to make an informed decision.

(4) In reaching its judgment, the foreign court must have obeyed the minimum standard of natural justice

A foreign judgment will not be enforced where it is shown – by the judgment debtor[165] – on the balance of probabilities[166] that the judgment was obtained contrary to the rules of natural justice.[167]

16.2.2 Enforcement pursuant to statute

16.2.2.1 *The regime for enforcement pursuant to statute*

The 1995 Act is, according to its long title, at least in part designed 'to provide for the enforcement in Zimbabwe of civil judgments given in foreign countries and territories and to facilitate the enforcement in foreign countries and territories of civil judgments given in Zimbabwe'. Therefore, the 1995 Act makes provision for a system of registration of foreign judgments, the purpose of which is to domesticate the foreign judgment and render it enforceable in Zimbabwe as if it were a judgment of the Zimbabwean court.[168]

The 1995 Act is additional to, and not a replacement for, enforcement of a foreign judgment at common law.[169]

The 1995 Act[170] repealed the Reciprocal Enforcement of Judgments Act 1974, the previous governing statute.

Despite the fact that the Reciprocal Enforcement of Judgments Act 1974 has now been repealed, the provisions of the High Court Rules (ie Order 37) dealing with the reciprocal enforcement of a foreign judgment, refer still to the previous Act. Hence, Order 37, rule 293, provides: 'An application under section 3 of the Reciprocal Enforcement of Judgment Act [Chapter 51] for leave to have a judgment obtained in a superior court in Great Britain registered in the High Court shall be made by a chamber application.' The provisions of the 1995 Act

---

[165] *Coluflandres Ltd v Scandia Industrial Products Ltd* 1969 (2) RLR 431 at 439. In that case, the judgment debtor alleged that it had not received notice of the trial in the foreign court; it bore the onus of proving that allegation.

[166] *Tiiso Holdings (Pty) Ltd v Zimbabwe Iron & Steel Co Ltd* [2010] ZWHHC 95, 2010 (2) ZLR 100 (H).

[167] For these purposes, the 'rules of natural justice' to be applied are those in force in Zimbabwe: *Steinberg v Cosmopolitan National Bank of Chicago* 1973 (3) SA 885 (RA: Rhodesia Appellate Division) (Macdonald ACJ, Lewis AJP and Goldin AJA) reversing the decision at first instance.

[168] Section 7(2). Certain provisions of the 1995 Act correspond closely to legislation of the United Kingdom on which the 1995 Act appears to have been based. In particular, ss 6 and 9 of the 1995 Act are in effect transpositions of ss 1(2), 2 and 4 of the Foreign Judgments (Reciprocal Enforcement) Act 1933. It is to be expected that a Zimbabwean court will refer to judicial and academic authorities on the construction of these provisions of the 1933 Act when deciding questions on the construction of corresponding provisions of the 1995 Act. In particular, reference should be made to: *Dicey, Morris and Collins on the Conflict of Laws* 15 ed (2012) vol 1, paras 14R183–14-195; Briggs *Civil Jurisdiction and Judgments* 7 ed (2021) paras 35.01–35.10.

[169] This being the effect of s 25 of the 1995 Act.

[170] See s 26(1) of the 1995 Act.

are not confined to judgments of superior courts of the United Kingdom (as the Reciprocal Enforcement of Judgments Act 1974 was),[171] but extend to the judgments given in any country designated by the Minister of Justice.[172]

It is likely that Order 37 will now be taken as referring to the provisions of the 1995 Act in view of the fact that both Order 37 and the 1995 Act envisage a process of registration leading to enforcement.[173]

The 1995 Act applies to international tribunals[174] and to judgments[175] given in a 'designated country'. A country becomes a designated country by the relevant Minister[176] making an order to that effect and publishing it in the *Gazette*. To date, it seems that only Australia, Dominica, South Africa, Bulgaria, Germany, Ghana, Portugal, Italy,[177] the Slovak Republic[178] and Zambia[179] have become designated countries for the purposes of the 1995 Act.

---

[171] In terms of s 3(1) of the Reciprocal Enforcement of Judgments Act, a judgment creditor, who had obtained a judgment in a superior court in the United Kingdom, was entitled, within 12 months from the date of judgment, to apply to the General Division in Rhodesia to have that judgment registered. Section 6(1) allowed the President, where satisfied that reciprocal provisions had been made by the legislature of any part of the dominions of the sovereign of the United Kingdom outside the United Kingdom or by the legislature of the Republic of South Africa for the enforcement of a Rhodesian judgment, he could extend the Reciprocal Enforcement of Judgments Act to judgments emanating from that country.

[172] Section 3(2) and (4).

[173] Section 25 of the 1995 Act provides: 'This Act shall be regarded as additional to, and not as limiting the provisions of any other law relating to the recognition and enforcement of foreign judgments ...'. Section 5(2)(b) provides that an application for enforcement 'shall be made in the form and manner prescribed in rules of court applicable to the appropriate court'. These provisions may provide a further basis for reading O 37 as now providing the machinery for the operation of the 1995 Act.

[174] Which term is defined in s 3(1) as 'any court or tribunal which, in pursuance of any international agreement or any resolution of the General Assembly of the United Nations' exercises jurisdiction or performs any function of a judicial nature, such as the Southern African Development Community Tribunal'. In order for a judgment of an international tribunal to fall within the registration regime of the 1995 Act, the relevant Minister must 'by order in the Gazette ... declare' that the Act shall apply to that tribunal (s 3(2)(b)).

[175] The term 'judgment' is defined in s 2 as 'a judgment or order given or made by any court or tribunal requiring the payment of money, and includes an award of compensation or damages to an aggrieved party in criminal proceedings'. The 1995 Act does not therefore apply to the enforcement of foreign arbitration awards (an extension which in the United Kingdom required amendment of the Foreign Judgments (Reciprocal Enforcement) Act 1933). The definition of 'judgment' also excludes judgments as to status (divorce, etc).

[176] Section 1 defines 'Minister' as meaning 'the Minister of Justice, Legal and Parliamentary Affairs or any other Minister to whom the President may, from time to time, assign the administration of this Act'.

[177] Civil Matters (Designated Countries) Order 1998 (SI 65 of 1998), art 4 of which repealed the Civil Matters (Mutual Assistance) (Designated Countries) Order 1997 (SI 185 of 1997), which had previously provided that Australia, Dominica and South Africa were designated countries for the purposes of the 1995 Act.

[178] Civil Matters (Mutual Assistance) (Designated Countries) (Amendment) Order (No 2) 1999 (SI 9 of 1999). This added the Slovak Republic to the list which had been contained in S1 65 of 1998. SI 9 of 1999 is cited in '"Recognition" under common law or "registration" in terms of the Act?: How to avoid the "confusion" fostered by the legislature with regards to the law of enforcement of foreign civil judgments', Godknows Munyaradzi Nyangwa of Mawere and Sibanda, Legal Practitioners: www.academia.edu/7413896/Recognition_under_common_law_or_registration_in_terms_of_statute_-_Enforcement_of_foreign_civil_judgments_in_Zimbabwe.

[179] Zambia was treated as a designated country in *Vehicle Delivery Services (Zimbabwe) (Pty) Ltd v Galaun Holdings Ltd* 2003 (2) ZLR 329 (H), *per* Hungwe J. The minister's order pursuant to which Zambia was designated was not referred to in the judgment.

16.2.2.2 *Procedure for registration*

The procedure for registration is as follows:[180] a judgment creditor under the foreign judgment may apply to the appropriate court[181] for registration of the judgment; the procedure for registration is prescribed by the procedural rules of the appropriate court; in the case of the High Court, these are the High Court Rules, Order 37;[182] an application for registration 'may' be made within six years of the date of either the foreign judgment itself or the determination of any appeal or review proceedings in respect of the foreign judgment.[183]

Registration of the foreign judgment is mandatory 'if the court is satisfied that it is just and convenient' for it to be enforced in Zimbabwe.[184] Therefore, a foreign judgment otherwise registrable will cease to be so if the court forms the view (on the evidence, it is to be supposed) that it is not just and convenient to register and enforce the foreign judgment in Zimbabwe.

In addition to those cases where it is not just and convenient to permit registration and enforcement of a foreign judgment otherwise registrable, section 6(2) of the 1995 Act provides that in certain prescribed circumstances the court is required not to register the foreign judgment. (The grounds in section 6(2) for mandatory non-registration also provide the basis for the setting aside of registration pursuant to section 8(4).)

There are 11 such circumstances (all but two of which also feature in the Foreign Judgments (Reciprocal Enforcement) Act 1933).[185] Therefore, where, in

---

[180] Section 5.

[181] This will be either the High Court or a magistrate's court, depending on whether the judgment in question would have been within the jurisdiction of a magistrate's court, had the cause of action arisen wholly within that court's province.

[182] Although O 37 remains drafted in terms applicable to the Reciprocal Enforcement of Judgments Act 1974 (Cap 51 of 1974; repealed by s 26(1) of the 1995 Act), it is to be supposed that the courts apply O 37 *mutatis mutandis* to applications for registration under the 1995 Act.

[183] Section 5(2). The six-year period is derived from s 2(1) of the UK Foreign Judgments (Reciprocal Enforcement) Act 1933. The terms of s 5(2) are not mandatory and appear to provide the court with discretion to permit registration outside the six-year period. In the 1933 Act the language used in relation to the six-year period is similarly permissive ('may apply … within six years'): Briggs *Civil Jurisdiction and Judgments* 7 ed (2021) para 35.10. In *Harman v Leaf* 1954 (2) SA 270 (SR), a decision under earlier Zimbabwe legislation for the reciprocal enforcement of foreign judgments which contained a one-year limit on registration subject to a discretion in the court to extend that time, dismissing an application for registration two years out of time, Beadle J held the plaintiff had failed to provide sufficient evidence that 'he has not in any way been dilatory in pressing for registration of his judgment' and dismissed the application. It may be that the extension of the registration period from one year to six years imposes an even greater burden on an application seeking to persuade the court that time should be extended.

[184] Section 6(1): 'an appropriate court *shall* direct the registration of the judgment concerned' (emphasis provided). The 'just and convenient' language used appears to be derived from s 9(1) of the Administration of Justice Act 1920, although that sub-section is permissive and not mandatory.

[185] The exclusionary provisions of the 1933 Act were based on the common law: 'The grounds of jurisdiction in the 1933 Act were deliberately framed so as to reproduce the rules of the common law as closely as possible' *Dicey, Morris and Collins on the Conflict of Laws* 15 ed (2012) vol 1, para 14-190.

analysing the circumstances in which the foreign court gave judgment, the court is satisfied of one of the following, it shall not permit registration of that foreign judgment.

(1) The foreign court which gave the judgment had no jurisdiction to do so.[186] The question whether the foreign court had jurisdiction is determined exhaustively[187] by the deeming provisions of section 9(4) of the 1995 Act.[188]

Section 9(4)(a) provides that the foreign court has jurisdiction[189] if the judgment debtor: (1) was a plaintiff in the foreign proceedings or submitted to them by voluntarily appearing for any purpose other than protecting or obtaining the release of property seized or threatened with seizure or contesting the jurisdiction of the court; or (2) was a defendant who had agreed to submit to the jurisdiction of the court in respect of the subject-matter of the proceedings; or (3) was a defendant and either (a) when proceedings were commenced was resident in the foreign country or, if a legal person, had its principal place of business in that country, or (b) at any time had an office or place of business in the foreign country through which or at which the transaction which gave rise to the proceedings was effected.

Section 9(4)(b)[190] relates to property and provides that the foreign court has jurisdiction in proceedings relating to movable or immovable property if that property was situated in the foreign country when proceedings were commenced.

Section 9(4)(c)[191] provides that in any other case the foreign court will be deemed to have had jurisdiction if the jurisdiction of the foreign court is recognised under the law of Zimbabwe.

---

[186] Section 6(2)(a); the equivalent of s 4(1)(a)(ii) of the Foreign Judgments (Reciprocal Enforcement) Act 1933.

[187] *Société Co-opérative Sidmetal v Titan International Ltd* [1966] 1 QB 828; *Sharps Commercials Ltd v Gas Turbines Ltd* [1956] NZLR 819 (a decision on the identically worded New Zealand Act).

[188] The provisions of s 9(4)(a) of the 1995 Act track the wording of s 4(2)(a) of the (English) Foreign Judgments (Reciprocal Enforcement) Act 1933.

[189] In s 4(2)(a) of the Foreign Judgments (Reciprocal Enforcement) Act 1933, the equivalent provision to s 9(4)(a) of the 1995 Act is qualified by the inclusion of a provision that the foreign judgment be given in an action '*in personam*', a term which does not appear in s 9(4)(a) of the 1995 Act. It is unclear whether this has the effect of expanding s 9(4)(c) to include foreign judgments that would be recognised at common law, but which do not satisfy the requirements of s 9(4)(a). The better view is probably that the words '*in personam*' should be implied by virtue of the subsequent provisions of the 1995 Act concerning movables and immovable property. However, the matter is not free from doubt because the draftsman of the 1995 Act clearly had in mind the provisions of the 1933 Act and it seems took a decision to omit the term '*in personam*' from the provisions of s 9(4)(a).

[190] The provisions of s 9(4)(b) track the wording of s 4(2)(b) of the Foreign Judgments (Reciprocal Enforcement) Act 1933.

[191] The provisions of s 9(4)(c) track the wording of s 4(2)(c) of the Foreign Judgments (Reciprocal Enforcement) Act 1933. It remains undecided whether this provision would entitle a court to recognise a basis for the jurisdiction of the foreign court not expressly provided for in the Act, but available at common law, such as presence of the defendant in the jurisdiction of the foreign court at the time of the commencement of

(2) The judgment is not a final and conclusive judgment of the court concerned.[192] The court may refuse to register a foreign judgment where an appeal against it is pending or the judgment debtor is entitled to appeal against it and intends to do so.[193]

(3) The judgment could not be enforced wholly or partly by execution in the relevant foreign country.[194]

(4) The judgment has been set aside by a court of competent jurisdiction.[195]

(5) The judgment has been wholly satisfied.[196]

(6) The judgment has become prescribed under the law of the relevant foreign country.[197]

(7) The enforcement of the foreign judgment would be contrary to any law or to public policy in Zimbabwe.[198]

(8) The judgment is for the payment of any tax, duty, rate or similar charge or a fine or penalty or maintenance for any person.[199]

(9) The judgment was obtained by fraud.[200]

---

proceedings. The discussion of this provision in *Dicey, Morris and Collins on the Conflict of Laws* 15 ed (2012) vol 1, para 14-190, suggests that this is not the case; in *Société Co-opérative Sidmetal v Titan International Ltd* [1966] 1 QB 828, Widgery J held (at 850C–D) that an action *in personam* not within s 4(2)(a) was also excluded from s 4(2)(c), 'It seems to me that an action *in personam* does not fall within subsection (2) unless it satisfies one or other of the conditions in paragraph (a). As I read the section, no action *in personam* could fall within paragraph (c) at all because all such actions are excluded by the terms of paragraph (c).' It is unclear whether the absence of the qualifying term '*in personam*' from the provisions of s 9(4)(a) means that s 9(4)(c) will be construed as providing a further means by which a foreign judgment may be registered.

[192] Section 6(2)(b); the equivalent of ss 1(2)(a) and 4(1)(a)(i) of the 1933 Act.

[193] This being the effect of s 6(5)(a) which contemplates non-registration on this basis; by contrast s 1(3) of the 1933 Act deems a judgment final and conclusive, notwithstanding that an appeal is pending or may be brought against the judgment. It is worth pointing out here that a judgment creditor who has successfully registered a foreign judgment may ask the court to attach assets of the judgment debtor (where such assets are within the jurisdiction) even though the judgment debtor's appeal against the foreign judgment is ongoing in the foreign country: *Siwela Holdings (Pvt) Ltd v Nyirongo* 1985 (1) ZLR 58 (H).

[194] Section 6(2)(c); the equivalent of ss 2(1)(b) and 4(1)(a)(i) of the 1933 Act.

[195] Section 6(2)(d).

[196] Section 6(2)(e); the equivalent of ss 2(1)(a) and 4(1)(a)(i) of the 1933 Act.

[197] Section 6(2)(f).

[198] Section 6(2)(g); the equivalent of s 4(1)(a)(v) of the 1933 Act. In *Dicey, Morris and Collins on the Conflict of Laws* 15 ed (2012) vol 1, para 14-191, it is stated of the equivalent provisions of the 1933 Act: 'The provisions with regard to fraud and public policy are the same as the common law rules. In particular, the common law rule that a foreign judgment can be impeached for fraud even though no newly discovered evidence is produced, and even though the fraud was alleged in the foreign proceedings, applies to enforcement and recognition under the 1933 Act. In *Owens Bank Ltd v Bracco* [[1992] 2 AC 443] the House of Lords held that the fraud exception in the 1920 Act was subject to the same rule, and indicated (obiter) that the same must be so under the 1933 Act.' The relevant rule is at r 51, paras 14R-152–14-158.

[199] Section 6(2)(h); the equivalent of ss 1(2)(b) and 4(1)(a)(i) of the 1933 Act.

[200] Section 6(2)(i); the equivalent of s 4(1)(a)(iv) of the 1933 Act. As mentioned above (see *The Conflict of Law* at para 14-191), it is likely that given the provenance of the 1995 Act, the English common-law rules will

(10) The applicant (ie the plaintiff) for registration is not a judgment creditor vested with a right to seek enforcement of the judgment.[201]

(11) The judgment debtor as defendant in the proceedings was not able to appear and defend the proceedings because he did not receive reasonable notice of them.[202]

16.2.2.3 *Setting aside registration of a foreign judgment*

Section 8 of the 1995 Act contains provisions concerned with the setting aside of a foreign judgment. Thus, inter alia: a judgment debtor may apply for registration of the foreign judgment to be set aside;[203] the judgment debtor requires the leave of the court to apply on the basis of a ground that was determined by the court on the original application for registration;[204] the court must set aside the registration of the foreign judgment if it is satisfied that registration should be set aside for any reason referred to in section 6(2) (public policy, fraud, etc);[205] if the court is satisfied that an appeal is pending or that the judgment debtor is entitled to appeal and intends to do so, the court may postpone the application to set aside the registration pending determination of the appeal[206] or it may set aside the registration, in which case the judgment creditor may bring further proceedings for registration under section 6 once the appeal has been determined.[207]

Finally, the 1995 Act provides that it does not prevent the court from recognising a foreign judgment as conclusive on any question of law or fact decided in the judgment, save in the case of foreign judgments that have been refused registration or have been set aside.[208]

---

be referred to on issues relating to the construction of the equivalent provisions of the 1995 Act. The rules relating to setting aside a foreign judgment obtained by fraud are comprehensively set out in *Dicey, Morris and Collins on the Conflict of Laws* 15 ed (2012) vol 1, r 50, paras 14R-137–14-145; the position in English law has not been followed in certain Commonwealth jurisdictions (eg Canada in *Beals v Saldanha* [2003] 3 SCR 416, (2003) 234 DLR (4th) 1; and New South Wales in *Keele v Findley* (1991) 21 NSWLR 444 (NSWSC); but in *Close v Arnot*, unreported, November 21, 1997 (NSW), the Common Law Division distinguished *Keele v Findley* and applied the traditional English standard of fraud in respect of a foreign judgment in a case where the defendant had, for good reason, allowed foreign proceedings to go undefended.

[201] Section 6(2)(j); the equivalent of s 4(1)(a)(vi) of the 1933 Act.

[202] Section 6(2)(k); the equivalent of s 4(1)(a)(iii) of the 1933 Act.

[203] Section 8(1). The fact that the 1995 Act imposes this condition makes it even more important that the registering court critically appraises the conditions in which the foreign judgment was secured.

[204] Section 8(3).

[205] Section 8(4).

[206] Section 8(5)(a).

[207] Section 8(6)(a).

[208] Section 10.

16.3 Interim Remedies

16.3.1 Jurisdiction to grant interim remedies

Section 176 of the Constitution enshrines the principle that the Constitutional, Supreme and High Courts 'have inherent power to protect and regulate their own process and to develop the common law or the customary law, taking into account the interests of justice and the provisions of this Constitution'.

Thus, like the South African Constitutional Court, Supreme Court of Appeal and High Courts,[209] the Zimbabwean superior courts have inherent jurisdiction to make orders for which no express statutory power is conferred, such as anti-dissipation orders, and to develop the common law in order to abolish, for example, attachment of the person, if that was considered to be required by the interests of justice and the terms of the Constitution.

The High Court Rules draw a distinction between interim relief and a provisional order. It is best to begin any explanation of that difference by reference to a provisional order. Hence, Order 32, rule 247, which describes the content and effect of a provisional order, makes it apparent that a provisional order is the functional equivalent of an order *nisi*: it specifies a time within which the defendant must file 'a notice of opposition' if he opposes the relief sought by the plaintiff. Presumably the court will or will not grant the relief sought in the intervening period (ie during the time within which the respondent must file his/her notice) on the basis of the merits of the individual case.

The relief sought by a plaintiff pursuant to an application for an interim order, on the other hand, will, if granted, take effect from the date of that order, subject only to any appeal against the order.

However, it seems that in practice the courts do not always maintain a strict terminological distinction between these two forms of order and the terms are often used interchangeably.[210]

16.3.2 Procedure for application

Any application for an interim interdict or provisional order (which distinction has been referred to above) or other interim relief is by way of an application under the High Court Rules, Order 32. Accordingly, below, is set out, first, the ways in which an application may be made.

---

[209] Section 173 of the South African Constitution is in materially identical terms to s 176 and provides: 'The Constitutional Court, Supreme Court of Appeal and High Courts have the inherent power to protect and regulate their own process, and to develop the common law, taking into account the interests of justice.'

[210] See, for example, the judgment of Mafusire J in *Northern Farming (Pvt) Ltd v Vegra Merchants (Pvt) Ltd* 2013 (2) ZLR 343 (H); and the judgment of Mtshiya J in *Stanbic Nominees (Pvt) Ltd v Remo Investment Brokers (Pvt) Ltd* 2013 (2) ZLR 413 (H).

Where an application is not made in the course of a hearing, an application must either be made as a 'court application' in writing to the court and on notice to all interested parties[211] or as a 'chamber application' in writing to a judge.[212] The documents required for a written application are the application itself, a draft order and any affidavit that it is sought to adduce in support of the application plus exhibits if appropriate.[213] Oral evidence is also admissible at the hearing of the application if the court considers it will be in the interests of justice to hear such evidence.[214]

In neither the case of a court application nor a chamber application is there a requirement that proceedings shall have been issued prior to the making of the application. Thus, an application may be made prior to the issuing of proceedings in an appropriate case. As a matter of practicality, if an application is sufficiently urgent to be made prior to the issuing of proceedings it is likely to be of sufficient urgency to satisfy the requirements of a chamber application. No doubt on the hearing of a pre-issue of proceedings chamber application, the court will seek an undertaking or order that proceedings be issued and served forthwith or as soon as reasonably practicable.[215]

A chamber application shall not be made unless one or more of five conditions is satisfied,[216] inter alia: the matter is urgent and cannot wait to be resolved through a court application; the relief sought is procedural or for a provisional order where no interim relief is sought; there are special circumstances which are set out in the application justifying the application. It is likely that, in practice, chamber applications will be of particular relevance to those practitioners and judges dealing with international commercial litigation and domestic litigation involving urgency.[217]

Order 32, rules 241–5 contain provisions which govern the making of chamber applications. A chamber application must be: made by entry in the chamber book; accompanied by the relevant court form (Form 29B) and supported by one or more affidavits setting out the facts upon which the plaintiff relies. The application must also be accompanied by heads of argument setting out the submissions and authorities relied upon.[218]

---

[211] Order 32, r 226(1)(a).

[212] Order 32, r 226(1)(b).

[213] Order 32, r 227. Detailed provisions are also set out at rr 230–40 for court applications and rr 241–5 for chamber applications.

[214] Order 32, r 229B.

[215] Indeed, in jurisdictions such as Namibia and South Africa, where interim relief is granted *pendente lite*, a party's failure then to institute proceedings within a reasonable time (or, as appropriate, by the date set by the court for the institution of such proceedings) can lead to the discharge of the rule *nisi* which had previously been granted in their favour.

[216] Order 32, r 226(2)(a)–(e).

[217] See the discussion below for what the threshold is for an 'urgent' application according to Zimbabwean law.

[218] Order 32, r 243.

A chamber application must be served on all interested parties unless the plaintiff reasonably believes one or more of the five matters set out in Order 32, rule 242(1) applies, inter alia: there is a risk of 'perverse conduct' in that any person who would otherwise be entitled to notice of the application is likely to act so as to defeat in whole or part the purpose of the application prior to an order being granted or served;[219] the matter is so urgent and the risk of irreparable damage so great that there is insufficient time to give notice to those otherwise entitled to it.[220] The basis of the plaintiff's belief must be set out in the affidavit(s) in support of the application.

The application must also be accompanied by a certificate from a legal practitioner, setting out with reasons that practitioner's belief that the matter is, inter alia, urgent[221] for one of the reasons set out in rule 242(1).[222]

There has been some controversy in Zimbabwe as to whether it is legitimate for the legal practitioner who is charged with the responsibility of producing the necessary certificate of urgency to come from the same law firm as that representing the plaintiff. The High Court[223] had originally held that legal practitioners from the same firm as that representing the plaintiff could not validly sign a certificate of urgency. However, while it is still an open question, it appears that the balance of judicial opinion[224] is in favour of allowing the legal practitioner representing the plaintiff to sign the certificate of urgency.

It is submitted that the latter (and now, it is submitted, prevalent) view is the better one. As Bere J stated in *Mudekunye v Mudekunye*,[225] the law puts in place certain safeguards to ensure the legitimacy of the certificate of urgency and leaves the final decision on whether the case is so urgent in the hands of the judge deciding the issue. Bere J continued:

> 'A legal practitioner who is representing a [plaintiff] in an urgent application is better positioned to prepare a certificate of urgency as opposed to any other legal practitioner who has not been favoured with direct instructions from the [plaintiff]. A legal practitioner

[219] Order 32, r 242(1)(c).

[220] Order 32, r 242(1)(d).

[221] The urgency of applications generally is considered under the sub-heading 'Urgency' further below.

[222] Rule 242(2)(b).

[223] *Chafanza v Edgars Stores Ltd* 2005 (1) ZLR 299 (H) (Cheda J). The report is slightly unusual, in that, while there is no doubt that Cheda J heard and decided the case, Ndou J (who did not hear the case) is also said to agree with the decision. This has given rise to a separate controversy, as to whether the judgment was a judgment of a two-judge High Court and so binding in instances where a single judge of the High Court sat. The case was certainly interpreted in that way by Kudya J in *The Attorney General of Zimbabwe v Chiriga Estates* (unreported) (case no HC 659/10). However, that interpretation has not been universal among the Zimbabwean courts: in both *Route Toute BV v Sunspun Bananas (Pvt) Ltd* [2010] ZWHHC 27 (Chatukuta J) and *Mudekunye v Mudekunye* [2010] ZWHHC 190, 2010 (2) ZLR 225 (H) (Bere J), the decision in *Chafanza* was not seen as binding.

[224] As is apparent from the authorities cited *supra* fn 223.

[225] [2010] ZWHHC 190, 2010 (2) ZLR 225 (H).

representing a [plaintiff] is in a better position to be of greater assistance to the court because he is familiar with the case. The question of bias or exaggerated interest, if ever it arises will be taken care of by the presiding judge in accordance with r 244. In coming to this conclusion I am among other things motivated by the fact that generally there is no legal practitioner worth his salt who would knowingly and intentionally conduct himself in such a way as to deliberately mislead the court particularly when he is fully aware that at the end of the day the discretion to confirm or decline urgency remains the prerogative of the court. As I earlier on stated there will be occasions when some legal practitioners will overstep but, again, our system has sufficient safeguards to deal with such a scenario.'

These are sound reasons, with which the authors respectfully agree.

However, it is important that a legal practitioner follows the relevant rules so as to ensure the validity of the certificate of urgency. Hence, in order for such a certificate to be valid, the legal practitioner must address his or her mind to the facts and circumstances of the case. Where she or he does not, the certificate will not be valid and the application will be dismissed. In *Chidawu v Shah*,[226] Gowora JA giving the judgment of the Supreme Court dismissing the plaintiff's appeal stated:

> 'In certifying the matter as urgent, the legal practitioner is required to apply his or her own mind to the circumstances of the case and reach an independent judgment as to the urgency of the matter. He or she is not supposed to take verbatim what his or her client says regarding perceived urgency and put it in the certificate of urgency ... it is a condition precedent to the validity of a certificate of urgency that a legal practitioner applies his mind to the facts.'[227]

In a similar way, as part of the legal practitioner's duty to exercise independent judgment when signing a certificate of urgency, s/he is not allowed to rely, uncritically, on a previous legal practitioner's point of view.[228]

If the application is accompanied by a certificate from a legal practitioner in accordance with the rules, the registrar 'shall immediately submit it to a judge, who shall consider the papers forthwith'.[229]

---

[226] [2013] ZWSC 12 (Malaba DCJ, Gowora JA and Omerjee AJA).

[227] Gowora J cited the decision of Gillespie J in *General Transport & Engineering (Pvt) Ltd v Zimbank Corp (Pvt) Ltd* 1998 2 ZLR 301 (H) where he stated (at 302E–303B): 'Where the rules relating to a certificate of urgency require a legal practitioner to state his own belief in the urgency of the matter that invitation must not be abused. He is not permitted to make as his certificate of urgency a submission in which he is unable to conscientiously concur. He has to apply his own mind and judgment to the circumstances and reach a personal view that he can honestly pass to a judge and which he can support not only by the strength of his arguments but on his own honour and name.' A legal practitioner who prepares and signs a certificate of urgency must set out reasons which have led to his or her belief that the application is urgent: *Triple C Pigs v Commissioner General Zimbabwe Revenue Authority* 2007 (1) ZLR 27 (H) (Gowora J), cited with approval in *Pascoe v Ministry, Lands and Rural Resettlement* [2017] ZWHHC 11 (Chitapi J).

[228] *Chidawu v Shah* [2011] ZWHHC 108, 2011 (2) ZLR 427 (H) (Uchena J), where the judge stated that the certificate of urgency should be based on the legal practitioner's honour. See, on appeal: [2013] ZWSC 12.

[229] Rule 244. While it is up to the legal practitioner to certify, in the above set out manner, that the matter is urgent, it is still up to the judge hearing the application to endorse or reject the legal practitioner's belief: *Laval Investments (Pvt) Ltd v BA Ncube Holdings (Pvt) Ltd t/a Airport Road Filling Station* [2004] ZWBHC 158.

16.3.2.1 *Urgency*

While the concept of urgency in the context of the making of chamber applications has already been partially considered, the Supreme Court in *Equity Properties (Pty) Ltd v Alshams Global BVI Ltd*[230] was able, when apparently speaking generally,[231] to state that the law governing urgency is settled in Zimbabwe: 'Urgency is manifested by either a time or consequence dimension'.

To understand what this means in practice, it is submitted that one needs to have regard to the case law which the Supreme Court cited with approval in the *Equity Properties* case.[232] Hence, in *Kuvarega v Registrar-General,*[233] the High Court explained: 'what constitutes urgency is not only the imminent arrival of the day of reckoning; a matter is urgent, if at the time the need to act arises, the matter cannot wait'. In *Document Support Centre (Pvt) Ltd v Mapuvire,*[234] the High Court cited *Kuvarega* with approval but provided further guidance on the test. In a passage which bears repetition in full, Makarau J held:

> 'I understand Chatikobo J in the above remarks to be saying that a matter is urgent if when the cause of action arises giving rise to the need to act, the harm suffered or threatened must be redressed or arrested there and then, for in waiting for the wheels of justice to grind at their ordinary pace, the aggrieved party would have irretrievably lost the right or legal interest that it seeks to protect and any approaches to court thereafter on that cause of action will be academic and of no direct benefit to the applicant.
>
> I need to digress a little at this stage and observe that it further appears to me that it is not every legal interest that is capable of protection by way of an urgent application no matter how compelling the circumstances. Thus, while the general position is that when the need to act arises, an applicant may approach the court for immediate redress without delay, it is not on every cause of action that such an approach may be made. An example that comes to mind is a spouse who may find her spouse committing an act that renders the continuance of married life insupportable and would want to end the marriage there and then. While the circumstances may be compelling, the aggrieved spouse may not approach the court for a decree of divorce on a certificate of urgency. The same observation can be made for most cases of damages for defamation, personal injury and /or accident damages to property.
>
> Without attempting to classify the causes of action that are incapable of redress by way of urgent application, it appears to me that the nature of the cause of action and the relief sought are important considerations in granting or denying urgent applications.

---

230 [2021] ZWSC 101 (SC) (Bhunu and Uchena JJA and Kudya J).

231 That is to say, while the Supreme Court was considering an urgent chamber application, their pronouncements on urgency did not appear to be confined to that context.

232 Namely: *Kuvarega v Registrar-General* 1998 (1) 188 (H) (Chatikobo J) 193E; *Document Support Centre (Pvt) Ltd v Mapuvire* 2006 (2) ZLR 240 (H) (Makarau J); *Gwarada v Johnson* 2009 (2) ZLR 159 (H) (Gowora J) and *Sitwell Gumbo v Porticullis (Pvt) Ltd t/a Financial Clearing Bureau SC* [2013] ZWSC 28 (SC) (Gwaunza JA).

233 1998 (1) 188 (H).

234 2006 (2) ZLR 240 (H) 243–4.

> Some actions, by their very nature, demand urgent attention and the law appears to have recognised that position. Thus, actions to protect life and liberty of the individual, or where the interests of minor children are at risk, demand that the courts drop everything else and, in appropriate cases, grant interim relief protecting the affected rights. The rationale of the courts acting swiftly where such interests are concerned is, in my view, clear. Failure to act in these circumstances will result in the loss of life or the liberty of individuals or the infliction of irreversible physical or psychological harm on children.
>
> It is now accepted that in some cases, even purely commercial interests can be protected urgently in appropriate cases. In *Silver's Trucks (Pvt) Ltd & Anor v Director of Customs & Excise* 1999 (1) ZLR 490 (H), Smith J considered the matter of the release of certain attached imports on the basis that the applicant would face bankruptcy and its 67 employees would lose their jobs as a result. In my view, the reasoning adopted by Smith J in this regard is still in line with the objective test that had the court waited, there would have been no need for the court to act subsequently. The applicants would have been liquidated and the return to it of the attached imports would not have reversed the effect of non-timeous action by the court. It will be of no further benefit to the applicant to pursue the legal interest.
>
> In my view, urgent applications are those where if the courts fail to act, the applicants may well be within their rights to dismissively suggest to the court that it should not bother to act subsequently as the position would have become irreversible and irreversibly so to the prejudice of the applicant.
>
> It is my further view that, the issue of urgency is not tested subjectively. Most litigants would like to see their disputes resolved as soon as they approach the courts. The test to be employed appears to me to be an objective one where the court has to be satisfied that the relief sought is such that it cannot wait without irreparably prejudicing the legal interest concerned.'

This reasoning was approved by the Supreme Court in *Equity Properties* and so sets out the approach which the court will take when faced with an urgent application.

In urgent applications made in the absence of the other party and, it seems, in urgent applications where 'short service' has been effected on the other party and that party is in attendance at the hearing of the application, the plaintiff has a duty of full and frank disclosure.

In *Bulawayo Dialogue Institute v Matyatya*,[235] Ndou J stated:[236] 'In urgent applications utmost good faith must be shown by the [plaintiff] to lay all the relevant facts before the court, so that it may have full knowledge of all the circumstances of the case before making its order' and:[237]

> 'The *audi alteram partem* rule as a principle of natural justice, applies in such urgent applications with merited exceptions. The respondents *in casu*, were served with

235 [2003] ZWBHC 87, 2003 (2) ZLR 79 (H).

236 At 82G–83A.

237 At 83D–G.

> application on the day of the hearing. This was indeed a very short notice. This short notice is a major constraint on the [defendants'] preparation of their response. The [defendants] did not have sufficient time to be heard from an informed position. An urgent application is an exception to the general rule and as such the [plaintiff] is expected to disclose fully and fairly all material facts known to him or her. This court has a discretion, even if non-disclosure is material, to grant or dismiss the application.'

The judge found that the plaintiff had acted in bad faith and dismissed the application as 'a seal of disapproval'.[238]

In this respect, it would appear that the law of Zimbabwe is in keeping with the law of Namibia and South Africa.[239]

16.3.3 Interim interdicts (provisional order/interim relief)

The Supreme Court in *Equity Properties (Pty) Ltd v Alshams Global BVI Ltd*[240] has recently set out and confirmed that the law in Zimbabwe governing the grant of interim interdict, such that a plaintiff must show:

> 'A. A clear or definite right - this is a matter of substantive law.
>
> B. An injury actually committed or reasonably apprehended - an infringement of the right established and resultant prejudice.
>
> C. The absence of a similar protection by any other ordinary remedy. The alternative remedy must (a) be adequate in the circumstances; (b) be ordinary and reasonable; (c) be a legal remedy; and (d) grant similar protection.
>
> In respect of an interim interdict, where the right sought to be protected is not clear, "a right which, 'though prima facie established, is open to some doubt'", suffices. See *Eriksen Motors (Welkom) Ltd v Warrenton & Anor* 1973 (3) SA 685 (A) at 691D.
>
> Where a clear right is established the applicant is precluded from establishing a well-grounded apprehension of irreparable harm but must do so where only a prima facie right open to some doubt is established. See *Pinkstone Mining (Pvt) Ltd & Ors v Lafarge Cement (Pvt) Ltd & Anor* HH 118/18 at p 3.'

It is, it is submitted, implicit in the above statement of the law that the balance of convenience must favour the granting of interim relief. That this is so follows from the materially identical nature of the law governing the grant of an interim interdict in Zimbabwe and the Republic of South Africa, as demonstrated by the Supreme Court's citation of South African authority in the above set out statement of the law.[241]

---

[238] At 83F–G.

[239] As to which, see the relevant parts of the chapters dealing with those jurisdictions.

[240] [2021] ZWSC 101 (SC) (Bhunu and Uchena JJA and Kudya J).

[241] For the position in the Republic of South Africa see, for example, *LF Boshoff Investments (Pty) Ltd v Cape Town Municipality* 1969 (2) SA 256 (C) (Corbett J) 267A–E, *Setlogelo v Setlogelo* 1914 AD 221

In the light of the material similarity between the law of Zimbabwe and the law of the Republic of South Africa governing the grant of interim interdicts, it may be useful to set out the way South African courts have approached each of the individual requirements found in the judgment of Corbett J (supra):

(a) Clear right or prima facie case

The requirement of a clear right or a right *prima facie* established though open to some doubt and the interrelationship between this requirement and the other requirements was addressed by Holmes J in *Olympic Passenger Service (Pty) Ltd v Ramlagan*,[242] where he stated:[243]

> 'It thus appears that where the plaintiff's right is clear, and the other requisites are present, no difficulty presents itself about granting an interdict. At the other end of the scale, where his prospects of ultimate success are nil, obviously the Court will refuse an interdict. Between those two extremes fall the intermediate cases in which, on the papers as a whole, the plaintiffs' prospects of ultimate success may range all the way from strong to weak. The expression '*prima facie* established though open to some doubt' seems to me a brilliantly apt classification of these cases. In such cases, upon proof of a well grounded apprehension of irreparable harm, and there being no adequate ordinary remedy, the Court may grant an interdict - it has a discretion, to be exercised judicially upon a consideration of all the facts. Usually this will resolve itself into a nice consideration of the prospects of success and the balance of convenience - the stronger the prospects of success, the less need for such balance to favour the plaintiff: the weaker the prospects of success, the greater the need for the balance of convenience to favour him. I need hardly add that by balance of convenience is meant the prejudice to the plaintiff if the interdict be refused, weighed against the prejudice to the defendant if it be granted.
>
> I have not overlooked the many Provincial decisions dealing with interdicts. Unfortunately they are disconcertingly inharmonious. Perhaps therefore I may be forgiven for respectfully refraining from garnishing the judgment with copious extracts from other decisions - a practice which sometimes serves only to burden the annotations and confuse the weary searcher after simple legal principles.'

At one extreme are the clear cases and at the other are the hopeless cases. In the former an interim interdict will usually be granted; in the latter an interdict will be refused.

The majority of cases will fall into the intermediate group of cases where the plaintiff establishes a *prima facie* right that is open to some doubt. The means by which this requirement is assessed has been the subject of various formulations,

(Innes JA) 227 and Prest *The Law and Practice of Interdicts* (1996) 49–51; Peté et al *Civil Procedure* 2 ed (2011) 409; Herbstein and Van Winsen *The Civil Practice of the High Courts of South Africa* 5 ed (2009) 1456–7.

[242] 1957 (2) SA 382 (D).

[243] Ibid 383C–G.

of which the most commonly cited is that of Clayden J in *Webster v Mitchell*,[244] where he stated:[245]

> 'The use of the phrase '*prima facie* established though open to some doubt' indicates I think that more is required than merely to look at the allegations of the applicant, but something short of a weighing up of the probabilities of conflicting versions is required. The proper manner of approach I consider is to take the facts as set out by the applicant, together with any facts set out by the respondent which the applicant cannot dispute, and to consider whether, having regard to the inherent probabilities, the applicant could on those facts obtain final relief at a trial. The facts set up in contradiction by the respondent should then be considered. If serious doubt is thrown on the case of the applicant he could not succeed in obtaining temporary relief, for his right, *prima facie* established, may only be open to 'some doubt'. But if there is mere contradiction, or unconvincing explanation, the matter should be left to trial and the right be protected in the meanwhile, subject of course to the respective prejudice in the grant or refusal of interim relief. Although the grant of a temporary interdict interferes with a right which is apparently possessed by the respondent, the position of the respondent is protected because, although the applicant sets up a case which *prima facie* establishes that the respondent has not the right apparently exercised by him, the test whether or not temporary relief is to be granted is the harm which will be done. And in a proper case it might well be that no relief would be granted to the applicant except on conditions which would compensate the respondent for interference with his right, should the applicant fail to show at the trial that he was entitled to interfere.'

Thus after consideration of the evidence concerning the existence and nature of the right in the manner set out by Clayden J, the court assesses whether the right, protection of which is claimed in the application, is a *prima facie* right though open to some doubt. If the right is open to serious doubt, this will not be sufficient to justify the grant of an interim interdict.

A question that has arisen concerns the disposability of issues of fact or law relating to the *prima facie* right prior to trial at the interlocutory stage. There is authority[246] for the view that factual issues should be remitted to trial but that issues of law may properly be dealt with in advance of trial, such that the question whether, as a matter of law, the plaintiff has a legal right should be resolved at an interlocutory stage. The better view is that legal (and factual) issues ought not to be resolved at the interlocutory stage unless they are straightforward and whether this is so is a question for the judge concerned:

[244] 1948 (1) SA 1186 (W). Affirmed as being the correct test by the Supreme Court of Appeal in *Simon NO v Air Operations of Europe AB* 1999 (1) SA 217 (SCA) (Smalberger, Howie, Plewman and Streicher JJA, Ngoepe AJA) 228F–H.

[245] Ibid 1189–90.

[246] *Fourie v Olivier* 1971 (3) SA 274 (T), *per* Viljoen J at 284–5; *Ex parte St Clair Lynn* 1980 (3) SA 163 (W), *per* Coetzee J at 164.

> 'If a legal issue could be disposed of at an interlocutory stage it would be sensible to do so. The problem, however, is that no hard and fast rule can be formulated to distinguish between difficult and not so difficult questions of law. A question of law, which at first blush, seems to be difficult, might not be so difficult depending on the expertise of the particular judge. The converse could also apply. It is submitted that the decision whether to dispose of a legal issue at the interlocutory stage should be left to the discretion of the Judge concerned in particular where situations of urgency require prompt decision. In those situations the English test for the first requirement, namely whether there is a serious question to be tried, seems to be the most apposite.'[247]

(b) Apprehension of irreparable harm

Once this assessment has been undertaken, the court will then consider both the evidence of irreparable harm to the plaintiff and the contention that there is no adequate ordinary remedy available to the plaintiff. If these requirements are satisfied then the court has discretion to grant an interim interdict. This discretion is to be exercised judicially in the light of all the facts.

In this regard 'irreparable' does not mean literally incapable of repair, but simply very difficult to repair and includes any prejudice suffered by the plaintiff as a result of the infringement of his rights.[248] Irreparable harm may comprise the prevention of the plaintiff from exercising his right at all, loss of money or the incurring of expenditure where sums are unlikely to be recovered.

It is not enough for the plaintiff simply to allege irreparable loss; the facts deposed to by the plaintiff must show that there is an actual or well-grounded apprehension of irreparable loss if no interdict is granted.

(c) No adequate ordinary remedy

The alternative remedy, the absence of which must be established by the plaintiff, must be: (1) adequate in the circumstances; (2) ordinary and reasonable; (3) a legal remedy; and (4) grant similar protection.[249]

---

[247] Herbstein and Van Winsen *The Civil Practice of the High Courts of South Africa* 5 ed (2009) 1463. The English test referred to being that set down by the House of Lords in *American Cyanamid Co v Ethicon Ltd* [1975] 1 All ER 504. See also, *Johannesburg Municipal Pension Fund v City of Johannesburg* 2005 (6) SA 273 (W), *per* Malan at 282–3.

[248] Herbstein and Van Winsen *The Civil Practice of the High Courts of South Africa* 5 ed (2009) 1464 (in the context of the test for a final order); *Bamford v Minister of Community Development and State Auxiliary Services* 1981 (3) SA 1054 (C), where Watermeyer JP granted an urgent interim interdict restraining the respondent from interfering with the plaintiff's access to certain land on which residences were being constructed and which was alleged to be part of a public park.

[249] Herbstein and Van Winsen *The Civil Practice of the High Courts of South Africa* 5 ed (2009) 1467–8; *Minister of Law and Order v Committee of the Church Summit* 1994 (3) SA 89 (BG), *per* Friedman AJP at 99F–H: 'Concerning the alternative remedy, the Courts have determined that it must be adequate in the circumstances, be ordinary and reasonable, be a legal remedy and also grant similar protection to a party. See *Free State Gold Areas Ltd v Merriespruit (Orange Free State) Gold Mining Co Ltd* 1961 (2) SA 505 at 524–5;

A question arises whether the absence of an alternative remedy is an essential requirement of the grant of an interim interdict or whether it is a matter to be taken into account in the exercise of the court's discretion. Herbstein and Van Winsen[250] categorise it as a matter to be taken into account in the exercise of the court's discretion. This is a view shared by Prest:[251]

> 'It has been held, correctly it is submitted, that the discretion of the court, apart from the position relating to the grant of interlocutory interdicts, where considerations of prejudice and convenience are of importance, is bound up with the question whether the rights of the party complaining can be protected by any other ordinary remedy. It is noticeable that in Van der Linden's exposition of the requisites, a discretion comes into play only in the case of his subsidiary rule relating to irreparable harm which applies to interlocutory relief.'

In *Candid Electronics (Pty) Ltd v Merchandise Buying Syndicate (Pty) Ltd*,[252] Cooper J stated:[253]

> 'The grant or refusal of an interdict is a matter within the discretion of the Court hearing the application and depends on the facts peculiar to each individual case and the right the plaintiff is seeking to enforce or protect' and, 'The rule that an interdict may not be granted when the plaintiff can obtain adequate redress by an award of damages is objectionable as it is an impermissible curtailment of the Court's discretion.'

The remedy that is usually proposed as an alternative to an interdict is damages. Damages will not be considered an adequate alternative remedy when: there is a continuing violation of the plaintiff's rights;[254] damages will be difficult or impossible to assess;[255] the plaintiff is not likely to be able to recover damages

---

Martin v Kiesbeampte, Newcastle Afdeling 1958 (2) SA 649 (D) at 654; *Cape Town Municipality v Abdulla* 1974 (4) SA 428 (C) at 440. Generally a [plaintiff] will not obtain an interdict if he can be awarded adequate compensation or amends by way of damages. The enquiry on this essential is whether an interdict is the only relief or remedy to help the [plaintiff], or is there a satisfactory alternative remedy. Furthermore, the circumstances relating to each case will indicate whether the award of damages is an adequate alternative remedy. The Court maintains a discretion. It is a factor in the general discretion of the Court.'

[250] *The Civil Practice of the High Courts of South Africa* 5 ed (2009) 1468.

[251] *The Law and Practice of Interdicts* (1996) 48 and 77.

[252] 1992 (2) SA 459 (C). Prest (at 78) quotes Sachs LJ in *Evans Marshall & Co Ltd v Bertola SA* [1973] 1 All ER 992 (CA) 1005d: 'The standard question in relation to the grant of an injunction, are damages an adequate remedy? might perhaps, in the light of the authorities of recent years, be re-written: is it just, in all the circumstances, that plaintiff should be confined to his remedy in damages?' EM Grosskopf JA in *Knox D'Arcy Ltd v Jamieson* 1996 (4) SA 348 (A) 362B–C (giving the judgment of the court), took the view that the availability of alternative remedies fell to be considered as a factor in the exercise of the court's discretion.

[253] 1992 (2) SA 459 (C) 464G and 465A, respectively.

[254] *Wynberg Municipality v Dreyer* 1920 AD 439; *Buitendach v West Rand Proprietary Mines Ltd* 1925 TPD 886; *Rivas v Premier (Transvaal) Diamond Mining Co Ltd* 1929 WLD 1.

[255] *Charney v Truebig* 1920 SWA 46.

from the defendant because, for example, he is a man of straw;[256] or the award of damages will otherwise be worthless.[257]

(d) Discretion/Balance of convenience

If the plaintiff establishes the requirements for an interdict, the remedy remains a discretionary remedy and the court may nonetheless refuse to make the order. In *Chirenje v Vendfin Investments*,[258] Chatukuta J stated that had the requirements for the grant of an interim interdict been satisfied in the case before him, he would nonetheless have refused the relief: the effect of the interdict would have been to mount a collateral attack on the decision of the court in earlier proceedings subject to an appeal by the plaintiff.

Chatukuta J cited the decision of Adam J in *Econet (Pvt) Ltd v Minister of Information, Posts and Telecommunications*,[259] in which Adam J had cited *Limbada v Dwarka*.[260] There, Holmes J, hearing an application for an interdict to restrain the defendant from alienating various properties he purchased using funds paid to him by the plaintiff for the purpose of effecting bribes, stated:[261]

> 'The Court always has a discretion whether to grant or refuse the extraordinary remedy of an interdict. The decisions are fairly unanimous on this point, from *Setlogelo v Setlogelo*, 1914 AD 221, down to *Olympic Passenger Service (Pty) Ltd v Ramlagan*, 1957 (2) SA 382 (D). This means that a [plaintiff] who establishes the requisites for an interdict is not necessarily entitled to that relief. I do not think that that proposition needs any authority, but as a matter of interest I quote with respectful agreement the following *obiter dicta* by Broome, J. (as he was then), in *Yusuf v Abboobaker and Pietermaritzburg Local Road Transportation Board*, 1943 NPD 244 at p. 247. After referring to three different sets of circumstances which afford grounds for an interdict, the learned Judge said:
>
> > "And I ought to add that the cases make it clear that a [plaintiff] who establishes one of the three propositions I have quoted above is not necessarily entitled to an interdict. The grant of an interdict is always in the discretion of the Court. Quite apart from the [plaintiff's] inability to establish any of the three propositions, I am not satisfied, for reasons which it would be undesirable to set out in view of the probability of this litigation going further, that the discretionary remedy of an interdict ought to be granted."

---

[256] *Aetiology Today CC v Van Aswegen* 1992 (1) SA 807 (W), *per* Cloete AJ at 815G–H: 'Even although an injury may be capable of pecuniary evaluation and compensation, a Court will generally grant an interdict if the respondent is a man of straw or if damages would be difficult to assess. In addition, the conduct of the respondents is likely to continue.'

[257] *Boiler Efficiency Services CC v Coalcor (Cape) (Pty) Ltd* 1989 (3) SA 460 (C), *per* Howie J at 475G: 'The value of a damages award in several years' time is of questionable adequacy in these inflationary times when in law one cannot obtain pre-judgment interest on the damages.'

[258] [2005] ZWHHC 4 (20/12/05).

[259] 1997 (1) ZLR 342 (HC).

[260] 1957 (3) SA 60 (N).

[261] Ibid 62B–G.

In exercising this discretion, I cannot shut my eyes to the [plaintiff's] unregenerate readiness to resort to bribery. His cynical disregard of the law for his own ends contrasts strikingly with his expectant recourse to the law when crossed in crime. All this may possibly not debar him from success at the trial, in view of the qualifications placed upon the *in pari delicto* rule in *Jajbhay v Cassim*, 1939 AD 537 at p. 544. But the overriding factor at this stage of the proceedings is that the relief which he seeks is discretionary and, in view of his turpitude, the Court is not prepared to extend it to him. At this discretionary stage he is not rescued by the fact that part, or even most, of the money may have been paid for innocent purposes, for the admitted taint of bribery casts its uneasy shadow over the whole application.'

Thus, where the plaintiff approaches the court without 'clean hands' or where, for some other reasons (such as collateral attack), the making of the order is not appropriate, the application for an interim interdict may be refused.

The Appellate Division of South Africa[262] further considered the appropriate way in which the court should exercise its discretion whether to grant an interim interdict in *Eriksen Motors (Welkom) Ltd v Protea Motors, Warrenton.*[263] Holmes JA recited the requirements for an interim interdict and stated:[264]

'In exercising its discretion the Court weighs, inter alia, the prejudice to the [plaintiff], if the interdict is withheld, against the prejudice to the respondent if it is granted. This is sometimes called the balance of convenience. The foregoing considerations are not individually decisive, but are interrelated; for example, the stronger the [plaintiff's] prospects of success the less his need to rely on prejudice to himself. Conversely, the more the element of "some doubt", the greater the need for the other factors to favour him. The Court considers the affidavits as a whole, and the interrelation of the foregoing considerations, according to the facts and probabilities; see *Olympic Passenger Service (Pty) Ltd v Ramlagan*, 1957 (2) SA 382 (D) at p. 383D - G. Viewed in that light, the reference to a right which, "though prima facie established, is open to some doubt" is apt, flexible and practical, and needs no further elaboration.'

Olympic Passenger Service (Pty) Ltd v Ramlagan[265] was an earlier decision of his own in which Holmes J (as he then was) elaborated on the exercise of the discretion to grant an interim interdict:[266]

'In *Setlogelo v Setlogelo*, 1914 AD 221 at p. 227, Innes, C.J., that great master of clarity and conciseness, had this to say about interdicts:

"The requisites for the right to claim an interdict are well known; a clear right, injury actually committed or reasonably apprehended, and the absence of similar protection by any other ordinary remedy ... The argument as to irreparable injury being a condition

---

[262] (Ogilvie Thompson CJ, Holmes, Wessels, Jansen and Muller JJA). Holmes JA gave the judgment of the court.

[263] 1973 (3) SA 685 (A).

[264] Ibid 691E–G.

[265] 1957 (2) SA 382 (D).

[266] Ibid 383A–G.

> precedent to the grant of an interdict is derived probably from a loose reading in the well-known passage in van der Linden's Institutes where he enumerates the essentials for such an application. The first, he says, is a clear right; the second is injury. But he does not say that where the right is clear the injury feared must be irreparable. That element is only introduced by him in cases where the right asserted by the applicant, though *prima facie* established, is open to some doubt. In such cases he says the test must be applied whether the continuance of the thing against which an interdict is sought would cause irreparable injury to the applicant. If so, the better course is to grant the relief if the discontinuance of the act complained of would not involve irreparable injury to the other party."

> It thus appears that where the applicant's right is clear, and the other requisites are present, no difficulty presents itself about granting an interdict. At the other end of the scale, where his prospects of ultimate success are nil, obviously the Court will refuse an interdict. Between those two extremes fall the intermediate cases in which, on the papers as a whole, the applicant's prospects of ultimate success may range all the way from strong to weak. The expression "*prima facie* established though open to some doubt" seems to me a brilliantly apt classification of these cases. In such cases, upon proof of a well grounded apprehension of irreparable harm, and there being no adequate ordinary remedy, the Court may grant an interdict - it has a discretion, to be exercised judicially upon a consideration of all the facts. Usually this will resolve itself into a nice consideration of the prospects of success and the balance of convenience - the stronger the prospects of success, the less need for such balance to favour the applicant: the weaker the prospects of success, the greater the need for the balance of convenience to favour him. I need hardly add that by balance of convenience is meant the prejudice to the applicant if the interdict be refused, weighed against the prejudice to the respondent if it be granted.'

If the right established by the plaintiff is a clear right and he can show that he has suffered or has a reasonable apprehension that he will suffer an injury and that there is no other remedy that will protect him, then he will be entitled to a final interdict (subject to any discretionary considerations).[267]

16.3.4 Freezing orders/Anti-dissipation interdicts

The Zimbabwean court has jurisdiction to grant an anti-dissipation interdict (or freezing order). In *Northern Farming (Pvt) Ltd v Vegra Merchants (Pvt) Ltd*,[268] the plaintiff had sold 709 tonnes of maize to the first defendant on 14-day credit terms with which the first defendant had not complied. The first defendant had taken delivery of the maize and had sold parts of the consignment on to various sub-purchasers. It appeared that the first defendant had received sums from sub-purchasers but had failed to pay the plaintiff out of such receipts. The credit terms

[267] *Mufakose Flats Residents Association v The Minister of Local Government and National Housing* (unreported) (case no HH 5-2002), *per* Chinhengo J.

[268] 2013 (2) ZLR 343 (H).

contained an arbitration clause, which the plaintiff had invoked and arbitration proceedings had been commenced. The plaintiff applied for what was termed an 'anti-dissipation interdict', to restrain the first defendant from disposing of the remaining maize, pending determination of the arbitration proceedings on the basis that the plaintiff feared that if the first defendant was not so restrained, any award in the plaintiff's favour would be unsatisfied because the first defendant was indigent.

Mafusire J set out his understanding of what an anti-dissipation interdict was, referred to the South African case *Knox D'Arcy Ltd v Jamieson*[269] and quoted the following passage from the judgment of EM Grosskopf JA:[270]

> 'The conduct sought to be interdicted
>
> The nature of the interdict sought by the petitioners is to prevent the [defendants] from concealing their assets. The [plaintiffs] do not claim any proprietary or quasi-proprietary right in these assets. It is conceded that the assets are the unencumbered property of the [defendants]. The interdict sought was therefore of an unusual nature. It is not the usual case where its purpose is to preserve an asset which is in issue between the parties. Here the [plaintiffs] lay no claim to the assets in question. They merely allege a general right to damages. Moreover, the conduct on the part of the [defendants] which is sought to be interdicted is *prima facie* lawful. It is therefore not surprising that both the name of the interdict and its essential content have been the subject of some debate.
>
> As far as its name is concerned, the [plaintiffs] referred to it as a Mareva-type interdict after the term used in English law. The Court *a quo* did not like this name since the use of the English term might suggest that English principles are automatically applicable (see 1994 (3) SA at 705A–706B). I agree with this criticism. The alternatives suggested by Stegmann J were not, however, much more felicitous. Thus he referred to an interdict *in securitatem debiti* and an anti-dissipation interdict. The former expression may suggest that the purpose of the interdict is to provide security for the [plaintiff's] claim. This is not so. The interdict prevents the [defendant] from dealing freely with his assets but grants the [plaintiff] no preferential rights over those assets. And 'anti-dissipation' suffers from the defect that in most cases and, certainly in the present case, the interdict is not sought to prevent the [defendant] from dissipating his assets, but rather from preserving them so well that the [plaintiff] cannot get his hands on them. Having criticised the names used for the interdict I find myself unfortunately unable to suggest a better one. I console myself with the thought that our law has recognised this type of interdict for many years without giving it any specific name.'

On the facts of the case before him, Mafusire J correctly found that the plaintiff was seeking an anti-dissipation interdict (although he characterised it as a simple prohibitory interdict). The judge proceeded to set out the requirements for such an interdict and make the order sought (citing *Setlogelo v Setlogelo*).

---

269 1996 (4) SA 348 (A) (EM Grosskopf, Nestadt, FH Grosskopf, Harms and Scott JJA).

270 Ibid 371G–372C; the other members of the court agreeing.

Mafusire J accepted the *Knox D'Arcy* case as an authoritative statement of the law relating to anti-dissipation interdicts for the purposes of Zimbabwean law. As such, it is appropriate to set out here the unanimous findings of the Appellate Division regarding the requirements for an anti-dissipation interdict:[271]

> 'What then must a [plaintiff] show in this regard? ... in *Mcitiki and Another v Maweni* 1913 CPD 684 at 687 Hopley J stated the effect of earlier cases as follows:
>
> > "... (T)hey all proceed upon the wish of the Court that the plaintiff should not have an injustice done to him by reason of leaving his debtor possessed of funds sufficient to satisfy the claim, when circumstances show that such debtor is wasting or getting rid of such funds to defeat his creditors, or is likely to do so." See also *Bricktec (Pty) Ltd v Pantland* 1977 (2) SA 489 (T) at 493E-G.
>
> The question which arises from this approach is whether a [plaintiff] need show a particular state of mind on the part of the [defendant], ie that he is getting rid of the funds, or is likely to do so, with the intention of defeating the claims of creditors. Having regard to the purpose of this type of interdict, the answer must be, I consider, yes, except possibly in exceptional cases. As I have said, the effect of the interdict is to prevent the [defendant] from freely dealing with his own property to which the [plaintiff] lays no claim. Justice may require this restriction in cases where the [defendant] is shown to be acting *mala fide* with the intent of preventing execution in respect of the [plaintiff's] claim. However, there would not normally be any justification to compel a [defendant] to regulate his bona fide expenditure so as to retain funds in his patrimony for the payment of claims (particularly disputed ones) against him. I am not, of course, at the moment dealing with special situations which might arise, for instance, by contract or under the law of insolvency.
>
> ... It is often said that an interdict will not be granted if there is another satisfactory remedy available to the [plaintiff]. In that context a claim for damages is often contrasted with a claim for an interdict ... That is not the question which arises here. In the present circumstances there is no question of a claim for damages being an alternative to an interdict. The only claim which the petitioners have is one for damages. There is no suggestion that it could be replaced by a claim for an interdict. The purpose of the interdict is not to be a substitute for the claim for damages but to reinforce it - to render it more effective. And the question whether the claim is a satisfactory remedy in the absence of an interdict would normally answer itself. Except where the [defendant] is a Croesus, a claim for damages buttressed by an interdict of this sort is always more satisfactory for the plaintiff than one standing on its own feet. The question of an alternative remedy accordingly does not arise in this sort of case. The interdict with which we are dealing is *sui generis.* It is either available or it is not. No other remedy can really take its place (except, possibly, in certain circumstances attachments or arrests). The question here is purely whether, in principle and on authority, such an interdict should be granted in cases where the [defendant] is in good faith disposing of his assets, or threatening to do so, and has no intent to render the [plaintiff's] claim nugatory.

[271] Ibid 372D–373H.

In view of the manner in which the present proceedings were brought it is however not necessary to pursue this matter further. The basis of the petitioners' claim as set out in the petition for leave to appeal and their heads of argument is that they have proved prima facie that the [defendants] had an intention to defeat the petitioners' claims, or to render them hollow, by secreting their assets. It was common cause that if these facts could be proved, together with the other requirements for an interim interdict, the petitioners would have a good case, and for the reasons given above I agree with this approach. There was some argument on whether the fact that assets were secreted with the intent to thwart the petitioners' claim had to be proved on a balance of probabilities or merely prima facie. However, it seems to me that here also the relative strength or weakness of the petitioners' proof would be a factor to be taken into account and weighed against other features in deciding whether an interim interdict should be granted.'

It is to be expected that the *Knox D'Arcy* case will be taken as the basis for the grant of anti-dissipation relief in the future.[272]

16.3.5 Search and seize orders

'Zimbabwean legal jurisprudence was characterised by a dearth of case law authority'[273] on the effect of an *Anton Piller* order until the decision of Devitte J in *Cooper v Leslie*.[274] In *Stanbic Nominees (Pvt) Ltd v Remo Investment Brokers (Pvt) Ltd*,[275] Mtshiya J considered the effect of an *Anton Piller* order on parties not named in the order and cited with approval passages from the decision in *Cooper*, which helpfully set out the principles on which the court will grant *Anton Piller* relief. Mtshiya J stated:[276]

> 'In the headnote to *Cooper v. Leslie & ors* 2000 (1) ZLR 14 (H) the following appears:
>
> > "An *Anton Piller* order is a modern legal remedy devised to cater for modern problems in the prosecution of civil actions. The procedure allows a party to make an *ex parte* application, without notice to the other side, for the attachment and removal of documents or other evidence. It has its genesis in English Law. Originally, its use was confined to cases involving intellectual property, but has since been extended to cover other civil cases. It has, after some initial reluctance and some contradictory judgments, been accepted by the courts of South Africa and should be accepted as part of the law of Zimbabwe.

---

[272] That the Zimbabwe High Court, in *Coverlink Insurance Brokers (PVT) Ltd v Kudzurunga* [2016] ZWHHC 150 (Tagu J), cited with approval the decision in the *Northern Farming* case only strengthens this view.

[273] *Dr Dish Ltd v Econet Media Ltd* [2020] ZWHHC 381 (HC) (Masithu J).

[274] 2000 (1) ZLR 14 (H).

[275] 2013 (2) ZLR 413 (H).

[276] Ibid 420A–E.

> An applicant [the plaintiff] for an *Anton Piller* order must *prima facie* establish:
>
> 1. that he has a cause of action against [the defendant] which he intends to pursue;
> 2. that [the defendant] has in his possession specific and specified documents or things which constitute vital evidence in substantiation of the [plaintiff's] cause of action, but in respect of which the [plaintiff] cannot claim a real or personal right; and
> 3. that there is a real and well-founded apprehension that this evidence may be hidden or destroyed or in some manner spirited away by the time the case comes to trial or to the stage of discovery.
>
> The remedy may, if used indiscriminately, become an instrument of oppression, so the court must proceed with caution and impose safeguards to protect the rights of the party against whom the relief is sought. In exercising its discretion, the court must pay regard to the cogency of the *prima facie* case established with reference to the three items listed above; the potential harm that will be suffered by the respondent if the order is granted, as compared to the potential harm to the [plaintiff if] it is not; and whether the terms of the order sought are no more onerous than is necessary to protect the interests of the [plaintiff]."
>
> Mtshiya J held that, because the applicant, being one of the persons against whom the order was sought, had not been joined to the original application for an *Anton Piller* order, the *ex parte* order obtained did not bind it and discharged the order against the applicant.'

It is noteworthy that the judge made no criticism of the terms in which the original order had been made, which included provisions for a supervising attorney to be present.[277] Thus it may be supposed that in making an *Anton Piller* order the court may order, inter alia, the appointment and attendance of a supervising attorney at the premises to be searched; that a list of items seized must be made; and that the items seized be held by the Deputy Sheriff or supervising attorney until further order.

One observation that may be made of the decision in the *Stanbic Nominees* case is that the order was directed at certain share certificates held by certain parties. Although the report does not set out the evidence on the basis of which the original application was made, it seems curious that an *Anton Piller* order was made in respect of movables which are capable of replacement and where an order *in personam* requiring the relevant addressee to procure the production of the certificates would have sufficed in place of the draconian remedy which is the *Anton Piller* order.

[277] The terms of the original order are at 415A–416D of the report and repay examination.

16.3.6 Third-party disclosure orders

There is an absence of judicial authority in Zimbabwe on the question of whether a court may make an order compelling, say, the defendant to disclose the identity of a wrongdoer, whose wrongdoing the defendant has facilitated. In those circumstances, it appears likely that a Zimbabwean court would follow the guidance which has been given by courts in the Republic of South Africa on this issue.

In *Kinekor Films (Pty) Ltd v B A Adami Films (Pty) Ltd*,[278] allowing the plaintiff's appeal, the court made an order compelling the defendant to disclose the identity of the source of the films in its possession of which the plaintiff was the copyright owner, with a view to the plaintiff bringing proceedings against those persons. Giving the judgment of the full bench of the Eastern Cape Division, Eksteen J held[279] that it was

> 'clear that the person or persons from whom the [defendant] had obtained the infringing copies of the films were, in the same way, infringing the [plaintiff's] copyright by supplying such films to the [defendant], and that the appellant would therefore, *prima facie*, have a cause of action against such suppliers. Such an action however cannot be brought unless the [plaintiff] knows who the person or persons are who are acting in breach of its copyright. It says that it does not know who these persons are, and the obvious place to seek this information is from the [defendant] who must be aware of their identity. To deny the [plaintiff] the relief it seeks would in my view not be in the interests of justice but would rather afford an unwarranted protection of the infringers of the plaintiff's] copyright in the pursuit of their illegal activity.'

In *Roamer Watch Co SA v African Textile Distributors*,[280] Cilliers AJ drew a distinction[281] between two types of disclosure cases: first, those where

> 'the [plaintiff] seeks to proceed against an unincorporated body or the officials of an unincorporated or incorporated body, and seeks disclosure of the names of the appropriate persons to cite from another person who is possessed of this information by virtue of his being an official of that body or standing in some other similar relation to that body';

and, second,[282] those where the plaintiff 'is concerned to obtain the name of a party whom he is unable to identify and against whom he may have a cause of action'. In the latter situation, the plaintiff is seeking discovery of the name from a party who may have sound commercial or other reasons for being reluctant to disclose it. Cilliers AJ stated[283] that in the second case the plaintiff would need to indicate at least the following in the papers filed for hearing:

---

[278] 1976 (4) SA 935 (E) (Eksteen, Kannemeyer and De Wet JJ).

[279] Ibid 939G–J.

[280] 1980 (2) SA 254 (W).

[281] Ibid 281F–G.

[282] Ibid 281H–I.

[283] Ibid 282A–D.

(1) A *bona fide* belief in his right of action against the party whose name he seeks to be disclosed and that he has reasonable grounds for believing that he has such a claim against such party. Here the strength of the plaintiff's case against the unknown alleged wrongdoer is relevant to the exercise of the court's discretion.

(2) There is no other complete remedy. Another appropriate remedy may consist either of an adequate claim against a party who is known to him in respect of the same damages which the plaintiff claims to have suffered, or in another procedural remedy to establish the same information which he seeks from the defendant.

(3) The defendant is able to supply such information.

In *Cerebos Food Corp v Diverse Foods SA (Pty) Ltd*,[284] giving the judgment of the full bench of the Transvaal Provincial Division, Van Dijkhorst J held:[285] 'Neither in the Roman law nor the Roman-Dutch law nor in our law as laid down by the Appellate Division is there any authority for an order that a defendant disclose the names or particulars of sources and retail outlets.'

However, the court in the *Cerebos Food* case also held[286] that South African courts had no jurisdiction to make *Anton Piller* orders (defined by the court as[287] 'orders for the attachment of documents and other things can be granted where no right is claimed to them except that they should be preserved and produced as evidence in an intended Court action'). However, the Appellate Division in *Shoba v Officer Commanding, Temporary Police Camp, Wagendrift Dam; Maphanga v Officer Commanding, SA Police Murder & Robbery Unit, Pietermaritzburg*,[288] subsequently held this decision to have been wrong. The authority of the *Cerebos Food* case on ancillary orders and disclosure orders must therefore be doubted.[289]

---

[284] 1984 (4) SA 149 (T; Boshoff JP and Van Dijkhorst and O'Donovan JJ).

[285] Ibid 168A–B. But the court also held that South African courts had no jurisdiction to make *Anton Piller* orders (defined by the court as, 'Orders for the attachment of documents and other things can be granted where no right is claimed to them except that they should be preserved and produced as evidence in an intended Court action' at 168B–C); see the passages at 170H–I and 173E–F. In view of the fact that this view has been held to be wrong by the Appellate Division (the *Shoba* case), the authority of the *Cerebos Food* case on ancillary orders and disclosure orders must be doubted.

[286] Ibid 170H–I and 173E–F.

[287] Ibid 168B–C.

[288] 1995 (4) SA 1 (A) (Corbett CJ, EM Grosskopf, Nestadt, and Steyn JJA and Nicholas AJA).

[289] In addition, the decision in *Roamer Watch Co SA v African Textile Distributors* 1980 (2) SA 254 (W) appears not to have been cited to the court in *Cerebos Food*. Further the Appellate Division assumed, without deciding the question, that a court may order a non-party to furnish information required by the applicant for the purpose of litigation: *Krygkor Pensioenfonds v Smith* 1993 (3) SA 459 (A), where a divorcee was entitled to part of her former husband's pension; he refused to pay her and she applied, inter alia, for an order requiring the pension fund to inform her as to her husband's pension. The Appellate Division held (at 462A–B): 'The Appellate Division had authoritatively affirmed that it was entitled to adapt its procedures in the interests of justice; that it could be accepted for the purposes of the present case (without so deciding) that a Court

The better view is that the court has power to make an order requiring a third party to disclose the identity of a wrongdoer.

The decisions of the South African courts which have been cited above all predate the enactment of the Zimbabwean Constitution in 2013. Section 62 of the Zimbabwean Constitution provides as follows:

> '1. Every Zimbabwean citizen or permanent resident, including juristic persons and the Zimbabwean media, has the right of access to any information held by the State or by any institution or agency of government at every level, in so far as the information is required in the interests of public accountability.
>
> 2. Every person, including the Zimbabwean media, has the right of access to any information held by any person, including the State, in so far as the information is required for the exercise or protection of a right.
>
> 3. Every person has a right to the correction of information, or the deletion of untrue, erroneous or misleading information, which is held by the State or any institution or agency of the government at any level, and which relates to that person.
>
> 4. Legislation must be enacted to give effect to this right, but may restrict access to information in the interests of defence, public security or professional confidentiality, to the extent that the restriction is fair, reasonable, necessary and justifiable in a democratic society based on openness, justice, human dignity, equality and freedom.'

At present, it does not appear that any such legislation has been enacted to give effect to this Constitutional provision. However, it is submitted that section 62 of the Constitution confers upon the court the jurisdiction to make an order for the disclosure of information, in the same way that courts in the Republic of South Africa may do.

16.3.7 Anti-suit interdicts (injunctions)

An anti-suit interdict (injunction) is an order restraining the injunction defendant from either commencing or continuing proceedings outside Zimbabwe in breach of a legal or equitable right on the part of the injunction plaintiff not to pursue litigation outside Zimbabwe or, conversely, restraining the injunction defendant

---

in appropriate circumstances had the jurisdiction to order a party against whom an applicant had no cause of action and who was not a party or intended party to litigation with the applicant, to supply the required information.' This goes further than previous authority in this area by extending the range of disclosure from the identity of a wrongdoer to 'information' generally. Referring to both documents and information, Wunsh J in *Eiser v Vuna Health Care (Pty) Ltd* 1998 (3) SA 139 (W) stated (at 148A–B): 'Our Courts have an inherent jurisdiction to come to the assistance of a litigant who, before proceedings are instituted, requires information from a third party, which is sparingly exercised (*Krygkor Pensioenfonds v Smith* 1993 (3) SA 459 (A)) and there are a few instances where a would-be opponent has been ordered to disclose documents before the institution of proceedings as in *Durban and District African Football Association v Dhludhla & Others* 1961 (3) SA 892 (D).'

from commencing or continuing proceedings inside Zimbabwe in breach of a legal or equitable right on the part of the injunction plaintiff to have the dispute between the parties litigated in a jurisdiction other than Zimbabwe.[290]

There is no reported judicial authority in Zimbabwe on whether or not an anti-suit interdict is a remedy available to the courts in Zimbabwe. That said, the courts of Ghana,[291] Nigeria[292] and, crucially, for present purposes, the Republic of South Africa[293] have concluded that this form of relief is available in those jurisdictions. Given the affinity which exists between the legal systems in place in Zimbabwe and the Republic of South Africa, it is likely that the Zimbabwe courts will be guided by the approach which the South African courts take with respect to this relief.[294]

16.3.8 *Mandament van spolie*

The protection from dispossession available in the Republic of South Africa is similarly available under Zimbabwe law, although certain differences exist between the principles applied in South Africa and those applied in Zimbabwe.

The Supreme Court in *Botha v Barrett*,[295] a case concerning the removal of movables (trucks, trailers and fuel tanks), relying on the decision of the Supreme Court of the Transvaal in *Nino Bonino v de Lange*,[296] held[297] that to obtain a spoliation order two conditions needed to be satisfied: '(a) that the [plaintiff] was in peaceful and undisturbed possession of the property; and, (b) that the [defendant] deprived him of the possession forcibly or wrongfully *against his consent*' (emphasis in original).[298] The burden of proof in showing a lack of consent was on the

[290] In similar vein, an anti-anti-suit injunction is an order restraining the injunction defendant from commencing or continuing proceedings to restrain the injunction plaintiff from applying to restrain the injunction defendant from commencing or continuing proceedings. The leading works on this topic are: Raphael *The Anti-Suit Injunction* 2 ed (2019) and Briggs *Civil Jurisdiction and Judgments* 7 ed (2021) ch 28. It is also conceptually possible to obtain similar relief in the context of arbitration but such relief is outside the scope of this work.

[291] *Quantum Oil Terminals Ltd v International Finance Corp* Suit No: Misc/00228/17 (unreported) 8 January 2018 and 23 February 2018 (H Ct) (Asiedu J).

[292] *United Bank for Africa Plc v Coker* (1996) 4 NWLR 239 (CA) (Muhammad, Ayoola and Pats-Acholonu JJCA).

[293] *Vedanta Resources Holdings Ltd v ZCCM Investment Holdings plc* 2019 JDR 1425 (GJ) (Adams J).

[294] For further guidance on the principles which a South African court would apply when asked to grant an anti-suit interdict, the reader is referred to the relevant section of the chapter on the Republic of South Africa.

[295] 1996 2 ZLR 73 (S) (Gubbay CJ, McNally and Muchechetere JJA).

[296] 1906 TS 120 (Innes CJ, Smith and Mason JJ) 122.

[297] 1996 2 ZLR 73, *per* Gubbay CJ (giving the judgment of the court) 79E.

[298] That these are still the requirements which a plaintiff (the applicant for the order) has to satisfy has recently been confirmed by the High Court of Harare: *Chimeri v Nguluve* [2017] ZWHHC 06 (Tsanga J) and *Betmon Inv (Pvt) Ltd v Dishtik Inv (Pvt) Ltd* [2017] ZWHHC 121 (Mwayera J).

plaintiff for the order. On the facts, the court held that the plaintiff had consented to the removal of the movables or at the very least had failed to show that he had not consented to the removal of the movables. It should be noted that the Supreme Court in *Minister of Mines and Mining Development v Grandwell Holdings (Private) Ltd*[299] has confirmed the correctness of the decision in *Botha*.

It must also be noted, as the Supreme Court has held in *Gateway Primary School v Fenesey*,[300] in Zimbabwe a spoilation order is 'a final form of interdict [and] cannot be granted as a provisional order. It cannot be granted as a provisional order'.[301]

The implementation of the Republic of Zimbabwe's land reallocation policies from 2000 onwards generated a number of cases in which the courts considered the question of *mandament van spolie*. In *Etheredge v Minister of State for National Security Responsible for Lands, Land Reform and Resettlement*,[302] Gowora J considered an application by a commercial farmer for relief in the form of a *mandament van spolie* premised on an alleged act of spoliation by persons acting on behalf of an individual to whom the plaintiff's land had been allocated pursuant to certain land resettlement legislation. The defendant contended that the plaintiff had no *locus standi* to bring the application because pursuant to the relevant legislation the plaintiff had no title to the land. The plaintiff contended that where a possessor of land is despoiled of the property then that gives the possessor the *locus standi* to bring the application. Gowora J cited, with apparent approval, *Mutsotso v Commissioner of Police*,[303] a decision of Robinson J where he stated:[304]

> 'I now turn to explain the basis on which a spoliation order is sought and granted.
>
> If, when this matter ultimately comes before it, the court were to find that the riot police had behaved towards the [plaintiffs] in the manner alleged and that the [plaintiffs] had thereby been cowed into leaving their dwellings and the Farm against their will, so that they had been dispossessed of their dwellings and, in the case of certain [plaintiffs], their household goods through the duress applied by the servants of the first [defendant], for the benefit of the second [defendant], then the law to be applied in such a situation is clear. The general principle was stated by Innes CJ in *Nino Bonino v. de Lange* 1906 TS 120 at 122 thus:

---

[299] [2018] ZWSC 34 (SC) (Patel, Guvava and Uchena JJA).

[300] [2021] ZWSC 63 (SC) (Hlatshwayo, Guvava JA and Bhunu AJ).

[301] In reaching this conclusion, the Supreme Court relied on the decision in *Blue Rangers Estates Ltd v Muduvuri* 2009 (1) ZLE 368.

[302] 2009 (1) ZLR 82 (H).

[303] 1993 (2) ZLR 329 (H).

[304] Ibid 332G–334B. Gowora J quoted only the passage up to the end of Millin J's judgment in *De Jager v Farah & Nedstadt* 1947 (4) SA 28 (W), set out above. However, in *Mutsotso*, Robinson J also made reference to *Fredericks v Stellenbosch Divisional Council* 1977 (3) SA 113 (C) 117C, where Diemont J stated that the court 'is not concerned with the nature of the [plaintiffs'] occupation. What it is concerned with is that the respondent should not take the law into its own hands ... Such conduct cannot be countenanced or condoned.' In so doing, Diemont J (and, by extension, Robinson J) set out the purpose of the remedy of *mandament van spolie*.

> "It is a fundamental principle that no man is allowed to take the law into his own hands; no one is permitted to dispossess another forcibly or wrongfully and against his consent of the possession of property, whether movable or immovable. If he does so, the court will summarily restore the *status quo ante*, and will do that as a preliminary to any inquiry or investigation into the merits of the dispute."
>
> As explained by Millin J in *De Jager & ors v. Farah & Nestadt* 1947 (4) SA 28 (W) at 35, a case where demolition of premises was undertaken without legal process:
>
> "What the court is doing is to insist on the principle that a person in possession of property, however unlawful his possession may be and however exposed he may be to ejectment proceedings, cannot be interfered with in his possession except by the due process of law, and if he is so interfered with the court will restrain such interference pending the taking of action against him for ejectment by those who claim that he is in wrongful possession. The fact that the applicants have no legal right to continue to live in this slum and would have no defence to proceedings for ejectment, does not mean that proceedings for ejectment can be dispensed with, nor does it make any difference to the illegality of the respondents' conduct that the occupation by the applicant carries with it penal consequences."
>
> In that case the court held that by their conduct in proceeding to demolish certain premises, which were dilapidated, verminous and generally unsanitary, without legal process in order to secure the ejectment of the occupiers, the respondents had committed acts of spoliation and they were therefore interdicted from further demolishing those premises.'

Gowora J stated: '[t]he question that then arises is whether as a result of the statutory provision even that right to protect himself from self helpers has been lost to him' and concluded:

> 'It is my view that a spoliator is in no better position tha[n] the former owner or occupier of farm land in the sense that in moving onto the land without due process he is equally guilty of an infraction of the law ... I do not accept that the applicant has been denuded of his right to approach the court for an order of spoliation to restore the *status quo ante*. The relief of *mandament van spolie* is a common law remedy and it is my view that its requirements have not been done away with by the promulgation of legislation to do with land acquisition.'

The plaintiff thus had *locus standi* to seek relief of *mandament van spolie* in relation to past acts of dispossession.[305]

In *Top Crop (1976) (Pvt) Ltd v Minister of Lands and Land Reform and Resettlement*,[306] Bhunu J reached a different conclusion, holding that because the plaintiffs' possession was a criminal offence under the relevant legislation the court could not come to their aid.

---

[305] On the facts, however, the judge refused the plaintiff's application for an interdict; because his land had been compulsorily acquired under land acquisition legislation, the plaintiff was unable to show that he had a *prima facie* right to be protected.

[306] Case no HH 74-09 (unreported).

A year later, in *Harland Brothers (Pvt) Ltd v The Minister of Lands and Rural Resettlement*,[307] Musakawa J reached a different conclusion for the same reasons as Gowora J gave in the *Etheredge* case when he made a spoliation order but refused an interim interdict.

Thus was the state of the authorities when these matters came before the Supreme Court. In *Commercial Farmers Union v Minister for Lands and Rural Resettlement*,[308] the Supreme Court closed the door on relief by way of *mandament van spolie*, holding[309]:

> 'Spoliation proceedings cannot confer jurisdiction where none exists. A court of law has no jurisdiction to authorise the commission of a criminal offence. In any event, spoliation is a criminal law remedy which cannot override the will of Parliament. A common law remedy cannot render nugatory an Act of Parliament.
>
> Apart from this, there is the principle that a litigant who is acting in open defiance of the law cannot approach a court for assistance. See *Associated Newspapers of Zimbabwe (Private) Limited v The Minister of State for Information and Publicity and Ors* SC 111/04. Indeed, if this point has been raised as a preliminary point, the probabilities are that this application would have been dismissed on that point alone. A former owner who is occupation of acquired land in open defiance of the law cannot approach the courts for assistance.'

Subsequently Bhunu J, relying on the decision of the Supreme Court in *Commercial Farmers Union v Minister for Lands and Rural Resettlement*,[310] dismissed an application for a spoliation order in similar circumstances.[311]

Based on the above, one may conclude that the application of the *mandament van spolie* remedy in Zimbabwe appears, therefore, to be limited to the following extent: a plaintiff cannot obtain this type of relief where his possession was at the time of his application a criminal offence.

It is unlikely that the decision of the Supreme Court in *Minister of Mines and Mining Development*[312] alters this conclusion. In this case, the plaintiff held special licences to mine diamonds. The defendant called a press conference at which it stated that the plaintiff no longer held the licences required to mine diamonds and that it had 90 days to vacate the mining site. As the plaintiff alleged, on the same day as the defendant held a press conference, the plaintiff's operations at the mining site were forcibly stopped and its employees forcibly evicted, prompting the plaintiff to seek relief. Guvava JA, speaking for a unanimous Supreme Court, referred to none of the jurisprudence dealing with land reform. Instead, the Supreme Court concentrated on the fact that the plaintiff was in possession of the

---

307 [2010] ZWHHC 6.

308 2010 (2) ZLR 576 (S) (Chidyausiku CJ, Malaba DCJ, Ziyambi, Garwe JJA and Cheda AJA).

309 Ibid 26, *per* Chidyausiku CJ (with whom the other judges agreed).

310 2010 (2) ZLR 576 (S) (Chidyausiku CJ, Malaba DCJ, Ziyambi, Garwe JJA and Cheda AJA).

311 *Heathcote v Matongo* [2011] ZWHHC 48.

312 *Supra* fn 299.

mining site.[313] While Guvava JA agreed with the proposition that 'lawfulness of [the plaintiff's] possession does not enter into it',[314] it was not argued before the court that the plaintiff's continued possession of the mining site after the press conference amounted to a criminal offence and the court was not asked to depart from its previous jurisprudence.[315]

16.3.9 Arrest of individuals *tanquam suspectus de fuga*

> 'Arrest *tanquam suspectus de fuga* owes its origin to Roman law. It was introduced in South Africa as part of Roman-Dutch law and was first reported as a part of the rules of court from as early as 1842. The procedure existed at common law as well as in a codified form in various rules of court. Arrest *tanquam suspectus de fuga* is ordered when a creditor on reasonable grounds suspects that a debtor, whose liability has not yet been acknowledged or proven in a court of law, is about to flee the country in order to prevent the adjudication of the dispute in this country. Only a court of law is, in terms of the common law as well as section 30(1) and (3) of the Act read with rule 56 of the Magistrate's courts Rules and section 19 of the Supreme Court Act read with rule 9 of the Uniform Rules of Court, entrusted with the authority to order arrest *tanquam suspectus de fuga*.'[316]

Order 36 of the High Court Rules contains provisions governing the issue of a writ of arrest against an individual *tanquam suspectus de fuga*.[317] Such a writ may be issued where the plaintiff proves to the satisfaction of a judge or the registrar of the High Court that[318] (1) he has a good cause of action against the defendant to the amount of 'five thousand dollars or more';[319] (2) there is 'good ground for believing that the defendant is about to remove from Zimbabwe';[320] and (3) the

[313] Ibid p 17 of the transcript.

[314] Ibid, citing the decision in *Yeko v Oana* 1973 (4) SA 735 (AD) 739G, *per* Van Blerk JA (giving the judgment of the court: Van Blerk, Wessels, Potgieter, Jansen and Rabie JJA).

[315] See too the decision of the Supreme Court in *Anjin Investments Ltd v Minister of Mines and Mining Development* [2020] ZWSC 39 (SC) (Bere JA), where the conclusion in *Minister of Mines and Mining Development* was endorsed.

[316] *Malachi v Cape Dance Academy International (Pty) Ltd* 2010 (6) SA 1 (CC), *per* Mogoeng J at para [17] (giving the judgment of the court: Ngcobo CJ, Moseneke DCJ, Cameron, Froneman, Jafta, Khampepe, Nkabinde, Skweyiya, Van der Westhuizen and Yacoob JJ).

[317] Currently, it is an open question whether these provisions would survive a constitutional challenge such as that which resulted in comparable provisions being declared unconstitutional in the Republic of South Africa (*Malachi v Cape Dance Academy International (Pty) Ltd* 2010 (6) SA 1 (CC)).

[318] Order 36, r 278(1).

[319] This monetary requirement is now otiose. The Zimbabwean dollar was demonetised between 15 June and 30 September 2015 (press release by Dr JP Mangudya, Governor of the Reserve Bank of Zimbabwe, 11 June 2015). Whether this means there is no financial requirement or whether the remedy is no longer available is uncertain.

[320] That this is a real requirement for the plaintiff to satisfy is demonstrated by *Galante v Summerfield* [2003] ZWHHC 75 (Makoni J). The plaintiff's inability to prove that the third respondent had anything to do with the removal of the relevant property meant that he could not obtain the order sought against her.

defendant's absence from Zimbabwe will 'materially prejudice the plaintiff in the prosecution of his claim'.[321]

Order 36 makes further provision for the mechanics of the writ of arrest *tanquam suspectus de fuga*, including: the requirement that the plaintiff give security for any damages that may be caused by the writ of arrest;[322] the release of the defendant if he pays the sum or delivers the thing referred to in the writ of arrest or if a bond or other security is given for the sums claimed;[323] the person arrested may anticipate the return day and apply to discharge the writ of arrest on 24 hours to the plaintiff.[324]

As has been mentioned above, in *Malachi v Cape Dance Academy International (Pty) Ltd*,[325] the Constitutional Court of South Africa abolished arrest *tanquam suspectus de fuga* in the Republic of South Africa. Mogoeng J (giving the judgment of the court) stated:

> '[32] The object of the arrest "is to ensure that [the potential debtor] remains within the jurisdiction of the court until the court has given judgment in the matter". As soon as judgment is given, a debtor would, however, be free to catch the next flight to any foreign destination even if this is done to evade payment and no realisable asset exists in the country, from the proceeds of which payment may be effected. Arrest does not, therefore, ensure the satisfaction of the judgment debt. Admittedly, the unfairly exerted pressure of incarceration may at times force the arrestee to pay the debt or provide security. But, that does not detract from the fact that the arrest does not necessarily render the judgment any more executable or beneficial to the creditor than would have been the case had the debtor left the country. It simply limits the fundamental right to freedom of the person for no just reason.
>
> [33] The order for the arrest of persons *tanquam suspectus de fuga* under the impugned provisions is ordinarily made at the time when their civil liability has not yet been established. Their debt is only alleged on affidavit, often in an urgent application brought *ex parte*. The potential debtor is often only afforded the opportunity to resist the severe curtailment of the right to freedom, by the order, on the return date. Potentially the detention may endure for as long as the action is pending. The effect of this deprivation was more aptly captured in *Segal v Diners Club South Africa* where we are warned that "[i]f the debtor has been wrongly deprived of his freedom it cannot be put right in the subsequent suit. The harm is irreparable." Nothing can undo the degrading effect of incarceration, particularly if the order were obtained *ex parte*. This is the position in which the plaintiff in this matter found herself for 16 days.

---

[321] Before the issue of the writ these matters must be deposed to in an affidavit made by the plaintiff or his agent or servant: O 36, r 278(2).

[322] Order 36, r 279.

[323] Order 36, r 283.

[324] Order 36, r 287.

[325] 2010 (6) SA 1 (CC) (Ngcobo CJ, Moseneke DCJ, Cameron, Froneman, Jafta, Khampepe, Nkabinde, Skweyiya, Van der Westhuizen, Yacoob and Mogoeng JJ).

> [34] Since there is no legal basis for the imprisonment of someone who has been found civilly liable, it is inconceivable that any legal justification can ever exist for putting behind bars a person whose civil liability is yet to, or will possibly never, be proven. Although an order for arrest is granted by a court, the intervention of the judicial process cannot legitimise the deprivation of freedom, since the arrest may stem from a debt which has itself not been established through the judicial process. I therefore conclude that there is no just cause for the arrest in terms of the impugned provisions.'

The present law has yet to be the subject of authoritative exposition by the Zimbabwean courts. The decision in *Malachi* turned on section 12(1) of the Constitution of South Africa, 1996, which is similar in terms to section 49 of the Constitution of Zimbabwe 2013:

> **'49 Right to personal liberty**
>
> (1) Every person has the right to personal liberty, which includes the right—
>
> *(a)* not to be detained without trial; and
>
> *(b)* not to be deprived of their liberty arbitrarily or without just cause.
>
> (2) No person may be imprisoned merely on the ground of inability to fulfil a contractual obligation.'

In addition to the right to not be detained without trial and the right not to be deprived of their liberty arbitrarily or without just cause contained in section 49(1), which are present in section 12(1) of the South African Constitution, section 49(2) prohibits imprisonment on the ground of an inability to fulfil a contractual obligation. Whilst the latter may not, properly construed, prohibit the arrest of a defendant *tanquam suspectus de fuga* alleged to be in breach of a contractual obligation, it gives an indication of the direction of travel of the constitutional principles contained in the Constitution as favouring individual liberty over private rights.

In the light of the persuasive nature of South African authorities in the courts in Zimbabwe, it is to be anticipated[326] that the courts in Zimbabwe will have regard to and adopt the reasoning of Mogoeng J, as set out above.

[326] Because of the affinity between Zimbabwe constitutional and private law and that of the Republic of South Africa, it is to be expected that the decisions of the Supreme Court of Appeal of the Republic of South Africa will be given weight by the Zimbabwean courts.

APPENDIX

Table setting out statutory regime for the enforcement of foreign judgments in place in each jurisdiction and the countries to which they are applicable.

Jurisdiction	Statutory regime(s) in place in that jurisdiction	Countries or territories to which that statutory regime has been extended
Botswana	Judgments (International Enforcement) Act 1981	Unclear* * Section 3 of the 1981 Act provides that where the President of Botswana is satisfied that if the benefits of Part II are extended to the superior courts of another country, substantial reciprocity of treatment will be assured; he or she may by statutory instrument order: *(a)* that Part II shall extend to that country; and *(b)* that such courts of that country as are specified in the order shall be the superior courts of that country for the purposes of Part II. As yet, no order under the 1981 Act so extending Part II has been made. Moreover, section 4 of the 1981 Act provides that the provisions of Part II apply to all countries to which the 'United Kingdom Judgments Act' applied immediately before the commencement of the part. However, it is not clear what the 1981 Act means when it says this – there is no 'United Kingdom Judgments Act'.

Jurisdiction	Statutory regime(s) in place in that jurisdiction	Countries or territories to which that statutory regime has been extended
Eswatini	Reciprocal Enforcement of Judgments Proclamation 1922	Basutoland (modern-day Lesotho) Bechuanaland (modern-day Botswana) Southern Rhodesia (modern-day Zimbabwe) Northern Rhodesia (modern-day Zambia) Zanzibar Nyasaland (modern-day Malawi) Kenya New Zealand Western Australia Tanganyika (modern-day Tanzania) Uganda New South Wales Victoria North Australia Central Australia
Ghana	Courts Act 1993	Brazil France Israel Italy Japan Lebanon Senegal Spain the United Arab Republic (a political union which existed between Egypt and Syria from 1858–1961 and not thereafter) United Kingdom

Jurisdiction	Statutory regime(s) in place in that jurisdiction	Countries or territories to which that statutory regime has been extended
Kenya	Foreign Judgments (Reciprocal Enforcement) Act 1984	Australia Malawi Seychelles Tanzania Uganda Zambia United Kingdom Republic of Rwanda
Lesotho	Reciprocal Enforcement of Judgments Proclamation 1922	Bechuanaland (modern-day Botswana) Swaziland (modern day Eswatini) Southern Rhodesia (modern-day Zimbabwe) Northern Rhodesia (modern-day Zambia) Zanzibar Nyasaland (modern-day Malawi) Kenya New Zealand Western Australia Tanganyika (modern-day Tanzania) Uganda New South Wales Victoria North Australia Central Australia
Liberia	No statutory regime is in place here.	N/A

Jurisdiction	Statutory regime(s) in place in that jurisdiction	Countries or territories to which that statutory regime has been extended
Malawi	Nyasaland Judgments Extension Ordinance 1912	Kenya Northern Rhodesia (modern-day Zambia) Tanganyika (modern-day Tanzania) Uganda Zanzibar
	British and Colonial Judgments Ordinance 1922	Basutoland (modern-day Lesotho) Swaziland (modern day Eswatini) Somaliland (modern-day Republic of Somaliland) New South Wales British Solomon Islands Gilbert and Ellis Islands (modern-day Kiribati and Tuvalu)
	Service of Process and Enforcement of Judgments Act 1957	Southern Rhodesia (modern-day Zimbabwe) Zambia
Namibia	Enforcement of Foreign Civil Judgments Act 1994	Republic of South Africa

Jurisdiction	Statutory regime(s) in place in that jurisdiction	Countries or territories to which that statutory regime has been extended
Nigeria	Reciprocal Enforcement of Foreign Judgments Ordinance 1922	England Republic of Ireland Scotland The Gambia Ghana Sierra Leone Newfoundland New South Wales Victoria Barbados Bermuda British Guiana Gibraltar Grenada Jamaica Leeward Islands St Lucia St Vincent Trinidad and Tobago
	Foreign Judgments (Reciprocal Enforcement) Act 1961	The power, as contained in section 3 of the 1961 Act, for the Minister of Justice to extend the provisions of Part I of the Act 1961 to judgments emanating from courts in other countries or territories has not yet been exercised.
Republic of South Africa	Enforcement of Foreign Civil Judgments Act 1988	Namibia
Sierra Leone	Foreign Judgments (Reciprocal Enforcement) Act 1935	Ghana Nigeria The Gambia United Kingdom

Jurisdiction	Statutory regime(s) in place in that jurisdiction	Countries or territories to which that statutory regime has been extended
Tanzania and Zanzibar	Tanzania Reciprocal Enforcement of Foreign Judgments Act 1935	Lesotho Botswana Sri Lanka Mauritius New South Wales Zambia The Seychelles Somalia Zimbabwe The Kingdom of Swaziland (modern-day Eswatini) The United Kingdom
	Judgments Extension Act 1921	Kenya Uganda Nyasaland (modern-day Malawi) Zanzibar
Tanzania and Zanzibar	Zanzibar Judgments Extension Decree 1908	Kenya Uganda Nyasaland (modern-day Malawi) Tanganyika (modern-day Tanzania)
	British Judgments Decree 1921	England Scotland Ireland Somaliland Lesotho Botswana Swaziland (modern-day Eswatini) New South Wales
The Gambia	Reciprocal Enforcement of Foreign Judgments Act 1922	England Northern Ireland Scotland
	Foreign Judgments Reciprocal Enforcement Act 1936	Nigeria

Jurisdiction	Statutory regime(s) in place in that jurisdiction	Countries or territories to which that statutory regime has been extended
Uganda	Judgments Extension Act 1908	Kenya Nyasaland (modern-day Malawi) Tanganyika (modern-day Tanzania)
	Reciprocal Enforcement of Judgments Act 1922	United Kingdom Republic of Ireland Botswana Lesotho Mauritius New South Wales Seychelles Sri Lanka Swaziland (modern-day Eswatini)
	Foreign Judgments (Reciprocal Enforcement) Act 1961	the Commonwealth (save those countries to which the 1922 Act applies) Grenada (specific provision has been made for this)
Zambia	British and Colonial Judgments Act 1922* * There is an issue whether the 1922 Act has been repealed such that its provisions are no longer operative. The authors, as more fully explained in the relevant chapter, take the view that the 1922 Act has not yet been repealed and that its provisions remain operative.	Zimbabwe Tanzania Malawi Lesotho Botswana Swaziland (modern-day Eswatini) Kenya New South Wales Victoria Scotland England Northern Ireland Republic of Ireland
	Foreign Judgments (Reciprocal Enforcement) Act 1937	Gilbert & Ellice Islands (modern-day Kiribati and Tuvalu) British Solomon Islands
	Service of Process and Execution of Judgments Act 1957	Nyasaland (modern-day Malawi) Southern Rhodesia (modern-day Zimbabwe)

➡

Jurisdiction	Statutory regime(s) in place in that jurisdiction	Countries or territories to which that statutory regime has been extended
Zimbabwe	Civil Matters (Mutual Assistance) Act 1995	Specific provision is made for international tribunals Australia Dominica South Africa Bulgaria Germany Ghana Portugal Italy Slovak Republic Zambia* * Zambia was treated as a designated country in *Vehicle Delivery Services (Zimbabwe) (Pty) Limited v Galaun Holdings Limited* 2003 (2) ZLR 329 (H), *per* Hungwe J. The Minister's Order pursuant to which Zambia was designated was not referred to in the judgment.

INDEX

www.ingramcontent.com/pod-product-compliance
Lightning Source LLC
LaVergne TN
LVHW060006210926
848481LV00013B/3661
* 9 7 8 1 4 8 5 1 5 0 4 3 5 *